Strategic

Retail

Management

text and cases

David E. Bell
Harvard University
Graduate School of Business Administration

Walter J. Salmon
Harvard University
Graduate School of Business Administration

SOUTH-WESTERN College Publishing

An International Thomson Publishing Company

Copyright © 1996
by South-Western College Publishing
Cincinnati, Ohio

I(T)P
International Thomson Publishing
South-Western College Publishing is an ITP Company. The ITP trademark is used under license.

ISBN: 0-538-84908-8

1 2 3 4 5 6 MT 0 9 8 7 6 5

Printed in the United States of America.

Library of Congress Cataloging-in-Publication Data

Bell, David E.
    Strategic retail management: text and cases / David E. Bell,
Walter J. Salmon.
        p. cm.
    ISBN 0-538-84908-8 (alk. paper)
    1. Retail trade—Management. I. Salmon, Walter J. II. Title.
HF5429.B4428 1995
658.8'7—dc20   95-32417
                                                          CIP

Production Editor: Sharon L. Smith
Cover and Interior Designer: Michael H. Stratton
Marketing Manager: Stephen E. Momper

P R E F A C E

The primary purpose of this book is to help attract and develop the human capital which retailers and related entities such as suppliers, landlords and bankers require to innovate and effectively operate distribution systems in free enterprise economies. To accomplish this goal, this book includes cases, readings, and "notes." The latter are in effect readings that provide supplementary knowledge and concepts to help resolve the challenges set forth in the cases.

The cases, which are the backbone of this publication, identify and provide information about critical and contemporary issues confronting retailers. How, for example, should a highly regarded operator of shopping centers, in view of major changes in shopping behavior, reposition two major regional malls to sustain and preferably improve their consumer appeal and profitability. Discussion and analyses of these cases in conjunction with the supplementary materials enhances interest and knowledge of retailing. Most importantly, it increases capacity to deal effectively with the critical issues confronting retailers and related parties.

To provide readers with a comprehensive overview of retailing, most of its major sectors are described in one or more of the cases included in this book. Thus some of the cases focus on the problems of some of industry's newer participants such as power retailers and electronic/mail-order retailers while others are concerned with more traditional branches of the industry such as discount and traditional department stores as well as supermarkets.

Although the nature of retailing issues, like the problems faced by most businesses, makes it difficult to write real and dynamic cases concerned only with one business function, the cases and other materials are grouped to provide a systematic examination of the industry. Three modules concerned with the strategic and tactical marketing and merchandising problems confronting retailers are at the beginning of the book. How the organization and systems have to be configured to deal with these problems is the subject of the book's fourth module. In view of the importance of "location" in retailing, the book's fifth module is dedicated to real estate issues. The final two modules focus on entrepreneurial issues in retailing with particular emphasis on international retailing and home shopping.

The issues set forth in this book should be of interest to able students of consumer marketing and distribution at various stages of their education. MBA students and executives at middle and upper management levels, however, usually benefit most from studying and discussing the intellectual challenges embedded in the cases.

In preparing for case discussions, students should review the study questions (provided by the instructor), and initially read the entire case quickly. Then they should endeavor, from a detailed and thoughtful review of the relevant information in the case, to prepare responses to the study questions. If time allows, class preparation should also include identification of important issues not necessarily addressed in the study questions and an overall plan of action to implement the suggested responses to the case issues.

To help guide the discussions of the cases, there is available, from the publisher, an associated instructor's manual. This manual includes suggested study questions, lines of reasoning that respond to these study questions, analysis, and teaching strategies.

ACKNOWLEDGMENTS

The authors are indebted to the Harvard Business School and its many supporters for the financial resources to research and write the cases and other materials in this book. We are equally grateful to the many organizations who allowed us to develop cases, who gave freely of their time, and often entrusted us with confidential information. They have done their best to help us contribute to the education of present and future retailers as well as those who are allied with retailers in helping to bring consumers a better standard of living.

David Bell
Walter Salmon
Boston, Massachusetts
June 16, 1995

C O N T E N T S

INTRODUCTION

RETAILING IN THE AGE OF EXECUTION

Evidence abounds that now, more than ever, retailing has become a business in which excellence in execution will distinguish winners from losers. Achieving excellence in execution, however, will require emphasis on different skills in the future than in the past.

This article first provides two kinds of evidence to show that skills in execution are of growing importance. Second, the paper explains why there is a shift in the mix of skills needed to achieve excellence in execution. Third, those skills of increasing importance in execution in retailing are described. Particular emphasis is placed upon attracting able rank and file employees and doing an outstanding job in motivating them.

IMPORTANCE OF EXECUTION

Evidence about the importance of execution in retailing arises from examining both old and new forms of retailing. While debatable performance has been a factor in the consolidation or recapitalization of four of the major department store groups, another department store company, Dillard's, remains a favorite of both consumers and investors. Dillard's installation of an on-line merchandise information system almost a generation before its department store competitors has been a major factor in its superior performance. This edge in execution helped Dillard's both improve the performance of its existing divisions dramatically and revitalize rapidly the sick department store operations which it acquired.

Wal-Mart's track record provides additional evidence of the importance of execution. Frequent service from nearby warehouses, an excellent management information and communication system, and store employees motivated by more responsibility than their counterparts in most other chains, as well as extra recognition and profit sharing, have helped make Wal-Mart an unusually cost effective competitor. The result has been lower Wal-Mart prices, higher sales per square foot, dramatically higher profits, and enviable growth in market share.

Exceptional skills in execution have also sustained the leadership of certain innovators in retailing. Price Club's superior performance compared to other warehouse clubs is in part due to its consummate concern with reducing expenses. Home Depot's leadership position among operators of warehouse home centers is related to exceptional skills in motivating employees to render attentive service. Similarly Toys R Us's ability to remain in stock more than its competitors has helped distinguish it from other toy supermarket chains. These pioneers have combined a unique strategy with excellence in execution. While most of their clones have adopted highly similar strategies, lack of comparable excellence in execution has been a major factor in their substantially inferior performance.

This article first appeared as "Retailing in the Age of Execution" by Walter J. Salmon, *Journal of Retailing,* Vol. 65 No. 1 Fall 1989, used by permission.

IMPACT OF ABUNDANT CAPITAL RESOURCES

Another factor that heightens the importance of execution in retailing is the abundant capital for innovators and their clones. The recent explosion in office supply warehouse operators is a case in point. Staples, a company headquartered outside of Boston, and financed largely by professional venture capitalists, originated the concept in 1985. Although Staples was only in the process of an initial public offering and revealing its operating results in the winter of 1988/89, there were already more than a half dozen clones in operation around the United States. Some were subsidiaries of established retailers seeking diversification and/or pursuing the "grass is always greener" theory. Most were financed by professional venture capitalists.

Retailing has obviously become an area of intense interest for venture capitalists. Some represent the traditional pools of venture capital money who perceive the rapid consumer acceptance of new ideas in retailing as an opportunity for a high return. Others, a newer breed, are venture capitalists dedicated to retailing, which puts additional pressure on them—maybe too much pressure—to put their money to work. The consequence of the abundant funds available for investment in retailing is the virtual elimination of the time period before which a new idea is cloned. Thus, even those who pioneer new concepts in retailing must almost immediately become excellent in execution if they are to enjoy the fruits of their innovations.

IS MERCHANDISING THE KEY?

Traditionally, the conclusion that execution was increasingly important for sustained success in retailing would have implied the need for further improvement in merchandising skills. While merchandising remains an important element in great execution, providing what the customer wants now demands more attention to other disciplines.

There are several reasons why merchandising skills are no longer as paramount in retailing success. More working women, who, like men, prefer traditional clothes for work, is one reason. Merchandising skills—particularly their taste component—may be less important in selecting apparel for women more interested in tradition than change.

Second, apparel as a means of self-expression may be less important today than home, health, food, cooking, fitness, and travel. If so, purveyors of taste in selecting apparel may have less magic than formerly in attracting consumer patronage.

Third, time constrained consumers may typically find shopping more chore and less pleasure than their predecessors. Instead, they want convenience. This can mean more shopping at home; witness the accelerated growth of mail order sales. If they continue to shop in stores, then quickly finding what they want in-stock, obtaining efficient sales assistance if required, and minimizing checkout or transaction time may be their goals.

Fourth, if consumers value home, health, food, fitness, and travel more and clothing less, they may have more interest in apparel retailers that emphasize low prices and less in those that are at the forefront of fashion.

Fifth, product changes may also be diminishing the importance of merchandising skill as a key to success in retailing. Technology that results in better products, government regulations that force publication of product content and assure product safety, and brand names that have important meaning to consumers all suggest that consumers may look less to retailers for assurance of product quality and taste. The names Liz Claiborne and Ralph Lauren may offer consumers more reassurance than the stores in which they are sold.

In combination with the transfer of responsibility for consumer reassurance from retailers to others, there is another "product factor" that changes the skills retailers need to satisfy consumers. The importance of brand names and the rapidity with which retailers can duplicate each other's selections may make differentiated assortments elusive for retailers to achieve and invisible for consumers to perceive. If consumers can find similar assortments of brand name merchandise in a number of stores, then which store they choose may no longer be primarily related to differences among retailers in merchandising skills.

Sixth, changes in technology as well as changes in consumers and products affect the environment in which retailers operate. The most significant technological change, of course, has been the explosion in information/communication systems.

Mastery of the information/communication explosion has profound implications for retailers. It can result in greatly increased spans of control, new ways of subdividing jobs, and significant shifts in responsibilities between headquarters and field or store organizations. It is possible to either centralize more responsibilities based on sound and current information or decentralize certain responsibilities without loss of control.

Together with the aforementioned changes in consumers, products, and technology, the changes in retailing itself dictate different emphasis on the skills the industry demands. Foremost among these changes is the replacement *first* of the individually owned and operated downtown emporium by the downtown store and its suburban branches, *and* the subsequent migration of this concept into regional, national, and now international chains of stores.

A second change of equal managerial significance in retailing is the explosion in types of retailing competing for consumer favor. Chains of discount department stores, specialty discounters, specialty apparel stores with selections equal in quality and fashion to department stores, and off price or non-continuity retailers have essentially arisen in the last thirty years or less.

Retailing has, in addition, been changed by the transformation of procurement practices. International sourcing has to a considerable extent replaced more proximate sources of supply. Changes in the scale and diversity of retailing, and now its internationalization on both the demand and supply side, mean that marketing, organization, and management information systems, as well as logistical and accounting skills, will be more important than ever before in achieving excellence in execution in retailing.

A final profound and more recent change in retailing has been the decline in the supply of labor. The implications of this development for such a labor intensive industry are not yet fully understood. Retailers who fail to adjust to this reality will find themselves increasingly threatened competitively.

NEW KEY SUCCESS FACTORS

What then are the key success factors to enhance retailing success in the future? They are:

1. Marketing skills
2. Organization skills
3. Logistical skills
4. Management information system skills
5. Accounting skills
6. Rank and file worker changes

A danger is, however, that retailers will go about improving their skills in these areas on a piecemeal basis and without recognizing how interrelated they are with each other and with the marketing mission of the firm. Future retailing success will demand more than excellence in each of these areas. These skills must be so interrelated with each other and the marketing mission of the firm that the totality represents a *culture*, which is outstanding in satisfying both consumers and employees.

Nordstrom is an example in certain respects of such a culture. Its marketing policies of overwhelming assortments crafted to the needs of each store, its excellent service, and its unique ability to attract and motivate outstanding people are highly interdependent. Without overwhelming assortments, it would be harder to attract great salespeople since such individuals regard these assortments as their principal selling tool. The motivation of these able salespeople is then additionally augmented by their involvement in the composition of their store's inventory. This psychological commitment to the inventory also means that employees will have a vested interest in helping Nordstrom minimize markdowns. In examining the individual skills and disciplines discussed below, the importance of the interrelationships among them which the Nordstrom example illustrates should not be forgotten.

Marketing Skills

First, although not necessarily foremost, among the skills required in this age of execution is marketing skill. Selecting a target market and articulating its needs and wants, even if the market itself cannot articulate them, and determining how to satisfy these needs and wants better than competition constitutes the marketing skill a retailer requires.

Why retailers need more marketing skills can be explained by two factors. The emergence of significantly different demands among target markets means that retailers have to choose more precisely which of these target markets they wish to serve. One formula that will satisfy most consumers for most lines of merchandise and most purchase occasions is an anachronism. Secondly, growth in the diversity of types of retailers means that analyzing competition is a far more complex task than formerly. The department store merchant who only compares the strength and weaknesses of his marketing offering to other department stores is probably failing to assess his most powerful competition. Thus the heightened complexity of competitive analysis demands more marketing skill.

More marketing skill should not be confused with more emphasis on merchandising. Retailers have often confused the two and emphasized unduly the latter. Formulating a market program is the essential point of departure for creation of a sound merchandising strategy. Too often retailers have floundered because their merchandise assortments and other elements of their merchandising program did not serve a specified target market better than competitors.

Organizational Skills

Perhaps even more vital than marketing skill for many retailers is more organizational skill. Department stores represent the most compelling example of the need in retailing for more organizational skill. At headquarters there are all sorts of organizational anomalies.

Low pay at all but senior levels, narrow spans of control in terms of range of merchandise being purchased and sometimes the number of stores for which it is being bought, purported responsibilities for buying, as well as planning, inventory management, and communication with the selling organization, intense supervision, and accelerated turnover characterize department store headquarters organizations. At the same time that headquarters personnel are overwhelmed, store level employees find themselves with too much grunt work and too little brainwork. The results have been catastrophic. Able young people often shun department stores, which they frequently confuse with the retailing industry; those that don't shun it, often leave it out of frustration. Opportunities for vendor clout and international procurement are not maximized. Turnover leads to inadequate familiarity with merchandise, vendors, customers, and colleagues. Finally, these organizations offset in numbers of bodies what they save in individual pay. The result is an expense albatross that succumbs only to LBOs, restructuring, takeovers, or the threat of these events. Instead of these currently calamitous arrangements, more organizational skill could lead to:

1. Buyers with professional status and pay, and with wider spans of control in terms of breadth of merchandise and number of stores for which they make purchases.
2. Delegation to able, other individuals within the merchandising organization of responsibility for inventory planning and management, and store communications.
3. A reduction in the intensity of supervision of buyers consistent with their higher pay, more professional status, and quite probably extended longevity in the same position.
4. A willingness to provide the remaining buyers and merchandise managers with the opportunity to formulate marketing, merchandising, and management strategies consistent with how consumers want to buy particular merchandise rather than having a consistent but less relevant strategy for the whole store.
5. Sharing of responsibilities in agreed upon ways, with store-line executives for the planning and execution of merchandising responsibilities.

Logistical Skills

Equal in importance to strong organizational skills are sound logistical skills. Except for the better managed food retailers and a few general merchandise retailers such as Wal-Mart and the Limited, these are in short supply in retailing. The result has been the twin curse of too much inventory and too many stockouts as well as excess inventories in one store when they are needed in another.

A higher order of logistical skills would manifest itself in a number of ways. On staple, longer life cycle merchandise, which includes items as disparate as toasters, women's hosiery, and men's white dress shirts, a manifestation of superior logistical skills would be just-in-time replenishment directly to the selling floor and the elimination of any store backroom stocks. Only this replenishment procedure provides assurance of a high in-stock condition, rapid inventory turnover, and minimization of handling costs. Resupply of such items directly to the selling floor from the retailer's own central stocks will, in nearly all instances, be the most cost effective means of both executing the just-in-time system and acquiring merchandise at the lowest landed in-store cost.

Contemporary logistical systems for fashion merchandise, on the other hand, demand different techniques. For this merchandise, post-distribution[1] from a responsive central distribution center with the assistance of planner-distributors would represent a state-of-the-art procedure. Only this procedure takes maximum advantage of recent sales history, and minimizes both the cost of merchandise from vendors, and receiving and marking expense.

To implement post-distribution, it may be essential to adopt one of the previously suggested organizational changes, namely the separation of buying from inventory planning and management. Moreover, post-distribution will only work well if also supported by management information systems (MISs) that incorporate on-line receiving, maintain computerized records of hanger or shelf capacity by merchandise class by store, and paradigms that suggest distributions of merchandise among stores based on anticipated sales and current inventories. The need to carefully coordinate changes in logistical arrangements with changes in organizational structure and MIS capabilities is an example of why retailers aiming at attaining excellence in execution cannot achieve this objective on a piecemeal basis.

---

1 Post-distribution is the allocation of merchandise among stores upon receipt from the vendor. It differs from pre-distribution, which is the allocation of merchandise among stores when the order is placed with the vendor, which usually takes place weeks or months before receipt of merchandise.

MIS Skills

While most retailers have crossed the Rubicon in accepting the rising importance of MIS systems, their indispensability in achieving excellence in execution may not be fully recognized. MIS is the key in retailing to performing a number of vital tasks quickly, accurately, and economically, and to linking and coordinating the activities of individuals increasingly separated by function and geography. MIS will be particularly important to excellence in execution through:

1. UPC and bar coding systems that collect accurately more detailed sales data by customer, SKU, and store. Sales information by customer and SKU will be a vital element in target marketing and in future combination mail order/retail businesses.
2. Exception reporting systems and other types of decision support systems that distinguish between actionable information and raw data, particularly for vendor reorder, markdown, and store replenishment decisions.
3. On-line, interactive systems that involve store personnel in sales and inventory planning.
4. MIS systems that, instead of centralizing decision making, empower rank and file employees to make certain merchandise decisions more accurately. Replenishment of staple items from central stocks is an example of this application.
5. MIS systems that provide data for sound employee scheduling and that provide employees with quantitative feedback about their individual performance, their performance compared to peers, and their work unit's performance compared to its counterparts in other stores.

Accounting Skills

Another area that is crucial to excellence in execution is the enhancement of accounting skills. Retailing has been afflicted by an accounting system, the retail inventory method, that while it is useful in arriving at realistic market values for inventories, has helped spawn a number of injurious by-products. Numbers or targets that frequently conflict with each other—such as the desire for both a higher percentage gross margin and for more sales—is one unfortunate example. Another is the attempt to hold individuals in one function responsible for one set of activities and individuals in another function responsible for different activities, when in fact the individuals in both functions are highly dependent on each other. Finally, the accounting goals to which retailers respond often are inadequately related to maximizing shareholder wealth. To overcome these problems, a number of changes in the accounting practices of retailers are required.

One improvement opportunity would be the frequent generation and dissemination to store personnel and others of accurate store contribution statements. Not only would such statements help retailers understand better their own economics; they would inspire store managers to supervise their stores in a manner more compatible with maximizing shareholder value.

A second accounting improvement would be to focus both buyers and sellers on maximizing contribution per unit of selling space (sales less cost of goods sold and variable expense). Both buying and selling executives must share the same goals to overcome the civil war that often characterizes the communication between them.

Finally, contribution to fixed expense must also be the main basis for performance evaluation and incentive rewards for most buying and selling executives. For buyers, this goal should supersede such fragmented and internally contradictory goals as maximizing sales, gross margin, and inventory turnover. For sellers, this goal would refocus them on what counts for stockholders rather than encourage them to minimize expenses or, even in the most centralized of organizations, to ignore their profound influence on gross margin.

Rank and File Worker Changes

More than any of the preceding means of achieving excellence in execution, however, attaining this goal will depend on the quality and motivation of rank and file employees. A labor shortage which will only get worse, and consumers who increasingly demand reduced transaction time, sales assistance on infrequently purchased, expensive, or psychologically risky purchases, and who even appear to succumb to friendliness, are the essential reasons for this emphasis. To overcome the shortage of people and productively and effectively render the help customers require, there is a need for employees who are:

1. Highly productive
2. Cooperative and competitive
3. Punctual and regular in attendance
4. Concerned with customer satisfaction
5. Loyal and thus familiar with their jobs

The devices available to produce this kind of behavior are:

1. Using people only for those tasks that customers prefer not to do themselves, and for which there are no MIS and/or logistical alternatives.
2. Recognizing that higher paid and higher caliber people typically more than offset their higher wages with higher productivity.
3. Using a variety of devices for raising productivity. These include:
   • Incentive pay such as piecework, commissions, gain sharing, or work unit profit sharing, depending on the circumstances, to stimulate productivity.
   • Examining the possibility of profit sharing and/or Employee Stock Ownership plans.
   • Allowing employees influence on how they do their work, and consistent with store needs, the scheduling of their work.
   • Providing employees with frequent quantitative feedback on their own performance and how it compares with comparable co-workers.
   • Substituting quality for quantity in the supervision of rank and file employees.
   • Using hoopla to enhance the fun and minimize the tedium of many of the tasks of rank and file employees.
   • Avoiding the layoff of all but seasonal employees.

Now, what kinds of organizational characteristics or cultures attract employees with this potential and then help instill it? These cultures usually:

1. Promote exclusively from within.
2. Have high initial attrition and then considerable loyalty from remaining employees.
3. Have few layers of management and wide spans of control.
4. Have an egalitarian environment with respect to pay and privilege.
5. Are at least partially insulated from short-run considerations such as quarterly earnings and high bank debt.

The aim of this kind of culture is to provide employees with excellent pay, a sense of creativity and participation, job satisfaction, and a sense of belonging. A quid pro quo for the retailer is customer satisfaction, and, because of high productivity, acceptable payroll costs. Achieving these goals will be the single most important element in achieving excellence in execution in retailing in the forthcoming years.

Case 1

HILLS DEPARTMENT STORES, INC.

As he reviewed 1988's performance, Steve Goldberger, president of Hills Department Stores, Inc., debated whether to alter Hills' unusual, enduring, and successful strategy. This strategy, which had helped make Hills a consistently profitable $1.7 billion powerhouse in the discount department store industry, stressed outstanding assortments of first quality (no seconds) soft goods, everyday low prices (EDLP), and a variety of techniques to convince customers that Hills offered consistently superior value. These techniques included clean, neat, but spartan store interiors, the refusal to accept credit cards, and advertising and in-store signing which informed customers that they were the beneficiaries of Hills' frugality. Supporting this marketing strategy was an operating philosophy that shunned ownership or operation of warehouses. Centralized responsibilities for execution of the merchandising plan and strict control of expenses were additional features of Hills' operations.

A number of factors had caused Mr. Goldberger to reappraise Hills' strategy. Sales growth of stores open more than a year had declined to 2.9% in 1988 compared to 3.8% in 1987. Operating Profit had declined from $103.5 to $97.7 million, the first such decline in Hills' history. Moreover, soft goods sales, in which Hills had always excelled, were flat while hard goods sales were up 5%. Goldberger acknowledged that there was no further room to expand soft goods assortments since selections may already have become too extensive. Finally, there was the intensification of competition among discount department stores in general and the prospect of increased competition with Wal-Mart in particular. Wal-Mart was commonly regarded as the most effective and aggressive competitor in the discount department store industry. Goldberger wondered what departures, if any, from Hills' historically successful strategy and the culture which reinforced it were desirable to sustain Hills' successful track record?

HISTORY AND PROFILE

The discount store format had been first introduced into the American scene in the mid-1950s. This then revolutionary concept, particularly in soft goods, offered merchandise which was directly competitive with the lower end of the department store range. The format grew rapidly in the '60s and '70s, surpassing traditional department stores as largest form of general merchandise retailing in United States.

Hills was founded in 1957 by Stephen Goldberger's father, Herbert, based on a strategy of everyday low pricing, outstanding assortments of soft goods and a full assortment of most other merchandise categories typically carried in discount department stores. The first store was opened in Youngstown, Ohio, and from there Hills expanded to include stores in smaller cities and towns in eastern Ohio, western Pennsylvania and northern West Virginia. In 1964 Hills was acquired by Shoe Corporation of America, Inc. (SCOA). Under the

Professor Walter J. Salmon and Research Associate David Wylie prepared this case as the basis for class discussion rather than to illustrate either effective or ineffective handling of an administrative situation.

leadership of Herbert Goldberger, who remained as president, Hills grew by 1981 to a chain of 93 stores in metropolitan areas as well as small towns in New York, Pennsylvania, Ohio, Virginia, West Virginia, Kentucky, Tennessee, and Indiana. Sales reached $747 million with operating income of $51 million. For a summary of sales and other operating results data, see **Exhibit 1**.

Stephen Goldberger took over the presidency from his father in 1981. Under his aegis the chain grew to 167 stores with sales of $1,670 million and operating profits of $97 million for the fiscal year ending January 28, 1989. By then Hills' territory included fourteen contiguous states and extended as far south as Alabama and Georgia and as far north as Michigan. Stores remained clustered in or near metropolitan areas and in small towns. By early 1989, 50% of all Hills stores were within major metropolitan areas, and 75% were covered by the TV signals emanating from these areas.

Although it had grown enormously in size and geographic coverage since 1957, Hills' target market had remained unchanged. Eighty percent of its customers were still female primarily from lower- to middle-income working class families.

Apart from the continuation of growth, two other rather recent events were of particular importance in the history of Hills. In 1985, a leveraged buyout resulted in the separation of Hills from the rest of SCOA. In 1987, Hills became a highly leveraged corporation with its own listing on the New York Stock Exchange. Then in the fall of 1988, Hills leased 33 former Gold Circle stores situated in Ohio and New York, which had been part of the discount store operations of Federated Department Stores. These stores were modified in layout and ambiance (all carpeting was removed) to conform to the Hills' mold, and reopened in early 1989. Together with eight new stores and one replacement which Hills also planned to open in 1989, this acquisition would raise the store count to 208.

THE STORES

In keeping with Hills' centralized operating philosophy, its stores had a standardized size, layout, decor and assortment of merchandise. The 82,000 square foot prototype was often an anchor tenant in a strip shopping center. The store facade was rather plain, adorned only by a large sign, lit at night, saying "Hills." Access to the store was through two center doors into a lobby that included a recessed small lunch counter featuring hot dogs,

popcorn and similar menu items. Although there were no chairs, a small stand-up counter was available.

As customers entered the 66,000 square foot store selling area from the lobby (see **Exhibit 2**, Store Planogram), they were welcomed by a "greeter" who also responded to any questions. They also found themselves in a clean, neat, utilitarian environment.

Gondolas and long, straight apparel racks designed to carry a maximum amount of merchandise and situated on a tile rather than carpeted floor emphasized the wide assortment and no frills merchandising policy. Signage in primary colors was adequate but not overwhelming, allowing categories of merchandise to be easily found, and reinforcing such themes as EDLP, "Made in the U.S.A.", or seasonal promotions. An occasional sign explained the savings accruing to customers from such Hills' policies as no credit cards and low level lighting. In point of fact the stores seemed adequately lit. The attention to detail stressed by Hills' executives was reflected in the well stocked condition of the racks and gondolas and the immaculateness of the stores.

For the price range in which Hills competed, there was both breadth and depth of family-oriented merchandise. In women's hosiery alone, for instance, there were more than 1,100 stock-keeping units (SKUs). The merchandise was quality name brand goods; there were no seconds or irregulars. In more basic merchandise categories such as underwear and health and beauty aids, Hills also offered lower priced private label products comparable in quality to name brand products. Hills' executives believed that use of private labels reinforced its image as a "provider of value" to its customers.

Excluding jewelry, 47% of the merchandise sold at Hills was still soft goods, which was substantially higher than at most other competing discount chains. This percentage, however, had been gradually declining from a high of about 60%. The increasing levels of hard goods were primarily in toys, health and beauty aids, housewares and home furnishings, electronics, greeting cards, and seasonal categories such as "trim a tree", garden, patio and grill and "back to school".

Hills' executives were inclined to reinforce this trend by shifting the merchandising emphasis to more hard goods particularly since they thought they had exhausted opportunities to add profitability to the soft goods assortments. This predilection, however, had sparked some internal controversy among Hills' executives. Soft goods both at Hills and in the discount department store industry in general had traditionally yielded better gross margins and faster inventory turnover than hard goods. Hard goods, on the other hand, had generated more sales per square foot (see **Exhibit 3**). Resolution of this controversy was one of the issues on Goldberger's agenda.

To offset its refusal to accept credit cards Hills had strongly promoted its layaway plan, which was an option for a person who could or would not pay cash for an item when originally purchasing it. To use this program a customer would take an item (or have it taken if it were too large, such as a patio set or grill) to a layaway counter at the rear of the store. There, they would register their name and payment schedule, pay a one dollar layaway fee and their first installment, and leave the item(s) until it was paid for in full during subsequent visits. There were four layaway registers, staffed according to demand so that there was never too long a wait. An employee would take the layaway item, place it into a special box, label it with the customer's name and then carry it into a secure and dedicated storage area. On average this area occupied 2,500 square feet of double decked first floor space or 5,000 square feet in total. This area could grow to up to 9,000 square feet (or 4,500 square feet of ground space) at the peak of the layaway season. Approximately 13% to 14% of Hills' sales were consummated on layaway at an average amount of $75 per transaction or five times the average cash sale (primarily in single items for hard goods and multiple items for soft goods). The maximum layaway period allowed was ninety days but the average was in the vicinity of 45 to 60 days.

There were obvious labor and space costs associated with the layaway program. Occupancy costs per store, which included rent, utilities, insurance, etc. for the average of 2,500 square feet of double decked ground space amounted to $11,000 annually. Labor costs per store including fringe benefits for operating the layaway department were estimated at $75,000 annually for the equivalent of five full-time employees.

Operation of the layaway plan also entailed determining what to do if a customer discontinued a layaway plan. Approximately 16% of the customers failed to complete their layaway plans in 1988. Ordinarily, the company kept the one dollar layaway charge, added to it a four dollar cancellation fee, and returned the balance of a customer's funds. Sometimes, however, the four dollar fee was waived if the customer had a valid reason for terminating the layaway or if the customer's goodwill was in jeopardy. Merchandise from terminated layaway plans was returned to inventory. Because Hills' executives did not allow layaway plans for seasonal merchandise to extend too far into the season, they believed that the markdown exposure emanating from terminated layaway plans was minimal.

Executives believed that the benefits of the layaway program to customers made it worthwhile, particularly in view of Hills' refusal to accept credit cards. It enabled Hills to avoid credit card expense, which, for bank credit, was about 1½% to 1¾% of credit transactions. Typically in discount department stores credit card transactions were two times an ordinary cash sale and amounted to 16% of total sales. This percentage had been on the rise in recent years.

A side benefit of the layaway program was that it boosted early sales of seasonal merchandise. Consequently, the Hills' central merchandising organization was able to obtain early feedback on merchandising trends and to make adjustments in purchases where possible to reflect more accurately customer demand.

While strongly committed to the layaway plan, Hills' executives did wonder whether they should continue their no credit card policy. In the spring of 1989, they had explored this issue in focus groups conducted in three cities. One was a major metropolitan area in which Hills had for a number of years been the leading discounter. The second market was a metropolitan area that Hills had only recently entered. The third city in which they had done research was described as a smaller mature market. Results did not vary by market and were inconclusive. When pressed, 52 of the 86 people included in the focus groups asserted that Hills should not accept credit cards. "Hills is guilt free shopping" said a customer in a major metropolitan area. Furthermore, the study confirmed that for the large majority of people, credit is not a critical factor in the decision to shop at a particular store. Pricing and selection continued to be the most important factors.

On the other hand, the study found that credit was a factor for those who already shopped in Hills stores. Most current customers admitted that if Hills did take credit cards, they would probably buy more. It appeared that some business was being lost, particularly at Christmas time. Summaries of focus group comments and of two customer surveys are reproduced as **Exhibits 4** and **5**.

Hills endeavored to communicate its unique characteristics to consumers through advertising that focused on the institutional messages of assortment, quality and EDLP rather than on the special sale pricing message embraced by many of Hills' competitors. Hills' strategy revolved around seasonal saturation of market areas with company produced television spots highlighting different features of the Hills' offering, stressing the family orientation and ending with "Hills! . . . Check us out!" The television campaign was coupled with a series of eleven circulars. By comparison, Hills' most important competitors, Wal-Mart and Kmart, distributed about 12 and more than 52 circulars respectively. Of Hills' eleven circulars, three were considered to be of major (Christmas, Back to School and Mother's Day), five of medium, and three of minor importance.

Hills allocated 50% of its advertising dollars to television, 35% to circulars, and the balance to newspaper, radio, and in-store signing. Advertising expense, after deducting cooperative advertising funds received from manufacturers, amounted to 1.9% of sales. A comparable figure for the typical discount department store was over 3%.

Hills' circulars articulated a seasonal theme while promoting appropriate products priced at EDLP. In addition Hills included in its circulars special purchases of merchandise which could be offered at especially attractive prices as long as quantities lasted, and limited time duration discounts, called "instant rebates," arising from passing through to customers manufacturers' promotional allowances. Hills' ads sometimes included price comparisons with competitors, but never the "regularly/now" comparisons so popular in discount department store advertising.

Hills distributed most of its circulars as freestanding inserts in Sunday newspapers, or, where newspaper coverage was inadequate, by direct mail. The increasing concentration of stores in and around metropolitan areas in recent years had helped Hills contain its advertising expense.

STORE OPERATIONS

To help its stores execute the company strategy, Hills had a rather conventional three tier store operations pyramid. At the close of fiscal 1988 (January 31, 1989), Hills' 167 stores were supervised by 23 district managers who reported to 5 regional managers who in turn were supervised by Ray Brinkman, the Senior V.P. of Store Operations. Brinkman was a veteran Hills' employee, having headed store operations since 1966. Also reporting to Brinkman were a vice president of loss prevention, a vice president of operations administration, and a vice president of field merchandising with a staff of soft and hard lines personnel. Their task was, in conjunction with the headquarters merchandising organization, to formulate planograms which showed where and how merchandise was to be displayed in the stores.

Hills' store managers were primarily responsible for achieving the sales budget, providing friendly and good customer service, making sure the stores were well stocked, neat and clean, and controlling shrinkage and store expense, particularly payroll. To achieve these goals, however, they had to engage in additional activities. For example, store managers were responsible for taking the third and subsequent markdowns to liquidate inventory on merchandise that had failed to sell even after the second markdown. Relative to store managers in such chains as Kmart and Wal-Mart, however, Hills' store managers were less involved in sales and merchandising and more focused on operating matters such as store conditions and expense control.

Another important responsibility was supervision of the receiving and marking room. Because Hills operated without warehouses, store receiving and marking rooms were where shipments from vendors were checked against orders to make sure that receipts corresponded with what had been ordered in style and quantity. Also, except for vendor pre-ticketed items, stores were responsible for affixing price tags or labels to the merchandise. Effective receiving and marking operations were vital for the control of shrinkage, the accuracy of inventory reports, and the maintenance of merchandise quality standards. Stores were encouraged, with head office authorization, to return to vendors any merchandise which did not meet quality standards. Speed as well as accuracy was also important in receiving and marking operations. Merchandise which was received but unprocessed was unavailable for sale and could hamper the receipt of other merchandise. Normally, Hills' stores processed vendor shipments within three days, but a backlog of up to seven days was common in peak periods.

The receiving and marking area occupied approximately 9,000 square feet of space in the typical Hills store. Payroll, including fringe benefits, for receiving and marking averaged about $100,000 to $125,000 per store.

Apart from the space for the receiving and marking area, the back room of a typical Hills store included 3,500 square feet of double decked ground space for storage of staple hard line items such as paper goods. The need for most of this space was the result of having vendors drop-ship numerous hard line items. Larger quantities were required to make drop-shipments economical and often there was inadequate space on the selling floor to accommodate an entire shipment.

Back room space in the typical Hills store was in particularly short supply just prior to publication of one of the three major circulars and at the beginning of the Christmas selling season. Therefore Hills rented and parked in the rear of its stores up to twenty 8' by 40' trailers to accommodate the overflow. Trailer rental expense for the chain averaged $300,000 annually. Storing extra inventory in trailers, furthermore, caused labor expense to rise and occasionally made it difficult to locate backup inventory.

Because Hills' store managers were perceived primarily as operations rather than profit center managers, their monthly performance report concentrated on the items for which they were primarily responsible (see **Exhibit 6** for a description of the main reports which store managers received monthly). In addition, their supervisors often discussed the implications of unsold merchandise with them even though they were not responsible for inventory turnover and gross margin. Furthermore, as part of their annual review, district managers usually showed the store manager a more complete profit and loss statement for his or her store.

Hills' store managers were paid at about the mid-point for their peers in discount department stores. Their pay was composed of two elements. Eighty to ninety percent was salary. The balance was bonus, which was based on both corporate profits and an assessment of how well they did in achieving their objectives. These objectives emphasized such matters as payroll control and shrinkage.

Although not exceptionally remunerated, Hills' store managers and, for that matter, most employees exhibited uncommon loyalty relative to their counterparts in other discount department stores. Senior management averaged over fifteen years with Hills. At store level, there was an average of 40 five-year veterans in each store open for five or more years. Consistency and simplicity in strategy, a commitment to organization building, promotional opportunities, the treatment of employees with compassion and dignity, award dinners each year hosted by top management for employees with five or more years of employment (7,000 attended in 1988) and 70% full-time hourly employees at store level all contributed to the human resources environment at Hills.

MERCHANDISING

The merchandise managers and buyers for most departments were headquartered at the main office in Canton, Massachusetts. The women's apparel lines divisional vice president, merchandise managers, and buyers were in New York City.

Hills' merchandising organization was headed by Eugene O'Donnell, Senior Vice President and General Merchandise Manager. O'Donnell had occupied that position since 1985 and previously was Vice President for Hard Goods. Reporting to O'Donnell were two vice presidents for soft lines and two vice presidents for hard lines. Under each of the merchandise vice presidents were 3 to 4 divisional merchandise managers. Several Hills' buyers and a merchandise controller reported to each of the divisional merchandise managers.

Each Hills' buyer was responsible for preparing and executing a seasonal merchandise plan for his or her department. The buyer worked closely with a planner, who set up a seasonal distribution plan on a store by store basis. This plan specified sales by store by week, inventories, receipts, and anticipated markdowns by store by month. The planners then monitored actual performance and adjusted replenishment shipments accordingly. The planners reported to a merchandise controller who, in turn, reported to a divisional merchandise manager.

The merchandising department bought all merchandise, set retail prices, arranged for delivery to individual stores, and determined the magnitude and timing of the first and second markdowns to be taken on particular items. The merchandising department also helped plan prototype product displays, planograms, standard and seasonal layouts and display guidelines. In this activity, they worked with the two directors for field merchandising and their staffs who reported to the vice president for field merchandising. The field merchandise managers then worked with the district managers to adapt the merchandise presentations to the needs of individual districts and stores. The field merchandise managers had the final say on displays.

Different categories of merchandise were bought and distributed in various ways. Soft goods were purchased directly from manufacturers by central buyers at offices in Canton and in New York City. Fashion sensitive merchandise was often drop-shipped to individual stores by United Parcel Service. The balance was distributed through consolidators. Consolidators never took title to the goods. They received shipments from each of the manufacturers in packets designated for individual stores, sometimes held them until the merchandise was needed for sales, and then combined them for delivery to the individual stores.

In contrast with soft goods, the purchasing arrangements for hard goods were somewhat more diverse. About 80% of hard goods were purchased direct from vendors and again, either drop shipped or routed through consolidators to individual stores. On hard goods also, the consolidators often performed a storage function, particularly for such seasonal merchandise as toys and Christmas trees and trimmings. The balance of the hard goods, particularly smaller items such as stationery, hardware and automotive, and some health and beauty aids (HBA) and candy, was replenished from wholesalers or jobbers as they were sometimes called. These organizations visited individual stores as frequently as weekly, ascertained the quantities needed for replenishment based on deducting stock on the shelves from "stock up to" targets established in Canton by headquarters merchants, and then shipped the merchandise to the individual stores. The use of wholesalers eliminated the need for backroom stocks in stores on merchandise which jobbers re-supplied.

Rapid and accurate communications between headquarters and stores was an essential element of Hills' merchandising and logistical arrangements. One facet of Hills' communication system was four or five headquarters connected CRTs, or terminals, located in the receiving and marking room, manager's office, and other locations in each store. This system enabled headquarters to keep each store abreast of what was on order for them and to communicate information to the stores on merchandise in transit. It also provided stores with initial retail price and markdown instructions. Headquarters personnel could electronically generate a receiving document in each store for impending receipts which included instructions for printing price labels or tags.

Store personnel used the same system to communicate to headquarters information on actual receipts. These data were essential for maintaining accurate information on the central computer for merchandise on order and on hand by stock-keeping unit (SKU) and by store. Such data also enabled Hills to pay its bills on a timely basis and earn the customary discounts for prompt payment. In addition to these merchandising purposes, this same communications system was used for two-way communication of a wide range of operating information and for electronic mail.

The other facet of the Hills' headquarters/store merchandise information and communication system was the point of sale (POS) terminals in the checkout lanes in each store. Since the price tags or labels for all merchandise included identification numbers, checkers recorded these codes for each item sold or returned, or entered a generic code when an item code was missing, illegible or unacceptable to the POS terminal. Every night the day's transaction data were automatically transmitted through a modem to the home office computer. This information provided the basis for weekly records of unit sales by SKU by store. By combining beginning inventories for the previous week with data on receipts from vendors and sales, the computer also generated inventory on hand by store by SKU.

Accurate store sales and inventory data were critical to Hills' centralized merchandising system. Executives were quick to admit, however, that the quality of that data could be improved with scanning systems which would, in addition to a number of other important advantages, vastly reduce failure or inaccuracy in entering SKU data. Hills was planning to introduce scanning systems experimentally in a few stores in 1989 and convert to scanning in all stores by 1991. Commenting on the usefulness of the POS system, Steve Goldberger said: "we rely primarily for sales and inventory information on our POS system although we also receive a continuous flow of information, corrections, and suggestions from store managers."

THE CHANGING BUSINESS ENVIRONMENT

The business environment in which Hills operated was undergoing a transformation as demographic, technological, and competitive changes converged to force Hills' management to consider changing the way in which they did business.

Demographically two issues confronted Hills. As marketers they were confronted with a decline in the number of teenagers. This decline was alleged to be an important factor in the industrywide decrease in junior sportswear sales beginning in the fall of 1987. The falloff in teenagers, however, had even more profound implications for Hills' store operations. Increasingly there was a shortage of entry level young people willing to work as full or part timers in stores.

Concurrent with these demographic changes was the technological revolution in information and communication systems which was changing the way retailers did business. Among these developments were sophisticated scanning systems, improved computer-related tools and decision support systems for the management of merchandising and inventories, and headquarters/store satellite communication systems. These and other developments created the potential for dramatically improved execution in store/headquarters/vendor communications, tighter inventory controls and more accurate and faster replenishment systems. Those retailers taking the fullest advantage of this potential were developing a competitive edge.

Among these retailers was Wal-Mart, an Arkansas headquartered chain of 1,250 discount department stores whose original stores were mainly in smaller southern cities. In more recent years, Wal-Mart had increased the size of its stores, migrated into larger cities, and had begun to expand northward. Wal-Mart was becoming an increasing threat to Hills. Historically, Hills had competed most directly with Kmart and Ames Department Stores. Hills had competed successfully against these retailers by having, for comparable merchandise, the most competitive prices and the best assortment of women's apparel in the discount industry. In addition, both of these competitors were sale price oriented as opposed to EDLP, which was another advantage for Hills.

As Wal-Mart expanded into more northern states, it was increasingly coming head to head with Hills. Furthermore, in January of 1989, Wal-Mart entered Ohio, which together with Pennsylvania, represented the heart of Hills' territory. Nevertheless in 1989 Wal-Mart and Hills would compete in only two Ohio trading areas. Wal-Mart had EDLP, credit, progressive human resource management (including profit sharing and considerable delegation of authority to the store level) and efficient and technologically advanced organizational and distribution systems. The latter was built around ten hard lines and three soft goods distribution centers strategically dispersed among Wal-Mart stores. Eighty percent of Wal-Mart's merchandise flowed through these distribution centers.

Wal-Mart and Hills differed in some important respects. Whereas soft goods constituted 47% of Hills' sales, only 35% of Wal-Mart's sales were in soft goods. Furthermore, Wal-Mart's soft goods were more basic, whereas Hills' were noticeably more fashionable. Wal-Mart, however, was trying to increase the proportion and fashion content of its soft goods.

Although both companies were proponents of EDLP, one Wall Street analyst estimated that on average Wal-Mart's prices were about 2% below Hills'. This difference was entirely attributable to lower Wal-Mart prices on HBA and some similar small hard goods items, on which Wal-Mart was the acknowledged discount department store price leader. This same analyst estimated that Wal-Mart priced 10% below Hills on HBA merchandise. He attributed this difference to Hills' method of acquisition of such items, which was through a combination of drop-shipping, consolidators, and wholesalers. In contrast, Wal-Mart bought all of its merchandise in these categories directly from vendors and routed them through its warehouse network. This analyst also concluded that on an everyday storewide basis Hills was priced 2% above Wal-Mart but 9% below Kmart and 10% below Ames.

Hills was already competing with Wal-Mart in southern Tennessee and other southern markets. Judging how Hills was faring in this competition involved separating the impact of Wal-Mart from Hills' overall southern experience.

Hills' average store sales in the south were typically lower than in the north. Less need on the part of southern customers for a cold weather wardrobe and the inclination of Southerners to remain loyal for apparel needs to smaller department stores which carried less expensive merchandise than traditional department stores were the reasons offered by Hills' executives. Because of the lower than average performance of many of its southern stores, Hills had refrained from opening new southern stores for the last several years.

When competing directly with Wal-Mart, Hills had experienced mixed results. Usually Wal-Mart had little impact on the sales of soft goods. On the other hand, when an existing Hills' store was confronted with Wal-Mart competition, for the first twelve months sales of hard lines fell but then resumed normal growth.

In addition to Wal-Mart, there were two other major national discount department stores which were growing and thriving: Kmart and Target. Kmart was a formidable competitor with its 2,273 stores, but it had been growing at only 1.0% per year in gross square feet and 6.3% in sales over the last five years. Equivalent numbers for Target were 14.2% and 17.1% as it pursued its national expansion strategy.

In addition to the intensification of competition within the discount store industry, new formats of category

Summary data for 1987 for Hills and some of its competitors are shown in the following table:

	Hills	Target	Kmart	Wal-Mart	Jamesway	Roses	Caldor	Venture
Sales	$1,512	$5,306	$22,140	$13,177	$701	$1,337	$1,502	$1,208
Number of stores	151	317	2,273	1,114	111	237	116	70
Compound growth (%)	3.8	4.0	3.6	11.0	6.0	3.2	7.7	0.9
Gross margin (%)	29.0	n/a	27.9	23.4	29.9	21.8	n/a	n/a
Profits before interest and tax (%)	7.5	6.1	5.6	8.2	4.0	2.9	3.7	5.8
Sales per square foot	$ 126	$ 168	$ 183	$ 213	$110	$ 113	$ 140	$ 163

dominant specialty discounters, power retailers, and off-price stores were growing in importance and threatening to erode Hills' market share in certain categories. Examples of such formats included Toys R Us, Kids R Us, Circuit City, Marshalls and T.J. Maxx. The strength of warehouse clubs, such as Price Club, and hypermarkets was also seen as a potential threat, as were the major chains such as Sears, which had recently switched to EDLP.

SUMMARY

Against the backdrop of this external environment, Hills' history and recent results, and its new status as a leveraged buy-out, Steve Goldberger wrestled with what changes Hills should undertake in strategy and operations. The issues of the future emphasis on hard versus soft lines, whether to alter Hills' no credit policy, and what implications, if any, these decisions had for Hills' approach to advertising particularly intrigued Goldberger. Moreover, Goldberger also did not regard Hills' operating practices as sacrosanct. In particular, he wondered whether Hills' growth and other factors argued for any departure from Hills' inclination to centralize most merchandise decision making.

Finally, Goldberger acknowledged that an argument could be made for departing from Hills' "no warehouse" philosophy. A consultant had recommended that Hills construct or acquire two 775,000 square foot warehouses for hard and basic soft goods at a cost of $35 to $40 million each. Almost all Hills' stores would be within 200 miles of one of these warehouses assuming they were correctly situated.

Lease financing could be arranged for these warehouses. What Goldberger didn't know, despite some reassuring estimates from the consultants, was whether the hard and soft savings from operation of the warehouses would justify the investment. Hard savings could arise from several sources. The use of two major warehouses would lower inbound transportation costs compared to the current system of the combination drop-shipping, consolidation, and resupply through wholesalers. Hills' executives estimated that in-bound transportation on hard lines currently amounted to $40 million, although this estimate was subject to error since some vendors included delivery in their selling prices.

The second source of hard savings would be a reduction in store space and personnel dedicated to receiving, marking, and storing and removing inventory from store reserve stocks. While this savings was hard to estimate accurately, it would come entirely from the 8½% of sales at store level now consumed by hourly labor.

Lower merchandise costs on goods bought from wholesalers was the third potential area of savings. Hills believed that the wholesalers who serviced them took a markup which ranged from 5% to 6% and from 12% to 14%, depending upon lines of merchandise. By buying directly from manufacturers, Hills believed it could recapture this markup or further reduce prices.

Apart from these hard savings, Hills' executives thought that central warehouses could also provide some more difficult to quantify advantages. One was lower purchase prices from vendors since they would now ship in bulk to warehouses rather than in quantities suitable for individual stores. The second advantage was the possibility of lower markdowns since reserve stocks would be more flexibly positioned in central warehouses rather than in the back rooms of individual stores. In a similar vein, fewer stockouts might occur because backup stocks could be rapidly shifted to stores with unexpectedly high selling rates on certain items.

In view of the reliance on distribution centers by Wal-Mart and other leading competitors for soft goods as well as hard goods, Goldberger wondered whether the consultant's proposal was sufficiently comprehensive. On the other hand, Goldberger recognized that trying to change too much too quickly at Hills could disturb a formula that had produced superior results since almost the advent of discount department stores. What changes, if any, Goldberger mused, would sustain and possibly further improve Hills' performance without jeopardizing the unique culture that for many years had helped deliver superior performance.

Exhibit 1
Summary Operating and Financial Information (in thousands)

	Fiscal Year Ended:					
	January 28, 1989		January 30, 1988		January 31, 1987	
Net sales	$ 1,670,866	100.0%	$ 1,514,329	100.0%	$ 1,343,102	100.0%
Cost of sales	$ 1,196,863	71.6%	$ 1,077,645	71.2%	$ 947,798	70.6%
Gross margin	$ 474,003	28.4%	$ 436,684	28.8%	$ 395,304	29.4%
Selling and administrative expenses[a]	$ 376,350	22.5%	$ 333,149	22.0%	$ 300,892	22.4%
Operating profit before nonrecurring inventory charge	$ 97,653	5.9%	$ 103,535	6.8%	$ 94,412	7.0%
Nonrecurring inventory charge					$ (41,344)	(3.1%)
Other expense, net (principally interest on long-term debt and capital leases)	$ (79,077)	(4.7%)	$ (69,688)	(4.6%)	$ (67,568)	(5.0%)
Net income (loss) before income taxes	$ 18,576	1.2%	$ 33,847	2.2%	$ (14,500)	(1.1%)
Inventories	$ 268,846		$ 232,675			
Total current assets	288,627		251,667			
Total assets	899,529		764,882			
Trade payables	111,953		125,774			
Total current liabilities	275,605		259,490			
All other liabilities	587,841		483,963			
Preferred stock	25,371		23,539			
Common equity	10,712		(2,110)			

a   Includes depreciation and amortization for 1989, 1988, and 1987 of $37,959, $34,459, and $35,507, respectively.

Exhibit 2
Store Planogram

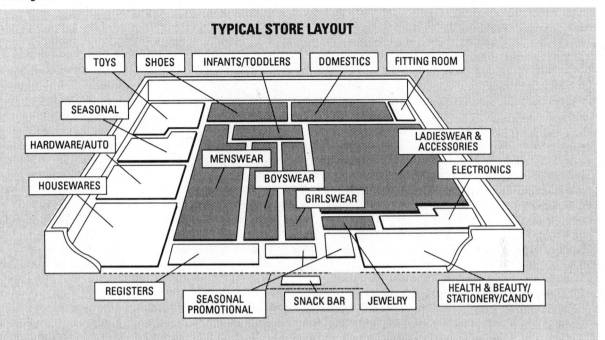

TYPICAL STORE LAYOUT

TOYS SHOES INFANTS/TODDLERS DOMESTICS FITTING ROOM

SEASONAL

HARDWARE/AUTO

HOUSEWARES

MENSWEAR

BOYSWEAR

GIRLSWEAR

LADIESWEAR & ACCESSORIES

ELECTRONICS

REGISTERS

SEASONAL PROMOTIONAL

SNACK BAR

JEWELRY

HEALTH & BEAUTY/ STATIONERY/CANDY

Note: In their more recent stores, the snack bar had been moved to a corner of the entryway where it was less prominently situated

Exhibit 3
Department Productivity Data—Fiscal Year 1989

Department	Sales (thousands)	Growth Rate[a]	Gross Profit (%)	Sales per Sq. Foot[b]	Inventory Turnover	GM/ROI[c]	GM/Sq. Foot
Ladies' Apparel and Accessories	$ 283,169	(3.3%)	31.8%	$151	5.4	2.52	$ 48
Girls' and Boys'	189,719	3.6	32.7	130	6.1	2.96	43
Men's and Basics	255,062	2.3	30.1	186	4.7	2.00	56
Total soft lines	729,954	0.4	31.8	154	5.2	2.42	49
Records, Christmas, and HBA	299,859	6.6	27.7	438	4.8	1.83	121
Toys	162,218	0.7	29.0	206	2.9	1.18	60
Jewelry and Home Entertainment	108,148	7.5	29.8	427	3.7	1.57	127
Housewares	142,073	10.4	27.0	161	4.5	1.66	43
Lawn, Auto, Hardware	109,793	1.7	28.9	143	3.3	1.34	41
Total hard lines	822,091	5.2	27.5	233	3.9	1.48	64
Total hard and soft lines	$ 1,552,041	2.9%	29.5%	$188	4.4	1.84	$ 55

a Growth rate in stores open for more than a year between 1988 and 1989
b Sales per square foot of selling space only
c Gross Margin Dollars divided by Inventory Dollars before deducting payables

Exhibit 4
Focus Group Comments[a]

- Consumers feel that "compare at" prices are not entirely believable. They feel that the retailer uses inflated original prices in order to make their regular prices look better than they actually are.

- Many people believe that American-made is not a reason to buy. They look for the best value for their money.

- Many people will use credit cards at Christmas, even though they may limit their use at other times of the year.

- The use of credit cards for gift giving is significant. Events that occur throughout the year, such as birthdays, baby showers, Mother's Day, Father's Day, etc., represent an unplanned purchase to the consumer. Hence, they may put purchases for these occasions on their credit card.

- Consumers will use their credit card to take advantage of an item which is currently on sale. Even though they may not be able to afford the merchandise at that time, they will buy it on credit in order to get the sale price.

- For the large majority of people, credit is not a critical factor in their decision to shop at a particular store. Pricing and selection continue to be the most important factors.

- The majority of people do use layaway. While there are some who would use credit instead of layaway, the majority would continue to use layaway. It gives them a good feeling to know that when they pick up that item, all payments have been completed. Layaway will still get extensive use, particularly at Christmas. Layaway is a way for parents to keep Christmas gifts out of sight of children.

- The number one criticism of retailers was a lack of visible and knowledgeable sales floor help. Many of the consumers cited their frustrations when there is no sales clerk available to answer questions. Also, many will not wait in line at the service desk when all they are seeking is information.

- A good return policy influences where the consumer will shop. This is particularly true for those who buy clothing for themselves and for their children. Many times, they will not try on the clothes while they are in the store; hence, they may return the items to get the proper size.

- People do not see major differences between discount stores.

a Source: In 1989, Hills conducted focus groups of discount store consumers in several cities where it had stores. Participants were selected by independent agencies and the groups moderated by Hills' employees, although participants were not aware of Hills' involvement in the research. The above comments summarize the results of this research.

Exhibit 5
Survey Results[a]

Who Is the Hills Customer?

The key characteristics of the Hills customer are:

- She is a woman (80% of our customers are women).

- She is between the ages of 18 and 49 (74% of our women customers are between 18 and 49).

- She is married (65% of our female customers are married).

- She has children (70% of our female customers have children).

- Her children are young (32% of these children are ages 6 or under).

- She works (60% or our female customers work, at least part time).

- She works full time (83% of our female customers who work, work full time).

- Her household income is slightly below the national median:

Less than $15,000	28%
$15,000 to $21,000	25%
$21,000 to $30,000	26%
$30,000 and more	22%

- She shops Hills frequently (60% of our customers shop at our stores at least every two weeks).

- She shops close to home (50% of our customers travel five miles or less to their Hills store).

a   Twice a year, Hills conducted 200 random exit interviews in each of its stores. The above profile of the "Hills customer" is a composite of all the exit interviews conducted at the 208 stores in 1989.

Exhibit 6
Reports Sent to General Managers

Accounting Department

Comparative Sales Ranking Store by Department (Monthly)
Bad Check Balances (Monthly)

Methods

Freight Processing (Weekly)

Field Operations

Snack Bar Sales (Monthly via General Letter)
Sales and Payroll Analysis (Weekly)
Management by Objectives Recap Report (Monthly)

Cashier Shortages
Apprehensions
Bad Check Totals

Consumer Affairs

Letters to President Recap (Monthly)
Exception Report Above Average Complaints (Year End)

Personnel

Targeted Job Tax Credits (Quarterly via General Letter)

Case 2

BABBAGE'S, AMERICA'S SOFTWARE HEADQUARTERS

Babbage's was a fast growing chain of retail stores that specialized in the sale of software for computers used in the home. Formed in Dallas, Texas, in 1983, by early 1989 there were 130 stores geographically clustered in high traffic regional shopping malls. They offered a broad, constantly changing selection of over 1,700 titles of entertainment, educational and productivity software at everyday low prices. The atmosphere was clean, modern and uncluttered. Babbage's emphasized responsive, enthusiastic customer service to make the shopping experience relaxed and enjoyable for new customers who were apprehensive about computer software and for repeat customers who appreciated complete selection and knowledgeable assistance.

Babbage's was formed by Gary Kusin, a former VP and general merchandise manager of a traditional department store division of a large retail group, and Jim McCurry, formerly a partner of a large international management consulting firm. Both had received their MBAs from Harvard. Their goal was to make Babbage's the dominant player in the retail home computer software market through a clustered expansion into all appropriate regional malls.

Although the expansion was challenging, it was manageable. McCurry and Kusin had been able to anticipate many of the problems usually associated with rapid growth, and had tried to build into the organization the ability to evolve with growth. They still had lingering fears, however, of unforeseen events which could blindside their strategy.

THE STORES

Babbage's had a distinctive store design as part of its merchandising strategy. The stores featured wide openings in order to be inviting to mall traffic. (See **Exhibit 1**.) Each had constantly running video monitors which showed brief excerpts from many of the popular software titles.

The stores catered to a broad range of customer types which generally represented the top end in economics and education of the mall shopper profile, and who had personal computers in the home. Women and children tended to be the buyers of educational and entertainment software, while professional men were more apt to buy productivity and higher end entertainment software. There were, however, numerous exceptions to this trend. In addition, some businesses were regular clients, but they represented only a minor segment of Babbage's business.

The typical store had 1,250 square feet of selling space and 250 square feet of office/back room space. Inventory was all on display and easily accessible to the public (with the exception of the Nintendo cartridges which,

Research Associate David Wylie prepared this case under the supervision of Professor Walter J. Salmon as the basis for class discussion rather than to illustrate either effective or ineffective handling of an administrative situation.

because they were apt to be stolen, were now kept behind the counter).

Because its stores were in a familiar, comfortable shopping environment, executives at Babbage's felt that the apprehension often associated with computer software purchasing was reduced. To the maximum extent possible, stores were clustered to allow for more effective district and regional management, which resulted in higher standards of store operations and customer service. (See **Exhibit 2**, Organization Chart. Locations of the stores are shown on the map in **Exhibit 3**.)

Each store had only two full-time employees: a salaried manager and assistant manager who shared in the daily operations of the store. They were expected to give friendly, informed advice to customers rather than to actively promote individual items. Indeed, there were no commissions or bonuses since it was felt that hard selling might result in excessively aggressive customer service. Overall compensation, however, was competitive with other specialty stores in each market. Given the focus of the product line and the arrangement of the store, much of the time one person could staff the store. During busier times on evenings and weekends, several part timers were scheduled to supplement the staff.

For stores which had been open for more than one year, fixed costs averaged $46,400 for store and district management payroll and benefits, $72,500 for occupancy expenses, and $15,600 for depreciation. Variable costs as a percentage of sales were: 1.92% for store part-time employees and benefits, .77% for store supplies and miscellaneous expenses, and .97% for distribution payroll and supplies.

THE BABBAGE'S PRODUCT LINE

At any one time the Babbage's assortment of software consisted of about 1,700 titles per store. These titles were categorized as entertainment, productivity and education, representing 53%, 27% and 5% of sales respectively. Computer supplies and accessories completed the offering, representing 15% of sales (no computers or other major hardware items were sold at Babbage's). Many of the more basic supply categories such as floppy disks and disk holders were sold under Babbage's private label. The average price of all items sold in Fiscal 1989 was $23.

Babbage's systematically discounted all of its merchandise from the publisher's list price. The top ten best-sellers in each category were priced at 25% off list

and were promoted monthly in store displays and mailings to a list of 450,000 recent customers. All other titles were discounted 15% to 20% with the exception of certain best-selling business software packages such as Lotus 1-2-3 and Microsoft Word which were discounted 40%. In addition, The "Babbage's Discount Club" provided customers with a $15 discount on a future purchase after they had made purchases of 10 items priced at $15 or more. The cost of this discount club program, including discounts and administrative expenses, was less than one percent of total sales.

Unlike many of its competitors, Babbage's had no computers on hand to use in sampling software. This arrangement relieved store personnel of the distraction of maintaining hardware and training customers on a specific software item. Thus they could devote their time to providing customers with more general advice. In addition, the temptation of mall shoppers to use the stores as free entertainment centers was eliminated. A very liberal return policy allowed customers to try out software at home rather than at the store and return it if they were dissatisfied.

The life cycle of software was partially dependent upon that of the host computer but also had characteristics, particularly in the entertainment segment, similar to the fiction section of bookstores. Many new titles were introduced each year. Having the best of the new titles in stock was essential to maintaining the interest of the mall customers.

In 1988, approximately 2,000 new titles were introduced into the Babbage's assortment. These titles were ordered for all the stores after a preliminary screening by Terri Favell, vice president of merchandising, to exclude easily identifiable losers. The POS system then tracked sales by item and by store. It adjusted target inventory levels for each title and store to seasonally adjusted multiples of prior weeks' sales. The MIS system generated semi-weekly replenishment orders which were then delivered from the distribution center.

The distribution center, situated in Dallas next to the corporate headquarters, tried to hold sufficient buffer inventories to avoid store stockouts. Orders to vendors were placed weekly and, except for Nintendo software, delivered within a period of three to ten days. Terms were net 30.

If a title did not meet the company's minimum rate of sale requirements, it was delisted. A reasonable number of unsold copies could be returned to vendors for a full credit. This return policy was typical in the software and music publishing industries and reduced the exposure to markdowns.

Seasonal demand characteristics varied considerably among categories, although sales of all software were heavily concentrated around Christmas, particularly entertainment software. In this category, there was always a buoyant market for new titles to gratify those consumers who tired quickly of a particular software item. The purchase of entertainment software, the prices of which ranged from $7.99 to $52.46, was often an add on or an impulse decision for the mall shopper.

Nintendo software was a part of this segment, but displayed unique characteristics of its own. "It is a toy, but it is more than a toy: it is a whole new medium, an immensely powerful agent for the dissemination of culture. Eleven million of them (special computer players required for the game) have been sold in the United States in the last three years, and by the end of the year they are expected to be in 20 million American homes. Nearly 50 million of the indispensable game cartridges are expected to be sold this year alone" (*Newsweek Magazine*, March 6, 1989).

The Nintendo Entertainment Systems sold, depending upon the model, for between $80 and $100, but Babbage's did not carry these systems because of the belief that any sales of hardware would detract from its specialty focus on software. Babbage's did, however, carry Nintendo software cartridges, priced from $25 to $40, for use on the Nintendo systems. Because of the dramatic growth in the market for these cartridges, they had grown to approximately 16% of the company's sales. Some market analysts expressed concern about Babbage's growing dependence upon such a potentially volatile product.

Although numerous companies designed and sold software for use on the Nintendo system, the manufacture of the cartridges themselves was controlled exclusively by Nintendo through licensing agreements, and the supply of cartridges was not always sufficient to meet demand. The popularity of Nintendo was such that a user would, even if other hardware was available, often choose to forgo an alternative entertainment purchase.

Home productivity software, representing approximately 22% of Babbage's total sales, consisted primarily of programs for home use and included programs such as those used for word processing, home finance, home record keeping, etc. Prices for home productivity software ranged from $8 to $80, life cycles were much longer than for entertainment software and selling was much more technically oriented.

Babbage's also stocked the best-selling business productivity software titles which represented approximately 5% of sales. Prices for business software ranged from $100 to $500, product life cycles tended to be much longer than those for all forms of home software and gross margins seldom exceeded 15%. Kusin and McCurry recognized that business software was not fully consistent with its specialty focus on software for home use, but believed that stocking the best selling titles in the business category was necessary to maintain the image of a complete software store.

Educational software, representing approximately 5% of Babbage's sales, had life cycles and selling characteristics similar to those for home productivity software. Prices ranged from $8 to $50.

ORGANIZATION AND MANAGEMENT

McCurry and Kusin maintained active control of the Babbage's organization. McCurry was Chairman of the Board, and responsible for store operations, finance, MIS systems design and personnel. Kusin was president and directed the company's merchandising, distribution, and real estate functions.

In a fast growing company such as Babbage's, an adequate inventory of individuals qualified to be store managers was critical. Mary Evans, VP Stores, focused her attention on this effort as well as store operations.

Prospective managers were recruited from the "Big Ten" and similar colleges. Management trainees received introductory training conducted by the company's field trainers and were assigned to specific stores to work with more experienced managers. All promotions to store managers, and from there district and zone management positions, were from within. Because of Babbage's rapid expansion, promotional opportunities were an important element in the company's incentive program.

Store managers reported to the central organization through district managers (DMs) and regional managers (RMs). The role of these individuals was to maintain operating and customer service standards, spread the "faith," disseminate merchandising and operations information and promote corporate belonging. They also gathered information about store operations for the headquarters staff.

All DMs and RMs had been store managers and understood the issues which faced the latter. In recent months, the issue of how to make the job of current store managers more fulfilling was receiving considerable attention, because it was apparent that the high incidence of promotional opportunities could not continue indefinitely.

Another element in Babbage's store operations was its MIS systems, which had been continually improved to handle as much of the routine information flow and processing as possible. Every night, sales information was transmitted by each store's POS system to the headquarters MIS system which twice per week would generate suggested replenishment orders.

An MIS systems design department reported directly to McCurry. This department reflected McCurry and Kusin's belief that software should support operations and thus should evolve in parallel with the growth of the business. This department was currently developing a new generation of software to more efficiently process the inventory, distribution and merchandising requirements of the 1,700 constantly changing titles.

Terri Favell, vice president of merchandising, reported to Kusin. The responsibilities of Favell and her staff included choosing new and delisting old titles, dealing with vendors, advertising, and screening both MIS generated orders intended for vendors and distributions suggested for the stores.

Babbage's purchased inventory from approximately 130 vendors. Orders were placed directly by phone with the larger software publishers or with distributors for the offerings of smaller publishers. No more than 8% of purchases were from a single supplier (including Nintendo cartridges, which were bought from a number of sources).

Babbage's was exceptionally important to software publishers and wholesalers as a channel of distribution. They therefore bought at advantageous prices, received promotional support, and received superior access to titles in short supply. Babbage's purchased 85% and 15% of their inventory, respectively, from these sources.

Favell found that sales themselves were the best criterion for making buying decisions. Virtually all titles were ordered for a trial period and kept in active inventory by the automatic replenishment system if sales were above a minimal level in any given store and above an aggregate level for all stores. Another basis for adding titles to active inventory was the daily store assessment sheets upon which store managers would note specific customer requests or questions. These sheets were forwarded to headquarters weekly for study by all management levels in operations and merchandising. Kusin and McCurry personally read all of these sheets to improve their insight into sales and operations.

The distribution function was led by Bob Young, who had started as manager of distribution in 1986. All merchandise was received into the new 38,000 square foot central distribution facility in Dallas, and distributed to the stores by common carriers twice each week.

Since up to 185,000 pieces of software or other items might be received and shipped in a busy week, effective receiving and distribution were critical. The distribution center was equipped with a state of the art "Flow-Rack System," which Babbage's executives believed had contributed greatly to increased picking efficiency and accuracy. The distribution center capacity was planned to accommodate requirements for the foreseeable future.

Acquiring new sites for expansion was of great importance to the company. Kusin worked personally with Ek Spieckerman, a real estate consultant who devoted virtually all his efforts to Babbage's growth. Most of the Babbage's new locations were obtained through his efforts. Spieckerman had been vice president of Real Estate and Construction for Radio Shack during its expansion from 180 to almost 6,000 locations.

Obtaining prime locations in high traffic malls and establishing good relationships with shopping center developers who might own malls in various locations around the country was critical. Within an environment in which only one or two software stores might be allowed in a mall, the preemptive advantage of an aggressive real estate expansion policy was exceptionally important.

Mall owners appreciated the high sales per square foot generated by Babbage's stores, the limited cannibalization of sales of other tenants and the diversity which they added to the mall shopping experience. A history of good comparable store growth added to Babbage's attractiveness.

COMMUNICATIONS

In the fast paced environment of Babbage's growth, communications between the various organizational elements was critical. During the first years, very informal, open-door meetings or telephone conversations provided the vehicle for discussing changes. But as the organization had grown this "phone culture" had become less feasible.

Now at 9:30 every Monday morning Kusin and McCurry both met with the heads of all departments to discuss ongoing projects and problems, plans for the week, sales and margin results, new store openings, and any other items of interest.

This meeting was followed by a real estate meeting which included Kusin, Spieckerman, Evans, the Vice President—Construction, the Personnel Manager and the Lease Administrator. The primary purpose of this meeting was to ensure that all factors relating to the opening of new stores (lease negotiation, construction, staffing, training, etc.) were properly coordinated.

At noon, McCurry met with Evans, the Manager—Store Administration (who reported to Evans), the Personnel Manager and the Manager—Special Projects. At 1:30, this group would have a conference call with the three RMs. Upon completion of this call, the RMs would call their six or seven DMs individually to discuss plans for the week and to gather responses or comments to communicate to headquarters through their superiors. After talking to the RMs, the DMs would call the store managers.

Several other devices were also used to facilitate communications. A new voice mail system had recently been installed, simplifying the dissemination of information among employees. The POS system in every store also produced a daily tape of price changes, news and announcements. Weekly, *The Babbage Bulletin* was published with news of rankings in store sales, employee promotions, and scheduled events. A more complete newsletter was distributed every other month.

Fundamental to communication at Babbage's, however, was an open-door policy. Any employee could always call managers on any level, including Kusin and McCurry.

PERFORMANCE

Since it was founded in 1983, Babbage's had grown to achieve net income of $2,772,000 on sales of $58,750,000 in fiscal 1989 (YE January 28, 1989). During fiscal 1989, the number of stores had grown from 58 to 108 and average sales per store had grown from $707,000 to $754,000. An additional 50 stores were scheduled to be opened in fiscal 1990.

Babbage's financed this growth initially with loans and then with venture capital equity totaling $11,000,000 and then with a 1988 public offering of $21,000,000 of which $7,000,000 was used to repay all outstanding debt.

Recent Performance	1986	1987	1988	1989
Net sales (000)	$5,211	$9,883	$29,340	$58,750
Net income (000)	$(670)	$8	$1,168	$2,772
Stores opened during the period	7	7	35	50
Stores open at end of period	16	23	58	108
Average annual sales per store (000)	$445	$511	$707	$754
Sales per sq. ft. selling space	$366	$428	$585	$623
Percent increase of comp. store sales	9.5	30.8	31.3	11.3

McCurry and Kusin believed that Babbage's success to date was due in large measure to a wide range of advice given to them in the company's early stages by H. Ross Perot, who guaranteed the initial debt financing, and Ralph Rogers, himself a 1947 graduate of Harvard Business School and the founder and Chairman Emeritus of Texas Industries, a large publicly traded company. In addition they credited each with specific advice which they considered critical.

To Perot, they gave credit for recommending that they start and operate the first store themselves, they personally conduct every aspect of the company's operations themselves and that they keep staff to a minimum. They continued to adhere to this advice. They had, for example, windowless offices next to the distribution center, and they prided themselves on there being no secretaries among the more than 1,000 employees. Kusin and McCurry, like all other employees, used only the personal computers at their desks for correspondence.

To Rogers, they gave credit for encouraging them to believe in the future of their market, even when short-term prospects made the company's survival appear questionable, and for recommending an EDLP (everyday low pricing) policy, which, when introduced in 1983, was unusual for a mall-based specialty store.

As of early 1989, the Board of Directors consisted of Kusin and McCurry and the following outside members:

John Friedman, 35, and Ernest Pomerantz, 46, managing directors of E.M. Warburg, Pincus & Co., an investment banking firm that provided specialized financial advisory and counseling services and owned approximately 28.8% of the Babbage's common stock.

W. Mitt Romney, 41, a general and managing partner of Bain Capital Partners and of Bain Venture Capital, who jointly owned about 7.4% of the Babbage's common stock.

David Waters, 56, CEO and director of Jos. A. Bank Clothiers, an apparel manufacturer and retailer. Waters had been executive vice president of General Mills, Inc. and president of its specialty retailing group.

THE AGGREGATE DEMAND FOR CONSUMER SOFTWARE

The market for consumer software was closely linked with the penetration of personal computers (PCs) into the home (IBM and compatibles, Apple, Commodore, and most recently the game-only computer, Nintendo). Demand for PCs was in direct proportion to their performance/price ratio. PCs installed in the home which sold for under $3,000 grew between 1984 and 1987 from 8% to 18% penetration of U.S. households or 18.1 million units, as prices dropped and performance increased. In, 1988, however, prices for PCs remained quite flat. The growth in penetration was commensurately reduced, despite continued improvement in performance and new software applications. Industry growth in software sales fell to under 10%. Industry analysts, however, expected increased performance and resumption of price reductions to be the dominant longer term trend, with a subsequent increase in the user base.

COMPETITION

Babbage's faced several kinds of competition which varied considerably by product category. In the entertainment category, Babbage's executives noted the presence of indirect competition in the form of alternate forms of home entertainment: television, cable and video cassette rentals and sales. More direct competition came from those retail and mail order competitors that sold computer software. These direct competitors included general merchandise stores, noncomputer specialty stores, other computer software specialty stores (which were generally, but not all, in shopping malls) and computer hardware stores, including the new arrival, the computer superstore.

General merchandise stores which sold computer software, primarily in the educational and entertainment categories, included discount stores such as Target and Wal-Mart and large department stores like Sears and Lechmere. Although some of these competitors had their own departments, many chose to lease out departments or turn them over to rack jobbers, who maintained the displays in exchange for a higher wholesale selling price. General merchandise stores generally had low retail prices but limited selection and service, and were losing market share of home computer software.

Non-computer specialty stores such as Child World and Kay-Bee Toys offered selections of Nintendo cartridges at prices comparable to Babbage's. Toys R Us additionally offered selections of the more popular entertainment and educational software for personal computers. In all categories except for Nintendo, however, the assortments and service at these stores were inferior to Babbage's and customers tended to purchase software only as add-ons to the toys for which the chains were known. Assortments of Nintendo titles at these stores, however, were equivalent to those at Babbage's and often represented destination purchases. These stores were not viewed as threatening competitors.

Babbage's executives believed that the most direct competition came from other software specialty stores located in regional malls (Electronic Boutique, Software Etc. and Waldensoftware). To a somewhat lesser extent Egghead Discount Software (Egghead), which was located in strip malls, offered competition as well.

There were already 505 mall located computer software specialty stores, with 300 more estimated to be in the pipeline. Many of the malls in which stores were located had more than one computer software specialty store. Babbage's currently had direct competition in thirty-four percent of its locations.

Although it appeared that specialty software stores were gaining market share, Babbage's executives thought that it would be those chains which could best improve their format, manage growth, and be most responsive to the changing consumer needs which would grow and prosper.

Egghead was a fast growing competitor, but was focused on the sale of business software in strip shopping

Computer Software Specialty Store Group

	#Stores 12/87	#Stores 12/88	Growth Rate
Egghead	97	176	81.4%
Elect Boutique	87	138	58.6
Software Etc.	133	230	72.9
Waldenbooks	8	31	287.5
Babbage's	58	106	107.8

centers. Only about $40 million of its $320 million in sales were in software intended for home use. Egghead's prices were very competitive and they offered "Egg"ceptional discounts, guaranteeing to beat any price by a dollar. Sales associates' incentives were heavily weighted toward commissions, and special incentives offered directly to salespeople by the various publishing houses, manufacturers and distributors.

Electronic Boutique was another mall-based competitor which sold computer books, magazines, accessories, hardware and software. This company had a less focused approach, was considered to have poorer service, had prices competitive with Babbage's, and presented a somewhat confused image to the shopper. Sales averaged about $400,000 annually per store.

Software Etc. was started by B. Dalton Booksellers, a subsidiary of Barnes and Noble. In addition to the same software categories carried by Babbage's, it carried a reasonably complete line of related books and magazines. Waldensoftware was a similar operation owned by Waldenbooks, a division of Kmart. The growth of Software Etc. had stopped.

Another class of competition, primarily in the business segment, was the computer hardware store, and now a new competitor, SoftWarehouse. This retail computer superstore had stores and corporate sales offices in Dallas, Houston and Atlanta and corporate sales offices in three additional cities. Eighty-five percent of their sales was derived from hardware sales and the remainder from software and accessories.

The computer superstore was a new format, and industry observers were in disagreement as to its potential effect on the market. The superstore was an approximately 25,000 square foot free standing facility in a secondary location. The interior was spartan, well lit and brightly painted with primary colors. Inventory was all on display in utilitarian racks or piled on the floor. Salespeople were easily identifiable by brightly colored vests, but, as in discount retail formats in other categories, not always available for customer assistance.

The SoftWarehouse (which later changed its name to CompUSA) was a so-called category killer, which offered an enormous selection of expensive hardware at very attractive prices. The software assortment emphasized business categories with educational and entertainment titles available for add-on purchases. Prices on all kinds of software were very attractive. Lotus 1-2-3, for example, was $289 compared to $297 at Babbage's. King's Quest IV, a popular entertainment program, sold for $29 versus $37.46 at Babbage's. Nintendo products were not carried.

The store was open only Monday to Friday from 9 to 7, and on Saturday from 10 to 6, and offered phone-in order service from a rather complete catalogue. Customers tended to be businesspeople. In-store traffic was particularly high at the lunch hour. The mood was one of hurried excitement. The superstore was obviously a destination shopping experience and positioned for expansion.

There were also a number of deep discount mail order companies which offered no service and a very limited return policy.

THE REMAINING CHALLENGES

So far, McCurry and Kusin had been able to either anticipate or deal with the challenges and uncertainties of growth. There remained, however, a number of unaddressed issues. As the industry matured, operational fine tuning would have a growing significance. New incentive plans would have to be developed as the opportunities for promotion decreased.

There was also uncertainty about growth in primary demand as PC penetration slowed, and concerns about how long Nintendo would remain popular. In addition there were newly evolving competitive forces such as the super warehouse which would have to be confronted. Were there opportunities in refining, expanding or improving the format?

These and other questions occupied the attention of Kusin and McCurry, but they thought that they could deal with the known issues which surrounded them. These uncertainties could be surmounted. Contingency plans could be developed. What remained was the vast range of unanticipated uncertainties. How could they identify and plan for these?

Exhibit 1A
Photograph of Store Facade

Exhibit 1B
Photograph of Store Interior

Exhibit 2
Organization Chart

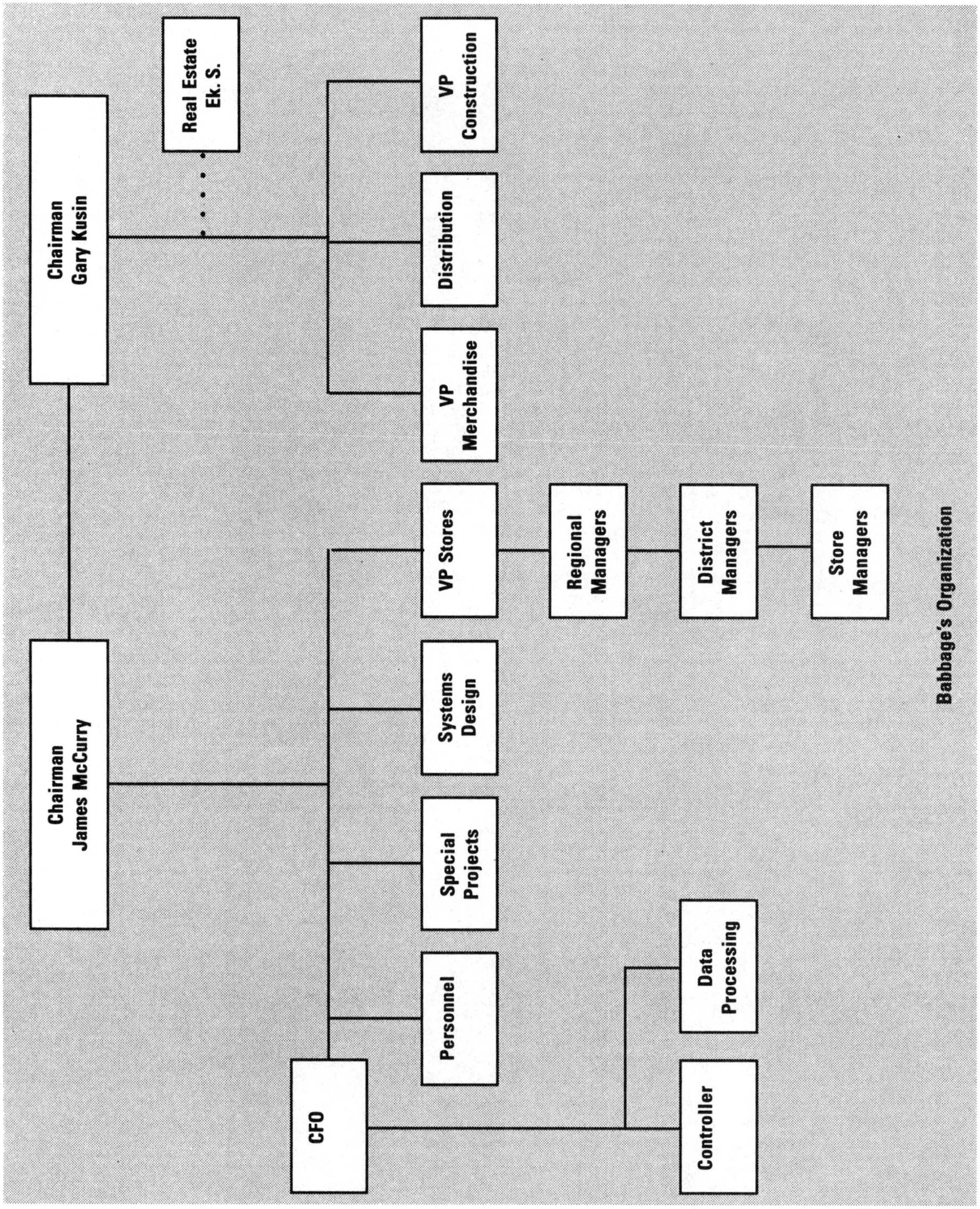

Babbage's Organization

Exhibit 3
Store Location Map

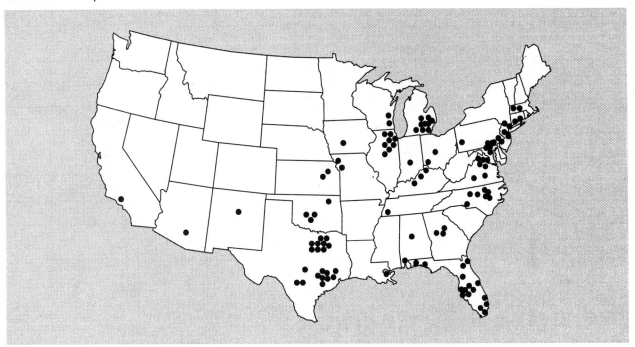

Exhibit 4
Cover of "Babbage's Top Ten" Mailer

EVERYDAY LOW PRICES ON EVERY ITEM.   MAY / JUNE 1989

Babbage's TopTen
25% OFF LIST PRICE

Entertainment	Productivity	Education
1. SPACE QUEST III IBM IBM 3.5" $37.46 $37.46	**1. PRINT SHOP** IBM IBM 3.5" Commodore $44.96 $44.96 $33.71 Apple Apple IIGS Macintosh $37.46 $44.96 $44.96	**1. MATH BLASTER / MATH BLASTER PLUS** IBM IBM 3.5" Commodore Apple $37.46 $37.46 $37.46 $37.46 Apple IIGS Macintosh $37.46 $37.46
2. 688 ATTACK SUB IBM IBM 3.5" $37.46 $41.21	**2. QUICKEN** IBM IBM 3.5" Apple Macintosh $37.46 $37.46 $37.46 $37.46	**2. READER RABBIT** IBM IBM 3.5" Commodore Apple $29.96 $29.96 $29.96 $29.96 Apple IIGS Macintosh $44.96 $44.96
3. HILLSFAR Commodore $29.96	**3. GEOS** Commodore Commodore 128 Apple $44.96 $52.46 $52.46	**3. SESAME STREET LEARNING LIBRARY VOLUME I** IBM IBM 3.5" Commodore Apple $18.71 $18.71 $18.71 $18.71
4. THE DUEL: TEST DRIVE II IBM IBM 3.5" $33.71 $33.71	**4. LEARNING DOS 2.0** IBM IBM 3.5" $37.46 $37.46	**4. MAVIS BEACON TEACHES TYPING** IBM IBM 3.5" Commodore Apple $37.46 $37.46 $29.96 $29.96 Apple IIGS Macintosh $37.46 $37.46
5. POOL OF RADIANCE IBM IBM 3.5" Commodore Apple $37.46 $37.46 $29.96 $33.71	**5. LOTUS 1-2-3** IBM IBM 3.5" $297.00 $297.00	**5. THINK QUICK** IBM IBM 3.5" Apple Apple IIGS $37.46 $37.46 $37.46 $37.46
6. ABRAMS BATTLE TANK IBM IBM 3.5" $29.96 $33.71	**6. BETTER WORKING RESUME KIT** IBM IBM 3.5" $29.96 $33.71	**6. MUPPET PRINT KIT** IBM IBM 3.5" Commodore Apple $11.21 $12.70 $11.21 $11.21
7. WHERE IN THE WORLD IS CARMEN SAN DIEGO? IBM IBM 3.5" Commodore Apple $29.96 $29.96 $26.21 $29.96 Apple IIGS Macintosh $33.71 $33.71	**7. MANAGING YOUR MONEY** IBM IBM 3.5" Apple Macintosh $131.99 $131.99 $89.97 $131.99	**7. ALF'S U.S. GEOGRAPHY** IBM Apple $11.21 $11.21
8. KING'S QUEST IV IBM IBM 3.5" Apple Apple IIGS $37.46 $37.46 $37.46 $37.46	**8. FLOORPLAN** IBM IBM 3.5" $37.46 $37.46	**8. MUSIC CONSTRUCTION SET** IBM Commodore Apple $11.21 $11.21 $11.21
9. JORDAN VS. BIRD IBM IBM 3.5" Commodore $29.96 $33.71 $22.46	**9. WORD WRITER 4** Commodore $29.96	**9. ALGEBLASTER** IBM IBM 3.5" Commodore Apple $37.46 $37.46 $37.46 $37.46
10. F-19 STEALTH FIGHTER IBM IBM 3.5" Commodore $52.46 $52.46 $33.71	**10. WORD PERFECT 5.0** IBM IBM 3.5" $249.99 $249.99	**10. DESIGNASAURUS** IBM IBM 3.5" Commodore $29.96 $29.96 $22.46 Apple Apple IIGS $29.96 $37.46

PICKS OF THE MONTH

THUNDER BLADE	PAINT SHOP	THE PUZZLE STORYBOOK
Commodore $26.21	IBM IBM 3.5" $22.46 $22.46	IBM IBM 3.5" $29.96 $29.96

125 Locations Throughout America.

DALLAS AREA STORES
NorthPark Center
(214) 368-0764
Collin Creek Mall
(214) 578-7649
Town East Mall
(214) 270-8865

Valley View Center
(214) 788-1707
Irving Mall
(214) 255-2129
The Galleria
(214) 701-9288

MID-CITIES AREA STORES
Northeast Mall
Metro (817) 589-0603
The Parks at Arlington
Metro (817) 784-1445

FT. WORTH
Hulen Mall
Metro (817) 654-3394

Babbage's
America's Software Headquarters

Dear Shareholders:

Babbage's continued to combine rapid growth with steadily improving operating results in fiscal 1989. At the same time, important steps were taken to make the Company better prepared for the challenges which lie ahead. Among the more important accomplishments for the year were the following:

- Sales doubled to $58,750,000.
- Net income increased by 137% to $2,772,000.
- Operating income more than tripled to $3,860,000.
- Gross profit improved as a percent of sales, while both store operating expenses and general and administrative expenses declined as a percent of sales.
- 50 new stores were opened, bringing total stores in operation to 108 at year-end, an 86% increase over the same time last year. By April 3, 1989, the Company had 122 stores in operation.
- An initial public offering, completed on July 21, 1988, enabled the Company to retire all debt and redeemable preferred stock and provided the funds to continue rapid expansion. We ended the year with over $7,000,000 in cash and cash equivalents and no outstanding debt.
- We moved to a new facility which more than tripled our distribution center square footage and provided us with the capacity necessary for continued fast growth.
- Enhancements of our management information systems, together with our disciplined approach to buying, permitted us to maintain inventory at satisfactory levels despite our rapid growth.

Because of the significant progress made in fiscal 1989, Babbage's is a much stronger company, better prepared to meet the challenges which lie ahead. Although we continue to believe firmly in the long-term growth of the market for consumer software, short-term market conditions are uncertain. As a result, it will be more critical than ever that we build upon our disciplined approach to cost and inventory management and maintain our commitment to day-in, day-out customer service at all Babbage's stores. These were our most important principles when we opened the first Babbage's store in May 1983. Our adherence to these principles, together with the hard work of hundreds of dedicated Babbage's employees, has made Babbage's one of the fastest growing, profitable specialty retail chains in the United States today. In meeting the challenges of the future, we intend to stick to these principles.

Fiscal 1989 was a year of tremendous progress for Babbage's, and we are committed to continuing that progress in the year ahead. We would like to thank all of those who contributed to the success of Babbage's in fiscal 1989, especially our customers and shareholders.

James McCurry   *Gary Kusin*

James B. McCurry   Gary M. Kusin
Chairman of the Board   President

April 3, 1989

Exhibit 5B
Five-Year Financial Summary from the 1989 Annual Report

(In thousands, except per share data and number of stores)

	Fiscal Year Ended				
	January 28, 1989	January 30, 1988	January 31, 1987	February 1, 1986	February 2, 1985
Net sales	$58,750	$29.341	$9,884	$5,211	$3,024
Gross profit	20,050	9,771	3,313	1,699	943
Operating income (loss)	3,860	1,239	(46)	(680)	(376)
Income (loss)before extraordinary item	2,634	641	5	(671)	(557)
Net income (loss)	2,772	1,168	8	(671)	(557)
Earnings (loss) per common share before extraordinary item	0.56	0.14	—	(0.67)	(0.56)
Earnings (loss) per common share	0.59	0.29	—	(0.67)	(0.56)
Average common equivalent shares outstanding	4,471	3,461	1,000	1,000	1,000
Working capital	$18,554	$ 3,823	$3,937	$ 827	$1,107
Total assets	35,844	13,540	7,060	2,679	2,212
Redeemable preferred stock	—	2,639	—	—	—
Shareholders' equity	30,782	7,776	6,276	2,287	1,964
Average annual sales per store	$ 754	$ 707	$ 511	$ 445	$ 439
Number of stores	108	58	23	16	9

Net sales (in thousands)

Net income (loss) (in thousands)

Exhibit 5C
Statements of Operations from the 1989 Annual Report

BABBAGE'S, INC.
Statement of Operations

(In thousands, except per share data)

	Fiscal Year Ended		
	January 28, 1989	January 30, 1988	January 31, 1987
Net sales	$ 58,750	$29,341	$9,884
Cost of sales	38,700	19,570	6,571
Gross profit	20,050	9,771	3,313
Store operating expenses (Note 5)	12,295	6,220	2,391
General and administrative expenses (Note 5)...................	3,895	2,312	968
Operating income (loss)	3,860	1,239	(46)
Other income (expense):			
Interest income	368	25	66
Interest expense	(122)	(59)	(12)
Income before provision for income taxes and extraordinary item ..	4,106	1,205	8
Provision (benefit) for income taxes (Note 4)			
Current...	1,533	37	—
Deferred	(199)	—	—
Provision in lieu of federal income taxes	138	527	3
	1,472	564	3
Income before extraordinary item................................	2,634	641	5
Extraordinary item–tax benefit from utilization of net operating			
loss carryforward (Note 4)	138	527	3
Net income	2,772	1,168	8
Preferred stock divident requirements (Note 6)..................	150	152	11
Income (loss) applicable to common shareholders	$ 2,622	$ 1,016	$ (3)
Earnings per common share (Note 7):			
Income before extraordinary item...........................	$ .56	$ .14	$ —
Extraordinary item...	.03	.15	—
Net income	$ .59	$ .29	$ —
Average common equivalent shares outstanding (Note 7)	4,471	3,461	1,000

Exhibit 5D
Balance Sheets from the 1989 Annual Report

BABBAGE'S, INC.
Balance Sheets

(In thousands, except share amounts)

	January 28, 1989	January 30, 1988
Assets		
Current assets:		
Cash and cash equivalents	$ 7,339	$ 458
Receivables:		
Trade	209	136
Advertising reimbursements	582	287
Merchandise inventory	14,508	5,694
Prepaids and other	968	373
Total current assets	23,606	6,948
Property and equipment, at cost, net of accumulated depreciation and amortization (Note 2)	12,192	6,543
Other assets	46	49
	$35,844	$ 13,540
Liabilities, Redeemable Preferred Stock, and Shareholders' Equity		
Current liabilities:		
Note payable (Note 3)	$ —	$ 700
Accounts payable	2,804	1,787
Income taxes payable (Note 4)	1,105	37
Accrued liabilities:		
Sales tax	316	199
Advertising	256	106
Other	581	296
Total current liabilities	5,062	3,125
Commitments (Notes 3 and 5)	—	—
Redeemable preferred stock (Note 6)	—	2,639
Shareholders' equity (Notes 6, 7, and 8):		
Convertible preferred stock	—	118
Common stock, $0.10 par value; 20,000,000 shares authorized; shares issues and outstanding: 1989—5,247,750; 1988—1,000,000	525	100
Paid-in capital	28,287	8,210
Retained earnings (deficit)	1,970	(652)
Total shareholders' equity	30,782	7,776
	$35,844	$ 13,540

Case 3

The Wholesale Club Industry

▶━◆◆◆━◀

"Value marketing means . . . giving more: an improved product with added features and enhanced service—all at a better price. It means changing the role of marketing itself. Rather than being a means to shape image, marketing becomes part of the system for delivering value to the customer. [Further], value marketing will be practiced by the leanest, toughest competitors with the greatest cost advantage."

—Business Week

"Maintaining profits is the trickiest part of a value-pricing strategy. Often the only way to lower prices without going broke is to redesign products or assemble processes from the bottom up to cut costs."

—The Wall Street Journal

It was early summer 1993 and John Boynton, a retail industry analyst, was reading with mixed emotions the most recently published quarterly financial statements by The Price Company, the originator of the "Membership Warehouse Club" concept.[1] On the positive side, the company had added 13 new stores as the comparable quarter ended December 20—nearly twice the number of new stores as in the comparable quarter last year. Also, revenues from membership fees were up, and gross margins had increased due to the higher percentage of sales attributable to items such as fresh meat, one-hour photo, and food services. On the negative side, total revenues were up less than 6% for the quarter— substantially below the comparable quarter last year. What really bothered Boynton and many other industry observers, however, were comparable store sales.[2] Sales for all Price Clubs that were operating during the same period last year decreased 5.6% in the first quarter.[3]

Paul Kennedy, an MBA student, class of '93, prepared this case under the supervision of Professor Walter J. Salmon as the basis for class discussion rather than to illustrate either effective or ineffective handling of an administrative situation.

1 "Membership Warehouse Club" and "Wholesale Club" are synonymous.
2 "Comparable stores" are stores in existence for more than one year. In their *Retail Monthly Monitor*, Goldman Sachs writes, "Comparable store sales comparisons are one of the most critical guides to a retailer's growth momentum. The ability of individual stores to increase sales over previous levels represents an excellent measurement of the retailer's ability, through successful merchandising and operating programs, to increase local market share in the sum of its stores."
3 The Price Clubs reported in their Form 10Q for the first quarter ended December 20, 1992, these comparable store results were due to the following: (1) the year's first quarter ended two days earlier than the first quarter of last year, resulting in less holiday sales; (2) a decline in the Canadian dollar relative to the U.S. dollar; and (3) the loss of sales at existing units caused by competitors' openings and a significant increase in the number of new Price Clubs located in existing markets.

Boynton wondered what actions The Price Company would take, if any, in response to these declines.

In reviewing wholesale club results through the end of 1992, Boynton learned that the other industry participants were having similar experiences in comparable store sales (**Exhibits 1** and **2**).[4] Potential explanations for these results included:

- the overall weakness in the North American economy,
- cannibalization from new club stores in existing markets,
- a more effective response from supermarkets,
- an absence of important new merchandising initiatives by the warehouse clubs,
- low food price inflation,
- diminishing benefits from fresh food sales,
- a weakened small business sector, and
- members shopping less often at wholesale clubs than previously.

To Boynton and other industry observers, the challenge was whether wholesale clubs should adhere to current policies or take action to improve their prospects.

WHOLESALE CLUB INDUSTRY OVERVIEW

In 1976, Sol Price and his son Robert opened Price Club in San Diego, California, which introduced the wholesale club concept to retailing. The 100,000 square foot cash-and-carry store, which sold products to customers at exceptionally low prices, was the only one of its kind for five or six years.

At first, Price Club limited membership to small-business customers. Because the club struggled to generate enough sales volume, Sol Price opened membership to individuals. In 1976, the company lost $750,000 on revenues of $16 million. From these modest beginnings, Price Club became a driving force in a new sector of retailing. In fiscal 1992 Price Club had revenues of $7.5 billion and earned $129 million.[5]

The wholesale club industry currently ranked among the fastest-growing sectors of retailing. In calendar year 1992, clubs accounted for an estimated $33.7 billion in retail sales through 625 warehouse units.[6] As recently as 1983 there were fewer than 25 clubs generating industry volume of less than $1 billion. The major industry participants included BJ's Wholesale Club ("BJ's"), Costco Wholesale Corp. ("Costco"), PACE Membership Warehouses, Inc. ("PACE," a unit of Kmart Corp.), The Price Company, Inc. ("Price Club"), and Sam's Clubs ("Sam's," a unit of Wal-Mart Stores, Inc.). Collectively, these five chains accounted for approximately 98% of the total sector sales (**Exhibit 3**). (See **Appendix 1** for more detail on each of these companies.)

THE WHOLESALE CLUB CONCEPT

Price Club's approach to retailing was "the intelligent loss of business." This approach is the foundation of the club industry. Instead of trying to be all things to all people, wholesale clubs focused on the fastest-moving products and the customers that bought the most. The products ranged from canned tuna to TVs, and from bananas to Big Wheels.

Selection of Items Carried by Wholesale Clubs

- Apparel
- Automotives
- Automotive Parts
- Books
- Candy
- Cigarettes
- Computers
- Fresh Baked Goods
- Fresh Cheese
- Fresh Flowers
- Fresh Meats
- Fresh Poultry
- Fresh Produce
- Fresh Seafood
- Frozen Foods
- Frozen Yogurt
- Furniture
- Hardware
- Health & Beauty Aids
- Home Improvement
- Home Security
- Hot Tubs

---

4 Note that among the various sources of historical wholesale club industry data, there are relatively slight inconsistencies.
5 Securities and Exchange Commission, *Form 10K, The Price Company Annual Report for the Fiscal Year Ended August 31, 1992* (Washington, D.C., 1993).
6 Goldman, Sachs & Co., *Warehouse Clubs: Still a Growth Industry?* (New York, New York: 1993).

- Household Products
- Housewares
- Jewelry
- Luggage
- Major Appliances
- Motor Homes
- Musical Instruments
- Office Equipment
- Office Supplies
- Pet Food
- Pizza
- Plants
- Small Appliances
- Sports Equipment
- Stationery Supplies
- Stereo Components
- Telephones
- Tires
- Tools
- Toys
- TVs
- Video Games
- Video Tapes
- Vitamins
- Wines

Source: *Packaged Facts*, 1992.

There was, however, generally only one bulk size or multi-pack SKU available within a product category,[7] or one model of a particular hard good, such as a 20 inch TV, resulting in a product mix of only approximately 3,500 to 4,000 SKUs. Further, as an item-based business, a club would usually stock the faster-moving given items (such as the TV), but would not always stock the same brand.

Roughly 55% to 65% of club industry revenues were from the grocery category, including perishable and non-perishable items. Non-grocery categories (appliances and electronics, giftware and housewares, office supplies and equipment, clothing, automotive, hardware, seasonal, and sporting goods) and membership fees accounted for the remaining revenues (see **Exhibits 4** and **5**).[8] Note that the data for these exhibits came from several sources, and represented 1991 as well as 1992 estimates. As a result, the aggregate sales values for these exhibits did not reconcile with total industry sales in **Exhibit 1**.

Another important tenet of the wholesale club concept was "everyday low pricing" on top quality, nationally branded merchandise. Merchandise buyers aimed to provide members with the best possible values, measured as price per unit volume. They tried to execute this objective by seeking the lowest possible prices from manufacturers and by operating on exceptionally low retail margins. The name of the game was low margins and high volume.

The club was a no-frills warehouse environment, where each SKU was available on a pallet, in a building of approximately 100,000 to 125,000 square feet. Clubs were also committed to minimizing operating costs and complexity, and maximizing inventory turns. Constant effort was also made to streamline distribution. Further, clubs were often located in areas where real estate costs were lower and access was not quite up to the standards of regional shopping centers.

Clubs also achieved low costs through vendor cooperation: UPC-marked packages, pre-palletized shipments, unique and large package sizes and multipacks, and powerful package graphics all helped to reduce operating costs.

The core of the club concept was membership. There were two main groups of members; wholesale/business members, and group members. Wholesale members were typically business owners or operators of restaurants, bars, caterers, gas stations, mini marts, and so on. Group members were defined as individual employees or retirees of "qualified" organizations (that is, government, universities, financial institutions, and so on). In reality, any individual consumer could become a group member. Membership also had the advantage of stimulating patronage, without the need for clubs to incur large media advertising expenses.

The typical industry annual fee for wholesale membership was $25, plus $10 each for from two to six additional cardholders. An individual group member, in contrast, could previously buy items without paying the $25 annual fee. This type of "member" would instead pay a 5% premium over the posted wholesale prices. All the wholesale clubs have eliminated free memberships, although several clubs offer a free trial membership

---

7 An SKU is a stock keeping unit. Each unique style, color, and size of an item represents one SKU regardless of how many are in stock.
8 James M. Degen and Company Inc., *Membership Warehouse Clubs: Industry Overview of the Distribution Concept of the 1990s* (Santa Barbara, Calif.: 1992); and The Food Marketing Institute, *Alternative Store Formats—Competing in the Nineties* (1992).

for new stores in communities in which they had not previously operated. Recently, Costco increased its annual membership fees to $30. Whether other clubs will follow is uncertain, but the move reinforces the view that paid membership will remain an important industry characteristic.

Exhibit 6 compares several key dimensions of the wholesale club format to the conventional supermarket, combination store, discount store, and hypermarket.

INDUSTRY PERFORMANCE

The main competitors in the already highly concentrated club industry continue to grow by competing with each other to build new units in untapped as well as established markets and by offering innovative products and services. Recent innovations include a shift in sales towards food and sundries by expanding into perishable foods, including bakery, fresh meats, and produce; additional services such as quick oil change, one-hour photo processing, a pharmacy, and one-hour optical departments; increased rotation of slower moving non-food items, which includes home furnishings, appliances, electronics, and office equipment; and enhanced information systems including scanning to reduce labor costs and enhance inventory turns. In 1992 the average annual sales per warehouse for the top five competitors ranged from approximately $44 million to $93 million; the industry average was $63 million (**Exhibit 7**).[9]

The club industry grew dramatically over the past seven years. Industry sales rose from $7.2 billion to $33.7 billion in the period 1986 to 1992, a compound annual growth rate (CAGR) of 26.5%. Industry revenues for 1993 were projected to be $40.3 billion, which represented growth of 19.6% over 1992 (**Exhibit 1**).[10] This growth rate was much higher than that of most competing retailing sectors which posted five-year growth rates ranging from 5% to 8%.[11]

Two factors accounted for the strong growth of the club industry: growth in number of clubs, and growth in sales per club. The number of clubs in North America went from 212 to 625 in the period 1986 to January 1993.[12] The number of units was expected to reach 768 by January 1994, an annual growth rate of nearly 23%. Unit growth was expected to average 15% annually from 1992 to 1997 (**Exhibit 1**). In the most recent two years, the Northeast saw the most rapid new unit growth of approximately 40% annually. The Midwest and South were next, with rates of 22% and 24%, respectively. The West's new unit growth rate since 1991 was 19%. As of the end of 1992, however, the Northeast still had the fewest clubs, with only 88. The Southern and Midwestern regions had 204 and 126 units, respectively.[13]

In 1993 alone, the top five wholesale club chains planned to open 134 new clubs.[14] With approximately 585 clubs in the United States in 1992, analysts predicted that the number of clubs could expand by another 500 before market saturation occurred (**Exhibit 9**).[15] By comparison, there were 30,400 supermarkets in the United States with revenues over $2 million.[16]

Exhibit 8 shows that average sales per club grew at a compound annual rate of 4% from 1987 to 1992. Furthermore, the forecasts were for the average sales per club to remain relatively flat through 1996. Industry observers attributed this forecast to the lower average sales within new clubs. Since the total number of club units was forecasted to grow over 20% through 1993, some believed the industry needed a period to "catch up" before growth in average sales per club resumed.

Rapid club construction meant many of the clubs were still very new and had relatively low sales. In 1992, average sales per club was $62.5 million.[17] By comparison some established, mature clubs generated more than $100 million in sales. For example, an analysis of Costco's club network revealed a strong relationship between maturity and sales per club. In 1992, Costco's clubs under two years old had average annual sales of $50.7 million; clubs two to five years old had average annual sales of $78.7 million, and clubs over five years had average annual sales of $88.8 million. Some of its oldest clubs exceeded $125 million in sales 1992.[18]

---

9   Dean Witter Reynolds Inc., *Membership Warehouse Club Review and Update—Industry Report* (1992).
10 Goldman, Sachs & Co.
11 U.S. Department of Commerce, *U.S. Industrial Outlook '92: Business Forecasts for 350 Industries* (Washington, D.C.: Government Printing Office, 1992), pp. 39 - 1:8, 32 - 1:3, 37 - 1:5.
12 Goldman, Sach & Co.
13 Dean Witter Reynolds Inc.
14 Goldman, Sachs & Co.
15 Dean Witter Reynolds Inc.
16 *Progressive Grocer*, April 1993.
17 Dean Witter Reynolds Inc.
18 Securities and Exchange Commission, *Form 10K, Costco Wholesale Corporation for the Fiscal Year Ended August 30, 1992* (Washington, D.C., 1993).

The dramatic growth of wholesale clubs has lead to a fundamental change in the relationship between clubs and their suppliers. Through the early 1980s, many important national brand manufacturers had concerns about the wholesale club channel. They feared both alienating existing trade channels and losing any remaining influence over pricing, display, and distribution. By the end of the 1980s, however, most major manufacturers were vying to gain access to or increase business with wholesale clubs. At the same time, clubs had begun to threaten competitive retailing formats, and none more so than traditional supermarkets.

A 1992 study financed by the Food Marketing Institute (FMI) reported that between 1986 and 1991, food and related sales to wholesale clubs, deep discount drug stores (such as Phar-Mor and Drug Emporium), and mass merchants (such as Wal-Mart and Target) grew from $14.8 billion to $33.0 billion of a total grocery-related retail volume of $537.4 billion. Wholesale clubs accounted for a large share of the $33 billion. End consumers, as opposed to business members, accounted for $11.3 billion of these sales.[19] The study estimated that 60% to 65% of club store food sales were to final customers, and only 35% to 40% were to business customers, of which only 55% to 65% was actually for business use (**Exhibit 10**). The growth rate of food sales in the clubs had exceeded the growth of total sales because clubs had expanded their food and related selections, especially items targeted at the final customer.

The wholesale clubs were estimated to have 2.1% market share of the $537.4 billion total grocery-related sales to end consumers in 1991, while supermarkets (with stores over $2 million in revenues) were estimated to have $260.1 billion, or 48.4% market share.[20] The 1992 FMI study estimated that by 2001, wholesale clubs could account for nearly 4.8% of the $812 billion in total grocery-related sales to end consumers, while the supermarket segment could slide to a 45.5% market share.

U.S. ECONOMIC DATA[21]

To put the wholesale club channel in perspective, the U.S. Department of Commerce reported total sales of retail stores exceeded $1.9 trillion in 1992—a gain of about 5% in current dollars over 1991. The Commerce department forecasted 1993 U.S. retail merchandise sales to increase by 5.4%, to more than $2.04 trillion. In the long term, the retailing sector was not expected to grow as fast as in the past, due to changes in consumer buying patterns and structural shifts in retailing. According to 1992 projections of the Department of Labor, retail sales, adjusted for inflation, would show an average annual growth rate of 2.5% between 1990 and 2005, compared with 3.5% annually during the previous 15 years. In addition, structural changes in retailing have resulted in increased market shares for the newer types of retailers and decreased shares for traditional retailers.

Retail food sales in 1992 (including grocery stores and most other retailers of foods and beverages for consumption at home but excluding food service) reached $387 billion—an increase of 1.6% over 1991 according to the Commerce Department. Sales in the retail grocery store segment, which accounted for more than 95% of all food retailing, rose by more than 1% in 1992 to about $362 billion. Sales of the larger retail grocery firms, however, advanced almost 2%, reaching $226 billion.

Other economic concerns affecting wholesale clubs included the weakness in the small-business sector. **Exhibit 11** shows that the percentage change in business formations declined 4.5% in 1991, while business failures *increased* 46% in the same period.

WHOLESALE CLUB CUSTOMERS

Estimates were that in 1992, approximately 17% to 25% of all households in the major U.S. and Canadian metropolitan areas—some 20.7 million people—were members of a wholesale club, including 13.4 million individual members and 7.3 million business members.[22] One-third of the club shoppers were classified as heavy users, spending over $100 per visit, while almost 60% were classified as light users, spending $53 per club visit.[23] These figures compared to the average supermarket spending of approximately $27 per visit.[24] The mean driving distance to a club was approximately 13 miles.[25]

19 The Food Marketing Institute, 1992.
20 Ibid.
21 U.S. Department of Commerce, *U.S. Industrial Outlook '92: Business Forecasts for 350 Industries.*
22 Dean Witter Reynolds Inc., 1992.
23 The Food Marketing Institute, 1992.
24 *Progressive Grocer,* April 1993.
25 Douglas J. Tigert, Stephen J. Arnold, and Terry W. Cotter, *Warehouse/Membership Clubs in North America: Are They Retailers or Wholesalers? And Who Is at Risk?* (Babson College, April 1992).

Most surveys of the club industry indicated that the average frequency of visits was once every two to three weeks. Of all the clubs, a 1992 Babson College survey reported BJ's had the lowest percentage of shoppers visiting more than twice per month, and Costco had the highest percentage (**Exhibit 12**). Business members tended to shop more often—approximately once every one to two weeks—while individual members shopped slightly less often, approximately every three to four weeks.[26]

Market penetration of warehouse clubs increased with time in operation. In markets where a club store had been operating for less than one year, 17% of households surveyed reported they shopped regularly for groceries at these outlets. This figure increased to 24% in markets where the clubs were more than three years old.[27]

Individual shoppers varied in the extent of their utilization of clubs and supermarkets for purchases of grocery items for personal, home use. The FMI data in **Exhibit 13** show that supermarkets captured $222 grocery dollars per month from their customers versus $120 per month for clubs. On a per-visit basis, however, shoppers spent $86 in clubs and $54 in these supermarkets. These data were substantially different than the April 1993 *Progressive Grocer* which cites an average customer transaction size of approximately $18 for a chain supermarket. **Exhibit 14**, from the Babson survey, elaborates further the spending habits and products bought for at-home use at clubs. **Exhibits 15** and **16** show the most frequently purchased grocery and non-grocery items at clubs for at-home use.

Shoppers who use a business/wholesale card have one of the most interesting patterns of shopping. According to the Babson survey, the average amount spent by business card members for grocery items for business was $42. The Babson data also indicate that 60% of these business cardholders did not buy any food for business purposes at wholesale clubs on their last trip. Moreover, the majority of grocery products bought for business use—coffee/tea, dairy products, candy, soda, salty snacks—are products that a business employee might normally buy at the retail level (see **Exhibit 17**).

Exhibit 18 shows non-grocery spending levels at clubs for business use, and it also shows the most frequently purchased major non-food purchases for business.

Although club shoppers are a subset of all supermarket shoppers, their demographics are substantially different (**Exhibit 19**). Club shoppers tend to be younger, more educated, earn higher income, have more than one income, and have larger families. The club customers' introduction to the club store is initiated more often by word-of-mouth than by formal marketing communications. Approximately 2/3 of all club shoppers either first went with a relative or friend, or heard about the store from someone else.[28] **Exhibit 20** shows how customers of warehouse clubs responded to characteristics of warehouse clubs and supermarkets.

The Babson College survey in **Exhibit 21** shows the frequency of visits club shoppers made to a particular club versus six months previous. The author of the Babson survey points out, however, that less frequent shopping may not translate into less spending, if the customer makes a larger purchase per visit. The results of the FMI survey, shown in **Exhibit 22**, appear to affirm stability of warehouse club purchases.

WHOLESALE CLUB BUSINESS STRATEGY

The success of the wholesale club business system is driven by innovation in distribution. There are several key elements of this business system, including:

- low everyday price on all items,
- locations which balance cost and access,
- efficient in-bound logistics,
- limited assortments,
- high inventory turns,
- emphasis on brand name merchandise,
- efficient store operations through minimization of operating costs and administrative overhead,
- high sales per square foot to meet gross margin dollar targets,
- shopping privileges limited to members only, and
- a large, high-quality membership base.

Lower Price

Although the business system allows clubs to offer many different benefits to consumers, lower price is the most significant. The 1992 FMI study compared a national

---

26 The Food Marketing Institute, 1992; Dean Witter Reynolds Inc., 1992.
27 The Food Marketing Institute, 1992.
28 Ibid.

market basket of grocery-related items carried by club stores, supermarkets, deep-discount drugstores, and mass merchandisers. The results showed the clubs had the lowest prices per measure among all the formats compared (**Exhibit 23**). Of the 26% difference between club prices and supermarket prices, approximately 14 points can be explained by the club's superior operating efficiency (**Exhibit 24**). Approximately 2 points are attributable to revenues earned from membership fees. The remaining 10 points are related to the lower cost of purchased product on a per-measure basis.

These figures are averages for a national market basket constructed at one time. The astute grocery store shopper, however, using coupons, buying the largest sizes available, and taking advantage of specials may be able to cut this 26% difference in half. Therefore, the difference between the lowest price in food stores and prevailing prices in wholesale clubs is approximately 12% to 13%, according to McKinsey's study.

Site Selection

Before a new club was constructed, a great deal of attention was paid to site selection. A new club required approximately 12 acres of land versus 4 acres for a supermarket.[29] The choice of location balanced several considerations, including real estate costs, proximity to small-business customers, and access to major highways.

Minimizing real estate costs helped clubs maintain a lean cost structure. For this reason, clubs were generally built on lower-cost, undeveloped land in suburban or slightly more remote areas. In addition, easy access to major highways was important to minimize logistics costs as well as to attract customers from greater distances. Recently, clubs have been opening closer to more convenient but somewhat higher-cost strip centers, and in some cases to regional shopping centers.[30] Clubs could justify the higher real estate expenses only if these locations generated higher sales per square foot.

According to industry observers, a typical wholesale club unit required between $10 million and $16 million in funds to build and start.[31] This figure included the ownership of land, building, fixtures and equipment, starting inventory and pre-opening expenses, but excluded any headquarters or non-store opening costs. Half of the beginning inventory was often financed with trade credit.

Originally, most wholesale clubs were approximately 100,000 square feet. They currently range up to 125,000 square feet to accommodate the fresh meat, fresh produce, bakery, and delicatessen sections.

Inbound Logistics

Once a club began operation, inbound logistics, merchandising, and store operations were the essentials of ongoing operational success. The inbound logistics process relied upon the smooth, efficient flow of products. Manufacturers gave clubs volume discounts for purchasing directly large quantities of a limited number of SKUs. Full truckload shipping and pallet-level handling minimized logistics costs. Sometimes, however, a truckload of merchandise was divided among several warehouse clubs belonging to the same chain in a single metropolitan area, or a truckload was delivered to one store serving as a redistribution point for other locations in the same market.

A close working relationship with the manufacturer helped clubs achieve logistical efficiencies. Clubs demanded from manufacturers strict adherence to delivery schedules, packaging guidelines, and other logistics requirements. Also, clubs had more recently demanded special bar codes for the multi-packs of small sizes and case packs.[32]

Merchandising

Club buyers strove to provide the best values to members by minimizing the price per unit of the products sold. They have been traditionally reluctant to accept price increases, and have switched among leading national brands whenever better pricing became available.

Clubs followed an "everyday low pricing" strategy, and were committed to a policy of thin markups. In most cases, club buyers set prices centrally, taking into account the difference between the wholesale club price and prices prevailing in other types of retail outlets. Wholesale clubs, however, almost never engaged in setting prices below the actual merchandise cost. Prices could be modified locally by store managers to meet competitive conditions, but the unique jumbo packs

29   Goldman, Sachs & Co., Industry Report, 1988.
30   The Food Marketing Institute, 1992.
31   Dean Witter Reynolds Inc..
32   The Food Marketing Institute, 1992.

helped clubs minimize direct item price comparison with supermarkets.[33]

On average, clubs had gross margins of 8% to 13%, including membership fees, compared to 25% to 30% for discount department stores and 20% to 25% for supermarkets. In supermarkets, however, fast-moving dry grocery items were often sold at gross margins of less than 15%.[34]

While quantity buying of large sizes from whichever national brand sellers offered the lowest prices lowered wholesale clubs' purchasing costs, it also significantly restricted the completeness of their merchandise assortments and their merchandise continuity. Typically, the average club carried 4,000 SKUs, compared to 18,000 for a traditional supermarket and 45,000 for a discount department store.[35] The new combination [supermarket] stores, which exceeded 50,000 square feet in gross space, also offered between 30,000 and 40,000 SKUs.[36] In contrast, club merchants emphasized wide product breadth and narrow product depth, preferring the "intelligent loss of business" to the urge to add incremental SKUs.

Club buyers worked with national manufacturers to create special extra-large club SKUs to increase price points and operating efficiencies. Specifically, since customer checkout was a relatively fixed cost activity, higher dollar transactions reduced labor costs as a percentage of sales. For example, the time to scan a $7 box of detergent versus a $20 box was roughly the same.

In all merchandise categories, the focus was on fast-moving brand name items. Especially in non-foods, entire categories of non-consumables might disappear from the shelves from time to time. Clubs rotated these items to generate excitement and take advantage of seasonal trends. These in-and-out items represented 20% of club sales.[37] Several club chains also carried a limited amount of private label items to enhance assortment.

Several wholesale club chains have begun to offer additional categories to enhance their assortments, provide services to their members, and build individual store volumes. Examples of these categories include pharmacies, optical shops, one-hour photo labs, and quick lube oil change service.

Club Operations

Clubs were very focused on effectively managing in-store operating costs. Labor costs were reduced by using forklifts and full pallet floor displays, and by limiting manual stocking of product. Further, most warehouse clubs were open fewer hours than traditional stores, which helped reduce payroll expenses as a percentage of sales. Lack of salespeople or customer service lowered labor overhead. Customers used flatbed trucks or large carriages to move even the largest purchases such as mattresses, furniture, and major appliances through the warehouse. Also, high-price point items and large transactions at the checkout reduced labor costs as a percentage of sales. Minimal but sufficient lighting and low maintenance costs were also characteristic of this environment.

Furthermore, there is minimal credit card use in clubs, although most clubs now take the Discover card, and PACE is experimenting with Mastercard in several markets. For the most part, clubs also do not accept coupons. In 1993, however, BJ's began to accept coupons.

Display techniques help to reinforce the low-price image of wholesale clubs. Fixtures are usually warehouse racks, extending from the sealed concrete floor to the exposed 20- to 30-foot-high ceiling. Merchandise was stored in multiple pallet quantities on these racks, maximizing utilization of floor space. Aisles were wide enough to allow forklifts to stock shelves. Placement of heavier products near loading docks at the back of the store minimized wear and tear on forklifts and damage to the product in transport. Warehouse rack systems also allowed quick replenishment of stock space accessible to consumers from storage space above, and minimized lost sales due to stock outs.

Inventory Turns and Sales per Square Foot

Since wholesale clubs offered limited selections of mainly fast-moving items at exceptionally low prices, inventory turns and sales per square foot were exceptionally high. A typical club operated at 16 to 20 inventory turns, generating more than $600 sales per gross square foot. A traditional supermarket operated at 12 to 14 turns and generated $320 sales per gross square

---

33 Ibid.
34 Marci Kosann Dew and Professor Walter J. Salmon, *Wholesale Club Industry* (Harvard Business School case 586-021), 1990.
35 *Progressive Grocer*, 1991.
36 Dew and Salmon, *Wholesale Club Industry*.
37 The Food Marketing Institute, 1992.

foot. Discount department stores operated at 4 to 5 turns and generated $188 sales per gross square foot.[38]

As a result of wholesale clubs achieving such rapid inventory turnover, accounts payable to suppliers often equaled or exceeded inventory investment. This "positive float from suppliers" lowered working capital requirements. Rapid turns also allowed clubs to maintain very high standards for product freshness. Furthermore, both the high inventory turns and sales per square foot enabled clubs to operate successfully with modest profits in relationship to sales.

Members-Only Shopping

The membership concept, a unique aspect of the club merchandising formula, was important for marketing as well as for economic reasons. Since the membership fee accounted for only 1 to 2 points of revenue, clubs could theoretically raise gross margins slightly, eliminate the fee, and open their doors to everyone. From a marketing perspective, however, the membership fee offered several advantages. First, it promoted loyalty to a particular club. Second, it drove higher volume per customer and per transaction as members modified their buying habits to justify the cost of membership. The membership concept also enabled clubs to spend less on advertising than other retailers.

Although start-up clubs may do some short-term advertising to build initial traffic and membership bases, mature clubs engaged in essentially no media advertising. Word-of-mouth became the main source of new members for established clubs.[39] The little marketing that mature clubs undertook was generally directed toward small-business members by means of direct mail.

Membership fees and policies may also result in a customer base not inclined to shoplift, therefore reducing shrinkage. In an interview, Sol Price said, "The customers identify [the club] as their place and that certainly helps keep shrink down. Also, one of our routine procedures is to have a security person at the door to verify each order as the customer leaves."[40]

Increase Members per Warehouse

One of the most effective strategies to improve sales productivity of clubs was to increase the number of members per club. Since there were a limited number of highly coveted small and medium-size businesses in any market, most new members would, by default, be individuals.[41]

Herein lies a risk to the wholesale club industry. Gregory Starzynski, director of retail marketing at Nielsen Household Services, figured clubs already were selling to nearly 60% of their most likely customers—families with two or more children with household incomes of more than $40,000.[42] Attracting new consumers with different shopping interests could add unaccustomed costs to operations that were built around high inventory turnover and narrow selection. If the club format became too much of a "retail" concept by increasing the number of brands and sizes carried to satisfy members, the club's pricing advantage over traditional retail formats could be reduced. Clubs, therefore, will need to balance the goal of increasing members per warehouse against increased costs of satisfying them through expanded assortments or possibly increased services.

COMPARISON OF WHOLESALE CLUBS AND PRIMARY COMPETITION

To determine the effectiveness of wholesale clubs, their performance needs to be measured against other kinds of retailers. Since clubs carry a wide spectrum of items, they compete with many different formats. For example, in general merchandise, clubs compete with "power retailers" such as Circuit City for household appliances and electronics, Home Depot for do-it-yourself and hardware products, and Staples for office supplies. Since 60% of club sales are grocery-related, however, supermarkets are their most important competitors.

Operating Expenses and Financial Performance: Supermarkets vs. Wholesale Clubs

The 1992 Food Marketing Institute study performs an in-depth comparison of mix-adjusted operating costs, including labor, facility, warehouse/transaction, and marketing costs between supermarkets and warehouse clubs (**Exhibit 25**).

Between supermarkets and wholesale clubs, labor is by far the largest difference in operating costs. Clubs

38 Ibid.
39 Ibid.
40 Compustat, Interview with Sol Price, November 1990.
41 Dean Witter Reynolds.
42 *Business Week*, 1993.

are able to lower labor costs by 6%, facility costs by 3.5%, warehouse and transportation costs by 1.5%, and advertising and marketing expenses by another 1.5% compared to supermarkets.

Another gauge of the relative performance of these two retail formats is return on invested capital (ROIC). It is a pre-tax and before-interest measure, and therefore excludes any effects that leverage has on financial performance. For mature stores, the FMI study estimated wholesale clubs earn 39.0% ROIC, while grocery stores earn a 21.2% ROIC (**Exhibit 26**). Economy of scale is an important driver of profitability. Costco's sales volume increased 364% from 1987 to 1992 (**Exhibit 27**), while its ratio of administration costs to sales volume declined substantially.

WHOLESALE CLUB SUPPLIERS

In the late 1980s, manufacturers began to recognize the rapid growth of the warehouse club channel. They viewed clubs as an opportunity to gain sales volume in a sluggish retail environment. Accordingly, manufacturers made capital investments to accommodate the packaging requirements of the clubs.

Clubs generally dealt with the leading branded manufacturers of fast-moving consumable and non-consumable products. These brand names also added to the reputations of clubs for carrying high-quality products. In addition, clubs generally did not emphasize private label merchandise, a practice that branded manufacturers found very appealing.

Another attractive feature of doing business with clubs was their "everyday low pricing" strategy. As a result, their buying patterns were predictable, allowing manufacturers to forecast production more accurately. Reduced uncertainties decreased the need for manufacturers to maintain excess capacity and carry large safety stocks. In addition, incremental volume from clubs led to higher utilization of fixed assets and to decreasing overhead expenses as a percentage of sales.

Manufacturers also realized cost benefits through packaging of larger "club size" products, on both a per-SKU and per-order basis. On a per-SKU basis, larger packages lowered costs per unit, since packaging costs as a percentage of total product costs generally decreased as the size increased. This effect was especially pronounced when packaging costs were a large percentage of total product costs, such as for household products. On a per-order basis, most clubs ordered multiple pallets of the same SKU, which resulted in further economies because of single-item pallets, and sometimes even single-item truckloads.

Manufacturers also incurred lower marketing costs in selling to clubs. Clubs bought on the basis of the lowest "dead net" cost, which meant net of any trade allowances. Consequently, lower manufacturer selling prices were offset by the avoidance of these trade allowances, which often amounted to 5% to 10% of factory selling prices.[43]

While the benefits of servicing the club industry seem compelling, internal support for club business among some manufacturers has occasionally been tepid because of special requirements for packaging, distribution, and order responsiveness. One of the manufacturers' biggest problems has been the special packaging requirements of clubs. New, larger SKUs, shrink wrapping, and palletizing often do not mesh with a manufacturer's traditional way of doing business.[44] One manufacturer was quoted as saying that "special items and packs don't fit our current lines, so we have to have it specially done and that costs a lot."[45] Another commented, "Knowledge of the business is needed, including merchandising practices, customer base, long-term strategic, and current tactical practices. The knowledge base needs to expand."[46]

COMPETITIVE RESPONSES

Competitive response to the clubs by supermarkets had been almost nonexistent prior to the 1990s. Throughout the 1980s, many supermarket chains augmented their merchandise mix with more discretionary, higher-margin grocery products and general merchandise products. With the benefit of a relatively strong economy and significant food price inflation, this strategy masked club competition.[47] Toward the end of the decade, as the economy slowed and the number of clubs exploded, the supermarket industry realized that clubs were indeed

---

43   The Food Marketing Institute, 1992.
44   James M. Degen & Company, Inc., *Selling and Marketing to Membership Warehouse Clubs.*
45   Ibid.
46   Ibid.
47   Dean Witter Reynolds Inc., 1992.

competitors. Over time, supermarket industry executives increasingly recognized the favorable prospects of the warehouse club industry (**Exhibit 28**).

Competitive response to clubs has not been limited to the United States. In Canada, Loblaw's, the respected Canadian supermarket operator, opened a 48,000-square-foot experimental "Real Canadian Warehouse Club" in Saskatoon that has proven to be effective competition for Costco in that market.[48]

The 1992 FMI study estimated that by 2001, warehouse clubs will increase their share of grocery-related sales from the 1991 level of 2.1% (or $11.3 billion) to 4.8% (or $39.0 billion), and supermarkets' market share will decrease from the 1991 level of 48.4% (or $260.1 billion) to 45.5% (or $370 billion).[49] This forecast was based on a relatively neutral scenario, where all participants share sales volume according to their relative capacity to sell each grocery-related category. If there is no competitive response by grocers to the current gains of the clubs, the results may be substantially worse for supermarkets, potentially cutting current profit margins in half.[50] If the competitive response by grocers is highly successful, warehouse club sales may be less buoyant.

Nearly 67% of club memberships were less than two years old in 1992.[51] Some industry observers consider this period too brief to shift shopping patterns permanently.[52] As a result, supermarket operators may have a window of opportunity to respond before new club shopping patterns are permanently ingrained among current shoppers.

One strong warning sign for supermarkets was that nearly one-third of upper-income shoppers (twice the proportion of other income groups) reported they now spend more at clubs, in comparison to their initial spending levels.[53] Upper-income households, however, also reported that they enjoyed supermarket shopping more than club shopping.[54]

Households with five or more people also spent more than two times as much at clubs as one- to two-person households, and exhibited nearly twice the shopping frequency.[55] These findings suggested potential opportunities for supermarkets to develop improved programs and merchandising activities to attract large families.

Competitive response from the supermarket industry intensified by 1993. Many chains responded by offering a limited selection of large-size "club pack" merchandise. One problem with club packs, however, was that they might adversely affect shopping frequency, consequently reducing the sales of high-margin, impulse items. Also, many independent supermarkets were quite small, which made stocking bulk items physically impractical.

Another response to clubs was suggested by a Cornell University study which found consumers rated supermarket perishables better in overall value than club store selections.[56] This study recommended that supermarkets emphasize superior fresh foods, friendly knowledgeable personnel, and one-stop shopping to differentiate themselves from clubs. Supermarkets were also encouraged to pursue a nonperishable pricing strategy that attempted to find the price point between supermarkets and clubs which equalized the value of the two stores' offerings, considering the other important aspects of the supermarket shopping experience.[57]

Most industry observers believe that the best strategic response to the clubs was a multidimensional strategy designed to reduce costs and strengthen merchandising and marketing. **Exhibit 29** is a road map suggested in the McKinsey FMI study, summarizing these options.

On the durable goods side, Circuit City, a large electronics and home appliance power retailer, and other similar chains have priced their opening price point products close to warehouse club price levels. These chains have also used their sales force to encourage consumers to buy more fully featured merchandise, as well as to purchase profitable extended warranties.

FUTURE PROSPECTS OF THE WHOLESALE CLUB INDUSTRY

Several industry observers predicted that approximately 325 to 600 additional clubs would open by the end of

---

48   Ibid.
49   The Food Marketing Institute, 1992.
50   Ibid.
51   Edward McLaughlin, et al., *Wholesale Club Stores: The Emerging Challenge* (New York: Cornell University, 1992).
52   Ibid.
53   Ibid.
54   Ibid.
55   Ibid.
56   Ibid.
57   Ibid.

the decade, based on a market saturation level of approximately 185,000 people per store.[58] Applying this market saturation level to the combined population of New York and New Jersey results in over 150 total possible clubs for the two-state area.[59] Comparing the New York/New Jersey projections of sales and stores for the year 2001 with the Goldman Sachs projections of additional stores for the nation (600) reveals that nearly 20% of the total growth in wholesale clubs projected for the U.S. will occur in New York and New Jersey. New York/New Jersey's saturation level, however, may be achieved at a higher population per club store than other areas due to higher rents, limited sites, zoning restrictions, different shopper preferences, and higher reliance on public transport, especially in metro New York/New Jersey.[60]

Competition within the club industry is expected to intensify as local markets reach saturation. As local markets become saturated, the ability to continue to generate large sales volumes per club becomes debatable.

Head-to-head warehouse club battles may change the nature of competition in the industry. Historically, clubs have competed with traditional retailers and each other on price. Will clubs lower or drop membership fees, endeavor to reduce prices even more, or shift to more non-price differentiation, such as product selection, service, and even image advertising? **Exhibit 30** presents the percentage of warehouses for each industry player that competed directly with other warehouses in 1991 and 1992.

As John Boynton thought about the implications of all the data he had before him, a new survey conducted by Custom Research Inc. arrived on his desk. (For excerpts see **Appendix 2**). He wondered whether this new information could add a different perspective to his understanding of the industry.

---

58 The Food Marketing Institute, 1992; Goldman, Sachs & Co., 1992; and Dean Witter Reynolds, 1992.
59 Edward McLaughlin, et al., *Wholesale Club Stores: The Emerging Challenge*, 1992.
60 Ibid.

Exhibit 1
Growth in Sales and Units, 1986–1997E ($ billions)[a]

YEAR	SAM'S CLUBS SALES	SAM'S CLUBS UNITS	PRICE[b] SALES	PRICE[b] UNITS	COSTCO SALES	COSTCO UNITS	PACE SALES	PACE UNITS	BJ'S SALES	BJ'S UNITS	OTHER SALES	OTHER UNITS	TOTAL SALES	TOTAL UNITS
1986	$1.7	49	$2.8	28	$0.8	37	$0.6	25	$0.4 E	15	$0.9	58	$7.2	212
1987	2.8	84	3.5	39	1.5	43	0.9	32	0.6 E	19	1.1	45	10.4	262
1988	3.8	105	4.3	41	2.4	50	1.3	39	0.8	22	1.3	49	13.9	306
1989	4.8	123	4.9	47	3.5	62	1.9[c]	56	1.0	23	1.8	55	17.9	366
1990	6.6	148	5.6	66	4.6	69	2.3	78	1.2	27	2.8	68	23.0	456
1991	9.4	208	6.9	77	5.8	82	3.6	87	1.4	29	0.3	14	27.5	497
1992	12.3	256	7.5	94	7.1	100	4.4	115	1.8	39	0.6	21	33.7	625
1993E	15.2	321	8.2	107	8.4	123	5.2	138	2.4	49	1.0	30	40.3	768
1994E	18.8	376	8.9	119	9.9	148	5.9	153	3.2	61	1.5	40	48.2	897
1995E	22.0	425	9.8	130	11.5	172	6.6	170	3.8	73	2.0	50	55.7	1,020
1996E	26.0	475	10.6	140	13.0	190	7.3	182	4.5	83	2.5	60	63.9	1,130
1997E	29.0	515	11.5	150	14.5	205	8.0	195	5.2	93	3.0	70	71.2	1,228
Historic growth[d]	34.4%	25.0%	16.5%	19.2%	36.5%	18.4%	37.4%	29.2%	24.6%	15.5%	(11.4%)	(14.1%)	26.5%	19.0%
Projected growth[e]	18.7%	15.0%	8.9%	9.8%	15.4%	15.4%	12.7%	11.1%	23.6%	19.0%	38.0%	27.2%	16.1%	14.5%

a All figures calendarized.
b Excludes Price Club Canada until fiscal 1991.
c Pro forma: Includes estimated $277 million in Makro sales.
d Five-year compound growth, 1987–1992.
e Five-year compound growth, 1992–1997.

Source: Goldman, Sachs & Co., 1993, Industry Report from *Warehouse Clubs: Still a Growth Industry?* by G. Strachan, 4/22/93.

Exhibit 2
Comparable Unit Sales Growth[a]

YEAR	SAM'S CLUBS FYE Jan.	PRICE CO. FYE Aug.	COSTCO FYE Aug.	PACE[b] FYE Jan.	BJ'S[c] FYE Jan.	AVERAGE
1986	16%	22%	28%	9%	32%	**21%**
1987	1%	12%	23%	16%	12%	**13%**
1988	10%	6%	25%	16%	12%	**14%**
1989	11%	12%	25%	12%	7%	**13%**
1990	15%	2%	20%	15%	9%	**12%**
1991	14%	4%	19%	17%	13%	**13%**
1992	9%[d]	3%	12%	7%	4%	**7%**
1993						
January	5%[e]	n/a	n/a	(2%)	(2%)	
February	(1%)	(6%) Q2	(4%) Q2	(3%)	(8%)	
March	(3%)	n/a	n/a	(6%)	(10%)	
April	0%	n/a	4%	(7%)	(10%)	
May	0%	n/a	3%	(5%)	(7%)	

a 1986–1992 data based on fiscal year.
b Estimated through fiscal year ended January 1991.
c Estimated through fiscal year ended January 1993.
d Adjusted to include extra day this year.
e Adjusted to include extra day last year.

Sources: Goldman, Sachs & Co.; Bloomberg Financial Systems.

Exhibit 3
Wholesale Club Industry 1992 North American Market Share (dollar sales)

Market Size = $33.7 Billion	
Wholesale Club	**Market Share (dollar sales)**
Sam's Club	37%
Price Club	22%
Costco Wholesale Club	21%
PACE Club	13%
BJ's Wholesale Club	5%
Other	2%

Source: Goldman, Sachs & Co.

Exhibit 4
Typical Warehouse Club Merchandise Mix: Grocery (sales dollars)

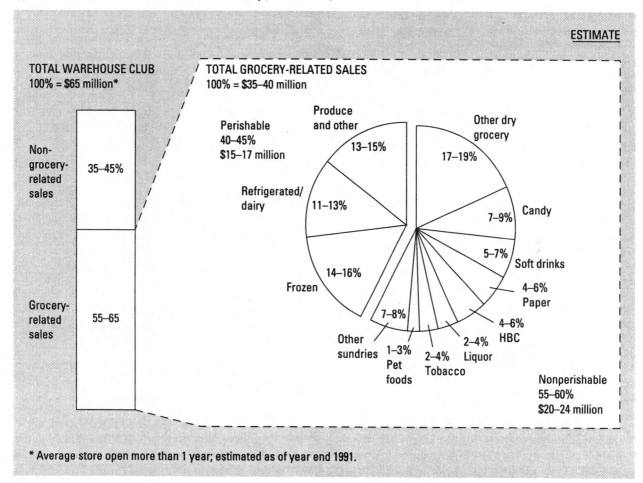

ESTIMATE

TOTAL WAREHOUSE CLUB
100% = $65 million*

Non-grocery-related sales   35–45%

Grocery-related sales   55–65

TOTAL GROCERY-RELATED SALES
100% = $35–40 million

Perishable
40–45%
$15–17 million

Produce and other
13–15%

Other dry grocery
17–19%

Refrigerated/dairy
11–13%

Candy
7–9%

Soft drinks
5–7%

Frozen
14–16%

Paper
4–6%

HBC
4–6%

Liquor
2–4%

Other sundries
7–8%

Pet foods
1–3%

Tobacco
2–4%

Nonperishable
55–60%
$20–24 million

* Average store open more than 1 year; estimated as of year end 1991.

Source: Used with the expressed permission of Food Marketing Institute, *Alternative Store Formats*, 1992.

Exhibit 5
Typical Warehouse Club Merchandise Mix: Non-Grocery (sales dollars)

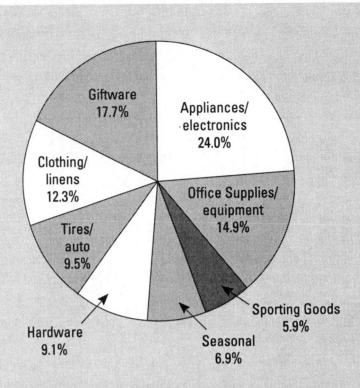

Section	Sales	%
Appliances/Electronics	$3,715 –$4,045	23.0 – 25.0%
Giftware/Housewares	2,800 – 2,900	17.4 – 18.0
Office Supplies/Equipment	2,350 – 2,450	14.6 – 15.2
Clothing/Linens	1,935 – 2,015	12.0 – 12.5
Tires/Automotive	1,480 – 1,580	9.2 – 9.8
Hardware	1,420 – 1,500	8.8 – 9.3
Seasonal	1,070 – 1,150	6.7 – 7.2
Sporting Goods	860 – 940	5.3 – 5.9
TOTAL	**$ 15,630–$16,580**	**97.0 –103.0%**

Source: James M. Degen & Company, Inc., 1992.

Exhibit 6
Estimated Financial Characteristics of Wholesale Clubs vs. Various Store Formats (millions, except where noted)

	Conventional Supermarket	Combination Store	Discount Store	Hypermarket	Wholesale Clubs with Sales of:		
					$40 M	$60 M	$100 M
Land (no. of acres)	4	6	8	25	12	12	12
Gross square feet	25,000	55,000	80,000	225,000	100,000	100,000	100,000
Sales	$8.0	$20.0	$15.0	$100.0	$40.0	$60.0	$100.0
Per square foot	320	364	188	444	400	600	1,000
Gross profit	$1.8	$5.0	$4.2	$14.0	$4.4	$6.6	$11.0
Gross margin	22.5%	25.0%	28.0%	14.0%	11.0%	11.0%	11.0%[a]
Expenses, excluding rent	$1.5	$3.8	$3.2	$11.0	$3.6	$4.5	$7.0
Expenses ratio	19.0%	19.0%	21.5%	11.0%	9.0%	7.5%	7.0%
Operating income	$0.3	$1.2	$1.0	$3.0	$0.8	$2.1	$4.0
Operating margin	3.5%	6.0%	6.5%	3.0%	2.0%	3.5%	4.0%
Return on investment:							
Land[b]	$1.5	$2.5	$3.0	$10.0	$6.0	$6.0	$6.0
Building	1.0	3.0	2.0	8.0	3.0	3.0	3.0
Fixtures	0.5	1.5	0.5	2.5	0.8	0.8	0.8
Fixed asset investment[c]	$3.0	$7.0	$5.5	$20.5	$9.8	$9.8	$9.8
Inventory (at cost)	$0.8	$1.5	$2.3	$8.0	$3.5	$4.0	$4.5
Less: Payables	0.5	1.0	0.8	8.0	2.5	4.0	5.0
Net inventory investment	$0.3	$0.5	$1.5	$0.0	$1.0	$0.0	($0.5)
Total investment, net	3.3	7.5	7.0	20.5	10.8	9.8	9.3
Pretax return on investment	10%	16%	14%	15%	7%	21%	43%

a Includes member fees.
b Land acquisition cost will vary significantly from these figures, depending on location. The figures here would be more typical of a California or East Coast location.
c Excludes investment in support facilities (distribution), which are minimal for wholesale clubs, but more extensive for the other formats shown.

Source: Goldman, Sachs & Co., 1990 Industry Report from February 12, 1990; *New Stores Formats: Changing of the Guard in U.S. Retailing* by Steve Mandel.

Exhibit 7
Wholesale Club Industry: 1992 Per-Store Average Sales

	Sam's	PACE	Price	Costco	BJ's
Millions of dollars	54.1	44.0	92.9	78.8	52.2

Source: Dean Witter Reynolds Inc., *Membership Warehouse Club Review and Update, 1992.*

Exhibit 8
Wholesale Club Industry: Average Annual Per-Store Sales

	Calendar Year							
	1986	1987	1988	1989	1990	1991	1992	1996(E)
Millions of dollars	54	51	52	58	61	63	63	65

Source: Dean Witter Reynolds Inc., *Membership Warehouse Club Review and Update, 1992.*

Exhibit 9
Saturation of U.S. Market

	Population per Club		Saturation[a]		Implied Potential New Stores Possible
	1991	1992	1991	1992	
Total U.S.			45	55	471
West	269	321	58	69	76
Midwest	345	422	44	54	109
South	299	370	50	62	126
Northeast	519	725	26	36	159

a Assumes 185,000 people/store is 100% saturation.

Source: Dean Witter Reynolds Inc., *Membership Warehouse Club Review and Update, 1992.*

Exhibit 10
Estimating Warehouse Club Grocery-Related Sales for Personal Use (%)

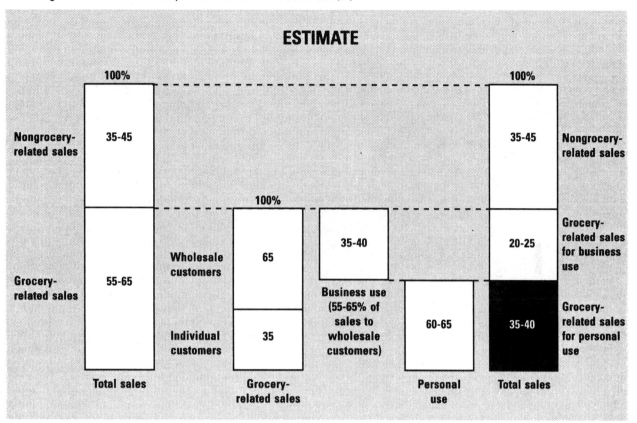

Exhibit 11
Evidence of Weakened Small-Business Sector

	1989	1990	1991	1992 E
BEA Index of Business Formations: Percentage change	+0.5%	-3.3%	-4.5%	+1.1%
Business failures	49,796	60,122	87,805	96,416
Percentage change	-13%	+20%	+46%	+11%

Source: Goldman, Sachs & Co., 1993 Industry Report, from *Warehouse Clubs: Still a Growth Industry?* by G. Strachan, 4/22/93.

Exhibit 12
Frequency of Shopping vs. Club Last Shopped for Family

| Frequency of Shopping | CLUB | | | | | | |
	Total	BJ's	Sam's	Warehouse Club	Costco	PACE	Price Club
Two or more times per month	38%	29%*	35%	34%	45%	39%	36%
Once a month	38	43	38	36	35	39	38
Once every 2 months	15	14	18	23	14	13	16
Once every 3 months	9	14	9	8	7	9	10
Total	100%	100%	100%	100%	100%	100%	100%
Sample size	1,852	143	331	53	378	443	475

* Read: Of those who last shopped at BJ's Wholesale Club for their family, 29% shopped two or more times a month for either food or non-food at any wholesale club.

Exhibit 13
Shopping Habits and Expenditures on Grocery Items

Q: Regarding purchases for food, household supplies, health and beauty care products, and paper products, approximately how many times do you go to buy these items in an average month at the following locations?

Q: About how much do you spend *per visit* on these items for your household at the following locations?

	Base	Visits per Month[b]	Average $ per Month[b]	Average $ per Visit[b]
All Shoppers				
Warehouse club	675	1.4	$ 120	$ 86
Mass merchandiser	769	2.5	$ 78	$ 31
Supermarket	1,218	4.1	$ 222	$ 54
Total[a]			$ 323	
Heavy Club Shoppers				
Warehouse club	242	2.2	$ 229	$104
Mass merchandiser	68	2.4	$ 99	$ 41
Supermarket	242	3.9	$ 281	$ 72
Total[a]			$ 530	
Light Club Shoppers				
Warehouse club	391	1.0	$ 53	$ 53
Mass merchandiser	146	2.7	$ 83	$ 31
Supermarket	391	3.8	$ 196	$ 52
Total[a]			$ 226	

a Not all shoppers shop at all formats listed. Therefore, total spent per month is less than the sum of individual items.
b Mean values exclude *Don't Know/None* responses.

Base: Alternative format shoppers

Source: Used with the expressed permission of Food Marketing Institute, *Alternative Store Formats*, 1992.

Exhibit 14
Family Food and Non-Food Spending

Amount Spent	Food Products	Non-Food Products
$0/Did not buy	8%	12%
$1 – $35	19	28
$36 – $50	19	23
$51 – $75	14	11
$76 – $99	7	5
$100 – $149	18	10
$150 – $199	7	4
$200 – $299	6	4
$300+	2	3
Totals	100%	100%
Sample size	1,818	1,797
Average—All	$83	$66
Average—Spend $1+	$90	$75

* Read: Of those who are family shopping for their household for food products at least once every three months, 19% spent $1 to $35 on food products the last time they shopped at a club. On average, respondents spent $83. The average among those who spent $1 or more was $90.

Source: Douglas J. Tigert, Stephen J. Arnold, and Terry W. Cotter, *Warehouse/Membership Clubs in North America: Are They Retailers or Wholesalers? And Who Is at Risk?* (Babson College, April 1992).

Exhibit 15
Top 20 Food Products Bought for Family at Warehouse Clubs

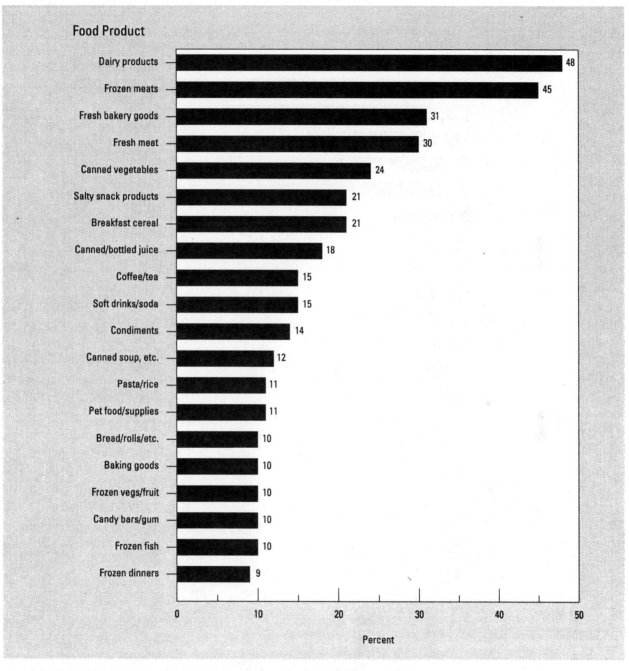

Food Product

Food Product	Percent
Dairy products	48
Frozen meats	45
Fresh bakery goods	31
Fresh meat	30
Canned vegetables	24
Salty snack products	21
Breakfast cereal	21
Canned/bottled juice	18
Coffee/tea	15
Soft drinks/soda	15
Condiments	14
Canned soup, etc.	12
Pasta/rice	11
Pet food/supplies	11
Bread/rolls/etc.	10
Baking goods	10
Frozen vegs/fruit	10
Candy bars/gum	10
Frozen fish	10
Frozen dinners	9

Percent

Source: Douglas J. Tigert, Stephen J. Arnold, and Terry W. Cotter, *Warehouse/Membership Clubs in North America: Are They Retailers or Wholesalers? And Who Is at Risk?* (Babson College, April 1992).

Exhibit 16
Top 21 Non-Food Products Bought for Family at Warehouse Clubs

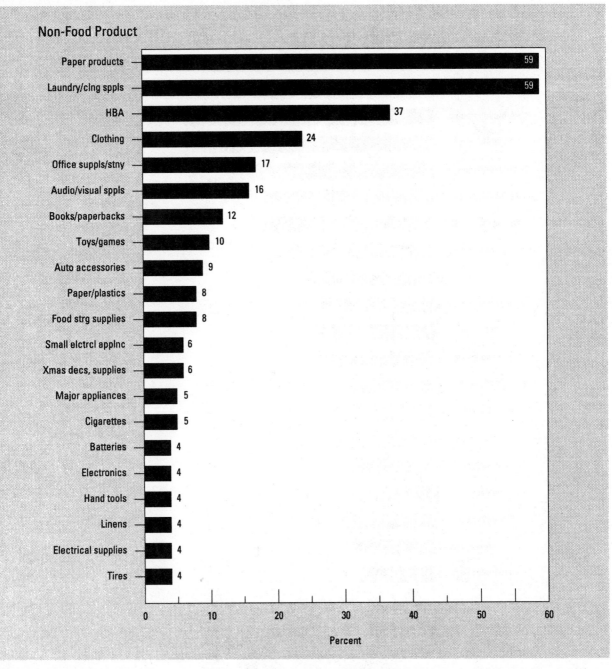

Source: Douglas J. Tigert, Stephen J. Arnold, and Terry W. Cotter, *Warehouse/Membership Clubs in North America: Are They Retailers or Wholesalers? And Who Is at Risk?* (Babson College, April 1992).

Exhibit 17
Top 20 Food Products Bought for Business/Organization at Warehouse Clubs

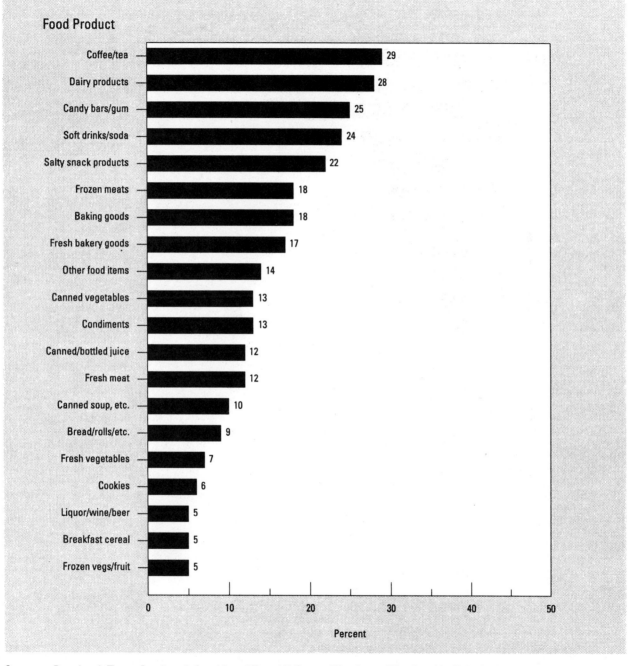

Source: Douglas J. Tigert, Stephen J. Arnold, and Terry W. Cotter, *Warehouse/Membership Clubs in North America: Are They Retailers or Wholesalers? And Who Is at Risk?* (Babson College, April 1992).

Exhibit 18
Top 20 Non-Food Products Bought for Business/Organization at Warehouse Clubs

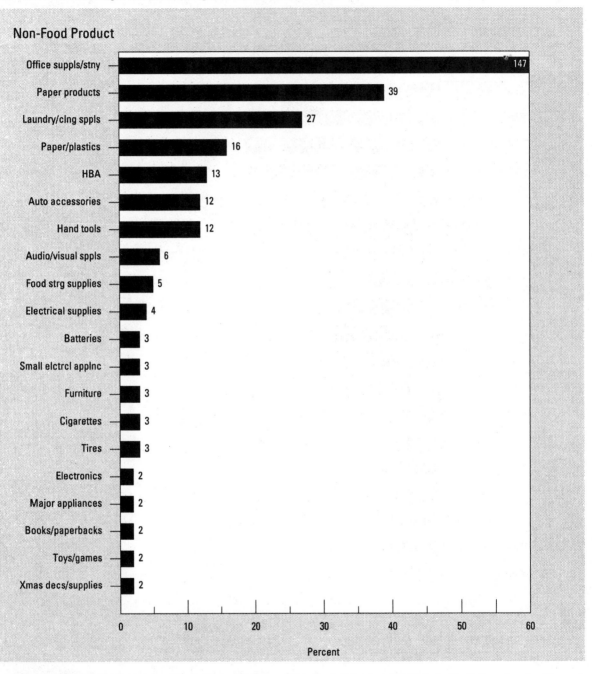

Source: Douglas J. Tigert, Stephen J. Arnold, and Terry W. Cotter, *Warehouse/Membership Clubs in North America: Are They Retailers or Wholesalers? And Who Is at Risk?* (Babson College, April 1992).

Exhibit 19
Demographics of Alternative Format Shoppers vs. Supermarket Shoppers

	Alternative Store Formats	Jan. 1992 Supermarket Shoppers[a]	Club Shoppers	
			Heavy	Light
Base	1,218	2,000	242	391
Sex				
Male	22%	23%	26%	23%
Female	78%	77%	74%	77%
Age				
18 – 24	8%	7%	5%	10%
25 – 39	39%	28%	43%	38%
40 – 49	21%	20%	29%	19%
50+	29%	35%	20%	30%
Education				
High school or less	47%	50%	43%	44%
Some college or more	52%	50%	56%	56%
Marital Status				
Married	68%	65%	80%	70%
Dual-income household	67%	49%	75%	65%
Household Type				
Children	47%	46%	61%	41%
No children	53%	53%	37%	58%
Size of Household				
One	12%	15%	4%	11%
Two	35%	31%	27%	39%
Three - four	38%	41%	42%	38%
Five or more	14%	12%	25%	12%
Income				
$15,000 or less	14%	18%	6%	12%
$15,001 – $25,000	17%	18%	12%	16%
$25,001 – $35,000	18%	17%	15%	19%
$35,001 – $50,000	20%	18%	24%	20%
More than $50,000	20%	16%	35%	22%
Mean	$36,000	$32,800	$44,900	$37,400

a Source: *Trends, 1992.*

Source: Used with the expressed permission of Food Marketing Institute, *Alternative Store Formats,* 1992.

Exhibit 20
Characteristics That Describe Warehouse Club Stores by Years Shopped

Q: For each characteristic, please indicate which one or more stores you feel fits that description. Would you say (CHARAC-TERISTIC) describes the supermarket where you do most of your shopping, does it describe the club, or does it describe none of them?

Base: Warehouse Club Shoppers

		Supermarket Total	Club Store Total	Years Shopped—Club Store		
				1 Year or Less	2–3 Years	More Than 3 Years
Base		1,218	675	239	191	231
Availability of large or institutional sizes	%	25	93	96	93	91
Good place to stock up	%	41	90	90	92	89
Clean store	%	85	72	74	74	68
Everyday low price	%	52	67	73	65	65
Good variety/wide selection	%	74	58	59	58	58
It's a fun place to shop	%	33	57	58	57	57
A place where I make many unplanned purchases	%	52	56	55	55	58
Availability of nationally advertised brands	%	80	56	60	52	54
Helpful employees	%	74	54	57	50	55
Fast checkout	%	58	47	52	47	44
Is easy to find things	%	81	46	45	45	49
Unadvertised sales/specials	%	55	41	47	36	39
Availability of quality fresh bakery items	%	83	35	32	31	41
Being able to do all my shopping in one store	%	64	32	30	33	36
Availability of fresh quality meat	%	87	28	25	30	32
Convenient location	%	87	28	26	27	32
Availability of fresh quality fruits and vegetables	%	92	18	17	17	20
A place I hate to shop	%	25	16	18	16	15
Advertised sales or specials	%	77	15	17	15	12
A place where I use coupons	%	85	7	6	9	8

Source: Food Marketing Institute, *Alternative Store Formats,* 1992. Used with the expressed permission of the Food Marketing Institute.

Exhibit 21
Club Shoppers' Frequency of Visits vs. Six Months Ago

Shopping More/Less	Total	BJ's	Sam's	Warehouse Club	Costco	PACE	Price Club
More often	15%	15%*	14%	14%	19%	17%	13%
About the same	60	60	61	61	58	57	62
Less often	25	25	25	25	24	26	25
Total	100%	100%	100%	100%	100%	100%	100%
Sample size	1,653	128	310	49	340	386	414

* Read: Of those who last shopped at BJ's Wholesale Club for their family, 15% said they are shopping more often at these stores compared to six months ago.

Source: Douglas J. Tigert, Stephen J. Arnold, and Terry W. Cotter, *Warehouse/Membership Clubs in North America: Are They Retailers or Wholesalers? And Who Is at Risk?* (Babson College, April 1992).

Exhibit 22
Change in Amount Purchased Since First Shopped at Warehouse Club Stores

Q: Are you buying more, less, or about the same amount of items for your household as you did when you first shopped at a given club store?

	Base	More	Less	Same	Don't Know
Total	675	33%	18%	46%	4%
Type of Shopper					
Heavy club	242	41%	13%	43%	3%
Light club	391	29%	20%	47%	3%
Market Maturity—Club Store					
New	179	35%	18%	43%	3%
Middle	212	34%	12%	49%	5%
Established	284	30%	22%	45%	3%
Time Shopped—Club Store					
1 year or less	239	33%	13%	48%	6%
2 – 3 years	191	35%	17%	46%	2%
Over 3 years	231	32%	24%	43%	1%

Base: Warehouse club store shoppers

Source: Food Marketing Institute, *Alternative Store Formats,* 1992. Used with express permission of the Food Marketing Institute.

Exhibit 23

Price Comparisons Between Alternative Retail Formats (supermarkets as benchmark)

		Retail Formats		
	Supermarket	**Discount Merchandiser**	**Deep-Discount Drugstore**	**Wholesale Club**
Percent of price	100%	85%	82%	74%

Exhibit 24

Overall Market Basket Comparison: Grocery vs. Wholesale Club

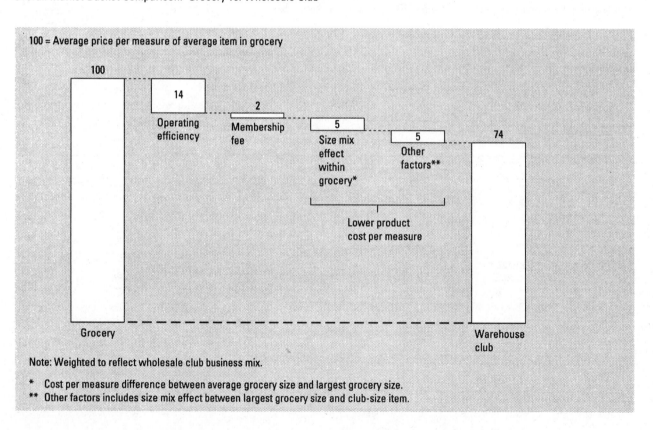

Note: Weighted to reflect wholesale club business mix.

*   Cost per measure difference between average grocery size and largest grocery size.

** Other factors includes size mix effect between largest grocery size and club-size item.

Source: Food Marketing Institute, *Alternative Store Formats,* 1992. Used with express permission of the Food Marketing Institute.

Exhibit 25
Supermarket vs. Wholesale Club Comparison of Operating Expenses (percent of sales)

	Supermarket	-	Wholesale Club	=	Difference
Labor	10%		4.0%		6.0%
Facility	5%		1.5%		3.5%
Warehouse/Transportation	2%		0.5%		1.5%
Advertising/Marketing	2%		0.5%		1.5%
Other	3%		1.5%		1.5%
Total	22%		8.0%		14.0%

Source: Food Marketing Institute, *Alternative Store Formats,* 1992. Used with express permission of the Food Marketing Institute.

Exhibit 26
Financial Returns Grocery vs. Wholesale Club

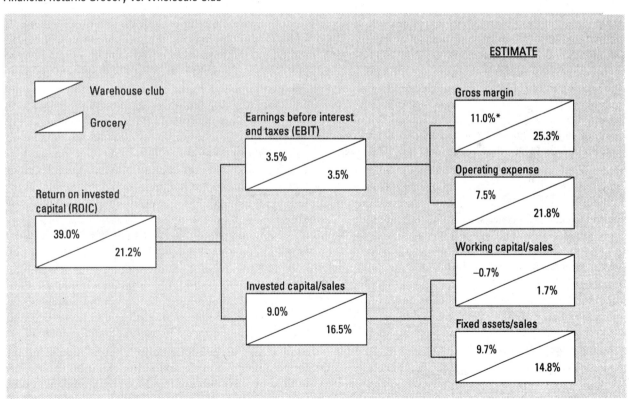

Source: Food Marketing Institute, *Alternative Store Formats,* 1992. Used with express permission of the Food Marketing Institute.

Exhibit 27
Costco Wholesale Corp. Sales, Operating Expenses, and Profitability

Year	Sales ($B)	Operating and Administrative Expenses as % of Sales	Return on Sales (%)
1987	$1.4	9.7%	0.4%
1988	$2.0	8.8%	0.7%
1989	$2.9	8.4%	0.9%
1990	$4.1	8.3%	1.2%
1991	$5.2	8.1%	1.6%
1992	$6.5	8.1%	1.7%

Source: Annual Reports, Costco Wholesale Corp.

Exhibit 28
Excerpt from Warehouse Club Industry Survey of Supermarket Executives

Q: How do you rate the future prospects for success of warehouse clubs?
(percentage rating future prospects excellent or good)

	1988	1989	1990	1991	1992
Supermarket chain response:	38%	42%	50%	58%	74%

Source: *Progressive Grocer*, April 1992, 1993.

Exhibit 29
Variety of Responses to Alternative Formats

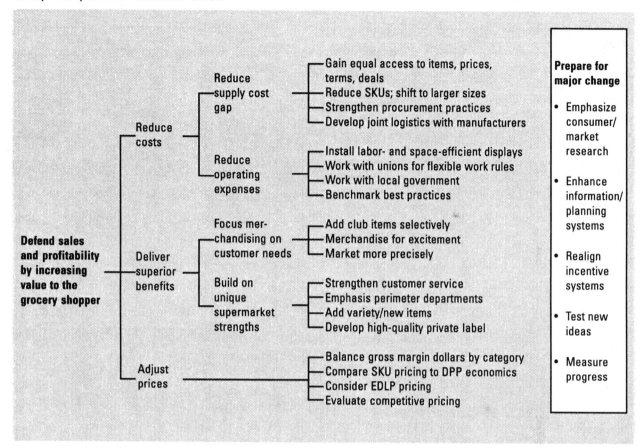

Source: Food Marketing Institute, *Alternative Store Formats*, 1992. Used with express permission of the Food Marketing Institute.

Exhibit 30
Percentage of Warehouses Competing Directly with Other Warehouse Clubs

Costco		1991	1992 E		Price		1991	1992 E
BJ's		12%	14%		BJ's		22%	23%
PACE		40%	54%		Costco		42%	47%
Price		37%	37%		PACE		58%	73%
Sam's		12%	33%		Sam's		3%	38%
	Total	63%	67%			Total	73%	80%

PACE		1991	1992 E		Sam's		1991	1992 E
BJ's		10%	18%		BJ's		5%	7%
Costco		25%	28%		Costco		2%	5%
Price		41%	44%		PACE		21%	30%
Sam's		51%	59%		Price		2%	12%
	Total	82%	90%			Total	25%	36%

Source: Dean Witter Reynolds Inc., *Membership Warehouse Club Review and Update*, 1992.

APPENDIX 1

MAJOR PLAYERS OF WHOLESALE CLUB INDUSTRY

Since the emergence of the wholesale club concept in the 1970s, the number of club chains grew rapidly, then fell steadily. In the early 1980s, new firms entered the industry and the number of players rose. Since then, the industry has consolidated, reducing the number of competitors by over 50%. By 1993, only seven companies competed in the wholesale club retailing segment.

Economies of scale and other advantages drove small chains out of business and forced intermediate chains to be acquired by larger players. Two of the top chains, Sam's and PACE, have both made multiple acquisitions over the last several years. In May 1993, Sam's acquired 14 PACE clubs, and in June, Price and Costco announced

their plan to merge. The top 5 firms (based upon Price and Costco still being separate entities) represented 98% of industry sales.[61] Each of these chains would rank in the 1992 *Fortune 250,* based on their sales revenues.[62]

Sam's Club

Sam's Club continued to be the dominant force in the industry, with 1992 sales of $12.6 billion and North American market share of 37% **(Exhibit 1)**. Sam's was part of Wal-Mart, named after the company's founder, Sam Walton. The division represented 28% of its parent's total sales.[63] Sam's was the largest club chain, and was

61 Goldman, Sachs & Co.
62 *Fortune*, "The Fortune 500 Special Report," April 1993.
63 Securities and Exchange Commission, *Form 10K, Wal-Mart Stores, Inc. for the Fiscal Year Ended January 31, 1992* (Washington, D.C., 1992).

growing at an above industry average rate in both sales and units.

Sam's opened its first unit in a former 100,000 square foot discount store in Oklahoma City in April 1983. It was one of Price Club's first imitators. The store lacked the warehouse look and configuration of subsequent locations, but offered Wal-Mart an inexpensive opportunity to test the concept.

With over twice as many units as any other competitor, Sam's has maintained its number one industry revenue position since 1990. Drawing on the retailing skills of its parent, Sam's expanded rapidly into new regions, following a cluster strategy. Its objective was to gain first-mover advantage by rapidly entering new regions and developing large, loyal membership bases. This strategy included opening as many stores as a local market could support in order to preempt potential competitors. For example, in 1992, Sam's had 45 clubs in Texas, with 10 in Dallas and 12 in Houston.[64] This strategy sacrificed some per-club sales and profits for long-term market share. Sam's had one of the lowest per-club sales in the industry at $54 million.[65]

Sam's has moved into the Northeast and expanded in the Midwest. In fiscal 1992 Sam's added 60 clubs. Twenty-eight were acquired from The Wholesale Club, and 32 new units were constructed. Sam's was also experiencing competition in Texas for the first time, where until late 1991 it had been the only club competitor.[66]

Sam's was lagging behind the other major competitors in introducing an expanded perishable goods program into its units. While new units included a fresh bakery, meat, and produce program, it was introduced into only 47 existing clubs by fiscal year 1992.[67]

In the fourth quarter 1992, Wal-Mart began operations of its first two clubs in Mexico City. Club Aurrera is the joint venture club between Sam's and CIFRA, Mexico's largest retailer.[68] In April 1993, Sam's had 272 stores, and planned to open a total of 65 stores during the year.

Price Club

Celebrating 17 years in business, industry pioneer Price Club boasted the most established club network in 1993.

Price Club had a formidable position in the California market, with a very strong membership franchise. Its operating policies had been widely imitated by other industry players. With sales of $7.5 billion and market share of 22%, it retained the number two position in the industry.

Price had the lowest number of clubs of the top 4 players with only 94 units. Its sales per club, however, were the highest at $92.9 million. Some of its oldest clubs in California generated $120 million in sales. In 1991, average sales per foot were $928, much higher than the industry average of $600.[69] Unlike most club operators, Price Club owned most of its real estate.

Before the Costco merger announcement, Price's expansion plans indicated its determination to stay an industry leader. It anticipated experiencing significant cannibalization in 1993, as the result of opening a large number of stores in existing markets. The result would be to augment the negative effects of a depressed California economy on Price's performance. Price operated approximately 40 of its stores in California as of 1992, or 43% of the total. It had 13 stores in the Greater Los Angeles area alone (out of 40 wholesale clubs there), a region with annual food-at-home sales of about $16 billion.

Price Club was also expanding into new markets such as Texas, Denver, and the Northeast, and it continued to expand outside the United States. Price had 11 units in Canada and a Mexico City unit as of year-end 1992.

Fiscal 1992 was a year of important improvements in merchandising and operations for Price Club, with substantial investment in existing facilities. Fresh meat departments were introduced in most Price Clubs. Major improvements were made in the produce, bakery, and delicatessen departments, which had been lagging behind the other competitors. Scanning was installed in nearly all warehouses. The Discover card is now accepted.[70] Price Club also expanded service options in 1992, including travel programs, new car buying programs, and oil lube centers in selected stores. In every case, the goal was to enhance the value of the Price Club membership card.

One of Price Club's Dallas stores was a prime example of their merchandising innovation. This store was

---

64 Dean Witter Reynolds Inc., 1992.
65 Ibid.
66 American Wholesale Club ceased operations in 1990 after just three years of operation.
67 Securities and Exchange Commission, *Form 10K, Wal-Mart Stores, Inc. for the Fiscal Year Ended Jaunary 31, 1992.*
68 Ibid.
69 Goldman, Sachs & Co.
70 Securities and Exchange Commission, *Form 10K, The Price Company for the Fiscal Year Ended August 31, 1992.*

among Price Club's largest, totaling 156,000 square feet, and included several new features: a brightly lit building with more of a retail store "feel" than its typical club; a "Tech center," with computers from Dell and other business machines; a sound room, where customers could listen to stereo, audio, VCR, and television equipment; and a "Touch & Shop" kiosk, which was the equivalent of an electronic catalog.[71]

To "stay ahead of competition," Price had developed several subsidiary businesses. These are managed under the umbrella of Price Club Industries (PCI).[72] Currently, PCI operated a state-of-the-art frozen ground meat packing plant, candy packaging operation, optical lab, and photo processing lab. The company also pursued quality private label opportunities, including Gibson's Gourmet Ranch ground beef, Hattie Brooks candy and ice cream, and Club Classic clothing. In each case the private label product was designed to compete in quality and sell at a significantly lower price than the national brands.[73]

Costco Wholesale Club

Costco ranked third in revenues behind Sam's and Price Club, with sales of $7.1 billion in 1992. Steady unit expansion over the past two years and the introduction of a major perishable program into all units pushed Costco nearer to the top for total and average club revenues. Costco achieved average sales per unit of over $75 million.

Costco has been an innovator in providing members with new products and services. It was the first to introduce an expanded perishables program chainwide and also the first to develop on-site pharmacy stores and optical shops. Costco was experimenting in 1992 with home improvement and green nursery products in selected warehouses, and also began testing a kiosk-based special-order program, whereby members select for home delivery from a wide range of "specialty high-end" products not carried in the warehouse.[74]

Costco had a relatively high percentage of its warehouses in smaller markets; only 20% of its warehouses shared markets with competitors. This location strategy may be an important competitive advantage, since profits from uncontested clubs in smaller markets could be used to subsidize clubs in competitive markets.[75]

Nearly 65% of Costco's clubs were located on the Pacific coast. It was especially strong in the Pacific Northwest, where its headquarters is situated, but a major issue for Costco is increased competition from new Sam's units in this area. In 1992, approximately 20% of Costco's warehouses and approximately 25% to 30% of operating profits came from the Oregon and Washington region.

Like the other major clubs, Costco has targeted the Northeast for further expansion. With an additional 23 units projected for 1993, Costco will have close to 125 units in operation in both the United States and Canada (where 12 of its units are in operation).

In 1993, Costco was expected to open 2 to 3 warehouse clubs in England, through a joint venture with Carrefour, the largest retailer in France and the originator of the hypermarket concept. (Carrefour was the owner of 22% of Costco's common stock.) If its test is successful, the joint venture could open another 2 to 3 clubs by 1994, and have at least 20 clubs operating by 1996. The warehouses were to be called Costco and look like their U.S. counterparts.[76]

The Costco/Carrefour joint venture was expected to have more long- than short-term value for Costco because of the same challenges U.S. warehouse clubs faced during the early 1980s, namely, consumer acceptance, vendor cooperation, and real estate availability.

PACE Club

In the late 1980s, Kmart decided to follow Wal-Mart into warehouse clubs. It built its presence through a series of takeovers, acquiring its flagship chain, PACE, from Kroger Supermarkets in 1989. Due to these acquisitions, PACE lacked a strong geographic focus, with stores spread across 25 states. Since many of its clubs were new, its sales per club were only $44 million— well below the three top competitors. In 1992, PACE continued to roll out its fresh foods program in existing units and equipped all new units with the expanded perishables program.

71 Dean Witter Reynolds Inc., 1992.
72 Ibid.
73 Ibid.
74 Securities and Exchange Commission, *Form 10K, Costco Wholesale Corporation for the Fiscal Year Ended August 30, 1992.*
75 Dean Witter Reynolds, 1992.
76 Ibid.

PACE has experienced steady growth over the past two years. With 1992 revenues exceeding $4.4 billion, it was the fourth-largest club operator. It operated 115 units at year-end 1992.

PACE's relatively low sales productivity reflected a debatable initial approach to expansion. It failed to cluster its warehouses by city or region. Instead, PACE opened one or two stores in many markets. The result was low name recognition and a lack of regional purchasing leverage with suppliers. This situation contributed greatly to lower warehouse volumes. Industry observers believed future expansion should focus more on existing markets.[77]

At the beginning of 1993, PACE planned to open 23 new clubs during the year.[78] This included expansion throughout the Northeast and Midwest as well as Texas, a new market for PACE. The company had also announced plans for a unit in Puerto Rico.

BJ's Wholesale Club

BJ's Wholesale Club was the largest of the other players in the industry. It was founded in 1984 by Zayre Corp., with the first store in Medford, Massachusetts. BJ's was spun off by Zayre as part of its restructuring in 1989 and is now a division of Waban, Inc. With $1.8 billion in 1992 sales, BJ's was a major club operator, but was very small in comparison to its larger rivals. Until recently, it enjoyed a relatively uncontested niche position in the Northeast, where over 80% of its clubs were located. It has pursued a slow-growth, regional cluster strategy, using strategically located cross dock facilities.

Outside of the Northeast, BJ's has a store cluster in metropolitan Miami. It retreated from its plans to expand into the Midwest when it closed all 4 of its clubs around Chicago in late 1991. BJ's has apparently decided to leverage the strengths of its East Coast base.[79]

New Entrant in the Industry

Meijer's Thrifty Acres was the newest industry entrant and may possess unique competitive attributes that increase its chances of survival. Meijer's was a private company, based in Grand Rapids, Michigan, operating 65 supercenters with estimated 1991 revenues of $3.5 billion, or $55 million per store. It was one of a very few retailers in the United States that profitably operated a chain of large-size combination food and general merchandise stores.[80]

Meijer's warehouse club format, Source Club, was similar to the industry standard with approximately 130,000 square feet of total space. The company opened 3 warehouses in 1992, all with fresh food sections. One of the clubs competed with Sam's in Lansing, Michigan, and two competed with PACE and Warehouse Club, a smaller operator, in Detroit. Source Club was expected to open at least 7 locations in 1993, all in the Midwest.

Despite its late entrance, Meijer had several competitive advantages, including a strong local reputation and loyal customer following, experience in successfully operating large-format food and general merchandise stores, and presumably strong financial resources.[81]

Source Club will have to compete with Sam's, which had plans for 14 clubs in Michigan by year-end 1993, as well as other sites targeted for the Detroit and Jackson Standard Metropolitan Statistical Areas (SMSA). Once these stores are in operation, the population per warehouse in Michigan's 10 metropolitan markets will have declined to approximately 190,000.[82]

77 Goldman, Sachs & Co.
78 Ibid.
79 Securities and Exchange Commission, *Form 10K, Waban, Inc. for the Fiscal Year Ended January 25, 1992.*
80 Meijer is sometimes confused as a hypermarket. Supercenters differ from hypermarkets in that supercenters carry a more narrow selection of high-priced durable goods.
81 Dean Witter Reynolds Inc., 1992.
82 Ibid.

APPENDIX 2

EXCERPTS FROM THE CUSTOM RESEARCH WAREHOUSE CLUB STORE OMNIBUS™

BACKGROUND AND PURPOSE

The growth of warehouse club stores has been extraordinary, from 25 stores and $1 billion in revenue nine years ago to over 450 stores and $28 billion in revenue last year.

Warehouse club stores are changing the way America shops and are representing a rising share of sales in numerous categories. Many of CRI's clients are increasingly interested in the dynamics of the club stores and how and what to market to the club shopper.

CRI developed the Warehouse Club Shopper Omnibus to learn more about the warehouse shopper and to size the market.

The Warehouse Shopper Omnibus is designed to provide base-line and ongoing tracking of warehouse club store shopping. The study measures awareness, attitudes, and usage information about warehouse club store shopping in general, as well as specific information about shoppers and shopping in the four major club store chains: Sam's, PACE, Price Club, and Costco.

The study is specifically designed to provide the following information from households:

- An overview of the warehouse club store phenomenon
- A profile of the warehouse club shopper
- Base-line data of awareness, shopping behavior, and category penetration
- Detailed profiles of purchasers of specific categories
- Answers to ad hoc questions relating to warehouse clubs

Starting in 1993, Custom Research Inc. will offer a profile of the business shopper and an ongoing Category Tracker to provide more detail on:

- Brands being purchased in various categories
- Impact of club purchases on brand preference
- Quality perceptions of brands in clubs
- Other ad hoc brand and category issues

RESEARCH PROCEDURE

To provide this information, telephone interviews were conducted among a national probability sample of *households*. The interviewing was conducted by CRI using computer-assisted interviewing and a random-digit dial sample.

One thousand one interviews were conducted as part of a representative national sample, 432 with club store shoppers and 569 with non-shoppers. Supplemental interviews were then conducted to find additional shoppers of the four major warehouse club store chains. In total, 863 interviews were completed with approximately 200 shoppers at each of the four major chains: Sam's, PACE, Price Club, and Costco.

Sample for the supplemental interviews was drawn to represent each of the franchise's geographical operating areas. (For example, for additional interviews with PACE shoppers, a supplemental sample was drawn to include only those states in which PACE operates.)

Interviews were conducted with the male or female head of household who does at least one half of the total shopping for their household. If there was a club store shopper in the household, the interview was completed with the primary warehouse club shopper (the person who does at least one half of the *club* store shopping for the household).

It should be noted that this sample is *household* based. As part of this, some shoppers were located who shop for business reasons, and their responses are included. Additional questions were asked of this group to learn more about business purchasers.

The telephone interviewing was conducted September 9–22, 1992. The interview was 12–25 minutes in length.

Source: Custom Research Inc. (CRI), July 1993.

MAJOR CONCLUSIONS

✓ This is big!

The warehouse club store shopping phenomenon is much larger than has been initially reported by industry sources. Nearly everyone is familiar with the concept (87% awareness), and membership is much higher than the 15% – 20% sometimes quoted. The real number is double this. Currently over four in ten households in the United States contain someone who shops at a warehouse club store. Many other households include members who have been to a store, but do not shop them regularly. Non-member shoppers have access to a club through a friend or relative.

✓ Not surprisingly, Sam's is the national leader.

Sam's has the largest number of stores (currently in 37 states) and, not surprisingly, is the most well known and most widely used on a national basis. PACE follows as a distant second in awareness.

✓ Price is the main reason for shopping warehouse club stores.

Shoppers go to the clubs primarily because of the good prices they can get there. The variety of merchandise offered and ability to buy in bulk are also appealing to many.

✓ Warehouse club store shoppers are not a single group of shoppers.

They are a cross section of all types of consumers. They share many attitudes in common with non-club store shoppers relating to shopping in general, liking bargains, being brand loyal, etc. In terms of their attitudes, club store shoppers are more interested in large-size packaging and less concerned about store decor or a store being too big.

✓ With club store shoppers, there are five distinct segments of shoppers, based on their attitudes toward shopping.

Although club shoppers and non-shoppers share many opinions about shopping *in general, within* the club store shoppers there are five distinct segments. These segments are:

- Frequent Freewheelers
- Hard-Core Shoppers
- Mission Shoppers
- Brand Buyers
- Grocery List Consumers

Three of these groups, the Frequent Freewheelers, the Hard-Core Shoppers and Grocery List Consumers, represent the best targets among warehouse club shoppers.

✓ Club store shoppers are different than non-shoppers in terms of their demographics.

The warehouse club store shopper is slightly younger, more likely to be employed outside the home, live in a dual income household, have a larger household size, have children at home, and, as a result, have less free time than the non-shopper. Shoppers and non-shoppers tend to be female, age 25–45, and live in single-family detached homes.

✓ A measurable segment of business shoppers exists within club households.

Among U.S. households, about one in five warehouse club store shoppers also shops for a business.

On average they spend $152 per trip and believe they are saving more than those buying for household or non-profit use. The businesses purchased for tend to be small offices, many of which have only one or two employees. Most purchases for businesses are supplies or snacks to be used around the office.

✓ Membership type (business vs. personal) is not a predictor of purchase purpose.

Nearly one half of members (44%) have a business membership (primary or secondary) but only one in five (21%) are making purchases for a business. On the other hand, nearly everyone is buying for personal/household use. This means that if the warehouse clubs attribute all sales from business memberships to be business purchases, they are greatly over-estimating the business component of their business, and under-estimating the household market size.

✓ **Significant volume in many different categories is moving through the club stores.**

Products sold in traditional retail outlets, like food and cleaning supplies, are almost universally purchased by club store members. Three fourths or more of shoppers have purchased paper products, cleaning supplies, and food and beverages in the clubs in the past year. Less commonly purchased items include furniture, jewelry, and appliances.

✓ **Club stores are still showing strong growth.**

The rapid growth of these outlets is far from over. One in five of shoppers joined within the past year, and memberships continue to expand rapidly. It is estimated that over 100 new club stores will be added in 1993, and some researchers now estimate the number of warehouses will double over the next 10 years. With these stores will come thousands of new members—and millions of dollars in sales.

✓ **Currently club stores are still a supplemental source of shopping for most consumers.**

Almost all club store shoppers buy grocery and household items in the clubs and make fill-in trips to their regular grocery store. But with current growth rates and expansion, the percent of total grocery purchases going through the clubs will increase. Some researchers estimate that clubs' share of grocery business could at least double in the next 10 years, unless grocery channels aggressively respond to the club threat.

✓ **Brand preferences are being affected, especially in certain categories.**

The research indicates that presence in warehouse club stores is affecting brand preference, more so in some categories than others.

In categories with strong brand preferences, many consumers will go elsewhere for a preferred brand if it is not available at the club, or they will wait until it comes to the club store. In other categories, consumers are more likely to accept whatever is on the shelf at the club. However, the on-shelf presence of weaker brands in the clubs can erode a stronger brand's position by generating some new trial and maybe even conversion.

✓ **Most shoppers are in the clubs at least once a month, shop with another adult, believe they are saving about 20%, and spend about $100 per trip.**

Although shopping clubs is not as frequent as a trip to the grocery store, many shoppers are making a club trip with considerable frequency. Most club shoppers are in these stores at least once a month.

A trip to the club store is expensive, though, with most consumers spending about $100 per trip, mostly on household purchases. Consumers believe that they are saving an average of 18%–20% on purchases made at the club stores.

✓ **It's okay to have your brand in the clubs. Shoppers do not perceive any loss in quality for brands sold in club stores.**

Most consumers believe that products bought in the club store are as good as or better than the same products sold in traditional grocery stores. Thus there does not appear to be a risk of any loss in brand image because products are included in this retail outlet.

A WAREHOUSE CLUB STORE SHOPPER OR MEMBER IS PRESENT IN OVER FOUR IN TEN U.S. HOUSEHOLDS.

Active, shopping members are present in about 36% of U.S. households. Another 7% shop, but don't have a membership.

It is also interesting to note that 5% of U.S. households have a membership available to them, but they don't take advantage of it by shopping the clubs. These may be individuals who have a membership through work, but don't use it.

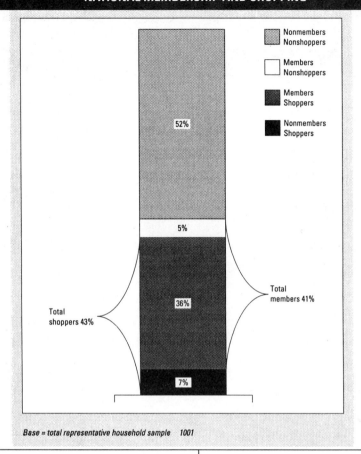

Nonmembers Nonshoppers

Members Nonshoppers

Members Shoppers

Nonmembers Shoppers

52%

5%

Total members 41%

36%

Total shoppers 43%

7%

Base = total representative household sample   1001

THERE IS NO SINGLE WAREHOUSE SHOPPER MIND-SET. RATHER, CLUB STORE SHOPPERS HAVE ATTITUDES ABOUT SHOPPING SIMILAR TO NONSHOPPERS.

Attitudinally, warehouse shoppers are much like nonshoppers, sharing many of the same beliefs and opinions about shopping in general. They do not stand out, for example, as being more "into" shopping or bargain hunting than nonshoppers.

Club store shoppers do have different attitudes than nonshoppers in a few areas. Shoppers are more prone to try to find low prices, to shop with someone else, to care less about attractive store decor, to not be put off by larger stores, and to have stronger interest in bulk packaging.

Although there is no clear pattern of stronger or weaker brand loyalty among shoppers, they are more likely to describe themselves as having strong brand preferences in many categories. On other topics related to shopping, they share similar beliefs with non-club-shoppers.

In addition to looking at responses to individual attitude statements, CRI completed a cluster analysis among the total representative sample. The purpose of this was to determine if club store shoppers had different attitudes about shopping than nonshoppers did. Could they be singled out from the general population by their attitudes?

This analysis included the 15 attitude statements about shopping in general. It showed that club store shoppers were quite similar in their attitudes to nonshoppers.

Because this segmentation showed no attitudinal differences between shoppers and nonshoppers, it is not reported here.

Although club store shoppers and nonshoppers are attitudinally similar, *within* warehouse club store shoppers there are several distinctly different segments.

PSYCHOGRAPHIC PROFILE OF NONSHOPPERS AND SHOPPERS				
Average Ratings*				
	Total	Non-Shoppers		Shoppers
Price Statements				
I try to shop where I can get the lowest prices	6.2	6.0	-S-	6.3
I just love finding a great bargain	6.2	6.2		6.3
**The main reason I shop at warehouse club stores is really great prices	n/a	n/a		5.7
**Just because something is offered at the warehouse club store doesn't guarantee it's the lowest price, so you still have to shop around	n/a	n/a		5.5
Variety				
**I like going up and down every aisle at the warehouse club store just to see what they have	n/a	n/a		5.0
**The main reason I shop at club stores is because I find some items that I don't usually find in my regular grocery store	n/a	n/a		4.1
Shopping Attitude				
I usually like to shop alone so I can get the job done quickly	5.0	5.3	-S-	4.7
Sometimes we go shopping just for fun—it's sort of entertaining	3.6	3.5		3.6
I love to shop	4.2	4.1		4.3
**Shopping at warehouse club stores is fun	n/a	n/a		5.0
Product Type				
**I wouldn't think of buying clothing at a warehouse club store	n/a	n/a		3.0
**I don't usually buy groceries at a warehouse club store	n/a	n/a		3.0
**I wouldn't buy big-ticket items like appliances or furniture at a warehouse club store	n/a	n/a		3.4

* Mean rating on a 7-point scale with 7 = completely agree and 1 = completely disagree.
** These statements refer specifically to warehouse club store shopping and were asked of club store shoppers only.
S = statistically significant at 95% confidence level or higher.

PSYCHOGRAPHIC PROFILE OF NONSHOPPERS AND SHOPPERS			
Average Ratings*			
	Total	**Non-Shoppers**	**Shoppers**
Time			
I like to allow plenty of time for shopping because I like to have enough time to look around	5.1	5.0	5.2
I like to get in and out of stores quickly, otherwise I spend too much money	4.9	4.8	4.9
I usually take a shopping list and try to buy only what is on the list	4.5	4.5	4.4
**When I go to the warehouse club store, I usually go just to find the items I need and don't spend time looking around to see what else they have	n/a	n/a	3.4
Brand			
I count on the stores I shop at to have the brands I am looking for	5.8	5.8	5.8
As long as a store has a major national brand of the product I need, I'll buy it, even if it's not the brand I prefer	3.6	3.7	3.5
I have a strong brand preference in many product categories. If a store does not carry that brand, I won't usually buy a substitute brand	4.4	4.2 -S-	4.6
Packaging			
I like buying large bulk packages of some products because they use less packaging which is better for the environment	4.9	4.6 -S-	5.4
I'm not very likely to try a new brand if the package size is too big	4.6	4.4 -S-	4.8
Store Facility			
I prefer to shop in stores that have an attractive decor	4.3	4.6 -S-	3.9
Some stores are just too big. I don't enjoy shopping in a store that is too big	3.7	4.0 -S-	3.4
Base = total representative household sample	*981*	*555*	*426*

* Mean rating on a 7-point scale with 7 = completely agree and 1 = completely disagree.
** These statements refer specifically to warehouse club store shopping and were asked on club store shoppers only.
S = statistically significant at 95% confidence level or higher

PRICE IS THE MOST IMPORTANT REASON FOR SHOPPING AT A CLUB STORE.

To help further understand what is important to club store shoppers, they were asked to react to a series of statements about shopping. These statements were developed from focus group discussions and covered a wide range of attitudes about shopping in general, including importance of price, time, product selection, branding, store facilities, and product packaging. Consumers indicated how much they agreed or disagreed with each statement, using a 7-point scale where 7 = completely agree and 1 = completely disagree.

Price

Getting a good price or finding a good bargain are most important to club store shoppers. Ninety percent of them agree that they love finding a great bargain and try to shop where they get low prices. Over 80% say the *main reason* they shop the clubs is the really great prices clubs offer.

Most shoppers are at least a bit skeptical, however, and say that just because something is in the club store does not necessarily mean it is the lowest price available, so they still have to shop around (76%).

Brands

Consumers overwhelmingly agree (84%) that they rely on the stores they shop to carry the brands they want, and most (59%) admit strong brand preferences in many categories.

Time

Consumers have diverse feelings about time involved in shopping. Most (68%) like to allow plenty of time to look around, while many (62%) want to get in and out quickly so they do not spend too much money. Some (59%) say they usually take a shopping list and try to stick with it instead of looking around to see what is available. Others, meanwhile, delight in going up and down every aisle and take the time to do so (67%).

Fun and Variety

The majority (64%) also describe warehouse shopping as fun and enjoy going up and down every aisle just to see what is offered (67%). Not quite one half (47%) agree that the main reason they shop the club is because they find unusual items they don't usually find in their regular store.

BASED ON THEIR ATTITUDES TOWARD SHOPPING, FIVE DISTINCT SEGMENTS OF CLUB STORE SHOPPERS EXIST.

In order to better understand club shoppers, they were segmented into groups according to attitudes about shopping. This process involved a Cluster Analysis, in which 24 different statements were evaluated by respondents. The statements were developed from focus group discussions and encompassed nine subject categories: shopping in general, price, variety, time, product type, brand, packaging, store facility, and shopping at warehouse club stores.

The segments were formed and appropriate names were given to each group based on their overall attitudes. Additional behavioral and demographic information was then examined to provide a more complete profile of each group.

The five segments are:

- Frequent Freewheelers
- Hard-Core Shoppers
- Brand Buyers
- Grocery List Consumers
- Mission Shoppers

Three of these groups (*Frequent Freewheelers, Hard-Core Shoppers,* and *Grocery List Consumers*) represent the best targets among warehouse shoppers because of group size, shopping frequency, and expenditures at the clubs.

Frequent Freewheelers are not very involved in shopping. Low prices, unique products, and bargains are not hot buttons to them. Despite this, they shop frequently, usually with others, and spend a lot per trip (an average of $154). They are slightly younger, have higher incomes, and include more men than the other groups of club shoppers.

The *Hard-Core Shoppers* and *Brand Buyers* are the two largest segments. Both of these groups are really "into" shopping, saying they love to shop and shopping is fun. Shoppers in both groups take the time to go up and down all aisles in the club store and are highly motivated to find bargains. Both like to shop the club stores, in part because they enjoy finding unusual items.

The key difference between these segments is that the *Brand Buyers* try to stick to their shopping list, while the *Hard-Core Shoppers* do not. Club store shopping is more of a social event for the *Hard-Core Shoppers,*

ATTITUDES TOWARD SHOPPING		
	% Who Agree**	**Mean***
I just love finding a great bargain	90 ←	6.3
I try to shop where I can get the lowest prices	90 ←	6.3
I count on the stores I shop at to have the brands I am looking for	84	5.8
The main reasons I shop at club stores is really great prices	83 ←	5.7
Just because something is offered at the ware house club store doesn't guarantee it's the lowest price, so you still have to shop around	76 ←	5.5
I like buying large bulk packages of some products because they use less packaging which is better for the environment	74	5.4
I like to allow plenty of time for shopping because I like to have enough time to look around	68	5.2
I like going up and down every aisle at the warehouse club store just to see what they have	67 ←	5.0
Shopping at warehouse club stores is fun	64 ←	5.0
I like to get in and out of stores quickly, otherwise I spend too much money	62	4.9
I'm not very likely to try a new brand if the package size is too big	63	4.8
I usually like to shop alone so I can get the job done quickly	60	4.7
I have a strong brand preference in many product categories. If a store does not carry that brand, I won't usually buy a substitute brand	59	4.6
I usually take a shopping list and try to buy only what is on the list	59	4.4
I love to shop	49	4.3
The main reason I shop at club stores is because I find some unusual items that I don't usually find in my regular grocery store	47 ←	4.1
I prefer to shop in stores that have an attractive decor	40	3.9
Sometimes we go shopping just for fun—it's sort of entertaining	40	3.6
As long as a store has a major national brand of the product I need, I'll buy it, even if it's not the brand I prefer	34	3.5
Some stores are just too big. I don't enjoy shopping in a store that is too big	35	3.4
When I go to the warehouse club store, I go just to find items I need and don't spend time looking around to see what else they have	35	3.4
I wouldn't buy big ticket items like appliances or furniture at a warehouse club store	34	3.4
I wouldn't think of buying clothing at a warehouse club store	26	3.0
I don't usually buy groceries at a warehouse club store	27	3.0
Base = total warehouse club store shoppers	*863*	*863*

*   Mean rating on a 7-point scale with 7 = completely agree and 1 = completely disagree
** Percent who responded in agreement (5, 6 or 7 on 7-point scale)

whereas *Brand Buyers* are more likely to shop alone. The *Brand Buyers* also are more likely than any others to have strong brand preferences in many categories.

Grocery List Consumers represent 18% of club shoppers. They visit the clubs fairly frequently with a list in hand to buy groceries and seek out the items they want, and then they try to get out of the store. They shop the clubs to get bargains and low prices are important to them.

They tend to be slightly older, have larger households, and are more likely to shop alone.

Mission Shoppers visit the club with a specific purchase in mind, go to get it and then like to get out. Because of this mind-set they buy fewer categories, spend less per trip, and visit clubs less frequently than other shoppers. They are older, with smaller households, and are more likely to buy for business purposes.

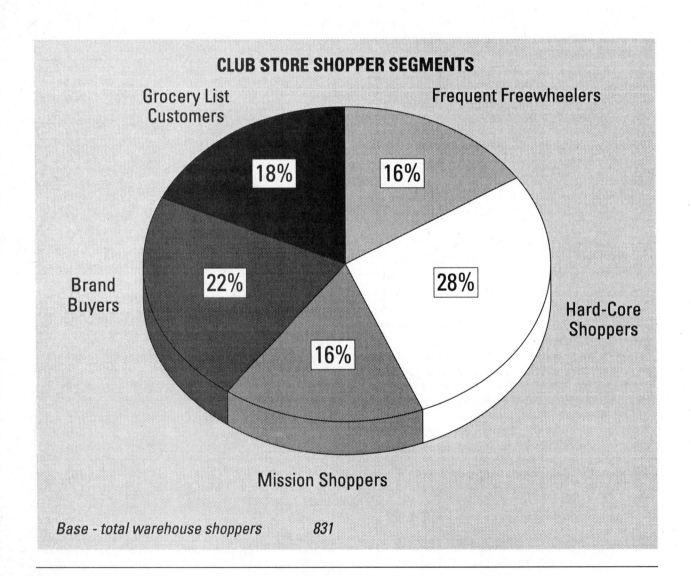

CLUB STORE SHOPPER SEGMENTS

Grocery List Customers — 18%
Frequent Freewheelers — 16%
Hard-Core Shoppers — 28%
Mission Shoppers — 16%
Brand Buyers — 22%

Base - total warehouse shoppers   *831*

HERE ARE THE CHARACTERISTICS OF THE FIVE CLUB STORE SEGMENTS:

SUMMARY OF CLUB STORE SHOPPER SEGMENTS					
	Frequent Freewheelers	**Hard-Core Shoppers**	**Mission Shoppers**	**Brand Buyers**	**Grocery List Consumers**
Percent of Market	16%	28%	16%	22%	18%
Demographics:					
Gender	-More men				
Age	-Slightly younger	-Slightly younger	-Oldest	-Slightly older	-Slightly older
Household size	-Average	-Slightly larger	-Smaller -Less likely to have kids	-Smaller -Less likely to have kids	-Larger w/kids
Income	-Slightly higher	-Average	-Highest	-Slightly lower	-Average
Shopping Behavior					
Memberships					
Length	-Shorter	-Longer			-Longer
Type	-More personal				-More business
Frequency of shopping club	-Most frequent every 10 wks	-Frequent every 12 wks	-Less frequent every 16 wks	-Least frequent every 15 wks	-Frequent every 12 wks
# of categories shopped (out of a list of 19)	7.1	-Highest 9.0	-Lowest 5.6	6.8	7.7
Shop alone/with others	-Shop with others	-Most likely to shop with others	-Most likely to shop alone	-Shop with others	-More tend to shop alone
Amount spent	Highest Mean $154 Median $83	Mean $108 Median $75	Mean $83 Median $70	Mean $88 Median $50	Mean $110 Median $75
Purpose of purchases			-Highest percentage on business purchases		

HERE ARE THE CHARACTERISTICS OF THE FIVE CLUB STORE SEGMENTS: (continued)

SUMMARY OF CLUB STORE SHOPPER SEGMENTS					
	Frequent Freewheelers	**Hard-Core Shoppers**	**Mission Shoppers**	**Brand Buyers**	**Grocery List Consumers**
Perception of savings		-Highest			
Shopping Attitudes:	-Don't love it	-Love to shop -Think it's fun	-Don't love it	-Love to shop -Think it's fun	-Don't love it
Price	-Less interest in low prices/ bargains	-Love bargains	-Less interest in low prices/ bargains	-Low prices important -W/C not always lowest prices	-Low prices/ bargains important
Variety	-Less interest in variety/ unusual items	-Go up and down every aisle -Shop W/C for unusual item	-Don't care about variety/ unusual items -Don't go up and down every aisle	-Go up and down every aisle -Shop W/C for unusual items	-Don't care much about variety/unusual items
Time		-Spend time looking around	-Don't take time to look around	-Like to get in/ out quickly	-Like to get in/ out quickly
List users	-No	-No	-Yes	-Yes	-Oh, yes!
Product type		-Interested in clothing big ticket	-Less likely to buy: clothing, groceries, big-ticket items	-Less like to buy clothing big-ticket items	-Buy groceries
Brand	-Not very brand loyal		-Any national brand O.K.	-More brand loyal	-Major national brand O.K.

POSITIONING

The positioning of a retail store is the totality of its offering to the public. Consumers vary in what they seek from a store, but the factors most people consider include product assortment, price, convenience, and service. Depending, in part, on the products that they offer, different stores will place different emphasis on these factors. Customers, too, will vary in the importance they attach to these factors, not only as a matter of personal taste but also as a function of their circumstances (in a hurry, for example) or because of the buying purpose (buying a scarf for oneself or as a gift). It is important that a store clearly communicate what a customer can expect from it, and that it deliver that offering in a consistent manner over time. This offering is its *positioning* with respect to its competition.

Inevitably no retailer can be all things to all people. Convenience stores, such as 7-Eleven, offer superior location but at the expense of a modest assortment and high prices. A category killer, such as Toys R Us, offers comprehensive assortment at good prices but, for the most part, with less than exceptional service. A warehouse club, such as Price Club, offers significantly reduced prices, forsaking virtually all else. Finally a boutique (a high-end specialty store) offers exceptional service, upscale ambience, but with modest assortment and high prices.

Consistency is important. A customer may travel several miles confident in the knowledge that a store will have exactly what he or she seeks. If it does not, then that trip was wasted and that person will be reluctant to make that trip again. Moreover the clientele that a store attracts likes the particular positioning that the store provides. The marketplace is voting with its feet. If the positioning of the store changes over time, either deliberately or accidentally, existing customers may be turned off. Of course, retailers must adapt to the realities of their competition and to the changing tastes or demographics of people in the trade area, but changes in positioning should be the result of a deliberate decision rather than as the unintentional result of a lack of consistency.

THE RETAILING MIX

The retailing mix of a store is the set of choices that reflect how a store chooses to implement its positioning.

Assortment

Choosing an assortment to carry requires decisions about major categories, about which brands, about which styles, and in what price range. The selection should be driven by an appreciation of customer requirements, competitor assortments, the willingness of suppliers to sell to you, customer expectations, the relation between your expertise and the customers' in the ability to select appropriate merchandise, and the availability of space, fixtures, and equipment. Last but

This note was prepared by Professor David E. Bell as the basis for class discussion.

Copyright© 1995 by the President and Fellows of Harvard College.
Harvard Business School case 593-105.

not least, your assortment will be influenced by your ability to make a profit. Major influences on profitability include not only the markup of the product above cost but also the speed with which the product is sold.

It is natural to think about an assortment as a hierarchy. Any given assortment may be represented by a variety of equivalent hierarchies but a very obvious one reflects the physical layout of goods in a store. There are some initial large groupings (possibly corresponding to departments in the store), sub-categories within those larger groupings, and so on. The last-but-one level of this hierarchy would be individual SKUs. The final level would represent the individual items carried in inventory for that SKU. As a result of this pictorial representation, it is common to talk of the breadth and depth of an assortment.

The *breadth* of an assortment usually refers to the range of goods carried in terms of categories, features, price levels, and so on. Breadth is important for customers who are not sure of exactly what they want. The *depth* of an assortment usually refers to the number of SKUs (colors, sizes) carried for a particular item. The terms vary in meaning by context and by the person using them. They reflect the speaker's personal mental classification of the goods. Depth is important for customers who come to your store knowing that you carry a particular item, expecting you to have, in stock, exactly the color, size, and brand that they seek.

Consider the shoe business. A shoe store may offer leather shoes, athletic shoes, boots, slippers, men's, women's, children's shoes, and so forth. A family shoe store such as Thom McAn carries all of these categories and so has great breadth. There are a very few large shoe stores, such as Bannister's, which operate in factory outlet malls. Otherwise, specialty shoe stores are mostly small (less than 5,000 sq. ft.) with a modest range of SKUs. Traditional boutique-style shoe stores carry a narrow assortment but emphasize what breadth they have by displaying one shoe per style. A customer selects a style and then reveals his or her shoe size and, perhaps, color preference. A store with depth is more likely to carry the size and color and to be in stock. Note that if the normal range of adult shoe sizes is 4 to 12 (proceeding by half sizes) with 3 or 4 width fittings, then a boutique must carry an inventory of at least $20 \times 3 = 60$ sizes for each style in order to have satisfactory depth. Given the space limitations, it is no wonder that the breadth is necessarily narrow. A small shoe store must cut back on inventory somewhere, either in depth (by not stocking the half sizes, or the very large or very small sizes, or by carrying only one pair in each size) or in breadth (by concentrating on men, women, or children or on formal, casual, or athletic.)

Larger, lower-end shoe stores are now displaying all of their inventory and by size rather than by style. This display emphasizes depth (by exhibiting the whole inventory), eases the process of self-service, and reduces disappointment for people whose sizes are not available (since they are likely to look at the selection carried in their own size first). Organizing the layout of the store is driven in part by retailer logistics, in part for ambience, but also to mirror the "hierarchy of needs" of the customer. Is a customer helped by organizing merchandise by brand, by function, by price, by size, or by some other criterion? This question is part of the larger issue of customer convenience.

Convenience

One may think of the total cost of a product to the customer as consisting of the manufacturer's price plus the retailer's markup plus the customer's cost of acquisition. Although many people regard some aspects of shopping to be enjoyable, for others it can be a time-consuming chore. The customer may wish to fulfill a shopping need within a minimum time and with the least frustration. The store can help by communicating clearly what may be obtained in a store (positioning plus depth), minimizing the travel time associated with a visit (clear directions to the store, a convenient location, ample parking). It also requires that the store be open at convenient times and that the in-store transaction time be low. We may summarize the time spent by a customer on a shopping trip as follows:

Shopping time = Planning time +
 Travel time +
 Parking time +
 Search time in store +
 Checkout time.

Added to this are the costs due to inconvenient opening hours, out-of-stock positions, or faulty merchandise requiring returns. The travel time will be reduced if more than one store is located at a given destination and search time will drop as the customer becomes familiar with the layout. Complaints from customers are the norm when a supermarket is remodeled. A chain will often ensure that the layouts of its stores are identical, thus simplifying the lives of both staff and customers.

Service

Customers vary in their knowledge of the products offered, in the cost of their time, and in their psychological need for attention. A customer who says "I'm just looking" may feel more knowledgeable than the sales help, may be gathering data before imposing on a salesperson, or may simply wish to avoid the rigors of a sales interaction. Some service personnel seem to be trained only to extol the features of a product rather than to try to match the products available to a customer's needs. Automated bank tellers work because most people know enough about routine banking that they do not need personal attention. Indeed, given the often inadequate responsiveness of bank clerks, many people would rather line up outside for a machine than inside for a human being. Service in a store might include valet parking, adequate information about product location, features and price, fast checkout, easy credit, carryout service, and delivery. As with all aspects of the retailing mix, the absolute level of service is important, but also important is the consistency with which it is delivered. Average checkout time might be 3 minutes, but can it be 10 minutes in busy periods? What are the credit arrangements if the credit card verification lines are down? What will the store do for a customer who wants a product that is out of stock, or a color that is never carried, or an item that a customer might reasonably expect that you would carry but which you don't?

Product Reassurance

"Caveat Emptor," "No returns," "All sales final" all give the same message—make sure you want it before you buy it! Such a position may be a sensible part of a retailing mix for special cases such as software, custom-made products, or clearance sales. But usually a customer will be wary of accepting all of the responsibility for satisfaction. Many products are warranted against defects by the manufacturer, and the retailer may accept the role of a go-between in ensuring satisfaction or may leave the search for satisfaction entirely up to the customer/vendor dialogue. Many retailers, such as Nordstrom's, will give their own guarantee. Often that is superior to the manufacturer's either because of more generous terms, greater surety of enforcement, or simply because it is more convenient to invoke. A customer may shop at a store not only because of the retailer's selection of goods but because of its role as guarantor of performance. Many stores will also allow customers to return a product for any reason at all, figuring that the value of such an offer in terms of increased goodwill exceeds the considerable cost of handling and markdowns associated with such returns. Such offers are often daring; one manufacturer offers installation of aluminum siding on this basis, an offer which comes close to an unconditional guarantee of satisfaction.

Ambience and Entertainment

If shopping is a chore, there are things that can be done to alleviate the discomfort. Ann Taylor now provides sofas for friends of customers. Play areas for children are provided at Circuit City stores. Nordstrom's has a piano player, Jordan's Furniture has its Mom ride. Supermarket music may not be to everyone's taste, but the attempt is always to provide low-cost touches that make the store a more inviting environment. Cable TV is promised for supermarket checkout lines; it is to be hoped that customers will still select the shorter lines.

Price

The general price levels charged by a store will inevitably reflect its cost of doing business. A store that tries to capture an excessive profit margin will open itself up to competition. But there is more than one way to secure a given return. Each product could be given a constant markup or, better still, a constant direct product profit (DPP). Or some products could serve as loss leaders. Or prices could vary by time of day—possible if items are barcoded, not individually price marked, and if electronic shelf price markers are used. Fashion products could be discounted heavily as the season progresses, or be placed on sale at frequent intervals. Service could be free, or charged for at or below cost, or regarded as a profit center. Off the rack, men's suits invariably require some individual tailoring; the first two forms are common, the last, sometimes an aspiration.

Even the labeling of price can be an element of the mix. At Boston's fabled downtown Filene's Basement store you know not only what the price of an item is now, but what it has been and, if it is not sold, what it will be next time you shop. In supermarkets, unit pricing is now common, and at Fretter's competitors' prices are posted (on some items). Many stores give "lowest price" guarantees. So long as you bring proof that an item you bought is readily available at a competitor, the store may be willing to refund you the difference, sometimes with a bonus: "plus 10%." Of course few customers may take the time to take advantage of such a guarantee, and where the savings may be significant, for example with new cars, extracting a competitor quote without purchase may be an improbable event. Another form of price guarantee promises a refund to the customer if an item is reduced in price by the store (or perhaps even by a competitor) within a certain time interval, say a month. This guarantee may reduce the practice of some salespeople who encourage customers to "come back next week when it's on sale."

Selecting the Retailing Mix

The positioning of a store represents an artful connection between the shopping needs of a segment of society and the financial realities of the marketplace. A successful retailing store must present a superior offer on some dimension of the mix—price, assortment, convenience, service—while achieving at least minimally acceptable standards on the other factors. Even the Durgin-Park restaurant in Boston has succumbed to requiring its servers to be polite to customers.

Case 4

DANTON'S,
THE SPECIALTY STORE MEN'S APPAREL BUSINESS

In February 1981, John Porter was considering what action he should take to revitalize Danton's, the Springton menswear retail company he had inherited nine months earlier. In April 1980 the then owner, Kevin Danton, John's bachelor cousin, had died in an accident. Kevin Danton himself had inherited the company only five years previously from his father.

John Porter, 38, most recently had been president of a small leather products company (luggage, briefcases, personal leather products) which was a division of Beatrice Foods. He was a 1964 graduate of the University of Illinois where he had majored in finance. After a couple of years in the Army, another couple with a bank, and two more in graduate school, he accepted a job at Quaker Oats as an assistant product manager. In 1973, he joined Beatrice Foods as a marketing manager in its leather products division. In 1976, he was named vice president marketing and in 1978 president of the same division. Porter and his wife, Sandy, 36, moved to Springton in July 1980 along with their three young children.

Danton's was founded in 1946 by Kevin's uncle Robert Porter Danton. The first store was located in downtown Springton, and it was still the anchor store of the operation. In 1960, Kevin's mother and father took over the business which still consisted of a single store. In 1963, they opened a second store, in 1967, a third one, and in 1970 a fourth one. After his father's death, in 1975, his mother turned the business over to Kevin. For the previous five years, Kevin had been employed as a regional sales manager for a Springton-based printing company.

The company that Kevin took over seemed in solid financial condition. With a book value of $1.6 million, it was fairly well capitalized. Bank loans amounted to $400,000. Payables were current. However, during the preceding few years sales had increased only slightly. Sales in 1975 were $5.4 million, and after-tax profits were $119,000. Return on net assets was 5.9%. For financial data, see **Exhibit 1**.

Kevin believed the company should have a higher level of profitability, and he was concerned about the flat sales performance for the individual stores in recent years. So, shortly after he took over the business, Kevin visited the credit manager of his major supplier, Hart Schaffner & Marx, who put him in touch with Peter Jones, a vice president in the company's retail division. Jones offered to visit Danton's and Kevin Danton accepted. After a two-day visit, Jones presented his observations to Danton and a few days later sent him a brief report.

In summary, Jones observed that the company was very well run on a day-to-day basis. The individual stores were well managed and salespeople seemed to be quite professional. Operating and financial systems were excellent.

This case, provided by a company that wishes to remain anonymous, was edited by Professor Richard S. Tedlow as the basis for class discussion rather than to illustrate either effective or ineffective handling of an administrative situation. The case does not represent an actual company but is rather a composite portrait of the specialty store men's apparel business. The consumer research data are strictly hypothetical.

Overhead was reasonable. Receivables were under control, although Jones noted that no interest was being charged for accounts past due. Inventory was current. The morale of the personnel was exceptional. The company had three very capable buyers (one each in clothing,[1] furnishings,[2] and sportswear). The warehouse and workroom[3] were well operated. Lease terms were quite favorable.

Jones observed, however, that the company and its image were not as contemporary as they could have been. The image of the store seemed to be somewhat stodgy and lacking in excitement. The appeal seemed to be to older, affluent men. Clothing and furnishings price points were quite high, and sportswear was not sufficiently emphasized. Store decor was old fashioned and not particularly inviting. Advertising, merchandise presentation, window display, and salesmen all projected a high-priced, high-quality, but overly conservative and unexciting image. Jones believed the net effect of this merchandising approach accounted for the lack of sales growth. He pointed out that the market growth was at moderate price points with younger men—the population of which was growing dramatically. Jones also observed that Danton's suffered from a common menswear retail problem—low inventory turn. Lastly, Jones felt the downtown store and one of the three suburban stores were too large.

Kevin Danton accepted Jones' observations and for the next five years he worked to revitalize the business. He pursued a multifaceted plan.

- The third floor of the downtown store was converted to office space and rented. One-third of the Eastbrook store was sublet.
- The downtown store also underwent a major renovation and all of the suburban stores received a cosmetic face-lift. All of the window fronts were opened up and new window displays emphasized contemporary settings. Fixtures enabling the customer to examine merchandise were installed.
- Danton attempted to broaden the appeal of the stores. Designer clothing lines were added. Moderately priced clothing was given greater emphasis.
- The furnishings offering was broadened in looks and price points.

- A larger inventory was made available for sportswear and several lines were added, including designer collections, an outdoor sportswear line, and active sportswear lines. In addition, the knit shirt and casual slacks lines were expanded.
- The advertising format was updated using photography instead of line drawings. An extra .5% of sales was allocated to advertising and half of all advertising dollars and window display space were used to support the new moderately priced lines.
- Past due charge accounts were charged interest at the rate of 1½% per month.
- To improve inventory turn, receipt of merchandise was more carefully scheduled.

Kevin Danton worked hard to implement these changes and, for the most part, they had been completed at the time of his untimely death. A month after his death, John Porter left his job at Beatrice Foods to run Danton's.

John Porter realized when he arrived that he knew virtually nothing about menswear retailing. Therefore, during his first nine months, he set out to educate himself.

- He carefully analyzed Danton's financial data. (See **Exhibits 1** through **3**.)
- He spent a week in each store talking to and observing employees and customers, visiting competitive stores in the immediate and surrounding area, and analyzing the sales trends and profitability of each store. (See **Exhibits 5** through **7**.)
- He spent a week with each of the three buyers discussing their merchandising strategy and philosophy and analyzing their advertising, merchandise trends, and current merchandise mix. He visited or talked with as many supplier salespeople as possible. He analyzed the lines carried and sales trends by line. (See **Exhibit 8**.)
- He visited the headquarters of his major clothing supplier, Hart Schaffner & Marx, and talked with some of its executives in the manufacturing and retail divisions, including Peter Jones.
- He visited the market research firm of the same company where he was presented an overview of the clothing and menswear retailing market.

---

1 In the apparel industry, the term "clothing" referred to men's suits, sportcoats, and tailored slacks.
2 "Furnishings" included shirts, ties, underwear, socks, and pajamas.
3 The workroom was where the alterations were carried out.

- He engaged a local market research firm to survey Danton's customers and those of leading competitors. (See **Exhibit 9.**)

After nine months of work, Porter evaluated what he had learned.

FINANCIAL CONDITION

Porter noted that the financial condition of the company appeared to be solid. Danton's actually was a wholly owned subsidiary of RPD, Inc. and, indeed was its only asset. As of January 31, 1981, Danton's represented an investment of $2,844,000. RPD, Inc. had loans outstanding of $1 million at an average interest rate of 12%. So the book value of RPD, Inc.'s equity was $1,844,000. In other respects, Danton's was also strong. Trade payables were current; leases were favorable. Profitability was somewhat better than the level of five years earlier. Profits were $254,000 on sales of $7,680,000. Profits as a percent of sales for the most recent year were 3.3%. Sales had grown at an annual rate of 6% since 1975. An index of price increases for major items indicated that Danton's prices had climbed about 6% per year during the same period.

MERCHANDISING

Generally, Danton's was merchandised as a quality, branded menswear store with conservative business styles. Tailored clothing was the backbone of the business, but sportswear was becoming more important. Danton's offered clothing, furnishings (and accessories), and sportswear. It did not sell shoes. There were no leased departments.

Porter learned from talking with the buyers that over the past few years, Danton's merchandising strategy had been modified in several significant ways.

First. In all categories, the number of lines offered had been expanded. For example, in suits, there used to be three lines—good, better, and best. The good-better-best concept was still observed, but now there were eight lines. In dress shirts, there were six lines. In sport shirts, about six lines were normally carried.

Second. Price points had been broadened. If they had not been, the suit price range would have been $200–$500. Now, it was $155–$500. The dress shirt price range would have been $20–$35. Now it was $15–$35.

Third. In all major classifications, an "operational line" had been created using the Kevin's label. This was a line initially priced at a 60% margin, and, after about a month, reduced to achieve a normal 52% margin. The purpose was to be able to appeal to the sale-oriented customer all year long.

Fourth. Danton's inaugurated a more aggressive policy on the clearance sales which it held January-February and July of each year. Formerly, the store had put only prior season merchandise and "problem" current season merchandise on sale. Now, however, all current season merchandise—not merely problem—was being put on sale. The store was continuing its long-standing practice of one special promotion sale each season.

Fifth. Danton's discontinued selling all quads,[4] all "highly shouldered"[5] goods, and all 100% polyester[6] suits and sportcoats. The store established a policy of not offering separates[7] by Levi Strauss, Haggar, or Farah. Kevin Danton strongly believed that Danton's customers did not want these items. They wanted "dress-up, business" looks.

Sixth. While selection had been broadened in terms of styles and price points, it had been reduced somewhat in terms of depth. Store policy was that 95% of the customers who came into the store should have at least 15 different suits in their size from which to select. In size 42 Regular (36 waist), the customer should have 75 different suits from which to select, except in the flagship store downtown where they should have 100. Previously these numbers had been considerably higher.

---

4 "Quads" referred to suits which consisted of a coat, a vest, and two pairs of slacks, one of which was cut from the same bolt of cloth as the coat and vest and the other of which was made of an unmatching fabric which was coordinated in color and finish with the coat and vest.

5 "Highly shouldered" goods referred to fashion forward merchandise. Heavily padded shoulders were a hallmark of suit coats of this style.

6 Polyester was a synthetic fabric less expensive than wool. Most better suits were made of wool or of blends of polyester and wool.

7 In the late 1970s, Levi Strauss, Haggar, and Farah vigorously began to market "separates." In the separately ticketed suit, the coat, vest, and slacks were displayed, priced, and purchased individually, rather than from the same hanger, as the traditional suit was. A three-piece "separate" suit retailed in major department stores at about $108 in 1980. Fabrications were mostly polyester and the construction of the coat was of a quality less exacting than some experts thought it should be. But these manufacturers had been advertising heavily and achieving significant sales.

MARKETING COMMUNICATIONS

Danton's marketing communications strategy, Porter learned, varied by type of communication. The general purpose of advertising had been primarily to create short-term demand for a particular item of merchandise (one-time traffic) rather than to create general traffic over time. In windows and exterior store design, the strategy had been to attract customers from the general traffic by making the stores "inviting." Inside the store, the communications strategy had been, in large part, based on a salesperson making direct contact with the customer. Window displays were thought to be excellent. Interior displays, on the other hand, were not always as effective as they should have been.

Over the past five years, expenditures on advertising averaged about 3.3% of sales and display 0.8%. Public relations expenditures had been minimal. Co-op money[8] boosted advertising expenditures to 3.8%. Newspaper advertising was the dominant medium (78%). About 10% of this total was made up of multipage four-color inserts which were purchased from the retail division of Danton's major supplier. The only other medium was direct mail (22%).

Advertising expenditures had been allocated between regular-priced merchandise (65%) and sales merchandise (35%). Institutional advertising had been minimal. After applying co-op allowances, 41% of the advertising funds had been spent on clothing, 25% on furnishings, and 34% on sportswear. With respect to clothing, expenditures had been disproportionately allocated to moderately priced lines.

In advertising clothing, the primary messages for the national brands were "quality" (first) and "conservative, tasteful fashion" (second). For the house brands, Danton's and Kevin's, the message was "price/value." For furnishings and sportswear, it was "branded, quality" merchandise, and during promotional periods, "price/value."

With respect to store design, until recently the stores had been designed and decorated to convey the message that the store was "a high quality, dignified men's store." In the past five years, the stores had been redecorated to convey a very different message, namely that they were "updated, relaxed and inviting."

PERSONNEL

Porter learned that Kevin Danton had been taking steps to improve personnel management. Susan Gross had been hired as the personnel manager in 1976. She had previously worked in personnel in the largest bank in town and had been well schooled in professional personnel practices. Among the areas she was emphasizing were systematic wage and salary administration, benefits, employee training, employee recognition and motivation programs, and employee communications. She had also worked on improving the selection process to reduce turnover which had been quite high. Her efforts had succeeded in bringing turnover within industry standards. Lastly, she had put together an informal management development program in which 16 management employees participated.

In general, Porter felt employee morale was quite good. The majority of full-time employees seemed to be conscientious, and most salespeople appeared to be meeting their quotas.

Porter learned that compensation at Danton's was within industry norms. Salespeople were paid a commission of 7.5% for clothing and 8.5% for furnishings and sportswear. The benefits package was quite attractive to employees and quite expensive for Danton's. Store managers and buyers were paid a straight salary. Store managers earned an average of $15,000 per year and buyers earned from $15,000 to $22,500. The company had 20 full-time clothing salespeople averaging $180,000 in volume annually and 20 part-timers averaging $75,000 annually.

CONTROLS AND INFORMATION

Porter was pleased with the controls in place at Danton's. The controller, Marty Feinberg, 58, seemed competent and had introduced excellent systems and procedures since joining the company in 1968.

Financial statements for each location and for the company as a whole were prepared monthly. A simple financial budgeting system was in place. Also, a detailed open-to-buy[9] system which accounted for clothing in units and sportswear and furnishings in dollars was in place.

---

8 "Co-op money" referred to money which a manufacturer paid a retailer when the retailer featured the manufacturer's merchandise in an advertisement.
9 "Open-to-buy" referred to funds budgeted but as yet unspent for the purchase of merchandise.

All the systems were manual, and Feinberg told Porter that Kevin Danton had been considering installing a small computer to improve the merchandising information. He had been particularly interested in tracking merchandise by style, size and color. Feinberg thought the system would be able to handle accounts receivable which now were being handled by an outside data processing service. There would be a net cost increase, but Feinberg thought the improved information would justify the additional cost.

METROPOLITAN SPRINGTON

Springton, Porter learned, was a relatively sophisticated, cultured city located in a large industrial state in the Northeast. The greater metropolitan area had a population of about 1.6 million with about 600,000 in the center city. The center city was comprised of middle-class and poorer households with minorities representing 40% of the population. It had been losing population at the rate of about 1% per year. The downtown business district was shrinking in employment and not much new construction occurred in the 1970s.

The suburbs, on the other hand, were largely middle and upper middle class with minorities representing 5% of the population. The growth rate of 3.5% per year was predominantly in middle-class suburbs on the far west and south sides of the area. Disposable income per household was $23,000, about equal to that of Chicago. Thirty-three percent of the suburban households had incomes greater than $25,000.

Altogether, there were nine major shopping centers[10] in the greater metropolitan area. There were plans for one additional center over the next three years and the outlook for the next decade was for perhaps an additional one or two more centers. Developers were investing in renovation in many of the existing centers.

The clothing market for the greater metropolitan area was estimated at 387,000 suit units representing $55 million at retail and 234,000 sportcoats representing $20 million at retail distributed by price points as follows:

Suits				Sportcoats			
Under $100	$100–149	$150–199	$200+	Under $50	$50–99	$100–149	$150+
96,000	124,000	118,000	49,000	63,000	121,000	30,000	20,000

COMPETITION

For the past nine months, Porter had been keeping a file on each of Danton's major competitors. Altogether, in the greater Springton area, there were three major department stores and 33 minor ones. Two of them represented significant competition and, combined, they operated 18 stores. There were 123 menswear specialty stores, but six of them, with 30 outlets altogether, stood out as relevant competition. Sears had eight stores in the area, JCPenney's six, Ward's four, Saks Fifth Avenue two, Lord and Taylor two, Bonwit Teller one, and Syms, a vigorous discounter, one.

Department Store A

This was a better full-line department store with a 400,000 square foot store in downtown Springton and six branch stores in the suburbs. It had a store in every shopping center in which Danton's was located except for Westpond. It attracted older, more affluent customers. In men's clothing, it carried Hart Schaffner & Marx as well as Dior and Cardin. It sold approximately $17 million worth of menswear annually. It advertised extensively. Its suit advertising was about one-third of Danton's, but its sportswear advertising was four times greater and its furnishings and sportswear inventories far surpassed those of Danton's.

10   A major shopping center was described as one with at least one department store or chain store.

Department Store B

This company operated moderately priced full-line stores. It had a large downtown store (320,000 square feet) and nine branch stores, six of which were in shopping centers. Only two of its branch stores were located in areas in which Danton's was also located. This company appealed to young to middle-aged, middle-income households. It sold about $21 million worth of menswear annually. It carried Botany, Johnny Carson, John Weitz, Pierre Cardin, and Bill Blass. It also carried Haggar separates. The store was highly promotional.

Specialty Store A

This was a better men's and women's specialty store with a downtown store and six suburban stores. All but one were in shopping centers. Its volume was about $14 million with menswear representing 45%. It featured conservative, quality clothing with its own labels. Its principal clothing resources were Schoeneman and Joseph & Feiss.

Specialty Store B

This was a moderately priced men's specialty store with nine branches, half of which were located in shopping centers. It sold a broad range of styles with suits priced at $125–$200. Its largest branded clothing lines were Palm Beach, Johnny Carson, John Weitz, and Phoenix, but the bulk of its sales were under its own label. This company was highly promotional and an extensive advertiser. It attracted a young to middle-aged customer from a broad variety of backgrounds.

Specialty Store C (Brooks Brothers)

Brooks Brothers operated one store in downtown Springton with annual volume of $4.5 million.

Specialty Store D

This was an upscale, traditional menswear store. It operated a store in the downtown area and a few years ago opened another in Fashion Square. Its volume was $4.0 million with 65% in clothing. It was high priced and offered pure natural shoulder clothing with Southwick the largest line.

Specialty Store E (Richman Brothers)

This moderately priced national chain operated seven stores in the Springton area. Its volume was estimated at $7.2 million.

Specialty Store F

This was a high-fashion shouldered clothing men's specialty store. It operated three outlets. Volume was estimated at $3.6 million with clothing representing almost 75%. Prices were high. The principal clothing lines were Louis Roth, Society Brand, and Phoenix.

Discount Store (Syms)

Syms operated one 40,000 square foot store north of the Westpond Center and did about $6 million in menswear. It was reported that Syms planned to open a second store in the southeastern suburbs. Syms displayed clothing with labels but removed them before the customer left the store. The brands included Austin Reed, Botany, Cerruti, Lanvin, Bill Blass, Chaps, Palm Beach, Phoenix, John Weitz, and Johnny Carson.

THE MARKET FOR BETTER MENSWEAR

In visiting Hart Schaffner & Marx, John Porter had the opportunity to talk with executives and managers in both the manufacturing and retail areas and in the corporate market research department. He formed the following picture of the market for better menswear.

- The total market for men's suits was growing in unit volume about 5% to 6% per year. The biggest growth was taking place in the better-priced area (sometimes referred to as Makes 4 and 6). The low-priced units (Makes X and 2) were declining while moderate-priced units were increasing.
- The total market for sportcoats was flat. Better-quality sportcoats had been selling slightly better than other Makes over the past few years.
- Specialty stores sold about 48% of suit units, department stores 21%, general merchandise chains (Sears, Ward's, JCPenney's) 18%, and the remainder belonged to discounters. The higher the price, the greater the specialty store's share.
- Specialty stores sold about 42% of all sportcoats, department stores 24%, the chains 13%, and discounters the remainder.
- Levi Strauss, Haggar, and Farah had begun selling separates in 1978, and by 1980 had captured 6% of the suit market. Separates were distributed mostly through department stores and chains, although specialty stores had about 20% of the market.

- Furnishings sales overall were flat, but sportswear was growing in real terms by 5% to 10% per year. Men's jeans had been leading the way.
- The performance of well-capitalized menswear retailers varied dramatically. For 90% of them, return on net assets (RONA) ranged from 2% to 3% to 20%. Sales growth ranged from minus 5% to plus 12%. The variance seemed to be attributable to the growth of the trading area and the level of competition, in addition, of course, to the capability of its management.
- Nationwide, most suits (91%), sportcoats (86%), and dress slacks (80%) were purchased by men, while women frequently purchased dress shirts (60%), ties (63%), and sport shirts (68%).

INTERVIEWS WITH DANTON'S PERSONNEL

Store Manager—Southlake

Gordon Campbell, 30, had been a store manager of the Southlake store for the past three years. Prior to that he had been the clothing department manager in the Westpond Mall store where he had started as a clothing salesperson at the age of 24.

Campbell said he enjoyed working at Danton's. It was a reputable company and sold high-quality products. In his opinion, the clothing department was the best not only in the mall but also in the immediate shopping area. He thought customers shopped at Danton's because of its large clothing selection and the excellent service rendered. Service to Campbell meant personal attention from a knowledgeable salesperson and skilled fitting from an experienced tailor. "Salespeople keep personal trait files on each customer, and each salesperson uses the files in accordance with his selling style." He thought men liked the idea of having their "own" salesperson just like they liked having their "own" barber. Campbell described a "typical" customer as "a middle-aged businessman who earns good money—perhaps $25,000 to $30,000 a year. He's a quality-oriented conservative dresser. His wife usually accompanies him to the store."

Campbell told Porter that Kevin Danton had tried to broaden the appeal of the store by offering more moderately priced clothing. Campbell was unsure of the results of this effort. "We're selling more lower priced clothing. But, overall I don't think we're selling more total units. I wonder whether we have attracted a different customer or whether we have traded down our old customers?"

Asked to assess the efforts to expand sportswear and furnishings, Campbell noted that:

We have boosted our sportswear sales somewhat, but not furnishings. I don't think we can compete with the department store in the mall in either category in terms of selection. Rather, we should compete on the basis of service. But, we should have basic styles in stock. Sometimes, we don't have basic blue oxford cloth shirts in 16–34s.[11] Lastly, our offering should be broader. We get many calls for Countess Mara ties which we don't carry.

Campbell was doubtful about the Westpond store's growth potential. "I think we will grow with the mall, but I don't think the mall's growth potential is very good. It is a mature center in an area whose population is stable."

Salesperson—Northstream Court Store

Glenn Patterson, 65, was a clothing salesperson in the Northstream store. He had formerly worked in the downtown store but had exercised his option (resulting from his seniority) to transfer to the newly opened Northstream in 1963 because it was located nearer to his home. Knowing that many of his downtown customers lived near Northstream and that the new corporate offices in the area had been accompanied by the building of many expensive new homes, he gambled that he could build his old volume back. Last year he had sold $200,000 in clothing and earned $15,000. He didn't know if he had met his last month's quota.

He thought the primary reason customers shopped at Danton's was the personal following the salespeople created. Further, he thought it was easy to satisfy potential customers because of the broad selection of better clothing in terms of styles, brands, sizes and price points and the good fitting and alterations the store offered. Patterson expressed concern about rising prices but said he had been able to keep his earnings even with inflation over the past several years. He also felt that he could significantly increase his earnings if he could take his clothing customers into the sportswear and furnishings departments.

---

11 These numbers referred to neck and arm measurements respectively.

Asked to assess the future sales growth potential of the store, Patterson said he thought it was "okay," but it depended on what was done. For example, he planned to retire at the end of the year and wondered how the company was going to retain his customers.

He also expressed concern about the level of traffic in the store. The problem on weekdays was especially serious.

> We are not getting a good flow of new customers. We seem to have a hard-core group of loyal customers who account for the vast majority of sales. But this group seems to be shrinking. The company needs to get more new customers to come into the store. We are pretty busy after 6:00 p.m. on weekdays and on Saturday and Sunday, but this place is like a tomb from 10:00 a.m. to 6:00 p.m. on weekdays.

Interview with Clothing Buyer

The clothing buyer for Danton's was Robert Hausch, 47. Prior to becoming the clothing buyer, he had been the store manager of the Eastbrook store from its opening in 1967. Before that, he had been a salesperson in the downtown store. He commented:

> Danton's is the largest, quality menswear specialty store in Springton when you consider menswear only. We are in every center where it makes sense, with the possible exception of one in the southwest suburbs. Our strategy is to go after the quality customer who wants tasteful fashions. From a fashion standpoint, our coverage is broad. We don't zero in on the conservative traditionalist like Brooks Brothers or the updated traditional customer like Richman Brothers or the high-fashion, "shouldered" customer like Specialty Store F. We can't afford to because five of our stores are in the suburbs where we have to appeal to as broad a market as possible to do the sales per square foot we need in order to achieve good profitability.
>
> I will be interested in the results of our consumer survey, but I think I know who our clothing customer is. He's the kind of man who likes our merchandise. You know, Hart Schaffner & Marx, Dior, Austin Reed, Cardin. Also, we attract a value or sale-oriented customer with our Danton and Kevin lines. He's probably a younger, less-affluent man than those who buy our other lines.

Asked why Danton's clothing volume had not grown in the past 10 years, Hausch said, "First, we have not opened enough new stores over this past decade; and second, we have really been hurt by discounters, especially Syms."

Interview with Sportswear Buyer

Rick Berman, 28, had been with Danton's for two years. Previously, he had been employed by Department Store B as an assistant sportswear buyer. He observed:

> Kevin Danton always thought we could do more sportswear business. And I guess it represents a bigger part of the overall business than it did when Kevin took over. But he told me he learned a lot trying to expand sportswear. For one thing, you can't just expand your lines and increase your open-to-buy. He suffered some big markdowns doing that. He said you have to get customers to come into your store. That's why a disproportionately large part of our advertising is allocated to sportswear.
>
> I am not sure who our sportswear customer is or who it should be. The consumer survey you are conducting, as I understand it, will only tell us who our clothing and furnishings customers are. Maybe we should do a survey of sportswear customers. I wouldn't be surprised if the type of customer varies by location. Now we merchandise each store the same, for all categories. Maybe we should merchandise each differently.

ALTERNATIVES

After spending nine months learning the business and studying its problems, Porter felt it was time for a decision. What was the best way to improve profitability? He felt that the business should earn a minimum of 12% and preferably a 15% return on net assets. Anything lower than 12% would mean the market value of the business would suffer. Eventually, Porter felt, he would want to sell the business to a larger company. Already he had been offered six times earnings for Danton's. (By the terms of this offer, the purchaser would not assume bank loans.) Indeed he had considered selling the business for that price but decided that he wanted to take a shot at increasing its value through increasing its earnings first.

In addition to realizing an acceptable return on investment, Porter strongly felt that the business should grow. This would not only enhance his personal wealth but would also provide opportunities for employees.

Besides, he thought it more fun to manage a profitable growing company than a profitable shrinking one.

Porter believed it would be difficult to improve Danton's profitability merely by doing better what the store was doing at present. He felt, as Peter Jones had five years earlier, that the store was well run. He felt he had either to improve sales, achieve a substantial reduction in expenses (so substantial that he was concerned that this option might change the nature of the store), reduce asset requirements, or implement some combination of the above. He was most attracted by the idea of increasing sales, and therefore most of the alternatives he considered dealt with ways of achieving that goal.

Alternative 1

To increase menswear volume by capturing a greater share of the market segments to which Danton's currently had strong appeal. Porter wondered how to achieve this objective. Was the store's competitive potential, for example, greater in clothing or in sportswear?

Alternative 2

To increase menswear sales by capturing a significant share of a market segment to which Danton's currently had weak appeal. Porter realized that this strategy ran the risk of diluting Danton's appeal to its current customers. For example, if Danton's became more promotional, to what extent would that negatively impact the store's relationship to its primary customer group?

Alternative 3

To increase sales by adding one or more major merchandise classifications not presently carried but which might appeal to Danton's present customers. Porter was familiar with luggage and such personal leather products as attache cases, and he thought they had potential. He was also considering adding men's shoes. Yet Porter wondered whether Danton's could attract sufficient customers to make this move significant.

In his more expansive moments, Porter considered repositioning the store entirely as one designed "to meet the businessman's every need." In addition to stocking the merchandise mentioned above, Porter contemplated products such as Electronic products including calculators and electronic games, pens and desk accessories, business-related books, gifts for wives/girlfriends, certain sports equipment such as tennis and squash rackets, and perhaps even insurance à la Sears. Porter felt that the grouping of all these products would make his store unique and create enormous appeal.

Alternative 4

To increase sales by adding a women's wear department. Danton's current self-definition was to sell businessmen the apparel they need for work. Perhaps this appeal should be broadened to "businessmen and businesswomen." No other local store was adopting this approach, and once again the idea of uniqueness appealed strongly to Porter. Yet he knew little about women's wear. How broadly based, he wondered, would the product offering have to be to achieve credibility? Should he try selling women's wear in only one or two stores at first to see how things went?

Alternative 5

To reduce assets or expenses even if that meant changing the nature of the business in a significant way. To reduce assets, Porter wondered whether a better inventory management system would improve inventory turn substantially without negatively affecting sales. He wondered whether he could eliminate Danton's own credit system by switching his customers to less expensive bank cards. He had been warned by some retail experts that discontinuing "own credit" was a very risky move. Porter wondered whether any major expense could be reduced without negatively affecting volume. For example, he wondered what would happen if advertising were cut from 3.3% to 1.0% or if furnishings, and sportswear departments were made self-service using a checkout counter.

These were the five alternatives which struck Porter as most plausible. But he was receptive to suggestions he might not as yet have considered. He knew that some of the above options involved more risk than others. He also realized that he was liable to be biased in favor of choices concerning which he already had a certain familiarity. Yet he was anxious not to limit himself. After all, a mere nine months previously he knew little about menswear, but now he felt quite comfortable about it. Most important, Porter felt, was to act decisively and to act soon.

Exhibit 1
Key Operating Performance Statistics, Years Ending January 21

	1971	1972	1973	1974	1975	1976	1977	1978	1979	1980	1981
Sales ($000)	$4,656	$4,866	$5,096	$5,321	$5,410	$5,408	$6,069	$6,576	$7,082	$7,640	$7,680
Cumulative Markup %	n/a	n/a	n/a	n/a	n/a	50.0	50.4	51.7	52.2	52.3	52.4
Shrinkage (%)[1]	n/a	n/a	n/a	n/a	n/a	1.7	1.3	1.2	1.2	1.3	1.5
Markdowns %[2]	n/a	n/a	n/a	n/a	n/a	7.6	7.4	7.9	8.0	8.2	9.0
Gross Profit %	41.5	41.8	42.5	42.6	42.4	42.7	43.3	43.8	43.9	44.5	44.0
Operating Expenses %	39.2	39.2	38.5	38.4	38.4	38.5	38.9	39.4	39.5	39.9	39.6
Total Payroll %	21.6	21.8	21.4	21.6	21.5	21.8	21.4	21.4	21.6	21.7	21.5
Operating Profit %	2.3	2.6	4.0	4.2	4.0	4.2	4.4	4.4	4.4	4.6	4.8
Other Income/Expense %	0.4	0.4	0.4	0.4	0.4	1.8	1.8	1.8	1.8	1.8	1.8
Pretax Profit %	2.7	3.0	4.4	4.6	4.4	4.6	6.2	6.2	6.2	6.4	6.6
After-tax Profit %	2.7	1.5	2.2	2.3	2.2	2.3	3.1	3.1	3.1	3.2	3.3
Investment Turn	2.7	2.7	2.8	2.9	2.7	2.8	2.5	2.6	2.6	2.7	2.7
RONA %	6.4	4.1	6.2	6.6	5.9	6.4	7.8	8.1	8.1	8.7	9.0

n/a = not available
1 Shrinkage usually ran about 0.6% to 0.8% for clothing; 1.5% to 1.9% for furnishings, and 1.8% to 2.3% for sportswear in comparable specialty stores.
2 Markdowns usually ran 6% to 8% for clothing; 5% to 6% for furnishings, and 7% to 9% for sportswear in comparable specialty stores.

Exhibit 2
Balance Sheet, January 31, 1981 ($000)

ASSETS

Cash	$ 75
Accounts Receivable (net of reserves)	895
Inventory (net of reserves):	
Clothing	1,542
Furnishings	232
Sportswear	348
TOTAL	$ 3,092
Deferred Charges and Other	11
TOTAL CURRENT ASSETS	$ 3,103
Fixed Assets	625
TOTAL ASSETS	$ 3,728

TOTAL LIABILITIES AND CAPITAL

Trade Payables	$ 548
Accounts Payable	200
Deferred Taxes on Installment Sales	136
Capital Employed*	2,844
Loan	1,000
Equity	1,844
TOTAL LIABILITIES AND CAPITAL	$ 3,728

INVENTORY TURN

Clothing	1.87
Furnishings	2.28
Sportswear	2.44
Average Combined	2.01

* The average net assets or capital employed in FY 80/81 was $2,844,000. This was the capital invested by the parent company RPD, Inc. of which Danton's was the sole subsidiary and, in fact, the only asset. The corporation had loans outstanding of $1,000,000 at an average interest rate of 12%.

Exhibit 3
Income Statement for Years Ending January 31, 1980 and 1981

	1980		1981	
	$000	% of Sales	$000	% of Sales
Sales				
Clothing	5,089	66.6	5,095	66.3
Furnishings	1,033	13.5	1,025	13.4
Sportswear	1,518	19.9	1,560	20.3
Total	7,640	100.0	7,680	100.0
Gross Profit				
Clothing	2,209	28.9	2,204	28.7
Furnishings	503	6.6	496	6.5
Sportswear	688	9.0	710	9.2
Total	3,400	44.5	3,410	44.4
Operating Expenses				
Administrative*	542	7.1	544	7.1
Accounting and Credit	313	4.1	307	4.0
Occupancy	711	9.3	722	9.4
Advertising	267	3.5	246	3.2
Display	61	0.8	61	0.8
Material Handling	76	1.0	77	1.0
Selling	917	12.0	922	12.0
Merchandising	161	2.1	162	2.1
Total	3,048	39.9	3,041	39.6
Operating Profit	352	4.6	369	4.8
Service Charge Income	107	1.4	108	1.4
Other Income/(Expense)	30	0.4	30	0.4
Profit Before Tax	489	6.4	507	6.6
Tax	244	3.2	253	3.3
Profit After Tax	245	3.2	254	3.3
Sales by Type of Payment				
Cash/COD Sales	2918	38		
Charge Sales	3379	44		
Outside Credit Sales	1383	18		
	7680	100		

* Includes interest on the one million dollar outstanding loan.

Exhibit 4
Metropolitan Springton

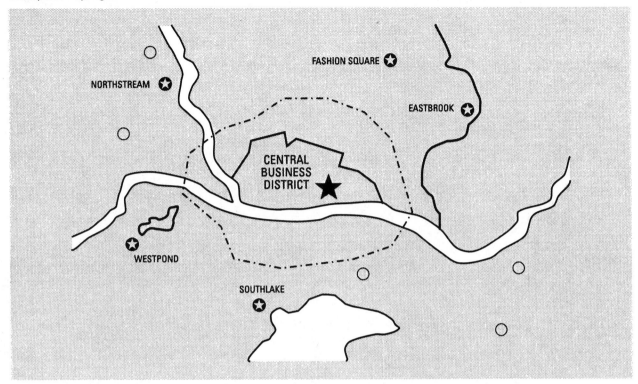

Exhibit 5
Store Information for Each Branch

Store	Location	Total SF / Selling SF	Sales 1980/81	Sales/SF Total / Selling	1980/81 Direct Profit Contribution[1]	Direct Investment Inventory & F.A.	Comments
Downtown	On main commercial street across from Dept. Store A	33,000 / 24,000	$2,997,000	$91 / $125	$551,000 18.4%	$950,000	Location excellent Condition of store excellent—remodeled in 1976; Downtown area declining
Northstream	Northstream Center 1.2 million sq. ft. Located lower level Opened 1963	10,000 / 8,500	$1,263,000	$126 / $149	$240,000 19.0%	$375,000	Location excellent Store remodeled in 1976. Mall mature; Upper middle class/affluent area
Eastbrook	Eastbrook Mall 700,000 sq. ft. Opened 1967	7,250 / 6,250	$872,000	$120 / $140	$147,000 16.9%	$250,000	Location good; Mall mature; Upper middle-class area
Fashion Square	Fashion Square 1.3 million sq. ft. Located lower level center; Opened 1970	8,400 / 7,500	$1,255,000	$149 / $167	$226,000 18.0%	$418,000	Mall still growing Location excellent Face-lift 1978 Surrounding area quite affluent
Westpond	Westpond Mall 600,000 sq. ft. Lower level Opened 1976	6,000 / 5,100	$585,000	$98 / $115	$70,000 12.0%	$300,000	Area still growing cation good; Mall lacks fashion image Young, middle-class area
Southlake	Southlake Court Opened 1978	6,200 / 5,200	$708,000	$114 / $136	$110,000 15.5%	$375,000	Area still growing; Mall lacks fashion image. Location fair; Middle class area
All Locations		70,850 / 56,550	$7,680,000	$108 / $136	$1,344,000 17.5%	$2,668,000	

1 Direct Profit Contribution is equal to sales for each category times average maintained gross margin by category less direct operating expenses including rent, payroll, fringes, occupancy expenses and local advertising and operating expenses.

Exhibit 6
Sales by Location, Years Ending January 31 ($000)

	1971	1972	1973	1974	1975	1976	1977	1978	1979	1980	1981
Fashion Square (1970)											
Clothing	$ 165	$ 570	$ 608	$ 660	$ 658	$ 679	$ 776	$ 787	$ 810	$ 805	$ 812
Furnishings	48	102	150	167	179	171	180	189	181	177	168
Sportswear	40	97	128	149	186	168	264	266	250	280	275
TOTAL	$ 253	$ 769	$ 886	$ 976	$1023	$1018	$1220	$1242	$1241	$1262	$1255
Downtown (1946)											
Clothing	$1925	$1804	$1849	$1940	$1921	$1923	$1994	$2068	$2042	$2072	$2089
Furnishings	479	448	526	481	457	432	427	433	402	388	406
Sportswear	295	302	300	311	346	387	426	476	501	507	502
TOTAL	$2699	$2554	$2675	$2732	$2724	$2742	$2847	$2977	$2945	$2967	$2997
Northstream (1963)											
Clothing	$ 817	$ 746	$ 708	$ 772	$ 751	$715	$ 745	$ 826	$ 898	$ 890	$ 876
Furnishings	142	140	131	141	146	135	143	146	139	141	135
Sportswear	120	105	98	105	117	126	153	173	198	251	252
TOTAL	$1079	$ 991	$ 937	$1018	$1014	$ 976	$1041	$1145	$1235	$1282	$1263
Eastbrook (1967)											
Clothing	$ 439	$ 369	$ 388	$ 412	$ 456	$ 468	$ 485	$ 540	$ 550	$ 552	$ 522
Furnishings	96	91	108	103	102	106	121	139	149	152	141
Sportswear	90	92	82	80	91	98	125	148	168	210	209
TOTAL	$ 625	$ 552	$ 578	$ 595	$ 649	$ 672	$ 731	$ 827	$ 867	$ 914	$ 872
Westpond (1976)											
Clothing							$ 136	$ 260	$ 320	$ 360	$ 391
Furnishings							36	50	62	67	72
Sportswear							58	75	78	118	122
TOTAL							$ 230	$ 385	$ 460	$ 545	$ 585
Southlake (1978)											
Clothing									$ 204	$ 410	$ 405
Furnishings									59	108	103
Sportswear									71	152	200
TOTAL									$ 334	$ 670	$ 708
All Locations											
Clothing	$3346	$3489	$3553	$3784	$3786	$3785	$4136	$4481	$4824	$5089	$5095
Furnishings	765	781	915	892	884	844	907	957	992	1033	1025
Sportswear	545	596	608	645	740	779	1026	1138	1266	1518	1560
TOTAL	$4656	$4866	$5076	$5321	$5410	$5408	$6069	$6576	$7082	$7640	$7680

Exhibit 7
Unit Sales by Location, Years Ending January 31

	1971	1972	1973	1974	1975	1976	1977	1978	1979	1980	1981
Fashion Square											
Suits	520	1,794	1,830	2,014	1,998	2,091	2,164	2,125	2,120	2,058	2,021
Sportcoats	246	850	867	954	945	995	1,030	1,011	1,042	1,005	990
Downtown											
Suits	5,625	5,602	5,642	5,631	5,590	5,569	5,599	5,589	5,544	5,505	5,492
Sportcoats	2,674	2,663	2,682	2,677	2,658	2,648	2,662	2,647	2,591	2,519	2,498
Northstream											
Suits	2,354	2,299	2,287	2,332	2,325	2,308	2,318	2,337	2,330	2,245	2,195
Sportcoats	1,141	1,114	1,108	1,129	1,126	1,119	1,128	1,120	1,102	1,091	1,097
Eastbrook											
Suits	1,354	1,321	1,344	1,380	1,402	1,363	1,350	1,381	1,352	1,280	1,240
Sportcoats	673	657	668	686	697	677	670	685	660	628	610
Westpond											
Suits							398	693	747	797	842
Sportcoats							195	338	360	382	437
Southlake											
Suits									589	927	905
Sportcoats									236	460	452
TOTAL											
Suits	9,853	11,016	11,103	11,357	11,315	11,331	11,829	12125	12,682	12,812	12,695
Sportcoats	4,734	5,284	5,325	5,446	5,426	5,439	5,685	5801	5,991	6,085	6,084

Exhibit 8
Suit Unit Sales by Brand

	1971	1972	1973	1974	1975	1976	1977	1978	1979	1980	1981
Hickey-Freeman	1,478	1,432	1,332	1,362	1,245	1,133	946	606	507	384	381
HSM	5,419	6,059	5,996	5,906	5,770	5,666	5,323	4,729	4,185	3,844	3,682
Christian Dior							355	727	888	1,025	1,016
Austin Reed							473	740	1,015	1,153	1,396
Pierre Cardin							340	606	761	897	975
Bill Blass							134	485	634	767	635
Danton's	2,956	3,525	3,775	4,089	4,300	4,532	4,,258	3,880	3,424	3,075	2,707
Kevin's								352	1,268	1,667	1,903
TOTAL	9,853	11,016	11,103	11,357	11,315	11,331	11,829	12,125	12,682	12,812	12,695

Exhibit 9
Market Research Report

TO: Mr. John Porter
         President
         Danton's

FROM: Specialty Retailers Consumer Research, Inc.

DATE: February 1, 1981

RE: Preliminary Report—Consumer Survey

We have just completed our computer analysis of the survey of 2,100 consumers/purchasers of men's suits and sportcoats. Eighteen hundred (1,800) of the respondents were randomly selected from the population of suit and sportcoat purchasers and three hundred (300) were selected from Danton's customers. This memo will briefly summarize our findings. A detailed report will be issued in about one week.

Approach

In the survey, we asked the respondents the following:

1. What they bought, where, and at what price (suits and sportcoats only).

2. Basic demographic information (age, income, etc.).

3. How many days they wore a suit and/or sportcoat to work.

4. The three most important product attributes (style, fit, etc.).

5. The three most important retail store attributes (selection, sales help, etc.).

6. An assessment of Danton's and several other stores for each of seventeen store attributes.

7. Various aspects of respondents' shopping behavior (e.g., whether they shopped around, bought mostly on sale, influence of wife, etc.).

On the basis of this, we were able to divide the customers into seven mutually exclusive groups. These groups have been labeled as follows:

Exhibit 9, continued

Nonwork Users	% of Clothing Market ($)
Fashion Interested	22
Fashion Indifferent	9

Work Users	% of Clothing Market ($)
Newcomers	·5
Utilitarian	14
Price-Conscious Emulators	19
Conservative, Quality Appreciators	19
Fashion Interested	12
	100

We were able to determine how important each group is in terms of the total clothing market, as shown above, and the share of each group's business held by Danton's and six other specialty stores, two department stores, and chains, Saks, Lord & Taylor and Bonwit's, the discounters including Syms, plus all other stores. More importantly, we were able to describe each group in terms of its demographics, product/store interests and appeals, and shopping behavior. Also, we were able to identify how each group rates Danton's compared to other stores in terms of the store attributes covered in the survey.

Findings

We found that Danton's has strong appeal to the CONSERVATIVE, QUALITY APPRECIATORS group, good appeal to the EMULATOR, group, fair appeal to the FASHION INTERESTED WORK USER group and the FASHION INTERESTED NONWORK USER group and virtually no appeal to the other three groups.

We found that each of the seven groups has distinctly different interests with regard to the clothing they buy and the stores they patronize. Also the shopping behavior of each group varies in significant ways. Lastly, each group has a different perception and evaluation of Danton's and the other stores covered in the survey.

The following exhibits summarize these findings. A more detailed analysis will be included in the final report.

Exhibit 9, continued
Segmentation of Men's Clothing Customers

Customer Type	% of All Men	% of Clothing Market—Units	% of Clothing Market—$	Description of Customers	Major Interests/Appeals	Shopping Behavior
Nonwork Users						
• Fashion Interested	31%	21%	22%	Does not regularly wear coats to work but uses frequently for social occasions. Household income: 35% over $25,000. Primarily resides in suburbs	Interested in distinctive, fashionable styling but not sophisticated styling; Appreciates attention from sales personnel; Wants versatile, mix and match clothing; Conscious of known brand names	Shops in stores with good "fashion" image. Many shop in better stores. Buys any time of year, but infrequently; Responds to advertising; Wife highly influential; Not particularly store loyal or salesperson loyal; 40% pay $175 or more for suit
• Fashion Indifferent	38%	12%	9%	Does not wear coats to work. Occupation: Service or factory worker generally. Age: Any age; Predominantly married with children; Very little discretionary income	Primarily interested in low-priced clothing. Buys basic items with versatility	Chain store customers. Wife frequently makes purchases. Few pay $175 or more for suit
Work Users						
• Newcomers	4%	7%	5%	Young men, new to buying clothing. Occupation: White collar. 68% single or married; No children	Interested in basic business styles. Interested in versatile styles to stretch dollars. Not particularly aware of brands	Lacks confidence; seeks out unintimidating salespeople, shopping environments; Fear of wasting his money; His cautiousness can be overcome through good selling but he will not return if dissatisfied; If satisfied, tends to develop store loyalty, more particularly salesperson loyalty; 10% pay $175 or more for suit

Exhibit 9, continued

Customer Type	% of All Men	% of Clothing Market—Units	% of Clothing Market—$	Description of Customers	Major Interests/Appeals	Shopping Behavior
• Utilitarian	9%	16%	14%	Lower level white collar worker; Does not meet the public; Clothing used only for utility; Little discretionary income; Any age	Interested in basic styles; Interested in versatile clothing; Heavy sportcoat buyer; Interested in low prices; Not interested in brands; Service of secondary importance	Chain store customer; Wife accompanies, influential; Loyal to stores, not sales personnel; Few pay $175 or more for suit
• Price-Conscious Emulators	8%	16%	19%	Regularly wears suits/sportcoats to work; Age: 25–45 (62%); Occupation: Managers, Sales Professionals; Works in fairly structured environment; Meets public, higher officials in company; Conforms to informal dress codes	Emulates conservative quality; Interested in basic business styles; Likes versatile garments for travel; Conscious of brand names Quality and fit of some importance; Will sacrifice sales service for lower price	No store/salesperson loyalty Shops around; 'Sale' buyer, responds to 'sale' ads especially for known brands; Wife not very influential; 20% will pay $175 or more for suit
• Conservative, Quality Appreciators	6%	15%	19%	Regularly wears suits/sportcoats to work; Occupation: Manager, Professionals, Executive high-level sales; Income: Primarily over $30,000; Good discretionary income; Age: Primarily 35–60 (72%); Concentrated in affluent suburbs, downtown 35% work downtown	Thinks of clothing as an investment in his career; Appreciates quality clothing; Interested in tasteful, conservative styles appropriate for work; Very interested in fit; Wants expert service; Does not need to rely on brands; Appreciates help in accessorizing	Prefers better stores primarily specialty stores; Develops store/salesperson loyalty; Wife not very influential; Not particularly responsive to advertising; Will only buy on sale if garment he wants is on sale; 75% will pay $175 or more for suit

Customer Type	% of All Men	% of Clothing Market—Units	% of Clothing Market—$	Description of Customers	Major Interests/Appeals	Shopping Behavior
• Fashion Interested	4%	10%	12%	High interest in clothing High discretionary income Lives downtown or in better suburbs (69%) Disproportionate number aged 45–55 Occupation: Proprietors, Sales, Professionals (61%)	Very persnickety, fastidious Two different types—Those wanting sophisticated classic or traditional styling and those wanting high-fashion, distinctive, sharp styling (½ of group) Not brand oriented Fit very important Sevice secondary to finding desired styles	A big spender Shops frequently Shops several stores regularly Develops salesperson loyalty within each store Wife not influential 60% will pay $175 or more for suit

Exhibit 9, continued

Customer Type	% of Clothing Market ($)	Danton's	Spec Store A	Spec Store B	Spec Store C Brooks	Spec Store D Traditional	Spec Store E Richman	Spec Store F Shouldered	Other Spec Store	Saks L&T Bonwit's	Dept Store A	Dept Store B	Chains	Syms & Other Disc.	Other	Total
Nonwork Users																
Fashion Interested	22	4	6	7	—	—	6	5	21	10	20	5	8	7	1	100
Fashion Indifferent	8	0	0	0	0	0	8	—	28	0	0	2	35	22	5	100
Work Users																
Newcomers	5	1	4	4	1	—	5	—	26	1	9	17	30	1	1	100
Utilitarian	14	0	0	5	—	—	12	—	25	0	7	9	35	6	1	100
Price-Conscious Emulators	19	7	8	12	6	2	5	—	18	4	12	10	12	4	—	100
Cons., Quality Appreciators	19	17	15	3	12	8	—	3	15	13	13	1	—	—	—	100
Fashion Interested	12	3	2	1	1	18	—	22	21	26	5	1	—	—	—	100

- Age distribution of Danton's clothing customers:

	% of Customers	% of Volume
18–24	5%	3%
25–34	16%	13%
35–44	24%	27%
45–54	25%	28%
55–64	17%	17%
Over 65	13%	12%
	100%	100%

- Household income of Danton's clothing customers: 68% have incomes greater than $25,000
- Percent buying clothing at Danton's in one-year period, 10/79 to 10/80, for first time in last five years: 30%
- Comments/Statistics by Consumer Group

Consumer Group	% Aware of Danton's	% Shopped at Danton's Last 5 Years	% Bought at Danton's Last 5 Years	What They Like About Danton's	What They Don't Like About Danton's
Nonwork Users					
Group I Fashion Interested	59%	34%	12%	1. Sales help (42%) 2. Alterations (21%) 3. Designer brands (9%)	1. The styles of their clothing (63%) 2. Prices too high (35%) 3. No mix & match clothing (18%)
Group II Fashion Indifferent	41%	12%	4%	1. The store looks (18%) 2. Charge account (8%) 3. Return policy (4%)	1. Prices too high (43%) 2. Sale price reductions too small (37%) 3. Sales help snobbish (9%)
Work Users					
Group III Newcomers	36%	7%	3%	1. Styles of clothing (27%) 2. Designer brands (22%) 3. Charge account (17%)	1. Sales help not friendly (37%) 2. Store too impersonal (22%) 3. Prices too high (19%)
Group IV Utilitarian	47%	12%	6%	1. "Sales" (21%) 2. Basic styles (18%) 3. Return policy (3%)	1. Prices too high (57%) 2. Sale price reductions too small (38%) 3. No mix & match clothing (14%)
Group V Emulators	73%	48%	26%	1. Selection (41%) 2. Sale prices (34%) 3. Fitting (27%)	1. Sale price reductions too small (36%) 2. Pressure from salespeople (14%) 3. Not enough selection in size (8%)
Group VI Quality Appreciators	82%	55%	48%	1. Quality clothing (52%) 2. Selection (38%) 3. Fitting (33%)	1. Not enough selection in size (32%) 2. The tie selection (31%) 3. Sales help (11%)
Group VII Fashion Interested	91%	81%	39%	1. Clothing selection (33%) 2. Fitting (30%) 3. Sales help (15%)	1. Clothing styles (34%) 2. Tie styles (26%) 3. Dress shirt styles (12%)

Case 5

THE CARTER AUTOMOTIVE GROUP

INTRODUCTION

Service had been the driving force behind the Carter Automotive Group (CAG), a chain of seven dealerships in Seattle, Washington. John Carter, president, was concerned, however, about the impact of a prolonged downturn in new car sales on his ability to maintain this service image while meeting the financial objectives of his new Swedish partner. This concern led to the question of whether the service image was strong enough to allow Carter to obtain a premium in new car pricing and, if so, how much.

Carter was also concerned about two other matters: first, was his current advertising program effective in communicating the service image, and second, in view of the commitment of each of the seven dealerships to the service image, had he optimally allocated organizational responsibilities to the dealerships and to the central organization for the implementation of this service orientation? Carter believed that resolution of these issues would clarify such secondary questions as expansion rate, required economies of scale to execute successfully his strategy, geographic focus, and whether to take on any additional brands (or name plates as they were called in the industry).

BACKGROUND ON AUTOMOBILE RETAILING

The role and character of automobile dealerships and service centers evolved slowly over the course of the twentieth century. In the first few years of the century, a car was a novelty and an expensive toy. A number of brands were available, but most bordered on being experimental. Urban department stores sold the new-fangled contraptions. Bicycle shops repaired fragile tires, hardware and general stores sold gasoline and blacksmiths maintained broken springs and "water jackets." Paved roads were virtually nonexistent until pressure from bicycle groups in 1905 began to force cities to pave some urban roadways. A suburban automobile jaunt was still, therefore, an adventure.

The introduction on October 1, 1908, of the Model T Ford opened the market to the masses. This car was more reliable and affordable and attempted to meet Henry Ford's goal "to build a simple low cost sturdy vehicle to replace the family horse." During the first year, Ford sold 10,600 passenger cars at $850 each, 17% of the total unit market. By 1911 the price had dropped to $525 and Ford had captured 40% of the 356,000 car market. Ford maintained this market share position until 1925.

Norval A. Hawkins was perhaps the father of the U.S. automobile dealership. As the first head of distribution and marketing for Ford, he founded the sales organization. The relationship which he forged with the dealers were to remain guiding principles for decades to come: territorial franchises to exclusive independent dealers, service as an integral role in supporting the manufacturers' reputation and goodwill, inventory shipped cash on delivery (COD) at a 10% discount from retail list price

David Wylie prepared this case under the supervision of Professor Walter J. Salmon as the basis for class discussion rather than to illustrate either effective or ineffective handling of an administrative situation. Locations and names in the case have been disguised.

Copyright © 1990 by the President and Fellows of Harvard College. Harvard Business School case 590-011.

in those days, and no volume discounts even to large dealers. Supporting this organization were teams of factory, trained mechanics who called upon the dealers from time to time to educate their service personnel.

Warranties were also a part of this equation, but had not always been so. In the early years when cars were sold primarily by urban general merchandise retailers, John Wanamaker, the Philadelphia department store giant, adopted the Model A Ford, made it a line leader, advertised it extensively, and backed it up with the store's respected guarantee against certain kinds of mechanical malfunctions. Ford, inspired by the success of this innovation, and, by the message it implied, added guarantees across all the models.

Automobile dealerships continued to thrive until the crash of 1929, a year in which 4,445,178 cars were sold and automobile registrations had grown to 23,060,421. Of the 38 million cars ever built in the United States up to 1929, 15 million were Model T Fords.

After a decline in sales in the early 1930s, the market returned to its former volume but then remained flat until World War II, when it virtually died. In 1943 and 1944, only 139 and 610 cars respectively were sold in the United States as production capacity was shifted to the war effort.

By 1950, however, a vibrant economy, pent-up demand and broad technological improvements arising from the war effort swelled sales to an all-time record of 6,665,863 cars. Manufacturers responded to this growth in demand with a breadth of different models and options. In 1966, the *New York Times* wrote:

Last year a Yale University physicist calculated that since Chevrolet offered 46 models, 32 engines, 20 transmissions, 21 colors (plus 9 two-tone combinations) and more than 400 accessories and options, the number of different cars that a Chevrolet customer conceivably could order was greater than the number of atoms in the universe. This seemingly would put General Motors one order higher than God in the chain of command.

Dealerships responded to this proliferation and to an intensely competitive marketplace with the format which remains prevalent today. This format included price as the primary competitive tool and, among certain automobile salespeople, high-pressure selling tactics. Emphasis on service varied among dealers, but was typically neither featured in advertising nor high in quality.

There was another dramatic shift during the years after World War II. A focus on developing a federally funded transportation infrastructure created a road network which gave the automobile owner immensely enhanced mobility. Along with suburban sprawl came dealerships which catered to a larger, more geographically dispersed base of customers. Among them the emphasis on "sales" grew immensely. Service departments concentrated more on new car setup and warranty work while repairs were increasingly the domain of the local service station.

The introduction of the foreign car into the United States also weighed heavily in the evolution of the postwar dealership. In 1953, Volkswagen (VW), to overcome a consumer concern for service and parts availability, offered a limited number of nonexclusive franchises to existing non-big three dealers (i.e., Ford, General Motors or Chrysler). Such dealers included, for example, the then-existing Nash-Rambler franchise of American Motors, a company subsequently absorbed first by a French automobile company and then by Chrysler Corporation. VW maintained, however, very strict standards of performance and standardized settings for service. Expert factory-trained mechanics worked in immaculate shops next to plate glass windows where customers could follow their progress. This degree of manufacturer control was hitherto unknown.

Toyota and Nissan soon followed using the VW formula. Their franchisees were for the most part dealers who had been waiting for VW franchises. These Japanese manufacturers added, however, large regional parts warehouses to avoid the long wait which had become associated with obtaining foreign car spare parts as individual items were ordered from abroad.

During the 1970s and 1980s, the traditional format of the service station was undergoing a transition as well. Gasoline prices increased dramatically and gasoline itself, historically the lifeblood of the service station, was increasingly being offered at self-service gasoline stations and convenience stores, where prices were extremely competitive. The result was the demise of many traditional service stations.

The driving consumer therefore had to turn elsewhere for automobile service. In addition to the remaining service stations and mechanics who operated independent repair shops, two formats evolved to fill this changing demand. First, specialty service providers such as Midas Muffler, AAMCO Transmissions, and Jiffy Lube arose.

Second, certain automobile dealerships reemphasized full-line service as part of their offering.

Service became an increasingly important component of the marketing strategy for these dealerships. Customers who previously had bought only on the basis of price and selection were encouraged to consider longer-term relationships with a dealership. Fulfilling this relationship meant offering higher quality and more convenient service. The previously effective hard sell and full-page price advertising were giving way to relationship building and word-of-mouth referrals.

As the last decade of the century dawned, the number of name plates available to the American consumer had grown to 35 and foreign manufacturers had captured over 35% of the U.S. market. The majority of dealerships were large, in easily accessible suburban locations and, particularly in large urban areas, owned by multidealer operations. The number of franchises in the United States had dropped 12% since 1979 while the number of dealer principals had fallen 29%. During this period, the percentage of dealers with a financial interest in two or more dealerships had jumped from 8% to over 22%. Almost half of all dealerships now belonged to individuals or corporations owning two or more dealers, and 20% were part of chains of four dealerships or more. The performance between large and small dealerships was spreading as well. Whereas in the late 1970s pretax net profit as a percentage of sales was about 1.7% for the two groups, by 1987 large dealerships averaged 2.5% while small dealers only 1.6% in pretax profit.

The consumer was changing as well. According to a survey by the National Automobile Dealers Association (NADA): The "consumer will demand greater convenience in auto shopping and servicing. . ." That consumer will also be much better informed about the product he or she wishes to buy, more deliberate about the buying process, and more focused on his or her total transportation outlays. Longer purchase cycles, already evident, will become a fact of life. Warranties, guarantees, and after-sale service will become more important. (See **Exhibit 1** for a summary of this survey.)

Carter Automotive Group represented the growing number of dealerships that emphasized service. It not only had to deliver excellent service but also convince prospective new car customers that it had the ability and intent to do so. Furthermore, either service had to stand financially on its own so that new car prices could remain competitive, or other aspects of Carter's operations had to subsidize service.

CARTER HISTORY

In 1965, John Carter's father and a group of investors acquired a Volkswagen dealership in Bellevue, Washington. In the 1970s, he purchased Audi and Porsche dealerships and opened new Nissan and Mazda dealerships in neighboring Renton and Auburn. These dealerships were operated separately and were held by different corporations, each with slightly different investment interests. Initially, the dealerships operated profitably, but in the late 1970s performance began to lag.

In 1978, John Carter joined, as controller, the CAG management company which was formed to oversee the operations. In 1980, the Carter family acquired the controlling interest in the group and John became president. The goal was to grow CAG to the point where it could go public. This objective was unique for American dealerships. The only other attempt to go public had been undertaken by a Rolls Royce and Yugo dealership in Kansas and had failed. Most dealerships remained privately held, many by families.

As controller, Carter had developed an appreciation for the potential of the business but an aversion to the high-pressure sales tactics and apparent lack of respect for customers which typically characterized dealers. He urged a different course upon CAG.

Carter thought that the CAG dealerships could differentiate themselves from competitors by offering high-quality service as well as competitively priced automobiles. Because he believed that excellent service and competitive new car prices would constitute an attractive package for consumers, he thought it would obviate the need for high-pressure sales tactics. Carter envisioned that prospects would not only return from their shopping to buy a new car but also return for subsequent new car purchases as well. Returning customers would open the prospect of greater margins since they would be less apt to shop around for price.

On February 1, 1985, Carter consolidated all the dealerships into a single ownership under "Carter Automotive Group. He then introduced this new direction into his dealerships, dubbing it the "Carter Difference." A brochure called *The Carter Difference: Ten Reasons Why It Matters"* described the 10 components of this offer:

1. **Selection and security.** A broad selection of vehicles from which to choose and an assurance that the dealership would be there for a long time.

2. **Loan cars at no charge.** For any mechanical service or mechanical warranty repairs, free loan cars or pickup trucks were available to customers who had purchased a new vehicle at CAG.

3. **No bull sticker policy and no gimmicks sales policy.** "All cars and trucks at Carter dealerships are priced at factory suggested retail or lower. *Every single day*. There is no additional dealer markup. *Ever*." There were therefore none of the extra markups sometimes used by dealers such as additional dealer markup, market price adjustment, or the inclusion of high-margin add-ons or accessories.

4. **No hassle salespeople.**

5. **Extended service hours.** Hours were extended to provide convenient pickup and drop-off. "We changed our hours so you won't have to."

6. **Toll free hot line.** An 800 number for comments, complaints, praises, etc. All comments were acted upon and/or passed along to constituent dealerships. (See **Exhibit 3** for copy of CEI report, also described below.)

7. **Carter Motorcars Club.** A membership which entitled those who purchased from Carter's a free car wash after every service, attendance at a seminar on your car or truck: its care and feeding, "a courtesy shuttle within a five-mile radius and other free services."

8. **Financing.** Vehicle financing or leasing could be initially consummated through the dealership. CAG qualified customers for financing, prepared the paperwork, and put a customer "on the road." Until financing was ultimately placed with a bank, CAG assumed the liability.

9. **Quality assurance used car guarantee.** CAG offered a free comprehensive six-month or 6,000-mile warranty on all used cars and trucks. Additional policies were sold for periods up to 30 months or 30,000 miles.

10. *On the Road Magazine.* A full-color, general-interest magazine with selected articles on new vehicles and announcements of events and sales at CAG was mailed quarterly to buyers for three years subsequent to their purchase of an automobile. By the end of 1989, circulation was almost 50,000.

In addition, the "Carter Difference" included a number of elements reflecting the company's commitment to "go the extra mile" to satisfy customers. These included such services as washing a vehicle inside and out after service, putting protective paper covers on the seats during service which were then, for emphasis, pulled off in view of the customer. All employees were encouraged to recognize customers' names and to put in "that extra touch." Carter calculated the out-of-pocket-cost of its special services to be $142 per new car sold, and another $130 for the used car warranty.

Carter also articulated the underlying philosophy, "The Carter Way" in the company mission statement:

Quality of service is our first priority: We will provide error-free service to each customer on time, the first time. Every employee will know the requirements of his or her job and conform to those requirements at all times.

Customer satisfaction is the goal of everything we do: We will deliver a level of service to our customers which is personal, courteous and unequaled in our industry. We will also keep abreast of our customer comments and trends in order to adjust our operations to the customer's wants and needs.

Integrity must never be compromised: We all must deal with our customers and employees alike with honesty and fairness. Our longevity as a company and our responsibility to our customer as a person require that we do business in an atmosphere of honesty and trust.

Innovation will make us grow: The only way to do things better is to do things differently. We must never fear change along the road to improvement.

Employees are always partners in our mission and the cornerstone of our success: Carter Automotive Group does not manufacture a product. We provide a service. Therefore, each employee is a member of our service team and only by working together will we achieve success.

We are a part of a greater community: Our efforts will better serve each customer, each employee and our community as a whole. Our good reputation is an asset to everyone, including our community.

Do it all over again: Continuous improvement and innovation are essential to our success. Whenever we believe we are doing everything right, we must reexamine the yardsticks by which we measure ourselves. Yardsticks as well as goals must always be updated.

And finally a note to skeptics: Carter Automotive Group genuinely believes in its mission statement. No one should doubt our resolve to accomplish each goal.

Carter realized that the success of this initiative depended both upon maintaining a helpful, low-pressure sales team and a reputation for quality service. He thought that by achieving a consistent, high service level across all the dealerships, he would gain the necessary economies to communicate effectively the message of the "Carter Difference." In addition, he thought the resulting good reputation would extend to all dealerships within the group. Most other multidealership chains lacked this consistency because they ran each dealership as a fully autonomous, self-contained entity.

A key component of the plan to achieve the required level of service quality and consistency was a central training program. All new employees were required to spend two weeks being introduced to all ramifications of the Mission Statement and, for new salespeople, details of the customer-oriented sales approach. Every six months all employees were required to attend a one- or two-day refresher course.

Each dealership placed full-page advertisements featuring low-priced specials in local newspapers to retain a competitive price image. These advertisements were lost, some said, in a sea of other dealer ads. They cost, on the average, $3,000 per week per dealership. In addition, a limited amount of radio advertising generated by the corporate office stressed the "Carter Difference." Since most radio stations reached the entire Seattle metropolitan area, however, sixty-second radio spots could cost up to $3,000. (See **Exhibit 2** for a typical radio script and sample printed advertisements.) Carter knew, therefore, that he could not entirely rely upon conventional price-oriented newspaper advertising to boost sales or upon corporate radio advertising to generate prospects. Prospective new car buyers would have to respond to the message of the "Carter Difference" at the dealerships and from direct marketing efforts.

Carter's total advertising expenditure was $1.9 million in 1989, of which $1,150,000 (61%) was spent on newspapers, $30,000 on radio (1.5%), and none on television. Of the remainder, $60,000 was spent on brochures which set forth "the Carter Difference" and $65,000 was for the quarterly publication and mailing of *On the Road Magazine*. Private sales,[1] direct mail, targeted outdoor advertising, brochures, referral services[2] and other direct marketing comprised the remaining $580,000 (31%) of the budget. Other dealers in the area tended to place somewhat more emphasis on either radio or TV and less on direct marketing. In contrast, the industry average for larger dealers advertising by media was 53.8% on newspapers, 16.3% on radio, 18.4% on TV, and 11.5% on direct mail, displays, demos and miscellaneous expenses. Carter's total budget for advertising was 1.2% of total dealership sales, or $256 per new car sold, whereas large dealers, average was 1.42% of sales, or $254 per new car sold.

There was also a central customer service center. Every work day, a selection of service and sales customers was telephoned and questioned about their experiences. From this survey, an internal "Customer Enthusiasm Index" (CEI) was generated which was sent to the dealerships. This information, in combination with the results from an industry survey rating various dealerships on a factory "Consumer Satisfaction Index" (CSI), was used to judge the quality of service at the dealerships. This customer service center also operated the "Carter's Hot Line." The content of the calls to the center were summarized in the CEI and distributed to the dealers. (See **Exhibit 3** for the CEI report.)

Control was a final issue which was coordinated centrally. Carter used a rather traditional control system to provide detailed information on the performance of each dealership. He made use of this information in working with the general managers to improve performance levels and maintain quality operations.

During the first part of the 1980s, the CAG service oriented marketing approach won immediate customer acceptance. Consequently, three additional dealerships were added to the group and two strategically located body shops were established to handle the group's entire needs. Sales grew from $63 million in 1980 to $138 million in 1986 and ratings for all the CAG dealerships

---

1 "Private sales" refers to direct mail limited time offers of special discounts on both new cars and service to employees of particular organizations.

2 "Referral services" means payment to others for referring customers to CAG.

soared. (See **Exhibit 4** for financial statements.) It was clear, however, that because economies of scale were not yet adequate to assure success of the group's strategy, it would have to grow.

During the last half of the 1980s, Carter began to explore obtaining capital for an expansion program. Not only was his apparently successful format ready for growth but marginal dealerships were becoming available as competition escalated among dealers offering a growing number of name plates.

In 1986 Carter was introduced to The Nilsson Group (Nilsson), which owned a Swedish chain of automobile dealerships. Nilsson wanted to ascertain whether its brand of service-intensive marketing would be well received in the U.S. market. It became quickly apparent that both CAG and Nilsson shared the same operating philosophy, and that a partnership could be attractive to both parties. Nilsson could enter the American market on an experimental basis and Carter could not only receive the funding it desired but also learn from Nilsson more about marketing and managing service-oriented automobile dealerships.

Nilsson was a public corporation with 1987 sales of $2.6 billion. Seventy percent of sales were derived from 75,000 new and used vehicles sold from 66 locations throughout Sweden. Franchises included Audi, Austin Rover, Citroen, Fiat, Ford, Jaguar, Lotus, Opel, Rolls Royce, Vauxhall, Volkswagen and Volvo. Nilsson was the sole Swedish importer of Volkswagen cars and parts. Nilsson attributed much of its success to a "commitment to customer service, emphasis on employee training and career development, and a disciplined approach to business planning and financial control." Seven thousand people were employed in the automotive division.

In 1988, CAG and Nilsson became equal partners in a new joint venture company. CAG contributed its existing organization and net assets at current valuation and Nilsson contributed an equal cash amount. Carter remained as president, with Nilsson providing management assistance in business planning and employee training, announcing that, "It is the intention of the joint venture to utilize the increased financial resources to expand and develop the Group and seek competitive advantage through the provision of high standards of service to customers. An important ingredient in the motivation of this venture is the strong commitment to customer service embodied within the corporate cultures of both parties."

The partnership with Nilsson was proving to be more fortuitous than Carter had expected. Not only was the balance sheet strengthened (see **Exhibit 4**) but the management contributions also transformed the way in which CAG did business.

Lars Ericksson, the Nilsson executive charged with adapting the strengths of the Swedish organization to CAG, moved into the office next to Carter soon after the partnership was formalized. He described the contributions of Nilsson as follows:

A critical piece of our management style lies in the way in which we relate to the general managers at the dealerships. We feel that they play a critical role in ensuring the profitability of each store so we give them all the support and information they need to do a good job. . . .

The most important element of our program is the CMI report (Carter Management Information). This monthly report compares actual performance against plan along a number of financial and statistical measures and includes details of the current CEI and the CSI ratings. . . .

Training and meetings are also important ways we keep the dealerships consistent and in line with objectives. . . .

The CMI report (see **Exhibit 5** for selected portions of the CMI report for the Carter's Ford dealership) was a detailed performance plan for each dealership by department. Its annual development started each October, when broad economic and market information was sent to each general manager. Over the course of the next month, he worked with his department heads to generate detailed plans, which were consolidated and returned to the corporate office for discussion, modification and ultimate approval.

During the year, the general manager of each dealership would receive the monthly CMI within several days of the end of the month. Carter, Ericksson, and the corporate chief financial officer would visit each dealership to review the performance against plan with the general manager. The general manager, in turn, would review the plan with all of his department heads who received complete CMIs as well as detailed CMIs for each subsection of their department.

Carter thought that the CMI and the meeting process had dramatically changed how he managed the business and the quality of decision making at the dealership level. In combination with the training program, the CMI and resulting discussions had significantly improved both the quality and performance of the dealerships. Whereas previously Carter had, as was the general practice in the industry, personally reviewed and interpreted performance results to guide his managers, now the feedback went directly to them. He no longer had to spend the majority of his time with the dealerships on daily operating matters.

Another major contribution of Nilsson was in the area of allocating costs to the dealerships. While a management fee was charged to each dealership to cover some of the corporate overhead, only expenses which could be reasonably identified with a particular business function were allocated to dealerships or departments. Consequently such items as corporate advertising and the Customer Service Center expenses were absorbed at the corporate level. Nilsson also introduced return on invested capital as a key performance measure for all levels of the organization.

Carter was eager to achieve the operating results expected by Nilsson of all their dealerships and affiliates. These objectives were ambitious in comparison to the reported performance range of most U.S. dealers. Nilsson generally expected a return on capital employed (ROCE)[3] of 25% before interest and taxes and a return on sales (ROS) before interest and taxes of 3.5%. In contrast, Carter estimated dealerships in the United States, which were mainly privately owned, to average an ROCE of 12.5% and a ROS of 1.7%.

By early 1990, CAG had seven dealerships and two body shops. (See **Exhibit 6**, Profile of Dealerships.) Sales in 1989 were $160 million and profits before taxes $609,000. Unit sales were 7,459 new cars and trucks, and 1,885 used vehicles. After several lackluster years, 1989 was profitable and 1990 was projected to meet industry averages (see **Exhibit 7**).

Results of the CSI were encouraging as well. The manufacturers' ratings of the CAG dealerships in comparison to competitors had consistently improved over the last four years. Moreover, the ratio of buyers to prospects (40% vs. 25% for the industry) was not only an endorsement of Carter's philosophy, but reduced the degree to which the CAG dealerships depended upon a large volume of shoppers.

CONCERNS IN 1990 AND THE FORD DEALERSHIP

Since affiliating with Nilsson, Carter had primarily devoted his energies to installing Nilsson management systems and training programs. Only recently had he begun to focus on acquisition opportunities in the Seattle metropolitan area. Carter recognized, however, that any acquisition could dilute management resources and stretch centralized services.

The one major project Carter had undertaken was the relocation of CAG's existing Ford dealership which had benefited from the recent popularity of the T-Bird, Taurus, Probe, and Escort models. The old dealership had been a relatively small, "neighborhood" dealership with limited growth potential and poor visibility.

Carter decided to develop this dealership into the flagship of the CAG fleet. He chose a highly visible and accessible location next to the Route 167 freeway on an "auto-mile," where six other major dealerships were located. The physical facility constructed on the site, although larger than the others within the group, represented Carter's vision of an ideal dealership.

The dealership was built on three acres along 1,200 feet of road frontage. In the center were a 20,000-square-foot, new car showroom and sales and administrative offices. The showroom was flanked on one side by the new truck and used car lot, and on the other side by a five-story, 116,000-square-foot garage which held the inventory of 400 cars. This garage was high enough to be visible from adjacent Route 167. Beyond was the service and parts facility. The service department boasted 24 bays. The parts department included an attractive showroom with a number of accessories on display. A 10,000-square-foot warehouse held inventory for the substantial wholesale and retail parts business. (See **Exhibit 8** for a photograph of the Ford dealership.) Since the move, total sales of both new and used vehicles had grown from $33.2 million in 1987 (2,358 units) to $55.4 million (3,670 units) in 1989.

Mase Bowen was the general manager. Having been promoted from the service side of the business, he felt

---

3 ROCE was calculated as: Net Income before Interest and Taxes/(Receivables + Inventory - Trade Payables + Depreciated Value of Fixed Assets). Fixed assets did not include land or buildings, since Nilsson management believed that the performance of a dealership should be judged excluding the value of real estate. Rent was charged, however, to the dealerships as an expense based on 10% of the market value of the property.

that at age forty-two, he had achieved his lifelong goal of operating his own dealership without the drawbacks of a financial commitment. General managers were paid a "good living wage" of between $80,000 and $105,000 in salary with a bonus based on the overall performance of the dealership. General managers could make in total from $100,000 to $130,000 in a good year. This range for total remuneration was slightly higher than for general managers in the industry, but competitive in the Seattle market.

Bowen was dedicated to the success of the dealership. Articulate and demanding, he had a reputation among his subordinates as being strict. Bowen spoke of his own style as: "I'm not out there to do their jobs. My job is to oversee this operation to make sure everything goes right. I stay out of their way, but I let them know it if anything is wrong. Then I try to work with them to find a solution."

Bowen saw himself as the intermediary between an undisciplined and moody sales force and the rational and disciplined corporate office. Although the excellent performance of his dealership allowed him to run his own show, he relied on headquarters for their "wealth of expertise." He had less independence than he might have at more traditional dealerships, but he thought the benefits gained from headquarters far outweighed this loss. Reporting to Bowen were Dan Jones, sales manager, John Thompson, service manager, a parts manager, and several administrative managers.

Jones was the son of a mid-western car dealer. A veteran salesperson, he had worked with a number of companies and thought that "the Carter Way, is the only way to go." Jones personally handled all inventory and ordering decisions directly with Ford. Reporting to him were two desk managers, one used car sales manager, four finance managers and two fleet and lease managers.

The 20-member sales force worked, after the required two-week training period during which they received a minimal salary, on a straight commission of 25% of vehicle gross margin. During the training period they spent a week in the headquarters classroom covering such topics as "the Carter Way," special selling techniques, and product information. They were then placed with a "mentor," an experienced salesperson for a week-long apprenticeship at a dealership. The sales force reported to the desk manager on duty for the shift, although Jones was ultimately responsible for training and performance.

A salesperson was trained to approach prospects in the lot and to follow them answering questions rather than pushing them in any particular direction. There was pressure, however, to close the deal on the spot. Carter's theory, confirmed by a 40% closing ratio (the industry ratio of purchasers to prospects was about 25%), was that prospects would appreciate the friendly and low-key treatment at Carter's. Indeed, once they had shopped around for price, some returning prospects were willing to pay an extra $100 to $400 for the service and treatment Carter's offered.

Salesmen were taught to sell (1) themselves, (2) the dealership and (3) the vehicle but to avoid discussion of price until it was introduced by the prospect. To assist in the introduction to "the Carter Difference," a brochure and a short video were available.

Once a vehicle was chosen, the salesperson introduced customers to the desk manager, the senior sales manager on duty under Jones. This individual, promoted from the rank of finance manager, was paid a small salary in addition to commission. A desk manager's total remuneration ranged from $60,000 to $75,000. His responsibility was to negotiate the final deals with customers and to qualify them for bank credit.

When the deal was finalized, the customer went to one of the four finance managers, each of whom had been promoted from the sales floor. His job was to prepare the contracts, complete the credit applications, which he would later place with a bank, and to sell "add-ons." Add-ons included alarm systems, extended warranties, the "Platinum Touch" (extra surface protection applied to fabrics and plastics) and a thirty-day insurance policy on the unpaid balance for the vehicle to protect Carter's from loss until bank financing was arranged. These add-ons, known as "F&I," generated about $150,000 per month of high-margin revenue, 16% of which constituted the finance managers' entire commission and only financial remuneration.

The used car sales manager devoted the majority of his time to wholesaling those cars traded in which were not good enough to merit the six-month warranty which Carter's extended on all used vehicles. The fleet and lease manager worked exclusively on multivehicle sales and arranging appropriate lease terms.

The service department was committed to providing the best quality repair and warranty work possible with a minimum of "comebacks" (cars returned for poor service). John Thompson, the service manager, was frustrated, however, in his efforts. He knew that excellent service was a critical component of the Carter's formula, yet he was struggling to keep up with demand.

Although the service department had 24 bays, availability of good mechanics in Western Washington was a major problem. Carter's paid competitive wages, yet Thompson had only been able to hire 16 mechanics and 24 support personnel. He had even tried advertising in several mid-western and Texan communities, but to no avail. A direct competitor in the area with equivalent volume dealerships had thirty bays and fourteen mechanics, and faced the same shortage of qualified help.

Mechanics were billed out at $52 per hour and paid an average of $15 per flagged hour, a standard time established by an industry association for the completion of specific jobs. A good performer could log a flagged hour in less than forty minutes on a routine job. The 24 service bays in use by the end of 1989 were divided by specialty. One, for instance, might be the exclusive domain of the automobile transmission specialist while another might be that of a brake or electrical specialist. Very few mechanics were qualified to do a number of different jobs.

A customer typically made a service appointment by telephone with a customer service manager who tried to assess the probable nature of the problem, schedule the repair time, and assign it when the car arrived to one or more mechanics. The customer service manager had to be particularly mindful of efficiently using the 36 available loan cars guaranteed under "the Carter Difference" since the department repaired up to 80 cars per day.

Thompson questioned whether his department could keep up with the demand generated by the 300 to 400 cars sold every month and by other customers who had not bought at Carter's but appreciated the convenience and quality of its service. In addition, much of the work was the "squeak and rattle" variety, which required extensive nonbillable diagnostic time and brought frequent comebacks. The more profitable work at which the mechanics excelled was increasingly going to the specialty franchises such as Midas Muffler or Jiffy Lube.

In spite of these problems, Thompson was able to keep his comeback ratio at 7%, well below what he said was the normal industry range of 15% to 29%. Labor on a comeback was not billed at Carter's. If a *customer* claimed a vehicle was inadequately serviced, it was defined as a comeback, unlike other dealerships which only withheld billing the customer if the *service department* acknowledged error. Carter equated this policy to Nordstrom's no questions asked return policy.

Recently the capacity constraints of the service department were starting to show. Over the course of 1989, the comeback ratio had been increasing. Customers could not always obtain a loan car. Often, scheduled completion times were missed, and occasionally the wash was omitted. Moreover, customer complaints had been rising through Carter's Hot Line. The general manager, Mase Bowen, said that the "sales department sells the first car, but it's the service department which sells the rest . . . and that's where the biggest margins are." He knew something had to be done.

THE FUTURE

Carter believed in the direction he had chosen, although the American market for automobiles had begun to soften during 1989. New car sales in the United States had declined from 10.6 million automobiles in 1988 to 9.9 million in 1989. Industry analysts expected a continued unit sales decline in excess of 2% in 1990 and no meaningful recovery before 1991. He knew this market environment would be the true test of "the Carter Difference." He believed, moreover, that in order to achieve the ambitious goals which Nilsson desired, the number of dealerships in the group would have to expand and results would have to exceed competition. He had not yet determined, however, the pace and nature of this expansion.

Carter had already made some strides in the expansion program. Construction of a new facility for the Buick dealership in Renton was under way. It would be similar to the Ford prototype which had proved to be so successful. The project would require an estimated $3.5 million for land and buildings, $3 million in inventory, $820,000 for furniture, fixtures and equipment, and $700,000 to finance receivables. Payables were expected to be about $600,000. Current levels of capital required for the existing Buick dealership were $170,000 in furniture, fixtures and equipment, $2.1 million in inventory and $700,000 in receivables. Payables were $500,000. Sales were expected to increase from their 1989 level of $12.3 million (745 units) to $22.5 million (1,600 units) by 1991.

In addition, General Motors had recently assigned Carter the market territories for two Saturn dealerships. Together, these new franchises would require approximately $2.25 million in new car and parts inventory, $500,000 for furniture, fixtures and equipment, and $400,000 for the total of used vehicle inventory and receivables net of payables. Sales were expected to exceed $20 million in 1991 and $25 million in 1992. Gross profits on new vehicles were projected to be about 10%, substantially higher than the 7% average for the CAG group. (The cost of land and buildings for the Saturn project were expected to be about $2.85 million. Ten percent of this amount would be charged to the dealership as rent.)

Saturn would be an interesting experiment. Each franchise would have one central new car sales dealership and a series of separate more conveniently located service centers. This arrangement intrigued Carter as a potential model for his other dealerships.

Acquisition was another possibility for Carter. Several underperforming dealerships within a few hours drive of Seattle were for sale. Carter thought that performance would improve with the adoption of "the Carter Way."

Carter attributed much of the recent improvement in CAG's performance to the Nilsson management and organizational system which allowed all the dealerships to make ongoing operating decisions, to benefit from cen-tralized resources and to achieve consistent quality and service levels. Carter felt that this organization gave CAG a real advantage over competitors. Single-dealership competitors had no centralized resources and most other dealership groups lacked the systems to achieve any kind of consistency among the various dealerships. Thus far for CAG, the extra costs incurred from high service levels had diminished the net contribution, but Carter felt confident that increased sales or margins would eventually justify the initial investment. On the other hand, he wondered what would happen during a declining market? Would he, like many others, have to weather the storm or could he take advantage of his strong balance sheet and acquire less fortunate competitors at attractive prices?

Exhibit 1
Summary of NADA Consumer Survey

THE CAR BUYING EXPERIENCE (by age group)					
	Total	**18–30**	**30–45**	**45–50**	**65+**
Satisfied	80%	78%*	78%	81%	89%
Neutral	2%	3%	1%	3%	2%
Dissatisfied	17%	18%	21%	15%	9%

WHAT'S IMPORTANT WHEN BUYING A CAR?			
	Total	**Expensive** **	**Not Expensive**
Good reputation	85%	82%***	85%
Quality of service	84%	85%	83%
Price	82%	68%	83%
Helpful sales staff	65%	60%	65%
Location of dealer	51%	54%	51%
Purchased car there before	40%	38%	40%
Advertising	29%	15%	31%

CAR BUYING INFORMATION SOURCES BY ORDER OF IMPORTANCE (by age group)					
	Total	**18–30**	**30–45**	**45–50**	**65+**
A visit to test drive car	44%	51%	46%	40%	29%
Friends and neighbors	35%	39%	41%	32%	17%
Magazines	20%	26%	26%	23%	11%
Television	23%	26%	16%	13%	13%
Newspaper	15%	18%	16%	13%	13%
Automobile sales staff	14%	13%	11%	18%	18%
Radio	3%	3%	3%	2%	5%
None/No 2nd mention	17%	9%	13%	21%	40%

THE SERVICES CONSUMERS LOOK FOR IN DEALERS BY RANK****			
	Total	**Expensive**	**Not Expensive**
Combined resources	51%	57%	51%
Service/maintenance	26%	21%	26%
Warranty	21%	21%	21%
Sales staff	13%	9%	13%
Price/financing/closing	5%	4%	5%
Others	2%	4%	2%
Reliability	2%	1%	2%
Demonstration	1%	1%	1%
Good selection	1%	1%	1%
No hassle	0%	0%	0%

* Reads: 78% of the 18–30 year old respondents were satisfied with their experience.

** Expensive cars were defined as those priced at over $20,000. Since less than 20% of those surveyed had purchased vehicles in this category, the percentages for "Total" were skewed toward "Not Expensive."

*** Reads: 82% of expensive car buyers cited a dealer's good reputation as important when buying a car.

**** The way in which the question was asked assumed that the dealer would have in stock the vehicle desired by the customer.

Source: *Automotive Executive*, March 1988.

Exhibit 2
Typical Radio Scripts

THE CARTER DIFFERENCE

In 1966, when the Carter family opened their first automotive dealership, they didn't like the way most other car dealers did business. They didn't like the high-pressure sales techniques, the one only price leaders, or the lack of service and follow-up.

So the Carters decided to do things differently. They set up their own training facility to teach salespeople how to make customers feel comfortable when buying a car. They offered Saturday service, free car washes, and a free Carter magazine to keep in touch. Today, if you ask any of their over one hundred thousand customers why they bought from Carter Ford, Nissan, Mazda, Mitsubishi, Porsche, Audi, or Volkswagen, they'll tell you the Carter Difference had everything to do with it.

For the location of a Carter dealer near you and a free brochure explaining the Carter Difference, call 1-800-962-CARS. That's 1-800-962-CARS. The Carter Automotive Group . . . it makes a difference.

KID'S STORY

Recently I went shopping for a car with my son. Have you ever seen a hungry car salesman deal with a six year old? I felt like Michael was a piece of luggage.

Then a friend told me about the Carter group of dealerships which include Ford, Nissan, Mazda, Buick, GMC trucks, Porsche, Audi, and Volkswagen. When we walked in the door I knew things were different. They showed us both around and gave Michael an activity book and a new box of crayons. Then they told us about Carter's toll free Hot Line, their magazine, extended service hours and free car washes. I also found out why Carter's salespeople are so nice. Carter has its own training school.

They call all this the Carter Difference, and I think it makes a big difference when you're buying a car. For the location of a Carter dealer near you and a Carter Difference brochure, call 1-800-962-CARS. 1-800-962-C-A-R-S. The Carter Automotive Group . . . it makes a difference. It *really* does!

WHY WE DON'T PLAY HIDE AND SEEK*

Frankly, we're a little annoyed by the new game a lot of automotive dealers are playing. It's called The Asterisk Game. It usually involves a giant headline which promises an incredibly low price or interest rate. Plus, a tiny little asterisk.

Of course, that little asterisk signals that the game has begun. You're on your own to find his rather mischievous twin brother - find the real facts of the offer - which are hidden elsewhere. In some out-of-the-way place, in much smaller type.

It's here that you discover what you really have to pay to get that lower-than-market interest rate. It's here that they tell you what the car will really cost. It's here - somewhere just above the bottom of the page - that you get the real bottom line.

AT CARTER AUTOMOTIVE GROUP, WE PLAY IT STRAIGHT

We don't believe in game playing. And we dont' think you want to do business with people who do.

We never make you search around in the corners of our ads or under rows of little boxes to find the key detail that makes our advertisement fair and complete. We don't stand it on end so you get a crimp in your neck trying to read it. Or print it upside down as if we were trying to conceal the answers to a crossword puzzle.

No way. We put all the facts in front of you in easy-to-read type. Right where they should be.

Together in one place.

Now, there are times when an asterisk is legally required. Then - and only then - we will use it. But, we won't abuse it to get your attention while hiding the real facts of the matter elsewhere.

IN OUR ADS AND IN EVERYTHING WE DO.
At Carter Automotive Group, we have our own way of doing things. We call it **The Carter Difference.**

It means we don't put "gimmicks" in our promotions. We don't advertise one-of-a-kind, we-just-sold-it price leaders. We don't add mysterious dealer mark-ups to the original factory sticker price.

And we don't play hide-and-seek with interest rates or pricing. We don't play games - period. With you. Or your money.

CARTER
AUTOMOTIVE GROUP

Exhibit 3
Copy of Customer Enthusiasm Index Report

CARTER FORD DEALERSHIP
CUSTOMER ENTHUSIASM INDEX—1989

	Prior Cal.Year	Jul	Aug	Sep	Oct	Nov	Dec	Current Cal.YTD
Sales								
Number of Contacts[1]	203	39	39	42	58	50	59	482
Received a telephone call[2]	87	92	82	74	79	78	88	83
Received thank you letter[2]	93	92	85	83	88	80	93	89
Received in working order[2]	91	97	97	95	100	98	100	98
Explained controls/manuals[2]	95	100	100	95	100	98	100	99
F&I courteous & helpful[2]		100	95	95	98	98	98	97
Internal CEI[3]	93	97	91	87	84	87	86	92
Factory CSI[4]	7.9	7.9	7.8	8.2	7.7	8.1	—	8.1
Shoppers[5]	—	—	69	—	—	—	82	76
Service								
Number of contacts[1]	1,368	107	69	80	168	143	150	1,740
Employees friendly[2]	99	99	96	100	98	99	100	99
Was your car washed 2	84	88	91	83	87	88	85	89
Was car ready when promised[2]	92	88	83	79	90	97	97	91
Was quality requirement met[2]	74	71	57	48	67	73	73	73
Comebacks[6]	89	85	75	68	83	89	90	87
INTERNAL CEI[3]	85	84	74	67	77	79	81	83
FACTORY CSI[4]	5.6	6.4	5.7	5.7	5.4	5.8	—	6.1
Negative Hotline calls	76	6	7	9	6	4	4	56
PARTS[7]								
Number of contacts[1]	—	—	—	—	—	13	19	32
Order taker helpful & friendly[2]	—	—	—	—	—	100	100	97
Del driver helpful & friendly[2]	—	—	—	—	—	100	100	100
Orders delivered promptly[2]	—	—	—	—	—	85	100	100
Quality requirement met[2]	—	—	—	—	—	85	100	97
Internal CEI[3]	—	—	—	—	—	91	91	91
Factory CSI[7]	—	—	—	—	—	91	91	91
Parts available on due bill[2]	—	—	—	—	—	92	100	96
Parts available for this serv[2]	—	—	—	—	—	83	94	89
Negative Hotline calls	—	—	—	—	—	—	2	2
Total Dealership Overall CEI	89	91	83	77	81	84	85	87

COMMENTS

Sales

POSITIVE MONTH
88% Empl helpful/courteous
37% Other pos. people
31% Vehicle pos. comments

SUGG/NEG MONTH
15% Other neg people
12% Vehicle has problem
8% F&I neg. comment

POSITIVE YTD
85% Empl. helpful/courteous
43% Other pos. people
24% Vehicle pos. comments

SUGG/NEG YTD
13% Other neg. people
8% F&I neg. comment
5% Other neg. tech

Service

POSITIVE MONTH
78% Empl. helpful/courteous
36% Car wash beneficial
31% Other pos. people

SUGG/NEG MONTH
22% Other neg. people
7% Not rep to satis.
3% Not informed of status

POSITIVE YTD
62% Empl. helpful/courteous
29% Other pos. people
25% Car wash beneficial

SUGG/NEG YTD
33% Other neg. people
12% Not rep to satis.
7% Not informed of status

Parts

POSITIVE MONTH
89% Empl.helpful/courteous
32% Receive order correctly
26% Other pos. people

SUGG/NEG MONTH
16% Other neg. people
5% Phone serv needs imp
5% Other neg. tech

POSITIVE YTD
88% Empl Helpful/courteous
41% Other pos. people
28% Receive order correctly

SUGG/NEG YTD
19% Other Neg. People
3% Not informed of status
3% Phone serv needs imp

1 Number of contacts: total customers contacted by the customer service center.
2 Percentage of contacts who answered affirmatively to the question.
3 Average of customers' ranking of the dealership by 100=excellent, 75=good, 50=fair, 25=poor.
4 Manufacturer's comparative rating of dealerships by customer survey--on scale of 1 to 10.
5 Rating given by professional shoppers hired by CAG.
6 Number of customers contacted who had returned their vehicles because of inadequate service.
7 The parts department had only recently been included in this survey.

Exhibit 4
Financial Performance of CAG from 1986 and Forecasts Through 1992

	1986	1987	1988	1989	1990	1991	1992
	Actual				**Forecast**		
Total Sales	$138,661	$136,713	$141,145	$159,657	$193,441	$250,000	$300,000
Gross Margin	18,223	19,225	19,994	20,181	26,887	30,800	35,434
Dealership Payroll	8,386	9,339	10,081	9,305	10,818	13,475	14,957
Dealership Advertising	1,571	1,544	1,937	1,888	2,131	2,891	3,180
Other Dealership Expenses	6,268	8,192	7,879	9,272	11,631	10,734	11,597
Total Dealership Expenses	16,225	19,075	19,897	20,465	24,580	27,100	29,734
Contribution from Dealership	1,998	150	97	(284)	2,307	3,700	5,700
Corporate Advertising	332	530	28	12	0	0	0
Other Corporate Overhead[a]	(1,645)	(1,105)	(2,191)	(2,132)	225	(300)	(300)
Earnings Before Lifo, Int., and Tax	3,311[d]	725	2,260	1,836	2,082	4,000	6,000
Interest Expense	1,413	2,177	1,659	1,227	762	2,000	3,000
Profit Before Lifo and Taxes	1,898	(1,452)	601	609	1,320	2,000	3,000
Profit Before Lifo, After Taxes	1,308	106	689	523	929	1,200	3,900
Capital Employed	18,783	21,942	20,687	26,136	37,000	49,500	58,500
Equity	9,372	9,478	23,617	24,120	25,049	26,249	30,149
Return on Sales[b]	2.4%	0.5%	1.6%	1.1%	1.1%	1.6%	2.0%
Return on Capital Employed[c]	17.6%	3.3%	10.9%	7.0%	5.6%	8.1%	10.3%

Dollars in thousands

a "Other Corporate Overhead" includes interest income and the internal rent on real estate charged to all the dealerships. This annual rent was based upon ten percent of the appraised value of the land and buildings. In 1989, for example, the total gross rent charged to dealerships was $1.8 million.
b "Return on Sales" is earnings before lifo, interest, and taxes, divided by total sales.
c "Return on Capital Employed" is earnings before lifo, interest, and taxes, divided by capital employed.
d Explanation: 3,311 = 1,998 - 332 - (1,645)
$$= 1,998 - 332 + 1,645$$

Exhibit 5A
Ford Dealership CMI Report

SUMMARY—CMI REPORT (excerpts)
1989
(dollars in thousands)
ALL DEPARTMENTS

SALES

New vehicles	$ 42,966
Used vehicles	6,649
Service	2,144
Parts	3,627
	$ 55,386

GROSS PROFIT

New vehicles	$ 4,324
Used vehicles	1,074
Service	1,289
Parts	770
	$ 7,457

DEPARTMENTAL PROFIT

New	$ 1,940
Used	504
Service	304
Parts	272
Total departmental profit	$ 3,020
Other income	509
Loan car expense	(154)
Administrative expenses	(2,096)
PROFIT BEFORE TAXES	$ 1,279

Exhibit 5B
Ford Dealership CMI Report

SUMMARY—CMI REPORT (excerpts)—1989		
ALL DEPARTMENTS (continued)		

STATISTICS

New units	3,032	
Used units	638	
Total units	3,670	
Gross per new unit	$ 953	
Gross per used unit (retail)	$ 1,072	
F&I per unit sold	$ 444	
Adv. per new unit sold	$ 188	New car advertising only
Adv. per used unit sold	$ 189	Used car advertising only
Adv. per total units sold	$ 216	Total dealership adv. (new, used, service, parts, general)
Flagged hours—service	38,535	
Labor efficiency—service	145%	
Parts and service absorbtion	27%	Profits of parts and service departments as a percent of administrative expenses
Personnel count	99	
Employee stability	63%	Percent of employees who have been with CAG for more than one year

CAPITAL EMPLOYED (December 31, 1989)
(dollars in thousands)

Furniture, fixtures & equip.	$ 776

INVENTORIES (before LIFO)

New vehicles	$ 6,396
Used vehicles	$ 600
Parts, accessories, other	$ 721
	$ 7,717

RECEIVABLES

Contracts in transit	$ 1,709
Customer receivables	86
Factory/warranty receivables	324
Other	29
	$ 2,148

PAYABLES

Accounts payable	$ 1,128
Accrued liabilities	444
Other	0
	$ 1,572

TOTAL CAPITAL EMPLOYED $ 9,069

YEAR TO DATE PERFORMANCE

Average capital employed	$ 8,313	
Annualized sales	$55,388	
Annualized profit before int.	$ 1,616	Profit before taxes plus interest expense on new car inventory ("flooring interest")
Return on sales	2.9%	
Return on capital employed	19.4%	
Capital turn	6.7	

Exhibit 5C
Ford Dealership CMI Report

SUMMARY—CMI REPORT (excerpts)
1989
(dollars in thousands)

ALL DEPARTMENTS
EXPENSE SUMMARY

	NEW VEHICLE		USED VEHICLE		SERVICE		PARTS		ADMIN.		DEALERSHIP	
Selling expenses	$ 911	37.3%	$134	23.4%	$ 89	9.0%	$ 21	4.2%	$ 81	3.9%	$1,235	18.9%
Personnel exp.	1,352	55.4%	400	69.9%	698	70.9%	369	74.3%	562	26.8%	3,382	51.8%
Operating exp.	104	4.3%	29	5.1%	110	11.2%	83	16.7%	180	8.6%	506	7.7%
Semi-fixed occ. exp.	18	0.7%	8	1.4%	88	8.9%	24	4.8%	438	20.9%	577	8.8%
Fixed expenses	$ 56	2.3%	$ 1	0.2%	$ 0	0.0%	$ 0	0.0%	$ 834	39.8%	$ 834	12.8%
TOTAL	$2,441	100.0%	$572	100.0%	$985	100.0%	$ 497	100.0%	$2,095	100.0%	$6,534	100.0%

Exhibit 5D
Ford Dealership CMI Report

CMI REPORT (excerpts)	December 1989		
NEW VEHICLE DEPARTMENT PROFIT & LOSS STATEMENT (000)			

SALES			**Units**
Cars	$ 19,596	45.6%	1,474
Trucks	22,539	52.5%	1,502
Fleet	830	1.9%	56
Total sales	$ 42,965	100.0%	3,032

GROSS PROFIT
Cars	$ 1,252	6.4%
Trucks	1,596	7.1%
Fleet	43	5.2%
Total gross profit	$ 2,891	6.7%
F&I reserve	$ 740	
Service contracts	495	
F&I and other	233	
Chargebacks	(35)	
F&I gross profit	$ 1,433	

DEPARTMENTAL PROFIT
Total gross profit	$ 4,324	10.1%
Departmental expenses	2,384	5.5%
Departmental profit	$ 1,940	4.5%

STATISTICS
Closing ratio	41.1%
Gross per unit	
Cars	$ 849
Trucks	$ 1,062
Fleet	$ 767
Total	$ 953
F&I per unit sold	$ 482
F&I penetration	
Reserve	45.0%
Service contracts	48.0%
Other	29.0%
Advertising per unit	$ 188
Salesperson's compensation as a percent of gross	19.6%
Days supply of new vehicles	55
Cars in inventory over 180 days	14
Vehicle receivables--balance	$1,261,000
Over 60 days	$ 31,000

CMI REPORT (excerpts)   **December 1989**

USED VEHICLE DEPARTMENT PROFIT & LOSS STATEMENT (000)

			Units
SALES			
Retail	$ 4,924	755	
Wholesale	1,725	600	
Total sales	$ 6,649	1,355	
GROSS PROFIT			
Retail	$ 684	12.4%	
Wholesale	196	10.3%	
Vehicle gross profit	$ 880	12.0%	
F&I reserve	$ 87		
Service contracts	111		
Other	6		
Chargebacks	(10)		
F&I gross profit	$ 194		
DEPARTMENTAL PROFIT			
Total gross profit	$ 1,074	15.5%	
Departmental expenses	(570)	8.1%	
Departmental profit	$ 504	7.4%	
STATISTICS			
Gross profit per unit			
Retail	$ 1,072		
Wholesale	$ 252		
F&I per unit sold	$ 305		
F&I penetration			
Reserve	32.0%		
Service contracts	48.0%		
Advertising per unit	$ 189		
Salesperson's compensation as % of gross	24.7%		
Inventory—Dollars	$ 586,000		
Units retail	83		
Units wholesale	34		
Units over 30 days	36		
Days supply	66		
Average cost—retail sold	$ 6,646		

CMI REPORT (excerpts)	December 1989	
SERVICE DEPARTMENT PROFIT & LOSS STATEMENT (000)		

SALES

Warranty	$ 727	
Customer paid	984	
Internal	30	
Sublet and other	404	
Total sales	$ 2,145	

GROSS PROFIT

Warranty	$ 509	70.0%
Customer paid	677	68.8%
Internal	13	43.3%
Sublet and other	20	5.0%
Discounts	71	
Total gross profit	$ 1,290	60.1%

DEPARTMENTAL PROFIT

Total gross profit	$ 1,289	60.1%
Departmental expenses	985	45.9%
Departmental profit	$ 304	14.2%

STATISTICS

Repair order count

Warranty	7,724	
Customer paid	8,736	
Internal	597	
Total	17,057	

$ per repair order

Warranty	$ 94	In-house work only
Customer paid	$ 113	In-house work only
Internal	$ 50	In-house work only
Total	$ 126	Includes sublet service sales
Available hours	28,192	Total potential hours (standard)
Attended hours	26,546	Actual hours worked—after training, sick & vacations
Flagged hours	38,535	Hours billed
Labor utilization (flagged/available)	137.0%	
Labor efficiency (flagged/attended)	145.0%	
Technical personnel	15	
Support personnel	20	
Total personnel count	35	
Technical/support ratio	75.0%	

Exhibit 5G
Ford Dealership CMI Report

CMI REPORT (excerpts)	December 1989	
PARTS DEPARTMENT PROFIT & LOSS STATEMENT (000)		

SALES

Warranty	$ 511	14.1%
Customer paid	544	15.0%
Counter	218	6.0%
Internal	329	9.1%
Wholesale	2,022	55.7%
Total sales	$ 3,627	100.0%

GROSS PROFIT

Warranty	$ 112	21.9%
Customer paid	201	36.9%
Counter	83	38.1%
Internal	39	11.9%
Wholesale	304	15.0%
Inventory adjustments	132	
Discounts	(102)	
Total gross profit	$ 771	21.3%

DEPARTMENTAL PROFIT

Total gross profit	$ 771	21.3%
Departmental expenses	499	13.8%
Departmental profit	$ 304	7.5%

STATISTICS

Lost sales	$ 49,636	Sales lost due to part unavailability
Level of service—(fill rate)	84.4%	Cost of stocked parts sold divided by:
Parts inventory	$ 582,000	the cost of stocked parts sold + cost of parts for lost sales
Gross turn	4.9	
Personnel count	13	

Exhibit 6
Profile of Dealerships in 1989[a]

	SALES					New Units Sold	Dealer Profit Before Taxes	Contrib./Sales
	New	Used	Service	Parts	Total			
TOTAL CAG	$108,376	$24,284	$11,781	$15,531	$159,657	7,459	$ 609	0.38%
Ford	42,966	6,649	2,144	3,627	55,388	3,032	1,277	2.31
Mazda—Bellevue (1/1–6/30)[b]	4,353	1,465	264	646	6,728	345	(111)	(1.65)
Mazda VW—Bellevue (7/1–12/31)[b]	6,186	1,533	394	1,007	9,120	440	(78)	(8.60)
Mazda—Renton	11,413	2,638	1,099	2,474	17,624	803	12	0.07
Buick/GMC Truck	9,771	1,580	440	549	12,340	745	(222)	(1.80)
Nissan—Renton (1/1–6/30)[b]	4,806	1,447	480	857	7,590	375	(305)	(4.02)
Nissan—Auburn	14,560	4,141	1,186	2,159	22,046	1,050	10	0.05
Nissan Porsche Audi—Bellevue (7/1–12/31)[b]	7,912	2,621	806	2,046	13,385	357	(310)	(2.32)
Porsche Audi Volkswagen (1/1–6/30)[b]	6,409	2,209	820	2,166	11,604	312	(157)	(1.35)
Body Shops			4,147		4,147		(16)	(0.00)
Headquarters[c]			340		340		534	157.06
Adjustments for intercompany transactions					(655)		(25)	

a Dollar statistics in thousands.

b Porsche Audi Volkswagen operated separately until 6/30, when VW went to Mazda—Bellevue and Porsche Audi went to Nissan—Bellevue. At year-end, there were seven dealerships.

c Headquarters sales includes profits on "Platinum Touch" service warranties only.

Exhibit 7
Historical Comparison of CAG Versus Industry Performance

	1980	1981	1982	1983	1984	1985	1986	1987	1988	1989
Industry Averages for New Car Franchises										
Total sales per dealer (000)			$6,136	$7,596	$9,063	$10,010	$10,585	$10,948	$12,009	
New units per dealership	408	404	411	493	574	621	639	598	616	
Net profit before taxes/sales			1.3%	2.1%	2.2%	2.2%	2.2%	1.9%	1.7%	
Net profit/net worth			18.9	29.6	35.7	35.3	37.7	28.3	27.3	

Source: NADA Industry Analysis.

	1980	1981	1982	1983	1984	1985	1986	1987	1988	1989
Carter Automotive Group[a]										
Total sales for group (000)	$63,013	$71,473	$63,375	$68,441	$93,191	$123,325	$138,661	$136,713	$141,145	$159,657
New unit sales for group	4,755	4,615	3,644	4,433	5,440	7,823	7,854	7,270	7,209	7,459
Net profit before taxes/sales	1.8%	1.1%	(0.2%)	2.1%	1.9%	1.7%	1.4%	(1.1%)	0.4%	0.4%
Net profit/net worth	21.9	10.3	(3.0)	9.7	15.3	15.7	14.0	1.1	2.9	2.2

a Data are for all of the Carter dealerships in each year.

Exhibit 8
Photograph of the Ford Dealership

RETAIL ECONOMICS

This note will describe many aspects of the economics of a retailer. It is organized into four broad topic areas.

- **Retail Statistics.** There are many quick calculations used by retailers to gain insight into the condition of their business. We provide definitions, examples and "normal ranges."
- **Retail Accounting.** Due to the special nature of their businesses, retailers have evolved an accounting procedure of their own.
- **Retail Financials.** What information can be gleaned from an inspection of company financials, both income and balance sheets?
- **Retail Decisions.** We examine the most common retail decisions and show how each should be analyzed. We relate these analyses to the information that is readily available to retailers.

RETAIL STATISTICS

Comparable Store Sales Growth

A closely watched statistic for any retailer is the rate of growth in dollar sales. A retailer whose sales are growing rapidly is presumed to be doing well; one whose sales are growing only slightly, or even falling, is deemed to be in trouble. The presumption, of course, is that a retailer with higher sales must have a strong retailing concept, or at least one that matches the current mood of the consumer.

The statistic can be misleading for a number of reasons:

(i) In periods of high inflation, that alone should lead to higher sales increases.

(ii) Increased sales may have been caused by a one-time sales promotion. For example, if Easter fell in March last year, and in April this year, April to April sales growth may look very good but not be indicative of a trend.

(iii) If the chain has added stores in the last two years, a net sales increase is to be expected, but it may not reflect an underlying strengthening of the retail concept.

The first two problems are finessed by judging a retailer's performance relative to others. This solves problem (i) and, at least within retail sectors, problem (ii) also. Problem (iii) is solved by calculating sales growth only for stores open throughout the periods involved—so-called comparable stores.

The following are the sales and comparable store sales growths comparing January 1992 to January 1991 for some well-known retailers:

Professor David E. Bell prepared this note as the basis for class discussion rather than to illustrate either effective or ineffective handling of an administrative situation.

	Total Sales Growth	Comparable Store Sales Growth		Gross Margin %
JCPenney	−1%	−2%	JCPenney	33
Dayton - Hudson	9	2	Dayton - Hudson	26
Toys R Us	11	2	Toys R Us	30
Home Depot	35	11	Home Depot	28
Circuit City	18	1	Circuit City	26
The Limited	17	3	The Limited	29
Wal-Mart	35	10	Wal-Mart	21
Kmart	8	4	Kmart	25
Stop & Shop	4	0	Stop & Shop	26
Costco	26	14	Costco	9

Gross Margin

One may think, simplistically, of retailing as buying products at one price and selling them for a higher price. The difference is "gross" profit, that is, profit before expenses other than cost of goods. Gross margin refers to the size of the gross profit as a percentage of the retail price:

$$\text{Gross Margin} = \frac{\text{Sales} - \text{Cost of Goods Sold}}{\text{Sales}}$$

$$= \frac{\text{Gross Margin Dollars}}{\text{Sales}}$$

While higher gross margins are to be preferred, realizable levels are dictated by the willingness to pay of consumers and the activities of competitors.

Examples of gross margin percentages for some retailers in fiscal 1992 were:

Inventory Turnover

A major expense for retailers is the inventory of unsold goods that they carry. Inventory costs have three components:

- the cost of capital tied up in the inventory.
- the cost of storing the goods, either in warehouses or in larger-than-necessary stores.
- the risk of obsolescence—the more inventory you have, the longer the period between purchase (by the retailer) and the sales (to the consumer). For fashion or date-sensitive items, this could be disastrous.

Inventory costs have been described as the "cost of poor information." The challenge of the retailers is to have the right goods in the right place at the right price at the right time. To the extent that a retailer cannot achieve these lofty standards, inventory results.

$$\text{Inventory Turnover} = \frac{\text{Retail Sales at Cost}}{\text{Average Inventory at Cost}}$$

Examples of inventory turnover levels in 1993 follow:

	COGS/Inventory
JCPenney	3.4
Dayton - Hudson	4.6
Toys R Us	3.1
Home Depot	5.6
Circuit City	4.7
The Limited	6.0
Wal-Mart	4.5
Kmart	3.0
Stop & Shop	12.6
Costco	11.8

Gross Margin Return on Inventory (GMROI)

Inventory turnover gives one view of the efficiency of a retail enterprise: how quickly goods are moved through the system. One can achieve a high turnover, at least temporarily, by giving goods away. But selection and an in-stock position are often the key to retail advantage. Surely, so the argument goes, what matters is whether the cost of inventory is reflected in superior returns. A second inventory statistic is

$$GMROI = \frac{\text{Gross Margin Dollars}}{\text{Average Inventory at Cost}}$$

Values for 1992 include:

	Gross Margin/Inventory
JCPenney	1.8
Dayton - Hudson	1.7
Toys R Us	1.3
Home Depot	2.2
Circuit City	1.6
The Limited	2.5
Wal-Mart	1.2
Kmart	1.2
Stop & Shop	4.5
Costco	1.2

Sales per Square Foot

We have discussed the problem of comparing sales growth as retailers expand; one way to standardize sales figures is to express them in terms of a common scarce resource—store space. As with other statistics, the assumption is that higher is better; a store with sales per square foot of $1,000 must be doing something right.

One detail to be checked is whether the square foot measure includes every square inch of the store, or just the selling area; and does the selling area include checkout counters, the garden center outside? Do the sales figures deduct returns, do they include mail order sales, sales to employees . . .?

Sales/square foot in 1992 for some retailers:

	Sales/Square Foot
JCPenney	$ 137
Dayton - Hudson	198
Home Depot	348
Circuit City	1,083
The Limited	302
Wal-Mart	279
Stop & Shop	614
Costco	670

Sales per square foot is also used to compare the effectiveness of departments within a store. If menswear is generating $600/square foot and children's only $250/square foot it may be worth trying to understand why this is, and what should be done about it. Assuming equal gross margins, the store would obviously rather have departments generating $600 per sq. ft. than $250/square foot.

If the menswear department were to be given more space at the expense of the children's section, would the moved space be more productive? The critical question is whether the *marginal* sales per square foot in menswear is higher or lower than that of children's. It could be that it is *lower!* This might occur if the explanation for the low sales per square foot in children's is due to its cramped space and poor selection. Men's might get the same total sales in half the space! As an example, the key kiosk in a Sears store has one of the highest sales/sq. ft. figures in the store, but a kiosk with twice the space may produce few extra sales.

Gross Margin Dollars/Square Foot

Though sales per square foot is a convenient indicator, we are more properly concerned with profit/sq. ft. High sales/sq. ft. and a gross margin of 0% will not make sense for long. Once more it is the marginal value of this statistic that is relevant to decisions concerning space reallocation.

Direct Profit

The key kiosk generates not only high sales per square foot, but also high gross margin per square foot. It may also serve as a generator of traffic since a person who has lost a key may select Sears as a destination. However, a key kiosk requires the continuous attention of a salesperson to cut the keys. Assuming this person is idle when not cutting keys we may readily see that a fairer indication of the department's profitability would subtract the cost of the key cutters' salaries, benefits, machinery cost, electricity . . .

But since menswear may have 8 dedicated salespeople shouldn't we subtract their salaries and commissions from the gross profit of the department?

Direct Profit is a measure of profitability after subtracting all identifiable costs directly associated with the operations leading to the profit. It does not include an allocation for fixed overheads. Examples include:

Direct Departmental Profit

The gross margin dollars generated by a department less salaries and commissions, the cost of advertising that is directly related to that department and the cost of capital associated with the inventory.

Direct Product Profit

The gross margin dollars associated with the sale of one item of a product. Subtracted from this would be the proportionate inventory cost, warehousing cost, personnel cost (stocking, checkout), transportation. . .

Direct Store Profit

The gross margin dollars associated with sales from the store, less all salaries and operating costs, less directly attributable costs outside the store such as warehousing and transportation. It should also take account of the fair rental value of the store itself.

RETAIL ACCOUNTING

Retailers face considerable difficulty in keeping track of the value of their inventory. The sheer number of items involved precludes frequent stocktaking, and the often fluid movement of prices makes the valuation of the physical inventory problematical. Today, computers can logically keep track of "assumed inventory" = initial inventory + deliveries - sales, but a physical counting is required on occasion (often once per year in January, when inventories are low) to account for losses due to theft, or mistakes (e.g., wrong quantity delivered but not noticed, sold items misidentified at checkout, returned items not reentered into inventory).

While it is possible to assess the actual "cost of goods" by adding up the cost of every item in the store, retailers prefer to account for their inventories in a way that reflects the realities of markdowns: sometimes it may be impossible to sell goods even for the price paid by the retailer. As we shall see, the method in effect revalues goods for inventory purposes whenever the sale price is lowered. In this way the *prospective* gross margin percentage is maintained. A more tangible advantage of this approach is that it is accepted by the IRS; as a result the profit impact of markdowns can be deducted for tax purposes at the time of the markdown, rather than at the time the goods are finally sold (i.e., sooner).

Here is an example. Let us suppose ABC retailer opens a new store on January 1, 1995, with $500,000 of inventory valued at cost. With an average markup of 42% the retail value of the goods is $862,069. To take an extreme scenario, suppose this retailer sells nothing during the first month and is forced to slash prices by a third. Using the *retail method* of accounting ABC would now carry the inventory on the books at $333,333, taking the $166,667 as a loss on current income. The retail price of the goods is now $574,713, still a markup of 42% on the inventory value of the goods.

Let us suppose that with these price reductions, the inventory starts to move. More cautious now, our retailer buys new goods but chooses to mark them up at a less aggressive rate of 30%.

By the end of the second month the inventory might consist of $100,000 worth of the original merchandise (markup 42%, retail value $172,414) and $350,000 of new merchandise (markup 30%, retail value $524,997.) The total, "blended" inventory is worth $450,000, has a combined retail value of $697,411 and, therefore, an average markup of 35.5%. If during the *third* month, no sales occur, and the retailer lowers prices across the board by 20%, the retail value will now be $557,929 ($697,411 x 0.8) with an inventory value of $360,000 ($450,000 x 0.8). The $90,000 loss on the inventory will again be taken as a loss against income.

If, at the end of the third month, the retailer conducts a physical inventory, and discovers $20,000 worth of goods (at book value) are missing, this fact would be recognized, and be a further expense against income.

The retail method of inventory accounting simplifies the potential headache of keeping track of the value of goods at the SKU level while allowing the retailer the privilege of recognizing the depreciation (or appreciation if the retail price is raised) of goods. Of course, the method has its drawbacks. The averaging method introduces distortions, and there may be an incentive for retailers to take excessive markups initially in order to more speedily take the tax advantages of the resulting markdowns.

With the increasing sophistication of computer tracking at the SKU level, there is no reason for averaging to persist; the retail method could be applied on an SKU by SKU basis.

RETAIL FINANCIALS

Reproduced below is the income statement for Wal-Mart, adapted from their 1993 Annual Report. The data relate to the fiscal year ending January 31, 1993.

Sales	$55,984,564,000
Cost of Goods	$44,174,685,000
Operating, Selling and General and Administrative Costs	$ 8,320,842,000
Interest Costs:	
Debt ·	$ 142,649,000
Capital Leases	$ 180,049,000
Income Taxes	$ 1,171,545,000
Net Income	$ 1,994,794,000

Wal-Mart's gross margin is 21%. (About 75% of the sales are from discount stores, and 25% from wholesale clubs (Sam's)). The operating expenses (payroll, warehousing, store operations, marketing, corporate overhead) amount to 15%, which is markedly lower than most retailers, who would consider themselves fortunate to be at 20%. Evidently, Wal-Mart leases many of its stores. Leases, which are long-term rental contracts, are usually capitalized as a long-term debt equal to the net present value of the contractual payments. The $180 million is the total of lease payments made during the year. Wal-Mart paid an effective tax rate of 37% (1.171/ (1.171 + 1.994)).

While it is hard to imagine any company that is earning $2 billion after tax being in bad shape, nevertheless, the question is, how profitable is this company? And how does it compare to other retailers? Let's take a look at the income statement of Kmart (for fiscal 1993).

Sales	$38,123,000,000
Cost of Goods	$28,485,000,000
Operating, Selling and	
Interest Costs:	
Debt	$ 244,000,000
Capital Leases	$ 187,000,000
Income Taxes	$ 485,000,000
Net Income	$ 941,000,000

Kmart's gross margin is 25%, higher than Wal-Mart's. This could be due to better merchandising (stocking more of what the customer wants), to better procurement (paying suppliers less) or due to a different mix of store types (the most plausible explanation). Operating expenses are also much higher, at 20.4% of sales; indeed Kmart's total operating expense is nearly equal to Wal-Mart's but on a third fewer sales dollars. Net income is 2.5% of sales compared to Wal-Mart's, 3.6%.

It may be misleading to compare net income figures; such comparisons may be distorted by the subtraction of interest on debt (a consequence of a financing decision) and taxes (which could be distorted based on depreciation activity). Thus it is more common to look at *operating income* (gross margin less operating expenses) as a percentage of sales. For Wal-Mart this is 6.2% (3.5/56) and for Kmart 4.9% (1.856/38.123). Operating income is also known as Earnings Before Interest, Taxes, Depreciation and Amortization (EBITDA).

Now let's look at the balance sheets for these two companies:

	Wal-Mart	Kmart
Assets		
Cash	12,363,000	611,000,000
Retail Receivables	524,555,000	1,146,000,000
Non-Retail Receivables	312,016,000	
Inventories	9,268,309,000	8,752,000,000
Pre-Paid Expenses	80,347,000	
Plant, Property, Equipment	8,254,277,000	6,405,000,000
Property Under Capital Lease	1,538,604,000	1,039,000,000
Other	574,616,000	978,000,000
Total Assets	20,565,087,000	18,931,000,000
Liabilities		
Short-Term Debt	1,602,674,000	707,000,000
Accounts Payable	4,063,951,000	2,959,000,000
Accrued Liabilities	1,042,108,000	1,583,000,000
Current Portion of Leases	45,553,000	
Long-Term Debt	3,072,835,000	3,237,000,000
Other Long-Term Liabilities		697,000,000
Capital Leases	1,772,152,000	1,698,000,000
Deferred Charges	206,634,000	514,000,000
Shareholders' Equity	8,759,180,000	7,536,000,000
Total Liabilities	20,565,087,000	18,931,000,000

The line items do not match precisely because of different reporting styles, but we can get some idea of their comparative financial health.

Most financial indicators take the following form:

$$\text{Performance Measure} = \frac{\text{Income Measure}}{\text{Measure of Capital Employed}}$$

As we have discussed, common measures of income are:

- Net Income (after interest, after tax)
- Net Income Before Tax
- Net Income Before Interest and Taxes
- Operating Income (or EBITDA)
- Cash Flow (excluding capital transactions)

Common measures of capital employed are:

- Total Assets
- Net Assets (Total Assets less non-financed liabilities such as Accounts Payable, less any cash over and above that needed to maintain the business.)
- Long-Term Capital (Long-Term Debt, Capital Leases, Shareholders' Equity)
- Equity

These measures are usually *averaged* over the current and previous year in order to more fairly reflect the fact that some of the earnings should be credited to the condition of the company as it was one year earlier.

Some commonly used ratios are:

$$\text{Return on (Total) Assets} = \frac{\text{EBITDA}}{\text{(Average) Total Assets}}$$

$$\text{Return on Invested Capital} = \frac{\text{EBITDA}}{\text{(Avg.) Long-Term Capital}}$$

$$\text{Return on Equity} = \frac{\text{EBITDA}}{\text{(Average) Equity}}$$

It is important to note that these terms have different meanings when used by different people. When people speak of "return" or "return on assets" the precise terminology should be clarified.

Statistics for Fiscal 1992 Include:			
	ROA	ROIC	ROE
Wal-Mart	25%	34%	26%
JCPenney	6%	9%	2%
Dayton-Hudson	12%	18%	14%
The Limited	22%	29%	23%

RETAIL DECISIONS

In this section we look at some typical retail decisions and describe the appropriate economic analysis for each. As with most quantitative analyses, it may be impossible to obtain exactly the numbers specified (how to estimate current inflation, for example), and some important unquantifiable issues are ignored (how a particular decision affects the overall image of the retailer.). The reader should, therefore, regard the following as the base economic input to the decisions.

1. Adding an SKU

Assuming for a moment that an additional SKU can be carried without it *replacing* another (and without overcrowding the store, etc.) then it should be carried if its direct product profit, less an allowance for any cannibalization, is positive. This is the amount by which the store's end of year earnings should increase as a result of a decision to carry the new SKU. If the new product is to displace an existing SKU then we need only demonstrate that the new product has a higher incremental DPP than that which it replaces.

Sometimes there is no explicit recognition of a product that is displaced. In this event some attempt must be made to establish the average profit per unit space generated by the least profitable items in the relevant department.

2. Changing the Location of an SKU

Should a particular SKU be given more prominent space in the store, say at the entrance of the department store or at an eye-level shelf of the supermarket?

In principle, we must judge whether the increased profit of the product in its new, better location is greater than the profit lost by the product it replaces.

However, as a general rule, it is useful to think of areas of the store as having certain profit-generating capacities, based on past history. For example, an area of the department store might generate $50 of DPP per square foot per year. A shelf might generate $20 of DPP per linear foot per year. A product should be placed wherever it creates the maximum value after subtraction of a "space charge."

For example, let's suppose a category is currently generating DPP of $29/sq. ft. in a quiet part of the store, but is expected to generate $42/sq. ft. if placed in a more favorable location. If the *marginal* value at the two locations is $15/sq. ft. and $30/sq. ft. respectively, then it is better to leave the product where it is. It generates an incremental $14/sq. ft. where it is ($29 - $15) but only $12/sq. ft. in the better location ($42 - $30).

3. Giving More Space to a Department at the Expense of Another

Two departments have the correct relative size if the *marginal* contribution of the space they occupy, in terms of DPP/sq. ft., is the same.

4. Adding a Store

Unless there are strategic aspects to the decision, a store should not be opened unless the gross margin less direct operating expenses, including rent and recoupment of fixed investments such as fixturing, is positive. There are two secondary considerations that should be factored in however. The first is that there may be an increase in overhead costs, such as warehousing and administration. The second is that the procurement leverage of the chain may be enhanced due to the increase in amount to be purchased.

To take account of these secondary factors one can estimate the *marginal* increase in overhead as a percent of marginal sales increases. Similarly one can calculate the marginal gross margin by seeing how cost of goods varies with volume.

As a simple example consider the following hypothetical figures for a retailer, over a two-year period.

	1994	1993
Sales	120	100
COGS	70	60
Overhead	22	20

Note that while the gross margin was 40% in 1993 and 42% in 1994 the marginal gross margin, the margin on incremental sales, was 50%. (Sales went up by 20, cost of goods only by 10). Similarly, though overhead was 20% of sales in 1993 and 18% in 1994, it was only 10% of the incremental sales ($2 out of $20).

Thus, if we plan to add a store that will generate $5 million of sales with an operating cost of $1 million, we should subtract only $2.5 million for cost of goods and $0.5 million for additional overhead, leaving $1 million of incremental profit, not the $200,000 that would have been estimated using *averages* from 1994.

Case 6

STAPLES, INC.

In August 1992, Staples continued on the fast track it had established since its founding in the fall of 1985. Store number 155 had just opened in Manhattan and stock analysts declared the shares to be a good buy at 30 times earnings. Henry Nassela, president of Staples (and former president of Star Market), spoke of their accomplishments: "The initial format of one-stop shopping for office supplies was such an instant success, we concentrated on expanding our store base, both to seize a first mover advantage and to build a critical mass of stores to make maximum use of our strategy of central distribution. But as the market begins to be saturated we must also continue to increase our same store sales in order to grow. Within the last year or two we have radically changed our approach to the merchandising of office equipment; we carry more brand names, a wider selection and we provide more knowledgeable sales help. Our next task is to fix the furniture department."

"We get good margins from furniture, but endless problems. Customers expect high quality furniture at low price points; it can't be done. To meet expectations we generally offer products at $300 and below, usually requiring assembly, and occasionally requiring delivery. As an experiment we have taken three stores in the Boston area and upgraded the furniture department considerably with price points anywhere from $100 to $1000. In these stores we display furniture in small office settings as you might see in a more formal furniture store

and in one store we even have carpeting. It remains to be seen whether this solves our problem."

Solving the "furniture problem" had strategic implications beyond pure merchandising. "In an 18,000 sq. ft. store we are allocating nearly 4,000 sq. ft. to furniture," said Tom Stemberg, founder and chairman of Staples. "We have not figured out whether this is the correct space allocation or if it should be halved, doubled or eliminated. The answer has implications for how big we make our stores going forward. Perhaps we should have one or two stores in a region dedicated to selling furniture, and drop the category from the others." "The problem is," added Henry Nassela, "*no one* knows how to sell office furniture."

BACKGROUND

In the spring of 1985, Tom Stemberg (HBS MBA '73) was fired as president of First National Supermarkets. The next day, Leo Kahn, the former owner of Purity Supreme supermarkets, who was now a retail venture capitalist, offered to back Tom in a new retail business: *any* retail business. Excluded by a non-compete clause from running a supermarket, Stemberg "walked the malls" looking for inspiration. He became convinced that the fragmented way in which office supplies were retailed offered an opportunity for a new category killer. The store would cater to the office supply needs of smaller businesses, those with

Professor David E. Bell prepared this case as the basis for class discussion rather than to illustrate either effective or ineffective handling of an administrative situation.

between one and 100 employees, who were not sizeable enough to generate much attention from the larger office supply distributors. The trick would be to change their habit of having small orders delivered, and convince them to come to the store; the bait would be everyday low prices.

In the fall of 1985, Stemberg raised $4 million to finance the opening (on May 1, 1986) of his first store, in Brighton, Massachusetts. "It wasn't so hard persuading vendors to supply me with basics," recalled Stemberg. "I told them not to think of me as a store but as the beginning of a whole new distribution method. There were exceptions. The Canon sales manager at first refused to cooperate, but I arranged to have lunch with him one day and then took him to the see the store. It was mobbed. I had the copiers within a week." Raising another $12 million in the fall of 1986, Staples rapidly opened new stores up and down the northeastern United States. "Our unique strategy of centralized distribution meant that we could not open stores in an opportunistic fashion. It was important for us to achieve an appropriate density of stores in order to gain scale economies from the warehouse. We had also discovered that once someone began shopping at an office products store, they were very hard to dislodge to a competitor. Last but not least, the store concept was so successful it made sense to open as many stores as soon as possible."

The success of Staples had not gone unnoticed. Within months of the opening of the Brighton store, copycat chains such as Office Depot, Office Max (since bought by Kmart) and Bizmart sprang up around the country. Indeed, by 1992 Office Depot was the leading office products chain with nearly twice the revenues of second-place Staples. "Office Depot took a different approach," said Stemberg. "Whereas we had gone with smaller stores supplied frequently from a central warehouse, Office Depot built larger stores with inventory direct-shipped from manufacturers. As a result, Office Depot stores tend to be in rural/suburban areas whereas Staples stores are in more high rent areas. There aren't many locations where we go head to head."

As of August 1992, the principal locations of Staples stores were Los Angeles and New York, each with about 35, and Boston, Philadelphia and Washington, each with about 20 (see **Exhibit 1**). Total sales for 1991 were $547 million with an operating profit (before interest and taxes) of $18 million, and a net income of $8 million.

THE STAPLES STORE

A typical store had 17,000 square feet, was located in a strip mall on a busy highway in an urban area with ample parking. The stores had the feel of a warehouse, with spartan fixtures and concrete floors. Upon entering, the customer was led down an aisle of basic items such as copying machine paper, manila folders and pads of lined paper. These served to reinforce the image of the store as a source of office "staples" and to establish favorable price imagery. The first aisle might also contain promotional items. In August 1992 these were of a "Back to School" nature. This aisle typically opened out close to the rear of the store where about 1,500 sq. ft. were devoted to a floor display of furniture. The furniture was loosely organized into three areas: computer, secretarial and executive. The care with which it was displayed varied from store to store. The shelf racks surrounding the display also contained furniture, such as chairs, filing cabinets and boxed inventory.

Leading back to the front of the store were several aisles forming the heart of the store. Along the aisle farthest from the entrance aisle lay the "store within a store" of office equipment. Finally, at the front of the store were the checkout counters, a copy center and a service desk **(Exhibit 2)**. "The copy center drives a lot of trips, so we've designed the stores not to allow that customer to bypass the rest of the store," said Luis Pepi, Executive Vice-President of Operations. "Some people are questioning that policy, indeed many of our California stores do allow the customer, upon entering the store, to go straight to the copy center. I guess our supermarket backgrounds really show."

"As with a supermarket the store is designed based on an assumption of self-service, but customers are always asking questions," continued Pepi. "They'll describe something they need for their desk, or they'll ask you if you have anything that could serve as a receipt book for some special purpose. People are not as familiar with office products as they are with groceries. One of our best selling items is the expandable pocket manila folder. People notice it and think to themselves 'I didn't know you could get those.' Who doesn't need folders that hold more stuff? So customer buying behavior is more of a blend between a hardware store and a supermarket than it is pure self-service."

Each store was run by a general manager, together with a merchandising manager, an assistant to the merchandising manager, a service manager and a business machines manager. In addition there would be between 25–40 sales "associates" (40% full-time) all of whom were non-commissioned. Part-time employees were often college or high school students. Full time employees were hired from other retail stores such as supermarkets and discount stores or direct from college (including some MBAs) and were typically aged in their 20s. A normal career pattern for full-time employees was to spend one year on the sales floor before moving into a management position, either at the store or elsewhere. The dropout rate among management trainees was about 30% in the first year but considerably less thereafter.

Salespeople were encouraged to approach customers with a view to problem solving. Traditionally associates had not been assigned to any particular part of the store, but with the increasing need for knowledgeable sales support in the business machines aisle, there was now a tendency for 3–4 associates to be assigned to that location. Training was an ongoing task for store management, particularly as turnover among the part-time associates ran at around 150% per year. Occasionally Staples would rent a hotel conference room for the day and run a training session for all merchandising managers and associates in the region. The sessions normally consisted of product demonstrations and lectures by vendors. One day per year (out of an average of 10) was allocated to furniture. "We try to send as many of our associates as we can spare," said Pepi, "but inevitably the depth of knowledge varies considerably from associate to associate. Some people naturally gravitate to one category of product or another. We make sure that business machines has good coverage and I'd be confident that one or two associates in any given store will be knowledgeable about furniture."

A typical store carried 5,000 permanent stock-keeping units (SKUs) plus many temporary SKUs for promotional, seasonal and short-lived items (such as business machines). Total in-store inventory averaged about $600,000 (at cost), $350,000 for the permanent SKUs and $250,000 for the others. The two distribution centers (one in Connecticut, one in California, each 130,000 sq. ft.), a bulk distribution center (100,000 sq. ft. in Plainfield, CT) and a delivery center (32,000 sq. ft. in Connecticut) contained an additional inventory equivalent to about $400,000 per store. Store sales averaged $85,000 per week (at cost) implying a turnover of around four and a half times per year. (Calculated as 52 weeks/year × $85,000/week ÷ [$600,000 + $400,000].) (For more detailed financials see **Exhibits 3** and **4**.)

Each SKU in a store was carried in sufficient quantities to allow the customer to find the product but also to convey the sense of an adequate supply. Most items had at least a three week supply. In-stock positions at the store level were close to 100%. Data on sales by SKU were transmitted to the distribution centers each night. The first store delivery of the week would be calculated to bring each SKU up to its target level at the time of the actual delivery.

As a trial, three "Express" stores had been opened in downtown Boston, New York and Washington. These stores, about one-third normal size, did not carry furniture, but emphasized the availability of delivery. As at all stores, customers could order from the United Stationers wholesale catalog, at 25% off the list price.

PROMOTION

A center piece of Staples' promotion strategy was the collection of point of sale information by customer. This was accomplished by offering small reductions for "members" on a modest number of visible items. Membership was free but required the presentation of a card for each purchase. This allowed identification of customers who, for whatever reason, had stopped shopping at Staples. "We find that after a year, some of our customers have moved or gone out of business' said Mary Leslie Ullmann of the direct marketing department. "But we find that a year is too long to wait. We target customers who have not made a purchase for three or four months. We send them a coupon good for $5, or notice of a special promotion."

Staples used a variety of promotional strategies for communicating with potential customers, including newspaper inserts, telemarketing, direct mail and, quite recently, television. Staples employees were known to go door-to-door in neighborhood office buildings handing out $50 coupons good towards any furniture purchase of $300 or more. "We get a good response rate out of those," smiled Ullmann. "At the other end of the spectrum, a direct mail no-coupon flyer gets us a fairly low response among prospects. We've tried upgrading our flyers to attract more attention to our higher end products such as computers. Our recent 4-color glossy pamphlet costs us about 60¢ to reach a prospect. It looks great, but it may conflict with our low price image."

BUYER BEHAVIOR

Jim Forbush (HBS MBA '78), Vice President of Marketing, recited some statistics about a typical Staples store: "It has a base of 10,000 customers (people who have shopped within a year) though many of these are occasional shoppers only. The repeat customer comes about twice per quarter and spends about $37.

"Behavior varies quite a bit by the size of the customer's company. Our bread and butter business comes from very small companies. A big surprise in this business is that a large portion of sales are to home offices with zero or one employees (see **Table 1**). I say zero because many homes now have computers, fax machines and desks even when there is no business conducted in the home. Add to that supplies needed for school kids and we have a pretty steady business. Companies spend about $400/year/employee (at Staples' prices) on office supplies (not including business machines or furniture). Once you get above 10 employees, the sheer volume of product daunts even the most price conscious customer. Who wants to carry 8 boxes of copy paper weighing 50 pounds apiece? So these people were using us only for emergency supplies. The boss is making a presentation in the morning and they need six binders, so someone gets into the car and goes to Staples. Or the person in charge of purchasing slips up and forgets Scotch tape; buying an emergency supply at Staples is acceptable because our prices are so low.

"Our old policy used to be to charge around $15 for next day delivery. The light, bulky stuff we shipped with UPS (who charge by weight) and the rest we would deliver with our own trucks. But few people wanted to pay the delivery charge. We tried explaining that even with a delivery charge they saved money over conventional suppliers but this argument carried no weight. Recently we went to free delivery for orders over $150 (excluding furniture). The average delivered order is now around $175.

"Small companies (between two and 10 employees) are perhaps the most interesting case. Typically, one person, possibly a secretary or receptionist, will be assigned to monitor a supplies cupboard, and to reorder as necessary. This person fulfills this role very conscientiously as stock outs are very public. On the other hand there's not a lot of incentive to be unduly economical unless the boss insists on a particular vendor such as Staples. The supplies person will use our catalog to buy in lots of $150 or more, but visit us in the lunch hour for emergencies. Actually you'd be surprised how often the boss is in the store doing the shopping. Maybe some receptionists are more vital than management.

"Mail order companies can have a cost advantage over us when postal rates are at a cyclical low, but they can't get you the product same day, or even next day. And some products you need to *see* before you buy. Once an order becomes *planned* though, you're going to want delivery. Delivery is maybe only 7% of our business at present but that's bound to grow.

"We do a round of 400 customer interviews 10 times per year. We do this without identifying our affiliation and ask, 'Where do you get most of your office supplies?' They answer, 'Staples.' But we know from our records what they spend at our stores. A typical example is a five employee firm that spends $1,000 a year with us. Therefore we are pretty sure that at least half of their expenditure is going elsewhere. I think what is going on is that some people think of office supplies as being only the kind of stuff you get in a stationery store."

FURNITURE

All but the Express stores carried furniture, with a typical floor display of around 1,500 sq. ft. plus adjoining shelving. Including all color and style variations, Staples offered nearly 200 SKUs in the furniture category. **Exhibit 5** illustrates pages from the Staples catalog including all of those that depict furniture. Most furniture skus are depicted or described. **Table 2** describes sales and profit information at a typical store. Furniture sales from the Staples catalog at Express stores were mostly of standardized items such as chairs, banquet tables and filing cabinets. Such orders were about 3% of Express store sales.

Table 1
Breakdown of Staples Revenue by Size of Customer

Personal	33%
1–20 employee	33%
≥ 20 employees	10%
Unknown business size	24%
	100%

Source: Company estimates.

Table 2
Sales and Contribution Information for a Typical Store—1991

	Sales $	Floor Space Sq. Ft.	Linear Shelf Space (Ft.)[1]	Turnover[2]	Gross Margin
Whole Store	6,000,000	17,000[3]	1,300	4.5×	24%
• General Supplies	3,250,000	6,500	900		27%
• Business Machines	2,100,000	1,500	240		19%[4]
• Furniture	650,000[5]	4,000[6]	160	5×	29%
• Files/Storage	180,000				22%
• Desks	160,000				30%
• Chairs	210,000				32%
• Other	100,000				36%

Notes:

1 The shelf space footage is only the floor length of the shelves: it does not reflect the additional space afforded by multiple shelves.

2 Turnover figures reflect inventory held both at stores and warehouses.

3 2,000 sq. ft. is used for copy center and checkout counters. 3,000 sq. ft. is used for back of the store purposes such as receiving, storage and sales support.

4 This figure represents both machines and accessories. The gross margin on machines alone was much lower.

5 Furniture sales include deliveries from the warehouse directly to a customer. In 1991 Staples had 45,000 such orders, averaging $175 each (not including delivery charges). Furniture sales per store were virtually unchanged from 1990 and were projected to be similar in 1992.

6 1,500 sq. ft. was the space actually used for floor display of furniture. The 4,000 sq. ft. number recognizes the surrounding aisles and the floor space occupied by the back wall shelves which displayed furniture.

"The buying occasions for furniture are quite varied," said Jim Forbush. "A small business starting out will need to equip two or three rooms with desks, chairs and filing cabinets. This can be accomplished in various ways, by buying or renting secondhand furniture, by visiting a mom and pop specialty store or by visiting Staples. Quite often a customer will come in looking for a desk but go out with a banquet table. Banquet tables may not look as formal as a desk, but they are cheap, functional and easy to move around.

"A second buying occasion is when the office expands, either with more space or simply to accommodate a new employee. It is natural, at that point, to furnish in the same style as the original furniture. Alternatively, the boss will often take this as an opportunity to get higher quality furniture for his or her office and pass the existing furniture on to the new hire. The third buying occasion is to satisfy the need for a single piece of add-on furniture, such as a filing cabinet, a computer table or to replace a broken chair."

"Perhaps our biggest obstacle to selling furniture is 'sticker shock,'" said Bill Paul, vice president for merchandising. "It doesn't matter whether you are buying for home or office, furniture always costs more than you expect. If you're on a budget, that means trading down on your expectations. People will often make that trade-off by accepting the need to assemble the furniture themselves. But that's very time consuming, and doesn't always get the best results. And, though I hate to say it, by assembling it yourself you become quite familiar with its quality.

"If the customer asks for delivery (at a charge of $25 per order) we can also perform any assembly required (for an additional charge of $15–$25 per item). An item in stock at the store can usually be delivered next day, or if from our warehouse, within a week.

"The second biggest problem is that there is no branding in furniture, or at least none that the customer is aware of. Thus the customer is confused as to both price and quality."

"The story isn't much better from our point of view" continued Paul. "Every furniture purchase claims some time from one or more of our assistants. The floor samples get scratched, dusty and damaged. We need special equipment at each store such as tailgate trucks, dollies, blankets and customized training to limit damage. Even so, perhaps 5% of all orders lead to a return of the merchandise because the goods have been damaged by the time they reach the customer.

"On top of all this, the support we get from manufacturers could be a lot better. Lead times for reorders are long and unreliable, and there's virtually no promotional backing. Staples has been successful in part by taking out layers of distribution in office products. But furniture is a different problem again. It doesn't lend itself to long production runs. Case goods furniture (pre-assembled) is bulky, heavy and delicate. And while the office furniture buyer is rarely thinking fashion, nevertheless personal taste is an important dimension in the purchase. I don't know if manufacturers will ever figure how to take cost out of their products."

SURVEY OF STAPLES CUSTOMERS

In the spring of 1991, Staples conducted a survey of its customers to discover their attitudes towards the stores in general and to the furniture department in particular. The survey team identified a sample of about 500 Staples members, each of whom had purchased some office supplies within the previous 12 months. The sample was constructed so that about half of the members had purchased office furniture ("Purchasers") from Staples in that period and half had not ("Non-Purchasers"). **Table 3** lists some results from the study. **Exhibit 6** illustrates where Non-Purchasers obtained their furniture. **Exhibit 7** describes why Non-Purchasers did not buy their furniture at Staples. **Exhibit 8** illustrates ways in which both groups initially learned that their primary source of furniture, sold furniture. Both categories in the sample regarded price, quality, selection, and ability to see the product as major considerations with respect to furniture. There were no significant differences between the groups with respect to secondary criteria.

THE OFFICE FURNITURE INDUSTRY

In 1992, office furniture was an $8 billion business[1] for U.S. manufacturers, with Steelcase ($2 billion) and Herman Miller ($850 million) the industry leaders. Until the fairly recent burgeoning of the home office market, distribution had been almost exclusively through wholesalers and dealerships. Wholesalers provided distribution and a warehousing function. Dealers were traditionally independently owned, though often tied to a particular manufacturer. Dealers had showrooms, knowledgeable and well motivated sales help, and provided extensive installation, delivery and repair services.

Manufacturer gross margins were thought to be around 33%, with payment usually required up front before the furniture was ever produced. Wholesalers added a margin to manufacturer prices of 25–30% (of which 15–20% would cover freight). Dealers had traditionally aimed to take a markup of 100% on wholesale cost.

A large organization, such as a Fortune 500 company or government agency, would work closely with a dealer, or through an interior design firm to furnish a new building. Once the choice of furniture had been made, the dealer would then contract with a manufacturer for the product. (The industry was often referred to as the *contract* furniture business as distinct from the retail trade.) Contract furniture manufacturers supplied about 70% of the office furniture market. Often the dealer would provide ongoing repair, service and replacement of the furniture after installation. (Such service might ultimately cost as much as the original furniture.) However, an aggressive customer with its own maintenance and design staff might purchase direct from the manufacturer for as little as 40% of the dealer list price.

The contract business tended to flourish with the advent of new innovative office furniture concepts. In the 1970s panel systems became popular. Large open plan rooms would be separated into cubicles with vertical panels from which desks and filing cabinets were suspended. In 1992 panel systems still represented 30% of all office furniture manufacturer sales. In the early 1980s modular furniture was the new idea, again with flexibility in

---

1 Not including carpeting and lighting. For comparison the total office products industry, including furniture, was estimated at $75 billion. In addition to furniture there was $21 billion of general office supplies, $12 billion in business machines (excluding computers), $20 billion in computers and $8 billion in business forms.

Table 3
Some Results From the Survey of Staples Customers

	Purchasers	Non-Purchasers
Percent self-employed	17%	19%
2–7 employees	46%	30%
More than 50 employees	9%	17%
Number of personal computers owned	4	31 (average)
% who have bought office supplies at Staples within 6 months	100%	67%
% who have ever bought office furniture at Staples	100%	22%
# of purchasing occasions at Staples (last 6 months)	8.36	6.24 (average)
Main drawback to Staples furniture department	Limited selection (16%)	Poor quality (27%)
Second drawback	Unhelpful staff (12%)	Limited selection (25%)
Main advantage of Staples furniture	Reasonable prices (44%)	—
Second advantage of Staples furniture	Selection (31%)	—
% orders delivered	37%	61% (average)
% respondents always using delivery	18%	66%
% requiring delivery within a week	60%	42%
% requiring delivery within a day	30%	18%
% willing to pay for delivery	65%	66%
% furniture bought with catalog	23%	31% (average)
% assembled by customer	60%	37% (average)

mind. Modular furniture and panel systems were often referred to as "systems furniture." Modular furniture accounted for about 5% of dollar manufacturer shipments in 1992. Other categories included seating (25%), filing cabinets (15%), tables (6%), desks (10%), and other storage units (4%). These categories include all computer furniture which was thought to be about 9% of the market.

A significant change in the office furniture industry began during the early 1980s. In the home furniture market, a number of manufacturers developed ready-to-assemble (RTA) furniture to meet a growing demand for lower price items. Many people first purchased these products to meet domestic needs of microwaves, VCRs and computers. Dealers were reluctant to carry RTA furniture because it was cheap, required no installation or delivery, and was not manufactured by their normal vendors. Those that did, often stocked only RTA computer furniture, since no comparable item was then available from the traditional vendors.

Frustrated by the lack of retail distribution, RTA manufacturers (such as O'Sullivan Industries) turned to mass-merchandise outlets such as Lechmere, Sears and Wal-Mart, and in due course, the office superstores. The RTA concept of offering good value at low price-points in a self-service format fit in well with the mass-merchandising philosophy. Mass merchandisers/superstores, who bought directly from the manufacturer, typically took a markup of only 30%. A desk selling in a superstore for $125 had typically been sold through dealers for around $350 pre-assembled. Even after superstore competition, dealer prices for the same desk were around $250. By 1992 mass merchandisers had 14% of the office furniture business with office superstores having an additional 7%. The traditional wholesaler/dealer network was reduced to 60% with catalogs (5%) and direct sales (7%) being other major channels.

Sales of RTA office furniture received their impetus from the home office market. As a consequence, cost-conscious executives, who were familiar with the availability of RTA furniture in their role as consumers, often found the same goods suitable for their office. The median RTA desk in 1991 sold for $199, as compared to $1,000 for a case goods desk bought through a dealer. Many home furniture retailers, such as Workbench or Crate and Barrel, offered a limited number of good quality case good desks in the $300—700 range.

The advent of personal computers, which for many was the impetus for a home office, created a consumer more educated about office furniture. At the same time, the workplace was becoming more specialized, requiring more individual tailoring of the office setup. Workers and even some state laws now insisted on "ergonomically correct" furniture. To be ergonomically correct, a chair or desk had to be designed for a particular body size and task.

Scrambling to adjust to the new environment, dealers responded in different ways. Some upgraded their showrooms emphasizing luxuriously appointed office displays. Those that did offer RTA furniture formed buying groups to increase price leverage with manufacturers. RTA manufacturers responded by providing traditional dealers and retailers with a brand name distinct from that supplied to the superstores, though the furniture itself was nearly identical.

Concerned at the weakened state of dealers, manufacturers became more active at the retail level. Steelcase offered 48-hour delivery and Herman Miller opened 50 of its own retail stores (Office Pavilion). Traditional manufacturers seemed reluctant either to distribute their own products through office superstores or to manufacture RTA products themselves. "Many of the chairs we sell have features that need to be pointed out to the customer" said Peter McDevitt, Vice-President of Eurosit Inc. (Chicago). "Discounters do not have the personnel or sales force necessary to do the selling job. We feel some of our chairs would be excellent for the superstore customer, but with no one there to sell them, discounters are wasting their time and our product."[2] "The superstore's product is junk," said Dave Petrick, Vice-President of Bretford Manufacturing (Schiller Park, IL). "They are trying to hit price points and will sacrifice the product's quality."[3]

Though some executives were content to buy RTA furniture for add-on items such as computer carts and temporary desks, most still wished their office to project a sense of taste and importance. The cost of contract furniture had tripled in real terms during the previous twenty years, and so there was good reason to expect the development of substitutes. But RTA furniture was often too fragile for the demands of commercial use. RTA manufacturers were anxious to develop furniture that was more durable and yet easier to assemble.

A furniture alternative for price-conscious business was used furniture. Many dealers traded in secondhand furniture. Even after extensive refurbishment, contract furniture could be bought at half its original list price. The used market was small, estimated at around $300 million annually.

A SUPERSTORE COMPARISON

The Office Max superstore in Somerville, MA., is located in a strip mall with adequate parking. It is close to the highway though not very visible from it. The store, at about 25,000 sq. ft., is slightly larger than the typical Staples store and has more space devoted to furniture, perhaps 2,000 sq. ft. Like Staples, the furniture

2 *Office Products Dealer,* June 1990.
3 *Office Products Dealer,* June 1991.

is displayed at the rear of the store, but unlike Staples, Plano-grams were used to lay out much of the furniture in small office displays. The furniture was rearranged nearly daily in an effort to achieve the best effect. Though prices were similar on directly comparable items, few items were identical (see **Table 4**). Variety seemed greater at Office Max, with some furniture at higher price points.

An Office Depot store in Hialeah, outside Miami, was considerably larger than a typical Staples store and had rather more of a warehouse feel. About 3,000 sq. ft. were devoted to furniture with individual pieces sufficiently spread out to allow a customer to walk around each item. Chairs and storage cabinets were carried on shelves. Prices were similar to those of Staples. Office Depot had appeared to be giving less prominence to furniture in recent months.

In addition to other office superstores, nearly all mass merchants and wholesale clubs carried some office furniture, as did some grocery stores and drugstores. At a Phar-Mor pharmacy in Hialeah, one full aisle was devoted to office products, though in small sizes inadequate for the business customer. In the center of half of the aisle was a two-tier display of RTA office furniture. Inventory was stocked on the lower of the two tiers with assembled models on the higher tier. Prices were low though the selection was limited. A nearby Wal-Mart carried very little office furniture in its small furniture department: a student desk, a computer workstation ($59.97) and a secretarial chair ($59.96). In another part of the store were two two-drawer filing cabinets (metal $19.97, wood $24.96).

At a BJ's Wholesale Club in Medford, MA., about 400 linear feet of shelf space (two levels of 200 linear feet of floor space) was devoted to furniture, including office furniture. Items included a four-drawer metal filing cabinet for $89.99, an O'Sullivan Computer Center for $169.99, a secretarial chair for $59.99 and a rolltop desk for $499.99.

A major foreign competitor in the RTA market was the Sweden-based IKEA. Their 200,000–300,000 sq. ft. warehouse style stores contain about 15,000 SKUs of RTA furniture plus housewares and furnishings. An exclusively self-service format, the stores had room displays with inventory held on shelves. The vast selection, low price points, and immediate availability created an air of excitement in the stores. IKEA was becoming an increasingly important competitor.

Table 4
Prices of Identical Items of Furniture from Staples and Competitors

	Staples	Office Max	Office Depot	Phar-Mor
Bush Computer Cart	119.99	119.99	—	—
O'Sullivan Two-Drawer File	38.99	39.99	—	36.45
O'Sullivan Radius (Oak Finish)				
Executive Desk	118.00	139.99	—	—
Hutch	49.99	49.96	—	—
Rolling File Cabinet	63.98	66.99	59.00	58.71
Sentry Fire Safe Office File	293.75	299.99	—	—
72" Metal Storage Cabinet	149.98	—	149.99	—

THE THREE-STORE EXPERIMENT

In May 1992, three Staples stores in Saugus, Shrewsbury and Weymouth, Massachusetts, were stocked with furniture at higher price points (up to $1,000). While occupying the original floor space, the furniture was set up in small office configurations. Sales associates with retail furniture experience assisted customers. All orders were delivered within a week if available in the Staples warehouse or, if ordered from the manufacturer, in about five weeks.

Most of the desk and computer furniture in these price points were case goods and as a result, required more space per unit at the warehouse, and more careful handling during delivery than an equivalent RTA product.

Early evidence suggested that revenues in the three stores were well ahead of normal.

OPTIONS

Tom Stemberg summarized the apparent alternatives for furniture at Staples: "At one extreme we could abandon it, except for very fast moving items like filing cabinets, chairs and banquet tables. At the other extreme we could open showrooms dedicated to displaying a wide range of furniture, with orders shipped directly to the customer from the manufacturer. This could be complemented by catalogs in all our other stores.

"Finally our three-store experiment seems to show us that if we offer a wider assortment of furniture, including higher quality goods, display it properly and generally give the category some attention, contribution will improve. That's all we did for business machines.

"Maybe furniture should not be part of the Staples assortment. The original logic, of course, was that offices buy furniture and therefore we should supply furniture. This would not be the first time we've dropped a category. We did forms printing (through a third party) when we started but quickly dropped it. We also offered software when we started out but then dropped it, though it has recently been reintroduced. There are so many categories that can do well for us once we figure out how to do them right."

Exhibit 1
Staples Stores by Market Area

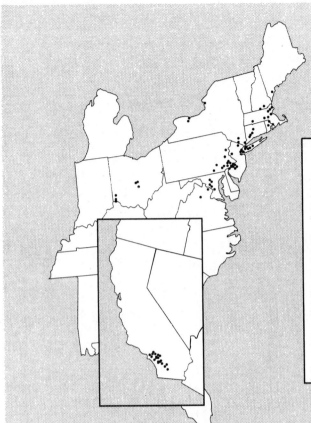

MARKETS	AS OF		PLAN
	1/26/91	2/01/92	1/30/93
New York	19	29	39
Philadelphia	11	17	21
Washington, DC	9	12	13
Boston	8	10	14
Southern Ohio	6	7	7
Baltimore	—	5	6
Southern California	9	27	45
Secondary markets	12	16	24
	74	123	169

Source: *Annual Report*

Exhibit 2
A Typical Staples Store

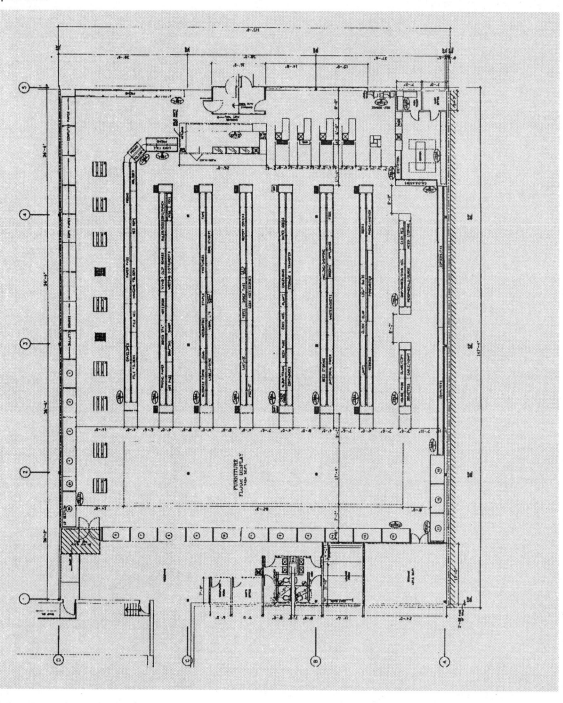

Exhibit 3
Consolidated Statements of Operations
(dollar amounts in thousands, except share data)

| | Fiscal Year Ended | | Twelve Months |
	February 1, 1992	January 26, 1991	Ended January 27, 1990 (Note B)
Sales	$ 547,080	$ 298,733	$ 181,699
Cost of goods sold and occupancy costs	419,068	225,490	135,702
Gross profit	128,012	73,243	45,997
Operating expenses:			
Store operating and selling	86,168	48,351	30,411
Pre-opening	2,798	2,467	1,000
General and administrative	20,608	14,458	9,362
Nonrecurring charges—Note I		2,053	
Total operating expenses	109,574	67,329	40,773
Operating income	18,438	5,914	5,224
Other income (expense):			
Interest income	1,966	3,625	1,678
Interest expense	(6,327)	(3,757)	(616)
Other	(1,139)	(157)	
Total other income (expense)	(5,500)	(289)	1,062
Income before income taxes and extraordinary credit	12,938	5,625	6,286
Income taxes—Note H	5,000	1,970	2,037
Income before extraordinary credit	7,938	3,655	4,249
Extraordinary credit—tax benefit from loss carryforward	1,200	1,545	1,496
Net income	$ 9,138	$ 5,200	$ 5,745
Earnings per common share—Note A:			
Income before extraordinary credit	$ 0.48	$ 0.25	$ 0.30
Extraordinary credit	$ 0.07	$ 0.10	$ 0.11
Net income	$ 0.55	$ 0.35	$ 0.41
Number of shares used in computing earnings per common share— Notes A and F	16,393,324	14,937,677	14,083,263

Source: *Annual Report* .

Exhibit 4
Consolidated Balance Sheets
(dollar amounts in thousands, except share data)

	February 1, 1992	January 26, 1991
ASSETS		
Current assets:		
Cash and cash equivalents	$ 50,378	$ 33,379
Short-term investments	2,000	25,532
Merchandise inventories	104,920	69,992
Receivables	13,884	7,728
Prepaid expenses and other assets	5,537	1,794
Total current assets	176,719	138,425
Property and equipment:		
Land	344	344
Building	3,215	3,215
Leasehold improvements	37,091	22,711
Equipment	23,354	14,310
Furniture and fixtures	17,704	10,135
Total property and equipment	81,708	50,715
Less accumulated depreciation and amortization	14,342	7,252
Net property and equipment	67,366	43,463
Other assets:		
Lease acquisition costs	35,093	18,036
Other	7,064	3,598
Total other assets	42,157	21,634
	286,242	203,522
LIABILITIES AND STOCKHOLDERS' EQUITY		
Current liabilities:		
Accounts payable	33,971	34,502
Accrued expenses and other current liabilities—Note C	17,207	17,167
Income taxes	2,910	606
Current portion of long-term debt	325	874
Total current liabilities	54,413	53,149
Long-term debt—Note D	5,922	4,233
Other long-term obligations—Note J	6,207	2,387
Convertible Debentures—Note E	75,000	75,000
Stockholders' equity—Notes F and G:		
Perferred stock, $0.01 par value—authorized 5,000,000 shares; no shares issued		
Common stock, $0.0006 par value—authorized 40,000,000 shares; issued and outstanding. 17,637,075 shares in 1992 and 14,397,568 shares in 1991	11	6
Additional paid-in capital	138,720	71,916
Retained earnings (deficit)	5,969	(3,169)
Total stockholders' equity	144,700	68,753
	286,242	203,522

Exhibit 5
Staples Catalog—Information

Why Should I Shop At Staples?

Every Day Low Prices
STAPLES prices average 30-70% off manufacturers' list. STAPLES can provide deep product discounts because we deal directly with manufacturers and purchase in volume, insuring the lowest possible cost.

Guaranteed Lowest Prices*
Find an item selling for less in any other supply store, STAPLES will match the price on your purchase.

* Proof of purchase required (recent advertisement, store catalog or sales receipt.) Must be a current local price on an identical item in stock. No rain checks. Ad errors, closeouts and clearance items not applicable. STAPLES reserves the right to limit quantities.

FREE Membership
STAPLES membership is free to all businesses and individuals. Membership privileges include: special discounts on selected items, our Guaranteed Lowest Prices and STAPLES' Next Day Delivery service. Becoming a member is easy-just sign up at a store near you or call 1-800-333-3330.

Phenomenal Product Selection
STAPLES carries copiers and computers, furniture and fax machines, pens, paper...everything you need for your office. In all, over 5,000 top quality items including the brand names you trust, like Panasonic, 3M, Canon, Xerox, AT&T, Hammermill, Bic and more!

Convenience
There are more than 120 STAPLES Office Superstores. See back cover for location nearest you. We are open extended hours to accommodate your busy schedule. Weekdays 7 a.m. to 9 p.m., and weekends. STAPLES accepts MasterCard, Visa, Discover, STAPLES Charge Card, American Express and Company checks.

Next Business Day Delivery
Staples' Next Day Delivery service saves you your most valued commodity--time. STAPLES members can shop by phone and get the same great prices and selection available in our stores. Next time you need anything for your office, just call (800) 333-3330, or fax your order to (508) 370-8958, before 4:00 p.m. EST, and you'll receive your order the next business day. Furniture may take up to five business days.

Shopping With The Staples Catalog

How To Use This Catalog More Effectively
In the front of this catalog, you will find a table of contents listing product categories. For a detailed index of specific products, turn to the back of the book. Throughout our catalog, look for these important symbols:

 Bulk Value Item. By purchasing a bulk pack, you save more.

 Extended Service Plan available. For additional details see page 73.

 Recycled Product. Recycling not only helps save the environment, it's smart business.

Need Help? Look To The Office Superstore!
Our courteous and capable customer service representatives have the answers to your office product dilemmas. When you have a question call (800) 333-3330 weekdays between 8:30 a.m. and 8:00 p.m. EST. This is the only telephone number you need. Call us to:

* Place an order.
* Check on a shipping date.
* Return an item.
* Get information you need about our products or services

What If An Item Is Out Of Stock?
It is a rare event when the STAPLES warehouse is out of a particular item, but it occasionally does happen. Fortunately STAPLES stocks over 5,000 items and usually, we can offer you a substitute product. Of course, you always have the option to order at another time. To keep our warehouse running smoothly and keep our prices low we do not back order items.

We're Not Satisfied Until You're Satisfied
At STAPLES, we do our best to prevent problems or misunderstandings. But, if they occur, you can be assured that we'll do whatever it takes to make things right.
If we make a mistake in filling your order, or if a delivered item just isn't exactly what you wanted, call us at (800) 333-3330 and we'll take care of you. Our business depends on your satisfaction.

★★★Staples Return Policy★★★
If, for some reason, you're dissatisfied with a product, return it within 30 days. If the item was delivered, just call us for a Return Authorization Number and we will pick it up. The item must be in its original packaging, with your receipt, for a full refund or replacement. All items purchased at a store must be returned to a store for refund. (If you paid by check and you return the item within ten days, you will receive a merchandise credit.)

74

See Back Inside Cover For A Complete Listing Of All Our Products.

General Index

File Cabinets

Premier Vertical Files
(No. 213975) Heavy duty, full suspension drawers glide smoothly on 10 nylon rollers. Heavy gauge steel reinforced frame. Full bottom for additional stability; follower block, label holders, thumb latch. Available in letter or legal size. 26.5" Deep. Optional lock No. 179580. Details below. List 230.00

26.5" Deep

109⁰⁰ Save 53%

GRAY	BLACK	SAND	SIZE	DIMENSIONS (H) x (W) x (D)	LIST	STAPLES PRICE	SAVE
4 DRAWER							
213975	179564	179572	Letter	52"x15"x26½"	230.00	109.00	53%
256867	179531	179523	Legal	52"x18"x26½"	275.00	139.00	49%
2 DRAWER							
256875	179549	179556	Letter	28"x15"x26½"	160.00	76.84	52%
256883	179515	179507	Legal	28"x18"x26½"	190.00	99.93	47%

Optional Vertical File Plunger Lock
Optional Plunger Lock (No. 179580) Plunger lock for above two and four drawer files. List 32.00

24⁹⁸ Save 22%

Premier Deluxe 4-Drawer File
(No. 268813)-Sand (No. 268821)-Black (No. 268839) Gray 52"(H) x 15"(W) x 26½"(D) Fully enclosed bottom for increased stability and security. Full suspension 10 rollers, 6 ball bearings. Hand hole at back of every drawer. Thumb latch prevents drawer from accidentally opening. Spring loaded follower block is easily adjustable to hold contents. Triple tie suspension. List 286.00

Includes Factory Installed Lock

149⁹⁸

Save 47%

Premier Lateral Files
Versatile lateral files can adjust for letter or legal size folders. Heavy duty 84 ball bearing suspension drawer system. Safety interlock system prevents tipping. Adjustable floor leveler, recessed handle. Lock included. On 5 drawer lateral only top drawer is a flip front drawer.

2 Drawer Lateral File
(No. 179606)-Sand, (No. 179598)-Black Two drawer. 28¼"x36"x18". List 425.00
218⁰⁰ Save 49%

4 Drawer Lateral File
(No. 179622)-Sand, (No. 179614)-Black Four drawer. 51"x36"x18". List 708.00
398⁰⁰ Save 44%

5 Drawer Lateral File
(No. 179648)-Sand, (No. 179630)-Black Five drawer. 64"x36"x18". List 900.00
466⁰⁰ Save 48%

(No. 267013). **Divider Kit.** List 17.00. **Staples 11.49. Save 32%**
(No. 267021). **Cross Rods.** List 16.00. **Staples 9.99. Save 38%**

Premier 4 Drawer Vertical File
(No. 221069) Heavy duty full suspension drawers. Heavy gauge steel reinforced frames. Full bottom block, label holders, thumb latch. Accepts letter-sized folders. Wire follower block. Sand. 52"Hx15"Wx25"D Non-member 83.30 List 200.00

25" Deep

MEMBER PRICE

92⁵⁶ Save 58%

*Accepts optional lock (No. 179580) List 32.00
24⁹⁸ Save 22%

Fire Safe Office File 6000
(No. 202556) 27⅜"(H) x 17¼"(W) x 23¼"(D) Accomodates legal, letter and A4 size file folders. Smooth suspension draw slides. Dual latch system, key lock for privacy. Fire and explosion tested. UL classified. List 499.00

SENTRY

293⁷⁵ Save 41%

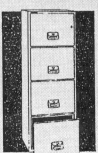

Schwab Fireproof 4 Drawer File
(No. 255232) Legal size file features Insulate - dry insulation, plunger lock, inner steel jacket and movable dividers. Full extension drawers. Both legal and letter folders can be filed. UL Classified. UL 350-1 hour Class C rating. Tested at 1700° for one hour internal temperature stay below 350° protecting documents inside. List 1350.00

699⁹² Save 48%

Exterior 19¾ Wx53½ Hx31 D
Interior Filing Depth 26
*Delivery only. Charges vary, please inquire.

Executive Chairs

Global Industries Gray Side Chair
(No. 251884). Fully upholstered chair includes scratch resistant frame, floor guides and welded steel frame. Grey. List 166.87

79⁹⁸ Save 52%

Global Industries Gray Midback Chair
(No. 251892). Adjustable seat with 4" range, tilts and swivels, includes 5 pronged base, twin wheel casters and upholstered back, seat and arms. Grey. List 233.70.

119⁹⁸ Save 49%

Global Industries Gray Executive High Back Swivel Chair
(No. 204032) Fully upholstered tilter. Manual seat height adjustment. 5 pronged black steel base. Dual wheel casters. Gray. List 422.56.

199⁹⁷ Save 53%

Global Industries Gray/Oak Sled Side Chair
(No. 262568-Gray). Comfortable spring seat. Sculptured seat and back cushions upholstery fabric. Solid hardwood frame. Easy to assemble. List 206.47.

99⁹⁸ Save 51%

Global Industries Gray/Oak Formula Low Back Swivel Chair
(No. 204016). Low back tilter with two cushion upholstered back. Solid wood arms. 5 pronged wood capped steel base. Oak finish. Gray. List 455.56.

217⁶⁵ Save 52%

Global Industries Gray/Oak Formula High Back Swivel Chair
(No. 204008). High back tilter with three cushion upholstered back. Solid wood arms. 5 pronged wood capped steel base. Oak finish. Gray. List 488.89

249⁰⁰ Save 49%

Global Industries Navy Thoro Side Chair
(No. 266973). Soft and durable upholstery. Floor glides are included at no extra cost to prevent floor and chair frame marring. Premium quality steel structure with epoxy coating for durability. Sled base design. 32"H x 24"W x 26" D. List 211.25

99⁹⁸ Save 53%

Global Industries Navy Thoro Hi-Back Chair
(No. 251850). Adjustable seat has 4" range. Includes tilt swivel mechanism, twin wheel casters, coated steel frame and durable fabric covered seat and arms. Navy. List 369.01.

179⁹⁸ Save 51%

Global Industries Economy Executive Swivel Chair
(No. 122705). 31½"(H)x22"(W) x22"(D). Swivel tilter chair with chrome arms and walnut finished wood armrests. Four pronged chrome base. Fabric seat and backrest. Manual seat height adjustment. Black. List 193.61.

89⁹⁹ Save 53%

Global Industries Brown Tufted Hi-Back Chair
(No. 251876). Adjustable seat has 4" range, tilt swivel mechanism, durable tufted fabric, twin wheel casters and genuine oak arms and base. Brown. List 594.50.

299⁹⁸ Save 49%

Wallace Gray/Oak Side Chair
(No. 238485). Sled base side chair with oak frame. Thick cushion on seat and back. Gray. List 84.00.

54⁹² Save 34%

Wallace Gray Executive Chair
(No. 265033). Executive arm chair with solid oak five star base. Adjustable tilt mechanism. Extra large cushioned seat and back. Gray. List 199.99.

99⁹⁷ Save 50%

chairs

Wallace Leather Hi Back
(No. 2G4457) Black. Seat tilt and lock mechanism. Pneumatic height adjustment. Reclining arms. Top grain imported leather and dual casters. List 600.00

299⁹⁸ Save 50%

Wallace Leather Executive Chair
(No. 238493) Executive highback natural grain leather arm chair. Includes locking tilt mechanism, large five star base with molding and dual wheel casters. Black. List 299.00

229⁹⁶ Save 23%

Global Oval High Back Chair
(No. 266981) Teal. (No. 266999) Grey. Oval tube frame provides extra durability. Upholstered arm tops give comfort. Sewn in upholstery stress relief panels. chair tilts, and height adjustments, dual wheel casters mean easy maneuverability. List 429.00

219⁹³ Save 40%

Global Oval Side Chair
(No. 266932) Teal. (No. 266940) Grey. Oval tube frame design for durability. Upholstered arms, back and seat. Four legs for stability. Sculptured upholstery for extra comfort. List 299.00

149⁹³ Save 49%

Wallace Drafting Chair
(No. 238436) Architect chair has pneumatic height adjustment from 18" to 26" with adjustable footring. Swivel seat. Back features manual height and angle adjustment. Five pronged nylon reinforced base. Black. List 169.00

129⁹² Save 23%

Global Super Drafting Chair
(No. 204073) Contoured, upholstered seat and back. Seat height adjustable. Footrest. 5 pronged steel base. Dual wheel casters. Gray. List 386.67

179⁹⁹ Save 53%

Galaxy Stack Chair
(No. 203984) Side stacking chair. Chrome tubing side frame. Black vinyl seat and back. List 68.33.

19⁹⁷ Save 71%

Galaxy Stack Chair With Arms
(No. 203976) Side stacking chair. Chrome tubing side frame. Walnut finished armrests. Black upholstered seat and vinyl back. List 86.67

24⁹⁹ Save 71%

Virco Plastic Shell Stacking Chair
(No. 260554) Blue. Anti-static plastic shell and chrome frame finish resists chips and scratches. Legs are capped with steel swivel glides. Back support tube prevents breaking. 30"(H)x19"(W)x21"(D). List 44.50

19⁹⁸ Save 55%

Global Key Stack Chair
(Nos. 122994 Gray. 122911 Burgundy) Side nesting chair with tubular chrome frame and nylon acrylic upholstery. Fabric seat and back seat. List 97.78

39⁸⁸ Save 59%

Virco Metal Folding Chair
(No. 229914) 4/PK. All steel. Bronze. Set of four. List 72.00

28⁸⁴ Save 60%

Task Chairs

Wallace Task Chair with Arms
(No. 268755). Burgundy. (No. 268763). Black. One-touch pneumatic height adjustment. Tension adjust tilt mechanism. 4" spring steel back support. Large seat and back for added comfort. List 229.99.

99⁹⁷ Save 56%

Wallace Ergosizer with Upholstered Arms
(No. 268722). Gray. (No. 268714). Burgundy. One-touch syncroseat and back support mechanism. One-touch pneumatic height adjustment. Upholstered arms. Waterfall seat and large back for continual comfort. List 249.99.

159⁹⁶ Save 36%

Global "Elation" Task Chair With Arms
(No. 266957). Plum. (No. 266965). Gray. Truly an ergonomic chair. Lumbar support for the back. Adjustable height, back and arm rest for user comfort. One touch seat tilt for keyboard and normal use. List 438.75.

219³⁷ Save 50%

Global Task Chair with Adjustable Arms
(No. 267005). Black. Height of arms are adjustable for user comfort. Back upholstery is designed to distribute weight evenly. Gas lift. List 273.00.

129⁹⁷ Save 52%

Global E-Z Manual Steno Chair
(No. 191080). Featuring plastic capped steel base with matching back upright and upholstered seat. Adjustable back and seat height. Five pronged base. Gray. List 148.22.

59⁹⁹ Save 59%

Wallace Task Chair
(No. 238426-Gray, 268748-Black). Task chair with pneumatic lift height adjustment. Contoured seat and flex back with vinyl covered five pronged base. Gray. List 89.00.

69⁹⁴ Save 21%

Global Economy Steno Chair
(No. 159046). Chrome base and back strap. Vinyl seat and backrest. Four way adjustable posture back. Manual seat height adjustment (17" to 22½"). Black. List 159.80.

73⁹⁹ Save 54%

Global Super Steno Chair
(Nos. 251413-Black, 122309-Burgundy, 122333-Gray). 35"(H)x20"(W)x22"(D). Non tilt seat with ergonomic seat height adjustment. Three way back adjustment. Contoured upholstery. Dual wheel casters. Chair arms sold separately. List 227.89.

95⁰⁰ Save 58%

Super Steno Arm
(Nos. 251421-Black, 146668-Burgundy, 123224-Gray). List 74.00.

29⁹⁹ Save 59%

Acco Task Chair With Arms
(Nos. 269415-Grey, 269407-Brown). Large seat and back of this multi function office chair tilts at the touch of a lever. Adjustable height. Soft molded arms. List 321.54.

179⁹⁸ Save 44%

Rubbermaid Econocleat Chairmats
(No. 124008) Chairmat. 45"x53". Clear. Non member 18.84. List 31.80

MEMBER PRICE
16⁹⁶ Save 47%

STAPLES NO.	DESCRIPTION	LIST	STAPLES PRICE	SAVE
124073	All Carpet Cleat	48.15	21.88	55%
176925	Anti-Skid	42.20	24.95	41%

Office Furniture/Accessories

BPI Panel Systems & Bookshelves

Fabric covered panels with metal frames use connectors to create workstations.

Desk not included.

Create An Office

STAPLES NO.	DESCRIPTION	COLOR	LIST	STAPLES PRICE	SAVE
224758	60"x60" Panel	Gray	165.00	79.99	51%
224766	60"x48" Panel	Gray	156.00	72.45	54%
224790	Straight Connector	Gray	9.00	4.49	50%
224808	90° Connector	Gray	9.00	4.49	50%
224816	3-Way Connector	Grey	13.00	6.49	50%
224824	4-Way Connector	Gray	17.00	8.49	50%
*224832	Stabilizing Foot	Gray	17.00	8.49	50%

*Order 2 feet for single free standing panel.

Virco Banquet Tables

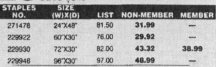

(No. 229922). 60"x30". Compressed hardwood walnut finished top with an 18 gauge steel apron. Includes rubber bumper edges. Steel legs fold up into table apron. 29" High. Brown/Walnut. No assembly required. List 76.00.

29⁹²
Save 60%

STAPLES NO.	SIZE (W)X(D)	LIST	NON-MEMBER	MEMBER
271478	24"X48"	81.50	31.99	—
229922	60"X30"	76.00	29.92	—
229930	72"X30"	82.00	43.32	38.99
229946	96"X30"	97.00	48.99	—

O'Sullivan Typewriter Cart

(No. 229898). 26⅛"(H) x25⅛"(W)x15¾"(D). Colonial oak laminate. Dual wheel casters. List 39.95.

24⁸⁷
Save 37%

Bush Typewriter Cart with Leaf

(No. 248682). 26½"(H)x26¾"(W)x15½"(D) with leaf 38¾" wide. Collapsable drop leaf side panel. Modesty panel. Softly shaped top w/rounded corners. Full ¾" board. Dual wheel hooded casters. List 69.95.

35⁹⁸
Save 48%

O'Sullivan Oak Finish 2 Drawer Vertical File

(No. 190959). 25"(H) x14⅞"(W)x19½"(D). Laminate compressed hardwood with oak drawer pulls. Assembly required. List 62.95.

38⁹⁹
Save 38%

Premier 5 Shelf 72" Step 1 Storage Cabinet

(No. 265637). Four Adjustable shelves. One Fixed. 3 point Locking system. 72"(H)x36"(W)x18"(D). Sand. No assembly required. List 252.00.

149⁹⁸
Save 40%

Edsal Five Shelf Storage System

(No. 736125). Heavy duty, sway free metal construction. Five adjustable shelves. Holds 150 lbs. if properly distributed. 70"(H)x36"(W)x15"(D). Gray. List 59.95.

39⁹⁸
Save 33%

☾omputer Furniture

Bush Workstation

Solid oak rails with rounded side panels. Pull-out tilt keyboard shelf. Wire management access opening. Low glare worksurface. Pieces available separately. Ready to assemble. List 1199.75

659⁶⁹
Save 45%

O'Sullivan Corner Workstation

(No. 261792,261800). Finished with colonial oak laminate. Includes two roomy bookshelves for storage, center computer shelf for easy viewing, portable printer cart with dual wheels and one box and one file drawer for letter size folders. Creates 90° work surface. Ready to assemble. List 240.95.

149⁹⁸ Save 40%

STAPLES NO.	DESCRIPTION	DIMENSIONS (H)x(W)x(D)	LIST	STAPLES PRICE	SAVE
250274	(A) Classic Desk	30"x48½"x28"	319.95	169.89	46%
250183	(B) Desk Hutch W/Doors	30"x48½"x13"	284.95	159.92	43%
250498	(C) Corner Unit	44½"x28¼"	114.95	59.96	47%
250191	(D) Printer Stand	30"x25"x28"	239.95	129.96	45%
253583	(E) Two Drawer File	27⅜"x16"x21"	239.95	139.96	41%

O'Sullivan Mobile Computer Cart

(No. 238410). Holds complete computer system in less than four square feet. Adjustable keyboard shelf and printer shelf feature high quality metal drawer slides. Four dual wheels with two locking casters. Colonial oak laminate. 33⅞"(H)x26¹/₁₆"(W)x23¼"(D). Ready to assemble. Non-member 63.33. List 99.95.

MEMBER PRICE
57⁰⁰ Save 42%

O'Sullivan Computer Workcenter

(No. 250167) (No. 250217) 48¼"(H) x 59¼"(W) x 23¾"(D). Colonial oak laminate. Complete workcenter. Roomy hutch with closed storage. Sturdy pull-out printer cart with caster. Pull-out keyboard shelf. Adjustable CPU shelf. Pull out dictation slide. Ready to assemble. List price 339.95.

199⁹⁶ Save 41%

Bookcases

CWI Commercial Bookcases

Solid core ¾" compressed hardwood with wood finished laminate. Adjustable shelves have wire support for maximum stability. Finished back panels. Floor levelers. Ready to assemble.

WALNUT	AMERICAN OAK	DESCRIPTION	DIMENSIONS (H)x(W)x(D)	LIST	STAPLES PRICE	SAVE
237495	237438	2 Shelves	30"x36"x12"	99.00	39.97	60%
237503	237446	3 Shelves	48"x36"x12"	129.00	59.97	53%
237511	237453	5 Shelves	72"x36"x12"	179.00	79.97	55%
237529	237461	6 Shelves	84"x36"x12"	209.00	99.97	52%

Exhibit 5, continued
Staples Catalog—Contemporary Office Furniture

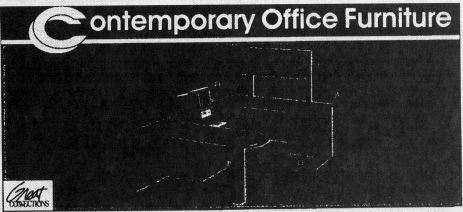

Contemporary Office Furniture

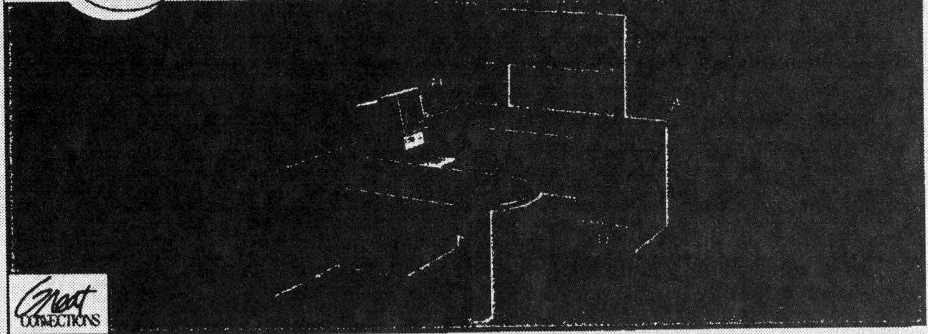

Great Connections "Spations" Computer Workcenter

A modular furniture system. Utilizing as few as 1 or as many as 11 modules, the "Spations" system can be tailored to create any workspace environment. Work surfaces are 1" thick with a Mica laminated finish. Radius edges for comfort. Full suspension drawer/pull-out shelf runners for smooth operation. Single lock secures all drawers. Convenient computer usage/storage option. Adjustable floor glides. Wire management grommets.

	STAPLES NO.	DESCRIPTION	DIMENSIONS	LIST	STAPLES PRICE	SAVE
A	*269902	Desk	66⅜"(W)x29¾"(H)x29¾"(D)	379.00	**174.92**	**53%**
B	*269910	Left Hand Return Base	48¼"(W)x28¾"(H)x22⅞"(D)	107.00	**49.98**	**53%**
C	269928	Right Hand Return Base	48¼"(W)x28¾"(H)x22⅞"(D)	107.00	**49.98**	**53%**
D	*269936	3 Drawer Pedestal	15½"(W)x21¼"(H)x21½"(D)	267.00	**129.98**	**51%**
E	269944	Return Top with Long Tubes	48¼"(W)x1"(H)x22⅞"(D)	169.00	**79.96**	**52%**
F	*269951	Return Top without Tubes	48¼"(W)x1"(H)x22⅞"(D)	113.00	**54.98**	**51%**
G	269969	Short Tube Accessory	1"(D)x22⅞"(L)	27.00	**14.99**	**44%**
H	*269977	Computer Work Center	26¾"(W)x21⅞"(H)x28½"(D)	132.00	**59.98**	**54%**
I	*269985	Hutch	40½"(W)x30½"(H)x14"(D)	267.00	**129.98**	**51%**
J	*269993	Conference Peninsula	65¾"(W)x29¾"(H)x29¾"(D)	463.00	**199.98**	**56%**
K	270009	Reversible Corner	29¾"(W)x1"(H)x22⅞"(D)	169.00	**79.98**	**52%**

*Represented in photograph

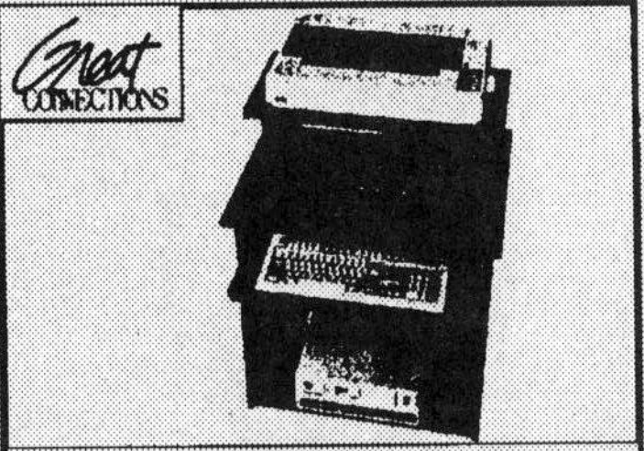

Great Connections Black Glass Computer Cart

(No. 269811). View-thru glass top with polished edges. Melamine thermal fused finish for durability. 1" thick sides for strength. Pull-out keyboard shelf for convenience. Adjustable shelf to accomodate different monitor sizes. Locking castors. List 299.00.

198.38 **Save 34%**

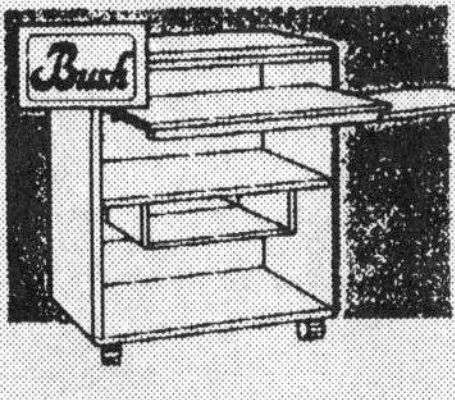

Bush Computer Cart

(No. 227835) Durable melamine finish. Convenient pull-out keyboard and printer shelves. Dual hooded casters. Specially designed back panel for easy paper management. Additional slide out shelf for extra work space. Black 30⅞"(H)x26½"(W)x 19⅜"(D) List 209.95

119.99 **Save 43%**

Great Connections Secretarial Desk with Return and Pedestal

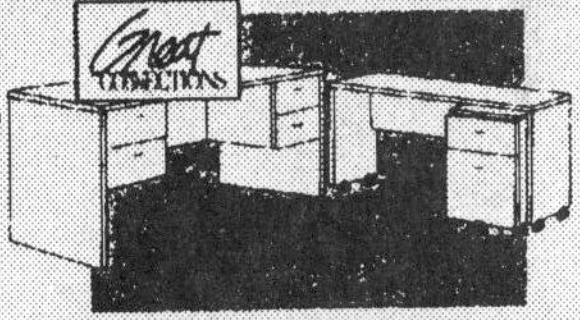

224.99 **3 PC SET**

A) Melamine 60" Desk
(No. 269852-Black, 269878-White) 1" thick Tops and sides. Durable and scratch resistant surface. Black or White. Pieces available seperately. Ready to assemble 59¾"(W)x29½"(H)x29¾"(D) List 174.00 **Staples price 96.28. Save 44%.**

B) Matching Return
(No. 269860-Black, 269886-White). Locking Casters. Ready to assemble. 47¾"(W)x26¾"(H)x18"(D) List 113.00 **Staples price 59.38. Save 47%.**

C) Matching Pedestal
(No. 237792-Black, 237768-White). Locking Casters. Two drawers, one box, one file. Fits under desk or return 15¾"(W)x24⅞"(H)x20½"(D). Ready to assemble. List 149.00 **Staples price 69.33. Save 53%.**

Pedestal With 2 Box Drawers
(Nos. 252809-Black, 252791-White) List 84.00 **Staples price 50.91. Save 39%.**

Contemporary Office Furniture

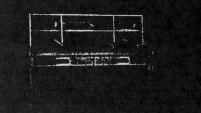

Lartech Executive Office Furniture

72" Granite Desk
(Nos. 269803, 269787, 269787). Charcoal grey granite look top with black sides. 29"(H)x72"(W)x38"(D). Sturdy vinyl edge banding in 1" thick top end panels. Easy to assemble hinge system. Unfold and slide in pedestals. List 664.85.

349.94 Save 47%

72" Granite Credenza
(Nos. 269795, 269787, 269787). Charcoal grey granite look. 29"(H)x72"(W)x24"(D). Keyboard adaptable for computer use. List 623.25.

329.94 Save 47%

Granite Lateral File
(No. 269779). Charcoal grey granite look. 29"(H)x36"(W)x28"(D). Full suspension file drawers. Safety interlock feature. List 484.75.

259.98 Save 46%

Trendines Mission Desk with Hutch and Rolling File
Birch color melamine laminated construction. Desk has two drawers, vinyl wrapped epoxy runners. Hutch has attractive sloping front, metal dowel and cam fasteners. File fits under desk and accomodates both letter and legal files.

STAPLES NO.	DESCRIPTION	LIST	STAPLES PRICE	SAVE
269704	41¼"Hx23⅜"Dx47⅞"W Mission Desk with Hutch	220.00	149.94	32%
269712	23¾"x15¾"x19⅝" Excutive File	99.00	69.94	29%

M&M Grey Computer Corner Workstation
(No. 256701). Angle design provides efficient workspace. Stain and scuff resistant laminated tops. Steel legs and backs baked enamel finish. Cantilevered legs. Recessed keyboard shelf. Grey. 29½"(H)x60"(W)x30"(D). List 249.95.

109.99 Save 56%

M&M Universal Printer Stand
(No. 269720). This stand can handle the largest printers, including a sloted top for bottom feeding printers. Open design steel frame and two sturdy, plated wire baskets allow for neater paper management. 24"Wx26½"Hx14"D (top dimension), 22 lbs. hardware and tools included. List 139.95.

69.98 Save 49%

M&M Acoustical Printer Stand
(No. 269761). Minimizes noise from printer. This cabinet will hold a variety of printers. A roll-out shelf provides easy access. Generous spacing between shelves facilitates paper loading. Smoked plexiglass panels permit viewing of the printing process. A unique cable management system restrains the computer cables out of the paper flow. Assembly required. 25" wide, 23" deep, 29" high. List 249.95.

119.98 Save 51%

Exhibit 5, continued
Staples Catalog—Wood Furniture

Wood Furniture

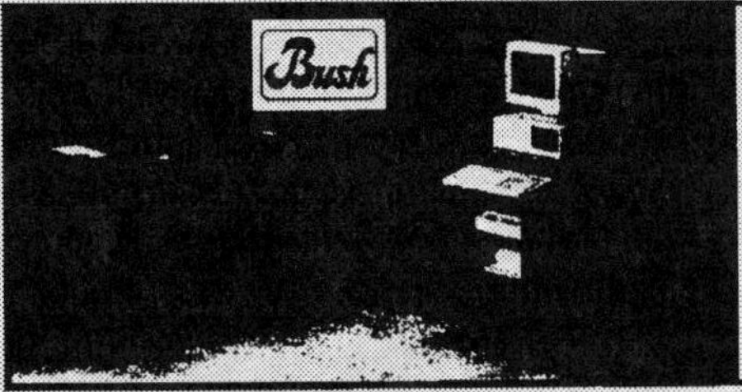

Bush Executive Desk

Desk is sturdy 1" thick work surface and sides with full suspension free drawers. Credenza has slide out keyboard and printer shelves and two box drawers. Return fits on left or right side of desk.

STAPLES NO.	DESCRIPTION	LIST	STAPLES PRICE	SAVE
263467	Oak Executive Desk	349.95	**199.98**	**43%**
263475	Credenza and Keyboard	349.95	**199.98**	**43%**
263483	Secretarial Return	119.95	**69.92**	**42%**

O'Sullivan Student Desk

(No. 203166). Desk features one box drawer and one file drawer. 27⅞"(H) x 49½"(W) x 23¾"(D). Oak finish. List 119.95. Ready to assemble.

69.00 **Save 42%**

O'Sullivan Oak Finish Panel Radius Furniture

Furniture pieces feature colonial oak laminates and a round-edge design. Executive desk includes twin box and twin file drawers. An optional center desk drawer is available. The matching file cabinet includes caster wheels and twin file drawers. All pieces are ready to assemble.

STAPLES NO.	DESCRIPTION	DIMENSIONS (H)x(W)x(D)	LIST	STAPLES PRICE	SAVE
203133	A). Executive Desk	28¾"x59"x29⅝"	229.95	**118.00**	**48%**
250209	B). Hutch/Organizer	15¼"x57"x11¾"	74.95	**49.96**	**33%**
203158	C). Rolling File Cabinet	28¾"x14⅞"x19⅜"	99.95	**63.98**	**36%**
229906	D). (Not Shown) Center Drawer Kit	2¼"x24¾"x20⅜"	39.95	**25.98**	**35%**

Anderson 72" Oak Desk

(No. 266460, 266486, 266486). 36"x72" desk. New hinged assembly system makes assembly as easy as 1-2-3. (1.) Unpack. (2.) Unfold hinged sides and modesty panel (3.) Attach optional pedestals to the shell. Includes melamine laminated surface with radius edge and full panel styling. Durable, scratch-resistant finish. List 725.00.

349.94 **Save 52%**

(No. 266452, 266486, 266486) **30"x60" Desk.** List 647.00. **Staples 299.94.** Save 54%

Anderson 22" x 72" Oak Credenza

(No. 266478, 266486, 266486). Knee hole style, hinged 3-step easy assembly system, expandable with additional components. Melamine laminated surface provides durable, scratch-resistant finish. Radius edge and full panel styling. List 725.00.

349.94 **Save 52%**

Anderson Optional Box/File Pedestal **64.98** **Save 57%**

(No. 266486) Pedestals fit either desk plus credenza. Metal glides. Letter size only files, front to back. Hinged 3-step easy assembly, expandable with additional components. Laminated surface provides durable, scratch-resistant finish. List 135.00

Anderson Deco Lateral File

(No. 234781) Matching file for letter or legal hanging files, 2 drawers with lock. 20"(D)x40"(W) x29"(H). List 502.00.

259.97 **Save 48%**

Exhibit 6
Type of Stores From Where Purchased Office Furniture (non-purchasers)

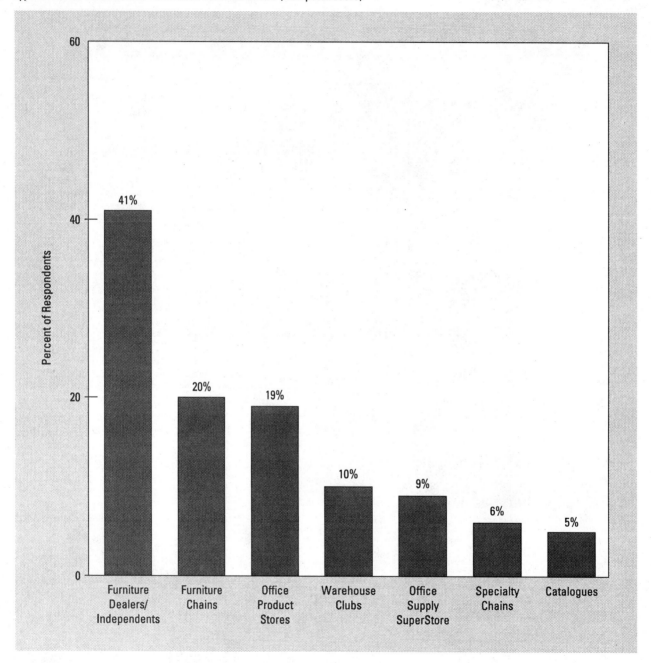

Exhibit 7
Reasons for Not Purchasing Office Furniture at Staples: Non-Purchasers (unprompted)

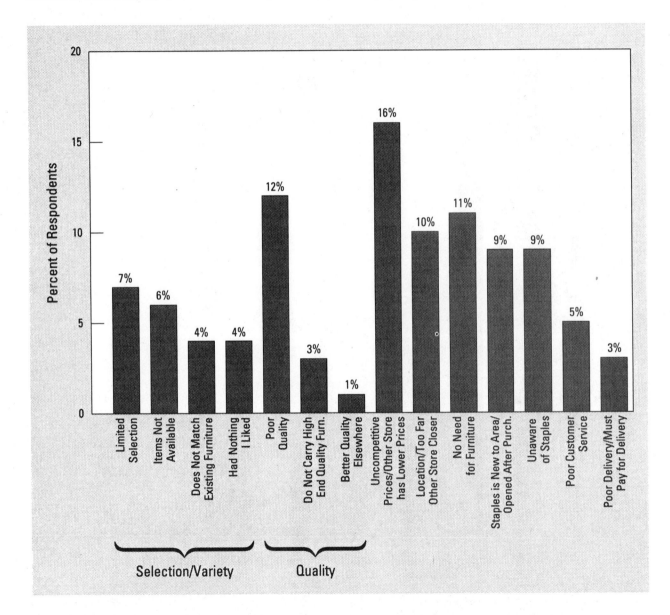

Exhibit 8
How Learned Primary Store Carries Office Furniture
(Staples vs. Other Stores Shopped)

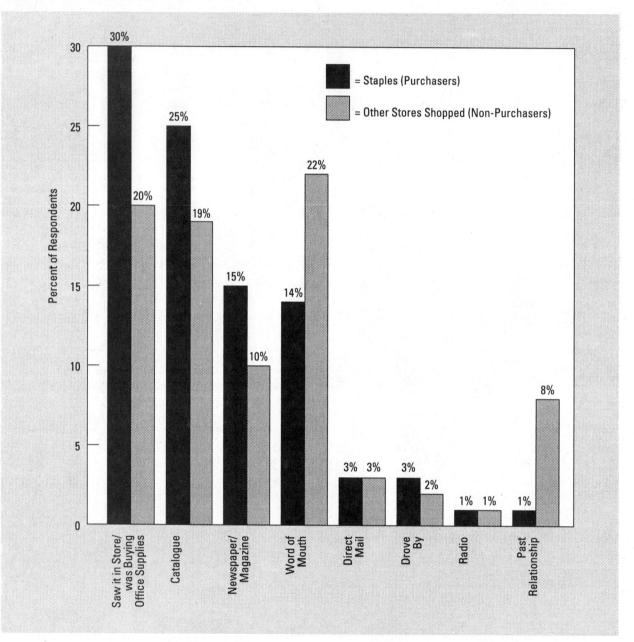

Case 7

PRIVATE LABEL AT DAYTON HUDSON DEPARTMENT STORE COMPANY

Steve Watson, chairman and chief executive officer of Dayton Hudson Department Store Company (DHDSC), met with Jim Stirratt, senior vice president, merchandise, to discuss DHDSC's private label business. Two issues were on the agenda. The first was whether buyers should continue to have considerable discretion for determining the emphasis on private label in their departments. This policy had led to substantial differences in private label emphasis, pricing, display, and promotion among departments. The second issue, which arose only if buyer discretion was to be curtailed, involved going beyond the current set of policies to establish a more stringent set of guidelines for private label programs at DHDSC. Although Watson and Stirratt recognized the merits of more stringent policy guidelines, they also believed that, given the wide range of merchandise sold, too much policy uniformity could be inconsistent with the character of the individual departments and could eliminate buyer flexibility, creativity, and independence.

Among the specific questions confronting Watson and Stirratt was how many private labels should DHDSC have and what should each represent? Currently, there were ten different private labels. Each was supposed to represent merchandise similar either in life-style, classification, price class or seasonality. For example, Boundary Waters was one of DHDSC "life-style" private labels.

The name was supposed to convey an image of an area in upper Minnesota known for a healthy, active, and casual life-style. The Boundary Waters label was found on different types of apparel, accessory, and home items as shown in **Exhibit 1**. Watson and Stirratt wondered whether the current set of labels covered the needs of the many merchandise departments and how much investment was required to support each label. Finally, Watson and Stirratt questioned what financial measures should be used to compare the profitability of private labels to that of national brands.

CORPORATE BACKGROUND

The Dayton Hudson Corporation, with sales of $12 billion, participated in four separate sectors of retailing in 1988. The Dayton Hudson Department Store Company (DHDSC), with sales of $1.7 billion, operated Dayton's and Hudson's traditional department stores in seven midwestern states. Target, an upscale discount department store chain, offered a broad assortment of hard and soft goods, and had achieved sales of $6.3 billion. Mervyn's, a highly promotional department store operation, with sales of $3.4 billion, sold lower- to moderate-priced merchandise and featured apparel, accessories and household softgoods. Lechmere, a competitively priced large store format retailer with sales of $800 million, sold

Marian Kremer, MBA '89, prepared this case under the supervision of Professor Walter J. Salmon as the basis for class discussion rather than to illustrate either effective or ineffective handling of an administrative situation.

major appliances, televisions, and audio equipment as well as small appliances and a variety of additional hard goods lines.

Dayton Hudson over the past ten years had divested a number of businesses that did not meet the corporate hurdle rate for pretax return on invested capital. These included bookstores (B. Dalton), jewelry stores, and department stores geographically not contiguous with DHDSC, and some new retail concepts that were also inconsistent with the company's long-term strategy.

From the late 1970s to mid-1980s Mervyn's and Target were the primary recipients of capital funds because they offered the greatest growth potential. Target had continued to be the recipient of the majority of funding but recent troubles at Mervyn's had resulted in at least a temporary diminution in the rate of investment in that business. Concurrently, the recent improvement in the performance of the traditional department stores had enhanced their future eligibility for more capital investment. **Exhibit 2** provides selected summary statistics of Dayton Hudson's divisional and corporate performance.

DHDSC STRATEGY

DHDSC consisted of 20 Hudson's stores in Indiana, Michigan, and Ohio and 17 Dayton's stores in Minnesota, North Dakota, South Dakota, and Wisconsin. **Exhibit 3** provides historical data on the number and size of stores as well as selected operating data. Both department stores offered a broad selection of moderate-to upper-priced merchandise. Relative to many other department stores, DHDSC has retained greater emphasis on certain departments such as furniture, floor coverings, and men's clothing. Both Dayton's and Hudson's had unusually dominant shares of local department store sales as well as a much stronger than average share of general merchandise, apparel, and furniture and appliance (GAF) sales in their respective markets.

Although both stores had retained their names, the two operations had been combined organizationally in 1984 to form DHDSC. Buying, finance, logistics, and advertising departments and more recently, credit operations, were consolidated.

Over the past few years DHDSC has increased its emphasis on customer service. In 1986 DHDSC began rolling out Performance Plus (PP), a major program aimed at improving customer service. By the end of 1989, PP was to be implemented in stores and departments which represented 66% of DHDSC sales. Under PP, the store organization and compensation system were restructured to provide employees with greater training, more career advancement opportunities, and the potential for increased pay. For example, most DHDSC salespeople, termed sales consultants, typically had earned in the $10,000 to $12,000 range and, with greater productivity, now earned under Performance Plus up to $18,000 to $22,000. In addition, under PP, awards were given at storewide sales meetings, often characterized as "pep rallies," to store employees with outstanding sales records. Management viewed PP as much more than a change in the compensation system. They believed PP had changed the "mind-set" of many of its employees, resulting in a greater customer orientation and an increased level of commitment to the company. In addition to PP, another major element of DHDSC's strategy was to be a leader in trend merchandising by offering customers "the latest and most wanted items."

DHDSC was also involved in efforts to change its approach to pricing. There were two elements to this effort. One involved a gradual reduction in the number of storewide promotional events. The second was the introduction of "ValuePlus," which offered consumers selected merchandise at everyday low prices. Management believed that ValuePlus, which represented 4% of all merchandise sold, generally worked most effectively on nationally branded items such as Fieldcrest towels because "customers could more easily recognize the value and quality of such names."

DHDSC CULTURE AND ORGANIZATION

Management viewed its strong, supportive culture as one of its greatest assets. At the heart of this culture was an energetic belief in maintaining a sense of teamwork, trust, and honesty, and a tradition of emphasizing the value and potential of employees. This tradition was reflected in the importance placed on the recruiting, development, and training of employees and, in most cases, promotion from within. Employee turnover was considerably less than at other large department stores. Management attributed this low turnover to a challenging and rewarding but "noncutthroat" environment.

Reporting directly to Steve Watson, chairman and CEO of DHDSC, were the following areas: Merchandise, Planning and Distribution, Stores, Marketing, Public Affairs, Human Resources, and Visual Presentation. The vice chairman also reported directly to the CEO. Reporting to the vice chairman were Finance, Operations, Properties, and MIS. A DHDSC organizational chart is shown in **Exhibit 4**.

Buyers reported to divisional merchandising managers (DMMs) who reported to general merchandise managers (GMMs) who, in turn, reported to the two senior merchants who reported directly to Watson. Buyers were evaluated on a number of measures. Achievement of sales, gross margin, turnover, and shortage objectives represented approximately 45 to 55 points of a 100-point evaluation scale. Objectives that were individually agreed upon between the buyer and his or her DMM accounted for another 25 to 35 points of the scale. Developing trend merchandise, negotiating better terms with vendors, and improving communication skills were examples of such objectives. The remaining 20 to 30 points of the evaluation scale were awarded for improvement of human relations and organizational skills. Compensation for buyers ranged from $38,000 to $70,000 annually. Management estimated that, on average, its buyers had 3 to 5 years of experience as buyers and spent up to four years in a particular departmental assignment. Buyers worked closely with the store executives who retained responsibility for their individual sales, the allocation of display space, and merchandise presentation.

The buyers also worked closely with individuals within the planning and distribution function. Distributors were responsible for informing buyers of the needs of individual stores and assisting them in allocating merchandise among the stores. Each divisional merchandise manager had a counterpart called a head planner to which the distributors that worked with the buyers in each merchandise division reported. The head planners reported, in turn, to the director of planning and distribution, who was on the same organizational level as the general merchandise manager.

GENERAL PRIVATE LABEL ISSUES

Retailers were confronted with a number of issues and challenges when they used private label. Good value for the consumer, higher margins, and exclusive merchandise were the attractions of private label. There were also, however, a number of problems or, at least, potential problems. With private label, retailers did not receive from vendors cooperative advertising allowances, markdown dollars, or the privilege of returning goods. The willingness of branded suppliers to offer such inducements varied by classification and vendor.

In addition, long lead times were often required to procure private label merchandise. These lead times, frequently 3–6 months longer than in the procurement of branded merchandise, required buyers to make early commitments and thereby increased the risk of markdowns.

Private label also required significant minimum quantity commitments for each private label product, and often larger individual orders to permit production of economic lot sizes. The consequence was typically larger inventories in relation to sales.

In addition, sourcing private label from abroad often proved risky because of fluctuating exchange rates, volatile political conditions, uncertain availability of import quotas, and quota surcharges. Quotas, or import limits in units of product, were determined annually by negotiation between the United States and individual supplier countries. A risk in purchasing merchandise for which there was a quota was the possibility of the retailer-owned goods being embargoed if the country's quota had been exhausted by the time the merchandise reached the port of entry. Furthermore, suppliers in countries which had nearly exhausted their quotas would often add substantial surcharges to their selling prices. To ensure continuity of supply many manufacturers (and some American retailers) were known to have purchased or "locked up" quotas in particular countries.

Another issue was that many department store buyers were not adequately trained in private label design and procurement. Buyers were often inexperienced regarding knowledge of product construction, materials, quality control, and vendor selection as well as scheduling, tracking, and costing of product. Given the high buyer turnover in the industry, retailers favoring private label were faced with the challenge of developing continuity of in-house knowledge in particular departments.

Recent Private Label Trends

The importance of private label to particular retail channels had shifted in recent years. Private label had gained share in traditional department and specialty stores but lost share in some national chains, such as Sears and JCPenney (see **Exhibit 5**). Nevertheless, more than 500 private label brands were identified by the KSA/NPD consumer purchase panel in 1988, more than double the number five years earlier.[1]

---

1 The Kurt Salmon Associates National Product Diary purchase panel consisted of 19,500 households.

Department stores had enhanced the role of private label in their merchandise assortment for several reasons. They wanted to differentiate their assortments from merchandise carried in other department and specialty stores, and, most particularly, off-price retailers. The latter now represented over 6% of total apparel sales and offered consumers savings of 20% or more on department store quality apparel.[2]

Second, department store interest in private label had been stimulated by the establishment of owned or franchised retail stores by certain manufacturers with strong consumer recognition such as Ralph Lauren, Laura Ashley, Coach, Benetton, and Burberry. These stores competed directly with the department stores themselves. Additionally, private label allowed retailers to fill unique merchandise needs in their individual marketplaces not met by branded manufacturers. Moreover, stores with considerable upscale appeal such as Bergdorf Goodman, Neiman Marcus, and Saks Fifth Avenue discovered that selling their own brand name often carried as much cachet as the branded merchandise of many lesser known designers.

Enthusiasm for private label among department stores, however, was not limitless. Macy's, which had one of the most aggressive private label programs among department stores, had recently reduced its private label emphasis when a substantial amount of private label merchandise, both classic and trendy, had not sold as well as anticipated.

Many specialty retailers had been extremely successful with private label as the foundation of their strategy. Over 70% of The Limited's merchandise was private label, and its Forenza private label was the #2 best-selling national brand of women's apparel behind Liz Claiborne. At The Gap, Levi's jeans were the only exception to an all private label offering. Because these retailers had narrowly defined target markets, they had been able to concentrate their private label design and procurement activities on a limited range of styles. Also, their volumes had enabled them to obtain excellent prices from manufacturers. Furthermore, their sophisticated information systems had allowed them to respond to trends more quickly as well as reduce order lead times and inventories. Finally, specialty retailers had also leveraged their private label brands by building cohesiveness between their merchandise and retail presentation.

In contrast, such retailers as JCPenney and Sears, and, in food retailing, Kroger and Safeway, had departed from a total or strongly private label-oriented focus. JCPenney's and Sears' private label apparel had allegedly become "dull," in part, because they tried to appeal to a broad customer base. Sears and JCPenney, however, have recently developed private labels with more "panache" (e.g. Halston for JCPenney) and added more national brands in order to give customers better selections in both private label and branded merchandise.

A partial explanation for more emphasis on national brands among certain food retailers may be their emerging thinking about item profitability. For years, they looked mainly at gross margin to measure item profitability. Direct product profitability (DPP), which measures item contribution per unit of selling space to fixed cost and profit, has been gaining acceptance in the food industry. DPP factors in not only gross margin, but differences in sales volume, inventory turnover, handling costs, trade promotion support, and credit terms from suppliers in measuring item profitability. This new yardstick of profitability may have encouraged food retailers to place greater emphasis on national brands.

Dayton Hudson Private Label Brands

In order to capitalize on the popularity of L.L. Bean-type products, in 1981 Dayton's Department Store created the Boundary Waters private label. The Boundary Waters label was used on authentic outdoor apparel and casual clothing for the entire family as well as housewares, sporting goods, and specialty foods. This merchandise could be found both in its usual departmental setting and in free-standing in-store Boundary Waters boutiques sometimes called "in-store outposts." Boundary Waters had become a strong, well-recognized brand name. **Exhibit 6** shows that Boundary Waters had aided awareness of 93% among Dayton's and 77% among Hudson's customers (Boundary Waters was not introduced into Hudson's stores until 1984).

Exhibit 7 gives a brief description of the ten private label brands at DHDSC. **Exhibit 8** shows their suggested product category usage. These labels stood for a lifestyle, a merchandise classification, a price line or seasonal merchandise. Their descriptions, as derived from a private label manual, are shown on page 2-182.

---

2 Kurt Salmon Associates.

Life-Style: The *Boundary Waters* label products were geared to the casual or active life-style and covered numerous merchandise classifications. Other brands such as *Woodward* and *Circle Square* were targeted to customers interested in traditional, conservative dressing in particular price ranges. Both the *Magnet* and *ICE* labels were geared to those who desired trendy merchandise. Magnet was generally targeted to juniors, and ICE was geared to a more fashion-forward, higher priced segment.

Classification: This type of private label included *Stork Club*—baby items and gifts; *Marketplace*—food products, food preparation, and casual entertainment items; and *Today/Tonight*—women's intimate apparel.

Price Class: The *Oval Room* label was used for women's apparel, shoes, and handbags offered at better prices.

Seasonal: *Santabear*, which had originated as a purchase-with-purchase stuffed bear for Christmas, had inspired the development of a Santabear line of Christmas private label merchandise in a number of product categories.[3]

During the mid-1980s management had strongly encouraged many private label programs, but private label had failed to meet expectations in a number of departments. Problems with design and manufacturing resulted in many items of poor quality. These problems were attributed to lack of experience among some buyers and the absence of appropriate "checkpoints" for procuring large amounts of private label merchandise. In addition, management had encouraged the creation of private label for "themed" events such as an "acorn" logo theme for Boundary Waters fall merchandise sold in freestanding in-store boutiques. Unfortunately, there were several inappropriate applications of this "themed" merchandise such as acorn "themed" cashmere sweaters.

In addition, the company had created a multiplicity of private labels which were not used consistently across classifications. Consequently, customers became confused about what particular labels denoted. DHDSC's response to the several private label problems which had arisen was to pare the number of labels to 10 and give the buyers responsibility to designate how much private label merchandise should be included in their departments. According to Steve Watson:

Currently, there is no DHDSC private label goal as a percent of sales. Private label is uneven by area on purpose; we allow it to seek its own level. The DMMs and buyers determine what should be the optimal mix of branded and private label in their own areas. Our philosophy is, however, that private label merchandise should be priced below equivalent national brands but be of at least equivalent quality.

Since DHDSC did not separately track private label merchandise, senior management was uncertain about the exact level of private label sales. They estimated, however, that private label constituted about 10% of sales in 1988 and had ranged from 10% to 15% of sales in recent years.

DHDSC Private Label Procedures

Several years ago there had been a committee of senior managers who had determined the characteristics of products which could use particular private labels. Currently, if a buyer recommended use of a new private label, it was Steve Watson's responsibility to approve it, for which he sought the advice of the vice president of Trend Merchandising. Known in other department stores as the fashion director, this vice president, who reported to the Senior Vice President, Marketing, had the Product Design department reporting to her. A buyer who wanted to use an existing label was supposed to contact and receive approval from this department.

Katherine McGraw, manager of Product Design, asserted that on many occasions, buyers used a private label without asking for approval. She also said that it was extremely uncommon to reject a buyer's request to use an existing label. McGraw also acknowledged that sometimes "DHDSC private labels were used on products somewhat inconsistent with the private label's image."

For example, the hosiery buyer used the Woodward label (considered a better traditional/conservative label) for private label hosiery and dancewear but dancewear consisted primarily of brightly colored, fashion-forward designs. The buyer realized that Woodward was less than the ideal label for trendy dancewear, but did not believe that any of the other DHDSC private labels were entirely appropriate either.

---

3 In 1987, retail sales of Santabear had reached $9 million. Because of a concern that Santabear was supplanting sales of other merchandise, the scope of the Santabear program was curtailed. Sales in 1988 were only $3 million.

Another example involved the choice of a label for a new men's sock. The buyer in men's socks introduced an orlon, moderately priced private label sock under the Woodward brand rather than under the suggested Circle Square label which had been designated as the name for traditional private label merchandise at moderate prices. The buyer currently used both Boundary Waters for rag wool socks and Woodward for 100% wool socks labels and hesitated to introduce a third private label in his department.

Measures were taken, however, to prevent or correct certain "misuses" of private label names. For instance, the Boundary Waters label was removed from ties since ties were considered inconsistent with the label's "casual, rugged and active" image.

Some DHDSC executives questioned whether the current set of labels was comprehensive enough to cover the needs of all departments. The question led to the issue of the range of merchandise, by life-style, classification, and price class which should be included under a single private label designation. Sears' "Kenmore" brand for major appliances, and "Craftsman" for hardware, for example, were restricted by product category but, within each category covered widely varying "good," "better," and "best" price points. The Limited's "Hunter's Run" and "Forenza," on the other hand, reflected life-style labeling within a limited price range. McGraw wondered what combination of labels would cover all of DHDSC's needs and still allow sufficient support for each private label so that it achieved consumer recognition, acceptance, or preference.

The Product Design and Advertising staffs worked closely with the buyers to plan companywide private label advertising and promotions. Past efforts which had often been funded from the Advertising department's budget rather than from individual department budgets, included magazine and newspaper ads, direct mail catalogues, in-store promotional pieces, and shopping bags. **Exhibit 9** shows an ad sponsored by the Advertising department promoting Santabear merchandise.

Santabear, Boundary Waters and Woodward had been the recipients of most companywide private label campaigns while lesser known labels such as ICE or Magnet were almost never promoted across departments. Classification-driven labels—i.e., Marketplace, Stork Club, and Today/Tonight were generally promoted from departmental budgets. The magnitude of companywide private label advertising efforts had declined substantially in the past two years in favor of programs to promote trendmerchandise.

Coordination and communication from the buyers and headquarters staff departments to the stores as well as store "buy in" were considered critical to the success of private label. For example, a store needed to allocate "key item space" for private label for in-store outposts and ensure dominant private label assortments within these outposts. In some instances, management believed private label programs and promotions had not reached expectations because inadequate coordination with the stores had resulted in a lack of strong in-store support.

An example of this problem arose when the Today/Tonight intimate apparel program and label were introduced. Product design had developed distinctive signs, shopping bags, tissues, etc., in order to create a "total specialty store environment similar to a Victoria's Secret." The GMM of women's intimate apparel, however, argued that the lingerie department had insufficient funds for this effort and that the stores should assume these expenses. Rather than fund it themselves, the stores continued to use the regular DHDSC bags and tissues.

Also critical to the success of its private label program, according to management, was the role of the Associated Merchandising Corporation (AMC), a buying organization headquartered in New York cooperatively owned by a number of department store companies that assisted buyers from DHDSC and other department stores in procuring private label merchandise. AMC, which had offices or representatives in large supplier countries around the world, sourced private label products for its clients, negotiated prices and ship dates, monitored production schedules and quality control, and tracked transportation, quota availability, and customs clearance. Departments had historically been charged an AMC processing fee, which was currently 1.65% of the factory cost of AMC- sourced private label merchandise, for inspection costs, and payment of the letter of credit. DHDSC had absorbed all other AMC private label-related charges without allocating these costs to the individual departments. To account better for the costs of private label, management decided to allocate the balance of AMC private label fees among departments which used its services. Effective May 1989, there would be an additional charge of 5.95% of the factory cost of all AMC private label merchandise which covered the balance of AMC services except for product design. A third fee of 1.6% of factory cost would be assessed if buyers purchased private label merchandise designed by AMC rather than by DHDSC buyers.

DHDSC Private Label Practices

As a result of the decentralization of responsibility for private label programs, DHDSC's private label activities varied substantially among departments. In fact, not all buyers separately summarized their private label sales. The variations included not only differences in the emphasis on private label but also differences in such matters as pricing, promotion, and display.

For example, as shown below in **Table A**, the men's undergarment buyer used Woodward as the label for opening price point briefs while a neighboring department used the Woodward label for its upper moderate price point men's dress shirts. Some buyers extensively used private label for DHDSC's ValuePlus program, which often offered starting price point merchandise at everyday low prices. Other buyers chose to sell private label at higher everyday prices but to reduce prices for a number of sale events.

Table A
Men's Undergarments

	Woodward	Munsingwear	Jockey	Christian Dior	Calvin Klein
100% cotton classic briefs—retail price	$11.50 (3-pack)	$13.00 (3-pack)	$13.50 (3-pack)	$13.00 (3-pack)	$15.50 (3-pack)
100% cotton full-cut solid boxers—retail price	$10.00[a]	$14.00 (50% poly/50% cotton, 3-pack)	$7.50	$8.00 (tapered)	$7.50

Men's Dress Shirts

	Woodward	Arrow	Geoffrey Beene	Christian Dior	Eagle
Poly/cotton solid men's dress shirt—retail price	$26.50	$25.00	$29.50	$32.50	[b]
100% cotton solid pinpoint Oxford—retail price	$39.50	[b]	[b]	[b]	$56.00

a Woodward boxers were offered in a broadcloth, a thicker, often more expensive fabric.
b Not sold at DHDSC.

Generally private label was not prominently displayed but there were exceptions. For example, in Marketplace, which was the name of the housewares department, as well as the designation of much of its private label merchandise, this merchandise was prominently displayed.

"Signing" for private label merchandise was another practice which varied substantially among departments. Only a few signs were apparent in the downtown Minneapolis flagship store which highlighted the features (i.e., quality, value, fashion) of private label brands. In this respect, the practice in private label adhered to general company policy which only used signs to draw attention to very well known brand names.

In order to understand better the varying uses of private label at DHDSC, the case writer talked with several buyers.

WOMEN'S MODERATES

Jocelyn Anderson was senior buyer of the Women's Moderate Sportswear department. Her 1988 departmental sales were $26 million, of which approximately 25% was private label. The Boundary Waters label was used for casual wear and Circle Square for career separates. Anderson said her private label merchandise filled two primary roles: (1) to give the customer needed product not supplied by current branded vendors, and (2) to offer private label at very low prices versus branded goods.

Twill skirts were an example of an unmet need. This department carried a 100% cotton Jordache twill skirt. Jocelyn introduced a similar polyester/cotton blend Boundary Waters twill skirt which was slightly longer in length. According to Jocelyn, she had introduced the blended private label item because many of her customers wanted (1) a blended product which was easier to care for, and (2) a little longer skirt to cover more of the leg. Anderson said that the Jordache and Boundary Waters skirts were comparable in make but the latter was significantly cheaper at cost and retail. The Jordache skirt cost $16.50 and retailed for $36.00 while the Boundary Waters skirt, cost $13.35 (exclusive of certain costs associated with private label procurement) and retailed for $30.00. According to Anderson:

> As a buyer of private label, I understand my customer, and I know she expects quality, value, and consistency. I begin with shopping the piece goods market. I check for consistent quality of fabric and have suppliers quote prices with strict standards, for instance, of fabric weight. And, if I "knock off" an item, I don't cut corners. I make sure that the vendor develops a product with the extra stitching, the same high quality buttons, zippers, etc. In addition, I use private label produced domestically versus overseas when speed and flexibility are important, fashion risk is high, or when there is no overseas supply.

Anderson priced private label generally 10% to 30% less than comparable national brands and often used it for opening price point apparel, which she sometimes designated as ValuePlus. Private label merchandise was plentiful and mixed in with the national brands. Anderson promoted private label during the three major storewide sales events and during monthly one- to two-day sales. Anderson estimated that 30% of private label and 35% of branded merchandise was sold on promotion. She also estimated that she spent 20% of her time working on private label. **Exhibit 10** provides an example of a comparable nationally branded and private label item—twill shorts.

According to Liz Williams, DMM for this department, "A sportswear buyer who sources basic or updated private label goods needs good visual abilities and solid design skills. Excellent design skills, however, are a prerequisite for fashion-forward merchandise."

Williams added that "plum assignments, additional administrative support, and higher pay within their pay scale are often essential to retain those buyers with excellent design skills." Since Anderson had been a buyer for over 10 years, with the past 3½ years in her current department, Williams believed that Anderson had acquired the necessary skills.

MEN'S DRESS SHIRTS

Men's dress shirts was a $21 million business at DHDSC, of which approximately 30% was private label, all under the Woodward label. John Rabson, senior buyer for Men's Dress Shirts, viewed the role of private label at DHDSC as: (1) providing customers with excellent quality merchandise in the upper moderate range, (2) creating exclusivity with the "trusted" Woodward label, and (3) developing products that capitalized on fashion trends.

In comparison to shirts in the upper moderate price range, Woodward shirts had additional features that were tailored to DHDSC customer needs. Examples included cutting extra room in the body of the shirt and sleeves, providing longer shirt tails, using finer fabrics, and finishing with more durable buttons. Rabson believed that customers trusted the Woodward name for shirts because quality was extremely consistent, unlike some national brands which sourced from numerous vendors in the United States and abroad.

Part of DHDSC's success in private label shirts had come from styles with features such as tab or spread collars inspired by higher-priced, fashion-forward, branded merchandise. These private label products were priced somewhat lower than their branded counterparts. Rabson believed, however, that there would be too much financial risk and not enough in-house design talent if he tried to push private label shirts beyond one-third of total sales. Furthermore, since private label products had to be designed 16 months prior to the start of the selling season, and ordered 3 to 6 months in advance of branded goods, limiting private label sales to about one-third of the total kept adequate flexibility in future inventory commitments.

Since Woodward shirts, like Geoffrey Beene and Yves Saint Laurent, were priced in the upper moderate price range, Rabson used Arrow for his opening price point merchandise. **Exhibit 11** compares the economics of a private label to a similar nationally branded item.

John promoted Woodward and national brands at approximately 25% off regular price about 36 to 40 days a year. Over 50% of both private label and branded merchandise was sold during these promotions. The case writer asked if he had considered everyday low pricing in this department. Rabson responded that promotions "drove" the men's dress shirt business and helped generate traffic and incremental business throughout the store. (For perspective, a Pinpoint Oxford in the Land End's mail-order catalogue was priced at an everyday low price of $33.50 plus $3.50 for handling and delivery per order while the regular price of the Woodward Pinpoint Oxford was $39.50 with periodic sales at 25% off.) Rabson and many of his salespeople strongly believed that dress shirt volume would drop sharply if he switched to everyday low prices.

John had been a buyer of men's dress shirts for approximately 20 years. He estimated that he spent approximately 50% of his time working on private label.

HOUSEWARES

In housewares, "Marketplace" was created to provide a specialty store atmosphere within DHDSC, similar in some respects to a combination of such specialty stores as Williams Sonoma and Crate & Barrel. Shopping bags and employees wearing "Marketplace" aprons reinforced the department's image. Marketplace was also used as a private label name in this department for food, food preparation, cookware, casual entertainment, and closet accessory items. The Marketplace brand, according to the department's several buyers, had consumer acceptance comparable to a number of well-known national brands. Private label accounted for approximately one-sixth of Marketplace's sales (excluding small electronics for which there was no private label merchandise).

Private label was used for various purposes in Marketplace. Marketplace high-quality private label plastic picnic cups with decorative designs filled a niche unexploited by branded manufacturers. These picnic cups were attractively and dominantly displayed. In storage and organization, which included closet accessories, a rather small product category, Marketplace was the only "brand" carried, since volume would not justify multiple brands. Marketplace cookware was used to create exclusive, distinctively designed products and deliver higher margins. It was more advanced in styling than comparable brands and similar in such characteristics as thickness, weight, etc.

Cookware was a heavily promoted category because well-known brands such as Farberware and Revere were sold by mass merchandisers as well as department stores. Regular and sales prices of Marketplace merchandise were slightly higher than were prices for Farberware and Revere. Karen Dodge, senior buyer for cookware, bakeware, and closet items, promoted branded and private label cookware at 20% to 25% off during frequent sale events. Over 70% of Revere and Farberware and 50% of Marketplace cookware was sold at reduced prices. **Exhibit 12** compares the economics of Marketplace to Farberware and Revere cookware.

In contrast to cookware, certain Marketplace bakeware items such as cookie sheets were offered at opening price points while national brands were slightly higher priced. Marketplace cookie sheets, however, were not priced on a ValuePlus basis although this approach to pricing was used for other private label and national branded items in the department.

Sales of the merchandise categories for which Karen Dodge was responsible were $13 million in 1988. In the last eight years, private label sales had risen from virtually zero to 30% of this total. Karen had been a buyer for over 10 years, seven of which were in Marketplace. She estimated she spent 20% of her time on private label.

LOOKING AHEAD

Watson and Stirratt reflected upon the private label programs at DHDSC, which they believed had, in recent years, generally met their expectations. An examination had, however, surfaced certain possible improvement opportunities. Watson and Stirratt realized that there were trade-offs in establishing additional guidelines and policies for private label. Their interest was in arriving at an optimal private label strategy.

Exhibit 1
Examples of Boundary Waters Merchandise

Exhibit 2
Dayton Hudson Divisional Operating Sales and Profits ($ millions)

	1988	1987	1986	1985	1984	1983
Sales						
DHDSC	$ 1,693	$ 1,552	$1,566	$1,448	$1,548[a]	$1,484[a]
Target	6,331	5,306	4,355	3,931	3,550	3,118
Mervyn's	3,411	3,183	2,862	2,527	2,141	1,689
Lechmere	769	636	476	349	280	227
Total	$12,204	$10,677	$9,259	$8,255	$7,519	$6,518
Operating Profit						
DHDSC	$ 159	$ 122	$ 166	$ 122	$ 107	$ 156
Target	341	323	311	278	236	177
Mervyn's	256	150	160	245	223	184
Lechmere	22	23	20	20	20	19
Total	$ 778	$ 618	$ 657	$ 665	$ 586	$ 536
Depreciation						
DHDSC	$ 33	$ 30	28	$ 27	$ 32	$ 33
Target	146	103	76	70	66	56
Mervyn's	91	82	68	54	43	30
Lechmere	15	11	8	5	3	2
Total	$ 285	$ 226	$ 180	$ 156	$ 144	$ 121
Assets						
DHDSC	$ 808	$ 761	$ 739	$ 738	$ 727	$ 863
Target	2,982	2,638	2,179	1,519	1,375	1,258
Mervyn's	2,166	2,114	1,817	1,615	1,329	1,064
Lechmere	484	431	317	210	151	105
Total	$ 6,440	$ 5,944	$5,052	$4,082	$3,582	$3,290
Capital Expenditures						
DHDSC	$ 31	$ 49	$ 31	$ 37	$ 33	$ 27
Target	457	501	598	138	110	143
Mervyn's	154	207	243	177	165	138
Lechmere	32	72	49	42	25	6
Total	$ 674	$ 829	$ 921	$ 394	$ 333	$ 314
Net Earnings from Continuing Operations	$ 287	$ 228	$ 256	$ 281	$ 259	$ 245
Net Earnings	$ 287	$ 228	$ 310	$ 284	$ 259	$ 245

a Department stores included Diamonds and John A. Brown stores through September 29, 1984.

Source: Dayton Hudson annual reports.

Exhibit 3
DHDSC Selected Operating Data for Comparable Store Sales

	Number of Stores	Average Square Foot (thousands)	Sales			Operating Profit			
			Amount ($ millions)	% Increase	Per Average Square Foot	Amount ($millions)	% Increase	% of Sales	Per Average Square Foot
1979	31	8,569	$1,009	3.1%	$118	$ 94.8	(7.2%)	9.4%	$11
1980	34	8,796	1,024	1.4	116	85.3	(10.0)	8.3	10
1981	35	8,739	1,068	4.4	122	83.7	(1.9)	7.8	10
1982	35	8,190	1,121	5.0	137	110.2	31.7	9.8	13
1983	36	7,934	1,242	10.8	157	146.7	33.1	11.8	15
1984	36	7,940	1,396	12.4	176	106.7	(27.3)	7.6	13
1985	37	7,904	1,448	3.7	183	121.8	14.2	8.4	15
1986	37	7,848	1,566	8.2	200	165.8	36.1	10.6	21
1987	37	7,791	1,552	(0.9)	199	122.4	(26.2)	7.9	16
1988	37	7,796	1,693	9.0	217	159.0	27.4	9.2	20

Source: Dayton Hudson annual reports and Goldman Sachs research.

Exhibit 4
Organizational Chart

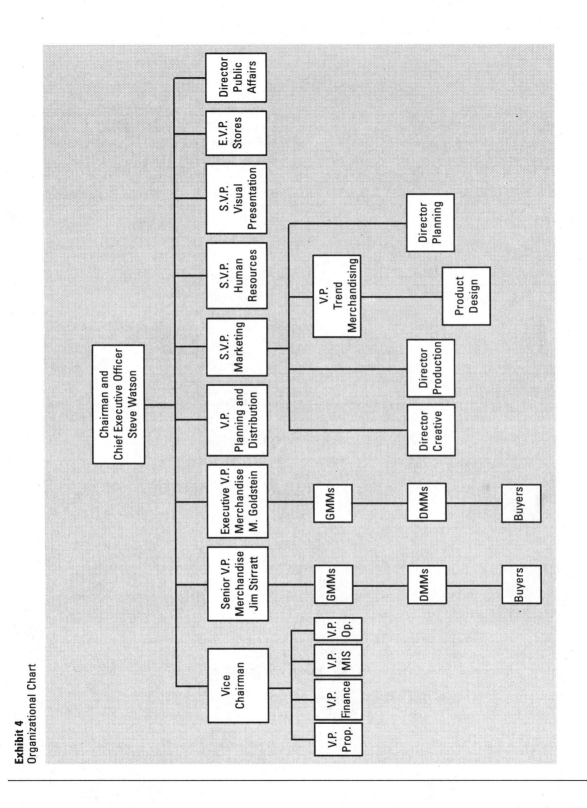

Exhibit 5
Shifts in Retail Shares of Total Private Label Apparel

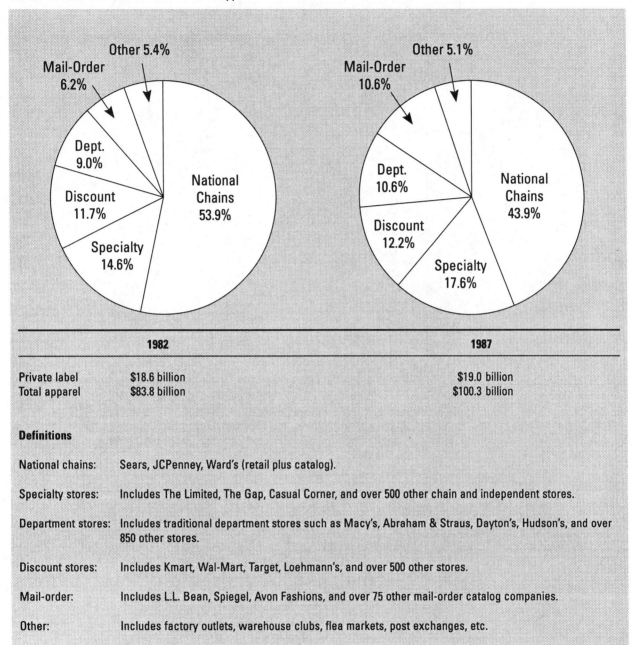

	1982	1987
Private label	$18.6 billion	$19.0 billion
Total apparel	$83.8 billion	$100.3 billion

Definitions

National chains: Sears, JCPenney, Ward's (retail plus catalog).

Specialty stores: Includes The Limited, The Gap, Casual Corner, and over 500 other chain and independent stores.

Department stores: Includes traditional department stores such as Macy's, Abraham & Straus, Dayton's, Hudson's, and over 850 other stores.

Discount stores: Includes Kmart, Wal-Mart, Target, Loehmann's, and over 500 other stores.

Mail-order: Includes L.L. Bean, Spiegel, Avon Fashions, and over 75 other mail-order catalog companies.

Other: Includes factory outlets, warehouse clubs, flea markets, post exchanges, etc.

Source: KSA/NPD Purchase Panel; dollar purchases reported by 19,500-member demographically representative consumer panel.

Exhibit 6
1986 DHDSC In-Store Survey[a] (percentage of DHDSC customers aware of selected "brands")[b]

	DHDSC Private Label Brands							National Brands				
	Boundary Waters	Woodward	Summit Hill[c]	Oval Room	ICE	Magnet	Stork Club	Liz Claiborne	Esprit	OshKosh	Gant	Generra
Dayton's	93%	38%	51%	45%	19%	15%	22%	85%	75%	68%	44%	35%
Hudson's	77	65	45	19	16	11	11	86	66	63	36	26

a Questionnaire distributed to customers while shopping at Dayton's and Hudson's.
b "Brand" names were listed on the questionnaire, and therefore, figures represent aided awareness of selected brands.
c Former DHDSC label which has essentially been replaced by the Circle Square label.

DHDSC Private Labels

Each label has a built-in appeal for a certain market segment of our customer base, ranging from traditional to fashion-forward, encompassing moderate and better price ranges.

Boundary Waters Products geared to a casual or active life-style. Outdoor themes in women's, men's, and children's ready-to-wear, accessories, shoes, home items, and gifts.

Woodward Traditional styling with classic appeal in all classifications, from women's and men's apparel, accessories and shoes to home furnishings.

Magnet Merchandise for juniors, young men, and children who want trend-right apparel, accessories, shoes, and home furnishings.

ICE Latest looks. Hottest trends. Upper moderate prices for advanced, fashion-forward customers in men's and women's apparel, accessories, and shoes.

Oval Room Women's career separates and suits, casual sportswear, handbags, and shoes. Emphasis on quality fabrication and design detail.

Today/Tonight All women's intimate apparel, from casual daywear and lingerie to fine sleepwear and accessories.

Stork Club Infants' merchandise. Emphasis on giftable items for the newborn.

Marketplace Products for food and food preparation and casual entertainment, including cookware, bakeware, serveware, and storage and organization products.

Circle Square Men's and women's updated traditional apparel and accessories within a moderate price range.

Santabear Wide variety of 4th quarter merchandise including bed and bath, tabletop, Marketplace, stationery, confections, women's, men's, and children's ready-to-wear, intimate apparel, trim the home, and toys.

Exhibit 8
Suggested Private Label Usage by Department—1989 DHDSC Product Development Manual (private labels)

Label	Boundary Waters	Woodward	Magnet	ICE	Oval Room	Today/ Tonight	Stork Club	Circle Square	Market- place
Men's									
Tailored:									
Updated				X					
Traditional		X							
Furnishings		X							
Accessories		X							
Gloves:									
Dress		X							
Sport	X								
Sportswear:									
Updated traditional	X	X							
Advanced & updated				X					
Young men's	X		X						
Outerwear	X	X							
Women's									
Oval Room					X				
Sportswear:									
Updated traditional	X	X						X	
Advanced & updated				X					
Active	X								
Juniors'			X						
Dresses/Suits:									
Updated traditional		X						X	
Advanced & updated				X					
Coats:									
Updated traditional		X						X	
Sport	X								
Juniors'			X						

Label	Boundary Waters	Woodward	Magnet	ICE	Oval Room	Today/ Tonight	Stork Club	Circle Square	Market-place
Special sizes	X	X							
Accessories		X			X				
Shoes:									
Designer					X				
Updated traditional		X						X	
Advanced & updated				X					
Juniors'			X						
Sport, boots	X								
Intimate apparel						X			
Children's									
Infants'							X		
Toddlers'	X								
Boys' 4–7	X								
Girls' 4–6X	X								
Boys' 8–20	X		X						
Girls' 7–14	X		X						
Pre-teen	X		X						
Accessories & furnishings	X								
Home									
Electronics				X					
Tabletop	X	X							
Home accents	X	X							
Stationery	X	X	X						
Bed & bath	X	X							
Marketplace	X							X	X
Furniture									

Exhibit 9
Advertisement for Santabear Merchandise

Santa's workshop was alive with the sights and sounds of hard-working elves. All busily preparing for the big day, while Santabear and his friends made music to help the time go by. Santa Claus watched his helpers tuning and tinkering with the many toys. But something bothered Santa...

"Toys break and are often lost," he thought. "There must be a gift that will give lasting happiness."

As Santa pondered this problem, he heard the music rise louder and louder above the rhythm of hammers and saws. Santabear, Miss Bear, Captain Jingle and Sneakers the Mouse were all playing wonderful music, making everyone happy. "Of course!" shouted Santa. "Music will be that special gift!"

Santa gathered the helpers to explain his idea of taking the music all over the world. And so they became the Polar Club Band and began their World Tour. Come along, they need your help to travel from place to place and page to page.

2A. Soft velour coverall with Santabear applique. Back snaps. Polyester/cotton in 3-9 mos. and 12-24 mos. Made in U.S.A. **$30.** Infants

2B. Choice of plush animals, each with ceramic mug to match: Miss Bear and Santabear. Also available, Bully Bear, Captain Jingle, Sneakers the Mouse. **$6 each.** Marketplace™

2C. Santabear and His Polar Club membership rally! Each comes with a booklet and official Polar Club membership card. Plush toys: 13" Sneakers the Mouse, 17" Captain Jingle, the penguin; and 12" Bully Bear, reg. 14.98, **sale 11.99.**

2D. Santabear and Miss Bear long sleeve P.J. in red cotton/polyester. S-M-L. Made in U.S.A. **$26.** Intimate Apparel

2E. Santabear flannel twin sheet set, with twin flat and fitted sheets, 1 std. case, all 100% cotton flannel. Imported. Reg. $38, **sale 28.99.** Matching comforter, twin size, reg. $88, **sale 69.99.** Bed and Bath

2F. Miss Bear puppet, reg. 14.98, **sale 11.99.** Exclusively ours. Plush Toys and Trim the Home

2G. Christmas Tree sweatshirt asks you to help Santabear and Miss Bear decorate their tree. Ink bottle is included. M-L-XL. White cotton/polyester. Made in U.S.A. **$22.** Stationery

3A. 5-pc. Santabear melamine set. Plate, bowl, mug, fork and spoon. **11.99.** Marketplace™

3B. Santabear and Miss Bear string bikini. S-M-L. 100% cotton. Imported. **$4.** Intimate Apparel

3C. Santabear boxers. 100% cotton. Imported. S-M-L. **$4.50.** Men's Underwear

3D. Santabear cookie tin filled with cookies. **10.95.** Marketplace™ Foods

3E. Santabear and His Polar Club ceramic cookie jar. **$20.** Marketplace™

2F. Sleep 'N' Play stretchie for infants 12-24 mos., 100% polyester, made in U.S.A. **$15.** Infants

3G. Santabear acrylic drinkware. 14 oz. double old-fashioneds or 19 oz. beverage glass. Reg. $12, **sale 9.90 each.** Marketplace™

3H. Fuzzy Santabear and Miss Bear 48" long fleece sleepshirt. 100% cotton. Grey or red, in sizes S-M-L. Made in U.S.A. **$36.** Intimate Apparel

3J. "1988 Santabear and his Polar Club" Fleece crewneck sweatshirt with puff-printed crest. Cotton/polyester. S-M-L-XL. Made in U.S.A. **$25.** Men's Active Sportswear

3K. Santabear puppet. Reg. 14.98, **sale 11.99.** Exclusively ours. Plush Toys and Trim the Home

Exhibit 10
Women's Moderates—Women's Twill Pleated Shorts to Be Sold During Summer 1989

	Nationally Branded Item "Essentials"	Private Label "Boundary Waters"	
Units purchased	2,400	2,400	
Vendor ship date	4/25/89	1/25/89	
Receipt date	5/07/89	4/25/89	
Initial selling date	5/14/89	5/02/89	
Invoices paid	6/10/89	1/25/89	
Budgeted markdown[a]	$8,000	$11,000	
Cost/item	$ 9.00	Factory cost	$ 4.50
Freight	0.09		
Total cost	$ 9.09	Total cost[b]	$ 6.63
Retail price	$22.00	Retail price	$20.00
Purchase MU	58.7%	Purchase MU	66.8%
Credit terms	8/10/EOM[c]		
Anticipated gross margin	54.4%	Anticipated gross margin	56.7%

Note: The cost of preticketing these items with DHDSC tickets was included in the private label cost. Branded resources did not preticket these items. DHDSC operations ticketed the branded merchandise at an estimated cost of $0.045/item.

a DMM worked with buyer to budget anticipated DHDSC markdown dollar amount for branded and private label.
b Total cost includes freight, duties, all AMC fees, and other internal fees.
c For goods delivered to the retailer by the 25th of the month, the retailer will receive 8% discount on the cost of goods, provided that payment is made by the 10th day of the next month. For goods delivered after the 25th of the month, the retailer will have until the 10th day of the next following month to pay and still receive the discount.

Exhibit 11
Men's Dress Shirts—Comparison of Geoffrey Beene vs. Private Label (1988 sales)

	Geoffrey Beene	Woodward
Order lead time	6 months	9 months
Ship date[a]	5/18/88	1/15/88
Receipt date[a]	5/25/88	4/01/88
Initial selling date[a]	6/01/88	6/01/88
Invoices paid[a]	6/25/88	1/15/88
Sales	$1.4 million	$6.3 million
Unit sales	30,673	138,370
Annual turnover	1.97	1.38
Minimum order size	None	300 dozen
Purchase MU	52.0%	61.4%[b]
Gross margin	44.7%[c]	47.7%

Notes:

1) Four percent of cost purchases were given by branded resource for advertising; this income item figure is not included in the gross margin calculation.

2) Both branded and private label resources preticketed items with DHDSC tickets, and costs are included in the cost of goods.

3) AMC fees were 7.6% of factory cost which amounted to approximately $127,000. Under the policy prevailing in 1988, only 1.65% of factory cost (which was approximately 72% of the landed cost of the merchandise on which the purchase markup was figured) was included in the cost of goods sold.

a   Items were received annually throughout the year. This represented average dates to ship, receive, etc.
b   Advertising expense of 5% for private label included in cost of goods.
c   Includes markdown allowances of 4% of cost provided by vendor.

Exhibit 12
Comparison of Revere and Farberware vs. Private Label (1988 sales)

Revere	Farberware	Marketplace	
Order lead time	3 weeks	3 week	3–9 weeks
Ship date[a]	5/15/88	5/15/88	3/15/88
Receipt date[a]	5/25/88	5/25/88	4/15/88
Initial selling date[a]	6/01/88	6/01/88	6/01/88
Invoices paid[a]	6/25/88	6/25/88	3/15/88
Sales	$540,000	$1,700,000	$486,000
Annual turnover	3.0	3.77	1.52
Purchase MU	45.6%[b]	40.2%[b]	52.8%[b]
Gross margin	39.9%	35.5%	41.1%

Notes:

1. Seven percent and 5% of cost purchases were given by Farberware and Revere, respectively, for advertising; these income item figures are not included in the gross margin calculations.

2. AMC fees were 7.6% of factory cost which amounted to approximately $10,000, but under the policy prevailing in 1988, only 1.65% of the factory cost was allocated to the department and charged to the merchandise.

a   Items were received annually throughout the year. This represented average dates to ship, receive, etc.
b   Advertising expense of 3% for both private label and branded items included in the cost of goods.

Case 8

DIRECT PRODUCT PROFITABILITY AT HANNAFORD BROS. CO.

———◆———

Hannaford Bros. Co., a northern New England supermarket chain, has utilized a Direct Product Profitability (DPP) system since the early 1980s to understand better the "true" profitability of nonperishable and perishable items. The chain has been a leader in recognizing that measuring a particular item's profit performance based only on gross margin data fails to reflect the warehouse, transportation, and store expenses incurred in selling that item to consumers. Because these costs are borne by the retailer, Hannaford's management believed that in order to maximize the chain's overall profitability, these costs should be accounted for when making merchandising and operating decisions.

Despite Hannaford's leadership in this area, several executives thought that the company might make better and greater use of DPP. Issues that concerned them included their use of DPP per unit rather than DPP per unit of shelf space as the most important quantitative element in merchandise decision making, the extension of the use of DPP to perishable departments, and the possible use of DPP for certain types of non-merchandise decision making. In addition, these executives recognized that even within departments currently using DPP, both headquar-

ters and store personnel often relied on more traditional measures of merchandising effectiveness such as gross margin percent or gross profit dollars for merchandise decision making. What changes, if any, they wondered, in organization, in incentives, and in the effectiveness and pervasiveness with which DPP data is disseminated, were required and desirable to enhance the use of DPP?

HISTORY OF DPP IN THE SUPERMARKET INDUSTRY

The idea that food retailers should consider product specific handling costs as well as gross margins and turnover rates in merchandise decision making goes back to 1963. The term DPP was created that year following the publication of a report known as the McKinsey-General Foods Study under the title "The Economics of Food Distributors" and another report entitled "Product Profitability and Merchandising Decisions" by three Harvard Business School professors, Robert D. Buzzell, Walter J. Salmon, and Richard F. Vancil.[1]

More recently the Food Marketing Institute has encouraged the use of DPP measures via their

---

Marci Kosann Dew prepared this case under the supervision of Professor Walter J. Salmon as the basis for class discussion rather than to illustrate either effective or ineffective handling of an administrative situation.

---

1 An article espousing applying similar thinking to decision making in general merchandise retailing authored by McNair and May had previously been published in the May/June 1957 issue of the *Harvard Business Review*.

---

development of an off-line computer model, the "Unified Direct Product Profit Method." While this model was initially developed for the grocery area of supermarkets, FMI later added other models for more difficult to measure departments like meat. FMI publications suggest that DPP measures can be used for a variety of merchandising decisions, including shelf space allocation, pricing, and selection of products for promotion.

A recent survey of major supermarket retailers suggests that while most retail food executives agree that DPP makes sense "in theory," the use of DPP remains rather limited. For the most part, its use within the industry consists of manufacturer sponsored studies of the DPP of specific product categories and items, off-line episodic studies done by retailers which often use cost data supplied by outside vendors rather than actual internal product handling costs, and periodic shelf allocation studies which are not integrated into the day-to-day merchandising and operating decisions.

Hannaford appears to be one of the few supermarket chains which has a DPP system integrated into its mainframe computer and uses this system not only for shelf allocation management but also for other merchandising decisions. This case summarizes the company's current DPP system and analyzes factors which have not only contributed to its success but also limited its utilization.

HANNAFORD BROS. CO.

Corporate History

At the end of fiscal year ended December 31, 1989, Hannaford Bros., which began business as a fruit and vegetable wholesaler in 1883 and first entered retailing in the mid-forties, reached $1.5 billion in sales and $39.2 million in net earnings. Over the last five years, the company experienced dramatic growth in sales and profitability. Sales grew at an average of 16.8% annually and earnings rose 28.5% per year. (See **Exhibit 1**.) In general, this performance is above the industry average. (See **Exhibit 2**.)

Hannaford operates two principal businesses: retail food and drugstores. By the end of 1989, Hannaford Bros. Co. was northern New England's largest food retailer with 76 supermarkets operating under the Shop N Save, Martin's or Sun Foods banner. These stores were located throughout Maine, parts of New Hampshire, Vermont, Massachusetts and more recently upstate New York. In addition, Hannaford operated 42 retail drug-

stores under the Wellby Super Drug name. Retail food sales were the most important part of the company's business, accounting for almost 88% of total sales in 1989. (See **Exhibit 3**).

Throughout the 1980s, Hannaford attempted to improve store formats in order to grow and compete successfully. In 1983, the company opened the first combination food and drug store in Maine. The 42,000 square foot prototype not only offered the convenience of a supermarket and pharmacy in one location but also added other one-stop shopping conveniences like deli, bakery, floral shop, salad bar, expanded general merchandise lines, a customer service center with banking services, utility bill payment and photo processing.

Since 1983, Hannaford has opened 15 combination food and drug stores ranging in size from 43,000 to 64,000 gross square feet. The company has also opened 12 combination food stores without pharmacies ranging in size from 38,000 to 69,000 gross square feet. In addition, Hannaford has opened 3 super warehouse stores operating under the name Sun Foods which range from 50,000 to 70,000 square feet. All of these stores represent Hannaford's commitment to developing stores which allow them to compete more effectively in existing markets as well as expand into new markets.

The changes which had occurred at Hannaford in the last decade were under the direction of a management team which had been part of the company for, in certain instances, more than twenty years. Jim Moody, the Chairman and Chief Executive Officer (CEO), was a Maine native, a graduate of Bates College, who after leaving college, participated in General Electric's financial management training program. He joined Hannaford in 1959 and advanced through a variety of financial, real estate, and planning positions to become CEO in 1972. Hugh Farrington, a native of New Hampshire, graduated from Dartmouth and received a Masters degree from the University of New Hampshire. He joined Hannaford's training program in 1968 and advanced through various operations and merchandising positions to become Chief Operating Officer (COO) and president in 1984. Jim Jermann joined Hannaford in 1978, after working with a midwestern grocery wholesaler, and advanced through various merchandising positions to become Vice President of Merchandising in 1983.

Systems Development History

The company's commitment to innovation and change is also seen in its systems and technological development.

Several of its systems were introduced in the late 1970s with additional systems and refinements of existing systems initiated in the 1980s.

In 1977, Hannaford installed its first Universal Product Code scanning system which tracked item sales information at the cash register. By the end of 1984, 33 stores had UPC scanners, and they were in 66 stores by 1989.

In 1978, the Company introduced an electronic ordering device in 65 stores. An individual uses this hand-held machine to scan shelf tags for product ordering information and record the number of cases of each item ordered. The device is then attached to a telephone to transmit the data to a central computer at the Company's distribution center which then prints the order and picking tickets for warehouse employees. The new system saved time and increased worker efficiency.

Other efforts to improve productivity also date back to the late 1970s when Hannaford instituted industrial engineering studies which enabled them to understand costs depending on cube and/or case movement, and utilized computerized reports which tracked these costs and movements. One outcome of these studies was the introduction of a labor scheduling system called Management Planning. This system identifies different labor functions in the store, assigns values to each of the different functions with variation around product categories, and then schedules store labor accordingly. For example, the stocking of shelves is a function which varies, depending on the bulk and pack of a case, i.e., paper towels take less time to stock than spices. If a store is receiving 10 cases of paper towels which take one minute per case to stock, and 10 cases of spices which take two minutes per case to stock, thirty minutes of time is then allocated to shelf stocking.

Hannaford also applied its commitment to improving operating efficiency and introducing systems to the warehousing and distribution functions. The company tracked warehouse handling and occupancy costs as well as transportation costs to each store, for each major merchandise department (grocery, frozen and dairy).

In 1981, Hannaford established the Direct Store Delivery (DSD) program to further assist the company in internal operations. The program was particularly important as DSD merchandise represents about 25% to 30% of all the products which stores receive. This system established centralized control, authorized item listings and vendor payments, and maintained accurate pricing and accurate cost data.

The DSD system was enhanced in 1984 through the test of a Honeywell in-store computer system for on-line processing of receiving data for DSD merchandise. Over the last five years, Hannaford installed mini-computers in all of its stores, not only to do on-line processing of DSD merchandise but also to do time and attendance accounting for payroll, in-store labor scheduling as a supplement to Management Planning, and to process videotape and VCR machine rentals.

Hannaford's ability to track item sales and actual product costs by store also dates back to the late '70s. The chain's warehouse withdrawal system captures case shipment data by item by store. In 1989, Hannaford's internal accounting systems were further improved to record more accurately manufacturer allowances and forward buy discounts by item. These enhancements enabled Hannaford to capture accurate product cost information for each item down to the store level.

DPP History

The Direct Product Profitability (DPP) system at Hannaford provides information to each store for the direct product profit of every non-perishable item, as well as some perishable items, regardless of the method of store delivery. The system measures the profitability of products after considering warehouse, distribution, and store expenses, in contrast to the traditional industry practice of looking only at gross margin as a measure of an item's profitability.

The evolution of DPP at Hannaford can be divided into several stages: conceptual development, initial design and introduction, and system implementation and maintenance. The conceptual development stage dates back to July 1980 when Ken Johnson, a bright, young MBA from the Tuck Graduate School of Business, was hired by Hannaford Bros. to study the Company's shelf allocation system and determine how to improve it. At that time, shelf management was based mainly on sales and gross margin data.

Initially, Ken reviewed shelf allocation systems used in the supermarket industry and found that few DPP-based systems existed. The reasons were lack of cost accounting systems which tracked product movement, an emphasis on precision in excess of what could be achieved with a DPP system, and, in companies that had experimented with DPP, strict adherence to DPP decision rules instead of combining DPP suggested decisions with logical, customer driven merchandising choices.

Despite these issues, Hannaford's senior management was committed to developing a DPP-based shelf management system which could be used on a regular basis and met once a month to accomplish this goal. Ken discovered that Hannaford's historical commitment to systems development resulted in good, basic sales and cost accounting systems which could be used to track profit data down to the store and item levels. A DPP model was developed in this early stage (see **Exhibit 4**) and the cost factors which were selected for this model are still currently used. (See **Exhibit 5**.)

Several important decisions were made during this initial period which were critical in developing Hannaford's DPP system. First, senior management drew from existing systems for their sales and cost inputs. Second, certain refinements of the DPP factors which would have been almost impossible to calculate were ignored until the systems could be introduced to uncover more easily these data. For example, the product costs which were charged to the stores often did not reflect forward buy allowances which extended beyond the store promotion period. These allowances were not incorporated into the system by item by store until 1989. In addition, it would have been extremely difficult to track warehouse inventory costs. It was determined that in groceries, days payable outstanding often approximated days of warehouse inventory, so on average these costs were relatively small and therefore not worth capturing.

Finally, DPP maximization was viewed as only one goal of shelf space management. Management believed that satisfying consumer demand was equally if not more important in making shelf space decisions. For example, if an item had a low DPP but generally was purchased by older consumers, the item was placed in a shelf position easily reachable by these customers even if a more profitable item could be used in its place.

By 1981, the conceptual development stage had been completed and DPP was more formally introduced at Hannaford. Bob Small, an 18-year store veteran, was brought in to spearhead the project's initial design and introduction. Bob reported to the Vice President of Merchandising and was responsible for designing retail reports, working with store personnel, and training grocery department and assistant grocery department managers in the stores to use the system. In addition, mainframe software was designed which integrated Hannaford's sales and cost data, and computed DPP dollars per unit. **Exhibit 6** highlights these computations using the DPP model and DPP factors shown in **Exhibits**

4 and 5. Over the next few years, Bob reset stores using the new DPP system. During this period, except at the subcategory level, very few overall planograms were actually developed as all work had to be done manually.

The third stage of development focused on system implementation and maintenance. Hugh Smith headed DPP development during this period. He was instrumental in fine-tuning the existing DPP system, introducing the Apollo software system in order to improve Hannaford's capability to produce planograms, and starting the manufacturer/broker employee program to provide the company with resources to formulate planograms and execute them at retail.

The refinement of the existing DPP system involved a simplification of the mainframe software, an examination of the actual data which went into the system, an analysis of the technical aspects of the DPP model and its calculations, and a modification of retail reports which were sent to the stores. At the same time, Hugh saw the need to introduce a computerized planogram system which would enable Hannaford to send planograms to the stores more frequently and thus reduce the possibility of error at store level in executing the suggested planograms. Apollo software and dedicated personal computers for planogramming were introduced during this period. While data are still manually input into the Apollo system from reports obtained from the mainframe computer, Hannaford's ability to implement and execute planograms was significantly enhanced from 1984 through the end of 1987.

Nonetheless, the need for manual data entry combined with the number of planograms needed for all the aisles in all of the stores overwhelmed the DPP department which was staffed by Hugh, a secretary, and a part-time employee. In response to this problem, senior management created the role of shelf management specialists and looked to brokers and manufacturers to supply employees who could help the company in this area at no charge to Hannaford. Initially, these employees were affiliated mainly with dairy and frozen brokers. Since these categories were more space constrained, Hannaford was easily able to convince brokers that they would benefit from having their employees influence shelf space and learn about competitive products. Instead of spending most of their time in stores, these broker representatives began to spend more time at Hannaford headquarters formulating planograms which maximized category DPP without inconveniencing consumers. The remainder of their time was spent in the stores helping store personnel implement the new planograms. This program was critical in solving a resource problem which would have hampered Hannaford's ability to implement and maintain the DPP system. The program has been so successful that it has been broadened to include representatives from the large grocery manufacturers, and is still in existence today.

Current Structure and Uses of DPP

Art Ledue became Manager of Product Management (which is the designation of the department responsible for DPP) in early 1988, and is now responsible for the DPP area. (See **Exhibit 7.**) Hannaford DPP personnel still consist of basically two people, Art Ledue and a secretarial assistant. Reporting to Art are approximately 15 specialists, 12 of whom are supplied by outside manufacturers and brokers and 3 of whom are private label specialists provided by a private label broker. The number of these employees varies at any point in time since they are assigned to these duties from six to eighteen months depending on the agreement worked out with their employers.

Current Store Uses. The DPP department's principal function is shelf management. Each specialist is assigned several product categories corresponding to the categories in which his or her employer has interests. They are responsible for updating information in the computer as items are added or deleted from their categories, and preparing revised planograms.

In preparing a planogram, each specialist works with the category buyer to understand the merchandising direction, current trends, specific manufacturer relations, and new ideas for the category. The specialist then works with a planogram which may already be on the system or actually goes to a store that has a complete offering and collects additional relevant information. The specialist then uses the Apollo shelf management program to put together a recommended planogram for the category. Planograms are developed for five indicator stores (one for each of Hannaford's geographic areas: Maine-North, Maine-South, New Hampshire, Vermont and New York).

These planograms are also done for varying linear feet so store personnel can more easily deal with the variety of store sizes which exist in each region. The planograms are then sent to the stores together with a current DPP report for the category for that store and a statement of category philosophy so this package can be used for resetting the category within the store. (See **Exhibits 8, 9** and **12.**)

Each specialist is also assigned a group of stores. This responsibility involves dealing with any shelf management problems which may arise at store level, working with store personnel and broker/manufacturer salesmen to reset the stores, making weekly store visits to ensure that scheduled planograms are in fact accomplished, and training store personnel in the usage of DPP. In the case of simple category resets, store department managers often manage the revisions themselves. In the case of more complex resets and/or resets which the stores do not have time to do, store personnel are urged to invite broker/manufacturer salespeople to help reset the stores and to monitor their performance.

There are several basic guidelines which are used to develop planograms and reset stores. First, unit DPP (i.e., DPP dollars per item sold) determines the location of the item on the shelf. In general, eye level in the center of a set is the best location and is recommended for the items with the highest unit DPPs. The bottom shelf is usually the worst location, especially the bottom corners, followed by the top shelf as the next worse location. Second, sales determine the amount of shelf space or number of facings. These facings are adjusted depending on the proper packout on the shelf, i.e., depending on the weekly delivery schedule, the shelf space should handle approximately 1½ cases of product so stores can reorder one case of product and restock a full case at one time. The limited number of products which move at the rate of several cases per day, however, require more space. Third, items should be grouped according to the category merchandising direction. In diapers, items are grouped by size, not brand, whereas in cereals, items are grouped by brand. Finally, items should be placed with consumer preference in mind. For example, even if gallons of vinegar are profitable, they will probably always be put on the bottom shelf because of their size and weight.

The Product Management department also sends stores a DPP report every 17 weeks with information for their store based on actual historical performance. This report includes a "Top 50/Bottom 50 Report" which shows those 50 items with the highest and lowest DPPs for the period, a "Management Summary Report" which highlights DPP performance for major family groups like canned fish and intermediate family groups like tuna and salmon, and an item specific report which is similar to a shelf allocation report and provides DPP detail for all items in a store for which DPP data is maintained. (See **Exhibits 10, 11** and **12**). The 17-week report (which stands 6 inches high) was supposed to be used to help stores add and delete items, as an aid to specific store resets, and for general DPP knowledge. Art Ledue uses these reports as well as the specific planogram reports when he conducts periodic training programs for district managers and store personnel.

The mainframe computer which prints this report, receives sales information on a weekly basis from three different systems: warehouse shipments, DSD receivings, and Progressive Distributors (Hannaford's HBA/GM Rack Jobber) shipments. These data are then fed into the software which uses the movement information to calculate DPP by item by store. In order to eliminate some of the sales peaks and valleys caused by store promotions, sales of particular items during the week they are included in a store circular are excluded from the analysis. (However, if an item is sold at the deal price beyond the circular period, these sales are not excluded from the analysis). The ability to collect data regardless of the method of store delivery, as well as the elimination of some of the effects of sales promotion activities, are unusual practices in the supermarket industry.

In addition to day-to-day shelf management activities, specialists work on special projects. These projects may include setting up a new store or resetting an existing store. Specialists also work with Art Ledue on specific analyses which have longer term implications such as how Hannaford determines what the exact footage should be in a particular category or whether DPP dollars per base foot should be used in shelf management.

The latter issue of whether to use DPP dollars per base foot in merchandise decision making is also the issue on which the FMI had not reached a conclusion. Its model suggested that DPP per unit or DPP per unit of shelf space were appropriate measures of profitability. The argument in favor of DPP per unit was that the amount of product Hannaford could sell within a product category or subcategory was determined by its overall market share.

Proponents of the "unit of space theory" argued that the hypothesis that category sales were determined by overall market share was incorrect. They argued that sensible merchandising could maximize share of market in a profitable category while minimizing share of market in an unprofitable category. Furthermore, they feared that an emphasis on DPP per unit would lead to giving the most prominent space to private label and slow-moving products because this standard failed to reflect the higher throughput per unit of space for the more profitable national brands.

Practically speaking, there was a major problem in endeavoring to ascertain DPP per unit of space since store managers were the final arbiters of how much shelf space was dedicated to any single SKU. Determining DPP per unit of space would require that store personnel keep the mainframe computer abreast of how many units of shelf space were actually dedicated to each SKU.

Current Merchandising Uses. The Product Management department also deals with the Merchandising department (i.e., the buyers) and the Pricing Department in addition to the stores. (See **Exhibit 7**. Buyers use DPP information when deciding to carry new items. (See **Exhibit 13**.) In the case of discontinued items, buyers do not typically use DPP data for discontinuing items that have no obvious merit, but may rely on this information for a dialogue with a major manufacturer before discontinuing one of their important items.

In addition to meetings with shelf management specialists for the development of category planograms, buyers also work with the DPP area (as well as other areas) in the course of their category reviews. These reviews, which occur every three months, entail variety checks versus competition, SKU counts, planograms and replanograms, item performance, and general category direction.

Buyers also rely on DPP performance to alter product strategy such as promotional policies or method of shipment. For example, paper towels are now recognized as an unprofitable category because of their low retail price and high bulk. As a result, Hannaford stopped promoting paper towels in its circulars and stopped putting paper towels on valuable end cap displays. Furthermore, in order to reduce losses, the buyer successfully negotiated with certain vendors to ship paper towels directly to the stores, thus eliminating Hannaford's warehouse and distribution expenses.

Finally, the Pricing Department, which also reports to the Manager of Grocery Merchandising (see **Exhibit 7**), uses DPP performance data. While competitive pricing is an important determinant of Hannaford's retail pricing, the Pricing Department uses DPP data to help set retail prices, particularly for less price sensitive items.

The use of a Pricing Department entirely separate from the Buying department emanated from Hannaford's conviction that prices, particularly on fast-moving items, should be established in relationship to local competition rather than the cost of the product. Hannaford's Pricing department, therefore, varied prices by item by store in comparison with the prices of leading local competitors.

Once these prices were established, Hannaford's computer systems enabled the company to bill each store at its own retail price as well as at cost for the items it actually received. This system enabled Hannaford to enjoy the benefits of both the retail inventory method and the competitive and gross margin advantages of local pricing.

Uses of DPP Among Departments

Progressive Distributors, Hannaford's subsidiary for the procurement, merchandising, and distribution of Health & Beauty Aids (HBA) and General Merchandise (GM), also works closely with the DPP department. In conjunction with the Product Management department, Progressive has developed DPP data for the HBA area but still relies on gross margin performance for most GM categories. Progressive carries 22,000 items for HBA and GM (7,000 of which are in HBA, 5,000 in cosmetics and 10,000 in GM). In the case of HBA, the combination of a large number of standard items combined with a constant flow of new items, pushed Progressive to institute DPP systems and use its own Apollo system to generate planograms in a more timely fashion. Progressive relies on its own personnel who service the stores to handle store resets and placement of new items.

Within GM, Progressive has developed DPP data for more price sensitive and competitive items like film and batteries. For other GM categories, which are less price-sensitive and often seasonal in nature, Progressive uses gross margin data for placement of items within a category.

For the most part, shelf management systems and DPP analysis have not been formalized in the perishable areas like meat, produce and deli. In the case of meat, many categories of product are still cut at store level with varying yields and sold in random weights. Hannaford has no systems which historically capture these varying yields and assign product costs to the sold items. In addition, spoilage is often high in these departments and this information is not regularly tracked. Third, meat and produce are sold on both an item and weight basis. Consequently, the company has not ascertained how to compare DPP within these departments. Should it be per unit of product, per pound of product, or if determinable, per unit of shelf space occupied by the product. Finally, meat and produce are agricultural items which are subject to volatile price swings. Despite these fluctuations, Hannaford must offer these items in the store even if they are unprofitable. Nevertheless, a DPP or contribution analysis is periodically done for more major product decisions. For example, a DPP analysis was used to determine whether Hannaford should continue cutting its own chicken or shift to prepackaged poultry.

In the case of the Deli and Bakery departments, which are now managed by Ken Johnson, DPP analysis is done manually on a periodic basis. Each department consists of seven categories with a narrow range of items (such as pies within the Bakery department). Retail prices and costs do not change as often as in other product categories and Everyday Low Purchase Pricing (EDLPP) arrangements exist with 90% of the vendors. By examining costs at the category level and assigning these costs to individual items, Ken believes that a periodic analysis is adequate. As in the case of other perishable departments, Ken uses DPP analysis to make certain procurement decisions such as whether to buy partially baked product and finish it in the store, or bake the product from scratch.

Potential Non-Merchandising Uses for DPP

Apart from the possibility of extending the use of DPP to other merchandise departments, its most zealous proponents envisioned several non-merchandising uses for these data. For example, they argued DPP should be used in helping to establish overall selling area size. Their theory was that, at the margin, the final square foot of selling space included in a new or remodeled store should produce a return equal to the cost of capital for constructing that square foot of selling space.

Another non-merchandising use contemplated for DPP was to measure labor efficiency. This use would measure department or store labor costs against the accumulation of direct product costs for any particular calendar period. A high percentage of direct product costs to total labor costs would reflect excellent efficiency in the use of labor while a low percentage of direct product costs in relation to total labor costs would suggest opportunities for enhancing the efficiency of store labor.

Benefits and Costs of DPP

Senior management at Hannaford firmly believes that the benefits of DPP far outweigh the costs of implementing the system. However, it was almost impossible for anyone to quantify accurately these benefits and costs.

Benefits. The benefits of DPP fall into several categories: a steady improvement in Hannaford financial performance, part of which management attributed to DPP, an analysis of the true profitability for selected items, a study of the incremental contribution resulting from remerchandising stores, and a general feeling that this logical analytical framework resulted in better overall management.

As shown in **Exhibits 1** and **3**, Hannaford's sales and profits have grown dramatically over the last five years. While this performance can be attributed to a variety of phenomena such as the upgrading of its stores, and constant systems innovation, management believes that basing merchandising and operating decisions on DPP has been an important contributor to net earnings after taxes as a percent of sales rising from 1.8% in 1985 to 2.6% in 1989.

This logic is also based on the fact that Hannaford's knowledge of an item's "true" profitability has resulted in decisions which fuel the sales of more profitable items. **Exhibit 14** compares the gross margin and DPP dollars per unit for a sample of different items. While traditional industry reliance on gross margin resulted, for example, in a misconception that paper towels were profitable relative to other grocery items, Hannaford's analysis revealed that these items were not as profitable as thought and changed policies significantly based on this knowledge. Cigarrest, a product aimed at deterring consumers from smoking, is another interesting example. Store managers refused to push this product because the gross margin was only 10%. A DPP analysis revealed that Cigarrest was one of the most profitable in the HBA/GM category due to a high retail combined with relatively low handling costs.

When Hannaford first began planogramming its stores, it did a test with twelve stores to track the store performance before and after planogramming. In this test, management discovered that they were able to improve store contribution by 1/4 of 1% to 3/4 of 1% of sales by remerchandising stores based on DPP.

Finally, senior management believed that examining profitability by factoring in warehousing, distribution and store costs was a logical framework for making decisions and dealing with problems. Traditional industry practices, Hannaford's management thought, hampered other retailers' performance, and Hannaford believed different thinking was required to be successful in the future. Consequently, DPP was viewed as a significant future competitive advantage.

Costs. The costs associated with implementing DPP at Hannaford were also difficult to quantify. The company's ability to develop a DPP system was facilitated by Hannaford's innovation in systems development and ac-

counting systems. The company would have introduced these systems even without a DPP system.

The major incremental DPP costs are those fixed costs and annual operating costs associated with the DPP analysis done on the mainframe, the Apollo shelf management program and other DPP-related expenses. Fixed costs include the initial software used to integrate the existing systems and calculate DPP data, as well as refinements to this software, and the Apollo software and computer network expenses. Whether, indeed, the Apollo costs should be considered a part of the DPP cost structure was an unresolved question. Numerous other companies also used the Apollo shelf management system but substituted gross profit percentages or gross profit per unit of space for DPP, as well as sales data, as the basis for shelf allocations.

Annual operating costs include MIS labor and computer time to produce the DPP reports, and the payroll and system maintenance costs of running the DPP department. **Exhibit 15** summarizes the fixed costs and annual operating expenses for the DPP system at Hannaford.

It is interesting to note that Hannaford's use of 15 outside manufacturer/broker employees significantly reduces the company's annual costs. This is particularly important because the system is still extremely time consuming in view of the manual data entry, manual manipulation of the planograms, the number of categories, and the updates required.

Barriers to Penetration of DPP

There are several barriers which limit the more extensive use of DPP at Hannaford Bros. Co. These barriers include the remains of a traditional supermarket mentality, daily operating reports which exclude DPP data, incentive systems geared to non-DPP performance measures, the off-line nature of the current system, the inability of the system to deal with certain product categories, and the lack of overall category management.

While store personnel and buyers are aware of DPP data, they regularly refer to item sales and gross margin when discussing an item's performance. In part, this continuing reliance on traditional measures reflects the fact that many managers have been in the supermarket industry for numerous years and find it difficult to change the way they have always looked at their business.

This traditional reliance is reinforced in their daily reports which often do not include DPP data, and still report only gross margin data. In the case of buyers,

DPP information is not in their normal day-to-day operating reports like out of stock, sales plans, sales reports, wholesale sales analysis, and item gross profits.

Store personnel also receive inconsistent communication as weekly sales plans and market notes often do not contain DPP data and their department reports do not compute DPP performance. In addition, the 17-week DPP report which they receive on a regular basis is somewhat intimidating, particularly for managers with a traditional supermarket mentality.

Incentive programs, instead of being geared to DPP, are measured for buyers on criteria like service levels (out of stocks), inventory turns, and department performance against plan, with sales and gross profit measures driving performance. Store personnel are also evaluated on department performance against plan using the same criteria, and expenses they can control like payroll and shrinkage.

The off-line nature of the DPP program makes it less timely to use and may deter more frequent usage. Buyers, for example, cannot request DPP performance data at their desktop computers, but instead must rely on the DPP department for this information. Since they operate in a hectic day-to-day environment, this inability to get a quick enough response discourages them from more actively using the information. In addition, the Apollo system is not tied into the mainframe computer which slows down the speed of producing planograms and limits the department's ability to do store-specific planograms.

While the existing DPP model and cost factors work well for most departments within Hannaford, there are certain perishable departments like meat, where it is difficult to apply the same model. Issues like varying yields and random weights need to be factored into the model in order to expand its penetration.

Finally, buyers are not category managers and consequently cannot be easily measured using DPP. Buyers are responsible for purchasing 1,200 to 1,500 items at best cost, and to the extent possible, on an everyday low purchase price (EDLPP) basis. They make item selection and deletion decisions, assist in sales and promotion decisions, have some control over shelf merchandising, but have no control over DSD items within the same category which are purchased by another buyer, and also have little influence over pricing, which is the responsibility of a separate pricing department.

Hannaford is considering a category management system in which a category manager would be responsible for negotiating with and buying from vendors for warehouse and DSD products. The category manager would also be responsible for a team of reorder buyers, pricing analysts, sales promotion personnel and shelf management specialists, all of whom would work to maximize category profitability. Senior management was wondering whether these organizational changes, as well as changes in incentive systems and the inclusion of DPP data in daily, weekly, and monthly operating reports, was necessary in order to implement DPP fully.

Exhibit 1
Selected Historical Financial Data

| | FYE 12/31: | | | | | 6 mos 6/30: | |
	1985	1986	1987	1988	1989	1989	1990
Net Sales	$816,775	$910,202	$1,033,418	$1,261,668	$1,520,600	$721,151	$812,271
% Change in Sales	14.4%	11.4%	13.5%	22.1%	20.5%	n/a	12.6%
Net Earnings	$ 14,399	$ 18,817	$ 24,083	$ 28,949	$ 39,202	$ 21,164	$ 22,002
% Change in Earnings	26.9%	30.7%	28.0%	20.2%	35.4%	n/a	4.0%
As % of Sales:							
Gross Margin	21.2%	22.3%	22.9%	23.0%	23.5%	23.8%	24.5%
SG&A	16.9	17.4	18.0	18.5	18.8	18.6	19.3
Net Earnings	1.8	2.1	2.3	2.3	2.6	2.9	2.7
Net Earnings as % of:							
Average Equity	16.3%	16.8%	18.5%	18.9%	19.6%	19.3%	18.3%
Average Assets	9.1	9.4	10.0	10.0	10.2	10.6	9.8

Note: Net earnings as % of average equity and assets for six-month results is based on the last 52 weeks.

Exhibit 2
Comparison with Other Regional Supermarket Companies (millions)

	Hannaford	Brunos	Delchamps	Food Lion	Giant Food	Ingles	Marsh	Ruddick	Smith's	Weis
Net Sales										
1989	$1,611.7	$2,330.9	$930.2	$5,112.2	$3,293.7	$999.5	$1,022.1	$1,399.1	$1,899.4	$1,261.4
1988	1,404.0	2,134.1	899.5	4,448.9	3,109.7	858.4	914.4	1,300.7	1,649.1	1,242.8
Net Income Continuing Operations										
1989	$ 40.1	$ 56.3	$ 14.9	$ 157.0	$ 110.3	$ 12.1	$ 11.5	$ 24.0	$ 31.2	$ 85.5
1988	34.2	47.8	12.1	127.3	105.9	14.3	9.4	20.2	23.6	85.6
5-Year Sales Growth										
1989	16.3%	24.4%	8.9%	26.3%	8.7%	14.0%	8.1%	12.2%	22.3%	5.3%
1988	15.0	24.4	8.9	26.6	8.8	13.3	7.0	15.3	21.8	5.9
After-tax Profit Margin										
1989	2.5%	2.4%	1.6%	3.1%	3.4%	1.2%	1.1%	1.8%	1.6%	6.8%
1988	2.5	2.2	1.3	2.9	3.4	1.7	1.0	1.6	1.4	6.9
Return on Tangible Equity										
1989	16.9%	20.6%	18.9%	26.4%	21.7%	9.4%	15.4%	13.3%	12.3%	14.7%
1988	17.3	20.1	17.1	25.5	23.1	12.0	14.4	12.7	10.0	15.7
Sales Per Square Foot										
1989	$ 545.0	$ 278.0	$281.0	$ 280.0	$ 595.0	$207.0	$ 323.0	$ 385.0	$ 340.0	$ 286.0

Note: Data are annualized based on most recent quarter results. For example, in 1989, Hannaford's results are based on the June quarter.

Source: A.G. Edwards & Sons, Inc.

Exhibit 3
Selected Supermarket Data (millions)

FYE 12/31:	1985	1986	1987	1988	1989
Net Sales:	$ 683	$ 761	$ 883	$ 1,094	$ 1,331
% Change in Sales:	n/a	11.4%	16.0%	23.9%	21.7%
% Change in Comp. Store Sales:	n/a	7.1%	10.3%	10.0%	8.9%
Number of Stores:	65	66	65	72	76
Sq. Ft. Selling: (000)	1,085	1,216	1,314	1,624	1,772
Sq. Ft. Selling per Store:	16,700	18,425	20,215	22,555	23,315
Sales/Store: (000)	$10,508	$11,530	$13,585	$15,194	$17,513
Sales/Sq. Ft. Selling:	$ 629	$ 626	$ 672	$ 674	$ 751

Exhibit 4
Direct Product Profit Calculation

Selling Price
- Cost

    = Gross Profit

- Product Buying Cost
- Warehouse Labor Cost
- Warehouse Occupancy Cost
- Transportation Cost
- Store Ordering Cost
- Store Unloading Cost
- Store Cutting/Pricing/Stocking Costs
- Store Checkout Cost
- Store Bagging Cost
- Store Inventory Cost

= Direct Product Profit

Note: The principal difference between the Hannaford and the FMI models is that the FMI model can use either DPP per unit (including a shelf space charge for a given item) or DPP per unit of shelf space (excluding the item's shelf space expense).

Exhibit 5
DPP Cost Factor Allocation Method

Factor	Basis	Allocation Method Detail
Product buying	Cases	Direct costs associated with merchandising depts (buying), A/P wages, and invoice processing costs divided by annual case movement by dept. (grocery, dairy, frozen).
Warehouse Labor	Cases Cube	Warehouse handling is broken down into variable and direct warehouse expense for each warehouse (grocery, dairy, frozen). These annual expenses are multiplied by the percentage of that wage associated with the cube of an item. The cube-based wage total is obtained by adding individual cube costs which are then subtracted from total wage costs to determine case-based wage cost. The warehouse handling/case cost was calculated by taking the variable and direct case-based wage costs and divided by annual case movement for each warehouse. The warehouse handling/cube cost was calculated by taking the variable and direct cube-based wage cost and divided by annual cube movement for each warehouse. (Cube movement was determined by multiplying each warehouse's case movement by an average cube factor, i.e., grocery = .98 cube/case, dairy = .47, frozen food = .71).
Warehouse Occupancy	Cube	Total fixed costs plus portion of forward buy and outside storage expenses related to the storage handling of turn inventory were added to determine total warehouse occupancy expense. These numbers were divided by total cube movement to arrive at a warehouse occupancy cost for each department.
Transportation	Cube	The transportation cost/cube factor is determined for each store based on a monthly average of actual store shipments and transportation costs by department. Each store's cost is expressed in cents per cube.
Store Ordering	Cases	This factor is determined by multiplying the time allowed to place an order by the order clerk's hourly wage and then dividing that figure by the average number of pieces ordered.
Store Unloading	Cube	This factor is determined by taking the average time it takes to unload a pallet of product assuming an average cube per pallet and multiplying this rate by an hourly unloading wage rate to arrive at a cost per cube.
Store Cutting/ Price/Stocking	Units	This factor is determined by taking each department's average labor cost per hour to handle these functions divided by the number of cases handled per hour divided by the number of units per case to arrive at an average cost per unit.

Exhibit 5, continued

Factor	Basis	Allocation Method Detail
Store Checkout	Units	Store checkout includes cashier costs (ring and tender time) and bagging costs (bagging and carryout time). This factor is calculated by taking an average hourly wage rate divided by the number of items that can be cashiered and bagged in an hour to arrive at an average cost per item.
Store Bag Costs	Cube	Store bag costs are calculated by taking the average cost per bag multiplied by the usable cube per bag to arrive at an average cost per cube. This factor is determined for paper and plastic bags and then weighted depending on the usage of paper versus plastic bags.
Store Inventory Costs	Units	Cost of capital times the product cost of the annual unit inventory recommended in shelf allocation costs divided by 52 weeks divided by weekly units sold.

Exhibit 6
Example of DPP Cost Factor Detail for a Grocery Item in a Typical Store

Item	14.5 oz Hunts Solid Tomatoes		
Cases Sold	68/year or 1.30/week		
Units Sold	1,632/year or 31.38/week		
Case Cube	0.60		
Units in Case	24		
Recommended Inventory Level	44 units		
Retail Price	$0.59		
Product Cost	$0.35		

Cost Factors:	Cube	Case	Unit
Warehouse Handling and Storage	0.210	0.08	0
Transportation (Varies by Store)	0.270		
Store Ordering		0.02	
Store Unloading	0.010		
Store Handling			0.00875
Store Checkout			0.00460
Store Bagging			0.00290
Store Bag Costs	0.047		
Store Inventory			0.00191
Total	0.537	0.10	0.01816

DPP Calculation:

Item Sales	$960.00
Product Cost	570.58
Gross Profit	389.42
- Cases (68 x 0.10)	6.80
- Units (1632 x 0.01816)	29.63
- Cube (68 x 0.60) x 0.537	21.91
DPP $	$331.08
DPP $/Unit	0.203

Exhibit 7
DPP Organization Chart

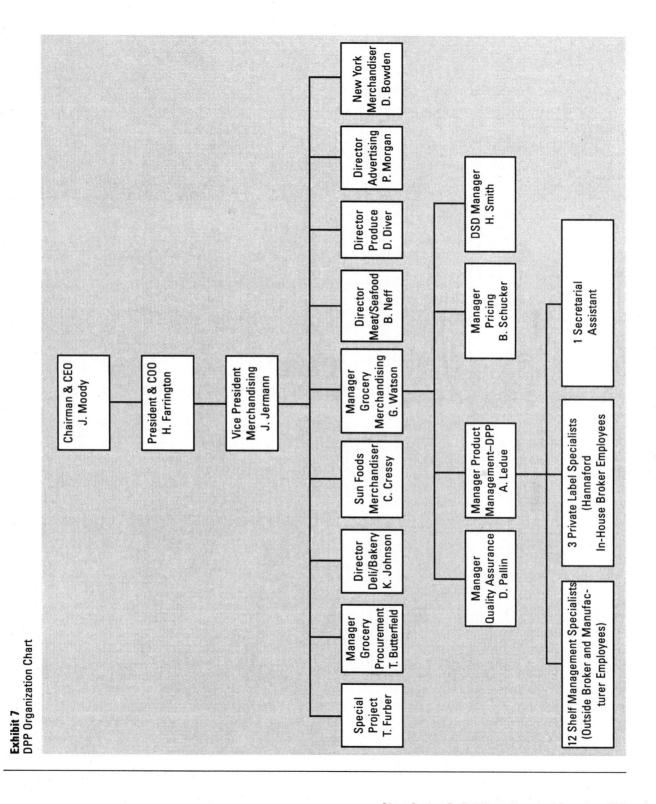

Exhibit 8
Sample Planogram

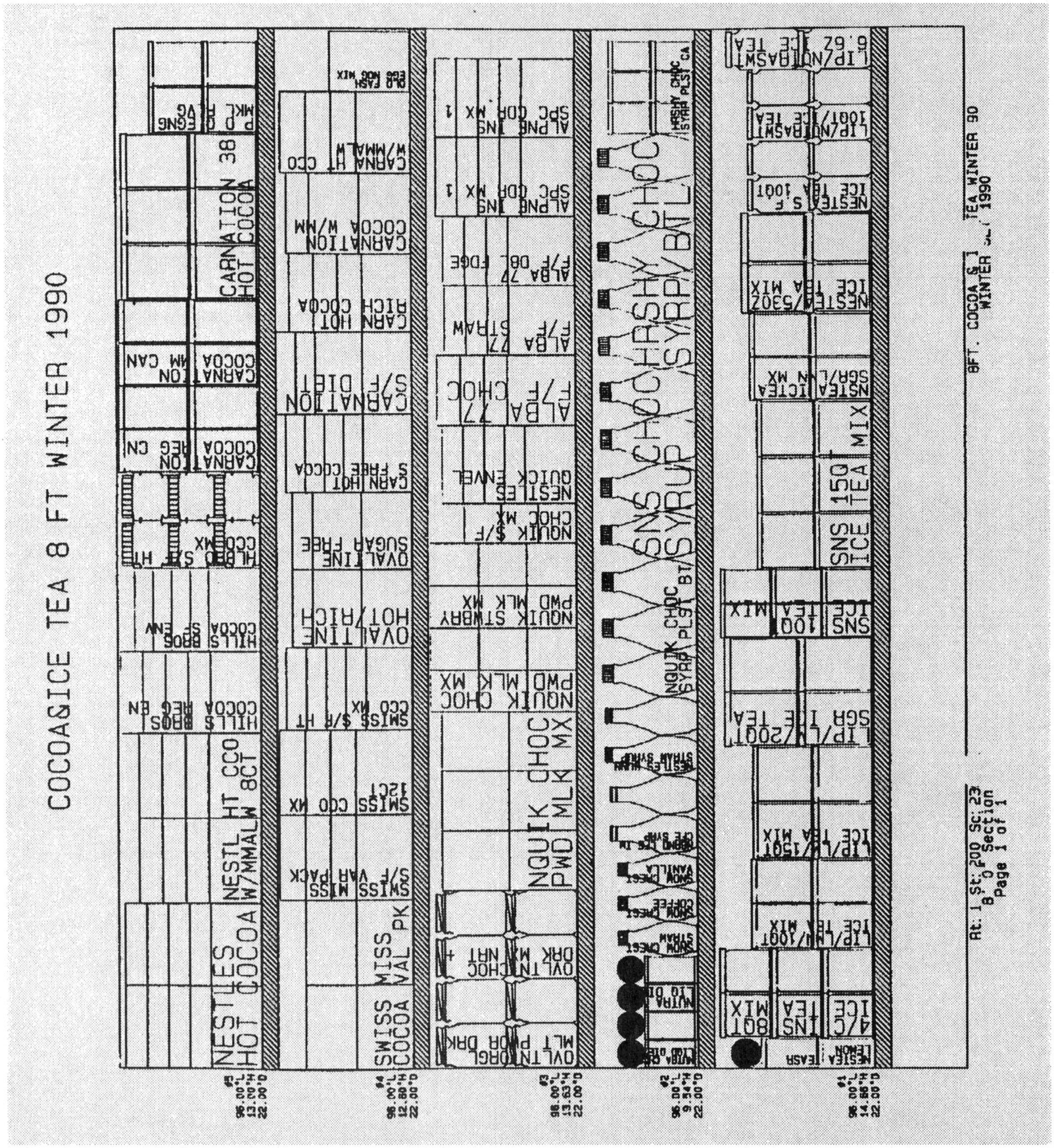

Exhibit 8, continued
Partial Sample Planogram Detail

SHELF # 1 L: 96.00 in. H: 14.66 in. D: 22 in. PRODUCT: 95.97 in. STANDARD

UPC Number	Stock Code	Long Description	Size	Casepk	Capacity	Facing
2800034540	3382430	Nestea Teasr Lemon	1.70 oz	12	18	1 fc
4138762255	2372712	4C Instant Iced Tea 8qt	24	12	30	2 fc
4100000845	2375525	Lip Lem/Sug 10qt	32	12	20	2 fc
4100000846	2375566	Lipton Lem/Sug 15qt	48	12	16	2 fc
4100000864	2375632	Lip Lem/Sug 20qt	64	6	16	2 fc
4126804574	2376184	Sns Ice Tea 10qt	32	12	42	2 fc
4126804575	2376192	Sns Ice Tea 15qt	48	12	24	3 fc
2800033960	2381804	Nestea Iced Tea 10qt	26	12	20	2 fc
2800033980	2381960	Nestea Iced Tea Mix 20qt	53	6	16	2 fc
2800034400	2381523	Nestea S.F. 10qt	3.30	12	24	2 fc
4100000872	2375319	Lip Nutrasweet 10qt	3.30	23	24	2 fc
4100000868	2375376	Lip Nutrasweet 6.6 oz	6.60	6	10	1 fc
					260	23 fc

SHELF # 2 L: 96.00 in. H: 9.54 in. D: 22 in. PRODUCT: 94.98 IN. STANDARD

UPC Number	Stock Code	Long Description	Size	Casepk	Capacity	Facing
1980017122	2396158	Nutrament Chocolate	12 oz	12	24	2 fc
1980017022	2396109	Nutrament Vanilla	12	12	24	2 fc
7355671420	13028	SNW Crst Straw Syrup	16	1	7	1 fc
7355671400	13026	SNW Crst Coffee Flv Syrup	16	1	7	1 fc
7355671410	13027	SNW Crst Vanilla Syrup	16	1	7	1 fc
7310330010	2397404	Coffee Time Coffee Syrup	12	12	20	2 fc
2800024460	2395879	Nestle Straw Syrup Bunny Bot	22	12	28	2 fc
2800024500	2397701	Nestle Quik Syrup Pl Bot	22	12	27	3 fc
4126804623	2397545	Sns Chocolate Syrup	28	12	22	4 fc
3400000312	2397644	Hershey Choc Syrup Bot	24	24	45	5 fc
3400031500	2397552	Hershey Choc Syrup	16	24	42	3 fc
					253	26 fc

Exhibit 9
Sample Planogram Category Philosophy

Hannaford Bros. Co.
P.O. Box 1000
Portland, ME 04104
Tel. 207/883-2911

Hannaford Retail Services

September 12, 1990

RE: COCOA AND ICE TEA PLANOGRAM WINTER 1990

Dear Retailer:

Please find attached 12' and 8' planograms for your Cocoa and Ice Tea section. You should utilize a current DPP report to compare your store's suggested allocation to the capacity column in order to insure that proper allocation is met. Remember, adjust facings as necessary but items should remain in the same location within the planogram.

   Stores with sections that fit the planograms should follow the planograms very closely while stores with smaller size sections should follow the intent of the 8' planogram, eliminating duplicate, slow moving and low DPP items as necessary. Stores with larger sections should follow the intent of the 12' planogram, expanding facings on high volume, high DPP items.

COCOA AND ICE TEA PHILOSOPHY:

The Cocoa and Ice Tea section has been divided into four subcategories including:

1. Ice Tea
2. Cocoa
3. Milk Additives
4. Drink Mixes

1. **Cocoa** is located on the top **two** shelves in the winter set due to high volume.
2. **Milk Additives** are on the middle two shelves as a permanent year-round item.
3. **Ice Tea** is located on the bottom shelf in the winter planogram due to low volume.
4. **Drink Mixes** representing a very small portion of the category are merchandised on the middle shelf on the right side.

   We have included a list of sales representatives to assist you in completing this project. Please feel free to call them for your assistance. Plan on having this set completed by Oct. 19. If you have any questions or comments, please call.

Doreen Lewis BUYER/MERCHANDISER	Mark Alexander BUYER/MERCHANDISER	Linda Gibbs BUYER/MERCHANDISER
Sue Shuman BUYER/MERCHANDISER	Art Ledue MANAGER PRODUCT MANAGEMENT	Gerry Laroche SHELF MANAGEMENT SPECIALIST

Exhibit 10
Sample Top 50/Bottom 50 Report

DP606-1 09/26/90 22.30   DIRECT PRODUCT PROFITABILITY TOP 50/BOTTOM 50   REPORT FOR—0387 ME MALL SUPER
SHOP N SAVE FROM 05/26/90 TO 09/15/90—17 WEEKS

Direct Product Profit			General Information			
Cat Rank	DPP $	DPP Unit	Item Number	Pck	Size	Description
1	4,311	5.200	029625-1	1	Carton	Marlboro Box
2	3,234	.222	41268-54030	1	Dozen	SNS Large Brown Eggs
3	3,032	5.192	029626-9	1	Carton	Marlboro Light Box
4	2,294	5.167	029711-9	1	Carton	Winston Filter King
5	2,198	.356	01012-00335	1	Book	Magazine 1.95
6	1,988	2.409	18200-11168	1	Stcse	Bud Stcse 122 C
7	1,949	.188	41268-77115	1	Gallon	SNS 1.5% Gallon
8	1,861	.351	562108-1	24	12 ounces	SNS Orange Juice
9	1,838	.305	41268-68024	1	22 ounces	SNS Giant Bread
10	1,619	.298	503030-9	36	16 ounces	Shop N Sav butter qtrs
11	1,545	5.201	029627-7	1	Carton	Marlboro Light King
12	1,516	2.407	11175	6	15.000	SNS Ultra Thin Chocolate
13	1,482	.262	73438-00027	1	Gallon	Oak 1.5% Pls Gallon
14	1,466	1.751	01012-00131	1	Book	Paperback 5.95
15	1,390	.556	01012-00360	1	Book	Magazine 2.36–2.95
16	1,356	.246	41268-54020	1	Dozen	SNS Egg X-Lg Brown
17	1,352	1.216	04601	8	7.400	Austin Toasty PB Ckr 8pk
18	1,352	.127	41268-04289	1	Gallon	SNS 1% Gallon Pls
19	1,347	.287	522664-2	12	12 ounces	SNS Shredded Mozzarella
20	1,322	.466	01012-00350	1	Book	Magazine 2.50
21	1,316	.362	27900-00045	1	19 ounces	Nis Brtop Wheat
22	1,286	5.205	029631-9	1	Carton	Marlboro King
23	1,283	.280	41268-68075	1	18 ounces	SNS Btrtp Wheat
24	1,271	.325	41268-68057	1	18 ounces	SNS Frank Rl 12pk
25	1,268	.134	41268-77113	1	Gallon	SNS Homo Plst Gallon
26	1,265	.276	41268-54010	1	Dozen	SNS Egg Jumbo Br
27	1,235	5.301	029632-7	1	Carton	Marlboro Light 100 Box
28	1,212	.197	41268-54035	1	Dozen	SNS Large White Eggs
29	1,202	.134	41268-04236	1	Gallon	SNS Skim Gallon Pls
30	1,193	.154	01012-00732	1	Book	Magazine .75
31	1,152	3.000	29905	48		Disp Neon Backpacks
32	1,143	4.968	029514-7	1	Carton	Pall Mall Reg Red
33	1,140	5.180	029673-1	1	Carton	Camel Cigarettes
34	1,139	.414	73402-10440	1	22 ounces	Ck Giant 22 ounces
35	1,088	5.204	029634-3	1	Carton	Merit Filter Kings
36	1,074	.709	18200-11047	2	12 Pack	Bud 12/12 Can
37	1,067	5.309	029628-5	1	Carton	Marlboro Light 100
38	1,066	5.199	029714-3	1	Carton	Winston Light King
39	1,036	5.313	029715-0	1	Carton	Winston Light 100s
40	1,025	5.281	029691-3	1	Carton	Now 100s Filter
41	1,015	5.258	029712-7	1	Carton	Winston 100s
42	983	.749	70438-16013	4	Quart	Gfrd Ice Cream
43	975	.368	73402-11350	1	16 ounces	Ck Scotch Ct Meal
44	956	1.054	70438-16011	2	HF Gl	Gfrd Ice Cream
45	952	.125	12000-00230	8	2 Liter	Pepsi 2 Liter
46	934	5.246	029685-5	1	Carton	Doral Lt Filter 100
47	933	.371	48121-10208	1	12 ounces	Thomas's English Muffins
48	896	5.303	0219630-1	1	Carton	Marlboro 100 Box
49	875	5.402	029501-4	1	Carton	Carlton 100s Cigars
50	847	5.326	029636-8	1	Carton	Merit Filter 100
	71,279	.455	TOP 50 TOTALS			

DP606-1 09/26/90 22.30 DIRECT PRODUCT PROFITABILITY TOP 50/BOTTOM 50 REPORT FOR—0387 ME MALL SUPER SHOP N SAVE FROM 05/26/90 TO 09/15/90—17 WEEKS

Direct Product Profit			General Information			
Cat Rank	DPP $	DPP Unit	Item Number	Pck	Size	Description
1	176-	.160-	106821-2	15	32 ounces	Hellmann's Mayonnaise
2	177-	.204-	363450-8	24	4 rolls	Northern TT Soft Print
3	179-	.932-	069137-8	4	32 count	Huggies for Her Large
4	179-	.141-	068643-6	24	13 ounces	Isomil Concentrate
5	184-	.137-	031060-7	24	1.76Z	Milky Way Dark Bars
6	184-	.084-	180592-8	24	16 ounces	B&M Baked Pea Beans
7	186-	.106-	068580-0	24	13 ounces	Similac W/Iron Conc
8	195-	.114-	364588-4	30	1 roll	Sparkle Design Paper Twl
9	196-	2.040-	582507-0	12	3.0 ounces	WW Sausage Biscuit
10	197-	.140-	364447-3	30	1 roll	Bounty Assorted
11	198-	.317-	362992-0	12	300 count	Mardi Gras Dec Napkins
12	198-	.097-	364690-8	30	1 roll	Scott Dec Towels
13	199-	.144-	364587-6	30	1 roll	Sparkle White/Brdr Print
14	201-	5.580-	270173-8	12	15.6 ounces	Kudos Peanut Bttr 12 ct
15	202-	.122-	646200-6	12	12 ounces	Lender's Bagels
16	206-	.286-	662830-9	12	28 ounces	Banquet Fried Chicken
17	210-	.087-	364170-1	30	1 roll	SNS 2Ply Paper Towels
18	211-	1.174-	069134-5	4	44 count	Huggies for Him/Medium
19	215-	.211-	303549-0	12	19.8 ounces	Ch. Chewy Brownie Fm Sze
20	218-	.188-	364443-2	10	3 rolls	Bounty Household Towels
21	223-	.039-	191050-4	48	6.5 ounces	Geisha Sol Wh Tuna/Wtr
22	229-	1.024-	069136-0	4	32 count	Huggies for Him/Large
23	230-	.177-	363448-2	24	4 rolls	Northrn Wh Bathrm Tissues
24	231-	.050-	363304-7	80	1 roll	Scottissue Bath Tis Asst
25	243-	.513-	069207-9	6	32 count	Pampers Ultra Pls Lg/Boy
26	247-	1.067-	069135-2	4	44 count	Huggies for Her/Medium
27	249-	.292-	362705-6	12	300 count	SNS 1Ply Napkins
28	249-	.138-	363515-8	24	4 rolls	Charmin White
29	252-	.779-	069212-9	6	44 count	Pampers Ultr Pls Med Grl
30	275-	.084-	210860-3	48	7.25 ounces	Kr Macaroni/Cheese Dinner
31	282-	.212-	277027-3	12	16 ounces	Sunshine Cheez-It
32	283-	.097-	364451-5	30	1 roll	Bounty Designer Towels
33	293-	2.711-	36065	1	2S	Evr Heavy Duty D 2Pack
34	319-	.193-	44600-00104	6	128 ounces	Clorox Bleach Regular
35	357-	.238-	37000-63037	30	1 roll	Bounty Wh Towel Mcro
36	357-	2.707-	663135-2	12	12 ounces	Barber Chicken Ital Style
37	358-	.101-	364442-4	30	1 roll	Bounty Wh/Micro Towels
38	393-	.489-	370060-6	6	128 ounces	Clorox Liquid Bleach
39	394-	.091-	512000-1	30	16 ounces	Blue Bonnt Margarine Qtrs
40	399-	1.664-	300207-8	24	16 ounces	SNS Dark Brown Sugar
41	452-	9.426-	29015	48		Disp Ninja Turtle Video
42	511-	.258-	174630-4	12	6 ounces	Near East Rice Pilaf
43	517-	3.314-	375213-6	12	40 count	Downy Sheets Reg 40 Count
44	526-	.054-	363303-9	80	1 roll	Scottissue Bath Tis Whte
45	560-	1.667-	300208-6	24	16 ounces	SNS Light Brown Sugar
46	571-	.238-	37000-63087	30	1 roll	Bounty Design Tw
47	599-	1.665-	300206-0	24	16 ounces	SNS Confectioners Sugar
48	992-	.195-	364643-7	30	1 roll	Mardi Gras Dec Towels
49	1,007-	.082-	191047-0	48	6.5 ounces	Geisha Ch Lt Tuna/Wtr
50	15,882-	35.769-	601744-6	12	7 ounces	V D Kamps L/C Had Fillet
	31.391-	.344-	BOTTOM 50 TOTALS			

Exhibit 11
Sample Management Summary Report

DP607-1 09/26/90 22.30 DIRECT PRODUCT PROFITABILITY MANAGEMENT SUMMARY REPORT FOR STORE—0387 ME MALL SUPER SHOP N SAVE, FROM 05/26/90 TO 09/15/90—17 WEEKS

006— BABY FOOD

Intermediate No.	Family Group Name	No. Items	DPP $	DPP $ Rank	DPP $ Pct to Tot	Average DPP Unit	Retail Sales	Sales Rank	Ret Sales Pct to Tot
06	Dinner, Regular	31	153	483	0.0165	.030	2,173.99	390	0.0422
12	Fruits	47	228	456	0.0246	.021	4,340.25	280	0.0842
18	Desserts	27	98	514	0.0106	.020	1,993.19	403	0.0387
30	Meats	14	218	462	0.0235	.090	1,679.76	425	0.0326
36	Juices	28	267	440	0.0288	.060	3,079.02	337	0.0597
42	Vegetables	39	220	460	0.0237	.026	3,381.27	321	0.0656
48	Cereal, Dry	10	125	500	0.0135	.110	1,424.52	445	0.0276
54	Dinners, Hi-Protein	5	52	540	0.0056	.090	377.28	532	0.0073
60	Cereal Combination	7	13	561	0.0014	.014	456.23	522	0.0089
62	Instant	1	1	571	0.0001	.083	8.28	583	0.0002
72	Bisc, Cook, Other Food	2	16	558	0.0017	.095	166.32	556	0.0032
78	Disposable Diapers	60	2,592-	626	0.2794	.403-	62,348.08	9	1.2098
79	Baby Wash Cloths	17	1,633	161	0.1760	.561	7,556.82	202	0.1466
85	Baby Formula	37	1,419-	624	0.1530	.138-	26,866.06	32	0.5213
**** Family Group Total ****		325	987-		0.1064	.017-	115,851.07		2.2479

008—PICKLES AND OLIVES

Intermediate No.	Family Group Name	No. Items	DPP $	DPP $ Rank	DPP $ Pct to Tot	Average DPP Unit	Retail Sales	Sales Rank	Ret Sales Pct to Tot
20	Pickles	54	2,532	111	0.2729	.309	13,547.60	105	0.2629
50	Pickle Specialties	13	357	410	0.0385	.356	1,481.22	443	0.0287
60	Olives	33	1,939	143	0.2090	.229	8,771.94	173	0.1702
65	Relishes	18	578	340	0.0623	.153	3,259.26	329	0.0632
**** Family Group Total ****		118	5,406		0.5827	.252	27,060.02		0.5250

Exhibit 12
Sample of DPP Category/Item-Specific Report

DP610-1 06/29/90 08.34   DIRECT PRODUCT PROFITABILITY REPORT FOR - 0351 FOREST AVE. SHOP N SAVE FROM 02/24/90 TO 06/16/90 - 17 WEEKS

36 - PAPER, FILM AND FOIL

Direct Product Profit			General Information				Shelf Allocation Units					Average		Pct
Cat Rank	DPP $	DPP Unit	Item Number	Pck	Size	Description	Sugg	Act	Facings	New	Variety from Sugg	Weekly Cases	Movmnt Units	Stores Carry
12 Facial Tissue														
1	96	.285	362501-9	24	280 ct	Scottie Facial Asstd Jbo	36					1	21	100
2	137	.238	362000-2	24	150 ct	Puffs Plus Asrt Fam Fclt	38					1	34	100
3	36	.214	361630-7	24	8's	Kleenex Pocket Pack Asst	36						10	100
4	154	.214	362340-2	24	280 ct	Scottie Facial Tissues	42					2	45	100
5	30	.206	361883-2	24	250 ct	Kleenex Fam Size White	36						8	100
6	84	.206	362001-0	24	250 ct	Puffs Fcl Wht/Asst Fm Sz	36					1	24	100
7	242	.198	361890-7	24	250 ct	Kleenex FS White PP 149	53					3	72	100
8	161	.197	361891-5	24	250 ct	Kleenex FS Asstd PP 149	43					2	48	100
9	53	.163	362330-3	36	175 ct	Tree Free Facials	54					1	19	100
10	11	.152	364360-7	36	6 ct	Hanks Paper Handkerchief	36						4	100
11	64	.136	362004-4	36	100 ct	Posh Puffs Scntd Cube	54					1	28	100
12	129	.133	362003-6	36	75 ct	Puffs Plus Cube Asstrd	59					2	57	100
13	43	.128	361640-6	24	60 ct	Klnx Man Size Tiss 3Ply	36					1	20	100
14	99	.125	362500-1	36	200 ct	Scott Asst Fac Tiss 2Ply	56					1	50	100
15	114	.113	362440-0	36	200 ct	Scott White Fac Tiss 2PLY	61					2	63	100
16	5	.110	361699-2	24	250 ct	Klnx Softique Family	36						3	100
17	128	.109	361892-3	36	95 ct	Kleenex Softique 100 99	83					2	68	100
18	51	.109	362009-3	36	100 ct	Puffs Free Unscented	54					1	28	100
19	168	.108	361680-2	36	100 ct	Klnx Boutique Asst PP 99	72					3	91	100
20	82	.108	362010-1	36	175 ct	Puffs Collated PP 109	54					1	44	100
21	38	.094	361701-6	24	250 ct	Klnx Softique FM Sz 1.49	36					1	23	100
22	403	.088	361530-9	36	175 ct	SNS 2Ply Facial Tissue	144					7	269	100
23	26	.076	362011-9	24	250 ct	Puffs Fam Colltd PP 1.49	36					1	20	100
24	95	.069	361717-2	36	175 ct	Klnx Foil White PP 109	88					2	80	100
25	4	.058	361678-6	36	100 ct	Klnx Boutique Tiss 2Ply	54						4	100
26	1	.035	361665-3	36	100 ct	Klnx Softique Facial Tis	54						2	100
27	12	.014	362584-5	21	140 ct	Sparkle Napkins PP 79	41					2	49	100
28	34-	.049-	362006-9	24	150 ct	Puffs Plus Asst PP 1.49	40					2	41	100
29	6-	.053-	362008-5	36	175 ct	Puffs Reg Wht Facial Tis	54						6	100
Total Items for—Facial Tissue	2,422	.117							29					
Cost per Cubic Foot of Shelf Space for This Reporting Period									.00					

Note: Recommended shelf allocation is in units.

Exhibit 13
Grocery New Item DPP Evaluation, Brand A Air Freshener—Line Extension

Description	7
Pack	12
Size	6
Case Cube	0.19
Regular Cost	$9.00
Deal Cost	$9.00
Weekly Movement (Cases)	0.50

Unit SRP	Portland Zone 1 $0.990	Bangor Zone 1 $0.990	Average Zone 2 $0.990	New York Zone 17 $0.990	Vermont Zone 16 $1.090
Gross Margins					
Total Sell	$ 5.94	$ 5.94	$ 5.94	$ 5.94	$ 6.54
Total Cost Reg.	4.50	4.50	4.50	4.50	4.50
Gross Margin	1.44	1.44	1.44	1.44	2.04
Gross Profit %	24.2	24.2	24.2	24.2	31.2
Total Cost Deal	$ 4.50	$ 4.50	$ 4.50	$ 4.50	$ 4.50
Gross Margin	1.44	1.44	1.44	1.44	2.04
Gross Profit %	24.2	24.2	24.2	24.2	31.2
Direct Product Costs					
Whse Handling Cube	0.022	0.022	0.022	0.022	0.022
Whse Handling Case	0.049	0.049	0.049	0.049	0.049
Whse Occupancy Cube	0.040	0.040	0.040	0.040	0.040
Buying Case	0.042	0.042	0.042	0.042	0.042
Store Order Case	0.009	0.009	0.009	0.009	0.009
Transportation	0.012	0.030	0.028	0.050	0.041
Store Unload Cube	0.001	0.001	0.001	0.001	0.001
Cut & Stock Unit	0.071	0.071	0.071	0.071	0.071
Store Inventory Cost	0.052	0.052	0.052	0.052	0.052
Cashier Cost Unit	0.067	0.067	0.067	0.067	0.067
Bagging Cost Unit	0.064	0.064	0.064	0.064	0.064
Bag Cost Cube	0.006	0.006	0.006	0.006	0.006
Total DPCs	$0.434	$0.452	$0.450	$0.472	$0.463
DPP $/Week Reg	$1.006	$0.988	$0.990	$0.968	$1.577
DPP $/Week Deal	1.006	0.988	0.990	0.968	1.577
Fresheners & Deodorizers:					
Average DPP/Unit	$0.350	$0.320	$0.400	$0.300	$0.460
New Item:					
DPP/Unit Reg	$0.168	$0.165	$0.165	$0.161	$0.263
DPP/Unit Deal	0.168	0.165	0.165	0.161	0.263

Exhibit 14
DPP Statistics for Selected Items

Item	Pack	Size	Retail	Gross Margin %	DPP/ Unit	Cube
Grocery						
SNS						
Potato Chips	9	16 oz	$1.89	31	6.7¢	High
Mardi Gras Paper Towels	30	1 roll	0.69	31	5.5	High
SNS						
Saltine Crackers	24	16 oz	0.89	27	2.0	Average to High
Durkee Potato Sticks	48	1.5 oz	0.39	41	15.7	Average
Purina Unique Can Cat Food	24	6 oz	2 for $1.00	24	8.8	Average
Dairy						
SNS						
Corn Oil Margarine	30	1 lb	0.67	29	18.5	Low
HBA						
Cigarrest	1	n/a	16.95	10	$1.00	Low
Listermint Trial Size	96	1.5 oz	2 for 89¢	44	(3.2¢)	High

Average Department Performance:

	Gross Margin %	DPP/ Unit
Grocery	20.5	31.7¢
Dairy	25.0	39.9
HBA	27.0	48.0

Exhibit 15
Incremental Costs Associated with DPP

Historical Fixed Costs:	
1981 DPP Software to Integrate Sales and Cost Systems	$ 50,000
Subsequent Software Enhancements	10,000
Apollo Software ($15,000/machine)	105,000
Apollo Hardware ($12,000/Machine)	84,000
Total Fixed	$ 249,000
Annual Operating Expenses:	
MIS Labor and Computer Time to Issue DPP Reports	$ 72,000
DPP Department Labor (including benefits) and System Maintenance	245,000
Total Annual Operating	$ 317,000

Note: Costs include the product management department at Hannaford as well as the DPP Department at Progressive.

RETAIL MARKETING
PART 1: THE COSTLY BARGAIN
OF TRADE PROMOTION

One of the most significant phenomena in retailing in recent years has been the shift in power from manufacturers to the trade. In frequently purchased, heavily advertised goods, the dominant players have become the big chains like Safeway, Wal-Mart, Kroger, Kmart, Toys R Us, Walgreen, CVS, Home Depot, and Circuit City.

Partly as a result of manufacturers' relative loss of clout, they have been reducing their commitment to advertising—especially national advertising—and spending much more on consumer and trade promotion. But systemic inefficiencies resulting from these short-term incentives have blossomed into huge problems: the high costs involved in paying slotting allowances, in forward buying, in diversion of goods, and in running promotion programs. These are problems for the trade and for manufacturers, but especially for manufacturers.

Manufacturers pay dearly for burgeoning promotional programs; for example, managers at Procter & Gamble estimate that 25% of salesperson time and about 30% of brand management time are spent in designing, implementing, and overseeing promotions. The costs are high for others too. In this promotion-intensive environment, consumers pay more for the goods they buy as distributors pass along the higher costs. In the food industry, for instance, increases in manufacturer and distribution costs from trade promotion alone amount to an estimated 2.5% or more of retail sales, including the costs of administering promotional programs.

The game playing and power playing inherent in promotions and related activities, like slotting allowances, have generated an enormous amount of mistrust in channels of distribution—manufacturers, wholesalers, and retailers have big bones to pick with one another. The mistrust has dominated the headlines in *Supermarket News* for two years or more. Here are sample news stories:

- Some consumer-goods producers have had to set up large reserves on their accounts receivable to handle expected retailer claims for damaged or spoiled merchandise and for promotion allowances for which they allegedly have not received full credit. These claims are not speculative; in 1988, for example, Kraft took a $35 million write-off. Such instances cause great friction because retailers have been known to file claims on merchandise as a way of getting discounts they could not have gotten otherwise. The number of contested claims has risen to an all-time high.

This article first appeared as "The Costly Bargain of Trade Promotion" by Robert D. Buzzell, John A. Quelch, and Walter J. Salmon in the Harvard Business Review, March–April 1990, used with permission.

Authors' note: The material on forward buying in this article is taken from a study sponsored by the Food Marketing Foundation, which we thank. Associate Professor Marie-Therese Flaherty and Professor Ramchandran Jaikumar of the Harvard Business School and Marci Dew of the consulting firm IAMCO were coauthors of the study.

- Last year, two of the largest grocery chains, Winn-Dixie and Kroger, boycotted some products of Pillsbury, Procter & Gamble, and other vendors after those companies refused to charge uniform prices for their goods throughout the chains' trading area. Winn-Dixie started the imbroglio by telling the big suppliers, "Everything we buy from you will be at the lowest promotion price offered throughout our entire system." The asserted motive: to smooth operations and save consumers money. Manufacturers took Winn-Dixie's demands as an infringement on their ability to engage in regional pricing. Winn-Dixie deleted from its shelves several hundred items of Pillsbury, P&G, Quaker Oats, and others. Negotiation eventually ended the standoff.
- For years, Kellogg has refused to pay slotting allowances—the fees mass merchandisers, mostly food chains, charge packaged-goods producers to allow new products into their stores—to Stop & Shop and other companies. These fees commonly amount to four- or five-figure numbers per item per chain. Countering Kellogg's stance, Stop & Shop for a time refused to carry its new cereal varieties.

Battles like these are a common occurrence today, now that retailers hold sway over manufacturers. Routinely, for example, department stores and other retailers demand from vendors cooperative advertising allowances, guaranteed gross margins, return privileges, reimbursement for the cost of fixtures, and in-store selling and stock-keeping help to promote their merchandise.

Deep-seated feelings about unfairness in today's promotion-laden atmosphere go hand in hand with the rising costs of promotions and the inefficiencies they produce. Mistrust inhibits industry cooperation on key issues like data exchange. The promotion practices also appear to be dispelling Washington's prolonged lack of interest in violation of laws upholding fair competition.

Here we will examine the by-products of the promotion explosion by putting under a microscope one widespread practice, forward buying, in key product lines sold in supermarkets: dry grocery products, health and beauty aids, and general merchandise. We examine the effects of forward buying and then of trade promotion in general on the entire distribution chain—manufacturers, wholesalers, retailers, and consumers. We suggest one pricing policy that not only helps get costs under control but also builds cooperation and trust among the parties.

Analysis of the costly inefficiencies that spill out of forward buying in food supermarkets may help manufacturers and distributors in other fields put the spotlight on practices in their own backyards. Although promotion practices are probably most widespread in the supermarket business, forward buying and diversion are also common in, say, athletic footwear, and slotting allowances are not unknown in the chain drugstores.

HIGH TIDE OF PROMOTION

At the expense of advertising, promotion has received a big lift in recent years. Just how much a lift can be seen in the responses to an annual survey of marketing managers in consumer packaged-goods companies showing the breakdowns of their marketing budgets. In 1978, advertising accounted for 42% of those budgets and consumer and trade promotion, 58%. By 1988, ad spending had slipped to 31% against 69% for promotion.[1] Trade promotion accounted for three-quarters of the shift.

There are some powerful forces in motion that explain the intensifying stress on sales promotion:

---

1 Donnelley Marketing, *Eleventh Annual Survey of Promotional Practices* (Stamford, Conn., 1989).

- The U.S. population is growing at only 0.8% annually, and growth in per-capita consumption of most mature products is modest. This situation, combined with excess production capacity, has aggravated competition for market share and the use of price promotions to secure it.
- Today's consumer is less interested in shopping, more likely to hold a job, under greater time pressure, and less inclined to prepare a shopping list ahead of a store visit. Hence today's consumer is more susceptible to prominent displays in the store and more likely to buy whichever of several acceptable brands happens to be on deal.
- As the technologies underpinning established products mature, the opportunities for product and quality differentiation shrink. That fact, combined with the weaker involvement of the consumer, makes development of creative advertising copy more difficult. The result: emphasis on price competition.
- While there is no shortage of new products, most are line extensions and me-too imitations. Given the proliferation of new products clamoring for finite shelf space and retailers' limited promotion capacity, distributors try to ration their sources. They turn to slotting allowances and press for more and better deals on all products in their stores.
- Many factors influence manufacturers and retailers in the direction of a short-term outlook. On the manufacturers' side, for example, top management's concern for meeting quarterly earnings targets, plus the fast career advancement that young managers expect, reinforces this orientation. A result is a preference for boosting sales through promotion instead of taking the time to strengthen the consumer franchise through advertising.

Of course, there are many good reasons for undertaking a serious promotion program. The insert "Why Sales Promotions?" lists several of them.

WHY SALES PROMOTIONS?

- They are useful in securing trial for new products and in defending shelf space against anticipated and existing competition.
- The funds manufacturers dedicate to them lower the distributor's risk in stocking new brands.
- They add excitement at the point of sale to the merchandising of mature and mundane products. They can instill a sense of urgency among consumers to buy while a deal is available.
- Since sales-promotion costs are incurred on a pay-as-you-go basis, they can spell survival for smaller, regional brands that cannot afford big advertising programs.
- Sales promotions allow manufacturers to use idle capacity and to adjust to demand and supply imbalances or softness in raw material prices and other input costs—while maintaining the same list prices.
- They allow manufacturers to price-discriminate among consumer segments that vary in price sensitivity. Most manufactures believe that a high-list, high-deal policy is more profitable than offering a single price to all consumers. A portion of sales-promotion expenditures, therefore, consists of reductions in list prices that are set for the least price-sensitive segment of the market.

A CASE: FORWARD BUYING

In our study of the important food distribution sector of the economy—accounting for super-market sales of $240 billion in 1988—we sought to discover how much trade promotion raises certain expenses. While our estimates of such cost effects apply only to food distributors and manufacturers, we believe that they will give a useful perspective on sales promotion broadly throughout the U.S. consumer-marketing system.

During the 1980s, marketers of food, household, and personal-care products offered more frequent and more attractive trade deals to food chains and wholesalers. These are induce-ments used to influence a distributor to stock or display more of a product or cut its price to consumers. The distributors respond by:

- Adding to their "forward-buy" inventories. These stocks—merchandise bought at cut prices in addition to quantities needed to sell at reduced prices or to sell through retailer advertising or end displays during the deal period—are held for later sale, usually at regular prices.
- Diverting goods from regions in which manufacturers offer especially deep discounts to higher priced areas when different deals are offered in different areas. The means of doing it include (1) transfer from one division of a multiregional or national retailer or wholesaler to another division, (2) sale and direct shipment from one distributor to another, and (3) consignment via "diverters" who make this their business.

Both practices add to the distributors' costs. Forward buying inflates inventories and thereby boosts interest expense, storage charges, and insurance costs. Forward buying also means extra transportation and handling outlays because forward-buy stocks are almost always kept sepa-rate from the "regular" inventories. Diversion of merchandise involves trans-shipment and double-handling, which of course cost money.

To estimate the added costs from diversion would have meant determining the normal paths followed by a sample shipment from suppliers to distributors. A comparison of actual shipping and handling expenses, including diversions, with normal costs would have yielded the de-sired numbers. But this would have been a monumental task given the large number of shipping points and warehouses in the United States, so we did not attempt it.

Even so, we believe that the added costs of diversion are substantial. Food-marketing con-sultant Willard Bishop, a longtime observer of the industry, estimates that the volume of merchandise involved amounts to at least $5 billion a year.

Impact on Distributor Inventories. We did estimate the impact of forward buying by comparing distributors' purchasing patterns with those that would have been expected if there had been no (or less) forward buying. ("Distributors" here means both retail chains and whole-salers.)

If trade deals did not exist, food chains and wholesalers customarily would order from their major suppliers about every two weeks. A company would order enough merchandise to cover the next two weeks plus a safety stock, typically about one week's supply, to accommodate unforeseeable variations in sales patterns leading to above-average sales. A distributor follow-ing this pattern would have an average inventory of two weeks' supply, as shown in the chart "No-Trade-Deal Distributor Inventory."

Now let's look at reality: distributors take advantage of periodic trade opportunities to forward-buy goods for later sale. Most well-run distributors use widely available computer programs to determine how much to buy on a given supplier's deal. The savings that distribu-tors realize normally more than offset the extra costs of buying, double-handling, and stocking enough merchandise to last perhaps until the next deal. Distributors usually have a good idea

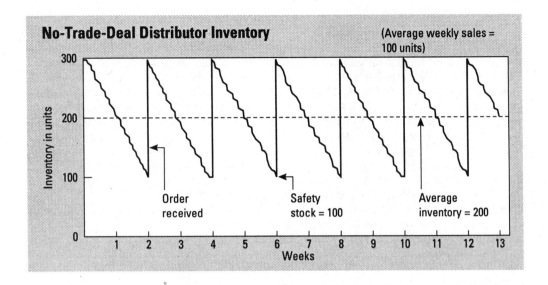

No-Trade-Deal Distributor Inventory (Average weekly sales = 100 units)

Inventory in units

Order received

Safety stock = 100

Average inventory = 200

Weeks

when the next deal will be offered because most suppliers schedule their trade deals well ahead. So a rational distributor will make nearly all purchases during deal periods.

How would average inventories then be affected? The answer depends on how often the price reductions are offered and the extent to which consumer purchases shift to the deal periods. The chart "Distributor Inventory on Trade Deals" illustrates a typical situation in which deals are offered during four weeks of each quarter, and 50% of consumer purchases are made during those weeks because the retailer features the manufacturer's merchandise. The effect on distributor inventories is drastic: year-round average inventory is 80% greater.

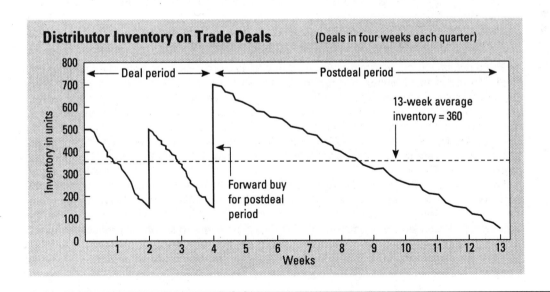

Distributor Inventory on Trade Deals (Deals in four weeks each quarter)

Inventory in units

Deal period

Postdeal period

13-week average inventory = 360

Forward buy for postdeal period

Weeks

While this estimate is based on just one set of assumptions about deal frequency and the size of deal discounts, this estimated increase agrees with information that food distributors gave us in our study. Their forward-buy inventories normally amounted to 40% to 50% of total stocks. If forward buying raised inventory by 80% over the level it would be under a no-dealing scenario, then 80/180, or 44%, of total inventory is attributable to forward buying.

Most forward buying in the retail food sector is in dry grocery goods, household supplies, and personal-care products. We estimate that supermarket sales of dry groceries, health and beauty aids, and general merchandise were $109 billion, or about $87.5 billion at wholesale values. In the absence of any forward buying, distributors' inventories of these goods would have neared $4.4 billion. If actual inventories included 40% to 50% of forward-buy stocks, the *increase* in distributors' inventories attributable to forward buying ranged from $2.9 billion to $4.4 billion. If these forward-buy purchases were usually bought at 10% below "normal" prices, the amount invested in them ranges from $2.6 billion to $4 billion.

Moreover, some forward buying in high-volume frozen foods and dairy products also goes on. Forward-buy stocks of these products represent a distributor investment of about $500 million. This brings the total to $3.1 billion to $4.5 billion.

The carrying costs on distributors' inventories—including handling, storage, and capital charges—were about 30% per year. Applying this figure to the added inventories in the system from forward buying yields an added system cost of between $930 million and $1.35 billion a year. While this is obviously a substantial amount, it represents only between 0.65% and 0.9% of total retail sales of the products affected.

Cost to the Manufacturers. Forward buying is a chief cause of fluctuations in a supplier's rate of shipment to distributors. How much does it contribute to the total "cost of uncertainty" for manufacturers? Our study shows that the impact of forward buying on suppliers' costs depends on:

- The fraction of total sales accounted for by forward-buy purchases. Not surprisingly, the more important forward buying is, the more it contributes to total uncertainty costs.
- The interval between promotions. The longer the interval, the greater the uncertainty about demand. (At the other extreme, continuous promotions would make forward buying unnecessary and, obviously, generate no uncertainty about it. A few heavily promoted categories, like ground coffee, nearly fit this description.)
- The number of items, or stock-keeping units (SKUs), in a supplier's product line. The more SKUs, the greater the demand uncertainty for any particular item.

For a manufacturer, distributors' forward buying is a serious factor, but only one of several factors (some of them having nothing to do with sales promotion) that generate uncertainty about demand and limit producers' ability to forecast sales accurately. So they maintain excess production capacity and carry safety stocks of finished goods, which cost money. Several leading food-industry suppliers are paying to price: they have undertaken large-scale plant closings. Among them are P&G, which in 1987 set up an $805 million reserve to "restructure" worldwide production operations, and Campbell Soup, which last summer scheduled a similar charge, to cost $343 million.

From discussions with several big food-industry suppliers, we estimate that for most food companies the incremental costs related to forward buying range between 1% and 2% of their costs of goods sold. If typical gross margins are around $33^1/_3$% for suppliers and 20% for distributors, this added cost represents 0.5% to 1.1% of *retail* prices of the products involved. Applying these figures to total 1988 retail sales of dry groceries and selected dairy and frozen products makes the incremental supplier costs from forward buying between $720 million and $1.58 billion.

Costs to the System. Adding the two figures yields the total of $1.6 billion to $2.9 billion, shown in the table "Total Added Costs Resulting from Forward Buying." Nonperishable food-store products represent some 5% of all retail sales. Forward buying is of course impractical for perishable merchandise, like fruit and vegetables, or short-life-cycle merchandise, like fashion apparel. But if all consumer goods are considered, forward-buying costs could total several times the $1.6 billion to $2.9 billion spread.

Moreover, these substantial amounts represent only a part of the true costs of trade promotion, let alone the total cost of all forms of sales promotion. Other expenses, which we have not tried to qualify, include:

- The added transportation and handling costs in diverting merchandise among regions.
- The higher administrative and selling costs that suppliers and distributors incur to operate increasingly complex selling and purchasing programs. We mentioned P&G's assertion that 30% of the brand management organization's time and 25% of field salespeople's time is absorbed by these tasks. The proportions are typical.
- The costs of the time that buyers and merchants spend evaluating deals, which would be better spent in competitive analyses and category management.

These hidden costs of promotion could easily equal or exceed the more tangible costs that we explored. The total cost is very high, both absolutely and relative to suppliers' and distributors' earnings. Reduction of these costs would produce savings that could greatly benefit consumers and retailers, wholesalers, and manufacturers.

SOME LIKE IT, SOME DON'T

In addition to impairing the efficiency of the distribution system, the explosion in sales-promotion expense has other important, harmful effects on the distribution chain.

Our analysis of the food industry yields estimates that the increase in manufacturer and distributor costs from more trade-promotion amounts to about 2½% of retail sales. Since there has been no noticeable decline of manufacturer and distributor *profits,* the consumer has presumably absorbed these costs.

This cost burden has not affected all consumers equally. Those with the time and inclination to shop for bargains, termed "cherry pickers" by the trade, have probably enjoyed lower prices as a result of the higher proportion of items offered on sale. But most consumers, whose shopping time is often constrained by work and other responsibilities, have probably seen their prices on affected items rise by somewhat more than 2%.

Other consequences of higher sales-promotion expenses have affected consumers too. Because it is harder to predict the rate of sale of merchandise offered at special prices, stock outs of preferred brands may be more frequent. This phenomenon would apply more to risky, short- life-cycle fashion merchandise offered at special prices than to staple items where

Total Added Costs Resulting from Forward Buying

	Millions of Dollars	Percent of Retail Sales
Distributors	$ 930 to $1,350	0.65% to 0.9%
Manufacturers	$ 720 to $1,584	0.50% to 1.1%
Total	$1,650 to $2,934	1.15% to 2.0%*

* Excluding added administrative costs

forward-buy inventories probably offset the less predictable sales rate of merchandise that is sold on specials.

Another probable effect of the availability of more merchandise at special prices is a deterioration of in-store service. Special sales exaggerate the normal peaks and valleys of store traffic and thus impair service, whether it is the availability of a salesperson in a department store or the length of a checkout line in a discount store or supermarket.

The extra costs that trade promotions impose on distribution channels do not affect all classes of trade equally. Such distributors as deep-discount drugstores and warehouse clubs—which carry few items in each category and have no commitment to item continuity—favor heightened manufacturer sales-promotion activity.

Warehouse clubs especially have this attitude. The burgeoning volume of trade deals, in particular, means that more items (or the same items more often) are available to them at sharply reduced prices. Moreover, since they usually offer only a few brands and sizes in a category, they can quickly dispose of the promoted items with no effect on the movement of competing items. Competitors allege that the frequency of trade deals, combined with relaxed enforcement of the Robinson-Patman Act and manufacturers' hunger for more volume, allows these limited-line distributors to buy at more favorable prices than traditional channels or to obtain other concessions, like direct store delivery of smaller quantities, at no extra cost.

Food wholesalers are ambivalent about promotion practices. While they vigorously condemn the allegedly better treatment that nonfood channels receive, they do not advocate elimination of these practices. Because quasinational or multiregional operators dominate food wholesaling, they have established their own internal diversion networks. Moreover, the difference between forward-buying income and expense gives them added flexibility. While passing on some of these funds to customers in proportion to their purchases, they can use a portion of the income to subsidize weak areas, underwrite new operations, support added services for retailers, or boost their own profits.

The wholesalers' ambivalent attitude toward promotion practices contrasts sharply with the views of some food retailers. They argue that the labor and storage costs of forward-buy inventories and the extra transportation costs in diverting merchandise, while more than offset by lower purchase prices for merchandise, nevertheless add to their costs of goods sold. These expenses, many retailers assert, undercut the advantages of just-in-time replenishment practices for their regular inventories. They fear that an overriding concern for buying at the lowest cost diverts their merchandising organizations from the primary goal of serving consumers better. What these retailers would prefer is a system that provides them with the lower purchase prices for merchandise *without* the added costs of forward buying and diversion.

Producers of health and beauty aids and food also take exception to these promotion practices. Apart from the incremental manufacturing or inventory costs they incur, they perceive serious, though nonquantifiable, consequences. Among them is a decline in brand loyalty arising from elevated consumer price sensitivity. Even consumers once faithful to certain brands may switch to other products that are on deal or time the purchase of their preferred products to coincide with available deals.

Food manufacturers also complain that retailers often fail to discharge their responsibility to provide temporary price reductions, special displays, or feature advertisements. Often retailers allegedly accept promotional allowances for more deals than they are able to fulfill. Manufacturers' attempts to enforce deal terms, however, may spur retailer retaliation, such as deducting unearned merchandise allowances from invoices, increasing claims for damaged merchandise, or delisting low turnover items.

The aforementioned trade-deal terms that favor limited-line distributors, like warehouse clubs, are another sore spot for manufacturers. Because the main goal of limited-line distributors is to sell merchandise at the lowest prices rather than have particular brands always in stock, their priorities inherently conflict with brand loyalty. Furthermore, limited-line distributors refuse to carry the slow movers in a manufacturer's line—but these are often the manufacturer's most profitable items.

The trade-promotion climate has had two disturbing effects. First, as we have indicated, it has aroused mistrust between manufacturers and distributors. This could inhibit cooperation on matters that benefit the whole distribution chain, including electronic-data interchange, modular packaging, and more use of direct product-profit accounting.

Second, today's climate invites political intervention to rid the system of the wasteful expenses of forward buying and diversion. The Federal Trade Commission has been studying slotting allowances for some time. If the Bush Administration decides to renew enforcement of the Robinson-Patman Act, manufacturers and distributors would be endangered. Running afoul of this law in the past has resulted in prolonged and costly litigation, stiff fines, and government-imposed sanctions and reporting requirements that are competitively disadvantageous. Improving sales-promotion practices ethically and legally would reduce this threat.

Despite their concern about the situation, manufacturers have not acted in concert to change matters. Competitive rivalries and fear of being charged with illegal price-fixing have inhibited them.

LIVING WITH PROMOTIONS

Forward buying, diversion, higher manufacturing expenses, and inflated selling and administrative expenses for manufacturers as well as distributors are costing consumers billions each year. And all indications are that the problem is becoming worse. Trade promotions cannot be wished away. But surely there must be a means to execute them at lower cost.

One way to smooth the expense peaks and valleys is a policy of everyday low purchase price (EDLPP). A retailer arranges to buy a particular product from a manufacturer on an as-needed basis at a weighted average price reflecting both the proportion of merchandise recently bought on a deal basis and the proportion bought at the regular price. In return, the retailer agrees to support the product with a certain number and type of promotional events or, more likely, a guarantee to "sell through" to consumers a given quantity of the particular item over a designated period. (Scanner tapes reveal whether the retailer has met the commitment.)

This arrangement has three great benefits. It avoids forward-buy inventory buildup for manufacturers and distributors. It reduces Selling, General, and Administration expenses for producers and sellers because they spend less time negotiating—the contracts run for six months to a year—or supervising performance—because the scanner tapes supply the evidence. Finally, it makes the relationship a collaborative, long-term effort and fosters a spirit of partnership that is seldom found in the monthly deal-buying frenzy.

True, wholesalers would lose some of the flexibility they now enjoy in the use of forward-buy income. In addition, since they have less influence over their retail customers than a chain store does, they could find it difficult to fulfill sell-through guarantees. EDLPP also violates tradition. Chain and wholesale buyers and suppliers' salespeople would have to be weaned away from deal-to-deal buying and selling. Moreover, performance evaluation and incentive systems geared to current practice would have to be changed.

Despite these obstacles, a number of distributors and manufacturers view EDLPP as a source of competitive advantage and are expanding their use of it. In New England, two leading supermarket chains, Hannaford Brothers and Shaw's, are doing business with suppliers on this basis. If EDLPP is superior to deal-to-deal transactions in executing trade promotions, it will gain greater acceptance. (Moreover, we believe, it leads to lower average prices for consumers because of pass-through of savings on handling costs and interest and transportation expenses, as well as administrative costs.)

Clearly, however, EDLPP does not constitute a panacea for all the problems associated with the current promotion climate. With EDLPP, friction among particular channel members will lessen but it will not disappear altogether. Manufacturers will therefore have to dedicate more resources than ever to evaluating their individual trade-promotion policies.

While for the most part trade power is rising, the balance of power between manufacturers and distributors depends on the industry, product category, and market shares. Formulation of a trade-promotion program should begin with an examination of what is practical and profitable for a particular manufacturer to do in lieu of trade promotion to market its products effectively.

We say "in lieu of" because trade promotion should be a last resort in the marketing mix. Product improvement, more effective advertising, and better packaging that more favorably differentiates the manufacturer's offering to the targeted consumer segments (that is, better marketing) are the best avenues for reducing promotion spending and its attendant costs. Investment in R&D is the best way to differentiate and to avoid the necessity of promotions. Even if the payoff is not immediate, discretionary funds can be invested in activities that strengthen a product's consumer franchise unless the present value of the resulting earnings stream is lower than the returns from comparable outlays on promotions.

If the manufacturer nevertheless concludes that it must continue to invest at lease some funds in promotions, we recommend adherence to the following guidelines:

- Focus on the particular support needed from the trade. What these are depends on an understanding of consumer buying behavior. In stimulating sales on impulse-oriented products—cookies, for example—displays are more effective than extra feature ads in retailers' circulars.
- Think through the ways that your trade-support needs differ by distributor. From one distributor, a manufacturer may want authorization for additional sizes and flavors; from a second, more shelf space for existing items; and from a third, better pricing on advertised items.
- Productivity improves when promotions complement distributors' merchandising thrusts. Money for a feature ad may work more effectively if it ties into a distributor's special-event promotion, while funds for a special display may spark more cooperation than a feature ad from a distributor committed to everyday low pricing. Provide a menu of promotions that distributors with different merchandising strategies can choose from.
- Look for ways to reduce the administrative burden imposed on distributors as well as on yourself. For example, there is much to be said for using scanner tapes to verify sell-through objectives instead of using hard-to-track measures like number of incremental end-aisle displays.
- Spread trade-promotion funds fairly among distributors. Fairness should take into account differences in the services they demand from you. A distributor that, say, wants a lot of help from your salespeople to do shelf resets will ordinarily be entitled to less trade-promotion support than a distributor that takes on this task itself. Therefore, be familiar with the components of your cost structure to know how many dollars to give an account in trade-promotion funds.

Effective use of trade-promotion funds means allocating them quantitatively and qualitatively on an account-by-account basis. A field sales organization that is close to the distributors is obviously better positioned to take on this burden than headquarters marketing personnel.

Sales force upgrading, training, and performance criteria that recognize trade-promotion profit as well as volume are therefore a necessity.

Of course, there are often ways to cut costs even in a full-scale promotion program. P&G has established product-supply managers for each of its products. They are charged with supervising the procurement and smoothing the logistics of getting P&G goods to market. The company has also eliminated special packs after discovering that the cost of running these promotions was far greater for distributors as well as for themselves than the cost of regular price promotions of equivalent value. For distributors, using special packs means removing regularly priced goods from the shelf and replacing them with the special packs, and then reversing the procedure at the end of the deal period. For P&G, the necessity of adding SKUs, for which demand had to be forecast, and the increased chances of residuals after the promotion ended were the villains in the cost structure of special packs.

The elimination of special packs has been a major factor in the dramatic improvement of P&G's relationships with wholesalers and retailers. We believe that P&G's success in taking this action is compelling evidence of what can be accomplished by a more rational approach to pricing and sales-promotion management. Many manufacturers are experimenting with EDLPP sales programs; we are confident that the resulting improvements in efficiency and trade relations can be even greater than those achieved by P&G via eliminating special packs.

Obviously, the responsibility for a more rational sales-promotion climate does not lie entirely with manufacturers. Retailers and wholesalers have to take advantage of their enhanced power in ways that do not encumber the distribution system with additional costs.

One way is through a switch in accounting systems so they can distinguish between "the most deal money" and acquiring merchandise at the lowest net cost, including their own expenses for storing and handling inventory. Accounting systems, however, are only as good as the people who use them. Therefore, reorientation and incentive programs that encourage their merchants and buyers to think in this manner are also necessary.

The balance of power in marketing is changing. Companies will best preserve and enhance their positions if they adjust their sales-promotion programs to reflect this reality without burdening the distribution system—and ultimately consumers—with additional costs.

RETAIL MARKETING
PART 2: RESTORING CREDIBILITY
TO RETAIL PRICING

In the 1980s, driven by excess retail space and only modest sales gains, retailers escalated their use of sale events. In 1988, for example, Sears sold 55 percent of its goods at sale prices.[1] Department store sales that used to begin after Christmas now start weeks beforehand. "Sales" in total accounted for over 60 percent of 1988 department store volume.[2] At the same time, retail list price margins as a percentage of the original selling price rose from an average of 47 percent in 1977 to 49.5 percent in 1987.[3] The increasing proportion of merchandise sold at discount and the rise in retail list price margins or "initial markup" have caused some to question the legitimacy of these promotional practices.

The use of inflated initial markups followed by alleged sales has become so severe a problem that some state and local consumer protection agencies are suing retailers. The Pennsylvania Bureau of Consumer Protection has successfully pursued retailers such as John Wanamaker for advertising misleading sale prices. In Massachusetts, regulatory changes have tightened rules for both price comparison claims and the availability of sale-priced merchandise. In addition, in May 1990, Massachusetts also required that sales advertised in retail catalogs state that the "original" price is a reference price and not necessarily the previous selling price.

Consumers as well as regulators are becoming increasingly suspicious of retailers' high "regular" prices and their frequent "sales." Retailers, concerned by the new regulations and the lack of consumer credibility for "high-low" pricing, are increasingly looking at the "everyday low pricing" (EDLP) strategy. This strategy establishes initial prices at or close to the competition's sale prices to both stimulate everyday business and dispense with most if not all sales. EDLP's use by rapidly growing and exceptionally profitable retailers like Wal-Mart, Home Depot, and Toys R Us has stimulated numerous others to consider shifting to EDLP. Typically, EDLP is accompanied by advertising claims such as Home Depot's "guaranteed low prices day in, day out."

This article first appeared as "Restoring Credibility to Retail Pricing" by Gwen Ortmeyer, John A. Quelch, and Walter J. Salmon *in Sloan Management Review.*
Copyrighted by the President and Fellows of Harvard College. Used with permission.

---

1 F. Schwadel and M.J. McCarthy, "New Sears Strategy on Display in Wichita," *Wall Street Journal,* 17 November 1988, p. B1.
2 D.R. McIlhenny, "Introducing the NRMA Retail Market Monitor," *Retail Control,* November 1989, pp. 9–14.
3 *Financial and Operating Results of Departments and Specialty Stores in 1987,* National Retail Merchants Association.

EDLP has caught on among certain grocery, general merchandise, and specialty retailers. Today, it is difficult to find a trade class without a retailer that has staked out an EDLP claim. Recent examples include Staples in office products, IKEA in contemporary furniture, and Paperama in paper goods. Sears' adoption of EDLP in 1989 focused special attention on it. On March 1, 1989, Sears closed its 824 U.S. stores for forty-eight hours to lower its shelf prices on 50,000 items. Sears spent $110 million in advertising during the subsequent three weeks to promote its new pricing strategy.

Apart from grocery retailing, most EDLP success stories represent retailers who either commenced operations as EDLP operators or converted to EDLP when they were first expanding geographically. Converting profitably to a credible EDLP policy overnight, however, may be very difficult for a historically high-low retailer for a variety of operational, consumer, and competitor reasons. We discuss these factors below and suggest an alternative means of price stabilization, "everyday fair pricing plus" (EDFP+). EDFP+ means three things: restoration of everyday prices to levels that represent good value to customers even though they do not purport to be the lowest in town; fewer sale events; and, most importantly, excellence in other differentiating elements of the merchandising mix, such as service and assortment. Following our discussion of the benefits and applicability of the two pricing policies, we analyze Sears' experience with EDLP. Finally, we offer prescriptive advice to retailers switching to a lower, more stable pricing policy.

BENEFITS OF EDLP AND EDFP+

Stable pricing can reduce inventory, personnel, and advertising costs, thus allowing retailers to keep their average prices lower and their profits higher than those of high-low retailers that artificially inflate nonsale prices. Furthermore, EDLP and EDFP+ offer the potential for improved customer service and merchandising, for better in-stock conditions, and for advertising that is image-, rather than price-, oriented. Finally, stable pricing gives a more honest pricing message to the consumer. All of these benefits (described in **Table 1**) are in addition to ultimately higher sales, which we discuss later.

Lower Costs, Better Service, and Better Merchandising

EDLP and EDFP+ stabilize the peaks and valleys in consumer demand caused by frequent, deep discount sales. Smoother demand means less forecasting error and thus fewer out-of-stocks on sale items. The result is less consumer dissatisfaction and, if rain checks were previously offered on out-of-stock advertised items, lower administrative costs. Additionally, the retailer faces fewer sale leftovers, or residuals, which must be marked down even further. This problem is particularly acute if items have been purchased specifically for sale events. Less forecasting error also leads to safety stock reductions, which means faster inventory turnover and less store back-room and warehouse space for inventory storage. Finally, better demand forecasting leads to improved distribution, as a stable flow of goods allows more efficient delivery scheduling.

These strategies can also reduce personnel costs. With fewer sales, less labor is required to reprice sale items, although this source of savings may decline as bar coding replaces individual item pricing. Still, stable pricing eliminates some of the labor that erects and removes temporary displays and that handles surges in consumer demand during sale periods.

Stable pricing has an additional important benefit, especially in merchandise categories where the customer needs sales assistance. Stable customer traffic patterns, unlike sale-stimulated throngs, allow salespeople to spend more time with customers. The high-low retailer could

Table 1 Benefits Associated with EDLP and EDFP+

Benefit	Operational Implication	Customer Implication
• Fewer stock outs	• Reduced costs of administering rain checks • Increased sales (if stock outs mean consumers shop elsewhere)	• Reduction in consumer dissatisfaction
• Fewer residuals	• Decreased margin loss due to leftovers from sales	
• More efficient inventory management	• Improved inventory turns • Less need for inventory safety stocks • Fewer inventory counts • Less need for store back-room and warehouse space	
• More efficient use of personnel	• Less need to pay additional personnel for reticketing and for handling demand surges • Less buyer time spent managing sale events and more time merchandising the entire line	• More salesperson time spent with customer • Better in-stock position on basics and better in-store merchandising
• More advertising flexibility	• Less need for weekly fliers announcing sales • More flexibility in media decisions • Catalogs less likely to become obsolete	• Potential for more image-oriented advertising
• More consumer appeal	• More sales to EDLP/EDFP+ store	• Pricing policy perceived as more honest • Less need to shop around, less need to postpone purchases, and more loyalty • Lower prices per unit

theoretically offer the same salesperson coverage as the stable pricing retailer but would need to hire additional salespeople for peak sale periods and then lay them off during nonpromotional periods. Both the cost and impracticality of hiring temporary salespeople strongly suggest that high-low retailers will have significant difficulty in providing sales assistance equal in quality to retailers with more stable prices.

Another source of advantage is in advertising. The stable pricing strategies limit the need for weekly sale advertising and allow advertising to focus on more image-oriented messages. This encourages the retailer to use such media as television and magazines, which can convey more visually appealing and distinctive messages than newspapers cluttered with sale advertisements. While EDLP or EDFP+ stores still occasionally publish store fliers, their size and frequency can be less than those of high-low chains. In addition, catalogs do not become obsolete as quickly because prices do not change as often.

EDLP and EDFP+ can also produce savings on advertising expense. Wal-Mart spent less than 1 percent of sales on media advertising compared to 2.5 percent for Kmart.[4] Retailers changing from a high-low to a stable pricing strategy, however, will not immediately realize advertising savings because they must communicate the strategy change to consumers. In fact, advertising costs typically rise as the retailer promotes consumer awareness and understanding of the new policy, but, if the strategy is sustained, advertising costs should eventually decline to a lower percentage of sales than before.

Stable pricing can also improve merchandising as buyers change their focus from managing sale events to managing their entire departments on a daily basis. Buyers should then be able to improve merchandise planning and assortments and create more attractive and organized displays.

Consumer Appeal

EDLP and EDFP+ also respond to emerging consumer attitudes. Many consumers—particularly younger consumers, with whom retailers must build relationships for their long-term future—are increasingly skeptical about shelf prices. They have developed the habit during the past decade of only buying during sales because they consider regular shelf prices inflated and unrealistic. They increasingly believe that the sale price is the legitimate price. When Workbench, the specialty furniture retailer, shifted to EDFP+ in 1988, it appealed to these sentiments in fliers that decried "the phony pricing policies of competitors that inflate regular prices."

Dual-income households are also disenchanted with sale prices. They are too busy to compare sale prices in newspapers and resent having to time their shopping trips to coincide with sales. Also, in some merchandise lines, retailers have deliberately complicated and discouraged shopping around by stocking derivative models, minor and often meaningless variations of national brands stocked by competitors. Yet, while these consumers resent having to study advertising and to shop around, they want the assurance that if they buy an item at regular price, the store or a competitor will not discount it soon thereafter. To summarize, despite their current sale-motivated shopping behavior, these consumers would prefer to shop at retailers offering *fair* everyday prices, assuming they found the price credible.

Once convinced that prices are fair, these shoppers enhance EDLP and EDFP+ store profitability in two important ways. They concentrate their purchases at their trusted chain by buying more each time and by buying more frequently. And for some types of merchandise they buy earlier, rather than postponing their purchases until an anticipated sale. Earlier purchasing particularly benefits fashion retailers. It gives them the jump on competition in ascertaining what to reorder and what to mark down, thus boosting sales and reducing markdowns.

Add to this emerging consumer segment those consumers whose purchase behavior is not currently sale influenced. This group includes higher income households, which are likely to patronize higher-end stores emphasizing assortment and exceptional service (admittedly, this segment may be small and declining given current economic conditions). The EDLP or EDFP+ retailer with appropriate product assortment that also offers exceptional service can expect continued patronage from this segment as well.

These two segments of consumers can be contrasted to more sale-oriented shoppers, often referred to as "cherry pickers" by the trade. This group frequently includes retired persons and two-parent families with only one working spouse. The distinguishing feature of cherry pickers

---

4 *Advertising Age,* 27 September 1987, p. 122; and *Advertising Age,* 23 November 1987, p. 548.

is that they usually have both the time and financial incentive to shop for the lowest prices. When sale-oriented stores adopt EDLP or EDFP+, cherry pickers will compare carefully the new price to competitors' sale prices. Thereafter, however, they will shop elsewhere most of the time (except during clearance sales), unless the new prices are truly the lowest in town. Thus the switch to more stable prices may well be accomplished by a loss in patronage from cherry pickers. These customers, however, are less profitable to retailers because they confine their purchases mainly to low- or no- markup sale merchandise. Furthermore, because cherry pickers buy mainly sale merchandise, they tend to spend less per shopping trip than other customers who prefer the convenience of buying everything they need at one location.

The eventual success of EDFP+ depends critically on whether the lost cherry picker volume is offset by business from remaining and new customers attracted by the fair prices, enhanced assortments, and better service. In markets, such as retiree communities, that are dominated by cherry pickers, high-low pricing may make sense for most if not all competing retailers. In such markets, if most retailers pursued stable pricing strategies, their costs might be lower but their profits would suffer, owing to substantial volume deterioration. In mixed markets, a high-low retailer may be successful at serving the cherry picker segment. Such a retailer, however, must recognize that it serves a less profitable and potentially shrinking customer segment.

There is an inherent interdependency between the successful implementation of EDFP+ and the reinforcement of its nonprice consumer benefits. With successful price stabilization comes greater demand predictability, fewer stock outs, better customer service, and the time to plan appropriate assortments. These advantages constitute the *plus* that, along with everyday fair prices, reinforces customer loyalty.

Applicability of EDLP

EDLP in its purest form—the same, noticeably lower prices every single day—is not feasible for most retailers. Five variables concerning the composition of the retailer's merchandise restrict EDLP's applicability: the proportion of comparable products carried, the proportion of frequently purchased products, the price of the merchandise, the percentage of merchandise that is fashion sensitive, and whether the retailer offers complete assortments within categories.

Carrying products and services that can be compared easily among retailers, such as national brands, commodity products (e.g., nails and similar building materials), and oil changes, is important to EDLP believability. So is carrying frequently purchased items; consumers have more knowledge about their prices and can, therefore, judge the fairness of an EDLP claim more quickly. And if the retailer carries a high proportion of lower-ticket items, consumers are more likely to value the convenience of shopping routinely at the EDLP store.

Another variable, the proportion of fashion merchandise, relates inversely to a retailer's ability to implement an EDLP policy successfully. Fashion retailers require sale events to sell the last few pieces of a season's line, soiled and damaged merchandise, and fashion mistakes. Such sales inhibit a retailer carrying predominantly fashion merchandise from adopting a pure EDLP strategy.

The final variable, the completeness within categories, affects an EDLP claim because it relates to the retailer's merchandise cost. Retailers with no commitment to complete assortments within a category can switch suppliers depending upon who offers the best deal. Their costs for merchandise are lower than for retailers committed to complete assortments. Moreover, since they may carry only one of several competing brands, they are not concerned with whether higher sales resulting from a very low selling price on one brand will adversely affect the movement of a competing brand. The result is that such retailers can offer consumers exceptionally low prices.

Table 2 juxtaposes the aforementioned factors against five classes of trade, including warehouse clubs, grocery stores, category specialists such as Home Depot, Circuit City, and Toys R Us, general merchandisers such as Sears and Montgomery Ward, and traditional department stores. We also included a retailer well known for its everyday low prices, Wal-Mart. Price stabilization takes different forms for these different classes of trade.

Warehouse clubs, such as Price Club and Costco, can truly promote EDLP as their main competitive advantage because their prices are both consistently and sufficiently low enough to substantiate this claim. Warehouse clubs offer prices 10 percent to 25 percent or more below competition, though at the cost of exceptionally limited assortments, minimal in-store service, no credit, and limited hours of operation. Furthermore, they essentially do not carry fashion merchandise.

Table 2 Applicability of EDLP

Type of Trade/ Retailer	Proportion of Comparable Products Carried	Proportion of Frequently Purchased Products	Merchandise Prices	% of Merchandise That Is Fashion- Sensitive	Category Completeness	Implications
Warehouse clubs	High	Both frequently /infrequently purchased products	Both high and low	0–5%	Incomplete	EDLP serves as sole point of difference
Grocery stores	High	Frequently purchased products	Low	0%	Complete	EDLP
Category specialists	High	Infrequently purchased products	Medium & high	0%	Complete	EDLP
General merchants Sears/ Montgomery Ward	Increasing	Primarily infrequently purchased products	Medium & high		Complete	EDFP+
Traditional department stores	High	Primarily infrequently purchased products	Medium & high	60–70%	Complete	EDFP+
Wal-Mart	High	Frequently purchased products	Medium & low	10–15%	Complete	Innovator in EDLP

Other trade classes have more difficulty using EDLP as their sole point of difference because their prices are not so clearly the lowest available. These include grocery stores and so-called power retailers such as Toys R Us and Home Depot.

Grocery retailers were among the first to convert successfully to EDLP. Their early and successful adoption relates to the high proportion of frequently purchased national brands they carry. Because customers have good knowledge of such merchandise, they can judge the fairness of the prices quickly. Furthermore, the frequency of grocery store visits encourages time-sensitive consumers to shop regularly at an EDLP retailer. For these customers, "one stop shopping" is preferable to a weekly newspaper and flier search and to multiple store visits to obtain the best available prices.

Nevertheless, because so many major grocery chains have adopted EDLP in at least some of their stores (*Supermarket News,* for example, lists nine major chains that have adopted EDLP[5]), they cannot use EDLP as their sole point of difference. Furthermore, since price differences between EDLP and more promotional grocery chains are small, consumers are unlikely to visit EDLP supermarkets just to secure the lowest available prices. If price was their only interest, such consumers could patronize warehouse clubs, which offer even lower prices. Thus EDLP food chains, like Shaw's and Hannaford Brothers, provide superior assortments in all departments, exceptional quality in their high-margin perishable departments, and fast and pleasant assistance in service departments and at the checkout counter as further sources of differentiation.

Even Wal-Mart, an early EDLP adopter, which continues to emphasize this strategy in its advertising and whose prices are considerably lower than competitors such as Kmart, supplements EDLP with other appeals. Particularly in competitive market areas, Wal-Mart offers sale-priced merchandise in its monthly circulars. It also provides exceptionally friendly customer service and an outstanding in-stock position. Consequently, 60 percent of Wal-Mart customers shop the chain "regularly" or "most often," a much higher percentage than the average chain store can claim, and probably much higher than Wal-Mart could claim if it offered only everyday low prices.[6]

Similarly, category specialists such as Toys R Us and Home Depot, which primarily sell products that are branded or otherwise highly comparable, higher priced, and less frequently purchased, provide EDLP but also offer other sources of distinctive customer value. Most power retailers offer prices perhaps 5 percent to 10 percent lower than those of noncategory specialists, but they are not *dramatically* lower. The absence of truly rock bottom prices requires these retailers to offer additional sources of customer value. Home Depot, for example, offers enormous selections and exceptional customer service. Toys R Us, in contrast, is in a category that does not require exceptional service; it needs breadth and depth of assortment and an excellent in-stock position. Therefore, Toys R Us not only provides everyday low prices but advertises that it has even the most popular toys in stock.

General merchandisers such as Sears and Montgomery Ward face an even more difficult task in adopting an EDLP strategy. They have been increasingly modifying their traditional disposition toward private labels by adding more and more branded merchandise in both hard and soft goods categories. As a result, these retailers have to meet or beat the prices of retailers carrying the same brands, such as Circuit City and Home Depot in some categories and Wal-Mart and Kmart in others.

An even more difficult problem confronts traditional department stores such as R.H. Macy and Company and Jordan Marsh. Their assortments include a higher proportion of

5 E. Zwiebach and D. Merrefield, "EDLP Gains Momentum," *Supermarket News,* 9 October 1989, pp. 1, 10.
6 K. Kerr, "Consumers Are Confused by Sears' New Policy," *Adweek's Marketing Week,* 12 June 1989, p. 30.

difficult-to-compare fashion goods of uncertain consumer acceptability. Because the merchandise is hard to compare, consumers find it difficult and time consuming to verify an EDLP claim. Moreover, the merchandise less acceptable to consumers must be sold at marked down prices. The almost unavoidable presence of marked down merchandise makes suspect any claim of everyday low prices.

These circumstances suggest that general merchandisers and traditional department stores will have trouble convincing consumers of their EDLP policy. Nevertheless, for the reasons cited above, such retailers must restore consumer confidence in their everyday shelf prices and overcome the disadvantageous economics associated with high-low pricing policies. For these retailers, we therefore advocate EDFP+, a reduction in both high initial markups and frequency of sale events, with concurrent improvements in other aspects of their marketing formulas to provide better customer value.

For example, Montgomery Ward, in its store-within-a-store concept departments like Electric Avenue for electronics and Home Ideas for home furnishings, offers fair, if not the lowest, prices, a broad assortment of brand names, plus some merchandise not immediately available at other retailers. Maytag introduces many of its newest models at Montgomery Ward because Ward's EDFP+ pricing policy stabilizes sales, enabling Maytag to predict demand for new models more accurately.

General merchandisers and traditional department stores must, therefore, accompany everyday fair pricing with excellent breadth of selection and, preferably, with informed and efficient personal service in appropriate merchandise categories. Nordstrom, a retailer known for everyday fair prices plus exceptional selections and customer service, exemplifies this strategy.

Switching to EDLP or EDFP+, however, is not without risk. We discuss these risks in the next two sections, first by reviewing the Sears experience and then by considering implementation issues.

RISKS OF A RAPID TRANSITION TO EDLP: THE SEARS EXPERIENCE

Sears' recent experience suggests that the risks of switching to EDLP are significant, particularly if a quick transition is planned. In the first half of 1990, approximately one year after announcing EDLP, Sears experienced flat sales of $15 billion, and its retail operations' net income fell by 63 percent to $73 million.[7] Sears' cost structure, for a variety of reasons, was not competitive when it introduced its new EDLP policy, and the company appeared unwilling to forgo short-term profitability. Its widely heralded 50,000 markdowns were not sufficient to make its price generally competitive, nor were its assortments or service much improved. Sears' cost structure continues to be a problem; costs rose $600 million in 1989 alone.[8] Moreover, Sears tended to compare prices to the other general merchandise chains, Montgomery Ward and JCPenney. It overlooked the need to compare prices, category-by-category, with discounters such as Wal-Mart and Target and power retailers such as Circuit City, Home Depot, and Toys R Us. Sears just did not drop its prices sufficiently, especially on fast-moving identicals, to achieve credible price comparisons.

As its prices were not sufficiently competitive, Sears continued to run sales after its EDLP announcement. Sears' weekly fliers often included brand name merchandise available in "limited quantities" or available only for limited time periods. Between March and October, 1989, Sears also ran two extensive, heavily advertised, in-store events involving sale merchandise and

---

7 K. Kelly and L. Zinn, "Can Ed Brennan Salvage the Sears He Designed?" *Business Week,* 27 August 1990, p. 34.
8 Kelley and Zinn (1990).

contests to build store traffic. The result: massive consumer confusion about the chain's pricing policy. By June 1989, because it heavily advertised its switch to EDLP, Sears was among the top ten companies in unaided advertising awareness. However, an *Adweek* poll that month found the following confusing perceptions of Sears' pricing among consumers:[9]

	Consumers Aware of Pricing Change	Consumers Not Aware of Pricing Change
Sears pricing policy is:		
• Always full price	16%	17%
• Full price with frequent sales	41	47
• Discount prices	16	11
• Discount prices with frequent sales	13	7
• Don't know	14	18

Only 16 percent of consumers who were aware of the policy change responded accurately that Sears offered discount prices—compared to 11 percent of those unaware of the change. Although further advertising may have decreased consumer confusion, the research indicates the difficulty that a major chain previously wedded to high-low pricing may have in changing consumer perceptions. If most ads promise everyday low prices, but significant sale advertising persists and much sale merchandise is available in the store, consumer confusion is inevitable. Successful EDLP implementation requires consistent practices and communications, particularly in general merchandising where it may take considerable consumer reeducation to make the price claim credible.

Sears' problems were compounded by the aggressive and predictable competitive response that its EDLP advertising inevitably stimulated. For example:

• T.J. Maxx ran ads that asked, "Why should Sears wait 102 years to cut prices?" and claimed that T.J. Maxx had carried brand name fashions at 20 percent to 60 percent savings "since day one."

• Wal-Mart ran ads that exclaimed, "Don't be fooled! There's always someone trying to imitate Wal-Mart's Everyday Low Prices."

Competitive advertising stimulated consumers to evaluate the relative attractiveness of Sears' retail prices. Had Sears not been so aggressive in its advertising, competitors might have been less vigorous in their responses and in slashing their own prices to meet or beat Sears on key items. Ironically, but predictably, Sears used a blockbuster advertising campaign to announce its EDLP program, which ignited a vigorous competitive response that, when combined with a confusing pricing strategy, successfully hindered the advertising's objective.

The Sears experience suggests the difficulty in quickly converting from a high-low pricing policy to EDLP. First, consumers' pricing perceptions have been conditioned by past pricing practices and may be hard to change, particularly for retailers well known for their weekly fliers and special events. As a result, even a retailer that switches to truly competitive everyday low prices may find that consumers initially perceive the new regular prices as higher than competitors' sale prices. Second, an aggressive adoption of EDLP may precipitate a

---

9 Kerr (1989), p. 30.

price war. Therefore, a retailer switching to EDLP should expect its profits to decline substantially for a prolonged period of time as a result of lower gross margins and higher advertising expense, and quite probably more price reductions and more advertising to combat competition. Thus the Sears example suggests that most general merchandise retailers will find price stabilization through EDFP+ preferable to a more dramatic shift to EDLP.

IMPLEMENTATION

EDFP+ versus EDLP

Figure 1 shows the time line for EDFP+ execution. If a retailer intends to adopt EDFP+, it must improve the other elements of its merchandising mix (service, assortment, etc.) *prior* to announcing EDFP+. It can make these improvements by gradually stabilizing demand: holding fewer sale events, reducing the number of sale items per event, reducing promotional fliers, and narrowing the gap between list and sale prices. Switching to EDFP+ also means using floor displays to highlight exceptional everyday values and redirecting the store's advertising —in particular, dropping the midweek sale events in favor of focusing on the nonprice elements of the merchandise mix. The resulting stability in the flow of goods improves costs, thus permitting lower shelf prices and further enhancements of service, assortment, and merchandise availability. Continuing improvements in cost position, in the availability of more products at everyday fair prices, and in the enhancement of nonprice elements should culminate in the official announcement of EDFP+.

For example, Montgomery Ward converted department by department, starting with automotive products. It reduced its operating costs, rationalized its product lines, and began changing its store environment *before* announcing its EDFP+ policy. Ward's success in automotive, a product category with many well-known brands, persuaded skeptical executives in other departments to accept the concept.

In **Table 3**, the requirements for a gradual implementation of EDFP+ are contrasted with those for a successful shift to EDLP. An aggressive EDLP announcement requires very competitive prices, particularly on fast-moving identicals. The new prices must be the focus of a heavy storewide and regionwide introductory advertising campaign designed to encourage customers to come in and compare prices. Few if any sale events should be planned; these are inconsistent with the EDLP claim. In contrast, the gradual adoption of EDFP+ emphasizes

---

Figure 1   Time Line for EDFP+ Execution

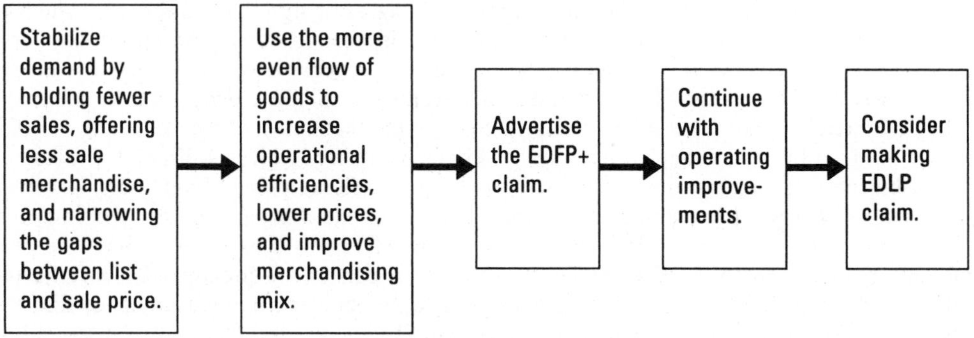

Table 3 Implementation of EDLP and EDFP+

	Dramatic Shift to EDLP	Gradual Shift to EDFP+
Prices (interim)	• Very competitive, particularly on fast movers.	• Decreasing initial markups and markdowns.
Advertising	• Heavy, with emphasis on price, including announcements of new pricing and price comparisons.	• Decreases in weekly sale fliers and midweek sale advertisements. Advertising emphasis is on elements of merchandising mix other than price.
Frequency of sale events	• Very low.	• Decreasing.
Price comparisons	• Essential.	• Comparisons made as prices stabilize and become lower.
Conversion	•. By store and by region.	• Flexible (geographic or department by department).
Other sources of differential advantage	• Not primary focus—consistent *low* prices are the primary focus.	• Excellent assortment and service are critical as prices decline and stabilize.

decreasing *but not eliminating* the retailers reliance on sales and, concurrently, focusing consumer attention on the retailer's other sources of differential advantage.

Profit and Sales Implications

These differences in execution suggest that the retailer adopting EDFP+ should not experience the sharp profit deterioration that Sears incurred when it aggressively reduced its shelf prices without concurrently improving its cost position. **Figure 2** compares our expectations of the sales projections for the two approaches. The intensive advertising campaign that heralds the switch to EDLP initially increases sales as customers (both those disposed to stable pricing and the cherry pickers) check out the new, lower prices. When the cherry pickers recognize that the new everyday low prices are not necessarily the lowest available, they are likely to decrease their patronage of the EDLP retailer, thus the drop in sales. Moreover, if the skepticism of the remaining customers is reinforced by significant availability of sale merchandise, which is difficult to avoid in fashion businesses, they too may be resistant to the new pricing policy. Eventually, however, with consistent everyday low pricing, consumers will accept the change, and sales will improve.

We hypothesize that the retailer gradually adopting EDFP+ will experience the same general sales trends but not the extreme highs and lows. Many consumers already will have adjusted to the new pricing and merchandising policies prior to the retailer's announcement of EDFP+. As cherry pickers take note of the retailer's decreasing frequency and intensity of discounting,

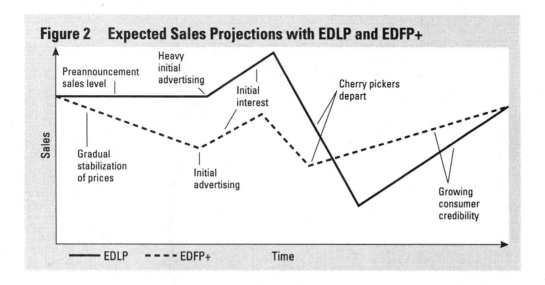

Figure 2 Expected Sales Projections with EDLP and EDFP+

Preannouncement sales level

Heavy initial advertising

Initial interest

Cherry pickers depart

Gradual stabilization of prices

Initial advertising

Growing consumer credibility

Sales

——— EDLP   - - - - EDFP+   Time

they may decrease their patronage. However, shoppers more interested in stable prices and better service and assortments may mitigate the effects of this loss. The EDFP+ announcement will generate less interest and less dramatic results than EDLP both because the claim is inherently less dramatic and because the introductory advertising is not as intensive. Sales will not decrease as steeply because many cherry pickers will have already departed. Sales may turn around sooner because customers will be recognizing the ongoing merchandising and service improvements. Since the EDFP+ prices are not intended to be among the lowest available, however, sales increases should not be as dramatic as they are for the EDLP retailer. Because introduction of EDFP+ will have a less pronounced and sudden effect on the marketplace, we also anticipate a less vigorous competitive response. Nevertheless, retailers embarking upon either an EDLP or EDFP+ policy should anticipate some competitor response. They should be prepared to take appropriate action, such as additional price reductions, stronger price guarantees, or increased advertising spending, at the expense of an additional adverse impact, in the short run, on both profits and cash flow.

As shown in **Figure 3**, we also hypothesize that the profit projections for the EDFP+ transition will be less traumatic than for the EDLP announcement. The EDFP+ announcement should not produce such a steep profit decline because of both less introductory advertising and less severe gross margin reductions. Profits may have declined in the preannouncement period, however, as margins decreased and the loss of cherry pickers was not offset by other business. During the EDLP transition, the retailer can expect substantial initial profit losses owing to a short-term escalation in advertising expenditures, a sharp decrease in average gross margin, and the certainty of aggressive competitor reaction. For both EDFP+ and EDLP, profits should eventually exceed those of the preannouncement period; the retailer can expect consumer demand increases and greater operating efficiencies. The turnaround is likely to happen sooner for the EDFP+ retailer who reduces operating costs, lowers prices, and improves assortments and service before the policy change announcement. EDFP+, in other words, represents an evolution in pricing, merchandising, and service policies rather than a pricing revolution.

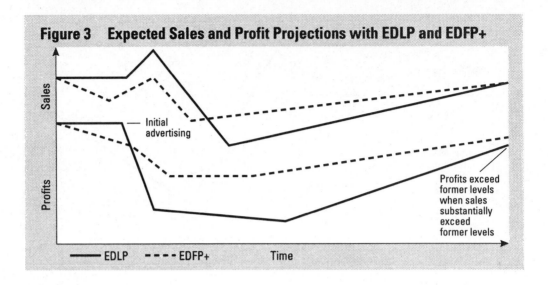

Figure 3 Expected Sales and Profit Projections with EDLP and EDFP+

Sales

Profits

Initial advertising

Profits exceed former levels when sales substantially exceed former levels

———— EDLP   - - - - EDFP+   Time

In-Store Communications

In implementing EDFP+, in particular, the retailer has to reconcile store communications that emphasize consistently low or fair prices with the merchandising realities that cause some prices to vary. Retailers often need to reduce prices to take advantage of manufacturer deals, to liquidate slow-selling or discontinued items, and to compete with the temporarily low sale prices of competitors.

Montgomery Ward has developed a logical price sign program to distinguish among these circumstances by using differently colored triangles that clearly communicate whether an item is an Extra Value (green triangle), a Super Buy (yellow), on Sale (red), or on Clearance (no triangle). At the inception of EDFP+, of course, there was a preponderance of green triangles. The Super Buy triangles were used to match competitors' prices when they had temporarily underpriced Montgomery Ward on branded items. Sale triangles identified temporarily lower prices arising from manufacturer deals on special purchases. This pricing structure, which was explained to consumers in handouts, on posters at store entrances, and in fliers, built trust in the store's new pricing policy. In addition, for six months after embarking on EDFP+, Montgomery Ward showed the previous retail prices of all merchandise marked down under the new program (see **Table 4**).

Also vital to the credibility of both EDLP and EDFP+ claims are price guarantees. A guarantee typically applies for a limited time period, usually thirty days, and protects the consumer against price reductions by the seller and competitors. The guarantee's credibility is often diluted, however, when competitors sell similar items with different stock numbers (derivative models) at lower prices. To sustain the guarantee's believability, Montgomery Ward draws up lists of derivatives considered equivalent to the specific models it carries and matches prices on them.

Retailers that pursue a more aggressive EDLP policy tend to place fewer restrictions on their guarantees and, like Home Depot, offer to beat competitors' prices by a stipulated percentage. They must, however, make sure that their price guarantees do not substitute for initially attractive everyday low prices on well-known brand items. Consumers will quickly lose faith in an everyday low price policy that relies unduly on the price guarantee to live up to its claim.

Table 4   Montgomery Ward Pricing Structure

Price Category	Description
Extra Value (green triangle)	"Compare our price! Buy with confidence! If you find this item advertised anywhere for less within thirty days, we'll gladly match that price!"
Super Buy (yellow triangle)	"We'll match anyone's advertised price! We'll never price it for less! Plus, if competition advertises it for less, we'll gladly refund the difference."
Sale (red triangle)	"Buy today and save! Reduced for a limited time only. If we advertise it for less within thirty days, we'll gladly refund the difference."

Monitoring of Price Perceptions

Longitudinal surveys to track consumers' changing price and other perceptions are essential to monitor the effectiveness of any newly implemented EDLP or EDFP+ program. Such tracking studies should evaluate:

- Whether consumers are aware of the retailer's new pricing policy, understand what it means, and can correctly identify the retailer's advertising slogan.
- How consumers perceive the retailer's current prices, on average and for key reference items, relative to its former prices, and whether they see current prices as higher or lower than those of other stores.
- The extent to which consumers both perceive and value the retailer's improvements in service, assortment, and display.

Internal Marketing

Before instituting one of these strategies, a retailer must ensure that executives and other employees are committed enthusiastically to it and recognize its importance and advantages. Internal acceptance is particularly important for EDFP+ because buyers, store managers, and salespeople will be responsible for developing the service and merchandising improvements that are key to EDFP+'s success.

- **Buyers** who are used to frequent sales and high-low pricing will have to be educated to the advantages of consistently attractive prices. The higher the percentage of a department's goods that have been sold on sale, the greater will be the buyer's anxiety. Montgomery Ward buyers are now very supportive of EDFP+ because they have witnessed its favorable effect on sales and expenses and can now devote time to important merchandising activities that used to be spent on changing prices and revising sales forecasts.
- **Store managers** who maintained only limited knowledge of other stores' prices will have to be trained to monitor carefully and frequently competitive prices on high-profile items. Wal-Mart, for example, insists that its store managers change prices in response to local

competition on the 300 to 500 fastest-moving items and on high-profile slow movers. Similarly, at Montgomery Ward, when a competitor prices an item below the Extra Value price, the store manager must reduce the item to a Super Buy.

- **Store salespeople** who are used to a high-low sale environment and a price-oriented sales pitch (e.g., telling consumers to "buy now before the sale is over" or not offering to call the customer when the item next goes on sale) need to understand the ramifications of the new pricing policy. Effective selling in an EDFP+ environment requires in-depth product knowledge and a customer service orientation. Salespeople must also understand the terms of any price-matching guarantees. Another concern is that salespeople compensated on commission will likely resist a switch to EDLP or EDFP+ because of the anticipated short-term drop in sales and the additional demands on them for professional selling. Because employee buy-in is critical to the new strategy's success, salespeople's earnings must be at least partially protected during the transition.

- **Suppliers** often support stable pricing because it encourages a sales pattern with fewer peaks and valleys of demand, which, if reflected in their production schedules, can reduce manufacturing and distribution costs. Some manufacturers, therefore, offer customers an everyday low price that is a weighted average of the trade deal price and the regular purchase price.[10] Vendors in fashion lines, however, sometimes resist EDFP+ and EDLP because they fear that the remaining high-low retailers will discontinue or de-emphasize the vendor's line. Overcoming this vendor resistance is an unavoidable problem for fashion retailers switching to a more stable pricing policy.

CONCLUSION

Our investigation has highlighted the difficulties that department stores and general merchandisers, in particular, have in switching to an EDLP claim. If they remain with high-low pricing policies, however, these retailers risk both a continuing decline in market share and lower sales. They also risk more prosecutions from regulatory authorities. These risks increase as additional retailers change to pricing policies that are both more attractive to most consumers and more cost effective, and as they begin to offer improved service, assortment, and display along with more reasonable list prices. Therefore, the issue is not whether to shift to an EDLP policy but how to shift to an EDFP+ policy.

A gradual transition to EDFP+ is more appropriate for most retailers for two reasons. First, only a limited number of retailers, such as warehouse clubs, can make a credible EDLP claim. From most other retailers, consumers want fair prices but also other benefits, such as complete assortments and excellent service. Therefore, most retailers who concentrate solely on low selling prices do not convey a desirable offering to a majority of consumers.

Second, switching to an EDLP policy for these retailers will be an expensive and unrewarding investment. They will be better served by exchanging their current high-low promotional pricing for everyday fair prices plus other consumer benefits.

---

10   R.D. Buzzell, J. A. Quelch, and W. Salmon, "The Costly Bargain of Trade Promotion," *Harvard Business Review*, March–April 1990, pp. 141–149.

Case 9

THE GAP, INC.

"Gap, Inc. was one of the hot stocks of recessionary 1991. Yesterday, investors got cold feet. . . ." From a high of 60 in the trailing 52 weeks, the stock had fallen to 35.50 on May 21, 1992.

Comparable store sales, which in the years 1989–1991 had risen at the rate of 13% to 15%, had risen only 5% to 6% through August 1992.

One big fear is that Gap will have to take more markdowns to attract penny-pinching shoppers. . . . Indeed, in the middle of August 1992 The Gap announced a 26% reduction in the prices of many jeans styles to respond to price cuts by makers and sellers of comparable products.

Expenses are also rising . . . this year's advertising budget is more than 50% higher than last year's $35 million, with most of the additional spending earmarked for national television in the second half. . . .

A portfolio manager . . . worries that Gap . . . could fall victim to the fashion cycle. As service sector employment rises, bringing more women back into the work force, career clothes could take off again and Gap's casual selection could languish, she reasons. . . .

Mr. Roth (a Merrill Lynch analyst) contends that trends still favor Gap, which sells moderately priced clothes. "We feel that most of the 1990s will be characterized by more of a 'value' orientation on the part of apparel consumers."

— Wall Street Journal, *May 15, 1992*

The Gap had adopted a relatively aggressive advertising strategy, unlike most other national chains of narrow line specialty stores. Indeed, if its advertising expenditures in 1992 amounted, as predicted, to over $50 million, Gap would be second only to Levi's in total advertising expenditures among all apparel specialty store retailers and manufacturers. Its advertising would also differ from that of almost all retailers in its emphasis on fashion rather than price. Other chains relied upon the mall traffic generated by anchor store advertising and the opportunity for shoppers to pleasantly and conveniently compare the offerings of a number of different stores to ensure a constant flow of shoppers to their stores. Conventional wisdom held that the high rent paid by a specialty store for a good mall location was a substitute for most media advertising.

The Gap, however, both paid the high rents for good mall locations and advertised on national television and in prestigious national magazines such as *Vanity Fair*, *Vogue*, and the *New York Times Magazine*.

This case explores if and why The Gap's more aggressive approach to advertising made sense and whether it should be modified. Should the addition of more nonshopping center stores and the more vigorous price competition in the jeans business affect the magnitude or character of the advertising effort. Another issue was whether The Gap's approach to advertising was

David Wylie prepared this case under the supervision of Professor Walter J. Salmon as the basis for class discussion rather than to illustrate either effective or ineffective handling of an administrative situation.

applicable to certain other narrow line specialty store chains and, if so, what might be their characteristics?

THE GAP[1]

The Gap was a specialty retailer of moderately priced casual apparel for men, women, and children. By April of 1992, it operated 1,226 apparel specialty stores, including 845 Gap Stores, 230 GapKids stores, and 151 Banana Republic stores in the United States and the United Kingdom. Sales for the year ending February 1, 1992, were $2.5 billion with net earnings of $230 million, representing increases from the previous year of 30% and 59% respectively. The success of The Gap was even more impressive within the context of lackluster performance of most retailers in a year of economic recession and low consumer spending. (See **Exhibit 1**, Financial Statements for The Gap).

The management of Gap attributed this success to a "continuing dedication to offering our customers well styled, casual clothing at affordable prices in a friendly environment," to its "knowledgeable, helpful sales associates," to its sophisticated internal systems, and to capable employees at all levels of the company.

Gap stores represented the major portion of The Gap's revenues with sales in 1991 estimated at almost $2 billion. Gap stores designed "in-house" private label casual and active wear for men and women to appeal primarily to the twenty to forty-five year old customer. Almost all merchandise sold bore the Gap label. The stores averaged about 4,000 square feet, with sales per square foot of about $475. The Gap owned no manufacturing facilities itself. It purchased 66% of its merchandise from overseas manufacturers.

FALL INTO THE GAP

Donald Fisher, then a 41-year-old California real estate developer, founded the Gap in 1969, naming it after the "generation gap." He "couldn't exchange a pair of Levi's that were an inch too short. Sensing a need for a place that sold jeans in a comprehensive array of sizes, he set up a shop in San Francisco on Ocean Avenue which sold a very broad selection of Levi products. Targeting the bulging population of young people from the 'baby boom,' the first ads touted the store's 'four tons' of Levi's. 'You couldn't get into the store' because it was so crowded, Fisher says."[2]

As the popularity of Gap stores increased, Fisher broadened the merchandise assortment by adding a limited number of Gap-brand products and as many as fifteen other national brands. Every effort was made to track the population bulge by adding merchandise which suited the tastes of its aging customers while maintaining its appeal to the youth market which had been its strength. As the merchandise assortment grew, Fisher experimented with a new breed of "superstores" as large as 10,000 square feet in selling space. By 1983, Gap had grown to a chain

Performance by Gap Stores

Year	Corp. Sales	Gap Store Sales[a]	No. Stores[b]	Avg. Size[c]	Sales/Sq. Ft.[d]
1987	1,062	811	681	3,102	261
1988	1,252	976	709	3,245	301
1989	1,596	1,288	741	3,380	381
1990	1,933	1,560	795	3,599	433
1991	2,515	1,953	849	4,114	475

a Estimated. Company does not publish divisional statistics.
b Number of Gap stores at end of fiscal year.
c Gross square footage of stores.
d Sales per average square foot for the year.

1 "The Gap" refers to the corporate entity; "Gap" or "the Gap" refers to the Gap division.
2 *Business Week*, March 9, 1992.

of 550 stores across the United States. Levi products then comprised only 23% of the merchandise sold.

In the early years, spot television was the backbone of Gap's advertising campaign. The "Fall into the Gap" campaign, focused on the wide selection of Levi jeans and denim shirts at excellent prices.

In the early 1980s, however, Levi started to sell its products through department stores and discount chains, placing increased pressure on Gap's margins. Fisher thought that a continuing dependence on national brands would force the Gap to continue competing on the basis of price, leading to constant price cutting and promotion. Thinking that the future would be brighter if the Gap could escape the lower margins inherent in such a strategy, he tried to upgrade the Gap image in parallel with the growing income of its customers. Even experimentation with some higher margin store brands, however, did not allow Gap to escape its primarily price-oriented image.

In 1983, Fisher recruited Millard (Mickey) Drexler to be the new president of the Gap stores division. Drexler had just successfully engineered the turnaround of the Ann Taylor specialty chain store which specialized in higher priced merchandise for the career woman. One of Drexler's first bold moves was to drop all non-Gap merchandise except for Levi's and to redirect the thrust of The Gap's appeal to a broader, slightly older, and more affluent group of customers. He ordered a new look for everything, selling more colorful sweaters, jerseys and shirts at moderate prices. Shunning fashion for fashion's sake, he described the new tone for Gap merchandise to be "basic, with attitude." The merchandise remained moderately priced, but since the fashions were casual and functional, since high quality cotton fabrics were used almost exclusively, and since an aggressive quality control program was introduced, the merchandise was thought to have far better value. In addition, ". . . because the company is integrated and is both the creator and retailer of its line, it is not only able to retain a greater portion of the available profit but also to provide the customer with 15% to 20% greater value than purveyors of competitive brands who are not similarly integrated and whose pricing must allow for profits for intermediaries as well."[3] Furthermore, the store interiors were remodeled to give them a more contemporary look.

Although profits suffered initially as a result of this transformation, plunging from $22 million after tax in 1983 to only $13 million in 1984, they had rebounded by 1987 to almost $70 million. Sales grew from $550 million in 1983 to $1.06 billion in 1987.

The Gap's advertising also changed during these early Drexler years. Although spot television commercials were still used extensively, a new medium was added. Advertising placed in national magazines with an upscale readership carried a high quality fashion image similar to those of higher priced designer labels. The models, however, featured the denim look of Gap merchandise. (See **Exhibit 2** for sample advertising from the pre-Drexler and early Drexler years, and **Exhibits 3**, **4**, and **5** for Gap's advertising expenditures from 1983 to 1991 and comparisons with other specialty retailers and apparel manufacturers.)

INDIVIDUALS OF STYLE

The Gap's management thought that it was important to stay "fresh" rather than merely maintaining established formulas.

> Blonde. Beautiful. Boring. That's how Maggie Gross, The Gap Inc.'s senior vice president for advertising and marketing, reacted to the woman modelling a white Gap turtleneck. The idea for this 1988 Los Angeles-area campaign was to show some L.A. trendies in Gap garb. But this Angelena, album designer Lynn Robb, looked like any other model.

It was in this spirit that a new promotional campaign was conceived in 1988 which was described as follows:

> Gross changed that. "Give me a shot of her with her own jacket on", she told photographer Matthew Rolston. Robb donned her well-worn motorcycle jacket, leaving it open to show the shirt. A fashion cliche was transformed into something that communicated, well, an individual sense of style.
>
> That photo launched the Individuals of Style campaign—a series of black and white photos of personalities from jazz great Miles Davis to neo-country singer k. d. lang, all mixing Gap threads with other clothes. The message was that Gap's fashions blended with everything from Armani sport coats to Greatful Dead headbands."[4] (See **Exhibit 6** for sample advertisements from this campaign.)

---

3 Dean Witter Reynolds Inc., March 2, 1990.
4 *Business Week*, March 9, 1992.

This new "Individuals of Style" campaign struck a chord with the "yuppie" generation of the 1980s, becoming the theme of Gap's advertising throughout the rest of the decade.

FOR EVERY GENERATION A GAP

A downturn in the economy in the early 1990s however, fostered more conservative consumer attitudes. Commenting on this shift, Jeffry Atlas, chairman of the Atlas Citron Haligman & Bedecarre advertising agency, said, "There's some feeling that the 80s were about celebrities and the 1990s are about real people."[5] Carol Farmer, a retail consultant, said, "The marketing challenge of the 1990s will be to sell more in an era of less." She noted that "shoppers' refocused attitudes (mean) they must end their obsession with evanescent fashion." "The consumer becomes an investor, prudently and cautiously guarding what little is left of his or her disposable income. That is the reason . . . for the sharply rising popularity of value brands, products that promise good quality at reasonable prices."[6]

In response to this shifting consumer attitude, the Gap developed a new campaign dubbed "for every generation a gap" with the advertising agency, Atlas Citron Haligman & Bedecarre. "This new campaign featured less well known individuals, with greater emphasis on fashion, functionality, pricing, quality. The people in the new advertising campaign are shown doing everyday things like shopping or driving, even wearing clothing from other stores."[7] The company's 10-K report for the year ending January 31, 1992, characterized the campaign as follows: "The Company's marketing strategy primarily involves advertising in life-style and fashion magazines, such as *Vanity Fair*, *Vogue*, *New York Times Magazine*, and *Los Angeles Times Magazine*. Advertisements . . . have also expanded into various outdoor media such as bus shelters, mass transit posters, telephone kiosks, and exterior bus panels. . . ."[8] In late 1990, it began to feature less well known people. "As we move into the Bart Simpson decade, young overachievers may be losing their mass appeal. Seen on attractive but blessedly anonymous models, the clothes can make an unmeditated appeal to our eyes."[9] (See **Exhibit 7** for sample advertisements.)

In 1991, the Gap also introduced a new black and white national television campaign. The intent of this new campaign was to communicate a fresh message and to reach a broader group of customers. One industry observer commented about the new campaign: "You can only speak in the same volume for so long before consumers stop hearing you."[10] In addition it would reach a wider audience and support smaller store formats in secondary locations. "Seventeen million dollars had been allocated to this campaign for the second half of 1992, and some industry observers estimated that it could grow to over $20 million."[11]

You glimpse a hand, a cup of coffee, then a blur as your eye moves to focus on her face. She has been waiting, but in that moment, she looks up; whomever she has been waiting for has arrived. The Gap's first TV work in almost a decade . . . is about moments like these: an instant of recognition or surprise; a knowing glance or a look of amusement . . . "you see a little glimpse and you want to know more."

"Some of the most prominent fashion shown is not from the Gap—a pair of sunglasses or a leather jacket. And some of the models are dressed in the clothes they arrived in, though there are Gap items worn throughout."[12] The Gap campaign used infants, children, teenagers, adults and the elderly.[13]

"As one scene dissolves, "For every generation" appears on the screen. Another street scene follows, then the words, "There is a gap." The spot closes with the retailer's name in white letters against a black background."[14]

GAP STORES AND MERCHANDISE

Meanwhile, the Gap's stores and merchandise had been undergoing a transformation. Joseph Ellis, an analyst with Goldman Sachs, commented:

5 *New York Times*, June 24, 1991, Section D, p. 3.
6 *New York Times*, January 16, 1992, Section D, p. 18.
7 *New York Times*, June 24, 1991, Section D, p. 3.
8 The Gap, Inc., Form 10-K, Year Ended February 1, 1992.
9 *Adweek Eastern Edition*, October 22, 1990, p. 46.
10 *Adweek's Marketing Week*, May 20, 1991, p. 13.
11 *Adweek's Marketing Week*, May 20, 1991, p. 13.
12 *Adweek Western Edition*, June 17, 1991, p. 6.
13 *New York Times*, June 24, 1991, Section D, p. 3.
14 *Adweek Eastern Edition*, June 17, 1991, p. 4.

... we were concerned during 1989 and 1990 that the company was in danger of reaching maximum penetration in its share of the basic pants, tops (shirts and T-shirts), and sweater market."

"Even though the company's extraordinary turnaround during the mid- and late 1980s has been a widely told story, The Gap, like any other high-achieving growth company, has needed to constantly reinvent itself in order to maintain its comparable-store sales growth and high profitability on already superior numbers. Indeed, as the Gap Division's outstanding comparable store sales growth of recent years began to strain the capacity of its smaller stores and as Gap customers filled their closets with more Gap sweaters in solid colors and stripes, the company might well have been unable to compound on its own success if management had not been aggressive in overhauling/reinventing/recreating its store format and merchandise assortment. Management has not only met this challenge but has moved the company to a whole new stage of performance by accelerating the sophistication and diversity of the Gap's merchandise assortment and by developing a larger and more dynamic store in an environment that complements its new merchandising posture. . . ."

Gap had expanded its merchandise selection and product categories. In 1991, Gap introduced a considerable array of new fashions and styles, including prints and plaids, in a variety of more textured fabrics. Equally important, it materially expanded its product categories. Gap now offers a wide array of unstructured blazers and outerwear (such as anoraks and parkas) in a variety of styles, a considerably broadened offering of men's and women's sport shirts, a new line of men's boxer shorts, and expanded offerings in classifications such as swimsuits and swim trunks, footwear, and miscellaneous accessories.

INCREASED CATEGORY DOMINANCE

Even in denim products (primarily jeans), where Gap many years ago already had a major market position, the company has substantially enhanced its market penetration by carrying greater *depth* of product. By far the best example of this is Gap's offering during the past two years of several distinct fits—four in women's sizes and three in men's—described on in-store signs as shown below:

This program has materially increased Gap's penetration of the denim market by not only appealing to a wider

Men's Jeans	Women's Jeans
TAPERED LEG The Original Gap Fit. Trim Throughout, Ever a Classic.	**STRAIGHT LEG** Great Slim Fit Throughout. Full or Ankle Lengths. Tapered at Bottom.
EASY FIT Comfortable Relaxed Fit. Roomier Than Tapered Leg. Easy to Wear.	**CLASSIC FIT** Great Slim Fit, with Slightly Curved Hip. Full-Length. Tapered at Bottom.
LOOSE FIT A Full Fit with Lots of Style. Slightly Looser Than Easy Fit.	**EASY FIT** Slightly Roomier Than Straight Leg or Classic Fit. Fuller Leg. Tapers to Bottom.
	RELAXED BUTTON FLY Our Roomiest Five-Pocket Jeans Fit. Full-Length. Very Relaxed Leg.

diversity of customer tastes but *body shapes*, an important step forward in appealing to the older demographic profile of today's customers.

The older, smaller stores, which averaged only 3,102 square feet in 1987 and 3,599 square feet in 1990, could no longer accommodate the expanded offering. The average store opened in 1990 had grown to 5,700, but ranged up to 8,000 square feet. The new stores not only accommodated the merchandise but also provided more area to improve the shopping experience for Gap customers.

Concurrently, the Gap was achieving a penetration in mall locations which would soon inhibit growth. A new breed of stores was therefore being developed for nonmall locations where rent was usually substantially lower. These stores were often located in upscale suburban town centers and in the downtowns of major cities. Often the suburban stores were smaller than the shopping center prototypes while the center city stores varied in size according to the estimated sales potential.

Exhibit 1
Financial Statements for The Gap ($000)

	1991	1990	1989	1988	1987
Operating Results					
Net sales	$2,518,893	$1,933,780	$1,586,596	$1,252,097	$1,062,021
Cost of goods sold and occupancy expenses, excluding depreciation and amortization	1,496,156	1,187,644	1,006,647	814,028	654,361
Percentage of sales	59.4%	61.4%	63.4%	65.0%	61.6%
Depreciation and amortization[a]	$ 72,765	$ 53,599	$ 39,589	$ 31,408	$ 24,869
Operating expenses	575,686	454,180	364,101	277,429	254,209
Interest expense (net)	3,523	1,435	2,760	3,416	3,860
Earnings before income taxes	370,763	236,922	162,714	125,816	124,722
Percentage of sales	14.7%	12.3%	10.3%	10.0%	11.7%
Income taxes	140,890	92,400	65,086	51,585	55,127
Net earnings[b]	229,873	144,522	97,628	74,231	69,595
Percentage of sales	9.1%	7.5%	6.2%	5.9%	6.6%
Cash dividends	41,126	29,625	22,857	18,244	17,328
Capital expenditures[c]	244,323	199,617	94,266	68,153	67,307
Per Share Data[d]					
Net earnings[b]	$ 1.62	$ 1.02	$ 0.69	$ 0.51	$ 0.49
Cash dividends	0.30	0.22	0.17	0.13	0.13
Stockholders' equity (book value)[e]	4.76	3.30	2.40	1.97	1.90

Note: While no published figures were available for Gap's occupancy expenses, they were estimated to be 8% to 10% of sales. Within "operating expenses," variable expenses including store payroll was estimated at approximately 12% of sales.

a Excludes amortization of restricted stock.
b 1989 includes a nonrecurring after-tax charge of $6,471 ($0.05 per share) taken in the fourth quarter for costs associated with closing the Hemisphere stores. 1988 includes a nonrecurring after-tax charge of $4,000 ($0.03 per share) taken in the first quarter for costs associated with restructuring of Banana Republic's operations.
c Includes property and equipment, as well as lease rights.
d Restated to reflect the 2-for-1 splits of common stock to stockholders of record on June 17, 1991, and September 17, 1990.
e Based on number of shares outstanding at year end.

	1991	1990	1989	1988	1987
Financial Position					
Property and equipment (net)	$ 547,740	$ 383,548	$ 238,103	$ 191,257	$ 156,639
Merchandise inventory	313,899	247,462	243,482	193,268	194,886
Total assets	1,147,414	776,900	579,483	481,148	434,231
Working capital	235,547	101,518	129,139	106,210	129,988
Current ratio	1.71:1	1.39:1	1.69:1	1.70:1	2.01:1
Total debt, including current installments	80,000	17,500	20,000	22,000	18,500
Ratio of total debt to stockholders' equity	0.12:1	0.04:1	0.06:1	0.08:1	0.07:1
Stockholders' equity	677,788	465,733	337,972	276,399	272,912
Return on average stockholders' equity	40.2%	36.0%	31.8%	27.0%	28.7%
Statistics					
Number of stores opened	139	152	98	106	110
Number of stores closed	15	20	38	21	19
Number of stores open at year end	1,216	1,092	960	900	815
Net increase in number of stores	11.4%	13.8%	6.7%	10.4%	12.6%
Comparable store sales growth (52-week basis)	13.0%	14.0%	15.0%	8.0%	9.0%
Sales per square foot[a] (52-week basis)	$ 481	$ 438	$ 389	$ 328	$ 292
Square footage of gross store space at year end	5,638,400	4,762,300	4,056,600	3,879,300	3,644,500
Percentage increase in square feet	18.4%	17.4%	4.6%	6.4%	8.0%
Number of employees at year end	32,000	26,000	23,000	20,000	16,000
Average number of shares outstanding[b]	142,139,577	141,500,888	141,080,200	144,589,120	142,918,052
Number of shares outstanding at year end, net of treasury stock[b]	142,523,334	141,264,030	140,551,404	140,525,456	143,479,852

a Based on average quarterly gross square footage.
b Restated to reflect the 2-for-1 splits of common stock to stockholders of record on June 17, 1991, and September 17, 1990.

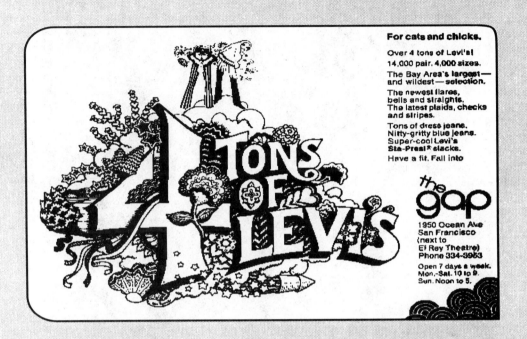

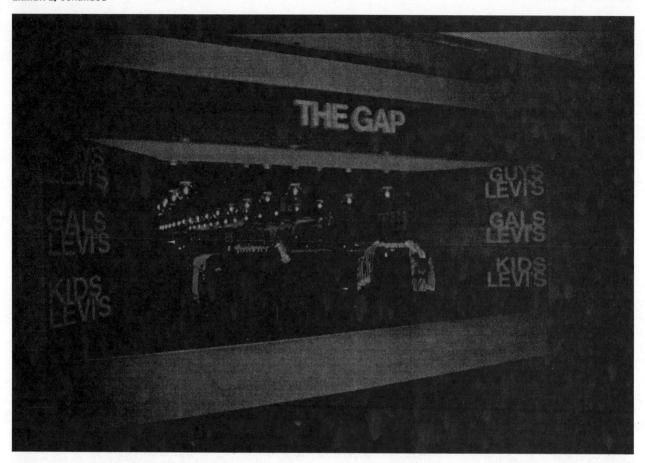

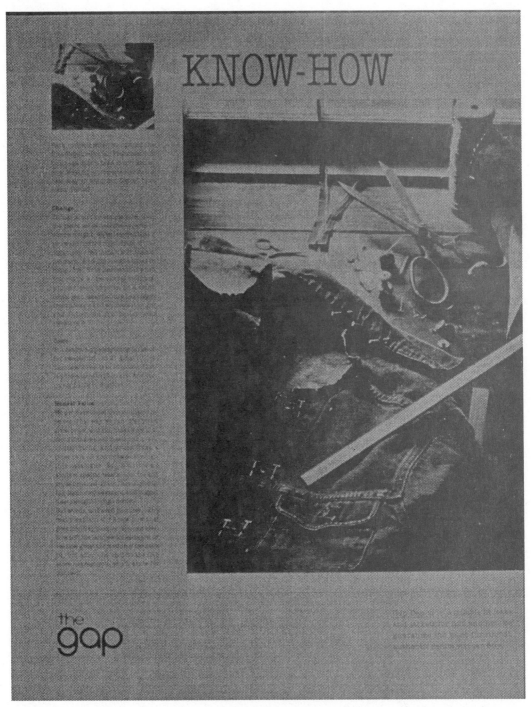

RUGBY

Exhibit 3
Advertising Expenditures, 1983–1990

	1983	1984	1985	1986	1987[b]	1990[b]	1991[b]
Total company sales (in billions)	$ 0.481	$ 0.534	$ 0.647	$ 0.848	$1.062	$ 1.933	$ 2.515
Total media[a] expenditures (in millions)	4.170	6.050	8.002	7.537	5.000	13.191	19.071
Magazines	0.50%	0.00%	65.80%	64.90%	61.80%	68.30%	27.16%
Sunday magazines	0.00	0.00	4.20	10.50	2.60	2.40	32.79
Newspapers	0.00	0.00	0.00	0.00	0.00	1.40	1.10
Outdoor	2.60	3.30	0.00	0.00	0.00	0.30	0.00
Network TV	0.00	0.90	0.00	0.00	0.00	0.00	20.29
Spot TV	96.90	67.60	28.90	24.60	35.60	20.00	2.16
Syndicated TV	0.00	0.00	0.00	0.00	0.00	0.00	13.85
Cable TV	0.00	0.00	1.10	0.00	0.00	5.70	2.62
Network radio	0.00	28.20	0.00	0.00	0.00	0.00	0.00
National spot radio	0.00	0.00	0.00	0.00	0.00	1.80	1.24
Media total	100.00%	100.00%	100.00%	100.0%	100.00%	100.00%	100.00%
% of sales	0.87%	1.13%	1.24%	0.89%	0.47%	0.68%	0.76%

a Source: Leading national advertiser. These figures may be considerably less than total corporate advertising expenses since other reliable sources estimated The Gap's advertising expenditures in 1991 at $35 million.

b These years are labeled correctly. Data for 1988 and 1989 are missing.

Exhibit 4
Advertising Expenditures for Apparel Retailers

Total Estimated Expenditures for 1991 as a % of Sales for Traditional Men's and Women's Specialty Store Chains

Ann Taylor	1.7%
Charming Shoppes	1.0
The Limited	0.5
Hot Seal	0.1
Merry-Go-Round	0.1
The Gap	1.2%

Source: Kidder Peabody & Company, Inc., November 12, 1991.

Leading National Advertisers Data for 1990

	The Limited	Melville[a]	L.L. Bean[b]	Burlington Coat[c]
Total sales (in billions)	5.253	8.687	0.6	0.887
Total media (in millions)	9.592	48.897	5.832	22.537
Magazines	0.14%	0.00%	0.35%	0.00%
Sunday magazines	0.03	0.01	0.03	0.00
Newspapers	0.01	0.27	0.00	0.58
Outdoor	0.00	0.00	0.00	0.01
Network TV	0.00	0.00	0.00	0.00
Spot TV	0.00	0.21	0.00	1.95
Syndicated TV	0.00	0.00	0.00	0.00
Cable TV	0.00	0.00	0.00	0.00
Network radio	0.00	0.00	0.00	0.00
National spot radio	0.00	0.07	0.00	0.00
Media total	0.18	0.56	0.39	2.54
Media % to total sales	0.2%	0.6%	1.0%	3.0%

a Operates CVS Drug Stores, Marshall's, Kay-Bee Toys, and numerous chains of specialty store retailers.
b Mainly a catalog retailer.
c Operates freestanding discount women's apparel stores with an emphasis on coats and suits.

Exhibit 5
Media Advertising of Apparel Manufacturers in 1990

	Levi	Polo/Ralph Lauren	VF	Liz Claiborne
Total sales (in billions)	$ 4.247	$ 0.180	$ 2.612	$1.728
Total media advertising (in millions)	66.059	16.552	23.653	4.736
Magazines	0.20%	6.04%	0.39%	0.22%
Sunday magazines	0.00	3.02	0.00	0.00
Newspapers	0.00	0.13	0.01	0.00
Outdoor	0.0	0.00	0.01	0.00
Network TV	0.52	0.00	0.08	0.00
Spot TV	0.25	0.00	0.31	0.04
Syndicated TV	0.29	0.00	0.01	0.00
Cable TV	0.30	0.00	0.02	0.00
Network radio	0.00	0.00	0.00	0.00
National spot radio	0.00	0.00	0.08	0.01
Media total as a % of sales	1.56%	9.20%	0.91%	0.27%

Exhibit 6
Sample Advertising from the "Individuals of Style" Campaign

Exhibit 7
Sample Advertising from the "For Every Generation a Gap" Campaign and Photos of Current Look of Gap Stores

Case 10

RANDALL'S DEPARTMENT STORES

Fiscal year 1989 (ending March 1, 1990) was successful for Randall's, a Billingsville retailer. Randall's operated a downtown department store and 12 Randall's branches. All were situated in an upper midwest state in a trading area of approximately 3.7 million inhabitants, that encompassed Billingsville, a major city and its surrounding area. The company enjoyed record-breaking results in 1989 (a 53-week year) in both sales and earnings. Pricing, however, was a source of continuing concern to Emily Randall, President, and Caroline Randall, Chairman of the Board. Like many other department store retailers, Randall's sold a high proportion of merchandise "On Sale." Over 50% of sales in many departments were at prices below the original price ticketed on the merchandise. "Extra Value Days," a sale event held by Randall's for four days each month, was particularly well known in the Billingsville area, and represented approximately 25% of store volume in the average 26-day shopping month.

Two of the store's more recent promotional events were troubling examples of how promotional Randall's had become. One was a promotional event called the "Pre-Season Sale." This event, which featured selected merchandise at reduced prices before the beginning of the regular selling season, had long been a standard promotional event in the women's coat business. The economic justification for offering pre-season reductions was that it provided both suppliers and retailers early indicators of the season's best-selling styles which resulted in additional production and reorders of best-sellers. Manufacturers, as a result, often provided additional discounts on coats that were featured in the pre-season sale events. Pre-season coat sales also allowed a customer to use a layaway plan to pay gradually for a big-ticket item before its purchase was completed.

More recently, retailers such as Taylor's, based on the East Coast, and Prescott's, one of Randall's competitors in Billingsville, had broadened the use of pre-season sale events to other women's apparel and accessories departments. Randall's, in response, had run an apparently successful spring pre-season sale in the women's shoe department. As a result, Kristen Olson, Vice President and General Merchandise Manager in charge of women's apparel, wondered whether she should institute a pre-season sale program throughout her area of the store.

The second innovative promotion, held in the spring, was a direct mail advertisement that included three "percent off" coupons. This advertisement, which was used to bolster the traditional spring anniversary sale, was very successful in generating sales volume. In addition, it stimulated 128,000 charge customers to reactivate their accounts and 4,700 new customers to open accounts. The profit implications of the coupon promotion, however, were debatable. Much of the store's merchandise was already marked down for the anniversary sale and the

Professor Gwendolyn K. Ortmeyer and Professor Walter J. Salmon prepared this case as the basis for class discussion rather than to illustrate either effective or ineffective handling of an administrative situation.

coupon discount further reduced the selling price of this merchandise.

To combat the disturbing increase in proportion of merchandise sold on sale over the past two years, "Everyday Low Pricing" had been tried in a number of departments, including women's fine jewelry, men's suits, and children's clothing. This policy meant that merchandise carried a lower initial markup than formerly and, at the same time, was promoted at discounted prices only once during the selling season. Children's clothing, however, was the only department that had experienced any success with this more stable form of pricing. In the other departments, lackluster sales indicated that customers did not give Randall's credit for everyday prices that were as low as, and in many instances even lower than, competitors' sale prices. Consequently, children's was the only department that continued to use everyday low pricing. Emily and Caroline Randall were determined to develop a cohesive pricing strategy even though they recognized that Randall's was committed to selling a wide array of merchandise that differed in its dollar value and frequency of purchase as well as other characteristics, such as the importance of fashion and brand names in influencing consumer buying behavior.

COMPANY BACKGROUND

Randall's Department Stores was founded by Elliot O. Randall, who opened the downtown Billingsville store in 1890. This location, still in operation, was the largest of Randall's stores in selling area and also housed the corporate offices. Descendants of the founder continued to play a major role in the management of the company. The Randalls took great pride in the continuity of the founding family's involvement and the store's long-standing presence in the Billingsville community.

Store Locations

Randall's aggressive expansion to the suburbs began in 1966, with the opening of the Donmore branch in the first covered mall in the state. **Exhibit 1** shows for each of the thirteen stores, its location, size, year of opening, and 1989 sales volume. **Exhibit 1** also lists key department store and general merchandise competitors with estimates of the volume done at the competing stores. Of the twelve branch locations, two of the older stores were in freestanding locations and the other ten were in malls. In the 1980s, all existing branch

stores were renovated and space reallocated among merchandise departments. The downtown store was scheduled for a major renovation beginning in 1992. Most often when a branch was renovated or a new store like Middletown opened, the budget departments, which offered the lowest priced merchandise, were removed in favor of departments featuring higher priced goods. In addition, furniture departments were either scaled back or eliminated entirely. Currently, furniture was carried only in the downtown store and eight of the branches.

While management felt that the department store competition faced in each of the locations was quite similar, the customer base differed across locations. The newer stores, including Middletown, Rosewater, and the newly renovated Donmore store appealed to a higher-end customer while the other branch locations and the downtown store continued to attract the moderate customer. This meant that these newer stores carried a somewhat different, more up-scale mix of merchandise, including Donna Karan New York and Ellen Tracy in women's apparel, and Ralph Lauren in home furnishings. Items from certain of these lines were also carried in the downtown store and some other branches.

The three newer or recently renovated branches also were more focused on soft goods such as apparel and home linens and did not sell furniture and electronics. Management believed that both the moderate and the furniture customers in the trading area of these branches would transfer their patronage to another nearby Randall's store. For furniture, this mobility was encouraged by stationing professional interior decorators in the downtown store and another branch to help in selecting furniture.

The Middletown store, which was located in an upscale mall, was notable in that it was the only branch with a commissioned sales staff. Incentive-based compensation was deemed necessary when Middletown opened to attract competent salespeople in a market with very tight labor conditions.

Randall's had succeeded in establishing a relatively more upscale image at Middletown, according to its store manager, because it had entered a suburban trading area in which the store did not already have a strong and well known image. Moreover, Extra Value Day sale events did not have the impact at Middletown that they did at the older branches and the downtown store. Of the thirteen stores, Middletown was currently one of the best performers in terms of sales volume, though, because of its incentive-based compensation system, it also had significantly higher selling costs.

Organizational Structure, Compensation, and Merchandising Objectives

The reporting structure within Randall's was similar to that in many traditional department stores. The three General Merchandise Managers (GMM) and the Vice Presidents for Sales Promotion and for Stores reported to Emily Randall (see **Exhibit 2** for Randall's Management Organization Chart). Theresa DiCarlo was the GMM responsible for Home Furnishings, Neal Smith for Men's, Children's and Intimate Apparel, and Kristen Olson for all of Women's Apparel and Accessories. A Fashion Director and several Divisional Merchandise Managers (DMM) reported to each of the GMMs. In turn, the buyers reported to the DMMs. Store managers reported to the Vice President for Stores.

Compensation for the merchants, including the GMMs, DMMs, and the buyers consisted of a base salary that was determined by comparing performance to merchandise plans and to the performance of other department stores in a buying cooperative of which Randall's was a member. Performance measures were sales, gross margin as a percent of net sales, gross profit dollars, initial markup, markdowns as a percent of net sales, inventory turns, and gross profit divided by inventory investment. According to Emily Randall, expense considerations, other than supplies and travel expenses, were not considered in evaluating the performance of the buying organization because the merchants had limited control over the advertising, selling, and distribution expenses.

Emily Randall considered her merchandising objectives to be maximization of net sales and gross profit dollars while maintaining an acceptable gross margin percent (including the cash discounts received from the vendors). This objective was consistent with building the store's volume and market share in key merchandise areas like fine jewelry and women's dresses, often at the expense of a lower gross margin percentage.

COMPETITION

Top management considered its major rivals to be Prescott's and D.H. Humphrey. As JCPenney (and to a much lesser extent Sears Roebuck) upgraded its stores physically and through adding important brand names to its assortments, however, it also became more directly competitive. In addition, more focused competitors threatened Randall's business in many merchandise categories. In children's clothing, for example, Kids R Us, a national chain of branded children's clothing owned by Toys R Us, was a key competitor. The Gap and The Limited were at least equally important threats in adult, particularly women's, apparel.

Prescott's

Prescott's first store in the Billingsville area was opened in the early 1960s in the Donmore Mall. It currently operated seven locations in the Billingsville area, three of which were in the same malls as Randall's biggest volume stores.

Prescott's was known for extensive merchandise assortments, aggressive advertising, and intensive promotional pricing. When it entered a market, Prescott's used aggressive pricing and promotion and its wide assortments, to build volume. In women's apparel, for example, Prescott's would often discount a vendor's entire line for a one-day sale event. Prescott's was described by a Randall's General Merchandise Manager as "the biggest off-price regular pricer in the world." Prior to Prescott's arrival, most competitors, including Randall's and D.H. Humphrey, were far less promotional, with less frequent sale events and more merchandise being sold at regular prices.

By the late 1970s, Prescott's had an important market presence in the Billingsville area. To combat this threat, Randall's became more promotional, and throughout the 1980s succeeded in achieving consistent increases in net sales and gross margin dollars. Prescott's, however, promoted more aggressively than Randall's, and often did up to twice the volume in a comparable location.

Prescott's also tended to be the market leader in store modernization and up-to-date merchandise assortments, according to Pete Stengel, Randall's Vice President for Stores. For example, Prescott's was the first area department store to abandon budget merchandise, followed by Randall's. More recently, Prescott's seemed to be abandoning furniture, placing less emphasis on the balance of the home store, and greater emphasis on apparel.

D.H. Humphrey

D.H. Humphrey had been a major force in Billingsville for over 80 years, but had failed to keep up with Prescott's and Randall's in renovating its stores. Many Randall's executives believed that its increased market share in the 1980s had been at D.H. Humphrey's expense.

D.H. Humphrey traditionally had carried better merchandise and offered good customer service, but its market position had deteriorated over the past ten years. The store was currently promoting aggressively. In women's dresses, for example, it had begun discounting its entire line for various sale events.

A–Z Retail

Although Randall's competed with A–Z Retail in two of its highest volume, higher end stores, A–Z Retail, with only two locations in the Billingsville area, was not considered a major competitor. A–Z Retail's lack of a substantial market presence precluded it from advertising aggressively. The chain had made a major commitment to home textiles (including sheets, towels, tablecloths and other home linens), however, and was considered a strong competitor by the divisional merchandise manager for home textiles.

JCPenney

JCPenney, having changed from mainly a national smaller city seller of utilitarian general merchandise to a big city department store company with a soft goods emphasis, now carried many moderately priced traditional department store brands. For example, in men's sportswear JCPenney carried an impressive assortment of Levi Dockers and in children's clothing they were rumored to be negotiating with Osh Kosh, a similarly prominent brand. In fine jewelry, JCPenney was known to have a strong diamond business. JCPenney was also using its large private label business to reinforce its position as a major competitor in home textiles.

Emerging Competitive Threats

Like other department stores, Randall's also now faced more narrowly focused competition in many merchandise categories. These included national specialty store chains, manufacturer's factory outlets and off-price stores in apparel, power retailers in home electronics and children's apparel, catalog showrooms in fine jewelry and certain other areas, and for lower priced merchandise, various discount department store operations. Of most concern to Randall's buyers were those competitors that carried name brands offered by traditional department stores. These included Marshall's, TJ Maxx, and Dress Barn in women's apparel, Coat Surplus Stores in coats and outerwear, and The Linen Drawer in home textiles. These so-called "off-price" retailers offered primarily last year's and the less popular of this year's styles and colors at sharply discounted prices. They were typically located in strip mall shopping centers, which had lower occupancy costs than comparable specialty store space in enclosed regional malls. Manufacturer's factory outlets also offered out of season, less popular and "second" or "irregular" branded merchandise at sharply reduced prices. Manufacturer's factory outlets were located in Lewiston, 50 miles from Billingsville. With over 50 factory outlet stores located in Lewiston, it had become a popular shopping destination for more price conscious consumers.

In contrast to manufacturer's outlets and off-price stores, power retailers that competed with Randall's included Kids R Us in children's apparel and Warehouse Electronics in home electronics. These national or multi-regional operations offered extensive assortments of current, branded merchandise at lower prices than traditional retailers and, if needed, also provided good to excellent service. Power retailers' lower prices resulted from substantial volume which enabled them to buy from manufacturers at very attractive terms and from high volume locations in lower cost strip malls. Randall's children's apparel department, which historically had dominated the greater Billingsville area, was particularly threatened by Kids R Us.

Catalog showrooms, including Service Merchandise and Best Products, were another form of retailing with which Randall's competed. They carried impressive assortments of fine jewelry, and, among other merchandise for the home, small appliances. Their prices were usually significantly below the manufacturer's suggested list price typically quoted by department stores.

National specialty store chains, which carried apparel bearing the retailer's own brand name, were also a competitive threat. Randall's buying staff were less concerned about them, however, since they did not compete head-to-head with the same brand names. In particular, Randall's faced competitors like The Limited in women's apparel, The Gap in men's and women's casual clothing, Victoria's Secret in lingerie, and Brooks Brothers in men's traditional clothing. The Limited (and its Victoria's Secret division) and The Gap were particularly strong competitors because their more efficient international procurement system enabled them to obtain wanted in-season fashion merchandise more quickly and at lower cost than department stores.[1]

Finally, for the sales of lower price point merchandise, Randall's competed with discount department stores. In small housewares, for example, Randall's would carry a Black & Decker coffee maker, while the same or a very similar Black & Decker model would also be carried in competing discount department stores.

CURRENT PRICING

Randall's currently employed three price designations for merchandise at its original selling price. Merchandise designated *Everyday Low Price* (EDLP) would never be marked down or put on sale except for end-of-season clearance sales or with the approval of the General Merchandise Manager for the department. Thus, the bulk of the inventory of an everyday low price item was sold at the full, undiscounted price. Everyday low priced merchandise was to be priced as low or lower than competitors' sale prices for the same or like items. Only the children's department continued to make significant use of this price designation, though it had been tried and discontinued in both fine jewelry and men's suits.

Value priced merchandise carried a price considered comparable to the competition's prices for the same item or a like item. Value prices could be adjusted to meet competition. This price designation was used throughout the store, almost exclusively for moderately priced merchandise, both branded and private label, and was meant to indicate exceptional value to the customer. High sellthrough at the value price was expected, though these items could be discounted for sale events. Value priced merchandise usually had a 95 cent ending, such as $12.95 for a basic women's pant.

Often, value priced merchandise were items that had been obtained from vendors at particularly attractive costs and the savings had been reflected in the retail prices. Moreover, Randall's would often take a lower markup on such merchandise with the expectation that substantial volume at the value price would more than compensate for the reduced percentage margin. Because of particularly attractive purchase prices, however, buyers were sometimes able to offer exceptional retail values while still maintaining the departmental target markup percentage. For example, the men's accessories department had value priced silk ties imported by Randall's itself and still achieved a 61% initial markup, which exceeded the average of 60% for neckware.

While most departments carried value priced merchandise, this designation, unlike the everyday low price designation, was not necessarily consistently communicated to the customer. For example, in women's apparel, value priced merchandise consistently had a 95 cent ending, while in home textiles value priced sheets and towels often had a 99 cent ending. Signs also differed across departments. Women's and men's apparel often used signs, such as "$79.95 for selected London Fog Jackets," that, according to the merchants, communicated exceptional value quickly and clearly. Women's dresses, however, used signs that read "Special Value" on fixtures that contained merchandise at several different prices. Senior management's view was that in the dress department, too many price signs would have resulted from specifying each special value price, thus cheapening the department's image. According to some store managers, customers seemed confused by value priced merchandise, often asking sales associates for the original prices of such items.

Merchandise that did not receive either of the above two price designations could be promoted at the discretion of Randall's merchants. Manufacturers of fashion apparel with strong brand images, however, sometimes discouraged "premature" markdowns of their merchandise.

Randall's reduced the price of "current" non-EDLP and non-value priced merchandise for a wide variety of

---

1 An executive from a prominent vendor provided a vivid example the retail price advantage enjoyed by The Limited. Assuming this vendor had historically operated on a gross margin of 33%, it could offer a dress, with a cost of goods sold of $40, to a department store at a purchase price of $60. The typical department store, however, had come to expect from the vendor a variety of discounts, including cooperative advertising dollars, allowances for returns, markdown protection, and even payment for fixturing. As a result, the vendor had raised his price to the retailer to approximately $75 to $80, to cover the cost of these additional discounts. The department store ordinarily then took a 50% initial markup at retail on the $75 to $80 purchase price, which would result in offering this dress to the consumer at an initial retail price of $150 to $160.

The Limited, however, could offer the dress at a much lower retail price, in part, because it avoided the inflation in price due to negotiated allowances. If The Limited, through its procurement arm, Mast Industries, had the same cost of manufacturing, and Mast's transfer price to The Limited included 20% added overhead, the dress described above would be transferred to The Limited at $50. The Limited, with a 50% initial markup could then offer the same dress as the department store at a retail price of $100!

store sales including Extra Value Day, Anniversary, Billingsville Saturday, and Bargain Weekend sales and departmental events such as the domestics department's White Sale. For these events, the merchandise typically was not physically marked down. Instead, the display might read "20% off the ticket price" with the discount calculated at the cash register. POS (point-of-sale) price reductions resulted in markdowns of only the merchandise that was actually sold. In contrast, permanent markdowns also caused the value of the remaining inventory to be reduced. Randall's typically took its permanent markdowns at the end of the season to reflect the decline in the worth of slow selling merchandise. Such "clearance" merchandise clearly showed the permanently reduced price on the price tag and was displayed on "Sale" racks, in the rear of the selling areas.

In any given department, the merchandise displays might indicate a number of different price designations including:

- Value priced merchandise, all at the same ticket price with this price highlighted on a "Value Price" sign.
- Value priced merchandise, of varying ticket prices, with a "Special Value" sign.
- Regularly priced merchandise, with no special sign.
- Clearance merchandise, with a "Sale" sign.
- Merchandise discounted for a special event like Value Days or the Anniversary Sale, typically with a sign indicating the percentage off the ticketed price at the register.

In addition, merchandise designated as everyday low price was available in the children's department and occasionally in domestics.

Randall's price guarantee program stipulated that it would match the price of any department store competitor and would reduce the price of a Randall's purchase if, within ten days of the purchase, Randall's lowered its price on the item. Such price adjustments created substantial logistical problems. Before the well known high-volume March and November Extra Value Day sales commenced, many customers purchased merchandise from the more complete selections, and then during the sale requested a price adjustment. Additional staffing and space (i.e., the room normally used for training at the branch locations) were needed for processing adjustments during these two sale periods.

ADVERTISING

Advertising at Randall's consisted of print (including inserts in local Sunday newspapers, other newspaper advertising, and catalogs), television, and radio (see **Exhibit 3** for Randall's Historical Advertising Expenditures, and **Exhibit 4** for some comparisons of Randall's media usage to that of selected competitors). Like many department stores, Randall's advertised primarily to announce sale events. Print media were mainly used for "sale" advertisements, because price reductions on numerous items could be communicated efficiently.

Randall's used both Sunday inserts and run of press (ROP) for its sale advertising. A typical Sunday insert consisted of up to sixty pages of color presentations of merchandise that showed both the sale price and the regular price. Value priced merchandise also was often included in Sunday inserts.

ROP ads were black and white advertisements within the body of the newspaper itself. ROP promotional advertisements often used a "boxes and liners" format with limited descriptions of merchandise such as "ALL SHORT SLEEVE SPORT SHIRTS," and the regular and sale prices within each box. The women's division also used ROP advertising, often with quarter- and full page illustrations or photographs of a single garment. These ads typically appeared on Mondays and Tuesdays, and emphasized in-season, full priced fashion merchandise.

Randall's advertising budget included both funds for "general" advertising and specific GMM allocations. General advertising expenditures included outlays for major storewide sale events, some of which were advertised on television as well as in newspapers, corporate and institutional advertisements, and expenditures for copy development and production, most of which was done in-house.

Funds allocated to the General Merchandise Managers were redistributed to their Divisional Merchandise Managers. These funds were used for focused events, like the Home Store's White Sale, and to pay for any additional Sunday inserts done at the discretion of the GMMs. A general merchandise or divisional budget might also pay for supplemental advertising done during a storewide sale period, for fashion ROP advertising, and for any catalog advertising.

Exhibit 5 shows 1989 advertising expenditures for selected merchandise divisions. The total advertising budget available to the DMMs, termed the "gross advertising budget" was composed of "net advertising dollars," which were funds allocated by the GMMs from their respective budgets, and cooperative advertising dollars provided by vendors. Cooperative advertising dollars could be quite substantial and, as shown in Exhibit 5, sometimes more than doubled a DMM's internally available advertising funds. Each division's and GMM's share of Randall's total net advertising dollars remained fairly constant from year to year.

In any given month, Randall's might have a number of storewide and divisional sale events, as shown, for example, in Exhibit 6, the promotion calendar for August, 1988 and 1989. Randall's 4-day Extra Value sale was its most important monthly sale event. This event had a long history at Randall's, and was a well known tradition in Billingsville. Extra Value Day had originally been a one-day event, which offered, at dramatically reduced and the lowest prices for the month, both clearance merchandise and stock ordered especially for the event.

Special red Extra Value Day signs were used to highlight Extra Value merchandise. In some divisions, additional merchandise might be put on sale during Extra Value Days, but, if the prices were not to be the lowest of the month, the merchandise was not displayed with Extra Value Day signs. The year's two biggest Extra Value Day sales were in November and March.

In addition to Extra Value Days, Randall's now also had a number of other storewide sales, including some specific to certain geographic locations, such as monthly Billingsville Saturday sales and the Bargain weekend sale in the suburban stores.

Randall's regularly received market research from its media suppliers, recent examples of which are shown in Exhibits 7–9. Exhibit 7, done by a local television station, shows demographic and psychographic data for consumers who had purchased women's clothing in the past year in Randall's and selected competitors. Exhibit 8 provides selected demographic data on Billingsville credit card holders. Data on the ninety-day shopping pattern of Billingsville adults for selected stores is shown in Exhibit 9.

Patricia Clarke, Vice President for Sales Promotion, was concerned both about Randall's reliance on sale advertising to drive store volume and the related emphasis on print advertising at the expense of television.

She argued that, because of reduced circulation and the tendency of younger consumers not to be heavy readers, newspapers had declined in effectiveness. In addition, she believed that the excessive use of ROP retail sale advertising and Sunday inserts had resulted in visual clutter and "insert junk," particularly in the Sunday newspaper.

Clarke was also concerned that Randall's relied too heavily on weekend sale events. "There is always something on sale on the weekend," according to Clarke. As a result, a substantial portion of advertising was done in the Friday newspaper and on television on Thursday and Friday. The consequence was a continuing shift of business to the already crowded weekend with correspondingly less business done during the week.

DETAIL ON SELECTED MERCHANDISE DEPARTMENTS

Specific data for the total store and selected merchandise categories for 1989 are shown in Exhibit 10. Randall's balance sheet, as of January 28, 1990, is provided in Exhibit 15. Exhibit 11 shows, for each of the selected merchandise departments and the total store, the percentage increases in net sales, against the previous year, from 1986 to 1989. Exhibits 12 and 13 provide the initial markup and total contribution, respectively, for selected departments and the total store from 1985 to 1989. Total contribution was calculated as gross profit, plus cash discounts, less salesforce, advertising, and inventory carrying costs.

Exhibit 14 provides a comparison of Randall's 1989 performance to the average among member companies of a buying cooperative to which Randall's belonged.

Children's Apparel

Randall's was, because of its strong reputation for superior assortment, good service and competitive prices, a major competitor in children's clothing. Children's clothing therefore represented 5.75% of overall store volume in 1989 compared to 4.9%, typical for department stores.

Competition in children's clothing traditionally had been Prescott's and D.H. Humphrey. Beginning in the mid 1980s, however, Kids R Us had entered the Billingsville area, offering extensive assortments of popular branded merchandise at everyday low prices. Prescott's responded by adopting everyday low pricing in children's clothing, and advertising aggressively that "Prescott's will not be undersold." In addition, Prescott's increased its assortment of private label merchandise, which, according to Jerry Cole, Divisional Merchandise Manager for children's clothing, was now up to 80% of its children's business. By comparison, only 25% to 35% of Randall's sales were private label. Many at Randall's believed that Prescott's had reduced its emphasis on children's clothing and had become less competitive.

To maintain competitive everyday prices when confronted by Kids R Us, Randall's adopted everyday low prices equal to Kids R Us on merchandise sold under twelve strong brand names. The merchandise was carried by most of Randall's competitors including Prescott's, D.H. Humphrey, and Kids R Us. Merchandise carried under the EDLP program was distinguished by its special price ticket and special EDLP signs on the displays.

Randall's new pricing policy caused the initial markup for the EDLP merchandise to decline to 28% to 33% compared to 48% to 50% for the remainder of the department's merchandise. The lower initial markup translated into a gross margin on EDLP merchandise of 28% to 29%, against the department's average of 35% of net sales.

Everyday low pricing was very successful for Randall's in children's, with substantial increases in volume more than compensating for the reduction in gross margin. Furthermore, the volume increases allowed Randall's to improve its already dominant merchandise selection.

Executives at Randall's offered a number of reasons for their success. Many believed that Randall's gains had been at D.H. Humphrey's expense. According to Cole, D.H. Humphrey, however, was now strengthening its business with increases in inventory and improvements in assortments. Still, Cole believed D.H. Humphrey would have difficulty regaining the share it lost over a ten-year period. Others argued that EDLP's success was attributable to most major competitors adopting it about the same time as Randall's. Conversely, Janet Lee, now Vice President of Planning, Development, and Research, who as DMM had instituted EDLP in children's clothing, believed that maintaining EDLP was tougher when it had been adopted by most competitors because there was a tendency for someone to start promoting off the EDLP prices.

Randall's emphasis on EDLP in children's clothing had recently declined from its 1988 high of 45% of sales.

Problems with Osh Kosh, a prestige brand name and an important EDLP vendor, were the major cause for the decline. In the early days of EDLP, Randall's would buy all fifteen Osh Kosh lines, everyday low price them very aggressively, and sell nearly all of its inventory at the everyday low prices. During this time period, Osh Kosh sales were increasing 40% to 50% per year and its inventory turns reached 6½. Osh Kosh currently, however, was a much less reliable resource, because of popularity-induced supply problems and its focus on much larger accounts such as Sears and potentially JCPenney. Perhaps due to supply problems, Osh Kosh merchandise had become stagnant and the number of lines offered to the trade had reached a low of six. Randall's sales of Osh Kosh slumped and markdowns were now often needed to clear inventory. Recently, customers seemed to expect to find Osh Kosh on sale. Cole, in particular, worried that other strong EDLP brands like Buster Brown would suffer a similar fate.

EDLP was becoming less appropriate for children's clothing for another reason, according to Cole. When it had been instituted, children's clothing had been a basic business. Now it was becoming increasingly more fashion driven, which required taking markdowns to clear obsolescent merchandise. Even Osh Kosh was becoming more fashion driven. Markdowns on EDLP merchandise had consequently risen from an average of 5% to over 10% of net sales.

Cole was contemplating revising the children's EDLP program. He particularly wanted to reduce the number of vendors in the program, keeping only the major ones, Carter, Osh Kosh, Health Tex, and Buster Brown at everyday low prices. Lesser brands, like Little Levis, which were becoming "hot," would still be priced competitively, but buyers could take advantage of their popularity by taking a higher initial markup of 45%. He also planned to take more seasonal merchandise like outerwear, swimwear, and sleepwear off EDLP to increase participation in storewide events like the pre-season and Columbus Day sales in early fall and the November Extra Value Days. He expected these changes to reduce EDLP merchandise to 25% to 30% of the department's sales compared to 45% a number of years ago.

Children's clothing also offered some value priced merchandise, especially when an advantageous purchase was obtained from a vendor. The average initial markup for value priced merchandise was approximately 40% compared to 48% to 50% for the overall department. In fall 1989, an attractively priced selection of children's coats had been offered at value prices. A selection of children's turtlenecks had also been value priced and had sold 38,000 units.

Children's clothing participated, to some extent, in nearly every storewide sale event but participated most heavily in the March and November Extra Value Days and in the Back to School sale. March and November Extra Value Day volume in children's clothing would exceed the storewide average of 25% of the month's total. Furthermore, Extra Value Days seemed to be a good traffic builder for regular priced business. For example, children's outerwear sales at regular prices were always quite strong during the November Extra Value Days. Moreover, only 25% of the markdowns in children's clothing were permanent. The balance were point-of-sale reductions.

In addition to storewide events, there were two departmental events in children's clothing, Back to School and Easter. The children's clothing business peaked more at Easter than did other departments. During this time of year, as much as 45% of girls' spring dresses were sold at the departmental initial markup of 48% to 50%.

Fine Jewelry

In the late 1980s Randall's had worked aggressively to improve its volume and market share in fine jewelry, a business management considered underdeveloped. Advertising was intensified and primarily used to announce frequent sale events including 45% discounts on gold jewelry, 30% discounts on better jewelry, and 35% discounts on precious stones. These price reductions were from the department's average initial markup of 65%, and resulted in dramatic increases in net sales and gross profit dollars, particularly in 1987.

Prescott's traditionally had been the dominant fine jewelry department store competitor as a result of its excellent assortments and intensive sale advertising. Other competitors, all of whom promoted their fine jewelry, included D.H. Humphrey, Hill's in some locations, JCPenney (particularly in diamonds), Sears, and, downtown, the jewelers on nearby Center Street. The latter's commissioned salespeople had authority to negotiate customer discounts of up to 25%. Catalog showrooms, including Service Merchandise, also had extensive fine jewelry assortments that were competitively priced and similar in quality to those of department stores.

In distinct contrast to the apparent success of EDLP in children's clothing, Kristen Olson, GMM for women's apparel and accessories described everyday low pricing in fine jewelry as a "two-year nightmare," which commenced in early 1988 and was concluded at the end of 1989.

Like many retailers, Randall's had been concerned about the increasing promotional intensity of departments like fine jewelry, electronics, and other areas of the Home Store. The State Attorney General was known to be prosecuting some retailers in these merchandise categories, claiming that their intensive "sale" advertising was deceptive. This concern had stimulated the decision to adopt EDLP in fine jewelry in 1988. Prices were reduced to a 50% initial markup, the salesforce was intensively trained in the benefits of EDLP and how to sell in this environment, and advertising expenditures to communicate the EDLP story were increased. During this time period, Randall's advertised everyday low price was always lower than the competition's (primarily Prescott's) sale price. Fine jewelry was promoted only during November Extra Value Days.

In 1988, the first year of the fine jewelry EDLP program, Randall's lost much of the volume gained in 1987. One explanation for poor 1988 sales was that, in anticipation of the change to EDLP, Linda Knowles, DMM for fashion accessories and the fine jewelry buyer, had bought in the Orient a substantial stock of precious stones. Sales of these stones were slow and by late 1988, much of this inventory was no longer new. Because it was everyday low priced, it was difficult to mark it down further and clear it. Thus the outdated inventory tended to exacerbate the 1989 difficulties in implementing EDLP. The additional sales decline in 1989 convinced many in the company that EDLP had significantly damaged a previously strong business.

Comments from the salesforce suggested that, regardless of their efforts to educate customers, they refused to believe that Randall's jewelry prices were at and often below the competition's sale prices. Incessant discounting by other retailers in the Billingsville area, in particular Prescott's, convinced customers that Randall's prices were no longer competitive. Customers would often ask when the EDLP merchandise was to go on sale and would dispute with the salesperson the policy of no further discounts.

Commenting on the fine jewelry experience, both Olson and Knowles believed that for it to succeed, the entire store needed to adopt EDLP. They acknowledged that fine jewelry presented a particular problem. Comparing the prices, or even determining the quality of the mainly unbranded merchandise was exceptionally difficult.

Now that EDLP had been discontinued, Knowles and Olson planned to promote jewelry about 50% of the time, most often at discounts of 25%. They planned to have 5 to 6 departmental sales, in addition to participating in most of the storewide sales, but to put the entire fine jewelry department on sale only for the Anniversary sale and some Extra Value Days and Billingsville Saturday sales. For the November Extra Value Days, they planned to run all fine jewelry at 40% off. They anticipated that Prescott's would nevertheless continue to out-promote Randall's in fine jewelry.

Men's Suits

Randall's offered men's suits in all but the Glenwood and Bellingham branches, but sales results differed substantially among stores. Sales were strong in the Middletown store partly because its commissioned salesforce provided superior customer service. In contrast to other stores, for example, its sales associates were much more inclined to sell among departments. Thus they often helped customers select a shirt and tie to match a suit. Since superior service stimulated greater loyalty, approximately 50% of Middletown customers were repeat buyers compared to an average of 25% in other stores.

In contrast with Middletown, several stores were underperforming in men's suits. Neal Smith, GMM for men's, children's, and intimate apparel, wondered whether men's suits should be discontinued at these stores. One reason to keep men's suits in a store, however, was to stimulate sales of other men's lines such as sportswear and furnishings.

Randall's major men's suits competitors were Prescotts, D.H. Humphrey and Bill's, a particularly strong men's specialty store in downtown Billingsville. In certain locations, including downtown and Middletown, another competitor was Brooks Brothers, a national specialty store chain carrying its own, conservative, primarily business clothing. Bob Wilson, DMM for men's clothing and furnishings, considered Prescott's to be his toughest competitor, though he believed that Randall's had a better selection of men's suits than either Prescott's or D.H. Humphrey. Both Prescott's and D.H. Humphrey, however, had commissioned sales staffs in men's suits.

Nevertheless, Wilson believed that Randall's service equalled that of its department store competition, although he acknowledged it was inferior to Bill's. Similarly, though Randall's dominated its department store competition in assortment, Bill's had a more complete selection in both styles and price points.

In August 1989, in recognition of the fact that 70% to 80% of men's suits already sold at 25% off during the Early Season Sale, Extra Value Days, and other storewide sales, everyday low pricing was adopted in the men's suit department. Smith and Wilson believed that sales of men's suits would benefit from EDLP because the merchandise was easy to compare across retailers. Therefore customers could judge the fairness of prices for themselves. They also believed that their customers would appreciate not having to shop around for sale prices when buying suits.

Randall's new EDLP prices represented a 25% reduction from the regular prices formerly prevailing in the department. They matched and sometimes were below the competitors' sale prices. Furthermore, if a customer found an identical suit priced lower in another department store, Randall's would match the lower price.

The change in pricing was accompanied by heavy advertising. In addition, salespeople were supportive of the change because they preferred a more even customer flow to doing the bulk of their business on sale days.

Because of a decline in gross profit dollars, everyday low pricing was discontinued at the end of January 1990. The reduction in initial markup from 54% to 39% when EDLP was adopted resulted only in sales remaining even with those of the previous fall. While EDLP improved Randall's day-to-day business, sales dropped significantly relative to sale periods. Also, when competitors were advertising discounts of 25% to 30%, customers often complained that Randall's did not discount men's suits. Smith and Wilson both feared that Randall's might lose market share if they continued EDLP. Another reason for discontinuing EDLP was that an important vendor, apparently pressured by its other retail accounts, suggested that it might stop selling to Randall's. The vendor said it did not want its brand name associated with EDLP.

Customers seemed to have trouble understanding the new pricing system. Smith and Wilson believed that the continuation of promotional pricing by other competitors and the adoption of EDLP in only a few departments at Randall's were sources of customer confusion. "It confuses the customer if you have suits at EDLP and men's dress shirts on sale," said Smith.

Additionally, Wilson wondered whether they had maintained EDLP in men's suits long enough. Perhaps if the program had been given a full year trial, instead of just the fall season, it might have worked. Wilson believed that the chances for EDLP to be successful should have been better in men's suits than in fine jewelry because of greater comparability of merchandise among competitors.

Now that men's suits were no longer everyday low priced, the department's initial markup had risen to 50% to 51%. Although the new regular prices were lower than Prescott's, 70% to 80% of the sales were nevertheless being done at a discount of 25% off regular price. To build volume, Wilson and Smith planned to include men's suits in the two men's wardrobe sales this year and in many of the Extra Value Day sales. They planned to offer particularly good values on Extra Value Days, including, for example, "30% off all sportcoats, trousers, and blazers."

OPTIONS

Emily and Caroline Randall and others in top management were worried about Randall's increasingly promotional profile. Over the past ten years, Randall's had been very successful in building volume and gross profit dollars by increasing the frequency and variety of its sale events. Some in the organization wondered, however, if further increases in the number of sale days and/or the discount percentage would continue to produce more volume and better bottom line results. Pete Stengel, Vice President for Stores said, "First our customers stopped believing that our regular prices represented good value and now they don't even believe our 20% off sales so we have to take an additional percentage off to move the merchandise. What will we have to offer next?"

An alternative Emily and Caroline were considering was more stable pricing throughout the store. One option was to reduce the number of storewide and departmental sale events, and concurrently reduce the initial markup for regular priced merchandise to the level currently used for value priced merchandise. Emily and Caroline believed a number of benefits would accrue from this approach. First, they expected to save on advertising expenses (primarily print) for sale

events. They wondered, however, how much of the money saved should be channeled into advertising to communicate the new policy and to help improve Randall's fashion image, at least in the short run. Second, they expected some savings in personnel costs. With fewer sale events they expected a reduction in the staff needed to process adjustments.

A third benefit they anticipated was better inventory turnover. They expected that with more predictable day-to-day sales, many departments could operate with less inventory. In addition, they expected a reduction in the quantity of residual merchandise from sale events, which was then sold at even lower prices.

A more predictable sales pattern could also lead to fewer stockouts. Stockouts were a particular problem during storewide sale periods in furniture, for example, but also led to lost sales in the fashion categories when a "hot item" was unnecessarily discounted.

Finally, Emily and Caroline expected that more stable pricing might enable the merchants to spend more time planning their assortments and merchandise presentations. They believed that improvements in merchandise assortments and presentation, along with improved service, were critical for reestablishing for Randall's a unique image that would stimulate greater store loyalty.

Though there seemed to be a number of good reasons for reducing Randall's reliance on sale events, Emily and Caroline were worried about the impact of such a move. The experience in fine jewelry and men's suits suggested the difficulty of convincing customers that a regular, undiscounted price was still a good value. Would a switch to more stable prices have to be accompanied by changes in assortment and service that would allow Randall's to compete with the best specialty shops?

On the other hand, in certain categories, like home electronics, Emily and Caroline worried whether Randall's could ever be on par with specialists like Warehouse Electronics. Did more stable pricing mean that Randall's should move out of categories where it was a rather weak and highly promotional competitor?

In other categories, like fine jewelry, the aggressive promotional posture of competitors like Prescott's would place Randall's at a significant disadvantage, particularly if customers could not be convinced to compare net prices. Still, many in the company believed that with storewide adoption of more stable pricing, Randall's could establish a reputation for good value even though competitors continued to promote aggressively.

Emily and Caroline wondered how they should quantify the potential benefits and risks of adopting more stable prices throughout the store. Implementation of the policy was also a concern. Which storewide sale events should they discontinue? If they kept a monthly event like Extra Value Days, should restrictions be placed on the merchandise that could be put on sale? How should they determine the initial markup that would be low enough to ensure customer acceptance of the new prices and high enough to operate profitably? What changes in assortment, service, and advertising might also be needed? Finally, if they didn't reduce their reliance on sale events, how could they better execute their emphasis on promotional pricing to enhance sales and operate more profitably?

Exhibit 1
Randall's Department Stores Branch Locations

Store Estimated Location	Retailers	Gross Square Feet	Year Opened	Volume,
				(millions)
Billingsville	Randall's	753,900	1890	64
	D.H. Humphrey			43
	Starr's			18
	JCPenney			19
Jamestown	Randall's	76,300	1935	11
	D.H. Humphrey			17
	Baylor's			9
Donmore	Randall's	178,500	1966	32
	Sears			29
	Prescott's			54
	D.H. Humphrey			20
	JCPenney			26
Watertown	Randall's	134,400	1969	31
	Prescott's			48
	D.H. Humphrey			20
Winston	Randall's	150,500	1971	27
	Sears			26
	Baylor's			6
	JCPenney			18
	Prescott's			42
	Furniture Express			40
	D.H. Humphrey			18
Raymond	Randall's	146,300	1973	27
	Prescott's			39
	Sears			29
	D.H. Humphrey			15
	JCPenney			18
Ellensburg	Randall's	170,800	1975	29
	Sears			35
	Starr's			7
	D.H. Humphrey			15
	JCPenney			19
	Prescott's			39

Store Estimated Location	Retailers	Gross SquareFeet	Year Opened	Volume
				(millions)
Astoria	Randall's	137,200	1978	29
Big Bear	Randall's	151,900	1983	34
	Prescott's			42
	JCPenney			20
Glenwood	Randall's	128,100	1987	17
	Sears			20
Goldendale	Randall's	108,500	1988	28
	Hill's			25
Middletown	Randall's	166,600	1991	32
	Prescott's			60
	A-Z Retail			32
	Sears			39
	JCPenney			19
	D.H. Humphrey			20
Rosewater	Randall's	165,200	1988	34
	A-Z Retail			25
	Sears			22
	D.H. Humphrey			13

Exhibit 2
Randall's Management Organization Chart

Board of Directors

President & Co-Chairman of the Executive Committee

Chairman of the Board & Co-Chairman of the Executive Committee

Chairman of the Board & Co-Chairman of the Exec. Committee

Merchandising & Stores

- Vice President GMM
  - Fash. Mdse. Director Home Furnishings
    - DMM Cosmetics
    - DMM Tabletop, Gifts, Housewares & Stationery
    - DMM Home Tex., Lamps & Notions
    - DMM Furniture & Rugs
    - DMM Appliances, Electronics, Candy/Gourmet & Luggage
- Vice President GMM
  - DMM Intimate Apparel
  - DMM Infants' Children's & Boywear
  - DMM Men's Clothing & Furnishings
  - DMM Men's Sportswear
- Vice President GMM
  - Fash. Mdse. Director R-T-W & Accessories
    - DMM R-T-W, Dresses & Coats
    - DMM Young Contemporary
    - DMM Better & Petite Sportswear
    - DMM Pop. Price, Mod. & Women's Sportswear
    - DMM Fashion Accessories
    - DMM Shoes, (ex. Mens)
- Vice President Sales Promotion
  - Advertising Director
    - Display Director
    - Special Events Director
- Vice President Stores
  - Store Managers

V.P. Treasurer & Secretary
- Assistant to the Treasurer

V.P. Planning & Development
- Research Director

V.P. Personnel
- Director Personnel Services
  - Director Organization Development
  - Director Compensation & Employee Benefits
  - Director Communications Empl. Relations & Activities

V.P. & Controller
- Asst. Cont. for Sales Aud., Accts. Pay. & COC
- Asst. Cont. for General Accounting Staff Services & Pay Ofc.
  - Director Mdse. Info. Organ.
  - Director of Credit
  - Director Assets Protection
  - Director Merchandise Planning & Quick Response

V.P. Operations & General Supt.
- Customer Relations Director
- Food Serv. Director
- Merchandise Handling Director
- Operating Service Director
- Long-Range Planning Director
- Planning Director
- Property Management Director

Exhibit 3
Randall's Advertising History (000s) (Total Advertising Expenditures, Exclusive of Cooperative Advertising Dollars)

	Spring	Fall	Total
1983	2,995.4	3,758.8	6,754.2
1984	3,620.3	5,887.0	9,507.3
1985	4,601.4	7,133.9	11,735.3
1986	5,505.1	8,068.9	13,574.0
1987	5,683.3	8,437.4	14,120.7
1988	6,590.8	9,971.2	16,562.0
1989	5,780.4	8,828.5	14,608.9

Exhibit 4
Comparison of 1989 Media Usage

	Randall's	Prescott's	D. H. Humphrey
Newspaper			
Billingsville Inquirer			
Number of inserts[a]	17	48	5
Daily space (inches)	81,636	42,203	79,038
Sunday space (inches)	17,921	21,848	14,736
The Daily Herald			
Number of inserts[a]	26	43	—
Daily space (inches)	7,722	19,138	4,588
Sunday space (inches)	1,367	7,006	1,217
Billingsville Times			
Number of inserts[a]	24	38	8
Daily space (inches)	23,916	24,480	16,218
Sunday space (inches)	6,656	12,789	2,910
Gross Radio Purchases	$ 766,301	$ 803,680	$ 615,058
Gross Television Purchases	$2,313,044	$4,140,794	$2,047,203

a Newspaper inserts are full-color catalogs that advertise sale merchandise primarily and can consist of 30 to 60 pages. Inserts are in addition to Sunday advertising space.

Exhibit 5
1989 Advertising Expenditures for Selected Divisions

	Sales Volume	% of Total	Gross Adv. Dollars (Including Cooperative Dollars)	Gross as % of Sales	Net Adv. Dollars (Excluding Cooperative Dollars)	Net as a % of Sales
Children's	$33,944,325	7.2%	$ 736,355	2.2%	$434,435	1.3%
Fine Jewelry & Fashion Accessories	44,067,315	9.1	1,531,275	3.5	678,810	1.5
Notions & Decorative Home Furnishings	24,142,125	4.9	2,203,795	9.1	901,170	3.7
Men's Clothings & Furnishings	30,622,440	6.3	1,076,185	3.5	525,045	1.7
Women's Coats & Dresses	33,928,611	7.2	1,123,700	3.3	636,055	1.9

Exhibit 6
Promotion Calendar, August 1988 and August 1989

Date		August 1988 Events	Date		August 1989 Events
S	31	Glenwood Sidewalk Sale Ends	S	30	Glenwood Sidewalk Sale Ends
M	1		M	31	
T	2		T	1	
W	3		W	2	
T	4	Bargain Weekend Begins	T	3	Bargain Weekend Begins
F	5		F	4	
S	6		S	5	
S	7	Bargain Weekend Ends	S	6	Bargain Weekend Ends
M	8		M	7	
T	9		T	8	
W	10		W	9	
T	11		T	10	
F	12	Billingsville Saturday Pre-Print	F	11	Billingsville Saturday Pre-Print Special Booklet for Middletown, Rosewater, and Donmore
S	13	Billingsville Saturday	S	12	Billingsville Saturday
S	14		S	13	Home Store Insert
M	15	Fall Fashion Catalog	M	14	
T	16		T	15	
W	17		W	16	
T	18		T	17	
F	19		F	18	Extra Value Day, Junior Catalog Mails
S	20	Extra Value Day	S	19	Extra Value Day
S	21	Extra Value Day, Combination Insert	S	20	Extra Value Day, Insert
M	22	Extra Value Day, Junior Catalog Mails	M	21	Extra Value Day
T	23	Extra Value Day	T	22	Extra Value Day[a]
W	24		W	23	
T	25		T	24	
F	26	Billingsville Saturday Pre-Print	F	25	Billingsville Saturday Pre-Print
S	27	Billingsville Saturday	S	26	Billingsville Saturday

March 13, 1989—Revised May 31, 1989

a Extra Value Day added.

Exhibit 7

Store Patronage Comparisons for Consumers Who Purchased Women's Clothing in the Past Year—Geographic Coverage: Billingsville and Surrounding Area

	Entire Sample	Purchased at Randall's	Purchased at Prescott's	Purchased at D.H. Humphrey
Number of Respondents	1,500	247 (16.5%)[a]	199 (13.2%)	171 (11.4%)
Male	47.1%[b]	21.1%[c]	27.1%	23.4%
Female	52.9	78.9	72.9	76.6
Average	44.0 Years	46.2 Years	39.3 Years	46.2 Years
18–49	64.3%	57.5%	75.4%	60.2%
25–54	56.1	53.8	63.8	58.5
50–64	18.7	24.7	18.1	21.6
65 Plus	17.0	17.8	6.5	18.1
Own	75.9%	81.8%	79.4%	79.5%
Rent	23.5	17.0	19.6	19.9
Average Income	$41,887	$45,012	$52,544	$41,783
Under $15,000	10.6%	8.1%	4.0%	8.8%
$15,000–$29,999	23.6	23.1	19.1	23.4
$30,000–$49,999	26.9	26.7	23.6	29.8
$50,000 Plus	25.7	30.0	39.2	25.7
Married	56.6%	58.7%	61.8%	51.5%
Unmarried	43.0	40.5	38.2	48.0
High School	11.5%	5.7%	5.0%	5.8%
High School Graduate	35.6	38.1	26.1	32.2
Some College	26.5	27.9	27.1	28.7
College Graduate Plus	26.1	28.3	41.2	33.3
Full-Time	55.9%	51.4%	55.3%	56.1%
Part-Time	12.3	15.8	22.1	13.5
Female-Employed (% of females)	59.0	63.6	73.1	64.9
White-Collar	42.2%	50.6%	57.3%	52.0%
Blue-Collar	24.3	15.0	17.1	16.4
Homemaker	8.9	11.3	10.1	9.9
Retired	17.0	18.2	7.0	17.5

a To be read: 16.5% of those surveyed purchased women's clothing at Randall's. **Note:** Not all of the 1,500 surveyed had purchased in the past year.

b To be read: 47.1.% of all respondents were male.

c To be read: 21.1% of those who purchased women's clothing at Randall's were male.

Survey sample included 1,500 respondents from the greater Billingsville area.

Source: Wesley Associates; survey done in 1989.

Exhibit 8
Selected Data on Billingsville Market Credit Card Holders

	Billingsville AMSA Total Adults		Randall's Credit Card Holders		Prescott's Credit Card Holders		D.H. Humphrey's Credit Card Holders		JCPenney's Credit Card Holders	
Total Adults	2,236,320	100.0%	632,580	100.0%	452,580	100.0%	513,780	100.0%	628,140	100.0%
Sex										
Male	1,035,416	46.3	222,668	35.2	182,390	40.3	175,713	34.2	271,356	43.2
Female	1,200,904	53.7	409,912	64.8	270,190	59.7	338,067	65.8	356,784	56.8
Age										
18–24	315,321	14.1	41,750	6.6	45,711	10.1	26,203	5.1	69,724	11.1
25–34	496,463	22.2	126,516	20.0	127,243	28.1	85,801	16.7	150,754	24.0
35–44	440,555	19.7	123,986	19.6	114,050	25.2	112,518	21.9	128,769	20.5
45–54	322,030	14.4	93,622	14.8	73,771	16.3	73,984	14.4	96,734	15.4
55–64	284,013	12.7	88,561	14.0	52,047	11.5	78,608	15.3	67,211	10.7
65 & over	377,938	16.9	158,145	25.0	39,268	8.7	137,693	26.8	118,090	18.8
Household Income										
$75,000 & over	243,759	10.9	96,152	15.2	69,245	15.3	77,067	15.0	78,518	12.5
$50,000–$74,999	360,048	16.1	132,842	21.0	118,123	26.1	117,656	22.9	124,372	19.8
$35,000–$49,999	545,662	24.4	149,289	23.6	136,227	30.1	116,114	22.6	176,507	28.1
$25,000–$34,999	469,627	21.0	93,622	14.8	75,128	16.6	80,663	15.7	111,181	17.7
$15,000–$24,999	362,284	16.2	99,315	15.7	38,469	8.5	69,874	13.6	84,171	13.4
Under $15,000	248,232	11.1	60,095	9.5	15,840	3.5	51,892	10.1	54,020	8.6
Place of Residence										
Billingsville	807,312	36.1	211,914	33.5	76,486	16.9	171,089	33.3	174,623	27.8
Billingsville Suburbs	941,491	42.1	279,600	44.2	251,634	55.6	243,018	47.3	288,316	45.9
Outlying Area	487,518	21.8	141,065	22.3	124,460	27.5	99,673	19.4	165,201	26.3

A probability sample was used with results projected to the entire Billingsville resident population.

Source: *Billingsville Times*, Spring 1990.

Exhibit 9
Ninety-Day Shopping Pattern: Number and Percentage of Billingsville Adults Who Have Shopped in Selected Stores in the Past Three Months

Adults	Number of Total Adults	Percent of Total Adults
Total adults in Billingsville PMSA	2,236,320	100.0%
Adults who, in the past three months, have shopped at:		
Randall's	856,080	38.3
Prescott's	939,040	42.0
D. H. Humphrey	704,280	31.5
Starr's	286,260	12.8
Sears Roebuck	969,360	43.3
Baylor's	94,140	4.2
JCPenney	735,240	32.9
Hill's	135,420	6.1
A-Z Retail	169,140	7.6

A probability sample was used with results projected to the entire Billingsville resident population.

Source: *Billingsville Inquirer*, Spring 1990.

Exhibit 10
1989 Key Sales and Contribution Data

	Total Store	Children's Apparel	Fine Jewelry	Men's Suits
Total net sales	470,195,310	33,944,443	8,224,957	5,299,461
Percent of total store sales	100.00%	7.22%	1.75%	1.13%
Markup percent	48.89%	48.14%	48.02%	47.53%
Markdowns	116,976,343	8,303,549	1,253,894	2,545,768
Gross profit & cash discount	186,996,181	13,833,367	3,094,592	1,084,662
Percent of net sales	39.77%	40.75%	37.62%	20.47%
Advertising expense	14,608,950	434,436	126,696	91,925
Salesforce expense	24,097,494	1,425,369	495,558	143,753
Inventory turnover	2.7	3.5	0.9	1.6
Inputted yearly interest on inventory	14%	14%	14%	14%
Inventory carrying cost	12,318,366	641,382	702,792	315,072
Contribution	135,971,371	11,322,178	1,769,544	533,911
Percent of sales	28.92%	33.36%	21.51%	10.07%

Explanatory Notes:

1. Advertising expenses were allocated to the divisional but not the departmental level. The data reported above allocated department level advertising expenses in proportion to the department's share of its division's net sales.
2. Total store advertising expenses include the general advertising expenses and those expenses attributable to specific merchandise areas through the GMM budgets.
3. Inventory carrying costs include consideration of payable terms with vendors. On average, payment for inventory received is due within thirty days.
4. Other department level variable expenses such as distribution, delivery, and net loss due to bad credit were not considered as they were unavailable at either the divisional or departmental level.

Exhibit 11
Net Sales Increases vs. Previous Year (Percent)

	1985	1986	1987	1988	1989
Total Store	–	10	11	12	2
Children's Apparel	–	9	10	44	1
Fine Jewelry	–	8	41	-16	-12
Men's Suits	–	17	-8	19	-1

Exhibit 12
Initial Markup (Percent)

	1985	1986	1987	1988	1989
Total Store	48	49	51	50	50
Children's Apparel	48	48	48	48	50
Fine Jewelry	50	50	62	50	50
Men's Suits	49	51	55	54	50

Exhibit 13
Contribution as a Percent of Sales

	1985	1986	1987	1988	1989
Total Store	29	28	28	28	29
Children's Apparel	36	32	34	32	34
Fine Jewelry	34	30	28	29	22
Men's Suits	14	14	15	18	10

Exhibit 14
Comparison of Randall's Performance to Buying Cooperative for Key Merchandising and Operating Statistics in 1989

	Randall's	AMC
Total Store		
Turnover	2.7	2.4
Percent initial purchase markup	53.9	52.8
Markdown, percent of net sales	24.8	22.6
Gross margin and cash discount	39.7	40.0
Total expense, percent of sales[a]	33.2	35.4
Children's (Total Infants through Young Teens, Includes Infant Furniture)		
Percent of department sales to total	5.75	4.96
Turnover	3.7	3.2
Percent initial purchase markup	53.7	52.6
Markdown, percent of net sales	22.3	25.5
Gross margin and cash discount	41.4	41.7
Total expense, percent of sales	33.1	37.7
Fine Jewelry and Watches		
Percent of department sales to total	1.68	2.56
Turnover	1.1	1.49
Percent initial purchase markup	51.9	53.8
Markdown, percent of net sales	15.1	13.0
Gross margin and cash discount	37.5	29.0
Total expense, percent of sales	33.2	32.7
Men's Suits		
Percent of department sales to total	0.69	0.84
Turnover	1.6	1.4
Percent initial purchase markup	51.2	55.6
Markdown, percent of net sales	49.5	45.5
Gross margin and cash discount	18.7	25.8
Total expense, percent of sales	32.7	32.3

a Defined in *Merchandising and Operating Results of Department and Specialty Stores Annual Report* (published by National Retail Merchants Association) as "Sum of selling, advertising, and buying expense expressed as a percent of net sales. It does not include interest on inventory at cost."

Exhibit 15
Randall's Department Store Balance Sheet as of January 28, 1990 ($000)

Assets

Current Assets

Cash and equivalents		$ 1,791
Accounts receivable	135,274	
(Allowance for doubtful accounts)	(3,200)	
		132,074
Merchandise inventories		67,826
Prepaid expenses and other		3,358
Total current assets		205,049

Property, Fixtures, and Equipment
(on the basis of cost)

Land	12,065
Buildings and improvements	156,219
Store fixtures, furniture, and equipment	103,157
Allowance for depreciation (deduction)	(101,213)
	170,228
Construction in progress	2,961
Other assets	4,426
Total assets	$ 382,664

Liabilities

Current Liabilities

Notes payable to banks	$ 17,680
Accounts payable	27,539
Accrued expenses	7,129
Federal, state, and local taxes	5,289
Deferred income taxes	4,010
Long-term debt and capital lease obligations due within one year	4,942
Total current liabilities	66,589
Long-term debt (due after one year)	80,219
Capital lease obligations (due after one year)	39,539
Other liabilities (principally deferred income taxes)	19,113
Preferred stock	623
Total common shareholders' equity	176,581
Total liabilities	$ 382,664

Case 11

RETAIL PROMOTIONAL PRICING: WHEN IS A SALE REALLY A SALE? (A)

The U.S. retail environment has become increasingly promotional over the past 10 years as exemplified by aggressive double couponing in the grocery trade, price discounting, rebating and special financing in retail auto sales, and nearly daily advertised sale events by general merchants, department stores, and specialty stores.[1] Over 60% of department store sales volume in 1988 was sold at sales prices, for example.[2] The intensive promotional policies of department stores, general merchandisers, and certain types of specialty stores, in particular, have come under close scrutiny by state and local agencies, who argue that the policies practiced by many of these retailers result in deceptive pricing to the end consumer. These pricing practices, often referred to as high-low pricing by the trade, entail setting prices at an initially high level for a brief period of time, then discounting the merchandise from the so-called original, former, or regular price for the bulk of the selling season. In this case, these price designations are referred to collectively as the *reference price* against which a sale price is compared. Typically, in-store signage and the item price tags continue to display the reference price along with the discounted price, so that customers can "compare the savings." Under such a pricing policy, very little of the merchandise is sold at reference prices.

The question raised by such promotional pricing is whether the consumer understands that the "sale" price, is, in fact, the price at which most of the goods are sold. Many state and local agencies have argued that customers overestimate the true value of merchandise priced this way because they compare the reference price to the sale price and interpret the latter as representing a real savings. This case documents the ongoing controversy, and presents a particular court case, *The State of Colorado versus The May Company.*

BACKGROUND

The increased promotional activity by department stores, as well as other classes of retail trade, can be traced to a number of industry changes, most notably increased competition. Continued expansion by department stores, the growth of specialty stores such as The Gap, The Limited, Toys R Us, and the movement upscale by discount

Professor Gwen Ortmeyer prepared this case as the basis for class discussion rather than to illustrate either effective or ineffective handling of an administrative situation.

1 Sears and Montgomery Wards are the most notable general merchants. These retailers carry both soft goods, including clothing, jewelry and accessories, housewares and linens, and hard goods, including, home appliances, tools, and electronics. In contrast, department stores tend to focus on the soft goods categories, often including furniture and some electronics as well.
2 Dudley R. McIlhenny, "Introducing the NRMA Retail Market Monitor," *Retail Control*, November 1989, pp. 9–14.

stores such as Target, has produced a dramatic increase in the number of retail options available to customers and, in many cases, has resulted in markets that are over-stored relative to the available retailer business. As competition has increased, many retailers have experienced modest or no sales gains in existing stores. Thus, in order to boost sales volume, and often to match the regular and sale prices of a broad range of competitors, retailers, across classes of trade, have resorted to incessant and extensive sale events. Most recently, many highly leveraged retailers including the Federated-Allied chain, Macy's, and Carter Hawley Hale have faced added pressure to boost sales volumes due to their debt-laden balance sheet. The result has been a further increase in promotional intensity in markets in which they operate.

Coinciding with the increased promotional activity has been an increase in the margins of retail list prices before they are reduced for sale events. These margins, termed *initial markup* by department stores and calculated as a percent of the original selling price, have risen from an average of 47.5% in 1979 to 50.9% in 1988. Over the same time period, department store markdowns, which are the dollar reductions from the originally set retail prices and are calculated as a percent of net sales, have risen from an average of 10.43% in 1979 to 16.27% in 1988.

Most product categories carried by department stores are susceptible to high-low pricing. For example, in the women's coat business, a seasonal category, department stores have resorted to more sale events and sale priced merchandise, partly in response to competition from coat discounters such as the Burlington Coat Factory. The women's coat business has traditionally had an annual Columbus Day pre-season event with perhaps the most popular coat in a number of lines promoted for the event, but the rest of the coats offered at full price. More recently, however, with increased competition, more sale events are offered throughout the season with a much greater proportion of merchandise offered early in the season at allegedly reduced prices. Fine jewelry is a product category that is well-known for high-low pricing, with 40% and 50% discounts off the reference prices being nearly a continuous event for many retailers, including department stores, jewelry stores, and catalog merchants.

Often the reference prices vary across retailers. For example, *The San Francisco Chronicle* reported the following in "Why Buyers Should Beware of 'Sale' Prices," (Wednesday, July 18, 1990):

A random survey of "sale" and "original" prices in Bay Area furniture stores found a difference of $1,680 between the highest and lowest "original price" for a single Henredon sofa.

Model No. 8670, with identical "E-grade" upholstery, was advertised at Noriega Furniture, a small furniture retailer, at an "original price" of $2,320, on sale for $2,170. A major department store offers the same sofa for $2,500—"35% off" the "original price" of $4,000. A major furniture chain advertised the same model, originally priced at $3,009 "on sale at 20% off" for $2,749. Another small furniture retailer in Marin County offers the same sofa at $2,476, 20% off its original price of $3,095.

Some department stores, Dillard's for example, are trying to reduce their reliance on sale events and sale-priced merchandise. In a speech to the American Apparel Manufacturers Association on October 18, 1989, James W. Sherburn, Jr., chairman of Dillard's Fort Worth Division, reported that the chain had "eliminated five major sale events this year to reinforce to our customer our commitment to sell merchandise at regular price," and had instituted a policy of pricing goods at "the prevailing market price." In the women's coat category, Macy's Northeast adopted everyday low prices in the fall of 1989, and in its advertisements promised to "cut through all the confusing sales, special buys, and clearances out there" by offering the lowest prices on an everyday basis. Like many retailers who have tried everyday low pricing on a limited basis, however, and have experienced significant short-term decreases in sales volume, Macy's reinstituted sale pricing in the coat category in the 1990 season.

REGULATORY PERSPECTIVE

Existing Federal and State Legislation

At the heart of the controversy surrounding high-low pricing policy, is the claim made by an increasing number of state and local authorities, that such pricing policies are deceptive. The FTC *Guides Against Deceptive Pricing*, initially adopted in 1964 and currently included as Part 233 in the FTC's *Code of Federal Regulations of Commercial Practices*, provide the Federal Trade Commission's guidelines as to what constitutes deceptive pricing policies (see **Exhibit 1** for an excerpt from the Guide's Part 233.1, which addresses comparisons to former prices specifically). The FTC is not currently playing a major role in enforcing deceptive pricing laws, however, and instead has left enforcement to state and local authorities. Barry J. Cutler, director of the FTC's Bureau of Consumer Protection, in an interview with Hal Taylor of *Women's Wear Daily* (October 3, 1990), offered the FTC's position, stating that deceptive pricing claims are "a hot topic among the states,' and that he felt "it would not be a good use of our resources to duplicate their efforts."

Many states have instituted regulations that correspond with the FTC Guides Against Deceptive Pricing. Others have statutes which specify that compliance with the FTC rules and regulations is "a complete defense" to allegations of deceptive pricing. Critical in the FTC Guides, as well as in the state statutes are statements of what is acceptable as a reference price. These definitions, which use various terms for the reference price against which the sale price is compared, include, for example:

- **Former price** as "the actual, bona fide price for which the article was offered to the public on a regular basis for a reasonably substantial period of time." (FTC Guides Against Deceptive Pricing)
- **Regular price** as "the price . . . at which the seller of merchandise has sold or offered to sell such merchandise for a reasonably substantial period of time in the recent, regular course of the seller's business." (Hawaii's Office of Consumer Protection—*Rules on Unfair or Deceptive Prices in Advertising*)
- **Reference price** as the "price at which the person, in the regular course of its business, made good faith sales of the same or similar goods or, if no sales were made, offered in good faith to make sales of the same or similar goods." (Administrative Rules of Oregon Department of Justice)

What is common to most of the definitions is that the reference price is legitimate if it has been offered for a reasonable amount of time *or* if it has resulted in significant sales. (Significant sales at the reference price are not appropriate as the *sole* indication of a legitimate regular price since retailers, on occasion, make buying mistakes which necessitate heavy discounting in order to clear out unpopular merchandise.) Neither the FTC Guides nor many of the state statutes, however, give concrete definitions of what constitutes "a reasonably substantial period of time" or what percentage of the overall sales of an item correspond to "good faith sales" at the reference price. Some states have provided concrete guidelines as listed in **Exhibit 2**. Most recently, for ex-

ample, Massachusetts, in May 1990, adopted retail advertising regulations stipulating that a reference price is legitimate if at least 30% of sales occur at that price *or* if the regular price is established for at least 15 days prior to the sale reduction and the item is not "on sale" for more than 45% of a 180-day period.

This lack of a concrete standard in most jurisdictions has created a great deal of confusion for retailers seeking to comply with federal and state regulations. Still, some in the industry maintain that "you know phony pricing when you see it" and suggest that if retailers offer merchandise at regular, everyday prices that represent a realistic and not inflated initial margin they will almost certainly be operating within both federal and state regulations.

Some retailers have added disclosures to their sale advertising that state that the reference price may not have resulted in actual sales. For example, an East Coast department store includes the following statement in small print at the bottom of its print ads:

> Regular, Original*, and Former prices reflect offering prices which may not have resulted in actual sales. Advertised items may be offered in future sale events. *Intermediate price reductions may have been taken.

Another department store on the east coast uses a similar disclaimer in its print ads:

> Regular and Original prices are offering prices only and may or may not have resulted in sales. Advertised merchandise may be available at sale prices in upcoming sale event. Intermediate markdowns taken.

Recent Litigation

Many states, including California, Georgia, New York, North Carolina, Pennsylvania, and Colorado, are currently active in prosecuting deceptive advertising claims against department stores. For example, in 1989, the Philadelphia-based John Wanamaker department store chain was accused, by the Pennsylvania Attorney General, of advertising special sales of 14-karat gold jewelry in late 1988 and early 1989—even though the sale prices were the same as the store's normal prices. The Georgia Governor's Office of Consumer Affairs has made similar allegations of deceptive pricing of jewelry against Macy's South and Rich's. Typically such cases are resolved out of court, with the retailer not admitting any guilt but still paying a fine and agreeing not to advertise sale prices unless the reference price can be substantiated.

Such agreements, as a rule, apply only to the category of trade that has been investigated. In some cases, local authorities have prosecuted retailers which have local stores in their jurisdictions. For example, the Los Angeles District Attorney, in 1990, settled a suit against Nordstrom, the headquarters of which was in Seattle, in which the retailer was charged with "making false or misleading statements of facts concerning the existence and amounts of price reductions." These and other recent examples of retailers prosecuted for deceptive pricing policies are included in **Exhibit 3**.

Retail Efforts at Self-Regulation

In response to both the increased investigation and tougher legislation by state and local authorities, a group of major retailers, under the auspices of the Council of Better Business Bureaus, has proposed a *Code of Advertising for Comparative Price Advertising*. The retailers involved included Sears Roebuck, Kmart Corp., Ames Department Store, Circuit City Stores, F.W. Woolworth Co., Goodyear Tire & Rubber Co., Home Depot, JCPenney Co., May Department Stores Co., Montgomery Ward, Service Merchandise Co., Best Products Co., Dayton Hudson Corp., Federated Stores/Allied Stores Corp., Marshalls, Mellart Jewelers, R.H. Macy & Co., Saks Fifth Avenue, and Woodward and Lothrop. The code, proposed in September 1989, provides guidelines for a range of comparative pricing tactics that includes comparisons to former selling prices and list prices, comparisons with the prices of competitors, and the use of terms such as *Factory to You*, *Emergency or Distress sale*, *imperfects*, *irregulars,* and *seconds*. The code also sets out some guidelines for price matching and lowest-price claims. Violations of the code, once it is approved, would be handled by the Council of Better Business Bureaus either through its local offices, or, in the case of national advertising, by the council's National Advertising Division. In either case, the council would ask the retailer to discontinue any inappropriate behavior, and if necessary notify the appropriate state or local regulatory agency for further action.

The section of the code that addresses comparisons with former selling prices, their term for reference prices, stipulates that: "An advertiser may claim a savings from its own former price if it can demonstrate that its former price is a bona fide or genuine price, that is, a price from which a reduction represents a genuine savings for the consumer." The criteria for establishing that a former price is genuine are similar to those offered in many of the state statutes and in the FTC Guides. Either "reasonably substantial sales" must have occurred at the former price *or* the retailer must have made a "good faith effort" to sell the merchandise at the former price. The latter is most often indicated by the time period over which the former price is in effect but could also be indicated by other factors including the initial margin relative to the retailer's customary margin (see **Exhibit 4** for the section in the proposed code that addresses comparisons with former prices).

The proposed code is reasonably specific about the appropriate time period for a legitimate reference price stating: "The offers of products at the former price for at least a majority of time during the relevant selling period presumptively meets the "reasonably substantial period of time" criterion, although lesser periods may meet this criterion depending on the circumstances." The code is not specific, however, in suggesting the percentage of overall sales that must be accomplished at reference prices.

In proposing the code and publicly committing to it, the major retailers involved in its development hoped to prompt other retailers to agree to it as well, thus creating a level playing field for all with a return to reasonable initial margins and less frequent sales. The concept of a level playing field is critical to any retailer's decision to discontinue high-low pricing. If competitors continue to promote aggressively and consumers remain responsive to sales, the retailer that reduces promotional activity risks losing substantial sales volumes. This fear has kept many retailers from attempting to stabilize their prices on an everyday basis and is often used as a defense when state and local agencies question high-low pricing policies.

THE STATE OF COLORADO VERSUS THE MAY DEPARTMENT STORES COMPANY

In June 1989, May D&F, a unit of the May Department Stores operating 12 department stores in Colorado, was charged with engaging in deceptive advertising practices in its Home Store department by the state attorney general's office. The Home Store department at May D&F includes housewares, cookware, mattresses, linens, textiles, small appliances, and electronics. The state alleged that since 1986, May had used fictitious or exaggerated reference prices as a basis for comparison against their sale prices. These reference prices included price designations such as "original" and "regular" price. The Colorado Attorney General gave several examples of suspect pricing, including:

- Bedding sheets that had remained on sale for eight months;
- A cutlery set advertised and displayed "on sale" for two years;
- A new style of luggage offered at its special "introductory price" indefinitely.

The case against May D&F, in contrast to most lawsuits alleging deceptive pricing by retailers, was not settled out of court. It went to trial in May 1990, with the Colorado Attorney General asking Denver District Court Judge Larry Naves to establish a standard for the proportion of overall sales volume that must occur at the reference price and to apply that standard in ruling on the legitimacy of May D&F's pricing policies. (See **Exhibit 5** for a *Wall Street Journal* article published at the start of the trial.)

May D&F's Pricing Policy— June 1986–August 1989[3]

During this time period, May D&F's pricing, specifically its comparative price advertising, the term used to reflect the retailer's promotional pricing, was dictated by the "Comparative Price Advertising" policy developed in 1986. This 1986 policy required that merchandise in the Home Store be offered at the so-called original price for at least 10 days at the beginning of each six-month selling season. Thereafter, the merchandise was discounted and advertising, in-store signage, and item price tickets indicated that it had been reduced from its original price. In addition, over the course of the six-month selling season, the merchandise could be discounted further for various sales of limited duration, including "15-Hour Sales" and "Three Days Only" sale events. After any such sale, prices were returned to the first discount level and not to the original price. At the end of the six-month selling season, the original prices were restored for a 10-day initial period.

More specifically, May D&F pricing was the responsibility of its buyers, who were also responsible for the advertising within their departments. Buyers set two prices when ordering merchandise, an initial markup price and a promotional markup price. The initial markup price reflected May D&F's usual or planned margin and was calculated using a formula that considered the cost of goods, the cost of doing business, and the company's profit goals. Merchandise was discounted to this price after being at the "original price" for 10 days. Thus, the initial markup price was the price for an item for the bulk of the selling season. The promotional markup price was significantly greater than the initial markup price and was used as the "original price," in effect for 10 days at the beginning of the season. Buyers set this price by taking into account competitors' prices, manufacturers' suggested retail prices, the quality, popularity, and brand name of the merchandise, and other subjective factors. Buyers who testified at the trial reported that this "original price" was a price at which some sales were expected, but they did not expect substantial sales at this price, nor could they provide a definition of what constituted substantial sales.

May D&F's Policy, After May 1989

In August 1989, May D&F introduced a new comparative price advertising policy. Promotional markup prices were lowered, though they were still determined subjectively, and were presented as "regular prices" on in-store signage and advertisements rather than as "original prices." In addition, these "regular prices" were to be in effect 28 out of each 90 selling days, with the 10 days at the beginning of the selling season counting toward the 28 days. This 28 out of 90 day standard was derived from the standards required by Connecticut and Wisconsin (see **Exhibit 2**). Customers who bought merchandise at the regular price were also able to return merchandise for a full refund under the store's new "Satisfaction Guaranteed" program even though prices had been subsequently reduced. Finally, May D&F hired a manager of Consumer Affairs in April 1989 to monitor and ensure the credibility of May D&F's advertisements.

May D&F reported that between October 1989 and March 1990, Home Store sales done at "regular price," for 55 top-selling items, ranged from 1% to more than 25% of total unit sales. However, in a sampling of 5,340 household items sold by May D&F between January 1989

---

3 Prior to the 1986 policy, in October 1982, May D&F had entered into an "Assurance of Discontinuance" with the Colorado Attorney General whereby it agreed to certain comparative advertising standards for a period of five years. Among these standards, according to May D&F, was the stipulation that an initial offering period for the reference price was an appropriate standard for judging the price's legitimacy. This offering period corresponds to the number of days, at the beginning of the selling season, that the merchandise is at regular or original prices. May D&F, on February 6, 1984, also received a letter from the Colorado Attorney General's office to all Colorado retailers advising them "to consider the enclosed copy of the Federal Trade Commission's *Guides Against Deceptive Pricing* when developing your advertisements...."

and March 1990, done by an investigator for the Colorado Attorney General, over 97% of the items were sold at sale prices. For example, of total sales of 2,257 units of a Braun coffeemaker, 79 units were sold either at its "original price" of $49.99 or its subsequent "regular price" of $46.99, and 2,178 were sold at the "sale price" of $35.24. Of total sales of 324 units for a Magnalite pot, one sold at the "original price" of $155, two sold at the subsequent "regular price" of $149.99, and the remaining 321 units sold at the "sale price" of $99.99 or less.

Specific Allegations Made by the State Attorney General

The Colorado Attorney General's office claimed that May D&F's comparative pricing policies, including both the 1986 and the August 1989 policies, violated the Colorado Consumer Protection Act, specifically the section dealing with deceptive trade practices. This section, 6-1-105, reads as follows:

6-1-105 Deceptive Trade Practices: (1) A person engages in a deceptive trade practice when, in the course of his business, vocations, or occupation, he:

(i) Advertises goods, services, or property with the intent not to sell them as advertised;

(ii) Makes false or misleading statements of facts concerning the price of goods, services, or property; or for the reasons for, existence of, or amounts of price reduction; and

(iii) Fails to disclose material information concerning goods, services, or property which information was known at the time of an advertisement or sale if such failure to disclose such information was intended to induce the consumer to enter into a transaction.

Assistant Attorney General James Lewis presented the state's position in the closing arguments of the trial saying, "May D&F violated the law every day for the last four years." "These were false, fictitious prices set not for the purpose of selling the items but for setting subsequent discounts," and "Consumers don't know what the original price of the item was nor the actual savings, if any, of the marked down sales item." The state asked the judge to award up to $20 million in civil penalties and to place new limits on the comparative price advertising used by May D&F.

State attorneys provided, along with other evidence, the testimony of customers, included as **Exhibit 6** and expert witness testimony by Associate Professor Joel Urbany of the University of South Carolina, a specialist in consumer behavior. Professor Urbany reported the results of a survey of Denver consumers he conducted for the attorney general. The executive summary from his study is given in **Exhibit 7**. Most notably, Professor Urbany's study indicated that when an "original" or "regular" price was advertised along with the sale price, respondents generally perceived greater savings and showed greater intention to purchase than when the advertisement contained no reference price. In addition, the majority of the respondents believed that "regular" or "original" priced merchandise represented at least 25% of the unit sales of a product in the previous 90 days and that the "regular" or "original" price was the price charged for the majority of the selling period. The Colorado Attorney General argued that both the customer testimony and the survey results showed that consumers had been deceived by May D&F's comparative pricing.

May D&F Defense

Attorneys for May D&F denied that the retailer had engaged in any deceptive advertising or trade practices and offered among a number of defenses the following:

1. Colorado law is vague on the issue of comparison advertising standards. Specifically the Colorado Consumer Protection Act (CPA) does not contain language requiring either an offering period during which the regular or original price must be in effect, or a standard for the percentage of sales that must be done at regular or original prices.
2. May D&F's compliance with the FTC Guides preempts the CPA.
3. May D&F's ads were not misleading and caused no injury.
4. The standards proposed by the Colorado Attorney General would hurt consumers and competition. Specifically, they argued that imposing any standard either regarding the proportion of time merchandise must be at regular price or the proportion of sales that must be done at reference price and applying that standard only to May D&F would place the retailer at a competitive disadvantage against retailers who continued to promote without such restrictions.

May D&F attorneys cited two consumer surveys, done for them by Leo Shapiro, a Chicago-based market research firm, as evidence that their ads were not misleading. In the first, done in October 1989, a random sample of 500 Denver households were surveyed by telephone to assess May D&F's reputation among area retailers and some specific advertising practices. A summary of the findings of this survey are reported in **Exhibit 8**. In a second survey, conducted in April 1990, 331 individuals were surveyed in a number of malls in Denver. Respondents in this survey were asked a number of questions designed to show what the term "original price" meant to them and whether respondents' perceptions of the term were influenced by the amount of merchandise actually sold at that price. The results of the second survey are also provided in **Exhibit 8**.

Finally, May D&F attorneys presented some mitigating circumstances that they hoped the judge would consider in determining penalties if he ruled that May D&F had violated the Colorado Consumer Protection Act. These included that May D&F, in August 1989, adopted a new policy for comparative price advertising which included a standard offering period for the regular price of 28 out of 90 days, which was consistent with the standard offered by the state of Connecticut, one of the few states offering a specific standard. Also cited as mitigating circumstances was the hiring of a Consumer Affairs director to monitor the chain's advertising and the establishment of the store's "Satisfaction Guaranteed" program. They also mentioned that the Home Store had operated at a net loss for the past three years.

Closing arguments for the case concluded on May 24, 1990. Retailers, state regulators, and state consumer protection agencies across the country had watched the progression of the case and were keenly interested in the judge's decision, particularly as it applied to the establishment of standards for the legitimacy of the references prices used in sale advertising. As noted by Clayton Friedman, an Assistant Attorney General in Missouri in a *Wall Street Journal* accounting of the case (see **Exhibit 5**), "The decision is going to dictate how the states act in enforcement and how retailers are going to advertise."

PART 233—GUIDES AGAINST DECEPTIVE PRICING

Sec.

233.1 Former price comparisons.

233.2 Retail price comparisons: comparable value comparisons.

233.3 Advertising retail prices which have been established or suggested by manufacturers (or other nonretail distributors).

233.4 Bargain offers based upon the purchase of other merchandise.

233.5 Miscellaneous price comparisons.

AUTHORITY: Secs. 5, 6, 38 Stat. 719, as amended 721: 15 U.S.C. 45, 46.

SOURCE: 32 FR 15534, Nov. 8, 1967, unless otherwise noted.

§ 233.1 Former price comparisons.

(a) One of the most commonly used forms of bargain advertising is to offer a reduction from the advertiser's own former price for an article. If the former price is the actual, bona fide price at which the article was offered to the public on a regular basis for a reasonably substantial period of time, it provides a legitimate basis for the advertising of a price comparison. Where the former price is genuine, the bargain being advertised is a true one. If, on the other hand, the former price being advertised is not bona fide but fictitious—for example, where an artificial, inflated price was established for the purpose of enabling the subsequent offer of a large reduction—the "bargain" being advertised is a false one; the purchaser is not receiving the unusual value he expects. In such a case, the "reduced" price is, in reality, probably just the seller's regular price.

(b) A former price is not necessarily fictitious merely because no sales at the advertised price were made. The advertiser should be especially careful, however, in such a case, that the price is one at which the product was openly and actively offered for sale, for a reasonably substantial period of time, in the recent, regular course of his business, honestly and in good faith—and, of course, not for the purpose of establishing a fictitious higher price on which a deceptive comparison might be based. And the advertiser should scrupulously avoid any implication that a former price is a selling, not an asking price (for example, by use of such language as, "Formerly sold at $————"), unless substantial sales at that price were actually made.

(c) The following is an example of a price comparison based on a fictitious former price. John Doe is a retailer of Brand X fountain pens, which cost him $5 each. His usual markup is 50 percent over cost; that is, his regular retail price is $7.50. In order subsequently to offer an unusual "bargain", Doe begins offering Brand X at $10 per pen. He realizes that he will be able to sell no, or very few, pens at this inflated price. But he doesn't care, for he maintains that price for only a few days. Then he "cuts" the price to its usual level-$7.50-and advertises: "Terrific Bargain: X Pens, Were $10, Now Only $7.50!" This is obviously a false claim. The advertised "bargain" is not genuine.

(d) Other illustrations of fictitious price comparisons could be given. An advertiser might use a price at which he never offered the article at all; he might feature a price which was not used in the regular course of business, or which was not used in the recent past but at some remote period in the past, without making disclosure of that fact; he might use a price that was not openly offered to the public, or that was not maintained for a reasonable length of time, but was immediately reduced.

(e) If the former price is set forth in the advertisement, whether accompanied or not by descriptive terminology such as "Regularly," "Usually," "Formerly," etc., the advertiser should make certain that the former price is not a fictitious one. If the former price, or the amount or percentage of reduction, is not stated in the advertisement, as when the ad merely states, "Sale," the advertiser must take care that the amount of reduction is not so insignificant as to be meaningless. It should be sufficiently large that the consumer, if he knew what it was, would believe that a genuine bargain or saving was being offered. An advertiser who claims that an item has been "Reduced to $9.99," when the former price was $10, is misleading the consumer, who will understand the claim to mean that a much greater, and not merely nominal, reduction was being offered. [Guide I]

Exhibit 2
State Standards Regarding the Legitimacy of Regular Prices

State	Time Period for Reference Price	% of Total Sales That Were at Reference Price
Connecticut	At least 4 weeks over the previous 90-day period	No standard given
Massachusetts	At least 15 days (unless seller discloses the original offering period) and over an 180-day period, the higher reference price must be offered at least 55% of the time	30% of the items sold at reference price
Minnesota	30 days preceding the comparison	No standard given
Missouri	Reference price must be in effect for some number of days initially, and in effect for 40% of the time during a period not less than thirty days, nor more than 12 months	10% of items sold at reference price
Wisconsin	At least 4 weeks during any 90-day period prior to the comparison	No standard given

Exhibit 3
Some Recent Litigation Regarding Deceptive Pricing

State	Retailer(s)	Product Category	Status
California-Los Angeles District Attorney	Nordstrom	Men's clothing	Settled out of court in August 1989 with Nordstrom paying a $200,000 fine.
California-Sacramento County District Attorney	Montgomery Ward & Co.	Paint	Settled out of court in February 1990 with Montgomery Ward paying a $160,000 fine.
Georgia-Governor's Office of Consumer Affairs	Macy's South and Rich's	Jewelry	The cases were settled in 1989. Both stores denied the allegations, but paid $37,500 each in fines and signed assurances saying they would refrain from "original/sale" price comparisons unless they could substantiate the reference prices.
Massachusetts-State Attorney General	Hit-or-Miss, Casual Corner, Anderson-Little, Caren Charles, Cherry, Webb & Touraine, Chess King, Cummings, and The Limited	Clothing	In May 1985, all retailers but The Limited agreed to pay fines, ranging from $500–12,000, and to refrain from deceptive pricing tactics in the future.
North Carolina-State Attorney General	Rhodes, Inc.	Furniture	Settled out of court in April 1987 with Rhodes paying a $10,000 fine and agreeing to refrain from deceptive pricing tactics in the future.
Pennsylvania-State Attorney General	John Wanamaker	Jewelry	In August 1989, Wanamaker's settled, paying $10,000 in fines and agreeing to refrain from deceptive pricing tactics in the future. They denied wrongdoing, however.
North Carolina-State Attorney General	JCPenney	Jewelry	No settlement reached as of May 1990.

Exhibit 4
Excerpt from Council of Better Business Bureau's Code of Advertising

1. Comparative Price, Value, and Savings Claims

Advertisers may offer a price reduction or savings by comparing their selling price with:

1. Their own former price;
2. the current price of identical merchandise offered by others in the market area;
3. the current price of comparable merchandise offered by others in the market area; or
4. a manufacturer's list price.

When any one of these comparisons is made in advertising, the claim should be based on, and substantiated in accordance with, the criteria set forth below. Savings claims should be substantiated on the basis of evidence existing when the claim is made, or, if the advertising must be submitted in advance of publication, a reasonable time prior to when the claim is made.

Most consumers reasonably expect that claims of price reductions expressed in terms of a percent "off" or a specific dollar "savings" are reductions or savings from an advertiser's own former price. Accordingly, unless the savings claim is in fact based on the advertiser's own former price, the basis for the reduction (item 2, 3, or 4 above) should be affirmatively disclosed, such as, "Buy from us and save $50. Sold elsewhere at $199. Our price $149." For example, it would be misleading for an advertiser, without explanation, to claim a savings from a "ticketed price" if the advertiser could not establish that the "ticketed price" was a genuine former price.

2. Comparison with Former Price

1. An advertiser may claim a savings from its own former price if it can demonstrate that its former price is a bona fide or genuine price, that is a price from which a reduction represents a genuine savings for the customer.

   A former price is bona fide when "reasonably substantial sales" were made at or above the price in the recent regular course of business. While it is reasonable to expect that a retailer's nonsale prices will usually result in sales of the product, there will be occasions where the nonsale prices do not produce substantial sales. The bona fides of a former price may also be established where few or no sales were made only if the advertiser openly and actively offered the merchandise honestly and in "good faith" for a "reasonably substantial period of time" in the recent regular course of business. A more detailed discussion of these criteria is set forth in (3) and (4) below.

2. If the former price was the price in effect immediately prior to the savings claim, the following usual and customary trade usages may be used to describe a former price: "Regularly," "Usually," "Formerly," "Was," "You Save $___," and "Origi-nally." If, however, the former price was not the price in effect immediately prior to the reduction, the advertiser should disclose this fact clearly and conspicuously by indicating that immediate markdowns have been taken Appropriate ways to do so include: "Originally $400, Formerly $300, Now $250;" or "Originally $400, Now 250, Intermediate markdowns taken." If the former price is one that was last used at a remote point in time, for example, more than six months earlier, the advertising should also indicate the time period in which the former price had been applicable. For example, "Now $250, Originally $400 in Fall 1988, Intermediate markdowns taken."

3. Establishing the Bona Fides of a Former Price Through Reasonably Substantial Sales

When substantiating a former price on the basis of reasonably substantial sales, the appropriate time period for evaluating the claim may vary depending on the product in question. If the product is seasonal, the "season" may be the appropriate time period in which to evaluate whether substantial sales were made at or above the former price. If the product is staple, up to a year could be an appropriate period for measurement.

An advertiser that establishes a uniform price over a national or regional trade area may rely on sales made at the price throughout that national or regional trade area in order to substantiate the bona fides of that price.

4. Establishing the Bona Fides of a Former Price Through a "Good Faith" Offer to Sell

The offers of products at the former price for at least a majority of time during the relevant selling period presumptively meets the "reasonably substantial period of time" criterion, although lesser periods may meet this criterion depending on the circumstances. If the product is seasonal, the "season" may be the period for measuring conformance with this criterion. If the product is staple in nature, up to one year could be an appropriate measurement period. In any event, the period during which discontinued products are permanently reduced for clearance or closeout from the advertiser's inventory should not be counted in measuring conformance.

A former price is not necessarily fictitious merely because "substantial sales" were not made at that price. In these situations, however, the advertiser should be especially cautious to assure that its former or offering price was a good faith offer to sell and not a price that has been inflated or exaggerated merely to show a large reduction.

Factors an advertiser may rely on in substantiating its good faith include, but are not necessarily limited to:

- Whether the advertiser had a reasonable expectation of selling the product at the offering price, based on demonstrated facts such as prior experience with sales of the same or comparable merchandise, and the appropriate time at or above the former price.
- Whether the offering price is realistic (i.e., whether it generally fell within the range of prices that the advertiser reasonably believes to be bona fide in the market area for the same or substantially similar products).
- The extent to which sales of the product were made at the former price, even if not "substantial," taking into account the nature of the merchandise.
- Whether the offering price is based on a markup that does not significantly exceed the advertiser's usual and customary retail markup for similar merchandise.
- Whether the product was openly and actively offered in the recent, regular course of business such as by devoting reasonable display space to the product during the period(s) in which it was at the offering price, maintaining reasonable inventory during former price periods, or advertising the product at the offering price, etc.

Exhibit 5
Wall Street Journal Article, May 15, 1990

Store's Concept of 'Sale' Pricing Gets Court Test

By Francine Schwadel
Staff Reporter of THE WALL
STREET JOURNAL

When is a sale truly a sale?

A state court judge in Denver could provide a precedent-setting answer in a widely watched case scheduled to go to trial today. The Colorado attorney general is asking Judge Larry Naves to define a standard for determining when a retailer promotes legitimate discounts.

Among the criteria suggested by the state: Retailers can advertise discounts only from higher prices at which goods actually were sold—not just offered for sale.

Any ruling would apply only to the Denver-based May D&F unit of May Department Stores Co., which stands accused of misleading Colorado consumers. But it could send shock waves throughout the retailing industry. The Colorado attorney general's suggested criteria are among the most detailed in the nation. And the defendant is the nation's largest operator of department stores.

"The decision is going to dictate how the states act in enforcement and how the retailers are going to advertise," predicts Clayton Friedman, an assistant attorney general in Missouri.

The Colorado case also provides a rare glimpse at how retail price promotions really work. The state alleges that May D&F deceives consumers by artificially inflating its "original" or "regular" prices, then promoting discounts from those prices to create the illusion of offering bargains on cookware, linens and other household goods. May denies the charges, claiming in part that its practices don't violate Federal Trade Commission guidelines.

But rather than settling out of court as other retailers have done in similar cases, May publicly is explaining how it establishes "original" and "regular" prices.

The case also comes as the Federal Trade Commission is taking its first comprehensive look at the subject in more than a decade. The agency is mulling comments on voluntary advertising guidelines drawn up recently by May and other big retailers, who are anxious to head off new state regulations. The FTC's current guidelines, which date from 1964, require that goods be offered for sale at regular prices "for a reasonably substantial period of time . . . honestly and in good faith and not for the purpose of establishing a fictitious higher price."

Sales are coming under more scrutiny today because they have become so common. As competition intensified in the 1980s, stores sought an edge by running more and more specials. That attracted the attention of state attorneys general, who investigated the claims, started writing more stringent rules and sued some of the most trusted names in retailing. Cases now are pending in other states against Sears, Roebuck & Co., J.C. Penney Co. and other big retailers.

Colorado prosecutors are cutting to the heart of the debate by suggesting that May be held to a standard of actually selling merchandise at the higher price. "That's a very important ques-tion," says Steven Cole, general counsel of the Council of Better Business Bureaus.

Neither prosecutors nor lawyers for May D&F would comment on the Colorado case. A spokesman for the parent company, based in St. Louis, also declined to comment.

In court documents, the Colorado attorney general argues that an actual sales standard is necessary to make any injunction against May enforceable and to match consumers' perceptions about what constitutes a special deal. The state says the majority of 400 Colorado consumers surveyed in March believed that at least 25% of a retailer's sales were made at the "original" or "regular" prices. The average consumer in the survey understood the terms "regular" and "original" to mean prices that were charged on 50 of the last 90 days, the state says.

In court documents, May D&F acknowledges that before last August, it made few sales in its Home Store departments at what is called "original" prices. At the time, the company says its policies required that household goods be offered for sale at an "original" price for at least 10 days at the beginning of each six-month season. After the 10 days, May says its policies allowed promotions touting discounts from the "original" price.

May changed its policies in August (two months after it was sued by the state) "to eliminate any doubt as to the legitimacy of its advertising," according to the company's court filings. Under the new policy, May says it establishes "regular" prices by offering Home Store merchandise for sale for at least 28 of every 90 days. And it says it instituted a "Satisfaction Guaranteed" program allowing shoppers to return merchandise for a full refund.

The company defends its new policy, contending it reduced the so-called "reference" prices the company uses to calculate discount claims on most Home Store merchandise. The price used to calculate discounts on a 12-cup Braun coffee maker, for example, slid to $64 from $69 as a result of the policy change.

May also says in court documents that it now makes "many sales" at its "regular" prices. In the six months ended in March 1990, May says it sold anywhere from less than 1% to more than 25% of the 55 best-selling Home Store items at its "regular" prices. Still, those levels may not be high enough to satisfy the state.

The company maintains that consumers aren't misled by its practices. In court documents, it cites surveys showing the majority of consumers understood the term "original" to mean "the first price of the season" and that 90% didn't care whether there were actual sales at that price.

May also argues in its filings that an actual sales standard is unworkable and would impede price competition. "May D&F cannot control how many products it will sell at a given price," the company says. "This will vary by the type of product, expectations of consumers about whether they might be able to obtain the merchandise on sale, the competitive environment for a given product, the economy" and other factors.

Exhibit 6
Summary of Testimony by Four Customers[a]

Consumer A had been watching ads for a Farberware rotisserie; and when it was "on sale" for "4 days only" at 40% off the "regular price" (stated as $119.99), she bought it at $71.99. She did no comparative shopping in advance. While shopping in a discount store, she saw the identical product in that store at $59.97 with a comparison price of $79.99 and a regular price of $64.97. She was angry. She checked a May D&F competitor and found a regular price of $74.99. She called the manufacturer in New York and found the suggested price was $109.99, $10 less than May D&F's "regular price."

Consumer B purchased a Scanpan saucepan at 25% off the regular price of $99.99, or $74.99, and then saw it in three competitor stores at a regular price of approximately $74. When she complained, May D&F gave her a full refund.

Consumer C had been watching some glasses priced at $15 and a set of mugs at $10. When she received a coupon with those glasses and mugs, it claimed "25% Off Last Sold Price with Coupon Only." At the store, the $15 glasses were now $21.99, the set of mugs, $13. Twenty-five percent (25%) off the glasses would be $16.50 on sale versus $15 before for the glasses and $9.75 versus $10 for the set of mugs.

Consumer D had been watching Krups coffee machines. Prior to January 1990, each time she checked they were at $79.99. In that month, when they were advertised at 30% off, she found that the 30% off sale price was $79.99 and the regular price was either $109.99 or $119.99.

a As reported in *Retailing Today*, January 1991, edited by Robert Kahn.

Exhibit 7
Executive Summary and Selected Results from "Comparative Price Advertising Effects in the Denver Market." Prepared by Joel Urbany, Ph.D., April 23, 1990

Study Description

- This paper reports the results of a study of whether/how comparative price advertising affects consumer perception and behavioral intentions. The study was conducted during the period March 19–28, 1990 in the Denver, Colorado, SMSA.
- The study involved mall intercept interviews of 400 Colorado consumers. Respondents were asked to examine and evaluate an advertised sale offer from the May Department Stores Company ("May D&F" or "May Company"), although the company name was removed from the ad. Of those surveyed, 46% said they recognized that the ad was from May D&F.
- Actual ads from two products recently advertised on sale by May D&F were used in the study: a Hoover canister vacuum cleaner and a Revereware frying pan.
- To examine whether the comparative prices (i.e., the "regular" or "original" prices stated in the ad) had any influence on consumer perception of savings and purchase intentions, half of the respondents were shown ads in which the comparative prices had been removed (these respondents are referred to as the "control" group).
- To examine consumer perception of comparative pricing terminology, respondents were additionally asked to explain their understanding of the terms "regular," "original," and "intermediate markdowns have been taken."

Selected Results

	Vacuum Cleaner		Frying Pan	
	Sale Price Only in Ad	Sale and Regular Price in Ad	Sale Price Only in Ad	Sale and Regular Price in Ad
% Who Agreed				
"I'll save a lot if I buy from the advertising store"	11%	35%	29%	44%
"The product is a bargain at the advertised sale price"	14%	27%	29%	44%
"The retailer reduced the price a lot for this sale"	11%	35%	13%	41%
Choice				
% who would consider buying today rather than comparison shopping	3%	13%	5%	9%
Chance				
Perceived chance of buying from the advertised retailer	22%	36%	43%	46%

Note: When the regular price was included, the sale price represented a 30% savings for the vacuum cleaner and a 35% savings for the frying pan.

Conclusions

1. The presence of the comparative price (i.e., regular) in the advertisements significantly increased both perceived savings and purchase intentions (the "comparative price effect").
2. This comparative price effect occurred in both the vacuum cleaner and frying pan product categories and for those respondents who knew that May D&F was the advertiser.
3. The majority of respondents believed that at least 25% of the products sold by the advertiser in the previous 90 days had been sold at the regular or original price.
4. Respondents believed that the terms "regular" and "original" referred to the price that was charged for the product when it was not on sale.
5. Respondents generally believed that the "regular" or "original" price is charged by the retailer the majority of the time during a given selling period.
6. The majority of respondents believed that, after the sale was over, the price would return to the regular or original level stated in the ad.
7. When respondents were asked the meaning of the term "intermediate markdowns have been taken," the most frequent answer was "don't know."

Exhibit 8
Summary of the Findings of Two Surveys Done for May D&F by Leo Shapiro and Associates, Inc.

Survey 1, October 1989

Selected Survey Responses

- And, on balance, do you feel that May D&F's advertised prices are generally higher or lower than the other stores in your area who sell the same things?

May D&F's advertised prices are higher	72% responding
May D&F's advertised prices are lower	6% responding
May D&F's advertised prices are the same	20% responding

- Specifically, when you see an advertisement from May D&F that says 50% off, do you believe that the item advertised from May D&F is going to be priced lower than any of the other stores in your area that sell the same thing?

No	70% responding
Yes	25% responding

- By the way, sometimes a store like May D&F will have a particular item or items that you can almost always find on sale in their store and in their ads. Do you believe that such an item from May D&F is going to be priced lower than any of the other stores in your area that sell the same things?

No	70% responding
Yes	21% responding

Expert's Conclusions

- The reputation that May D&F has among the retailers who serve Denver area households can be described as a store whose prices are relatively high while offering good quality products and good service to their customers.
- Denver area households expect May D&F to advertise specials and sales which bring their prices more in line with other area retailers; however, a majority believe that May D&F's advertised sales prices are generally higher than those of other area merchants.
- When confronted with a claim for 50% off in a May D&F ad, nearly three in four (70%) report that they do not believe that this means May D&F is priced lower than other area retailers.
- When asked how they felt about items which are almost always offered on sale in their advertisements and in their store, a similar majority (70%) report that these items are not lower priced than can be found at other area retailers.
- Taken collectively, the results of this survey indicate that May D&F's advertising is not misleading for households in the Denver metropolitan area. In fact, few households believe that May D&F advertised prices are better than those which they can find at other area retailers, even when advertising claims (e.g., 50% off) are for substantial reductions.

Survey 2, April 1990

Selected Results

Respondents were shown a graph which showed the price at which May D&F offered a Cuisinart Mini-Mate for sale over a three-month period (see **Exhibit 9**). They were then asked the following questions:

"Please take a look at this chart. It shows what the price was that a department store charged for a specific item over the course of three months. Thinking about the advertising where they show the original price for an item and then show the sale price, please point to or read aloud the price or point on the graph where the price is what you would consider to be the original price for this item."

$49.99	56% responding
39.99	19% responding
37.99	8% responding
34.99	9% responding
33.49	3% responding
29.99	4% responding
Other	1% responding

"And when you consider what they mean by the original price, does it make a difference to you how much merchandise, if any, they had sold at that price?"

No	88% responding
Yes	12% responding

"Thinking about advertising for bedding, clothing, household appliances, jewelry, home electronics, and other things for your home and family, about how often do you check the ads before you shop for items like this?"

All of the time	41% responding
Some of the time	31% responding
Not much at all	17% responding
Never	11% responding

"Thinking about the way stores advertise, when you see an ad, how can you tell whether the price of an item is really very good? What tells you this is a really super price for something?"

Compare to other stores	47% responding
I know the price/previous experience	31% responding
Compare to the original price	12% responding

Expert's Conclusions

- Consumers have a very clear idea of what the word "original" means when looking at department store advertising. When shown the actual prices at which a typical May D&F housewares product was offered for sale by date, over a three-month period, a majority of consumers report that the price which they themselves would judge to be the "original" price was, in fact, the price which the May D&F advertisement said was the "original" price.
- In addition, when asked whether or not it makes any difference in their assessment if any products are sold at the original price point, nine out of ten consumers report that it does not make any difference whether any sales occur at that price.
- It is also clear from this study that most Denver-area consumers feel that the most important thing to look for when trying to judge a price is to compare that price with other stores, while few feel that the store's reference or original price holds great importance for them.

Exhibit 9
Cuisinart Mini-Mate—Three-Month Price History

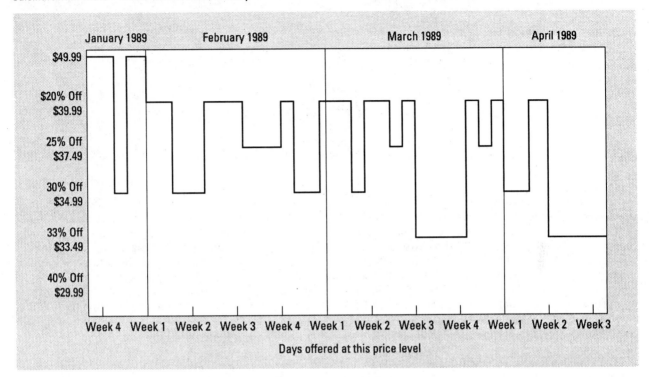

CATALINA MARKETING CORPORATION

In 1983 the idea was hatched. Five friends, with extensive experience in market research, scanner technology, and the packaged goods industry, were discussing the problems of consumer products promotions in the supermarket industry while sailing out to Catalina Island off the coast of Long Beach, California. Their conversation revolved around the clutter and inefficiency of most supermarket promotional vehicles, such as freestanding inserts. "How could marketers more effectively reach their target markets?" they debated. "Isn't there a straightforward way to find the right customer?" For the five entrepreneurs on the boat the answer lay in the emerging point of sale scanner technology in use in an increasing number of supermarket chains. "How could they harness this technology?" they asked themselves. "Could they use that technology to trigger coupons at the time that a customer was making a purchase? What were the advantages of this type of marketing to the customer, retailer, and the manufacturer?" By the time they reached port, the foundation for Catalina Marketing Corporation had been created.

That was 1983. Now, in the spring of 1993, the management team at Catalina Marketing Corporation, which had become a well-established, very successful marketing service firm, had to make some important decisions about the company's future. With plenty of cash in the bank,

Tommy Greer, the chief executive officer, thought there were many opportunities to pursue. The company could sell more advertising cycles, it could expand its geographic market both within the United States and internationally, it could provide its marketing services to non-supermarket retailers, it could use its proprietary technology to provide direct store delivery information to manufacturers, or it could enter the coupon redemption business.

CATALINA BACKGROUND

Catalina Marketing Corporation, located in St. Petersberg, Florida, was a leading supplier of in-store electronic marketing services. Through its proprietary software and communications network, it had the ability to reach 81 million shoppers a week. Since 1988 the company had distributed close to two billion coupons nationally through approximately 5,600 supermarket chain stores. Revenues for 1992 were about $70 million and were expected to reach $85 million in 1993. The company provided both consumer-products manufacturers and retailers a cost-effective, targeted, promotions-delivery system. The technology was based on point of sale information gathered through a scanner in the supermarket checkout lane.

The printing of Catalina coupons, unlike freestand-

Research Associate Dinny Starr prepared this case under the supervision of Professors David Bell and Walter Salmon as the basis for class discussion rather than to illustrate either effective or ineffective handling of an administrative situation.

1 Freestanding inserts are full-color collections of coupons printed on glossy paper and usually distributed in Sunday newspapers. These promotions, also known as circulars, are printed as a separate section of the publication. They are then inserted in, and distributed with, a newspaper or magazine.

ing inserts (FSIs)[1] or other general promotional vehicles, was based on a consumer's actual purchase. For example, as a cashier entered a customer's purchase, the UPC code[2] was scanned into the register. This information then went directly into the Catalina computer system in the store. If the customer purchased a targeted product, a six-pack of Coca-Cola for example, a coupon would then be printed at the register and handed back to the shopper at the end of the sale. The coupon printed might be for a six-pack of Pepsi, or for a two-liter bottle of Coca-Cola, or perhaps for a bag of Frito Lay or Safeway brand potato chips. The content of the coupon would depend on who was sponsoring the promotion. Because of this direct connection to purchasing behavior and the ability to respond immediately, a manufacturer or retailer could target specific consumers for its promotions.

Catalina distributed its coupons through small printers that sat on top of, or next to, the cash register in a supermarket checkout lane. The coupons took less that three seconds to print. The stores that were signed onto the program included supermarket giants such as Ralphs, Lucky, Safeway, Pathmark, Giant, Shoprite, Winn-Dixie, and Dominicks. In all, there were over 89 supermarket chains in a network which represented an estimated 42% of the national *All Commodity Volume* (ACV)[3] as of January 1993. Catalina had the best coverage in the Denver and Baltimore-Washington markets, with 89% and 83% ACV in those two areas, respectively. (See **Exhibit 1** for additional information on market statistics by regional supermarket chain.)

In 1992, Catalina generated 985,840,484 coupons for its consumer products manufacturers and supermarket retailer clients. This represented an average of 18.9 million coupons printed per week, 4,110 coupons printed per week per supermarket, and 0.284 coupons printed per shopper transaction. The most current redemption rates for these coupons, derived from 1991 circulation, averaged 11.2%. In comparison, the national consumer redemption rate for all coupons was approximately 2.3%. More specifically, newspaper and magazine coupons, found within the pages of the media, redeemed at 1.6%; FSI coupons, found in newspaper or magazines inserts (not within the editorial content of the media), redeemed at 2.5%; and direct mail coupons redeemed at 4.3%.[4] The national redemption of

coupons, moreover, had been falling at a rate of about a tenth of one percent annually, while Catalina's coupon redemption had been increasing.

PRODUCTS AND SERVICES AVAILABLE

Catalina offered several different marketing services and products to its customers. All Catalina products worked in conjunction with the network of printers connected to a register's UPC scanner. The original and most prevalent product was the Checkout Coupon (see **Figure 1**). Other products offered by Catalina, all of which were based on the same technology, included Quick Cash, Shopping List, Checkout Direct, and Cross Retail Coupons. In addition, detailed redemption information was available as part of these programs. Catalina created these reporting services in partnership with its clients.

Checkout Coupon

Checkout Coupon, Catalina's major product offering (representing 97.6% of FY92 revenues), was a service offered to manufacturers and retailers alike as a strategic marketing tool. The coupon was issued when the shopper bought a "trigger product" at the checkout stand. The trigger product was set up in advance by the manufacturer or retailer. And, the type of coupon issued was designed with some type of marketing goal in mind. As of 1992 there were six basic categories of Checkout Coupon. *Competitive* coupons, the major portion of Checkout Coupons were designed to reach and switch over competitive-product purchasers. The second coupon type, *Continuity* coupons, were used to reinforce brand purchases by existing customers. In contrast, the third coupon type, *Own User* coupons, were designed to increase purchase quantities among already loyal customers. The fourth coupon type, *Cross Category* coupons, were distributed for one category of product (such as jelly) but were triggered from the purchase of another category of product (such as peanut butter). These coupons were issued to expand the brand and/or manufacturer franchise. *Ad Message* coupons, the fifth coupon type, were a nonredeemable coupon with a message on it only. Finally, *Tie-In* coupons were a program that tied in a manufacturer's trigger item to a retailer's

---

2 Universal Product Code (UPC) is the black-and-white bar code on products used for scanning. It is generally printed on the product packaging by the national brand or private label manufacturer, or printed in the store for meats, produce, and deli items.
3 All Commodity Volume (ACV) is a designation used to establish the sales penetration that a supermarket (or other establishment) has in a given market. Higher percentage ACV indicates greater coverage of a market.
4 Source: Catalina Marketing from Nielsen Clearing House Promotional Services, 1991.

Figure 1
Sample Checkout Coupons

couponed item. Often, the retailer's couponed item was either a coupon for a private label product, a discount on the next purchase at a service counter (such as the deli), or a coupon redeemable for cash. Tie-In programs had to be supported by the retailer by some advertising such as a newspaper ad, an in-store circular, a flyer, banner, or mailer, etc. (See **Table A** for a breakdown of the distribution of the different types of Checkout Coupon. **Exhibit 2** shows the 1991 distribution of coupons in detail.)

The Checkout Coupon was distributed based on the purchase by a consumer. Because the exact purchase

Table A
1992 Checkout Coupon Distribution By Sales Type

Sales Type	% of Distribution
Ad Message	5.9
Competitive	61.7
Continuity	0.6
Own User	12.3
Tie-In	3.6
Cross Category	15.8

was known, the incentive was targeted to a specific customer. The coupon could then be used during the customer's next shopping trip, but was valid only at that supermarket chain. This stimulated trial and brand switching among manufacturers as well as promoted loyalty to the supermarket chain. The coupon itself specified what the client was offering: a certain amount off the next purchase, a two-for-one deal, a free product with the purchase of another item, or a combination of several promotions. In addition, Catalina coupons had extra space where a unique message, up to 32 characters long, could be printed. The average face value of a printed Checkout Coupon in 1991 was $0.84. However, because higher value coupons were redeemed more frequently, the average redeemed value of a Checkout Coupon was $0.86. (**Exhibit 3** shows two advertisements promoting Catalina's Checkout Coupon services.)

There were several advantages to Catalina's electronic in-store couponing over more traditional ones. Checkout Coupons were more efficient and effective. First of all, they were printed only as needed, cutting down on waste. In addition, the coupons were hand-delivered to the customer. Because the coupons were valid only at the store chain where they were printed, the Catalina coupons promoted retailer loyalty, something retailers were constantly trying to strengthen and which they considered to be a competitive edge. Moreover, the type of coupon printed was flexible and it could be tailored to fit the goals of the client. For example, of the several types of coupons currently printed, Continuity coupons had a redemption rate of 33.3%, Own User coupons 14.5%, Competitive coupons 6.3%, and Cross Category coupons 3.1%. Since Catalina coupons redeemed four times more often than the national average, the final advantage was that Catalina coupons appealed to consumers. (**Exhibit 4** shows a chart outlining the benefits of Checkout Coupon for a manufacturer.)

Quick Cash

A second product provided by Catalina was Quick Cash. This program, which was an ancillary service to the Checkout Coupon system, allowed the retailer to use the printer as a delivery vehicle for a performance-based cash coupon. For this service retailers negotiated with manufacturers to select products to be included in the program. Each product was then assigned a value. When checking out at the register, if a consumer purchased one of these products the assigned value was recorded and a monetary credit was given. After all the shopper's items

were scanned, a single Quick Cash coupon was issued for the total amount of the credits. This coupon could then be used toward the shopper's subsequent purchases in that store, or redeemed for cash. Manufacturers usually paid for the cost of running the Quick Cash promotion through their trade promotion budgets. In addition, they usually supported the merchandise in the Quick Cash program with in-store shopping lists, in-store advertisements and circulars, shelf signs or end-aisle displays. The length of time of the promotion was flexible, depending on the retailer's marketing strategy.

During the pilot stage of Quick Cash, Catalina found that on average, approximately 40% of the coupons issued were redeemed. The company believed, therefore, that Quick Cash could have significant impact for the retailers who used the service. In 1991, Catalina decided to offer the Quick Cash service to all of its retailers. However, the company did not believe that Quick Cash would become a significant new product for the future.

Shopping List

Shopping List, a newer addition to Catalina's product line, offered an incentive for volume customers. For all shoppers who purchased over $25 worth of merchandise (this was approximately 25% of all supermarket transactions), a Shopping List coupon was printed at the end of the transaction. The coupon displayed up to five non-competing incentives that would be generated at the time of the shopper's next purchase at the store.

Shopping List helped to promote store loyalty and to quickly build manufacturer volume. A typical offer was "buy two, get one free," "buy two, get a companion product free," or, "buy two, get $1 off next purchase." Catalina initiated the Shopping List program in six retail grocery chains in the fall of 1992. The company found that from a manufacturer's point of view the program generated sales equal to those generated by FSIs at approximately one quarter of the cost.

Checkout Direct

Checkout Direct was a companion product to Checkout Coupon that added a time dimension to the targeting ability of a promotion. Checkout Direct used the printer at the register to distribute incentives based on the historical purchasing behavior of the consumer. The program was based on the link between the Catalina network and the retailer's in-store card-based programs such as check-cashing cards or frequent shopping club cards, and more recently, bank debit cards and credit cards such as Visa, Mastercard, Discover, and so on. When a shopper used his or her identifying card, which Catalina tracked by number only, a manufacturer could create an incentive based on that customer's shopping history. For instance, a shampoo manufacturer using the Checkout Direct program might track the purchasing behavior of a customer who used a competitive shampoo. Toward the end of the estimated product usage time period, the manufacturer could distribute a coupon to that customer to encourage him or her to switch shampoo brands. If timed correctly, the customer would receive a shampoo coupon at the end of a shopping trip just prior to making a decision to purchase more shampoo. In this way a manufacturer could time a coupon to meet the needs of a consumer.

Catalina believed that the Checkout Direct product was more than a typical frequent-shopper program. Unlike a traditional frequent-shopper program, the Checkout Direct program combined customer loyalty with a manufacturer's ability to attack competitive users and brand switchers. The one drawback to this program, however, was that it relied on the customers both to consistently use their identifying card and to shop at the same store when making their purchases.

Cross Retail Tie-Ins and MarketMatch

Catalina had several other services that either tied in local merchants and schools to the supermarkets in their community or tied in a non-supermarket product promotion to a grocery purchase. The community-based programs were usually initiated by the local merchant and the retailer. The programs included School Bucks and SportsCheck—both promotions that raised money for school supplies or sporting equipment for the local school. The funds were raised when shoppers purchased specific products included in the promotion. A certificate was issued to the customer at the end of his or her purchase. These certificates were collected at the schools and then presented to the retailer for cash redemption. The manufacturer reimbursed the retailer for the amount donated to the school.

School Bucks and SportsCheck programs were supported by the retailer or manufacturer with newspaper advertisements, in-store signage, shopping lists, broadcast advertisements, and school bulletins. Although these programs were entirely set up and managed by the retailer, the Catalina network was essential for the implementation of the program. Catalina assisted in developing all facets of the program, from presenting the concept to local and national vendors to helping with copy ideas for the coupons.

The second type of cross retailer tie-in, called Market-Match, was a nongrocery-related product promotion. This program allowed manufacturers the opportunity to move product by generating coupons for a giveaway item or service. Several programs had been tested out. These included generating coupons to send away for a Fig Newton T-Shirt when Fig Newtons were purchased, coupons to call for a free lighter when cigarettes were purchased, and coupons for credit to a Sears Portrait Studio sitting when baby food, diapers, or a child-size toothbrush was purchased. The manufacturer, such as Sears Portrait Studios, paid the cost of the distribution and redemption of these coupons.

Marketing Reports Generated

Each of the different programs offered by Catalina also provided real-time cumulative data about coupon distribution for that promotion. Several types of reports were available with each promotion, as well as the ability to customize the reports for each individual client. On a normal basis, clients could receive their first coupon distribution report one week after the program commencement and their first coupon redemption report three weeks after the program start date. Most programs ran 12 weeks. All clients were furnished with cumulative reports at the end of their programs.

Two typical reports are shown in **Exhibit 5** and **6**. The first one, **Exhibit 5**, *Checkout Coupon Trigger Analysis by Program*, identified the time frame of the report, the number of coupons distributed, and the number redeemed grouped by the individual trigger SKU that was scanned. This data can also be provided at both market and region levels. The second report generated was the *Speed of Distribution and Redemption Report*. As the name suggested, this document identified how quickly coupons were distributed and redeemed over the lifetime of the program. (An excerpt of this report is shown in **Exhibit 6**.) Both reports were available within a few days of the actual transactions.

COUPON/PROMOTION INDUSTRY

Traditional Promotional Activities

Coupons, in any format, were primarily used by manufacturers to promote awareness or trial of a new product or to increase the volume of an existing product. For the majority of consumer product manufacturers, coupon advertising was a significant component of their advertising budgets. According to Donnelly Marketing, Inc., in 1992 the typical consumer products manufacturer spent 50% of its promotional budget on trade allowances (discounts and cooperative advertising), 25% on straight image advertising, and 25% on consumer promotions (the area in which coupons fall). This represented a shift over the past several years away from consumer advertising dollars toward trade dollars for the typical brand advertising budget.

There were several traditional types of coupons currently being used for promotional purposes. These included four major coupon categories: Magazine and Newspaper coupons (appearing in the editorial content of the medium); On/In Product coupons; Direct Mail coupons; and freestanding inserts (separate "coupon only" publications which were inserted into newspapers and magazines). Of these, FSIs were the major group, comprising approximately $1.8 billion of the $2.1 billion coupon industry in 1992. These four categories differed in several ways, the most important of which was how they reached the end consumer and the rate at which they were redeemed. According to Nielsen Clearing House Promotional Services (NCH), an estimated 310 billion coupons of all varieties were distributed in 1992, 90% of which were FSIs.

Magazine and Newspaper Coupons.

Only occasionally did manufacturers and other promoters use coupon advertising, such as rebates, two-for-ones, or sweepstakes in newspapers and magazines. More often, newspaper and magazine advertisements did not contain coupons. Magazine or newspaper advertising with a coupon was not particularly effective because of both high media costs and low redemption rates, with redemption running at 1.6% in 1991. However, coupons in newspapers and magazines had the advantage of enticing readers to a product that they might never have considered buying before.

On/In Product Coupons.

Unlike less-targeted newspaper or magazine coupons, promotions found on or in a product had the advantage of already reaching the end consumer. Advertising campaigns that used this medium often did so in order to promote a line extension, such as the "garden style" spaghetti sauce instead of the regular sauce, or to increase trial of a new product, such as a box of pasta to accompany the spaghetti sauce. Coupons that were on or in a package might also be used to create an event that would continue customer loyalty to the product over time. This type of event, often called a "continuity" program because it promoted repeat purchases of a product, was based on sending in one or several "game piece(s)," (the lid, UPC code, or special sticker located on the package). The event itself might have been a sweepstake, a cash or special prize, a chance to meet a celebrity, or a chance to do something unusual, like be an honorary bat boy or girl at a professional baseball game. Coupons on or in a product might also offer some amount off of the customer's next purchase of the product. No matter what the deal offered on the On/In Product coupon, however, the customer had to purchase the product first in order to receive the coupon.

Direct Mail Coupons.

Of the traditional coupon programs, Direct Mail coupons were probably the most flexible and effective at reaching a particular type of consumer. As the name implies, Direct Mail coupons arrived at a consumer's home through the mail. The mailing could be arranged to fit the desired profile of the recipient. Because the ability to target the end consumer was greater than in either newspapers or magazines, Direct Mail coupons had a higher redemption rate. In 1991 it was 4.3%.

Freestanding Inserts.

The most prevalent of all couponing methods was the freestanding insert (FSI). FSIs were the separate newspaper circulars most often found in the Sunday edition of the local or regional newspaper. The advertisements were usually grouped according to manufacturer and product type. Typically, each advertisement included a coupon that could be clipped out and taken to a participating supermarket to be redeemed for the face value of the coupon. Some FSIs however, had to be mailed directly to the manufacturer or a manufacturer's clearinghouse where a rebate, prize, or whatever the coupon indicated would be issued. FSI promotions were a traditional element of most consumer product manufacturers' annual brand budget. (For more information about FSIs see the section titled "FSIs: Nuts and Bolts.")

The Coupon Redemption Cycle.

With a national average redemption rate of 2.3%, most coupons in 1992, once printed, ended up in landfill. Those coupons that did make it back to the store for redemption, had a long and complex excursion to their final resting place. The cycle went as follows: Retailers accepted coupons for their face value and typically sent them to a retail clearinghouse (RCH) that sorted the coupons by manufacturer.

The clearinghouse calculated the total value of the coupons and issued a check for that amount to the retailer, essentially "buying" the coupons. At the same time, the retail clearinghouse invoiced each manufacturer for the value of the coupons received plus a service and handling charge. The retail clearinghouse then sent the actual coupons to the manufacturer's clearinghouse. At this establishment, the coupons were then sorted by brand and type. The cumulative information based on these sortings was then forwarded to the manufacturer, usually for the benefit of the brand manager and other marketing executives.

The whole coupon redemption cycle took 3 to 6 months to complete. Therefore, a manufacturer who ran a coupon with a 3-month expiration date would not receive formal information until 6 to 9 months later! Catalina, whose coupons currently went through this process, believed that there was some opportunity to automate and expedite this system using scanner technology. However, there were already several major players in the industry. There was a reluctance, moreover, to increase the amount of space used for bar coding information on a coupon.

FSIs: Nuts and Bolts

Freestanding inserts were the traditional vehicle for consumer product manufacturers to promote their brands. Many of the larger manufacturers contracted with advertisers months, or years, in advance to guarantee space in each circular. Usually the manufacturer purchased space several times over the course of the year. Most of these arrangements included exclusivity contracts with the advertiser. However, because there were several marketing companies producing FSIs (see the section titled "Catalina Competitors") and because most Sunday newspapers distributed more than one company's circular, exclusivity could not be guaranteed. As an example, although Coke may have purchased exclusive category rights to advertise one week in the Sullivan Marketing circular, Pepsi would probably be advertising in a competing circular, both of which would arrive on the consumer's doorstep in the same newspaper.

With FSIs, manufacturers could neither control who was advertising in other FSIs, nor could they target precisely particular classes of consumer. Industry research[5] has suggested that when the objective of an FSI was to stimulate trial by users of a competitive product, only 3 out of every 1,000 FSI coupons reached that goal. For example, on average, of the original 1,000 coupons distributed, only 25 were redeemed. Of these, 8 were mis-redeemed. (Mis-redemption occurred when coupons were used against non-matching products, often as a result of not scanning the UPC code properly or at all.) This left 17 remaining coupons, 14 of which were estimated to be redeemed by people who already used the couponed product. Therefore, of the original 1,000 coupons distributed, only 3 were actually redeemed by the targeted consumer.

The average cost for running an FSI was approximately $5.00 per 1,000 coupons distributed in a Sunday circular. If the face value of the coupon was $0.50 (the approximate value of an average FSI coupon in 1992), with a processing cost of $0.09 each, then the total cost to the manufacturer was $19.75 per 1,000 coupons printed. Given industry redemption patterns, each manufacturer spent between $6 and $7 for each of the 3 new users it had reached. Therefore, although the exposure of FSIs was great, the effectiveness seemed to be limited. **Table B** shows comparative statistics between typical FSI costs versus Catalina's Checkout Coupon costs for the distribution of competitive user coupons.

Table B
Couponing to Competitive Users: Checkout Coupons vs. FSIs

	FSIs	Checkout Coupons
Distribution cost, 1,000 coupons	$ 5.00	$ 90.00
Number redeemed	25	65
Value of coupon	$ 0.50	$ 0.75
Expense of coupons	$12.50	$ 48.75
Processing at $0.09/coupon	$ 2.25	$5.85
Total program cost per 1,000	$19.75	$144.60
Number of competitive user trials	3	65
Cost per competitive user trial	$ 6.58	$ 2.22

Source: Catalina Marketing from Morgan Stanley report, "*U.S. Investment Research,*" July 27, 1992.

Information Captured by FSIs. The type of information captured by the use of FSIs, although limited,

---

5 Information in this section has been adapted from research performed by Morgan Stanley for their report "*U.S. Investment Research,*" July 27, 1992.

---

was useful and traditionally the only data available for analysis. However, FSIs had several shortcomings. First, because of the long, drawn-out coupon redemption process, full disclosure of redemption rates and associated information was not available to the manufacturer until anywhere between 3 to 6 months after the expiration date of the coupon. Second, the type of information captured was limited to the basics, such as the total value of the coupons redeemed, how many were redeemed, and how quickly they were redeemed. There was no indication of where the redemption was made. Finally, even if a brand manager wanted more detailed redemption information and was willing to pay for it, given the nonautomated nature of current FSI processing, it would be impossible to generate.

FSIs, Retailers, and Manufacturers. Traditionally, retailers and manufacturers have had an adversarial relationship. Supermarket buyers have tried to find those manufacturers who would negotiate the best prices and biggest trade allowances. They tried to locate those who supported their products with in-store promotions, merchandising, signage, and consistent delivery. Manufacturers on the other hand, negotiated aggressively with retailers and fought with each other for retailer shelf space and for prime end-aisle displays. In the past manufacturers and retailers had failed to share consumer purchasing information.

Cooperative advertising, where a manufacturer would help to pay for a retailer's promotional piece in exchange for the display of its product or logo, was a key element in manufacturer/retailer negotiations. At one time, manufacturers had the upper hand in these negotiations. More recently, however, since share of market among supermarket chains has become concentrated and scanner data have made them more knowledgeable about product movement, the supermarkets have gained more advantage in these negotiations.

CATALINA OPERATIONS

Technology. The lifeblood of Catalina's organization was the computer system. Each one of the *Checkout Coupon* machines, located at every register in the 5,628 stores in the Catalina network, was linked to the company's main database. In the corporate "computer lab," the transactions going on in any store, whether in southern California or across the country, could be monitored on a computer screen at any time. This was essential for maintaining and troubleshooting the system.

For example, from the Anaheim office one morning in April 1993, the computer lab dialed up one of the Minneapolis supermarkets in the Catalina network. From the technician's computer screen, which displayed the activity going on in the store, the following information was immediately available. The store had been open for two hours. Five registers were currently in operation: lanes 1, 2, 5, 8, and 12. Seventeen *Checkout Coupons* had been distributed so far that day. Seven of the coupons printed were triggered from purchases made in the soft drink category, the other ten were mixed over several product categories. Also shown were the particular coupons which had been printed. The computer link remained open for about 10 minutes. During that time two more coupons were generated. With this computer link, Catalina was able to monitor and accumulate data on each coupon printed down to the SKU level of both the triggering product and the couponed item. (**Exhibit 7** shows a typical computer readout for a store in operation as seen from Catalina's computer lab.)

Each night, the on-line store PCs sent that day's coupon distribution information to the main computer data centers located in Anaheim, California, and Atlanta, Georgia. This information, down to the register level and the UPC code being scanned, was then compiled and stored for various reports generated for Catalina's clients. Depending on the type of program being offered to the customer, information was available within a week.

Economics

Revenue Generation. Catalina set up advertising cycles similar to those used for purchasing newspaper advertisements. There were 13 cycles per year, each four weeks long. Cycle dates had been designated for the remainder of the 1990s. A manufacturer or retailer could purchase these cycles, as late as 8 weeks before the cycle start date (depending on the program), or up to three years in advance of the cycle date.

When a cycle was purchased by a manufacturer or retailer, Catalina guaranteed exclusivity for that product's coupon distribution. In order to maintain this advertising exclusivity, Catalina grouped each product by category. The company used the product categories defined by Information Resources Incorporated (IRI) as a guideline for these category definitions. There were approximately 550 categories in all. (**Exhibit 8** shows a list of sample categories.) The definitions were updated every six months. Categories could be considered for revision or sub-division at the request of a manufacturer.

In addition, to increase carryover business, if a manufacturer purchased three or more cycles for a product category in a given year, that client had the right of first refusal on those cycles the following year. Catalina estimated that it was currently using only 11%–13% of its cycle/product category capacity.

A client who purchased a cycle had to commit to pay a minimum category fee in order to have the right to distribute coupons in that category. These fees depended upon the category volume and assumed that the more items purchased, the more coupons distributed, and therefore, the more it would cost the client to participate.

In June 1993, the category fee calculation started with the total households reached by the Catalina network. This figure was decreased by the percentage of households buying the product category (this was often referred to as category penetration). The number of households buying the category was then annualized by identifying the number of household purchases of this product category made during the year. Once this number was generated, it was whittled down further by deducting the percentage of private label share for the product category. The new number, the total number of annual brand purchases in the category, was then multiplied by the price to purchase a Catalina coupon. This showed the total value of the annual coupon dollars for a product category. This amount was then divided to equal the length of one cycle (four weeks). The minimum fees were based on 30% of the value of the cycle period. Any coupons distributed beyond the original 30% number were charged to the client on a per-coupon basis. In the early 1990s, the minimum category fee was $15,000 (expected to be $25,000 by 1994); however, the minimum full program or contract fee was $35,000 (expected to remain the same in 1994). Very few programs were run for only one cycle; therefore, meeting the program fee, even if it was a low value category, was not too difficult. If necessary, a client could add markets, cycles, triggers, or different coupon types to reach the minimum levels.

All Catalina manufacturing clients were pre-billed for the minimum amount to be spent during the advertising cycle. This amount was due six weeks prior to the cycle's commencement. The final billing took place at the end of the cycle. Quantity discounts, regional rates, and other supplementary services and price reductions were also available. (**Exhibit 9** outlines these prices.)

Cost of Installation. Catalina spent approximately $10,000 to install its system in a new store. About 75% of this cost was for hardware (PCs, printers, interface cards, cables, and so forth). This expenditure was amortized over five years. The remaining 25% was for third-party installation costs, which were amortized over the life of the contract with the store (generally 3 to 5 years). Any maintenance necessary, which was usually limited, was expensed as incurred.

Cost of Distribution. Once the computer network and printers were installed, there were several costs associated with the use of the Catalina system. The first was the cost of the coupon itself: the paper, printing, and handling costs. Catalina had estimated this cost to be approximately $3.33 per 1,000 coupons distributed. A second cost was the ongoing upkeep of the printers, which was the responsibility of Catalina's technology services.

The last category of cost was payment to retailers who had installed the Catalina network. Each retailer was paid a small service fee for distributing Catalina coupons. The payment was based on the number of coupons printed and was made in a lump sum, payable at the end of each quarter.

Organizational Structure

Corporate. Catalina's corporate office was plain vanilla in character. The atmosphere was informal and fast-paced. The feeling was of a company that had a lot of future potential. Almost all employees were stockholders and stood to make a significant amount of money if the company remained successful. According to several employees the benefits package was good, including—among other items—a 401K plan. In addition, more than one employee stated that Catalina was "a great place to work, where people were treated like family." All executives were familiar with people in all departments and areas. As of June 1993, there were 294 employees—92 in the corporate offices and 202 in 24 field offices throughout the United States.

The Field Organization. Catalina's "heart" was its field organization. Currently, field employees worked in either of two areas—Retail Marketing Services (RMS) or Manufacturer Sales. Each area focused directly on the market it served—either the supermarket chains or the consumer products manufacturers. Although run separately, the two field organizations exchanged information regularly and helped to coordinate the promotions between the manufacturers and the retailers.

In July 1992, the reporting structure of the field organization had successfully been revamped in order to bring the two sides of the house closer together, as well as put more emphasis on the sales side of retail operations. At that time, Helene Monat became the senior vice president of Sales and Retail Marketing Services, formally joining the two sides. (Prior to that, each area had its own senior vice president.) Reporting to her were four regional vice presidents, each with responsibilities for both Manufacturing Sales and Retail Marketing Services in their own areas of the country.

Because of the difficulty of selling a new and nontraditional promotional service to both consumer products manufacturers and supermarket chains, Catalina had proactively built a well-compensated, high-powered sales force. Catalina's salaries and commissions for both Manufacturing Sales and RMS employees were considered to be higher-than-market.[6]

On the Manufacturing Sales side of the business, Catalina's strategy was to expand its market penetration; therefore, commissions were focused more on securing new, larger clients, new product categories, and higher-volume programs, rather than on client renewal. In addition, Catalina believed that most customers would be very satisfied with their products and services and would renew their contracts. This emphasis on new, larger accounts gave many of the Manufacturing Sales people the opportunity to more than double their base salaries in commissions. New hires were generally given a few months of on-the-job training to learn the business. This entailed going out on sales calls with a seasoned salesperson and understanding Catalina's philosophy of objective-based selling. After that time they were given a territory and assigned their own quota amount.

Supporting the team of manufacturing salespeople were the field client service executives. These employees had the responsibility to set up, document, and implement the manufacturer's advertising program. The process was completed through a series of documents and information sent to the corporate office where the program specifics were entered into the main database. The client service executives were as critical to the smooth functioning of the program as they were the administrative interface with the manufacturer. In the words of one salesperson, the client service executives were essential, "picking up the pieces" once a salesperson had struck a deal with a manufacturer.

On the RMS side of the business, the focus of the organization was different. RMS account executives, although always trying to both sign up new retailers and sell new ideas to retailers already in the network, considered themselves more in the business of servicing their clients. Because Catalina required its retailers to sign on to a least a five-year contract, the RMS executives were constantly trying to improve and maintain the services and relationship with the retailers.

CATALINA COMPETITORS

Catalina had three major categories of competitors: (1) traditional FSI distributors, (2) direct mail coupon distributors, and (3) in-store electronic, non-electronic, and broadcast-oriented promotional services. At the time, however, Catalina was the only company generating coupons based on point-of-sale information captured at the register. Several other in-store marketing companies, however, were offering other innovative advertising programs. (**Exhibit 10** shows a brief chart of different types of coupon programs available in supermarkets.)

Freestanding Insert Distributors

Several companies were in the freestanding insert business, the predominant form of couponing in the United States. They included Product Movers, Quad, Valassis, and Sullivan Marketing, to name a few. As a group they reached a total circulation of 55 million households. In general, the cost for an FSI promotion was $3.50–$4.00 for a half page, and $6.50–$7.50 for a full page, per thousand printed. Drop dates varied among the different companies, ranging from 46 times per year for Valassis, to 34 for Product Movers, and 28 for Quad. Sullivan Marketing, as the newest entrant to this market, had only 2 drop dates in 1992. For most of these organizations, the lead time to run a manufacturer promotion was approximately 12 weeks. And, although each firm offered category exclusivity for its client, more than one of these marketing companies might be running their circulars in the same newspaper at the same time. The reported redemption rate for FSIs was 2.3% in 1992, with about 80% of those redeemed coupons gauged as "own users" redemptions.

Although offering basically similar products, some of the FSI distributors were trying to differentiate themselves. Valassis, for example, recently introduced two new programs—a county-based program and the "Heart Beat"

---

6 According to one Catalina executive, prior to July 1992 there was a perception of inequity between the salaries of the manufacturer sales side and the retail operations side of the field organization—the retail side considered the "stepsister" in the organization. The restructuring in July 1992 attempted to address this issue.

program—both aimed at newspapers that distributed to a more targeted readership. The "Heart Beat" program, for instance, distributed FSIs in newspapers with circulations that served particular groups of people such as French- and Spanish-speaking people, African-Americans, military personnel, and upscale communities.

Direct Mail Distributors

Val-Pak was the largest direct mail cooperative[7] network in the United States, with a 42-million, non-duplicated household circulation. Val-Pak provided its clients with a sorting capability of over 70 demographic groups. It also offered a Neighborhood Trade Area program based on postal carrier routes so that retail tie-ins could be more effectively executed. The lead time for these programs was 4–7 weeks, which was considered to be the shortest in the industry.

Jane Tucker's Supermarket of Savings was another direct mail marketer and Catalina competitor. It had a circulation of 42 million households[8] and offered several mailing options based on different demographic characteristics. The cost for its targeted FSI was $14.75 per thousand coupons mailed, with some occasional discounting on the price available. Most of these coupons were direct response promotions, (i.e., they had to be returned to the manufacturer via the mail for redemption). Only a small percentage were redeemable at a store.

The last of the major direct mail competitors was Carol Wright, a company that offered a cooperative direct mail program to manufacturers. The circulation of Carol Wright's promotions was 30 million households nationwide taken from a database of 90 million households. The database could be tailored to the needs of the manufacturer and it included data sorts based on ethnic background and age, such as "Hispanic" and "New Age" (the 50+ market). Programs were run 10 times per year with additional mailings and services available. The cost to run the program in 1992 was approximately $16 per thousand coupons distributed. In addition, the mailings could be coordinated with sampling programs and retailer advertisements.

In-Store Marketing: Non-Electronic

ActMedia had several in-store marketing services available for its clients. The first of these, the ActMedia Instant Coupon Machines (ICMs), were currently located in 6,894 grocery and 4,000 drugstores. These plastic boxes dispensed pre-printed coupons. The boxes were mounted on the shelves in front of the product that the coupons were promoting. Usually there was a flashing light on the box to catch the attention of the shopper. A customer simply pulled the protruding coupon from the machine. After a 15- to 40-second delay, a small, battery-operated motor in the box issued another coupon for the next shopper. The coupon had no additional tracking information on it other than a bar code similar to a traditional FSI. The face value of the coupon was fixed. Unlike the Catalina coupon, the ActMedia coupon was not triggered by the different purchases of a shopper, since the machine would distribute a coupon to anyone who walked by. ActMedia reported its redemption rate was 15%–22%, with a 30% increase in unit sales for the participating manufacturer. ActMedia rented its ICM machine to manufacturers for $40 per store for each four-week purchase cycle and guaranteed category exclusivity.

A second ActMedia service available was the ActNow Co-op. This was an in-store cooperative coupon and sampling program. In-store demonstrators distributed coupon booklets, solo coupons, samples, and premiums. The program was run 5 times per year in 19 top retail chains. Programs provided two-day, three-day, and weekend activities with each product displayed at a kiosk with point-of-sale signs. In 1992, 13,000 stores participated in the ActNow Co-op program. ActMedia reported a 22% average increase in sales of the promoted items during the promotion period. The ActNow-targeted shopper however, was limited to the demographics of the particular store in which the promotion was being run. In addition, the costs of this service were substantial and varied, depending on the type of sampling done and the number of extra personnel needed. Moreover, many distributed coupons were left behind in the store.

Similar to the ActNow Co-op program was ActMedia's Impact program. This was a customized, solo in-store sampling, demonstrating, and couponing event. A brand or a family of brands constituted the items usually selected for this type of program. In addition, ActMedia provided training and supervision of the demonstrators as well as program results for the retailer. However, this program was quite expensive, running approximately $160 per day. Sales of the promoted items

---

7 In this instance "cooperative" means that several manufacturers were participating in a single mailing.
8 Although both Val-Pak and Jane Tucker's Supermarket of Savings had the same circulation number, Val-Pak's circulation was non-duplicating, whereas the Jane Tucker's circulation had some overlap in names.

allegedly increased by 15%–20% during the promotion period.

ActMedia offered several other non-electronic in-store promotional programs. These included small billboards on carts, shelf posters that displayed product information without any price indication, small spring-loaded coupon dispensers that attached to a shelf, and two-sided posters that could be displayed in conjunction with the store directory signs.

Advanced Retail Marketing's Super End Aisle (SEA) was a brand new in-store marketing program, currently in the testing phase and designed to coordinate promotions with end-aisle (end cap) displays. A coupon dispenser was located at the end of the aisle where the promoted product was stocked. This arrangement was particularly appealing to retailers, who used the end cap shelf space to sell high margin or highly promotional merchandise. Unlike the majority of other marketing companies that sought business primarily from manufacturers, SEA considered the retailer its customer. SEA signed up retailers who would notify it when they were planning their regular cents-off end-aisle displays. SEA then had the right to approach the national manufacturer of the products the retailer planned to display, to add to the discount by installing its SEA coupon dispenser on the end cap. Because the program was in test phase, its selling prices to the manufacturer were unknown. Catalina executives, however, believed that this type of program gave an added advantage to the manufacturer, by marrying its trade and consumer promotion dollars to move product in the stores.

In-Store Marketing: Electronic

One of the latest in-store marketing vehicles was the VideOcart, an interactive computer display screen mounted onto a shopping cart. The machine offered an item locator which told the shopper where an item was located in the store. In addition, when the shopper approached the products being promoted, a shelf sensor would trigger product messages and offers viewable on the VideOcart screen. An optional feature of the VideOcart was that customers could indicate on the screen if they were interested in a coupon for that product. This resulted in a coupon being printed by the register.

In the spring of 1993, the VideOcart was being tested in 220 stores. The company was experimenting with charging the retailer for installation and maintenance—considered to be substantial—which the retailer would recoup by selling VideOcart programs to local vendors. Catalina believed that this selling technique indicated that VideOcart was having less success in selling national advertisements than it had expected. (National advertisements were the initial way VideOcart had expected to generate revenues.)

Feedback from retailers who were testing the system indicated that they were having difficulty selling the program to local vendors. An additional drawback to the VideOcart system was that retailers could not install the machines throughout their chain as some stores were in high cart-theft areas.

Another in-store competitor for Catalina was In-Store Advertising, owned by Cap Cities. In-Store installed electronic light-emitting diode (LED) billboards in supermarkets. The billboards were 57" wide by 7" high and were usually placed in high-traffic areas (but not near the registers). Each billboard (there were between 4 and 7 signs per store) played a six-minute loop with five minutes for manufacturer advertising and one minute for the retailer advertising. Usually the messages promoted products without mention of the item's price. About 5,400 stores had In-Store billboards in operation. The charge to manufacturers for participating was $50 per store per four-week cycle.

A third in-store electronic competitor was Advanced Promotion Technology (APT). APT was in the process of testing out a new marketing program called Vision and a companion program called Vision Value Club. The Vision machine, an in-store electronic promotion delivery system, combined a consumer-activated, touch-sensitive screen with computer graphics and compact disc (CD) technology, located at the checkstand. The installation also included a coupon printer and a card reader. The machine printed coupons upon customer request via the computer screen.

The Vision Value Club was a frequent-shopper program tracked by a smart card swiped through a Vision card reader at the register. APT, owned in part by Procter & Gamble, Schlumberger, and more recently, Vons Supermarkets, was currently testing the Vision machine and Vision Value Club programs in 34 stores. The cost to trigger each coupon ranged from $0.01–$0.09. However, Catalina believed the initial cost for the equipment was probably quite high and was most likely a major impediment to expansion.

In-Store Marketing: Broadcast

Fame/Muzak was an in-store radio system that broadcast advertisements as customers shopped. The promotions were tied into the store merchandising program with shelf signs and other materials to support radio advertisements. Each advertisement was about 30 seconds long and was aired every 6 or 7 minutes. Catalina believed that Fame/Muzak would be installed in approximately 2,000 stores by the end of 1993. The company itself was a joint venture between Fleming Foods, one of the largest food wholesalers, and Muzak. The two companies would be selling and manufacturing the system on a joint basis. Currently, the selling price of the system to a manufacturer was $20 per store per four-week cycle to run the program. The number of participants per cycle was limited to 24.

Checkout Channel, a joint venture between Turner Broadcasting and ActMedia, was a program that aired news and advertisements shown on TV monitors located at the checkstands. The broadcasts were 70% CNN live newscast and 30% paid advertisements, both delivered via satellite. A sensor on the machine could tell when a customer was in the checkstand line and would automatically turn on the sound. This system was designed to take advantage of a captive audience and at the same time alleviate shopper boredom in the checkout line. Initially, there were approximately 1,000 stores involved in the pilot program, but the preliminary testing was disappointing. The cost was $6 for the broadcast of one thousand 30-second spots and included category exclusivity. The installation and start-up costs, however, proved to be too substantial and Checkout Channel was forced to discontinue operations in the beginning of 1993.

OTHER CATALINA VENTURES— CURRENT TECHNOLOGY USES

Catalina was also involved in several ventures outside of the supermarket in-store promotion industry. The first of these, Catalina Information Resources (CIR), a subsidiary of Catalina, was created in 1992 as a joint venture with Information Resources Incorporated. The goal of CIR was to help manufacturers decrease the cost of their product delivery services to retailers, as well as to optimize inventory control. The CIR application worked by tracking approximately 3,000 items at the store level. These items, which manufacturing clients ordered by UPC code, were tracked until 11 P.M. At that time data relating to the movement of the products during the day were captured and sent to the CIR facility to be validated and stored. The information was available to CIR clients by 5 A.M. the following morning. Several predefined reports and queries were available that allowed manufacturers to immediately react to individual store out-of-stock conditions, react to new product introductions, and forecast store inventory needs.

A second new venture for Catalina was a licensing agreement established with the creation of Catalina Electronic Marketing Ltd. of Oxford, England. In the fall of 1992, this company tested out the use of the Catalina network in five supermarkets belonging to Asda, a British supermarket chain. At least 100 more stores were scheduled to come on line during 1993. Like the operations in the United States, Catalina was optimistic about the future of the British and European market.

A third venture established in the beginning of 1993 was a relationship with a music company called the Intouch Group, Incorporated. Intouch sold an interactive album sampling station kiosk, called the "i-station," that was used to allow customers to listen to songs prior to purchasing a CD. The i-station was installed in Wherehouse Entertainment, Streetside Records, and Tower Record stores. Through the joint venture, Catalina's coupon distribution technology was integrated with the i-station kiosk. Coupons related to the customers' recording selection were printed at the kiosk. The partnership with Intouch represented Catalina's first venture outside of the consumer products industry.

The fourth and most recent addition to Catalina's ventures outside of supermarkets was the company's move into drugstore promotions. As of April 1993, Catalina was installing the Checkout Coupon Network into selected Thrifty Drug Stores in southern California and Longs Drug Stores in northern California. This program, which was not a joint venture, offered Catalina the potential of moving into a large new area of sales. In addition, Catalina believed that the drugstore operations would attract new manufacturing clientele from the health and beauty-care product categories.

FUTURE OPTIONS

By the spring of 1993, Catalina Marketing was at a crossroad. There were several avenues for future expansion that the management could pursue. (For selected financial information see **Exhibit 11**.)

The most straightforward of these options was to *expand the cycle/product capacity* of the existing Catalina network. Currently, the network was running at about 12% capacity, seemingly leaving a lot of room for growth. One senior executive suggested, however, that increasing capacity would be great, but that there were some technological challenges that would first have to be overcome. As an example he mentioned a period in the fall of 1992 when, in certain regions, the network had "maxed out," creating an inability to print all coupons triggered. Until some information was flushed out of the system, not all programs ran completely. By 1993, however, the system was updated and cleaned out more frequently. Program information from 12 weeks to 24 weeks prior was considered "old" and therefore in need of purging. Even with these changes, the executive was skeptical about Catalina's ability to increase capacity without augmenting its current computer system.

Catalina's second possibility for expansion was to *increase its geographic markets* both nationally and overseas. There were an estimated 22,000 supermarkets in the United States alone, only 25% of them currently part of the Catalina network. According to the National Coverage statistics, however, many of the major supermarket chains had already joined the Catalina network. In fact, senior executives discouraged signing up single store and small chain store supermarkets.

On the international front, with the licensing agreement going well in the United Kingdom, perhaps there were other opportunities in countries around the world. This expansion option, however, posed many technological and operational challenges which would have to be addressed.

The third option was to provide either *additional marketing services* to existing customers or *expand services to new types of retailers*. Catalina already had the technology and infrastructure set up to augment the services that it provided to current clients. In the same vein, Catalina could increase the number of ventures with nongrocery store retailers. The Intouch joint venture, although in its beginning stages, could be just the beginning of Catalina industry expansion.

The *CIR venture* highlighted the fourth possible area of expansion. To date, the direct store delivery program that was in its test phase was well-received by both retailers and manufacturers. The program itself went hand-in-hand with many manufacturers' and retailers' current attempts to improve the supplier/retailer relationship. The program significantly decreased the out-of-stock position in stores and allowed for less than 24-hour turnaround of product movement information. This was considered a breakthrough in restocking procedures.

Lastly, Catalina could *expand its operations into the redemption area* of the coupon business. Although there were several large coupon redemption houses currently in operation, they were not fully automated, nor were they as well connected to both the retailers and manufacturers as Catalina. In addition, much of the data-capture technology and know-how that Catalina had created and learned for coupon distribution could be transferred to the coupon redemption process. Catalina was already collecting redemption information on a limited basis as a service to some of its present customers. Given Catalina's current technology, a move into coupon redemption and clearing services would seem to be an easy transition.

Catalina had many possible expansion options from which to choose. However, whatever avenue Catalina management decided to pursue, it ran the risk of altering its current success. As Tommy Greer said, "Given the technology, the opportunities are limitless. The objective, however, is to expand profitably while minimizing the risk."

Exhibit 1
Checkout Coupon National Coverage

Region	Market	Retailer	No. of Stores	ACV[a]	No. Shopping Baskets	No. of Households
1. Pacific	S. California	Ralphs	159			
		Lucky	242			
		Alpha Beta	134			
		Boys	14			
		Food 4 Less	16			
		Major	3	58%	8,291,664	4,145,832
	Arizona	ABCO	75			
		Fry's	42	39%	1,707,966	853,983
2. Northwest	N. California	Safeway	192			
		Lucky	189			
		Raley's	63	65%	6,481,512	3,240,756
	Seattle	Safeway	113			
		QFC	3	43%	1,693,368	846,684
3. Mountain	Denver	King Soopers	68			
		Safeway	68			
		Cub Foods	8	89%	2,102,112	1,051,056
4. Central	St. Louis	Schnucks	60			
		Dierbergs	14			
		National	55	65%	1,883,142	941,571
	Nebraska	Baker's	10			
		Cub Foods	1	21%	160,578	80,289
5. North Central	Chicago	Dominick's	86			
		Cub Foods	16			
		Eagle	107			
		OMNI	15	35%	3,269,952	1,634,976
	Indiana	Kroger	116			
		Cub Foods—North[b]	21			
		Cub Foods—South[b]	8	46%	2,116,710	1,058,355
	Minneapolis	Cub Foods	16			
		Coburn's[b]	14	16%	437,940	218,970
	Wisconsin	Cub Foods	7			
		Dick's[b]	7	8%	204,372	102,186
	Columbus, OH	Kroger	87			
		Cub Foods[b]	16	50%	1,503,594	751,797
	Michigan	Farmer Jack	72			
		A & P	15			
		Meijer	70	60%	2,291,886	1,145,943

a All Commodity Volume (ACV) is a designation used to establish the sales penetration that a supermarket (or other establishment) has in a given market. Higher percentage ACV indicates greater coverage of a market.
b Installations in Process/Updated 1/93.

Region	Market	Retailer	No. of Stores	ACV*	No. Shopping Baskets	No. of Households
6. Southwest	Dallas/Ft. Worth	Tom Thumb	62			
		Winn-Dixie	79			
		Food Lion	59	36%	2,919,600	1,459,800
	Houston	Randall's	46			
		Apple Tree	50			
		Food Lion[b]	8	33%	1,518,192	759,096
	Louisiana	Winn-Dixie	91			
		Schwegmann	15			
		Food Lion[b]	5	41%	1,620,378	810,189
	Oklahoma	Food Lion	13	5%	189,774	94,887
7. Southeast	Florida	Winn-Dixie	453			
		Food Lion	108			
		Kash n' Karry	111	42%	9,809,856	4,904,928
	Georgia	Winn-Dixie	92			
		Cub Foods	9			
		Food Lion	50	24%	2,204,298	1,102,149
	Alabama	Winn-Dixie	114			
		Bruno's	6	21%	1,751,760	875,880
8. Carolinas	Kentucky	Winn-Dixie	55			
		Food Lion	9	24%	934,272	467,136
	Charlotte	Winn-Dixie	104			
		Food Lion	193	51%	4,335,606	2,167,803
	Raleigh	Winn-Dixie	88			
		Food Lion	150	62%	3,474,324	1,737,162
	South Carolina	Winn-Dixie	94			
		Food Lion[b]	98	36%	2,802,816	1,401,408
	Virginia	Food Lion[b]	158	31%	2,306,484	1,153,242
	Tennessee	Food Lion	69	6%	1,007,262	503,631
9. Mid-Atlantic	Balt./Wash.	Giant Food	157			
		Safeway	141			
		Shprs Food Whse	31			
		Food Lion	55	83%	5,605,632	2,802,816
10. Northeast	New England	Purity	58	17%	846,684	432,342
	New York Metro.	Pathmark	145			
	Philadelphia	Shoprite	153			
		Foodtown	50			
		King Kullen	47			
		Kings	18	41%	6,028,974	3,014,487
	Upstate NY	Tops Friendly	60	23%	875,880	437,940
All Markets			**5,506**	**42%**	**80,376,588**	**40,197,294**

Exhibit 2
Manufacturer Coupons Redeemed and Distributed by Program and Cycle, 1991

Program Type	Cycle	No. of Programs	Distribution	Redemption	% Redemption
Competitive	1	271	31,861,219	2,036,227	6.4%
	2	205	44,785,916	2,494,659	5.6%
	3	202	45,264,800	3,490,459	7.7%
	4	147	29,778,954	1,978,755	6.6%
	5	186	24,305,450	1,373,274	5.7%
	6	209	31,073,569	1,934,779	6.2%
	7	209	32,622,983	1,751,009	5.4%
	8	197	42,357,421	2,965,869	7.0%
	9	210	30,764,194	2,294,801	7.5%
	10	225	49,405,615	3,154,773	6.4%
	11	160	41,980,526	2,304,181	5.5%
	12	154	21,299,711	1,102,261	5.2%
	13	123	18,314,394	1,240,099	6.8%
	Total	2,498	443,814,752	28,121,146	6.3%
Continuity	1	196	1,033,690	345,010	33.4%
	2	136	796,898	250,090	31.4%
	3	139	1,034,517	398,736	38.5%
	4	125	672,714	257,060	38.2%
	5	111	438,397	146,456	33.4%
	6	118	425,698	169,173	39.7%
	7	94	405,559	137,267	33.8%
	8	71	538,589	210,644	39.1%
	9	116	504,879	145,484	28.8%
	10	72	936,896	242,984	25.9%
	11	52	379,548	98,632	26.0%
	12	67	171,701	51,164	29.8%
	13	40	63,261	15,358	24.3%
	Total	1,337	7,402,347	2,468,058	33.3%

Program Type	Cycle	No. of Programs	Distribution	Redemption	% Redemption
Own-User	1	52	4,332,546	734,578	17.0%
	2	60	5,307,965	803,947	15.1%
	3	12	2,021,610	236,419	11.7%
	4	27	3,978,795	688,636	17.3%
	5	34	2,011,173	301,086	15.0%
	6	58	2,722,219	482,986	17.7%
	7	48	4,040,670	766,098	19.0%
	8	39	4,897,446	955,026	19.5%
	9	33	5,729,490	470,082	8.2%
	10	51	6,664,673	859,829	12.9%
	11	47	7,987,817	988,353	12.4%
	12	47	2,155,076	389,743	18.1%
	13	41	4,777,388	549,095	11.5%
	Total	549	56,626,868	8,225,878	14.5%
Cross Category	1	39	9,833,444	283,377	2.9%
	2	32	6,602,854	149,510	2.3%
	3	28	7,402,739	191,720	2.6%
	4	19	5,696,791	132,760	2.3%
	5	56	7,612,879	293,705	3.9%
	6	22	4,609,336	170,511	3.7%
	7	36	12,965,256	311,790	2.4%
	8	18	5,348,820	117,394	2.2%
	9	29	13,384,687	461,056	3.4%
	10	63	24,540,815	942,867	3.8%
	11	30	6,629,698	201,571	3.0%
	12	16	3,367,318	73,801	2.2%
	13	19	2,978,297	54,996	1.8%
	Total	407	110,972,934	3,385,058	3.1%

Exhibit 3
Advertisement for Checkout Coupon

You're Looking At The Reason The FSI Is An Obsolete Medium.

FSI's have no idea what's in a consumer's head. Or on it. Lacking the capacity to identify your target customer, they just throw themselves at everyone. Talking to people who'd never want to buy your product.

This kind of mass waste was completely unavoidable in the old days. But now, with Checkout Coupon® you can pick out the customers you want, and deliver coupons only to them. On a national basis reaching 65 million shoppers each week.

Far too many FSI's go to waste. Checkout Coupon eliminates waste by issuing coupons based solely on purchase behavior.

Using scanner data right at the checkstand, we issue coupons only when a shopper buys a product you've specified in advance. Such as a competitive brand.

So instead of promoting where there's no growth potential, call us about Checkout Coupon. Catalina Marketing, 721 East Ball Road, Anaheim, CA 92805. (800) 955-9770.

CHECKOUT COUPON III®

© 1992 Catalina Marketing Corporation

Exhibit 4
Checkout Coupon Presentation to a Manufacturer

Checkout Coupon®
Our Network Can Accomplish a Variety of Different Objectives Simultaneously

We Reach Over
70MM Shoppers Each Week

Merchandising
- instant rewards
- guaranteed pay for performance

Advertising
Equity Building
- 70MM transactions
- educational
- entertainment
- nutritional
- public service

Learning
- blind trigger

Brand Loyalty
- multi-unit purchasing
- ad messages
- heavy user
- size trade-up

Competitive Promotion
- sampling
- competitive trial
- continuity

LONG-TERM STRATEGIC ADVANTAGE
Build Brand Share Through System Ownership

Non-Price Promotion
- contests
- sweepstakes

Own User Promotion
- size trade-up
- multiple purchases

Niche Consumers
- two-tier triggers

New Distribution
- cross category
- competitive
- own user
- did not buy

Exhibit 5
Checkout Coupon Trigger Analysis by Program

Report Run On:
Date: 3/18/93
Time: 8:53 am

Client: Nabisco, Inc.
Program: NBC Fleischmann V. Other Blends
Offer: Fleischmann's or Move Over Butter
Message: Margarine/Spread - Any Size

Cycle(s):   302   Start Date: 25 - Jan - 93
Coupon Value: $0.50   Stop Date: 14 - Feb - 93
Offer Number: 80209   Expire Date: 12 Rolling Wks
Deal Number: 29000-793394   Fin. Exp. Date: 9 - May - 93

Trigger Description	Total Coupons Distributed	Estimated Redeemed	Redemptions Percentage
Primary to CT MC# 80210			
ICBINB[a] STICK (X-LT Stick)	484,706	16,412	3.4
ICBINB SOFT (X-LT & 3LB BOWL)	978,790	25,135	2.6
ICBINB SQUEEZE	128,478	3,400	2.6
ICBINB LT STICK/SOFT	207,527	5,098	2.5
ICBINB REG 3LB BOWL	14,960	140	0.9
LO'L[b] SWT CRM REG 1LB STICK	173,082	4,123	2.4
LO'L SWT CRM UNSALT 1LB STICK	169,272	2,491	1.5
LO'L SWT CRM REG 1LB S/V	60,515	877	1.4
LO'L SWT CRM REG 1LB BOWL	154,218	3,918	2.5
TOTAL	**2,371,548**	**61,594**	**2.6**

a I CAN'T BELIEVE IT'S NOT BUTTER
b LAND O'LAKES BUTTER

Exhibit 6
Speed of Distribution and Redemption Report

Report Run On:
Date: 8/18/93
Time: 11:11 am

Client: Nabisco
Program: NBC Fleisch V. Blends
Offer: Fleischmann's or Move Over Butter
Message: Margarine/Spread - Any Size

Cycle(s):	302		Start Date:	25 - Jan - 93
Coupon Value:	$0.50		Stop Date:	14 - Feb - 93
Offer Number:	80209		Expire Date:	12 Rolling Wks
Deal Number:	29000-793394		Fin. Exp. Date:	9 - May - 93

Week Ending	Total Coupons Distributed	Estimated Redeemed	% of Total Redeemed	Cumulative % Redeemed
1/31/93	790,457	2,977	2.22	2.2
2/07/93	779,821	9,875	7.38	9.6
2/14/93	801,270	14,761	11.02	20.1
2/21/93	0	18,871	14.09	34.7
2/28/93	0	15,395	11.50	46.2
3/07/93	0	13,160	9.83	56.0
3/14/93	0	10,337	7.72	63.8
3/21/93	0	8,711	6.51	70.3
3/28/93	0	8,434	6.30	76.6
4/04/93	0	6,412	4.79	81.4
4/11/93	0	6,716	5.02	86.4
4/18/93	0	6,053	4.52	90.9
4/25/93	0	5,156	3.85	94.7
5/02/93	0	3,948	2.95	97.7
5/09/93	0	2,581	1.93	99.6
5/16/93	0	363	0.27	99.9
5/23/93	0	146	0.11	100.0
Total	2,371,548	133,896	Redemption %	5.6

Exhibit 7
Computer Screen Readout of an On-Line Supermarket

1-Ready[a]	2-Ready	3-Ready
4-Ready	5-Ready	6-Ready
7-Ready	8-Ready	9-Ready
10-Ready	11-Ready	12-Ready
13-Ready	14-Ready	15-Ready
16-Ready	17-Ready	18-Ready
19-Ready	20-Ready	21-Ready

COUPON STATISTICS

Coupons Triggered	796
Coupons Printed	791
Coupons Flushed	
• End Trans	5
• Printer Error	0
• Paper Jam	0
• Paper Out	0
• Inoperative	0
Coupons Redeemed	50
Blind Triggers[b]	1,636

Note: This computer screen shows the progress of a supermarket's distribution of coupons. Each night (or whenever the computer is shut down, usually only once a day) the total counts are stored and then reset to zero.

a Signifies that the coupon printer in that checkout lane is ready to print.
b Blind Triggers are programs set up to capture additional consumer purchasing behavior information. The data are used for internal analysis.

Exhibit 8
Category Fees for Sample Categories, 1991

Category Name		Category Fee	12-Week Flight Fee
01	**Baby Foods**		
0103	Cereal Baby Food	$ 28,600	$ 85,800
0104	Juice Baby Food	25,000	75,000
0105	Formula Baby Food	27,000	81,000
0106	Baby Food	60,500	181,500
02	**Baking Mixes**		
0201	Cake Mixes	129,700	389,100
0202	Brownie Mixes	44,300	132,900
0203	Pie Crust Mix	15,000	45,000
0205	Biscuit Mix	45,200	135,600
0206	Muffin, Bread, Roll Mix	48,700	146,100
0214	Pancake Mix	36,900	110,700
03	**Baking Needs**		
0302	Baking Chocolate & Bits	56,500	169,500
0203	Cake Decorations	15,000	45,000
0204	Baking Extracts	28,300	84,900
0305	Baking Powder & Soda	15,000	45,000
0308	Dry Yeast	23,800	71,400
0309	Coconut	24,500	73,500
0310	Baking Nuts	28,100	84,300
0311	Ready-to-Spread Frosting	62,500	187,500
0312	Dry Mix Frosting	15,000	45,000
0313	S/S Pie Shells	17,400	52,200
04	**Candy**		
0401	Candy Bars Single/Multi Pack	262,800	788,400
0403	Hard Roll Candy & Breath Fresheners	63,100	189,300
0405	Marshmallows	41,000	123,000
0407	Licorice	15,000	45,000
0424	Packaged Candy	88,300	264,900
05	**Cereal**		
0502	Fruit & Granola Bars/Rolls/Bits	150,900	452,700
0507	RTE Cereal Adult-A	70,600	211,800
0507	RTE Cereal Adult-B	70,600	211,800
0508	RTE Cereal Family-A	70,600	211,800
0508	RTE Cereal Family-B	70,600	211,800
0509	RTE Cereal Children	141,400	424,200
0510	Wheat Germ	15,000	45,000
0511	Hot Cereal—Instant	105,300	315,900
0512	Hot Cereal—Canister	15,000	45,000
0513	Hot Cereal—Wheat	15,000	45,000

Exhibit 9
Catalina "Rate Card"

1. Distribution Fee per Coupon

	Regional	National
Competitive Triggers, Continuities, Multiple Coupons	$0.10	$0.09
Cross Category, Retailer Tie-In	$0.06	$0.05
Own User	$0.045	$0.035

2. Advertising/Trailer Messages

Trailer Messages: Any message or communication that is connected to a printed Checkout Coupon offer during a cycle.

Advertising Message: Any message or communication that prints separate and unrelated to any Checkout Coupon offer during a cycle.

Fee: Per message costs equal to coupon type, i.e.: what triggers coupon:

	Regional	National
• Competitive	$0.10	$0.09
• Order Size	TBD	TBD
• Cross Category, Retailer Tie-In	$0.06	$0.05
• Own User	$0.045	$0.035

3. Set-Up Charge

Up to five (5) coupon variations per category per cycle are provided at no charge. ("Variation" means different couponed brands, face values, expirations, trailer messages, or trigger lists.) A set-up charge of $500 per coupon variation is charged for each variation beyond five (5).

4. Category Fee

These fees are the minimum dollars that a client must commit to in order to have the rights to distribute coupons in that category. These fees are listed on the category fee schedule.

5. Multi-Year Contracts—Discount Policy

All *multi-year* proposals must be approved by the Sales VP and Executive VP of Sales before going to the client.

6. Clients will have rights to first acceptance for all categories that they buy and that they operate for 3 or more national cycles.

7. Clients are permitted to contract for a category or subcategory that they may not have existing products or brands in. All standard policies and fees will be in effect.

8. Clients contracting for a category or subcategory are not required to trigger within the category that they have contracted for. All standard policies and fees for the contracted category will be in effect.

Exhibit 9, continued
Quantity Discounts, 1993

All quantity discounts for 1993 will be based on the clients' individual company volume as opposed to total corporation volume (i.e., Kraft vs. Phillip Morris).

Quantity Distributed	Distribution Cost per Coupon
up to 13,000,000	$ 0.10
over 13,000,000	$ 0.085
over 25,000,000	$ 0.08
over 48,000,000	$ 0.075
over 71,000,000	$ 0.07
over 94,000,000	$ 0.065

1. All types of coupons distributed by your client can be included to reach the quantity breakpoints. *The discounted price applies only to competitive coupons.*

2. The quantity discount is an annual calendar year program. If your client's contract for the year includes enough cycles/categories to earn the discount, the discount rate will be the invoice rate throughout the year.

3. If your client does not contract for enough coupons up front before January 1, all contracts during the year that get you over the breakpoint will reflect the discount rate.

4. The discount plan is *not* to be published or placed in any sales brochure or presentation. Each Catalina representative should discuss the program with his/her applicable clients to generate additional volume during the year.

5. Any additional questions about the quantity discount program should be addressed to the Regional Sales VP or the VP of Marketing.

6. There will be *no discounting of minimums or discounts on coupon rates* without approval from the President.

	Checkout Coupon	FSI	Co-Op Direct Mail	Direct Mail	Solo In-Store Couponing
Household Circulation	34,000,000	52,000,000	30,000,000	30,000,000	18,050,000
Determining Target	Actual Purchase Behavior	None	Surveys Conducted 6–12 Months Prior to Drop Mail Date		Random Delivery
Category Exclusivity	Yes	By FSI Company	By Direct Mail Vehicle		Yes
% Misredeemed	Virtually Zero	33%	Virtually Zero	Virtually Zero	5%
% Redeemed New Users (Incremental)	100%	20%	35%	35%	43%
Targeting Flexibility	Complete	By Market	By Demo.	By Demo.	By Market
Clutter (Coupons/HH)	Low 0–2	High 60–80	High 10–20	Medium 5–10	Medium 5–10

Exhibit 11
Consolidated Balance Sheets ($ in thousands)

	March 31,	
	1993	**1992**
Assets		
Current Assets		
Cash and cash equivalents	$ 25,613	$ 6,538
Accounts receivable	9,131	10,449
Receivable from public offering, net	—	6,938
Allowance for doubtful accounts	(552)	(837)
Inventories	311	306
Prepaid expenses	1,704	172
Deferred tax benefit	3,647	2,254
Total current assets	39,854	25,820
Furniture and Equipment		
Furniture and office equipment	1,949	1,526
Store equipment	44,271	32,729
	46,220	34,255
Less accumulated depreciation & amortization	(25,796)	(16,666)
Total furniture and equipment	20,424	17,589
Other Assets	918	1,090
Total Assets	$ 61,196	$ 44,499
Liabilities and Stockholders' Equity		
Current Liabilities		
Obligations under capital leases	—	592
Accounts payable	5,853	5,113
Taxes payable	809	1,896
Accrued expenses	15,775	7,796
Deferred revenue	9,422	7,910
Total current liabilities	31,859	23,307
Obligations Under Capital Leases, Long-Term	—	2,365
Commitments and Contingencies	—	—
Stockholders' Equity		
Preferred stock; $0.01 par value; 5,000,000 authorized shares; none issued & outstanding		
Common stock; $0.01 par value; 30,000,000 authorized shares; 9,514,920 and 9,233,105 shares outstanding at March 31, 1993 and 1992, respectively	95	92
Paid-in capital	24,196	21,918
Retained (deficit) earnings	5,046	(3,183)
Total stockholders' equity	29,337	18,827
Total Liabilities and Stockholders' Equity	$ 61,196	$ 44,499

Exhibit 11, continued

	Fiscal Year Ended March 31,		
	1993	1992	1991
Revenues	$71,947	$51,710	$33,138
Costs and Expenses			
Direct operating expenses	27,100	24,510	17,084
Selling, general and administrative	19,391	13,092	10,200
Headquarters relocation	3,875	—	—
Depreciation and amortization	9,266	7,847	4,874
Total costs and expenses	59,632	45,449	32,158
Income from Operations	12,315	6,261	980
Other Income (Expense)			
Interest (expense)	(68)	(349)	(318)
Other income, net	1,034	759	1,116
Income Before Provision for Income Taxes	13,281	6,671	1,778
Provision for Income Taxes	5,052	1,911	356
Net Income	$ 8,229	$ 4,760	$ 1,422
Net Income per Common and Common Equivalent Share	$ 0.81	$ 0.51	$ 0.16
Weighted Average Common and Common Equivalent Shares Outstanding (*in thousands*)	10,132	9,411	9,125

	Common Stock		Paid-in Capital	Retained (Deficit) Earnings	Total Stockholders' Equity
	Shares	Par Value			
Balance at March 31, 1990	8,503	$85	$12,637	$(6,733)	$5,989
Net proceeds from issance of common stock	135	1	37	—	38
Amortization of option-related compensation	—	—	61	—	61
Common stock/warrant repurchase	(12)	—	(2)	(529)	(531)
Net income				1,422	1,422
Balance at March 31, 1991	8,626	86	12,733	(5,840)	6,979
Net proceeds from issuance of common stock	530	5	9,390	—	9,395
Net proceeds from exercise of warrants	77	1	164	—	155
Amortization of option-related compensation	—	—	30	—	30
Common stock/warrant repurchase	—	—	—	(2,103)	(2,103)
Equity transaction costs	—	—	(389)	—	(389)
Net income				4,760	4,760
Balance at March 31, 1992	9,233	92	21,918	(3,183)	18,827
Net proceeds from issuance of common stock	310	3	889	—	892
Amortization of option-related compensation	—	—	92	—	92
Stock grants to employees and directors	6	—	260	—	260
Tax benefit from exercise of non-qualified stock options	—	—	2,285	—	2,285
Common stock/warrant repurchase	(35)	—	(1,248)	—	(1,248)
Net income				8,229	8,229
Balance at March 31, 1993	9,514	$95	$24,196	$5,046	$29,337

MANAGING THE ORGANIZATION

Retailing remains a labor intensive activity. In this module introduction we describe some common forms of organization in retail firms, giving descriptions of the duties of various positions, both traditional and innovative.

FORMS OF ORGANIZATION

We may think of a retailer performing several day-to-day tasks:

 (i) buying merchandise for sale in stores
 (ii) operating stores for the selling of merchandise
(iii) operating warehouses and trucks for the receiving, storage and transshipment of goods

In addition, a retailer must perform all the usual tasks of a corporation such as financial control, marketing and personnel management. We will concentrate, however, on the first two tasks listed above, since these are the ones most characteristic of a retailer.

The organization form most often used by department stores is shown in **Figure 1.** Its main feature is a distinct chain of command for the buying and selling processes. This separation recognizes the reality that the buyers are typically at headquarters whereas the sellers are scattered across the country in the stores.

It is most desirable, however, that the buyers and sellers should be in close contact with one another; buyers so that they understand the opinions of the people who are in day-to-day contact with the customer; sellers so that they understand the attractive qualities of products procured by the buyers.

Since it often happens that the buyers are located at a flagship store, in some organizations the salespeople at the main store report to the buyers, all other salespeople report to their respective store manager.

The problem of opening up channels of communication between buyers and sellers is of paramount importance; in what follows we will describe some procedures that have been devised to overcome the barriers to such communication:

 (i) the physical separation of buyers and sellers and
 (ii) there may be a handful of buyers but many hundreds of store merchandise managers.

THE ROLE OF A BUYER

A buyer is given responsibility for procuring goods for some department within the store. To do this, a buyer will be in frequent contact with potential vendors, attending trade shows and fashion shows as appropriate. The buyer will negotiate with the vendor as to prices, quantities,

Professor David E. Bell prepared this note as the basis for class discussion rather than to illustrate either effective or ineffective handling of an administrative situation.

Copyright © 1994 by the President and Fellows of Harvard College.
Harvard Business School case 595-009.

Figure 1

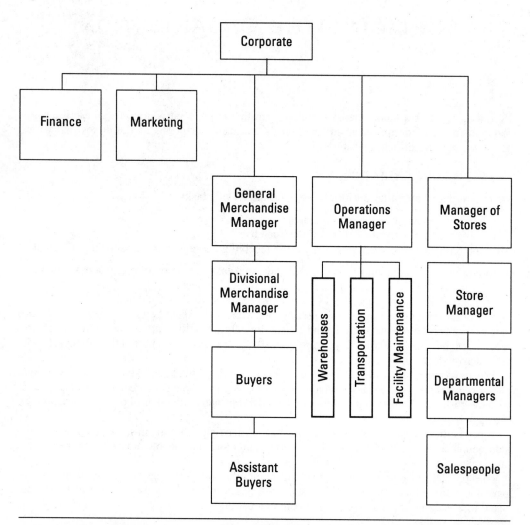

sizes and delivery dates. The buyer might well suggest modifications to the product, either to suit the store's particular customer profile or to maintain distinctiveness with respect to the competition.

Though practices vary, the buyer has typically been responsible for allocating a total purchase order among stores based on their current inventories and likely demand for a particular item. This allocation may be done at the time of the order (known as pre-distribution) or at the time the goods are delivered to the retailer's distribution center (known as post-distribution). For a retailer with hundreds of stores, the allocation process is a complex and laborious one. For this reason a buyer may have an assistant (sometimes called a *planner*) to perform this role.

The buyer is responsible for setting prices and deciding upon price reductions as necessary. Retailers differ in the license granted to store department managers to modify prices to match local demand and competition. Traditionally, almost all price decisions are taken centrally.

Although given considerable autonomy with respect to individual items, the buyer must adhere to a total inventory budget that may vary by season, even within season. The budget is negotiated from time to time with the divisional merchandise manager who, as the buyer's superior, also supervises the general strategy for the department. The difference between the budget and the anticipated inventory (the dollar value of current inventory plus outstanding orders less expected items sold in the interim) is called the *open-to-buy*. The buyer can increase the size of the open-to-buy by marking down items in current inventory thus lowering their cost (by the *retail method* of accounting). This tactic is often necessary towards the end of a season in order to make way for new merchandise.

Finally, the buyer must act as an advocate of the goods he or she has bought, perhaps convincing skeptical store managers of the attractiveness of items allocated by the buyer to the store. At the same time, the buyer must listen to the market information available from people in the stores. The logistics of staying in touch with perhaps several hundred store departmental managers are overwhelming.

THE PLANNER

With the advent of scanning and the memory and computing power of the desktop computer, it is possible to automate somewhat the process of predicting demand, and allocating merchandise, particularly for more staple items. In principle one might guess that next month's demand will be similar to last month's but this simple rule is distorted by

- fashion trends
- seasonality
- promotions
- price changes
- competitive actions

Accurate measurement of historical demand is made complicated by stockouts and inaccuracies in scanning. Multiply all of these problems by the number of SKUs and by the number of stores and the enormity of the problem becomes apparent. Some retailers now rely on vendors to perform their own reordering for basic items. While the vendor can achieve some economies by not having to maintain inventories due to uncertainty about the reordering decisions of the retailer, the vendor is inevitably less well informed about the various idiosyncrasies that have led to particular sales figures.

THE REGIONAL MANAGER

In order to solve the communication problem between the buyer/planner/allocator and the stores, many retailers have between 10 and 100 people whose only responsibility is to ensure that the two-way channel between headquarters and the stores remains open.

At Wal-Mart the regional managers have an exhausting schedule. Each one lives in Bentonville, Arkansas and spends each Monday through Thursday visiting stores in his or her region. At a Friday lunch meeting they meet with the buyers both to communicate what they have learned from store managers and to hear the buyers' plans for the next few weeks. A regional manager is more senior than a buyer, and the meeting is conducted in the presence of the CEO, so the needs of the store managers are well attended to.

DIVISIONAL MERCHANDISE MANAGER/GENERAL MERCHANDISE MANAGER

These two positions, of which the GMM is the more senior, are not directly responsible for buying, but instead for planning and budgeting. A GMM at a department store might be in charge of all hard goods, at Toys R Us, in charge of all apparel. A DMM might supervise five or six buyers and be responsible for establishing a sales forecast and appropriate inventory levels for the category of goods covered by the buyers.

CATEGORY MANAGER

In recent years the buyer's role has evolved at some retailers, particularly in supermarkets, into that of a category manager. Traditionally, a buyer has been a very vendor-focussed person. The buyer prized his or her long standing relationships with key vendors and tended to regard the job of actually selling the goods as of somewhat secondary importance (hence the proliferation of planners/allocators/regional managers). This was in part a by-product of the evaluation system which rewarded bargaining skills with respect to procurement more than it did the satisfaction of the customer.

The category manager's role is conceived as that of the head of a profit center defined over a set of goods viewed as coherent by the *customer* rather than the vendor. Whereas a supermarket buyer might be in charge of all frozen goods, or all Procter and Gamble products, a category manager might be in charge of all household cleaning products, or all pasta (whether fresh, frozen, packaged or tinned). By taking the customer's perspective of the store's offering and by being rewarded on the basis of category gross profit less attributable expenses, it is thought that the category manager will be more likely to eliminate slow movers and duplicated products while ensuring that essential niche products are included. The category manager is the head of a team that is entirely responsible for the profitability of that category.

SALESPERSON

The salesperson can be viewed as either the low person in the retail hierarchy—or as the one person whose job it is to directly satisfy the customer, an exceedingly important role. Salespeople are expected to ensure shelves are kept stocked (if additional supplies are available in a backroom), to keep displays tidy, to help customers find the things they need, and to perform sales transactions. From time to time they will also represent the first point of contact for a customer who wishes to complain.

Some people find the challenge of satisfying customers and interacting with them to be intrinsically rewarding. Others take the job because it pays the rent. Motivating this second group is a major challenge for most retailers. Sales commissions are common for items requiring considerable sales skill and intensive service per customer; examples include shoes, men's suits and automobiles. A growing number of companies are following Wal-Mart's idea of giving all employees (after some minimal initial employment period) some stock in the company, or some share of annual profits. This is thought to produce substantial employee goodwill, at least when the company is profitable, but there are questions as to the actual degree of incentive it provides.

Non-financial incentives include various styles of peer pressure; from posting sales/hour by employee in the staff rest area to prizes for the salespeople who have given especially good service. Most successful retailers now try to create a climate of positive thinking, both about the company and the customers it serves.

Nothing is more detrimental to salespeople's morale than a store that is not able to satisfy its customers no matter how hard they may try. Out of stock positions, a restrictive return policy, poor quality merchandise ... even the best salesperson has to have something to work with.

And while the financial incentives of the corporation are always, in the short term, to keep salespeople's wages at a low level, low wages inevitably lead to a poor selection of job applicants, low morale and high turnover. In short, the recipe for failure.

DEPARTMENTAL SALES MANAGER

This person supervises and trains salespeople within a department of a store, tries to convey market information and stock problems to the buyer, and monitors the competition.

STORE MANAGER

There are two major responsibilities of a store manager; managing the facility itself and managing the sales operation that occurs within it. Thus the store manager must ensure that salespeople are available at the times needed, that the checkout or sales counters do not have long lines, that the store is not too warm or too cold and so on. The store manager's position can be quite junior (at a small specialty store in a mall) or worthy of vice-president status (at the flagship store of a department store chain). The relative influence of a store manager and a buyer can have a substantial impact on the character of the store.

A store manager is often judged on the basis of the operating expenses of the store (mainly labor, utilities and repairs), though if the manager has significant merchandising responsibility it is appropriate to reward the manager based on total gross margin less operating expenses and a fair rental value.

CAREER PATHS

It is generally believed that in retailing *everyone* has to start on the sales floor. A person with management potential would quickly be moved to the position of departmental manager and then either to a position as assistant buyer, then buyer, or alternatively to assistant store manager, then store manager. These may be terminal positions, as the ranks of long-serving buyers and store managers will attest.

A buyer or store manager may be promoted to DMM (or regional manager) and then GMM. A GMM is one of the most senior people in the corporation. Indeed, traditionally the path to the CEO's position has been through the GMM post. In recent years it has become more common for others, from finance or logistics, to reach the top.

CONCLUSION

One of the central dilemmas of retailing concerns the trade-off between centralization and standardization (leading to a low cost structure) and responsiveness to local customer tastes (leading to high sales figures). The constant experimentation with organizational formats reflects this tension and also, to a certain extent, the changing technological possibilities.

With interactive telecommunication nearly commonplace, it should soon be possible for departmental managers not only to communicate their sense of likely sales by SKU in their store, but also to convey more subjective opinions ("people here are becoming more concerned about value", "red is becoming more popular").

As always however, the more responsibility expected of a member of the retail organization, the higher education level it requires, and the higher salary that typically will be required.

Over the last several decades self service, scanning, and sophisticated cash registers have all served to reduce the number of salespeople required to run a store of a given volume. Perhaps the time will come when paying for goods is automatic and when sophisticated video screens match customer needs to available products. Until then, however, the central problem of the retailer will remain; the lowest paid employees are the ones most responsible for satisfying the customer.

Case 13

NORDSTROM

Bruce Nordstrom, age 45, cochairman of Nordstrom, and the eldest of the Nordstroms, typified the modest, unassuming attitude of the company's management. "There is nothing special or difficult about what we do," he said. "I mean, none of us has been to Harvard, Stanford, etc. We are all graduates of the University of Washington here." He almost painted a picture of being "just plain country boys."

However, there was nothing modest about Nordstrom's success. It had grown from sales of $67 million in 1970 to sales of $250 million in 1977 (January 31, 1978); 1978 sales were just under $300 million. Earnings too had increased from $2.8 million in 1970 to $13.7 million in 1978. From 1970 to date (April 1979) the company had built three Nordstrom stores and four Place Two stores in Washington State and three Nordstrom stores and one Place Two in Oregon. It had also expanded and remodeled existing stores. And in addition to its growth in its traditional trading areas, Nordstrom had acquired a department store company in Alaska in 1975 and had opened its first store in California in 1978. In May 1979 the company planned to open its first store in Utah. Nordstrom also operated leased shoe departments, but it was gradually phasing out this business. By the end of 1978, Nordstrom maintained only eight leased shoe departments, all in Hawaii. About 90% of its business came from its 16 Nordstrom stores,

6% from its 10 Place Two Units, and the balance from its leased departments. **Exhibit 1** provides a five-year summary of financial results and other data.

All through their expansions, the Nordstroms had maintained their philosophy of offering a wide selection, exceptionally attractive shopping surroundings, good service, and competitive prices. At the same time, the organization offered its employees a decentralized management environment where initiative tended to be directly and strongly rewarded. If only one word could be used to describe the atmosphere within Nordstrom, it would have been "vitality." An extract from management's written statement of philosophy is shown in **Exhibit 2.**

The Nordstroms were confident that their philosophy and methods of operation could be transferred to their new locations. They recalled that a noted West Coast retailer had told them to "wait until you are a hundred million dollar company," implying they could not maintain their philosophy in a larger organization. Yet the Nordstroms noted with pride that they were at $300 million and still going strong.

Could they continue to use this philosophy successfully? What should they be alert for? What changes should they expect, and what effect would they have on Nordstrom's performance? To answer these questions, it was important to identify why Nordstrom was successful.

Associate Fellow Manu Parpia prepared this case under the supervision of Professor Walter J. Salmon, as the basis for class discussion rather than to illustrate either effective or ineffective handling of an administrative situation.

NORDSTROM'S BACKGROUND

In the late 1880s, a 16-year-old boy left Sweden for the United States, arriving in the Midwest with five dollars in his pocket and a determination to succeed. His name was John W. Nordstrom. The young immigrant worked in the mines, in the logging camps, and at manual labor in Michigan, Colorado, California, and Washington before heading north to the Alaskan gold rush in 1896. He returned to Seattle two years later with a $13,000 stake, ready to settle down.

Carl F. Wallin, a Seattle shoemaker he had met in Alaska, offered Nordstrom a partnership in a shoe store, and in 1901 the store opened in downtown Seattle. The first day it made one sale and took in only $12.50, but the two men worked hard and lived thriftily, and gradually the business grew. In 1929 Wallin sold his interest to Nordstrom, and in 1930 John W. sold the company to his sons, Elmer, Everett, and Lloyd. Although the three had worked for Nordstrom earlier, they were not working for him in 1930. As Jim Nordstrom tells it, "Grandpa rang up Everett, who was working here in Seattle, and asked him if he and his brother would like to take over the business. Once they took over the store, Grandpa handed over the keys and just walked away."

The three brothers had built the single shoe store into a 27-unit operation with sales of $12 million by 1963. At this stage the next generation, Bruce and John Nordstrom, as well as their brother-in-law Jack McMillan, were working for the company, and Jim Nordstrom was about to join on a full-time basis. Each of the young Nordstroms had worked from stock boys on up in the shoe stores. They knew the fashion shoe business intimately. However, it was clear that to employ the young Nordstroms gainfully, the company would have either to expand the shoe business to other geographic regions or diversify into another business within the state. An expansion of the shoe business would mean, for at least some of the young Nordstroms, a permanent move to another region—the idea of establishing stores elsewhere without the presence of a Nordstrom was, at that time, unthinkable. But all the family enjoyed the outdoor life in Washington. They were very comfortable in Seattle and really didn't want to move. So Nordstrom had to diversify out of shoes.

In 1963 Nordstrom purchased Best's Apparel in downtown Seattle and in Lloyd Center in Portland, Oregon. Best's had an established reputation in fashion apparel and was considered one of Seattle's leading fashion stores.

The Nordstroms reasoned that because they were familiar with shoes, a highly fashion-related business, fashion apparel would be relatively easy for them to retail successfully. It did not, however, turn out to be as easy as they had expected, and, in Bruce Nordstrom's words, "We took some tremendous markdowns." However, the family learned quickly, and profits soon recovered. In the late sixties, Nordstrom began to introduce men's clothing into some of its stores, and it found good customer acceptance. By 1971 there were seven Nordstrom-Best stores, with sales of nearly $80 million.

Nordstrom management again changed hands in 1970. Since 1963 the present generation of Nordstroms had been prominent in the management. Their fathers wanted to retire, and they faced three alternatives: sell to their sons as their father had done, sell out to an established company, or let their sons take over. They also wanted their estates to have an easily established market value. The first alternative was not feasible; it would have required more funds than the young Nordstroms had. The senior Nordstroms were inclined to sell out, but the younger Nordstroms prevailed on them to—as Bruce put it—"entrust their fortune to us." Once this decision was taken, the older Nordstroms quickly withdrew from day-to-day responsibilities—in fact, Elmer and Everett retired and Lloyd became chairman of the board. The company also went public, thus fulfilling the senior Nordstroms' desire for a market value to their estate. Thus, once again the transition between generations was accomplished smoothly, leaving the younger generation in full control.

The Nordstroms attributed their success in apparel to having applied the principles of the shoe business. Nordstrom shoe stores had offered an exceptionally wide selection of merchandise, attractive surroundings, a high level of service, and competitive prices. A broad selection of merchandise was a must for a successful, family shoe store. Operators had to ensure (within reason) that any customer who walked in could choose from a variety of appropriately styled shoes that would fit. As shoes were often branded merchandise, operators also had to ensure in catering to the mass market that they met competitors' prices. Finally, selling shoes is a service-intensive business. Store salespeople had to be willing to identify a customer's needs and tastes, locate appropriate shoes, and finally try them on the customer's feet.

The Nordstroms believed that they had effectively transferred these principles to apparel retailing. Nordstrom stores stocked a wide variety of depth of merchandise. Their inventory per square foot averaged almost twice that of comparable classifications in department stores. Nordstrom also had an established policy of meeting competitors on price. If a customer told a Nordstrom salesperson that he or she had seen the same item of apparel at a competitor's for $25 and the store was selling it for $26, the salesperson was authorized to sell the customer the merchandise for $25. After a suitable (but quick) check on the validity of the customer's claim, the entire stock would be marked down. Finally, Nordstrom management took pride in the fact that a customer would always find helpful and knowledgeable salespeople in their stores. Salespeople were encouraged to develop client lists and telephone their "regular" clients if new merchandise that would suit them had been delivered to the store. If merchandise to suit a customer's needs was not available, salespeople were encouraged to follow up with the buyers.

Even the Nordstrom policy of decentralized decision making was an offshoot of its shoe store origin. As a family shoe store operator, Nordstrom had believed that it had to allow the store manager flexibility in ordering, and particularly reordering, because Store A might have clientele with different tastes and different size needs than Store B. Initially the Nordstroms exercised control by having a "Nordstrom in every store," but soon this was not possible, so they had to delegate responsibilities to the store managers. As one Nordstrom put it, "Our objective is to transmit the entrepreneurial feeling to the store level—that's why we keep it decentralized." Another "transfer" from the shoe business was Nordstrom's policy of paying the majority of its salespeople commissions—common practice in shoe retailing.

The success of these transfers was apparent, and Nordstrom-Best continued to grow. In 1971 it substantially remodeled the headquarters store in downtown Seattle. Though it continued to expand, the company faced constraints, particularly in 1974. Concern about the environment resulted in a slowdown in building of new shopping centers and expansion of old ones. Money, too, became scarce. The Nordstroms found few opportunities to grow. They did note that many customers from smaller towns in the Northwest often asked why Nordstrom did not "come to their town." These towns could not support a full-fledged store, so Nordstrom examined what it could transfer, in its entirety, from its larger stores.

The examination culminated in the establishment of Place Two Stores. These were 15,000–20,000 sq. ft. stores to be located in towns with populations of 25,000–50,000. The stores stocked young men's and women's clothing. Ultimately they were placed under a separate general manager and given their own buying organization. The Nordstroms found this concept successful in locations with exceptionally high concentrations of young people, including college communities and locations in large standard metropolitan statistical areas where Nordstrom could not find a site for a full-scale store. Nonetheless, in the changed environment of the late 1970s, management felt that they should concentrate on the larger stores and that Place Two expansion should basically be limited to what the Place Two organization could itself finance.

In 1979 Nordstrom was recognized as Seattle's leading women's apparel store and a strong second choice in men's clothing. The store offered a wide variety of apparel, accessories, and, of course, shoes. It was Seattle's leading store for fashion shoes for both men and women. In fact, Nordstrom inevitably dominated the fashion shoe market once it was established in a location. The store did not offer major appliances, furniture, health and beauty aids, and the like, nor did it intend to.[1] In addition to its own charge cards, Nordstrom accepted Master Charge and VISA. Some idea of Nordstrom's market strengths can be gained from the results of a survey conducted by a marketing organization (**Exhibit 3**). The survey covered six counties around Seattle-Tacoma and consisted of 1,000 interviews over the telephone, lasting approximately 20 minutes each.

Nordstrom's advertising strategy emphasized image advertising. Although the company used newspaper advertising to help achieve its goal, it did not aim to dominate newspaper advertising in its merchandise categories. Nordstrom also used direct mail advertising, sending catalogs and brochures to its active accounts about five to six times a year. And the company always inserted a few pamphlets advertising merchandise in its monthly customer statements. Nordstrom spent 2.1% of sales on advertising in 1978 and 2.2% in 1977—these figures excluded suppliers' promotional allowances.

Nordstrom had gone public in 1971; its stock was traded in the over-the-counter market. In 1976 and

---

1 The Alaska division, which had been acquired in 1975, had sold a range of major appliances, but the Nordstroms had gradually phased out the appliances. The Alaska division stores still offered televisions and microwave ovens but did not sell refrigerators, cooking ranges, and so on. The company intended to move out of this category altogether.

in 1978, the company had tapped the equity market, issuing 900,000 shares of common stock on each occasion.[2] As of January 31, 1979, the company believed it was in a strong financial condition with a long-term debt to capital ratio of 29%.[3] The company also believed that it could sustain a growth rate of two to three stores a year with internally generated funds. As its store base increased, the company believed it could accelerate its growth rate if it desired. As of April 1979, the Nordstrom family owned 57% of the common stock.

THE ORGANIZATION

The Nordstroms did not have an organization chart. As one of them put it, "It would be too confusing." However, all the managers knew that the top management consisted of "the five": the three Nordstroms—referred to widely in the company as "Mr. Bruce," "Mr. John," and "Mr. Jim"; John A. (Jack) McMillan, related to the Nordstroms by marriage; and Robert E. Bender, a close family friend. Each was responsible for a merchandise group. (**Exhibit 4** gives their individual backgrounds and responsibilities.)

The company was divided into four regions: Washington, Oregon, Alaska, and California. There were three regional managers; the Washington division reported to "the five." Except in Washington State, all the store managers reported to the regional manager. There Ray Johnson, the downtown store manager, was considered more equal than the others (mostly because he was Nordstrom's personnel manager, too). However, if a store manager had any questions, he or she would ring up one of "the five," or, as Mr. Jim put it, "talk to any one of us who picks up the phone."

The regional managers were given a great deal of autonomy, including, in general, buying autonomy. There was, however, no hard and fast rule on the degree of buying autonomy delegated to the regions and, within each region, how much the buying was centralized.

Under each store manager were department managers and a personnel manager. Although department managers did report to the store managers, they also had to work with and work within guidelines given by their merchandise managers or buyers.

Nordstrom's buying organization was unusual if not unique in the industry. Four of "the five" had working for them general merchandise managers for each of the merchandise categories for which they were responsible. The organization within each category varied according to its needs. However, the guiding principle was to ensure the greatest extent of decentralization to allow initiative at the lower levels. The organization under John Nordstrom typified the variations that existed within the buying pyramid.

Mr. John was responsible for the men's clothing and the men's shoe divisions. In men's clothing, buying was completely centralized. One buyer bought for the whole company and was responsible for the inventory levels at each store. The company had tried to decentralize the buying function by delegating authority to regional buyers, but it had found that this did not work. The company kept experimenting, though, by giving buying authority to the regions. One of the possible reasons for this lack of success was that quality men's clothing still had a large handmade element. This meant that buyers had to be highly trained in the cuts and stitches used in the industry. Also, buyers had to decide on color and patterns on the basis of swatches of material, making buying a very specialized field. Possibly another reason was that very few vendors produced desirable merchandise, and thus vendor relations were more important than in most other merchandise lines.

The shoe department, however, was the very epitome of decentralization. There was a general merchandise manager and four regional merchandise managers (because the California division was still small, the regional manager held the title of buyer). Each store had a department manager with the authority to purchase shoes for the store. The department managers' open-to-buy (OTB) was controlled by the regional merchandise manager, whose OTB was, in turn, controlled by the general merchandise manager.

The delegation of buying authority ranged between these two extremes. For instance, in women's sportswear (under Mr. Jim) in Washington State there were two buyers—one for the downtown store and three additional stores in the state, the other for the Tacoma store and the other three stores. In the other divisions (regions), there was only one buyer each. The department managers in every store had an OTB controlled by the buyers. Whenever sportswear vendors visited a region, all department managers attended a showing of the merchandise and

---

2 Adjusted for stock splits.
3 (Long-term debt + capitalized leases) ÷ (Long-term debt + capitalized leases + equity).

made purchase decisions. If the department managers were unsure of their choices, the buyers would help. Only the buyers and the general merchandise managers would travel to out-of-town buying trips and make all the purchase decisions. The bulk of women's sportswear was purchased by the buyers.

Cosmetics, on the other hand, was more centralized. There were four regional merchandise managers, and the department managers at each store did not have the authority to reorder. **Exhibit 5** summarizes the organization and the delegation of responsibilities in the buying organization for key merchandise categories. This organization amplified the diversity in structure. One women's clothing buyer half-jokingly noted that her stiffest competition came from within—other women's departments in the company. Indeed, in recognition of this situation, the company enforced a rule that women's apparel buyers in different departments (as outlined in **Exhibit 5**), could not buy from the same vendor. One modification not noted in **Exhibit 5** was that the regional manager in Oregon felt he needed a merchandise manager for John McMillan's area, and he made one of the buyers into a regional merchandise manager, coordinating all the buyers of women's clothing in Oregon.

Despite its decentralized organization, Nordstrom's management believed that there was good coordination between buyers where necessary. For instance, there were two women's sportswear buyers for Washington State. If they were going to advertise and/or promote merchandise, they had to concur on which merchandise to advertise and which to mark down. Because it was in each one's best interest, the Nordstroms had found that they always reached an agreement. The difference was that if the buyers were on good terms, agreement was reached sooner; if they weren't it took longer. Thus, even though theoretically the buyers could advertise different merchandise in the same region or not carry advertised merchandise, this rarely happened.

When Nordstrom produced a catalog, all the buyers got together and agreed on which merchandise should go into it; they were then required to carry all the merchandise in the catalog.

KEY SUCCESS FACTORS

There appeared to be three key factors to Nordstrom's success in operating an unorthodox system—getting good people and paying them well, a good and up-to-date financial information flow, and its control system.

People

Nordstrom adhered strictly to a policy of promoting from within. Salespeople were hired at each store by the store manager or department manager. Except for certain stores in Washington (including the downtown store), Nordstrom's stores were not unionized. The company, except where restricted by union rules, met if it did not exceed hourly salaries paid by competition in the area of operation. Salaries within each of the four regions tended to be uniform. The company provided comprehensive health insurance coverage that included dental benefits. All employees who worked over 1,000 hours per year participated in the profit-sharing plan.

The amount paid under the profit-sharing plan depended on three factors—the total amount set aside by the board, length of service, and the employee's income during the year. Monies allocated to the employee were paid into a trust fund administered by a bank, which invested the funds in equities, bonds, and cash equivalents. Thus, an employee would share in any increase (or decrease) in the portfolio in proportion to the amount invested on the employee's behalf. The employee was entitled to the amount in the fund depending on his vesting percentage, which in turn was determined by duration of service. The vesting percentages ranged from 20% after 2 years' service to 100% after 10 years. The amount forfeited by employees who left the company before 10 years was reinvested in the portfolio. Management was proud of this plan, which had been instituted in 1951, and believed it to be an integral part of its philosophy of treating its employees well.

The hourly wages formed the base salary for most sales personnel, who were paid on a commission basis. The commissions varied by department, ranging from 5% to 10%; the median was 6¾%. A commission was not paid unless the amount due an individual exceeded the base salary on a semimonthly basis. Salespeople in departments such as women's accessories and children's apparel did not receive commissions because merchandise management (which included the concerned Nordstrom)[4] believed that, barring an unacceptably high percentage rate, these salespeople would not earn com-

---

4 Here Nordstrom means one of "the five" Nordstroms.

---

missions given their relatively low volume.

Generally, salespeople in the noncommission departments moved to commission departments as soon as there were openings. Nordstrom expected salespeople to reach their commission earning level fairly rapidly. The company maintained a daily record of sales per hour by individual. In fact, department managers, store managers, regional managers, and even the Nordstroms kept track of these data. If salespeople's performance lagged, the department manager would counsel them and point out their weaknesses. If they showed no improvement, then the department manager, after consultation with the store manager and the store personnel manager, would fire the employee. Employees' base wages were between $3.10 and $5.10 per hour. An employee with no previous retail selling experience earned the minimum. An employee with 700 hours of experience earned $3.50; 1,400 hours of experience earned $3.90, and everyone with over 2,100 hours of experience earned $5.10 per hour. Full-time salespeople on commission averaged annual earnings between $12,000 and $15,000.

Turnover at the salesperson level, although fairly high, was not considered a problem. The company estimated salesperson turnover at around 50–60%, most of which was accounted for by seasonal needs.[5] Turnover among permanent salespeople was estimated at around 15–20%, with family situations the primary reason for voluntary resignation. Termination by the company for poor performance or improper behavior accounted for up to 50% of the turnover of permanent employees.

Successful salespeople formed the basis of Nordstrom management. One had to achieve reasonable success as a salesperson to be promoted to department manager— the next step up the ladder. In keeping with the policy of hiring from within, all department managers had been salespeople. The store manager decided whom to promote after taking the advice of the department manager under whom the employee worked. In some instances, the store manager might also ask the advice of the department buyer. However, the decision was made by the store manager. Often an employee would approach the store manager or department manager and express a desire to become a manager.

Department managers received a salary plus a commission on any sales they made. They were also eligible for a bonus, which was generally 1% of the sales increase over the previous year. Department managers' salaries ranged between $14,000 and $40,000; only $6,000 to $8,000 constituted base salary. The average department manager was estimated to earn around $18,000, of which $7,000 was base, $9,500 earned commission, and $1,500 bonus for increased sales. Store managers called on department managers to cover for them when they were not in the store.

The department managers had a dotted line relationship with their merchandise managers or buyers. Although they reported to the store manager, in many instances they had buying authority and had to work closely with the buyers. Store managers were responsible for recommendations on the promotion of department managers, but they always consulted the regional merchandise managers or buyers first.

A department manager could be promoted in two ways: to a larger department or to the position of buyer. The buyer, depending on the degree of autonomy in the department, bought for the region or just bought imports and merchandise not available locally (some merchandise categories had only department managers and regional merchandise managers). Buyers earned between $15,000 and $50,000 per year including bonuses. They earned one bonus on the percentage increase in sales over the previous year and another on gross margin performance. However, the latter bonus was not awarded for all merchandise categories. For instance, none of the buyers under Mr. Jim received it because he did not believe that this was appropriate for his merchandise categories. The regional manager was responsible for all the buyers in the region and decided on salary increases and, where necessary, the performance criteria for bonuses. However, the regional manager never decided on buyer remuneration without consulting the general merchandise manager. In addition, the regional manager generally informally discussed the buyer's salary increase with the Nordstrom in charge of the merchandise category.

A buyer could be promoted to either merchandise manager or store manager. Most store managers earned between $30,000 and $60,000 per year, with one or two earning more, of which up to 30% could be bonus based. The bonuses were paid on three criteria:

1. Sales increase—averaged 1% of the sales increase over the previous year. In some cases a lump sum was paid for achievement of a dollar increase target.

5 Excludes movement due to promotion.

2. Expenses goals as a percent of sales.
3. Shortage target—a relatively new target.

"The five" felt free to add to or subtract from the bonus criteria as the need arose. For example, if they felt personnel turnover was a problem, they might offer a manager a $5,000 bonus if he or she could achieve a lower specified rate. Regional managers were evaluated for regional performance on basically the same criteria as store managers.

Merchandise managers (general and regional) were evaluated using basically the same criteria as buyers, except they were responsible for inventory turns and in some cases for advertising expenses (net of vendors' promotion allowances) as a percent of sales. Even the general merchandise managers under Mr. Jim were responsible for gross margin and inventory turns. Thus, although the buyers in departments under Mr. Jim were not paid a bonus on gross margin, they were under pressure from their merchandise managers to ensure that gross margins did not get out of line.

Information Flow

"The five" received the following information in the form of printouts:

1. Sales by department by store (daily basis). This printout had daily sales this year; last year; this year as a percent of last year; and month to date this year, last year, and this year as a percent of last year. In summary, the printout gave the combined data for the department for all stores and also provided a comparison with the company as a whole (**Exhibit 6** amplifies).
2. Gross margin and inventory by department by store (monthly): The printout provided this year's and last year's figures for the month. The department data included beginning-of-the-month inventory, end-of-the-month inventory, percent change of end-of-the-month inventory, this year/last year, amount on order, sales by month and year to date, percent change in sales over previous year, markdowns, employee discount shown as a percent of sales, stock-to-sales ratio, and inventory turns (see **Exhibit 7**). The departmental data were also totaled by the merchandise division.
3. Gross margin and inventory by department for the company (monthly): The printout listed the same data breakdown as that in Item 2 except for the company as a whole.
4. Sales per hour performance by employee (semimonthly): The printout gave employee name and number, store

and department, hours worked, gross sales, returns, net sales, and sales per hour (**Exhibit 8**).

To ensure that the printouts were up to date, the company had installed a point-of-sale system. Each time a salesperson made a sale, he or she input the following information:

1. Salesperson employee number
2. Department number
3. Classification number
4. Charge account number (if any)
5. Price

Also, Kimball tickets were used at the merchandise manager's request. The following additional information was keypunched on these tickets: vendor, style, month merchandise arrived, color code, and size. However, the printout used by senior management was not dependent on Kimball ticket information. For the future, management was experimenting with a point-of-sale system that would provide information by stockkeeping unit. Here, too, the company expected that these details would not be given to top management and indeed would be provided to the merchandise manager only if he or she requested.

Using the information on the printout, management could quickly pinpoint problem departments and keep track of their progress. However, "the five" rarely intervened directly in a problem. Rather, they waited to be contacted. Because the printouts were also sent to the respective merchandise managers, the "five knew" that the merchandise managers too must be aware of the problem. Store managers received similar printouts, giving them the sales breakdown by department within their stores as well as an overall sales comparison with other stores in their region and the company as a whole. This meant the store managers, too, would be aware of the data reaching corporate. Management reasoned that they would also react to correct a problem. The delegation of responsibilities ensured that top management managed through exception—and generally those exceptions were requests for help or clarification by regional managers, store managers, or merchandise managers.

"The five" met with their respective merchandise managers to work out planned sales and inventory figures for their department categories. They also met with store managers in the state on a monthly basis. Other meetings included regular visits to regions and stores.

However, although important, these meetings were only a part of the information flow. The Nordstroms maintained a very informal atmosphere and were readily accessible to their employees. As one of them noted, they had their own offices, but the offices had no doors—this symbolized the openness of the company.

Employees had access to department performance data. For instance, in the downtown store any employee could view the daily sales performance printout for all departments for all stores on microfiche. These data were also made available in other stores, but with a lag for delivery of the fiche. Allowing employees access to sales information helped them feel a part of the team. As one employee put it, "In the company I used to work for, buyers used to get upset but we never knew why they were upset. Here we know if sales aren't doing well and we can do our best to improve sales."

Sales per hour by employee were posted semimonthly by each department manager for the department. Some store managers made available semimonthly sales per employee figures to all employees. In all stores the top sales per hour performances were publicly commended through a letter sent to all employees. In addition to the individuals' names, their sales per hour were shown.

The Control System

The diversity of the Nordstrom organization, the significant variation in responsibilities and duties for the same level of personnel in different merchandise departments, and the extent of decentralization were in the casewriter's opinion quite unusual, if not unique, for an organization of Nordstrom's size. To keep it all functioning smoothly and to ensure that the key management people kept in touch with significant events, the company relied on some equally unique control mechanisms.

Both buyers and store managers were paid bonuses on their percent increase in sales over the previous year. Achievement of a target increase as a prerequisite for the bonus was not a part of the system, but goal setting was achieved through peer pressure. Every year a meeting attended by all regional buyers and store managers was held at each region's headquarters. The regional manager, or in Washington State the Nordstroms, would call on each manager (or buyer), in turn to present his or her sales target for the year. As the figures were called out, the regional manager wrote them beside the individual's name on a large chart. Next to the figures was a space on which the regional manager had written his target for each manager. That figure was kept covered during the initial part of the meeting. Then, amid great suspense, the regional manager tore off the slip of paper that covered his or her target for each manager. If the manager's sales target was under that of the regional manager, the assembly would boo the unfortunate manager. However, if the manager's target was above that of the regional manager, the group would break out in cheers. One manager described the scene as being like a classroom before an exam, or perhaps during an exam, with all the store managers and buyers doing feverish calculations as they heard their peers' targets and were tempted to revise their own. The meeting held in Washington at Nordstrom's headquarters was the largest because, in addition to the managers in Washington State, the regional managers attended. Any employee was welcome at the meetings in each region.

To arrive at their targets, store managers consulted with their department managers. This process was similar to that of the larger meeting. Each department manager read out the target figure for sales in his or her store. Then the store manager revealed his or her figure for each department manager, accompanied by boos or cheers. The store manager, however, did not use the department manager's targets as the only basis for his own goals, but made adjustments wherever he thought necessary. For instance, if the store manager considered a particular department manager's target unrealistic, he/she would scale it down in arriving at a total target for the store.

The buyer, too, would ask each store's department manager for a target. However, this was generally done over the telephone or in individual conversations. This was because a department manager did not report directly to the buyer or the merchandise manager. Once again, the merchandise manager or buyer would use the department manager's target as a guide and adjust it as he/she thought it necessary. Thus, if all the buying organization's targets were totaled, they would give a different figure from the sum of all the store managers' targets. This discrepancy was not important, however, because neither the buying organization nor the store managers or regional managers used these targets as their criteria for planning. The buyers or merchandise managers had already agreed or planned on certain open-to-buy figures for the next six months based on more conservative planned sales figures, and the store managers used different and, again, more conservative figures in their expense budgets.

In addition to the annual sales target meeting, there were monthly meetings in each region attended by buyers, all store managers, and all department managers. Various awards were distributed during these meetings. For instance, there was a customer service award in each region. Every store had to enter the contest for this award. Each store submitted an entry backed up by documentation. There were no set criteria for the entry; selection was left to the store manager. Among the documentation required were all complaint letters received by the store during that month. Two or three stores won prizes, which ranged from $300 to $1,500. These were collected by the store managers who in turn distributed them to outstanding customer service salespeople in their stores.

Also presented was the all-star award. For this each store manager brought a salesperson who had done something to deserve this award. The store managers then described their salespeople's activities to the meeting. A cash award of $100 was presented to the winning individual. A Nordstrom always attended these monthly meetings; they shared attendance responsibilities on a rotating basis.

Buyers, too, were eligible for awards. Each division held a Make Nordstrom Special contest every month, which awarded cash prizes of $200, $100, and $50. The judges looked for good value, unique merchandise, good sales, good promotion, or some combination of the above.

Another award, the Pace Setters Club, recognized outstanding selling performance. Sales targets required to qualify for membership were posted early in the year. To help employees pace themselves, store managers often broke down goals into sales per hour terms. Some department managers asked salespeople to set sales targets and then helped them keep track of their progress. It is important to note that all salespeople who were on commission had the same commission rate, whether or not they achieved targets and/or became a Pace Setter. Pace Setters were recognized through circulation of their names and a separate meeting over a meal with the Nordstroms.

The Nordstroms believed that these cash prizes, although not important in money terms, played an important role in keeping the organization vital and boosting employee morale.

NORDSTROM IN CALIFORNIA

To see how Nordstrom's philosophy worked when transplanted to a distant region where the Nordstrom name was not so well known, the casewriter visited Nordstrom's first (and only) store in California. The company had invested a great deal in the California store because it was their first move outside the Northwest. Management commented on the significance of their move in the 1979 annual report. "Never before had we devoted so much time and money in the planning of a new store because this was a totally new market area for us and it was vital that we get a strong start." The store was located in the South Coast Plaza Mall in Costa Mesa, in southern California. The casewriter interviewed Betsy Sanders, the regional manager for California.

Conversation with the Regional Manager

Sanders recalled with a twinkle in her eye her first interview with Nordstrom. She had returned to Seattle after a long spell in Europe, where she had obtained a degree in German in Munich and a graduate degree in Naples. In Seattle her husband had decided to return to college and Sanders had agreed to support them. However, because she could not get a teaching job she considered retailing. A friend gave her a letter of introduction to Mr. Bruce. She almost didn't go to the interview because she thought she wouldn't enjoy the work. Mr. Bruce almost didn't hire her because he thought she wouldn't be able to work in a department store given her, as he now recalls with a laugh, "dilettante" background. Until her husband completed his studies, Sanders was a salesperson and discovered that she enjoyed her work a great deal. When her husband got his degree, she decided to stay on at Nordstrom and make it a career. She recalled with pride that four years and two days after that decision she was a store manager. When she was offered her present position, her husband agreed to move to Southern California.

Sanders exuded confidence and vitality. It appeared to the casewriter that the employees found working for her a joy and a challenge. She knew most of her employees by name. Because there was only one store, Sanders also filled the role of store manager. She discussed various aspects of her job:

- On selection of personnel for the California store Sanders said, "It was my decision on who to have as the buyers for this region. In keeping with our policy of hiring from within, all the buyers have worked for Nordstrom in one of the other three regions. I sent out a bulletin to various people in the divisions and then reviewed the responses. My criteria were basically that the people had to be successful in the positions they were in at that time. They had to prove to me they had knowledge and competence to buy. They also had to be able to manage constructively. By that I mean having the ability to get people to work together and not exercise their authority by fear. I looked for people who had a history of developing people because we will need people here to meet our growing needs. I also looked for a strong record of being customer oriented. Obviously I did not know all the people before and depended on regional managers and store managers to give me their recommendations. I think it worked and worked pretty well because a manager is interested in promoting his or her people, and they [managers] know that if they recommend someone who does not measure up to requirements, the next time I would regard their recommendations with a certain amount of skepticism. Of course, if this were to happen often, I just wouldn't ring them up.

- "We have strictly adhered to the policy that all managers must have been salespeople at Nordstrom. We don't hire from outside for two major reasons. On the one hand, we know they (in-house people) can perform because we have their record. On the other hand, they understand the company and the atmosphere within it and have obviously grown comfortable with that atmosphere. Just the other day two buyers from _____ came here to discuss a job at Nordstrom. I told them that I was very interested but that they would have to work on the floor and prove themselves before they could become buyers at Nordstrom. They were rather shocked and horrified. I think that many buyers in other stores regard selling as an operation they don't want to have anything to do with. In this store particularly, we have our buyers on the floor selling."

- Expanding on the previous statement, Sanders noted that the buyers in the Costa Mesa store spent a great deal of time on the floor. She felt this was particularly useful because it helped them to get to know the California customers better. Another unusual feature of the California region was that buyers, too, earned a commission on sales they made. Although Sanders had to present the case to corporate to institute that policy, corporate's agreement reflected the extent of decentralization and therefore diversity in Nordstrom's organization.

- Another difference in California was that all salespeople could earn commissions; even the accessories and children's apparel salespeople earned commissions if their percent of sales exceeded their base salary. In instituting this change, Sanders reasoned as follows: She believed that noncommissioned status reflected the union's concern that salespeople in certain departments would never really earn their commission and therefore should not be expected to work on a commission basis. However, because the California store was not unionized, Sanders did not believe it necessary to follow Seattle's policy. She also noted that sometimes a salesperson sold 80 handbags and put in a creditable performance yet she would not feel rewarded when her paycheck came around unless she was allowed to earn a commission.

- Some of Sanders's other decisions also reflected the degree of freedom given to the regional manager. She determined the level of base pay for sales employees in California, and she decided to keep the union rates used in Seattle (these were much higher than those offered by the competition in California). When this became known to the competition, they expressed their unhappiness at Nordstrom's higher rates because most salespeople Nordstrom hired had substantial experience and therefore earned $5.10 an hour. Another change was Sanders's decision to advertise in magazines, such as *The New West* and *Los Angeles*. Nordstrom had always advertised in newspapers, but Sanders felt that this market required advertisement in magazines. Although corporate questioned her decision, it was her right, she noted, to control advertising within the region.

- On the budget process, Sanders commented that Nordstrom worked its budget forward and not backward. By this she meant that she decided on what raises to give various individuals, then worked out the total salaries to arrive at an expense figure for the year. She then looked at the sales target for the year and unless expenses as a percentage of sales were unacceptably high, that was the base she used for expenses. She noted that other stores often estimated their sales increase and then, using a target percentage, worked out the expense level in terms of dollars available for the year. After that they calculated the raises they could give to keep within that expense level. Sanders believed the difference in approach reflected Nordstrom's concept of treating and paying good people well.

- On goal setting, she recalled with obvious pleasure the scene at the previous February meeting (1978). She had set a goal of $15 million for the first nine months of operation. When she had given the figure, the Nordstroms had asked if she wished to revise it downward, because they felt it was very ambitious. Their own figure had been $10 million. (**Note:** for the first year or two of operations the manager of a new store earned a bonus based on a percentage of the amount by which the store exceeded the target.) Sanders noted, "Of course we achieved $15 million in sales last year. Incidentally, in our first full year of operation we achieved sales of $21 million. This year I set a target of $27 million, whereas their target was $25 million. Mine is the highest target for any branch store in the company."

- Sanders was asked to comment on the possible dichotomy between customer service and the measurement of employees by sales per hour and the fact that salespeople received a commission on sales. Might that make them less responsive to a customer's needs and more eager to make a sale? Sanders disagreed that a dichotomy existed because the employees' remuneration was dependent on satisfying customers and therefore they had to behave responsibly. She did agree that a few employees became too eager to generate sales and paid less attention to giving customers what they wanted. However, there were at least two means of controlling this. First, the department manager would notice the salespeople's behavior and counsel them to change their pattern; and second, customers would begin to avoid these salespeople and turn to others who were less pushy. Thus, such an aggressive stance was unlikely to pay off in the long run. Sanders added that it was the department manager's role to improve salespeople's customer service posture.

- Sanders noted with pride and perhaps a little regret that she had had 7 Pace Setters in the previous year. She had expected only 2 or 3 in the first year and therefore had promised them a breakfast in Seattle with the Nordstroms. Although she was pleasantly surprised that there were 7, she noted that next year she expected 30, and the division overhead would not support a visit to Seattle for breakfast.

Some miscellaneous reflections:

- Regional managers could influence the percentage markup for merchandise in their region. Sanders had decided to aim for the same markup as in Seattle, even though she believed that it was lower than that of competition in the area and that the merchandise might support a higher markup.
- Sanders noted that a big difference between Nordstrom and other stores in the shopping center was that once

you walked into the store and were looking at merchandise, someone would ask if you needed help. That sort of inquiry, she believed, was almost a thing of the past with other stores.

- The key to Nordstrom's success, Sanders thought, was the Nordstroms' ability to put people in key positions who knew and understood the company's philosophy and were comfortable in the environment. The role of every manager was to ensure that the atmosphere of vitality and drive was maintained. This was a particularly important goal for store managers because each of them set the tone for a whole unit.

- Sanders noted that her store got responses from 1,500 people to its ad for help in the local newspaper (see **Exhibit 9**). Three people (including herself) did the initial interviewing. Selected applicants were called for a second round of interviews by department managers, who made the final decisions.

- Nordstrom did not have a formal training program; it believed in on-the-job training. "We hire what we consider good people and let them get on with their job. Of course the managers are there to help and provide guidance, but we encourage people to take initiative and reward them for doing so."

Other Interviews

The casewriter then talked with some of the buyers. Although at the time they bought only for one store, in a few years their responsibility would grow during Nordstrom's California expansion.

Jeff Cox, buyer of women's shoes, had left the military and joined Nordstrom in 1970 as a salesperson for shoes. He noted that the shoe business was tough. Unlike a buyer of dresses, a shoe buyer had to commit to purchases almost eight months in advance of delivery. This commitment consisted of decisions on style, color, size, and quantities. Cox noted that to order a shoe of one style and color in every size available would result in 72 pairs.

At the moment Cox was the only California buyer for shoes, but once the Brea store opened, each store would have a department manager who would buy the style, color, and size that he or she wanted for the store.[6] Cox would guide them and control their open-to-buy. Cox would buy direct imports, which constituted approximately 5% of total sales.

---

6 Brea would be Nordstrom's second store in California, scheduled for opening in October 1979.

The shoe department took a weekly inventory by style and size. Stock time was paid for separately, and the hours used were not included in an individual's sales per hour computation. However, setting up displays and keeping them tidy was not paid for separately and had to be done on employees' time.[7] Cox agreed that some employees might avoid their share of this "maintenance" work in their desire to maintain their sales per hour. It was his job to see that the load was distributed equitably.

As a buyer, Cox would be evaluated and paid a bonus on (1) gross margin—the bonus on achievement of a gross margin above a certain percentage; and (2) sales increase—1% of the sales increase over the previous year. He also had to watch his expense ratio as a percent of sales, but this was an informal measure on which no bonus was paid. He noted that if the merchandise manager felt a particular department manager's expense ratio was too high, he or she might pay the department manager a lump sum bonus to reduce the percentage below a certain targeted figure.

Michelle Carrig, buyer for cosmetics, had been with Frederick & Nelson and had worked as a fine jewelry buyer. She believed she couldn't achieve growth in that company, and had joined Nordstrom five years before. She had been a buyer in Washington State before moving to California.

In discussing her operating procedures, she noted that she kept an open-to-buy line by vendor, for instance, Estée Lauder, and so on. Inventory by stockkeeping unit count was taken monthly. Every year case space and length were measured and sales per linear foot calculated for every store. If a supplier was not performing satisfactorily in terms of sales per linear foot, its space allocation tended to be reduced. Similarly, if a company did well, it might be granted more space.

Carrig noted that promotional allowances were a key factor in achieving profitability in her business. To encourage aggressive follow-up, the person who processed the invoices allowance was paid a bonus if able to keep promotional allowances above a certain percentage of sales. Such follow-up was necessary because some vendors did not pay promotional allowances unless prodded. Similarly, department managers, although not rewarded through a bonus on promotional allowances, were evaluated informally on this percentage. Thus, they were encouraged to report accurately all sales by vendor.

Department managers also supervised the monthly stocktaking.

Carrig noted that although a department manager did not have an open-to-buy for cosmetics, she as a buyer nevertheless expected good feedback from the department manager through notes and comments. She felt that department managers would be eager to provide good feedback because they would receive a bonus on sales and thus were anxious to ensure that the right products were available at their stores. She also noted that she often tailored needs to suit a department manager's taste. For instance, if a department manager felt more comfortable with pink and other lighter-colored lipsticks it was in Carrig's interest to ensure that she had a better variety of lighter shades.

Carrig herself was evaluated and received a bonus on sales increases, achievement of a gross margin target, and inventory turns. She also had to keep an eye on selling expenses as a percent of sales although she was not formally evaluated on that criterion.

E. N. Goodson, buyer of juniors' coats and dresses, had joined Nordstrom in 1974. There were only six or seven buyers for juniors in the company, and department managers did not have an open-to-buy. Goodson made frequent visits to New York along with the other buyers for U.S. purchases. All imports were bought by the general merchandise manager.

When asked about her buying philosophy, Goodson said she generally bought two to three months in advance. She believed this gave her a great deal of flexibility in timing. She and her merchandise manager mutually agreed every six months to an open-to-buy plan, but she could adjust this in line with sales by telephoning the merchandise manager. She had done this frequently as sales had outstripped all expectations in the first year of operation in California. Goodson characterized her method as buying a few items of each style, but purchasing a wide variety of styles. She compared this with other department stores, which bought a large quantity of items in a certain style. She believed her policy was more effective for juniors, because few juniors wished to wear the same thing as the person next door. If an item was hot Goodson did buy it in somewhat greater depth. Nonetheless, she believed it was worth being unable to reorder a hot item for the sake of providing a wide variety of fresh merchandise. She was

---

7 All departments required salespeople to do "maintenance" work on their own time. Exceptions were made for substantial changes and stocktaking.

not evaluated on gross margin and received a bonus on sales increases.

When asked to comment on working for Nordstrom, Goodson said that the main thing is "you are left to yourself. If you want help, you ask for it. If not, you are on your own. The sales goal is a personal commitment and not really a means of evaluation. It is really up to you what you make of it."

Salesperson Interviews

Person A. This employee was a fairly senior woman. She had worked for Bullock's for three and a half years before coming to Nordstrom. She expressed herself freely.

> The company (Nordstrom) has a very positive attitude. Everyone is working for the same excellent top management, and I have to say we are paid very well. I think the company takes pride in the people that work for them. For instance, it is a small thing, I know, but everyone was invited to the Christmas party, not just department managers and buyers.
>
> I also like the fact that the buyers are on the floor selling. I think the people like the feel of our store. I know there is a fine line between being helpful and being pushy, and we are very much aware of that.
>
> I keep a book of customers who shop regularly and who have expressed their tastes and desires to me. Whenever there is new merchandise which I feel will suit their needs, I call them up and tell them that it is available. I think there are very few other stores that offer this kind of service.
>
> In terms of rules, I feel there are only two hard and fast rules here: take good care of customers and do not steal. We are allowed a great deal of freedom within these constraints. Just the other day a lady came and bought a dress. Then she wanted a pair of shoes which would match the dress. I could go down and get those shoes for her, so that she had a complete shopping trip without having to move up and down. Besides, I knew that shoes matching her dress were available downstairs, something she may not have known.
>
> Comparing them (Nordstrom to Bullock's), without trying to run down Bullock's, I feel Bullock's almost felt that customer service was not important. They really weren't concerned about employees at the sales level. There was a great deal of emphasis on who was who and following the chain of command. There is no such constraint here, I feel.

Person B. I used to work in I. Magnin and May Company on a part-time basis. I really enjoy working for Nordstrom. They treat employees differently and treat them well. When I used to work for I. Magnin, I didn't know the people on the second floor. Here we get to meet everyone.

> Also, in both the (other) companies we didn't know any of the figures (financial data). Therefore, we didn't know why managers got upset at certain times. Here we get a good flow of information. We know how each line is doing and our opinions are often asked for. We are treated like people who can think, and I find this very encouraging.
>
> Our buyer involves us in almost everything. She tells us about new fashions that are coming out, what is in, what we should expect in the future, and what will be moving out. Every month we meet on Sundays for breakfast. In the May Company we never even met on a yearly basis.

Nordstrom managers and employees stressed the fact there was no one organization structure method for doing things. Individuals were given responsibility and left to work things out for themselves in a manner they thought suitable—as long as it was not outrageous. The employees and managers appreciated this freedom and enjoyed working in such an environment.

Conversation with Jim Nordstrom

To conclude his interviews, the casewriter spoke with Mr. Jim, the youngest of the Nordstroms:

> We (Nordstroms) have been moving away from the merchandising end of the business, even though we are the nominal merchandise managers. Yes, I guess I do feel a certain sense of loss, but I am really not that unhappy about it. After all, our business has improved since we have moved away, so maybe the people who have taken over are doing a better job than we were.
>
> A great deal of our time now is spent looking for opportunities to locate new stores. However, our number one responsibility is our employees. In fact, normally an organization is depicted as a pyramid with the top management controlling the whole chain of command going down. We look at it the other way. We believe we are at the bottom of the pyramid here to ensure that our employees have everything that they need in order to do a good job, and not that the employees are here for us to supervise.

What Mr. Jim said tied in closely with the feelings expressed by the other Nordstroms. Mr. Jim also confirmed the view held by the other Nordstroms that store managers were more important than buyers, though of course both were valued. The Nordstroms viewed buyers as providing a service to the store managers, whose role was to service the customers and conclude the sale.

The casewriter asked if "delegation of responsibility" was the correct expression to use in describing Nordstrom's philosophy. Mr. Jim felt that it was not the best, because "delegation" implied that the Nordstroms retained a certain degree of control, which by and large they didn't have. He said quite candidly:

> If I proclaim an edict, I don't know if it will get implemented. For instance, there have been signs in stores which said we don't take merchandise back unless accompanied by receipt. This is just not true. It is our policy to take back merchandise if the customer says they bought it from us, unless we had a valid reason to reject it. I have taken down the signs personally and told several people that this is not our policy. Yet time and again I see the signs. Well, that's life.

Mr. Jim also acknowledged that there was often a certain amount of conflict among buyers and sometimes among buyers and department managers, or others. But he felt very comfortable with the conflict. In fact, he said that "sometimes if there are no conflicts, particularly between buyers, I feel that they are being too kind to each other and not being critical. The conflict, as long as it is within reason, provides a means of competition."

Finally, Mr. Jim said that he didn't think the Nordstrom children would particularly enjoy working for the firm. "By the time they take over we'd be a large company and I think all the fun of growing and expanding will have gone."

CONCERNS FOR THE FUTURE

Summarizing Nordstrom's modus operandi, Mr. Bruce said:

> We offer the customer great variety and depth of merchandise displayed in an attractive environment, with high levels of customer service. All these elements cost money and add to expense, so we compensate that by generating volume. We have to move the merchandise off the floor. We depend on good salespeople to help us do it and we take markdowns whenever we see that merchandise isn't moving as expected.

Nordstrom's sales per square foot figures reflected the emphasis on turnover. Sales per square foot of total space (excluding leased departments operated in other stores) rose from $127 in 1973 to $163 in 1977 and approximately $180 in 1978. This compared with a rise from $58 to $74 per square foot for department stores between 1973 and 1977.[8] Between 1973 and 1978 Nordstrom had more than doubled its space. Total sales had almost tripled in the same period.

Could Nordstrom maintain its pace of growth without detracting from the factors that contributed to its success? Growth would inevitably involve two components: number of stores and geographic dispersion.

Nordstrom had hitherto been identified with the Northwest, and even as late as the mid-sixties the Nordstroms had resisted growth outside the region. The casewriter asked Mr. Bruce, "Why grow?" "We have always had a fairly competitive nature," he said, "and growth is a yardstick of success. We've always had, you might call it, an instinct to do the best we can. Besides, we owe it to our employees to do the best we can for them. By growing we offer them opportunities and succeed in attracting good people."

Profitable growth had been essential to Nordstrom. The company had been able to maintain a conservative balance sheet by tapping the equity markets twice in the last three years in addition to generating funds through retained earnings. The Southern California "experiment" had been a success, and the company planned to build four more Nordstrom stores there over the next two to three years. In addition it planned to open two stores in Oregon, one in Washington, and one in Utah and to expand some existing stores.

The board had set a long-term debt to capital ratio target of 35–40%. (Long-term debt included capitalized leases.) The company estimated that every 100,000 square foot required an investment in land, building, fixtures, and inventory of approximately $10 million in 1978–79 dollars. Of this total, approximately $2–$2.5

---

8 F.O.R. for department stores and specialty stores, published by the National Retail Merchants Association. Figures relate to sales per gross square foot. The 1973 figure is for department stores with sales over $50 million, 1977 for department stores with sales over $100 million.

million consisted of inventory (at cost).[9] Accounts receivable were estimated at 15%–18% of sales and working capital needs at 25%–30% of sales. Thus, to maintain a conservative balance sheet and still take advantage of all the opportunities available, it was likely that Nordstrom would have to tap the equity markets again. To do this at reasonable cost, it had to continue to be successful.

Was continued emphasis on a decentralized organization, with maximum possible freedom to individual managers, the correct approach? Or would the company run into problems as it expanded?

---

9 If payables were taken into account, investment in inventory was estimated at $1.5 million at cost.

Exhibit 1
Operating Statement and Balance Sheet (amounts in thousands)

Year Ended January 31,	1979	1978	1977	1976	1975
Operations Sales	$ 297,629	$ 249,690	$ 209,882	$ 179,229	$ 130,512
Cost of sales and related buying and occupancy costs	195,348	165,561	137,510	119,944	87,475
Selling, general and administrative expenses	72,626	59,099	50,597	43,115	31,510
Interest expense	3,343	2,893	2,641	2,845	2,116
Earnings before income taxes	26,312	22,137	19,134	13,325	9,411
Income taxes	12,645	10,440	9,288	6,375	4,343
Net earnings	13,667	11,697	9,846	6,950	5,068
Net earnings per average share of common stock	1.80	1.60	1.38	1.08	.79
Average shares outstanding	7,579,482	7,318,170	7,123,662	6,418,170	6,418,170
Dividends per share of common stock	.30	.24	.19	.15	.13
Net earnings as a percent of net sales	4.59%	4.68%	4.69%	3.88%	3.88%
Financial Position					
Accounts and notes receivable (net)	$ 56,599	$ 46,855	$ 36,927	$ 31,916	$ 22,269
Merchandise inventories	45,200	33,737	29,047	27,594	20,303
Property, buildings and equipment (net)	66,382	53,718	39,248	38,008	32,069
Total assets	180,950	138,896	116,688	98,864	77,579
Long-term debt	13,367	14,339	14,563	14,636	14,705
Working capital	70,589	51,699	49,256	32,268	28,623
Ratio of current assets to current liabilities	2.61	2.54	2.75	2.13	2.67
Shareholders' Equity					
Book value	$ 97,230	$ 67,618	$ 57,677	$ 39,620	$ 33,654
Per common share	11.83	9.24	7.88	6.17	5.25
Earnings per share of common stock as percentage of book value per share at beginning of year	19.5%	20.3%	20.5%	20.6%	17.2%
Stores and Facilities					
Company-operated stores	26	24	20	17	14
Total square footage	1,585,000	1,406,000	1,167,000	1,114,000	907,000

Exhibit 1, continued
Consolidated Balance Sheets (amounts in thousands)

| | January 31, | |
	1979	1978
Assets		
Current Assets:		
Cash	$ 80	$ 1,216
Short-term investments, at cost (approximates market)	11,025	2,029
Accounts and notes receivable—Customers (net of allowance for doubtful accounts of $1,600 in 1979 and $1,227 in 1978)	53,724	40,798
Licensors and others	2,875	6,057
Merchandise inventories	200	33,737
Prepaid expenses and other assets	1,664	1,341
Total Current Assets	114,568	85,178
Property, Buildings and Equipment	66,382	53,718
	$ 180,950	$ 138,896
Liabilities and Shareholders' Equity		
Current Liabilities:		
Accounts payable	$ 22,146	$ 15,732
Accrued salaries, wages and taxes	9,181	7,490
Accrued expenses	1,452	1,472
Accrued taxes on income—		
Currently payable	2,276	1,341
Deferred	7,413	5,685
Current portion of long-term liabilities	1,511	1,759
Total Current Liabilities	43,979	33,479
Long-Term Debt	13,367	14,339
Obligations under Capitalized Leases	26,374	23,460
Shareholders' Equity	97,230	67,618
	$ 180,950	$ 138,896

The accompanying financial review and the summary of significant accounting policies are an integral part of these statements. Merchandise inventories are stated at lower of cost (first in/first out basis) or market using the retail method.

Exhibit 1, continued
Financial Position (amounts in thousands)

| | Year Ended January 31, | |
	1979	1978
Working Capital Was Provided by:		
Net earnings	$ 13,667	$ 11,697
Charge not affecting working capital—provision for depreciation and amortization	6,285	4,721
Working capital provided by operations	19,952	16,418
Proceeds from long-term borrowings	—	1,060
Obligations under capitalized leases	4,929	10,228
Proceeds from sale of stock	18,216	—
Disposition of property and equipment	1,643	2,636
	44,740	30,342
Working Capital Was Used for:		
Additions to property, buildings and equipment	15,663	11,599
Property leased under capitalized leases	4,929	10,228
Cash dividends paid	2,268	1,756
Reduction of long-term debt	972	1,284
Reduction of obligations under capitalized leases	2,015	3,032
Fractional shares redeemed on share distribution	3	—
	25,850	27,899
Net Increase in Working Capital	$ 18,890	$ 2,443
Changes in Components of Working Capital:		
Cash	$ (1,136)	$ 939
Short-term investments	8,996	(8,628)
Accounts and notes receivable (net)	9,744	9,928
Merchandise inventories	11,463	4,690
Prepaid expenses and other assets	323	809
Accounts payable	(6,414)	(2,983)
Accrued salaries, wages and taxes	(1,691)	(1,468)
Accrued expenses	20	(301)
Accrued taxes on income	(2,663)	225
Current portion of long-term liabilities	248	(768)
Net Increase in Working Capital	$ 18,890	$ 2,443

The accompanying financial review and the summary of significant accounting policies are an integral part of these statements.

Exhibit 2
Extract from "The Nordstrom Philosophy"

Offering an in-depth selection of quality merchandise and exceptional customer service, Nordstrom has earned a reputation for value and reliability that is perhaps unsurpassed in the Northwest. So, too, has Nordstrom grown to become a fashion leader, gathering together in tasteful contemporary settings a spectacular array of the most sought-after fashions of the day.

Central to the Nordstrom philosophy is a strong belief in an *individualized* approach to fashion. Each Nordstrom store has been carefully tailored to reflect the lifestyles of customers in the surrounding area, showcasing a wide selection of shoes, apparel and accessories in a variety of distinctive "shops" that are rich in color, texture and design. Nordstrom buyers work closely with top-quality manufacturers from both here and abroad to obtain the best values, most unique items and widest selections for their customers; and salespeople, who keep notes on their personal customers' sizes and preferences, are quick to let their customers know when something that may be of interest arrives in the store. It is, in fact, this type of customer service which is perhaps the company's greatest strength—for Nordstrom is a place where friendliness, courtesy and a sincere desire to help are the rule rather than the exception.

An individualized approach is evident *within* the company, too—in a decentralized management structure where ideas and initiative are generated from the bottom up rather than filtered from top management down. Salespeople and department managers are encouraged to implement their own ideas; buyers, who have a great deal of autonomy, are encouraged to seek out and promote new fashion directions at all times. As a result of this distribution of responsibility, Nordstrom employees possess a remarkable amount of enthusiasm—both toward their company and their customers—and motivation is often quickly rewarded, as promotions are made almost exclusively from within.

There is little doubt that the Nordstrom philosophy of selection, value and service—begun in 1901 when John W. Nordstrom opened his first shoe store in Seattle—has contributed tremendously to the company's growth throughout the Northwest and Alaska. It is also the reason Nordstrom believes it can enter new market areas with confidence in the years to come.

Exhibit 3
Results of Marketing Organization Survey

WOMEN'S APPAREL

When you think of fashion, what store comes to mind first?

STORE	%
Nordstrom	29.3
Bon Marche	24.2
Frederick & Nelson	10.4
Penney's	7.8
Jay Jacobs	3.3
Lamonts	3.3
Sears	3.1
Kmart	2.7
I. Magnin	1.6

Description of Competition

1. Bon Marche	=	Full line, middle of the road, department store—division of Allied Stores
2. Frederick & Nelson	=	Full line, better department store with middle to higher price points—division of Marshall Field's
3. Jay Jacobs	=	Specialty store catering to apparel for young men and women, juniors oriented. Promotional stance. Line includes shoes.
4. Lamonts	=	Middle of the road department store, similar to Bon Marche but more "bread and butter" oriented.
5. I. Magnin	=	Women's specialty store, with upper-middle price points—division of Federated Department Stores.

Location of Last Purchase

Active Sportswear	%	Denim Jeans	%
Bon Marche	18.2	Bon Marche	19.9
Nordstrom	17.2	Nordstrom	10.5
JCPenney	11.7	JCPenney	9.1
Frederick & Nelson	6.5	Sears	5.8
Sears	6.2	Kmart	5.8
Lamonts	4.5	Jay Jacobs	5.8
Kmart	4.1	Bernies & Bottoms	4.0
Sportswest	4.1	Lamonts	3.3

Tops & Blouses	%	Pants	%
Bon Marche	24.0	Bon Marche	20.5
Nordstrom	14.4	JCPenney	14.2
JCPenney	11.8	Nordstrom	13.6
Frederick & Nelson	7.4	Lamonts	6.0
Lamonts	7.4	Sears	5.7
Kmart	6.0	Kmart	5.1
Sears	4.3	Frederick & Nelson	4.3
Lerner	1.9		

Dress	%	Coat/Jacket	%
Bon Marche	20.5	Nordstrom	18.5
Nordstrom	15.5	JCPenney	12.0
Frederick & Nelson	11.5	Bon Marche	11.7
JCPenney	8.7	Frederick & Nelson	9.7
Lamonts	6.2	Sears	6.2
Kmart	6.0	Kmart	4.5
Sears	4.7	Peoples	2.3
		Jay Jacobs	2.3

Lingerie/Foundations	%	Hosiery/Pantyhose	%
JCPenney	23.1	JCPenney	16.3
Bon Marche	21.9	Safeway	16.0
Nordstrom	11.8	Grocery Store	9.8
Sears	10.3	Bon Marche	8.3
Frederick & Nelson	9.0	Frederick & Nelson	6.0
Lamonts	6.3	Sears	5.3
Fred Meyer	3.3	Kmart	4.3
Kmart	2.8	Nordstrom	3.8
		Pay'n Save	3.8

Fashion Accessories	%	Shoes/Boots	%
Bon Marche	20.3	Nordstrom	34.1
Nordstrom	18.2	JCPenney	7.7
JCPenney	12.7	Bon Marche	7.7
Frederick & Nelson	6.5	Sears	5.0
Lamonts	4.8	Frederick & Nelson	4.8
Fred Meyer	3.8	Kinney Shoes	4.1
Kmart	3.8	Leed's	3.6
Sears	2.7	Kmart	2.6
		Lamonts	2.6

MEN'S CLOTHING

When you think of fashion, what store comes to mind first?

STORE	%
Bon Marche	21.7
Nordstrom	17.3
JCPenney	9.2
Sears	9.2
Frederick & Nelson	6.6
Klopfenstein's	4.0
Squire Shop	3.8
Lamonts	1.7
Finkelstein Goldberg & Feldman	1.4

Location of Last Purchase

Suits	%	Top Coat/Rainwear	%
JCPenney	13.6	Bon Marche	13.6
Bon Marche	13.3	Sears	10.0
Nordstrom	10.9	Frederick & Nelson	9.3
Frederick & Nelson	8.5	JCPenney	7.9
Sears	8.2	REI	7.1
Klopfenstein's	6.7	Nordstrom	6.4
		Klopfenstein's	5.0

Sport Coat		Shoes	
Bon Marche	16.4	Nordstrom	29.4
JCPenney	13.1	JCPenney	13.9
Nordstrom	11.3	Sears	10.5
Sears	6.9	Bon Marche	8.7
Klopfenstein's	5.8	Kinney Shoes	8.0
Frederick & Nelson	5.8	Florsheim	4.3
Fred Meyer	2.2	Thom McAn	3.4
		Fred Meyer	2.8
		Raff's	2.8

Dress Slacks	%
Bon Marche	20.7
JCPenney	13.8
Nordstrom	10.1
Sears	10.1
Frederick & Nelson	5.2
Squire Shop	3.7
Lamonts	3.2
People's	1.7
Fred Meyer	1.4

Exhibit 4
Brief Background Information on "The Five"

	Salaries[a]	Insurance benefits as reinvestments, profit sharing, and personal benefits
Bruce A. Nordstrom—Cochairman of the board of directors. Graduated from the University of Washington in 1955 with a degree in economics. Started as a shoe salesman; was then responsible for the shoe operation in Portland. Now merchandise manager for the Women's Shoe Division.	$135,500	$16,411
John N. Nordstrom—Cochairman of the board of directors. Graduated from the University of Washington in 1958 with a degree in accounting. Started as a shoe salesman and has since managed several departments and stores. Is now merchandise manager for Men's Clothing and Shoe Division.	$135,500	$15,859
James F. Nordstrom—Director and President. Graduated from the University of Washington in 1962 with a degree in business. Worked as a shoe salesman and manager of shoe stores. Is merchandise manager for Junior Apparel, Women's Sportswear, Children's Apparel, and Women's Shoe divisions.	$135,500	$17,133
John A. McMillan—Director and Executive Vice President. Graduated from the University of Washington in 1957 with a degree in economics. Started in Budget Shoe Department; now merchandise manager for the Women's Ready-to-Wear Division.	$135,500	$17,380
Robert E. Bender—Director and Senior Vice President. Graduated from the University of Washington in 1958 with a degree in marketing. Worked for JCPenney for six years. Was hired as manager of the Northgate store in 1964. Now merchandise manager for the Accessories and Cosmetics divisions.	$104,500	$10,430

a Proxy statement, April 20, 1979.

Exhibit 5
Buying Organization

Department	Member of "The Five" in Charge	Description of Department Organization
Juniors	Jim Nordstrom	A general merchandise manager, under Mr. Jim, two buyers in each region, one each for Sportswear and Ready-to-Wear (RTW). There were two department managers (Sports and RTW) in large stores and one department manager in smaller stores. The department managers had no buying authority.
Children's Clothing	Jim Nordstrom	A general merchandise manager, one buyer in each state (division), except in Washington, where the department was broken down into Infants, Boys, and Girls with a buyer for each. Only one department manager per store, and they did not have buying authority.
Cosmetics	Robert Bender	A general merchandise manager, a regional merchandise manager for every division except Washington, where there were two buyers, who divided the buying responsibility by vendor. One department manager per store, who did not have the authority to buy. However, they had to take a monthly inventory.
Shoes (men's) Shoes (women's)	John Nordstrom Bruce Nordstrom	The organization for each, though separate, was similar. Each had a general merchandise manager, and each region had a merchandise manager who controlled the open-to-buys of the department managers in each division. Thus, department managers had full authority to buy for their stores except for imports, which were bought by the merchandise manager in each region.
Men's Clothing	John Nordstrom	Entirely centralized; one buyer bought for the whole company.
Women's Accesories	Robert Bender	No general merchandise manager, but a buyer in each region. Department managers in each store had the responsibility and authority to reorder.
Women's Ready-to-Wear[a]	Jack McMillan	No general merchandise managers. However, women's clothing was broken down into several departments by name:
		1. Point of View: Three buyers in Washington State (broken down by coats, knits, and dresses). Two buyers in Oregon, and one each in California and Alaska.
		2. Town Square: (Modern Missy) Same structure as in Point of View except in California, where there were two buyers—one for Sportswear and one for RTW.
		3. Gallery: Two buyers in Washington (dresses and coats), two buyers in Oregon, one buyer each in Cal. & Alaska.
		4. Collectors: (Better Sportswear) One buyer in Washington (who also bought for Alaska), one buyer in Oregon, and one in California.
		5. Savvy One buyer for whole company (a new department).
Women's Sportswear	Jim Nordstrom	A general merchandise manager, then broken down as follows:
		1. Blouses: Five buyers—two in Washington (divided by region), and one each in other divisions.
		2. Active: Four buyers—one in California, one in Oregon, and two in Washington, the latter also buying for Alaska.
		3. Sportswear: Same structure as in Blouses.
		4. Equipment: (skis, etc.) One buyer in California, one in Washington, and one in Alaska.
		One dept. manager per store, who handled all four categories. Dept. managers in Washington had the authority to buy for their stores from local vendors.

a There was a department manager in each store for each department, however, they did not have buying authority.

Exhibit 6
Daily Sales by Department Store

REPORT NAME	DAILY DEPARTMENT/DIVISION COMPARATIVE NET SALES		REPORT NUMBER	SA000009
REPORT RUN DATE AND TIME	04/03/79	05:11:24	REPORT PAGE NUMBER	67
DATE AUDITED THROUGH	03/25/79			

DAILY COMPARATIVE DATES		MONTH TO DATE INCLUSIVE DATES		DATES EXCLUDED FROM MONTH TO DATE
THIS YEAR	04/02/79 MONDAY	THIS YEAR	04/01/79 THROUGH 04/02/79	THIS YEAR
LAST YEAR	04/03/78 MONDAY	LAST YEAR	04/02/78 THROUGH 04/03/78	LAST YEAR

| | | DAILY NET SALES | | | | MONTH TO DATE CUMULATIVE NET SALES | | | |
| | | | | DIFFERENCE | | | | DIFFERENCE | |
DEPT. NO.	DEPARTMENT DESCRIPTION	This Year	Last Year	Amount	% of Last Year	This Year	Last Year	Amount	% of Last Year
STORE 0001	DOWNTOWN SEATTLE								
0045 MENS	POLO SHOP								
0075 MENS	BRASS RAIL								
0076 MENS	CLOTHING								
0077 MENS	SPORTSWEAR								
0078 MENS	FURNISHINGS								
0080 MENS	LUGGAGE/WORK CLOTHES								
MENS WEAR	TOTAL								
0024 MENS	CASUAL SHOES								
0025 MENS	DRESS SHOES								
MENS SHOES	TOTAL								
MENS WEAR AND SHOES	TOTAL								
STORE 0001									
STORE 0002	NORTHGATE								
0045 MENS	POLO SHOP								
0075 MENS	BRASS RAIL								
0076 MENS	CLOTHING								
0077 MENS	SPORTSWEAR								
0078 MENS	FURNISHINGS								
0080 MENS	LUGGAGE/WORK CLOTHES								
MENS WEAR	TOTAL								

Exhibit 6, continued

REPORT NAME: DAILY DEPARTMENT/DIVISION COMPARATIVE NET SALES
REPORT RUN DATE AND TIME: 04/03/79 05:11:24
DATE AUDITED THROUGH: 03/25/79
REPORT NUMBER: SA000008
REPORT PAGE NUMBER: 88

DAILY COMPARATIVE DATES
THIS YEAR 04/02/79 MONDAY
LAST YEAR 04/03/78 MONDAY

MONTH TO DATE INCLUSIVE DATES
THIS YEAR 04/01/79 THROUGH 04/02/79
LAST YEAR 04/02/78 THROUGH 04/03/78

DATES EXCLUDED FROM MONTH TO DATE
THIS YEAR
LAST YEAR

| | | DAILY NET SALES | | | | MONTH TO DATE CUMULATIVE NET SALES | | | |
| | | | | DIFFERENCE | | | | DIFFERENCE | |
DEPT. NO.	DEPARTMENT DESCRIPTION	This Year	Last Year	Amount	% of Last Year	This Year	Last Year	Amount	% of Last Year
	MENS WEAR AND SHOES	TOTAL							
	PLACE TWO	TOTAL							
	DIVISION ALL GROUPS								
0045	MENS POLO SHOP								
0075	MENS BRASS RAIL								
0076	MENS CLOTHING								
0077	MENS SPORTSWEAR								
0078	MENS FURNISHINGS								
0080	MENS LUGGAGE/WORK CLOTHES								
	MENS WEAR	TOTAL							
0024	MENS CASUAL SHOES	TOTAL							
0025	MENS DRESS SHOES	TOTAL							
	MENS SHOES	TOTAL							
	MENS WEAR AND SHOES	TOTAL							
	DIVISION ALL GROUPS	TOTAL							

Exhibit 7
Monthly Gross Margin and Inventory by Department by Store

MERCHANDISE INVENTORY REPORT | REPORT AS OF: FEBRUARY 28, 1979 (TY/LY AMOUNTS IN HUNDREDS) | REPORT NUMBER: MIR00020 RUN DATE: 03/14/79 10.56.44 PAGE NO. 1

STORE	INVENTORY				M.T.D. NET SALES		Y.T.D. NET SALES								
01	BEG. MONTH	END OF PERIOD	% CHG END INV TY/LY	ON ORDER	AMOUNT	% CHANGE TY/LY	AMOUNT	% OF STORE TOTAL	% CHANGE TY/LY	YTD MD AS % OF SALES	YTD MD %	YTD EMPL DISC SHRINK %	GROSS MARGIN OF SALES	STOCK TO SALES RATIO	INVEN TURN
DEPT													01		
20															
26															
33															
36															
02															
09															
29															
32															
39															
43															
10															
46															
47															

Exhibit 8
Semimonthly Sales Performance by Employee

PAY PERIOD ENDING 03/31/79
LADIES SHOES

EMPLOYEE NUMBER	EMPLOYEE NAME	STORE /DEPT	SELLING HOURS WORKED	GROSS SALES	RETURNS	NET SALES	SALES PER HOUR
19554		5 0020	9.00	1,784.20	152.80	1,631.40	181.26
6410		5 0020	83.00	15,831.38	1,307.15	14,524.23	174.99
1622		6 0020	43.40	17,561.62	2,280.80	15,280.82	163.60
6703		1 0001	80.50	11,843.95	624.45	11,219.50	139.37
6518		5 0020	57.60	9,581.83	1,844.32	7,737.51	134.33
1194		21 0020	20.00	2,835.90	182.75	2,653.15	132.65
819		7 0020	35.50	5,035.33	340.45	4,694.88	132.25
22		1 0030	112.60	17,692.31	3,165.64	14,526.67	129.01
4830		21 0020	87.50	12,363.80	1,252.35	11,111.45	126.98
10036		1 0026	96.50	12,861.71	1,128.11	11,733.60	121.59
906		6 0020	35.00	4,352.18	237.60	4,114.58	117.55
4004		25 0020	26.80	3,731.37	654.10	3,077.27	114.82
808		7 0020	96.00	12,260.89	1,313.70	10,947.19	114.03
7408		21 0020	84.00	10,757.49	1,190.57	9,566.92	113.89
6779		1 0001	84.40	10,546.85	1,064.20	9,482.65	112.35
9578		1 0001	97.70	4,688.40	464.50	4,223.90	112.03
2152		1 0036	106.70	14,766.44	2,822.55	11,943.89	111.93
163		21 0020	47.00	5,539.95	282.55	5,257.40	111.85
2449		60 0026	85.70	10,334.93	1,113.56	9,321.37	108.76
8726		25 0020	30.10	3,734.97	473.10	3,261.87	108.36
813		1 0036	91.80	11,775.16	1,850.57	9,924.59	108.11
5666		5 0020	67.10	8,009.15	853.76	7,155.39	106.63
9240		9 0001	73.78	8,361.73	511.40	7,850.33	106.51
229		5 0020	68.00	7,229.72	569.06	6,660.66	105.72
7410		21 0020	48.50	5,738.05	613.20	5,124.85	105.66
2040		1 0026	92.00	11,925.83	2,259.97	9,665.56	105.05
6368		6 0020	39.60	4,179.73	24.95	4,154.78	104.91
2862		4 0020	82.00	9,549.13	976.61	8,592.52	104.78
1608		6 0020	80.80	9,422.11	969.72	8,452.39	104.60
10544		5 0020	68.20	8,103.12	977.15	7,125.97	104.48
4455		20 0020	4.33	513.00	62.00	451.00	104.15
47		4 0020	68.30	7,849.53	855.36	6,994.17	102.43
6204		5 0020	82.50	9,529.24	1,098.25	8,430.99	102.19
811		7 0020	112.10	12,489.02	994.25	11,414.77	101.82
9197		5 0020	83.50	9,549.31	1,095.89	8,453.42	101.23
6163		1 0036	54.50	6,624.78	1,131.15	5,493.63	100.80
627		8 0020	34.70	4,517.81	1,023.85	3,493.96	100.69
3250		1 0036	74.80	8,842.03	1,366.41	7,475.62	99.94
4661		21 0020	61.30	6,832.72	713.95	6,118.77	99.81
7493		25 0020	46.90	4,922.83	285.65	4,637.18	98.87
8352		73 0026	47.30	4,943.49	340.40	4,683.09	97.31
72		21 0020	35.30	3,991.51	560.10	3,431.41	97.20
1838		21 0020	80.80	8,131.67	321.45	7,810.22	96.66
97		1 0036	94.70	10,713.81	1,569.59	9,143.42	96.55
8338		8 0020	68.60	7,651.16	1,064.55	6,586.61	96.81
404		4 0020	71.10	8,065.25	1,254.15	6,811.10	95.79
108		21 0020	38.38	4,157.40	493.25	3,664.15	95.66
9868		9 0001	63.00	6,449.16	436.37	6,012.79	94.68

Exhibit 9
California Store Help Wanted Advertisement

WANTED:
people power

it's something nordstrom feels very strongly about. on
may 8 we will be opening our exciting new south coast
plaza store at costa mesa. .and we are now taking
applications in our search for the best possible people
to staff it.
we are looking for experienced people who want to
learn, grow and expand with us, people who genuinely
like people: who find satisfaction in helping others, in
going out of their way to be of service.
we need people with an eye for detail, a brain for
figures, a will to succeed, experienced people to handle
sales, to alter and wrap, to maintain the building
and keep it stocked. people to lead and people
to follow.
we need people to make things go smoothly. people
with ideas, all kinds of people with all kinds of potential
people power, it's the difference at nordstrom. help us
make it happen at south coast plaza.
APPLY IN PERSON ONLY.

10:00-5:00 daily beginning march 20.
use n.e. entrance to store, follow signs in stairways.

an equal opportunity employer

nordstrom

Case 14

NATIONAL EXPANSION AT NEIMAN-MARCUS

When a store had no branches, it was much easier to keep up with customer demand, service, and fashion trends. The boss was there and he could make personal observations of what was going on instead of having to read reports from his subordinates. He could even get behind the counter to wait on a customer, and in the course of doing so, learn more about his business than the computer printouts tell him today.

The elephantine growth of stores has forced the managements to devote a large portion of their working hours to budgeting and the solution of operational problems. Expansion programs demand attention for review with the architects and interior planners. The result is that there is an inadequate amount of time left over to devote to the two most important elements of a retail business: merchandise and customers. Under these conditions, it is inevitable that the quality of both goods and services will deteriorate sharply.

In the above words, from his book *Quest for the Best*, Stanley Marcus, retired chairman of Neiman-Marcus, reflected on some of the changes that had taken place during the years since he entered retailing.[1] Neiman-Marcus had changed dramatically since he had been involved in all aspects of the business. Following its acquisition by Carter Hawley Hale in 1969, Neiman-Marcus had embarked on an aggressive expansion program, growing from its original 4 Texas-based stores to the current 12 spread from coast to coast in April 1980.

Long-term plans called for opening new stores at an average of two per year. (See **Exhibit 1** for store expansion history and plans.) The challenge of managing Neiman-Marcus in this expansionary phase fell on Stanley Marcus's son, Richard, chairman and CEO, who viewed two issues as critical challenges.

There are two paramount issues facing any expanding retailer: development of human resources and development of sound logistical and information systems. In terms of human resources, we have to continue to improve our ability to attract and develop people. Although we are committed to an aggressive program of in-house development training, our buyer turnover shows we haven't mastered the problem.

Recently, there has been a concerted effort to improve information systems in all stores by September 1980. Our new POS (point-of-sale) system will be the spinal cord for future information systems. Although we have improved our information systems, there is still a long way to go. Especially, we must make sure that the information systems are user responsive. Also, we will have to focus our attention on organization structure—centralized versus decentralized buying environment.

Professor Robert G. Eccles prepared this case as the basis for class discussion rather than to illustrate either effective or ineffective handling of an administrative situation.

---

1 New York: Viking Press, 1979.

The key questions facing Marcus were

1. Could Neiman-Marcus maintain its "exclusive" image in light of its aggressive expansion and efforts to increase operating profits?
2. What was the potential for information systems at Neiman-Marcus? For what specifically should they be used?
3. How could the turnover of buyers be reduced? What should their responsibilities actually be?

EXPANSION ISSUES

Carter Hawley Hale's commitment to aggressive expansion for Neiman-Marcus also included pressure on Neiman-Marcus's profit margins: plans called for a doubling of net profit margins before taxes. Although the expansion raised many issues, the two most immediate concerns to Philip Miller, president, were upper-teens interest rates and improving profit margins:

> The single biggest factor affecting our plans is the cost of borrowed capital. We are in the most capital-intensive part of Neiman-Marcus's life. In the next 18 months we will have 4 more stores on top of the current 12. This will require new inventory and accounts receivable funding. We have to improve pretax profit margins while nurturing the new stores along. The margin for error, given the interest rates, is very small.

Its expansion program and emphasis on improving net profit margins influenced the company's merchandising strategy. In particular, the challenge was to maintain high standards of quality, exclusivity, and customer service while adapting to local markets. Some at Neiman-Marcus felt that other high-fashion specialty chains had changed their images through national expansion. They maintained that stores like Saks Fifth Avenue and Lord & Taylor had extended the price range of their goods and become more like traditional department stores. Wary of these precedents, Miller defined Neiman-Marcus's task simply: "Our single biggest challenge is preserving our image while creating new and distinctive stores." Others at Neiman-Marcus shared Miller's concern.

Two basic tendencies, both problematic, confronted buyers when making purchases for stores in different locations while trying to preserve the Neiman-Marcus image. First, a buyer could seek merchandise that would be acceptable to customers of all the stores, minimizing variation and risk. Ann Keenes, general merchandise manager, described this problem: "The more stores a buyer has, the greater the tendency to buy for the lowest common denominator. A low-risk buying strategy can lead to a dull inventory." Such buying could easily cause a decline in the image of Neiman-Marcus.

Image problems also surfaced when buyers attempted to obtain merchandise specifically for certain stores. Ed Bodde, Chicago store manager, described this aspect of the issue: "It is hard to keep quality and expand. The pressures of expansion can force a lowering of quality as one caters to local life-styles and weather conditions."

COMPANY BACKGROUND

History

The Neiman-Marcus organization had been established by Al Neiman, his wife, Carrie Marcus-Neiman, and her brother Herbert Marcus in Dallas in 1907.[2] At that time wealthy Dallas women had their clothing custom-made in Paris or New York; other women went to a local dressmaker. The three young entrepreneurs were convinced of the Dallas market's potential for fine-quality ready-to-wear women's apparel, even though their concept was a daring innovation. But they were quickly proven right. Neiman-Marcus grew with the Texas economy. Throughout the expansion, however, the Neiman-Marcus image as a specialty store was maintained. During this period Marcus bought out Neiman's share of the business and became president.

In 1950 Herbert Marcus died. Among his unfulfilled plans was a geographic expansion program. His son Stanley was subsequently elected president. Mr. Stanley (as he was called to distinguish him from his father) immediately began the expansion his father had wanted.

By the mid-1960s Neiman-Marcus had four stores in Texas and an international reputation. As with all expansions, financing had been an important issue, and Mr. Stanley had questioned whether internally generated funds would be sufficient to support an ambitious program. Furthermore, the sale of company stock to generate funds for expansion would reduce family control of the business. He had wondered how the problems of management succession typical of family businesses that are sold

---

2 Some information in this and the subsequent section was obtained from *Minding the Store* by Stanley Marcus (Boston: Little, Brown, 1974).

would be handled. As an outgrowth of these concerns, Marcus had concluded that the best course of action was to seek a merger.

The decision had not been easy to implement; he had insisted on finding a partner who would want Neiman-Marcus to continue its traditional high style. In 1969, after turning down several offers, Neiman-Marcus was sold to Carter Hawley Hale, which had promised Marcus the autonomy he sought. (See **Exhibit 2** for a list of other Carter Hawley Hale stores.) In the period 1968-1974, Carter Hawley Hale had exhibited a "hands-off" policy, demonstrating its faith in Neiman-Marcus's management.

In 1972, in a move designed to allow time to work with a new president, Stanley Marcus had become chairman of the board while Richard Marcus who was 35 years old and had moved through a number of positions in buying, merchandising management, and store management, had been elected president.

In 1974 Stanley Marcus had retired as chairman and chief executive officer, and Richard Hauser had been brought in from Bloomingdale's (a non-Carter Hawley Hale store) as chairman sharing the responsibilities of chief executive officer with Richard Marcus. This arrangement had lasted one year; Hauser had left to become president of the Broadway division of Carter Hawley Hale. He had been replaced by Angelo Arena from the Emporium division of Carter Hawley Hale, who had been given the titles of chairman and chief executive officer. Arena, in turn, had left in 1977 to become president of Marshall Field. One month before Arena had left, he and Richard Marcus hired Philip Miller, then the vice chairman of Lord & Taylor. Miller had been brought in as president in charge of merchandising and stores in an attempt to integrate the buying and selling functions better. After Arena's departure, Marcus and Miller had run the business as equals for 15 months. In January of 1979 Marcus had been appointed chief executive officer.

Philosophies and Policies

Herbert Marcus had defined Neiman-Marcus policies in the company's early years. The store was to concentrate on quality, exclusivity, value at all price levels, and customer satisfaction. Quality meant selling the finest and most fashionable merchandise in the world. He also wanted the store's selection to be unique. Stanley Marcus referred to this selection as "editing."

Exclusivity meant more than sole representation and reliance on manufacturers' workmanship. It included the improvements in style and fabrication that Neiman-Marcus buyers insisted on and paid extra for—such as silk linings and handmade buttonholes. The principle was always to improve the actual merchandise, never to reduce its quality in order to lower cost.

Herbert Marcus felt that price was a poor indication of value. Whether merchandise cost $5 or $50,000, he expected it to represent a true value to the customer. Thus, despite its image of catering only to affluence, the store actually carried much popular-priced merchandise. Stanley Marcus called it "a store with a split personality," selling fur coats or jewelry items at $50,000 but also doing a large business in $50 dresses. Neiman-Marcus sought to maximize the value of its moderately priced merchandise by having it be better selected, better made, better displayed, and better styled then similar articles in other stores.

Customer satisfaction was Herbert Marcus's final maxim. He believed that there was a right customer for every piece of merchandise and that a merchant should match customers and goods, even if this meant losing a sale, rather than selling an inappropriate product. Stanley Marcus quoted his father: "There is never a good sale for Neiman-Marcus unless it is a good buy for the customer." His comment became the Neiman-Marcus "Golden Rule."

COMPETITION

Neiman-Marcus competed against other high-fashion specialty chains (such as Saks Fifth Avenue, Lord & Taylor, and I. Magnin), similar regional and national narrow-line stores, and local specialty shops ("carriage shops" or "boutiques"). Narrow-line specialty stores emphasized a few merchandise lines that ranged from good to high quality. Carriage shops were typically owned by one or a few people and carried high-fashion goods in a limited number of product areas. Philip Lundell, senior vice president and director of stores, commented on recent changes in the competitive environment:

There has been a general strengthening of small boutiques. New people are going into this business and coming at us harder in high-end goods. In the moderate price ranges we face increased competition from the big chains. They have more volume and profits. They will want to remain in the moderate end. Thus, we want to compete in the end where the department stores consider it risky.

Exhibit 3 provides data illustrating the difference in price for merchandise lines carried by Neiman-Marcus and a typical department store. **Exhibit 4** outlines the national, local and specialty competition as well as major department stores in 10 cities in which Neiman-Marcus operated.

Although Neiman-Marcus customers also shopped at other specialty chains, department stores, and boutiques, Joel Rath, general merchandise manager, suggested the following approach to the customers:

> Ideally, a really bright merchant wants to find out what the customer wants rather than what the competition is offering. Our first responsibility should be to analyze what that customer wants to find.

Exhibit 5 outlines how widely customer characteristics varied by store.

ORGANIZATION STRUCTURE

Corporate

Neiman-Marcus employees referred to Neiman-Marcus corporate headquarters in Dallas as the "multi-organization," or simply "multi" because of its integration of multiple functions. The company operated by what is called a "two principal" structure, with a president, in charge of the merchandising functions (buying and selling) and sales promotion, reporting to a chairman, who also had responsibility for merchandise-support functions (finance, operations, personnel). (See **Exhibit 6** for a corporate organization chart.)

As chairman, Richard Marcus managed the president; the finance, operations, and personnel functions; and relationships with Carter Hawley Hale. Under Marcus, the finance function had been considerably strengthened. He had hired John Gailys, executive vice president-finance, in September 1978 from Dayton-Hudson (a department store chain with a good financial reputation). Gailys described his experiences at Neiman-Marcus:

> When I came here the financial function lacked credibility. Everything was manual; there was no point-of-sale computer system. Even sales checks were done manually.
>
> It used to be that Neiman-Marcus people didn't trust numbers. Now the numbers are taken as true and attention is focused on trying to understand the business reasons behind them.

The operations function had been created in 1976 to consolidate planning and management of security, merchandise handling, transportation, communications, alterations, purchasing (of nonresale items), packaging systems and engineering. Previously these functions had been either under the corporate controller or managed solely at the store level. But operations now managed all of them at headquarters directly, or with some strong dotted lines to the stores.

Operations was considering construction of a national merchandise handling center in Dallas, which would receive most of the incoming merchandise before shipment to the stores. (Currently, merchandise was shipped directly to all stores except those in the Dallas area.) This would improve shipping costs through full loads and control of merchandise receipts. The basic operations concept was more centralization of activities that were not directly customer related to permit economies of scale.

Philip Miller, president, saw coordination as critical for strategic reasons. He described his role:

> My major responsibilities are bridging the buying and selling functions and providing the company with a strategy and working structure that positions us in the marketplace vis-à-vis competitors and our required bottom line. I think this is important—to have one office make things happen at both ends. It has to happen at the principal level, not the EVP [executive vice president] level. It is an overview job that can't be done by an operating person. The director of stores is a full-time job at the operating level. My office can affect things by mandate if necessary. If I perceive a merchandise deficiency I can point this out by getting information from the stores to tell the buyers.

Reporting to the president were three senior general merchandise managers, the director of stores, the executive vice president for marketing, the director of mail order, and the directors for the furs and precious jewelry divisions. The directors responsible for furs and precious jewelry reported directly to the president because of their importance in sustaining the store's high-status reputation and their unique buying roles.

The director of stores was responsible for personnel and expense planning in the stores, refining plans for new stores, and overseeing total store performance. This position was a link between senior management and the stores. It was anticipated that by 1981 a director of merchandising strategy would be added. This person would report to the director of stores and would have a dotted-line relationship to the stores to prevent adding yet another layer of management between the stores and senior management.

Marketing was responsible for every aspect of Neiman-Marcus exposed directly to the customer except merchandise. It included advertising, public relations, the fashion office and fashion show presentations, displays, and marketing services.

Mail order was responsible for Neiman-Marcus's Christmas catalogue as well as the new **N.M. by Post**, which sent out catalogues of merchandise some of which was available through mail order only.

The Buying Organization

The buying organization was composed of three basic levels: general merchandise managers (GMMs), divisional merchandise managers (DMMs), and buyers. In most cases buyers had associate and/or assistant buyers reporting to them. (See **Exhibit 7** for the organizational chart of the buying organization.) General merchandise managers were responsible for setting the merchandising strategy for the future and increasing market share, taking advantage of and exploring new businesses, developing the businesses under them, and developing people.

Divisional merchandise managers had the same set of responsibilities for a narrower line of merchandise categories. They were most directly involved with the buyers. Buyers had the same responsibilities for an even narrower line of merchandise, with more emphasis on the buying task and less on developing people. Miller estimated that GMMs spent 30% of their time dealing with the market (vendors or resources), 50% with the DMMs and other "multi" functions such as operations and finance, and 20% working with the stores. For DMMs the time allocation was 40% with vendors; 35% with nonstore personnel such as GMMs, buyers, and operations people, and 25% with store personnel. For buyers the allocation was 60% with vendors (in person or by phone), 20% with the "multi" organization, and 20% with the stores.

The buying role was critical at Neiman-Marcus. It included defining the market needs (through information on trends, customer awareness, and store input), selecting the merchandise to fulfill these needs, and identifying the resources available both domestically and abroad to supply the merchandise. A key responsibility of buyers was to cultivate relationships with resources in the United States, Europe, the Far East, and even other areas, that provided unusual merchandise. These activities were important for giving Neiman-Marcus convincingly distinct merchandise relative to that of traditional department stores.

In selecting merchandise, buyers considered fashion quality, value, initial markups, and inventory levels; they did all initial ordering. Buyers planned sales and inventory levels for all merchandise items on a store-by-store basis. For fashion-sensitive, short-cycle items, timely reordering was essential to have the merchandise available for purchase before demand declined. Reordering of this merchandise required close contact with the resource and was the buyer's responsibility. For less fashion-sensitive, longer cycle merchandise, some reordering could be done by the stores.

Fashion, quality, and value were critical for Neiman-Marcus's reputation and customer satisfaction. Initial markups and inventory had significant impacts on profitability. When merchandise was not selling as expected, buyers took "markdowns." These were typically 33-40% of the initial retail price for first markdowns and, if still not sold, 50% of the initial retail price on second markdowns. The final gross margin, a key measure of buyer performance, was a result of planned gross margins less markdowns, shortage, employee discounts, and workroom costs.

Buyers made their purchases according to the two basic seasons of retailing: spring (February 1 to July 31) and fall (August 1 to January 31). Initial purchases for a season were made months in advance. They involved shopping many resources or vendors. In some cases merchandise was specially made according to the buyers' specifications. After an initial purchase buyers remained in constant contact with resources about deliveries and reorders. When it was not possible to reorder identical merchandise, substitutions had to be made. Buyers were also involved in selecting merchandise for special promotions.

Store Management

Responsibility for selling was located in the stores. Each store was under the direction of a vice president and store manager. Store volumes ranged from $12 million to nearly $42 million. (**Exhibit 8** reports sales volume and square foot data by store.) Norbert Stanislav, store manager of the Atlanta store described his job:

My responsibility is to produce a favorable P&L [profit and loss statement] while maintaining the image and the integrity of the store. There are four subgoals: (1) achieve sales goals, (2) achieve expense goals, (3) control shortages, and (4) maintain morale. The last is certainly not least in importance. We can't overlook management of our human resources. Every two weeks we have employee discussion groups. Employees are picked at random. People open up. They talk, I listen. It is difficult to be successful if you don't have good morale. There is a strict open door policy in this company.

Both Marcus and Miller considered the store managers an especially capable group and one of Neiman-Marcus's competitive advantages. Store managers were expected to communicate merchandise needs to buyers. Philip Lundell, senior vice president and director of stores, observed: "The more that our stores can influence the mix of merchandise the better."

Reporting to the store manager in a typical store were an assistant store manager merchandise (ASMM), an assistant store manager operations, a personnel manager, a security manager, a public relations manager, a credit manager, a food service manager, and a display manager. (See **Exhibit 9** for a typical store organizational chart.) The ASMM was responsible for the department managers, who managed the sales personnel. (The total number of employees at individual stores ranged from 235 to 692, with an average of 375. The number of department managers ranged from 12 to 21, with an average of 17. Nonselling managers ranged from 7 to 22, averaging 11. The range in sales personnel by store was from 104 to 322 and the average was 178.) The ASMMs were also responsible for coordinating with the buying side of the organization on displays, merchandise levels, and merchandise needs. The stores had final authority on displays, and buyers made the final determinations on merchandise selection and inventory levels. The assistant store manager for operations was responsible for receiving (and marking) merchandise, shipping, maintenance (and cleaning) services, and accounts. This position had a strong informal relationship with the director of operations.

Division of Responsibility: Buying and Store Management

At the top of the organization Philip Miller resolved issues between buying and selling, the merchants and the stores. However, a great deal of communication, conflict, and mutual problem solving occurred across the buying and selling organizations at lower levels. The GMMs communicated directly with the director of stores on buying, inventory levels, merchandising strategies, receipts of on-order merchandise, and markdowns. They also communicated directly with store managers on these issues. The DMMs communicated directly with store managers, ASMMs, and even department managers. Communication from the merchants to the stores was to give the latter the fashion and other merchandise information they needed to service their customers. Communication in the opposite direction was intended to give merchants information on merchandise needs and performance. Marilyn Kaplan, general merchandise manager, discussed the buyer-store interface:

> We continue to struggle with the relationship between buyers and merchandise people in the stores. We've tried everything from fashion directors, to videotapes, to visits, to training people in the stores. We experiment with all kinds of ideas to train store salespeople. I have concluded that the best thing I can do is travel more people. This costs money and takes time but I can get excitement going in merchandise ideas this way. I accomplish more by sending divisional merchandise managers than buyers.

The buyers themselves communicated directly with department managers, ASMMs, and sometimes store managers. Although store people had final authority on displays and buyers on merchandise, each influenced the other; sometimes there was conflict, although less in 1980 than in the past.

A store manager typically communicated with one or more DMMs 8 to 10 times per week. A buyer typically communicated with a store at some level five times per week. An ASMM communicated with three to four DMMs per day and in the course of a week spoke to all DMMs. Department managers talked to the buyers responsible for the lines under their direction (four to ten buyers with an average of about six) around three times per week. Department managers could spend 25% of their time communicating with the merchants in Dallas. Both the merchants and the stores initiated these conversations.

Philip Miller commented on the buyer-seller interface:

> The sellers should have input to buyers on an "up-front" basis. Dialogue between buyer and seller is tough to get. We don't provide for it. We also don't have a system for assessing lost opportunities from what we did *not* buy. We measure only results of what we did buy.

Currently we don't have good input from the stores on what they think sales opportunities are by division. We need a better interface at the buyer-department manager level.

Norbert Stanislav, store manager in Atlanta, emphasized the importance of effective communication between the buyer and the stores:

Communication is a great problem—one of the greatest problems the company has in general. When you have 12 stores and are buying for all of them, unless there is a communication link you don't know where to take your business.

Another important issue was the extent to which buying responsibility should be given to the stores. On decentralized buying Marcus commented:

We have permitted delegation of some buying and reordering responsibility to the stores and we continue to talk about decentralization of buying, but we haven't really sat down and looked at this. I don't have an intuitive feel yet on if and when to try decentralized buying. We don't yet fully understand the technological opportunities of information processing. If I had to hazard a guess I would say that at between 20 and 22 stores we probably will have to come to some decision points on the buying decision.

Miller also viewed technology as an important factor in the decision to decentralize buying:

Merchandise information systems are the key to giving stores some buying autonomy (such as reordering). Stores might even be permitted to do original buying on a test basis. We may let them continue that vendor relationship if the buy is peculiar to that region. If all stores carry it we may centralize it.

Ed Bodde, Chicago store manager, felt regional differences in taste weren't sufficiently important to justify decentralized buying:

It would make sense to have some buyers in Chicago for cold weather goods, but it is better to have a broader perspective. Except for reordering capability, I don't think centralized buying is wrong.

He went on to consider the specific issue of reorders:

Stores could have more reorder responsibility. It depends on the area. You also have vendor reactions to consider. Maybe they won't want to take separate orders from various stores. This would also affect markdown responsibility. Right now we are reordering some basics. The buyer makes the initial selection in terms of fabric and color. Based on historical data we can set up inventory levels and reorder when necessary. Decentralized reordering is a good way to go. Decentralized initial selection would be a mistake. Neiman-Marcus would become 12 companies.

Other reasons given for centralized buying were the necessity of having knowledge of worldwide markets, greater bargaining power with vendors, and the fact that most merchandise was the same in all stores, the variations being in the mix of this merchandise. Stores varied in the relative importance of all the different merchandise lines. (**Exhibit 10** gives percentage figures on retail sales by product line and store.)

Planning

Planning at Neiman-Marcus focused on (1) merchandise planning—sales, markups, inventories, markdowns, employee discounts, cash discounts, workroom costs, shortage and miscellaneous expenses, and (2) financial or expense planning for the stores and multiorganization. This resulted in two plans: a merchandise plan and a financial plan. Different sales goals were established for each. Sales goals for the financial or expense plan were established by Marcus and Miller on a total company basis and then allocated on a store-by-store basis with the input of Philip Lundell. Against this sales plan, target expenses were budgeted for the individual stores and multifunctions. The merchandise plan was based on sales targets 3%–4% higher than those in the financial plan. Again, this aggregate number was determined by Marcus and Miller and communicated to the GMMs. They, in turn, worked with the DMMs, who worked with the buyers, to distribute these sales projections across the various merchandise lines and individual stores.

For all practical purposes people worked towards the merchandise plan numbers; in other words, the sales goals of department managers were derived from the merchandise plan. The company's objective was to achieve the incremental sales difference between the merchandise and financial plan targets at a "conversion ratio" of expenses less than the percentage of expenses to sales in the financial plan. The current conversion ratio or target for variable expenses on incremental sales was 15%.[3] Philip Miller explained the philosophy behind this planning system as follows:

The merchandise plan is our goal numbers; it is an optimistic plan. If we achieve this we should beat the pretax margin targets by a lot (if we achieve our conversion ratio). By planning our expenses at a lower number we have some slippage. If we used financial plan sales targets only, it would inhibit our expansion of the business because buying would be done on a more conservative basis. If we planned to only the optimistic numbers, it would be hard to cut back expenses.

Buyers were responsible for merchandise planning, which was done on a six-month seasonal basis and then updated monthly with three-month rolling projections. Targets were established for sales, end-of-month inventories, retail receipts, markdowns, employee discounts, shortage, and markups. Markups typically ranged between 40% and 55%.

Currently, the initiative in merchandise planning rested with the buyers. They varied in terms of how much input they sought from the stores. Time constraints limited the degree to which the stores could be involved in merchandise planning. However, Miller stated:

Within five years we hope to have completely installed an interactive computerized approach to planning where the stores and buyers are all involved in the process. Right now we don't have good input from the stores on what they think the sales opportunities are by division.

MANAGEMENT INFORMATION SYSTEMS

Marcus discussed part of his philosophy of management information systems:

One of the great curses of management information systems is the tendency to circulate a lot of information to secondary users. The question is, who is the primary user and who else *really* needs to get this information? There is a difference between getting information for revelation and getting information for decision making. What do people need to know to run their business better? Another risk is that when secondary users get information they start calling the primary users to ask them what they are going to do. This simply interferes with their ability to do it.

Miller agreed:

Our information needs are essentially very basic. We need to know on-order and on-hand versus selling trends, whether by line, by vendor, by style, by color, or by size.

Director of Merchandise Information Systems Linda Powers, a recent Harvard Business School graduate, argued for better coordination between systems: "The problem with retailing is that there are lots of systems but they don't all connect."

The major system used to generate information on merchandise owned and sold was the Fashion Merchandise Management (FAMM) system. This included about two-thirds of the departments, most of which were apparel related. An internal company document on the FAMM system stated:

Fashion Merchandise Management (FAMM) is a system that produces reports about merchandise that's currently in stock at all Neiman-Marcus stores. Since Neiman-Marcus buyers base most of their merchandising decisions on FAMM information the accuracy of these reports is of special importance. Both the department manager and the selling staff have a major responsibility in maintaining the accuracy of FAMM reports.

The three-part ticket that is attached to all new merchandise that arrives in your department is the heart of the FAMM system. Knowledge of what has been received, sold, and remains in stock is dependent upon these three parts—the receipt stub, the credit stub and the sales stub. The department number, class number, style number, vendor number and, of course, price are identified on all three parts of the ticket.

Powers observed two problems with the system: it provided information "after the fact," and it was inaccurate. Part of the difficulty was in the use of ticket stubs as the basic information input. Information on the ticket would often be incorrect, garments would arrive without tickets, customers would return garments without tickets, and problems would arise with intra- and interstore transfers of merchandise. When an item was

---

3 For example, the sales volume on the financial plan would be $10 million, with expenses of $3 million or 30%. The merchandise sales plan would be $10.4 million, with additional expenses of $60,000 (15% of $400,000), for total expenses of $3,060,000.

sold, the sales stub was removed and placed on a spindle. These were collected daily and sent by overnight delivery to Dallas.

Recently, a number of efforts had been made to improve these systems. Don Robson, senior vice president and controller, who had joined Neiman-Marcus in November 1978, discussed some of these:

When I came here I saw that a lot of work was needed in systems development. People needed information to do their jobs properly. We immediately began to put things in place by working on the "defense," the traditional control functions in a retail environment: accounting, subsidiary systems, sales processing, accounts receivable, payroll, gross margin, et cetera.

The emphasis of this effort was on producing timely reports for users. Automated billing was introduced for the over 1 million customers responsible for 40,000 transactions per day.

Two major computer system development efforts were point of sale (POS) and purchase order entry (POE). Marcus referred to POS as the "spinal cord" of future information systems. He expected installation in all stores by late 1980. Robson commented:

The POS register we are installing is a fairly smart, programmable terminal. The total system will contain 1,400 terminals. Richard [Marcus] wants to start using SKUs [stockkeeping units] as input to POS so that we can use the system to generate our merchandise reports.[4]

Management expected that many of the FAMM system's shortcomings would be eliminated when the POS system was installed in all stores and used for generating merchandise information. As of February 1980, the POS system was only producing an associate sales report and a department sales report. The associate sales report was a daily summary showing dollar sales, numbers of transactions, dollar value and number of returns, and other information for each salesperson. The department sales report, run at scheduled times during the day to gauge peak traffic in the stores, showed for each department, sales, returns, and net sales (sales less returns) in dollars and units. With more timely and accurate POS figures

from all stores, more information could be generated than through the tickets of FAMM.

Miller noted other opportunities of technology for satisfying information requirements:

We need more input from the selling organization into the buy. We also need specific information broken out by store location. Right now we have stock and sales data by store and are in the process of developing on-order by location data. This will enable us to generate open-to-buy by location—then we would really have something.[5]

We also need a system for providing the buyer with instantaneous information. This is critical to this business—to know what is selling and what is not. We are installing on-line terminals to have instantaneous information on inventory by location for precious jewelry and furs. In general, we need to get away from all this hard copy and make more *use* of this type of technology.

PERSONNEL

Philip Miller placed great emphasis on systems development as a means of improving employee performance. In his words: "I'd rather have a few good people with a lot of support systems than a lot of average people."

Recruitment and Training

Most people entering the Neiman-Marcus organization with aspirations toward managerial positions were college graduates, although a degree was not a requirement. (See **Exhibit 11** for data on the age and experience of personnel.) Labeled executive trainees, these individuals immediately entered a 15-week-long executive development program that included buyer training (merchandise math, FAMM, budgets, gross margins, foreign buying, theory, and so on) and management training (motivation, time management, productivity, systems, merchandising the floor, selection and review of staff, and so on). This program involved both classroom instruction and on-the-job rotations in the buying offices, stores, mail order, market research, finance, and personnel. Upon completion of the program the trainee became an assistant buyer or department manager for one to two

---

4 Stockkeeping unit refers to a unique item of merchandise, such as a woman's blouse of a certain style, size, and color. The SKU numbers identified a particular item of merchandise.

5 Open-to-buy is dollars in a buyer's budget not yet committed for goods.

years. (**Exhibit 12** provides data on retention of executive trainees.) Sales associates were recruited from the communities in which stores were located and would typically either work for a year or two before leaving or become sales professionals for a longer term.

Recently there had been a campaign to recruit MBAs from well-known business schools. Management hoped that these individuals' education could be combined with the training and development provided by Neiman-Marcus to produce professional managers who were sensitive to the requirements of high-fashion retailing. It was acknowledged that finding people who could develop both sets of skills was difficult.

Within the past year a great deal of emphasis had been placed on developing training programs. In addition to the executive trainee program, there were programs for leadership, communications, selling, POS conversion, merchandising, secretaries' skills, department management, merchandise coordination, buyer education, POE conversion, and executive secretaries' skills. Programs existed for nearly all levels in the buying and selling organizations. With the exception of the executive trainee program, most of these had been developed since March 1979 under the direction of Bruce Matza, vice president of training and personnel development.

Performance Appraisal

Formal performance appraisals were conducted throughout the organization on an annual basis. All GMMs, DMMs, and buyers were evaluated on the basis of sales, gross margin, people skills, and their own promotability. Salary increases were tied to these reviews.

Larry Elkin, senior vice president and director of personnel, commented on salaries and performance reviews:

Salaries are tied to performance reviews. We are heading towards extending incentive pay in some form. It is an effective but difficult method to use. There are annual guidelines on salary increases for a given performance rating. A formal interview process is used for performance appraisals.

Store managers were evaluated on the basis of sales and expenses by the director of stores with input from the directors of operations, personnel, and finance. (**Exhibit 13** provides 1980 data on salary ranges by job level.) There was some debate over whether store managers should also be held partially responsible for gross margins. Speaking to the store managers at their April 1980 meeting, Marcus addressed this issue:

Two thoughts. First, store management has to adopt the attitude that it can affect gross margin in ways such as turnover of goods and multiple selling. Second, store management can influence markup by creating an awareness of items that carry better than average margins.

Miller disagreed:

The gross margin should not be the seller's primary concern. This is a hot issue right now. But it doesn't work for fashion buying and selling. The seller should only have a voice in the selling price of an item vis-à-vis the competition.

In this case store personnel would have input on the selling price only if the Neiman-Marcus price was higher than that of local competition for an identical item.

The ASMMs and the department managers were evaluated primarily on the basis of sales and people skills. Sales personnel were paid on a straight commission basis. Assistant store managers for operations were evaluated primarily on the basis of expense control, cost reduction programs, and people skills.

Career Paths

Debate also existed on the types of career paths available. For years the traditional promotional sequence had been assistant buyer to store department manager (or vice versa) to buyer, to ASMM, at which point an individual would choose a career either in selling by becoming a store manager or in buying by becoming a DMM.

Miller commented on the limitations of such career pathing:

I believe less now in the cross-fertilization of buying and selling. Some years ago the industry was heavily emphasizing career paths and job titles and is still doing it. One reason for buyer turnover is we've career-pathed ourselves so that once a person was made a buyer, he or she already had expectations for the next step. In adding stores we create a need for new assistant managers, especially in merchandising. Lots of the buyer turnover is caused by internal needs for store expansion. Maybe we should have parallel career paths rather than a diagonal one between buying and selling. The diagonal one would only be for people you want to turn into general managers.

Elkin, however, felt that diagonal career paths continued to make good sense:

The career path is still basically the same—a diagonal. We don't send as many people out of Dallas as we used to. A new piece is trying to think through career paths for store people that do not include merchandising. And the newly activated financial division needs career paths.

I feel we should not establish a career path in buying only. Buyers need to know what the stores are all about. By and large there is a consensus on diagonal career ladders. The DMMs and GMMs have been supportive in sending people to the stores.

Buyer Turnover

With expansion had come increasing numbers of buyers. In 1977 there had been 63 buyers, in 1980, 72. Miller commented on some of the buying problems resulting from expansion:

We are trying desperately to hold down the number of buyers. As we get bigger geographically, we have to have communication lines that are as streamlined and efficient as possible.

With expansion there is a tendency for responsibility to go to the top of the organization. Twenty years ago the buyer was a "big deal" position—it had a lot of autonomy. Today the buyer is more often regarded as a least common denominator. Many of our resources only want to do business at the DMM level or higher.

Problems resulting from the increased number of buyers were exacerbated by buyer turnover, which itself contributed to the lack of experience in the buying group and the diminution in the buyer's role. (See **Exhibit 14** for executive personnel flow data and **Exhibit 15** for thoughts from Stanley Marcus on buyers and their promotions as well as other related issues.)

Richard Marcus expressed concern over turnover:

One challenge of expansion is, how do you ensure the same quality of buying if growth has accelerated turnover? In my mind turnover is the curse of retailing. It is a real problem since buyers need to have high expertise. We've had a great demand for people as we've expanded.

With more buyers and stores, it had become less possible to travel to the stores (because of expense and time). Buyers knew individual markets less and lost some of the influence of their expert knowledge. Ann Keenes, GMM, commented on the difference between buyers in carriage shops and buyers geographically remote from their sales organizations:

In the carriage shop the buyer can be on the floor to know what's selling. She can know by lunch and move quickly. At Neiman-Marcus buyers have to rely on computer reports. They can't react as quickly, so to be responsive we have to narrow the product lines. One of the disadvantages of narrower departments is duplication of fabrics and looks. To avoid this we need careful merchandise direction.

Marilyn Kaplan GMM commented on the industrywide problem of lack of professionalism in the buying function:

There is a tremendous lack of professional buyers. This is an industry problem. Sometimes we as senior managers demean buyers—but don't mean to. When I started in buying you could earn $40,000 to $50,000 per year and be promoted up the buying ladder. We are only beginning to do this here.

Jim Guerra, DMM for men's clothing, confirmed Keenes's and Kaplan's thoughts:

The area I was buying in when I joined the store 19 years ago as a buyer is now being bought by five buyers. In the last six months the feeling has been that emphasis on growth has caused buying to be looked at as a way station. The responsibilities of the buyer kept being divided. The amount of control I used to have was a lot more than buyers have today. It's gotten to the point where the buyer is just performing mundane tasks. But to build our business on a national scale, buying is the backbone. The kind of retailing we're in—national high fashion retail—is in its first generation.

Guerra also observed:

Buyers used to think they had to keep moving. Ambitious buyers would get disappointed. A lot of responsibility fell on the shoulders of DMMs. We got to the point of having 40% of the buyers new in their positions. When there is a change in buyers there is a loss of momentum. The interpretation of the market by a new buyer will be different.

A task force composed of Richard Marcus, Philip Miller, Larry Elkin, Joel Rath (a GMM), Ann Keenes, Philip Lundell, and Bruce Matza was examining the problem of buyer turnover. Company plans were to control the growing number of buyers by increasing the scope of buyer jobs through the addition of product lines. At the same time, management hoped that an increase in buyer responsibility would help reduce turnover because buyers would feel less need to move out of their positions as a sign of career progress.

Elkin commented:

We are moving toward getting broader-based buyers rather than buyers of narrow product lines. We are looking for minimal growth in the number of buyers—two to three per year.

Guerra stated:

There is a commitment to upgrade the position of the buyer. One year ago there was a total of 12 buyers in the men's division. Two left, and rather than replace them we combined their responsibilities.

Several buyers also commented on this plan. Bill Allan, group buyer for china, silver, and porcelain, said: "I hear talk about upgrading the buyer role. I first heard about it six months ago from Phil Miller. There is no evidence of it yet." Jan Bryant, buyer for robes and loungewear, observed: "I have heard of upgrading buying roles but I haven't seen evidence of it yet. People laugh about it."

Tied to increasing the scope of buyer's responsibility was increasing the amount of time buyers spent in a job. Elkin suggested that "the optimal time for a person in the buyer role is about three years." Allan thought this too short:

Buyers are less professional than years ago. Staff is turning over far too quickly. Every three years all buyers change on average. We should look for at least five years in a buyer.

In addition to improving the professional expertise of buyers, management also thought it necessary to improve their business skills. Elkin explained: "We probably need to have buyers who can be better managers of the business—using systems to make decisions."

Bryant commented:

Ten years ago there were lots of old-timers—the emphasis was on quality and taste. Maybe the business wasn't too profitable. Now the staff is larger and younger on average. Maybe there is some change—buyers put more emphasis on gross margin than quality. I'm more concerned with gross margins than I used to be. This is good—it makes the job more interesting.

CONCLUSION

In discussing Neiman-Marcus's expansion over the next five years and the pressures that would accompany it, Philip Miller emphasized two factors:

The first priority is keeping people in specific responsibilities over longer periods of time by reducing job turnover. We must make jobs more challenging. With expansion there is a pull of responsibility toward the top of the organization. But if buyers were given more responsibility they could transact business directly with resources without the incessant intervention of DMMs!

The second key factor is ensuring that people have pertinent information to do their jobs. This doesn't come from adding layers of management and people. Retailing continues to be light years behind in taking advantage of technology.

Exhibit 1
Expansion History and Plans, 1980

Existing Stores	Opened	Number of Floors	Total Square Feet[a] (000)	Selling Square Feet[a] (000)
Downtown Dallas, Texas	1907	7		
Houston, Texas	1955 (69) (present store)	4		
Fort Worth, Texas	1963 (77) (present store)	1 2		
Northpark (replaced Preston Center in Dallas, Texas)	1965	2		
Bal Harbour, Florida	1971	3		
Atlanta, Georgia	1972	3		
Saint Louis, Missouri	1974	2		
Chicago, Illinois	1976	2		
Washington, D.C.	1977	3		
Beverly Hills, California	1979	4		
Newport Beach, California	1978	2		
Prestonwood (Dallas, Texas)	1979	2		
Proposed Stores				
Westchester, New York	1980	4	138.0	105.0
Las Vegas, Nevada	1981	2	105.2	79.0
Oak Brook (Chicago, Illinois)	1981	3	112.0	85.0 (approx.)
San Diego, California	1981	3	105.0	78.0 (approx.)
Michigan Avenue (Chicago, Illinois)	1982-83	4	194.0	135.0
San Francisco, California	1982-83	5	170.0	111.0 (if selling in basement)
Houston, Texas	1982	2	—	—
Fort Lauderdale, Florida	1982	2	—	—
Palo Alto, California	—	2	—	—

a This information is deleted for existing stores to preserve the confidentiality of the data in **Exhibit 8.**

Exhibit 2
Stores of Carter Hawley Hale, Inc., 1979

Department Stores

The Broadway
Los Angeles   47 department stores in southern California, Arizona, Nevada, and New Mexico

Capwell's
Oakland   6 department stores in northern California

The Emporium
San Francisco   12 department stores in northern California

Thalhimers
Richmond   26 department stores in southern Virginia and North Carolina

John Wanamaker
Philadelphia   16 department stores, primarily in the greater Philadelphia area

Weinstock's
Sacramento   10 department stores in California, Nevada, and Utah

High-Fashion Specialty Stores

Bergdorf Goodman
New York   High-fashion specialty stores in New York City and White Plains, New York

Holt, Renfrew
Montreal   18 high-fashion specialty stores throughout Canada

Neiman-Marcus
Dallas   12 high-fashion specialty stores in Texas, Florida, Georgia, Missouri, Illinois, California, and Washington, D.C.

Specialized Merchandising Operations

Sunset House
Los Angeles   38 gift stores and nationally distributed catalogues

Walden Books
Stamford   500 bookstores in 44 states

Exhibit 3

Comparative Price Point Information for Selected Merchandise Lines

	Neiman-Marcus	
	Price Range	Peak Price
Women's Dresses		
Junior	$ 30 – 80	$ 55
Misses Trendsetter	60 – 210	100
Misses Moderate/Better	50 – 500	90, 200
Designer	260 – 460	400
Couture and Evening	200 – 5,000	500, 1000
Men's Sportscoats and Slacks		
Moderate/Better Sportscoats	100 – 460	190, 290
Designer Sportscoats	200 – 450	300
Better Sportscoats	140 – 800	500
Dress Slacks	50 – 500	100, 160

	Department Store	
	Price Range	Peak Price
Women's Dresses		
Junior	$ 25 – 60	$ 40
Better Dresses Apparel	150 – 250	160
Misses Specialty and Better	150 – 300	185
Misses Moderate	60 – 120	95
Misses Budget	30 – 60	45
Women's Dresses	40 – 50	45
Men's Sportscoats and Slacks		
Men's Sportscoats	$ 100 – 185	
$140		
Men's Dress Slack	32 – 68	45

Note: Information provided by Neiman-Marcus. Department store data are estimates for a typical department store. Peak price is the price at which the largest number of units is sold.

Exhibit 4
Major Competing Stores in Some Neiman-Marcus Markets

	National Specialty Store	Local Specialty Store	Major Department Store
Dallas, Texas	Lord & Taylor Brooks Brothers	L. Blum L. Lattimore M. Leuvell W. Brothers J.K. Wilson	Sanger Harris Joske's
Fort Worth, Texas		Clothes Horse Clyde Campbell John L. Ash Monnigs Cox's	Sanger Harris Dillards
Houston, Texas	Lord & Taylor Saks Fifth Avenue	Frost Bros. Sakowitz Battelstein's	Joske's Foley's
Atlanta, Georgia	Lord & Taylor Saks Fifth Avenue Brooks Brothers	Muse's Zachry's	Rich's Davison's
Saint Louis	Saks Fifth Avenue Brooks Brothers	F.B. Limited Boyd's Wolff's	Famous-Barr Stix Bear and Fuller
Bal Harbour, Florida	Saks Fifth Avenue	Baron's Chester's	Burdine's Jordan Marsh
Chicago, Illinois	I. Magnin Saks Fifth Avenue Lord & Taylor Brooks Brothers	Baskin's Fells	Carson Pirie Scott Marshall Field
Washington, D.C.	Lord & Taylor Saks Fifth Avenue I. Magnin Brooks Brothers	Garfinckel's Raleigh's	Bloomingdale's Hecht's
Newport Beach, California	I. Magnin	Nordstrom	Bullock's Wilshire Robinson's Broadway Bullock's May Co.
Beverly Hills, California	I. Magnin Saks Fifth Avenue Bonwit Teller	B. Silverwood's	Bullock's Wilshire Robinson's Broadway Bullock's May Co.

Exhibit 5
Major Customer Characteristics in Neiman-Marcus Stores

Store Number Code[a]	1	2	4	5	6	7	8	9	11	12
Survey Data[b]										
Men	23[c]	28	24	27	22	16	20	21	18	19
Women: Employed	48	19	39	59	44	40	33	52	30	24
Not employed	29	52	37	14	55	44	47	27	52	76
Median Age	37.0	48.5	43.0	34.0	43.8	32.9	43.1	35.0	37.4	38.1
Median Income	$39,100	$39,500	$46,700	$27,800	$27,400	$29,600	$35,200	$31,200	$26,900	$35,300
Avg. Persons/Household	2.7	2.7	3.2	2.4	2.9	3.0	2.6	2.7	2.8	2.5
Percent College Graduate	63	40	53	47	41	53	50	54	49	70
Proportion of Households with Children										
Under Nine Years	22	18	22	47	40	27	32	18	20	35
Nine-Fourteen Years	39	8	12	25	25	10	40	7	12	31
Fifteen Years and Over	30	24	22	51	45	18	61	19	34	62
Frequency of Shopping N-M										
Once a Week or More	19	21	18	27	19	18	13	25	19	10
1-3 Times a Month	41	40	35	39	38	41	31	43	38	36
Less than Once a Month	40	60	47	33	43	41	56	32	43	55
On Present Visit to N-M										
Planned Specific Purchase	66	46	64	59	76	63	43	74	58	64
Did Not Plan Such Purchase	34	54	36	41	24	37	57	26	42	36
Saw Item Advertised	17	5	8	13	35	12	5	8	8	18
Bought Planned Item	60	59	52	69	75	70	45	74	43	81
% Unplanned/Impulse Items	44	40	48	28	17	43	35	34	43	35

Note: Store 10 is omitted for lack of data.

a Numbers have been randomly substituted for store names to preserve confidentiality of data. Number codes correspond to the same store in all exhibits.

b In the September 1980 revision of this case, data from the most recent surveys were used. All data in this exhibit were supplied by Neiman-Marcus.

c Numbers are percents except for median income and average persons/household.

Exhibit 6
Neiman-Marcus Organizational Chart (July 1, 1980)

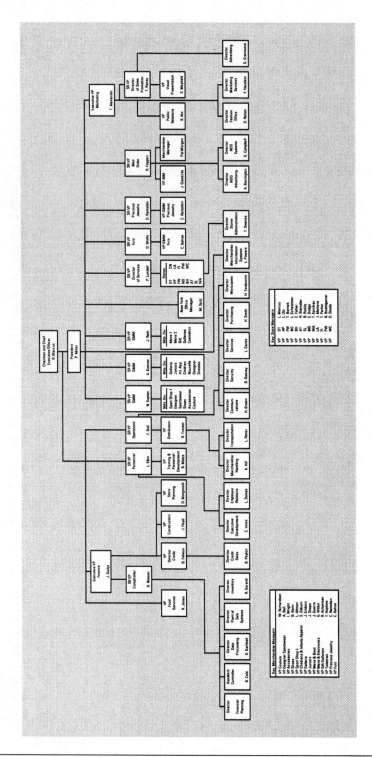

Exhibit 7
Merchandise Organizational Chart (October 1980)

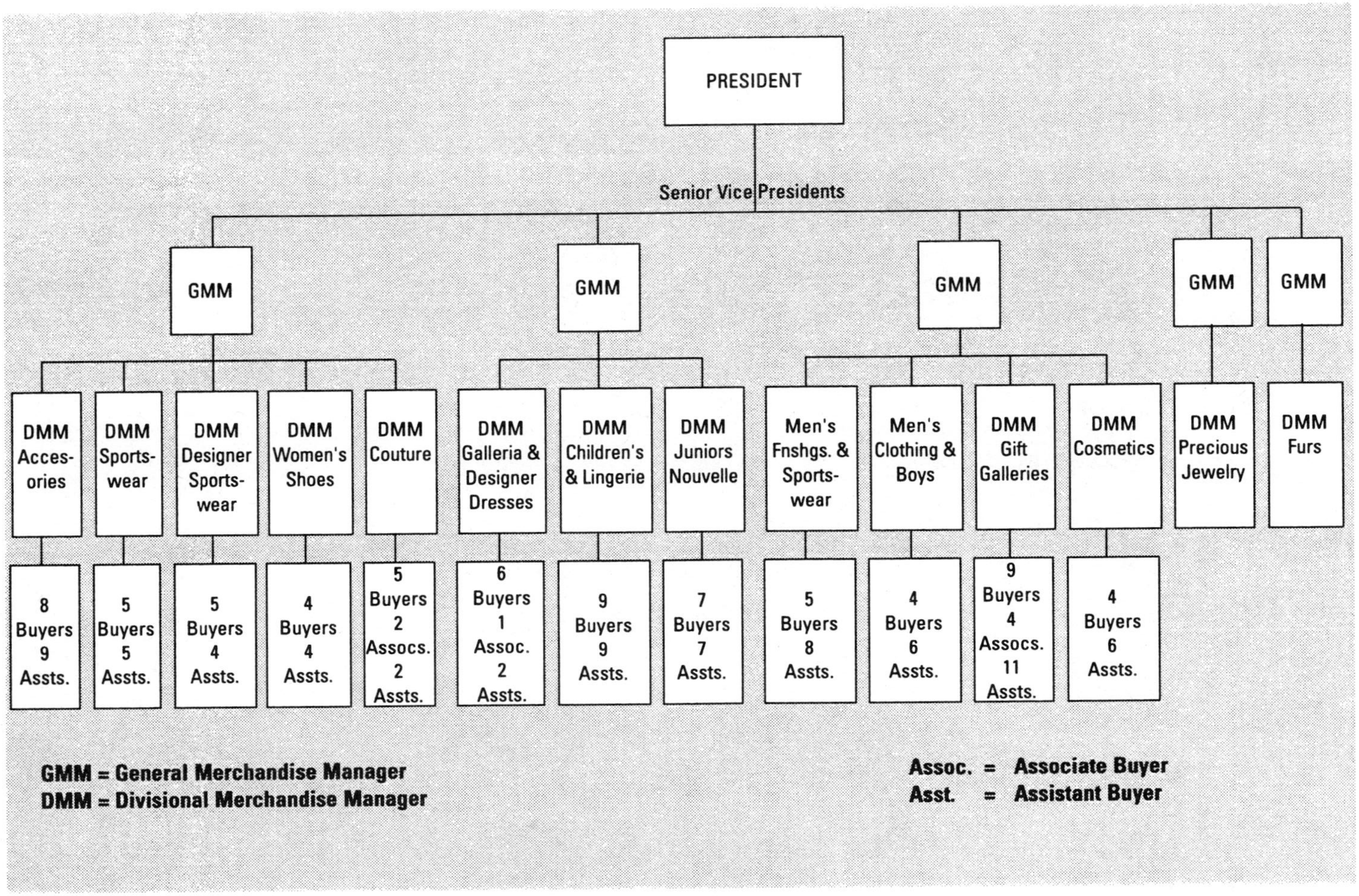

PRESIDENT

Senior Vice Presidents

GMM
- **DMM Accessories** — 8 Buyers, 9 Assts.
- **DMM Sportswear** — 5 Buyers, 5 Assts.
- **DMM Designer Sportswear** — 5 Buyers, 4 Assts.
- **DMM Women's Shoes** — 4 Buyers, 4 Assts.
- **DMM Couture** — 5 Buyers, 2 Assocs., 2 Assts.

GMM
- **DMM Galleria & Designer Dresses** — 6 Buyers, 1 Assoc., 2 Assts.
- **DMM Children's & Lingerie** — 9 Buyers, 9 Assts.
- **DMM Juniors Nouvelle** — 7 Buyers, 7 Assts.

GMM
- **Men's Frnshgs. & Sportswear** — 5 Buyers, 8 Assts.
- **Men's Clothing & Boys** — 4 Buyers, 6 Assts.
- **DMM Gift Galleries** — 9 Buyers, 4 Assocs., 11 Assts.
- **DMM Cosmetics** — 4 Buyers, 6 Assts.

GMM
- **DMM Precious Jewelry**

GMM
- **DMM Furs**

GMM = General Merchandise Manager
DMM = Divisional Merchandise Manager

Assoc. = Associate Buyer
Asst. = Assistant Buyer

Exhibit 8
Store Characteristics: Square Feet and Sales Volume, 1979

Store Code	Total Square Feet (000)	Selling Square Feet (000)	Annual Sales ($ millions)
1	136.4	97.0	19.2
2	100.4	78.8	23.1
3	178.0	117.2	29.4
4	147.9	112.3	18.5
5	287.4	178.8	38.2
6	127.3	99.7	15.6
7	200.6	131.0	39.5
8	133.6	99.6	12.4
9	160.3	130.4	41.7
11	138.0	101.6	13.0
12	125.0	88.9	14.2

Note: Store 10 is omitted for lack of data.

Exhibit 9
Typical Store Organization

Exhibit 9
Typical Store Organization

Store Manager

- Assistant Store Manager Operations
  - Sales Support Managers (5-8)
    - Nonselling Personnel (81-178)
- Food Service Manager
- Security Manager
- Credit Manager
- Public Relations Manager
- Personnel Manager
  - Personnel Assistants (2) Training/Employment
- Assistant Store Manager Merchandise
  - Department Managers (13-18)
    - Sales Coordinators (12-15)
      - Salespeople (85-232)
  - Display Manager

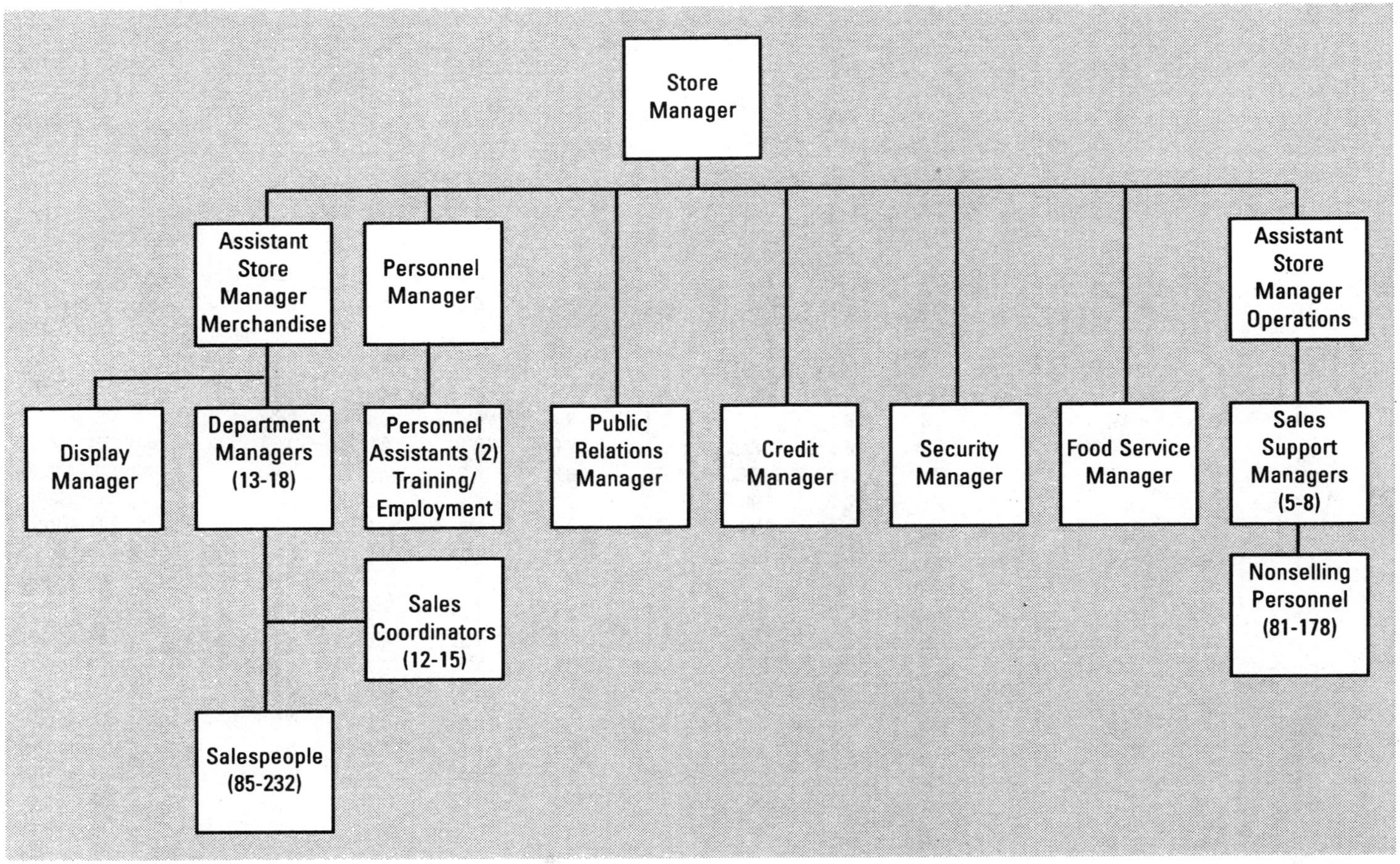

Exhibit 10
Percent of Individual Store Retail Sales by Product Line, 1979

Product Description	Store Number Code											
	1	2	3	4	5	6	7	8	9	10	11	12
Sports Shop	7.6	9.6	2.3	7.4	4.5	6.4	6.2	8.4	5.1	8.3	8.8	7.8
Designer Sportswear	4.0	8.9	6.3	7.1	3.3	4.0	4.4	6.0	3.8	2.8	2.9	3.7
Shoes	7.8	8.9	8.6	9.1	6.6	6.4	7.1	5.1	7.8	5.8	6.1	6.5
Accessories	7.6	10.4	12.5	9.8	8.8	6.0	8.8	7.7	8.1	7.8	8.6	9.3
Nouvelle	2.0	2.3	2.9	2.1	2.3	2.4	2.0	2.8	1.8	0	2.0	2.0
Intimate	3.0	4.1	4.0	4.8	2.7	3.6	3.2	3.8	3.1	3.0	4.0	4.0
Galleria	7.4	7.2	6.8	7.6	5.2	6.4	7.9	7.0	8.8	6.6	9.2	10.4
Children's	3.6	4.0	3.0	4.1	2.5	3.9	4.2	4.3	4.8	4.4	4.7	3.6
Juniors	4.3	3.1	4.4	4.4	2.5	6.1	4.5	5.2	6.1	6.6	7.6	3.2
Couture	7.1	7.6	7.7	6.2	13.9	7.8	9.9	6.7	4.8	6.8	8.6	10.0
Toiletries	1.2	12.2	7.1	7.9	12.3	24.7	12.2	7.8	22.9	20.4	6.3	6.2
Gifts	9.4	9.4	10.7	12.2	13.0	9.6	9.8	11.7	10.4	10.4	12.9	14.0
Men's Furnishings	4.2	3.3	3.9	2.9	4.4	2.8	4.0	4.3	2.7	4.3	4.1	4.1
Sportswear	2.6	3.7	3.6	2.6	1.7	1.9	1.9	3.6	1.9	3.0	2.3	2.4
Electronics	1.0	.7	.5	.8	1.1	.6	1.2	1.4	.9	1.0	1.6	1.0
Men's Clothes	5.6	5.1	3.0	3.0	5.8	3.3	3.6	4.3	2.1	3.0	3.8	3.6
Men's Designer	.6	.5	1.6	3.8	.7	.3	1.0	1.2	.5	.8	.4	.8
One Up Shop	2.4	1.6	2.5	1.6	1.4	1.7	1.6	2.1	1.6	2.0	2.0	1.9
Boys	1.4	.4	.6	.9	.6	1.0	.8	.8	.9	1.2	1.1	.7
Furs	6.8	3.3	4.6	5.0	7.8	3.1	5.6	5.4	2.7	3.1	3.6	7.6
Precious Jewelry	7.6	17.5	5.6	6.1	10.6	7.3	11.7	6.8	3.9	3.4	8.1	10.0

Exhibit 11
Personnel Demographics

	Age			Years at Neiman-Marcus			Years at Current Job		
	Youngest	**Average**	**Oldest**	**Least**	**Average**	**Most**	**Least**	**Average**	**Most**
Buyers	24	30	64	0	4	43	0	1	28
Divisional Merchandise Managers	27	33	52	1	9	28	0	6	6
Assistant Store Managers	28	32	62	0	7	28	0	6	11
Store Managers	34	41	63	1	5	44	0	2	14

Exhibit 12
Executive Trainee Retention, 1974-1979

Executive Trainee Class	Internally Generated Candidates			Outside Hires			Total		
	Number Trained	**Number Still Employed**	**%**	**Number Trained**	**Number Still Employed**	**%**	**Number Trained**	**Number Still Employed**	**%**
Spring 1974	26	9	34.6%	10	3	30.0%	36	12	33.3%
Fall 1974	9	2	22.2	24	10	41.6	33	12	36.3
Fall 1975	19	11	57.9	14	8	57.1	33	19	57.5
Spring 1976	14	7	50.0	5	3	60.0	19	10	52.6
Fall 1976	12	9	75.0	13	2	15.0	25	11	44.0
Fall 1977	14	8	57.1	9	6	66.6	23	14	60.9
Spring 1978	15	9	60.0	11	9	81.8	26	18	69.2
Summer 1978	1	1	100.0	10	5	50.0	11	6	54.5
Fall 1978	16	12	75.0	2	1	50.0	18	13	72.2
Spring 1979	10	8	80.0	9	7	77.7	19	15	78.9
Summer 1979	8	8	100.0	10	10	100.0	18	18	100.0
Fall 1979	8	9	100.0	8	8	100.0	16	16	100.0
Total	152	92	60.5%	125	72	57.6%	277	164	59.0%

Exhibit 13
Salary Levels, 1980

	Salary Range	Medium
Department Managers	$11,000–40,000	$18,000
Buyers	$16,000–45,000	$26,000
Divisional Merchandise Managers	$40,000–70,000	$53,000
Assistant Store Managers	$24,000–43,000	$31,000
Store Managers	$40,000–94,000	$62,000

Exhibit 14
Executive Personnel Flows

	1977	1978	1979
Promotions (to new job level)			
Senior Management	3	4	8
Division Merchandise Managers	3	3	3
Buyers	12	16	14
Store Managers	2	2	1
Assistant Store Managers	6	7	8
All Others[a]	17	13	15
New Hires			
Senior Management	2	2	1
Division Merchandise Managers	0	0	0
Buyers	7	8	10
Store Managers	2	1	0
Assistant Store Managers	0	4	1
All Others[a]	8	6	12
Transfers (at same level)			
Senior Management	2	2	0
Division Merchandise Managers	0	0	1
Buyers	10	10	8
Store Managers	2	3	3
Assistant Store Managers	4	1	0
All Others[a]	0	0	6
Terminations			
Senior Management	5	4	1
Division Merchandise Managers	2	0	1
Buyers	9	8	16
Store Managers	1	0	0
Assistant Store Managers	0	0	2
All Others[a]	11	12	7
Total Personnel	**4,863**	**4,780**	**5,660**

a All others—personnel, finance, operations, construction, sales promotion, mail order, miscellaneous.

Exhibit 15
Post Retirement Thoughts of Stanley Marcus

ON BIGNESS IN BUSINESS

Bigness in itself is a destructive influence on high-quality operations, because it not only diminishes the personal involvement of top management in many vital areas but brings with it other distractions that are an even greater threat. Bigger businesses entail bigger problems in finance, labor relations, building programs, employee training, executive development. The ultimate solution often leads in the direction of public ownership, either through the marketing of capital stock or merger. The moment an entrepreneur of fine quality takes in an outside partner or three thousand stockholders, the quality of his business will be affected, for the shareholders invest for three reasons only: security, dividends, and growth. They are notoriously unsentimental about their investments; they are not interested in the architectural style of the factories or the cleanliness of the lavatories—they want increased dividends and higher market prices, and they are perfectly willing for the operating standards of the business to be bent in favor of their own priorities. No longer is the entrepreneur the complete master of his business; to meet the demands of his stockholders, he starts making compromises with his traditional quality. New status as a publicly held company may force him to become more efficient, which is one of the pluses of having outside stockholders, but when he starts to depreciate the quality of his product by the elimination of two of the ten coats of lacquer on a chair or the pinking of the seams of a dress, or the substitution of plastic for fresh-water-pearl buttons on a sportshirt, he defaults in his position as a quality-maker.

Today, most stores follow a personnel-promotion program dictated by both their own internal requirements and the pressure of young buyers for quick advancement and new assignments. Too many able trainees are opting for rapid job changes in the mistaken belief that the largest number of job experiences in the shortest period of time is the best qualification for the first management job available. Barely has a shoe buyer learned the difference between calf and kidskin when he is promoted to buy men's clothing. I questioned a newly appointed men's neckwear buyer to ascertain how much he knew about ties, asking the origin of the words "paisley" and "Tremlett," and the significance of a handmade bar tack on a tie. He was unable to answer any of these questions. Of course, this does not prove that he won't eventually be a successful tie buyer, but for at least two years the quality of his neckwear stock may possibly suffer as he learns. By that time he will be moved into another area, in which, again, he has no expertise.

ON SERVICE PROBLEMS OF CHAIN OPERATIONS

As department and specialty stores have expanded with branch operations, they have done a good job of mastering their merchandising problems with the assistance of computers, but because of cost pressures, they have staffed their stores inadequately and they have failed to adopt modern training techniques, already developed by other service industries, to prepare their salespeople to serve their customers satisfactorily. The reason there are so many stores in shopping centers can be attributed in great part to the number of lost sales that each store engenders. They prosper on each other's failures.

Large retailers have a higher turnover rate of employees than smaller ones, partly self-induced by the rapid movement of executive trainees, partly imposed upon them by voluntary departures of employees who choose to move to a more personalized store environment, and partly caused by staff layoffs that are orchestrated to coincide with lags in business. Whatever the reasons, it is difficult to build an esprit de corps that is prevalent in smaller stores where the owner is available to answer questions which are not written out in the book of standard operating procedures. The owner is apt to fight for each sale even if it involves an immediate long-distance phone call to determine the availability of a special order. He takes a "can do, will do" attitude which becomes contagious to his sales force, whereas, in large stores, both salespeople and supervisors shrink from going through the red tape involved with "specials." The large institution is apt to consider its role as being that of a quartermaster, dispensing what it has in stock on any given day; the smaller store regards itself as a supplier to the needs of the individuals who are its customers.

Case 15

DUNKIN' DONUTS (E): 1988 DISTRIBUTION STRATEGIES

The signs and buttons prominently displayed through-out the Dunkin' Donuts corporate headquarters read, "Time to Make the Profits," a reference to the long running advertising slogan, "Time to Make the Donuts." It also expressed a sense of urgency with respect to franchisee profit levels. Dunkin' Donuts was a pioneer in business format franchising[1] and the management placed great value on the long-standing harmonious relationship with its franchisees. The company had achieved 50 consecutive quarters of sales and earnings growth, and many franchisees had become wealthy by expanding their operations as the company grew. By early 1988, however, deteriorating sales to capital ratios, stiffening competition, and uneven expansion threatened not only the level of company profitability, but also its relationship with the franchisees. A number of options which related primarily to increased distribution were being explored. Any change in strategy would require careful examination of its effect on both the franchisees and the company.

DUNKIN' DONUTS

William Rosenberg opened his first coffee and dough-nut shop in Quincy, Massachusetts in 1950. In 1955 he began licensing the right to imitate his retail operation to independent owner/operators called franchisees. Business format franchising, as this type of cloning relationship came to be known, was in its infancy in the early 1950s. By the late 1980s, however, business format franchising had become a major force in retailing in the United States. Meanwhile, Dunkin' Donuts had experienced similar growth. As of the end of 1987 there were 1,478 Dunkin' Donuts units in operation in its North American Region (i.e., United States, Canada, and Puerto Rico) of which 1,449 were franchised. Dunkin' Donuts licensed an additional 191 units throughout the rest of the world.

THE DUNKIN' DONUTS CUSTOMER

In addition to the fresh doughnuts signified in its name,

Assistant Professor Patrick J. Kaufmann prepared this case as the basis for class discussion rather than to illustrate either effective or ineffective handling of an administrative situation. Company data have been disguised and should be used for purposes of class discussion only.

Copyright © 1988 by the President and Fellows of Harvard College.
Harvard Business School case 589-017.

---

1 Business format franchising is distinguished from product franchising in that the product franchisor is typically a manufacturer seeking contractual outlets for its branded goods. The product franchisor may offer some advertising and managerial assistance, but the franchisee generally conducts business as an independent distributor. The business format franchisor is typically an operating retailer who licenses the right to reproduce the franchisor's business fromula and systems in another location. In return for a one time franchise fee and an ongoing royalty based on a percentage of gross sales, the franchisee not only receives the right to use the business format franchisor's trademark, but also operates under specific guidelines covering all aspects of the business; including marketing, operations, finance, accounting, and design of the premises.

Dunkin' Donuts sold other related products, such as muffins, croissants, cookies, soup, and croissant sandwiches. Nevertheless, customers strongly associated the stores with doughnuts and coffee. In a nationwide sample of customers who lived within 15 minutes of a Dunkin' Donuts shop, 86% had purchased doughnuts on their last visit to a Dunkin' Donuts shop (75% in the Northeast), and 30% had purchased coffee (52% in the Northeast).

To aid in their market analysis company managers categorized purchases by location of consumption (see **Table 1**).

Dunkin' Donuts also categorized purchases by type of occasion; social (11%), work (19%), and family (70%). Family and social occasion purchases were consumed primarily at home, while 70% of work related purchases were consumed in the workplace. Customers for all types of purchase occasions chose Dunkin' Donuts primarily because of the freshness and consistency of the product. Convenience of the locations was another major reason for shopping at Dunkin' Donuts. For work related purchase occasions convenience often meant, "on the way to home or office."

Another method of analyzing the Dunkin' Donuts customer was by time of purchase (see **Table 2**).

Of the sampled consumers, 22% were heavy users (i.e., visited a Dunkin' Donuts shop once a week or more), 48% were medium users (once a month but less than once a week), and 30% were light users (less than once a month). Heavy users accounted for 86% of all coffee purchases, 53% of all doughnut purchases, and 68% of all croissant purchases. For all usage level segments product quality and freshness were the most important reasons for shopping at Dunkin' Donuts. However, for heavy users superior coffee and quick service played a greater role in their decision to stop at Dunkin' Donuts than for less frequent purchasers. Heavy users also differed from light and medium users along several other dimensions (see **Table 3**).

Among the sampled consumers, product awareness was highest in the Northeast and lowest in the Southwest/West. Trial of all non-doughnut pastry items was also lower in the Southwest/West. Purchasers in the Southwest/West were less likely to be purchasing for themselves, more likely to be purchasing on the weekend, and much less likely to eat at the shop or order coffee than Northeastern consumers.

THE COMPETITION

Dunkin' Donuts competed with other doughnut shops, bakeries, supermarket bakeries, restaurants, and convenience stores. Fast food restaurants generally were not considered direct competitors. However, the strong entry of McDonald's into the breakfast market had changed that viewpoint somewhat. Dunkin' Donuts also competed indirectly with "snack" franchises such as Dairy Queen (ice cream) and the various gourmet cookie shops.

Competition from convenience stores and supermarket bakeries was becoming increasingly acute. In 1988 there were over 20 thousand supermarket bakeries, and the second largest selling item in those bakeries was doughnuts. Moreover, convenience stores were expanding into food service at an alarming rate, and had become

Table 1 Doughnut Consumption Locations

	In Shop	In Car	At Work	At Home
% Purchasers*	20%	12%	17%	46%
% Volume Purchases*	16%	9%	23%	47%
% Volume Purchases Which Were Sold in Dozens	—	60%	92%	88%
Competitive Set	other shops, restaurants, convenience stores	other shops, convenience stores	bakeries, other shops, some convenience stores	bakeries, supermarket bakeries

* Does not sum to 100%; consumption in "other" locations not included.

Table 2 Time of Last Purchase Occasion

	Weekday				Weekend	
	Breakfast/ AM Snack at Shop	Breakfast/ AM Snack Takeout	Noon Snack Takeout	Late Night Snack Takeout	Breakfast/ AM Snack Takeout	Late Night Snack Takeout
Percent Purchasers	11%	39%	7%	11%	25%	7%

Table 3 Degree of Usage Comparison

	Light/Medium Users	Heavy Users
Planned Visits	44%	66%
Purchased for Self Only	19%	30%
Weekday Breakfast/AM Snack	34%	45%
Consumed at Shop	18%	38%

a serious threat. In 1988, approximately 12% of convenience store revenues were from food service sales. Many, if not most, convenience stores offered coffee and fresh or packaged doughnuts, and because of their ubiquitous locations (approximately 65,000 nationwide) and long hours, they competed vigorously for commuter and impulse purchases.

Dunkin' Donuts managers were convinced that consumers who purchased doughnuts at a convenience store were looking primarily for convenience, not product quality. Convenience stores purchased packaged doughnuts from bakeries and fresh doughnuts from local doughnut shops, but often kept them on the shelves until sold out, sometimes long after they had lost their freshness. Many Dunkin' Donuts franchisees sold wholesale unbranded doughnuts to the local convenience outlets.

Dunkin' Donuts franchisees also competed with one another. New franchisees and those seeking to expand would occasionally pick new locations which would draw some customers away from an existing franchisee.

Dunkin' Donuts franchise agreements typically granted the franchisee the right to operate only at a specified location and provided no territorial exclusivity. In other words, an operating franchisee could find that another franchisee had been granted the right to open an outlet in close proximity to its previously operating outlet. The company had adopted and published to the franchisees a policy which provided for a formal grievance procedure if the company had developed the property for the new outlet (i.e., if the company had found the site, purchased or leased the land and building, and sublet the property to the franchisee). The grievance procedure allowed an existing franchisee to object to the location of the new outlet before a committee of company executives and other franchisees. In preparation for the formal hearing, the company would gather extensive evidence of the expected effects of the new location on the existing franchisee's shop. The committee, after hearing all of the company's and franchisee's evidence, would attempt to shape a compromise solution, or recommend either that the shop be opened or not. However, the company retained the right to open the shop against the recommendation of the grievance committee.

If the new outlet was entirely franchisee developed (i.e., if a prospective franchisee found the site, and purchased or leased the land and building directly from a third party), the grievance procedure did not apply. Under those circumstances, antitrust law made it illegal for the company to "conspire" with existing franchisees to preclude another franchisee from opening a shop in an otherwise suitable location. Any such determination had to be made unilaterally by the company according to some uniformly applied criteria. The company, therefore, carefully screened all potential new locations, examining the competitive environment, sales and profits of nearby Dunkin' Donuts shops, shopping activity, demographics, and the physical attributes of the site in an attempt to optimize Dunkin' Donuts' penetration (i.e., distribution) pattern in each market without jeopardizing the businesses of existing franchisees. If the company disagreed with the franchisee's choice of locations, it sent a "site deficiency letter" outlining the reasons it would not approve the site.

THE FRANCHISEES

While many business format franchisors approximated a balance between the number of company owned and franchised outlets, Dunkin' Donuts was almost exclusively a franchising company. In 1979 the franchisor, Dunkin' Donuts of America, operated 110 shops. Staffing problems and increasing administrative costs led the company to reduce the number of company operated shops, and of the 1478 units in operation in North America at the end of fiscal 1987, the company operated only 29 units. Although Dunkin' Donuts itself operated relatively few units, throughout its history, it had been very active in acquiring real estate (either by extended lease or purchase) and developing units to be operated by its franchisees. In fact, the company derived more revenue from rental income from franchisees operating company developed units than it did from its total ongoing franchise royalty fees. Franchisee rental fees were calculated as either the "base rent" (determined by the capitalized cost of acquiring and developing the property) or 12% of the franchisee's gross sales, whichever was greater; and were in addition to the royalty (4.9% of gross sales) and advertising fees (5% of gross sales). Table 4 presents some details on company developed and controlled real estate. (See **Exhibits 1** and **2** for franchisee and company operating results.)

Table 4 Company Developed and Controlled Real Estate 1983–1987

		1987	1986	1985	1984	1983
Lease Land and Building		382	392	395	416	437
Lease Land and Own Building		345	332	316	299	288
Own Land and Building		215	219	216	200	168
	Total	942	943	927	915	893
Total Number of Shops in N. America		1,478	1,397	1,321	1,260	1,210

Although still heavily invested in real estate, in 1988 Dunkin' Donuts was actively attempting to reduce the percentage of company developed shops. In the early 1980s, approximately 80% of all new franchisee operated shops were company developed. Between 1980 and 1987, escalating development costs and a sales growth decline from 8% to 2% led to a drop in the sales to capital ratio for a typical shop from 1.1:1 to less than 1:1. Assuming the 2% sales growth rate remained constant, average rental income per store (because of the base rent calculation) and projected ROI for Dunkin' Donuts would decline significantly. Moreover, the number of franchisee objections to planned development was increasing and the company's Development Group was spending approximately 40% of its time and a substantial amount of money fighting formal grievances (**Table 5**). The return on investment in shop development, therefore, became marginal to the publicly held company, and in order to free capital for more attractive alternatives,[2] senior management began to shift the development burden to the franchisees.

Franchisees with fewer investment alternatives than the company and an opportunity to build personal equity in the property, often found the returns on developing their own real estate very attractive (assuming they had sufficient capital to do so). Franchisees who developed and controlled their own real estate also proved to be more committed to the business and managed the operation more closely, thereby achieving better returns than for company developed stores. However, in some rapidly appreciating real estate markets, franchisees were willing to develop marginal sites and run close to breakeven, with the intention of eventually selling the franchise and retaining the real estate as landlord. This provided for much more intensive distribution in those markets. Some franchisees wishing to expand or to protect their areas from the expansion of other franchisees, but lacking the capital to develop their own property, became frustrated by the company's growing unwillingness to develop sites for lease to franchisees.

Table 5 Formal Grievance Procedures 1982–1987

	1982	1983	1984	1985	1986	1987
Number of Grievances	15	10	18	28	20	8

By 1987 nearly 80% of all new shops were franchisee developed. This was much easier to accomplish in Region I (the eastern United States and Canada) where 75% of all domestic Dunkin' Donuts shops were located, where the average store sales were significantly higher than in Region II (the western United States), and where existing franchisees were much more active in purchasing real estate and developing stores in order to expand their existing operations. (**Exhibit 1** presents franchisee operating results by sub-Region.)

REGIONAL DIFFERENCES

In 1978, the company had adopted a highly focused strategy of growing in markets where it already had the greatest penetration, and further development of Region I naturally became an integral part of that strategy. Between 1983 and 1987, 74% of all new shops were opened in Region I. Although widely considered a national chain, Dunkin' Donuts had shops in only 168 of the 334 U.S. Standard Metropolitan Statistical Areas. In 1987 there were 1,100 Dunkin' Donuts shops concentrated in 96 of the 156 SMSA's of Region I. In Region II there were 378 shops in 71 of the 178 different SMSAs. The 423 new shops opened from 1983 to 1987 were located in only 75 different SMSAs, almost all of which already had operating shops. The highly focused development strategy had significantly increased the concentration of shops in a relatively small number of markets.

In areas such as Boston, Massachusetts and Providence, Rhode Island where many of the oldest and most successful franchises were located, franchisee development was almost frenetic, and by 1988 overpenetration had become critical. In some areas of Region I, Dunkin' Donuts shops were located within 4 blocks of each other. New franchisees, however, accounted for only 20% of the franchisee developed units. Existing franchisees, responding to what company managers referred to as the "fear and greed" factors, sought to expand their own businesses and preclude development in their area by competing franchisees. By developing good properties wherever they could find them, they were sometimes forced to "leapfrog" over other franchisees, and different multi-unit franchisees' shops became intermingled within the same small market areas. By 1988, some managers felt that development in parts of Region I were out of control. Overall sales in those markets were increasing and the

---

2 In 1986 the company acquired the rights to Chili's Restaurant and Bar for all of New England. The acquisition of a Chili's area franchise reflected the first diversification move since the company had divested several subsidiaries in the early 1970's to concentrate on growing the doughnut business.

region contained many of the most profitable stores, but some individual store sales were suffering. Although overall system morale remained high, some franchisees were getting increasingly angry with the company for approving sites which increased total market sales and franchise royalties but hurt their individual businesses, and some lost faith in the company's willingness to look after their interests. By contrast, in Region II, where there was relatively little franchisee expansion activity, when increased market penetration took place, it was most often because the company had developed the property itself.

The differences between Region I and II were due primarily to the historical development of the company, and to the experience and sophistication of the local franchisees. The original base of operations had been in the northeastern United States, and development there had been intensive. Early franchisees expanded with the company, often forming partnerships with family members to open additional stores. Many of the most successful original franchisees had strong connections to their Portuguese heritage, and were part of a substantial local Portuguese community. When they succeeded as Dunkin' Donuts franchisees, they attracted a significant number of relatives, friends, neighbors, and other recent Portuguese immigrants into the franchise system. The resulting network of interconnected ownership among extended families and friends led to a continuity of experience and investment in the system in that area of the country which solidified the company's leading market position.

Expansion in other areas of the country was somewhat haphazard. In the 1960s when Dunkin' Donuts was experiencing a 40% growth rate, a belief that the company could do no wrong led to completely undisciplined development. For example, in 1968, a Dunkin' Donuts real estate manager in the Southwest was reported to have rented a Lear jet and approved 11 new shop sites without ever landing.

The spotty development of Region II had left Dunkin' Donuts with little trademark recognition and no marketing or operational efficiencies in most market areas. This put the company at a distinct disadvantage when faced with a serious competitor willing to invest heavily to achieve market penetration. For example, Dunkin' Donuts had opened 8 stores in Kansas City. Winchell's, a California based doughnut chain with 600 stores, expanded eastward into the Kansas City market and met Dunkin' Donuts head on. Within two years, Winchell's had opened 23 shops, and Dunkin' Donuts had closed all of its stores.

Average store sales were significantly lower in Region II than in Region I, and there were more than twice as many shops in Region II on rent relief (i.e., the practice of allowing a struggling franchisee to sign a note for the accruing rent in order to relieve cash flow problems and avoid closing the shop). One of the greatest contrasts between the two Regions was in the amount of coffee sold. Northeastern Dunkin' Donuts outlets were primarily coffee shops where customers came to buy one or two doughnuts and a cup of coffee. Everywhere else in the country, Dunkin' Donuts was primarily a doughnut shop where customers purchased doughnuts by the dozen. Shops in the Northeast averaged about 235 dozen doughnuts and 1900 cups of coffee a day while elsewhere the shops averaged 260 dozen doughnuts and 850 cups of coffee. The differences had a significant sales and profit impact. Doughnuts averaged $ .45 a piece, but sold for approximately $3.00 by the dozen, and coffee was a high margin item.

The continuity of ownership characteristic of Region I was noticeably absent in Region II. One company operations manager estimated that ownership of all shops in the region turned over about every 4 years. However, there was some indication that the same type of extended family networking observed in Region I was beginning to take place in Region II. A large percentage of Region II franchisees were recent immigrants to the United States, and many had family and friends in their native countries who also wished to immigrate. U.S. immigration policy generally granted preferred status to individuals assured of a job in the United States. Dunkin' Donut's franchisees, as independent owners of their own businesses were able to offer jobs or partnerships to friends and relatives, thereby increasing their chances of attaining permanent residency status.

In 1987 38% of the franchisees in Region II were Indian, Pakastani, Cambodian, or Korean. Long hours and thin profit margins were acceptable to many of these franchisees who had experienced much more difficult conditions in their native countries. The use of family members to work behind the counter and to bake the doughnuts helped solve the most serious problem facing all Dunkin' Donuts' franchisees, staffing the shop. Having trusted family members at the cash register also served to reduce theft, sometimes estimated to reach 2% to 3% of gross sales system wide.

In some markets, however, Dunkin' Donuts' managers had sensed a negative consumer reaction to the widespread use of recent immigrants as franchisees. Language barriers and cultural differences also created managerial challenges. The solidarity of the various ethnic communities was often reflected in the reticence of one franchisee to adopt a program unless his or her friends were also going to adopt it. Moreover, in order to protect Dunkin' Donuts' reputation for quality, company policy required that doughnuts and other baked goods be discarded after a specified time period. Reverence for food, however, led some franchisees to retain the products beyond their freshness limit.

SHOP OPERATIONS

Unlike many fast food franchises, Dunkin' Donuts shops did not just prepare the product they sold, they manufactured it. Although the franchisees received extensive training at Dunkin' Donuts University, most had no previous food service experience, and yet had to manage the retail business (or front of the shop), as well as the baking business (or back of the shop). Most shops were open 24 hours a day, 7 days a week. This was a very demanding job, and as one Dunkin' Donuts manager put it, "our franchisees are real roll-up-the-sleeves, hands-on managers."

In order to meet the company's freshness standards, Dunkin' Donuts recommended 3 production shifts; 11 p.m. to 6 a.m., 7 a.m. to 11 a.m., and noon to 7 p.m. Frequent baking was vital to maintaining the company's reputation for freshness and the company set shelf life limits on the sale of various products (e.g., 5 hours for cake doughnuts, 8 hours for yeast doughnuts, and 12 hours for muffins). Staffing the baking positions was extremely difficult (particularly in Region II), and the people attracted to night-shift baking jobs frequently proved not to be dependable. In Region II on average night-shift bakers failed to show up for work 1 out of every 6 nights. This often required franchisees either to come in at night to fill in, or to put on extra help, thereby decreasing their profit margin. Many of the franchisees ignored the company's recommendation of 3 shift baking entirely. In Region I where the wage rate for bakers was very high, operators could save over $300 a week by running on two shifts. Because two-shift baking jeopardized Dunkin' Donuts reputation for freshness, one way the company attempted to mitigate this problem was through its research and development effort to extend the shelf life of the product.

Front of the store staffing was also a serious problem. In some areas of Region I where there was an especially low level of unemployment, franchisees found attracting reliable counter personnel and assistant managers very difficult. Most franchisees employed at least one other family member in the operation of the business to help ease the supervisory burden. In markets where unemployment levels were higher and employees more readily available due to depressed economic conditions, the shops' revenues tended to be lower as well. Increases in labor costs, like capital investments, therefore, were severely squeezing franchisee profits.

Although the on-the-premises production of doughnuts made the operation difficult, the original product line was narrow enough that franchisees were able to concentrate on making fresh doughnuts and good coffee. Because of changes in consumer attitudes towards health and diet, however, there were fewer doughnuts sold in 1988 than in 1968. Meanwhile, the product line had been extended to include specialty baked goods (e.g., croissants), soup, and sandwiches. The four most recent major line extensions had required additional franchisee investment in equipment totalling over $20,000. In addition to the broadening product line, the company had expanded its marketing programs significantly, adding a wide variety of price, product, and premium promotions of which the franchisee had to be aware. These changes added new levels of complexity to the concept, and the franchisee could no longer be just a good "doughnut person." Senior management at Dunkin' Donuts was acutely aware of the dangers presented by making the concept more complex, both in terms of customer confusion and the burden on the franchisees. Consequently, the company was committed to finding other ways to increase sales and franchisee profits.

One way to increase sales without increasing the complexity of the concept was to increase distribution, i.e., put more Dunkin' Donuts shops in existing or new markets, in locations convenient to consumers. One of the most serious problems already facing the franchisees, however, was the overcapacity of the existing full-producing units. In the weaker markets the excess capacity was often due to lack of trademark recognition. However, as the strong Dunkin' Donuts markets became more and more saturated with full producing shops, the overcapacity problem intensified there as well. A Dunkin' Donuts' kitchen with the standard configuration provided the production capacity for up to 250 dozen doughnuts per shift. However, shops were typically staffed with one baker per shift who was also required to finish the products (i.e., glaze or fill the doughnuts after baking them), and to prepare muffins and croissants. The maximum doughnut production capacity under these conditions was, in reality, approximately 140 dozen per shift. Production was not spread evenly across the 2 or 3 shifts.

Two thirds of the baking was done at night because 60% of each day's business was done between 6 and 10 a.m.

MARKETING AT DUNKIN' DONUTS

There were three distinct components to the marketing effort at Dunkin' Donuts. The corporate marketing department had primary responsibility for the development of marketing programs. These programs were sold into the franchise organization by 14 field marketing representatives, who also managed and monitored the execution of the programs.[3] Finally, the franchisees implemented the marketing programs at the shop level.

Franchisees contributed 5% of gross sales to an Advertising and Promotion Fund. Because of the uneven distribution of Dunkin' Donuts shops nationwide, there was no national media purchased, and all television and radio advertising was on a market or regional basis. In addition to advertising, marketing field representatives were constantly alerting the franchisees to new Dunkin' Donuts promotions. The franchisees bore the entire expense of the promotions, and could choose to participate or not. Recently, approximately 20% of the advertising budget was being spent promoting new products such as sandwiches which were designed to shift Dunkin' Donuts away from its dependence on doughnuts and spread demand more evenly throughout the day.

Senior managers at Dunkin' Donuts were concerned about the way in which some franchisees were executing the marketing programs. Moreover, customer satisfaction levels, although high, were flat; and the lowest scoring product category was doughnuts. Many believed that there was a serious need to either attract more sophisticated franchisees or to simplify the marketing programs and the production processes. As franchisee profit margins decreased along with the sales to capital ratio, however, it was increasingly difficult to attract the more sophisticated investor.

DISTRIBUTION STRATEGIES

Dunkin' Donuts management was convinced that the decreasing sales growth, stiffening competition, and worsening sales to capital ratio faced by the company and its franchisees required a new emphasis on expanding distribution. Three distinct approaches emerged; (1) the development of new and/or previously underdeveloped markets (which could include the revitalization of the company operated stores division), (2) the sale of branded products through convenience stores, and (3) opening satellite (i.e., non-producing) retail outlets. Dunkin' Donuts corporate policy was to test all new programs and strategies thoroughly before asking the franchisees to adopt them. Managers disagreed, however, on which strategy should receive the highest priority.

New Markets. Some managers favored expanding distribution by opening new stores in less saturated markets, either through focused company development of specific markets, or through the use of area franchising. Area franchising could take two forms; subfranchising—where the master franchisee purchased the exclusive rights to subfranchise to individual owner operators in a particular territory, or exclusive development franchising—where the franchisee purchased the exclusive rights to a territory and agreed to open and operate a specified number of shops in the area within a specified time period. In subfranchising, the franchisees paid a master franchisee a royalty percentage of sales and the master franchisee, in turn paid a royalty to the franchisor. Unlike exclusive development franchising, therefore, subfranchising added another layer between the franchisor and the operating franchisee. The master franchisee typically assumed all or most of the duties of the franchisor in its territory. Exclusive development franchising retained the direct connection between operating franchisee and the franchisor, but when the areas were large, the individual shops resembled company owned shops in that they were operated by salaried managers instead of the franchisees themselves. Both types of area franchising allowed the franchisor to expand quickly into new markets. Also, area franchising did not require the company to invest in the development of the properties.

Dunkin' Donuts had tried exclusive development franchising in Region II several times, but had never been successful. For example, in 1978 the rights to develop all of San Diego were sold to three brothers who owned a large chain of furniture stores (as large as Dunkin' Donuts itself). The franchisees opened 6 stores. Only 1 was in a location approved by Dunkin' Donuts, and it was the only one ever to reach breakeven. The other stores experienced extremely high turnover of employees and

---

3 In addition to the marketing representatives, the field management force of Dunkin' Donuts consisted of district and area managers. Each district manager was responsible for overseeing the operations of either 17 franchised outlets *or* 5 company operated stores depending on the division to which he or she was assigned.

consistently lost money. The exclusive development agreement eventually was terminated, and the individual stores (not the territory) were sold to another franchisee who doubled their sales.

Focused sequential development of new or underdeveloped markets was another alternative. Under that strategy, Dunkin' Donuts would enter new or currently underdeveloped markets sequentially, opening as many new stores in each market as was necessary to achieve economies of scale in marketing and operations before moving on to the next market. This approach would avoid the haphazard development currently characteristic of Region II, while providing for efficient growth in the less saturated markets. However, it was likely that such a strategy would require Dunkin' Donuts to take an active role in the development of the real estate for the various sites. There were some who favored not only continued company site development, but also revitalization of the Company Operated Store Division.

Branded Products. Another approach would be to expand the distribution of existing stores. Some managers proposed that Dunkin' Donuts contract with convenience store chains to supply branded products to participating outlets. It was expected that a local franchisee could deliver fresh Dunkin' Donuts' products twice daily to between 10 and 15 convenience stores. The products would be displayed in illuminated Dunkin' Donuts self-serve display cases. It was estimated that a typical branded product route would involve an additional investment by the franchisee of $19,000 for cases and other equipment (usually financed by a five-year note). It was assumed that the franchisees would lease the delivery vehicles, and there would be no additional franchise fee.

Dunkin' Donuts management knew that the branded products strategy could cause additional friction between franchisees in the more saturated markets unless some system was designed to allocate specific convenience chain outlets to each participating franchisee. The question remained as to whether to protect nonparticipating franchisees from having the convenience store next door selling another franchisee's branded Dunkin' Donuts. Quality control also would be a significant problem. It would be necessary for the supplying franchisee to carefully monitor the convenience stores and ensure that products which had passed their freshness limit were removed and discarded. Convenience stores were likely to want the products early in the morning, the same time the shops needed to be fully stocked. There was also a

question as to which products would be made available under this program.

Franchisees who were already supplying the local convenience stores on an individual basis with unbranded products did not see the benefit to them of switching to branded products. Margins were not expected to improve, and unlike the current arrangements, the franchisees would have to deliver the products to the convenience stores. Other franchisees did not like the idea of "competing with themselves." Company managers believed that the convenience store doughnut customer was different from the doughnut shop customer, but found it hard to convince some franchisees of that fact.

Another possibility was for the company to supply the convenience stores in each market from a local central commissary. The commissary would be for production only, and would not sell to retail customers. Therefore, it could be placed in a relatively inexpensive central location without concern for its ability to attract retail customers.

Exhibit 3 presents a pro forma income statement for a hypothetical branded products route in the Northeast, and reflected the current sales and cost estimates of the Dunkin' Donuts' Development Group.

Satellites. Dunkin' Donuts' management believed that in many operating markets there were "seams" of consumer demand which existed between the full-producing shops, but which could not support an additional producing unit. To preempt competition from gaining a toehold in those locations, one option was the use of satellite outlets. Satellites were non-producing units which were serviced from nearby full-producing units. They could take the form of a storefront, a stall in a shopping mall, or even a cart in a train station.

Company managers were convinced that a good business case could be made for investing in the non-producing units. Although there was wide national variance in real estate costs, for purposes of comparison the company's Development Group compiled some scenarios which compared the pro forma operating results for a typical full producing unit in the Northeast to those of a hypothetical satellite network (see **Exhibit 4**). Full producing units typically required an investment of about $455,000 for the land, site improvement, and building, plus $115,000 for the ovens and other equipment. Satellite sites were generally leased, but for purposes of comparison the company assumed that an 800 square foot satellite with some seating and finishing capacity would require $20,000 for the lease hold improvements, and $80,000 for capitalized land and building costs. The satellite's equipment would cost an additional $55,000. Development Group managers estimated the average weekly sales of a satellite to be $6,100.

Although shrink was expected to be greater at the satellite unit, food costs as a percentage of sales were expected to be the same as for the producing unit because a greater proportion of the doughnuts would be sold as singles. Similarly, the payroll costs as a percent of sales were expected to be approximately the same for satellites as for the producing units. Although the satellites would be charged with the additional payroll expense of a delivery person, the baker's payroll expense for the satellite was lower because it was taken as an incremental cost over and above the regular baking expense for the producing unit.

Although coordination would be difficult, if these units could be supplied from a shop with excess capacity, Dunkin' Donuts' management believed that the franchisee should be able to substantially increase his or her profits. In the strong Dunkin' Donuts markets, however, some franchisees did not see how it was possible to supply a satellite from their full-producing shops. Although they had excess production capacity, many were already stretched to the limits with respect to their management of the business.

Most company managers thought that in order to obtain the optimal mix of producing and non-producing units, it would be necessary to sell exclusive micro-territories to qualified existing franchisees. Under this plan, the company would assess how many and what type (full-producing, satellites, carts) of outlets would be optimal for the micro-territory surrounding a particular franchisee (typically 1–2 producing shops and 1–3 satellites). The franchisee would be offered the exclusive rights to the territory in return for a prepaid fee equal to the cumulative franchise fees for that combination of outlets. (In Region I, full-producing unit fees were $27,000 and non-producing units were $10,000; in Region II, they were $20,000 and $7,500). The franchisee would agree to find the specific sites and develop the specified outlets within a 5 year time period. If the shops were not opened according to schedule the franchisee could lose the territory, and forfeit the fees.

Dunkin' Donuts management believed that exclusive territories would appeal to both the greed and fear factors. The more aggressive franchisees viewed it as a way to open more outlets, while more conservative franchisees expressed a begrudging willingness to purchase territories simply to protect themselves (at least temporarily) from competition from other Dunkin' Donuts franchisees. Some franchisees who had been with the company for a long time were thinking about retirement. Although typically they did not have the energy or willingness to build the business in a new shop, they saw the exclusive territory as a way to protect their existing investment until they were ready to sell.

Some of the most successful franchisees had individual shops with sales twice the system average or more, generating substantial profits. Extremely high sales and profits could be interpreted by the company to mean that the market was underdeveloped, and that requests from other franchisees to open shops in that area should be approved. Although purchasing a micro-territory would protect these profitable areas from other franchisees, opening additional shops would mean an increase in the franchisee's investment and a possible decrease in the sales of his or her successful shop. Some franchisees remained unconvinced that the satellites would increase their return on investment. The sale of micro-territories, therefore, did not automatically ensure the smooth opening of the planned additional shops.

Implementation of an exclusive territory strategy would be difficult and would divert most of the Development Group's efforts from other projects. Although some company managers believed that for the program to be successfully sold to the franchisees a high level of flexibility must be exhibited, others felt that it would be necessary to strictly enforce the development schedules. This raised a number of issues. For example, would the franchisee automatically lose the exclusive rights to the territory if he or she did not comply with the development schedule? Would there be any allowance for reasonable delays such as difficulty in finding appropriate sites or in obtaining zoning permits? Would lack of available funds be an excusable delay?

One of the most serious problems facing Dunkin' Donuts management was the development of a policy regarding the design of the exclusive development micro-territories. How big should territories be? Should they require more than one or two additional shops? Should territories be designed without regard to existing franchisees' desires to purchase them? What criteria should be used to determine whether to permit a franchisee to buy a territory? If the franchisee is not operationally or financially qualified to purchase a territory or is not interested in buying, should the territory around his or her shop be held open or sold to another franchisee? A particularly difficult issue involved those markets where there had already been significant development. Should territories be defined so as to include more than one franchisee's existing shop, or should some markets be immune from exclusive territory development?

CURRENT SITUATION

Tom Schwarz, president of Dunkin' Donuts, commented on the current situation:

"It's our job to enhance shareholder value. That depends on how well we use our capital, both human and financial, and grow the company. We're in great shape, but we have to continue to satisfy our customers, and to do so we have to make sure our franchisees are successful. Recently, the franchisees haven't been as profitable as we'd like, and if they aren't profitable, they won't invest in their shops to maintain standards or introduce new products. We know we're not going to get people to eat a lot more doughnuts, but by increasing our distribution we can get a lot more people to eat our doughnuts. We've got some work to do."

	Franchisee Operated:				Co. Oper.:
	Region I		Region II		
	Northeast	Southeast	Central	Western	Northeast
Sales (Annual)	530,387	435,791	392,215	354,868	597,187
Cost of Sales					
Food Cost	121,989	109,334	100,810	93,744	157,527
Payroll	134,187	104,474	92,571	87,973	142,640
Supplies	24,928	15,847	16,541	13,323	26,776
Total Cost of Sales	281,104	229,655	209,922	195,030	326,943
Operating Expenses					
Weekly Franchise Fee	25,989	20,627	19,298	17,202	0
Advertising Contribution	26,519	20,903	19,619	18,452	27,057
Payroll Taxes	14,320	10,743	10,721	8,737	19,791
Other Operating Expenses (1)	30,763	26,207	20,857	18,385	37,952
Total Operating Expenses	97,591	78,480	70,495	62,776	84,800
Occupancy and Financing Expenses					
Rent and Real Estate Taxes	50,988	45,398	41,311	34,514	38,508
Utilities	17,366	18,116	14,938	13,485	24,740
Insurance	6,223	6,745	4,382	4,861	10,019
Interest	10,073	9,188	6,150	6,307	9,519
Total Occupancy and Financing Expenses	84,650	79,447	66,781	59,167	82,786
Total Depreciation and Amortization	19,327	19,439	15,033	14,211	14,640
Net Operating Profit/Loss Before Owner's					
Draw and Income Taxes	47,715	28,770	29,984	23,684	88,018
Addbacks: Total Depreciation and Amortization	19,327	19,439	15,033	14,211	14,640
Rent	45,889	40,858	37,180	31,063	34,657
Interest	10,073	9,188	6,150	6,307	9,519
Adjusted Cash Flow	123,004	98,255	88,347	75,265	146,834
(1) Other Operating Expenses Include:					
Professional Services	4,243	3,600	2,700	2,526	483
Municipal Taxes and Related Charges	1,061	1,935	1,948	2,395	205
Travel and Freight	530	1,982	746	1,015	908
Cleaning, Maintenance and Repairs	17,503	12,394	10,113	8,631	29,247
Administrative and Office Expenses	3,713	3,279	3,118	2,556	2,847
Other Expenses	3,713	3,017	2,232	1,256	4,262
Total Other Operating Expenses	30,763	26,207	20,857	18,379	37,952

Exhibit 2
Contribution to Corporate Income by Division

	October 31, 1987	October 25, 1986
Franchise Division (Does not include International Licenses)		
Revenues		
Rental income	$37,780,000	$35,356,000
Continuing franchise fee income	32,126,000	28,829,000
Sales by temporarily operated shops	1,025,000	2,141,000
Other [1]	6,664,000	4,458,000
	77,595,000	70,784,000
Expenses		
Expenses related to rental properties	18,218,000	16,324,000
Exp. related to temporarily operated shops	1,092,000	2,292,000
Selling, general and administrative expenses directly related to Franchise Division	14,738,000	11,217,000
	34,048,000	29,833,000
Contribution to income before taxes and prior to corporate selling, general and administrative expenses	$43,547,000	$40,951,000
Number of Shops	1,449	1,353
Company-Operated Shops Division		
Revenues		
Sales	$17,042,000	$27,453,000
Other [2]	3,583,000	2,978,000
	20,625,000	30,431,000
Operating costs and expenses	15,774,000	25,996,000
Gross profit from operations	4,851,000	4,435,000
Selling, general and administrative expenses directly related to Company-operated Shops Division	1,157,000	1,823,000
Contribution to income before income taxes and prior to corporate selling, general and administrative expenses	$ 3,694,000	$ 2,612,000
Number of Shops	29	44

1 includes initial franchise fees and sales of real estate and temporarily operated shops
2 includes sales of company-operated shops

Exhibit 3
Pro Forma for Branded Product Operations in Northeast Region

	Full Producing Unit		Branded Product Route		Combination Network	
Sales	530,387		140,110		670,497	
Cost of Sales						
Food Cost	121,989	(23.0%)	30,124	(21.5%)	152,113	(22.7%)
Payroll—Production	49,326	(9.3%)	23,819	(17.0%)	73,145	(10.9%)
Payroll—Sales	80,088	(15.1%)	—	(0.0%)	80,088	(11.9%)
Payroll—Maintenance	4,773	(.9%)	5,044	(3.6%)	9,817	(1.5%)
Payroll—Delivery	—	(0.0%)	14,291	(10.2%)	14,291	(2.1%)
Suppliers	24,928	(4.7%)	—	(0.0%)	24,928	(3.7%)
Total Cost of Sales	281,104	(53.0%)	73,278	(52.3%)	354,382	(52.9%)
Operating Expenses						
Weekly Franchise Fee	25,989	(4.9%)	9,808	(7.0%)	35,797	(5.3%)
Advertising Contribution	26,519	(5.0%)	7,006	(5.0%)	33,525	(5.0%)
Payroll Taxes	14,320	(2.7%)	5,044	(3.6%)	19,364	(2.9%)
Professional Services	4,243	(.8%)	—	(0.0%)	4,243	(.6%)
Other Taxes (Not R.E.)	1,061	(.2%)	140	(.1%)	1,201	(.2%)
Travel, Freight	530	(.1%)	—	(0.0%)	530	(.1%)
Cleaning, Maint., Repair	17,503	(3.3%)	420	(.3%)	17,923	(2.7%)
Admin. & Office Exp.	3,713	(.7%)	1,121	(.8%)	4,834	(.7%)
Other Expense	3,713	(.7%)	1,261	(.9%)	4,974	(.7%)
Delivery Cost	—	(0.0%)	10,500	(7.5%)	10,500	(1.6%)
Total Operating Expense	97,591	(18.4%)	35,300	(25.2%)	132,891	(19.8%)
Occupancy and Financing Expenses						
Rent and R.E. Taxes	50,988	(9.6%)	—	(0.0%)	50,988	(7.6%)
Utilities	17,366	(3.3%)	1,121	(.8%)	18,487	(2.8%)
Insurance	6,223	(1.2%)	2,662	(1.9%)	8,885	(1.3%)
Interest	10,073	(1.9%)	5,200	(3.7%)	15,273	(2.3%)
Total Occupancy/Fin. Exp.	84,650	(16.0%)	8,983	(6.4%)	93,633	(14.0%)
Total Depreciation & Amort.	19,327	(3.6%)	—	(0.0%)	19,327	(2.9%)
Profit before Owner's Draw and Income Taxes	47,715	(9.0%)	22,549	(16.1%)	70,264	(10.5%)
— ADJUSTMENTS —						
Addbacks						
Depreciation & Amort.	19,327	(3.6%)	—	(0.0%)	19,327	(2.9%)
Interest	10,073	(1.9%)	5,200	(3.7%)	15,273	(2.3%)
Rent	45,889	(8.7%)	—	(0.0%)	45,889	(8.7%)
Adjusted Cash Flow before Owner's Draw and Income Taxes	123,004	(23.2%)	27,749	(19.8%)	150,753	(22.5%)

Exhibit 4
Pro Forma for Satellite Operations in Northeast Region (One Satellite)

	Full Producing Unit		Branded Product Route		Combination Network	
Sales	530,387		319,185		849,572	
Cost of Sales						
Food Cost	121,989	(23.0%)	73,413	(23.0%)	195,402	(23.0%)
Payroll—Production	49,326	(9.3%)	20,109	(6.3%)	69,435	(8.2%)
Payroll—Sales	80,088	(15.1%)	51,389	(16.1%)	131,477	(15.5%)
Payroll—Maintenance	4,773	(.9%)	1,596	(.5%)	6,369	(.8%)
Payroll—Delivery	—	(0.0%)	7,980	(2.5%)	7,980	(.9%)
Suppliers	24,928	(4.7%)	15,002	(4.7%)	39,930	(4.7%)
Total Cost of Sales	281,104	(53.0%)	169,489	(53.0%)	450,593	(53.0%)
Operating Expenses						
Weekly Franchise Fee	25,989	(4.9%)	15,640	(4.9%)	41,629	(4.9%)
Advertising Contribution	26,519	(5.0%)	15,959	(5.0%)	42,478	(5.0%)
Payroll Taxes	14,320	(2.7%)	9,256	(2.9%)	23,576	(2.8%)
Professional Services	4,243	(.8%)	1,277	(.4%)	5,520	(.7%)
Other Taxes (Not R.E.)	1,061	(.2%)	319	(.1%)	1,380	(.2%)
Travel, Freight	530	(.1%)	—	(0.0%)	530	(.1%)
Cleaning, Maint., Repair	17,503	(3.3%)	4,149	(1.3%)	21,652	(2.5%)
Admin. & Office Exp.	3,713	(.7%)	638	(.2%)	4,351	(.5%)
Other Expense	3,713	(.7%)	1,915	(.6%)	5,628	(.7%)
Delivery Cost	—	(0.0%)	10,500	(3.3%)	10,500	(1.2%)
Total Operating Expense	97,591	(18.4%)	59,653	(18.7%)	157,244	(18.5%)
Occupancy and Financing Expenses						
Rent and R.E. Taxes	50,988	(9.6%)	27,075	(8.5%)	78,063	(9.2%)
Utilities	17,366	(3.3%)	6,078	(1.9%)	23,444	(2.8%)
Insurance	6,223	(1.2%)	4,408	(1.3%)	10,271	(1.2%)
Interest	10,073	(1.9%)	9,403	(2.9%)	19,476	(2.3%)
Total Occupancy/Fin. Exp.	84,650	(16.0%)	46,604	(14.6%)	131,254	(15.4%)
Total Depreciation & Amort.	19,327	(3.6%)	—	(0.0%)	19,327	(2.3%)
Profit before Owner's Draw and Income Taxes	47,715	(9.0%)	43,439	(13.6%)	91,154	(10.7%)
— ADJUSTMENTS —						
Addbacks						
Depreciation & Amort.	19,327	(3.6%)	—	(0.0%)	19,327	(2.3%)
Interest	10,073	(1.9%)	9,403	(3.7%)	19,476	(2.3%)
Rent	45,889	(8.7%)	24,368	(7.6%)	70,257	(8.3%)
Adjusted Cash Flow before Owner's Draw and Income Taxes	123,004	(23.2%)	77,210	(24.2%)	200,214	(23.6%)

Case 16

VANITY FAIR MILLS
MARKET RESPONSE SYSTEM

＊＊＊＊

VF's Market Response System is a new way of doing business accompanied by a climate that promotes optimum performance.

- L.R. Pugh, Chairman, VF Corporation

In February 1993 Tom Wyatt, President of Vanity Fair Mills (VFM), received a progress report on the company's "flow replenishment" and "quick response partnership" programs. The report, prepared by Marty Abercrombie (Manager of Flow Replenishment), summarized VFM's accomplishments during 1992 in implementing flow replenishment agreements with retailers. Retailers who participated in these partnerships sent sales data from their point-of-sale systems (POS) via electronic data interchange (EDI) to VFM periodically. The POS data were used, either by VFM or by a retail buyer, to develop a replenishment order. The system was designed so that orders for "never-out" items (a core group of high-volume products) would be received by retailers within 5 days, assuming they were shipped by VF direct to stores. The ultimate objective of the system was improved operating performance for both VFM and its retail partners.

As Wyatt reviewed Abercrombie's report, he wondered what questions he should raise with his management team about the impact of flow replenishment on VFM, and how the effectiveness of retail partnerships might be improved.

VF CORPORATION BACKGROUND

With 1992 sales of $3.8 billion, VF Corporation was the largest publicly-owned apparel manufacturing company in the United States. The company, established in 1899 as the Reading (PA) Glove and Mitten Company, entered the lingerie business in 1914 and adopted the Vanity Fair brand name in 1917.

In 1969, Vanity Fair acquired the Lee Company, one of the world's leading producers of jeanswear. Subsequently—until the mid-1980s—jeanswear represented 75% or more of VF's sales, which first exceeded $1 billion in 1983.

Beginning in 1984, VF made a series of acquisitions aimed at diversifying the company's product lines. Bassett-Walker, a leading producer of fleecewear, was acquired in 1984 as was Modern Globe, a producer of knit underwear. A major step in the diversification program was the acquisition of Blue Bell in late 1986. Blue Bell's product lines included Wrangler, Rustler, and Girbaud jeanswear; Jantzen and JanSport swimsuits and sportswear; and Red Kap, a producer of occupational apparel. As a result of the Blue Bell acquisition, VF sales increased from $1.54 billion in 1986 to $2.57

Professor Robert D. Buzzell prepared this case as the basis for class discussion rather than to illustrate either effective or ineffective handling of an administrative situation.

Copyright © 1993 by the President and Fellows of Harvard College.
Harvard Business School case 593-111.

billion in 1987. Subsequent acquisitions included Health-Tex, a children's wear producer (1990); Valero, a French lingerie manufacturer, Green Cotton Environment, a producer of "organic" cotton sportswear, and Vivesa, a Spanish lingerie producer (all in 1992).

Exhibit 1 summarizes VF's financial performance for the years 1988–92 and **Exhibit 2** shows changes in the distribution of VF's sales and operating profits by product group for the years 1990–92.

VF CORPORATE STRATEGY[1]

In 1992, VF top management described the company's strategy as one based on several key elements:

1. *Concentration on "basic" and "basic fashion" apparel products.* Basic apparel products were those, like 5-pocket jeans in a traditional fabric and color, that remained in a company's product line for years—in some cases, indefinitely. "Basic fashion" apparel products, in contrast, had limited lives—possibly lasting only one season, but usually several seasons. The fashion element in basic fashion jeans or intimate apparel might consist of fabric, finish, color, or trim.

   With rare exceptions, VF did not participate in true *fashion* apparel categories such as women's sportswear. Management believed that competing effectively in the fashion apparel business required a different set of resources and skills than those needed for basic and basic fashion.

2. *Well-known brands that offer superior customer value.* VF considered its brands to be "among its most important assets." Management believed that the company's extensive, modern domestic manufacturing base enabled it to achieve superior customer value, i.e., to produce high-quality garments at reasonable costs while providing superior service to retailers. In the early 1990s some VF divisions were developing "megabrands" by extending their strongest brand names to additional product categories. The Lee jeans brand, for example, was used to market fleecewear produced by Bassett-Walker.

3. *Multiple brands for different distribution channels.* Traditionally, VF had relied primarily on full-service department and specialty apparel retailers for the distribution of brands such as Lee, Wrangler, and Vanity Fair. During the 1980s other types of retailers, especially discount department stores such as Wal-Mart, grew in importance while conventional department stores lost ground. In response to shifting distribution channels, VF adopted a strategy aimed at ensuring that the consumer would be able to find VF products "wherever he or she chooses to shop." Among the new brands acquired or developed by VF to implement the multi-brand strategy were Vassarette (intimate apparel for distribution through discounters) and Timber Creek (non-denim casual pants for the discount channel).

4. *Market Response System.* In 1989 VF began implementing, on a company-wide basis, its Market Response System (MRS). As explained in the company's 1990 *Annual Report*:

   The traditional apparel product development cycle (is) a lengthy and cumbersome process . . . the development of a garment routinely begins as long as 18 months before the scheduled shipment date . . . (As a result) consumer preference changes faster than the time required to complete the line development cycle. Without the flexibility to modify products during a season, manufacturers can often do little more than bear the expense of excess inventory. The situation is equally complicated when products sell well; in-season reorders may be required and out-of-stock positions may result for retailers.

   In contrast to the traditional system, VF characterized MRS as "a completely new approach to conducting our business." When MRS was initiated, VF Chairman Larry Pugh established as its goals (1) a 40% reduction in product development cycle time, (2) a 30% reduction in total inventory, and (3) a 20% reduction in garment cost. Shorter development cycles would, Pugh reasoned, allow the company's product groups to utilize "continuous merchandising," by which new styles could be conceived, designed, produced, and put on retail shelves *within* a given selling season.

   Another key element of MRS was flexible or modular manufacturing. In a modular manufacturing system, production workers were organized in small groups or "modules," with each module being responsible for the complete sequence of operations required to produce a small batch of garments. This system allowed more flexible scheduling of production and greatly reduced

---

1 This section is based in part on a description provided by the company in a Registration Statement (Form S-3) filed with the Securities and Exchange Commission on December 22, 1992, and on other company documents.

manufacturing throughput times. This allowed quicker fulfillment of incoming orders than was possible under the traditional "progressive bundle" production system in which bundles of garments are passed through a series of steps, at each of which a specialized operator performed a distinct sewing operation.

The third key element of VF's MRS system was its proprietary Flow Replenishment System. To implement Flow Replenishment, VF divisions formed partnerships with key retailers. The retailers transmitted point-of-sale (POS) data from individual stores to the supplying VF division via electronic data interchange (EDI). Based on the POS data, the VF division prepared appropriate replenishment orders and sent them to the retailers, often to individual stores, within 5 days.

Although each VF division managed its own replenishment system, all of the divisions utilized the corporation's central information and communications systems. During 1991–92 VF had invested substantial sums in these systems; a major reason for upgrading and expanding the systems was to accommodate the growing volume of EDI and other communications with retailers, which included order entry, purchase order confirmation, advance notice of shipment, electronic funds transfer, and other types of transactions.

The implementation of MRS at Vanity Fair Mills, VF's intimate apparel product group, is described in some detail in later sections of this case study.

Both Lee and Wrangler had long-established international operations, including manufacturing facilities in Europe. As noted earlier, VF acquired the Valero and Vivesa intimate apparel companies in Europe in 1992. VF's other product groups were not significantly involved in international markets. It was expected, however, that international operations would grow in importance in the future.

THE INTIMATE APPAREL INDUSTRY

Consumer purchases of intimate apparel in 1992 were estimated at 1.2 billion units with an aggregate retail value of $7.54 billion. Trends in retail sales for the six major categories of intimate apparel are shown in **Exhibit 3**.

Sales of intimate apparel grew very little from 1990 to 1992—shapewear and daywear unit sales actually declined slightly. The market was generally regarded as mature, with the likely prospect of only modest year-to-year growth during the balance of the 1990s.

INTIMATE APPAREL CONSUMERS

All women were users of some or all categories of intimate apparel. The distribution of total purchases by consumer age varied significantly among the different product categories, as shown in **Table A.**

A market segmentation study conducted for VFM in 1989 suggested that consumers differed greatly in their attitudes toward intimate apparel. The study was based on personal interviews with 765 women, each of whom had made one or more purchases of both bras and pants during the preceding year. Topics covered in the interviews included brand awareness, purchasing patterns, and the importance of various product characteristics and benefits.

The segmentation study indicated that the Vanity Fair brand name enjoyed a "strong consumer franchise," with high levels of unaided brand awareness in the bras, pants, and slips categories. Awareness of Vanity Fair advertising was, however, low. According to the researchers, the implication was that the brand had achieved its high awareness level primarily through its extensive distribution. Vanity Fair was ranked second only to Playtex as a brand that consumers "would consider if they were to make a purchase today."

Table A   Per Cent of Dollar Purchases of Intimate Apparel Product Categories, by Age of User, 1992

	34 or Younger	**35–54**	**55 or Older**
All Intimate Apparel	36.9%	35.1%	28.0%
Bras	41.9	35.3	22.8
Shapewear	14.3	26.8	58.9
Pants	42.2	36.3	21.5
Daywear	39.5	34.6	25.9
Sleepwear	35.2	36.3	28.5
Robes/Housecoats	22.2	32.6	45.3

Consumer attitudes toward intimate apparel were evaluated in the study by giving each respondent a list of 68 product benefits and asking her to rate their importance on a 5-point scale. All of the consumers participating in the study rated product quality, comfort, and fit as very important. There were significant differences, however, in their ratings of other product benefits. Based on these benefit importance ratings, the study identified six attitude segments. Among these, four were of particular interest: "Brand Buyers," "Sensuous Buyers," "Romantic Buyers," and "Cost-Conscious Buyers." These four consumer segments are described briefly below:

- *Brand Buyers* placed great importance on a product being "a brand I have bought before," "from a well-known company," and "a brand sold in department stores." Vanity Fair's brand franchise was strongest among this consumer group. Brand buyers tended to be older and more affluent than women in other segments.
- *Sensuous Buyers* were the heaviest buyers of lingerie. These consumers gave above-average importance ratings to the fabrics, colors, and appearance of intimate apparel. They also gave high importance to such emotional benefits as "feminine," "romantic," "provocative," "elegant," and "reward myself," among others. Consumers in this group were younger and less affluent than Brand Buyers. Familiarity with and ownership of the Vanity Fair brand was below average in this segment.
- *Romantic Buyers* were similar to sensuous buyers, but displayed less emotional involvement in lingerie purchases. They were especially interested in products that were "pretty" and "silky."
- *Cost-Conscious Buyers* ". . . seek only one benefit—inexpensive. They express no emotional needs in

selecting lingerie." Consumers in this group spent the least on intimate apparel and were the most likely to buy in discount stores. Vanity Fair brand did not enjoy a strong position in this segment; private-label products did, however.

One conclusion of the segmentation study was that Vanity Fair (as well as several other well-established brands) was seen as pretty, high quality, well-known, "but not sensual or sexy." In contrast, the Victoria's Secret and Lily of France brands were seen as different, exciting, sensual, romantic, and fun.

VANITY FAIR MILLS

In late 1992 VFM operated 7 manufacturing facilities in Alabama and employed 6,000 persons. The company was vertically integrated, with fabric knitting, dyeing, and finishing operations as well as garment cutting and sewing. Less than a third of VFM production came from facilities outside the United States, primarily in Mexico and the Caribbean.

Prior to 1990 VFM's product lines included only the Vanity Fair brand and private label garments. In 1990 VF Corporation acquired the Vassarette brand and the production facilities of the Form-O-Uth company, a private label supplier with low-cost manufacturing facilities in Mexico. Also in 1990 VF entered into a licensing agreement with Eileen West, a designer and producer of "upscale, natural fiber products." Diversification of VFM's product lines continued with the 1991 acquisition of Barbizon, a 75-year old producer of branded lingerie whose operations included a chain of 44 factory outlet stores.

As a result of the company's acquisitions and its repositioning of the Vassarette brand, VFM's offerings in early 1993 spanned the full range of intimate apparel price points and distribution channels, as shown in **Table B:**

Table B   Vanity Fair Mills Brands, 1993

Brand	Price Level/Distribution
Queen Anne's Lace by Eileen West	Designer bras and pants
Eileen West	"Bridge" Line (between Designer and Mainstream)
Vanity Fair	Mainstream, Department and Specialty Stores
Private Label	National Chains and Lingerie Specialty Stores
Vassarette	Discount Department Stores

VFM was the only domestic producer that marketed products in all six intimate apparel product classifications. Within the Vanity Fair *Brand* (VFB), the product assortment in each classification (i.e., the number of different *styles*) was among the broadest in the industry. As a result of the broad assortment of styles, the VFB product line was extraordinarily complex. Tom Wyatt explained that intimate apparel was a "SKU-intensive business," in that each style was produced in a range of sizes *and* a choice of colors and prints. The complexity was especially great for bras, which were typically offered in from 3 to as many as 8 girth sizes (32, 34, 36, etc.) and two to four cup sizes (A, B, C, etc.). Taking into account all of the various combinations, the Fall 1991 VFB line of bras included:

- 50 different styles
- in an average of 10 sizes (strap/cup combinations)
- in an average of 6 colors or patterns

The result was a grand total of approximately 3,000 distinct SKUs. Wyatt pointed out, however, that a relatively small number of the SKUs accounted for a majority of total unit sales.

Compared with bras, sleepwear and robes were relatively simple categories with relatively few SKUs. In addition, sales of sleepwear and robes were highly seasonal, with the bulk of consumer purchases being made in the fourth quarter.

VFB's retail price points were similar to those of other mainstream manufacturers' brands: for example, bras ranged from $17 to $29 and daywear from $10 to $29. In contrast, bras sold in discount department stores were typically priced at $4.99 to $9.99. VFB selling prices to retailers, for all of its products, were set at 45% of the suggested retail prices.

COMPETITORS

Although there were many small producers of intimate apparel, VFM's competition came primarily from two large companies, Sara Lee and Warnaco. According to Tom Wyatt, Sara Lee was by far the most formidable of the two.

Of Sara Lee's 1992 sales of $13.2 billion, nearly half was accounted for by food products, the company's original line of business. Among the food brands were Sara Lee baked goods and Jimmy Dean, Hillshire Farms, and Kahn's meats. Other Sara Lee divisions included Coach Leatherware, Champion apparel, and Hanes and L'Eggs hosiery. In the intimate apparel field, Sara Lee brands included Hanes Her Way, Playtex, and Just My Size (distributed via discount stores) as well as Bali and Henson (department store brands). The company also marketed men's underwear, with the Hanes brand reportedly ranking second only to Fruit of the Loom.

Exhibit 4 compares Sara Lee's market shares with those of VFM, Warnaco, and private label products for the years 1990–1992. Sara Lee's competitive position was strong-est in bras, panties, and shapewear, with only a token presence in sleepwear and robes.

Sara Lee's competitive position was strongest in lower-priced distribution channels; it was a relative newcomer to full-service department and specialty outlets. List prices of the Hanes Her Way brand were 5%–10% higher than VFM's Vassarette, but frequent promotions made the actual average price about the same.

Well over half of Sara Lee's intimate apparel production was sourced outside the United States. VFM executives believed that Sara Lee was the lowest-cost producer in the industry.

Warnaco, with 1992 intimate apparel sales of $384.8 million (80% in the U.S.), competed primarily in full-service retail channels. Warnaco produced and marketed the Warners and Olga brands of bras and pants. The Warners brand was priced 10%–15% below Vanity Fair while Olga was about 10% above Vanity Fair. Almost all of Warnaco's bra production was foreign sourced; as a result, their costs were believed to be lower than Vanity Fair's. A mid-1992 study indicated that consumer quality ratings for Vanity Fair, Warners, and Olga were very similar.

According to a report prepared by Salomon Brothers, Warnaco's intimate apparel sales nearly doubled from 1986 to 1992, and the company's share of U.S. brassiere sales had increased steadily during the same period.

In 1992, Warnaco entered the discount department store channel via its licensing of the well-known Fruit of the Loom brand name. VFM executives expected Warnaco to be an aggressive competitor for Vassarette in this channel.

Warnaco's total sales in 1992 amounted to $625.1 million. Besides intimate apparel, the company's products included Hathaway, Christian Dior, Chaps by Ralph Lauren, and other menswear lines.

DISTRIBUTION CHANNELS

At one time the dominant channels of distribution for "mainstream" intimate apparel were full-service department stores, such as Macy's and Hecht Company, and full-service multi-line specialty stores, such as Lord & Taylor and Filene's. Private brands available from Sears, JCPenney, and Ward provided lower-priced alternatives to the department and specialty store lines.

Throughout the 1970s and 1980s, discount department stores gained steadily in importance as outlets for intimate apparel. As shown in **Exhibit 5**, by 1992 discounters accounted for 44% of unit volume and 25% of retail sales dollars. The average price per garment in discount stores was $3.63, compared with $9.79 in department stores. (The gap in average unit price reflected differences in both product mix and selling prices for a given type of garment.) It seemed likely that by 1995 the dollar share of discount stores would, for the first time, exceed that of department stores. (Note that in **Exhibit 5**, department store sales are included in the category "Department and Specialty Stores.")

Another shift in intimate apparel distribution was the rapid growth of national specialty chains and catalog marketers, notably Victoria's Secret and Frederick's of Hollywood. Victoria's Secret consisted of four stores and a small mail-order operation when it was acquired by The Limited in 1982. By the fall of 1992 there were more than 500 Victoria's Secret stores in shopping malls throughout the United States as well as a thriving mail order business. Salomon Brothers estimated Victoria's Secret sales at $750 million in 1991. Victoria's Secret sold only private label garments (some of them supplied by VFM), and emphasized more fashionable and romantic styles than those typically carried in department stores.

VFB products were distributed through full-service department and specialty stores as well as JCPenney. During the late 1980s Penney had repositioned its stores and merchandise assortments for greater fashion appeal. As a result, many or most Penney stores were basically moderate-priced department stores. Altogether VFB products were present in 2,400 accounts and 7,700 "doors" (store locations) nationwide.

Prior to the acquisition of Vassarette in 1990, VFM products were not represented in discount stores. By 1992 Vassarette garments (which included all six product categories) were sold in Wal-Mart and 18 other discount department store chains.

Another change affecting intimate apparel distribution in the early 1990s was that of consolidation in the retailing industry. Reflecting a wave of bankruptcies and

acquisitions, an ever-decreasing number of large firms controlled a steadily increasing proportion of total apparel sales. Examples of the consolidation process included the 1990 bankruptcy of the Campeau group, owner of the Federated and Allied department store groups; the 1990 acquisition of Marshall Field by Dayton-Hudson; the 1992 bankruptcy of Macy's; and the acquisitions of several regional department store companies by Dillard's. Not only were there fewer, larger retail companies, but many of them were moving toward more centralized corporate buying. Until the late 1980s, each of the local or regional companies (e.g. Hecht's or Famous Barr) within a retail corporate group (May Company) had maintained strict local autonomy in buying. The tradition of local buying autonomy could be traced to the originally independent ownership of the regional divisions. Maintaining local autonomy, even after two decades of decline in department stores' share of retail sales, was typically justified by the claim that consumers' apparel tastes varied significantly among the various divisions' territories. But in response to continued competitive pressure from national specialty chains and discounters, department stores were gradually adopting more centralized approaches to merchandise planning and buying. For example, May Company's 1991 *Annual Report* indicated that the company had established "corporate-wide steering committees" to coordinate the operating divisions' merchandise selections.

THE QUICK RESPONSE MOVEMENT[2]

"Quick Response" was the term used by textile and apparel manufacturers and retailers to describe buyer-seller "partnership" relationships in which (1) the buyer transmitted orders via EDI and (2) the seller promised to fill orders quickly (relative to traditional standards). Numerous other features or practices could be added to these two basic elements, depending on the preferences and capabilities of the partners. One of VFM's major department store customers, Mercantile Stores, had identified the following possible components of a Quick Response relationship:

- UPC code symbols attached to product by the manufacturer, and scanned at point of sale by the retailer
- Electronic Purchase Orders (EPO) transmitted to vendor

---

2 For an extended discussion of Quick Response in the apparel industry, see "Quick Response in the Apparel Industry," HBS Case Services No. 9-690-038.

- Vendor marking of retail prices on garments ("pre-retailing")
- POS data, by store, transmitted to vendor
- Advance Shipping Notices received from vendor in advance of shipment
- Shipping containers marked to allow scanning at receiving point
- Electronic Invoicing
- Electronic Funds Transfer

The Quick Response movement had grown out of the activities of an industry group called the Crafted with Pride in the U.S.A. Council (CWP).[3] CWP was formed in 1984, with the objective of strengthening the competitive position of the domestic manufacuturing industries in the "fiber-textile-apparel" chain. One of CWP's programs was an advertising campaign that encouraged consumers to buy U.S.-made apparel. A second program, which evolved into Quick Response, was intended to improve U.S. producers' position vis-à-vis imports by improving the flow of merchandise through the production and distribution systems. Technical committees were set up to develop industry standards for EDI, shipping container marking, etc. (The bar code symbols used for POS scanning and more generally for identifying items had been developed earlier in the food industry.) By early 1993, industry standards had been widely adopted by textile producers, apparel manufacturers, retailers, and transportation companies.

With industry standards in place, retailers and suppliers were able to develop partnerships whose basic objective was "to have the right quantities of the right goods in the right place at the right time."

Manufacturers and retailers who adopted Quick Response trading practices had strong incentives to encourage others—including competitors—to adopt them too. For any one company, it was desirable to spread the costs involved in QR systems over as much of total sales or purchases as possible. For this reason, many manufacturers and retailers actively promoted QR via speeches, interviews, press releases, and other forms of communication.

VFM'S MARKET RESPONSE SYSTEM

VF Corporation's Market Response programs began with a company-wide conference held in the fall of 1989. At that time Chairman Larry Pugh established the goals

mentioned earlier: a 40% reduction in cycle time, 30% reduction in inventory and a 20% cut in unit cost. Pugh also called for a new spirit of cooperation between apparel producers and retailers. Traditionally, he said, their relationship had been largely adversarial, resulting in increased costs for both sides. Implementation of QR, however, would require mutual trust. **Exhibit 6** is a VF advertisement in the trade publication *Women's Wear Daily* conveying this message.

In response to Pugh's challenge, VFM Chairman Peter Velardi set up several task forces to explore different aspects of market responsiveness. These included, among others:

- Flow replenishment systems (see below)
- Continuous product development (see below)
- In-store testing of new products
- Sales forecasting
- Distribution center requirements
- Partnerships with fabric and trim suppliers
- Modular manufacturing
- Activity-based costing (to provide better measures of product costs)
- Improved workplace ergonomics

Each of the task forces developed recommendations, and by July 1990 Velardi had authorized implementation of many of the proposed changes.

FLOW REPLENISHMENT

By late 1992 all of VF Corporation's domestic divisions were utilizing flow replenishment systems and the company's subsidiaries in Europe were developing similar systems. At VFM, the elements of the flow replenishment system were as follows:

1. VFM and the retailer agreed on a *model stock* of Vanity Fair, Vassarette, or private label products. The model stock specified, for individual stores, for a specific season, the quantity of each stockkeeping unit or SKU (style, color, and size) that should be on hand. As products were sold, it would be replenished back up to the model stock level. Model stocks were established by analyzing a store's sales history over a preceding 12–24 month period. For each SKU, the model stock quantity was set at a level sufficient to cover expected demand, 95% (or any other selected percentage) of the time, during the time between

3 See "Crafted With Pride in the U.S.A. Council," HBS Case Services No. 9-587-110.

placement of the order and arrival of the replenishment goods at the store. On average, model stocks for VFB products were set at levels that were expected to yield an annual inventory turnover rate of 4 times.

For stores that carried the VFB line, extra stocks were needed to meet demand during promotions. The VFM account manager worked with the retail buyer to estimate the additional stock needed.

2. The retailer transmitted POS data, by SKU and by store, to VFM via EDI. POS data were transmitted by most accounts weekly; one discount department store chain sent POS data to VFM daily.

3. VFM guaranteed to ship "never out" styles, colors, and sizes in its product line within 5 days. Other items would be shipped within 30 days. This quick response made it possible to replenish retail inventories sooner, thereby reducing the frequency of being out of stock on an item. (Studies made in the early stages of the QR movement indicated that the incidence of out-of-stock conditions for specific SKUs in a typical department store was nearly 30%).

The "never out" SKUs in the VFB catalog were the *core basics* of the product line: high-volume items with relatively long life expectancies. In the Fall 1991 catalog, for example, about 400 of the nearly 3,000 SKUs in the bra category were designated as never-out items. Core basics accounted for about 75% of VFB sales and an even higher proportion of Vassarette sales.

4. Replenishment of SKUs under the model stock program was "automatic." For some accounts, VFM handled the automatic replenishment while others utilized their own in-house systems. In the latter case, VFM still received POS data, to be used for establishing model stock quantities and for sales forecasting and production planning. Retailers utilizing VFM's replenishment system fell into two groups: for *flow accounts*, VFM not only determined how much to ship and when, but also released the replenishment shipments under a "blanket release." A second group, designated as *ARP accounts*, also utilized VFM's system to determine replenishment quantities, but reviewed the recommendations before approving the shipments.

In addition to model stocks, EDI, and POS data, VFM could also provide Advance Shipping Notices, Shipping Container Marking, Pre-Ticketing, and Electronic Invoicing to accounts that were equipped to handle these procedures. A diagram used by VFM to explain the Flow Replenishment System is reproduced as **Exhibit 7. Exhibit 8** compares the steps involved and time required for traditional retail ordering as compared with flow replenishment.

A significant improvement in the flow replenishment system that was scheduled for 1993 was the adoption of "INFOREM" III (INventory FOrecasting and REplenishment Module), an IBM software package. Utilizing INFOREM III would enable VFM to design and continuously update "dynamic model stocks" for each store that participated in the system. In a dynamic model stock, the number of units of each SKU to be carried was modified over time, based on trends and seasonal patterns that were detected in actual sales. Maxine Cofield, who was responsible for implementing the dynamic model stock capability, explained that model stocks were presently being set on the basis of an SKU's sales history during the preceding year. One problem with this approach was that when sales of a high-volume style started to decline, excess inventory would gradually build up. The INFOREM III software would detect the declining trend earlier than the existing system and make corresponding changes in the model stock.

Agreeing on the terms and conditions of a replenishment partnership called for substantial changes in the traditional buyer-seller relationship. As Larry Pugh had pointed out in his keynote address at the 1991 Quick Response Conference,[4]

> The most important ingredient in our Flow Replenishment System is the new form of alliance we must establish with our retail partners...without this alliance, all the technology in the world won't accomplish Quick Response.

It was recognized that many of the efficiencies that were achieved in a flow replenishment partnership depended on the partners trusting each others' intentions and capabilities. A retailer needed to trust VFM to ship the SKU quantities needed to replenish an agreed-upon model stock. Historically, it was not uncommon for an apparel producer to substitute one color or size or even style for another in a shipment. Such substitutions were incompatible with accurate tracking and replenishment of a model stock. A significant reduction in a retailer's

---

4 Quick Response Conferences, co-sponsored by AIM (Automatic Identification Manufacturers) USA and the Voluntary Interindustry Communications Standards (VICS) Committee, were held annually beginning in March 1989.

receiving cost could be achieved by eliminating inspection of incoming shipments. This, however, required reliance on the supplier's honesty and near-error-free order fulfillment.

Because partnerships required so many changes and so much trust, they were invariably set up by "top-to-top" meetings between Larry Pugh and/or the head of a VF division, such as Tom Wyatt, and the CEO of a retail company.

CONTINUOUS MERCHANDISING

A second element of VFM's Market Response System, and—according to Larry Pugh "arguably the most important," was Continuous Merchandising. Traditionally new intimate apparel styles (and most other apparel products) had been designed for introduction during well-defined retail *seasons*. Thus, VFB produced catalogs twice a year, for its Spring and Fall seasons. Within the two major seasons were "sub-seasons"—new Fall styles were shown to retail buyers in March and May, and new Spring styles were shown in August, November, and January.

The planning process for a new style involved several distinct steps, as shown in **Exhibit 9.** Jennifer Falconer, VFM's Vice President–Product Development, explained that traditionally the steps in the process were carried out in strict sequence. Each task was the responsibility of a specialized department (Design, Pattern Making, Sewing, etc.) and functional specialists were not assigned to specific product lines. Projects moved through the sequence with delays at each "handoff" point; in addition, considerable time was spent monitoring the status of a project. Priorities were not clearly established, and one project was often moved ahead of another because one designer clamored for attention more than another one.

Beginning in 1990, product development for VFB was reorganized around a *modular* system. Three modules or "mods" were formed, one each for Body Fashions/Shapewear, Daywear/Pants, and Sleepwear/Robes. The composition of a mod is shown in **Exhibit 10,** along with a job description for each member. Each mod met about every two weeks, with more frequent meetings at critical stages in the calendar. The Product Development Manager in each mod was responsible for allocating resources and establishing schedules for all projects within his or her product area.

Members of each mod were cross-trained to some extent in each others' specialties. This enabled them to fill in for one another during absences due to illness, vacation, etc.

Adopting the mod system had enabled VFB, according to Jennifer Falconer, to compress the product development cycle—from initial design to large scale shipments to the trade—from 42 weeks to 26 weeks. About half the 26-week period was devoted to design and testing, and the remainder to production.

A major benefit of the mod system was its enhanced ability to develop new products "off-line," i.e., outside the normal seasonal calendar. An example cited by Tom Wyatt and Greg Stephenson, VFB's Manager of Line Development, was the "slender-slip" introduced in mid-1991. The product was a pettiskirt with stretch fabric for shaping. It was developed in response to the success of a similar product from a small competitor. The sales force had requested a comparable item in mid-April. A design was created and samples were prepared by May 1. By June 25 30,000 units had been shipped; the product was a major success.

Another change in VFM's product development process was the use of Computer-Assisted Design (CAD) technology. CAD systems, acquired in 1991 were used to create color pictures of garments. A fabric could be scanned into the CAD system and "cut and pasted" into an outline drawing of a garment. A book of pictures created in this way, representing possible colors and patterns for an upcoming season, could then be shown to retailers and used as a basis for initial evaluation of a product line.

VFM SALES FORCE

As the retail industry became more concentrated during the late 1980s, the number of VFM field sales representatives declined from a high of 75 to 48 in early 1993. Sales representatives were called *account managers* to emphasize the idea that their function had shifted from "getting real estate and protecting turf" to helping retailers manage a product line. Part of the reduction in sales force head count was achieved by shifting smaller accounts (under $10,000 annual purchases) to service via telemarketing only.

Miriam Bakker, a VFM District Sales Manager, explained that an account manager's responsibilities included:

- Developing a sales and inventory plan for each account, for each six-month season.
- Making sales projections for new products.

- Developing plans for advertising and sales promotion events.
- Monitoring actual results vs. plan on a continuous basis.

Prior to the introduction of the flow replenishment system, the account manager's planning and monitoring had to be carried out manually. Bakker expected that flow replenishment would relieve the account manager of much of the routine, repetitive work of stock checking. But, she said, the account manager would still need to review the performance of each account regularly to determine needed changes in model stock levels and to facilitate the introduction of new products.

In 1990 VFM had adopted a sales compensation system in which 65% of total compensation was in the form of base salary, 17.5% a bonus based on dollar volume, and 17.5% a bonus based on service. ("Service" included achieving targets in distribution, control of promotions, and expense control.) In January 1993, however, VFM revised the sales compensation system to 40% base salary, 10% service bonus, and 50% commission. The commission rate increased as shipments to an account manager's accounts went up; there was a cap on the dollar amount of commission income at 135% of the target level. Tom Wyatt commented on the change in the compensation method:

> We went too far in emphasizing service, and lost sight of the reality that the job is still to make sales.

ADVERTISING AND SALES PROMOTION

Traditionally, intimate apparel manufacturers had relied primarily on "push" from retailers to generate sales. "Pull" created by media advertising was of little importance in comparison with in-store displays, local retail advertising, and personal sales support. Marketing communication programs were changing, however, with national advertising outlays rising. Manufacturers' advertising was heaviest for bras, which were increasingly marketed in ways similar to so-called "packaged goods" such as soft drinks. Estimated national advertising expenditures by intimate apparel manufacturers are shown in **Exhibit 11**.

Among department store brands Maidenform was the leading advertiser, accounting for almost 40% of total expenditures by this group. Vanity Fair was second with a 30% "share of voice." Bali had been heavily advertised up to 1989, but its budget was then reduced sharply,

reportedly in order to fund major in-store fixture programs. Most advertising for department store brands was devoted to print ads, especially in fashion-oriented magazines such as *Glamour*, *Seventeen*, and *Elle*. VFB and other major brands provided cooperative advertising allowances (up to around 3% of purchases) to retailers.

Advertising budgets were significantly larger among brands distributed through discounters, with three brands spending more than $5 million each. Advertising support for the Vassarette brand was still in its early stages in 1991 as the brand gained increased distribution.

Consumer awareness of the Hanes and Playtex brands was very high, at 98% and 95%, respectively. Awareness of the Hanes brand was bolstered by advertising for Hanes hosiery and men's underwear. Altogether, advertising for Hanes products amounted to some $30 million in 1992.

As **Exhibit 11** shows, very little national advertising was devoted to the Warners brand. The Warners and Olga brands were supported by frequent manufacturer-sponsored promotions, however, often using the theme "Buy 2, Get 1 Free." Other department store brands (but not Vanity Fair) had copied this type of promotion.

All of the major intimate apparel brands, including VFB, periodically sponsored retail promotions of their products. During a promotion retail prices were typically reduced by around 25%. The manufacturer reduced wholesale selling prices and also provided special allowances to fund retail advertising of the event. For Vanity Fair, shipments at promotional prices had historically represented less than a third of annual shipments. According to Tom Wyatt, the frequency of promotions for Warners and Bali had increased dramatically during 1992. Promotional sales of the two brands were estimated at 50% or more of total sales. Wyatt believed that VFB probably should have responded to the competitors' promotions earlier in the season. But when VFB did "fire back" with its own promotion in November, it appeared that some account managers had gone too far in encouraging retailers to increase their orders. As a result, some accounts had complained about unsatisfactory inventory turnover results in the quarter ended January 31, 1993.

Sales of intimate apparel were very responsive to promotions. **Exhibit 12** shows weekly retail sales of a specific style in a department store group that heavily emphasized sale events. All of the "spikes" in the chart represent promotions.

STATUS OF FLOW REPLENISHMENT IN EARLY 1993

Marty Abercrombie's progress report indicated that the volume of business handled under VFM's flow replenishment/quick response programs had increased dramatically in 1992. The number of stores (doors) participating in the programs was up by 20%, and shipments made under the VFM-managed replenishment system had more than doubled. Altogether, more than 60% of VFM's 1992 shipments were to Quick Response partners, either flow accounts (pre-approved shipments) or ARP accounts (who reviewed each recommended replenishment order). (The 60% figure included shipments of *all* products to the QR partner accounts, not just shipments of the basic merchandise covered by automatic replenishment.)

VFM's shipments to flow accounts had increased significantly in both 1991 and 1992, while shipments to ARP and other accounts had actually declined slightly in 1992, as shown in **Table C.**

For each Flow Replenishment account, Abercrombie compiled various measures of progress and performance. Some of these measures are summarized in **Exhibit 13,** which covers 24 department store accounts belonging to three national department store groups, "Alpha," "Beta," and "Gamma" and 3 discount department store chain accounts. For each account, the exhibit shows:

- How long the account had been covered by the VFM-managed Flow Replenishment System.
- The frequency with which orders were placed.
- Whether replenishment orders were covered by an automatic release agreement or were reviewed by the retail buyer before shipment ("Manual" release).
- The percentage difference between the account's *actual* inventory of replenishment merchandise and its *model stock* inventory. The figure of +79% for Alpha-1, for example, showed that in this account the actual dollar amount of inventory was 79% greater

than the amount specified by the model stock plan. (Abercrombie explained that in 1992 most accounts still had inventories in excess of their model stocks, primarily because it took some time to sell merchandise that was in store inventories at the time the model stock was set up.) Some retailers' year-end inventories had also been built up as a result of a promotional push by VFM in the fourth quarter.

- The percentage of model stock SKUs that were in stock (according to the POS data) as of December 31, 1992.
- The account's 1992 rate of inventory turnover for replenishment merchandise.
- The percentage of the account's total purchases that were covered by the Flow Replenishment System. (Because fashion styles and colors were not suitable for automatic replenishment, Abercrombie thought the maximum possible coverage for department stores was 70% or less, depending on the account.)

As the exhibit shows, the discount stores had generally achieved higher in-stock levels and turnover rates than the department store accounts. Wyatt recognized, however, that the discounters also had simpler product assortments. He also pointed out that the Vassarette product line had been introduced in the discount stores during 1990 and 1991. As a result, the discounters started on the Flow Replenishment System with a "clean slate," i.e., without any accumulations of "old" inventory.

DIRECTIONS FOR THE FUTURE

As he reviewed Marty Abercrombie's report, Tom Wyatt wondered how VFM could derive the greatest benefit from flow replenishment and other forms of Quick Response trading relationships. Wyatt was convinced that flow replenishment had produced significant gains for VFM. The most visible benefit was the successful repositioning of the Vassarette line. VF's flow replenishment

Table C Changes in VFM Shipments, by Type of Replenishment System

Replenishment System	% Change in Shipments	
	1991 vs. 1990	1992 vs. 1991
Flow	+18.5%	+16.6%
ARP	+9.8	−4.5
None	+2.5	−8.4

capability had been an important factor in achieving placement of the Vassarette line at Wal-Mart and other discount department stores, according to Wyatt. It was more difficult to show the value of flow replenishment for VFB's performance in traditional retail channels. As Wyatt reviewed the figures in **Exhibit 13,** he reflected on the many variables that affected performance in individual retail accounts. These included, in addition to the replenishment system, the fashionability of VFB's products; changes in retail buyer assignments; changes in a store's merchandising strategy; and trends in consumer spending in particular regions of the country.

Another area of concern was the impact of promotions, which created problems for the flow replenishment system because they led to large fluctuations in sales rates. Under the present system, the retail buyer and/or VFM account manager estimated the extra quantities needed for a promotion and added these quantities to the normal order. Wyatt wished that he could cut back on promotions, but he saw no evidence that Warnaco or Sara Lee would follow suit. Since both competitors relied on foreign manufacturing sources, it seemed unlikely that either could match VFM's Quick Response capabilities. Perhaps, Wyatt mused, they were compensating for slower response with heavier promotion.

Another area where change might be needed was that of sales force compensation. While VFM had just shifted back to a system that emphasized commission incentives, Wyatt was still not sure that he had found the proper balance between rewards for sales and rewards for service.

Related to the question of sales force compensation was that of performance measures for retail buyers. Traditionally buyers had been evaluated (and rewarded) on the basis of (1) the percentage gross margin they achieved and (2) growth in sales volume. These measures took no account of the amount invested in inventories. As a result, buyers in many stores were notorious for carrying massive stocks. (One speaker at an industry conference, referring to buyers at a well-known department store, said "their idea of safety stock was 48 weeks' supply!") In recent years some retail executives were putting greater emphasis on inventory turnover, and a few companies had adopted Gross Margin Return on Investment (GMROI) or Contribution per Dollar of Average Inventory as performance measures. GMROI was the ratio of Gross Margin Dollars to Average Inventory Dollars in a specified time period. "Contribution" was defined as the gross margin for a department or merchandise classification, *minus* its direct sales payroll and advertising expenses. Some stores, following the lead of specialty chains and discounters, were also paying greater attention to sales or contribution dollars per square foot of selling space. Wyatt was confident that products handled under automatic replenishment systems would outperform other lines when evaluated in terms of such measures as GMROI or sales per square foot. But most retailers still paid little or no attention to these concepts.

Another issue related to flow replenishment was how products should move through the steps in the distribution system. Shipments from VFM's distribution center (DC) could reach retail stores in any of four different ways:

- Direct to individual stores (doors). This was the fastest method, but it was also the most costly because shipping costs were considerably greater per unit for the small quantities involved. In the case of one discount department store chain, the minimum shipment quantity was only two dozen units. VFM prepaid the costs of all shipments of Vanity Fair Brand products, but freight costs for Vassarette were usually paid by the retailers.
- To the retailer's distribution center, prepacked in orders designated for specific stores. Under this system the orders were moved directly from the DC receiving area to its shipping area ("cross-docked"). Costs of shipping under this method were considerably lower than direct store shipments.
- To the retailer's DC in a single order, which was assigned to individual stores *after* receipt at the DC ("post-distributed"). This gave the retailer an opportunity to modify the quantities designated for the stores, but it involved a delay of at least one day in the arrival of the merchandise at the stores.
- To the retailer's DC for holding there as reserve stock. Most retailers were reluctant to carry significant reserve stocks of apparel at their DC's because of the extra handling costs and the risks of obsolescence.

Related to the choice of shipment paths was the question of who could best manage an automatic replenishment system. For accounts served by VFM's flow replenishment system, VFM was authorized to make replenishment shipments (within the framework of the model stock agreement) without any review or approval. An alternative approach, favored by most department stores, was in-house management of the automatic replenishment system by the retailer. In-house management was required for logistics systems in which merchandise was post-distributed after receipt at the retailer's DC and/or held in reserve DC stocks. When shipments went direct to stores or were cross-docked, either vendor management or in-house management of the replenishment could be adopted.

Advocates of vendor management claimed that a manufacturer had a greater incentive to pay careful attention to sales trends and other changes in a specific product category than a retailer, who carried dozens or hundreds of different categories. Retailers who preferred in-house management argued that they knew more than their suppliers did about marketplace trends in a local or regional trading area. In addition, retail buyers were likely to be more fully informed about the marketing activities of all the suppliers in a given category than any one of the suppliers was.

Wyatt knew that the various suppliers and retailers participating in QR programs were utilizing different combinations of management systems (vendor vs. in-house) and shipment patterns (direct to stores, cross-docked, etc.). He wondered which approach would produce the greatest benefits for VF and its retail accounts in terms of inventory turnover, in-stock position, markdowns, and operating costs.

Exhibit 1
Selected Financial Data, VF Corporation, 1988–1992
(In Thousands, Except Per Share Data)

	1988	1989	1990	1991	1992
Net Sales	$2,516,107	$2,532,711	$2,612,613	$2,952,433	$3,824,449
Operating Income	304,601	312,864	207,253	304,054	429,380
Net Income	173,660	176,011	81,124	161,330	237,031
Earnings per Share (primary)	$ 2.55	$ 2.72	$ 1.35	$ 2.75	$ 3.97
Total Assets	$1,759,862	$1,889,764	$1,852,829	$2,126,913	$2,712,380
Shareholders' Equity	1,095,383	819,777	823,126	938,078	1,153,971
Capital Expenditures[a]	64,137	125,294	110,143	110,762	207,202

a Excluding acquisitions.

Source: Company Annual Reports

Exhibit 2
VF Corporation Sales and Operating Profit by Business Group, 1990–1992
(Amounts in Thousands)

	1990	1991	1992
Net Sales			
Jeanswear	$ 1,191,327	$ 1,371,978	$ 1,896,258
Casual/Sportswear	487,556	505,804	652,571[a]
Intimate apparel	360,062[b]	452,899	420,200[a,b]
International	245,932	272,524	420,278
Other apparel	327,736	349,228	435,142
	$ 2,612,613	$ 2,952,433	$ 3,824,449
Operating Profit			
Jeanswear	$ 85,494	$ 173,640	$ 274,256
Casual/Sportswear	14,778	37,889	52,184[a]
Intimate apparel	52,411	42,289	53,425[a]
International	36,830	35,937	34,253
Other apparel	43,215	42,103	46,483
	$ 232,728	$ 331,858	$ 460,601

a Sales and operating profits of the Modern Globe business unit were classified under Intimate Apparel in 1991 but reclassified into the Casual/Sportswear segment in 1992. This reflected a shift of Modern Globe's activities from knit underwear to tee-shirts. Shearson Lehman Brothers estimated Modern Globe's 1991 sales at $60-$65 million.
b Vassarette was acquired in 1990. Shearson Lehman Brothers estimated Vassarette sales at $16 million in 1990, increasing to $60 million in 1992.

Exhibit 3
Estimated Retail Sales of Intimate Apparel, United States, 1990–1992 and Average Retail Price Per Unit, 1992—($ Million)

	Retail Sales			Average Retail Price (1992)
	1990	1991	1992	
Product Category				
Bras	$2,362	$2,414	$2,591	$ 8.85
Shapewear	347	315	338	10.05
Pants	1,189	1,257	1,333	2.17
Daywear	670	625	633	9.42
Sleepwear	1,761	1,798	1,918	12.68
Robes/Housecoats	716	695	728	20.46
TOTAL	$7,045	$7,104	$7,542	
Average Unit Price	$ 6.13	$ 6.17	$ 6.31	

Exhibit 4
Market Share of Leading Intimate Apparel Brands, 1990–1992
(Share of Dollar Purchases, All Outlets)

Brand	1990	1991	1992
VFM:			
Vanity Fair	5.6	5.4	4.9
Vassarette	0.3	0.6	1.2
Sara Lee:			
Bali	3.7	3.6	3.4
Hanes Her Way	3.0	3.6	4.1
Playtex	5.1	4.4	5.2
Just My Size	0.5	0.6	0.5
Warnaco:			
Warner	2.3	2.5	2.6
Olga	1.3	1.5	1.5
Fruit of the Loom[a]	1.1	1.3	1.4
Private Labels	28.3	26.7	26.4

a Licensed.

Source: NPD Consumer Panel data.

Exhibit 5
Estimated Shares of Retail Sales by Distribution Channel, 1990–92
(Units and Dollars)

Retail Channels	Share of Units			Share of Dollars		
	1990	1991	1992	1990	1991	1992
Department & Specialty	26%	25%	24%	41%	39%	39%
National Chains[a]	18	18	16	20	20	19
Discounters	42	42	44	23	24	25
Direct Mail	4	4	4	5	6	6
Others[b]	10	11	12	11	11	11
TOTAL	100%	100%	100%	100%	100%	100%

a Sears, JCPenney, & Montgomery Ward

Source: NPD Consumer Panel Data

Exhibit 7
Diagram of VFM Flow Replenishment System

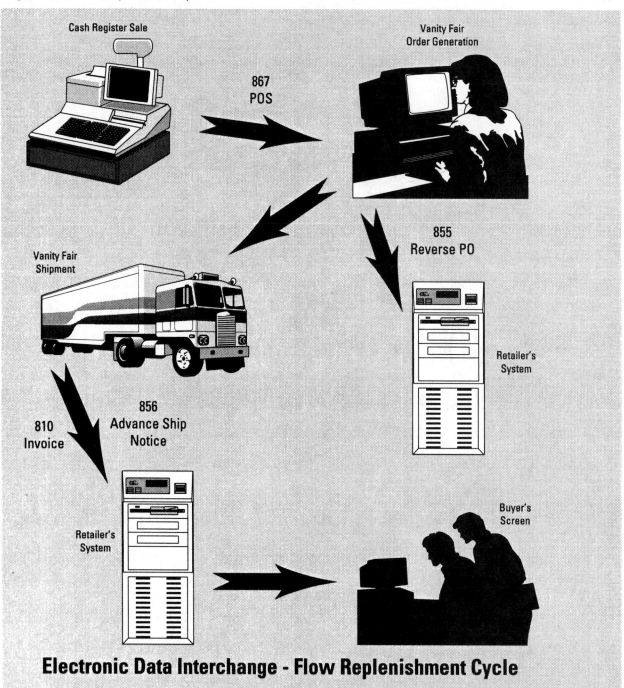

Cash Register Sale

Vanity Fair
Order Generation

867
POS

855
Reverse PO

Vanity Fair
Shipment

810
Invoice

856
Advance Ship
Notice

Retailer's
System

Retailer's
System

Buyer's
Screen

Electronic Data Interchange - Flow Replenishment Cycle

Exhibit 8
Comparison of Conventional Order Processing with Flow Replenishment

Day	CONVENTIONAL ORDER PROCESSING	FLOW REPLENISHMENT[a]
1	• Manual inventory in store	• POS scanning—data transmitted to VFM
1-2		• VFM generates purchase order and ships merchandise
3		• Retailer's D.C. notified
4	• Purchase order mailed to VFM	
5	• VFM inputs order into computer	• Merchandise replaced on sales floor
	• VFM sends acknowledgement	
8	• VFM sales rep receives acknowledgement • Retailer notified of changes in order	
9	• Order changes made • Order shipped	
10	• Order at retailer's D.C.	
12	• Merchandise replaced on sales floor	

a This comparison assumes cross-docking of individual store orders at the retailer's distribution center (see page 18 for an explanation of cross-docking).

Source: Company records.

Exhibit 9
Traditional New Product Development Process

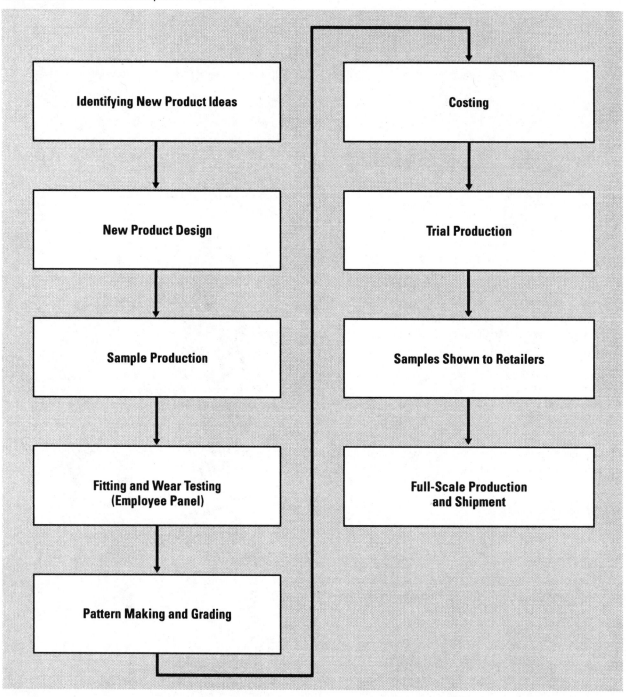

Identifying New Product Ideas

New Product Design

Sample Production

Fitting and Wear Testing
(Employee Panel)

Pattern Making and Grading

Costing

Trial Production

Samples Shown to Retailers

Full-Scale Production
and Shipment

PRODUCT DEVELOPMENT MANAGER

Primary Responsibility — Ensure focus and direction of product development team to meet consumer demands.

ASSOCIATE PRODUCT DEVELOPMENT MANAGER

Primary Responsibility — Utilizing consumer/retail research information to conceptualize and guide product development process.

PRODUCT DEVELOPMENT FACILITATOR

Primary Responsibility — Purchasing and costing for module.

PRODUCT DEVELOPMENT DESIGNERS

Primary Responsibility — Design and fit product within format as directed by direct Product Development manager.

SENIOR PRODUCT PATTERN SPECIALISTS

Primary Responsibility — To make patterns and grade them (modify patterns for various sizes).

PRODUCT PATTERN SPECIALIST

Primary Responsibility — To assist in making patterns and grading.

PRODUCT LINE COORDINATOR

Primary Responsibility — Disseminate product information for module.

MARKETING SERVICES ASSISTANT

Primary Responsibility — Maintain product information and record for module.

PRODUCT SEWING COORDINATOR

Primary Responsibility — Oversee sewing module and the making of prototype garments.

Exhibit 11
Estimated National Advertising Expenditures, 1989–91
($000)

Brand	1989	1990	1991
Vanity Fair	$ 1,482	$ 2,501	$ 2,768
Maidenform	2,591	2,888	3,715
Bali	2,286	1,314	382
Jockey for Her	1,400	521	1,298
Other Department Store Brands[a]	3,055	2,732	1,426
Vassarette	—	—	1,690
Hanes Her Way	13,121	5,881	5,677
Playtex	10,481	9,083	6,103
Fruit of the Loom	5,078	5,322	8,601
Gitano	95	—	73
Category Total	$42,818	$33,072	$32,743

a Includes Calvin Klein, Christian Dior, Lily of France, Warner's, and others.

Source: Company reports, based on LNA data. The estimates cover only "major media"—national newspaper advertisements, magazines, television, spot radio, and outdoor—and do not include local retail advertising.

Exhibit 12
Weekly Sales

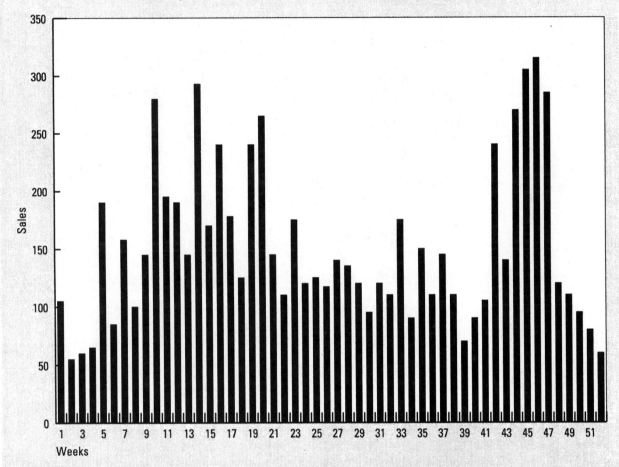

Weekly Sales Of An Individual Style-Promotional Store

Exhibit 13
Status and Performance Measures for Flow Replenishment Accounts—Department Stores and Discount Department Store Chains

	ACCOUNT STATUS				INVENTORIES			TURNS			IN STOCK		SHIPMENT	SALES
	1	2	3	4	5	6	7	8	9	10	11	12	13	14
Account Name	Months on System	Order Period	Order Release	% of Ship on System	Avg. Inventory 1991	Avg. Inventory 1992	% Chg. 92 v 91	Annual Turns 91	Annual Turns 92	% Chg. 92 v 91	% in Stock EOY 91	% in Stock EOY 92	Ship Chg 92 v 91	Sales Chg 92 v 91 OTC
Department Stores:														
ALPHA 1	7	2 wks	Manual	22	n/a	48,784	n/a	n/a	2.56	n/a	n/a	90	-21	n/a
ALPHA 2	36	2 wks	Manual	45	69,223	91,997	33	3.24.	2.36	-27	83	95	-6	+23
ALPHA 3	36	2 wks	Manual	40	60,429	80,350	33	2.89	3.09	7	86	88	+15	+38
ALPHA 4	36	2 wks	Manual	49	62,707	141,519	126	3.22	2.32	-28	83	88	-37	n/a
ALPHA 5	12	2 wks	Manual	26	n/a	60,193	n/a	n/a	2.33	n/a	n/a	92	-5	n/a
ALPHA 6	36	2 wks	Manual	34	94,460	126,164	34	2.81	2.71	-4	82	92	-6	n/a
ALPHA 7	36	2 wks	Manual	47	92,797	120,836	30	2.31	2.11	-9	91	92	+17	+36
ALPHA 8	36	2 wks	Manual	39	14,601	31,138	113	2.72	2.16	-21	73	96	-31	n/a
ALPHA 9	(New)	2 wks	(New)	(New)	n/a	n/a	n/a	n/a	2.24	n/a	n/a	92	+1	+14
BETA 1	24	2 wks	Manual	33	135,425	177,984	31	3.09	3.17	3	79	87	+24	n/a
BETA 2	7	1 wk	Manual	53	111,765	138,401	24	3.84	3.06	-20	93	90	-40	+6
BETA 3	(New)	2 wks	(New)	64	n/a	53,265	n/a	n/a	3.22	n/a	n/a	80	-24	n/a
BETA 4	36	1 wk	Auto	64	112,417	114,452	2	3.49	3.66	5	81	90	+8	+5
BETA 5	8	2 wks	Manual	39	n/a	73,023	n/a	n/a	3.17	n/a	n/a	87	-8	n/a
BETA 6	36	1 wk	Auto	44	58,318	65,561	12	2.35	2.65	13	93	86	+7	+25
GAMMA 1	26	1 wk	Auto	66	41,904	72,021	72	3.06	2.70	-12	88	96	+6	+32
GAMMA 2	36	1 wk	Auto	72	51,205	55,457	8	3.15	3.59	14	82	91	-2	+20
GAMMA 3	36	1 wk	Auto	63	66,525	94,363	42	2.37	2.66	12	92	95	+38	+71
GAMMA 4	36	1 wk	Auto	67	30,840	56,367	83	2.76	3.14	14	91	96	-2	+17
GAMMA 5	36	1 wk	Auto	64	34,032	35,003	3	2.57	2.53	-2	84	97	-9	+12
GAMMA 6	36	1 wk	Auto	41	26,256	49,598	89	3.07	2.71	-12	90	91	+8	+21
GAMMA 7	36	1 wk	Auto	68	27,974	39,547	41	2.54	2.62	3	95	95	+26	+42
Discounters:														
COMET	24	2 wks	Manual	41	n/a	6,712	n/a	n/a	5.95	n/a	n/a	96	N.M.	N.M.
METEOR	24	1 mo	Manual	54	16,943	45,369	168	2.81	3.04	8	97	97	N.M.	+240
NOVA	24	1 wk	Auto	75	1,706,000	3,141,479	84	3.04	3.62	19	94	93	N.M.	+95

- n/a due to account not being on replenishment system during period or account not sending point-of-sale data for the entire period
- The following divisions' 1991 figures are the sum of two divisions that are reflected as merged in 1992: Alpha 2, Alpha 6, Beta 1, Gamma 7
- Columns 5 and 6 are unit figures; column 13 is based on wholesale dollars; column 14 is based on units
- Column 13 is the percent change in VFM shipments to the customer
- Column 14 is the percent change in over-the-counter sales
- Meteor and Nova divisions were new customers in 1991 and therefore had significant increases in average inventory and over-the-counter sales
- Gamma 2 added 3 stores in 1992
- Gamma 3 added 16 new stores in 1992

Case 17

ITO YOKADO

The Ito Yokado Group was a Japanese chain of department stores, 7/11 markets and other retail stores and restaurants with 1988 sales of over 2,096 billion yen ($16 billion, based on an exchange rate of 128 yen per dollar—see **Exhibit 1**). Masatoshi Ito, its president, had presided over almost three decades of rapid growth from its beginnings as a 66-square-foot family-owned specialty store. He had taken full advantage of the explosion of consumer purchasing power in Japan and had more recently responded to a decline in the growth opportunities for the company by massively improving its retail operations. He attributed much of the credit for the success of Ito Yokado in the 1980s to the "Reform Program," and in 1988 wondered how far to extend the reaches of this program (see **Exhibits 2 and 3**).

BACKGROUND ON JAPANESE CONSUMER GOODS DISTRIBUTION

Japan had survived and often prospered within the constraints of being an island with only limited land resources. By 1988, it had become one of the more densely populated countries of the world (120 million people on 60,000 square miles of habitable land).

The historic combination of small houses with very little refrigeration and storage space and very few consumers with automobiles allowed the traditional distribution pattern of many small neighborhood specialty shops to prosper.

There was one exception to distribution through small shops: a limited number of large central city department stores carrying both food and general merchandise (e.g., Mitsukoshi and Takashimaya). These stores catered, however, to the affluent consumer and for gift shopping rather than for everyday requirements. Among the owners of other traditional central city department stores (Tokyu, Seibu and Hankyu) were the railroad companies who leveraged their real estate in the center of the great cities to develop some of these stores on top of their centrally located train depots.

THE 1950s AND EARLY 1960s

In the 1950s, the Japanese became exposed to the temptations and conveniences of the "modern" world. Coupled with rising income, rapid urbanization and increased mobility from automobile ownership, a new consumer market was developing. Not only did demand grow in the aggregate for consumer products, but the demand for variety grew as well. To meet this swelling demand, contemporary retailing formats borrowed from abroad began to become popular.

Under the influence of these changes, chains of contemporary retailers arose, somewhat replicating American and European supermarket and general merchandise chains such as supermarkets and discount department stores. But unlike in the United States, the major Japanese chain stores carried reasonably complete

Research Associate David Wylie prepared this case under the supervision of Professor Walter J. Salmon of the Harvard Business School and Professor Kosei Furukawa of Keio University Business School as the basis for class discussion rather than to illustrate either effective or ineffective handling of an administrative situation.

Copyright © 1989 by the President and Fellows of Harvard College and Keio University Business School.
Harvard Business School case 589-116.

lines of both food and general merchandise and were called superstores in Japan.

Among the chains started in the fifties and early sixties were Ito Yokado, Daiei, Seiyu, and Jusco. These four companies distinguished themselves from the more traditional department stores by catering to a wider socioeconomic profile with a broad assortment of everyday items. The atmosphere was less luxurious and more utilitarian. Merchandise was for personal use rather than gifts, although in more remote geographic areas the stores would fulfill more complete roles. Stores were often located near the terminals of suburban railroad stations.

Under pressure from traditional small businesses which felt threatened by the explosive growth of chains of large stores, the Japanese Diet enacted the "Department Store Act" in 1955. This law was the first in a series of regulatory measures intended to protect small stores by limiting the growth of the new large store chains.

FROM 1964 TO 1970

In 1964, the Olympics were held in Tokyo, home for over 10% of the Japanese population. The country had come into its own, and the capital was to be the showplace to introduce the world to a great country, a new member of the world's industrial community, poised for meteoric growth. This opportunity was a catalyst to improve Japan's strained infrastructure. Roads were paved, modern highways were built, and the city of Tokyo acquired a major new addition to its subway system.

From 1964 to 1970, hourly compensation in Japan grew 131% while prices only rose 38%. GNP was growing at an annual compound rate of over 10.4%. Modern manufacturing methods permitted costs for consumer durables to drop and prices to fall commensurately. The consumer was enjoying buying power previously unknown in Japan. Much of this higher income was diverted to savings to meet the dream of home ownership, but the remainder was available for cars, televisions and a plethora of consumables. The new retail chains, especially those which had started in the late fifties and early sixties, were, despite the 1955 legislation, able to expand to meet this demand, replacing many of the smaller traditional shops.

FROM 1970 TO 1982

The 1970s were tumultuous years in Japan. At the beginning of this period, consumer buying habits were rapidly changing. The percentage spent on the necessities of food, clothing and shelter was declining while spending on products such as cars, appliances, electronics, general merchandise and apparel was increasing rapidly.

While the period began on a positive note, the oil shocks of 1973 and 1978 had an adverse impact on consumption. Rising prices put a damper on the growth in demand. Retailers found themselves in a profit squeeze as their energy-related costs increased due to Japan's reliance on expensive Middle Eastern oil. Oil prices pegged to the dollar and the strong value of the dollar relative to the yen in 1978 compounded this negative impact. Imports became prohibitive in price and exports commensurately attractive. By the end of the period, per capita income and consumer prices were both growing at 6.2% per year and the GNP at only 4.4%.

Large retailers, in particular, had to confront this issue as well as additional legislative curbs on growth. As the rate of economic growth declined, the pressure from traditional small retailers increased. The result was modifications of the 1955 department store act in 1974 and 1979 in ways which further inhibited the expansion of large store chains without the consent of their small store neighbors. The time required to obtain approval for and construct a large new store rose to anywhere from three to fifteen years. The period of rapid expansion was over.

As a result of such pressures, in 1982 Ito Yokado found itself in a reasonably severe profit squeeze. This squeeze, combined with the dim outlook for traditional growth, was the origin of what became known as the "Reform Program" (RP).

ITO YOKADO—BACKGROUND

Masatoshi Ito was the founder, president, and leading stockholder of the Ito Yokado Group. From relatively humble beginnings, he developed the Ito Yokado Group into a retail conglomerate with over two trillion yen in sales and in so doing became one of the wealthiest individuals in the world.

By 1960, he had grown the 66-square-foot family clothing store in Tokyo where he went to work after World War II into a 384 million yen company over which he had sole control. It was then that National Cash Register, given his status as a customer, invited Ito to the United States.

On this trip Ito visited some notable retail chains including JC Penney, A & P, Safeway and Sears. He was confident that Japan was ready to embrace large store retailing, and, upon his return to Tokyo, moved quickly to open a superstore which carried a full range of food and general merchandise catering to the mass markets.

By 1965, this endeavor had grown to a chain of eight superstores under the new banner of Ito Yokado.

Tokyo was growing dramatically during the 1960s with the suburban explosion being serviced by the new subway system, the spread of automobile ownership and a massive population shift into urban areas from agricultural communities. Ito moved to capitalize on these changes by opening free-standing suburban stores with abundant parking.

By 1988, Ito Yokado itself had grown to 131 stores with sales of over one trillion yen and 27,779 employees. The stores featured high-quality food and a full range of household goods and apparel with emphasis on the basics.

In addition to its combined food and general merchandise stores, Ito Yokado began to diversify into other forms of retailing. The 7/11 stores were among the earlier forms of diversification and became a means for Ito Yokado to expand without challenging the department store acts since independent businesspeople became Ito Yokado's 7/11 franchisees. Since the first stores opened in 1974, the 7/11 division had become, in proportion to sales and investment, the most profitable unit in the Ito Yokado empire with 3,304 stores and net profits of 18.9 billion yen on sales of 599.1 billion yen (see **Exhibit 4**).

Other forms of diversification included supermarkets (York-Benimaru, York Mart, Life, Sanei), upscale department stores (York-Matsuzakaya, Robinson's), specialty stores (Mary Ann, Steps, Oshman's), a hard goods discount store chain (Daikuma), restaurants (Denny's, Famil, York Bussan), food processing (Kanseien, Nihon Nosuisan, Daily Foods, York Seika), and real estate.

While the Ito Yokado Group weathered and indeed prospered during the tumult of the 1970s, its profitability was not exceptional compared to that of its competitors. Moreover, external conditions were dimming the outlook for more traditional forms of growth (higher consumer spending or increases in the number of Ito Yokado stores). Thus, the "RP" was initiated. In an address to investors in June, 1985, Mr. Ito elaborated on the reasons for and the nature of the RP:

As you know, retailers in Japan and probably elsewhere are facing a situation in which the market has reached a ceiling, and in which fierce competition is generally worsening an already difficult environment. Add to this the fact that retailers must keep abreast of consumers. They have new lifestyles, they are expressing their needs in unprecedented ways. In short, retailing is not what it used to be, when customers were willing to purchase just about whatever the retailer put on the shelf. They are spending, but they are now much more careful.

For this reason, then, it is more important than ever before to know the customer.

These past three years have been momentous for us. In 1982, we formed a management committee to identify and address the implications of the factors I've just traced. Focus has been on reducing inventory, and then salesfloor inventory levels. After about a year of very thorough efforts at every level of Ito Yokado, results came through. In addition to improving our operating margin, the emphasis on inventory management has also succeeded in making us give closer, more thorough and more meticulous attention to identifying customer needs. Everyone is energetically involved in this area—from managers and employees to part-time sales clerks.

Inventory management is part of a program at Ito Yokado to firm up its operations, become leaner, and make sales increases count more in generating earnings increases.

Changes at Ito Yokado are evident in three general areas. These are:

1. Merchandising
2. The image of Ito Yokado in our customers' eyes
3. The physical presentation of our stores

Our actions in each area have served to further distinguish us from other Japanese retailers. Let me briefly touch on these.

Half of merchandising is choosing merchandise that will be popular. The other half is knowing which items are not, and eliminating those from the shelf. We've been working to identify and eliminate slow-moving items from our stores, and as a result have reduced inventory and eliminated the need to resort to price cuts.

Just as important is the identification of the right products. This depends, of course, on knowing your customers and his or her needs, and it is here that retailing becomes something of an art. We encourage our salesfloor employees to feel responsible for the merchandise in their department, in other words, to get a sense of what their customers are looking for. Input from these employees helps us make merchandising decisions. Better decision making distinguishes us from our peers, as is indicated by improved comparable store sales levels.

We are managing the consumer perception of Ito Yokado as a provider of value. There was a time when our franchise was based on our ability to provide low prices. Price, of course, is only one of the variables that go into value, and we are carefully making sure that our customers are thinking about more than low price when they think of Ito Yokado. We are upgrading the tone and content of our advertising, using TV and quality printed media. And we are improving the appearance of our stores and presentation of merchandise, which brings me to the third area in which we are making important changes.

We are remodeling store interiors and exteriors, and upgrading our displays to match the leaner, fresher sense of our merchandise selections.

Recent store remodels are far more extensive than previously, and they are costing several times more. But the higher profitability stemming from inventory improvements means that these investments in our stores can be financed internally. . . .

Now that our house is in good order, we are entering new, diversified business areas in which we also expect high growth. This year, we will open an Oshman's sports store and our second department store, Robinson's. In both ventures, we are adapting the proven concept and know-how of U.S. retailers to conditions in Japan. These are other investments that we will be handling with retained earnings.

THE "REFORM PROGRAM"

The RP commenced as an innovative way to motivate, empower and so leverage the expertise of all employees, including the rank and file, to identify customer needs and take advantage of opportunities to manage the stores and inventories more expertly. Ultimately the RP would also include the rationalization of distribution systems and the utilization of a sophisticated MIS system.

THE ORGANIZATION

The organization chart of Ito Yokado (**Exhibit 5**) showed those employees who were closest to the customers on the top. These were the full- and part-time store employees who were responsible for the sales and inventories of specific lines of merchandise (since 1965, the percentage of work done by part-timers had increased from 9% to 58%). Everyone in every store and in every category had ordering or reordering responsibility for a select number of items. The younger people just out of school who were either just entering a long term career at Ito Yokado or who would work only until they started families had responsibility for fewer less critical items. The more experienced employees were charged with the more

difficult, sensitive or important lines. (Later in this case study the employees responsible for fish eggs and salmon and for young women's bottoms for one store are introduced and their roles are discussed in more detail.)

These part-time and full-time employees reported to a category manager, a more experienced full-timer. For fish, for example, this was a fresh fish manager or, for apparel, a women's apparel category manager. These individuals reported to one of three department managers for each store who were in charge of apparel, household goods and food.

Ito Yokado's philosophy was that employees worked for the company rather than in any specific capacity. Therefore, it would not be unusual at Ito Yokado or other Japanese companies for an employee to move laterally or vertically within an organization without concern for status. Status was largely derived from seniority and from the variety of roles which an individual had assumed. The department manager of the apparel department at the Tsudanuma store, for instance, had been a senior buyer for the entire company's women's clothing department and was soon to leave to become the store manager of a new and very important store near downtown Tokyo.

The Ito Yokado stores were grouped into eight zones of approximately sixteen stores each. Store managers within each group of sixteen stores reported to a zone manager, who in turn reported to the division manager of store operations. On the same organizational level as this division manager were the heads of the merchandising groups at the central office in food and general merchandise. All three reported to the executive vice president of operations.

The headquarters merchandising organization included department general managers (buyers on a level more or less equivalent to that of zone managers) and, reporting to them, buyer managers. There was, for example, a fresh fish department general manager with a fresh fish buyer manager reporting to him. Each buyer manager had a number of specialized buyers reporting to him. Distributors coordinated the receipt of orders from the stores as well as the movement of merchandise from company warehouses and suppliers to the stores.

The Ito Yokado organization also included three levels of supervisors:

1. Category supervisors (CS) acted as the primary intermediaries between buyers at headquarters and the stores. The role of these individuals, who reported to the Department General Manager, was to inform, support and advise the store category managers on such topics as fashion trends and merchandising and to

inform headquarters merchandising personnel about individual store needs. There were 146 CS's, generally organized by category and by zone. In this way a communications link was formed between the buyers at headquarters and those at the stores who, depending upon the product category, made some or all of the ultimate ordering or reordering decisions.

2. Department supervisors (DS) acted as liaison between the heads of the central office merchandising pyramids and department managers at the stores (food, household goods or apparel). There were fifteen DS's who reported to the division manager of store operations.

3. Finally there were five store manager supervisors (SMS) who reported to the division manager of store operations. These individuals were the senior communications link between headquarters and store managers on matters relating to store operations (see **Exhibit 6**).

Communications among all supervisors was very frequent and informal since all supervisors shared the same office at headquarters (see **Table A**).

HUMAN RESOURCES AND THE EMPOWERMENT OF THE EMPLOYEE

Responsibility for sales and inventory management was delegated from headquarters to store level executives and through them, to both full- and part-time rank and file employees. Managers viewed themselves as teachers and advisors more than as decision makers. A part-timer, for example might be given responsibility for monitoring sales and ordering, displaying and managing the inventory for a limited number of SKUs. The idea was that people on the firing line in individual stores were in the best position to understand the subtleties of consumer demand and competitive conditions in their local areas. This element of the RP became known as "store-by-store, item-by-item" sales and inventory management. The result was fewer stockouts, higher sales, lower inventory levels, less inventory loss, higher profits, higher quality (particularly in the highly sensitive and visible area of perishable foods) and higher commitment levels on the part of employees.

RATIONALIZATION OF DISTRIBUTION

Another element of the RP was the rationalization of distribution. The traditional Japanese distribution system involved numerous intermediaries between producer and consumer. This multilayered intermediary system had a role in absorbing people who would have otherwise been unemployed and in enabling small stores to offer both variety and credit to their customers. The latter was facilitated by the credit which the intermediaries extended to small stores. In addition, these intermediaries allowed small stores to be relieved of inventory risk by accepting the return of slow selling merchandise. For chain stores with state-of-the-art inventory control systems, however, this multilayered system provided redundant services, added unnecessarily to final selling prices and, with respect to perishable foods, detracted from product quality.

Historically, domestic manufacturers and producers had also delegated almost the entire marketing function to intermediaries. Observers of the Japanese economy believe that this fragmented intermediary system had, in recent times, in addition to contributing to high retail prices, become an obstacle to introducing new products for both domestic manufacturers and importers.

Table A Supervisors

Supervisor	Store Contact	Reports to:	Number
CS	Category Manager	Department General Manager	146
DS	Department Manager	Division Manager of Store Operations	15
SMS	Store Manager	Division Manager of Store Operations	5

(More detail on the role of supervisors is presented later in the case.)

That part of the RP which dealt with the rationalization of distribution was meant to streamline the channel of distribution between manufacturer and end consumer. Thus, Ito Yokado was exercising its power over intermediaries to become more efficient and responsive. It was specifying high-quality merchandise, the transportation and distribution system that was to be used to move the merchandise from manufacturer to the stores and absolute adherence to a policy of on-time delivery with no stockouts. The resulting efficiencies allowed Ito Yokado to charge lower prices for those products, make more profits, or often improve product quality, particularly if the products were perishable.

Initially, Ito Yokado had concentrated its efforts in rationalizing distribution on large volume products which were of high importance to the consumer. Other characteristics of these products were predictable demand, the potential to reduce product and inventory costs, and to improve quality by changes in procurement practices.

THE ROLE OF THE MIS SYSTEM

As the RP gathered steam, it also encompassed a commitment to a new state-of-the-art MIS system. The MIS system tracked sales and inventories by item and by store, provided accurate information to the employee on the selling floor to enable him/her to make the best decisions possible, and allowed rank-and-file employees to enter and communicate orders directly to an Ito Yokado central warehouse or to selected vendors. Although recognizing the underlying importance of the MIS system to the success of the RP, Ito Yokado executives maintained it was less important than the innovative human resource program and the rationalization of distribution.

MANAGEMENT OF THE REFORM PROGRAM

The RP was considered by Ito Yokado executives to be an on-going initiative, reflective of an attitude which considered all employees as vital intermediaries between customers and vendors. The leader of the RP was Mr. Suzuki, who also was the president of the 7/11 division and executive vice president of administration of Ito Yokado.

Mr. Suzuki instilled the spirit of the program through weekly store managers meetings where he stressed the importance of both delegation to those employees closest to the customer, and of encouraging innovation through constant questioning of ways of doing business. Indicative of his commitment to delegation was the corporate myth (and perhaps fact) that he had never visited an Ito Yokado store.

Recited at the beginning of each day and at each meeting, and posted conspicuously in the employee areas of each store and headquarters was the credo of the RP:

Our Principles:
1. Our sincere pledge to our customers—honesty and sincerity.
2. Our sincere pledge to our shareholders, business associates, and community—honesty and cooperation.
2. Our sincere pledge to our employees—honesty and respect.

An incentive program for full-time and about a third of part-time employees rewarded successful efforts with a bonus which was directly tied to the profitability of the company, and which could amount to half of normal pay. This bonus was funded by a company policy that normally allocated one-third of profits to employees, one-third to stockholders, and one-third to retained earnings.

DIALOGUE ABOUT THE REFORM PROGRAM

Communication between the headquarters, the stores and among employees was a critical element for the implementation of the RP. Employees had always been linked to each other and to the headquarters through a series of regular meetings but these meetings were now particularly important. Direct verbal interaction was encouraged as a more valuable medium for transmitting information, and, in general, informal meetings were preferred to the formal meetings which were required.

Among the formal meetings was the Reform Committee Meeting which was held every Tuesday afternoon at headquarters (see **Exhibit 7**). This meeting was chaired by Mr. Suzuki and lasted for ninety minutes. It was attended by about 100 people including all zone managers, senior members of the merchandising organization, representatives from the other IYG subsidiaries, senior management and staff from headquarters, and members of the board of directors. In addition, several category, department, or store managers might be invited to give presentations.

The zone managers also held weekly Zone Meetings at headquarters with their store managers to transmit information about the RP and other matters. On the same day, all zone managers and store managers would gather at a Store Manager's Meeting run by the five SMS's and attended by different senior executives. This meeting was for the introduction of new items, the review of advertising and promotion programs and the exchange of information among personnel.

In addition to presentations by the headquarter's staff, these meetings facilitated communications among store managers and let headquarters know how they could be better served. Store managers were occasionally called upon to give a presentation on a particular area of interest or success. In these cases, appropriate department heads came as well to hear or to participate in these presentations as well as to exchange ideas with each other. When the executive vice president, Mr. Suzuki, was present at these meetings, he used this format for an in-depth inquiry into the rationale for traditional ways of doing business by asking employees the "why, why, why?" of current practices. This persistent inquiry resulted in numerous innovative ways of conducting business.

Department managers met with DS's twice every month, once at headquarters and once at the stores. Category managers gathered weekly with their CS's.

At the stores, formal meetings were kept very brief. Every Sunday morning each store manager held a ten-minute meeting with all store employees to pass on information from his weekly meeting at headquarters, to provide information about the results of the previous week, to announce goals for the following week, and to collect questions, problems, or innovations to introduce at his next store manager's meeting.

Department managers held meetings on each floor every other morning to pass on information from the weekly meetings, to provide information about the success of the previous day, and to announce goals for the upcoming day. After these meetings, the category manager would gather several full- and part-time employees together to discuss the subtleties of forecasting demand and ordering inventory in their particular lines.

Formal meetings facilitated the dissemination of information, but managers at all levels were quick to add that the most valuable information came through informal meetings and networking.

RESULTS OF THE REFORM PROGRAM

Presented in the next several pages are examples of the impact of the RP on certain categories within the fresh fish and apparel departments. Interviews with employees of these departments were conducted at the Tsudanuma store. This store was one of the largest Ito Yokado stores, accounting for almost 2% of the Ito Yokado division's sales. It was located just east of Tokyo near two railroad stations. **Exhibit 8**, as well as other exhibits, reflect the changes in operational results since the initiation of the RP.

TUNAFISH

One of the first foci for the RP was the fresh fish department, particularly raw tuna, a prime ingredient for traditional Japanese sushi. The consumer wanted only the very freshest fish of the best quality. The magnitude of their demands, however, changed dramatically depending on the time of day, the proximity to a holiday, the weather, etc. (see **Exhibits 9A** and **9B**).

The sale of tunafish represented almost 10% of total sales in the fish department. The consumer judged freshness on the basis of color, which changed quite rapidly after the tuna was thawed and started to oxidize. The process of controlling the color was difficult since the fish came from distant oceans and went through many processes before it reached the shelf. The problem was compounded by the sensitivity of tuna to each step in the process.

Ito Yokado undertook a study of the oxidation process from the ocean to the store and discovered that while most of the color transformation occurred on the store shelf, the speed of that process was directly related to the product's previous treatment (see **Exhibit 10**).

Therefore, Ito Yokado's RP for tuna concentrated its purchases from a limited number of large wholesalers and trading companies and specified where the fish was to be caught, how soon it must be frozen, when it must be cut into what size, how it was to be packaged, the temperature at which it must be stored, and the methods of transportation. This control, combined with the store clerks' control of the product from the store freezer to display and sale, reduced the amount of inventory loss or spoilage from 6.0% to 2.8% of sales, provided higher quality to the consumer, and increased the profitability of the department commensurately.

INTERVIEW

The following summarizes an interview with Mr. Suzuki, the category manager for the fish department at the Tsudanuma store and with Mrs. Ichikawa, a part-timer responsible for the salmon and fish eggs department.

Her role in managing fish was similar to that of the individual responsible for tuna, although, since tunafish was more sensitive to deterioration, a more experienced full-time employee had that responsibility.

Mr. Suzuki was an articulate man of about 40 who had been with Ito Yokado for twelve years in the fish department. Like most full-time employees, he worked five days and fifty hours a week. He was paid a salary that was substantially augmented by an annual bonus based on the performance of the company. Mr. Suzuki came to the interview wearing the standard uniform of the department: yellow shirt and hat, green apron, and white rubber boots.

He arrived at the store each day at 8:30 in time for the regular ten-minute morning meeting with all employees in the department. During this meeting, after the recitation of the pledge, he identified items to push for the day, targeted sales goals, and encouraged good flow of product. He also asked about new ways to improve the performance of the department and encouraged his staff to share any questions or problems.

On Saturday and Sunday mornings at 9:30, Mr. Suzuki joined the meeting of all category and department managers with the store manager to receive any relevant information from the Tuesday morning Reform Committee Meeting at headquarters and to pass along any information for the store manager to take back to the next meeting.

After the morning meetings, Mr. Suzuki moved around the department to answer questions, encourage performance, question ways of working, and to lend his expertise to those in charge of ordering. In the fish department, most of the packing, stocking and preparation was done on a team basis as demand required, with the exception of tuna which required the constant vigilance of an experienced full-timer.

Mrs. Ichikawa was a good-natured woman of about fifty who had been with the company for nine years. She had a grandmotherly demeanor, was somewhat heavyset, had a rather glorious display of gold front teeth, and obviously enjoyed her work. Her family responsibilities necessitated her part-time role. She took a good deal of pride in the responsibility which she had assumed in the last two years for six kinds of salmon and twelve varieties of fish eggs. She expressed a sense of accomplishment arising from the accuracy with which she could project demand and stock the shelves. The job was "fun," she added, except that she had developed a recurring nightmare about "the day she stocked and shelved and nothing sold."

All fish orders were entered into the departmental computer terminal two days prior to delivery. The order would specify whether a product should be delivered at 8:00 a.m. or 2:00 p.m. on the designated day. Orders would go either through headquarters' buyers or directly to a vendor. Deliveries were made straight from the fish piers, and most items came from that day's early morning or noon catch. In this way the fish was freshest and inventory was minimized. It did, however, require an accurate demand forecast to avoid stockouts or waste.

At 8:00 each morning, Mrs. Ichikawa checked the inventory remaining on the shelf from the previous day (which, for the tuna, would have to be thrown away). Then, after the morning department meeting, she stocked the shelves for the morning opening rush at 10:00. During the day, she stayed in the back preparation room only to emerge to check and resupply stock and to confer with the salesperson on the floor about what items should be pushed through sales demonstrations. Between 4:00 and 5:00 she prepared the order.

Mrs. Ichikawa first took a 4:00 p.m. inventory to compare against the computer, which, although she claimed not entirely to trust, seemed quite accurate. She also felt that counting the inventory herself gave her a better feel for demand. In planning the order, she went to the computer terminal for the food department, printed and reviewed the following reports (see **Exhibit 9A** and **9B** for samples of these reports):

1. ABC Analysis, within class of product, in ABC order, with detail on price, unit sales last week and current week to date, yen sales last week and current week and waste. ("ABC" was a categorization of product by sales volume.)
2. Graph of average unit sales per hour during the last week in all stores.
3. Graph of unit sales in the store by product combined with chart of sales, purchases and loss rate by hour by yen and by unit.
4. Graph and chart of units taken to the shelf and sold in the store by hour.

On the basis of this information and her intimate knowledge of the season, day of the week, competitor's prices and weather, she calculated the required order for all eighteen SKUs in her charge and entered it into the computer terminal.

The procedure for tuna was similar except that it called for hourly attention to stock and required, therefore, an extra level of demand forecasting. Tuna arrived at the store frozen, required twenty-four hours to defrost in water in the refrigerator, removal from water thirty minutes before cutting and a final thirty minutes before going out to the shelf in order for the color to "mature." Any tuna left on the shelf for more than two hours was discarded.

APPAREL

In addition to food, the RP had also impacted other merchandising areas including apparel. Apparel at Ito Yokado was divided into seven categories: traditional kimonos and accessories, specialty store apparel (which was a series of seasonally changing specialty categories), underwear, children's clothing, menswear, suits and accessories and women's clothing. The selections were quite broad and concentrated in basic to moderately fashionable lines.

Mr. Kijima was the manager of the women's clothing category. He was 42 and had been with the company for fourteen years. Initially he had been on the selling floor for six years, then had transferred to buying at headquarters, and eventually became responsible for buying all women's clothing. He then had planned and opened the first new store in western Japan, an important new marketing frontier for Ito Yokado before he was transferred to his current position at the Tsudanuma store. He was to depart soon to become store manager at a smaller, older store near the center of Tokyo. The store to which he was moving was growing rapidly and was important since it was on the fringe of an expanding high-income area. It therefore represented an opportunity for Ito Yokado to move somewhat upscale.

Ito Yokado maintained its own brands of more basic clothing items for which demand could be forecast rather accurately. Although it purchased some fabrics for these items, it relied upon independent manufacturers to produce finished products according to specifications. It did, however, commit to firm purchases and assume the risks of excess inventory. The traditional Japanese system relied upon wholesalers who took back unsold inventory. This program allowed Ito Yokado to negotiate substantial savings.

The typical Ito Yokado store carried approximately 4000 styles in all of the categories which comprised its clothing department over the course of a year. Since the average style might be available in five sizes and four colors, the result was 80,000 SKUs. No more than approximately 25% would be carried, however, during any one season.

The clothing department of the Tsudanuma store was staffed with 80 full-time employees and 60 part-timers. The sole function of six of the part-timers was order responsibility for certain fashion lines. Twelve were experienced salespeople who also assumed line-ordering responsibilities for less fashionable merchandise. The rest were younger women just out of high school who worked only from 10:00 a.m. to 4:00 p.m., had less than a one-year commitment, and did not share in the bonus program.

It was in departments which were most susceptible to fashion changes and fluctuations in aggregate consumption that the effect of the RP was most pronounced. In some of these departments, lead time for ordering was longer than the seasons in which the fashions might be sold. Accurate forecasting of demand by style, color, fabric and size was critical, as was the allocation of the right mix of merchandise to each of the various stores.

An example of such a line within women's clothing was young ladies bottoms. It included skirts, pants and shorts. Demand for these items was volatile. Bottoms for the young ladies spring line, for instance, had very heavy sales, but only during the two-week spring high school holiday in early April. The season was too short for in-season adjustments. In the spring of 1988, for example, there was an unexpected explosion in demand for bottoms in brilliant peppermint green, a fad which took buyers totally by surprise. Although some of the color was in stock as a normal part of the line, the unanticipated demand forced otherwise loyal customers to frequent competitors' racks.

The process of building the spring line for women's bottoms began the summer before among the buyers in the merchandising division at headquarters. The buyer whose responsibilities included women's bottoms kept in close contact with the trends and fashions in the industry and was aware of the relative strengths of various vendors. For fashion trends, the buyer consulted with his superior, the buyer manager for women's clothing, and also relied on fashion consultants, shows, media and other sources. After comparing his vision of trends with past seasons' sales, consulting again with the buyer manager and his distributor (the individual in charge of allocating initial stock to each store and filling replenishment orders), and several meetings with his superiors, he developed a line of approximately 25 styles of slacks and shorts and 50 skirt styles. In early September, he placed a preliminary order with appropriate vendors.

In November, the CS who acted as a liaison between

headquarters and stores met at headquarters with all the category managers, the distributor and buyers. At this meeting, he described the line and its life cycle, showed samples and provided a printed catalogue (see **Exhibit 9C**) of all units available, presented recommended merchandising and advertising strategies, and gathered complaints or suggestions for the buyers at headquarters. Initial store allocations were suggested according to six different "store profile mix types" as defined by the buyer manager for clothing. After this meeting, the headquarters buyers assessed the feedback and developed a final order to submit to the vendor.

Three weeks prior to the annual introduction of a line, the category supervisor once again met with the store category managers to provide more detailed information about the items, merchandising and initial allocations. At this point the category manager, with the approval of the store department manager, could choose to reject any items as inappropriate for his store. Companywide, the refusal rate at this point ranged from 4% to 8%.

Once the season started, it was up to the full- and part-time employees at the store to reorder the more staple styles for replenishment. Mrs. Nomoto, the line specialist responsible for the women's bottoms at the Tsudanuma store, was a pleasant woman of about forty who worked part time while her children were in school. Mrs. Nomoto had been with Ito Yokado for nine years in the same department, and took great pride in her work. The number of SKUs in women's bottoms since the advent of the RP had been reduced by 50% and the department was ranked number two in sales among all 131 Ito Yokado stores. She was responsible for ordering 132 items (about 15 SKUs per item) during the winter season and 330 during the peak summer season.

Orders were delivered twice a week on Wednesdays and Saturdays. Mrs. Nomoto prepared the order on Monday and Thursday evenings and entered it into the departmental computer terminal during a one-hour period

the following morning for delivery the next day. (see **Table B.**)

The calculation of the order involved synthesizing information from a number of sources including an element of intuition. After checking the physical inventory, the weather report, the life cycle section of the catalogue, the supervisor's memo on new items arriving, storewide trends, and what happened last year, Mrs. Nomoto would print out the following reports from the department computer terminal (sample copies of these printouts are included as **Exhibits 9D** and **9E**):

1. Corporate life cycle summary by line and subclass (fabric) in chart and graph form.
2. ABC analysis report including inventory available, store sales history, vendor, price and seasonally oriented qualitative ordering and display suggestions.
3. Sales by subclass and style in order of sales volume for prior four weeks, current week to date, percentage of total department sales, inventory by percent of total in store by unit and by value, number of days available in the warehouse at current sales rate for all stores, units delivered year-to-date, margins and markdown rates by unit and by value.
4. Weekly sales summary for store with last years' comps, accessible in various levels of detail.
5. Distribution of sales bar graphs and charts by price point, sub-class (fabric), color and size.

Armed with this information, she would complete the order. The order form included additional information: sales information for the prior two weeks, current inventory available and notation if SKUs were discontinued (life cycle over) or out of stock. If she ordered discontinued items, which she might if they were selling particularly well at this store, she would have a 60% chance of having it fulfilled (up from 23% prior to the RP). For available items, the fulfillment rate was 99%. Ten to fifteen percent of items would be ordered weekly.

Table B Routine for Preparation of Ladies Bottoms Orders

Monday evening	Prepare order for next day
Tuesday at 8:00 A.M.	Place order for Wednesday delivery
Wednesday	Receive order
Thursday evening	Prepare order for next day
Friday at 8:00 A.M.	Place order for Saturday delivery
Saturday	Receive order

Since Mrs. Nomoto had started preparing the orders, sales were up about 10%, the number of SKUs had dropped 43%, inventory value was reduced by 40%, markdowns were down to 5% from 8%, and average unit price was up 20% as customers relied upon Ito Yokado for consistent high quality with an adequate yet more limited selection. The ongoing challenge was to identify and eliminate slow stock and to replace it with fast-moving new items.

THE REMAINING CHALLENGE

By early 1989, the RP had had an impact, to at least some extent, on nearly all the merchandise categories in Ito Yokado and had also been implemented in most other companies of the Ito Yokado Group. The company regarded the RP as a never-ending quest for improvement in execution and therefore intended to adhere to it for the foreseeable future. The issues before Mr. Ito and his senior colleagues were what further improvements could be made in the RP and what if anything beyond the RP were the next evolutionary steps in the growth of Ito Yokado.

Exhibit 1
Exchange Rate (Yen/$)

Year	1982	1983	1984	1985	1986	1987
Rate	249	234	233	244	165	147

Exhibit 2
Ito Yokado Group and its Competition (¥ billions)

	1982	1983	1984	1985	1986	1987	1988
Ito Yokado							
Sales	¥862.0	¥923.6	¥996.1	¥1,057.3	¥1,203.3	¥1,281.0	¥1,371.0
Income after taxes			¥24.5	¥30.4	¥37.9	¥42.6	¥53.6
Return on sales			2.5%	2.9%	3.2%	3.3%	3.9%
Return on assets	4.5%	4.3%	5.8%	6.7%	7.2%	7.2%	8.2%
Daiei							
Sales			¥1,394.1	¥1,443.6	¥1,534.4	¥1,631.0	¥1,764.4
Income after taxes			¥.1	¥5.1	¥10.2	¥10.8	¥11.8
Return on sales			0.0%	0.4%	0.7%	0.7%	0.7%
Return on assets			-1.3%	-1.0%	0.1%	0.3%	0.6%
Jusco							
Sales			¥775.3	¥834.4	¥881.3	¥937.1	¥992.8
Income after Taxes			¥8.2	¥8.3	¥10.1	¥12.0	¥15.2
Return on sales			1.1%	1.0%	1.1%	1.3%	1.5%
Return on assets			1.7%	1.9%	2.0%	2.2%	2.4%
Average of Five Top Companies							
Sales			¥867.6	¥909.5	¥954.0	¥1,003.8	¥1,069.9
Income after taxes			¥4.6	¥6.5	¥8.6	¥10.1	¥11.6
Return on sales			0.5%	0.7%	0.9%	1.0%	1.1%
Return on assets			1.0%	1.2%	1.6%	1.8%	1.8%

Exhibit 3

Financial Statistics for the Ito Yokado Division (¥ in billions except for sales per square foot which is expressed in tens of thousands of ¥)

Total Ito Yokado	1982	1983	1984	1985	1986	1987
Net sales	¥669.9	¥708.2	¥740.1	¥779.9	¥809.7	¥861.4
Gross margin	¥171.2	¥192.7	¥211.7	¥228.5	¥241.6	¥262.9
Gross margin percent	25.7%	27.2%	28.6%	29.3%	29.8%	30.5%
Net profit	¥17.6	¥24.1	¥29.9	¥36.1	¥39.1	¥49.0
Net profit percent	2.6%	3.4%	4.0%	4.6%	4.8%	5.7%
Inventory—end of month average[a]	¥70.3	¥64.2	¥61.9	¥59.3	¥58.1	¥59.3
Inventory turnover	9.5	11.0	12.0	13.1	13.9	14.5
Sales per square foot	¥8.7	¥8.5	¥8.6	¥8.8	¥8.8	¥9.0
Return on inventory[b]	25.1%	37.5%	48.3%	60.9%	67.2%	82.6%
Food Department						
Net sales	¥273.8	¥294.9	¥306.2	¥316.9	¥320.9	¥336.4
Gross margin	¥59.3	¥67.5	¥72.6	¥75.8	¥78.9	¥84.6
Gross margin percent	25.7%	27.2%	28.6%	29.3%	29.8%	30.5%
Net profit	¥9.5	¥10.5	¥9.9	¥9.0	¥8.8	¥10.1
Net profit percent	3.5%	3.6%	3.2%	2.8%	2.7%	3.0%
Inventory—end of month average[a]	¥7.4	¥6.6	¥6.1	¥6.2	¥5.8	¥5.4
Inventory turnover	37.3	44.7	50.0	51.3	55.4	62.3
Sales per square foot	¥17.9	¥17.9	¥17.8	¥17.5	¥16.9	¥17.1
Return on inventory[b]	129.3%	159.2%	162.3%	145.5%	152.0%	187.6%
Apparel Department						
Net sales	¥235.2	¥249.8	¥265.4	¥286.4	¥303.2	¥324.7
Gross margin	¥70.9	¥80.8	¥89.8	¥100.0	¥106.0	¥116.4
Gross margin percent	30.1%	32.3%	33.8%	34.9%	35.0%	35.8%
Net profit	¥10.3	¥15.4	¥20.1	¥25.1	¥26.7	¥32.1
Net profit percent	4.4%	6.2%	7.6%	8.7%	8.8%	9.9%
Inventory—end of month average[a]	¥35.9	¥32.6	¥32.1	¥30.5	¥30.2	¥31.1
Inventory turnover	6.5	7.7	8.3	9.4	10.0	10.5
Sales per square foot	¥6.6	¥6.4	¥6.6	¥6.8	¥6.9	¥7.6
Return on inventory[b]	28.7%	47.2%	62.6%	82.2%	88.4%	103.3%

a Inventory is expressed at retail rather than at cost
b ¥ net profit/¥ inventory

Source: Company records.

Exhibit 4
Ito Yokado Financial Summary—by Major Divisions (¥ billions)

	1982	1983	1984	1985	1986	1987	1988
Superstore and Other Retail							
Revenues	¥783.0	¥827.0	¥887.0	¥931.0	¥1,057.0	¥1,121.0	¥1,205.0
Operating profits	¥36.7	¥35.3	¥44.6	¥53.7	¥64.4	¥68.2	¥79.1
7-11 and Convenience Stores							
Revenues*	¥37.7	¥49.2	¥59.7	¥69.8	¥83.8	¥94.7	¥94.0
Operating profits	¥9.3	¥12.0	¥16.3	¥22.5	¥29.3	¥34.9	¥42.8
Restaurants							
Revenues*	¥41.0	¥47.2	¥49.3	¥55.6	¥60.2	¥65.3	¥72.5
Operating profits	¥2.2	¥2.4	¥3.6	¥5.4	¥5.5	¥6.3	¥7.2
Ito Yokado Group							
Total ROE	11.6%	10.3%	12.6%	13.2%	13.6%	13.3%	14.5%
Total ROA	4.5%	4.3%	5.8%	6.7%	7.2%	7.2%	8.2%
Inventory Turnover	11.9	13.0	14.4	16.4	18.1	18.1	18.9

* The numbers shown mainly represent the fees, which were a percentage of the franchisee's markup, that the franchisees paid to Ito Yokado for services and products which they received.

Exhibit 5
Organization Chart

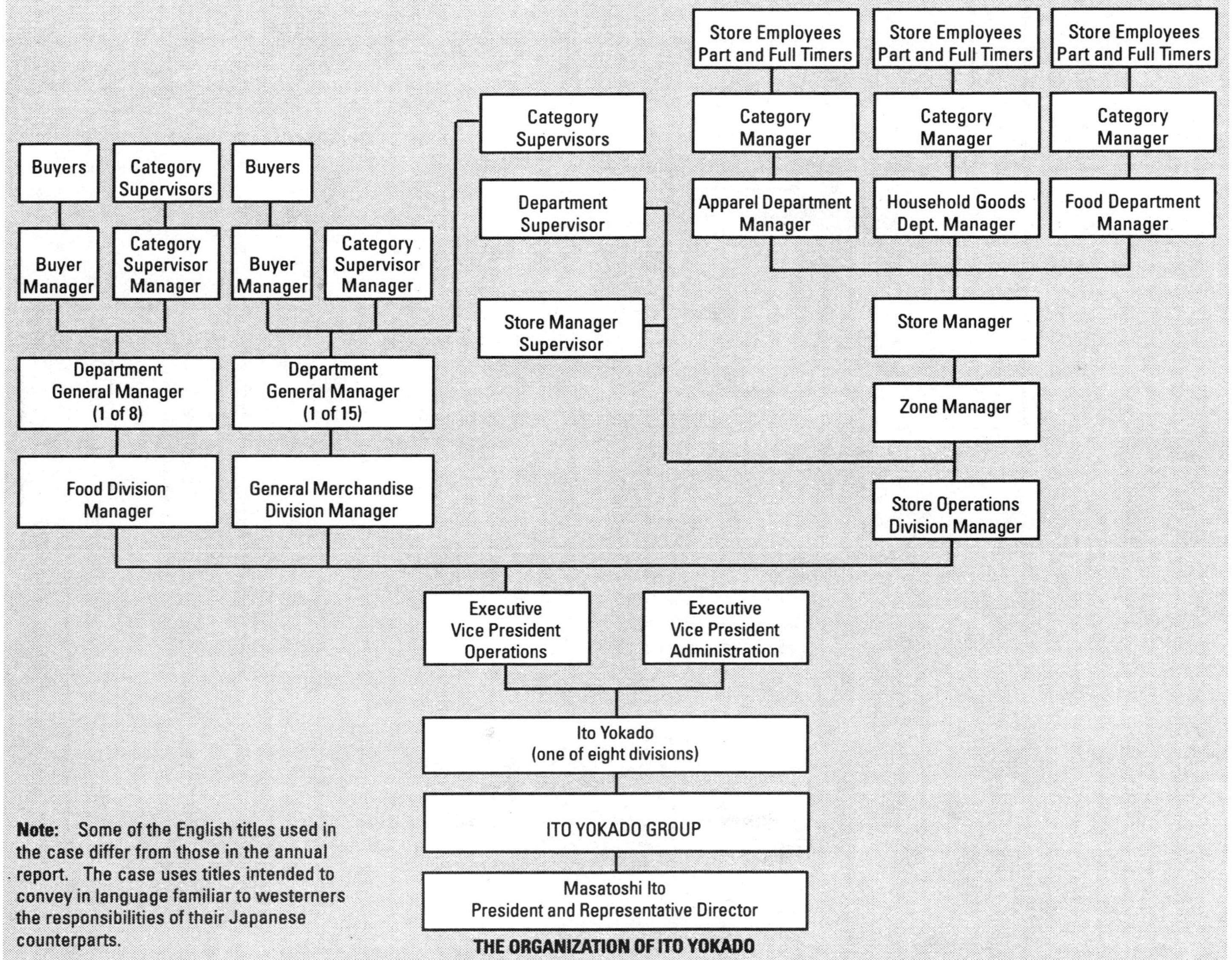

THE ORGANIZATION OF ITO YOKADO

Note: Some of the English titles used in the case differ from those in the annual report. The case uses titles intended to convey in language familiar to westerners the responsibilities of their Japanese counterparts.

Exhibit 6
Communication at Ito Yokado

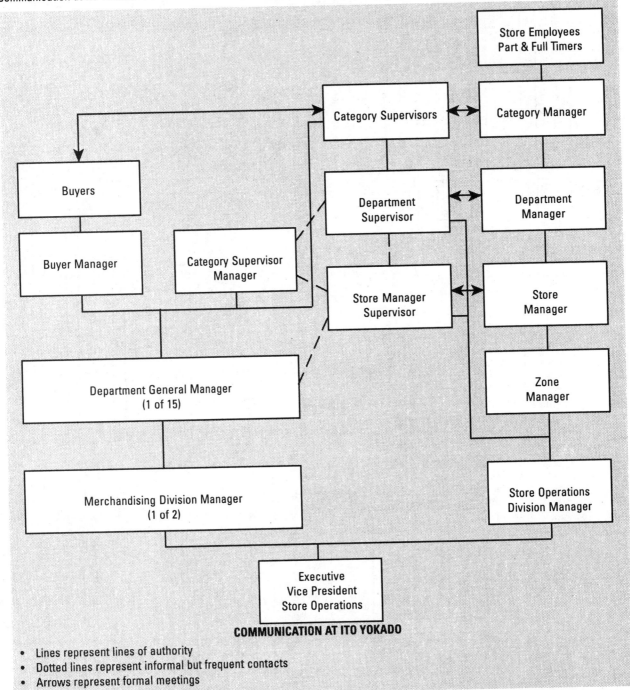

COMMUNICATION AT ITO YOKADO

- Lines represent lines of authority
- Dotted lines represent informal but frequent contacts
- Arrows represent formal meetings

Exhibit 7
Meetings at Ito Yokado

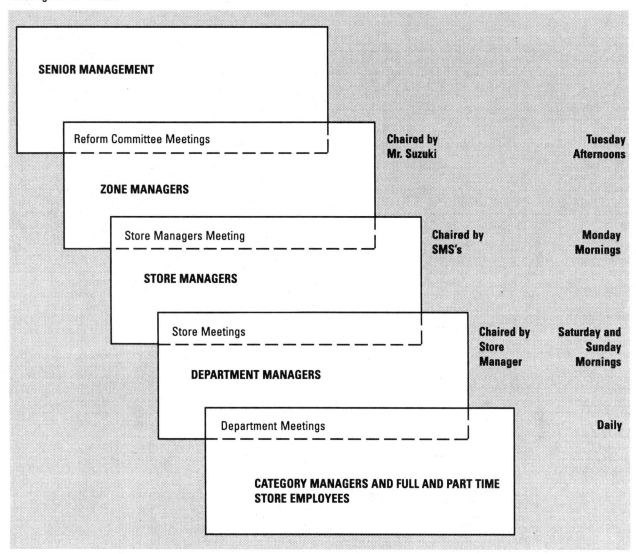

SENIOR MANAGEMENT

Reform Committee Meetings — Chaired by Mr. Suzuki — Tuesday Afternoons

ZONE MANAGERS

Store Managers Meeting — Chaired by SMS's — Monday Mornings

STORE MANAGERS

Store Meetings — Chaired by Store Manager — Saturday and Sunday Mornings

DEPARTMENT MANAGERS

Department Meetings — Daily

CATEGORY MANAGERS AND FULL AND PART TIME STORE EMPLOYEES

Exhibit 8
Days Inventory

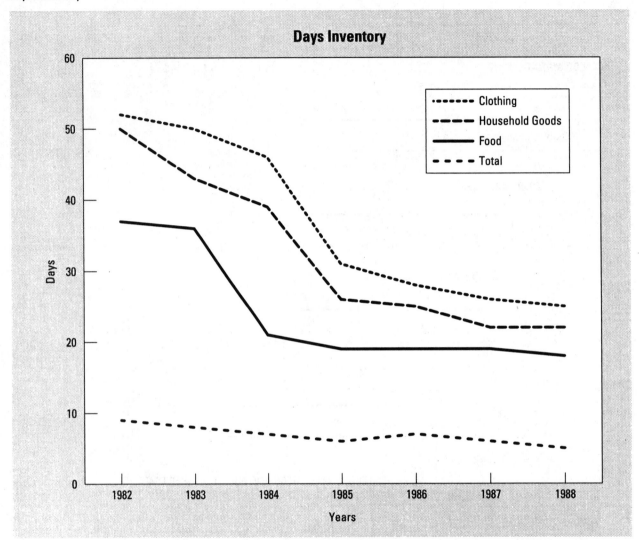

Days Inventory

Exhibit 9
Samples of Information Available to Ito Yokado Staff Through the Computers Located in Each Department

Exhibit 9A
Chart of hourly sales of fish at the Tsudama Store, by number of packages (above). The bottom chart outlines the focus of work in the department by hour (order processing, markdowns, packing, stocking and preparing, and other). Used by various staff members of the department.

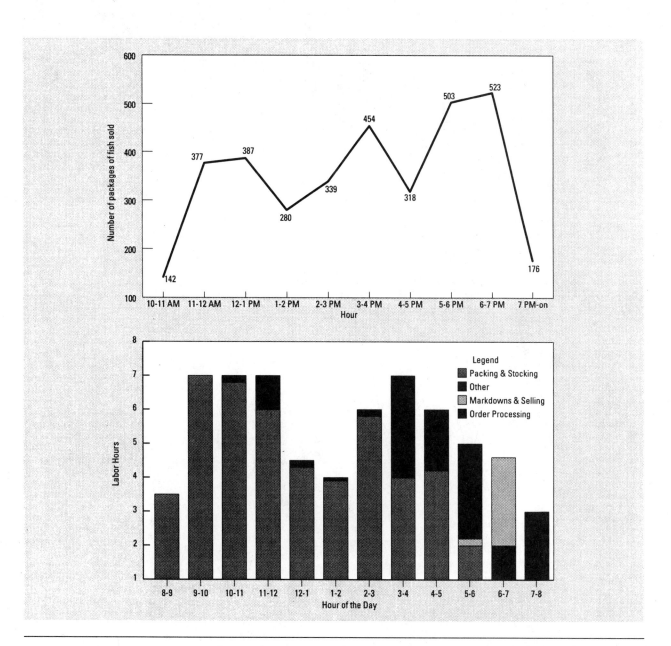

Chart of average hourly sales of various kinds of tuna for the trailing ten days. Detail provides information on the weather, unit sales, ¥ sales, purchased quantities and loss rate

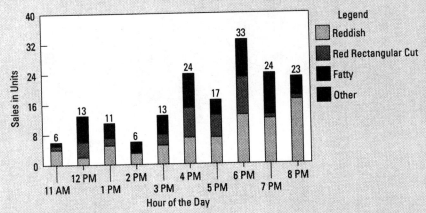

Total Sales in Units = 170
Purchase Unit = 193
Loss Rate in ¥ = 8,858

Sales in ¥ = 83,564
Purchase Unit Value = 111,165
Loss Rate in Units = 10.6

Information on the units of one kind of raw tuna taken from the back room to the shelf compared to the number of units sold. By hour from the equivalent day of the prior week

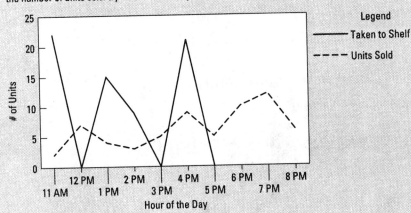

Total Sales in Units = 61
Purchase Unit = 65
Loss Rate in ¥ = 3,958

Sales in ¥ = 43,668
Purchase Unit Value = 50,701
Loss Rate in Units = 9.1

Both of these chart types are used by Mrs. Ichikawa in her order planning.

Exhibit 9C

Sample of catalogue which is presented to the store for reordering apparel. When reordering, Mrs. Nomoto used this catalogue for information on vendor, prices, availability dates, sales season, etc.

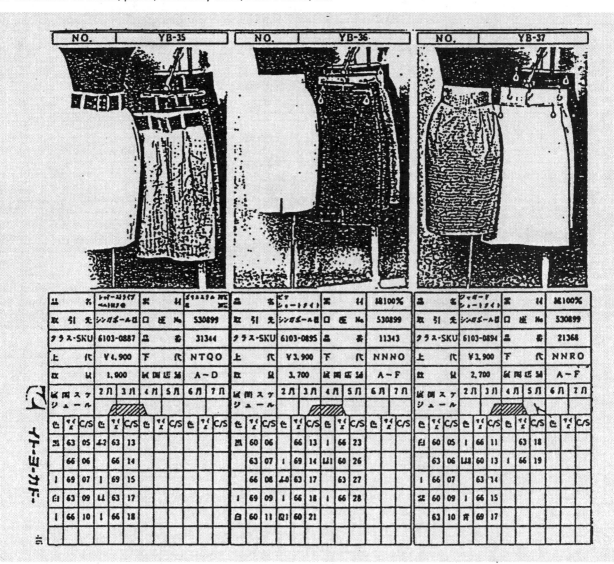

Exhibit 9D
Chart of weekly sales and inventory levels on a particular young ladies skirt. Included is comparison to previous year's performance.

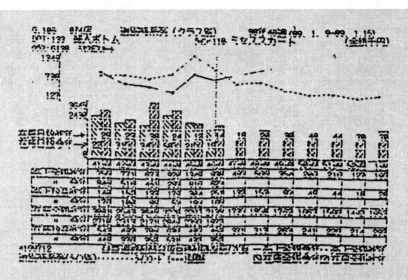

Distribution of prior weeks sales by size for a particular skirt style. Information also available by fabric, color, price in various levels of aggregations.

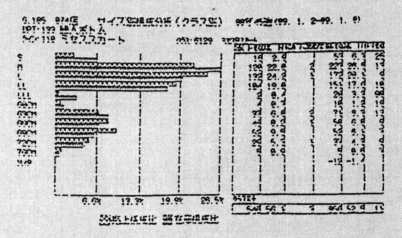

Mrs. Nomoto used both of these screens when preparing an order.

Exhibit 9E

Graph of sales of various types of fabric in young ladies bottoms sold during a 26-week period in all of the stores in a particular zone, along with qualitative merchandising suggestions. This information is available to the staff as needed in varying levels of aggregation by various categories (fabric, color, price, etc.).

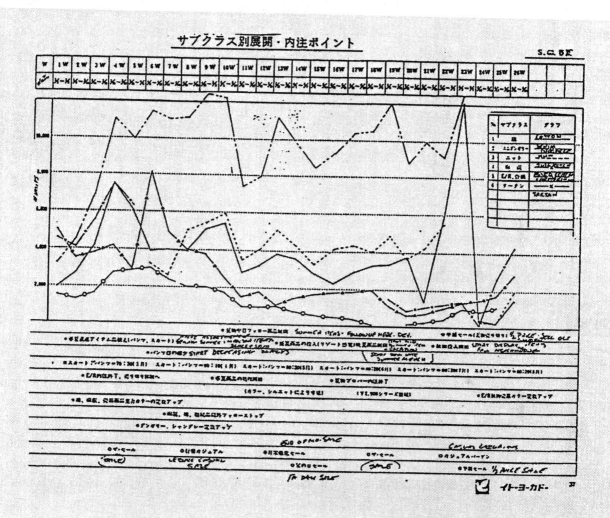

Exhibit 10
Oxidation of Tuna

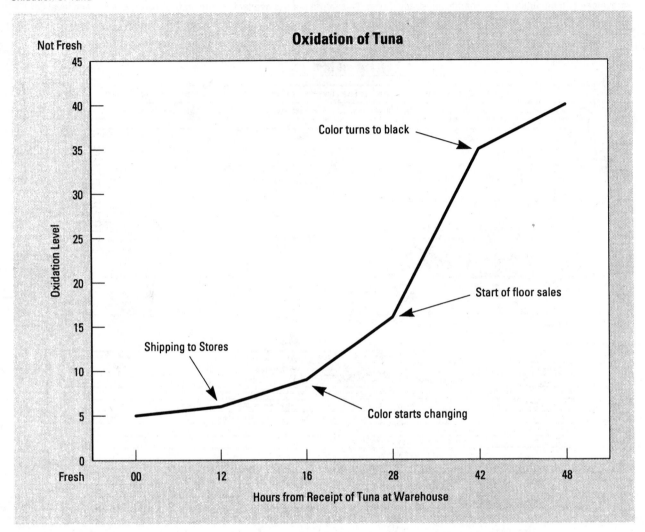

Oxidation of Tuna

Not Fresh

Oxidation Level

Color turns to black

Start of floor sales

Shipping to Stores

Color starts changing

Fresh

Hours from Receipt of Tuna at Warehouse

CHOOSING THE RETAIL LOCATION

Selecting a location for a retail store is a critical undertaking. A store needs to be in a building of adequate size, that is appropriate for the nature of the offering, and that is in satisfactory condition. It needs to be in a location that is convenient for a suitably large number of potential customers and preferably in a very visible location so as to serve a promotional role. All of these attributes must be available at a cost consistent with the profit potential of the business and involve a level of commitment that is compatible with the riskiness of the venture.

Despite all these provisions, store siting is one of the most well understood aspects of retailing. Roughly speaking, one may think of store siting issues in terms of macro conditions, that is, how attractive is the region around the store, and micro conditions, that is, how attractive is the store itself and its immediate vicinity. The macro issues determine the potential of the store to attract customers, the micro issues determine, in part, the willingness of those potential customers actually to visit the store.

IDENTIFYING CANDIDATE REGIONS

The first Wal-Mart store was opened in Rogers, Arkansas. This location decision was not because that was the world's most attractive location for such a store, but because it was close to Sam Walton's home and had an affordable rent. But when a chain is thinking about its 20th or 30th store, a more systematic approach to finding good locations may be justified.

DEMOGRAPHICS

Assuming your store concept has been well thought out, it should be possible to describe the target consumer. For example for a do-it-yourself store the target consumer might be a homeowner whose home is worth more than $100,000 and which was built before 1963. Where in the United States are there agglomerations of such people?

Information is available from a number of sources about the population in a region of interest. The United States conducts a population census every decade and the results are publicly available on computer tapes and CD ROM discs. In addition to the basic head count that is requested of every household, extensive census questionnaires are filled out by every 10th household. This means it is possible to compute accurate statistics concerning home ownership, home assessed value, major possessions, nature of employment, and family income. Many consulting firms incorporate these data in sophisticated programs that allow the user to print out census statistics on any region of the United States, defined even down to the level of city blocks. A region of interest may even be defined by using a light pen to sketch out a rough contour on a map shown on a monitor screen.

This note was prepared by David Bell as the basis for class discussion rather than to illustrate either effective or ineffective handling of an administrative situation.

Copyright © 1993 by the President and Fellows of Harvard College.
Harvard Business School case 593-112

Census data is, on average, about six years out of date at the time it is used and is inconvenient to use if the U.S. tapes are used directly, or expensive if a research firm is hired. Two publications provide more up-to-date and convenient access to demographic information. *The Survey of Buying Power*, published annually by the magazine *Sales & Marketing Management*, gives current demographic information at the city level including extensive data about retail sales, by product type, and estimated buying power in the region. It also estimates future values of these statistics. The *Editor & Publishing Market Guide* gives far less information of a statistical nature but more physical information about a region such as the number of cars, banks, and a description of local industries. It also provides an extensive list of retail stores, which is invaluable for a first cut at the second key regional characteristic of a candidate region: the competition.

COMPETITION

Perhaps your store is sufficiently new to have little meaningful competition, or perhaps it is a vastly superior rendition of an existing format. In these cases it may suffice to ignore existing competition. Otherwise it makes sense to reevaluate the buying potential of a region in light of the sales that are likely to be drawn off by competing formats. For example, suppose that we wish to open a bookstore in a city that we calculate has a book-buying potential of $25 per capita per year. (We might draw this conclusion by noting that regions with similar demographics have per capita sales at this level.) If we calculate that the city already has bookstores whose cumulative sales are equivalent to $24 per capita then there may be little left over for a new entrant. In summary, a first cut method for assessing potential demand is

Total Regional Buying Power – Existing Sales = Unmet Demand.

A simpler measure of regional attractiveness is the sales per square foot in existing competing stores. If sales are substantially higher than needed to make a satisfactory profit, it may mean there is enough to share with a new entrant. If a region is overstored, that is, has too small a population to justify the stores currently open, this will show up as a low average sales per square foot.

Even if there is unmet demand in a region, it is necessary to consider whether that demand will gravitate to your store. If the unmet demand is in one section of town, it makes sense that a store located there will pick up some of that potential. If the unmet demand is concentrated among a segment of customers, say children's books, parents may be prepared to drive past existing stores to benefit from your superior selection. But if the unmet demand is spread throughout the region and across all segments, it may mean that this region is less book-oriented than others. Or perhaps existing bookstores are poorly merchandised, but not so poorly as to encourage a person to drive across town to take advantage of your store.

A major issue in determining regional sales potential is to consider whether sales are "leaking" out of the region. Residents may be making purchases outside of the boundaries of the region, perhaps at a regional mall, perhaps through mail order, or perhaps on annual pilgrimages to a major metropolis. The question for a potential entrant to the area is whether the leakage will reduce, and by how much, once customers appreciate the entrant's offering.

COSTS

The potential profitability of a region depends not only on the unmet demand, but also on the costs that would be incurred to operate there. A region might have very high store rental rates, or local taxes, or onerous regulations about opening hours in the evenings, on Sundays and on holidays. A region might be a great distance from an existing central warehouse. In particular it might fall just beyond a one day drive for company trucks.

A region might also offer operating economies if it is close to existing stores in a neighboring region. For example, if they are in the same television market then customers in the new region may already be familiar with your advertising, and, moreover, no new expenditures will be necessary. Existing store managers can more easily train and supervise staff for the new stores. A critical mass of stores might also increase bargaining leverage with state or local suppliers.

EVALUATING TRADING AREAS

For screening purposes we have considered regions as a totality, but a store will be at a specific site and so it is important to consider the potential demand at that particular location.

The trading area of a store is that region from which most of its customers are drawn. While terms are not precise, the primary trading area normally means an area responsible for about 70% of sales. The secondary trading area is that responsible for about the next 20% of business. Of course, such definitions do not lead to precise definitions of a zone; there are many possible ways to draw a region responsible for 70% of sales. A circular trading area may not make sense if barriers such as mountains, a river, or an expressway distort travel times or population densities. The Mall of America in Minneapolis, currently still a tourist attraction, may have a secondary trading area that encompasses most of the United States. The intent of course is to describe a region from which it is reasonable to suppose most of your customers live.

For an existing store, calculating trading areas is relatively simple by use of "customer spotting" techniques. It is straightforward to interview a sample of customers as they enter or leave the store. More dangerous (statistically speaking) is to interview a sample of people at some other location and ask them where they shop and where they live. The sample gained may not be representative of the customer base. At least one store asks customers at checkout to give their zip code. Stores with in-house credit cards already have plenty of information about charge customers, though cash customers may have different demographics. Those that take only bank credit cards might ask customers for their phone numbers (which can be used to identify residence). In some countries, car license plate numbers give away the owner's town of residence. In many U.S. states, the department of motor vehicles will provide, for a fee, the name and address of a car owner if the license plate number is known. This can be useful for determining not only your own trading zone but those of your competitors, or for a mall that you may be considering. While zip code information is a little too aggregated, individual addresses may be too precise to be useful without laborious map reading. One device in customer interviews is to ask them which major road intersection they live near.

Estimating the likely trading area at a new location is much harder. It helps greatly if one knows the trading area of stores similar to that which is to be opened. Such stores might be others in the same chain or competitor stores. Statistics of interest from existing stores include the distribution of distance (in terms of time or some other measure of degree of difficulty) traveled by customers, their demographics, and average purchase amount. Of course, travel time need not be the right measure of difficulty for commuting to a store. For example, customers of a specialty store at a mall may have traveled, not from home, but a few feet from the mall anchor store. Some customers of a supermarket may be stopping on their way home from work, having made a detour of one block. Shoppers at a downtown store may be workers in local office buildings. Finally, and most intriguingly, customers may prove to be those of your competitors, doing some comparison shopping.

There are a few theories that predict where people will shop, based on simplified issues such as distance to stores, and the relative sizes of competing stores. Reilly's Law of Retail Gravitation considers a customer deliberating between journeying to one of two towns (or malls). William J. Reilly posited that a customer's attraction to a shopping complex went up as the square root of the selling space available. (Actually his formulation was in terms of the population of towns, but the principle is the same.) The relative attractiveness of each town is equal to the square root of its selling space divided by its distance away. D. L. Huff proposed a model in which a customer's *probability* of shopping at a particular location was proportional to a ratio of selling space to the travel time required to get there. Of course, such theories are useful only in making rough guesses in the absence of more concrete sources of information.

Reilly's Law relates only to the relative attractiveness of store locations. The distance a person will travel to shop at a store varies greatly by person and by the nature of the purchase. For a small purchase such as a newspaper or a soda (a *convenience* good), there is rarely a need to travel far since most neighborhoods have a local store that carries such items. A customer has no incentive to travel even a mile or two in order to save 5¢ or 10¢ on such a purchase. For a washing machine, or a television (a *shopping* good), a customer might feel that it is worth traveling many miles to have the benefit of a more comprehensive selection and/or lower prices. People are known to travel up to 50 miles to visit regional shopping malls and warehouse clubs.

As Reilly suggests, people will travel further if there are more stores to choose from when they get there. This idea is sometimes called the *principle of cumulative attraction*. For shopping goods, a consumer will usually prefer to go to a single location where two or more stores may be shopped so as to compare selections and prices. Automobile dealers often congregate in a single location (the "automile"). Furniture stores also cluster together. If there are three stores of a competing nature in a town, two in one location and one some distance away, the two may have an advantage. Though the isolated store is presumably closer to more consumers, many people may prefer to drive past the isolated store in order to have the benefit of one-stop comparison shopping. Power retailers can afford to capture the advantage of the lower rents of isolated locations if they can convince potential customers that comparison shopping is unnecessary on the grounds that they carry a wide selection of goods at prices that are competitive.

EVALUATING THE LOCATION

Store locations are usually classified according to the following hierarchy of association:

Free Standing (or Isolated): A store that is not close to any other stores. A store is free standing if, for example, a customer of that store is unlikely to walk from it to another store. Such stores make sense if in a residential neighborhood or office complex where for some set of people the location happens to be convenient. This includes isolated locations that have good *interceptor* qualities (for example, a supermarket that is on a commuter route).

Strip Malls: A set of stores having a common parking lot usually arranged in linear fashion. Often leased from a common owner, the mall may have developed in incremental fashion. It will usually include stores selling routine goods such as a supermarket and drugstore and services such as dry cleaning and photo developing.

Downtown Shopping District: A store that is one of many on streets near a city center. There is usually no common ownership of the buildings and only rarely some kind of effective association formed to tackle common concerns such as, perhaps, street cleaning. A neighborhood shopping district is similar but on a smaller scale. A small town might have two or three such centers.

Local Malls: A set of stores, usually managed and owned by a single company, organized around an enclosed, possibly covered, common space. Typically having 20–30 stores and 100,000 to 250,000 square feet of gross leasable space, such a mall will have a trading area of some portion of a city and include a branch store of a local department store, a variety store, and a category killer such as Toys R Us.

Regional Malls: Larger than a local mall, perhaps 300,000 to 800,000 square feet, and situated near highways to attract customers from a considerably wider area. The stores contain primarily shopping goods and include two or more anchor stores such as a department store (e.g., Dillard's) and a mass merchandiser (e.g., Sears). Such malls do not make sense as locations for supermarkets. Supermarket customers are not apt to combine their trip with a tour of the department store and they also need to park close to the store entrance (not always possible at a regional mall on a busy day). Neither are department-store shoppers likely to decide impulsively to pick up a week's groceries, especially if they are 20 miles from home. A mall is effective (and affordable) only if there is a sharing of customers among the member stores (i.e., there are economies of scale derived from the principle of cumulative attraction).

Super-Regional Malls: Those having more than about 800,000 square feet, referred to as super-regionals or mega malls. They are intended to attract customers from a 50-mile radius. Since customers may have spent upwards of an hour getting to these malls, it is important to include rest areas, food courts, and entertainment.

A site can be unacceptable if rush hour traffic snarls access for four hours per day, or if access is otherwise inhibited say by a median strip, or unhelpful one-way signs. A major store will often negotiate new traffic systems with the local authorities before signing a lease. A site is enhanced if the store or its sign can be easily seen for some distance away, or at the very least as one is driving by. Such visibility provides advertising and encourages impulse stops. A site's visibility might be latent: if the previous occupant of a free standing location made the place a local landmark, customers will be able to refer others to it quite easily.

As with any real estate purchase, it makes sense to do one's homework about any local problems: Is the local army base closing? Is a new mall opening up? Is traffic being rerouted? How do the demographics of the immediate neighborhood compare to the overall demographics of the trading area? If the store happens to be located in the one run-down part of town, customers may feel unsafe visiting the location. It is worth hanging around the store location for a week or more. Is the parking lot a hangout for local gangs, a flea market on Sundays, does it flood when it rains? Which brings us to the question of the lease.

THE LEASE

While some free standing stores may choose to buy their own building, most stores are leased from the owner. This eliminates the need for up-front capital and reduces the time a store owner needs to spend on maintenance issues. There is some rationale for separating one's aspirations for riches via merchandising and via real estate speculation. Owning the building may make sense in a few circumstances, for example, if the financial success of the building is inexorably intertwined with the store in it. This may occur if the store has special architectural demands, or if the store is to be in a very isolated or otherwise risky location. While leasing a store requires no up-front capital, many companies capitalize the lease on their balance sheet, recognizing that the lease payments are just as much a liability as long-term debt. Analysts and lenders typically capitalize retail leases when calculating debt-coverage ratios.

A lease commonly covers the following issues:

Price: It is usual for the price to be quoted in dollars per square feet (usually total square feet) or as a percentage of sales. Many stores have leases that require payment of the higher of some base rent per square foot and a percentage of sales. By this device a landlord can effectively evict a store with low sales (because the rent is high relative to the sales) or participate in the store's success.

Length: A lease might be for a fixed period of time with options for renewal. If the renewal option is not automatic, the contract might spell out conditions about how the lease is to be renegotiated at the end of that time. The store might have first right of refusal on any deal the landlord offers to another store, for example.

Contingencies: Of great importance are the terms under which a store may break a lease. Even successful chains sometimes err in their choice of location. A lease is an operating commitment and the lessor is highly placed in the hierarchy of claimants in bankruptcy proceedings. A lease will often require that a store not "go dark," that is, the lessee cannot simply close down operations and make lease payments on an empty store. A lease might, however, permit the store to sub-let the building or to operate a different format; for example, Woolworth's might close its variety store but re-open as a World Foot Locker.

Details of lease negotiation should not obscure the fact that no lease is favorable enough to make a poor location viable.

FORECASTING DEMAND

Estimating likely demand at a location is not an easy task. Every location seems to have, at least after the fact, some special circumstance that makes it out of the ordinary. If the store is the first of its type, rough estimates may be gained by considering the sales per square foot in neighboring stores, or by estimating per capita revenue from population in the trading area. But evidently such estimation techniques do not consider the effects of poor assortments or indifferent customer service.

The task is a little easier if the new store is one of a chain, for then the new location can be compared to existing ones, and sometimes to that of a competitor's store. The analogy method (sometimes called the peer method) proceeds by identifying that store which, all in all, seems to be the closest, demographically, to the candidate.

It may be that no store seems sufficiently similar to make an immediate comparison plausible. Perhaps, though, by understanding patterns of sales across existing stores a useful extrapolation might be made to the new location. For example, sales per square foot or sales per capita or sales per household might be found to be more or less constant at existing stores. More likely is that a complex theory is developed in which, say, sales per capita varies with average income per capita and/or other factors.

Regression analysis is the methodology most often used to provide specific relationships between sales and measurable explanatory factors. Regression analysis is particularly useful for aiding understanding. An analysis might suggest that "all else being equal" stores that share a parking lot with a supermarket have higher sales than those that do not. Or it might reveal that stores open 24 hours per day do no better (in sales per square foot, say) than those open 18 hours per day.

There are two main drawbacks to the use of regression analysis. The first is that the value of the conclusions depends critically on the number of stores in the sample. Twenty stores might be a minimum for gaining anything more than a rough insight into any relationships between factors. Fledgling chains need siting help long before they reach 20 stores. The second drawback is that the scientific trappings of the computer output often leads users of regression to place too much faith in the predictions that arise from the model. With a database of 20 stores, say, it might well be true that the 5 stores sited near a church did better than the others, but will this relationship really hold up for the next 20 locations?

A common result is that the model works beautifully on existing stores, but not on new stores. A model is not validated until it has successfully predicted sales of stores not originally in its database. To avoid the delay that this step inevitably entails, it is useful, if possible, to "hold back" 2 or 3 existing locations from the sample of stores included in the analysis. These may then be used as a check on any conclusions drawn by playing the role of "new" stores—that is, new to the model.

FORECASTING PROFITABILITY

Unless sales are important for strategic purposes, the primary forecasting job should be that of predicting the profitability of a location. It makes sense to set up a spreadsheet that accounts for initial costs, operating costs including lease costs, cost of goods, and so on. These should be expressed in relation to sales as appropriate. Note that sales may not equal demand if out-of-stocks are common, or if service is slow. The analysis should indicate that the store will provide a cashflow that exceeds the company's cost of capital, that is, has a positive net present value.

Many people will analyze the "expected case" scenario, but retailing is a risky affair. It makes some sense to consider the costs incurred of opening in a location that fails to be profitable. On the brighter side it also makes sense to consider the costs of expansion should the location prove even better than expected.

Case 18

VALUPLUS SUPERMARKETS, INC.

ValuPlus Supermarkets, Inc. (VPS), a Wisconsin-based company, operated 124 retail food outlets throughout Wisconsin and Minnesota under two names: 112 Best Buy Supermarkets and 12 Price Rite Food Warehouses. In February 1983 William MacDonald, president of VPS, was reviewing the performance of a recently opened Price Rite Food Warehouse in Walton, Minnesota. This outlet differed from VPS's other Price Rite stores. It was much larger and offered not only low warehouse prices, but also substantial brand name selection in groceries, an excellent selection of perishables, a number of specialty food departments, and some of the amenities of a conventional supermarket. Initial performance was excellent, with dollar sales volume almost 100% above the objective set by VPS management. Given this success, MacDonald wondered if he should rethink his decision to build Best Buy superstores rather than warehouse stores on two recently acquired sites in Minnesota.

COMPANY BACKGROUND

ValuPlus Supermarkets realized sales of $909 million in fiscal year 1982,[1] down from 1981 sales of $932 million. The decline resulted from the closing of a substantial number of small stores during fiscal years 1981 and 1982.

As **Exhibit 1** shows, the company's fiscal year 1982 operating income declined $1.1 million, from $10.6 million to $9.5 million. Sales and gross margins were depressed in two of the company's major trading areas because of high unemployment associated with the recession in Minnesota and intense competition in most of its trading areas. **Exhibit 2** provides VPS's 1982 balance sheet.

The company's 112 Best Buy stores were grouped in three divisions based on geographic location: the Northern Division had 36 stores, the Southern Division 36 stores, and the Central Division 40 stores. As **Exhibit 3** indicates, store operations for all divisions were consolidated under Harold Stratton, senior vice president of store operations. Buying and merchandising for Best Buy stores were consolidated under James Morrison, also a senior vice president.

The Price Rite Division was organized differently; Walter Tennant, vice president and general manager, was responsible for both store operations and merchandising for all 12 stores. The Price Rite stores were organized into a separate division in early 1982 as a result of management's perception that for the new Walton Price Rite retailing concept to be profitable operations and merchandising had to be closely associated. Tennant reported

---

This case was prepared by Research Associate Alice M. Court, under the supervision of Professor Walter J. Salmon, as the basis for class discussion rather than to illustrate either effective or ineffective handling of an administrative situation. Names and data have been disguised.

---

1 ValuPlus's fiscal year ended June 30, 1982.

---

to Morrison, as did the various buying pyramids Price Rite used.

RETAIL FOOD INDUSTRY

In 1982 retail food store sales in the United States totaled $252 billion, up 4.6% from 1981, while net profit percentage for the industry remained constant. This represented the lowest sales increase since 1966, and was mainly the result of a slowdown in inflation; the food-at-home portion of the Consumer Price Index advanced only 3.6%, the lowest increase in over 10 years. As **Exhibit 4** illustrates, real growth in the industry had been minimal for the past 10 years.

The number of stores in operation increased only slightly in 1982, because high construction and interest expenses restrained new store openings and unprofitable and marginal units continued to be closed. However, the stores opened in 1982 were invariably larger than the abandoned units, so the square footage of supermarket space per capita increased. See **Exhibit 5** for the 1981 margin, expenses, and earnings of an average supermarket.

Store Formats

Conventional supermarkets continued to dominate the retail food industry, accounting for 79% of total outlets. However, as **Exhibit 6** illustrates, other store formats did expand their share of units in operation in 1982, with warehouse stores increasing by almost one-fourth and combination stores increasing about 14%. The superstore remained the most popular alternative to the conventional supermarket, while limited assortment units suffered a decline of about 25% in total. A description of each of these formats follows.

Warehouse Stores. These stores offered retail food prices as much as 20% lower than those of conventional supermarkets. Their store operations were characterized by a reduction or elimination of customer services such as bagging, carryout, and check cashing; fewer store aesthetics; merchandise sold directly from shipping cartons, which were placed on warehouse-type racks with inventory stacked on top of the racks for easy restocking; and a greater proportion of merchandise purchased on deal. Because of fewer customer services and higher volumes, warehouse stores were able almost to double labor productivity over the supermarket industry average. Where possible these stores also used more part-time and fewer full-time employees to reduce fringe benefit payments.

By the 1980s a number of forms of the warehouse store existed, differing primarily in breadth of product assortment. The older warehouse stores were usually smaller, housed in converted conventional supermarkets. They tended to stock a limited assortment of basic perishables and a narrower assortment of total items, usually 2,000–3,000, compared with the 14,000 items in a typical supermarket.

The new warehouse stores, which often were housed in custom-built facilities, tended to carry a much greater assortment of merchandise. For example, Super Valu's "Cub" warehouse stores averaged 55,000 square foot and carried a selection of dry groceries equal to or better than that of a conventional supermarket. In addition, these stores had an extensive assortment of perishables, including many specialty perishable departments, such as cheese and sausage shops, fresh fish marts, and hot and cold delicatessens. An aggressive everyday low pricing policy was adopted throughout these stores, with an emphasis on national brands.

Limited Assortment Stores. These stores or box stores were like warehouse outlets but carried a very narrow product selection. These stores were characterized by very small or often no perishable departments and as few as 500 dry grocery items, which were skewed toward lower-quality and private label items. Retail prices averaged as much as 30% below those of conventional supermarkets, but part of this savings was attributable to the lower quality of many dry grocery items.

Superstores. Superstores were retail food outlets that offered a full line of grocery items in addition to an extensive range of frequently purchased general merchandise, such as stationery, garden supplies, records, and photographic supplies. The Superstore concept aimed to serve consumers' total needs for all types of routine purchases. These stores averaged 40,000–50,000 square foot and carried extensive perishables, a full assortment of brand name dry grocery items, and 4,000–10,000 general merchandise items. Most superstores offered full customer service, and their prices were comparable to those of conventional supermarkets.

Combination Stores. Like superstores, they offered a complete assortment of food products. Combination stores were larger, however, averaging 50,000–60,000 square foot, and included pharmacies as well as more extensive assortments of general merchandise. Their pricing was comparable to that of conventional supermarkets.

Because of their higher proportion of general merchandise, both combination and superstores realized a higher total gross margin. Some industry analysts believed the greater gross margin on general merchandise was offset by slower inventory turns and lower sales per square foot. Nevertheless, these analysts agreed that the more complete assortment of routinely purchased merchandise enhanced the total store's consumer appeal.

Consumer Characteristics

According to a 1982 national consumer research study commissioned by *Progressive Grocer* (see **Exhibit 7**), store cleanliness was the most important factor in choosing a food outlet. The second most important factor was low prices, supporting industry analysts' observations that, despite disinflation, consumers would remain acutely price conscious in the foreseeable future. Industry executives also anticipated no letup in the importance of games, coupons, and other promotions.

The study also revealed that women continued to take the main responsibility for grocery shopping in families: 93% of women versus only 33% of men and 15% of children reported that they participated in a major weekly grocery shopping trip. The average number of grocery shopping trips had remained virtually constant over the past five years at two and a half per week.

VALUPLUS OPERATIONS

In February 1983, VPS was operating three store formats—the Best Buy Supermarket, the conventional Price Rite Food Warehouse, and the expanded Price Rite Food Warehouse in Walton. Additionally, VPS management had developed complete operating plans for a fourth store format, the Best Buy Superstore.

Best Buy Supermarkets

The Best Buy Supermarkets were older facilities (most had opened in the late 1950s and 1960s), ranging in size from 12,000 to 28,000 square foot. Their customers tended to be middle-income, older consumers with small families, most of whom were loyal to Best Buy because of its convenient locations. Management believed these stores had an excellent image for meats, a fair image for private label products, and a poor to fair image for produce.

Best Buy stores were open from 9:00 a.m. to 9:00 p.m. Monday through Saturday and, where permitted, 9:00 a.m. to 6:00 p.m. on Sunday. They offered full customer service, including front-end bagging and carryout, check cashing, and film processing. Their selection of dry groceries was competitive with that of other traditional supermarkets, and pricing was also in line with that of supermarket competition. **Exhibit 8** provides sales and markup by merchandise type for all VPS's store formats.

Since 1980 VPS had closed a number of unprofitable Best Buy stores. It began to remodel many of the remaining stores and upgrade the merchandise. Although these efforts did improve performance, sales per square foot for the chain remained low in early 1983 because many small, older, unprofitable facilities still existed. The average order size in Best Buy Supermarkets, at $14 a visit, was well below those of the Price Rite chain at $21 and the Walton Price Rite at $32.

The old, advantageous lease arrangements that most Best Buy stores enjoyed were offset by higher than average labor and transportation costs. Labor costs were 5–10% higher than those of competitive independents because Best Buy personnel were unionized. Additionally, Best Buy's personnel were on average ten years older than the industry average, and most had been with the company for a number of years. As a result, these employees received top union-scale wages and benefits.

Transportation costs were high because of the geographic dispersion of Best Buy's stores, which were all serviced by VPS's single, centrally located distribution center. ValuPlus had made an effort to reduce its geographic coverage as well as its number of stores in the past two years.

Conventional Price Rite Food Warehouses

The conventional Price Rite Food Warehouses utilized the facilities of converted Best Buy Supermarkets, ranging from 19,000 to about 29,000 square foot. Before conversion all these stores had been losing money, despite management's judgment that they were in excellent locations. In 1979 VPS changed the signing on these facilities, eliminated front-end service, reduced assortments of dry groceries to mainly more rapid turnover items that could be purchased on deal, and instituted an everyday low-price policy that made them competitive with other warehouse operations. Performance began to improve, and by 1982 these stores were profitable. Their customers were younger than Best Buy customers and had larger families and middle incomes.

Management believed their conventional Price Rite Food Warehouse stores had a good lower-price image, an excellent image for meat and private label, but a poor image for breadth of assortment and produce. In late 1982, however, all the conventional Price Rite Food Warehouses adapted the merchandising concepts proven successful in the Walton store. The result was an improved image for produce and assortment.

The Price Rite Warehouses were open from 8:00 a.m. to 10:00 p.m. Monday through Saturday and, where permitted, 8:00 a.m. to 6:00 p.m. on Sunday. They offered check-cashing and film-processing services, but did not provide bagging and carryout. The selection of dry groceries was limited, with 97% purchased on deal, versus 85% for the Best Buy Supermarkets, and only basic perishables were available. Advertising was limited to "item and price" print advertising only and represented 0.96% of sales versus 1.5% for Best Buy Supermarkets.

The Walton Price Rite

The Walton Price Rite had opened in May 1982. ValuPlus had purchased the site in 1981 and initially was unsure what to do with it. Management believed the site was unsuitable for a Best Buy store because it was seven to ten minutes away from the main population (the city of Walton had 46,000 inhabitants). On the other hand, nearby competition was not particularly strong, and the site was at an exit of an important north-south freeway, which made it accessible to 175,000 people living in nearby cities. ValuPlus's research also indicated that warehouse stores had an 18% share of the market in the entire trading area, well above the 11% share industry analysts believed to be the saturation point.

Management felt the Walton store would have to have a special draw to be successful. To gain further insight, they sponsored consumer research on the current perceptions of warehouse stores. It revealed the following:

- The limited selection of brands at warehouse stores did not bother consumers for most products, but there were a number of critical purchases for which consumers would accept only a particular national brand.
- Consumers were dissatisfied with the quality and assortment of perishables in warehouse stores.
- Consumers were very concerned about cleanliness.

ValuPlus management believed that if they could create a retail warehouse store that satisfied these concerns, they could capture a significant share of market. They organized a meeting with VPS's top store managers, buyers, and merchandisers to develop a list of products that they felt had to be carried at all times. Using store movement figures as well as published sources, they agreed on over 800 items and over 200 national brands to be carried at all times in at least one size. These items would be made available at warehouse prices, even if VPS buyers had to purchase them at full manufacturers' list prices. The list of mandatory items was to be reviewed and updated twice a year.

To house the new warehouse store, a 53,000-square-foot facility with 37,000 square foot of selling area was custom-built at a cost of $3.5 million. The interior, although deliberately stark with a dark ceiling, utilized large, bold graphics and posters for decoration. Cleanliness was a top priority. The store provided 24-hour operation, rest rooms, an extensive and complete produce department, in-house bakery, sausage shop, floral shop, gourmet section, and a cheese shop with the largest selection of imported and domestic cheeses of all the VPS operations. As **Table 1** shows, the Walton Price Rite carried over 8,000 items, including 65% of the dry groceries carried by a conventional supermarket.

In addition, Walton carried over 200 bulk food items, including a wide variety of pastas and beans, dried fruits,

Table 1
Items in the Walton Store

Department	Dairy	Health and Beauty Aids	Dry Grocery	Frozen	Direct Store Delivery[a]	Nonfoods[b]	Total
Number of items	295	480	3,068	623	1,618	2,273	8,357

a Direct store delivery items include beverages, cookies, and crackers delivered directly from the manufacturer.
b Nonfoods include magazines, greeting cards, socks, hardware, and household items.

cookies, baking needs, chocolate pudding, pancake mixes, jellies and jams, peanut butter, cake and muffin mixes, and many other items. These were stored in wooden barrels from which consumers could scoop the exact amount they needed into a plastic cup or bag. Weigh stations, located in the bulk food area, weighed and ticketed the items. Bulk items were priced as much as 50% below similar branded packaged products. The bulk foods averaged $24,600 per week in sales, but management believed that the consumers drawn into the store by the bulk items accounted for close to $62,000 in extra sales.

Because of the Walton store's unique retailing concept, VPS management believed a major advertising campaign was an important part of their initial promotional program. The company's advertising agency recommended an introductory five-week campaign utilizing heavy television and radio media supplemented by a strong newspaper schedule. The plan was designed to capture a dominant share of voice in the Walton trading area, resulting in high initial trial of 44,000 shoppers in the first week and 22,000 additional new shoppers in each of the following three weeks. The consequences would be trial by 110,000 unduplicated shoppers in the first four weeks. The plan's objective was to reach 100% of potential consumers ("reach") about 25 times each ("frequency") in the first month. The sustaining media plan delivered a 100% reach and 40 frequency on a quarterly basis. The total plan had a projected cost of over $450,000 in the first year and delivered a 35% share of voice which, as **Exhibit 9** shows, was above competitive TV expenditures and share of voice in the Walton market before Price Rite's opening. The messages stressed the quality and variety of perishables as well as the brand name selection available at low warehouse prices.

An in-store survey of 496 Walton Price Rite customers revealed that 66% lived within a six-mile radius of the site. Sixty-eight percent of customers lived within a 15-minute drive from the store, and 87% lived within a 20-minute drive. The typical Price Rite customer was middle income, between the ages of 26 to 55, and part of a larger-than-average family. The survey also revealed that there was an average of 1.9 wage earners per family among Price Rite customers, versus a 1.6 average among Minnesota families.

The Walton store was performing well above management's sales projection of $525,000 per week, which they estimated was necessary for profitability. During the first six months of operation, sales had averaged $835,000 per week.

Walter Tennant, vice president and general manager of the Price Rite Division, believed a high-volume store required a very special type of store manager. "When you operate a store with sales of $200,000 to $250,000 a week, you get involved in every decision, but with a store the size of Walton, you just can't do that. That manager has to be good at delegating—and good with people." Tennant estimated that Walton had 350 employees, including part-time help. He also felt that the store manager's merchandising skills were very important in a store like Walton and could affect sales by as much as 5%.

There were only two VPS stores within the Walton Price Rite's six-mile primary trading area. These were both conventional Best Buy Supermarkets. Neither was high volume, and although sales dropped in both stores immediately following the Walton Price Rite opening, they had rebounded to their previous levels within two months.

The Best Buy Superstore Concept

Although VPS had not yet executed the Superstore concept, management believed this format had significant potential, and had therefore formulated complete operating and merchandising plans for such a store.

The Best Buy Superstore would offer consumers complete "one-stop" shopping. Its decor would be upscale, and the store would provide full front-end service, check cashing, and film processing. The merchandise selection would be broad, including an estimated 14,000 food items in addition to 8,000 general merchandise items. The perishables departments would be the most extensive in any of the VPS operations and would include a number of specialty shops, such as cheese, sausage, bakery, cooked foods, deli and fish market, as well as a floral shop, bulk food section, and gourmet shop. Pricing would be competitive with that of traditional supermarkets.

Store hours would be 8:00 a.m. to midnight Monday through Saturday, and 8:00 a.m. to 6:00 p.m. on Sunday. ValuPlus management believed they could build a superstore in 50,000 gross square foot. They thought that the superstore would attract younger (aged 20–45) consumers with large families in the middle- and upper-income brackets. They estimated that average order size would be just slightly below that of the Walton Price Rite store, but shopping frequency was expected to be higher.

Competition

Although VPS management considered all grocery outlets in the Minnesota area as potential competition for their proposed new stores, they identified three chains as particularly strong competitors—LoCost Goods, Sunnyside, and Park-N-Shop.

LoCost Goods was a bare-bones warehouse store. Its pricing was slightly higher than that of the Walton Price Rite, but its price image among consumers was very good, probably because of weekly newspaper advertising that emphasized item and price. LoCost had limited grocery assortments and poor produce, but its meat departments were considered good.

Sunnyside was a traditional supermarket chain. Its stores were quite modern, with good management and merchandising. Pricing was comparable to that of Best Buy, but Sunnyside's "specials" were lower priced. In addition, it utilized double manufacturers' coupons as a very successful merchandising tool. Its grocery selection, meat, and produce were all considered good by VPS management. Sunnyside advertised on television and radio as well as in a weekly newspaper circular outlining its specials.

Park-N-Shop was managed and merchandised similarly to Sunnyside. ValuPlus management believed, however, that Park-N-Shop's pricing on "specials" was below Sunnyside's.

NEW SITES

Markam

ValuPlus had recently obtained two sites, which management planned to utilize for new grocery outlets.

The first site was in a strip shopping center on the main shopping street in the northeastern section of the city of Markam. It was approximately 10 miles from the Price Rite in Walton. The Markam store was planned to have a total of 44,000 square foot and 31,592 square foot of selling area.

The population of Markam in 1980 was 90,874, a 4.4% decline from 1970, versus an increase for Minnesota as a whole. The estimated median household income was $18,400 in 1982, considerably below the Minnesota average of $23,000. The average family size in 1980 was 2.5, versus 2.7 for the state, and the average age was 35, slightly higher than the Minnesota average of 32. Markam looked old, and many of its buildings were deteriorating. The percentage of blue-collar workers was much higher than the norm for Minnesota.

ValuPlus management estimated that the primary/secondary trading area for the new site would be the surrounding two-mile radius. This included the town of Willow, with a population of 11,400. The limited size of the trading area was related to an inferior road system compared with that of Walton. ValuPlus did not operate any other stores within this area. However, there were six other major competitive grocery outlets, as shown in **Table 2**.

ValuPlus conducted an image study of its principal competition in the Markam area, the results of which are shown in **Exhibit 10**. According to the author of the study,

What is particularly important in this exhibit is the relationship of a particular supermarket to various image factors. For example, if 40% of the respondents shop most often at Park-N-Shop but only 15% think that Park-N-Shop has the best quality meat, that difference is significant. Conversely, if 5% of the respondents shop most often at Markrite, for example,

Table 2
Competitors in the Markam Trading Area

Store Name	Selling Area (sq. ft.)	Estimated Weekly Sales
Park-N-Shop	33,800	$374,000
Ben's Market	14,256	74,800
Sunnyside	16,104	202,400
Sunnyside	13,640	176,000
Markrite	33,000	352,000
LoCost Goods	19,360	123,200

but 20% think Markrite is the dirtiest supermarket, **that** relationship is important. The fact that a particular supermarket is shopped most often by a particular percentage of respondents is due not only to the popularity of that supermarket but to the particular geographic area in which the telephone interviews were conducted.

As **Exhibit 11** indicates, sales projections for this site were estimated at $308,000 per week for a superstore and $455,612 per week for a warehouse store. **Exhibit 11** also shows operating expenses and income generation for the two proposed store formats. Total investment for a superstore was $2,608,350, of which $2,147,200 was required for fixtures and leasehold improvements and $461,150 for working capital. Expected internal rate of return (IRR) was 50.38%, well above the company's hurdle rate of 20%.

The required investment for a warehouse store was $2,523,851; only $376,651 in working capital was required. The expected IRR for this format was 20.33%, and payback was expected in 4.35 years.

White Falls

ValuPlus purchased both the land and building of its second new site, located in White Falls, Minnesota. The site was approximately six miles away from the Walton Price Rite store. The White Falls store was planned to have 43,120 square foot of total area and 30,350 square foot of selling area.

The population of White Falls was 64,980 in 1980, up 2% over the 1970 figure. A full 46% of White Falls was composed of first- to third-generation immigrants who had been attracted to the numerous factories that opened in the area through the 1900s. The predominant ethnic groups were Polish, accounting for 14% of the population, and Italian, 10%. The median annual family income was $20,500, and the average family size was 2.5. The 1981 weekly per capita expenditures for groceries in the area was $20.75.

ValuPlus management estimated that the primary/secondary trading area for the proposed store would include the city of White Falls and the surrounding townships within a two-mile radius. This area included 77,350 people.

There were three existing Best Buy stores in this trading area which ValuPlus planned to close. All three were small, older facilities with combined sales of only $211,200 per week. Because of their close proximity to the new site, it was expected that 70% of their current business would transfer to the new store. The first five stores shown in **Table 3** were major competitors in the trading area. The remaining three were located on the fringe of the area but drew 50% or more of their sales from the trading area.

As **Exhibit 12** indicates, sales projections for a Best Buy Superstore were estimated at $308,000 per week in White Falls also. **Exhibit 12** also shows projected operating expenses and income generation for a superstore. Total investment would be $1,142,759, of which $712,259 was required for land, building, and fixtures, with the remaining portion for working capital. The balance of the fixed capital in White Falls was to be landlord supplied. The IRR was projected at 35.2%.

Table 3
Competitors in the White Falls Trading Area

Store Name	Selling Area (sq. ft.)	Estimated Weekly Sales	% of Sales Allocated to the Trading Area
LoCost Goods	12,400	$154,000	90
Sunnyside	19,400	202,000	90
Family Place	7,300	48,400	100
MacIntyre's	11,500	74,000	90
Good Deal	14,800	141,000	90
MacIntyre's	8,800	66,000	75
Park-N-Shop	19,300	154,000	50
Better Way	17,600	440,000	50

Because White Falls was within the Walton Price Rite's six-mile trading radius, management had not considered a Price Rite format for this site. However, MacDonald wondered whether the area could support two super warehouse stores and how much the new store would cannibalize the Walton store's business.

CONSUMER RESEARCH

In an effort to understand consumer reactions to and acceptance of the two store formats, management commissioned three research studies:

1. A quantitative analysis of perceptions of the Walton Price Rite among 186 Walton and 176 White Falls consumers.

2. Two qualitative focus groups conducted among White Falls homemakers (most of whom had been exposed to the Walton Price Rite store) to analyze the concept of the superstore.

3. An analysis of Markam by a real estate research company.

Results of the research were as follows:

As **Table 4** reveals, 20% of Walton respondents identified Price Rite as their primary grocery store. It appeared that the store's success was a result of its unique combination of price, selection, and quality. As **Table 5** indicates, Price Rite scored above the average established by all Walton stores on price, cleanliness, meat, and produce, and equal to the average on selection.

Table 4
Walton Store Research—Walton Customers: Primary Grocery Store

Store	Number	Crude Share
Price Rite (Walton)	38	20%
Park-N-Shop	80	43%
Good Deal	29	16%
Others	39	21%

Table 5
Walton Store Research—Walton Customers: Respondents (%) Indicating "My Store Is Best For"

	U.S. Norms	Walton Average	Price Rite	Park-N-Shop	Good Deal	Others
Price	(41)	52	85	40	60	30
Selection	(18)	26	26	28	22	27
Cleanliness	(6)	14	17	16	4	16
Location	(44)	29	12	40	25	39
Meat	(11)	11	12	5	0	21
Produce	(7)	8	11	10	4	4
Quality	(4)	10	4	14	7	12
People	(11)	9	5	20	8	13
Store	(4)	5	6	7	2	2

Although Price Rite made share gains by cannibalizing sales of all stores in the Walton area, it realized its greatest gains from Park-N-Shop, which received the lowest rating for price image of any of the major stores.

As **Table 6** indicates, 8% of White Falls' respondents identified Price Rite as their primary grocery store.

Price Rite's lower share in White Falls was mainly caused by location; 0% of the respondents indicated that Price Rite was their closest store. Second, as **Table 6** indicates, competitive warehouse stores were well entrenched, with an 18% share, versus only a 2% share in Walton. However, as **Table 7** shows, White Falls consumers were not satisfied with the selection, perishables, or cleanliness in warehouse stores. It is important to note that Price Rite also ranked below the White Falls average. ValuPlus management believed these findings might indicate that White Falls consumers had higher expectations on these attributes, or that the competition was more intense.

Both the focus group and the quantitative studies agreed that a new store was required to protect VPS's share in White Falls, because the Best Buy stores had a low overall image, ranking below the city average on both price and quality. However, the authors of these two studies had different recommendations.

Authors of the focus group study recommended that VPS build a Price Rite Food Warehouse; they believed it would have a stronger immediate impact because of

Table 6
Walton Store Research—White Falls Customers: Primary Grocery Store

Store	Number	Crude Share
Price Rite	14	8%
Park-N-Shop	37	21%
Sunnyside	38	22%
Warehouse Stores	32	18%
Better Way	17	
LoCost Goods	13	
Save Plus	2	
Best Buy	25	14%
Others	30	17%

Table 7
Walton Store Research—White Falls Customers: % Respondents Indicating "My Store Is Best For"

	U.S. Norm	White Falls Average	Price Rite	Park -N- Shop	Sunnyside	LoCost Goods	Best Buy	Others
Price	(41)	50	28	20	35	72	33	44
Selection	(18)	18	11	14	35	17	17	25
Cleanliness	(6)	14	8	28	10	10	11	14
Location	(44)	48	14	75	48	36	66	60
Meat	(11)	10	8	12	2	8	17	14
Produce	(7)	9	15	4	2	8	10	5
Quality	(4)	8	4	7	2	12	5	13
People	(11)	8	3	9	2	2	10	13

White Falls consumers' exposure to the Walton store. Their focus groups indicated that it would be more difficult to communicate the advantages of a Best Buy Superstore because of the current low image of existing Best Buy Supermarkets and the residents' lack of experience with the superstore concept. Additionally, they felt a Price Rite could attract a major portion of White Falls consumers who were shopping at warehouse stores because of price, but had indicated they were dissatisfied with selection and quality.

Authors of the quantitative study, on the other hand, believed that VPS should introduce a superstore. Their primary reason was the current "negative" image of warehouse stores in the area. They believed it would take too long to dispel this image.

The Markam analysis, conducted by a real estate research firm, revealed that a full 72% of the 285 residents who participated were very satisfied with their present supermarket, well above the 52% average generally found in this type of survey. Additionally, only 52% of respondents indicated that a well-operated new supermarket was needed in the area, well below the usual average of 75%–80%.

However, as **Table 8** indicates, when respondents were asked what a new store would have to offer to cause them to do most of their shopping there, 55% responded that lower prices would cause them to switch.

DECISION ISSUES

The major question facing MacDonald was which of the two potential store formats would be of the most benefit to VPS in White Falls and in Markam. MacDonald believed the decision required a thorough examination of the management, marketing, and financial implications of both formats.

He wondered whether VPS could successfully manage a fourth retailing format within its organization. He was concerned that it could strain his merchandising and buying staff. What were the implications of introducing a format that required significant merchandising and buying skills for general merchandise—an area in which the company had little experience?

MacDonald also wondered if there were enough potential sales in either White Falls or Markam to support a Price Rite Food Warehouse. He knew he needed sales of over $450,000 a week to obtain a satisfactory rate of return on a Price Rite, versus only $300,000 a week for a Best Buy Superstore.

Finally, what effect would these new stores have on his current operations? MacDonald knew that a new store tended to improve the consumers' image of all the stores in the chain. Would a Best Buy Superstore improve the performance of the company's Best Buy chain? How would his competition react to these new stores?

Table 8

Low prices	55%	Pleasant help	13%	Good parking	8%
Good specials	28%	Quality products	12%	Name brand items	5%
Good meat	23%	Clean	7%	Bakery	3%
Good produce	18%	Fast checkout	10%	Double coupons	4%
Large variety	18%	Convenient to home	10%	Deli	3%

Note: Respondents were permitted multiple responses.

Exhibit 1
Financial Highlights, Fiscal Years 1981 and 1982 ($000)

For the Fiscal Years Ended	June 30, 1982	June 30, 1981
Sales	908,751	931,516
Operating Income	9,465	10,555
Income before extraordinary items	3,836	5,701
Per common and common equivalent share:		
Income before extraordinary items	1.19	1.44
Working capital provided from operations	10,084	15,791
Working capital	15,731	27,476
Increase (decrease) in working capital	-12,304	2,128

Source: ValuPlus 1982 annual report

Exhibit 2
1982 Balance Sheet

ASSETS	1982	1981
CURRENT ASSETS:		
Cash	$ 9,558	$ 7,084
Accounts receivable, less allowance of $168 (1982), $235 (1981)	5,425	6,716
Merchandise inventories:		
FIFO cost	76,585	76,426
Less: LIFO reserve	- 14,097	- 12,161
	$ 62,488	$ 64,265
Other current assets	4,557	3,842
Total current assets	$ 82,028	$ 81,907
PROPERTY AND EQUIPMENT		
net of depreciation:	30,014	25,112
LEASED PROPERTY UNDER CAPITAL LEASES		
net of amortization of $17,361 (1982), $16,539 (1981):	38,131	38,734
OTHER ASSETS	1,806	1,750
TOTAL ASSETS	$ 151,979	$ 147,503
LIABILITIES AND SHAREHOLDERS' INVESTMENT		
CURRENT LIABILITIES:		
Accounts payable	$ 39,739	$ 27,963
Accrued expenses	23,400	23,715
Current portion of long-term obligations	3,717	2,752
Total current liabilities	$ 66,856	$ 54,430
LONG-TERM DEBT	$ 20,583	$ 28,395
OBLIGATIONS UNDER CAPITAL LEASES	28,372	28,012
OTHER LONG-TERM LIABILITIES	8,337	3,352
SHAREHOLDERS' INVESTMENT	27,831	33,314
TOTAL LIABILITIES AND SHAREHOLDERS' INVESTMENT	$ 151,979	$ 147,503

Source: ValuPlus 1982 annual report

Exhibit 3
Organization Chart

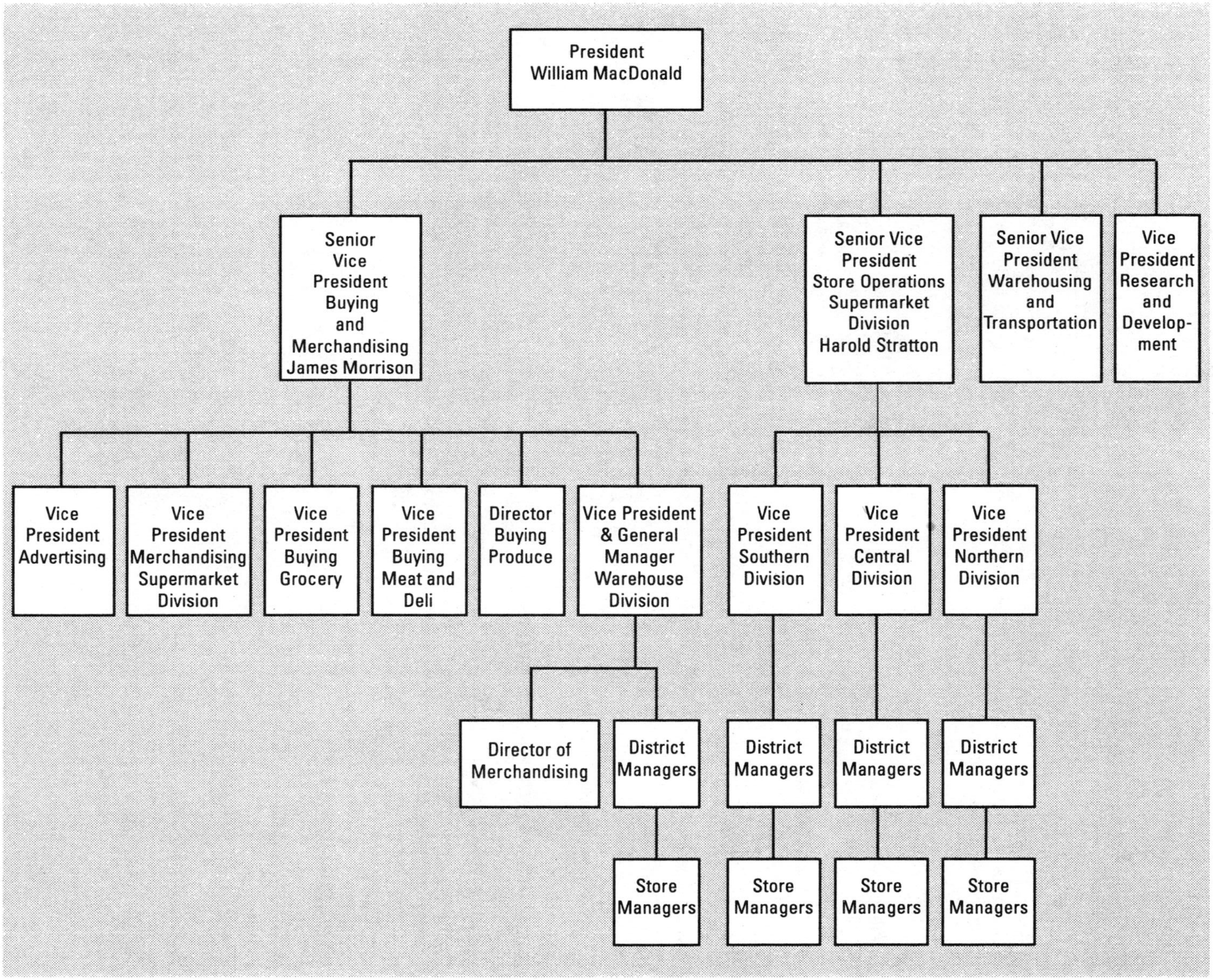

President
William MacDonald

Vice President Research and Development

Senior Vice President Warehousing and Transportation

Senior Vice President Store Operations Supermarket Division
Harold Stratton

Senior Vice President Buying and Merchandising
James Morrison

Vice President Northern Division

Vice President Central Division

Vice President Southern Division

District Managers

District Managers

District Managers

Store Managers

Store Managers

Store Managers

Vice President & General Manager Warehouse Division

Director Buying Produce

Vice President Buying Meat and Deli

Vice President Buying Grocery

Vice President Merchandising Supermarket Division

Vice President Advertising

Director of Merchandising

District Managers

Store Managers

Exhibit 4
Total U.S. Food Store Retail Sales

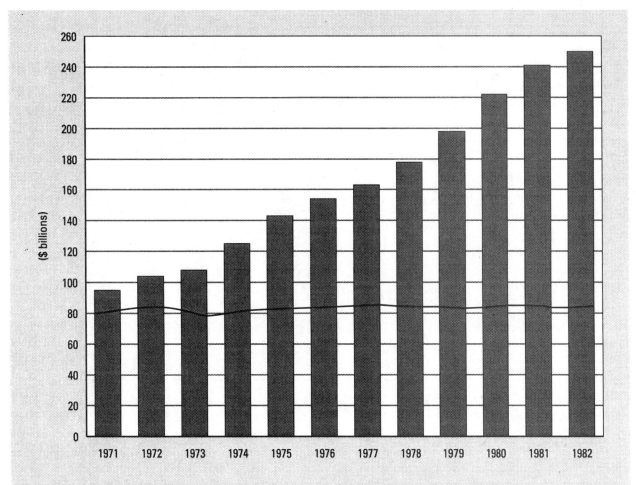

Note: Bars represent current dollar growth; the line represents constant dollar growth.

Source: *Progressive Grocer*—reprinted with permission.

Exhibit 5
Average Supermarket Margin, Expenses, and Earnings, 1981

	1981
Gross Margin	22.3%
Expenses	
Payroll	12.66
Supplies	1.07
Utilities	1.24
Communications	0.07
Travel	0.08
Services purchased	1.20
Promotional activities	0.41
Professional services	0.05
Donations	0.01
Insurance	1.02
Taxes and licenses	1.04
Property rentals	1.28
Equipment rentals	0.14
Depreciation and amortization	0.87
Repairs	0.64
Unclassified	1.14
Credits and allowances	−1.33
Total expenses before interest	21.60
Total interest	0.19
Total expenses including interest	21.79
Net operating profit	0.53
Other income or deductions	
Credit for imputed interest	—
Cash discounts earned	0.56
Other revenue, net	0.34
Total net other income	0.91
Total net earnings before income taxes	1.44
Total income taxes	0.56
Total net earnings after income taxes	0.88

	1981–1982
Net earnings after taxes as a percent of net worth	11.53
Stockturns	13.59
Sales per store (000s)	$ 8,216
Square feet per store, selling area	19,788
Sales per sq. ft. of selling area	$ 415

Source: *Progressive Grocer*, April 1982—reprinted with permission.

Exhibit 6
Units of Various Store Formats

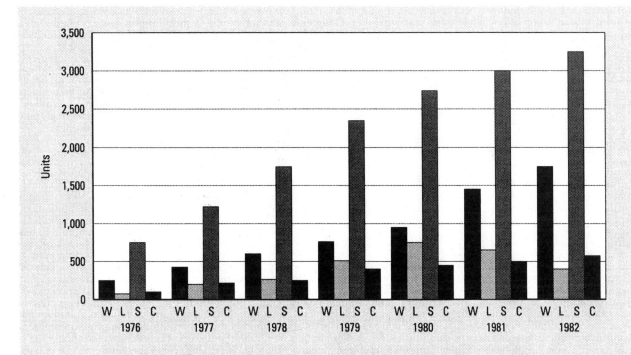

Key: W = Warehouse stores
      L = Limited assortment stores
      S = Superstores
      C = Combination stores

Source: *Progressive Grocer*, April 1982—reprinted with permission.

Exhibit 7
Forty Factors in Choosing a Supermarket

Rank	Characteristic	Extremely Important (% rating)	Not Important at All (% Rating)
1	Cleanliness	81.5	0.3
2	All prices clearly labeled	74.0	—
3	Low prices	76.1	0.3
4	Good produce department	69.1	—
5	Accurate, pleasant checkout clerks	69.4	0.3
6	Good meat department	70.9	2.3
7	Freshness date marked on products	68.7	0.5
8	Shelves usually kept well stocked	58.7	0.3
9	Convenient store location	58.7	0.5
10	Good parking facilities	57.0	0.5
11	Frequent "sales or specials"	56.5	1.3
12	Good dairy department	55.2	0.8
13	Don't run short of items on "special"	54.8	1.3
14	Helpful personnel in service departments	51.0	0.8
15	Short wait for checkout	47.1	1.0
16	Good layout for fast, easy shopping	49.6	1.0
17	Good selection of nationally advertised brands	39.6	1.5
18	Aisles clear of boxes	42.0	2.8
19	Good selection of low-priced store-brand items	39.6	3.3
20	New items I see advertised are available	36.0	2.3
21	Baggers on duty	40.6	4.1
22	Pleasant atmosphere, decor	34.8	2.8
23	Good frozen-foods department	34.6	1.8
24	Manager is friendly and helpful	35.6	5.6
25	Check-cashing service	40.8	14.3
26	Not usually overcrowded	20.4	4.8
27	Unit pricing signs on shelves	29.8	6.9
28	Good selection of budget-priced generic (no brand name) products	26.6	11.9
29	Open late hours	25.8	12.4
30	Store has customer restroom facilities	28.1	18.7
31	Good drugs and toiletries section	15.5	20.3
32	Good assortment of nonfoods	9.8	15.4
33	Carry purchases to my car	20.4	26.7
34	Have deli department	11.9	23.4
35	Have in-store bakery	9.4	23.4
36	Store has UPC scanning registers	13.2	28.2
37	Eye-catching mass displays	7.2	24.9
38	People know my name	10.2	41.9
39	Trading stamps or other extras	7.8	49.0
40	Sell hot foods to take out or eat in store	3.6	52.3

Source: *Progressive Grocer*—Home Testing Institute Study, 1982. Questionnaires were mailed to a stratified, representative sample of 500 homemakers throughout the United States—reprinted with permission.

Exhibit 8
Sales and Markup by Merchandise Type

	Best Buy Supermarket		Conventional Price Rite		Price Rite Walton		Best Buy Superstore	
	% of Total Sales	% Markup	% of Total Sales	% Markup	% of Total Sales	% Markup	% of Total Sales	% Markup
Produce	10.7	32.9	11.2	28.5	14.2	22.7	15.0	33.0
Meat	17.5	23.7	19.1	19.5	20.4	19.0	18.5	24.0
Dry Grocery	67.6	25.0	64.4	17.6	58.6	14.8	59.5	25.0
Deli	4.2	35.9	4.4	29.3	5.1	21.6	5.0	36.0
Bakery	na	na	0.9[a]	29.0	1.7	25.0	2.0	33.0
Total	100.0	26.2	100.0	19.7	100.0	16.3	100.0	26.7

a The percent is low because only 2 of the 11 traditional Price Rite stores had bakeries.

Note: Percentages for the Best Buy Supermarkets, conventional Price Rite Warehouse stores, and the Walton Price Rite were all based on an average of actual figures for all stores within each category. Percentages for the Best Buy Superstore were estimates based on management judgment.

Exhibit 9
Competitive TV Expenditure—Walton Market (July 1981 to June 1982) ($ thousands)

Outlet	Projected Yearly $	Estimated Monthly $	Share of Voice (%)
Good Deal	$284.4	$23.6	31.7%
Sunnyside	226.9	18.9	25.3
LoCost Goods	129.6	10.8	14.5
ABC	26.5	2.2	3.0
Park-N-Shop	191.6	15.9	21.3
Quality Stores	19.8	1.7	2.2
Better Way	17.6	1.5	2.0

Exhibit 10
Image Factors for Major Competitors in the Markam Area (%)

	Park-N-Shop	Ben's Market	Sunnyside	Markrite	LoCost Goods
Supermarket shopped most often	27	20	21	9	17
Other supermarkets shopped frequently	24	20	31	13	21
Lowest everyday grocery prices	28	22	19	2	1
Lowest everyday meat prices	11	16	8	5	25
Highest everyday grocery prices	11	16	8	5	25
Best advertised special	40	20	14	6	4
Best quality meat	7	33	20	3	6
Worst quality meat	17	—	6	8	7
Best quality produce	24	18	24	8	14
Worst quality produce	3	3	4	2	4
Cleanest	32	20	11	—	2
Dirtiest	—	1	10	10	9
Most friendly, courteous help	20	24	16	1	8
Worst speed of checkout	19	3	17	15	4
Best variety and selection	50	16	21	6	4
Out of stock on specials	10	3	20	—	2
Worst parking	8	6	3	3	6
Worst operated supermarket	4	2	5	4	3
Where buys most meat	10	31	13	2	10
Where buys most produce	25	25	20	4	16

Exhibit 11
Comparative Economics of Potential Store Formats in Markam

	Best Buy Superstore	Price Rite Food Warehouse
Weekly sales	$ 308,000	$ 455,612
Grocery sales	11,164,753	14,696,281
Produce sales	1,784,182	2,548,146
Meat sales	2,288,686	4,740,736
Deli sales	778,378	1,706,665
Total Sales	$ 16,015,999	$ 23,691,828
Grocery gross	$ 2,657,211	$ 2,204,442
Produce gross	562,017	611,555
Meat gross	514,955	900,740
Deli gross	291,892	401,066
Shrink	− 55,824	− 73,482
Cash discount	122,812	161,660
Total Gross	$ 4,093,063	$ 4,205,981
Total worked wages	1,277,809	1,650,521
Fringes	383,343	497,302
Other variable	200,200	237,037
Rent	172,480	218,126
Fixture depreciation	150,700	150,700
Leasehold amortization	62,773	62,773
Total depreciation and amortization	213,473	213,473
Other fixed	145,200	145,000
Utilities	164,120	164,120
Net before Direct Corporate Charges	$ 1,536,438	$ 1,080,402
Warehousing	219,419	324,740
Transportation	102,502	151,111
Advertising	160,160	237,037
Net before Burden	$ 1,054,357	$ 367,514
Days open	7	7
Hours open	80	158

Exhibit 12
Economics of a Potential Best Buy Superstore in White Falls

	Best Buy Superstore
Weekly Sales	$ 308,000
Grocery sales	10,906,896
Produce sales	1,329,328
Meat sales	2,882,880
Deli sales	890,736
Total Sales	$16,009,840
Grocery gross	2,508,590
Produce gross	451,971
Meat gross	634,234
Deli gross	336,336
Shrink	− 43,628
Cash discount	119,976
Total Gross	$ 4,007,479
Total worked wages	1,200,382
Fringes	368,612
Other variable	200,200
Rent	308,880
Fixture depreciation	110,000
Leasehold amortization	2,200
Total depreciation and amortization	112,200
Other fixed	142,542
Utilities	132,000
Net before Direct Corporate Charges	$ 1,542,663
Warehousing	349,430
Transportation	147,741
Advertising	204,248
Net before Burden	$ 841,244
Days open	7
Hours open	80

C a s e 19

FILENE'S BASEMENT

In January 1993, four executives of Filene's Basement sat in the board room at the company's headquarters in Wellesley Massachusetts, examining a map of metropolitan Chicago. On it were marked the locations of four existing Filene's Basement stores. Sam Gerson, Chairman, Jim Anathan, President, Gary Crittenden, Chief Financial Officer, and Brian Bootay, Vice President of Real Estate, were considering adding two new store locations. The first three Chicago stores had opened in October 1991, and were currently performing strongly, especially the downtown store. While there was always the danger that new stores could cannibalize existing sales, the expectation was that sales at existing stores could be enhanced by the increase in overall customer awareness created by the larger number of stores.

The two sites in question were located just outside of downtown Chicago, in the towns of Naperville and Mount Prospect. It was Brian Bootay's responsibility to recommend to the senior executives whether the company should open one, both or neither of these stores. Whatever they decided, they needed to do so quickly, in order that the company could keep pace with its midwest expansion strategy.

BACKGROUND

The year was 1908. The place was Boston, Massachusetts. Edward A. Filene, a successful Boston businessman, had a revolutionary idea: to use the basement of his store as a place to sell retail store overstocks and manufacturers' overruns of merchandise—and sell it at great bargain prices.

In order to keep merchandise moving, he designed the Automatic Markdown Plan. This innovative premise was simple but effective: the longer an item remained on the selling floor, the more its price would decrease; if it remained unsold after thirty-five days it was given to charity.

Thus it was that Filene's Basement opened its doors and introduced a new and unique retailing concept to the world. The bargain basement was born.

- Filene's Basement Annual Report 1991

In 1908, when Edward A. Filene opened the doors to his store's basement, the primary purpose was to carry the leftover merchandise from the parent store upstairs as well as to provide manufacturers with a way to get rid

---

Research Associate Dinny Starr wrote this case under the supervision of Professor David E. Bell as the basis for class discussion rather than to illustrate either effective or ineffective handling of an administrative situation. Some confidential information, in particular store figures, have been disguised.

of their unsold merchandise. Mr. Filene was not concerned about product mix or display, customer demand, or profitability. In fact, it was ten years before the basement showed any profit at all. The Basement of old simply fulfilled the need to dispose of slow-selling merchandise.

As part of the Basement operating policies, Mr. Filene created the Automatic Markdown Plan. This determined the price reduction schedule of each item based upon the length of time the item remained unsold. All merchandise was initially marked with a date indicating when the item was first offered for sale. The price of the merchandise was then automatically reduced by 25% after 14 selling days, 50% after 21 selling days, 75% after 28 selling days, and, after 35 selling days, if it remained unsold, it was given to charity. This pricing policy was still in force, but only in the downtown Boston store.

As the Basement grew and matured, so did its buying and merchandising policies. Instead of relying solely on surpluses from the upstairs store, management actively sought deals from outside resources such as brand-name manufacturers and other retailers. Also, more focus was placed on buying *groups* of coordinated products instead of unmatched items. During the 1970s and early 1980s, the market for discount specialty stores experienced significant growth. The Basement, already operating as a discount specialty store on a one-store basis, opened stores in regional malls around the Northeast. Management continued to pursue buying opportunities with outside resources and to display categories of product in department-store style.

By 1988, Filene's Basement was at a turning point. The Basement's operating philosophy had fueled significant growth and success. Because of this, management wanted to expand aggressively in the off-price apparel market. Nevertheless, the Basement's parent company, Federated Department Stores, wanted to continue to focus on its more traditional department store strategy. This led to the opportunity for some organizational change. In 1988, Filene's Basement, led by Chief Executive Officer Sam Gerson and President Jim Anathan, became an autonomous entity through a management leveraged buy-out.

After the buy-out, management followed through on their projected expansion plans, opening at least one store per quarter. From fiscal years ending 1988 to 1992 (the Basement fiscal years ended in either the end of January or beginning of February of the following calendar year—for example, FY92 ended on January 30, 1993) the Basement grew from 22 stores to 49 stores; expanding down the northeast coast and to the Midwest, with nine new stores in Chicago and Minneapolis. The Basement funded this expansion using cash from operations and through two public offerings, one held in May 1991, which raised $46.9 million, and the other held in October 1991, which raised $14.2 million.

Filene's Basement had become one of the leading off-price specialty apparel chains in the United States. They employed over 1,700 people and had stores in 11 states. Sales per selling square foot were among the best in the industry. The downtown Boston store generated almost six times the sales per square foot of the nearest competitor. The branch stores, with average selling space of 25,000 feet, generated nearly twice the sales per square foot of the nearest competitor (see **Table 1**). Despite an unfavorable economic environment, sales and earnings kept pace with the company's growth. Sales increased approximately 40% from fiscal years 1989 to 1992, while net income rose from $3.6 million in FY1987, to $14.0 million in FY1991, and to $33.9 million in FY1992. See **Exhibit 1A** for Financial Statement Highlights from FY1989–FY1992 and **Exhibit 1B** for full FY1992 Financial Statements.

Commenting on expansion plans, Jim Anathan said, "the 1993 expansion program remains consistent with our long-term strategy of back-filling within our existing markets, coupled with geographic diversification in metropolitan markets that offer multiple store opportunities."[1] Twelve new stores were scheduled to open in 1993—three stores in the spring, and nine in the fall. Following 1993, ten to twelve new stores were slated to open each year through the mid-1990s. Future possible expansion markets included Washington D.C. (opening in 1993), Cincinnati, Cleveland, Detroit, and Pittsburgh.

PRODUCT, PRICES & SERVICES

In the early 1990s, Filene's Basement carried medium- to high-quality, current-season, brand-name merchandise in the latest colors and styles at discount prices. It sold a range of items, from Men's and Women's apparel and accessories to Children's and Infant's clothing in the larger format stores. All merchandise was offered in many sizes and styles, with plenty of back stock available of all items. Prices ranged from 20% to 60% below

---

1 As cited in PRNewswire, Bloomberg Information Services, February 10, 1993.

Table 1[2]

Store	1991 Sales/Sq. Ft. of Selling Space
Filene's Basement—Downtown	$ 1,560
Filene's Basement—Branch store	520
T.J.Maxx	266
Marshalls	254
Ross Stores	206

typical department and specialty store prices. CEO Sam Gerson explained why people shop at Basement stores: "Price is just one component of the value equation. Quality and taste, having the right names and having them at the right time, are just as important."[3]

Unlike the original store's operations, which relied in large part on the overstock received from "upstairs," Filene's Basement in the 1990s had an aggressive buying department that purchased value-oriented merchandise from a variety of outside resources. The Basement's buyers acquired merchandise from brand-name manufacturers, at low prices through both volume purchases and special deals. These deals consisted of manufacturer's pre-season merchandise programs, in-season overruns and cancellations, and post-season surpluses. The opportunistic purchases, called "packaways," were usually warehoused until the following season. Unlike many of its competitors, the Basement had ample warehouse and distribution space, with two distribution centers of 320,000 and 457,000 square feet, and adequate financial resources to inventory this merchandise for at least a year.

Brand-name merchandise, both current and from earlier seasons, comprised approximately 75% of the Basement's inventory. In addition, the Basement acquired excess or slow selling merchandise from other retailers at particularly favorable prices. This merchandise, called Retail Stock, made up 12–13% of the merchandise assortment. The remainder was the Basement's own private label program. The company developed and implemented a private label program, called The Basics, revolving around basic fashion apparel. The Basement planned and committed for this merchandise

program well in advance of the selling season, which allowed it to create savings that were passed along to the customers.[4]

Unlike some off-price "pipe-rack" retailers, Filene's Basement tried not to sacrifice ambiance for price. Accordingly, merchandise in the Basement stores was creatively displayed with a layout similar to traditional department stores. There were distinct department areas such as Men's Furnishings and Women's Designer Apparel. In addition, most merchandise was displayed on 4-way or rounder fixtures (typically found in department stores) and grouped according to style and classification. For instance, the skirt, jacket and blouse of a suit from a typical designer or brand-name manufacturer would be merchandised on the same fixture, instead of being separated by product type in different areas of a store. According to the 1991 Annual Report, the Basement's "display standards are on a par with the fine department and specialty stores and (the) merchandise is carefully coordinated into collections. . . . (the) in-store display is deliberately crafted to make shopping both enjoyable and convenient for the customer."[5]

FILENE'S BASEMENT CUSTOMER

Filene's Basement customers were thought to look for both high-quality fashions and good value. Washington, D.C., which had been targeted as the newest trading area for development by the company, represented a high potential market. Jim Anathan noted: "Washington has long been recognized for its quality demographics, fashion orientation and sophistication—all important ingredients for a successful market entry program."[6]

2 Sales per square foot figures were calculated by Alex. Brown & Sons, Inc. in the Growth Retailers Report on Ross Stores, Inc. March, 1992.
3 As cited in Discount Merchandiser Vol: 31, Issue: 10 October, 1991 p. 31.
4 Discount Merchandiser vol: 31 Issue 10: October 1991 p. 31,
5 Filene's Basement 1991 Annual Report p. 6.
6 As cited in PRNewswire, Bloomberg Information Services, February 10, 1993.

According to industry analysts, the majority of Filene's Basement customers were between the ages of 25 and 49. Of these, slightly over half were female. In addition, the Basement attracted an educated consumer, with at least 40% of their shoppers having attended college. Over three-quarters of the customer base came from households with incomes of over $25,000 a year; the targeted average annual household income was between $35,000 and $45,000.

COMPETITION

As part of the $11 billion off-price retail apparel industry segment, Filene's Basement faced strong competition from many different retailers. The biggest threat came from other off-price retailers that had a similar merchandising mix. These included Marshalls, T.J.Maxx, and Loehmann's, Ross Stores (on the west coast), and Nordstrom Rack. Like Filene's Basement, these stores offered brand-name merchandise for less than suggested retail prices. **Exhibits 2** and **3** show some comparative statistics.

Narrow-line off-price specialty stores, such as the Dress Barn and Hit or Miss, also represented competition for Filene's Basement. Although not carrying the same broad selection of product, these stores also offered deeply discounted prices on a narrower range of product categories. Their ambiance tended to be less attractive, with little attention paid to merchandising details. Products were displayed on long racks with the shopping atmosphere taking a back seat to low prices. This often led to the impression that merchandise from these stores was not of the highest quality or the latest fashion.

In terms of competitive advertising, the Basement focused mostly on item/price promotions. These were typically run in daily newspapers and Sunday inserts. The advertisements depicted particular items at special prices for a limited period of time. Most of the Basements competitors, however, did institutional advertising. This image advertising, usually on television or on the radio, promoted the store concept as a whole, and did not include any specific pricing information. See **Exhibit 4** for a recent Filene's Basement advertisement.

Marshalls

Marshalls, one of the largest off-price family apparel retailers in the United States, was formidable competition for Filene's Basement. In December 1991, it had 405 stores in operation in 39 states. Most of the stores were located in suburban strip shopping centers where it was usually an anchor tenant. As part of the Melville Corporation, whose sales at the end of the 1991 fiscal year were $9.88 billion, it enjoyed the resources and network of a major U.S. retailer. Marshalls sales of approximately $2.37 billion represented 24% of Melville's total volume.

The merchandise offered at Marshalls was similar to that of the Basement. Both offered brand-name and private-label apparel. Both priced items at 20% to 60% below department and specialty stores' prices. Marshalls however, carried apparel for all members of the family, including children, toddlers, and infants, as well as housewares and giftware, in all of its stores.

T.J.Maxx

In 1993, T.J.Maxx had over 440 stores in operation in 46 states. The average store size was 25,000 square foot and was located in a suburban shopping area. T.J.Maxx stores targeted women with families between the ages of 25 and 50. The pricing strategy was similar to the Basement's but the merchandise mix was broader. The mix included women's, men's, and children's apparel and accessories, women's shoes, domestics, and giftware. Furthermore, neither Marshalls nor T.J.Maxx carried as much merchandise from upscale stores and designers as the Basement. Like the Basement, T.J.Maxx also followed an opportunistic buying pattern used to deliver greater values to the customer.

Like Marshalls, T.J.Maxx was part of a larger corporation, The TJX Companies, Inc. Among its other retail operations, TJX owned Hit or Miss, Chadwicks of Boston (an apparel mail-order operation) and Winners, a T.J.Maxx-like operation in Canada. Of the corporation's total sales of $2.76 billion for the year ending January 1992, the family apparel stores accounted for $2.21 billion, the women's apparel stores $377 million, and the mail-order division $173 million.

Ross Stores

There were over 200 Ross "Dress For Less" Stores in operation in 18 states by the end of 1992. Although headquartered in California, Ross Stores had a presence throughout the United States. In addition to California, major clusters of stores operated in Florida (30 stores), Texas (14 stores), Arizona, and Washington (10 stores each). Ross' sales for the fiscal year ending in January 1992, were $929 million.

Ross Stores specialized in quality, in-season branded apparel, accessories, and footwear for the entire family. The stores averaged 24,000 square foot and merchandise was displayed in a department-store style. The divisions included (1) Ladies (34% of sales), comprised of Misses Sportswear, Juniors, Petites, Women's World, Dresses, Lingerie, and Accessories departments, (2) Men's (24%), comprised of Traditional Men's and Young Men's departments, (3) Children's (10%), (4) Shoes (12%), and (5) Fragrances (20%). The target customers were women and men between the ages of 25 and 54. Like its competitors, Ross Stores also promoted product prices at 20–60% below department and specialty stores' prices.

SITE SELECTION

The General Process

Given management's aggressive expansion plans, selecting well-located new store sites was essential for the Basement's future success. An internal group, headed by Brian Bootay, coordinated store siting efforts and, in particular, handled most siting issues in the company's own backyard of Boston. Outside of the Boston Metro area, the Basement used a Wisconsin-based consultant, Ralph Chiodo, of Economic Research Corporation. Chiodo had helped the Basement with its expansion strategy by determining which trading areas, such as Chicago and Washington D.C., had the highest sales potential and concentration of typical Basement shoppers. This information was based in part on demographic information purchased from other market research firms, and in part on the competitive conditions in the particular markets. The presence of a competitor in a market could be a good sign, indicating a promising customer base, or a liability because of the direct competition they represented. To be viable, a candidate region had to be able to support a cluster of stores so as to create a critical advertising presence.

Of 140 metropolitan areas considered within the U.S., 18 were identified as being able to support multiple Basement stores. An additional 33 regions were thought to be able to support a single store.

Once this priority list had been established, Chiodo identified individual sites within particularly promising markets. "It's usually fairly clear where in a city the major demographic centers are, and then it becomes a question of finding available locations in those centers. Once a candidate site has been identified, I compare the local demographics to previous Basement stores to see if there is a close analog. A few years ago we conducted a zip code check on a sample of Basement customers. This information is invaluable in helping us to understand how far Basement customers were travelling and how this varied with the demographics of their zip code. I can overlay this information on the candidate site and so get some idea of the likely trading zone and potential sales.

"I also monitor the competitive presence around a potential site. We do a lot of work for all kinds of retail chains and so I have a good idea of how much of that potential is already being soaked up. Estimating store sales is as much an art as it is a science. The numbers can only take you so far. It's important to take account of the characteristics of the particular site, such as access and the next-door retailers."

For each candidate region, Ralph provided Basement management with reports on available locations in different sub-markets of interest. "Site Analysis Reports" highlighted data on the region and gave some specifics for each site available. Information included square footage of the site, parking facilities available, the consultant's view on the mix of other stores in the mall or area, and the competitors in the vicinity, as well as a rough estimate of likely sales. **Exhibit 5** shows excerpts and demographic information from Site Analysis Reports for the two locations under consideration in the Chicago area.

Once several sites had been identified in a region, Crittenden and Bootay would visit the sites. Bootay then analyzed the locations based on the economics of each deal. The likely success of the store was estimated by its cost structure weighed against its likely sales. The final selection of sites came from the marriage of the estimated sales and costs figures.

When back-filling in an existing market, Chiodo used zip code demographics to estimate the degree of cannibalization at other Basement stores. Consideration was given to the total net effect of a new store introduction, though sometimes a new store could be justified for competitive reasons: it might be better to open a marginally profitable store than watch a competitor take the site.

IN-HOUSE MODELING EFFORTS

The 1987 Computer Model

In 1987 Gary and Brian constructed a sales forecasting model to help with the site selection process. Enormous amounts of data were collected at the store level, covering what the Basement considered to be the critical aspects of store location. These included market size, the number of households, the level of education in the market area, the selling space available and the competition in the area. Over 50 variables were collected on 15 stores for use in the model. The model took over five months to develop and complete. (**Exhibit 6** displays the model parameters, regression analysis, and projected sales).

The variables having the greatest cumulative association with sales per square foot were:

1. Fair Rental Rate per square foot. The fair rental rate was not necessarily equal to the actual rental rate since this might be distorted by non-price aspects of a lease, such as building allowances and discounts, or due to the age of lease.
2. Market impressions per household. This was a weighted summation of the advertising history in a location, taking into account several factors such as the cost of the media, the effectiveness of the advertising, the circulation of the media used, etc.
3. Competition square feet per household. This calculation was based on locations within a 20-minute travel time of the site.

The resulting regression model suggested that sales per square foot could be estimated by assuming a base of $59 per square foot plus a location-specific multiple of the fair rental rate per square foot. The Multiple was calculated as $19 plus .001 times the Market Impressions per household squared, minus 3.2 times the logarithm of the Competition square feet per household. **Exhibit 6** also shows how this model performed on the 15 stores in the sample together with 6 other stores not included in the sample.

Despite the effort put into the model, it never became a formal part of the site selection process. Although management thought that the findings of the computer model were interesting, they felt that the value used for the fair market rent element in the model was subjective. Therefore, they used the model infrequently, and then only in conjunction with a number of the other site selection tools available to them.

New Modeling Efforts

Nearly 6 years later, in 1993, many new stores had been opened, providing a richer database from which to extract sales patterns. Gary, Brian Bootay and Donna

Capichano from the Real Estate Department, and Joan O'Hare from the Advertising Department met to reexamine the site selection issue. The objective of the meeting was twofold; (1) to outline the critical factors of a successful Filene's Basement location and, (2) to consider whether these factors might be combined into a new model.

The meeting started with the discussion of what each participant thought were the key factors for selecting a successful site. Much of the discussion centered on the considerations that were being used in the current site selection process, such as population, income, and education.

About twenty minutes into the two-hour meeting, a theory was introduced about the Basement's sales in specific markets. There seemed to be a wide range in sales per household between the different major markets. It was postulated that this fluctuation was due at least in part to the following factors: (1) the length of time that Basement stores existed in the market, (2) the cumulative marketing effect of advertising and promotions in the given area, and (3) the education level of the population. As a market became more mature, or if the level of education in the market was high, household spending increased in what might be considered a fairly predictable manner. Spending per household in a new market seemed always to hover around the same amount, whether the new market was on the East Coast or in the Midwest. But this tended to increase as the market matured. The speed with which a region matured might be explained by the longevity of the Basement in that region and the level of marketing activity. In the same way, an increase in the level of education of the population tended to increase the average base amount of spending per household. If these predictions could be validated, then estimating sales for a given store would be reduced to a question of quantifying the magnitude of these factors, and then modifying the prediction to allow for any physical or access peculiarities of the site itself.

It seemed plausible that a new effort along these lines could be productive, but it would take some time to collect the necessary data and do the analysis. Meanwhile Brian still had to resolve the more immediate decision of what to do in the Chicago market and make his presentation to the senior executives. Should they open two more stores in that area, or, should they wait to see how the existing Chicago stores matured over time?

THE CHICAGO MARKET

In October 1991, Filene's Basement opened three stores in the Chicago area. Management had targeted Chicago because it was the largest market of the 140 studied in the preliminary screening of June, 1990. The city's estimated population in 1989 was 6.7 million. This compared to a population of 4.1 million in greater Boston. In addition, Chicago was considered to be an upscale, white collar market, two prime characteristics of the Basement target customer. The average 1989 median household income in Chicago was $31,556. This income level was 15% higher than the national average, but 8% lower than the income level in Boston at the same time. For more information see **Exhibit 7** which outlines some comparative market demographics of Chicago, Boston and the United States.

For the Basement management, expansion into the Chicago area marked a new phase in the company's growth. Chicago was the first new market to open beyond the Basement's East Coast base. It also represented the test site for expansion in other major national markets. The quick success or failure of the Chicago stores would help to determine the company's future expansion policy. The original store sites, therefore, were chosen only after thorough research and investigation.

Of the three stores opened in Chicago in 1991, one store was located in the heart of the downtown area on State Street. The second one, in an area called Schaumberg, was situated in one of the city's upscale suburbs. The third location, Gurnee Mills, was located north of the city at the edge of the greater Chicago area in an outlet mall. **Exhibit 8** (a zip code map) shows the area surrounding the three existing sites, as well as a fourth site, Vernon Hills, which was opened in April 1992. The locations of the two proposed sites are also identified on the map. **Exhibit 9** shows projected and actual sales, and advertising dollars spent, by region, for selected stores. The final exhibit, **Exhibit 10**, shows Chicago demographic information by zip code.

The Two Prospective Sites

One of the two prospective areas, a suburb in the north central section of the Chicago market, called Mount Prospect, had three locations available. Mount Prospect was situated between two existing Basement store locations, the Vernon Hills store to the north and the Schaumberg store to the south. The other area under consideration was in a town called Naperville. This area of Greater Chicago had been part of the original group of sites targeted in 1991. However, at that time there had been no appropriate space available in the Aurora/Naperville area for the Basement to lease. See **Exhibit 5** for more information about these locations.

The Chicago market was a critical proving ground for Basement management. Brian was particularly concerned about this second round of store openings as they had the potential to add significantly to the profitability of the Chicago market by defraying the total Chicago market's advertising and operating expenses. Although the consultant's view about these new sites was optimistic, Brian wondered whether the greater Chicago area could support more stores. Was the market already saturated? If not, were these the optimal places to situate more stores? How would these new stores affect the stores that already existed in the market? He wondered what information was necessary to make this decision.

Exhibit 1A

Filene's Basement Financial Information, FY1989 –1992—Highlights

Dollars in millions, except for per share amounts

	FY 1/93	FY 2/92	FY 2/91	FY 2/90
Income Statement Data:				
Net Sales	529.5	465.4	400.8	357.7
Operating Income	33.9	32.9	26.6	20.6
Income (Loss) before extraordinary				
Gain (Loss)	18.7	16.3	9.1	3.0
Net Income	18.1	14.0	12.3	5.5
Operating Data:				
Number of Stores	49	37	31	25
Comparable Store Net Sales				
Increase (decrease)	0.0%	(0.7)%	0.7%	11.5%
Balance Sheet Data:				
Total Assets	215.7	188.7	148.4	132.2
Long-term Debt	25.9	30.9	77.6	82.1
Total Stockholders Equity	114.8	93.5	13.6	1.0

Exhibit 1B
Filene's Basement Financial Information

Consolidated Statement of Operations
For year ending January 30, 1993, dollars in thousands

Net Sales	$ 529,468
Cost of Sales	381,657
Gross Profit	147,811
Selling, general & admin. expenses	111,595
Amortization of intangible assets	960
Amortization of beneficial operating lease rights	1,314
Operating income	33,942
Interest expense, net of $359, $935, $438 of interest income	3,586
Income before income taxes and extraordinary gain (loss)	30,356
Provision for income taxes	11,693
Income before extraordinary gain (loss)	18,663
Extraordinary loss: loss on debt repurchase	(550)
Net income	$ 18,113

Consolidated Balance Sheets
For year ending January 1, 1993, dollars in thousands

Current Assets:	
Cash and cash equivalents	$ 4,473
Inventories	113,001
Other current assets	8,996
Deferred income taxes	6,289
Total current assets	132,759
Property, plant and equipment, net	56,675
Beneficial operating lease rights, net of $5,912 and $4,598 of accumulated amortization	20,066
Intangible assets and goodwill, net of $14,495 and $13,536 of accumulated amortization	6,234
Total assets	$ 215,734
Current Liabilities:	
Accounts payable	53,178
Accrued expenses	21,497
Obligations under capital leases, due within one year	331
Total current liabilities	75,006
Long-term debt	21,359
Obligations under capital leases less portion due in one year	4,528
Stockholders' equity:	
Common stock, $.01 par value; authorized 70,000,000 shares; 20,098,040 and 19,782,081 issued and outstanding	201
Additional paid-in capital	83,832
Retained Earnings	30,824
Cost of 75,000 common shares in treasury	(16)
Total stockholders' equity	114,841
Total liabilities and stockholders' equity	$ 215,734

Consolidated Statements of Cash Flow
For year ending January 30, 1993, dollars in thousands

Cash flows from activities:	
Net income	$ 18,113
Adjustments to reconcile net income cash provided by operations:	
Depreciation and amortization	11,481
Amortization related to debt financing costs and discounts	138
Loss on repurchase of subordinated debentures and term notes	550
Forgiveness of stock subscription receivable	—
Changes in operating assets and liabilities:	
Inventory	(11,681)
Other current assets	(3,413)
Deferred income taxes	(653)
Accounts payable	10,562
Accrued expenses	724
Net cash provided by operating activities	25,821
Cash flows from investing activities:	
Purchase of property, plant and equipment	(25,917)
Net cash used in investing activities	(25,917)
Cash flows from financing activities:	
Principal payments on long-term debt	—
Principal payments on capital lease obligations	(445)
Repurchase of subordinated debentures and term notes	(5,748)
Proceeds from sale of common stock, net of issuance	—
Proceeds from sale of stock to employees	1,395
Tax benefit resulting from exercise of stock options	1,798
Purchase of treasury stock	—
Net cash provided by financing activities	(3,000)
Net increase (decrease) in cash and cash equivalents	(3,096)
Cash and cash equivalents at beginning of year	7,569
Cash and cash equivalents at end of year	$ 4,473
Supplemental disclosures of cash flow information:	
Interest paid	$ 3,392
Income taxes paid	$ 10,025

Exhibit 2
Store Location Comparison In States Where Operations Overlap

State As of	Filene's Basement 12/30/92	Marshalls Stores 12/30/91	T.J.Maxx 1/25/92	Ross Stores 2/1/92	Hit or Miss 1/25/92
Connecticut	2	14	14	0	22
Illinois	4	22	34	0	38
Maine	1	0	3	0	2
Massachusetts	14	32[1]	29	0	46
Minnesota	5	8	12	0	9
New Hampshire	3	0	3	0	6
New Jersey	2	0	11	3	53
New York	11	34[2]	16	0	35
Pennsylvania	4	11	22	4	38
Rhode Island	1	6[3]	3	0	10
Vermont	0	0	1	0	1

1 Includes Manchester, New Hampshire
2 Includes New Jersey stores in New York metro area
3 Includes New Bedford, Massachusetts

Exhibit 3
Comparative Financial Statistics[7]

	Ross[1]	T.J.Maxx[1]	Marshalls[1]
Sales (millions)	$ 798.40[2]	$1,937.40	$2,183.00
Operating Profit (millions)	$ 32.70	$ 161.00	n/a
Operating Margin	4.10%	8.30%	n/a
Avg. Operating Margin (1986–1990)	4.30%	8.40%	n/a
Number of Stores	185	393	386
Average Number of Stores	171	373	367
Average Store Size (sq. ft.)	24,000	25,000	29,300
Avg. Selling Space (sq. ft.)	22,650	19,500	23,440
Total Avg. Selling Space (Thous. sq.ft.)	3,873	7,274	8,602
Revenue per Avg. Sq. Ft. of Selling Space	$ 206.15	$ 266.36	$ 253.76
Revenue/Avg. Store (millions)	$ 4.67	$ 5.19	$ 5.95
Compound Annual Growth 1985–1990:[2]			
Sales	16.8%	18.5%	10.5%
Operating Profit	20.6%	18.5%	n/a
Number of Stores	11.6%	15.5%	10.3%
Total Avg. Selling Space (Thous. sq. ft.)	8.5%	16.5%	n/a
Revenue per Avg. Sq. Ft. of Selling Space	7.0%	1.7%	n/a
Geographic Distribution of Stores:			
Northeast	4	90	116
South	41	97	93
Midwest	0	124	72
West & Southwest	140	82	105
Total	185	393	386
Financial Statistics:[3]			
Current Ratio	1.6x	1.6 x	1.8x
Long-Term Debt/Equity	46.8%	114.1%	23.1%
Return on Average Equity	14.7%	29.7%	22.2%
Inventory Turnover[4]	4.0x	3.8x	3.6 x

1 T.J.Maxx and Ross figures are for their fiscal periods ended January 1991; Marshalls figures are for its calendar period ended in December 1990.
2 Excluding income from brand departments.
3 T.J.Maxx and Marshalls statistics are for their respective parent organizations The TJX Companies, Inc. as of Jan. 1991 and Melville Corporation as of Dec. 1990. The Ross figures are as of Jan. 1991.
4 Calculated using cost of goods sold divided by average inventory.

7 As cited in Alex. Brown & Sons, Inc. p.18.

Exhibit 4
1993 Filene's Basement Newspaper Advertisement

Exhibit 5
Excerpts from Site Analysis Reports

FILENE'S BASEMENT
Site Analysis
CHICAGO, ILLINOIS

1) RANDHURST/MOUNT PROSPECT

Background

Three Filene's Basement store expansion opportunities have been identified in the North Central Chicago market (the Mount Prospect area). They include the Randhurst Shopping Center, the Sugar Grove Mall, and a site across the street from the Longwood Center. Economic Research Corporation has been asked to evaluate the viability of these Chicago locations and to estimate first-year sales.

Findings

Randhurst Shopping Center is located at the intersection of Rand Road and Elmhurst Road. This center has 1.35 million square feet of selling space and is anchored by JCPenney, Carson Pirie Scott, Montgomery Ward, Kohl's and Spiess. The center is clearly attempting to appeal to a more upscale population. All of the anchor stores have been updated and traffic levels appear high. Randhurst is a very attractive center.

The Filene's Basement location is assumed to be between Spiess and Wards. It is in the downstairs area served by escalators from the middle of the mall.

The Randhurst Center trade area is large and demographics are very good. The trade area has an estimated 1990 population of 465,500 people. The median household income is $53,167.

One issue with the Randhurst site has been the proximity to the Schaumberg Place Filene's Basement store opened in 1991. The Schaumberg trade area has comparable demographics and 526,000 people. While overlap between the trade areas of the two locations is estimated at 20 percent, the market is large enough that Filene's Basement can do well in both locations.

Sugar Grove Mall is a possible alternative to the Randhurst Center location. Sugar Grove is a 1 million square foot center located south of Central Road, west of River Road and east of Wolf Road. The center is anchored by JCPenney, Sanders and Sears. Sears is in the middle of the center with Sanders and Penney's on opposite ends. Mall customers have to pass through the Sears to get from one end of the center to the other. This layout is a serious impediment to customer convenience.

The center is well leased with a lot of small tenant space. The Filene's Basement location is a below ground site on the Sanders side of the center. Most of the small tenant space is on the Penney's side. Filene's Basement customers would enter at the main level of the center and take an escalator down to the store. Of the two centers, we consider the Randhurst Center to be a much stronger site opportunity.

The third site is across Highway 53 from the *Longwood Center*. It is a small center on the northeast corner of Palatine Road and Highway 53. Tenants in the center include Book Closet Book Shop, United Audio Centers and 13 small, mostly local tenants. The space identified for Filene's Basement is believed to be in the middle of the center.

Longwood Center is a large, upscale center anchored by Bonwit Teller, I. Magnin, Lord & Taylor, Marshall Field's, Neiman Marcus, Saks Fifth Avenue and Sears. Nordstrom's will enter the center in the near future. Unfortunately, the Filene's Basement site across Highway 53 is not visible from the Longwood parking lot. We do not believe that Filene's Basement will benefit from its proximity to Longwood. For all practical purposes, Filene's Basement would be a single anchor in a weak center with inadequate parking. For this reason, we do not recommend this site option.

In summary, the Randhurst Shopping Center presents an excellent opportunity for Filene's Basement. We would not anticipate any major transfer problems associated with developing both the Schaumberg Place and Randhurst locations. The Sugar Grove Mall location and the site across from the Longwood Center are not seen as viable options for Filene's Basement.

Sales Analysis

A store in the Randhurst Shopping Center can be expected to show $6.7 million for its first full year of sales. This is equivalent

Exhibit 5, continued

to the sales projected for Schaumberg Place. Again, the 20 percent overlap between the two trade areas should not present serious transfer problems. The demand in these two areas should easily support two Filene's Basement stores.

2) AURORA/NAPERVILLE

Filene's Basement has identified a location in a strip center to be constructed at the northeast quadrant of Route 59 and Aurora Avenue (Route 65). This center is located kitty-corner across the street from the Fox Valley Mall which is anchored by JCPenney, Marshall Field's, Sears and Lord & Taylor. The proposed location for the Filene's Basement will be with Montgomery Ward which will have a two-level 111,000 square foot store. The visibility and access to this center is good. It is my understanding that Filene's Basement will have signs on the front and the back area of their building and also on the northern edge of the shopping center building.

There is a considerable amount of additional retail on the other two intersections and on the property to the north and east of the proposed strip center. Other tenants in the area include Builder's Square, Marshalls, SportsMart, Kids R Us, Electric Avenue (Wards), Kohl's, Service Merchandise, T.J.Maxx, Highland Appliance, Wal-Mart, Sams, F & M Drug, Venture, Spiegel's, Cub Foods and Kmart. This area clearly is the retail focus for Aurora, Naperville and the surrounding townships.

In the June, 1990 analysis it was assumed that Filene's Basement would open in the Fox Valley Center in 1993 and would have first-year sales of $5.4 to $6.1 million in 1994. It is our understanding that the proposed strip center will be constructed to allow for a 1993 opening for Filene's Basement. Based on the change of the site from the mall to the strip center, we would estimate the sales range for this store to be $4.7 to $5.4 million for its first full year of operation. This is an excellent strip center location, and it is recommended that Filene's Basement pursue this opportunity.

FILENE'S BASEMENT
Proposed Location Data Sheet[8]
CHICAGO, ILLINOIS

Characteristic	Randhurst/ Mount Prospect	Aurora/ Naperville	Filene's Basement 1990 Store
	70% Trade Area	70% Trade Area	Median
Population	465,464	351,568	432,562
1990 % HH with income $50,000 and Above[1]			
- Number	115,738	70,330	62,553
- Percent	68.9%	60.1%	39.3%
Median HH Income	$53,167	$45,350	$45,268
Adults with 4 or More Years of College ('80)			
- Number	80,117	37,423	61,834
- Percent	32.5%	25.2%	22.1%
White Collar Employment ('80)			
- Number	163,379	79,534	128,578
- Percent	72.8%	59.9%	65.4%
Manager/Professional ('80)			
- Number	84,082	41,235	67,977
- Percent	39.3%	31.5%	33.4%

1 For Aurora/Naperville area, income based on number of households with incomes greater than $35,000 in 1989.

8 Figures in this exhibit have been disguised.

Exhibit 6
Information from 1987 Computer Model[9]

Sales Estimate Formula from Model

Sales/Sq. Ft. = $59 + Rent/Sq. Ft. times Multiple

Multiple = [$19 + .001(Market Impressions/Household)^2 − 3.2 ln (Comp. Sq. Ft./Household)]

For Households and Competitors within 20 minutes drive time of site

Regression Statistics		Std Error of Coeff:		
Std error of Y est	= $48	19	+/−	7.5
R Squared	= 0.76	.001	+/−	.0005
No of Observations	= 15	3.2	+/−	1.7
Degrees of Freedom	= 11			

Projected and Actual Store Sales Using 1987 Model

Store	FMR	I/HH	MLF-HH	(I/HH)^2 *FMR	LN(MLFHH) *FMR	Forecast	Actual	Error
Willow Grove	$12	24	0.32	6912	−13.9	$341	$312	-29
Framingham	$16	80	0.42	102400	−14.0	$510	$487	-23
Burlington	$12	73	1.39	63948	3.9	$340	$383	44
Saugus	$12	80	0.60	76800	−6.2	$384	$358	-25
Danvers	$12	73	0.85	63948	−1.9	$358	$340	-17
Methuen	$10	30	1.68	9000	5.2	$244	$253	8
Manchester	$8	29	1.19	6728	1.4	$216	$205	-10
Holyoke	$14	43	0.31	25886	−16.5	$406	$350	-56
Corbins Corner	$14	40	0.52	22400	−9.1	$379	$410	31
Paramus 17	$14	42	1.08	24696	1.1	$349	$307	-43
Cherry Hill	$12	24	0.82	6912	−2.5	$305	$303	-2
Copaigue	$8	63	1.66	31752	4.1	$231	$236	5
Fresh Meadows	$12	35	0.15	14700	−22.7	$376	$470	94
Manhasset	$14	63	1.28	55566	3.4	$372	$440	68
Worcester	$10	39	0.69	15210	−3.7	$278	$235	-43
Paramus 4	$11	42	1.18	19404	1.8	$284	$317	33
Scarsdale	$14	18	0.27	4526	−18.3	$391	$448	56
Warwick	$12	43	0.39	22188	−11.4	$348	$353	5
Huntington	$10	63	1.91	39690	6.5	$270	$335	65
Braintree	$16	80	0.55	102400	−9.6	$496	$704	208
Dedham	$12	73	0.53	63948	−7.7	$376	$464	88

9 Figures in this exhibit have been disguised.

Exhibit 7
Comparative Market Demographics

1989 Characteristics	Greater Chicago[1]	Greater Boston[2]	United States
Population	6,739,960	4,106,478	246,849,740
% HH with Incomes $ 35,000 & Above	44.8%	48.9%	37.6%
Median HH Income	$31,556	$34,242	$27,310
% Adults with 4 or more Years College (1980)	18.8%	22.4%	16.2%
% White Collar Employment (1980)	58.9%	61.1%	53.0%
% Mgr/Prof/Tech (1980)	27.6%	32.1%	25.7%

1 Greater Chicago includes the Chicago and Lake County PMSA's
2 Greater Boston includes the Boston-Lawrence-Salem-Lowell-Brockton NECMA

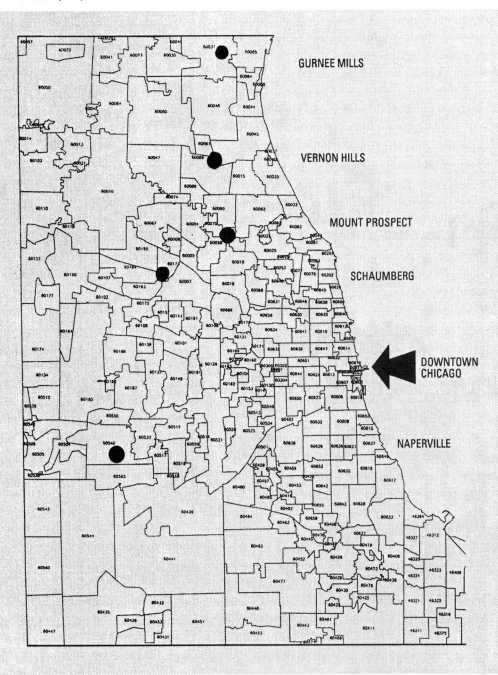

Exhibit 9
Selected Stores Projected and Actual Sales, and Advertising Dollars by Region[10]

Opening Date	Store	Region	Estimated Sales[1] Vol.	Annualized or Actual '93
Boston Metro Region (8 Stores)				
3/93	Watertown, MA	BOSM	B	Not yet open
3/93	Wellesley, MA	BOSM	C	Not yet open
11/92	Peabody, MA	BOSM	A	A
10/90	Newton, MA	BOSM	B	A
Total Advertising FY89–92		BOSM	$ 18,954,200	
Boston Remote Region (8 Stores)				
3/92	Taunton, MA	BOSR	C	C
3/91	Nashua, NH	BOSR	B	B
6/91	Salem, MA	BOSR	A	A
10/90	Attleboro, MA	BOSR	B	B
10/90	Hyannis, MA	BOSR	B	A
11/89	Plymouth, MA	BOSR	C	B
Total Advertising FY89–92		BOSR	$ 5,719,200	
New England Remote (4 Stores)				
4/90	Orange, CT	NER	B	A
8/89	Portland, ME	NER	C	B
Total Advertising FY89–92		NER	$ 5,757,360	
New York Metro (10 Stores)				
8/92	White Plains, NY	NYM	A	C
3/91	Lake Grove, NY	NYM	B	C
4/90	Carle Place, NY	NYM	A	A
Total Advertising FY89–92		NYM	$ 12,905,760	
New York Remote (3 Stores)				
4/92	Middletown, NY	NYR	C	C
9/91	Buffalo, NY	NYR	A	B
10/90	Syracuse, NY	NYR	C	B
Total Advertising FY89–92		NYR	$ 1,767,920	

10 Advertising figures have been disguised.

Exhibit 9, continued

Philadelphia Region (4 Stores)					
9/92	St. David's, PA		PA	A	A
8/89	Franklin Mills, PA		PA	C	B
Total Advertising FY89–92			PA	$ 5,535,000	
Chicago Region (4 Stores)					
4/92	Vernon Mills, IL		CHI	B	C
10/91	Chicago, IL		CHI	A	A
10/91	Gurnee Mills, IL		CHI	B	B
10/91	Schaumberg, IL		CHI	A	A
Total Advertising FY91–92			CHI	$ 3,965,100	
Minnesota Region (5 Stores)					
8/92	Mall America, MN		MIN	B	B
8/92	Minnetonka, MN		MIN	A	C
8/92	Edina, MN		MIN	A	C
8/92	Minneapolis, MN		MIN	A	B
8/92	Roseville, MN		MIN	B	C
Total Advertising FY92			MIN	$ 965,200	

1 In this chart the estimated and actual volumes are represented by a letter. The range of sales volume is approximately $4 million to $15 million. The letter "A" represents roughly the top third, "B" the middle third, and "C" the lower third.

Exhibit 10
Chicago Area Demographic Information By Zip Code[11]

ZIP Code	% of Shoppers at Gurnee* #82 Vernon Hills * #84 Schaumberg* #83			Population	Age	Median Income	% Households Income 50K+
	#82	#84	#83				
60002	2.01			9,044	32.5	38,321	31.2
60087	1.53			17,815	32.5	43,047	39.9
60099	1.05			25,038	29.8	36,436	28.1
60096	0.63			7,358	30.9	42,818	40.3
60083	0.18			5,489	33.2	47,989	47.4
60085	3.44			55,776	29.9	31,114	23.6
60031	4.02			32,125	31.2	46,486	44.4
60046	1.04			20,636	31.4	46,315	43.9
60030	0.86			8,022	31.9	40,872	36.1
60073	0.77			28,918	27.9	37,476	28.6
60020	0.36			10,366	33.1	33,617	28.6
60041	0.87			4,228	33.2	36,797	31.6
60084				11,150	33.4	39,875	35.9
60060	0.68	7.84		22,817	31.0	44,971	42.5
60061	0.52	7.44		19,711	30.2	46,627	45.2
60048	0.45	9.11		37,708	36.5	49,080	48.9
60064	0.26			26,541	22.9	28,522	20.0
60088	0.74			8,779	20.7	26,697	9.2
60044	0.22	3.30		8,087	37.2	49,165	49.2
60045		9.27		17,948	37.6	78,184	70.0
60037		0.97		2,639	27.5	40,350	36.6
60040		0.65		3,953	35.0	32,250	29.4
60035		2.89		29,320	38.2	70,059	65.0
60015		6.26		22,296	35.5	69,206	70.1
60069		3.12		3,785	40.4	82,333	78.5
60074			0.56	11,805	28.8	40,076	35.9
60089		6.87	0.22	39,986	32.0	55,394	57.4
60090		1.15		31,816	32.6	39,556	34.1
60062		2.75		39,980	40.1	62,090	62.6
60022				8,168	41.1	76,304	69.8
60082				388	40.8	60,776	61.0
60026				700	24.2	24,308	10.7
60025		1.45		44,805	37.7	50,108	50.1
60070		0.47		14,549	32.2	38,417	35.4
60004		1.67	2.10	53,994	34.7	48,800	48.4
60056			0.57	54,888	34.5	42,579	40.0

Source: United States Census Bureau

11 The figures for the percent of shoppers from each zip code have been disguised.

ZIP Code	% of Shoppers at Gurnee* #82 Vernon Hills * #84 Schaumberg* #83			Population	Age	Median Income	% Households Income 50K+
	#82	#84	#83	TTL			
60067			6.04	54,162	32.6	47,108	46.2
60010			3.42	36,477	36.2	60,273	60.2
60008			2.82	21,035	32.3	42,768	39.5
60005			2.44	26,434	37.2	46,265	45.4
60016				54,695	35.4	36,263	31.5
60018				28,890	34.6	36,158	29.4
60007			6.53	34,164	33.2	46,250	44.2
60173			4.76	9,655	31.1	43,982	41.5
60195			4.59	29,700	30.9	47,693	46.7
60118			0.52	11,983	33.3	43,416	39.9
60120			1.14	43,375	28.8	32,764	22.8
60107			1.97	29,376	29.0	43,279	35.8
60194			4.24	37,721	30.8	40,955	35.3
60193			7.83	39,450	32.5	46,735	44.2
60103			3.09	52,346	29.4	45,006	40.1
60172			1.31	22,769	31.6	47,537	45.5
60108			1.42	16,753	31.7	47,747	45.9
60143			0.73	8,850	33.1	50,371	50.5
60191			0.88	14,011	33.3	45,707	42.7
60106			1.11	20,024	32.3	42,527	36.6
60666				262	37.7	30,000	26.7
60176				11,189	31.7	33,867	26.3
60126			0.89	43,635	36.2	46,932	45.2
60101			0.80	34,802	31.7	44,121	40.5
60181			0.43	27,092	34.4	41,878	36.2
60148			1.11	52,416	33.0	44,281	39.7
60139			0.17	27,308	29.3	45,837	41.4
60137			1.01	35,444	33.6	50,103	50.1
60188			0.98	34,908	28.8	44,240	38.2
60187			0.40	57,898	32.8	50,771	50.9
Around Mount Prospect							
60093				19,312	40.5	68,079	64.3
60091				26,579	40.3	60,420	60.7
60053				22,480	42.5	48,612	48.1
60648				54,794	32.1	40,693	37.3
60068				37,022	41.5	50,563	50.6
60631				25,171	41.6	36,624	32.4

ZIP Code	% of Shoppers at Gurnee* #82 Vernon Hills * #84 Schaumberg* #83			Population	Age	Median Income	% Households Income 50K+
	#82	#84	#83	TTL			
Around Naperville							
60185				23,878	34.4	43,752	38.6
60555				12,420	30.1	45,127	40.9
60515				27,068	36.0	44,188	40.9
60514				16,923	35.0	46,025	43.0
60559				42,606	34.7	47,790	46.5
60516				36,131	32.9	51,176	51.6
60517				23,754	29.5	45,608	41.9
60540				35,177	32.8	57,993	60.9
60504				15,480	28.0	49,216	49.0
60505				51,349	27.5	32,824	20.0
60544				10,401	33.1	41,307	51.9
60565				32,692	31.4	54,992	57.1
60439				19,914	32.1	38,022	32.1
60441				55,299	30.6	41,255	34.8
60563				26,268	31.6	54,739	56.0
60506				42,674	31.4	36,396	28.5
60564				8,548	30.7	48,987	48.0
60440				34,688	27.8	42,463	35.7
60543				9,651	33.0	41,416	36.4
60510				19,284	32.8	40,397	35.3
60538				14,058	30.9	40,474	31.7
60542				6,617	32.3	37,697	30.7
60134				13,648	34.4	46,140	44.5
60539				371	33.1	40,250	35.0

* Represents percentage of shoppers from that zip code.

Case 20

WARDS CO., INC.

In June 1981 Alan Wurtzel, president of Wards Co., Inc., was preparing a presentation for his board of directors and paused to consider the company's expansion plans. Wards, a publicly held company, had achieved sales in the 1981 fiscal year (ending February 28, 1981) of approximately $130 million. Its net profit, after taxes, had been in the range of $2.3 to $2.7 million for three years. The company operated, among other businesses, two warehouse showrooms called Loading Docks in Richmond, Virginia which sold major appliances and audio and video equipment.[1] It was planning to expand by building warehouse showrooms elsewhere in the Sunbelt.

Mr. Wurtzel had three specific questions on his mind:

1. Was success in expanding the warehouse showroom concept more likely in an intermediate-size city such as Birmingham, Alabama (population approximately one million) or in a smaller city such as Winston-Salem, North Carolina (population approximately 300,000)?
2. If Wards chose an intermediate-size market, should it build one or two stores? How far would people come to shop?
3. In either case, what would be the optimum-size facility to maximize sales at an acceptable return on investment?

HISTORY AND CURRENT SITUATION OF WARDS

Wards Co. was founded in 1949 in Richmond by S.S. Wurtzel (father of Alan Wurtzel) to sell newly available televisions.

By 1954 the company had grown to a chain of four conventional appliance stores in Richmond selling television sets and major home appliances. Over the next 20 years, it developed, acquired, and disposed of a number of other retail businesses. Alan Wurtzel joined Wards in 1966 as company counsel. After graduating from Oberlin College and Yale Law School, Wurtzel had practiced in a prestigious law firm in Washington, D.C. By 1981 the company Wurtzel headed had three primary operations.

Wards' three main businesses were leased departments in Zody's, a large discount department store chain on the West Coast; Circuit City, free-standing stores selling audio, video, and other consumer electronics products; and Loading Dock, the warehouse showrooms.

Although organized by division, Wards had two executive vice presidents above the divisional level. Both were long-term company employees and shared the store operations and support functions in a scheme based more on experience, work loads, and history than on a logical

---

This case was prepared by Kristina Cannon-Boventre, Research Associate under the supervision of Professor Walter J. Salmon, as the basis for class discussion rather than to illustrate either effective or ineffective handling of an administrative situation. The nonpublic financial data in this case has been disguised to protect company confidentiality. They are sufficiently realistic, however, for class discussion.

---

1 In 1981 Wards decided to call both its existing Loading Docks and its newly opened warehouse showrooms, "Circuit City Super Stores."

---

structure. One executive vice president was responsible for the Circuit City stores, merchandising, distribution and service; and the other, William Rivas, was responsible for the Zody's departments, the Loading Docks, advertising, and sales training. These two executives, together with the president and other members of senior management, coordinated strategic and important operating decisions for all three businesses. **Exhibit 1** shows an organization chart for the business, and **Exhibit 2** presents a condensed operating statement and balance sheet.

Zody's Leased Departments

Since 1969 Wards had operated departments averaging 3,000 square foot in the Zody's full-line, discount department stores, primarily in southern California. By 1981 there were 39 such departments selling major appliances and audio and video equipment. Among discount department stores in southern California, Zody's was second only to Kmart. Wards's management felt, on the basis of market surveys, that its leased departments were a significant factor in the Los Angeles television and major appliance market.

Circuit City

The Circuit City division, four years old in 1981, featured a large selection of audio equipment for home and auto use and also sold popular consumer electronics, such as portable televisions, video recorders, radios, tape recorders, and telephone-answering equipment. Video and a wide range of consumer electronics had been added with the opening of the division, thereby offsetting the ill effects of the 1980–81 industrywide softness in audio sales. Circuit City stores, approximately 4,500 square foot in size, were clustered in middle-size, southeastern cities. In 1981 there were 37 locations.

Loading Dock

As of 1981 there were two Loading Docks in Richmond and plans for expansion in the Sunbelt. Each facility was approximately 35,000 square foot, with approximately 12,000 square foot devoted to the showroom. In addition to televisions and major appliances, audio and other consumer electronics equipment was sold from the Circuit City departments within the Loading Dock stores. In the 1981 fiscal year, the sales of both Richmond Loading Docks were $14 million, approximately 11% of Wards's total business.

Loading Dock Origins

In the middle 1970s Wards had opened the first Loading Dock in Richmond to replace Wards TV. The typical Wards TV store had sold televisions and major appliances from floor samples at more or less conventional prices in about 3,000 to 5,000 square foot of selling space. The stock on display had been limited to approximately 50 to 60 units of major appliances and 100 units of televisions. Wards TV was, in almost all respects, standard for its time as a retailer of major appliances and televisions.

In contrast, Loading Dock was a substantial innovation in big-ticket, hard-goods marketing. It presented, in a warehouse showroom format, a large selection of high-quality, national brand appliances and audio and video equipment. Major appliance brands included Whirlpool, Norge, Rheem, Frigidaire, Hotpoint, Magic Chef, Maytag, KitchenAid, Jenn-Air, Litton, and Amana. Video equipment brands offered were RCA, Zenith, Sanyo, Magnavox, Panasonic, Sylvania, Sony, MGA, Advent, Toshiba, JVC, GE, and Hitachi. Brands of audio equipment were Technics, Pioneer, Sharp, Onkyo, BIC, Micro-Acoustics, Sansui, Concept, Hitachi, Shure, Altec, HiComp, BASF, Advent, Maxwell, TDK, Electrobrand, Audiovox, and JVC. Wards provided professional sales assistance, sold at the lowest prices in its local market, and had on-premises service facilities, visible to customers, that provided both in-store and in-home service. Loading Dock's presentation was similar to the approach used by Levitz Furniture. Merchandise was warehoused on site and customers, following purchase in the showroom, could pick up their choices at the warehouse door. Wards would also provide home delivery, and, where necessary, installation, for additional fees.

The showroom comprised approximately 12,000 square foot of selling space with about 3,400 square foot devoted to major appliances, 3,900 for video equipment (primarily televisions), and 2,500 for audio equipment. The balance of the selling space was dedicated to nondisplay uses. Other nonselling areas in the facility included a service operation (3,400 square foot), cooking school, customer lounge (400 square foot), credit counseling area (600 square foot), sales training area (720 sq. ft), and a nursery for children of customers, called the Kiddie Dock (250 square foot). In the warehouse, with approximately 100,000 cubic feet of net useable volume, the following cubages were devoted to each major merchandise category:

Merchandise	Cubage
Major appliances	50,000
Video equipment	16,000
Audio equipment	16,000
Accessories and other	20,000

The costs of opening the second Loading Dock in May 1979 had included a $1.2 million initial investment for the building, land, and fixtures, and approximately $800,000 for inventory. The building and land were subsequently sold and leased back by Wards. Exterior and interior views and a simplified sales floor plan of the facility are presented in **Exhibit 3**.

The appearance of the Loading Docks was a combination of an attractive, open, well-lit design and an attempt to convey the feeling that prices had not been unduly inflated by store overhead. The selling area included bold graphics, indirect lighting, and carpeted floors, but the overall effect was more functional than decorative—more like a contemporary discount department store than a traditional department store operation.

Marketing Approach

Loading Dock's marketing approach was based on what Wards referred to as the four S's: selection, savings, services and satisfaction.

Selection. Wards' aim was to be unequivocally dominant in each of its markets. Therefore, in each key merchandise category, such as televisions, refrigerators, and so on, the selection included multiple models of most leading national brands. In categories that were side-lines for Loading Dock, such as lawn mowers, the selection was adequate to give a range of choices, but not necessarily the most extensive in the market. The approximate number of models of selected merchandise categories on display are presented in **Exhibit 4**.

Regarding Loading Dock's assortment philosophy, Wurtzel noted that

> Our expertise is in selling big-ticket consumer products that require salesmanship and service. Audio and video equipment and white goods (refrigerators, ranges, laundry appliances, etc.) are the heart of our business. We are also allotting space in our Loading Docks to a section called Advanced Consumer Electronics (ACE), containing telephones, telephone-answering equipment, tape recorders, radios, TV games, smoke detectors, calculators, home security equipment, and, in the future, possibly personal computers.

Savings. Low prices were another aspect of Loading Dock's marketing approach. It strove for the lowest prices in its local market. Loading Dock offered with each sale a written, 30-day "Lowest Price Guarantee." If the same item became locally available for less within 30 days, the guarantee offered the customer a refund of the difference. William Rivas, executive vice president, noted that: "We are our own toughest competitor since we make refunds to our customers resulting from our own markdowns."

Wards' capacity to offer low prices was enhanced by its membership with a number of retailers in a buying group (NATM). The company purchased about 35% of its requirements through this group. By buying in concert from manufacturers, the group received discounts or other advantages, such as larger advertising allowances or confined models, which would have been difficult to obtain had group members purchased separately.

Service. Loading Dock offered a variety of services. On entering the store, consumers initially viewed the warehouse, which emphasized the immediate availability of merchandise. They then passed the service operation, where they could see merchandise being repaired. Immediately before the showroom, they passed the supervised nursery.

Excellent selling was another aspect of Loading Dock's service. To stay current on new products, models, and features, the sales personnel, known as sales counselors, spent a minimum of six hours per week in training.

To facilitate having one shift of full-time professional salespeople available at all times, Loading Dock was open only from noon until 9 p.m. daily and from 9 a.m. to 9 p.m. on Saturday. (Individual salespeople, however, worked only a five-day week.)

Satisfaction. To assess their satisfaction or additional needs, most customers were telephoned by their sales counselor within 10 days of a purchase. Loading Dock also had a liberal return policy.

THE RICHMOND MARKET

The two Loading Docks were located in Richmond, Virginia. The first, Thalbro, was next to Wards' corporate headquarters in a mixed industrial and older retail area.

The second, Midlothian was to the south in a major shopping district located in a rapidly growing suburban residential area (see **Exhibit 5**).

The Richmond (SMSA), Standard Metropolitan Statistical area—including Chesterfield, Hanover, Charles City, Powhatan, New Kent, Goochland, and Henrico counties and the City of Richmond—had a population of approximately 611,000 in 1980. It was the financial, insurance, manufacturing, and distribution center of Virginia and tended toward conservative governments favoring economic growth. Retail trade in the Richmond SMSA represented 13% of Virginia's total retail sales; the annual growth of sales in the SMSA was estimated at 10.4%. The Richmond SMSA had effective buying income per household estimated at $21,968 in 1979.

Pertinent additional data about Loading Dock customers and Richmond are presented in **Exhibit 6**. **Exhibit 7** briefly describes Loading Dock's competitors in Richmond. Operating results for the two Loading Dock stores are presented in **Exhibit 8**.

Loading Dock's strongest competition in Richmond came from Sears and from independent TV and audio centers and neighborhood stores. The rest of the market was distributed among discount department stores, such as Kmart and Woolco; Best Products, a catalog showroom; traditional department stores; such as Miller and Rhoads; and other types of stores, such as furniture stores. Market share data obtained through an independent market survey are shown in **Exhibit 9**. This survey also indicated that even most noncustomers were aware of the Loading Dock stores, regardless of age, income, employment, or education.

SELLING, SERVICE, AND PROMOTION

Sales Force

The Thalbro and Midlothian (Southside) Loading Docks had 22 full-time equivalent and 16 full-time equivalent sales counselors, respectively, during the 1981 fiscal year. Most employees were full time, with additional help hired during peak periods. Salespeople were assigned to specific merchandise lines as follows:

	Thalbro	Midlothian
Major appliances (including TVs)	16	11
Audio equipment	6	5

Salespeople were guaranteed hourly pay of 1.5 times the minimum wage. The bulk of their remuneration, however, came from commissions (2% of *all* sales) and "spiffs." *Spiffs* were additional incentives associated with the sale of service contracts or specific items of merchandise selected by Wards.[2] They averaged 3% of the sale price of the items to which they applied but the percentage varied depending on management's emphasis on specific services or merchandise. Individuals who surpassed predetermined volume goals were also eligible for various incentives, such as membership in Wards's Century Club, recognition at awards dinners, shopping sprees, and resort vacations. **Exhibit 10** summarizes sales counselor earnings by merchandise category.

The compensation system promoted competition within the sales force and provided frequent and concrete feedback on performance. Individual performance ratings were regularly and publicly posted.

Service

Customer Credit. In addition to cash and checks, customers could use Visa and MasterCharge cards or make extended credit arrangements through General Electric Credit Corporation (GECC), in the form of a payment coupon book. GECC's participation in these arrangements, however, was not generally visible to the customer. Furthermore, all credit arrangements were without recourse to Wards. Wards paid approximately 1.5% of credit sales in fees for the use of credit cards and 1% to 4%, depending on the prime rate, for GECC's coupon book system. Credit transactions accounted for approximately 55% of Loading Dock's sales in fiscal year 1981.

Delivery. Following purchase, Loading Dock customers could take merchandise with them or pay a fee for delivery. Delivery services showed a small net

2 Other retailers allowed manufacturers to pay spiffs directly to the retailer's salespeople, but Wards prohibited this practice.

operating loss for 1980–81. Wards anticipated changing the fees and structure of the delivery operation to reach a break-even point.

Service Contracts and Operations. At the time of purchase, customers were offered a service contract at the following average rates (duration varied with product and length of manufacturer's warranty):

Major appliances	$35
Video equipment	80
Audio equipment	25

Loading Dock service operations were marginally profitable; but management believed that the principal purpose of the service operations was to enhance sales.

Service personnel were paid on the basis of the actual repairs they satisfactorily accomplished. Total annual remuneration for experienced repair persons ranged from $16,000 to $25,000.

Of the total service calls generated, approximately 20% were repairs in customers homes and 80% were brought to Loading Dock by customers.

Advertising. Loading Dock's advertising spending, including cooperative advertising allowances from suppliers, in 1980–81 was approximately 4.5% of the combined sales of both Richmond locations ($610,000). Before the opening of Midlothian in 1979, advertising spending had been 5.7% ($443,000) of sales for the Thalbro location. Wards's purchase arrangements were such that very little of Loading Dock's advertising expenditures were defrayed by supplier advertising allowances. **Exhibit 11** presents a typical television storyboard and **Exhibit 12** shows a sample print advertisement.

Television accounted for approximately 30% of the advertising budget. The balance was spent on radio and print (newspaper and mailings). Before the 1980 recession, about 50% of Loading Dock's television advertising had been institutional in nature, focusing on the four Ss. However, with the economic downturn, that percentage dropped to 10%. The bulk of current advertising was price and event oriented. Loading Dock featured sales events on all holidays (for instance, Washington's Birthday, July 4 and Columbus Day). In addition, one or two events of Loading Dock's own creation (Midnight Madness Sale, Warehouse Sale, and so on) were scheduled each month.

EXPANSION BEYOND RICHMOND

By the end of 1981, Wards planned to open Loading Docks in Raleigh (June 1981), Greensboro (August or September 1981), and Durham, North Carolina (October 1981). The stores were to have the following selling areas and warehouse cubages:

	Approximate Selling Area	Approximate Warehouse Cubage (net usable)
Raleigh	12,000	100,000
Greensboro	12,000	100,000
Durham	9,400	70,000

In addition, in 1982 Wards contemplated opening one warehouse showroom in Winston-Salem, North Carolina[3] and two showrooms in the Birmingham, Alabama market (in 1982). Competitive, economic, and demographic information for these two communities are presented in **Exhibits 13** and **14**.

In Winston-Salem, Wards had identified an available parcel of land located near, but not in, a large shopping mall in the southwestern section of the community. The site was near the intersection of several major highways, as shown in **Exhibit 15**. The estimated costs of building and opening this store are presented in **Exhibit 16**. Subsequent to its construction, Wards would have the opportunity to sell and lease back this store.

Wards contemplated opening one store directly east and the other south of central Birmingham. The eastern

---

3 Downtown Winston-Salem was only approximately 25 miles from downtown Greensboro; indeed, the Census Bureau considered them part of a single SMSA.

site was an existing 120,000-square foot building, larger than Wards's needs, which would be remodeled and fixtured as a Loading Dock with a 12,000-square foot selling floor, the support space (sales training, office, service, and credit) of a large store such as Raleigh or Greensboro, and a large warehouse. The large warehouse was considered necessary because of Birmingham's distance from Wards's central warehouse in Richmond. The company planned to drop-ship a larger percentage of goods to Birmingham to avoid freight from Richmond. The warehouse could also serve the second Birmingham store. The landlord would take responsibility for leasing the remainder of the building.

The southern location was a parcel of land to be purchased by Wards on which a store could be erected. This store could, subsequent to construction, also be sold and leased back. Cost breakdowns for the two Birmingham stores are presented in **Exhibit 16**. A map of the Birmingham area is presented in **Exhibit 17**.

In view of his experience with the Loading Dock operation thus far, Wurtzel wondered whether the contemplated Winston-Salem and Birmingham operations represented, in pace and character, appropriate expansion opportunities.

Exhibit 1
Corporate Organization

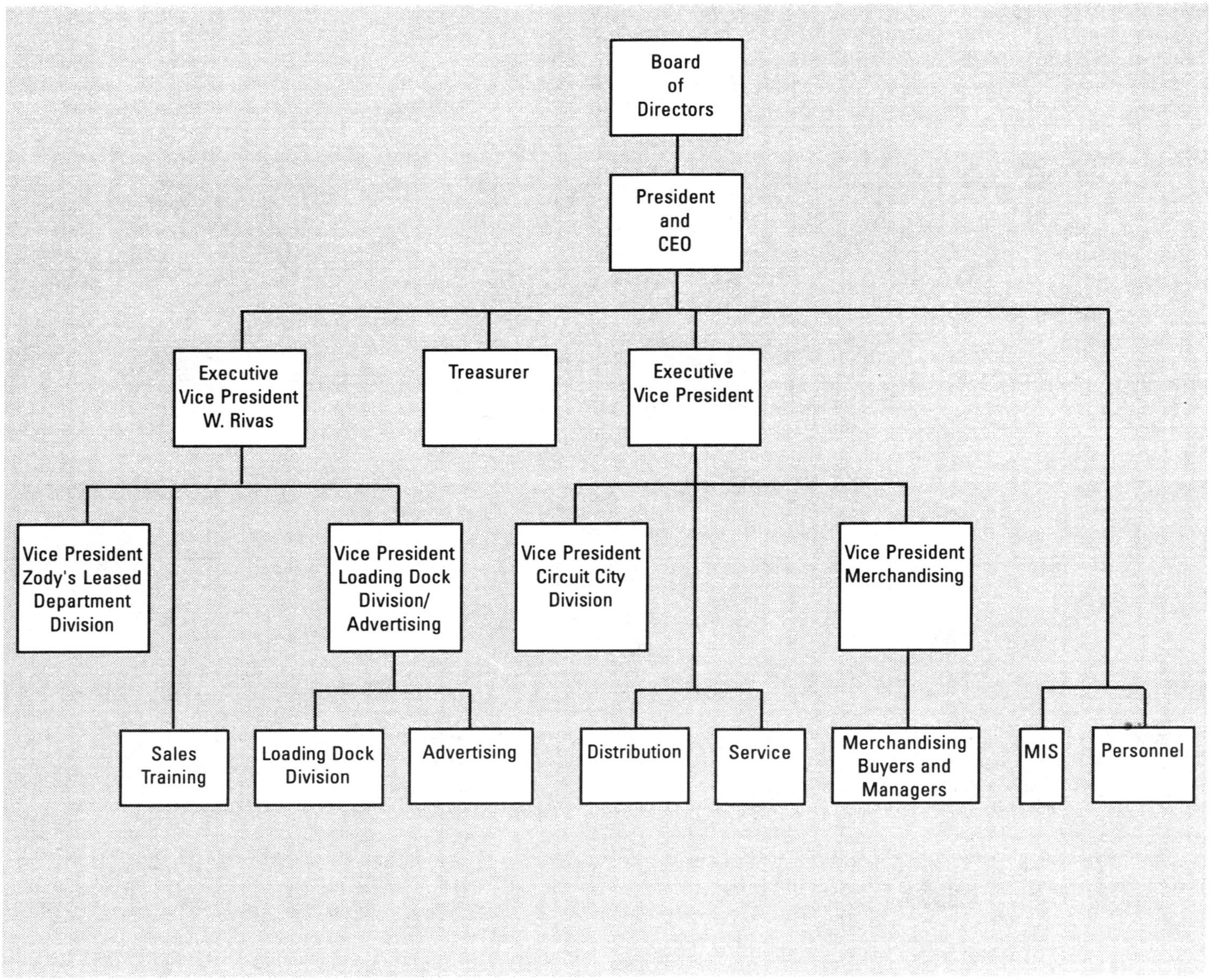

Organization chart:

- Board of Directors — President and CEO
- President and CEO connects to: Treasurer, Executive Vice President W. Rivas, Executive Vice President
- Executive Vice President connects to: Vice President Merchandising, Vice President Circuit City Division, MIS, Personnel
  - Vice President Merchandising — Merchandising Buyers and Managers
  - Vice President Circuit City Division — Distribution, Service
- Executive Vice President W. Rivas connects to: Vice President Loading Dock Division/Advertising, Vice President Zody's Leased Department Division
  - Vice President Loading Dock Division/Advertising — Advertising, Loading Dock Division
  - Vice President Zody's Leased Department Division — Sales Training

Exhibit 2
Wards' Statement of Earnings and Balance Sheets

Consolidated Statements of Earnings
Years ended February 28, 1981; February 29, 1980 and February 28, 1979 (Amounts in thousands except per share data)

	1981	1980	1979
Net sales and operating revenues	$ 131,881	$ 119,609	$ 111,534
Cost of sales, buying and warehousing	96,764	88,568	83,157
Selling, general and administrative expense	29,885	26,105	22,821
Interest expense	1,194	740	656
Total expenses	$ 127,843	$ 115,413	$ 106,634
Earnings before income taxes	4,038	4,196	4,900
Provision for income taxes:			
Current	1,418	2,029	2,277
Deferred	(81)	(119)	53
Total income taxes	$ 1,337	$ 1,910	$ 2,330
Net earnings	$ 2,701	$ 2,286	$ 2,570
Net earnings per common share:			
Primary	$ 3.53	$ 3.04	$ 3.41
Fully diluted	$ 3.31	$ 2.80	$ 3.03

Condensed Consolidated Balance Sheets
February 28, 1981 and February 29, 1980 (Amounts in thousands)

	1981	1980
Assets		
Current Assets:		
Cash	$ 2,211	$ 2,316
Accounts and notes receivable,		
less allowance for doubtful accounts	3,821	2,374
Merchandise inventory	20,129	18,182
Other assets	1,298	877
Total current assets	$ 27,459	$ 23,749
Property and equipment, net	6,626	5,896
Notes receivable and other assets	3,856	739
Total assets	$ 37,941	$ 30,384
Liabilities and Stockholders' Equity		
Current liabilities:		
Current installments of long-term debt	$ 486	$ 83
Accounts payable	10,441	8,335
Accrued expenses	2,384	2,603
Total current liabilities	$ 13,311	$ 11,021
Long-term debt	7,396	4,633
Deferred items	1,866	1,703
Stockholders' equity	15,368	13,027
Total liabilities and stockholders' equity	$ 37,941	$ 30,384

loading dock

BRAND NAME TV, APPLIANCES & ELECTRONICS AT FORK LIFT PRICES

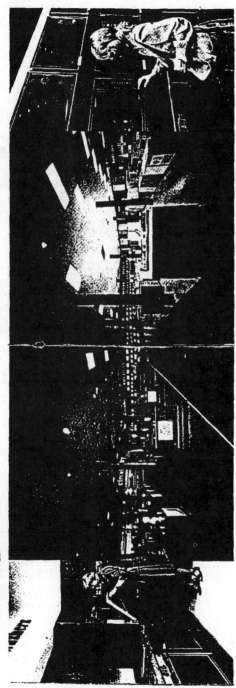

The Loading Dock merchandises a full line of kitchen appliances. Built-in fixtures designed for stove tops, dishwashers, and floor and wall ovens all create a realistic kitchen atmosphere.

Massive Displays In Every Department Command Instant Attention. The Loading Dock's 12,000 square foot showrooms contain the area's largest display of televisions, appliances, and electronics. A complete Circuit City Sound Shop with full-line audio displays is incorporated into the Dock's operation. More than a hundred and fifty portable and over fifty console TV's, each in operation and tuned to the same channel, reinforce the image of massive selection while creating a functional atmosphere for comparative product evaluation. Similarly, all types of major appliances from every important quality supplier are also found on the showroom floor, with features ranging from basic functions to the most advanced. Angled aisles provide improved traffic circulation and better visibility for side-wall merchandise.

A large selection of microwave ovens complete the full line of kitchen appliances. The Loading Dock sponsors frequent Cooking Schools to improve the customer's product knowledge.

loading dock

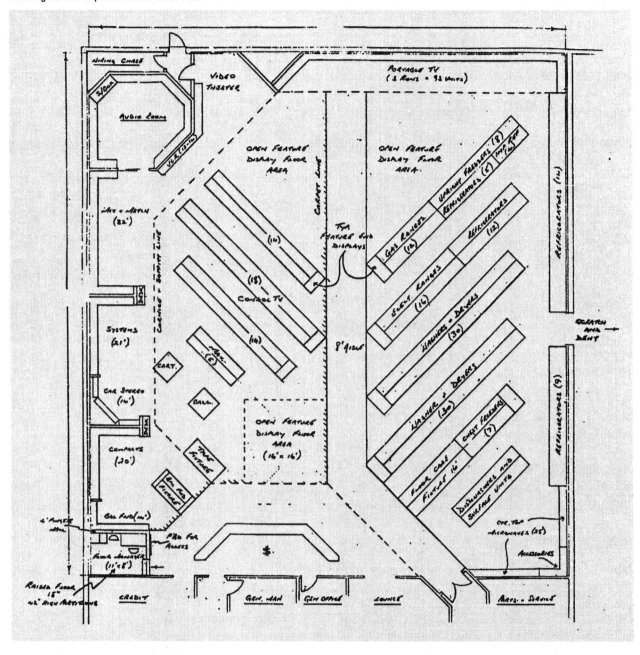

Exhibit 4
Numbers of Brands and Models Offered by Loading Dock in Selected Merchandise Categories

Merchandise Category	Number of Brands	Number of Models
Major Appliances		
Refrigerators	3	50
Ranges, electric	3	20
Ranges, gas	2	15
Microwave ovens	6	25
Clothes washers	3	30
Clothes dryers	3	20
Dishwashers	5	23
Freezers	2	11
Audio Equipment		
Stereo Components		
Receivers	8	19
Speakers	9	29
Turntables	8	16
Cassette Decks	7	17
Portable tape recorders and players	6	24
Video Equipment		
Televisions, black and white	5	12
Televisions, color		
Portable	1	60
Console	4	49
Televisions, projection	4	7
Home video cassette recorders	7	11

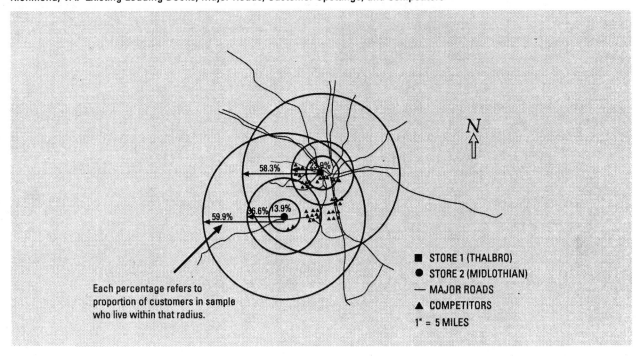

58.3%

24.9%

59.9%

36.6% 13.9%

Each percentage refers to
proportion of customers in sample
who live within that radius.

N

■ STORE 1 (THALBRO)
● STORE 2 (MIDLOTHIAN)
— MAJOR ROADS
▲ COMPETITORS
1" = 5 MILES

Exhibit 6
Demographic and Economic Characteristics of Richmond Loading Dock Customers

Zip Code	No. of Customers from Sample	% of Customers	Approximate Distance from Store (miles)	Loading Dock Sales ($000s)	Total Sales L.D. Merchandise (all stores) ($000s)**	Market Share of L.D. (%)	Pop. 1980 (000s)	Pop. % Change 1970	Number of Households 1980 (000s)	Change since 1980	Household Income ($000s)	% Households moved into zip in last 5 years	% SF* Dwelling Units
THALBRO LOCATION													
23229	23	8.2	1.2	616	3,270	19	32.7	-6	11.2	+8	29.6	54	79.0
23228	19	6.8	2.6	511	2,702	19	27.2	+11	10.4	+26	19.4	52	58.7
23221***	19	6.8	1.8	511	1,380	37	13.8	-19	7.3	+1	25.4	54	47.2
23220***	17	6.1	3.3	458	3,130	15	31.3	-22	14.7	-1	12.0	67	38.3
23111	16	5.7	11.2	428	2,750	16	27.5	+46	8.4	+54	22.3	50	93.5
23226	14	5.0	1.3	376	1,800	21	18.0	-10	7.1	+7	28.9	42	84.1
23227	14	5.0	3.3	376	2,430	15	24.3	+7	10.3	+26	19.4	56	57.3
23223***	13	4.7	6.6	353	4,510	8	45.1	-15	15.9	+4	13.7	53	74.6
23222	12	4.3	4.6	323	2,910	11	29.1	-11	11.1	+9	14.9	48	75.3
23230	11	3.9	Store location	293	580	51	5.8	-17	2.5	-3	19.4	55	68.7
23860***	8	2.9	6.9	218	1,120	19	11.2	0	3.7	+16	26.3	56	97.0
23150	7	2.5	13.2	188	900	21	9.0	-1	3.1	+14	19.8	50	93.1
23235***	5	1.8	7.6	135	3,930	3	39.3	+117	11.9	+141	22.9	61	88.9
23005	4	1.4	10.6	105	1,180	9	11.8	+37	3.5	+47	16.4	57	80.8
23103	4	1.4	n/a	105	180	58	1.8	+11	0.5	+29	20.9	59	99.8
23225	4	1.4	4.3	105	3,930	3	39.3	+4	15.9	+25	19.1	65	65.2
TOTAL	190	67.9		5,101	36,702	14	367.2		137.5				
MIDLOTHIAN LOCATION													
23235***	40	13.9	Store Location	887	3,990	22	39.3	+117	11.9	+141	22.9	61	88.9
23224	37	12.9	5.9	823	3,530	23	35.3	-10	13.4	+11	17.4	59	70.5
23234	34	11.8	9.2	753	4,520	17	45.2	+29	15.8	+41	20.2	60	83.5
23225	28	9.8	5.3	625	3,930	16	39.3	+4	15.9	-25	19.1	65	65.2
23113	24	8.4	8.3	536	1,570	34	15.7	+90	4.6	+108	22.9	78	95.7
23832	12	4.2	10.9	268	1,110	24	11.1	+16	3.1	+27	17.6	79	95.7
23308	9	3.1	21.0	n/a	n/a	n/a	n/a	n/a	n/a	n/a	n/a	n/a	n/a
23831	9	3.1	15.8	198	1,900	10	19.0	+28	6.0	+39	22.5	55	89.9
23860***	9	3.1	22.0	n/a	n/a	n/a	n/a	n/a	n/a	n/a	n/a	n/a	n/a
23139	9	3.1	21.5	198	770	26	7.7	+64	2.0	+94	13.7	57	99.1
23223***	7	2.4	12.0	153	4,510	3	45.1	-15	15.9	+4	13.5	53	74.6
23834	7	2.4	19.0	n/a	n/a	n/a	n/a	n/a	n/a	n/a	n/a	n/a	n/a
23221***	5	1.7	6.9	108	1,380	8	13.8	-19	7.3	+1	25.4	54	47.2
23220***	4	1.4	8.3	89	3,130	15	31.3	-22	14.7	-1	12.0	67	38.3
TOTAL	234	81.3		4,638	30,340	15	303.3		110.6				

Note: Data obtained from Donnelly Marketing (Stamford, CT). Sample for Thalbro was 280 customers; sample for Midlothian was 288 customers.

** Assumes per capita annual spending of $100 for Loading Dock merchandise. Source for spending figure is *1977 Census of Retail Trade*, Merchandise Line Sales, Bureau of Census. The 1977 figure of $100 per capita has not been adjusted for the inflation between 1977 and 1981. The reason is that the 1977 figure includes several items, such as sewing machines, that Loading Dock does not sell. Therefore, it is assumed that the figure for 1977 was sufficiently overstated to offset the effect of subsequent inflation.

* SF = Single Family.

*** Zip code included in trading area of both stores.

Exhibit 6, continued
Summary of Customer Characteristics

Loading Dock Customers	Mean Zip Code Characteristics*			
	Income (1980)	Population (1980)	Number of Households	% Moved in during 1979
Thalbro	17.2	15.4	5.5	18
Midlothian	17.4	15.9	5.9	18
Noncustomers	13.7	2.0	0.6	12
Number of Purchases in Zip Code				
THALBRO				
None	13.8	1.7	0.6	12
Less than or equal to 8	16.0	12.7	4.3	17
More than or equal to 9	21.3	25.0	9.5	21
MIDLOTHIAN				
None	13.9	2.0	0.8	12
Less than or equal to 8	16.8	11.6	4.5	16
More than or equal to 9	19.7	33.5	11.2	23

* Figures for income, population, and number of households are in 000s. They are averages (weighted by population) for the zip codes from which Loading Docks did and did not draw business in Richmond.

Exhibit 7
Loading Dock Competitors in Richmond

National General Merchandise Chains

SEARS, ROEBUCK AND CO.: Appliances, video and audio equipment offered in Sears' traditional value-oriented format.

JCPENNEY: Appliances, video and audio equipment offered in Penney's usual format.

JEFFERSON WARD (Montgomery Ward): Video equipment and appliances offered.

Other Large-Store Competitors

KMART: Video equipment and appliances.

WOOLCO: Video equipment and appliances.

MILLER AND RHOADS: Appliances and video offered. Traditional department store.

THALHIMERS: Video equipment. Traditional department store.

BEST PRODUCTS: Appliances, video and audio equipment offered. Catalog showroom.

MEMCO: Video and audio equipment and appliances. Membership discount department store.

LOWE'S: Appliances offered. Approximately five national brands available. Prices comparable to Loading Dock's. Delivery for a flat fee. Scant attention to attractive, clean displays.

Specialty Stores

AUDIO ASSOCIATES: Audio store.

AUTO SOUND OF VIRGINIA: Car stereo store.

HARVEYS: Video and audio store. Approximately 2,500 square foot of selling space. No service offered. Free five-year warranty on audio components; customer required to ship back to factory in original boxes. Trade-ins allowed. Negotiable prices. Systems offered at a discount from individual components. Small number of televisions offered.

MOLLENS AUDIO: Car stereo store.

RADIO SHACK: Audio equipment offered in Radio Shack's usual format.

GARY'S: Audio store.

ATLANTIS: Audio store.

APPLIANCE BARGAIN MART: Appliance store.

DON WOOD TV: Appliance and television store.

LIPSCOMB APPLIANCE: Appliance and television store.

BLAKES TV: Appliance and television store.

Exhibit 8
Approximate Loading Dock Operating Results for Year Ending February 28, 1981

	Thalbro	% of Sales	Midlothian	% of Sales	Total	% of Total
Sales						
Video	2,600	34.6	2,100	32.8	4,700	33.8
Appliances	2,600	34.6	2,300	35.9	4,900	35.2
Audio	1,900	25.3	1,600	25.0	3,500	25.2
Other	(200)	(2.5)	(100)	(1.5)	(300)	(2.1)
Service	600	8.0	500	7.8	1,100	7.9
Sales, Total	7,500	100.0	6,400	100.0	13,900	100.0
Cost of Sales	5,450	72.7	4,550	71.1	10,000	71.9
Gross Margin	2,050	27.3	1,850	28.9	3,900	28.1
Expenses, Variable						
Selling	450	6.0	400	6.3	850	6.1
Advertising and promotion	430	5.7	370	5.8	800	5.7
Other	250	3.3	150	2.3	400	2.9
Variable, Total	1,130	15.0	920	14.4	2,050	14.7
Expenses, Fixed						
Occupancy	100	1.3	150	2.3	250	1.8
Store management	250	3.4	250	3.9	500	3.6
Allocated division overhead	50	0.7	30	0.5	80	0.6
Other	40	0.5	20	0.3	60	0.4
Depreciation & amortization	10	0.1	100	1.6	110	0.8
Depreciation & amortization (deferred)*	—	—	20	0.3	20	0.1
Fixed, Total	450	6.0	570	8.9	1,020	7.3
Total operating expenses	1,580	21.0	1,490	23.3	3,070	22.0
Corporate overhead	150	2.0	130	2.0	280	2.0
Net income	320	4.3	230	3.6	550	4.1

*Preopening.

Exhibit 9
Market Shares in Richmond of Loading Docks and Major Competitors

Retail Store	Market Share (%)
Loading Dock	23
Sears, Roebuck and Co.	13
Independent TV and audio and neighborhood stores	18
Discount department stores (e.g., Kmart and Woolco)	8
Best Products (catalog showrooms)	8
Department stores (e.g., Miller and Rhoads)	5
Others (e.g., furniture stores)	25

Source: The Southeastern Institute of Research, Inc., October 1980.

Exhibit 10
Summary of Loading Dock Sales Counselors' Earnings by Merchandise Category (1980)

	Store Location				
	THALBRO			MIDLOTHIAN	
Merchandise Type/ Earnings Source	Monthly Average	Range		Monthly Average	Range
Major Appliances (including TV)					
Commissions	$ 654	$481 – 782		$ 722	$ 561 –1,525
Spiffs	950	280 –1,148		1,178	662 –2,736
Earnings (total)	1,604	761 –2,200		1,900	1,223 –4,261
Audio Equipment					
Commissions	620	368 – 913		496	361 – 635
Spiffs	950	472 –1,740		653	296 –1,079
Earnings (total)	1,570	840 –2,653		1,149	657 –1,714
Store Average					
Commissions	646	—		652	—
Spiffs	949	—		1,017	—
Earnings (total)	1,595	—		1,669	—

Note: Although the majority of Loading Dock sales force was full-time these figures also include the earnings of some part-time sales counselors.

Exhibit 11
Loading Dock Television Storyboard

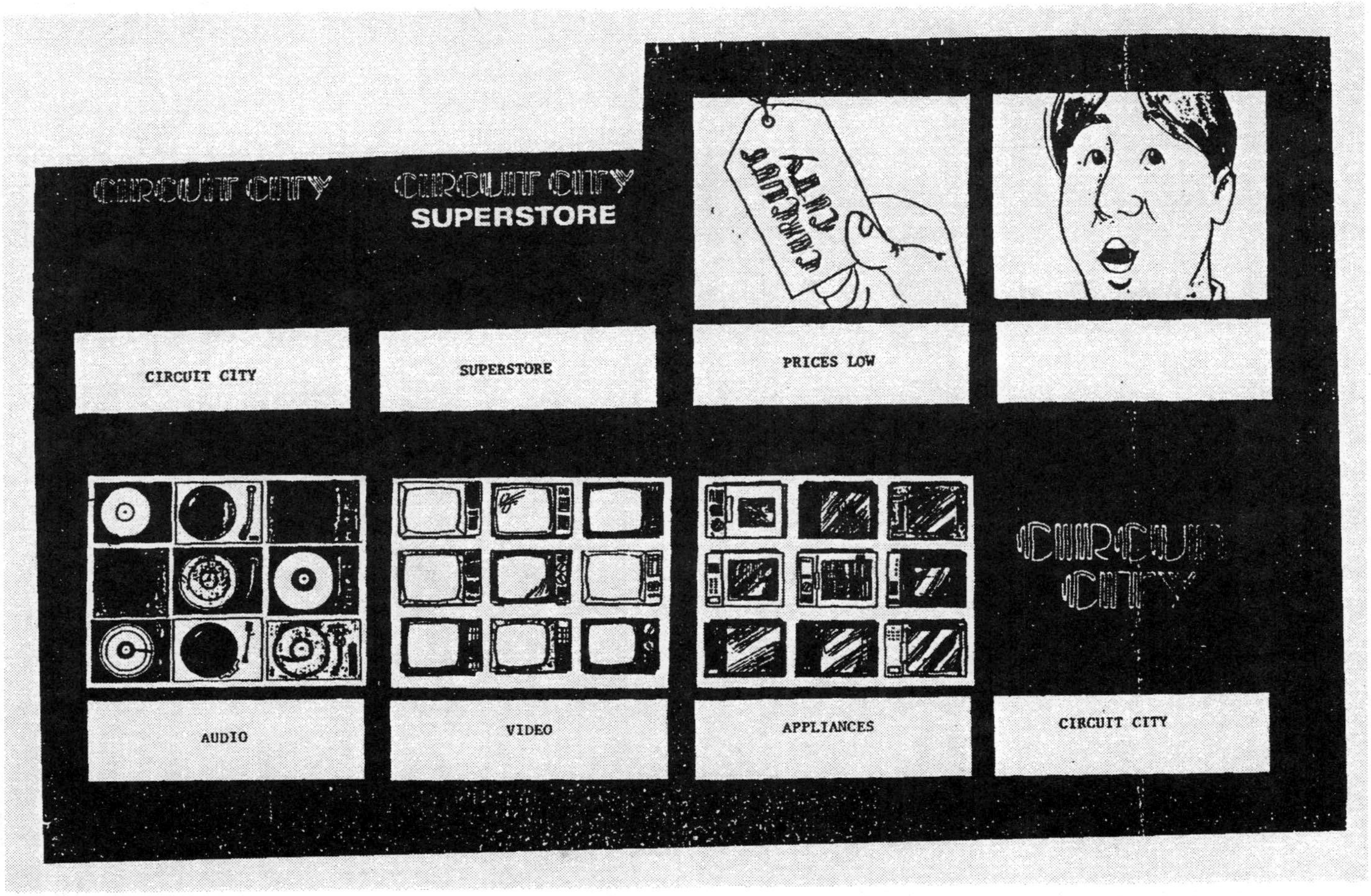

Exhibit 12
Loading Dock Print Advertising

Exhibit 13
Demographic and Economic Characteristics of Selected Zip Codes in Winston-Salem Area and Loading Dock's Potential Sales

Zip Code	Approx. Distance from Store (miles)	Pop. 1980 (000s)	Pop.% Change Since 1970	Number of Households 1980 (000s)	Pop.% Change Since 1980	Total Sales L.D. Merch. (all stores) ($000)	Potential Sales with L.D. Market Share = 21% ($000s)*	Potential Sales in Codes with Income $15K and 21% Market Share ($000)*	Mean Household Income ($000s)	% Households Moved into Zip in Last 5 Years	% SF*** Dwelling Units
27103	Store Location	22.1	25	8.4	37	2,210	464	464	15.9	59	71.5
27104	2	19.6	15	7.1	29	1,960	412	412	27.1	54	68.0
27107	4	45.1	9	15.7	22	4,510	947	947	17.4	55	85.6
27101	4	18.0	3	7.2	15	1,800	378	—	12.9	59	64.7
27106	5	26.9	44	9.0	63	2,690	565	565	22.0	62	69.7
27105	6	38.3	-1	13.5	12	3,880	815	—	14.2	52	82.7
27012	7	10.3	2	3.6	16	1,030	216	216	22.8	79	93.4
27010	8	0.5	14	0.2	28	50	11	11	23.6	74	96.8
27040	8	6.4	-5	2.2	7	640	134	134	24.2	85	94.5
27373	8	0.4	14	0.1	21	40	8	8	16.8	75	100.0
27023	9	5.5	16	1.9	30	550	116	116	21.0	72	93.1
27374	10	2.1	68	0.7	79	210	44	44	16.0	55	100.0
27045	10	6.0	3	2.1	16	600	126	126	20.1	69	95.7
27051	12	4.9	7	1.7	20	490	103	103	20.1	75	94.1
27050	13	2.7	0	0.9	12	270	57	57	23.6	91	100.0
27284	14	24.0	-1	8.4	12	2,400	504	504	21.1	71	87.3
27021	15	11.4	34	4.0	50	1,140	239	—	13.9	64	99.6
27019	15	3.4	2	1.1	15	340	71	—	12.7	82	100.0
27009	16	1.3	-12	0.4	-1	130	27	27	20.5	91	98.5
27018	17	5.4	14	1.8	22	530	113	113	14.6	40	100.0
27052	17	7.3	27	2.4	42	740	153	—	13.2	32	100.0
27360	17	32.8	5	10.8	12	3,280	687	667	15.4	57	87.5
27292	18	52.5	8	17.4	16	5,520	1,102	—	14.8	58	90.1
27299	18	3.3	12	1.0	21	330	69	—	14.7	87	100.0
27043	18	3.6	19	1.3	34	360	76	—	13.6	47	100.0
27055	21	8.6	7	2.9	15	860	181	—	14.0	50	100.0
TOTAL		362.9		125.8		36,290	7,618	4,514			

Note: Demographic and economic data supplied by Donnelley Marketing (Stamford, Conn).

* Figure of 21% approximates Loading Dock's total share of market in Richmond. Exclusion of zip codes will mean family incomes less than or equal to $15K reflects Wards' belief that it obtains only limited sales from such areas.

** Assumes per capita annual spending of $100 for Loading Dock merchandise. Source for spending figure is 1977 Census of Retail Trade, Merchandise Line Sales, Bureau of Census. The 1977 figure includes several items, such as sewing machines, that Loading Dock does not sell. Therefore, it is assumed that the figure for 1977 was sufficiently overstated to offset the effect of subsequent inflation.

*** SF = single family.

Large Store

MEMCO: Membership discount department store. Appliances, video, and audio merchandise offered.

Specialty Stores

STEREO STATION: Video and audio store.

STEREO SOUND: Audio store.

ED KELLY INC.: Loading Dock's major competitor. Approximately six stores in Winston-Salem, Greensboro, and High Point area. Aggressive expansion. Large selection of nationally branded (60 brands) merchandise priced generally higher than Loading Dock's. Service contracts offered. Thirty-day lowest price guarantee identical to Loading Dock's. Free and next-day delivery offered. Plans to expand through franchising and by miniaturizing the concept in smaller towns in the surrounding area.

BRENDLES: Appliance, video, and audio store.

ARDAN'S SHOWROOM: Appliance and video store.
JOYCE BROS. SHOWROOM: Appliance and video store.

BOBBY TEAGUE APPLIANCE: Appliance and video store. Substantial selection of nationally branded merchandise, free delivery, no service contracts, service performed in-house. Prices generally higher than Loading Dock's.

HAROLD GIBSON TV AND APPLIANCE: Appliance and video store.

Exhibit 14
Demographic and Economic Characteristics of Selected Zip Codes in Birmingham SMSA

Zip Code	Approx. Distance from Site 1 (Miles)	Approx Distance from Site 2 (Miles)	Pop. 1980 (000s)	Pop. % Change since 1970	Number of Households 1980 (000s)	% Change since 1980	Total Sales L.D. Merch. (all stores) ($000s)	Potential Sales with L.D. Market Share of 21% and Mean Income >$15K (000s)**	Mean Household Income ($000s)	% Households Moved into Zip in Last 5 Years	% SF *** Dwelling Units
35216	Store Site	7	35.5	130	11.5	140	3,550	746	25.6	65	59
35209	3	7	35.0	36	12.6	44	3,500	735	15.2	62	52
35226	4	10	26.1	133	7.7	141	2,610	548	23.9	59	87
35223	4	3	12.0	31	4.2	39	1,200	252	55.7	48	83
35243	4	6	14.8	77	5.5	133	1,480	311	26.8	68	87
35213	5	2	14.6	16	5.4	32	1,460	307	45.2	50	84
35204	6	8	20.8	-18	9.7	15	2,080	437	16.7	46	78
35222	6	3	9.9	-16	4.9	19	990	208	16.6	55	73
35210	7	Store Site	13.7	4	5.3	27	1,370	288	17.7	62	78
35228	8	13	13.0	1	4.5	13	1,300	273	16.8	45	92
35064	9	13	15.1	-1	5.0	4	1,510	317	18.8	45	83
35244	9	16	3.3	49	1.2	75	330	69	17.5	62	83
35206	10	3	23.6	-16	10.5	13	2,360	496	15.6	44	85
35217	10	5	19.1	-6	6.7	5	1,910	401	15.2	48	89
35214	11	12	24.7	-1	8.5	16	2,470	519	17.7	47	89
35224	11	14	6.5	-24	2.8	6	650	137	16.1	38	93
35015	12	5	0.5	6	0.1	10	50	11	20.0	63	100
35060	12	14	1.6	-1	0.5	2	160	34	23.7	42	99
35127	12	16	5.6	20	2.3	69	560	118	21.6	54	95
35124	13	20	5.8	54	2.1	84	580	122	15.5	74	88
35235	13	5	7.1	-28	2.8	-6	710	149	18.0	54	91
35071	14	10	12.7	4	3.9	8	1,270	267	21.8	48	94
35080	14	21	3.1	100	1.1	139	310	65	16.7	68	98
35215	14	7	46.4	27	17.3	65	4,640	974	19.3	58	76
35005	15	16	11.2	4	3.4	8	1,120	235	19.5	68	97
35036	15	15	0.6	8	0.2	12	60	13	16.5	28	100
35119	15	9	0.4	10	0.1	6	40	8	17.8	47	93
35181	15	13	0.3	14	0.1	18	30	6	16.4	63	100
35041	16	16	0.3	24	0.1	28	30	6	16.5	68	97
35111	16	24	4.6	17	1.4	21	460	97	18.4	57	100
35114	16	22	1.8	69	0.6	100	180	38	16.8	74	99
35117	16	14	4.4	14	1.4	18	440	92	19.2	95	99
35118	16	19	3.7	-18	1.4	4	370	78	18.9	61	98
35073	17	17	3.9	21	1.2	25	390	82	19.3	57	99
35094	17	11	17.4	10	5.6	15	1,740	365	17.0	64	91

Zip Code	Approx. Distance from Site 1 (Miles)	Approx Distance from Site 2 (Miles)	Pop. 1980 (000s)	Pop. % Change since 1970	Number of Households 1980 (000s)	% Change since 1980	Total Sales L.D. Merch. (all stores) ($000s)	Potential Sales with L.D. Market Share of 21% and Mean Income >$15K ($000s)**	Mean Household Income ($000s)	% Households Moved into Zip in Last 5 Years	% SF *** Dwelling Units
35173	17	10	10.0	2	3.3	8	1,070	225	18.5	57	90
35116	18	13	3.7	9	1.2	13	370	78	18.0	90	99
35059	21	14	0.2	-2	0.1	1	20	4	15.2	56	100
35091	22	16	1.3	-2	0.4	2	130	27	15.2	56	100
35123	22	15	0.4	48	0.1	52	40	8	17.6	63	100
35126	22	15	13.7	19	4.2	22	1,370	288	17.6	73	97
35048	23	15	0.2	-4	0.1	2	20	4	18.0	95	100
35180	24	20	8.6	0	2.8	4	860	181	15.2	61	94
Total			457.9		163.7		45,790	9,619			

Note: Demographic and economic data supplied by Donnelley Marketing (Stamford, CT). Includes only those zip codes in the Birmingham SMSA with mean household incomes greater than or equal to $15K annually and located 24 miles or less from the proposed store locations. The distance reflects the size of the primary trading area of Richmond Loading Docks.

* Assumes per capita annual spending of $100 for Loading Dock merchandise. Source for spending figures is *1977 Census of Retail Trade, Merchandise Line Sales*, Bureau of Census. The 1977 figure of $100 per capita has not been adjusted for the inflation between 1977 and 1981. The reason is that the 1977 figure includes several items, such as sewing machines, that Loading Dock does not sell. Therefore, it is assumed that the figure of $100 per capita for 1977 was sufficiently overstated to offset the effect of subsequent inflation.

** Figure of 21% approximates Loading Dock's total share of market in Richmond. Exclusion of zip codes with mean family incomes less than or equal to $15K reflects Wards' belief that it obtains only limited sales from such areas.

*** SF = Single Family.

National General Merchandise Chains

JCPENNEY: Appliance, video, and audio.

SEARS, ROEBUCK AND CO.: Appliances, audio, and video offered in Sears' traditional value-oriented format.

Other Large-Store Competitor

WOOLCO: Appliances, video, and audio available. Discount department store.

Specialty Stores

BARR-SEAL TV AND APPLIANCE: Appliance and television store.

BILLINGSLEY-DUDDY APPLIANCE: Appliance store.

A AND H APPLIANCE CO.: Appliance store.

SWINNEY'S HOME APPLIANCE CENTER: Appliance store.

JACK'S TV AND APPLIANCE: Appliance and television store owned by Handy TV (see description following). Value approximately $2.5-$3.0 million.

ERWIN TV AND APPLIANCE: Appliance and television store.

MAYER TV: Television store.

STEREO CITY: Audio store.

GOOD HOUSEKEEPING SHOWROOM: Nine stores in Birmingham metropolitan area. Owned by Zenith distributor. Approximately eight national brands carried. Consumer-oriented image. Service available, including service contracts. Middle- to upper-class customers. Low prices and strong promotion. Small stores.

APPLIANCE DISTRIBUTORS WAREHOUSE: Appliance and television store.

VIDEO BOX OFFICE: Video store.

BIRMINGHAM VIDEO AND PHOTOGRAPHY: Video equipment available.

THE VIDEO CENTER: Video store.

VIDEO TECHNOLOGY: Video store.

MODERN ELECTRONICS: Video store.

HARVEY'S WAREHOUSE: Video and audio equipment. Approximately 2,500 square foot of selling space. No service offered. Free five-year warranty on audio components; customers required to keep original boxes for shipment to factory. Trade-ins allowed. Negotiable prices. Systems offered at a discount from individual components. Small number of televisions.

HANDY TV WAREHOUSE: Appliance, audio, and video store (also owns Jack's TV). Approximately nine national brands offered. Good customer relations; family oriented. Ninety percent of sales by cash or credit card; time payment available. Recently introduced extended service. Warehouse showroom operation.

STATHAM TV: Appliance, video, and audio store.

GODWIN RADIO CO.: Appliance and video store.

Others Not on Birmingham Map

SERVICE MERCHANDISE: Opened in 1979. Audio and video equipment.

ALABAMA POWER COMPANY: Appliances only. Three national brands. Premium prices. Statewide chain (80 stores).

PIZITZ: Birmingham's major department store (six locations). Similar to Miller and Rhoads.

STEREO WAREHOUSE: Retail stores and mail-order business. Approximately eight brands of audio equipment.

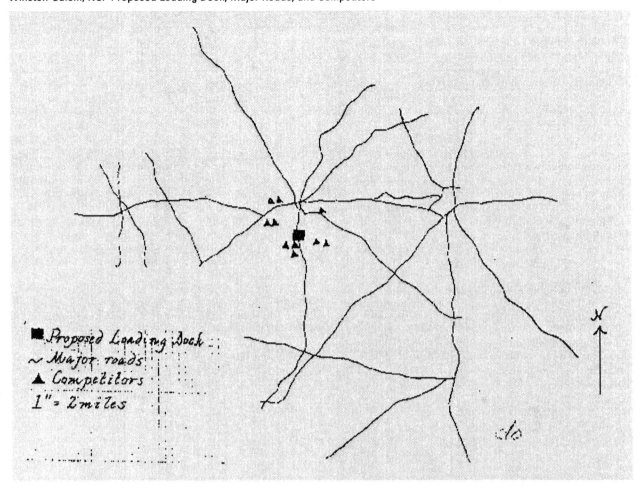

■ Proposed Loading Dock
~ Major roads
▲ Competitors
1" = 2 miles

Exhibit 16
Cost Estimates

Winston-Salem Expansion Cost Estimates

Land purchase	$375,000
Building construction	750,000
Fixturing*	300,000
Opening inventory	1.1–1.2 million
Sell building and land	1.175 million
Leaseback of land and building**	150,000 /year

Birmingham Expansion Cost Estimates (two locations)

Birmingham (South)

Land purchase	$400,000
Building construction	750,000
Fixturing*	1.1–1.2 million
Opening inventory	1.2 million
Leaseback of land and building**	156,000 /year

Birmingham (East)

Rent existing building	$140,000 /year
Lease extra warehouse space	25,000 /year
Fixturing	200,000
Opening inventory	1.1–1.2 million

* Wards to retain ownership of store fixtures
** This figure is for five years, with limited escalation thereafter.

Source: Wards Co.

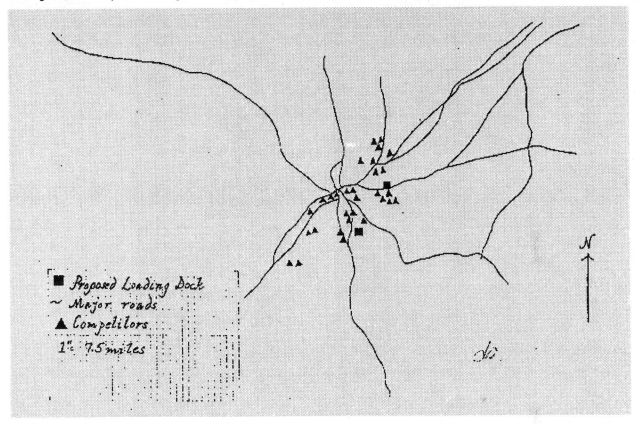

■ Proposed Loading Dock
~ Major roads
▲ Competitors
1" = 7.5 miles

N

COIN DEPARTMENT STORES

COIN was a chain of thirty-four department stores located in and around larger cities and towns throughout Italy with sales in 1989 of $400 million. In addition to operating its own stores, COIN provided merchandise and advertising support to twenty-five COIN franchisees. COIN was owned by Piergiorgio and Vittorio Coin and their sister Paola, members of an old and distinguished Venetian family.

After a period of lackluster performance during the early eighties, Coin had repositioned its stores by focussing on fewer merchandise categories, a narrower price range, a stronger emphasis on private label, and a concept which they called "shops within a shop."

Together with operating reforms, the repositioning had resulted in a turnaround in profitability and accelerating sales growth. Whereas COIN had planned for a growth in sales in 1990 of 12% for stores open for more than a year (6% of which represented inflation), it now appeared that growth would be in the vicinity of 17%. (See **Exhibit 1**.) Piergiorgio and Vittorio Coin recognized, however, that much remained to be done to achieve satisfactory profits for the COIN division.

In September of 1990, they had opened a new store in Florence, the first new store to reflect fully the new positioning. Sales for the rest of the year at this store were almost 25% over projections. Pleased with these results, COIN executives realized that this store's performance might provide insights into what kind of stores they should operate in the future and the related issues of private label positioning and procurement, as well as the role of franchising

The COIN stores served very different regional markets. Although living standards in Italy were equivalent to other western European countries, consumers in the north were much more affluent and cosmopolitan than in the south.

RETAILING IN ITALY

Retailing in Italy was still far more traditional than in most northern European countries and the United States. Independently owned specialty stores dominated retailing for the sale of almost all commodities from food to general merchandise. There were two traditional department store companies, COIN and La Rinascente, but their stores represented only 1.5% of the apparel business although they also engaged in other lines of business. Furthermore, although some of the specialty store business was in the hands of chains, independents (operators of less than ten stores) accounted for 82% of the Italian apparel trade.

Change, however was now accelerating in Italian retailing. In the food business, smaller supermarkets (averaging less than 20,000 square feet) were finding sites in or near the city centers. On the outskirts there were both larger supermarkets and hypermarkets. The latter carried, besides food and other routine needs, an almost complete assortment of general merchandise.

David Wylie prepared this case under the supervision of Professor Walter J. Salmon with the special assistance of GEA as the basis for class discussion rather than to illustrate either effective or ineffective handling of an administrative situation.

While the hardgoods within the general merchandise assortments included many well-known and respected brands, the softgoods, or textiles as they were called, were generally lower in price, quality and fashion content. (See **Exhibit 2**.)

Power retailers were a newer addition to the Italian retailing scene. Some were owned by existing retailing interests such as Brico, a do-it-yourself retailer which was an offshoot of La Rinascente, the largest of the Italian food and department store groups. Others, like the Swedish furniture chain, IKEA, had invaded from a foreign home base. Among these was Toys R Us which was considering adding Italian stores to its current chain of European toy supermarkets.

Two factors were mainly responsible for the changes occurring in Italian retailing. Laws and traditions that had enabled local communities to refuse licenses to prospective operators of large surface stores were becoming less effective and, in some instances, even abolished. Secondly, in 1992 Italian rules and regulations governing retailing were to become harmonized with the more liberal regulations of other Common Market countries. Thus an acceleration of the transformation of Italian retailing was anticipated, stimulated by both Italian retailers themselves and new entrants from the remainder of the Common Market and the United States.

Labor unions still played a major role in Italian retailing, often placing constraints on the ways in which a retailer could organize and expand. Unions often regulated such details as organizational hierarchies and incentive structures in stores.

BACKGROUND OF THE COIN GROUP

The COIN Group currently consisted of several entities. One was the thirty-four COIN department stores. The second, which operated as a branch of the department store entity, were the COIN franchisees. The third entity within the Group was Oviesse, a successful chain of one hundred limited service, lower priced, promotional apparel stores which also carried some other categories of merchandise such as cosmetics, household textiles, dishes and glassware, cooking utensils and seasonal merchandise such as toys, trim-a-tree, etc. Finally, the group also included a real estate company which owned or leased all the group's properties and in turn rented them to the operating divisions.

COIN first entered the department store business shortly after World War II. Oviesse was established in 1972 and the holding company structure was finalized in 1990. Over the years, the COIN Group had also engaged in activities such as equipment leasing and receivable factoring for other companies. They had, however, withdrawn from these activities to concentrate on what they considered their core businesses: the COIN and Oviesse stores.

Oviesse had been from inception a very successful operation entirely independent of the COIN department stores. It had, for example, its own management information systems (MIS), warehouses and made its own domestic and overseas procurement arrangements.

COIN real estate activities were also now dedicated almost entirely to retail and retail related properties. The current policy of the group was to charge the retail operations rent equal to 5% of the market value of their premises. Periodically these properties were reevaluated so that rents assessed were based on their approximate updated market value.

COIN department stores were mainly located in northern Italy (see map, **Exhibit 3**) and in or near major cities in the south. The stores averaged 26,657 square feet in size of selling area. In contrast, the franchised COIN stores averaged only 5,722 square feet in selling space. Some were as small as 2,000 square feet. The size of the COIN stores depended upon the size of the market, the ability to assemble retail real estate that was difficult to obtain, and the acquisition of a license from local authorities to operate a department store of a given size.

Unlike Oviesse, the department store group had a checkered history. Until recently, the department stores had sold a wide range of merchandise in many price brackets ranging from just below medium to upper price points. Given the limited size of many COIN department stores, the result had been exceptional breadth of merchandise, but little depth. In addition, much of the merchandise had not been private label and was consequently available in numerous competitive stores. The former merchandising policy had limited consumer appeal and, together with certain operating problems, had resulted in significant losses for the department store operation from 1980 to 1985.

Beginning in 1985, Piergiorgio and Victorio Coin (then forty-three and forty-one years old respectively) had taken a renewed interest in the department store division. With new management, consulting assistance from Management Horizons Europe, a major retail consulting firm headquartered in London, England, and GEA, a large and respected Italian consulting company, they had refocused and reorganized the business.

Table A
COIN Selected Data 1989

	Fully Owned[a]	Franchised[b]	Other[c]	Total COIN Co.
Sales ($ millions)	376	20	12	408
Outlets number	34	25	16	75
Total retail surface (square feet)	906,328	143,054		
Average retail surface per outlet (square feet)	26,657	5,722		
Sales per square foot[d]	415	140		
Sales personnel	1,430	145		
Square feet per sales personnel	634	986		
Sales per sales personnel	262,937	137,931		
Total personnel				2,279
Number of SKUs handled annually				53,404
Number of suppliers of which:				1,837
Italy				1,465
non Italy				372

a Retail prices
b Wholesale prices
c Sales to customers who have not yet signed franchising agreements or been authorized to sell under the "COIN" brand.
d Excluding new openings 1989, retail price

Note: Statistics denominated in lira have been converted to U.S. dollars at 1,200 Lira per dollar throughout the case.

Now COIN was concentrating on fewer merchandise categories, a greater proportion of medium-priced merchandise, and a stronger private label emphasis that offered the customer appealing merchandise at attractive prices. It was increasingly associating its private labels, which now accounted for 15% of COIN sales, with particular lifestyles such as J.C. Twidd (pronounced "Tweed") which stood for a conservative English look in its men's shop, Miss Twidd which represented a similar look in its women's departments, and Twiddy Bambino (pronounced, "Tweedy") for the children's department. (See **Exhibit 4** for photographs of some of these fashions copied from magazine advertisements.) Despite the improvements brought about by the merchandising changes and operating reforms, profits were still not satisfactory. In addition, Piergiorgio and Vittorio Coin had other objectives. These included providing more "equilibrium" for the entire COIN Group. Equilibrium was to come from a reduction in corporate debt to 50%, the possible establishment of specialty stores

that included only a limited number of the shops now represented in most department stores, and changes in governance for each of the operations within the Group. In the future, each entity within the Group would have its own board of directors, including the Coin brothers, the division general manager and one or more able nonfamily business people. Conceivably, each entity could eventually offer stock to the public.

The Coin brothers also thought that the addition of nonfamily members to the boards of the various entities would provide a more constructive and objective environment for their four offspring should they want to enter the family business.

THE COIN ORGANIZATION

The COIN Group was headquartered in Venice. Both Coin brothers were actively involved in the operations of all aspects of the Group. Formally, the entire Oviesse and real estate group reported to Vittorio Coin and to

Sergio Bianchi, general manager and chief operating officer, while the COIN department store pyramid reported to Piergiorgio Coin. (See **Exhibit 5**, Organization Chart.) Below this level, there was very little organizational overlap between Oviesse and COIN. There was, in fact, an effort to keep these organizations distinctly apart since the management of Oviesse did not always share the Coins' enthusiasm for the now blossoming department store division.

Angelo Barozzi, general manager and chief operating officer of COIN, was the senior executive responsible for the department store division. Directors of customer services, promotion, merchandising, and stores reported to Barozzi.

Three "world" directors, equivalent to American general merchandise managers, were responsible for the worlds of women and children, men, and home, as they were called. Reporting to them were area managers responsible for individual merchandise categories such as, in the women's world, women's traditional, juniors, or special sizes. Senior and junior buyers were in turn responsible for individual subcategories such as elegant traditional wear, casual classics, or accessories. One hundred and forty people worked within this buying organization. Area managers were responsible for approximately $40 million of merchandise, senior buyers $17 million, and junior buyers $9 million.

The thirty-four managers of individual stores, most of whom had been promoted from within the store organization, reported directly to the director of stores. Although there was some variation according to the size of the store, as a rule four shop managers, generally organized in parallel to the headquarter's merchandising group, an administrative manager, and a visual merchandise manager reported to these store managers. Salespeople all reported directly to shop managers. Everyone at the stores was paid a competitive salary and a bonus which was based on achieving a sales and contribution goal for the entire store. For store managers, this bonus ranged between 15% to 25% of total gross salary. For shop managers, it ranged from 25% to 30% although it was virtually assured. This bonus, however, only comprised two to three percent of a salesperson's total compensation since labor unions in Italy imposed rather severe limitations on such incentives. The bonus arrangement, constrained as it was by the labor unions, was thought to encourage teamwork within the store. In some stores where allowed by the unions, salespeople received an additional income opportunity. Before a sale officially began, a salesperson could earn an amount equal to the planned discount on an item if a salesperson sold an item at the pre-sale price. Turnover of employees stayed at only five percent to six percent for two reasons. First, COIN human resource policies were considered attractive, and second, Italian law made it very difficult to fire or lay off anyone. In many respects, something approaching lifetime employment was guaranteed.

Although many guidelines were dictated to the store managers from Venice, the managers had considerable autonomy in operating the stores within these guidelines. When something needed to be changed, however, such as the reallocation of space, different store fixtures, or the deletion or addition of certain items in stock, the manager could petition the director of stores, the general manager of COIN, and the appropriate headquarter's expert on the subject to make modifications. Although the complexity of this procedure discouraged minor changes, major changes were more often than not modified or approved entirely.

THE MERCHANDISING AND DISTRIBUTION CYCLE

All COIN merchandise was bought by the headquarter's buyers. The role of the stores was to sell merchandise, not to buy it. The merchandising cycle began almost a year before the beginning of each of four seasons when the stores would estimate sales volumes for the following season by merchandise area. These estimates were adjusted and approved by the area managers. The world directors would then in turn approve these projections and pass them down to the buying organization along with general design and fashion objectives for the season. Area managers would then further define the "architecture" of the merchandise (by this they meant the depth and breadth of each merchandise line). The buyers would then develop lines with their suppliers for both private label merchandise and with COIN's important branded vendors. They worked with outside "style" consultants to design the lines of more fashionable private label merchandise such as Miss Twidd or Leiluna. Finally, the buyers would develop suggested allocations of the merchandise for each of the stores.

To insure quality, all private label merchandise in the past had been purchased, mostly from Italian vendors, by SIREMA, a design and procurement company owned by the COIN Group. Some limited production in the Far

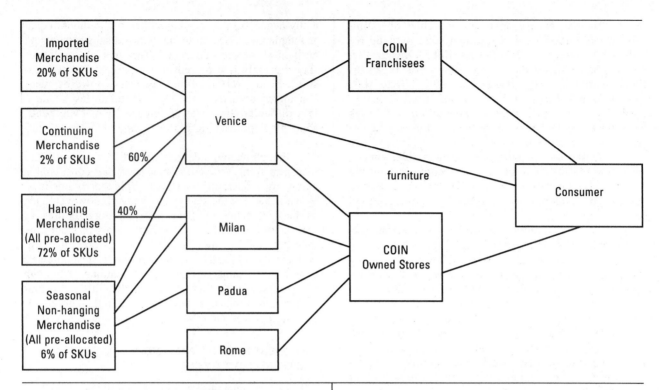

East, however, was now under consideration. Several trips to Hong Kong had resulted in the identification of a production agent, a quality control agent, fabric suppliers, and how to develop prototype merchandise for far eastern production. In spite of the cost advantages of this production, caution was thought to be important since poor quality private label merchandise could compromise the COIN image. In addition, payment terms would be very different from those of Italian suppliers, whose terms allowed COIN's day's payables to be 115 days. Generally, imports from the Far East had to be paid for on the date that the vessel or airplane carrying them from abroad left the port of embarkation.

Six months prior to the beginning of the season, the shop managers of all the stores would converge upon Venice to attend a fashion show of all the new merchandise. Armed with this introduction and a knowledge of their markets, they could modify the mix of merchandise allocated by the buyers to their stores by as much as 30%. The buyers would then place final orders with their suppliers. Since buyers were always on the lookout for fast breaking fashions which might come to their attention after the "show," they were authorized to buy and distribute a limited quantity of additional

merchandise. This prerogative was, however, infrequently exercised.

Merchandise was categorized as seasonal hanging, seasonal non-hanging, and continuing (longer life cycle.) Eighty percent of the 53,404 stock keeping units (SKUs) offered by COIN was pre-allocated to individual stores in accordance with the managers' orders, including all of the seasonal merchandise, and was delivered to the stores in predetermined waves. Pre-allocated meant that the requirements of individual stores were determined when vendor orders were placed and not when merchandise arrived at the distribution centers, which could be several months later. Some adjustments could be made to pre-allocated merchandise deliveries if an item was selling particularly well or poorly at particular stores. In such a case, a shop manager would contact the buyer responsible for the item and negotiate an adjustment or possible transfer from another store.

COIN maintained its own distribution center in the mainland of Venice through which all imported and continuing merchandise, sixty percent of pre-allocated hanging goods, and all merchandise bound to franchisees was channeled. All seasonal nonhanging pre-allocated merchandise bound for the COIN-owned stores flowed through one of three independently owned and operated regional distribution facilities in Milan, Padua, and Rome. The Milan distributor also had the capability of handling hanging merchandise and distributed about forty percent of the pre-allocated hanging merchandise. The Rome distributor was installing equipment meant to handle hanging goods and would absorb some of the merchandise now flowing through Milan and Venice. The stores all received two deliveries per week from both Venice and one of the distributors. Franchisees only received weekly deliveries. Basic merchandise was all replenished from vendor stocks or from the central warehouse maintained by COIN in Venice by the buyers, based on point of sale (POS) data.

Furniture was handled differently. The stores only maintained samples on the sales floor and purchases were shipped directly to the customer from the Venice warehouse.

ADVERTISING AND PROMOTION

Advertising and promotion programs were all developed and implemented centrally. Beyond a heavy public relations emphasis to attract positive media coverage, COIN concentrated its advertising in popular national women's fashion magazines. Every effort was made to produce advertising which would be appropriate for all the stores across Italy, transcending climatic and cultural differences.

The advertising message changed according to the season, but now consistently attempted to promote the stores' more fashionable image as exemplified by the private label lines. Frequently up to ten pages of full color photographs in one monthly issue of a magazine were alternated with a ten percent discount card in the next. Recently, COIN marketing executives were experimenting with the regular use of television, but had not yet come to any conclusion as to what role it might play in the future.

The phrase "in giro per negozi" (meaning browsing through the shops) was used to promote COIN's new merchandising position of being more a collection of specialty stores than a traditional, broad-based department store. Several years before, the message of "COIN is in" was used. It had generated a lot of traffic as people came to check out the new and more fashion-forward image implied by this message. Because the merchandise did not meet consumer expectations resulting in more disappointment than new sales, this advertising message was abandoned.

Local promotional programs were the exception rather than the rule. Posters, local radio, newspapers and other media were used only to promote local events such as the opening of a new store. In addition, if a store manager wanted to have a local promotion, he could make that request of headquarters. The central promotional organization was quite responsive to reasonable requests and often agreed to proceed with implementation.

THE NEW FLORENCE STORE

In March of 1986, the Coin family purchased "Duilio 48", one of the oldest discount stores in Florence along with the license to operate a retail store. It was located on one of the busiest and most prestigious shopping streets in the city, Via de' Calzaiuoli, with entrances on all side streets. (See Map of Florence, **Exhibit 6**.) This street was the main walking thoroughfare between the Piazza del Duomo and the Piazza della Signoria. The volume of pedestrian traffic every day on this street was similar to that in popular American regional malls on a busy weekend.

This location's history as a retail center commenced in 1834 when the Bazar Buonajuti was founded. In the early part of the twentieth century it had become Duilio 48, and had the distinction of being the largest private retail space in Florence. The structure itself dated to the early Renaissance. The design of some of the early details was attributed to Filippo Brunelleschi (1337–1446), the famous sculptor and architect.

Wanting to take full advantage of this prime location while preserving the integrity of the building, the Coins proceeded cautiously in deciding what the new store should look like. For over a year they continued to operate a discount store there, while studying their options. The new COIN store opened on September 29, 1990. Over $18,000,000 had been spent on its purchase, renovation, and fixturing.

THE FLORENTINE MARKET, DUILO 48, AND COIN OBJECTIVES

Florence was known as the birthplace of the Italian Renaissance and one of the most beautiful cities in Europe. It was an international destination for tourists and students, a preeminent artistic and cultural center, and one of Italy's more sophisticated cities. Outside the city, grand villas dotted the countryside while village populations concentrated on producing the traditional crops of olive oil and wine.

The population of Florence was about 420,000, with an additional 250,000 living within three kilometers of the city. Retail sales for those items which were typically carried by COIN in Florence were estimated to be 631 billion Lira ($526 million) in 1987, 20% of which was tourist trade.

Via de' Calzaiuoli was closed off to all vehicular traffic, to give shoppers full access to the wide street. Surveys revealed that fifty-one percent of the foot traffic was Florentine, nine percent from within three kilometers of the city limits, and ten percent from the countryside beyond. Thirteen percent were Italians from other regions of the country and sixteen percent foreign tourists. Of the Florentines, two-thirds were between the ages of twenty-five and thirty-five, and seventy percent from middle- to high-income families. They were in the area for the purpose of shopping, and sixty percent shopped there at least once each week. The socioeconomic profile of tourists was equivalent to that of the Florentines. The results from additional surveys conducted by COIN are as follows:

Profile of Florentine shoppers from COIN random intercept survey on ViaCalzavola near the COIN store.

Age of Shopper	15–24	25–39	40–45	Total
Merchandise Category				
Women's apparel	17%	46%	37%	100%
Men's apparel	18	59	23	100
Women's lingerie	16	48	36	100

Survey of Florentine Shoppers	Percentage of Sales		Average Price of Merchandise in $[a]	
	Women	Men	Women	Men
Styles				
Classic modern	36%	39%	$120	$157
Traditional	23	30	127	137
Basic	14	17	61	77
Up to date	21	12	165	69
Fashion forward	6	2	102	121
	100%	100%		
Occasion for use	**Men and Women**			
Special occasion	74%		143	183
Casual use	26		69	54
	100%			

a Merchandise refers to women's skirts and men's dress shirts.

Retail stores in the area were almost exclusively small specialty shops carrying leather goods, candy, perfume, fashion apparel and other higher priced merchandise. Several discount department stores such as Upim, Standa, and Oviesse provided a selection of low-priced housewares, basic clothing such as underwear, and clothing which was below the quality level desired by most Florentine shoppers.

Very little was offered in medium price ranges in women's apparel in Florence, especially in more up-to-date styles and in intimate apparel. There was much wider representation in men's apparel, yet the quality of items in the medium price range was low. The inefficiencies of a specialty store distribution system dominated by independent operations was the main explanation for this situation.

In housewares, there were two classes of competition similar to that in women's apparel. Low-priced goods were offered by the discount stores and high-quality goods were offered by specialty stores.

Given the consumer profile and the characteristics of the competition, and encouraged by the success of the COIN department store's recent repositioning in other locations, the Coins decided to transform the Duilio 48 into a COIN store which would concentrate on the underrepresented middle market. It would offer wide assortments of predominantly "classic modern" and, early in each season, "up-to-date" styles. Thirty percent of the merchandise would be priced in the high range, fifty percent in the middle range, and twenty percent in the low range. While presenting a coherent overall look, the new store would cater to the traditional consumer preference for small specialty stores. It would contain a series of "shops within a shop", each with its own distinctive atmosphere.

The following table outlines some of COIN's primary competitors in different merchandise categories in Florence.

Table B
Competition in Florence

Style	Women	Men
Basic	Chiarini Principe Roberta Benetton G.D.	Mattucci
Traditional	Bera Chic Max Mara G.D.	Principe Centro Moda
Classic modern	Luisa Max Mara Amica	Principe Eredi Chiarini
Up to date	Raspini Max Mara Amica	Mulas
Fashion forward	Amica	

Note: Also see **Exhibit 2**.

THE NEW STORE

The Florence store had women's, men's, children's, and home departments, categorized in the same way as all COIN stores. Each department was further broken down into subcategories, such as traditional, teen and casual in women's, or gourmet and textile in home. **Exhibit 7**, "Data on Florence Store," shows the performance of the Florence store within the Florence market, the various departments with the square footage allocated to each at the Florence store, as well as other sales and productivity data.

The store's 25,420 square feet of selling space in several interconnected buildings was situated on three floors surrounding an open courtyard that was covered by a skylight (see **Exhibit 8**, sketch of Florence store), plus a full basement which had been renovated to provide an another 5,350 square feet of selling space. The first floor (12,230 square feet of selling space) featured the men's department, women's hosiery and knitwear, accessories, and, as an experiment in a separate area directly accessible from a side entrance, the perfumerie. The main entrance opened into the courtyard where leather goods and accessories were displayed. Various shops were arrayed around this courtyard and accessible from side entrances. A chrome and glass elevator connected the floors.

The second floor (7,840 square feet of selling space) featured women's apparel. Since this department was thought to draw most customers, it was located so that customers would be drawn through the less popular departments on the first floor. In such a way, sales for these other departments might be bolstered. The third floor (2,600 square feet) was reserved for services and offices. The basement contained the children's and home departments.

The entire store was airy, clean, and open. Most of the walls were painted white and fixtures varied from department to department, but were predominantly chrome or dark wood.

Merchandise in each department was displayed in several ways. Racks and counters in more open spaces were used to display more basic items such as men's shorts or women's hosiery where it was important to emphasize the broad selection. Departments like the perfumerie (cosmetics and health and beauty aids) where service was important were arranged to look like traditional specialty stores. Much of the private label merchandise was displayed in intimate spaces to create distinct atmospheres for such shops as the Miss Twidd or the Leiluna Shops. Other shops, such as women's special sizes which might be a destination for a customer, were easy to find in appropriately decorated rooms. In addition, exceptionally attractive window displays visable from the street featured merchandise from the various "shops."

Each shop had a distinct atmosphere which mirrored the merchandising emphasis of the category. The result was a store which allowed customers to find more easily basic items, feel pampered and explore the worlds of fashion in service-intensive areas. On the whole, the store gave the impression of ample selection and assortment in all categories.

Prices for more basic items were between those of discount stores and specialty stores in the area. Men's button-down shirts, for example, ranged from about $25 to $40 at COIN, whereas Upim, a discount store around the corner, had shirts which ranged from $20 to $35. A typical men's apparel specialty store in the area carried shirts from $38 to $75, and some ranged as high as $250. COIN's more fashionable goods were almost as high in quality as the specialty stores, yet at more reasonable prices.

Service was thought to be an important component of the merchandising mix and included alterations, acceptance of a wide range of credit cards as well as a "COIN CARD," liberal return policies, exceptional signage and layout, free home delivery, buying on approval, installment buying, acceptance of U.S. dollars, gift wrapping, bridal registry, adequate and clean toilet facilities, and, in accordance with the law, no value-added tax for foreigners.

THE EARLY RETURNS

Since it had opened, the new Florence store had enjoyed sales almost 26% above projections. Women's was up 16%, men's 38%, children's 28%, and home 23%. The ten best and the ten worst performing categories of merchandise were as follows in **Table C**:

Table C
Early Performance of Merchandise Categories in the Florence Store

Merchandise Category	Percent Over (Under) Budget
Leather goods	140
Perfumerie	138
Men's night apparel	124
Women's teen	119
Men's sweaters	110
Women's night wear	75
Young men	63
Men's accessories	59
Women's casual classics	52
Men's teen	49
Sheets and towels	49
Furniture	(42)
Elegant traditional	(20)
Classic apparel	(21)
Classic bottoms	(20)
Boutique	(19)
Women's leather	(18)
Evening wear	(18)
Lingerie—day	(10)
Women's outer wear	(10)

Table D
Projected Income Statement for the Florence Store

	1990 Projected from Actual Sales of the First Four Months[a]		1991 Projected		1992 Projected		1993 Projected	
	$	%	$	%	$	%	$	%
Sales	16.3	100.0	20.5	100.0	22.5	100.0	25.0	100.0
Gross margin	6.3	39.0	8.4	40.8	9.2	40.8	10.2	40.8
Labor	1.7	10.7	2.1	10.1	2.4	10.4	2.8	11.4
Rent and occupancy costs	1.5	9.2	1.8	8.5	1.9	8.2	2.0	7.9
Other operating expenses	1.4	8.4	1.2	5.7	1.3	5.6	1.5	6.2
Goodwill	0.7	4.1	0.7	3.3	0.7	3.0	0.0	0.0
Total expenses[b]	5.3	32.4	5.7	27.6	6.1	27.3	6.4	25.4
Contribution	1.1	6.6	2.7	13.1	3.0	13.5	3.8	15.3

a Dollars in millions, calculated at 1,200 Lira per dollar
b Does not include allocation of central office overhead

REMAINING QUESTIONS

While pleased with the results from the Florence store, COIN executives nevertheless wondered what might have been done to make even better use of the available space. Furthermore they also wondered how far to take the "shop within the shop" concept. Should they, either purposely or in attractive locations where there was only a limited amount of space available, open stores that consisted, at the extreme, of perhaps only a single shop? They had just completed some draft guidelines for how the different departments should be represented in stores of varying sizes. What additional considerations, they wondered, should they address in order to create the best stores in other locations, varying according to size, character, and competition within the market, real estate availability and other variables which made each situation unique. What might be the implications in the field or at the store level as well as at headquarters for the management of the stores which varied substantially in departmental composition.

Related to this management issue was a concern about the future of the franchise division. While the division's volume increased COIN's buying power for private label merchandise and allowed the company to be represented in communities and locations too small or remote for COIN itself, it also represented a potential threat to COIN's image if franchisees failed to adhere to COIN standards. In addition, the financial instability of certain franchisees raised questions about investing in funding the accounts receivable necessary to sell them.

Finally, COIN's management had concerns about the procurement challenge brought about by the reliance on private label. COIN management believed that, for economic reasons, it would increasingly have to source many styles of its private label merchandise overseas which, given the limited quantity it required in any one style, could pose significant difficulties. How might this affect the positioning of COIN's private label merchandise?

It was in this context that the Coin brothers were trying to grapple with the future of the department store division. What kinds of stores should operate under the COIN name? While they had no intention of abandoning their existing larger stores, both difficulties in acquiring real estate and a trend towards specialization in general merchandise retailing raised questions about what types of stores they should operate. The Coins thought that settling the issue of store positioning would place the related issues of private label merchandise and the role of franchising into clearer perspective.

Exhibit 1
COIN Financial Projections (in U.S. dollars)

	1990 Actual			1991			1992			1993		
	Stores	Franchise	Total	Stores	Franchise	Total	Stores	Franchise	Total	Stores	Franchise	Total
Sales[a]	492.0	$72.2	$564.1	$527.1	$94.9	$621.9	$597.5	$119.3	$716.8	$689.7	$149.2	$838.9
Net sales	440.8	45.6	486.4	478.1	58.5	536.6	550.9	73.8	624.8	638.2	92.3	730.5
Gross margin	171.6	8.4	180.0	189.2	10.9	200.0	221.0	13.5	234.5	259.2	16.9	276.1
Variable costs	89.2	2.9	92.1	98.7	3.9	102.5	117.8	4.1	121.9	135.9	4.6	140.6
Fixed costs	23.7	0.1	23.8	26.8	0.1	26.9	31.0	0.1	31.2	36.6	0.1	36.7
Allocated costs[b]	10.4	1.7	12.1	12.6	2.0	14.6	15.7	2.4	18.1	18.1	2.9	21.0
Contribution to corporate overhead	48.3	3.7	52.0	51.1	4.8	56.0	56.5	6.8	63.3	68.6	9.3	77.9

Notes: Dollar amounts throughout the exhibits are in millions and based upon an average rate of 1,200 Lira per dollar

a Florence store not included.

b Certain headquarters costs which were associated with the operations of the stores were allocated to the stores. Allocated costs were: Buying organization (allocated by cost of sales), Distribution (allocated first by costs directly attributable to a specific store and then on the basis of net sales), Technical Services (allocated like Distribution), and Advertising (allocated by net sales). Thirty percent of all allocated costs were attributable to the buying organization, and 13.5% to distribution.

Exhibit 2
Apparel Distribution in Italy

Channel	Structure	Main Firms	Trend (last 5 years)	Mkt. Share (Apparel)
Independent	• Very low con-centration (5% more than 1BN Lira sales) • 124,000 privately owned outlets		• Overall slight decrease of tradi-tional outlets • Increase of special-ized boutiques	70.0%
Specialized Chains	• Franchising: 65 chains and 6,100 outlets • Fully owned: 50 chains and 400 outlets	Benetton, Stefanel, Max Mara, Armani, etc. Duca d'Aosta, Boggi, E. Zegna, etc.	• Sharp increase • Stable	10.8% 1.2%
Department Stores	• 49 outlets; 60% apparel sales (13 BN Lira per outlet on average)	Rinascente (14 Out.) COIN (33 Out.)	• Apparel share increasing • Total sales decreasing (-1.3% p.a.)	1.5%
Popular Stores	• 3 chains; 492 fully owned outlets and 327 franchising • 30% sales in apparel business, (2 BN Lira per outlet on average)	Standa UPIM OVIESSE	• 1% p.a. decrease in sales	3.5%
Hypermarkets	• 120 outlets • Average outlet dimen-sion: 44,000 sq. ft. • Share apparel sales: 7% (2 BN Lira on average)	Citta Mercato (Rinascente Group) Euromercato (Standa) Panorama COOP	• Outlets number tripled in 3 years	0.6%
Supermarkets	• About 2,500 outlets, but only 15% offering apparel • 3% apparel share of total sales	GS, Standa, PAM, SMA, COOP: 30% Independent: 20% Associated: 50%	• + 8% sales p.a.	
Mail Order Distribution	• Apparel equals 40% of total sales	Vestro, Postal Market, Euronova	• Slight increase	1.0%
Other	• Hawkers, discount, etc.		• Stable	11.4%

Exhibit 3
COIN Locations in Italy

COIN FRANCHISEES ○
AVELLLINO
BARI
BASSANO
BRINDISK
CAMPOBASSO
COMO
COSENZA
ESTE
FORMIA
GROSSETO
LATINA
LECCE
MONSELICE
OLBIA
ORBETELLO
ORISTANO
PALERMO
PISTOLAPOTENZA
REGGIO EMILIA
ROSSANO CALABRO
SALERNO
SASSARI
SORRENTO
TRENTO
VIGEVANO

● **COIN OWNED STORES**
BERGAMO
BOLOGNA
BOLZANO
BRESCIA
FERRARA
GNEOVA
LIVORNO
MANTOVA
MILANO
MONTECATINI
NAPOLI
PADOVA
PARMA
PIACENZA
PORDENONE
RIMINI
ROMA
TARANTO
TORINO
TREVISO
TRIESTE
UDINE
VARESE
VENEZIA
VENEZIA-MESTRE
VERONA
VICENZA

coin
In giro per negozi.

Exhibit 4
Photographs of Private Label Fashions from Typical Magazine Advertisements

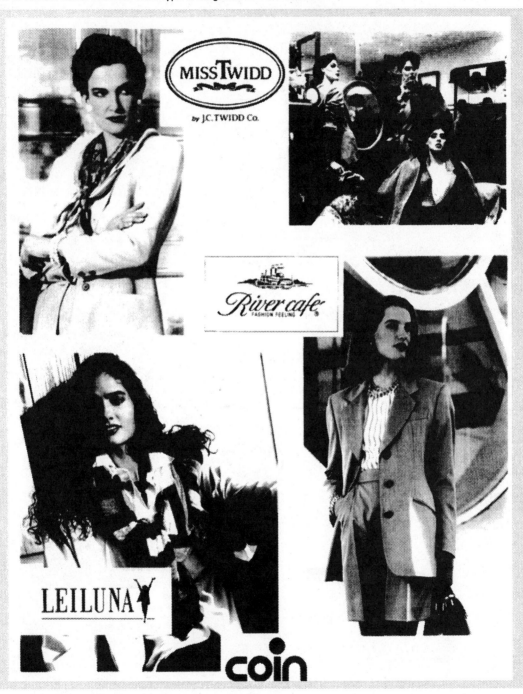

Exhibit 5
COIN S.p.A. Organization Chart

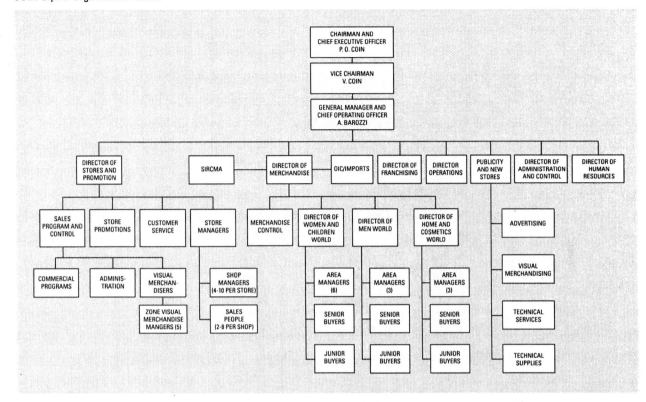

Exhibit 6
Map of Florence

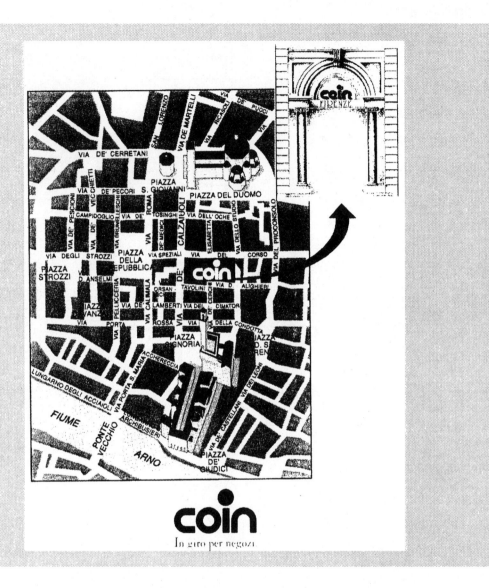

Exhibit 7
Data on Florence Store

Merchandise Categories	The Florence Market			The Florence Store		Sales and Productivity Data			
	Total Market for Category[a]	COIN Sales Est.[a]	COIN Market Share	Selling Space Square Ft.	Sales-People	Sales per salesperson[c] Florence Store	Sales per salesperson[c] The Rest of COIN	Sales per square ft. Florence Store	Sales per square ft. The Rest of COIN
Women's apparel	$159	5.3	3.3%	7,858	15	$353	$289	$674	$449
Outerwear		0.6	n/a	775	2	312	263	800	449
Accessories	30	1.1	3.7	2,411	4	275	227	456	488
Lingerie	16	1.6	10.0	2,497	5	326	226	653	387
Perfume shop	67	0.3	0.4	764	2	130	192	340	612
Men's wear	131	4.9	3.7	5,856	14	352	286	844	449
Children's	33	1.1	3.3	2,282	4	265	194	465	395
Home	90	1.4	1.6	3,185	5	282	206	443	248
Total	**526**	**16.3**	**3.1%**	**25,629**	**51**	**319**	**242**	**636**	**387**

a Millions of dollars
b Florence store statistics are estimates of annual sales based on first four months of sales (September 1990–December 1990).
c Thousands of dollars

Category Performance in all COIN Stores

	Gross Margin Percentage[a]	Inventory Turnover	Value-Added Tax[a]
Women's apparel	41.7%	3.3	11%
Sweaters	41.9	2.6	11
Accessories	37.8	3.0	11
Lingerie	42.1	2.9	11
Perfume Shop	34.8	2.2	19
Men's Wear	39.7	2.2	11
Children's	37.7	2.5	11
Home	35.0	1.7	19
Total Company Average	39.0	2.4	

a Gross margin percentages are expressed after the value-added tax has been deducted. Before the tax is included, for example, women's apparel would have a gross margin of 52.7% and perfume 53.8%.

Source: Company Records

Shop	Florence[a] Annual Sales	As % of Total	Rest of COIN[a,b]	As % of Total
Women's world				
Women's traditional	$1.70	19.7%	$21.67	17.3%
Young women and teen	2.00	23.2	28.06	22.4
Special sizes	1.58	18.3	22.17	17.7
Outer wear	0.62	7.2	9.67	7.7
Accessories	1.10	12.8	24.70	19.7
Lingerie	1.63	18.9	18.96	15.1
Total women's world	**$8.64**	**100.0%**	**$125.23**	**100.0%**
Perfume	**$0.26**	**100.0%**	**$19.82**	**100.0%**
Men's world				
Traditional	2.08	42.1%	29.05	32.5%
Young men and teen	0.93	18.8	22.07	24.7
Accessories	0.99	20.2	17.49	19.6
Seasonal	0.53	10.7	11.48	12.8
Outer wear	0.40	8.2	9.34	10.4
Total men's	**$4.94**	**100.0%**	**$89.42**	**100.0%**
Children's world				
2–5 years	$0.27	25.8%	$6.66	21.6%
Infant's underwear and accessories	0.19	18.3	10.75	34.9
6–13 years	0.59	55.8	13.40	43.5
Total Children's	**$1.06**	**100.0%**	**$30.82**	**100.0%**
World of Home				
Gourmet	$0.36	25.4%	$13.03	33.9%
Textiles	$0.80	56.8	19.48	50.7
Furniture	0.25	17.8	5.94	15.4
Total World of Home	**$1.41**	**100.0%**	**$38.44**	**100.0%**
Total	**$16.30**		**$303.73**	

a Millions of dollars
b Sales data for "Rest of COIN" is based upon 1988 sales.

Exhibit 8
Sketch of Florence Store

C a s e   22

THE NORTHRIDGE AND SOUTHRIDGE MALLS

SYNOPSIS

In May 1992, Martha J. Matthews stared out the window of JMB Realty Corporation's North Michigan Avenue offices and reviewed the alternatives before her. Since JMB had acquired two major regional malls in the Milwaukee area, the firm had invested heavily in capital improvements, retenanting and increased marketing, achieving some very favorable results. Now, however, retailing was undergoing a subtle shift as discounters and other value-oriented merchants proliferated. Further, JMB faced the threat of the potential closing of one of the malls' key anchor stores. The company was under pressure to develop a contingency plan for the space. Matthews knew that in the face of increased costs, competitive pressures from new retailing sectors, and a national recession, the negotiation for a replacement tenant would have a critical impact on the profitability of the mall.

SHOPPING CENTERS IN THE UNITED STATES

Since the first free-standing suburban shopping centers were developed in the 1950s, regional malls have played a significant role in determining how America shops. In the last 25 years over 2 billion square feet of new shopping centers have been developed, reordering local shopping patterns and reshaping our commercial cores. The United States today contains 18 square feet of retail space in shopping centers for every inhabitant—a doubling of space since 1975. As highly visible fixtures of their communities, shopping centers have a significant impact on the local environment, providing goods and services, recreation, jobs, and sales and property tax revenues.

By 1992, fundamental retailing norms were being challenged by new economic and demographic realities and a maturing stock of shopping centers. A soft investment climate reflected in lack of credit, saturated markets, over-building, and declining real estate values, provided little opportunity for new development. For the next decade, investment in the revitalization of older centers is expected to equal or exceed the total contract value of new mall construction as aging centers demand upgrading. The profitability of many existing malls will depend on competitive re-positioning, revitalization, renovation, and expansion.

Changes in demographics and consumer demand, and a slowdown in population growth and household formation will continue to have an effect on the traditional retail landscape. In spite of recent government efforts to energize the economy, industry analysts predict that real growth in consumer spending for the first half of the decade will be negligible (averaging 1.5% annually). Disposable income is expected to increase more slowly and consumers are expected to save more. An aging population, particularly the baby boom generation, is expected to spend and borrow less (as a percent of income), and have less time to shop. The tremendous influx of women into the work force has further influenced

Research Associate Elizabeth H. McLoughlin prepared this case under the supervision of Adjunct Professor William J. Poorvu as the basis for class discussion rather than to illustrate either effective or ineffective handling of an administrative situation.

buying habits, and has reduced so-called "recreational" shopping time. The 1990 shopping center customer, for example, spent an average of 4 hours per month in malls, compared to 12 hours in 1980.[1] This, combined with a recessionary economy, will cause mall shop owners to compete for increasingly scarce time and dollars.

MALL DYNAMICS

Regional malls face unique competitive challenges as well. One of the biggest challenges to mall managers is keeping a high occupancy rate, particularly in the face of the escalating cost structure of most malls, the often uncertain health of the retail tenants, and a changing competitive climate.

New product types from strip centers to urban marketplaces compete for market share with conventional regional malls. In some markets, particularly smaller, less vibrant areas, malls are losing ground to free-standing retailers who offer both lower prices and convenient shopping, garnering a large share of the "destination" business. As discounters and off-price stores attract more consumer dollars, the market dominance by department store anchors (which have historically drawn traffic to the malls) can be threatened, particularly the business of mass merchants.

Department stores, whose strong credit and retailing muscle has historically "anchored" most malls, are experiencing problems of their own. The department store industry has undergone significant change in the last decade. The 1980s fueled investment interest in retail real estate, as sales and profitability forecasts followed a straight northeast path. An industry once dominated by developer owners has given way to ownership structures which include pension funds, other institutional investors, and partnership groups. Acquisitions and mergers in the department store sector often funded through increasingly onerous leverage have created a situation whereby merchandising decisions are often a function of the capital constraints of the parent company. Consolidated department store groups, sometimes owning several anchors at a given center, face enormous marketing challenges as consumers have difficulty differentiating competing merchandise offerings.

Finally, operating costs for many malls increased dramatically during the late 1980s. High acquisition prices resulted in inflated property assessments, which translated into major increases in tax bills. As real estate taxes and other expenses are typically passed through to tenants, these charges forced some specialty retailers to cut costs in other areas, or close altogether. Needless to say, for mall owners there is not only the possibility of lost rents, but the burden of assuming the tenants' pro rata share of operating costs and taxes.

JMB REALTY

JMB Realty Corporation, based in Chicago, is one of the largest full service real estate companies in the country. JMB began developing income properties in the mid-1970s, and, together with its affiliates, has since become one of the foremost developers and owners of shopping centers and other commercial property in the United States and Canada.

JMB Institutional Realty Corporation, formed in 1979, provides real estate investment advice and management for pension and profit sharing plans, trusts, endowments, foundations, and other tax exempt entities. JMB Institutional manages a portfolio of about $10 billion. JMB Realty, JMB Institutional, and their respective affiliated portfolios include approximately 79 million square feet of retail malls, 71 million square feet of office and industrial buildings, 19,400 units of residential apartments, 16 hotels containing 8,000 rooms and 79,500 acres of land held for development.

Throughout the 1980s JMB aggressively pursued retail acquisitions. By 1992, with 79,523,000 square feet of mall space under management, the firm was the dominant manager of shopping centers in North America.

Though, industry wide, real estate returns have eroded relative to those of other asset classes, the retail property segment has performed better than other real estate product types. From an investment standpoint, the total (income and capital) return on retail property has outperformed the overall Russell-NCREIF[2] index in every quarter since 1982 (see **Exhibit 1**). JMB was confident that its management strength, its development capacity, and its strong national presence would allow it to profitably operate its retail assets despite a recessionary climate.

---

1 MAS Marketing Survey, cited in *Emerging Trends in Real Estate 1992*, by Equitable Real Estate.
2 The Russell-NCREIF index is compiled quarterly by the National Council of Real Estate Investment Fiduciaries, a non-profit research organization, and the Frank Russell Company as part of its larger data base which tracks the performance of institutionally owned real estate over time.

Table A
Top Shopping Center Managers in North America

The Firm	Retail Square Footage Under Management
JMB Properties/Cadillac Fairview	79,523,000
Edward J. DeBartolo	74,929,093
Melvin Simon & Assoc.	70,320,907
General Growth Center Cos., Inc.	61,000,000
The Rouse Company	47,440,000
Jacobs, Visconsi & Jacobs, Co.	40,113,250
The Hahn Co.	35,056,400
The Cafaro Co.	33,395,306
Crown American Corp.	29,139,807
Leo Eisenberg Co.	26,731,070

Source: *Shopping Center World*, March, 1991, and *Canadian Directory of Shopping Centers*, 1991

THE INVESTMENT—NORTHRIDGE AND SOUTHRIDGE MALLS

An affiliate of JMB Institutional acquired the Northridge and Southridge Malls, both located in the greater Milwaukee area, for $225 million ($200 million in equity, and $25 million of debt) in April, 1988. JMB had assumed management of the two centers in the prior year and was attracted to the investment for several reasons. First, the centers had not been aggressively managed prior to JMB's takeover, and there was an opportunity to create value through lease-up, lease rollovers and selected physical improvements, including the additional of food courts and renovations of the interiors. The centers were the dominant regional shopping malls in a slow-growing, but stable, market and synergies were anticipated from the collective marketing and operation of the properties. Furthermore, 100% interests were being offered (a somewhat unusual circumstance), and the acquisition could occur outside of an auction environment, a setting which tended to inflate prices. The centers are two of the eight in the Milwaukee Metropolitan Statistical Area which are considered regional malls (see **Exhibits 2** and **3**). Both were built in the early 1970s as two-level super-regional centers.

The Northridge Mall has a total of 1.0 million square feet containing 142 specialty shops which surround an enclosed common area, with four anchors at the periphery—Boston Store, Sears, JCPenney, and Prange's. Southridge Mall is Wisconsin's largest shopping center—with 148 specialty stores, and four anchors—Boston Store, JCPenney, Prange's, and Sears, and an additional major tenant occupying 66,000 square feet of mall space—Kohl's Department Store. The gross leasable area at Southridge including the specialty retail shops and department store anchors approaches 1,300,000 square feet (see **Exhibit 5**). The approximate breakdown of space at both malls is as follows: [3]

	Northridge	Southridge
Specialty stores (sq. ft.)	398,415	443,800
Department stores (sq. ft.)	619,260	820,260
Total	1,017,675	1,264,060

3 JMB owned the space occupied by specialty store tenants, and the common areas. JMB had no ownership interest in the department store space, though it did have contractual operating and reciprocal easement agreements with each anchor.

Both Northridge and Southridge are considered to be solid, "meat and potatoes" centers, committed to maintaining a popularly priced tenant base. The malls are typically marketed together, using the blended marketing theme, "Nobody Offers You More" to express dominance in the market, and emphasize what is perceived to be their key strengths—selection, convenience, and value. As two of the largest regional malls in the greater Milwaukee area, Northridge and Southridge enjoy a competitive advantage in the variety of their stores, and the breadth of their merchandise offerings. Customer surveys show that consumers at both centers shop different categories of stores at price points across the board, a fact which JMB feels shows the range of taste at the malls, and the malls' ability to attract a diverse customer base. Further, it feels that the malls' positioning as family oriented shopping centers works singularly well in Milwaukee's conservative "value oriented" market.

THE MILWAUKEE CUSTOMER

Milwaukee is Wisconsin's largest city and the 17th largest in the nation. Its Metropolitan Statistical Area includes four counties and covers 1,462 square miles on the shore of Lake Michigan. The 1990 population of the MSA was 1,436,000, up a moderate 2.5% since 1980, and is expected to continue with slow growth through 1995. Compared to the rest of the United States, Milwaukee households are relatively affluent. Milwaukee's median household effective buying income is $5,000 higher than the Midwest median, and $2,000 higher than the U.S. median. (See **Exhibit 4** for trade area demographics.) Milwaukee shoppers, however, are typically described as middle of the road, value conscious consumers who emphasize the importance of quality at a price.

The compound annual growth rate of department store sales in the Milwaukee MSA during the late 1980s was less than a third of that of the U.S. average during that time. However, department store sales in both 1990 and the first four months of 1991 showed increases of close to 8% over prior periods.

MALL MANAGEMENT

At the time that JMB acquired Northridge and Southridge, occupancy rates ranged from 85–90%. It was expected that a well conceived renovation and upgrade program would bring vacancy rates down to more

Table B
Population Profile 1991

| | Milwaukee MSA (4 County)[a] | | | | | ADI[b] |
	Milwaukee County	Waukesha County	Washington County	Ozaukee County	Total MSA	Rest of ADI (6 counties)
Population	958,700	308,000	96,500	73,600	1,436,800	629,100
Households	372,800	107,200	33,400	26,000	539,400	228,700
Retail Sales(000s)	$ 7,359,491	$2,810,454	$ 554,372	$ 490,679	$ 11,214,996	$4,026,000
Effective Buying Income (000s)	$14,248,820	$5,755,035	$1,342,037	$1,283,918	$ 22,621,810	$8,743,260
EBI per household[c]	$ 38,200	$ 53,685	$ 40,181	$ 49,381	$ 45,361	$ 38,230

a Milwaukee MSA includes Milwaukee, Ozaukee, Washington and Waukesha counties.
b The ADI (Area of Dominant Influence) includes the Milwaukee MSA and 6 surrounding counties
c EBI (Effective Buying Income) = Household spendable income after taxes

Source: 1991 Survey of Buying Power Demographics U.S.A.
© Copyright 1991 Sales and Marketing Management Magazine

profitable levels and improve the product mix of the centers. (The average vacancy in U.S. enclosed malls was around 6.5% in 1990.) Additional growth in revenues was expected to come partially from real income growth, but more significantly from increased market share, extended reach (the trading area from which the mall draws customers) or improved productivity (defined as sales dollars per customer).

The first major capital expenditure for renovations was the addition of a food court at each center.[4] In other malls food courts had been a proven consumer draw, lengthening the amount of time shoppers spent at a mall, and increasing the amount of spending in other mall shops. And, in and of themselves, typical food court sales per square foot of GLA[5] pegged them as some of the most productive mall tenants. In November, 1988 the 450-seat Skyridge Cafe was opened on Northridge's upper level, in concert with the renovation of common areas which included new fountains, skylights, and improved mall entrances. (See **Exhibit 6** for food court sales figures.) Two mall anchors—Prange's and Sears—completed major renovations at Northridge in 1990 as well. At Southridge, in addition to major renovations to the center court atrium, a $3.7 million 33,000 square foot multi-tenant food court addition was added in 1990. The total cost of renovations at both malls was $10.8 million. By the end of 1990, combined mall net operating income to JMB was up 14.6% from 1989 levels, and occupancy rates had increased to 96% at Northridge and 97% at Southridge.

However, by late 1990 some problems had become apparent, particularly at the Northridge Mall, where sales had begun to decline. Management attributed the fall off in part to negative trends which were happening nationwide—the lack of population growth, uncertainty in the department store market, and consumer votes of no-confidence in the economy. Additionally, Northridge was plagued by a growing image problem, and a perception that it was a haven for groups of loitering teens. This was exacerbated by a change in municipal bus routes which placed Northridge squarely between a major high school and home, and the decline of the more urban Capitol Court center which had a fairly sizable share of the youth market. According to trade area surveys, the Northridge customer shopped more often at higher end—moderate to better—stores, but it was becoming difficult to attract these shoppers to the mall because of the perceived youth problem. As the mall increasingly became the focus for after school and weekend socializing for teens, store managers feared that these groups would drive other shoppers away. JMB management discovered that often, by late Saturday afternoon, groups of teens would constitute a major presence in the mall, and act as a damper to other center traffic.

A second problem confronting both malls was their escalating expense structures. Often, the sale of property triggers a revision in its assessed valuation; the acquisition of the malls at Northridge and Southridge was no different. The tremendous escalation in taxes which often ensues—passed through as an occupancy

Table C
Northridge and Southridge
Net Operating Income (in 000s)

	Actual 1989	Actual 1990	Actual 1991	Projected 1992
Northridge	$ 7,157	$ 8,547	$ 7,835	$ 8,490
Southridge	7,686	8,469	9,980	9,614
Total	$ 14,843	$ 17,016	$ 17,815	$ 18,104
Increase over Prior Year	5.2%	14.6%	4.7%	1.6%

4 A food court is a collection of vendor stalls arranged in arcade fashion around a shared eating space. A typical one million square foot mall might have 8–12 food vendors.

5 The gross leasable area (GLA) of the mall is the total floor area allocated for tenant use. Mall-owned GLA is differentiated from that occupied by anchor stores, which typically own their own space.

cost to tenants—can distort the expense structure for smaller tenants, sometimes making it difficult for enclosed malls to compete with free-standing stores or with less costly strip centers. It also can limit a center's ability to raise rents. Though specialty retail chains such as The Limited and The Gap also are affected by the increased tax expense, their size allows them to spread operating costs over a larger base of stores. In addition, chains like The Limited often own multiple stores under separate names in a single mall; thus, they are often able to negotiate favorable lease terms with mall managers to offset other rising costs.

According to the International Council of Shopping Centers, in 1991 average taxes per square foot of non-anchor center owned GLA in U.S. enclosed malls of 1,000,000+ square feet were approximately $3.00 per square foot, with mean operating expenses totalling $13.63 per square foot. Tenants at Northridge and Southridge paid cumulative charges of more than $20.00, driven in large part by the high taxes. By 1991, the breakdown of charges to tenants was as follows:

Table D
Average Cumulative Charges to Tenants (PSF)

CAM Charges [6]	4.54
Real Estate Taxes	11.02
Merchant Association	1.65
Marketing	2.50
Trash/utilities	0.50
Total	**20.21**
Average 1991 Market Rents	25.00
Total Cumulative Charges	**45.21**

Industry standards suggest a healthy percentage of costs to sales is in the 10–12% range, with anything over 18% a red flag for concern.

JMB felt that there were several management implications to the high occupancy costs at the centers. The firm was concerned with maintaining stability in the malls, both in terms of retaining current strong retail performers, and attracting a new tenant base. High fixed costs could inhibit JMB's ability to attract more "value-oriented" tenants to the mall. Demand for space was further shrunk by the pressure on retailers to conserve capital, and more timely distribution practices which led to lower inventory levels and less need for storage at individual stores. And, as the rental cost of real estate had increased more rapidly than the price of merchandise, there was pressure on existing tenants to downsize. For the leasing managers who approached decisions about tenant space needs as they would a giant jigsaw puzzle, the problems of re-configuring space were augmented by the structural constraints and unusual depth of most mall stores (almost 100'), which precluded too much downsizing without losing valuable frontage (see **Exhibit 5**).

From an income standpoint, JMB had a strong incentive to attract and maintain a tenant base which generated maximum foot traffic and sales per square foot. The profitability of JMB's investment was based on derived demand; rents paid by retail tenants were typically calculated as the greater of a predetermined base amount or a stated percentage of sales. JMB feared that as retailers sought to trim costs by measures which included leaner staffing, fewer frills, and most likely, less service, they would more closely resemble the increasingly prolific discounters who competed on a lower cost basis, and from whom they were trying to differentiate themselves.

COMPETITIVE STRATEGY

In 1989, JMB commissioned a series of customer exit surveys to help it better identify the trade area, market profile, shopper preferences, and the mall's performance relative to the local competition and other industry norms. JMB had identified some areas of improvement. It was found that at both malls the incidence of entering a department store and making a purchase was low relative to other regional centers. For example, 71% of Northridge customers entered a department store versus a JMB norm of 79% with, on average, 32% making a purchase (a conversion ratio of 45% versus a norm of 49%).[7] At Southridge all four department stores had a conversion ratio of 33% or lower, though Kohl's was the exception at 42%. Any department store with a conversion ratio below 40% is not considered a strong performer.

This translated into sales per square foot in the department stores which were below industry averages.

---

6 CAM, or common area maintenance charges, were assessed to tenants on a pro-rata basis based on square footage, and included all expense items related to maintenance of common spaces, excluding major capital expenditures.
7 A conversion ratio is the percentage of shoppers making a purchase divided by the percent entering the store.

Industry averages range from $150 to $200 per square foot for traditional department stores such as Boston Store or Prange's, and somewhat lower for mass merchants such as Sears or JCPenney. Fashion stores, on the other hand, like Nordstrom and Saks Fifth Avenue, achieve productivities in the $290–$400 per square foot range. At the Northridge Mall, total department store sales were approximately $75.3 million in 1990, and at the Southridge Mall, $100.9 million. The aggregate department store sales at Southridge were significantly higher than at Northridge; however, the extremely large size of the Southridge stores resulted in only moderately higher per square foot sales.

Although the department stores owned their own space and therefore paid no rent to mall owners, they contributed to CAM charges, and typically drew shoppers to the mall through their own promotions, advertising, and a strong consumer franchise. Whereas once the attraction of a strong anchor ensured the success of the center, JMB felt that it was increasingly the specialty stores which were driving profitability. Mall owners, locked into 10–15 year leases with anchor stores, were often faced with the fact that department stores which had negotiated profitable agreements with minimal contribution to CAM, or low base rents, were not the strong performers they had been in the past.

Part of the problem was attributable to ex-mall factors affecting individual department stores. Balance sheets bogged down by unprofitable divisions in other markets resulted in the filing for Chapter 11 protection by Boston Store's parent company, P.A. Bergner and Co., in August, 1991. Though management was confident that it could restructure its debt, and return the business to profitability, the company has not made needed renovations at many of its Milwaukee locations.

Prange's also was encountering problems with its Milwaukee operations. It had never been able to achieve the sales volume of the extremely profitable Gimbel's Department Store, which occupied the stores at both centers until 1986. Gimbel's had a strong name recognition in the area and a deliberately lean cost and management structure. Consumers in Milwaukee responded favorably to its orientation towards moderately priced merchandise and its aggressive promotional programs. A brief and unsuccessful takeover of the Gimbel's stores by Marshall Field's in 1986 (accompanying a divestiture of the Gimbel's chain by its parent company BATUS) caused sales to plummet dramatically, with the better business going to Boston Store, and the "price" traffic migrating to Kohl's. In February 1989, Prange's took over both stores, presumably hoping that a favorable acquisition price, and a strong promotional merchandising strategy would allow it to establish a new presence in Milwaukee, and regain the patronage of the Gimbel's customer. Unfortunately, the increasing strength of Kohl's, the difficulty of establishing an identity with only two stores in the Milwaukee area to share the promotional and advertising expenses necessary to achieve strong penetration in the market area, over-expansion by other divisions, and management turnover combined to put Prange's into an increasingly precarious position.

The two anchors with lower price points—JCPenney and Sears—were doing proportionally better with their programs of selling more moderately priced merchandise, particularly in apparel, than the traditional department stores. JCPenney is considered to be one of the largest U.S. department store chains with $16.2 billion of sales in 1991, and 1,312 stores. Sears was pegged as America's third largest retailer with 1991 corporate sales of $31.4 billion from its 868 department stores and other retail outlets.

Sales per square foot (mall wide) were somewhat higher at Southridge than at Northridge, attributable to several key factors. One was the presence of Kohl's Department Store as a major tenant, which in 1990–1991 averaged $270 in sales per square foot. Kohl's was a successful value oriented department store which offered the central checkout and the self-service emphasis typical of discount department stores. JMB executives thought that Kohl's Department Store was a strong draw to the more moderate income residents of the trading area. With 13 stores in the greater metropolitan area, Kohl's had the market presence to support a significant promotional campaign and out-advertise its competitors. Its weekly circulars drew shoppers both into its own stores, and into the mall. In an area where the consumer was known to be particularly value conscious, Kohl's deeper (close to 33%) discounts attracted a loyal following. As a major tenant in the mall (unlike an anchor), Kohl's was a significant rent payer, whose successes favorably impacted average per square foot sales mall wide (see **Exhibit 6**).

The "value sensitivity" of Milwaukee shoppers was clearly revealed by JMB's market research. Exit surveys of current shoppers showed that in both trading areas, households shopped most often at a discount/value store, such as Kohl's, Target, or Kmart. Traditional department stores, such as Boston Store or Prange's were

Table E
Department Store Shopped Most Often—1990

Type of Store	Exit Survey Southridge	Exit Survey Northridge	Telephone Survey Southridge	Telephone Survey Northridge
Discount/Value Oriented	**41%**	**36%**	**58%**	**45%**
Kohl's	25%	18%	27%	16
Target	9%	10%	17%	14
Kmart	7%	6%	11%	12
Chain Department Stores	**25%**	**29%**	**18%**	**17%**
JCPenney	12%	16%	9%	8
Sears	13%	13%	8%	9
Traditional Department Stores	**34%**	**33%**	**19%**	**26%**
Boston Store	28%	25%	14%	23
Prange's	6%	8%	5%	3
Better Stores	**1%**	**4%**	**1%**	**4%**
Marshall Field	1%	4%	1%	4

the next most frequently shopped, followed by the chain stores. In wider surveys conducted by phone to consumers throughout the respective trade areas, shoppers were found to prefer discount stores to department stores by an even greater margin, implying that reinforcing the centers' value oriented positioning would most effectively attract and retain a large customer base. Correspondingly, JMB's marketing programs began to focus on the centers' size and "value for the money."

JMB management was well aware of the strength of the discounters. Discount stores, on the operational end, typically have lean management groups, low overhead, and a multi-store national presence. An enormous store base allows them to invest in technological systems that greatly increase merchandising efficiency, and reduce operating costs. Database marketing programs, distribution systems, communication and inventory networks, and performance monitoring technology—all give these firms a competitive edge over many other department stores. National marketing economies and sourcing leverage with vendors further bolster gross margins. With the top ten discounters controlling 85% of discount sales in 1991, they were in a strong competitive position, particularly relative to the financially strapped department stores. JMB was aware that many industry analysts felt that the three strongest discounters—Target, Wal-Mart, Kmart—might eventually replace department store anchors in some markets. Each had a strong balance sheet and was aggressively expanding.

Table F

Discount Store	1991 Sales	Number of Stores
Wal-Mart	$43.9 billion	1,573
Kmart	$34.6 billion	2,205
Target	$ 9.0 billion	463

However, many at JMB felt strongly that a discounter would not fit in with the image at either mall. And, though the public appeared to want more value oriented stores, JMB was not convinced that mall-wide, there would be greater dollars flowing to the bottom line. Some felt that the more appropriate issues to focus on were; how could department stores provide what consumers were increasingly demanding—value, service, and convenience? Many at the firm felt that one of the critical tasks facing mall owners was how to maintain the health of the retailers. How could Prange's or other stores continue to operate profitably relative to the threat of discount stores? How would this affect the merchandising decisions at Northridge and Southridge? And most importantly, how would this decision affect the all-important rents of the mall stores?

THE SPECIFIC DILEMMA OF PRANGE'S

Simultaneously with its agreement to acquire the two locations from Marshall Field's at Northridge and Southridge in 1989, Prange's management sold the two buildings (approximately 370,000 square feet) to a local investor/developer for $15 million, taking back a 10-year lease at $4.00 per square foot. The investor, in turn, financed this acquisition with a short term bank note. Prange's also made an agreement with JMB management to complete major renovations at both stores, which it hoped to fund with profits from the building sale. Renovations were completed at Northridge in 1990, though by the spring of 1992, renovations at Southridge had yet to be planned.

In May 1992, the investor's short term bank note which had funded his acquisition of the Prange's space was soon to come due. Although Prange's could continue to operate by fulfilling its lease obligations, JMB felt that it was possible that the bank would call the investor's short term note, finding Prange's balance sheet insufficient collateral for extending its loan commitment. Should the investor be unable to repay the loan, the bank could foreclose on the property and become the sole owner.

Martha Matthews, responsible for negotiations with all anchors at the center, was becoming increasingly concerned with the possible ramifications of Prange's uncertain financial future. What were the added complications arising from third party ownership of the space? Typically, a department store directly owns or leases space in a shopping center, with the arrangement governed by an operating agreement between the mall owner and the retailer. These agreements ensure the owner or occupant of the department store easement rights to the parking and the common areas for access to its building, and ensures for all parties to the agreement that the center will be operated in a unified and consistent manner. The mall owner also executes with each anchor store separate lease or supplemental agreements (in the case of fee ownership by the retailer) which frequently provide the mall owner the right to approve transfer of ownership or assignment of the lease, or in the event of disapproval, provide the mall owner the option of buying the store (usually at the department store's unamortized cost). In this case, however, because of the sale/leaseback of the Prange's store, JMB had few contractual rights regarding approval of a replacement tenant.

In theory, Prange's had, in addition to the lease with the investor, a non-disturbance agreement with the bank which required it to honor Prange's lease in the event of a foreclosure. However, JMB had heard that Prange's might be in default of certain provisions of its lease obligations, which gave the owner or lender the right to terminate. Matthews wondered, if the bank foreclosed, would it allow Prange's to remain in the space, or would it look for a stronger tenant? If so, how would the situation impact the marketing of the center, particularly if the anchor went "dark"? JMB's contractual agreements were with the store—not the fee owner or the bank; what kind of leverage would JMB have in the selection of a new tenant for the space under the bank's stewardship? How could the terms of the reciprocal agreements affect its negotiating strategy?

One preemptive option Matthews had considered was to negotiate with Prange's for a buyout of its lease, or with the building owner for outright ownership of the space, which would give JMB more control over the successor tenant. Both Prange's and the investor had indicated a willingness to negotiate. Matthews had been told, however, that it would be difficult to financially justify putting additional dollars into the malls at this point.

An additional complication was the potential threat that Prange's itself might declare Chapter 11. Currently, operating covenants between Prange's, the other anchors, and JMB provided that all four department stores and JMB had approval rights over who could occupy the Prange's space. While theoretically these covenants would remain in effect throughout the bankruptcy proceedings, in a similar instance involving JMB, another judge had overruled these contractual agreements, and had allowed JMB to disapprove only those operators who were dissimilar to the stores currently anchoring the mall. Matthews was concerned that should Prange's go bankrupt, the court's sole interest would be to sell the lease to the highest bidder, although there was the possibility that the property could be purchased at auction at a lower price than could be negotiated with the current owner.

JMB's first priority was to identify alternative users for the space; one of its key considerations was the selection of an appropriate tenant. Though JMB might not be a part of the active negotiations, Matthews saw her role as that of creating a market, and demand for the space, which would hopefully lead to the best possible mix of retailers, thereby preserving and ensuring the value of JMB's investment.

Matthews had spoken with several prospective anchors, knowing that the anchor ultimately selected could affect existing anchors and specialty stores. What type of merchandiser would complement mall stores? How, for example, would adding a retailer with lower price points and/or a discount orientation change the mall's image? Would it ultimately create specialty store pressure for reduced rents? Could JMB expand the breadth of price points and product offerings in the mall, and thereby expand its customer base, and increase sales? Would power retailers in such categories as television and appliances, sporting goods, books, or records attract more customers to the centers than a more traditional department store?

Could the store design be modified to reflect changing market conditions i.e., the tendency of stores to want smaller space? What implications would each option have for the merchandise mix and financial performance of the center? How would each of the options affect JMB's future negotiations with other mall tenants?

MONTGOMERY WARD

One of the retailers whom JMB had approached was Montgomery Ward. Montgomery Ward was, in many respects, similar to Sears, offering similar merchandise at comparable price points. It had, however, floundered after World War II and had had difficulty regaining momentum. More recently, a management team had taken over in a leveraged buy-out, successfully slashed expenses, and modified the merchandising of the stores. Each store was typically about 90,000 square feet. While sales in stores open for more than a year had not been outstanding, Montgomery Ward had been solidly profitable.

Montgomery Ward had no stores in the Milwaukee area and had expressed a strong interest in the entire space occupied by Prange's in Northridge—165,200 square feet on two levels, plus one of the two floors of the Prange's space at Southridge, preferably the 100,000 square foot upper level. Montgomery Ward felt that it would do approximately $20 million in sales at each center, compared to estimates of Prange's current productivity which pegged sales at no more than $17 million. Up until now, the chain had not been in better centers and had catered to largely lower-middle to middle income households, and was not perceived as a particularly exciting retailer by some of Matthews' colleagues.

Montgomery Ward appeared willing to move quickly, however. As part of its strategy for penetrating the market, it had already negotiated to take over a Woolworth's in the Milwaukee area. Matthews knew that Prange's had been negotiating with Ward's for a buyout of its lease, though Prange's was reputed to be asking for an unreasonable amount of money. Aware that Prange's lease might be terminated, Matthews felt that there might be an opportunity for Montgomery Ward's to obtain better terms by dealing with the building owner directly. She wondered how JMB could facilitate a deal structure. Additionally, Montgomery Ward's proposal for space use still left the problem of the 100,000 square foot lower level at Southridge.

KOHL'S

Kohl's had expressed interest in moving from its current 66,000 square foot location in the Southridge Mall to one floor of the vacated Prange's space. Since Kohl's sales per square foot were one of the highest in the mall, the company felt that the move would provide the opportunity to expand into a more visible location, and to significantly increase sales by having a larger store. Kohl's had been doing close to $18 million in sales in 66,000 square feet, and expected to bump that up to at least $20 million in sales. Additionally, it hoped that more favorable lease terms or less burdensome common charges in the new space would further bolster profit margins.

The move, however, would present some financial disadvantages for JMB, because Kohl's space would have to be back-filled, and because it was currently a significant contributor to common area expenses and real estate taxes and a strong rent payer—albeit at a lower per square foot price than some of the other specialty stores. On the plus side, however, there was the possibility that should negotiations with Montgomery Ward not work out, Kohl's also might be persuaded to give up its present free-standing store near the Northridge Mall, and take at least one floor of the Prange's space there.

At Southridge, JMB had made it clear that Kohl's would have to find an acceptable retailer to whom it could assign its lease. Matthews was aware that, at least in part, the success of any such negotiations would depend on favorable lease terms. The high expense structure at the mall was a significant negotiating hurdle. She had met with Kohl's management to discuss a possible strategy. Would Kohl's commit to defray some of the expenses for the replacement store? What could JMB offer in the way of incentives, or concessions? How would that affect negotiations with other tenants in the mall? How pro-active should JMB be?

PHAR-MOR AND OTHER DISCOUNTERS

Should negotiations with Montgomery Ward not proceed as hoped, Matthews felt that the time might be right for bringing in non-traditional retailers to the mix of anchors. It was her belief that a mix of anchors offering different price points would draw a wider range of customers, and increase sales mall-wide. Kmart was beginning to garner a presence in some regional malls. Wal-Mart was another long-term tenant that had recently entered the Milwaukee market, although it basically wanted free-standing stores. Another retailer with whom JMB was talking was the Phar-Mor discount chain. Phar-Mor was a privately owned chain of deep discount drug stores which also carried selected items of food and general merchandise. Some merchandise was carried consistently, but most items were featured on an "in and out" basis at exceptionally good prices. It was expanding rapidly and was allegedly profitable. Phar-Mor was confident that it could generate close to $20 million in sales in 100,000 square feet.

Matthews foresaw at least two problems. First, the occupancy cost of the mall was significantly higher than many discounters typically paid. Secondly, very few discounters wanted more than one floor of space at either mall thus leaving the second floor vacant. This problem might be solved by allowing Prange's to remain on one floor at each location. Matthews thought that downsizing Prange's, and adding a new discount retailer might be a creative merchandising alternative, though it would not necessarily resolve Prange's operational or financial concerns.

OTHER DEPARTMENT STORES

Though several department stores had expressed tentative interest in entering the Milwaukee market, JMB felt that obtaining commitments from a strong department store anchor would not be an easy task. Industry studies had reported that it takes up to two years from first negotiations with a new anchor to store opening. Matthews felt that 2–4 years was more typical of actual situations. As well, she felt that the retailing challenges for any prospective tenant would be the same as those faced by Prange's—how to effectively compete with only two stores in the metropolitan area, and to generate sufficient store volume to justify advertising expenses and the enormous square footage occupied.

Dillard's, based in Little Rock, Arkansas, was known to be considering entering the Milwaukee market. Dillard's, operating primarily in the South, was considered by many to be the strongest traditional department store in the country in large part due to its advanced technological systems which enabled it to merchandise a large assortment of goods, and at the same time maintain an efficient cost structure. Unlike almost all other traditional department stores, Dillard's was aggressively championing an everyday low price (EDLP) policy. In recent years, Dillard's had far outdistanced most other traditional department stores in increases in both comparable store sales and sales per square foot. On average, however, Dillard's sales per square foot still trailed other traditional department store operations such as Dayton's, Macy's, and May department stores. It was rumored, however, that Dillard's was adopting a wait and see attitude with the Boston Store, which, with seven locations in greater Milwaukee, might be a better strategic target.

The Dayton Hudson Corporation owned several chains of department and discount department stores which represented possible tenants. In addition to Marshall Field's (which continued to operate stores in Milwaukee's downtown Grand Avenue Mall and Mayfair), it also operated Dayton's and Hudson's, traditional department stores in seven mid-western states. It also operated Target, an upscale discount department store chain which offered a broad assortment of hard lines and soft goods, and Mervyn's, a highly promotional department store which sold lower to moderately priced merchandise and featured apparel, accessories, and household soft goods. There were already seven Target stores in the Milwaukee metropolitan area, with trading areas which, in some cases, overlapped those of the Northridge and Southridge malls.

Other potential tenants for larger store spaces included Venture Shopco, and Yonkers Inc. Venture was a very successful upscale discount department store operation headquartered in St. Louis. Shopco was an equally successful, more hard goods oriented operation, headquartered in Minneapolis, that had concentrated on smaller community locations. Yonkers Inc. is a Des Moines-based, traditional department store that serves many smaller midwest markets, primarily Iowa, Nebraska, Minnesota, Illinois, and South Dakota. It currently has 29 stores, which generated $330 million in sales in 1991.

A final category of retailers under consideration were electronic and appliance superstores such as Circuit City. Such stores typically occupy 30,000–40,000 square feet. Circuit City was aggressively expanding and had already entered the St. Louis and Chicago markets. Might Circuit City or another superstore operation already in Milwaukee be interested in the space?

SUMMARY

Rumors of the uncertainty of Prange's future were beginning to circulate throughout the industry, making the decision to identify a replacement more urgent. JMB was already encountering some leasing resistance on the part of prospective specialty retailers, who, before making a commitment to specific locations within the centers, wanted assurances as to the anchor store alignment and ongoing operations. These prospects were unwilling to risk the cost of building, staffing, and stocking a new store in a center with an uncertain anchor base.

JMB, on behalf of its investors, had capitalized effectively on most of the opportunities anticipated with the mall acquisitions. Through improved leasing and physical improvements, the centers had realized substantial increases in NOI, despite an increasingly difficult retail environment. On a broader level, however, JMB now faced merchandising issues that were confronting mall owners around the country. How could they maintain or continue to attract new tenants? Would a changing set of economics force them to become more price oriented? How could malls maintain their viability in the face of strong new competition? How is the role of the owner/developer/manager changing? JMB felt a strong responsibility to its investors to maximize long term returns, and did not want to overreact to what might be short term economic pressures. Still, retailing is a dynamic industry where adaptability is crucial.

Exhibit 1
Real Estate Returns by Property Type

Year	Office	Retail	Warehouse/Industrial	Total
1978	21.2%	10.9%	14.3%	16.1%
1979	19.6	12.3	20.4	20.7
1980	26.0	12.8	16.2	18.1
1981	20.9	11.0	15.2	16.9
1982	9.9	7.0	9.0	9.4
1983	12.3	15.1	10.8	13.3
1984	12.1	16.2	12.4	13.0
1985	8.8	11.9	12.5	10.0
1986	4.2	11.4	8.6	6.5
1987	5.6	11.4	11.5	5.4
1988	2.9	13.4	10.2	7.0
1989	3.2	10.3	10.2	5.8
1990	−2.5	6.0	2.7	1.6
5-Year Average 1986–1990	1.6	10.5	8.6	5.2
13-Year Average 1978–1990	10.4	11.5	11.8	10.9

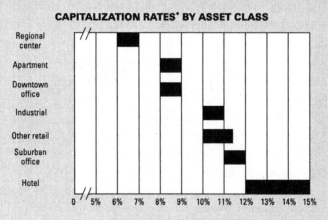

CAPITALIZATION RATES* BY ASSET CLASS

* Ranges represent the most likely rates for premium properties.

Exhibit 2
Major MSA Shopping Centers

Shopping Center		Total Square Footage	# of Stores	# Parking Spaces	Anchor Store	Anchor GLA
Northridge Mall	1972 1989 (R)	1,017,675	142	7,500	Boston Store Sears JCPenney Prange's	152,730 148,110 153,220 165,200
Bay Shore	1954 1987 (E)	552,000	90	2,000	Boston Store Sears	137,000 89,000
Capitol Court	1956 1978 (E/R)	780,000	85	4,600	Target	n/a
Mayfair Mall	1958 1986 (E/R)	1,046,000	160	7,167	Marshall Field's Boston Store	290,000 156,000
The Grand Avenue	1982	845,000	160	1,350	Marshall Field's Boston Store	290,000 250,000
Brookfield Square	1967 1991 (E/R)	884,000	95	4,700	Boston Store Sears JCPenney	221,000 228,000 202,800
Southgate Mall	1951 1971 (E) 1985 (R)	421,200	54	1,997	Boston Store Woolworth's	196,000 47,233
Southridge Mall	1970 1990 (R)	1,264,060	148	7,223	Boston Store Prange's Kohl's JCPenney Sears	219,400 210,280 66,000 175,880 214,700

Note: E/R is the date of Expansion/Renovation

Source: Top Shopping Centers, 1991, Updated 2/1992, and company information

Milwaukee Metro Area Retail Chains

Major Department and Fashion Stores	Major Discount Stores	Major Food Stores
Boston Store (7,7)	Kmart (13)	Cub Foods
JCPenney (6,3)	Shopko (2)	Kohl's
Kohl's (13,1)	Target (7)	Pick'N Save
Marshall Field's (2,2)	Sam's Wholesale Club (5)	Piggly Wiggly
Prange's (2,2)	Wal-mart (6)	Sentry
Sears (5,4)		Town and Country

Note: Numbers in parentheses refer to the number of area stores for each chain followed by the number of regional mall stores.

Source: Automated Marketing Systems, Inc. 1991, Top Shopping Centers

Exhibit 3
Major Competitive Centers and Trade Area Profile

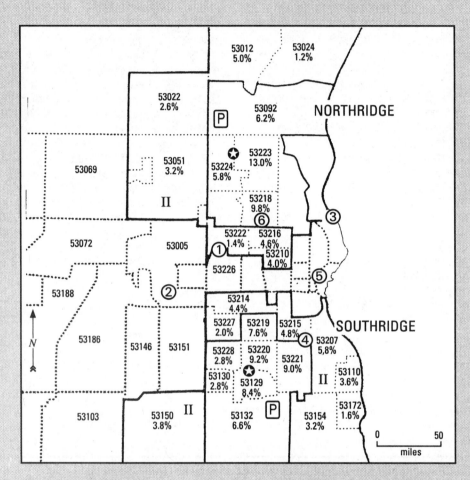

53012 5.0%
53024 1.2%
53022 2.6%
53092 6.2%
NORTHRIDGE
53069
53051 3.2%
53223 13.0%
53224 5.8%
II
53218 9.8%
⑥
53222 1.4%
53216 4.6%
①
53072
53005
53210 4.0%
53226
③
53188
②
⑤
53214 4.4%
SOUTHRIDGE
53227 2.0%
53219 7.6%
53215 4.8%
④
53207 5.8%
53186
53146
53151
53228 2.8%
53220 9.2%
53221 9.0%
II
53110 3.6%
53130 2.8%
53129 8.4%
53103
53150 3.8%
II
53132 6.6%
53154 3.2%
53172 1.6%

N

0   50
miles

⊛ SOUTHRIDGE MALL

⊛ NORTHRIDGE MALL

P PRIMARY TRADING AREA

II SECONDARY TRADING AREA

% PERCENT OF INTERVIEWS

○ MAJOR COMPETITIVE CENTERS

1. Mayfair Mall
2. Brookfield Mall
3. Bay Shore Shopping Center
4. Southgate Mall
5. The Grand Avenue
6. Capitol Court

Exhibit 4
Trade Area Demographics

	Northridge Total Trade Area	Southridge Total Trade Area	Milwaukee MSA [1]	United States
NORTHRIDGE VS. SOUTHRIDGE				
Population				
1996	386,062	387,295	1,474,040	263,148,992
1991	379,712	385,685	1,439,264	251,139,808
1980	372,853	386,292	1,397,143	226,545,856
% Change 1991–96	0.3%	0.1%	0.5%	0.9%
% Change 1980–91	0.2%	0.0%	0.3%	0.9%
Households				
1996	150,661	160,246	574,178	100,503,872
1991	144,306	155,785	545,335	93,665,984
1980	134,103	143,226	500,684	80,389,688
% Change 1991–96	0.9%	0.6%	1.0%	1.4%
% Change 1980–91	0.7%	0.8%	0.8%	1.4%
Income				
Average HH Income, 1991	$44,349	$36,868	$40,242	$38,413
% 50,000+	33.1%	24.6%	28.7%	26.1%
% 35,000+	55.5%	48.3%	50.6%	44.2%
% Professional/Managerial	24.0%	17.8%	22.2%	22.7%
% College Graduate	19.4%	11.3%	17.1%	16.2%
Average Age	36.5	37.5	35.6	35.6
Females Working				
% Females w/Child under 18	60.9%	58.5%	57.9%	55.3%
Population by Race & Spanish Origin				
White	84.4%	98.1%	87.0%	83.2%
Black	14.1%	0.3%	10.8%	11.7%
American Indian	0.3%	0.5%	0.5%	0.6%
Asian Pacific Islander	0.6%	0.5%	0.6%	1.6%
Other Races	0.6%	0.7%	1.2%	3.0%
Spanish Origin	1.1%	1.9%	2.5%	6.5%
Housing				
% Owner Occupied	65.6%	63.1%	60.1%	64.4%
% Single Unit	74.5%	70.0%	69.4%	71.1%

1 The Milwaukee MSA includes Milwaukee, Ozaukee, Washington and Waukesha Counties.

Source: Equifax Marketing Decision Systems.

Exhibit 5
The Northridge Mall

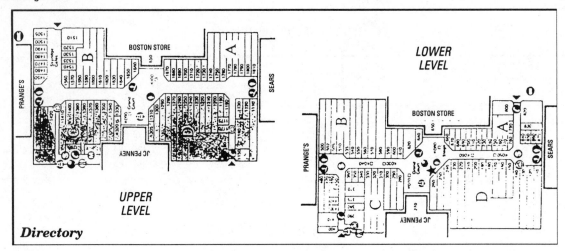

Directory

Women's Fashions

Lower Level		Upper Level	
B620	Au Coton	B1590	American Eagle Outfitters
B535	Designs-Levi Strauss & Co.	D1420	Caren Charles
C330	Eddie Bauer	C1390	Contempo Casuals
D200	Foxmoor	D1300	County Seat
A760	The Gap	A1810	Deb Shop
C300	Jay Jacobs	C1360	Express
D220	Jean Nicole	A1780	Frederick's of Hollywood
B500	Lane Bryant	B1580	Gantos
D130	The Avenue	C1410	Id
	(Lerner Woman)	B1600	Madison's
B570	The Limited	A1770	Marianne
C290	Paul Harris	C1340	Merry Go Round
A750	Petite Sophisticate	D1150	Motherhood Maternity
B502	Richman Brothers	C1400	Networks
B540	Ups 'N' Downs	D1290	Womans World Shops
D250	Victoria's Secret		
D230	Wilsons Suede & Leather		
	(Bermans)		

Men's Fashions

Lower Level		Upper Level	
D180	Attivo	B1590	American Eagle Outfitters
A720	Chess King	B1270	Bachrachs
B535	Designs-Levi Strauss & Co.	D1300	County Seat
A850	Desmond's Formal Wear	C1360	Express (Structure)
C330	Eddie Bauer	D1170	Gingiss Formalwear
A760	The Gap	C1370	Jay Jacobs
B590	Oak Tree	C1350	J. Riggings
B502	Richman Brothers	A1730	Merle Harmon's Fan Fair
D230	Wilsons Suede &	C1340	Merry Go Round
	Leather (Bermans)	B1620	Webster Men's Wear

Children's Shoes

Lower Level		Upper Level	
C310	Foot Locker	D1260	Kinney Shoes
A710	Stride Rite Shoes		
A740	Thom McAn		

Food Specialties

Lower Level		Upper Level	
C450	Fanny Farmer	D1190	Buddy Squirrel Nut Shop
C470	General Nutrition Center	B1640	Original Cookie Co.
A840	Mrs. Field's Cookies		
A680	Quality Candy		

Restaurants

Lower Level	Upper Level
A820 Ponderosa	Corn Dog on A Stick
	Freshen's Yogurt
	Gyro Wrap
Upper Level	1 Potato 2
Boston Store Garden	Sbarro Italian Eatery
Skyridge Cafe's	Subway Subs
A&W Hot Dogs & More	Taco Bell
Chick-fil-A	Wong's Wok
Cinnabon	

Home Furnishings & Gifts

Lower Level		Upper Level	
A790	Aftaire (Gift Warehouse)	C1430	Arcadia
D240	Amy's Hallmark	D1305	AT&T Phone Center
B580	Ashbys	C1440	Everything's $1.00
C460	Legacy Shop	D1180	Expressly Portraits
A770	Milwaukee Music Box	A1690	Prints Plus
C375	Oriental Art	D1740	Spencer Gifts
A700	Things Remembered	D1760	This End Up Furniture Co.
		A1720	Wicks 'N' Sticks

Women's Accessories

Lower Level		Upper Level	
D260	Accessory Place	A1680	Afterthoughts
A790	Aftaire (Gift Warehouse)	A1710	Claire's Boutique
B550	Bejeweled	K090	Earring Tree

Women's Shoes

Lower Level		Upper Level	
B610	Bakers Shoes	B1660	Cobbie Shop
A670	Connie Shoes	C1330	Joyce Selby
C310	Foot Locker	D1260	Kinney Shoes
C480	Payless Shoe Source	B1630	Naturalizer
A740	Thom McAn	B1570	9 West

Men's Shoes

Lower Level		Upper Level	
C310	Foot Locker	D1260	Kinney Shoes
A780	Jarman Shoes		
A690	M/K Florsheim Shoes		
C480	Payless Shoe Source		
A740	Thom McAn		

Jewelry

Lower Level		Upper Level	
D260	Accessory Place	A1680	Afterthoughts
A790	Aftaire (Gift Warehouse)	B1650	Bailey Banks & Biddle
B550	Bejeweled	A1710	Claire's Boutiques
B600	Fox's Jewelers	K090	Earring Tree
A660	Merkaamer Jewelers	D1310	J.B. Robinson Jewelers
C375	Oriental Art	D1130	Rogers & Hollands Jewelers
B510	Osterman Jewelers	B1560	Shaw's Jewelers
K030	Time Square	A1670	Zales Jewelers

Beauty & Health

Lower Level		Upper Level	
C470	General Nutrition Center	D1120	Mr. Dino's (Hair Stylists)
A870	Regis Hair Stylists		
C400	House of Fashion/Best Cuts		
C350	Merle Norman Cosmetics		
A830	Trade Secret Beauty Products		

Children's Fashions

Lower Level		Upper Level	
D110	Children's Place	A1810	Deb Shop
B535	Designs-Levi Strauss & Co.	A1770	Marianne
		A1730	Merle Harmon's Fan Fair

Books, Cards, Stationery

Lower Level		Upper Level	
D240	Amy's Hallmark	C1430	Arcadia
B505	B. Dalton Booksellers	A1740	Spencer Gifts
		D1110	Waldenbooks

Music, Electronics & Photography

Lower Level		Upper Level	
D1200	Black's Photography	A1750	Babbages
K080	Captron/Nintendo	D1210	Radio Shack
D160	Musicland	D1220	Sam Goody
C370	One Hour Photo	C1380	Suncoast Motion Picture CO.
		B1610	Tape World

Sports, Specialties

Lower Level		Upper Level	
C330	Eddie Bauer	B1590	American Eagle Outfitters
C310	Foot Locker	A1800	Herman's Sporting Goods
K070	Sunglass Hut	A1730	Merle Harmon's Fan Fair

Drug, Variety, Tobacco

Lower Level	
C320	Walgreens

Toys & Hobbies

Upper Level	
D1250	Kay-Bee Toy & Hobby

Services

Lower Level		Upper Level	
D1200	Black's Photography	D1305	AT&T Phone Center
C380	Bob Cook's Vagabond Travel	C1320	D.O.C. Optical
A860	Crystal Gardens Florist	C1395	Lein Spiegelhoff
A870	Regis Hair Stylists	D1120	Mr. Dino's (Hair Stylists)
C400	House of Fashion/Best Cuts		
C430	M & I Bank		
C350	Merle Norman Cosmetics		
A800	Mutual Savings		
C370	One Hour Photo		
C440	Shoe Fixers		
D120	Stein Optical		
D150	Sterling Optical		
K070	Sunglass Hut		
A830	Trade Secret		

Entertainment

Lower Level		Upper Level	
D140	Northridge Movies 1,2, & 3	D1160	Northridge Movies 4,5, & 6
C410	Time Out Amusements		

Exhibit 5, continued
The Southridge Mall

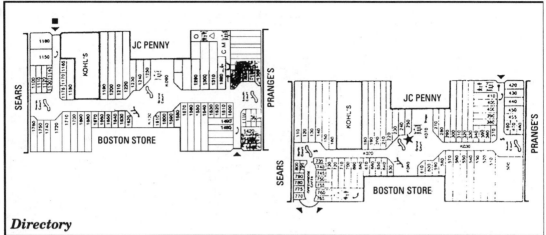

Directory

Department Stores

620	Boston Store	490	Prange's
260	JCPenney	100	Sear's
170	Kohl's Department Store		

Women's Fashions

1300	American Eagle Outfitters	280	Id
1570	Au Coton	300	Jay Jacobs
1120	August Max Woman	1320	Lane Bryant
310	Brooks	1220	Lerner of New York
220	Caren Charles	540	Limited, The
210	Casual Corner	1560	Madison's
1280	Contempo Casuals	1210	Marianne
120	County Seat	570	Merry Go Round
1310	Deb	440	Motherhood Maternity
1220	Designs Exclusively Levi	510	Paul Harris
1540	Express	600	Petite Sophisticate
1600	5-7-9	1390	Richman Brothers
520	Florence Tanners	680	Susie's
1720	Frederick's of Hollywood	140	Wilson's
1330	Gantos	290	Woman's World Shops
1210	Gap, The		

Men's Fashions

1300	American Eagle Outfitters	1210	Gap, The
1290	Bachrachs	1430	Gingiss Formalwear
690	Chess King	560	J. Riggings
240	Coda	730	Merle Harmon's Fan Fair
120	County Seat	570	Merry Go Round
530	DJ's Fashion Center	650	Oaktree
1220	Designs Exclusively Levi	1390	Richman Brothers
390	Desmonds Formal Wear	150	Webster Men's Wear
520	Florence Tanners	140	Wilsons

Children's Apparel & Shoes

1190	Children's Place	1100	Payless Shoe Source
1220	Designs Exclusively Levi	1165	Stride Rite
1180	Foot Locker	200	Thom McAn
1200	Kinney Shoes		

Women's Shoes

1580	Baker's Qualicraft Shoes	1200	Kinney Shoes
640	Cobbie Shop	1510	Naturalizer
1270	Connie Shoes	1100	Payless Shoe Source
1180	Foot Locker	200	Thom McAn
1650	Joyce-Selby Shoes		

Men's Shoes

660	Father and Son	1100	Payless Shoe Source
1180	Foot Locker	200	Thom McAn
1200	Kinney Shoes		

Fine Jewelry

270	Fox's Jewelers	1740	Osterman Jewelers
1175	JB Robinson Jewelers	460	Rogers and Hollands
1620	Merksamer Jewelers	630	Shaw's Jewelers

Restaurants

380	Arby's	1160	McDonald's
500	Harvest House Coffee Shop	1450	Ruby Tuesday

Food Specialties

1130	Buddy Squirrel's Nut Shop	350	Mrs. Fields Cookies
1590	Confectionery	450	Nutrition World
1500	Fannie May Candies	735	Original Cookie Company
1520	General Nutrition Center	250	Quality Candy
1640	Gloria Jean's Coffee Bean		

Home Furnishings

330	Ashbys	1395	Legacy Shop
1260	AT&T Phone Center	1170	Pagoda Imports
610	Bombay Company, The	1630	Prints Plus
1240	Carlton Cards	670	Things Remembered
130	Gourmet Center, The	1700	Wicks 'N' Sticks

Books, Cards & Gifts

580	Arcadia	590	Lang Collections
1340	B. Dalton Bookseller	1550	Suncoast Motion Picture Co.
230	Barbara's Hallmark	800	Toonville
1240	Carlton Cards	190	Waldenbooks
1660	Crazy about Cars		

Music, Electronics & Photography

1260	AT&T Phone Center	1690	Musicland
1680	Babbage's	160	Radio Shack
1410	Ritz Camera Center	710	Sam Goody
K080	Captron - World of Nintendo	1550	Suncoast Motion Picture Co.
360	Expressly Portraits		
455	Mike Cirvello's Cameras		

Sport Specialties

1300	American Eagle Outfitters	1760	Herman's World of Sporting Goods
1180	Foot Locker		
		730	Merle Harmon's Fan Fair

Toy's, Hobbies & Pets

K080	Captron - World of Nintendo	550	Kay Bee Toys

Drugs & Variety

1360	Everything's $1.00	500	Woolworth
320	Walgreens		

Entertainment

1150	Time Out Amusements

Finances and Services

1325	Lein/Spiegelhoff	$	TYME Machine - North
1440	M & I Bank	$	TYME Machine - South
480	Mutual Savings	1460	Vagabond Travel
1420	Shoe Fixers		

Jewelry and Accessories

1530	Afterthoughts Boutique	1140	Gifts Plus
340	Claire's Boutique	K030	Time Square Watch Shop
K090	Earring Tree, The		

Beauty, Health & Hair Styling

420	Barber, The	1110	Merle Norman Cosmetics
1520	General Nutrition Center	450	Nutrition World
1470	Hair Care Harmony	1480	Trade Secret
410	House of Fashion		

Optical

1350	DOC Optical	
180	Stein Optical	
720	Sterling Optical	
K070	Sunglass Hut	

Customer Service Symbols

Telephones . . . . . 📞

Security . . . . S

Lockers . . . . 🔑

Restrooms . . . . 🚻

Drinking Fountains . . . . △

Stairs . . . .

Escalators . . . .

Elevators . . . .

TYME Machine . . . . $

Marketing Office . . . . M

Mall Office . . . . O

Community Room C

Access Door for Handicapped . . . . ♿

★

Customer Service Center

Information

Stroller Rental/Wheelchair

Gift Certificates

Exhibit 6
Tenant Mix Analysis Based on GLA June 1990–June 1991

Southridge Mall					
Category	# of Stores	Square Feet	% Total GLA[2]	% of Sales[2]	$ Total Sales[3]
Food Specialty	8	7,023	2.7	3.7	2,510,005
Food Services (Restaurants)	1	3,620	1.4	1.1	726,311
Food Court[1]	0	0	0.0	0.0	0
Clothing	31	115,747	44.2	41.4	27,757,856
Shoes	9	17,873	6.8	6.5	4,388,342
Home Furnishings	3	7,242	2.8	1.3	896,127
Appliances/Music	3	8,836	3.4	4.0	2,682,744
Hobby	4	17,010	6.5	6.6	4,439,844
Gifts/Specialty	8	21,318	8.1	9.6	6,466,479
Jewelry/Cosmetics	9	9,318	3.6	13.0	8,690,062
Drugs	2	11,633	4.4	4.5	3,045,641
Other	3	3,162	1.2	2.2	1,494,175
Personal Services	5	6,452	2.5	2.9	1,962,640
Recreation	1	3,000	1.1	0.5	309,625
Financial	2	5,129	2.0	n/a	n/a
Offices	2	2,136	0.8	n/a	n/a
General Merch.	1	22,546	8.6	2.8	1,707,115
Total (excluding Kohl's)	92	262,045	100	100	67,076,966
Kohl's Department Store		66,002	18.4	20.2	17,846,583
Total		**328,047**			**84,923,549**

1 Food court tenants are non-comparable until November 1991.
2 Excluding Kohl's Department Store
3 Comparable sales reflect the performance of stores in operation for at least the prior 24 mos.

Northridge Mall					
Category	# of Stores	Square Feet	% Total GLA	% of Sales	$ Total Sales
Food Specialty	5	4,375	1.4	2.0	1,288,326
Food Services	1	5,900	1.9	0.7	466,780
Food Court[4]	8	4,610	1.5	4.5	2,871,976
Clothing	36	157,018	51.3	43.7	27,889,788
Shoes	10	21,541	7.0	6.4	4,102,602
Home Furnishings	2	2,325	0.8	0.7	446,199
Appliances/Music	5	12,709	4.2	4.3	2,735,837
Hobby	4	13,030	4.3	5.7	3,629,054
Gifts/Specialty	8	18,923	6.2	6.7	4,298,209
Jewelry/Cosmetics	8	17,097	5.6	14.7	9,367,535
Drugs	2	10,526	3.4	4.0	2,534,137
Other	2	2,889	0.9	1.5	969,098
Personal Services	7	8,483	2.8	2.5	1,594,575
Recreation	1	3,028	1.0	0.5	293,687
Financial	2	3,914	1.3	n/a	n/a
Offices	2	2,322	0.8	n/a	n/a
General Merch.	1	17,407	5.7	2.1	1,367,422
Total	**104**	**306,097**	**100**	**100**	**63,855,225**

4 Food court square footage included only vendor stalls; common seating area was not included.

Source: Comparable Sales Rolling 12 month report, June 1991, JMB Retail Properties Co.

Exhibit 7
Profile of Competition—Northridge

Shopping Center	# of Stores	Total Footage	Location	Distance	Anchor/Lead Stores	Market Position
Mayfair	160	1,046,000	Wauwautosa	10 m.	Marshall Field's, Boston Store	Fashion Upscale
Bay Shore	85	500,592	Glendale	7 m.	Boston Store, Sears	Regional/Traditional
Brookfield Square	95	1,008,000	Brookfield	14 m.	Sears, Boston Store, JC Penney	Regional/Traditional
The Grand Avenue	160	845,000	Milwaukee	13 m.	Marshall Field's, Boston Store	Fashion/Specialty
Pavillion At Mequon	70+	211,000	Mequon	6 m.	Kohl's Emporium, Mequon Serv-U Warehouse Shoes, Porters of Rac	Convenience/Specialty
Northwest Fashion	18+	123,290	Milwaukee	.25 m.	F & M, Marshalls	Value Oriented
American Plaza	3		Milwaukee	2 m.	Land's End, Warehouse Shoes, American of Madison	Discount Center
Northridge Plaza	22	137,000	Milwaukee	.25 m.	Kohl's Food Store	Convenience
Highland Plaza	15	78,000	Milwaukee	Perimeter	Kids R Us, Lenscrafters, Office Depot	Discount Center
Northpoint Plaza	8	10,000	Milwaukee	Perimeter	Children's Palace, Bartz, USA Baby	Neighborhood/Strip
Unnamed Plaza	8	50,000	Milwaukee	1.5 m.	Blockbuster Video, Kinko's, Radio Shack	Neighborhood/Strip
Brown Deer Center	20+		Milwaukee	2 m.	Country Buffet, Groundwater	Community
West Bend Outlet	30	45,000	West Bend	20 m.	Outlet stores	Outlet Center
Paradise Mall	22		West Bend	20 m.	Kohl's, JCPenney, Shopko	Community/Regional
Gurnee Mills	240	2,200,000	Gurnee	63 m.	10 Anchors, Outlet stores	Mega Mall/Outlet

Shopping Center	# of Stores	Total Footage	Location	Distance	Anchor/Lead Stores	Market Position
Brookfield Square	95	1,000,000	Brookfield	12 m.	Sears, JCPenney, Boston Store	Regional/Traditional
The Grand Avenue	160	845,000	Milwaukee	12 m.	Marshall Field's, Boston Store	Fashion/Specialty
Greenfield Fashion Center	35	187,000	Greenfield	.25 m.	Marshalls, F & M, Fashionation Lenscrafters, Old Country Buffet	Value Oriented
Fashion Outlet Center	110	338,000	Kenosha	34 m.	Kids R Us	Outlet Center
Lakeside Market Center	60	153,000	Kenosha	35 m.	Liz Claiborne, other designers	Designer Outlet
Mayfair Mall	160	1,046,000	Wauwautosa	11 m.	Marshall Field's, Boston Store	Fashion/Upscale
Regency Mall	110	960,000	Racine	24 m.	Target, JCPenney, Sears Boston Store, Prange's	Regional/Traditional
Southgate Mall	54	421,000	Milwaukee	5 m.	Woolworth's, Boston Store	Community/Regional
Spring Mall	23	230,000	Milwaukee	1.5 m.	Movie Theatre, Walgreen's T.J. Maxx, Pick n Save	Neighborhood/Strip
Gurnee Mills	240	2,200,000	Gurnee	43 m.	Outlet stores	Mega Mall/Outlet

Source: JMB Retail Properties Co.

EXPANSION STRATEGIES

Typically a retail business starts out with one store, often in the owner's home town. After early difficulties, fine-tuning the concept, the business takes off and the thought then naturally arises as to whether the concept could be expanded, eventually across the USA, and ultimately to the rest of the world. Here we lay out some issues that need to be thought through before a roll out occurs.

APPRAISING THE ORIGINAL BUSINESS

The first step should be to examine the fundamental premise behind the thoughts of expansion, namely that the current business is a success. An owner-run start-up store may appear profitable but only because the owner-manager is not drawing out a salary that a professional manager might require (the owner is "leaving the equity in the business"). More subtly, the sales revenue may be increased due to a loyalty by local consumers that can be attributed to the larger societal efforts of the owner. Perhaps the owner has a sweetheart deal on a lease that has never been renegotiated or in some other way the business does not bear the true "market" expense of operations. In short, the business must be evaluated independently of idiosyncratic initial conditions.

Even with a fair appraisal of the business in hand there is a second, more general issue to be considered. It is quite likely that a given concept will achieve different successes in different locations. If two people were by coincidence to open the identical concept in two different towns, they would have different experiences. However it is the owner of the more successful of the two who would be motivated to roll out the concept. This person is necessarily going to have a more optimistic impression of the venture's likely prospects. The moral is that one should always recognize that site-specific luck is a component in any business and this will not carry over to subsequent sites.

Finally, and on a similar theme, an important element in the success of a roll out is that the fundamental reasons for the success of the original store be understood. Is it the selection, is it the location, is it a fortuitous synergy between the concept and unusual demographic conditions?

PERFECTING THE CONCEPT

Opening the second store can be an acid test of the viability of the concept. But possibly not. To the extent that the new site shares synergies with the existing store (same neighborhood, same landlord, half of the owner's direct management time) the second site may not provide a true test of the independent viability of the concept.

Professor David E. Bell prepared this note as the basis for class discussion rather than to illustrate either effective or ineffective handling of an administrative situation.

Copyright© 1994 by the President and Fellows of Harvard College.
Harvard Business School case 595-005.

A true test would be the ability of the store to go to a second, entirely different location and be successful. Somewhere where the owner is not conversant at first hand with the intricacies of local real estate and their players, somewhere where the owner cannot rely on his/her clout with local regulators.

DANGER OF PREEMPTION

Despite all of these cautions about perfecting the concept, a very real danger for the owner with a good concept is that a competitor will copy the idea and roll it out first. The competitor may have advantages in this regard, say for example spare capital or unused retail sites. It is no consolation if the competitor is unable to implement the strategy successfully, for it may nevertheless serve to reduce the impact and viability of the original chain.

HOW TO EXPAND

There are three major components of the expansion strategy: geographic strategy, ownership strategy and rate of expansion.

Cluster v Flagship

One geographic strategy calls for the second store to be as close to the first without creating undue cannibalization of customers. The third is opened in a similar manner until the chain gradually creeps across the country. The advantages of this strategy are several. Organizationally, not only can the owner divide his/her time more easily among the different outlets, but the same applies to other employees. Managers can be moved from store to store without the considerable inconvenience and expense of relocation. Training is easier for this reason. Advertising can benefit from the economies of scale from operating in a single media market. Word of mouth from contented customers will not be wasted on people who have no access to a store. Finally there will be economies of scale in distribution. A warehouse can be built to serve the cluster of stores, or a wholesaler will find it easier to deliver to 10 stores in a limited region.

A second geographic strategy calls for a store in each major metropolis. The first store, say in New York City, is followed by one in Los Angeles, then Chicago and so on. Two principal advantages are (i) there is some geographic diversification of risk; an economic downturn in Georgia could bankrupt a retailer who had begun rolling out a new concept there. (ii) Assuming the concept will roll out across the country and if the store has special siting needs, it makes sense to lock up leases on good sites in major markets early.

An important third geographic strategy is an amalgam of these two primary approaches—jump and back fill. The idea here is to practice creeping incrementalism for a while but then jump to a second flagship location and then back fill by opening stores as needed between the original region and the new flagship. For example, one might start in Boston and expand out to a radius of 30 miles but then jump to New York City, back filling in Connecticut and Rhode Island at a later time.

Ownership Strategy

It is an expensive proposition to build up your chain to 100 stores if all the while you are paying for the building of stores, their fixtures and the necessary warehouse infrastructure. If the company is not sufficiently well capitalized, leasing retail stores is the first step to overcoming this hurdle. Since most retail leases involve a substantial long term commitment, the lease payments are usually capitalized as a corporate debt and hence place a curb on the borrowing capacity of the organization that is approximately equal to that which you would have paid to own the building. Thus the issue of building ownership is of secondary importance to that of selecting the best site and selecting the most suitable building type for the purpose. Ownership is to be preferred if the mere fact of your retail presence will cause local real estate prices to rise (as might occur if an upscale department store reinvigorates a depressed downtown area), or if flexibility of building use is critical. An unexpected liability of building ownership may arise if local real estate prices rise above that explained by their retailing value. If the site is not sold, (it could be leased back to maintain retail continuity) the chain may become a takeover target by those eager to capture the true economic value of the sites. The moral in favor of leasing is "retailers are not in the business of real estate speculation."

A radically different ownership strategy is to consider franchising the concept. Under this system entrepreneurial store owners pay royalties (or some other payment formula) for the right to use the business concept that you have developed. All stores will appear very similar to the customer, but each will be owned separately. Certain functions are handled centrally, possibly marketing, procurement, training, distribution, and site selection. One of the central problems of chain management, namely the incentivization of the store manager is solved in one step, since the store manager owns the profit stream from the store. On the other hand the lack of central control can lead to a dilution of the concept and an inertia with respect to bold new initiatives.

The Rate of Expansion

We have discussed the dilemma of waiting to perfect the concept versus waiting too long and being preempted. A second dilemma is the decision about how rapidly the roll out should occur. A company that grows in fits and starts may be handicapped in many ways. The management talent hired to operate a 40-store chain may not have the savvy to run a 600-store national chain. Time is wasted changing the crew along the way. The financial investment may have been sufficient for phase 1 but new investors may be brought in before phase 2, each phase taking its own cut of the equity. The information processing superstructure may have to be revamped along the way, as might the warehouse and logistic system. To be sure there are no easy answers to this problem; their solution depends upon an artful tradeoff between the risk reduction in taking small steps versus the long term economic advantages of a single roll of the dice. A similar element concerns the length of leases. At start up the desire is inevitably to sign short leases to avoid exposure should the venture fail. However if those early leases run out just when the concept is taking off it might be very expensive to renew those flagship location leases.

Ultimately the rate of expansion depends on the intrinsic attractiveness of the opportunity; the sooner the stores are functioning, the sooner profits can be made. If it is capital intensive, it may take longer to convince enough investors to participate. If time is of the essence it may be worth accepting heavy dilution of equity rather than to allow the first mover advantage to slip away.

PREDICTING COMPETITIVE RESPONSE

In addition to the danger of having your innovative concept copied, it is essential to consider the potential reaction of entrenched competitors to your expansion. No matter how novel your concept, someone else will be hurt and as your business starts to create inroads against theirs, they may start to compete more proactively than at first. In particular they are almost certainly likely to imitate all or part of your strategy in an attempt to share in your idea. If the idea is easily copied it is essential that you saturate each market that you develop. For example your store in Poughkeepsie may be doing $550 per square foot and a source of great pride in the organization, but if a competitor opens the identical concept next door, reducing your sales by half at a stroke, you may wish you had had the presence of mind to cannibalize your own sales. The limiting rule is that you should open as many stores in a region as are necessary to eliminate the potential for a competitor to earn its cost of capital. This advice is hard to follow if the competitor is Sears, and if all they need to do is renovate 1,000 square foot in each of their stores.

AFTER THE MARKET IS SATURATED

Wal-Mart, the most successful retail concept ever, has been growing its sales at 25% per year for many years. It is clear that there are limits to this growth. There is a finite market size in the general merchandise category in the United States. It stands to reason that at least one of the following predictions will prove to be true:

(i)   Wal-Mart will stop growing at 25%
(ii) Wal-Mart will take its concept overseas
(iii) Wal-Mart will diversify into other (retail) businesses.

Of course we know it has already diversified somewhat into a Wholesale Club (Sam's) and into the grocery business (its Wal-Mart supercenters).

Diversification bears the drawbacks true for any business that tries to repeat success in a new area: it may have been "lucky" the first time (lucky rather than shrewd in selecting the right retail mix) and/or the diversification may prove to be a distraction to management and ultimately a detriment to the health of the original business. On the other hand advantages are numerous. Retail sites may be converted (subject to lease provisions) from one concept to the other. Scale advantages may be obtained from amortization of warehouses, computers, and contacts. Customers may accept the transfer of reputation from one concept to the other (as is apparent in the case of Wal-Mart and Sam's.

International expansion also conveys economies of scale and in addition does not bring with it the distractions of a diversification. The disadvantages of international expansion are all those of any business expanding overseas, namely, will the concept transfer readily to a foreign culture, can the differences in operating procedure (regulations as to labelling food content etc.) be overcome, can key employees be prevailed upon to travel frequently abroad, is there a significantly different competitive environment, as well as a myriad of similar problems. The question of foreign expansion however is essentially similar to the problem faced by the retailer who, having saturated the Philadelphia market wonders if it is too big a step to enter Baltimore. As the barriers of international trade continue to fall and as international communication continues to homogenize standards of living and tastes across the globe so international expansion will become the norm for any truly successful concept.

Case 23

GEORGETOWN LEATHER DESIGN

GEORGETOWN LEATHER DESIGN

Georgetown Leather Design (GLD) was a chain of 13 retail stores that specialized in the sale of fine leather apparel, business cases, handbags and accessories. Ten stores were clustered in malls around the Washington/Baltimore area and three new stores had been opened in late 1988 in suburban malls in Philadelphia, New Jersey and Boston. They offered an assortment of quality merchandise which emphasized basic enduring styles at prices which constituted an excellent value. Their well trained staff could provide customers with considerably more product knowledge than either department stores or apparel chains.

William McCormick, president and CEO of GLD and a 1961 graduate of the Harvard Business School, had purchased the company in 1984. He was a veteran of seventeen years in specialty retailing, most recently having built Jordan Kitts Music into one of the largest chains of keyboard retailers in the country with sales of over $30 million. The center of the Jordan Kitts Music business was the Baltimore/Washington metropolitan area, but the company had stores as far north as Wilmington, Delaware and as far south as Virginia Beach, Virginia.

In the four years since he had purchased GLD, McCormick had positioned the company for growth and consequently thought it was ready for aggressive expansion. The store format and merchandise mix had been refined, and effective sourcing relationships in the Far East and Europe developed. A state of the art point of sale system and a new distribution center were in place. McCormick also thought the team of senior managers at headquarters were qualified to guide the company from 13 to 62 stores in the next five years.

McCormick still harbored lingering doubts, however, about the character and pace of the proposed roll-out strategy. He wondered how it might be affected by such issues as: (1) continued growth and long term stability of the leather apparel market, (2) applicability of the formula in different markets, (3) evolving competitive forces, (4) the availability of appropriate real estate and (5) the risk reward ratio implied by the five-year plan (see **Exhibit 7**).

BACKGROUND

GLD was founded in 1968 by Mary Vinton and Toni Ray. Originally called the "Sandal Shop," GLD's roots went back to the thousands of leather craft shops that proliferated in the Vietnam era. GLD was one of the few successful survivors and had become the dominant specialty leather products retailer in the Baltimore/Washington market.

Vinton and Ray had successfully developed six GLD stores by the late 1970's. The company developed an excellent reputation for high quality leathers and distinctively designed products. Their successful basic handbag collection was one of the first made of apparel

This case was prepared by David Wylie, Research Associate, under the supervision of Professor Walter J. Salmon as the basis for class discussion rather than to illustrate either effective or ineffective handling of an administrative situation. Numbers in the case have been disguised but are nonetheless useful in assessing the economics of the situation.

quality leather, and they were among the first to develop leather separates and sportswear.

During the early 1980's the company expanded to ten stores by stretching its existing financing to cover the resulting capital expenditures and working capital requirements. By 1984, sales volume exceeded $6.8 million or $350/square foot or about 2.5 times the prevailing specialty store averages. From 1982–1984, however, GLD incurred annual losses of about $200,000.

The founders also realized that their original MIS and control procedures were inadequate for the increased size of the company, and that, in order to compete, they would have to achieve adequate volume to buy directly from contract manufacturers who were often located overseas. In December of 1984, GLD was acquired by Bill McCormick, who had the resources to realize these objectives.

McCormick thought that there was a growing market for quality leather products. His strategy was to offer customers good value by passing on savings from direct sourcing and by supporting top quality merchandise with knowledgeable in-store sales support. His goal was to become a major player among higher end consumer leather goods retailers.

Toni Ray remained with GLD as senior vice president and in that role, retained much of the responsibility for product design and skin selection. Her apparel designer and buyer, Harley Chappel, remained with the company as well, assuming the role of vice president. Both were still with GLD in 1989.

THE STORES

GLD stores typically had about 1,600 square feet of selling and 400 square feet of back room space. Actual size varied from 1,500 to 2,400 square feet of selling space based on mall space availability. Typically GLD stores had excellent mall locations with wide openings to the mall, allowing easy access to shoppers. The designs featured well-lit areas and a mixture of brass, granite, and rough wood which was intended to reflect the classic quality of the business cases and accessories and complement the basic leather handbag collection and the more fashion-forward apparel offerings. The dominant feature of the stores, however, was the pungent smell of fresh leather (see **Exhibit 1**).

When McCormick acquired GLD in 1984, the merchandise mix included handbags, business cases, accessories, apparel, belts and footwear. Footwear had been dropped, however, because of the abundance of mall competitors. GLD also refocused more on upscale, mature customers.

GLD stores had different display arrangements for each merchandise category which accentuated its unique characteristics. Apparel was on open displays so it could be easily touched and tried on. Handbags were festooned over rough hewn wood to demonstrate their wide selection and natural quality. Business cases were distinctively offered in a more private space of nicely finished conventional shelves. Accessories were displayed in or behind the checkout counter.

Quality of skins, design and craftsmanship, although consistently high for all GLD lines, was not always apparent to customers, and required some explanation. Without this explanation, customers could not always justify GLD's prices. Staffing the stores with knowledgeable staff was, therefore, critical.

Every store had a manager, an assistant manager, an associate manager, one or two full time and several part time salespeople. Each new employee received sales training and an introduction to leather at headquarters, and was expected to attend monthly headquarters sessions on leather, fashion and selling techniques. The stores were open 75 hours per week. There was always an experienced manager and a salesperson on hand, and, during peak holiday periods up to ten salespeople to answer any customer questions.

In addition to the retail stores, McCormick had created a mail order catalog with about 150 selected items. The catalog was intended as an introductory mailing piece for new markets, a way to capitalize on the growing mailing list of prior retail customers (120,000 names by 1989), and, through the use of rental mailing lists, as a stand-alone channel of distribution.

The catalog was in its third season. As an advertising piece to current customers and an introductory piece for new stores it was proving to be very valuable, but as a profit center, results were quite disappointing. Mailings in 1988 of 1.7 million catalogs generated losses of $400,000 partly due to the unusually high percentage of cancellations and returns. McCormick was scaling down the catalog considerably for 1989 and, indeed, was reconsidering the future viability of this channel for GLD.

By the end of 1988, the number of stores had increased from 10 to 13. One older, less successful store had been closed, and four new stores opened. One of these new stores was an outlet store through which all closeouts and discontinued lines flowed.

By April of 1989, McCormick had negotiated a real estate deal with a major national mall developer for the acquisition of five new store sites to be opened in 1989 through 1991. Early returns from the new 1988 stores and the five planned new 1989 stores would be critical in determining the viability of the overall expansion plan.

Performance improved significantly from 1985 to 1988. Comparable store sales increased 25%, 23%, and 19% in '86, '87, and '88. Average sales per square foot for stores open more than a year exceeded $570 in 1988, ranging from $360 to over $850. Forty percent of sales were in November and December (see **Exhibits 3, 4,** and **6**). Earnings before catalog losses, interest and taxes had grown from a loss of 1% of sales in 1985 to a profit of over 5% in 1988, as gross margins grew from 39.6% to 46.3%.

THE MERCHANDISE MIX

GLD's merchandise consisted of men's and women's apparel and accessories (handbags, business cases, and small leather goods). Depending on their appetite for somewhat more fashionable merchandise, stores were divided into A (fashionable), B and C (least fashionable) groups for allocation of merchandise. The different categories of merchandise at GLD appealed to a broad range of customers who appreciated classic or contemporary styling, quality materials and workmanship, and designs stressing durability and functionality.

Apparel

The growing popularity of leather garments in America was largely attributed to increasing consumer preference for longer lasting merchandise and to new tanning technology which results in soft and supple textures for finished leather. Thus leather became acceptable as a material for sportswear.

Women's apparel, although emphasizing the more enduring classic and contemporary styles was still the most fashion sensitive component of the GLD mix. Women's sportswear was priced from $95 to $495. Outer wear prices ranged from $225 to $975. In both categories, however, sales were concentrated at the lower to mid range (see **Exhibit 2**).

Prices for men's apparel ranged from $135 to $625. Variations on the bomber jacket theme and other outerwear comprised the bulk of sales. The mix included some fashion forward styles, but tended to be more classic.

Handbags

There were four lines of handbags: the GLD classic, the GLD Italian line, the Coach line (an independent manufacturer of natural leather handbags and small leather goods), and other miscellaneous branded bags.

The basic handbag, which had been one of GLD's early stars, was still the top seller in unit sales. It was the only item which GLD continued to manufacture in its own workshop (28% of handbags were made offshore). The basic handbag line had been expanded in numerous ways. It now included more fashion forward items, higher priced items, bags which spanned the difference between handbags and informal business cases, and unisex all-purpose bags. Prices ranged from $50 to $200.

Based on 1988 Sales	Sales ($000)	Gross Mgn. %	% of Mix	Sales/ Sq. Ft.	Inv. Turns	Selling Space
Women's Apparel	3,751	48.3%	31%	$573	2.6	30%
Men's Apparel	3,464	46.2	29	598	2.4	27
TOTAL Apparel	7,215	47.3	60	585	2.5	57
Handbags	2,123	46.4	17	503	2.5	20
Business Cases	1,568	45.5	13	501	1.9	15
Other Accessories	1,254	47.1	10	759	2.5	8
TOTAL Accessories	4,945	46.3	40	550	2.3	43
TOTAL	12,160	46.3%	100%	570	2.4	100%

Note: Early returns from the new stores outside the Washington/Baltimore area indicated a mix closer to 70% apparel and 30% accessories in these markets.

Business Cases

Business case sales also peaked around Christmas, but brisk sales for other occasions made it GLD's least seasonal category. Styles were more classic, and prices ranged from $125 to $400. The customer was older and more affluent whether purchasing for self of as a gift.

Sales of business cases required much more explanation than other categories. The quality of material and craftsmanship (stitching, fittings, linings, hinges, etc.) was not entirely apparent to the average buyer. The usefulness of available features (number of pockets, thickness, expandability, etc.) and the appropriateness of different styles for different occasions also often required clarification. Sales assistance, therefore, was more critical in this category.

Other Accessories

Other accessories included gloves, wallets, desk and business accessories, change purses, key chains, leather care products and other small leather goods. These items were primarily gift, add-on or smaller "trial" purchases, and represented almost 50% of total unit sales. Such accessories were therefore disproportionately important in developing new and repeat customers.

Quality Leather Products

There were three basic ingredients required to achieve the specified premium quality of the products in the GLD mix: the raw skins themselves, preparation in the tannery, and the workmanship in the finishing room. As part of the effort to educate their customers, GLD provided a booklet *About Fine Leather* which describes these elements of the final product:

"**Premium Quality Leather**—Any great garment or accessory begins with good leather, and good leather begins with nature. Whether it's lambskins from the lush pastures of New Zealand, France and England, calfskin or cowhide from the U.S. and Canada, or pigskin from Japan, we search the globe for superior leathers. Each type of leather has its own special use. Cowhide belting leather goes into business cases that last a lifetime. Fine grained lambskin is perfect for fashion apparel. Oxhide makes durable yet elegant items for personal use. Regardless of the type of leather or its ultimate purpose, GLD selects only the finest full-grain and top-grain skins available anywhere . . . . We individually inspect every single skin for size, density and imperfections before tanning . . . Our skins are individually drum-dyed, a process which takes up to six weeks. Even if it means several treatments, each finished piece can only pass inspection if it matches our sample exactly."

"**Workmanship**— . . .Unlike fabric where many layers are cut at once by computerized equipment, each skin is hand cut, one at a time . . . Some garments require up to six separate skins to achieve a perfect match of color and grain, so the cutter must position his pattern perfectly . . . Finally the individual pieces are assembled . . . Of course, GLD thoroughly examines every item before it leaves the workroom . . . After our products meet these standards, there is still one more: value. We give you the best price in high quality leathergoods obtainable anywhere. Top-grain and full-grain leather is definitely more expensive, but the unique appearance of each piece and meticulous hand-crafting make the finished product worth the investment."

"**Taking the Guess-Work Out of Buying Leather**— Why wonder if you are making a sound investment? Georgetown Leather Design has spent a generation refining its skills to an art. Leather is our only business. Our exclusive designs, specially selected and tanned leathers, and old-fashioned hand work make all our products special... apparel and accessories of unsurpassed quality which will bring you years of pleasure. We're confident you won't find a better value anywhere. In fact, we guarantee it. Unconditionally!"

In order to achieve quality at reasonable cost, GLD specified the origin and quality of most of its own skins, how and where they were to be tanned, and developed good relationships with manufacturers. Independent inspectors were hired in each country from which product was purchased to maintain quality control. McCormick thought the GLD's vendor relationships were key to both the growth and competitive advantage of the firm.

Prior to 1984, about 80% of GLD merchandise was purchased from importers and wholesalers (who generally operated on 40% markups) while most of the balance was manufactured by GLD. In 1985, GLD started direct sourcing. GLD's direct factory purchases represented 5% of volume in 1985, 30% in 1986, 50% in 1987, and over 80% in 1988. Cost effective design and direct purchasing had allowed GLD to offer better values to its customers while at the same time enhancing gross margins from 39% in 1984 to 46% in 1988.

To benefit further from direct purchasing, GLD was under pressure to concentrate on fewer SKUs and to place larger orders. There was also an interest in importing more fashion forward merchandise but there were concerns about the potential markdown exposure from fewer and more fashion forward styles.

THE YEARLY PRODUCT SOURCING CYCLE

Exclusive design and direct sourcing had somewhat different implications for the different elements of the GLD mix, but long lead times and limited possibility for reordering for the two-month peak season were common characteristics.

Because of these long lead times and the highly seasonal sales, inventory risk could be quite high, but was mitigated by concentrating on the more classic fashions. Some competitors offered fashion forward lines but in so doing assumed an inventory risk which forced them into much higher price brackets than GLD, particularly if they chose to combine high quality leather with high fashion styling.

Buying for a Christmas season began in the fall of the previous year when McCormick, Harley Chappell, vice president and garment merchandise manager and Toni Ray, senior vice president for accessory merchandising and fashion coordinator, attended the annual Paris Leather Show. At this show, new leathers and fashion lines for all categories were introduced.

Both Chappell and Ray would purchase promising new skins and styles at this show and send them to manufacturers to produce samples. Very often the items would be substantially modified to meet GLD cost and fashion criteria. The manufacturers frequently would pass on helpful design information about competitors' lines since they sold a wide range of international retailers and had an excellent feel for the market.

During November and December, GLD would further develop their idea for the next Fall season almost a year away. Fashion information would come from shopping competitors' lines and from sales results that Fall. Chappell developed about 160 styles annually, while Ray developed over 400.

The basic designs were then approved. In January design and production specifications were finalized and production schedules and contracts negotiated. Shipments would start to arrive in the U.S. during May and June. After an August pre-season sale, there was some ability to order items for October and November delivery if justified by early demand. During 1988, just under 30% of the merchandise was ordered during this period.

The cycle from reviewing the European lines to arrival of finished goods was almost a year for merchandise which GLD specified and imported. This time could be reduced somewhat by sourcing from domestic importers or wholesalers, as GLD did with some higher margin lines, but costs were significantly higher and availability uncertain.

INFRASTRUCTURE—POISED FOR GROWTH

In anticipation of the planned growth, McCormick had developed an infrastructure to handle staffing, distribution and information requirements for the foreseeable future.

In 1986, GLD moved its headquarters into a new 26,000 square foot facility. This facility housed corporate offices, a catalog telemarketing center, a training center, a warehouse and distribution center and a small workshop for handbag production and merchandise repair.

In 1987 a state of the art point of sale system was installed. It provided for individual item control (style, skin, color, size) with daily register polling. Accurate sales and inventory information allowed for better performance evaluation and commission incentives as well as daily stock replenishment from the central warehouse. Based on results from the previous day's sales, merchandise could be replenished from the 12,000 square

Category	Fashion/Basic	1988 percent of category sourced from:		
		GLD Shop	Domestic Vendor	Direct Import
Women's Apparel	Classic/Contemp.	0	25	75
Men's Apparel	Classic/Contemp.	0	15	85
Handbags	Basic/Classic	15	20	65
Business Cases	Basic/Classic	0	20	80
Accessories	Basic	15	65	20

foot distribution facility within 24 hours. This post-distribution system allowed valuable and sometimes scarce inventory to be allocated to the right locations. As a consequence, there was only minor need for inter-store transfers.

REAL ESTATE

Since GLD relied heavily on mall traffic and reputation for customer generation rather than on advertising, obtaining excellent locations within the best malls in the Northeast was a critical matter. In 1989, such space was at a premium and sometimes lease negotiations required compromises. In order to acquire space in a premier mall in New Jersey, for instance, GLD had had to agree with a national developer upon a five store package including one location due to open in 1991 in a mid-sized southern city in a less attractive mall.

THE ORGANIZATION

Bill McCormick, the president of GLD, had responsibility for organization development, merchandising strategy, financial planning and real estate. Reporting to him were Toni Ray, Harley Chappell, Anne-Marie Swartz, director of operations, Bob Schwartz, CFO, and Tom Benner, financial analysis and planning (see **Exhibit 5** for organization chart).

Ray had been one of GLD's founders and remained as somewhat of a guiding spirit behind GLD. As senior vice president, her responsibilities included fashion co-ordinator, general merchandise manager for accessories, catalog merchandise manager and advertising manager. She worked very closely with Chappell, vice president, in his role as garment merchandising manager.

Swartz had been with the company for just over a year, having been manager of personnel for one of the country's major apparel chains. Although she had been hired by GLD in a similar capacity, she had recently been promoted to her current role as director of operations, an indication of McCormick's awareness of the importance of human resources to the growth of the company. McCormick and Swartz had previously developed a rather innovative incentive plan for store personnel which smoothed commission income over the course of the year. In recognition of the importance of personal selling, the objective of the incentive plan was to encourage exceptional motivation.

Store Managers. Almost all GLD store managers were college graduates, and had been promoted from within. They reported to a district manager. The average age was 26. The median base salary was $25,000 per year and the median annual bonus (paid quarterly based on achievement of planned sales, MBO objectives, shrinkage and payroll levels) was $5,000. This compensation level exceeded that of most comparable positions in other retail stores in the malls where GLD was located. There had been no turnover in store managers during the 18 months ending in April, 1989.

Salespeople. Full time salespeople, assistant managers and associate managers received an average base wage of $7.00 per hour plus seasonally adjusted commissions of 1% to 4% of sales. These rates were geared to achieve average commissions of $2.00 per hour. Compensation levels were very competitive.

Other incentives included contests which awarded the winners trips to well known resorts, special individual and store performance prizes, employee discounts which encouraged employees to wear GLD garments at work, employee referral awards and an annual banquet.

To further ensure competent sales assistance, GLD had an extensive training program. Sessions included seminars at headquarters for all store personnel and extensive store follow up by the store manager. Training included communication of knowledge about leather, fashion and selling techniques.

THE COMPETITION

GLD competed in two fairly distinct markets in the apparel and accessories categories. The retail market for leather apparel was estimated to be about $2 billion in 1988 and had been growing at a rate of 16% per year over the last five years. Growth was attributed to the acceptance of leather as a durable alternative to other materials, and, according to a GLD customer survey, it was perceived as attractive, having a soft, supple feeling and having become chic.

Most leather apparel was sold through general apparel retailers (i.e. non-leather stores). Of about 20,000 estimated retail outlets for leather garments, less than 1,000 were specialty leather stores. These specialty stores represented about 20% of total sales.

Department stores had the largest share of leather apparel sales, with the more upscale chains making the heaviest commitments (Saks, Nieman Marcus, Bloomingdales and Nordstroms). The regional/middle to upper-middle chains such as the May Company and Federated offered a relatively smaller selection of lower priced leather apparel which was usually promoted on a "was/is" basis early in the season and was largely sold out by November/December. Several specialty apparel chains such as Chess King, Merry Go Round, T. Edwards and Ann Taylor were aggressive sellers of leather apparel, but they too promoted and often sold out early.

There were four dedicated leather apparel chains operating on a national or multi-market basis. These were:

	GLD Est. of Store Size	# of stores in 1988	Est. 1988 Sales	Locations
Berman's	2,800	210	$170,000,000	Mainly Mid-West
Wilson's	2,500	270	160,000,000	National
Tannery West	1,500	30	24,000,000	National
North Beach Leather	3,000	10	24,000,000	National

The Melville Corporation, a $6.7 billion highly thought of operator of 6,540 specialty retail stores in various segments of retailing, represented the most formidable competition. It had owned Wilson's for some time, but in 1988, it had also acquired Berman's and Tannery West. In early 1989, it still was expanding all three operations.

Berman's offered a broad selection of men's and women's apparel at popular price points (men's outerwear from $149–$299). Styles ranged from basic/contemporary (flight jackets) to more fashion forward (motorcycle related). About 15% of sales were accessories.

Wilson's Suede and Leather price points were similar to Berman's while the focus was a bit more fashion forward. Accessories only represented about 10% of sales. Both Berman's and Wilson's shared two successful fundamental strategies: category dominance and, like GLD, design and specification of their own merchandise and direct procurement mainly from foreign suppliers.

Tannery West was positioned at higher price points and more fashion forward styles than GLD (jackets from $300–$700).

North Beach Leather offered a still more fashion forward presentation, bordering on "kinky." It was believed, however, that a substantial portion of sales were more classic or contemporary. Price points for jackets ranged from $350 to $800, featuring better quality leathers. Like the other chains, it had much of its merchandise manufactured for it, and like GLD, prepared a catalogue but used it primarily for store promotion.

In addition to the above multi-regional chains, there were dozens of smaller local leather apparel chains operating in major markets which offered actual or potential competition to GLD.

Leather accessories were sold through a diverse array of retail channels presumably exceeding 100,000 store outlets. The most significant competition was from department stores and specialty luggage stores.

Department stores competed principally in handbags and personal leather goods but not significantly in business cases or related business accessories. According to GLD customer surveys, 40% of GLD customers perceived department stores as the best alternative for quality/value and for selection in handbags and small leather goods. Department stores did not provide, however, a level of service or product knowledge equivalent to GLD.

A secondary but important source of competition was Coach, an upscale manufacturer which sold through its own outlets and mail order catalog, upscale department stores and specialty stores and from which GLD sourced a line of accessories, and The Compliment, a regional mass-market and heavily promotional retailer. GLD considered the Coach line to have a quality and fashion position similar to their own.

Specialty luggage stores were the principal competitors for business cases and related accessories and, to a lesser extent, personal leather goods. There were several such chains in the GLD market with broader selections of more promotionally priced business cases and accessories. In addition, there were usually one or two "old line" specialty luggage stores in each major market that offered extensive selections of high quality classic business cases and accessories (e.g. London Harness in Boston, Crouch and Fitzgerald in New York, or Robinson in Philadelphia).

THE EXPANSION PLAN

McCormick felt that the basics were in place for implementing his plan to expand the number of stores to 62 over five years. McCormick estimated that each new store required an investment of $250,000 in leasehold improvements, fixtures and equipment. In addition, inventory requirements per store ranged from a low of $150,000 to a high of $300,000 at the beginning of the peak season (see **Exhibit 7** for financial projections). Early returns from the new stores would be instrumental in judging the pace of the intended roll-out. For the first four months of 1989, sales from these stores yielded annualized projections of $1.2 million per store. Through

expansion, GLD could develop economies of scale which could ensure a prosperous future.

GLD, McCormick knew, would have to move fast enough to pre-empt the competition, but not so fast as to falter. He knew his own financial resources might be stretched if he tried to fund the capital investment projected by the five-year plan himself. He wanted to be sure that he was not pressured to make marginal and potentially destructive real estate deals. He also knew that he would have to expand the management group at both headquarters and stores as the company grew. The financial controls, moreover, would have to survive the test of accelerated growth. Unknowns included whether the GLD formula would prosper in warmer climates and the adjustment in the merchandise mix required for other geographic areas with different weather conditions and tastes.

Exhibit 1A
Photograph of Exterior of One of the Stores

Exhibit 1B
Photograph of Interior of One of the Stores

Exhibit 2
Sample Items from the Catalog

E'RE PROUD OF OUR PERSONAL TOUCH.

From the moment we opened our retail doors in 1968, we realized that the best way to achieve a personal sense of quality and craft was by keeping the entire process of leather design under our own watchful eye. These leathers are the most superbly tanned skins we can find, hand selected from the finest tanneries. Designs created in our workrooms are by artisans who excel in their craft. From start to finish, we control the design, cost and quality of our products. We can offer them to you at remarkable prices because we deliver our special creations direct from our workshops to you.

We now operate 11 stores in Washington D.C., Maryland, Virginia and Pennsylvania. We are pleased to offer our unique leather products for purchase by mail or phone.

We look forward to a long lasting relationship with you. We personally guarantee your total satisfaction and will refund or exchange with never a question asked.

Sincerely yours,

William J. McCormick, Jr.
Chairman

© Georgetown Leather Design 1988

TALIAN
LEATHERS

The tanneries of Italy are
world-renowned for producing
the finest leathers.
Georgetown Leather Design
takes these superb skins to
our workshops, where our
devotion to quality and value
brings these exclusive
designs to life.

A. Long and buttonless, our
supple coat of Italian tanned
lambskin features shawl collar,
taped leather seams and generous
patch pockets. Brown or black.
Sizes XS(3/4), S(5/6-7/8), M(9/10),
L(11/12-13/14). (#104) $595.
B. Matching 24" Italian tanned
lambskin skirt is fully lined. Brown,
black, red, cobalt or taupe.
Sizes 3/4-13/14. (#105) $165.

Buttero calfskin handbags, tanned
and glazed in Italy to a deep
burnished glow.
C. Tailored shoulder bag has top-
zip compartment, exterior gusseted
pocket. Mocha, caramel or black.
13 × 9 × 4½". (#302) $115.
D. Remove the shoulder strap and
you have a tailored clutch. Four
interior pockets, magnetic closure.
Caramel, mocha or black.
10½ × 7 × 2". (#303) $80.

FORWARD FASHION

Our contemporary silhouettes highlight the inherent beauty of the richest plonge leather available. Each is a superb value, found only at Georgetown Leather Design.

A. Our traditional rucksack in smooth naked cowhide features two buckled gusset pockets, roomy drawstring compartment and two pleated snap pockets under the flap. Black or tan. 13 × 11 × 5". (#329) $135.

Luxurious and warm, our 4-way jackets in drum-dyed plonge leather have a New Zealand opossum fur vest to wear as a liner, over the jacket or alone. **B.** Women's 4-way jacket. Black. Sizes S(5/6-7/8), M(9/10), L(11/12-13/14). (#118) $495. **C.** Men's 4-way jacket. Black. Sizes S(36). M(38-40). L(42-44). XL(46) (#219) $495.

D. Handsome ¾ length coat in drum-dyed plonge cowhide has a 2-way zipper, wrap belt and Thermolite® insulation. Black. Sizes S(36). M(38-40). L(42-44). XL(46). (#220) $375. Long sizes ML(38L-40L). LL(42L-44L). XLL(46L). (#221) $395.

E. Traditional Danish book-bag's many compartments expand to meet your every-day needs. Main compart-ment zips on 3 sides. Made from durable cowhide. Black. 15 × 11 × 4". (#330) $125.

F. Sleek shawl lapel jacket of the finest Italian lambskin has a 3-button front and side stash pockets. Cobalt. Sizes XS(3/4), S(5/6-7/8), M(9/10), L(11/12-13/14). (#119) $495.
G. 24" drum-dyed plonge skirt is fully lined. Black. Sizes 3/4-13/14. (#120) $135.

H. Plonge leather trenchcoat. Classic details include epaulettes, cuff straps and inverted back pleat. Removeable red lining. Black. Sizes 3/4-15/16. (#121) $575.

J. Our popular "feed bag" tote has an adjustable shoulder strap, functional D-ring belt, magnetic closure and roomy interior zip pocket. Made of naked cowhide in our workshop. Black or taupe. 14½×10½×5½". (#331) $120.
K. Top-zip naked cowhide shoulder bag from our Workshop Collection has two outside pockets with magnetic tab closures. Black or taupe. 12½×9×5". (#332) $105

L. Our generously oversized clutch has a zippered interior compartment, large open back pocket, detachable shoulder strap and magnetic security closure. Black or taupe. 15×10×5" (#333) $125.

XECUTIVE APPOINTMENTS

When every detail counts, our Italian leather business cases, bags and accessories meet the demands of your professional standards.

A Briefbag in full grain Italian cowhide has a 5 position lock which opens to reveal a roomy 5 compartment and 3 partitie. The back has a full-zip compartment. Brown 17 x 11 x 5 #401 $195

B Our classic soft bag in Italian nappa calfskin is a compact organizer with 5 interior compartments and a zipper pocket. Solid brass turn-lock closure. Mocha, caramel or black 10 x 7 x 3 #324 $95

C This exclusive legal-size file case unzips on 3 sides for easy access. Crafted of full-grain Italian cowhide with 4 file compartments and 2 inside zip pockets. Brown 16 x 11 x 3 #400 $160

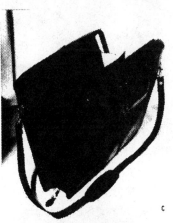

The rugged look of natural grain tanned cowhide complements our Rugato cases for men.
D Maxi Bag has 2 large inside compartments, rear zip pocket and 38" detachable shoulder strap in cognac or dark brown 9 x 11 x 4 #326 $135
E Wrist strap clutch with main compartment and outside open pocket in cognac or dark brown 9 x 5 x 2 #345 $55

F Legal size briefbag of leather from Italian cowhide with comfortable handles, inside file, 2 under two exterior pockets and detachable shoulder strap. Burgundy or brown 16 x 11 x 4 #402 $165

Italian Rugato cowhide accessories are exclusively ours. Available in cognac or dark brown.
G Portfolio holds legal documents, has rear zipper pocket 15 x 7 x 1 #403 $85
H Pocket organizer has a place for names, numbers, and more 4 x 4 #464 $30
J Address book #507 $20
K Business card holder #508 $15
L Letter pad 12 x 9 #485 $65

16

OUR TRADEMARK HANDBAGS

The Georgetown Leather Design Workshop Collection has enjoyed a loyal following for over 20 years. Made from the finest cowhide by our skilled artisans, these classic bags age beautifully

G. Oversized tote will carry daily essentials and much more with style. With structured bottom, reinforced handles, four exterior pockets and inside zip pocket. Tobacco, earth or black. 14 × 11 × 7". (#310) $125

H. Our roomy drawstring tote has adjustable shoulder strap, reinforced bottom and inside zipper pocket. Tobacco, taupe or black. 11½ × 13 × 8". (#311) $95

J. Generously sized flap over bag has a comfortable extra-wide shoulder strap plus a zippered expansion pocket in front, open back pocket and inside hanging pocket. Earth, tobacco or black. 13 × 11 × 5". (#312) $125

K. Roomy companion bag features pleated side gusset pockets and unique shoulder tabs, plus inside and outside zip pockets. Tobacco, taupe, black or navy. 11½ × 8 × 5". (#313) $80

L. Everything fits in our large flap over clutch. Inside, two open and two zippered pockets. Earth, taupe or black. 15 × 8 × 2". (#314) $70

M. Spacious top zip bucket bag features unique stitching and styling details. Specially designed double-rolled shoulder straps, interior pocket and reinforced bottom for comfort and durability. Taupe, earth or black. 11 × 9½ × 6". (#315) $80

We guarantee your satisfaction
If you are not pleased with your purchase, simply return it to us for full refund or exchange.

Exhibit 3
The Merchandise Mix Based on 1988 Sales

Ladies' Garments	30.85%
Men's Garments	28.49%
Handbags	17.46%
Business Cases	12.89%
Other Accessories	10.31%

Exhibit 4a
Total Sales by Month (1988)

February	4.82%	August	7.59%
March	4.75%	September	10.26%
April	3.30%	October	9.81%
May	3.71%	November	11.10%
June	4.87%	December	28.54%
July	4.35%	January	6.89%

Exhibit 4b
Sales Category by Month (1988)

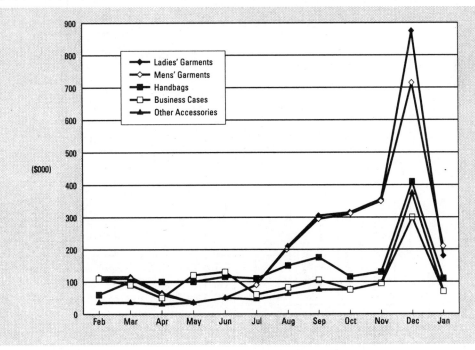

Exhibit 5
Organization Chart

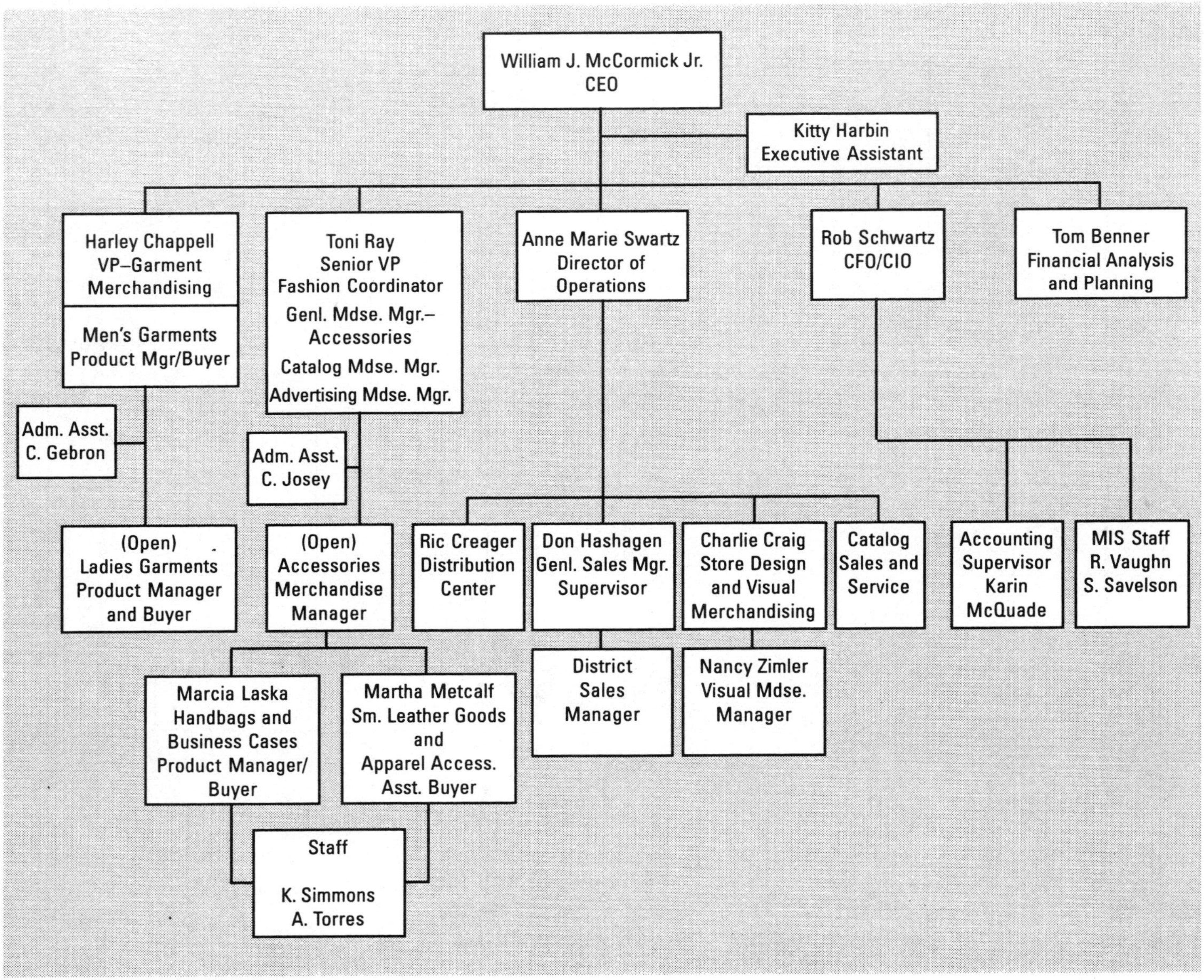

William J. McCormick Jr.
CEO

Kitty Harbin
Executive Assistant

Tom Benner
Financial Analysis
and Planning

Rob Schwartz
CFO/CIO

Accounting
Supervisor
Karin
McQuade

MIS Staff
R. Vaughn
S. Savelson

Anne Marie Swartz
Director of
Operations

Charlie Craig
Store Design
and Visual
Merchandising

Nancy Zimler
Visual Mdse.
Manager

Catalog
Sales and
Service

Don Hashagen
Genl. Sales Mgr.
Supervisor

District
Sales
Manager

Ric Creager
Distribution
Center

Toni Ray
Senior VP
Fashion Coordinator
Genl. Mdse. Mgr.–
Accessories
Catalog Mdse. Mgr.
Advertising Mdse. Mgr.

Adm. Asst.
C. Josey

(Open)
Accessories
Merchandise
Manager

Martha Metcalf
Sm. Leather Goods
and
Apparel Access.
Asst. Buyer

Marcia Laska
Handbags and
Business Cases
Product Manager/
Buyer

Staff
K. Simmons
A. Torres

Harley Chappell
VP–Garment
Merchandising

Men's Garments
Product Mgr/Buyer

Adm. Asst.
C. Gebron

(Open)
Ladies Garments
Product Manager
and Buyer

Exhibit 6
Financial Statements

(as of January 31)	1985 Actual		1986 Actual		1987 Actual		1988 Actual	
NUMBER OF STORES	10		10		10		13	
INCOME STATEMENT								
Sales—Store	$ 7,361	100.0%	$ 8,362	95.6%	$ 9,661	89.3%	$12,160	88.3%
Sales—Catalog	$ 0	0.0%	$ 381	4.4%	$ 1,153	10.7%	$ 1,607	11.7%
TOTAL SALES	$ 7,361	100.0%	$ 8,743	100.0%	$10,814	100.0%	$13,767	100.0%
Gross Profit—Stores	$ 2,914	39.6%	$ 3,498	40.0%	$ 4,152	38.4%	$ 5,554	40.3%
Gross Profit—Catalog	$ 0	0.0%	$ 204	2.3%	$ 544	5.0%	$ 814	5.9%
TOTAL GROSS PROFIT	$ 2,914	39.6%	$ 3,702	42.3%	$ 4,696	43.4%	$ 6,368	46.3%
Payroll—Stores	$ 606	8.2%	$ 711	8.1%	$ 899	8.3%	$ 1,005	7.3%
Payroll—Catalog	$ 656	8.9%	$ 744	8.5%	$ 771	7.1%	$ 930	6.8%
TOTAL PAYROLL	$ 1,263	17.2%	$ 1,455	16.6%	$ 1,670	15.4%	$ 1,935	14.1%
Occupancy	$ 716	9.7%	$ 767	8.8%	$ 828	7.7%	$ 1,002	7.3%
Depreciation	$ 130	1.8%	$ 205	2.3%	$ 330	3.0%	$ 402	2.9%
Advertising	$ 145	2.0%	$ 159	1.8%	$ 286	2.6%	$ 198	1.4%
Travel & Entertainment	$ 117	1.6%	$ 82	0.9%	$ 105	1.0%	$ 146	1.1%
Supplies & Displays	$ 121	1.6%	$ 163	1.9%	$ 179	1.7%	$ 258	1.9%
Other	$ 478	6.5%	$ 605	6.9%	$ 697	6.4%	$ 816	5.9%
TOTAL OPERATING EXP.	$ 2,970	40.3%	$ 3,435	39.3%	$ 4,095	37.9%	$ 4,758	34.6%
Operating Profit(Loss)*	$ (56)	-0.8%	$ 63	0.7%	$ 57	0.5%	$ 796	5.8%
Catalog Income(Loss)**	$ 0	0.0%	$ (410)	-4.7%	$ (163)	-1.5%	$ (397)	-2.9%
E.B.I.T.	$ (56)	-0.8%	$ (347)	-4.0%	$ (106)	-1.0%	$ 399	2.9%
Interest & Other Expense	$ 180	2.4%	$ 186	2.1%	$ 295	2.7%	$ 581	4.2%
Taxes	$ (103)	-1.4%	$ (250)	-2.9%	$ (169)	-1.6%	$ (66)	-0.5%
NET INCOME	$ (133)	-1.8%	$ (283)	-3.2%	$ (232)	-2.1%	$ (116)	-0.8%

* Excludes catalog gross profit

**Sum of Catalog Gross Profit and Catalog Expenses
  Interest includes interest on seasonal working capital

BALANCE SHEET

	1987 Actual	1988 Actual
ASSETS		
Inventories	$ 2,007	$ 2,289
Other Current Assets	$ 649	$ 643
Property and Equipment	$ 3,948	$ 5,312
Accumulated Depreciation	$(1,440)	$(1,792)
Other Assets	$ 125	$ 93
Goodwill	$ 329	$ 319
TOTAL ASSETS	$ 5,618	$ 6,864
LIABILITIES AND OWNERS' EQUITY		
Accounts Payable*	$ 151	$ 192
Accrued Expenses**	$ 972	$ 1,421
Current Portion of L/T Debt	$ 93	$ 134
Income Taxes Payable	$ (88)	$ (69)
Long Term Debt	$ 2,151	$ 2,963
TOTAL LIABILITIES	$ 3,279	$ 4,641
STOCKHOLDERS' EQUITY	$ 2,339	$ 2,223
TOTAL LIABILITIES & EQUITY	$ 5,618	$ 6,864

* Most inventory was received in summer months and paid for by letter of credit.

**Accrued expenses include payroll payable, sales tax (5%), bonuses payable, percentage rent payable, negative cash float and other miscellaneous accrued expenses and accounts payable.

(All amounts expressed in thousands of dollars)

Exhibit 7
Financial Projections

	1989 Plan		1990 Plan		1991 Plan		1992 Plan		1993 Plan	
# of Stores	18		26		36		48		62	
INCOME STATEMENT										
Sales—Stores	$18,595	93.3%	$26,200	89.7%	$38,309	91.4%	$54,154	92.6%	$74,256	93.7%
Sales—Catalog	$1,330	6.7%	$ 3,000	10.3%	$ 3,600	8.6%	$ 4,300	7.4%	$ 5,000	6.3%
TOTAL SALES	$19,925	100.0%	$29,200	100.0%	$41,909	100.0%	$58,454	100.0%	$79,256	100.0%
Gross Profit—Stores	$8,743	43.9%	$12,396	42.5%	$18,180	43.4%	$25,747	44.0%	$35,358	44.6%
Gross Profit—Catalog	$ 701	3.5%	$ 1,569	5.4%	$ 1,883	4.5%	$ 2,249	3.8%	$ 2,615	3.3%
TOTAL GROSS PROFIT	$9,444	47.4%	$13,965	47.8%	$20,063	47.9%	$27,966	47.9%	$37,973	47.9%
Payroll—Stores	$1,625	8.2%	$ 2,245	7.7%	$ 3,416	8.2%	$ 4,901	8.4%	$ 6,799	8.6%
Payroll—Corporate	$1,410	7.1%	$ 1,756	6.0%	$ 2,124	5.1%	$ 2,485	4.3%	$ 2,811	3.5%
TOTAL PAYROLL	$3,035	15.2%	$4,001	13.7%	$ 5,540	13.2%	$ 7,386	12.6%	$ 9,610	12.1%
Occupancy	$1,625	8.2%	$ 2,568	8.8%	$ 3,924	9.4%	$ 5,685	9.7%	$ 7,883	9.9%
Depreciation	$ 591	3.0%	$ 775	2.7%	$ 1,087	2.6%	$ 1,472	2.5%	$ 1,913	2.4%
Advertising	$ 252	1.3%	$ 415	1.4%	$ 540	1.3%	$ 680	1.2%	$ 870	1.1%
Travel & Entertain.	$ 182	0.9%	$ 192	0.7%	$ 216	0.5%	$ 233	0.4%	$ 261	0.3%
Supplies & Displays	$ 340	1.7%	$ 433	1.5%	$ 633	1.5%	$ 900	1.5%	$ 1,238	1.6%
Other	$1,170	5.9%	$ 1,683	5.8%	$ 2,314	5.5%	$ 3,061	5.2%	$ 3,961	5.0%
TOTAL OPERATING EXPENSE	$7,195	36.1%	$10,067	34.5%	$14,255	34.0%	$19,417	33.2%	$25,737	32.5%
Operat. Profit(Loss)*	$1,549	7.8%	$ 2,329	8.0%	$ 3,925	9.4%	$ 6,330	10.8%	$ 9,621	12.1%
Catalog Inc.(Loss)**	$ (80)	-0.4%	$ 0	0.0%	$ 100	0.2%	$ 200	0.3%	$ 300	0.4%
E.B.I.T.	$1,469	7.4%	$ 2,329	8.0%	$ 4,025	9.6%	$ 6,530	11.2%	$ 9,921	12.5%
Interest & Other Ex.	$ 984	4.9%	$ 996	3.4%	$ 1,070	2.6%	$ 1,201	2.1%	$ 1,415	1.8%
Taxes	$ 185	0.9%	$ 506	1.7%	$ 1,234	2.9%	$ 2,158	3.7%	$ 3,388	4.3%
NET INCOME	$ 300	1.5%	$ 827	2.8%	$ 1,721	4.1%	$ 3,171	5.4%	$ 5,118	6.5%

* Excludes catalog gross profit
**Sum of Catalog Gross Profit and Catalog Expenses

BALANCE SHEET

	1989 Plan	1990 Plan	1991 Plan	1992 Plan	1993 Plan
ASSETS					
Inventories	$ 3,094	$ 4,190	$ 5,636	$ 7,416	$ 9,528
Other Current Assets	$ 548	$ 865	$ 1,122	$ 1,444	$ 1,842
Property & Equipment	$ 7,805	$ 9,722	$ 13,172	$ 17,182	$ 22,162
Accumulated Depreciation	$ (2,432)	$ (3,203)	$ (4,380)	$ (6,005)	$ (8,146)
Other Assets	$ 93	$ 93	$ 93	$ 93	$ 93
Goodwill	$ 309	$ 299	$ 289	$ 279	$ 269
TOTAL ASSETS	$ 9,417	$ 11,966	$ 15,932	$ 20,409	$ 25,748
LIABILITIES & OWNERS' EQUITY					
Accounts Payable*	$ 350	$ 304	$ 409	$ 538	$ 691
Accrued Expenses**	$ 1,272	$ 1,957	$ 2,750	$ 3,730	$ 4,906
Current Portion of L/T Debt	$ 134	$ 134	$ 134	$ 134	$ 134
Income Taxes Payable	$ 116	$ 455	$ 949	$ 1,749	$ 2,824
Long Term Debt	$ 5,022	$ 5,767	$ 6,622	$ 6,019	$ 3,834
TOTAL LIABILITIES	$ 6,894	$ 8,617	$ 10,864	$ 12,170	$ 12,389
STOCKHOLDERS' EQUITY	$ 2,523	$ 3,349	$ 5,068	$ 8,239	$ 13,359
TOTAL LIABILITIES & EQUITY	$ 9,417	$ 11,966	$ 15,932	$ 20,409	$ 25,748

* Most inventory was received in summer months and paid for by letter of credit.

**Accrued expenses include payroll payable, sales tax (5%), bonuses payable, percentage rent payable, negative cash float and other miscellaneous accrued expenses and accounts payable.

(All amounts expressed in thousands of dollars)

C a s e   24

LOWE'S

INTRODUCTION

Lowe's was a chain of 306 stores spread mainly over smaller towns in the southeastern United States. The stores offered full lines of "everything imaginable to repair, improve, or enhance the homes and apartments of America." These lines included building supplies, do-it-yourself materials and consumer durables such as home appliances and electronics. Sales in the year ending January 31, 1990 were over $2.6 billion. (See **Exhibit 1**, Map of Store Locations.)

Lowe's had recently embarked upon a program to build new forty and sixty thousand square foot stores. These stores, although considerably larger than their other stores, were significantly smaller than those being constructed by Home Depot, a major competitor whose stores ranged from one hundred to one hundred and forty thousand square feet. Were Lowe's new stores large enough to serve the smaller city and town do-it-yourself (DIY) and contractor constituencies which were Lowe's primary market? Should the eighty to one hundred thousand square foot stores being considered for the limited number of larger markets be considered in smaller markets? Furthermore was departmental emphasis correct? Currently, Lowe's was in several categories of merchandise such as white goods (major appliances) and brown goods (electronics) which Home Depot eschewed. Finally, there was the issue of Lowe's pricing practices. Home Depot religiously adhered to an everyday-low-pricing (EDLP) policy. Lowe's had always priced aggressively on an everyday basis, but had supplemented this policy with various kinds of weekly newspaper and other promotions. It now was being forced to fine tune and more explicitly communicate its pricing policies. How could they better communicate the attractiveness of their day in and day out prices as well as their promotions when confronted with Home Depot's highly publicized EDLP policy?

THE INDUSTRY

Lowe's competed in both the building contractor supply and the fast growing and highly competitive DIY industries. The total U.S. market for both industries in 1990 varied considerably with some analysts judging the market at around $100 billion and others at as high as $200 billion. The following table shows estimates of Lowe's total market potential.

Competition in the contractor segment had always been primarily from small, mainly independently owned lumber yards and other distributors such as electrical and plumbing wholesalers. Their prices generally were somewhat higher than Lowe's and they did not always have the same depth or breadth of merchandise. They did however, offer high levels of personalized service, and like Lowe's, extended credit. Lowe's competition in this market segment had not dramatically changed over the years.

This case was prepared by David Wylie under the supervision of Professor Walter J. Salmon as the basis for class discussion rather than to illustrate either effective or ineffective handling of an administrative situation.

Copyright © 1990 by the President and Fellows of Harvard College.
Harvard Business School case 590-013.

National Market Potential for Lowe's Type Merchandise (billions $)

Home Center

	Contractor New Housing	R&R[a]	DIY	Homeowner Durables	Total
1995(est)	60	48	99	43	250
1990	47	35	72	33	187
1985	40	25	54	29	148
1980	24	16	38	14	92
1975	22	8	22	8	60

a R&R refers to Repair and Remodelling

Although lumber yards had always done a limited amount of business with ultimate consumers, the post World War II building boom and the resulting explosion in home owners had given birth to the DIY business. Not surprisingly, the original retailers in this industry were mainly regional chains of lumberyards such as Grossman's, Scotty's, Central Hardware and even Lowe's who continued to do a substantial amount of contractor business as well. The promotional strategies of these original DIY competitors evolved, however, to focus more on the retail consumer with tabloids featuring seasonal merchandise, often supported by cooperative advertising funds from manufacturers.

During the formative years of the DIY industry, retailers had enjoyed a ground-swell of consumer demand as their businesses became more consumer oriented. More recently, companies which catered solely to the DIY trade had arisen. Such competition came both from somewhat more fashion oriented stores like Hechinger's and from large warehouse stores like Home Depot.

Hechingers operated seventy-five stores on the northern fringes of the Lowe's territory and was headquartered in the Washington/Baltimore area. The Hechinger stores offered comprehensive assortments of DIY merchandise and were particularly strong in areas such as housewares and related DIY merchandise such as wallpaper and floor tiles. Prices, while not as low as Home Depot, were competitive. Hechingers promoted through frequent sales, relying upon aggressive newspaper and direct mail advertising, and TV and radio where appropriate. Their prototype store was 60,000 square feet, with an additional 20,000 square feet of outdoor selling and storage space. In addition to the "Hechingers" format, Hechingers also operated several other format stores. One was "Home Quarters," a Home Depot clone, and another was "Triangle," a chain of six 21,000 to 70,000 square foot stores which catered to the small contractor trade.

By far the most heated competition for Lowe's and indeed the entire DIY industry came from Home Depot, and, so far, its less successful clone Builder's Square (a division of Kmart). In 1986, Home Depot had begun a rollout of stores up to 140,000 square feet in size. These stores had no exterior selling space except that devoted to nursery products and offered outstanding customer service and everyday low prices (EDLP). Having started in Atlanta, Home Depot now had nine stores in the Greater Atlanta area. Home Depot described its stores as "DIY warehouse stores which carried a wide range of building materials and home improvement products." Home Depot sales in 1989 were $2.75 billion which represented a 38% increase over 1988. Sales of stores open for more than a year had increased thirteen percent and earnings were up by 46%. (See **Exhibit 2** for Home Depot operating statements.) By early 1990, Home Depot operated 118 stores ranging in size from 67,000 to 140,000 square foot in major cities in the East from Connecticut to Florida, and across the South to California. The plan for 1990 included thirty new stores.

A typical Home Depot store carried 30,000 items. Their formula included highly competitive everyday low prices, which was stressed in its aggressive advertising program, combined with depth and breadth of assortment and high in-store service levels. In its 1987 Third Quarter Report, Home Depot stated:

As important as technology is, the Home Depot's success is founded on people and this is reflected in our corporate culture. By moving decision-making down to the lowest levels, we avoid a chain-store mentality and give our employees a sense of ownership which is uncommon in corporate America today. We encourage free expression, risk taking, personal initiative and teamwork.

Home Depot accepted all major consumer credit cards and, in addition, offered its own card. (See **Exhibit 3** for a sample Home Depot advertisement.)

In the United States, there were 283 home center warehouses similar to the Home Depot concept, 66% of which were in markets with populations greater than 1 million. In contrast, only 8% of Lowe's stores were in these major markets.

Other retailers also competed with Lowe's in particular merchandise categories. They ranged from specialty stores such as hardware stores, wallpaper stores and home and garden centers, to discount stores for smaller tools and housewares, and power retailers such as Circuit City which offered an outstanding selection of brown goods (such as televisions, VCRs, and audio equipment) and white goods (major appliances such as refrigerators, stoves, washers and dryers).

LOWE'S

Although Lowe's could trace its origins to before World War II, it began to take on its current characteristics in the mid 1950s. Then it was a chain of six small stores which catered to the needs of the building contractor, offering building materials at good prices. There was little display space and proportionately large back room inventories. Locations were secondary and the ongoing relationship between contractor and salesperson was very important for maintaining business and for extending credit. Competition was mainly small, local, independently owned lumberyards. During that period, Lowe's established an employee ownership and profit sharing plan which, in a revised form, in 1990 owned 26% of its stock. In 1955, Leonard Herring, the current president and CEO, was hired. Robert Strickland, currently chairman of the board, joined the company directly from the Harvard Business School in 1957. While Herring presided over everyday operations, Robert Strickland was more concerned with long range planning and relations with outside constituencies such as the financial community. In addition, he tried to remain close to government bodies which influenced laws and regulations pertaining to the employee stock ownership plan (ESOP).

Lowe's grew rapidly in the sixties and early seventies with the focus of the business on small contractors and a product line featuring building materials and appliances. By 1975, there were 141 stores in operation with sales of nearly $400 million.

To cater to contractors, Lowe's took telephone orders, often gathered merchandise from stock or selling areas, and delivered it at an extra charge. Because of the substantial quantities of merchandise they bought, contractors often negotiated for lower prices than Lowe's charged ultimate consumers.

Lowe's also provided contractors with credit. Store managers' judgement and relationship with contractors was a very important component in assessing the creditworthiness of contractors and in monitoring the resulting accounts receivable.

In 1978, spurred by the beginnings of one of the sharpest declines in housing starts in U.S. history and by the continuing boom in the DIY market, Lowe's began shifting its primary emphasis from contractor to DIY business. The move was expected both to provide higher margins and reduce the volatility of being tied so closely to the housing market.

This shift was not into an entirely new market for Lowe's. In the '50s, brand name appliances and other durables had been added to the line, mainly for contractor sales, but the clients of contractors often came to Lowe's to select fixtures, appliances, models and finishes, and thus had become familiar with the store. Lowe's, therefore, had developed a growing popularity with ultimate consumers.

In order to cater to the different demands of the consumer, Lowe's had to adapt the merchandise mix, the store layout and the kind of services being offered. These included (1) the addition of more consumer oriented lines such as brown goods, lawn and garden, wall coverings, light fixtures, DIY supplies, etc., (2) more display space in proportion to back room space as manufacturers responded to consumer demand for choice with a proliferation of models, finishes and colors, and (3) service levels which were more responsive to the needs of relatively less knowledgeable ultimate consumers.

The move was successful. From 1980 to 1984 retail sales increased from $420 to $881 million. Growing consumer business offset the continuing decline in the building industry. By 1984, consumer sales constituted 52% of total sales and became Lowe's core business. Contractor sales were considered "plus" business, although still extremely important. (See **Exhibit 4**, Lowe's Financial Performance showing trends of consumer vs. building contractor business since 1980.)

In 1984, to protect the successful consumer business, Lowe's decided to construct larger stores. Home Depot and others were a growing threat and Lowe's stores were stocked beyond capacity. The decision was made to increase breadth and depth of existing lines while increasing total company selling square footage 10% and the number of stores 5% annually. The smaller, older stores were to be retrofitted into larger 20,000 to 30,000 square foot retail units. New stores were designed with 30,000 square feet of selling space. In conjunction with this move, inventory was moved from the back room to the sales floor to encourage self service and thereby reduce the need for so much store personnel.

The focus was on existing smaller city and town markets where competition was mainly limited to independent operators and local chains of small stores. In addition, this focus avoided confronting the intensification of competition around major metropolitan areas. By introducing the larger store format into smaller towns, Lowe's was offering non-urban customers something which they never had before: choice. By 1989, retail sales represented 62% of total sales.

Consumer research completed in 1989, however, indicated that Lowe's had perhaps not gone far enough. The customer wanted more convenient locations, bigger assortments of merchandise, low prices every day, knowledgeable help and advice when they needed it, and reduced transaction time. The competitive climate was heating up as well, posing a serious threat to future growth. Competitors were offering wide assortments and low prices without sacrificing customer service by being deeply committed to high volume, low cost operations.

Management decided, therefore, to open larger and more powerful stores, to widen assortments by adding full ranges in every category to the basics they had focused on, to adopt an everyday low pricing policy, and to become more responsive to customers in each market by moving more merchandising authority to the stores. They hoped to achieve double digit annual sales increases by increasing sales volume in existing stores and generating even higher volumes in the newest stores. Achieving these goals was expected to lead to parity or better in sales per square foot compared to Home Depot.

Lowe's newest prototypes were 40,000 to 60,000 square foot stores plus 10,000 to 20,000 square feet of outside storage of bulky building materials to replace the 9,000 to 20,000 square foot models plus outside storage of yesteryear. For the largest markets and in those areas where zoning prohibited outside storage of building materials, even 100,000 square foot stores were contemplated. The accelerated store replacement program was scheduled for three years. While some stores would be immediately replaced, others would be remerchan-dised to reflect the new vision until new stores could be built.

At this time, chains like Home Depot were saturating the urban markets and planned to expand into secondary markets which were Lowe's stronghold. Lowe's management thought that Home Depot's resounding success in their first stores in new markets in the Northeast, however, may have temporarily diverted them from an interest in secondary markets. Lowe's thus might have a window of opportunity to consolidate their position in current markets. In the states in which Lowe's operated, there were 343 cities with populations more than 50,000 and less than 100,000, and 200 cities with populations over 100,000.

During 1989, Lowe's completed twelve new stores, twelve relocations and seven retrofits representing 1,210,153 square feet of incremental retail space. By end of 1989, stores with over 40,000 square feet constituted about twenty-four percent of the chain's floor space, and by 1991, almost thirty-nine percent of floor space would be in these stores. Plans for 1990 called for 1.5 million square feet of new construction, comprised of four new stores in existing markets, a contractor only yard in Nashville, Tennessee, and twenty-two relocations into 40,000, 60,000 and 100,000 square foot stores. The capital investment required in 1990 for these new stores, including investment in inventory, would be approximately $167 million, adding 1,225,624 square feet of incremental retail space.

Land costs for each new store would vary depending upon size and location but would range from $250,000 to over $1 million. Building, fixtures and equipment costs would approach industry averages for comparable construction of about $58 per square foot. Since accounts receivable were primarily from the contractor business, they were not expected to increase with the increased retail sales the larger stores would generate. Inventory levels were expected to increase somewhat, however, given the smaller proportion of high volume contractor business.

The new Lowe's stores were located in easily accessible areas with abundant parking. The facades featured wide entrances flanked by displays of seasonal merchandise. (See **Exhibit 5** for photographs of store.) Upon entering past the check out stations, the sense of space and selection was pervasive. Easily readable signs directed the customer to various supplies, tools and fixtures in the center of the store; to electronics, appliances, kitchen and home decor on the left; and seasonal, bath, and plumbing on the right. Millwork and enough lumber and building materials to service the retail trade were all to the rear of the store. The fast growing category of lawn and garden was in an open but roofed outside area on the right side. The aisles of the store itself were concrete, and wide enough for customers easily to push carts of lumber or for employees with fork lifts to replenish the shelves with inventory as it was delivered. The top portion of the twenty foot high industrial shelving was filled with back stock, lending an atmosphere of abundant inventory. There was no back room inventory space.

Throughout the store were easily readable product information signs, designed to lessen the need for customer assistance. There were still, however, two staffed information centers on the selling floor and a number of salespeople in the aisles. (See **Exhibit 6** for Store Plan.)

Near the rear loading dock was a separate entrance to the contractor sales department, where a dedicated staff handled orders and scheduled delivery for this important segment of Lowe's sales. Most contractor sales were telephone transactions. In some markets, the old smaller stores remained open as "contractor only yards" to supplement the contractor departments in the retail stores.

Within any given merchandise category, the offerings included a wide range of price points. Kitchen faucets, for instance, ranged from a basic fixture at $17.99 to a high end designer faucet at $129. In expanding stores, the goal was to move from a limited range of basic items to a full range which appealed to a much wider clientele. The same enhanced breadth of selection could be found in such categories as electronics, lighting fixtures, power and hand tools, nails, millwork, and lumber. By adding more selection, Lowe's aim was to generate both higher margins and increased sales. The new forty and sixty thousand square foot prototypes carried about 20,000 SKU's compared to the 12,000 carried in the older ten to twenty thousand square foot stores.

The stores were all managed by well paid store managers who had considerable autonomy, assuming growing responsibilities for advertising, pricing, reordering and other aspects of the business which required adaptations to local market conditions. The average manager was forty years old, had been a store manager for six years, and had been with the company for thirteen years. Salaries were competitive and augmented by a substantial bonus based on store performance. The top performing store managers could earn in excess of $100,000. Store managers reported through area general managers (each with about fifteen stores) to one of three regional vice presidents of store operations, who in turn reported to Wendell Emerine, the senior vice president store operations. (See **Exhibit 7**, Organization Chart.)

Like all employees, the managers participated in the ESOP to which the company contributed Lowe's stock at a rate determined annually by the board of directors. In recent years, this had been at a value equal to thirteen percent of gross annual salary, and had historically ranged from twelve to fifteen percent. This fund could produce net worth at retirement of over $1 million for long tenure store managers.

Other innovative programs also inspired employees to greater performance. One such program was the "Swing for a Million" contest for store managers and area general managers. Stores were grouped by budgeted sales and given points for meeting various milestones based on sales and margin budgets in the period between March and August, 1990. Managers of the most successful stores in each group were invited to a four-day vacation and golf tournament at a nearby resort. A manager who made a hole-in-one on the eighteenth hole received $1 million and an additional $1 million to be divided among all the store employees. Lowe's covered its exposure to one or more managers attaining this bonanza prize with insurance.

In the new 60,000 square foot stores, one or two assistant store managers and, when required, a contractor sales manager reported to the store manager. Reporting to the former were four floor managers responsible for various categories of merchandise. One, for example, might be responsible for bath, plumbing, lighting, and electrical while another might be responsible for lumber and millwork. Responsibilities, determined by the store manager, varied from store to store depending on the skills and interests of the floor managers and the needs of the market area. Some variation existed as well in the structure of the store organization among different size stores.

Reporting to the floor managers were salespeople who helped customers and restocked shelves. The policy for all employees was: "say 'yes' with enthusiasm to what-ever our customers ask." "The only person who can say 'no' to a customer at Lowe's is the store manager" stated this 1990 policy.

All full time and part time employees were eligible to participate in the ESOP after a two year waiting period, and all were paid competitive wages. Personnel who participated in the ESOP were given name badges which identified them as "manager-owners" or "employee-owners." Although turnover among many of the sales-people was substantial, management turnover was low.

Replenishment reorders were generated by the head-quarters computer system based on point of sale (POS) data. Store managers, assisted by floor managers, moni-tored the stores daily, noted any inventory shortages, and compared this information to the replenishment orders making any adjustments deemed appropriate. Often adjustments might be made in response to such local conditions as a favorable weather report or a special lo-cal "run-of-press" (ROP) advertisement. Warm weather in the entire Southeastern United States during a late winter week in 1990, for instance, prompted sales of 2,200 riding mowers compared to only 700 for the equivalent week the previous year. This unexpected shift would not have been anticipated by computer generated reorders.

Just as nobody except the manager was allowed to say "no" to a customer, nobody in the central buying office was allowed to say "no" to store managers. Ev-ery effort was made to supply them with whatever they wanted, even if it went against the better judgement of a buyer.

The computer system also was able to track the gross profit, and the direct buying and distribution expenses of all items by SKU. This system gave valuable infor-mation which the store staff used to help gauge the proper allocation of selling space. At times, however, execu-tives were concerned that this information prompted too much attention to detail while bigger perspectives such as displaying seasonally correct, dominant merchandise assortment were overlooked.

Fifty-two percent of the merchandise, mainly the more bulky commodities which would fill a truck load (such as lumber), usually were shipped directly from suppliers to stores. The remaining forty-eight percent flowed through two strategically located distribution centers which shipped merchandise to stores a minimum of two times per week. These orders from the distribution cen-ters arrived in the stores within, on average, five days.

The use of distribution centers significantly reduced both shipping cost and required smaller store inventory levels. In many instances it also lowered purchase prices from vendors. Indeed, some Lowe's executives thought that Lowe's 60,000 square foot stores could approach the selling capacity of Home Depot's stores since Home Depot did not make extensive use of distribution centers and therefore had to accommodate more inventory in the stores.

Lowe's management thought that training was a par-ticularly important element in executing its customer driven vision. It therefore offered management, sales, and product training seminars to all levels of the organi-zation. A six-member training team at headquarters spearheaded this effort. In addition to conducting some courses at a headquarters training facility, it conducted traveling seminars and demonstrations, and focused par-ticularly on training managers to train subordinates. In-store training was particularly important. Therefore the in-store library of training aids included videotapes and self-instruction manuals on such subjects as cash register operation, blue print takeoffs and specific prod-uct information. A satellite system to provide a video broadcast link between headquarters and the stores, which would enhance training efforts, was to commence operations in August, 1990.

Advertising was an area in which the stores had always played an important role. Thirty percent of the advertising budget was devoted to ROP printed adver-tising in local newspapers, over which the store man-ager had complete control. Suggested formats were prepared at headquarters from which the store manager could cut and paste an advertisement suitable for his or her market. (See **Exhibit 8** for sample advertisements.) For many items, prices were left to the discretion of the manager to meet local competition, while prices for oth-ers were established centrally to be consistent with prices in the weekly newspaper inserts produced by headquar-ters. These weekly advertisements absorbed another fifty percent of the advertising budget.

The quest for market penetration and a current shift towards image advertising meant that television was likely to become a more effective advertising tool. In 1989, television had grown from six percent to eleven percent of the advertising budget while radio (three per-cent), billboards, magazines, and direct marketing (six percent) made up the balance. Concurrent with the in-crease in television advertising was a reduction in the budget percentage allocated to newspaper inserts.

In contrast to Lowe's expenditures, Home Depot was supposed to be spending forty percent of their advertising budget on large (sixty page) monthly newspaper inserts, thirty percent on ROP generated regionally by headquarters, and eighteen percent on television. The latter focused on new store openings. It featured specific products at very attractive everyday low prices and, like Lowe's, was often supported by manufacturers "coop" funds. The remainder of its advertising budget was used for radio and other advertising. Whereas Lowe's spent three percent of non-contractor sales on advertising, Home Depot allegedly averaged less than two percent.

HEADQUARTERS ORGANIZATION

The new organization of the headquarters buying pyramid reflected the attitude of being "there to support the stores" rather than the older attitude of the stores "being there to move the goods." Bob Tillman, the senior vice president of merchandising, had recently been promoted from the role of regional vice president of operations, previously having been the store manager of the first "twenty million dollar store." Vice presidents responsible for distribution, advertising, store merchandising, and merchandising administration reported to Tillman as well as five merchandising vice presidents.

Tillman described his new organization in a memorandum: "This new merchandising organization focuses increased emphasis on the marketing side of the business, while continuing to provide the very best replenishment service possible. Most important, this organization will help create a pro-active, market driven Merchandising Department, with a highly focused management team with greater responsibility, as well as authority, to run the business."

Rather than having buyers be responsible for sourcing and distribution as before, a marketing manager and an operations manager now reported to each of the merchandising vice presidents. "Marketing specialists" (formerly buyers), who reported to the marketing manager, managed each merchandise category as a profit center. They were responsible for sourcing, marketing, vendor negotiation, and planning. They provided the big "vision." The operations department, which was headed by the operations manager, was staffed by operations specialists assisted by "replenishers." The operations specialists had responsibility for inventory management, administration, re-buying, daily operations, and providing service to the stores. Both marketing specialists and operations specialists were encouraged to spend at least twenty-five percent of their time in the stores.

In addition to Tillman and Emerine, the senior vice president of store operations, senior vice presidents of real estate and of finance reported to the president and chief executive officer, Leonard Herring. These officers had quite traditional functions. A vice president of human resources reported to the senior vice president of finance.

FUTURE CONSIDERATIONS

While Lowe's management was confident that the format of the new stores was ready for the full scale rollout, it was still being refined. The process of expanding the merchandise assortment in the stores, for instance, had been progressing department by department but was not yet complete. Lowe's was adding wider assortments in all categories of merchandise including those which Home Depot shunned such as home electronics and appliances. Home Depot focused almost exclusively on wide assortments in the do-it-yourself category. This aggressive expansion of Lowe's assortment was still in process, and management was not yet sure of its ultimate form.

Another issue which attracted the continual attention of Lowe's executives was the activity of competitors such as Home Depot and Circuit City in home electronics. While Lowe's was holding its position in Atlanta where Home Depot was so dominant, it was moving as quickly as possible in smaller and large cities alike to replace smaller stores with bigger facilities fully capable of competing with new competition such as Circuit City and Home Depot. In addition, however, Lowe's was giving added attention to smaller markets where its unique synergistic blend of contractor and retail business allowed it to prosper. Did that mean it should continue to carry in smaller communities more categories of merchandise but fewer SKU's in each category?

As the merchandise mix changed to be increasingly responsive to the retail customer, attention had to be given to maintaining assortments attractive and accessible to the core contractor trade. (See **Exhibit 9**, Sales by Category and Customer Type.) There was certainly temptation to emphasize the more profitable new categories at the expense of the more historically successful, but less profitable, assortments of basics. How far, management wondered, could this emphasis go without jeopardizing the blend of consumer and contractor business upon which Lowe's had thrived? (See **Exhibit 10**, Comparative Product Category Statistics.)

Lowe's was also facing some pricing and advertising policy issues. Lowe's had always had everyday low pricing in certain parts of the business. Advertising, however, had historically focused on frequent promotions and sales. Now it had to emphasize wide selection and good service as well as attractive prices. What media would best convey this multifaceted message?

Lowe's was anxious to take advantage of its "window of opportunity" to expand and modernize its store network. On the other hand, management wondered what additional changes they should make in the stores to strengthen them even further.

Exhibit 1
Map of Store Locations

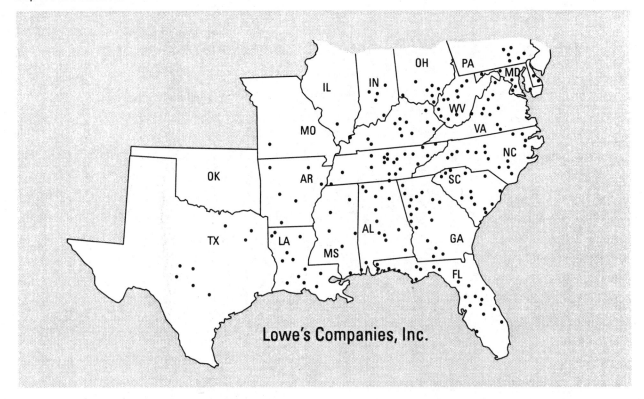

Lowe's Companies, Inc.

Exhibit 2
Home Depot Operating Statements (dollars in millions)

	1980	1981	1982	1983	1984	1985	1986	1987	1988	1989
Number of stores	4	8	10	19	31	50	60	75	96	118
Square footage (thousands)	249	507	696	1,449	2,381	4,001	4,828	6,161	8,216	10,424
Avg. square footage per store	62,250	63,375	69,600	76,263	76,806	80,020	80,467	82,147	85,583	88,339
Avg. sales per square foot	$ 88	$ 101	$ 170	$ 177	$ 182	$ 175	$ 209	$ 236	$ 243	$ 265
Total sales	$ 22	$ 51	$ 118	$ 256	$ 433	$ 701	$ 1,011	$ 1,453	$ 2,000	$ 2,758
Gross margin	30.7%	28.6%	28.4%	27.3%	26.4%	25.9%	27.5%	27.7%	27.0%	27.9%
Expenses										
Selling and stores	20.6%	19.0%	16.5%	17.0%	17.3%	19.2%	18.7%	18.1%	17.9%	18.3%
Pre-opening	0.1%	1.5%	0.4%	1.0%	0.4%	1.1%	0.3%	0.3%	0.4%	0.3%
G & A	4.3%	3.7%	3.3%	2.9%	2.9%	2.9%	2.7%	2.6%	2.4%	2.4%
Operating income	1.2	2.3	9.7	16.7	25.1	19.0	58.3	98.2	126.7	185.0
Operating income %	5.5%	4.5%	8.2%	6.5%	5.8%	2.7%	5.8%	6.8%	6.3%	6.6%
Net inc. bef. extraord. items	$ 0.5	$ 1.2	$ 5.3	$ 10.2	$ 14.1	$ 8.2	$ 23.8	$ 54.1	$ 76.7	$ 111.9

Balance Sheet (dollars in millions)

Assets	1988	1989
Cash & short term invest.	$ 16	$ 135
Accounts receivable	18	39
Merchandise inventory	294	381
Prepaid expenses	9	11
Total current assets	337	566
Fixed assets	354	535
Other assets	7	16
Total assets	$698	$1,117

Liabilities	1988	1989
Total current liabilities	$194	$ 292
Long term debt	108	303
Deferred income tax	14	10
Total liabilities	316	605
Shareholder equity	382	512
Total liabilities and equity	$698	$1,117

Exhibit 3
Sample Page from Home Depot Newspaper Insert, Cover Page

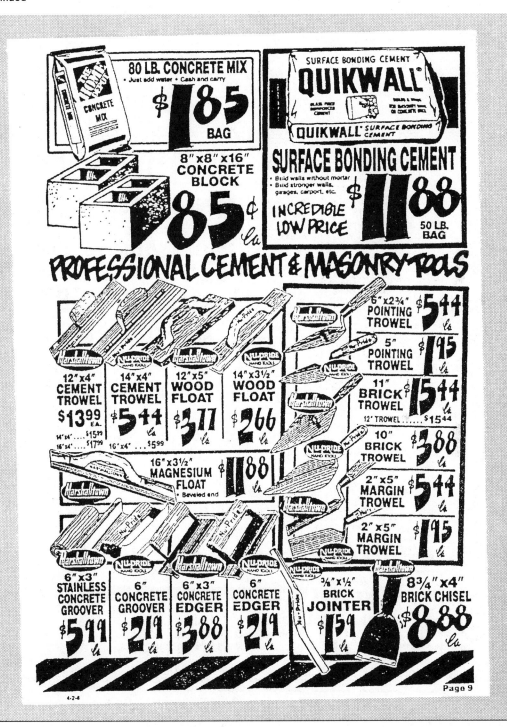

Exhibit 4
Lowe's Financial Performance (dollars in millions)[a]

	1980	1981	1982	1983	1984	1985	1986	1987	1988	1989
Number of stores	214	229	235	238	248	282	300	295	296	306
Square footage (thousands)	1,998	2,232	2,337	2,529	2,980	3,641	4,452	4,773	5,062	6,219
Avg. square footage per store	9,336	9,747	9,945	10,626	12,016	12,911	14,840	16,180	17,101	20,324
Avg. sales per square foot	$442	$397	$442	$565	$566	$569	$513	$511	$497	$426
Sales										
Retail	$419	$460	$570	$723	$881	$1,098	$1,261	$1,374	$1,484	$1,649
Building contractor	464	427	463	706	807	974	1,021	1,067	1,032	1,001
Total Sales	883	887	1,033	1,429	1,688	2,072	2,282	2,441	2,516	2,650
Gross Margin	$205	$220	$261	$359	$426	$512	$559	$583	$600	$646
Gross Margin Percent[b]	23.2%	24.8%	25.3%	25.1%	25.2%	24.7%	24.5%	23.9%	23.8%	24.4%
Expenses										
SGA	$144	$164	$187	$231	$269	$343	$382	$403	$410	$447
Depreciation	10	10	11	12	14	21	30	38	41	46
Employee retirement	10	9	10	17	20	23	24	21	22	24
Other								9[c]		
Total expenses	164	183	208	260	303	387	436	462	473	517
Earnings before int. and taxes	41	37	53	99	123	125	123	121	127	129
Interest	4	3	4	1	2	11	13	19	21	19
Taxes	17	15	22	46	58	53	53	34	36	34
Net inc. bef. extraord. items	19	18	25	50	61	60	55	56	69	74

Balance Sheet (January 31) (dollars in millions)

	1980	1981	1982	1983	1984	1985	1986	1987	1988	1989
Assets										
Cash	$15	$32	$25	$74	$84	$87	$50	$44	$60	$66
Accounts receivable	68	48	75	94	97	127	118	118	127	122
Merchandise inventory	125	113	167	205	248	313	368	373	379	408
Other current assets	1	2	3	3	3	7	10	7	9	0
Deferred income taxes								9	1	1
Total current assets	$209	$195	$270	$376	$432	$534	$546	$552	$578	$596
Fixed assets	$91	$110	$121	$141	$195	$308	$413	$453	$479	$508
Other assets	$1	$1	$1	$1	$6	$13	$9	$22	$28	$44
Total assets	$301	$306	$393	$519	$634	$856	$969	$1,027	$1,085	$1,147
Liabilities										
Accounts payable	$52	$48	$90	$110	$125	$168	$163	$157	$203	$210
Other current liabilities	29	32	44	58	64	83	94	44	44	98
Total current liabilities	80	80	134	169	189	252	257	232	286	308
Long term debt	51	49	56	52	92	184	153	186	190	168
Total liabilities	$133	$129	$194	$228	$293	$449	$429	$445	$499	$502
Shareholder's equity	$169	$177	$198	$291	$341	$407	$540	$582	$586	$645
Total Liabilities and Equity	$301	$306	$393	$519	$634	$856	$969	$1,027	$1,085	$1,147

a Totals may reflect rounding errors.
b Gross margins were several points higher for the retail business than for contractor business.
c The 1987 other expense represents the estimated total of closing a group of stores.

Cash Flow	1986	1987	1988
Cash from operations	$87	$103	$115
Changes in assets and liabilities			
Accounts Receivable	9	1	(9)
Merchandise Inventory	(55)	(6)	(5)
Accounts Payable	(5)	(6)	46
Employee Retirement	12	15	21
Other	7	1	1
Net Cash from operations	55	108	168
Cash from investing activities			
Fixed assets acquired	(131)	(92)	(82)
Cash from sale of fixed assets	5	2	5
Other long term assets	4	4	3
Total cash used in investing	(123)	(86)	(74)
Net cash from financing activities	31	29	78
Net increase in cash	(37)	(6)	16
Cash at end of year	50	44	60

Exhibit 5
Photographs of Lowe's Store

Exhibit 6
Plan of 60,000 Square Foot Store

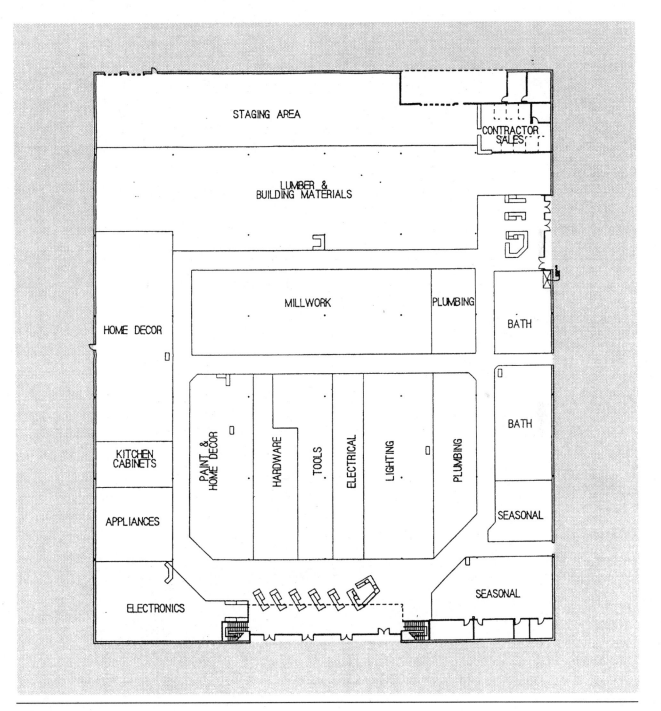

Exhibit 7
Organization Chart

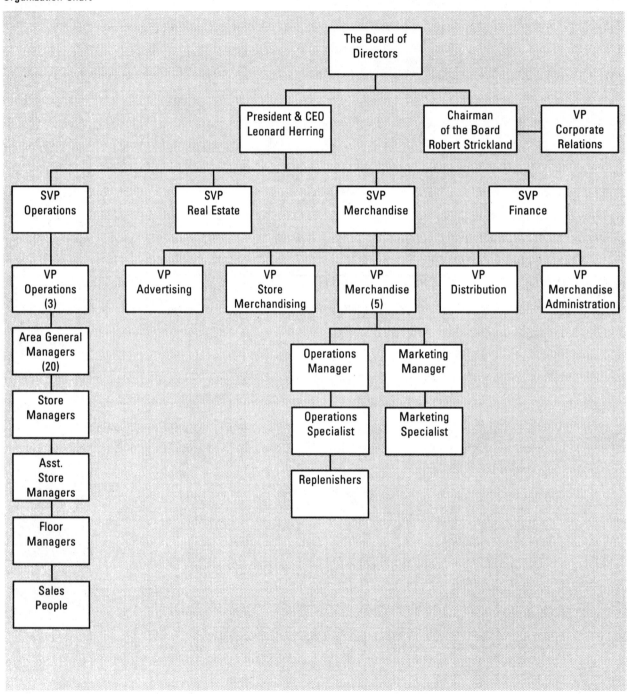

Exhibit 8
Sample Advertisements, Suggested ROP Advertisement

Exhibit 8, continued

$19⁸⁷
8" Electric String Trimmer #96571

$28⁸⁸
12" Electric String Trimmer #95557

$69⁸⁷
15" Gas-Powered String Trimmer #91578

$89⁶³
McCULLOCH
17" Gas-Powered String Trimmer #96546
2-Cycle Engine Oil
67¢
8 oz. #91406,93467

$128
18" Gas-Powered String Trimmer/ Brushcutter
Comes with 2 blades. #96544
Replacement Trimmer Line
$8⁶⁷
400 ft. .080 line. #91582

$166
18" Gas-Powered String Trimmer/ Brushcutter
52" straight shaft. 30cc 2-cycle engine. 8" wheel blade. #96545

$28⁷³
14" Electric Hedge Trimmer
2.2 amp motor. 3,600 cutting strokes per minute. #98010
19" Hedge Trimmer   #98014 $38.45

Gas-Powered Yard Blower
21.2 cc 2-cycle engine. Includes 12½" concentrator nozzle. Solid state ignition. #91560
$83⁷⁷

Electric Yard Blower
Achieves up to 125 mph air velocity. 8.5 amp motor switch. 2 speed. #91598
$39⁸¹

WEED EATER

$218
Commercial Duty 3 HP Gas Lawn Edger
Up to 3" cutting depth. 11 cutting angles that can be adjusted from handle. Grease fittings for maintenance. #91592

YOUR CHOICE
$8⁴⁶ Each

Lawn And Garden Tools
Poly rake, round point shovel, warren hoe, 4-prong cultivator, 14-tooth rake, garden hoe. #90635;94322,8;99681,764,9
4   *Credit Terms On Page 15

$25⁶²
36"x 50' Vinyl-Coated Fence
Green vinyl coating helps resist rust and corrosion. 2"x 3" mesh. #92253

48"x 50' Vinyl-Coated Fence	#92254	$32.62
4' Fence Post	#92063	$2.04
5' Fence Post	#92064	$2.43

$19⁸³
42"x 3' Gard-N-Gate®
Lets you make a gate with the same fabric as your fence. Includes hardware. #92261

| 42"x 4' Gate | #92262 | $22.83 |

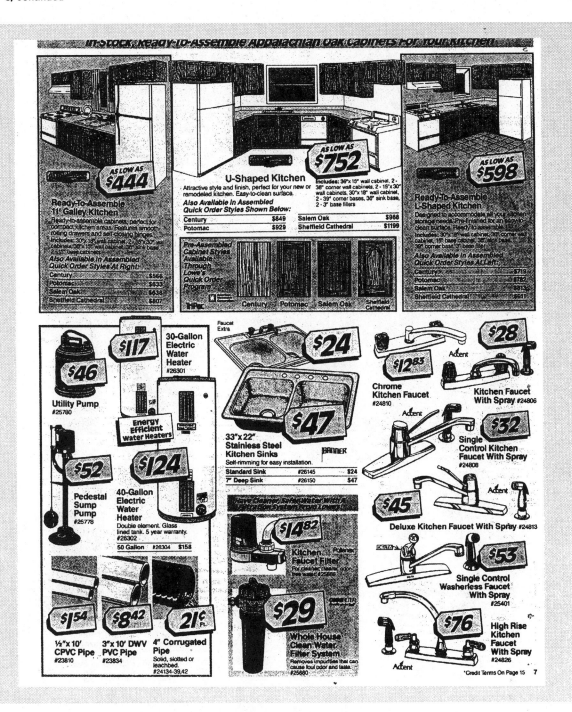

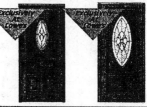

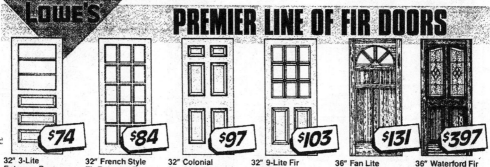

Exhibit 8, continued
Page from Regional Newspaper Insert

24" Or 48" Decorative Fluorescent Fixture — $34 / $27
Both have acrylic diffuser for soft, even lighting. Ideal for kitchen, bath, work area or any room. Both have oak ends. #75423,4

48" Or 96" Fluorescent Ceiling Fixture — YOUR CHOICE $19 88
48" fixture has acrylic diffuser. 96" fixture is perfect for garage or basement. #75406,74645

Brass Piano Lamp — $19
Polished brass finish. #78718

Swing Arm Table Lamp — $19
Polished brass finish. Includes shade. #78716
Bulbs Extra For All Light Fixtures

Chrome, Polished Brass Or Antique Brass Finish Bath Bar Light — YOUR CHOICE $12
#73400,7,15

Oak And Polished Brass Bath Light — $15
#73425

Pendant Light — $21 88 #79181
Beveled Glass Chandelier — $44 #79175

12" Ceiling Light — $4 77 #74125
6" Round Light — $6 87 #74437

3-Light Brass & Glass Ceiling Fixture — $26 #79177
4-Light Fixture #79176 $39

Photo Sensor Floodlight — $14 #72665

Dusk To Dawn Security Light — $26 #74011

Fluorescent Entrance Light #74002 — $15

Solar Walklight — $28 #71407

75 Or 150 Watt Outdoor Flood Lamp — YOUR CHOICE $1 92 #75229,31

3-Pack Light Bulbs — YOUR CHOICE 79¢
Choose 40, 60, 75 or 100 watts. #75220-3

200 Amp 20-Space Panel Box — $79 #71776

YOUR CHOICE 15, 20 Or 30 Amp Single-Pole Breaker — $3 82 #71922,4,6

12/2 With Ground Copper Cable — $29 36
250' roll. 20 amp. #70111

½"x 10' EMT Electrical Conduit — $1 51 #72711
¾"x 10' Thinwall EMT Electrical Conduit #72713 $2.16
½"x 10' PVC Electrical Conduit #72808 $1.19
¾"x 10' PVC Electrical Conduit #72809 $1.87

Weatherproof Floodlamp Holder — $1 88 #72164

PVC Electrical Box — 19¢
16 cu. in. #70991

Ceiling Electrical Box — 67¢
Non-metallic. #70976

¾" Clamp Connector For Conduit — $1 46
Bag 10 per bag. #75637

Duplex Outlet — 45¢
Brown or ivory. #70500,695

Single Pole Switch — 45¢
Brown or ivory. #70400,605

6-Outlet Strip With Surge Protection — $8 87 #70387

Outdoor Extension Cord — $9 87
100' cord. #70372

14   *Credit Terms On Page 15

I—

Video:
We open with a shot of a woman working in a garden—Mary. The voice-over (VO) speaks to her, and she looks up and smiles.
Audio:
VO: Mary, Mary, oh so merry, how does your garden grow?
Mary: With pretty plants and flowering shrubs, all from down at Lowe's!
VO: I didn't know they had at Lowe's so many plants to see.
Mary: Yes, indeed, if you need plants, Lowe's is the place to be.
VO: But I need trees, and healthy seeds, and rosy bushes, too.
Mary: Then go to Lowe's and find them all—they're waiting there for you.
VO: Thank you, Mary, now I'm merry, because now I, too, know. . .
Mary: That anything that blooms or grows, you can find right now—at Lowe's!
VO: Lowe's garden center—it's growing everyday.

II—

Video: Mother-type lady standing in front of a freshly painted wall.
Audio: Mother: Would you ever think of doing this to your wall?
Video: She draws on the wall with lipstick or crayon.
Audio: Or this?
Video: She smears a handful of mud on the wall.
Audio: Or even this. . . !
Video: She takes a slice of tomato and flings it against the wall.
Audio: You probably wouldn't, you probably wouldn't, but if you have kids, you know they might.
Video: She holds up a can of "One and Only" paint.
Audio: That's why you need "One and Only" interior paint from Lowe's. With "One and Only," stains like these wash away. . .
(she washes one or more of the stains off the wall) time after time after time. . .
Video: Close-up of can of "One and Only."
Audio: Lowe's "One and Only" interior paint. The one and only paint you'll ever need.

Exhibit 9
Sales by Category and Customer Type

1989 Dollars in millions	Contractor $	Sales %	Consumer $	Sales %
Structural Lumber	$ 268	26.8%	$ 187	11.3%
Building commodities and millwork	400	40.0	361	21.9
Home decorating and illuminating	60	6.0	286	17.3
Kitchens, bathrooms and laundries	46	4.6	191	11.6
Heating, cooling and water systems	19	1.9	125	7.6
Home entertainment	6	0.6	119	7.2
Recreation, yard, patio, garden and farm	16	1.6	245	14.8
Tools	16	1.6	96	5.8
Special order sales	170	17.0	40	2.4
Total	$1,001	100.0%	$1,650	100.0%

Exhibit 10
Comparative Product Category Statistics

Department	General Industry All Firms		Lowe's		
	% 1987 Sales	% Space	% '88 Sales Ret.	Total	% Space
Lumber/building materials/millwork	56%	25%	34%	53%	27%
Hardware/tools	12	22	8	6	9
Plumbing/electrical/heating/cooling	10	13	12	9	16
Paint/Paint Sundries	6	11	4	3	5
Kitchen/bath/other decor	11	15	12	9	18
Lawn and garden	3	5	14	9	8
Other	2	9	16	11	17

Source: *Home Center Magazine*, "1988 Market Profile," Spring 1988, Lowe's Marketing Research.
Note: Numbers for "all firms" category were taken from survey information and generally represent respondents' estimates. Lowe's numbers were calculated using Lowe's sales figures but do not necessarily represent core groups.

Department	General Industry—1987, Among Firms With					
	10+ Stores		26-74% DIY[a]		75% DIY	
	% Sales	% Space	%Sales	% Space	% Sales	% Space
Lumber/building materials/millwork	48%	27%	60%	26%	41%	13%
Hardware/tools	14	20	11	22	16	22
Paint and Sundries	8	10	5	11	8	14
Plumbing/electrical/heating/cooling	13	15	8	14	16	16
Kitchen/bath/other decor	12	18	11	15	13	12
Lawn and garden	4	4	2	5	5	8
Other Merchandise	1	6	3	7	1	15

Source: *Home Center Magazine*, "1988 Market Profile," Spring 1988; Lowe's Marketing Research
a This means that DIY sales were 26% to 74% of the total. The balance were contractor sales.

Department	Home Quarters % of Sales For Year Ended			Lowe's % '88 Sales	
	Jan. 26, 1986	Jan. 25 1987	Jul. 26 1987	Ret.	Tot.
Lumber/building materials/millwork	30%	27%	28%	34%	53%
Plumbing/electrical	33	33	32	12	9
Hardware/tools	11	11	10	8	6
Paint/wallpaper/furniture	9	9	9	4[a]	3
Decor/storage/housewares	4	5	5	12[a]	9
Lawn and garden/seasonal	13	15	16	14	9

Source: Competitor Files, Lowe's Marketing Research.
Prototype store: 100,000 total sq. ft.
Average Number of Items: 25,000 sku's

Note: This is the most recent information available for Home Quarters as a separate unit.[a]
a Also, some product categories may not match exactly. For instance, Lowe's paint numbers do not include wallpaper and furniture and Lowe's decor numbers include kitchen and bath products. From the information available, it is not clear where kitchen and bath products plus other miscellaneous products are included in HQ's numbers. Since we have put many of these miscellaneous products in an "other" category, Lowe's numbers do not add to 100% on this table.

Department	Home Depot % of '88 Sales	Lowe's % of '88 Sales	
		Retail	Total
Lumber/building materials	27%	34%	53%
Plumbing/heating/electrical	31	12	9
Hardware/tools	13	8	6
Lawn & Garden/Seasonal	14	14	9
Paint	15	4	3

Source: Competitor Files, Lowe's Marketing Research. (Most information from Prudential-Bache analyst report on Builder's Square.)

Average Store: 90,000 - 100,000 sq. ft.

Average Number of Items: 30,000 sku's.

Note: Some product categories may not match exactly. For instance, these numbers for Home Depot do not break out miscellaneous products which are included in an "other" category for Lowe's. From the information available, it is not clear which of the above categories for Home Depot have absorbed these "other" products. For this reason, Lowe's numbers do not add to 100% in this table.

Department	Builder's Square % of '88 Sales	Lowe's % of '88 Sales	
		Retail	Total
Lumber/building materials	41%	34%	53%
Plumbing/heating/electrical	20	12	9
Hardware/tools	20	8	6
Lawn & Garden/Seasonal	11	14	9
Paint	8	4	3

Percent of space: 40% of the store devoted to Lumber & Building Materials according to management (versus 27% of Lowe's space).

Source: Competitor Files, Lowe's Marketing Research. (Most information from Prudential-Bache analyst report.)

Average Store: 80,000–90,000 sq. ft.

Average Number of Items at Builder's Square: Started at 35,000 sku's then dropped to 22,000 and reportedly will go down to 17,000–18,000 (no mention of when).

Note: Some product categories may not match exactly. For instance, these numbers for Builder's Square do not break out miscellaneous products which are included in an "other" category for Lowe's. From the information available, it is not clear which of the above categories for Builder's Square have absorbed these "other" products. For this reason, Lowe's numbers do not add to 100% in this table.

Case 25

TALBOTS

Talbots was a specialty retailer and mail order seller of updated classic women's apparel headquartered in Hingham, Massachusetts. In 1988 it was purchased by the Japanese retail company JUSCO Co., LTD., a core company of the conglomerate, ÆON, and in February of 1990 opened the first Talbots store in Japan. Talbots' senior executives were reviewing the events and decisions which had led to this international expansion. They were also, in view of Talbots anticipated growth in the United States and increasing involvement in Japan, appraising the extent to which Talbots should engage in further international expansion. Might critical energies be diffused? Was the Japanese model appropriate for further international expansion, and indeed right for Japan?

TALBOTS

Talbots was founded by Rudolf and Nancy Talbot in 1947 as a single store retailer in the Boston suburb of Hingham. In 1973, it was purchased by General Mills and by early 1988 had grown to 119 stores. It categorized its stores as village, urban, and mall, depending upon location. With few exceptions, the stores were all very similar. The typical store size was approximately 4,600 square feet, 3,700 of which was selling space. The decor conveyed an informal country look through extensive use of attractively finished maple leasehold improvements and fixtures. The front door of every Talbots store featured a bright red door. Annual store sales averaged $2.1 million. In addition, catalog sales in the fiscal year ending January 1990 accounted for just over a third of total sales of $453 million. (See **Exhibit 1** for photo of a store and **Exhibit 2** for recent financial performance.)

The merchandise assortment included weekend, classic and career clothing and special occasion clothing for misses and petites. In addition, a complementary line of accessories was offered. Pricing was identical in the Talbots stores and catalogs. Prices ranged from $9 for color coordinated knee socks to over $350 for a wool wrap coat. Blouses were clustered in the range of $50 to $100, while dresses ranged from $100 to $200. This assortment represented an offering in the mid to upper range.

By 1990, over 60% of the merchandise was private label. This percentage was increasing steadily with the growth of the company. Much of the remaining merchandise was designed exclusively for Talbots by major American resources such as Alpert Nipon, Herman Geist, Jones New York and Susan Bristol. Thirty percent of the private label merchandise was directly imported through Hong Kong, while the remainder was ordered through U.S. vendors.

There were 24 catalogs published annually, with a combined circulation in the United States and sixteen foreign countries of more than seventy-eight million. Complete catalogs offering the entire assortment for each

This case was prepared by David Wylie under the supervision of Professor Walter J. Salmon, with the special assistance of Professor Hiro Takeuchi, as the basis for class discussion rather than to illustrate either effective or ineffective handling of an administrative situation. Certain numbers in the case have been disguised but are nonetheless useful in assessing the economics of the situation.

of the four main selling seasons were mailed to most of the active customer list. A variety of specialty catalogs targeted more focused groups within the list.

The merchandise offering in the main catalogs for each season generally paralleled that of the stores with a somewhat broader assortment of apparel. Specialty catalog series focused on narrower fashion spectra. One such series, for instance, was the "Resumé" series featuring career clothing. (See **Exhibit 3** for representative pages from several catalogs.)

Catalog customers could return merchandise to any store, and items not normally available or out of stock in the stores could be ordered by catalog from within stores via Talbots "Red Line Phone," which connected the customer directly to a telemarketing sales associate. This procedure effectively extended the merchandise selection at the stores to all that was offered in the catalogs.

According to an independent survey commissioned by Talbots, the profile of its typical customer was a well educated woman with a household income of over $75,000. Her median age was forty-three (ranging from twenty-five to sixty-five). Sixty percent of the customers surveyed had college degrees, sixty-seven percent were married and fifty percent were employed.

Competition for this affluent segment of the population was intense in both catalog and store channels. Major direct competitors included, in addition to department stores like Lord & Taylor and Marshall Fields, specialty stores such as Ann Taylor, Eddie Bauer, The Gap, and Carroll Reed. Well established catalog operations such as J. Crew, Eddie Bauer, Lands End, and L.L. Bean also targeted this segment. In addition, a host of less well known catalog operations and a plethora of regional specialty stores competed in all of the markets in which Talbots operated.

Talbots growth in the 1970s and early 1980s had created capacity constraints in information systems, distribution and telemarketing. Beginning in 1987, expansion continued more cautiously while an infrastructure for a much larger Talbots was developed. A distribution and catalog fulfillment center was built in Lakeville, Massachusetts. This facility had a 360,000 square foot footprint and a two-story working area of 550,000 square feet. It was expandable to over 2 million square feet, and incorporated the latest computer and material handling technologies to enable five hundred associates to process 25,000 items per day. Ultimate capacity, if expanded, would be triple this volume. A computer system with greatly expanded capacity was installed in a Florida facility. Finally a second 25,000 square foot telemarketing center was built in Knoxville, Tennessee. Coupled with these efforts was the opening of a product office in New York in 1987 and a buying office in 1989 in Hong Kong for the purpose of improving gross margins, providing liaison with vendors as well as undertaking product research, development, and quality control activities.

Underlying Talbots organizational structure (see **Exhibit 4** for organizational chart) was a powerful corporate culture which was conducive to maintaining a strong customer orientation and dedication to the Talbots long standing creed of: "do what is right for the customer."

Both a buying pyramid and a merchandise administration pyramid reported to the executive vice president and general merchandise manager, who reported to the president and chief executive officer, Arnold Zetcher. Six planners within the merchandise administration pyramid developed aggregate seasonal sales plans by department for the stores. These plans, or "open-to-buys" as they were called, included inventory levels, sales, markdowns and receiving objectives for calendar periods within each season. The buyers would then negotiate with vendors, choose merchandise, and determine quantities according to their open-to-buys. When the merchandise arrived at the distribution center, the nine distributors (who reported to the planners) allocated the merchandise to the various stores. (This method of allocating merchandise was called post-distribution. In contrast, pre-distribution referred to the practice of allocating merchandise to the stores as it was ordered from the vendors.) Distributors, who were mainly entry-level employees just out of college, used sophisticated computer software to assist them in their efforts.

Ten to 15 stores deemed to be underperforming their potential were always designated as "opportunity" stores, and given special attention. Representatives from among the planners, buyers and distributors met weekly to discuss these stores' unique requirements. Talbots executives felt that such attention not only helped the stores, but gave headquarters representatives a valuable added perspective.

Initial prices and markdowns for sale events were established within the central buying pyramid as well. Each store put any unsold seasonal merchandise on sale at sharply reduced prices at the end of each season. Goods still unsold at the conclusion of the seasonal sales were transferred to designated regional "surplus stores," which had a clientele especially interested in reduced price merchandise. Management felt the other alternative of deep additional markdowns at all stores detracted from the image of consistent quality and price points. Sales confined to the end of a season were not felt to detract from Talbots image of quality.

Store managers at Talbots enjoyed a considerable amount of autonomy with commensurate accountability compared to many other retail operations. Although initial inventories and operating guidelines were set by headquarters, managers were completely responsible for the display of merchandise and for the entire operation of the stores. Their incentive package included, in addition to a competitive salary, a bonus tied to corporate targets for the store's sales, sales per square foot and shrinkage. Sales associates were all paid competitive hourly wages but no commissions.

Store managers reported, through twenty-two district managers and four regional managers, to the senior vice president of stores who reported to Zetcher. They were counseled by roving visual merchandise managers who reported to this senior vice president. Also reporting to Zetcher were senior vice presidents of operations (whose responsibilities included store design and construction, catalog distribution, and the operation of the merchandise distribution center), human resources, marketing (customer service, telemarketing, list management, catalog mailing control and public relations), catalog development (design, layout and production), finance, MIS, and legal/real estate.

Talbots maintained a warm and friendly working environment for their 4,000 plus "associates," referring to the organization as a family. The headquarters staff of about 750 worked in a campus-like facility in Hingham. Although lines of communication were well defined, informal communications were important in maintaining the "hands-on" team approach to doing business.

More aggressive expansion resumed during the last part of the 1980s. Talbots had 157 stores by the end of 1989 with 28 new stores planned for the United States in 1990. Sales of stores open for more than a year ("comp stores") had been growing at a rate of 5.8% in 1988 and 5.2% in 1989. By comparison, The Gap had 909 stores in 1988, sales of $1.25 billion, and comp store growth of 7.7%. Equivalent numbers for The Limited were 3,381 stores, sales of $4.1 billion, and comp store growth of 8%.

ÆON

The ÆON Group was one of Japan's leading retail groups. By 1989, it was a broadly diversified retailer with superstores which operated under the "JUSCO" name, department stores, specialty stores, restaurants and service operations extending across Japan. Sales were ¥1.2 trillion (US$9.6 billion). The name of the group had recently been changed from JUSCO to ÆON on its twentieth anniversary in September 1989. Takuya Okada, chairman and chief executive officer of JUSCO Co., LTD. and head of the ÆON Group thought that long-term prosperity depended upon maintaining a strong corporate philosophy. A company without such a philosophy "may be able to achieve short-term profit, but it will not be able to sustain its performance in the long run. The word 'ÆON', with its connotation of eternity, symbolizes our group philosophy perfectly."

ÆON had wanted to acquire an American retail chain for a number of reasons. First, it wanted to keep the organization fresh and vital by introducing the long term challenge and perspective arising from a cooperative international venture. Second, it sought to learn the subtleties of American retailing to apply internally, especially in fashion. Finally, it wanted a company which could be introduced to Japan without requiring a great deal of adaptation.

ÆON was not a stranger to operating specialty formats in Japan imported from abroad. Indeed, ÆON executives considered their commitment to globalization to be of paramount importance in direct importing, cross border partnerships and international mergers. In 1982, for example, it had formed a partnership with General Mills Inc. to develop a chain of "Red Lobster" restaurants in Japan. These western style restaurants featured Maine lobster and Alaskan king crab. The chain had grown to thirty-two restaurants by the end of 1989. ÆON had also formed a partnership with Laura Ashley and had opened 22 stores in Japan by the end of 1989. In addition, it operated 404 other specialty stores in Japan.

When ÆON executives first considered the possibility of acquiring Talbots, they immediately felt an affinity to the Talbots philosophy and culture: a people orientation, a dedication to autonomy and responsibility, and a belief that the customer comes first. In addition, they thought they both spoke the common language of "retailing" and shared a long term focus. They thought these attributes were critical to Talbots' becoming a successful member of the "ÆON Family."

The positioning of Talbots as a retailer of totally co-ordinated high quality, classic and tasteful merchandise appealed to ÆON executives as well. They thought that the fashions which appealed to women in their thirties and forties in the United States would appeal to the growing segment of Japanese working women without requiring a great deal of adaptation.

Other aspects of Talbots were also attractive: the state of the art infrastructure, a history of good profit performance, and its retailing expertise. In the 1989 ÆON Annual Report, the Talbots acquisition was introduced as follows:

> Cross-border partnerships and mergers . . . have the potential to improve the competitiveness of all concerned parties. ÆON purchased Talbots with just this intention, and has emphasized that, as a highly successful store in its own right, Talbots offers its new parent company a wealth of vital retailing know-how.

Soon after the acquisition, Talbots hosted an ÆON team to work with and learn from Talbots, followed by a similar visit by a Talbots team to Japan.

ÆON/TALBOTS

ÆON managed its subsidiaries according to what they termed the "Federated Management System." Chairman Okada of ÆON described this system in the ÆON Company Charter as follows:

> ÆON values autonomy and responsibility.
>
> The initiative of ÆON's member enterprises is the fundamental support of the company. Autonomy is forever accompanied by individual responsibility. Every management in the federation, operating autonomously, works to serve the community, to expand its business operations and to strengthen its corporate structure. Each formulates its own management goals and long term strategy, and by achieving these fulfills its managerial responsibilities for growth, profit, and the development of human resources.
>
> The Federated Management System comes into flower only when its participating enterprises live up to their full potential for independence and responsibility.

Based on ÆON's Federated Management System, it was natural, therefore, for Talbots to operate on its own with very little direct control from its parent. There was

an ÆON office of JUSCO (U.S.A.) (a subsidiary of JUSCO Co., LTD. established as a holding company for Talbots). Located in New York City on the top floor of the new New York Talbots flagship store on Madison Avenue, it worked with Talbots on certain specific questions and projects. It acted mainly, however, as a liaison office. Representing JUSCO (U.S.A.) was Executive Vice President and General Manager Masaharu Isogai, a graduate of Harvard Business School's AMP program and the sole JUSCO employee dispatched directly from Tokyo, and his staff. Major strategic issues were discussed with the new Talbots board. The board was comprised of Chairman Okada from ÆON, President Zetcher and Executive Vice President Hinkley of Talbots, and, as an outside director, President Willes of General Mills. Otherwise Talbots operated completely autonomously.

Based on its recent performance and on the strength of the partnership with the new parent company, the Talbots Executive Operating Committee developed a five-year business plan, coined: "Agenda 1994: Our Billion Dollar Blueprint." This plan featured goals of sales of $1 billion, profitability considered high by industry standards, 275 domestic Talbots stores (28 stores in 1990 and 35 in 1991), a new chain of Kid's Stores complete with its own separate catalog, and a chain of stores throughout Canada and perhaps Europe. In addition, catalog sales were planned to grow substantially.

Talbots growth continued unabated after the acquisition. In the seven month stub year (July 1988 to January 1989) that was created after the acquisition to change the timing of the fiscal calendar, total sales grew 27%, with comp store sales increasing 9%. During this same period, operating profits more than doubled compared to the previous comparable seven month period. In the first full fiscal year after the acquisition (ending in January 1990), total sales reached $453 million. Store sales rose 18% to $306 million with comp stores increasing 5%, while catalog sales increased 10% to $147 million. Operating profits increased over 50%. Talbots executives noted that they really felt no modification in philosophy from the change in ownership other than greatly increased support and enthusiasm for long term growth. The transition had been smooth.

TALBOTS JAPAN

Both the Talbots and ÆON management were eager to introduce Talbots to Japan. They realized, however, that the Japan project could be a major distraction to both

Talbots domestic and other expansion plans. The challenge, therefore, was to define roles and responsibilities for all participants which would maximize their contribution without detracting from the ambitious agenda set forth for the core business, U.S. Talbots.

A separate partnership called "Talbots Japan Co. LTD" with Motoya Okada, chairman Okada's son, as president was established to develop and manage the operations in Japan (80% JUSCO Co. LTD and 20% Talbots U.S.). This was the first case of a Japanese-owned American retail company "landing" in Japan. ÆON and Talbots executives realized they had to address some very fundamental differences between doing business in Japan and the United States, differences which touched on many of the basic operating and merchandising issues to be settled. The basic guidelines for addressing these issues were to (1) maintain the image and the format of the U.S. stores, (2) do the merchandising and design in the United States, and (3) allow the operations to be Japanese. There were no concrete expectations of short-term profit performance, although the goal was to break even within the first three years with twenty-two stores in and around Tokyo. Within five years, they planned to have fifty stores open in several regions with sales of ten billion yen (about $80 million, or $1.6 million per store). All those concerned realized, however, that the first store was an experiment out of which would flow more specific objectives. Nothing, therefore, was rigidly structured and a "wait and see" attitude prevailed.

ÆON management was also aware of the unique characteristics of operating retail ventures in Japan. Executives stationed in Japan would have to play an important role in real estate, pricing, advertising, store operations, distribution and certain aspects of merchandising.

The intention was to virtually reproduce an urban Talbots store in the Japanese locations. In recent years, foreign fashions were becoming in vogue in Japan, and ÆON management felt that the ambiance of its American format would be popular. Internationally well known labels such as Brooks Brothers, Ralph Lauren, Dunhill and Burberry had become prestigious and fashionable in Japan. The American concept of "wardrobing" offering complete coordinated outfits such as tops, bottoms, sweaters, scarves, etc.) which Talbots espoused was relatively new in Japan. Management thought this concept would add a competitive edge to Talbots Japan.

Talbots merchandise did not appeal to the same age woman in Japan as it did in the United States. The older Japanese woman (similar in age to the U.S. customer) preferred much more traditional Japanese fashions. The large and growing segment of younger working women, however, could find the line appealing. This initial positioning was not considered to be fixed. Indeed, the initial thought had been to position Talbots Japan at the high end of the market, but results from early focus groups had convinced executives to position Talbots Japan at slightly lower prices. Although still twenty to thirty percent above equivalent U.S. prices, they were still significantly lower than the prices of most other Japanese retailers for equivalent imported apparel. ÆON management thought such a conservative pricing strategy responded to being a responsible corporate citizen in an era of inflated costs of living in Japan. Management also recognized that merchandise positioning would be a constantly changing learning process.

Because of the subtleties of the Japanese real estate market, initial site selection for the first stores was made by experts from the ÆON organization. Final site approval was a joint process between both Talbots and Talbots Japan which included both Zetcher and Paul Kastner, the Talbots vice president of new business ventures and strategic planning. They relied heavily upon the input from their Japanese counterparts, however, since even potential sites in secondary locations appeared to enjoy heavy traffic by American standards. ÆON then completed the lease negotiations and made final arrangements for occupancy.

The location for the first store was near the Jiyugaoka railway station, about 40 minutes from the center of Tokyo. This emerging fashion center, well known for its stores such as Laura Ashley and Charles Jordan, was thought to be an excellent location for the first of the planned Tokyo stores. By early 1990, four other sites in and around Tokyo had already been acquired.

Once the sites were selected and leases signed, the leasehold improvements and fixtures were designed in the United States but made in Japan. As in the United States, each store was to be designed individually to fit different spaces and locations. Store sites being considered ranged from 1,600 to over 3,000 square feet. The high cost of real estate in Japan necessitated downsizing the store from what might otherwise have been considered ideal by U.S. standards. The first store in Jiyugaoka, for instance was only 2,350 total square feet (2,100 square feet of selling and fitting room space) while a U.S. store in a comparable location would have had perhaps 5,000 total square feet. This constraint required reducing the size and number of dressing rooms, limiting the size of the back stockroom, and offering a somewhat narrower assortment of merchandise. Every effort was made, nevertheless, to retain the ambiance and quality of the U.S. stores. Prior to opening, each new store was subjected to the scrutiny of an American Talbots representative.

The selection of merchandise for the stores was a far more involved issue which required substantially more collaboration. Such factors as reduced store size, different size characteristics of the Japanese customer and slightly different standards of quality required joint participation by members of the U.S. merchandising organization and that of Talbots Japan. Although the objective was to maintain the same assortments in Japan as in the United States, certain exceptions were unavoidable.

In Japan, women required a different size range and fit than American women. Nippon Hinshutsu Kyokai (literally translated as "Japan Quality Association") mandated the place of production and standard sizes, labelling and specifications of all clothing manufactured for sale in Japan. Since none of the Talbots line was manufactured in Japan and since U.S. petite sizes were close enough to the mandated specifications, the Nippon Hinshutsu Kyokai approved American sizing for the Talbots stores.

Since the goal was to develop and maintain a single merchandise assortment which would be acceptable in any country, the buyers were all located in Hingham. English-speaking merchandising representatives from Japan were scheduled to visit the United States each season to meet with Beth Thomas, the director of import merchandise operations. After reviewing the current U.S. assortment, they chose the lines which they thought were appropriate for the Japanese stores. They also suggested minor cosmetic changes in make and fitting which would have a substantial impact on acceptability to Japanese customers. Since the Japanese consumer had a different perception of what defined "quality," they might suggest, for instance, slightly different and higher quality buttons, lined skirts, or a different kind of lining. Thomas would also make suggestions based upon her twelve years' experience as an apparel buyer. Often, the Japanese suggestions revealed opportunities for quality improvement, in which case enhancements might be made to the entire Talbots line. Otherwise, existing specifications were maintained. One hundred percent quality inspection was ordered, however, for all merchandise bound for Japan.

The limited range of sizes required by the Japanese consumer (five Petite sizes in Japan compared to the six Missy and seven Petite sizes required in the United States), the reduced number of styles which the Japanese representatives thought were appropriate for the Japanese market (see table below) and the policy of only carrying Talbots private label merchandise lessened selling space requirements in the Japanese stores. In addition, the number of imported shoes was strictly limited by government regulation, necessitating a sharply curtailed assortment. Those shoes which were offered were displayed in the traditional Japanese fashion in low shelves under hanging goods, unlike the space intensive custom in the United States of having a separate shoe department. To reduce further the number of units to be carried in the smaller Japanese store, assortments of more basic items such as jewelry, swimwear, hosiery and slickers were reduced or eliminated, and the number of colors represented in a style was limited.

Store Type	No. Styles	No. Units
Village store	517	12,000
Urban store	591	14,000
Upscale specialty store	498	11,000
Jiyugaoka store	350	4,000 + 2,000 back stock

Note: A single style included different colors and sizes. These figures represent the average styles and units which would be in a store type at any given time.

Once the assortments were chosen, Thomas placed orders with the manufacturers for the merchandise to be directly imported into Japan from the same suppliers used by Talbots U.S. This procedure eliminated any double handling, reduced shipping costs and avoided imposition of double duties. In addition, it circumvented the traditional multilayered Japanese distribution system.

For the first stores in Japan, an arrangement had been made with the shipping company to store reserve stocks in their warehouse. The Talbots Japan employee responsible for inventory management was to replenish the stores twice per week or as often as required from this reserve stock. Since the life cycle on the more fashionable merchandise was so short and since, for the time being, only limited backup inventory was held by the manufacturer, there was virtually no possibility of in-season replenishment from manufacturers' stocks. Occasionally, however, reorders could be filled from the regular catalog or store inventories, particularly if the style was slow moving in the United States. Because Talbots U.S. had a financial interest in Talbots Japan, merchandise was charged to Talbots Japan at cost with no overhead charge.

The Jiyugaoka store and its successors were to be managed by members of the Talbots Japan organization. Consistent with the policy of keeping the stores American, however, the Jiyugaoka store manager was trained by a top rated store manager from the United States.

Advertising was to be handled by means of a three-way partnership between Talbots Japan, Talbots U.S. and Yomiko, an advertising agency which had been hired to perform the creative service in Japan. Advertising in Japan was primarily through subway posters, monthly magazines targeted towards an over 25-year-old audience and an active public relations effort. Shopping bags, gift wrapping and other packaging were those designed and being used in the United States. They were, however, to be manufactured in Japan.

A separate information system was installed which linked ÆON, the store, the warehouse and Talbots Japan with the Talbots information system in Florida. The plan was to develop a real-time network which would allow for the possibility of global expansion.

Introduction of a mail order catalog in Japan was on the back burner, pending a successful introduction for the stores. One problem was that mail order operations in Japan generally had a lower class image than in the United States. A catalogue-like brochure was, however, being produced for distribution in the stores. Currently, Talbots had 1,200 mail order customers in Japan. More than half of these were American, however, and would most likely maintain the U.S. connection since only smaller sizes were to be offered in the stores in Japan.

OTHER INTERNATIONAL EXPANSION

Talbots executives had also been actively exploring the potential of expansion into Canada. Initially this notion had seemed straightforward, but consultants who were still working on a final report had pointed out significant challenges.

One was consistency with the policy in the United States that stores were to be "clean" coming out of each season. (This referred to the policy of avoiding any residual seasonal inventory at the end of the selling season.) For a Canadian operation, transfers to U.S. "surplus stores" (as described above) would not be duty free. This implied a minimum number of stores to support a separate Canadian "surplus store."

Another challenge was that if any merchandise was shipped to Canadian stores on a post distribution basis from the central distribution center in Lakeville, Massachusetts, it would be subject to duty both into the United States if it had been imported, and into Canada as it was distributed. This issue suggested the need for economies of scale adequate to support a Canadian distribution center. Another issue arising from expansion into Canada was the requirement of certain provinces for bilingual labeling and signage which, of course, also implied certain economies of scale.

In order to overcome these obstacles, Talbots had explored the possibility of sharing distribution centers with other retailers which had established outlets in Canada such as Laura Ashley, Pier One, The Gap, The Body Shop, and others. Talbots management was concerned, however, about the practicality of such shared endeavors. Failing any such cooperative solutions, early indications were that a minimum scale for a Canadian operation might be in the 10 to 15 store range. The consultants final report was expected soon.

European expansion was also a direction which Talbots was considering. Some preliminary explorations had been made and management felt that there might be opportunities particularly in England, Germany, and some Scandinavian countries. There were no specific plans, however, to enter the European market.

The notion of international fashion retailing was not new, but by and large had been either less than successfully undertaken by U.S. giants such as Sears or JCPenney or initiated by foreign firms coming into the United States such as Benetton and Marks and Spencer. Exceptions among U.S. companies included The Gap. It was a very successful chain of 900 plus U.S. casual fashion apparel stores catering to fifteen- to thirty-year-old customers that had recently added ten stores in the United Kingdom, one in West Germany, and one in Canada. Fifteen more were in the pipeline for 1989, including eight in Canada.

REMAINING QUESTIONS

ÆON and Talbots executives approached the upcoming year with confidence. The first store in Japan had opened in February and had enjoyed a reception even more positive than expected. Nevertheless, executives of both organizations were aware that there would always be an element of uncertainty around which they would have to adjust their plans. Such questions as the continued availability and affordability of real estate, the possible threat from new competitors and the sustained acceptance of the Talbots line by Japanese consumers remained unanswered. Executives of both ÆON and Talbots were also uncertain about the applicability of the formula to an expansion into Europe since any other international expansion would require active management from some level of the U.S. Talbots organization and might prove to be a significant distraction to existing operations. Under these circumstances Talbots U.S. executives wondered how much more effort they should dedicate at the present time to international expansion.

Exhibit 1
Photographs of Talbots Store

Exhibit 2
Talbots Financial Performance

	1986	1987	1988	1989	Budget 1990
Number of stores at year end[1]	101	119	137	157	187
Selling square feet (000)[2]			416.6	488.5	562.6
Average square feet per store[2]			3,655.0	3,701.0	3,726.0
Average sales per store (000)[2]			$1,949.0	$2,036.0	$2,071.0
Average sales per square foot[2]			$ 533.0	$ 550.0	$ 556.0
Comp store sales growth[3]			5.8%	5.2%	2.8%
Store sales (millions)	$185.5	$219.5	$ 258.9	$ 306.2	$ 353.7
Catalog sales	$ 93.6	$112.3	$ 132.9	$ 146.6	$ 157.4
Total sales	$279.1	$331.8	$ 391.8	$ 452.8	$ 511.1
Direct profit-stores			$ 48.5	$ 53.7	$ 63.9
Direct profit-catalog			$ 11.8	$ 18.5	$ 21.3
Total direct profit			$ 60.3	$ 72.2	$ 85.2
Direct profit percent-stores			18.7%	17.5%	18.1%
Direct profit percent-catalog			8.9%	12.6%	13.5%
Indirect expense[4]			$ 37.2	$ 37.3	$ 44.9
Indirect expense percent			9.5%	8.2%	8.8%
Operating profit[5]			$ 23.1	$ 34.9	$ 40.3
Operating profit percent			5.9%	7.7%	7.9%

1 This includes an additional two "Kids" stores which were planned for 1990 plus four Kids catalogs. During this period, five surplus stores were open with a sixth planned for 1990. New U.S. stores required investments averaging $220,000 in working capital and inventory and $400,000 in fixed assets exclusive of land and buildings which were rented.
2 Statistics only apply to stores open for one full year or longer.
3 Comp store growth rates are somewhat diluted by the effect of opening new stores in existing markets.
4 MIS followed by merchandising comprised the single biggest components of indirect expenses. It also includes distribution center and other joint facilities expenses, executive salaries, legal and real estate, human resources and finance and credit department expenses, offset by finance charge income.
5 Operating profit is calculated after deduction of rental expenses but before interest, income tax, royalty payments, goodwill, and amortization of acquisition related expenses. While the method of calculating operating profit used by Talbots was not directly comparable to that of most other specialty retailers, the performance was generally well above other women's specialty retailing chains. Talbots management acknowledged, however, that it was still several percentage points behind industry leaders such as The Gap and The Limited.

Exhibit 3
Sample Pages from Catalog

TODAY'S CLASSICS

Classically inspired clothes are evolving into a comfortable new style for the nineties. Traditional patterns and colors in soft new fabrics, adorned in exciting new ways.

A. Our exclusive velvet dress from Nancy Johnson has the special elegance of a satin portrait collar trimmed with rosettes. Fitted with princess seams. Full, flare skirt, back zipper. Dress acetate/rayon; collar polyester. Dry clean. Made in U.S.A. Burgundy (27), hunter green (18), black (78). **$280.00** Mass. residents add $4.25 tax.
A 248. Sizes 4-16
Aa 248. <u>Petite</u> sizes 2-14

B-C. Carolee's faux pearl necklace and faux pearl/gold shoulder-duster earrings in 18 kt. electroplate settings. Three-strand necklace adjusts from 15" to 17". Earrings are 2¾" long. Pearl (82).
B 248. Necklace. **$44.00**
C 248. Clip-on earrings. **$30.00**
Ca 248. Pierced earrings. **$30.00**

D. Our graceful leather pumps have a detachable bow for two distinct looks. 2½" self-covered heels. Black peau de soie (76), black patent (77), black velvet (78), bone (81). Whole and half sizes. **$76.00**
D 248. Sizes 7-9 Narrow
Da 248. Sizes 5½-10 Medium

E. Joan Leslie Evenings creates this dazzling party dress exclusively for Talbots. Paisley-print brocade bodice with goldtone metallic-braid trim. Metallic-striped taffeta skirt with crinoline. Back zipper. Shoulder pads. Bodice is lined. Acetate/metallic. Dry clean. Made in U.S.A. Burgundy/multi (27). **$240.00** Mass. residents add $3.25 tax.
E 348. Sizes 4-16
Ea 348. <u>Petite</u> sizes 2-14

AND EVERYTHING'S
GUARANTEED
It's this simple. . . if you're
not satisfied with your
purchase, we'll replace it or
refund your money. No time
limit. No exceptions. Our
credo is "Do what's right for
the customer."

Exhibit 4
Organizational Chart

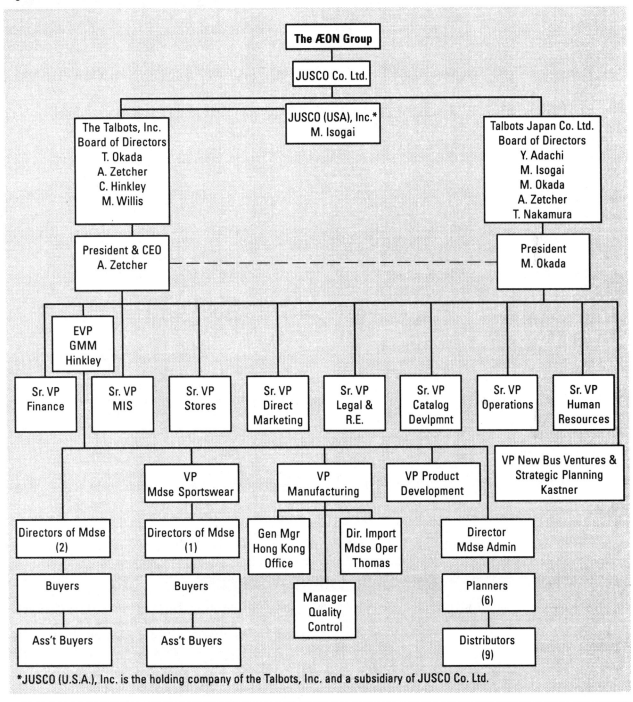

*JUSCO (U.S.A.), Inc. is the holding company of the Talbots, Inc. and a subsidiary of JUSCO Co. Ltd.

The Internationalisation of Retailing

——◄•••►——

Manufacturers have already developed an international view of their markets, and the largest among them have prepared themselves for worldwide marketing of their products: this is the concept of a global market, which has evolved because the consumer cultures of the western nations are becoming increasingly interlinked.

Paradoxically, retailing retains a strong national character. The internationalisation of retailing is not a new phenomenon, but it remains partial and marginal. However, during the past three decades, retailers have increasingly concerned themselves with the international market, which has broadened its scope. The retailers' interest extends across both food and nonfood sectors, and involves a wide range of business formats. For some companies, international operations already represent a significant proportion of their activities and income.

Many obstacles have restrained the internationalisation of retail:

- the size of the firms, often small-scale and independent, and without either the financial capacity or the managerial culture necessary for international expansion;
- the high priority given to national expansion through geographical diversification and through a wider range of activities;
- insufficient knowledge of foreign conditions and markets;
- the drive for productivity, particularly by concentrating purchases on a national scale.

Today these obstacles have been reduced. Large retail firms have the financial and human resources available. They have saturated their national markets, and have attained the limit of the benefits of mass production. They are better informed about their foreign customers, whose behavior and expectations are becoming more closely aligned with those of their own domestic market.

Apart from the homogenization of the groups of consumers, there are other reasons which explain the rapid internationalisation of retail, and which flavor the export of the business formats, as well as the products themselves. The development of international commerce and the opening up of national frontiers encourage the export of capital and of business acumen. Technological progress in the fields of transport and communication enable merchandise and information to be circulated at very low cost.

An evolution of the strategies used has accompanied this acceleration in the internationalisation of retailing. Retailers first developed the investment strategy. This

Reprinted from *International Journal of Retailing*, vol. 4, No. 2, 1989, by Walter J. Salmon and André Tordjman. Reproduced by permission.

involves obtaining a financial stake in retail abroad, and thus consists of a transfer of money from the country of origin to the host country, with the intention of buying all or part of a working retail chain.

Among the reasons for this international investment strategy, one should note: the search for a rate of growth and viability superior to that obtainable in the country of origin, the diversification of financial and political risks, and rapid acquisition of part of the existing market in those countries where the creation of shops would be costly and risky, and the learning of business know-how for those types of retail not mastered by the foreign investor.

The retailers which employ such an investment strategy are generally large-scale companies, nationally diversified, which are looking for new growth opportunities abroad. Vendex International, a Dutch group with a turnover of more that 15 billion Florins in 1986, illustrates well this approach. With interests in more than ten national sectors, involving 80 different enterprises, it added interests in the USA, Brazil, Japan and the UK, all effected by buying a stake in an existing retail chain. Certain French hypermarket groups have also obtained stakes in American firms. For example, Promodès bought Red Food Stores supermarket chain; Docks de France, which controls 183 (Lil' Champ Food) convenience stores; Rally has diversified its portfolio of businesses with a stake in Athlete's Foot; and Carrefour now owns 20 percent of the capital of Costco.

More recently, retailers have made use of two other strategies for their international development. They are, on the one hand, the multinational strategy, which involves the implantation of autonomous affiliates operating comparably to the parent company, but adapted to the local market; and, on the other hand, the global strategy, which corresponds to a reproduction outside their national frontiers of a formula which is known to be successful in the country of origin.

This article concentrates on the analysis of multinational and global strategies in order to study the marketing and managerial implications of each one.

THE GLOBAL STRATEGY

The global strategy is defined as the faithful replication of a concept abroad. Those who have decided to use a global strategy operate beyond national borders, as if their targeted market was homogenous, thereby ignoring all national or regional differences. Global retailers address those groups of consumers who, independent of the country in which they live, have similar lifestyles and expectations.

The chains of specialized stores, such as Benetton, Laura Ashley, Conran, IKEA, and Marks & Spencer have in particular developed a global strategy. Others, within the franchise sector, are joining in strongly with global strategies of their own (Yves Rocher, Speedy, McDonalds).

A STANDARDIZED MARKETING STRATAGEM

Global retailers are faced with two potentially conflicting forces (Waldman, 1978). The first is the need to adapt to the local market conditions in order to better satisfy consumer expectations. The second is the desire to utilize their corporate resources in order to benefit from economies of scale. Buzzell (1968) and Quelch and Hoff (1986) suggested that rather than taking an extreme position, the marketer should balance between the advantages of standardization and the necessity of responding to the heterogeneous nature of national markets. In contrast, Levitt (1983) advanced the idea that, because the needs and expectations of consumers around the world are becoming irrevocably more homogeneous, the multinational strategies will become obsolete and will be replaced by global strategies.

The global retailers have mainly followed Levitt's approach. Even if they have occasionally adapted to local market conditions at a very superficial level, they have a global definition of their segmentation of customers, and a single market posture for all their shops. The standardization of their marketing techniques is a consequence of choosing a global strategy. The range of products, the store decor, the advertising, the prices, and the level of service are all comparable (**Table I**).

Vertical Integration

The global retailers possess another distinctive characteristic: their vertical integration is accentuated. For some of them this extends from the conception of the products, through production and quality control, to retailing.

The original concept, together with good business sense, is often at the root of the success of the global retailers. Terence Conran, Giuliana Benetton, Laura Ashley, and Ingar Kamprad (IKEA) have personally marked their companies with a particular style, and Marks & Spencer is working in collaboration with its suppliers on a more elaborate range of exclusive products. This interaction between the products and the shops which sell them confers a significant advantage, based on a

Table I
Standardization of the Marketing Mix of Global Retailers

	Benetton/Laura Ashley	IKEA/Conran	Marks & Spencer
Assortment	The stores have the same assortment sold under a brand name.	The products are the same, but the size of assortment varies according to the country.	The products are much the same. Only the size of the store influences the range of choices.
Service	Identical standard of service and sales method.	Identical standard of service and sales method.	Identical standard of service and sales method.
Price	Pricing policy decided by the head office in each country.	Pricing policy decided by head office and local representatives in each country.	Standard pricing policy throughout Europe, but discounts decided nationally.
Promotion	Same "united colors of Benetton" theme, and same advertising and catalogue.	Same slogans but adapted to the local market—IKEA uses four separate catalogues in the world.	Determined by country, based essentially on the stores themselves.
Decor	Identical presentation and display.	Identical presentation and display.	Comparable presentation and display.

unique and distinctive product line. Under a brand name or a private name, global retailers are developing a choice of merchandise which matches the particular expectations of the consumers whom they wish to attract. They are concentrating on products with a long life-cycle, thereby limiting the uncertainty attached to fashion forward products.

Certain global retailers are also mastering the techniques of production. They guarantee the manufacture and design as well as the quality of the merchandise. Because they work with a longer lead time than the retailers who are supplied by industry, the global retailers take more inventory risk than the less well-integrated retailers. In order to reduce this risk, and to gain greater flexibility in their production management, they subcontract a part of their manufacturing. Benetton makes use of a network of 220 subcontractors, who contribute 40 percent of the weaving of the wool, 60 percent of the garment fabrication, and ten percent of the finishing. Each of these subcontractors uses the same know-how, standards, and technology as Benetton. In contrast, Marks

& Spencer does not integrate the production, but all its goods carry its brand name, St Michael.

Finally, logistics play an important role in the global strategy. Shops around the world are supplied from several centralized warehouses, which are fully automated and integrated. The success of the specialized international chains depends upon the combination of a global marketing strategy supported by a modern, flexible production system, and by an effective supply network.

There are, however, other retailers, who have integrated neither the conception of their products, nor their manufacture, but are developing global strategies. Toys R Us, the leading toy retailer in the United States, has recently set up stores in Europe (Britain, Germany, and soon France) using its successful toy-supermarket concept. The shops offer a wide range of brand name products sold at a low price throughout the year. Toys R Us has reproduced the global concept, and it seems that by acting as the retailer for many multinational toy manufacturers, Toys R Us will benefit from negotiations at an international level.

Managerial Implications

Putting a global strategy into effect has many managerial implications. First of all, the organization of operations becomes strongly centralized. All decisions involving the company are made at the highest level. Little initiative is allowed of the representatives from the shops, whose role is reduced to following the regulations and procedures laid down by the head office. They have practically no influence on the tactical and strategic organization of the retail outlets. All policies covering the product line, the merchandising, service and communication are defined in detail by the head office. Even for variables as sensitive as prices or discounts, the local representatives cannot act of their own accord, since these things are decided at a national level.

After that, an effective, permanent information system is required in order to control the activities of the network. This system, which is usually computerised, enables detailed data to be collected on sales and required restocking, so that special offers can be evaluated, and the product line can be adjusted if necessary (especially such things as style and colors).

The global retailers, because they reuse an already proven formula, with a centralized organization of their operations, are capable of very rapid expansion. Benetton, Laura Ashley, IKEA, as well as Yves Rocher, McDonalds, and Speedy, have been able to develop their networks largely because their standard formula can be replicated cheaply and swiftly. The market studies carried out prior to the opening of a shop, the necessary financing, and the recruitment of management do not slow down the expansion of these chains abroad. Retail units can therefore be made operational and viable quickly. Benetton, which today controls nearly 5,000 shops around the world, doubled its network between 1983 and 1987 (see **Table II**). Laura Ashley multiplied the number of its shops eightfold between 1980 and 1987 (see **Table III**). IKEA has opened more than 60 outlets since 1974, and now operates in 17 countries (**Table IV**). For other global retailers, such as Marks & Spencer, the expansion of their network is complicated by difficulties in finding appropriate large retail spaces in city centres. Finally, the standardization of their activities enables retailers to benefit from economies of scale as much from the point of view of sales, as for production, distribution, shop management, advertising, and personnel training.

Many factors explain the successful expansion of the global retailers. These retailers concentrate their efforts in those sectors of the market with clearly defined expectations. They present a single front, linking the shop to its merchandise and they benefit from reduced costs in various parts of their network. Further expansion is likely to occur if these advantages are maintained. However, there are two principal dangers: first, their strong specialization makes them vulnerable to changes in

Table II
Benetton's Internationalisation (1987)

Countries	Stores (%)	Sales (%)
Italy	34.8	38.4
Germany	10.2	12.8
France	13.2	10.0
Great Britain	7.3	6.4
Austria	1.8	1.8
Switzerland	2.6	3.0
Spain	3.4	1.0
US	15.4	15.1
Other countries	11.3	11.5
Total	100.0	100.0

Source: Annual Reports

Table III
Laura Ashley's Internationalisation (1987)

	Stores (%)	Sales (%)	Retail Space (%)	Profit (%)
UK	37.7	42.9	44.0	37.0
North America	36.3	42.8	32.0	55.0
Europe	20.3	12.2	20.0	5.0
Others	5.7	2.1	4.0	3.0
Total	100.0	100.0	100.0	100.0

Source: Annual Reports

Table IV
IKEA's Internationalisation (1987)

Countries	Sales (%)	Surface (%)
Scandinavia	30.7	30.0
West Germany	33.0	28.0
Rest of Europe	22.0	26.0
Rest of World	14.3	16.0
Total	100.0	100.0

Source: Annual Reports

consumer attitudes and to attacks by their competitors; and second, their incapacity to take the nuances of local markets into account can prevent them from keeping up to date with the market trends.

THE MULTINATIONAL STRATEGY

Contrary to the global retailers, the multinational retailers consider their subsidiaries to be a portfolio of geographically dispersed retail businesses, for each of which they adapt their standard formula to fit the local market conditions. The basic concept remains the same, but certain alterations are necessary to suit specific expectations in each national market. The internationalisation of the hypermarkets is definitely the best illustration of the multinational strategy. "One-stop shopping" (all types of products sold at a discount under one roof) has been reproduced in all sorts of countries, but the types of produce and the brands sold vary according to the expectations of the consumers in each country. This multinational approach is practised by C&A, but with a much higher degree of standardization under the control of each country. While consumer homogenization inspired the global strategy, other reasons are at the origin of the multinational strategy of the French hypermarket chains:

- the restrictions imposed by the Loi Royer have been the decisive factor which has led these firms to look abroad for growth opportunities, because their national markets have been restrained;
- the mastery of technical and commercial know-how, together with satisfying results from diversification in their home market, have encouraged French

entrepreneurs to make their initial concepts more viable, and to spread out their financial risks;

- a search for new challenges, and an international image, has perhaps influenced the choice of country made by successful market leaders.

The internationalisation of the hypermarkets started in the countries bordering on France (Belgium, Switzerland, Germany and England). It then spread to those countries with a large potential for growth, but where modern retailing was almost nonexistent (Spain, Portugal, Italy, Brazil, and Argentina). Today international hypermarkets exist in other countries as well, such as the U.S. and Taiwan.

With the exception of the U.S., where their success has not yet been proven, the hypermarkets have basically developed in those countries where they have a competitive advantage over the local retailers. The mastery of business know-how in a favorable environment has enabled the French chains to realize increased profits and remarkable rates of expansion. Today group results show a significant contribution from abroad, which is likely to continue to increase (**Tables V** and **VI**).

Adapted Marketing Strategy

The multinational retailers have a global definition of their formula; but they adjust certain important aspects of it to suit local situations.

The hypermarkets have tried to preserve the causes of their success—a tight control over management costs, a limited provision of service to their customers, and the use of very small profit margins, which are offset by the large volume of sales. C&A has preserved the kernel of its strategy in all the countries in which it operates; namely a recognizable line of clothing for men, women and children, all at reasonable prices. In addition to the reproduction of these key elements, each marketing variable is adapted to suit their clientele and to face up to the local competition.

The product range may vary from country to country, and even between different shops, depending on local

Table V
Carrefour's Internationalisation (1988)

	France	Brazil	Spain	Other
Stores (%)	64.0	10.0	20.0	2.0
Selling area (%)	66.0	12.0	20.0	2.0
Sales (%)	80.0	8.0	11.0	1.0
Profit (%)	66.0	13.0	19.0	1.0
Investments (%)	58.0	12.0	27.0	3.0
Profit (% sales)	1.24	2.3	2.6	2.6

Source: Annual Reports

Table VI
Promodès' Internationalisation (1986)

	France	Abroad
Sales (%)	70.0	30.0
Profit (%)	23.0	77.0

Source: Annual Reports

market conditions and the exigencies of supply. The choice of products at C&A is determined at a national level, each shop being obliged to follow the national guidelines. This is in contrast to the hypermarkets, where the range of goods is decided by each individual outlet for two reasons: firstly, each outlet must adapt itself to the micro-market conditions of the zone in which it operates; secondly, for goods which are perishable, bulky or require rapid turnover, the services offered by national or local suppliers become of prime importance.

Pricing policy varies according to the country (at C&A), and according to each outlet (for the hypermarkets). C&A devises its policy and profit margin at a national level, and requires all outlets within each country to follow the national guidelines. The hypermarkets (which essentially sell basic and brand name products for which prices must be adjusted carefully to attract customers and to face up to local competition) allow their shop managers more autonomy in deciding price levels.

Advertising policy is specific to each country. The amount of advertising varies, as does the choice of media, depending on cost, availability and relative effectiveness. Advertising for C&A is national; it is regional for the hypermarkets. The level of service offered does not vary between countries, but evolves with consumer habits.

The Managerial Implications of a Multinational Strategy

The multinational retailers manage decentrally much more than their global counterparts. While the parent company approves major strategic options, such as localization of the sales outlets, or recruitment of executives from abroad, it allows a considerable degree of autonomy to the local national teams, who decide upon the marketing mix at the sales outlets. This decentralization of responsibility is very marked in the case of the hypermarket managers, who choose the product line and the suppliers, fix the profit margins according to the local competition, determine the level of service offered, decide upon the advertising themes, and select the advertising media. Such a delegation of power requires those concerned with the definition and operation of the marketing policy of their department to be competent, well trained and capable of acting swiftly. Such delegation is very limited for the managers of C&A, who have little independence within the guidelines set by the national executive (**Table VII**).

In order to remain true to their original concept, while taking local nuances into account, the multinational retailers use mixed management teams, composed of both native and expatriate executives. The corporate culture of each company, which is crucial if the original formula is to be adhered to, is transmitted by the home country executives to the local management during training programs.

The choice of a multinational strategy has three principal strategic consequences. First, the multinational retailers have a weaker development capacity than their global counterparts. The scale of investment required for each shop, and the difficulty of recruiting high-level managers to run each sales outlet limits the replication of their formula. During the past 20 years, Carrefour has opened fewer that 40 sales outlets abroad, compared to over 1,000 for Benetton between 1984 and 1986.

Secondly, the multinational retailers do not benefit much from economies of scale. They profit from their acquired experience, but, in contrast to the global retailers, the international expansion of their network does not invoke a reduction in the costs of retailing, supplying and advertising. The multinational retailers concentrate their activities in a few countries in order to achieve a large presence at a local level, sufficient to significantly reduce supply and management costs. However, C&A benefits from a concentration of its purchases from certain international suppliers.

The diversity of experience encourages a transfer of techniques and an enrichment of the global know-how of the organization. The French hypermarket chains have exported their formulae, but have learned in return new techniques from the countries in which they have set up operation (fish retailing from Spain and the handling of funds from Brazil). The head offices of the countries in which C&A operates exchange information about local markets and suppliers. Finally, the development of an international image has stimulated executive recruitment, and opened up new career prospects for those ready to take on new challenges.

In the future, multinational retailers, in contrast to global retailers, will gain market share in businesses in which the bulk, weight, or perishability of the merchandise inhibits international procurement. In addition they will become more important in the retailing of product categories less subject to abrupt changes in lifestyles and fashion. Food and related lines of merchandise are, therefore, sectors of distribution in which multinational retailing will grow.

Table VII
Marketing and Management of International Retailers

M a r k e t i n g		Management	
		Decentralized	Centralized
	Standard	C&A*	Benetton Laura Ashley
	Adjusted	Carrefour Auchan	IKEA Conran Marks & Spencer

* The management of C&A is decentralized at the international level but strongly centralized inside each country.

The multinational retailers will expand in those countries where they possess a competitive advantage over the local competition, and where they can find good retail space for their shops, which limits the number of suitable development sites.

CONCLUSION

The internationalisation of retail should continue to accelerate. The homogenization of consumer groups around the world, the reduction in costs of transportation, improved circulation of information and especially the retailers' international vision of their marketplace should favor this trend. With a unified European market, which reaffirms the wish of those countries to effect a single large market as envisaged by the Treaty of Rome (1957), it is to be expected that the internationalisation of retail firms will be strengthened, and that retailing will thus experience the same evolution as production did in the 1970s.

All three strategies outlined previously and summarized in **Table VIII** will be used, but the global strategy will realize the strongest growth rate. In effect, the global retailers will benefit more than the others from consumer homogenization around the world, and from the harmonization of standards, which will facilitate the distribution of products between countries.

Several consequences should follow from retail internationalisation. For the retailers themselves, oppor-

tunities and threats from outside national frontiers will have to be studied. Retailing on the European scale began in the 1970s, with the export of certain successful marketing formulae. However, in comparison with the exchange of products, this development remains limited. Will it be spurred on by the unified European market? If not, will the Europeanization of retailing come about thanks to American retailers, motivated by a new market without trade barriers? Those American retailers who began the internationalisation of retail after the war by setting up operations in Europe have had difficulty in penetrating certain countries. These difficulties have been linked to the cost of suitable premises, over-restrictive legislation concerning the opening of shops, local management problems and the need for capital to finance the national expansion of the parent company. Firms such as Jewel Company, JCPenney, Sears Roebuck, Safeway and Woolworth have progressively reduced, and in some cases totally stopped their investments on the other side of the Atlantic. With the opening of a single unified market in Europe, American firms are expected to retain their interest there. Toys R Us, The Limited, and The Gap are some examples of chains which will affect the European competition.

The European retailers, as well as defending their home markets, are aiming to move into other markets in Europe, as well as in the rest of the world. Their international expansion will make use of alliances between traders of different expertise in different countries, and by

Table VIII
International Retail Strategies

	Global	Multinational	Investment
Definition	Replicate the same formula worldwide.	Adapt the formula to local conditions.	Transfer of money for buying partially or totally an existing retail company in a foreign country.
Business formats	Speciality chains	Hypermarkets, department stores, variety stores	Retailers/non-retailers operators
Marketing	Global segmentation and global positioning	Reproduction of the concept but adaptation of the content	
	Standardization of marketing mix	Adaptation of marketing mix	
	Uniform assortment, price, store design, service, advertising	Similar worldwide definition of store decor, price strategy, service strategy	No real marketing implications
		Adjustment of assortment and advertising strategies	
Organizational implications	Vertical integration of design function, production process, distribution system	Multidomestic approach	Portfolio of foreign operations
Management implications	Centralized management	Decentralized management	Partially controlled management
	Excellent information system	Frequent communications with HQ	
	Rapid capacity to growth	Average capacity to growth	Fast international expansion
	Large economies of scale	No economies of scale	Lower risk
	Very little transfer of know-how	Important transfer of know-how	Transfer of skills

grouping companies together to achieve greater concentrations.

Even though the European retailers are actively concerned with the European market, many of them will continue to invest in the USA, for the following reasons:

- the size of the market and the level of disposable income far exceeds that in any single European country;
- the comparatively low cost of land and leases enables rapid expansion;
- the stable political climate and the relative absence of restrictive legislation reassures all foreign investors;

- the observation of new techniques and concepts which can then be used in the European market.

In 1985, Europeans invested $5.55 billion in American retailing, in contrast to the $2.5 billion invested by Americans in European retailing. Just three countries, the UK, the Netherlands and Germany accounted for 90 percent of this investment (**Table IX**).

The globalization of retailing will have other consequences. It will probably encourage independent traders to form associations with each other in order to pool their expertise and resist the multinational retailers. It will speed up the replacement of backward equipment in southern Europe, often at a large social cost.

Table IX
Foreign Investments in U.S. Retailing

	Belgium	France	Germany	Netherlands	UK	Switzerland	Others	Total
Million dollars	112	136	610	1099	2989	73	36	5055
%	2.7	2.7	12.0	21.7	59.0	1.4	1.0	100.0

Source: *Foreign Direct Investment Position in the United States*, U.S. Department of Commerce, Bureau of Economic Analysis (1985).

The manufacturers will be equally affected by this internationalisation. In certain sectors, well-integrated retailers will be able to compete with them. In others, manufacturers will have to negotiate with multinational retailers whose economic size will force them to make extra concessions. There will be a large demand for high level executives who can interpret changes in consumer expectations, manage operations abroad, and negotiate at an international level both for the retailers and the manufacturers.

Finally, more intense competition together with the transfer of techniques between various markets should provide the consumer with better quality service and an improved range of available goods.

REFERENCES

Buzzell, R.D. (1968), "Can You Standardize Multinational Marketing?," *Harvard Business Review*, November-December.

Levitt, T. (1983), "The Globalization of the Markets," *Harvard Business Review,* May-June.

Quelch, J.A. and Hoff, E.J. (1986), "Customizing Global Marketing," *Harvard Business Review,* May-June.

Waldman, C. (1987), *Strategies of International Mass Retailers*, Praeger Publishing.

SOURCES

"Actualités mondiales," *LSA*, No. 985, 7 June 1985, p. 134.

"Actualités mondiales," *LSA*, No. 831, 5 February 1982, p. 85.

"Actualités mondiales," *LSA*, No. 993, 20 September 1985, p. 172.

"Actualités mondiales," *LSA*, No. 1008, 10 January 1986, p. 80.

"American Retreat," *Dun's Business Month,* August 1984, p. 69.

"L'Andalousie de Continente," *Points de Vente*, 15 March 1986, p. 48.

Benetton, *Annual Report 1985*.

Benetton, "Retail Basic Study," *Morgan & Stanley,* Walter F. Loeb, 29 October 1986.

"BHS to Harness the Habitat Image," *Investors Chronicle*, 27 November 1985, p. 74.

"Bilan de Santé de 29 Enterprises de Distribution," *LSA*, No. 957, p. 90.

"Brésil, Argentine, Terre de Croissance Pour les Hyper," *LSA*, 19 June 1981, p. 76.

Carrefour, *Annual Report 1986*.

"Carrefour Hypermarkets Slated for 2 US Locales," *Supermarket News,* 17 November 1986.

"Companies On The Move—February," *Investors Chronicle*, 11 March 1983, p. 59.

Conran Stores Inc., Retail Research, *Capel-Cure Myers*, 5 November 1981.

"Conran's Grand Design," *Market Place*, Spring, 1984.

"Conran's Recipe for Mothercare," *Advertising Age*, November 1983, p. 7.

"Continent Madrid, du Meilleur cru," *Points de Vente*, 15 September 1984.

"Continent Porto," *LSA*, 4 January 1986, p. 19.

"Destination L'Espagne," *Hyper*, July 1984.

"La Distribution Francaise a l'étranger," *LSA*, No. 957, p. 90.

Euromarché, *Annual Report 1985*.

"The Europeanization of American Retailing," *Standard and Poor's Industry Surveys*, 7 November 1985.

"Europe's US Shopping Speed," *Fortune*, 1 December 1980, p. 83.

"European Target Specialty Chains," *Chain Store Age Executive*, January 1982.

"Fnac," *Market Place*, Summer 1986.

"Foreign Retail Companies Operating in the UK," *Retail & Distribution Management*, January-February 1987.

"France-Etats Unis, Promodés arbitre le match de la productivité," *Points de Vente*, March 1985.

French, Nigel, *A Global Perspective of Consumer Changes*, NRMA conference, New York, 13 January 1987.

"French-based Carrefour Tests US Hypermarket," *Discount Store News*, 10 November 1986.

"French Trend to Hypermarkets Gains Momentum," *Supermarket News*, 13 February 1987, p. 13.

Galeries Lafayette, *Annual Report 1985*.

"Habitat Acquires Stake in French Leisure Group," *Financial Times*, 29 June 1985, p. 10.

"Habitat France prend le contróle de la Maison de la Redoute," *LSA*, No. 859, 1 October 1982.

"Habitat/Heal," *Investors Chronicle*, 25 February 1983, p. 41.

"Habitat Mothercare," *Investors Chronicle*, 8 June 1984, p. 68.

"Habitat Mothercare," *Investors Chronicle*, 15 July 1986, p. 48.

"Habitat Mothercare," *Investors Chronicle*, 9 December 1983, p. 61.

"Habitat Mothercare," *Investors Chronicle*, 10 June 1983, p. 66.

"Habitat Mothercare—Globe Trotting," *Investors Chronicle*, 6 July 1984, p. 44.

"Habitat Mothercare—Widely Spread," *Investors Chronicle*, 12 July 1985, p. 52.

"Habitat Posts 19% Profit Gain From Fiscal 1985," *Wall Street Journal*, (Europe), 7 June 1985, p. 5.

"Habitat Steps in on Richard Shops Deal," *Financial Times*, 1 October 1983, p. 1.

"Habitat to Buy 34% of FNAC, GMF Boosts Stake to 50.1%," *Wall Street Journal* (Europe), 1 July 1985, p. 4.

"Habitat to Open Two Stores in Netherlands," *Financial Times*, 22 May 1985, p. 8.

Harvard Business Case, Benetton case (A) & (B).

Hollander, Stanley C., *Multinational Retailing*, MSU International Business and Economic Studies, Michigan State University, East Lansing, 1970.

"How A Major Swedish Retailer Chose a Beachhead in the US," *The Wall Street Journal*, 17 April 1987, p. 37.

"IKEA, le choc des prix," *LSA*, December, 1981, p. 48.

"IKEA, Premier magasin en France," *LSA*, No. 811, p. 11.

"IKEA et coopcréent un magasin en commun," *LSA*, No. 987, p. 79.

"IKEA, développement et Strategie," *LSA*, No. 866, p. 10.

Kacker, Madmar P., *Transatlantic Trends in Retailing*, Quorum Books, 1985.

Kuin, Pieter, "The Magic of Multinational Management," *Harvard Business Review*, November–December 1972.

Laura Ashley, *Annual Report 1986*.

"Laura Ashley,", *Investor's Choice*, 29 November 1985, p. 22.

"Laura Ashley Inc.," *Market Place*, Autumn 1986.

"Laura Ashley, Retail Research," *Capel-Cure Myers*, April 1986, October 1986.

"Laura Ashley Aims for Retail Rating for its Rag Trade Hybrid," *Investors Chronicle*, 29 November 1985, p. 22.

"Laura Ashley, Welsh Lessons from Business," *The Economist*, 15 December 1985, p. 88.

"Laura Ashley to Seek Full Listing on London Exchange," *Wall Street Journal*, (Europe), 11 July 1985, p.5.

"Laura Ashley Dies, Leaving Company's Plan in Limbo," *Wall Street Journal*, (Europe), 18 September 1985, p. 5.

"Laura Ashley Plans Initial Public Share Offering of $91 Million," *Wall Street Journal*, 25 November 1985, p. 4.

"Laura Ashley, Investors Scramble to Buy Shares in LA Group," *Wall Street Journal*, (Europe), 29 November 1984, p. 9.

"Laura Ashley's Pattern," *Financial Times*, October 1986, p. 9.

"Laura Ashley Opts for Welsh Expansion," *Financial Times*, 11 December 1984, p. 8.

"Laura Ashley to Open Clothes Factory in Wrexham," *Financial Times*, 24 November 1985, p. 6.

"Le Cas Promodès: de Caen a Chicago," *Sciences et vie économique*, 9 October 1985, p. 57.

Le Printemps, *Annual Report 1986*.

"Le Redeploiement International: une éxigence pour le commerce Francais," *Institut du Commerce et de la Consommation*, Paris, September 1985.

"Made in Wales," *Market Place*, Winter 1985–1986.

Marks and Spencer, *Annual Report 1985*.

"Market Place," Laura Ashley Inc., Autumn 1986.

"Market Place," Laura Ashley Inc., Winter 1985/86.

Marketing Review, Spring 1986.

Martenson, Rita, *Innovation in Multinational Retailing*, University of Gothenburg, 1981.

"The New Immigrants: Europeans are Changing the Face of American Retailing," *Chain Store Age Executive*, February 1986, p. 16.

"Non Stop Meubles," *LSA*, No. 883, 1 April 1983, p. 79.

"Now Conran's Magic Misses its First Trick," *Financial Times*, 12 June 1986, p. 12.

"L'Offensif Orientale du Printemps," *LSA*, No. 943, p. 111.

Porter, Michael E., *Competition in Global Industries*, Harvard Business School, 1986.

"Promodès, Hors de l'Exagone," *CPA Management*, 1 Trimestre 1981.

"Promodès, Poursuite de la Restructuration," *LSA*, No. 1030, p. 22.

"Promodès sans Frontières," *Points de vente*, 1 June 1984, p. 48.

"Promodès, évolution très Positive des Activités Etrangères," *LSA*, 24 May 1985, p. 85.

Promodès, *Annual Report 1986*.

"Red Food Stores, le Succès d'une forte image de marque," *LSA*, 13 November 1987.

Salmon, Walter J., *Is the Balance of Power between Manufacturers and Retailers in the United States Changing?*, World Conference of Retailers, 22 October 1986, Zurich, Switzerland.

"Sir Terence Calls His Customers to Heal's," *Financial Times*, 18 February 1987, p. 8.

"Storehouse View," *Market Place*, Summer 1986.

Survey of Current Business, *Direct Investments Abroad*, August 1985–86.

Tordjman, A., *A Comparative Study of Distribution in Six European Countries*, Esomar, June 1986.

Tordjman, A., *L'Appareil Commercial Francais, Structures, Evolutions, Tendances*, Cahier de Recherche du Centre, HEC/ISA, 1985.

"A Touch of Class, It's Paid Off for Habitat-Mothercare," *Barron's*, 3 December 1984, p. 68.

"UK Mothercare Gets US Operation on its Feet," *Advertising Age*, 6 February 1984, p. 32.

"Une Grande Aventure pour Promodès, son internationalisation," *LSA*, 7 June 1985, p. 20.

HOME SHOPPING
THE MAIL ORDER INDUSTRY

Catalog shopping dates back to the colonial times when, in 1744, Benjamin Franklin printed a catalog offering nearly 600 books for sale. The modern mail order catalog industry, however, did not truly develop until the 1880s with the establishment of the Montgomery Ward Catalog by Aaron Montgomery Ward. His catalog, a one-page price list, was first printed in August 1872. Most of the merchandise available for sale was listed at $1.00. Shortly thereafter, Richard W. Sears, the other great catalog retailer of the time, established the Sears watch catalog in 1886. Originally, Sears sold a shipment of watches by mail that had been mis-shipped to a local jeweler. Because of his success with the first batch of watches, Sears continued and expanded his mail order business. By 1924, the Sears catalog sales had reached $220 million.

In general, mail order sales are focused either on an end consumer, or, on a business. Direct marketing to a company is referred to as business-to-business sales. Business-to-business mail order tends to concentrate on office and computer equipment, office supplies, and furniture. The typical end consumer mail order retailer tends to sell either general merchandise, like J.C. Penney, specialty products, such as J. Crew or L.L. Bean, or products available on a seasonal basis only, such as Godbee Pecan Company, which sells merchandise only during the holiday season. In addition, a catalog or mail order[1] piece might represent a company's only retail outlet, might be part of a larger strategy that combines mail order sales and a few stores, or, might be an offshoot of a major retail chain. Finally, mail order products, although almost always delivered by mail, may be ordered in a variety of ways, such as by mail or telephone, by in-store transaction, by computer, or, by a separate catalog sales outlet.

UNITED STATES MAIL ORDER INDUSTRY

From 1990–1992, the United States mail order industry generated $80–$90 billion in revenue annually. Over the years from 1985 to 1990, the industry experienced a compound annual growth rate of 12.5%.[2] Mail order sales, as part of the larger direct marketing industry, included several channels of distribution, such as sales via the mail, the telephone, the television, and the computer. According to the Direct Marketing Association, in 1991, 13.4 billion catalogs were distributed compared to 5.8 billion catalogs in 1980. In 1991, 52.6% of the population in the U.S., or 95.9 million adults, shopped by mail. See exhibits for additional statistics on the mail order industry.

For 1992, Catalog Age Magazine, in conjunction with the Marketing Logistics Company, put together a listing of the leading one hundred mail order houses, both business-to-business

---

Research Associate Dinny Starr Gordon prepared this note under the supervision of Professor David Bell as the basis for class discussion rather than to illustrate effective or ineffective handling of an administrative situation.

---

1 For the purposes of this note the terms "mail order" and "catalog order" are synonymous.
2 Cathy Dybdahl, "Catalog Retailing Cools Down after Growth of 1980s; State of the Industry Overview," *Chain Store Age Executive with Shopping Center Age*, August 1992, p. 38a.

and end consumer, in the United States. (See **Exhibit 1** for the top 25 companies.) The top 100 companies were responsible for approximately $29 billion in mail order sales during 1992. The top 10 companies on the list, on a cumulative basis, experienced a 20% increase in revenues over the prior year, while half of the top 100 companies registered sales gains of at least 10%. For the 100 mail order firms on the list this represented, on average, an overall sales increase of 15% from 1991.[3]

Over half of the sales volume of the top 100 companies, moreover, comes from three product categories; computer products, apparel, and business supplies. According to industry experts, the reason that these categories dominate mail order sales differs by product category. Computer products and business supplies, for example, are benefiting from the growth of small businesses and the increasing number of home offices. These two product categories are also experiencing significant worldwide growth, especially in the area of computer supply sales. Direct mail computer companies, such as DEC Direct, Dell Computer, and Gateway 2000, in fact, are growing at a rate of 80% a year or better. The other leading product category, apparel, has reached the top of the chart primarily through its longevity and breadth in the mail order market. The well-established apparel companies, nonetheless, face slower growth in the future due to over-saturation in their industry segment.

WORLDWIDE MAIL ORDER INDUSTRY

According to a report released by Euromonitor,[4] a London-based market research and analysis firm, worldwide mail order and home shopping was a $135 billion market in 1991. This represented about 3% of total global retail sales. The mail order share of the global retail market will, it was estimated, increase to 3.5% by 1995, and to 4% by the year 2000. Of the major players in the current global arena, Germany has the largest share of the market. However, nearly half of global mail order sales come from the United States, 34% of sales from Europe, and 11% of sales from Asia (mostly Japan). **Table 1**, below, outlines the world's mail order leaders.

Table 1
The World Mail Order Leaders

Company	Country	1991 Sales ($ millions U.S.)	% World Mail Order Market
Otto Versand[a]	Germany	$13,330	9.9
La Redoute	France	4,065	3.0
Quelle	Germany	4,000	3.0
GUS	U.K.	3,110	2.3
JCPenney	U.S.A.	3,000	2.2
Sears	U.S.A.	2,215	1.6
Les Trois Suisses	France	2,150	1.6
Bertelsmann	Germany	2,065	1.5
Littlewoods	U.K.	1,810	1.3
Reader's Digest	U.S.A	1,500	1.1

a Otto Versand worldwide holdings include Spiegel

3 These statistics are based on an article by Harry Chevan titled, "The Catalog Age 100," *Catalog Age Magazine,* August 1993, pp. 74-85.
4 Statistics for this section are based on the article "World mail order growing faster than retail," *Catalog Age,* August. 1993, p. 7.

Although there seems to be much opportunity in the global mail order market, each country, however, has its own mailing and marketing regulations. Germany, for instance, has strict privacy laws that limit the amount of database marketing that can be performed, reducing the ability to fine tune catalog mailings. Because of these limitations the countries that have the most potential for mail order growth include Spain and Portugal, some newly industrialized countries such as those in the Pacific region, and some of the wealthier Latin American countries, such as Argentina, Brazil and Mexico.

CATALOG CUSTOMERS

According to the Direct Marketing Association's *1993/94 Statistical Fact Book*, the typical catalog shopper (not a business-to-business customer) in 1992 was a married female, between the ages of 45–54, from the midwest region of the United States. These customers were well-educated, having graduated college, were employed at the professional/managerial level, and owned a residence valued at $60,000 or more. The highest volume of catalog purchases were of apparel, which accounted for 26.7% of the 1992 total. Other larger product categories were home furnishings, which made up 8.6% of the sales volume, housewares which accounted for 7.3% of sales, and, toys which made up 6.3% of sales.[5]

CATALOG OPERATIONS AND COSTS

Most catalog operations offer mail, phone, and fax ordering service. Some companies operate their phone lines 24 hours a day while others offer a toll free 800 number to place orders. Catalog Age Magazine, in an attempt to illuminate typical mail order operations, surveyed 2000 catalog company executives in 1992 and produced "The Catalog Age Report, 1992" (383 executives responded). The report stated that 66.4% of the companies responding offered a regular business telephone number for ordering, 69.9% offered an 800 number, and 65.3% offered a fax number. Only 2.5% of the respondents (down from 4.5% in 1991) offered no telephone number at all for customer ordering. In addition, the majority of the respondents, 71.6% only offered telephone service during normal business hours.[6]

In earlier research, Catalog Age and Directel, a market research company, conducted another survey to identify the average costs associated with fulfilling a catalog order. These costs are outlined in **Table 2**, on page 686. The figures do not include the actual cost of the product ordered.

In addition to the cost of fulfilling a catalog order, the actual cost of the product, and the postage cost associated with sending that product to the customer, it is essential to understand the cost of acquiring a customer name and the value of that name. According to the "Catalog Age Report, 1992," 58% of the respondents surveyed spent less than $10 to acquire a new customer; 21% spent between $10–$20 to acquire a customer name, 14% spent $21–$30, 2% spent $31–$40, and 5% spent more than $40. The respondents also disclosed that when they charged a customer for a catalog that customer was more likely to buy from that catalog. Only 13% of the respondents said that free catalogs resulted in a higher than 25% purchase rate, while 21% of the respondents replied that a paid-for catalog resulted in a higher than 25% purchase rate. Once a customer has made a purchase, moreover, their value increases over time. Of the companies that responded to the Catalog Age survey, almost half of their customers (49%) represented at least $200 or more, of lifetime value. In general, therefore, the value of a catalog customer increases significantly as time goes on.

---

5 Direct Marketing Association, *1993/94 Statistical Fact Book*, 1993, pp. 87, 88.
6 Direct Marketing Association, *1993/94 Statistical Fact Book*, pp. 119, 120.

Table 2
Average Fulfillment Costs[7]

Cost Category	Avg. Cost as % of Sales	Avg. Cost per order	% of Total Fulfillment Cost
Direct Labor	4.2%	$4.48	24.1%
Overhead	2.7%	4.80	15.8%
Facilities	1.2%	1.63	7.0%
Supplies	0.9%	1.02	5.3%
Equipment	0.4%	0.51	2.3%
Data Processing	1.6%	2.04	9.4%
Transportation	4.0%	3.99	23.5%
Communications	1.1%	1.60	6.2%
Miscellaneous	1.1%	0.82	6.4%
Total	17.2%	$20.89	100.0%

RESPONSE RATES, RETURNS AND BACK ORDERS

Response rates to a mail order piece are a critical factor for determining not only the success of a mailing, but also the inventory requirements for the catalog. The average sale cycle indicates that the most activity from a mailing comes during the first four weeks after a catalog has been "dropped" (put in the mail). Approximately 95% of sales will be registered by the sixteenth week of the catalog life cycle. Because mail order houses have limited ability to substitute products and/or reorder items, forecasting is very important. In 1992, over 82% of catalogers had back order rates of 15% or less, and 81.5% had merchandise return rates of less than 5%. **Table 3** outlines the typical catalog response curve.[8]

MAIL ORDER TRENDS AND CHALLENGES

One of the major problems facing mail order retailers of the 1990s is the over saturation of the market. The average U.S. household is receiving, on average, 100-150 catalogs every year. In addition, while 80% of the primary shoppers in the United States will flip through a mail order catalog at least every six months, only about 56% actually make a purchase from a catalog that frequently.[9] Of those people who have made mail or phone purchases, moreover, only about half have spent $74 or more on mail order purchases over a twelve-month period.[10]

The problem of market saturation raises a second issue that mail order retailers must face over the long term. This challenge, how to create and develop a productive customer mailing list, will be critical to the success of any mail order company. Most firms purchase lists on a regular basis from other direct mail companies and/or credit card firms. Although this process helps establish a customer list, it does not guarantee sales. In that light, many direct marketers are now spending more time and effort analyzing their target customer data in order to more

---

7   This table, adapted from a Catalog Age/Directel report, is based on the responses from a questionnaire sent to several hundred consumer catalog companies in 1990. About an 11% response rate was achieved.
8   Direct Marketing Association, *1993/94 Statistical Fact Book*, pp. 100, 101, 123.
9   Laura Richardson, "Consumers in the 1990s: no Time or Money to Burn; The State of the Industry," *Chain Store Age Executive with Shopping Center Age*, August, 1993, p. 15a.
10   Direct Marketing Association, *1992/93 Statistical Fact Book*.

Table 3
Catalog Response Curve

End of Week #		Weekly % of Sales
1	(in the mail)	0.0%
2		14.7%
3		15.8%
4		15.8%
5		12.0%
6		8.0%
7		6.3%
8		5.6%
9		4.0%
10		2.1%
11		2.0%
12		1.7%
13		1.7%
14		1.7%
15		1.7%

effectively focus their mailings.[11] Database technology, in addition, is making it easier to refine existing mailing lists, targeting only customers who are most likely to make a purchase.

A third challenge that all direct marketers face is the issue of forecasting. Most catalogs are produced six months to a year prior to the season in which the products will be sold. Like in-store retailers, this means that direct mail companies must try to forecast demand months in advance of the first sale. But, unlike store retailers who often use pricing controls to help decrease inventory levels, the catalog firms have no flexibility on merchandise pricing once a catalog has been distributed. No matter how much inventory is sitting in the warehouse, printed prices must be honored. On the flip side, if a mail order company oversells a product, it cannot as easily substitute products as an in-store retailer, making back-orders another facet of the mail order firm's forecasting responsibility. A well-managed, direct mail organization must, therefore, be able to find alternative ways to react to inaccurate forecasting and pricing structures.

To be successful in the increasingly competitive mail order market many of the major direct marketers are finding new and innovative ways to both reach more, and better targeted, end consumers, and to reduce costs. Many catalog retailers are paring their mailing and shipping costs by reducing the number of catalogs sent out per year, reducing the number of pages per catalog, or, using lighter weight papers to qualify for lower postal rates. Some firms, such as the Fingerhut Companies, Inc. (the fifth largest catalog retailer in the nation in 1992), moreover, attract and retain more customers by offering them very attractive financing terms for their purchases.

Another alternative to the highly competitive U.S. market is for mail order retailers to develop business overseas. Several larger mail order houses have chosen this route over the

---

11   Dybdahl, *Chain Store Age Executive with Shopping Center Age* p. 38a.

past few years. In 1991, L.L. Bean's catalog sales to Japan reached $14 million, representing a 20% increase over the prior year. Lands' End has also been testing the European market, mailing three catalogs to the United Kingdom in 1991, as well as planning a test mailing in France. As of August 1992, J. Crew was also planning to expand overseas. Many U.S. mail order retailers consider the overseas market to be the best opportunity for sales growth.

The following section outlines, in general, some advantages and disadvantages of the mail order industry.

ADVANTAGES OF DIRECT MAIL[12]

1. *Reduced Costs*:   Initial start-up costs and investment for a mail order business are low as a new company may be started out of a garage (such as Dell Computers) or a small warehouse site. Reduced inventory levels may be maintained, no fixtures are needed for display, a high traffic, retail location is unnecessary, and usually no sales force is needed.
2. *Lower Prices/Larger Market*:   Relative to a store's selling price, a catalog retailer can maintain lower prices on the same products because of the cost advantages listed above. In addition, a larger geographic market can be reached more efficiently and effectively using direct mail than from a traditional store location.
3. *Convenience*:   Direct mail offers a more convenient channel for shopping. There is no need to leave your home, there are no crowds, no parking congestion, no lines at the cash register. As the trend for dual income families grows, moreover, the convenience aspect of mail order shopping becomes more potent as there continues to be less time available per household for in-store shopping.
4. *Target Marketing*:   Potential customers can be pinpointed by specific market. Direct mail pieces can be tailored to each market segment. New technology can now customize each catalog/mailing piece to a particular household.
5. *No Taxes*:   A customer can legally avoid paying sales tax by purchasing products by catalog from companies that do not operate facilities in the consumer's home state. (For more information on tax issues, see below).
6. *Additional Sales*:   A store-based retailer can augment its regular business and expand its geographic market by using direct marketing techniques highlighting the current product offerings without having to open additional storefronts.

DISADVANTAGES OF DIRECT MAIL

1. *Touch & Feel*:   One of the largest disadvantages of direct mail retailing is the customers inability to touch the products that they are buying. Although this is not a critical issue for some general merchandise categories, it can be a barrier to the sale of apparel and other high fashion items.
2. *Returns*:   Because a customer may not be totally confident of the quality of a product without seeing it "in the flesh," direct mail retailers may feel the need to offer a very liberal return policy in order to assuage a customer's resistance to nonstore purchasing.
3. *Operational Costs*:   Although start-up costs are low, the on-going costs of a catalog business need to be addressed. An average catalog (20–40 pages) costs about $2–$3, or more, to print and mail. There may be a need, moreover, for a computer system to facilitate placing orders, tracking shipments, monitoring purchases and returns, and keeping mailing lists up

---

12 This section on the advantages and disadvantages of the mail order business is adapted from several sources including Barry Berman and Joel R. Evans, *Retail Management: A Strategic Approach* (New York: Macmillan Publishing Company, 1989), pp. 116-120.

to date. In addition, both an 800 telephone number and a 24-hour telephone staff may be required as the business grows.

4. *Postage & Paper*: Both third class mail rates and paper prices are volatile and continue to increase. These two items, which can make up a significant portion of the cost structure of the average mail order business, could notably impact the bottom line of a mail order business.[13]

5. *Efficiency*: The average catalog conversion rate for the most successful mail order retailers is less than 10%. In addition, with the growth of the industry in the past decade, there is increased evidence of direct marketing clutter and over-saturation of the market.

6. *Taxes*: Currently, mail order companies must only charge customers sales tax on their purchases when the purchase is made in a state where the mail order company has a facility. (For example, L.L. Bean charges sales tax when a customer in Maine buys a mail order item; no sales tax is charged if the customer makes the purchase from Alaska.) However, this ruling has been under debate in the courts and may change in the future. (The ruling is referred to as the National Bellas Hess ruling.)

---

13 According to the Direct Marketing Association, since 1980 the income generated by third class mail to the U.S. Postal Service has increased more than 235%—from $2.4 billion in 1980 to $8.1 billion in 1990. In 1990 more than 20% of USPS revenue was generated by third class mail.

Exhibit 1
1992 Mail Order Industry Leaders[14]

Rank	Company	Market Segment	'92 Sales (millions)	Comments
1	JCPenney	General Merchandise	$ 2,992	Includes Thrift Drugs
2	Sears[a]	General Merchandise	2,135	No catalog desk orders
3	DEC Direct	Computer Products	1,800	
4	Dell Computers	Computer Products	1,610	
5	Fingerhut	General Merchandise	1,394	Includes Figi's, COMB
6	Spiegel	Apparel	1,322	Includes Eddie Bauer
7	Gateway 2000	Computer Products	1,100	
8	Lands' End	Apparel	697	
9	L.L. Bean	Apparel	662	
10	The Limited	Apparel	600	Inc. Lane Bryant, Lerner, Victoria's Secret, etc.
11	Hanover Direct	General Merchandise	586	Publishes 15 catalog titles
12	Omega Scientific	Industrial Electronics	500	
13	J.Crew Group	Apparel	475	Inc. Clifford & Wills and Popular Club
14	Deluxe Corp	Business Supplies	437	Includes Current
15	Premier Industrial	Industrial Electronics	436	Inc. Newark Electronics
16	Everex Computer	Computer Products	436	In Chapter 11
17	IBM Direct	Computer Products	400	
18	Viking Office Products	Business Supplies	394	
19	Henry Schein	Medical Supplies	360	
20	Quill Corp	Business Supplies	341	
21	Inmac	Computer Products	315	
22	McMaster Carr	Industrial Electronics	308	
23	New Hampton	Apparel	300	Inc. Newport News, JRT Brights Creek
24	Chadwick's of Boston	Apparel	291	Owned by TJX Co.
25	Damark International	Electronics	270	Bought COMB in '93

a Sears' Spring '93 was its last full line catalog.

14   Chevan, *Catalog Age Magazine*, pp. 74-85.

Exhibit 2
Examples of some Selected Nonstore Retailers and their Methods of Operation and the Various Types of Participants

Method of Operation	Nonstore retail specialist	Retailers with separate nonstore retailing divisions	Retailers with catalogs/ direct mail used to supplement store sales	Nonstore retailing by companies whose primary business is not retailing
General Merchandise Catalog[a]	The Fingerhut Companies, Hanover Direct.	Catalog division of JCPenney, Wards, Sears (prior to spring 1993).	Seasonal and special promotional catalogs of conventional department stores such as Marshall Fields, Bloomingdale's, Jordan Marsh.	Reader's Digest, catalogs of trading stamp companies, (S & H), American Express.
Specialty Catalog	Figi's, The Paragon, Hammacher Schlemmer, Hanna Anderson, New Process Company.	Catalog divisions of Lane Bryant, L.L. Bean, Talbots, Victoria's Secret.	Seasonal and special catalogs of specialty retailers such as Gumps, Bonwit Teller, Eddie Bauer.	Time Warner, In-flight shopping catalogs of major airlines.
At-home Personal Selling	Residential door-to-door selling, (Avon), party plan selling (Tupperware), "Pyramid" selling (Amway).	Outside salespersons of conventional retailers for products such as appliances, carpeting, home improvements.		At-home selling of publishers of encyclopedias and other book sets.
Electronic Retailing	Merchandisers of gadgets, CDs and tapes not available in stores; Home Shopping Network.	Use of interactive cable TV as means of ordering merchandise from retailers such as JCPenney or R.H. Macy's.		Emerging home shopping on cable television, such as QVC.
Borderline Nonstore Retailing Situations	Duty-free shops at airports; concession stands at amusement parks and resorts; roadside stands of produce; auctions; merchandise sold at non-store locations such as golf and tennis clubs; personal care products sold at barber shops and beauty salons; photofinisher drive-throughs; garage or yard sales, etc.			

a A number of general merchandise catalogers may also sell specialty products using the same catalog name or under a separate name.

Exhibit 3
Mail Order Sales To Consumers —Merchandise Trends

Category	1980	1985	1990
(in billions)			
Apparel	1.478	2.844	8.624
Auto Clubs	0.900	1.317	1.954
Automotive	0.198	0.367	0.575
Books	1.531	1.708	2.017
Collectibles	1.015	1.514	2.063
Cosmetics	0.176	0.276	0.432
Crafts	0.577	0.894	1.240
Educational Services	0.430	0.743	1.239
Electronic Goods	0.364	0.900	2.650
Food	0.550	0.694	0.892
Gardening/Horticultural	0.414	0.432	0.561
Gen Mdse/Housewares/Gift	2.978	4.750	9.515
Health/Nutrition	0.469	0.614	0.902
Insurance/Financial	4.412	7.773	13.329
Jewelry	0.121	0.231	0.436
Magazines	2.096	3.406	5.790
Photofinishing	0.400	0.724	0.987
Prescriptions	0.165	0.306	0.658
Records & Tapes	0.459	0.673	1.143
Sporting Goods	0.860	1.669	3.559
Tools/Home Repair	0.331	0.584	1.085
Major Catalog Retailers	5.026	5.705	6.146
Department Stores	2.688	5.077	11.667
Unclassified Mdse	1.108	2.075	4.236
TOTAL CONSUMER SALES	28.746	45.276	81.700

Source: Adapted from Maxwell Sroge Report, "The United States Mail Order Industry."

Exhibit 4
Selected Financial Information

	Lands' End January, 1993	Fingerhut December, 1992	Spiegel[b] December, 1992	JCPenney[c] January, 1993
Revenues:				
Net Sales	733,623	1,470,628	1,972,283	18,009,000
Finance income, net	266	135,486	174,025	570,000
Other income	00	00	72,424	506,000
	733,889	1,606,114	2,218,732	19,085,000
Costs and expenses:				
Product cost[a]	426,964	711,764	1,344,711	12,040,000
Administrative and selling expenses	251,065	558,416	714,132	5,160,000
Provision for uncollectible accts.	00	186,372	00	00
Discount on sale of A/R	00	22,325	00	00
Other costs and expenses	497	00	00	368,000
Nonrecurring charge	00	00	14,467	00
Interest expense	1,330	33,307	76,055	258,000
	679,856	1,512,184	2,149,365	17,826,000
Income before income tax provision	54,033	93,930	69,367	1,259,000
Provision for income taxes	20,533	32,124	30,244	482,000
Net income	33,500	61,806	43,224	777,000

a The line item description for "Product cost" is different for each company, as follows: Lands' End is "Cost of sales," Finger Hut is "Product cost," Spiegel is "Cost of sales, including buying and occupancy expenses," and, JCPenney is "Cost of goods sold, occupancy, buying, and warehousing costs."

b Spiegel financial information includes both store and catalog sales. Spiegel owns retail stores including For You From Spiegel, Crayola Kids, and Eddie Bauer stores, among others.

c JCPenney financial information includes both JCPenney store and catalog sales. Of the $18 billion in total company revenues, $3.166 billion is from catalog operations.

Exhibit 5
1991—Total Amount Spent on Merchandise and Services Ordered by Mail or Telephone, per Year

Amount Spent	Percent[a]
Less than $20	4.4%
$20–$29	4.1%
$30–$49	5.5%
$50–$74	5.3%
$75–$99	4.7%
$100–$149	7.2%
$150–$199	5.8%
$200–$499	9.6%
$500–$999	3.8%
$1000 or more	2.2%

a Based on interviews with a sample group of 23,555 adults.

Source: Adapted from: Simmons Market Research Bureau: 1991 Study of Media and Markets.

Exhibit 6
Percentage of Mail or Catalog Orders that Resulted in Back-Orders

Range of back-orders	Percent in range
15% or less	82.5%[a]
15%–25%	11.3%
25%–35%	2.6%
35%–50%	2.2%
More than 50%	1.3%

a This means that 82.5% of the respondents to the survey said that 15% or less of their orders resulted in a back-order.

Source: Adapted from: *Catalog Age*, The Catalog Age Report, 1992.

Exhibit 7
Excerpts on How Two Companies are Addressing the Challenges of Mail Order Retail

Spiegel

"For Spiegel, the well-known mail-order catalog company, the economics are simple: Every catalog mailed out represents $5 in creative, production, and postage costs. To mail four million catalogs costs $20 million. If, say, 82% of the recipients don't respond, that's $16.4 million wasted. No wonder Spiegel relies heavily on database marketing to slim down its mailing lists by identifying the most promising prospective customers.

"We needed to eliminate as much unproductive catalog circulation as we could" said Cynthia Wolter, Merchandise Control Manager for Spiegel. "This was difficult since what people buy is largely determined by whim. So we gauged the likelihood of their purchasing by using a type of scoring model.

"The model Spiegel applied was a refined version of the so-called Recency-Frequency-Monetary methodology. This is a cell matrix, in which a customer is assigned to a cell based on how often they make purchases, how much money they spend, and how recently their last purchase occurred. Since some 75% of Spiegel's customers use the company's private label credit card, demographic data from the credit card application is added to the equation. Data can be included such as the age and income of the customer, or whether the region of the country they come from responds to Spiegel catalogs better than others.

"From that matrix, we rank the customers, and decide whether they're profitable to continue going after . . . Database marketing has enabled us to better plan our sales, which also helps us to better plan our inventory levels." Wolter concluded, "We have become very accurate, through our modeling, in predicting how our customers will respond."

Source: "Spiegel Gains Through Database Marketing. . .", *Chain Store Age Executive with Shopping Center Age*, October, 1993, p. 138.

Talbots

"We took a lot of steps to strengthen our catalog operation over the past nine months" said president and CEO Arnold B. Zetcher. Those steps included consolidating the catalogs, adding pages, cutting back on prospecting and further enhancing catalog/retail synergy. The plan apparently has worked: Catalog sales improved by nearly 13 percent in the second half of 1991, and are up 14 percent in the first quarter of 1992.

"We decided to look inward and see if there were things we were doing wrong or to make things even stronger," Zetcher explains.

According to Ronald Ramseyer, Talbots' Senior Vice President of direct marketing, response rates "are improving dramatically" thanks in part to those adjustments, which included:

- combining smaller catalogs into larger, dominant ones;
- adding pages to the base catalog and indexing the larger editions to make it easier for customers to find merchandise;
- redoubling efforts to provide clear and accurate product descriptions;
- re-emphasizing classic apparel;
- introducing larger sizes up to 18 and 20;
- expanding intimate apparel offerings.

"Talbots catalogs reached 75 million people worldwide in 1990, $65 million in 1991, and $63 million in 1992, but as Zetcher explains, "the goal was not to decrease circulation but to give the books longer lives and be more efficient." He continued, "We have a real good fix where our [catalog] customers are by ZIP code. That gives us a competitive edge. We don't have to just rely on demographics—we already know where our business is going to be."

"Virtually all the clothing found in the Talbots stores is offered in the catalog, which generally has a wider selection in terms of color. New styles are introduced in the catalog first, giving retail executives an indication of how store sales will fare.

"Staffing and systems reflect how closely the two operations work. Retail and mail order use the same merchandising-buying personnel; creative staff, public relations and accounting MIS for both are handled out of a data center in Tampa; and, catalog orders and customer service are handled by two telemarketing centers in Hingham, MA and Knoxville, TN.

"Integral to the retailing/catalog base is Talbots' charge card, held by roughly half of Talbot's catalog customers, and Talbots foresees further growth from its retail base now that it is developing a name-and-address database of store patrons."

Source: "How Talbots Turned Pain Into Gain in '92", *DM News*, June 22, 1992, p. 4.

Case 26

CALYX & COROLLA

Well, it's two botanical parts of the flower—the calyx (the guard leaves that protect the bud) and the corolla (the flower itself). It was on the very first list of names that a good friend and I brainstormed and we liked it right away. I liked the way it sounded and the way it looked and its uniqueness. But a lot of people didn't like it—too hard to pronounce and nobody would know what it meant. So we went back to the drawing board, and brainstormed a second and third and fourth list. Each time we'd get a consensus on a name, we couldn't clear it with the trademark office. Finally, so much time had elapsed, we were ready with a catalog layout but had no company name and no logo . . .

One Friday evening, we all unenthusiastically agreed on using the name: "The First Flower Company." That Sunday, I was leafing through some trade magazines and turned to a full-page ad by a new consortium of South American flower growers: "The First Flower Corporation"!

That was it—I walked in on Monday morning, showed the ad to my staff and said: "We're going to be Calyx & Corolla."

—Excerpt from Owades speech

It had been two and a half years since Calyx & Corolla had pioneered the concept of selling fresh flowers by mail. During 1990, it had consummated over 150,000 transactions, yielding revenues in excess of $10 million.

The company's results had surpassed the plan that Ruth Owades, its founder, had presented to the 18 investors who had provided the original $2 million in capital. In fact, the results were sufficiently positive to enable Owades and her management group to raise another $1 million in the Spring of 1991, mainly from the original investors. (See **Exhibit 1**, Five-Year Summary Financial Statements and Projections.)

Nevertheless, stimulated by their success in introducing a new distribution channel for flowers, Owades and her two key associates, Fran Wilson and Ann Lee, were reassessing the firm's long-term growth strategy. Was Calyx & Corolla more a mail order operation or should it compete directly against more traditional outlets, such as retail florists, and wire services, such as Florists Telegraph Delivery (FTD)? How fast did it have to grow to protect its initial success? What would be the financial implications of various growth strategies? How should its personal objectives and those of its investors and employees influence the character and pace of growth?

Calyx & Corolla was an exceptionally innovative direct mail concept. Besides mailing six yearly color catalogs and having an 800 telephone number, its distribution and transportation arrangements were unique. Orders from customers were received by telephone, fax, or mail at the central office in San Francisco and then sent via fax or computer to the 30 flower growers who supplied Calyx & Corolla. They, in turn, packed and shipped individual orders and sent them directly to consumers

---

This case was prepared by David Wylie under the supervision of Professor Walter J. Salmon as the basis for class discussion rather than to illustrate either effective or ineffective handling of an administrative situation. Certain numbers in the case have been disguised.

by Federal Express. Calyx & Corolla customers thus received much fresher flowers, often fresher by as many as seven to ten days, than were available through conventional retailers. Prices, which included the cost of delivery, were competitive with conventional florists. (See **Exhibit 2**, letters from customers.)

> *If the goal of most entrepreneurs is to build a business that's better than what's already out there, Ruth Owades has done it in spades. In fact, you could say she has created a new market. . . .*
>
> *Until Calyx & Corolla came along, the hugely lucrative $8.4 billion American flower industry had encountered few innovations. There had been flowers by wire, but not garden-fresh, exotic flowers displayed in a beautiful catalog (you actually get to see what you're ordering), with a money-back guarantee.*
>
> *But as Owades realized early on, having a revolutionary idea is one thing; executing it is something else again. To make her brainchild work, she had to get major industry players to disrupt their established routines and see things her way.*
>
> *Working Woman,* February 1991

THE CALYX & COROLLA MANAGEMENT TEAM

Ruth Owades was no stranger to the mail order business. Upon graduation from the Harvard Business School in 1975, she joined the CML Group as director of marketing. The CML group then owned a number of retail and direct mail businesses. Within two years, Owades proposed to CML executives that they launch a direct mail business focused on garden implements and accessories. When they declined, Owades resigned and, under her own auspices, launched "Gardener's Eden." Very quickly, the business grew and prospered.

In 1982, Owades sold Gardener's Eden to Williams-Sonoma, an upscale direct mail and retail seller of cookware, serving pieces, and other merchandise associated with the kitchen. For four and a half years Owades directed the Gardener's Eden division of Williams-Sonoma, during which time it continued to grow and prosper. Since the price Williams-Sonoma paid for Gardener's Eden was based in part upon a multiple of sales in the years subsequent to the purchase, the funds Owades ultimately received for Gardener's Eden reflected her stewardship during these years.

After about a year of relaxation and rejuvenation following her resignation from Williams-Sonoma, Owades decided to establish Calyx & Corolla. This time, she enlisted Fran Wilson, a 1983 graduate of the Harvard Business School and a former employee of Williams-Sonoma, as vice president of operations.

After about a year of operation, Ann Hayes Lee joined Calyx & Corolla as vice president of marketing. Lee was a veteran of the catalog business. She had spent almost twenty years in the industry, most recently with the Roger Horchow Company, a catalog seller of both home goods and apparel, where she was creative director.

> *I was fortunate to convince two of the most talented and experienced people in our industry to join the Calyx & Corolla start-up team—Fran Wilson became vice president of operations and created the unique yet crucial systems that make this business work. Ann Hayes Lee became vice president of marketing, creating six spectacular catalogs a year, while overseeing all merchandising and other marketing programs.*
>
> —Excerpt from Owades speech

As in many small businesses, titles did not fully define responsibilities at Calyx & Corolla. Owades herself took a major hand in the selection and pricing of flowers and other merchandise that appeared in the catalog. She also set the critical strategy for the catalog mailing plan. Wilson was responsible for customer orders and service, day to day communications with growers, systems development and management, and finance and accounting. Lee took responsibility for merchandise development and catalog creation and production. She was also responsible for a number of nondirect mail initiatives aimed at accelerating the growth of the business (described in more detail later).

The entire management team of Calyx & Corolla was dedicated to the success of the business. Owades realized that the ultimate success of Calyx & Corolla would hinge on the efforts of this team. They had adapted their lifestyles to the rigors of a start-up venture but each executive appreciated the congenial corporate culture and found job satisfaction and the promise of a substantial payout at some future date to be powerful incentives.

THE FRESH FLOWER INDUSTRY

Retail flower and plant sales were almost a $9 billion business in the United States in 1990, having grown at a rate of 7.7% since 1985. While most flowers were grown domestically, over half of the carnations, almost a third of the roses, and a variety of other flowers were imported from over 50 countries around the world. Colombia was the major source of imported flowers, representing over 60% of the total.

The horticulture industry was extremely fragmented at all levels, with small, family-operated companies dominant among growers, distributors, wholesalers, and retail florists. Although there were some larger organizations, they did not represent a major share of the business. The typical channel of distribution was from growers to distributors located in the growing regions to geographically dispersed wholesalers who sold to florists, supermarkets, and other retailers in geographic proximity to them. Of the retailers, the 25,000 florists had the largest market share, selling 59% of all floriculture products (flowers, seeds, and potted plants) in 1987, the last year for which government retail statistics were published. Supermarkets had about 18% of this market, while nurseries, mail order companies (such as seed companies), and other miscellaneous retailers accounted for the balance. In most major cities there were flower markets in which a number of wholesalers would gather to sell their goods to retailers.

Often industry participants would not confine themselves to a single role. For example, most growers distributed some flowers directly to local or more distant wholesalers and retailers. Many distributors and wholesalers engaged in some of their own production. In addition, direct purchasing relationships often existed between growers and distributors and larger retailers such as supermarket chains.

Distributors generally paid growers in 60 to 90 days and then extended the same terms to wholesalers. Retailers usually paid wholesalers in cash. They shopped for availability, quality, and freshness from the many wholesalers who serviced them. Distributors typically marked up flowers 50% on cost to wholesalers who in turn marked them up, on cost, 100% to retailers. Florists took a markup of another 150% to 200% on cost. A flower that a grower would sell for approximately $5, for example, would thus cost the ultimate consumer about $40. **Exhibit 3** includes summary financial data for FTD affiliated florists as well as additional data on their sales and advertising expenditures.

Retail florists were very service oriented. Often they prepared custom bouquets and, for major events such as weddings, provided flower arranging services, usually as part of the cost of the product. It was not unusual, for example, for the bill for flowers used in a large wedding to amount to several thousand dollars.

Flowers were purchased by consumers for a variety of occasions. Flowers were an essential part of most weddings and funerals and were often given as manifestations of love and caring for occasions such as birthdays, anniversaries, convalescence, Valentine's Day, and Mother's Day. Cynics often claimed that flowers were given to assuage guilt rather than to demonstrate affection. Many Americans also bought flowers for occasions such as dinner parties or regularly kept fresh flowers or plants in their homes.

Fresh flowers were more ubiquitous in Europe than in the United States. Per capita consumption of flowers and plants in the United States was $36 annually, whereas in Holland it was $60, which approximated the average in Europe. Americans were only beginning to acquire the European propensity to purchase flowers for themselves year round.

Flowers varied in their perishability. Roses, for instance, could last as long as one to two weeks from the time they were picked until they would have to be discarded, while anthurium could still be acceptable for sale two to three weeks after picking. Time, however, was not kind to flowers, and quality deteriorated steadily from the time of picking. Each day a flower remained unsold diminished its remaining value.

Efficient distribution was thus key to the flower industry. The almost infinite variety of species, colors, and growing locations on the supply end, however, and fragmentation within the channels of distribution resulted in a rather inefficient distribution system. A flower might, therefore, be as much as seven to ten days old before it was available for sale in a retail store.

Although some flowers were bought and taken from the store by purchasers, most were delivered to the recipient. Typically, florists made deliveries themselves for an extra charge within a radius of several miles from their store. For delivery beyond their own service areas, florists usually used FTD or one of the several competing service organizations that had cloned FTD.

FTD was a member-owned, worldwide cooperative of 25,000 florists. Its members took orders from local customers for delivery by member florists at other locations. Although there was a catalog of "FTD Bouquets" at each member florist, there was no guarantee that the delivery florist would deliver the freshest flowers in inventory. The consumer to whom FTD historically had appealed represented a wide cross-section of households with incomes in excess of $35,000. Typically a consumer would pay an extra $3.50 order transmission fee and, depending on location and distance, an additional $6.50 for delivery. During holiday periods, incoming wire orders accounted for 21.7% of the revenues of FTD florists, while outgoing wire orders accounted for another 18.7% according to a 1989 FTD survey. During nonholiday periods, these proportions were 17.9% and 15.1% respectively. FTD processed almost 21 million orders in 1990, including more than 500,000 orders and messages daily during holiday periods. Of the total order (including flowers, transmission fee, and delivery charge), the florist who originated the order received 20%, the florist who delivered the order 73%, and FTD 7%.

In addition to its clearing service, FTD offered its members promotional and advertising support, supplies, educational programs, marketing research, publications, and credit card processing. With the total value of orders from U.S. florists of over $700 million (almost three times its nearest competitor) and revenues of approximately $49 million, FTD spent over $24 million on advertising in 1989, 55% of which was concentrated in holiday periods.

According to *Leading National Advertisers*, an Arbitron publication, FTD concentrated most of its advertising on network television spots (73%), newspaper advertising (14%), and network radio (8%). The balance was spent on a mixture of magazines (4%), outdoor advertising, and cable and local television spots. The image promoted in electronic media had been "FTD, the feeling never ends," featuring ex-Ram's defensive tackle, Merlin Olsen. FTD was shifting, however, to a theme of "It's as easy as FTD" and shifting the percentage spent on more costly prime time television to newshour spots. The intention was also to reallocate significant advertising dollars to magazines and major regional newspapers. Print advertising was much more product oriented. FTD even planned to put a mini-catalog in magazines featuring six everyday products and a selection of seasonal bouquets. (See **Exhibit 4** for sample FTD advertisements and **Exhibit 5** for monthly advertising media expenditures of FTD itself.)

One of the largest FTD members was a 1984 start-up called "800-Flowers," which was becoming increasingly popular. When customers called 1-800-FLOWERS, one of 300 salespeople in its telemarketing center would take an order and transmit it by FTD or another service to a network of florists around the country. Minimum orders were $35 and went up in $5 increments. The retail customer was charged a $2.96 relay fee and a $5.99 handling fee in addition to the price of the flowers. 800-Flowers received as its fee 25% of the flower order from the delivering florist. Revenues of 800-Flowers in 1990 were about $16 million. 800-Flowers advertised primarily through billboards, subway posters, and on CNN television. Its advertising expenditures in 1990 totaled $5 million.

Supermarkets were also becoming increasingly important flower retailers. Recently their florist departments were moving price points upwards from under $10 to compete more with florists whose average order was over $32. In addition, larger supermarket chains were purchasing directly from growers, distributors, and importers. Although many florists considered supermarkets to be a serious threat, they felt that supermarket employees lacked the sensitivity and expertise required to handle, package, maintain, and sell flowers effectively. Flower shops in supermarkets often, for example, were placed next to produce departments where fruit, as it ripened, produced ethylene gas, a chemical which hastens the deterioration of flowers. Sixty-five percent of the nation's 17,460 chain and 35% of the nation's 13,290 independent supermarkets sold flowers in 1990. The average annual sales for supermarket floral departments was $104,950, having grown almost fourfold in the past 10 years.

CALYX & COROLLA

Calyx & Corolla represented a true departure from traditional channels of distribution by directly linking the consumer with growers and, through Federal Express, growers with consumers. Calyx & Corolla was able to reduce very substantially the time it took to deliver flowers to the consumer's door. Calyx & Corolla typically delivered roses to the consumer within one to two days from the time they were cut. Anthuriums were delivered within three to four days. FTD deliveries of roses and anthuriums, in contrast, often occurred one to two weeks and two to three weeks, respectively, following cutting.

Owades and her colleagues realized that Calyx & Corolla was an entirely new concept which revolutionized the distribution of flowers. In order to succeed, however, they also had to understand the emotions that consumers tried to convey with flowers and to maintain critical relationships with both growers and Federal Express. Owades said in a speech about the Calyx & Corolla concept: "I envisioned a table with three legs, and

Calyx & Corolla was only one of them. The second was the best flower growers available, and the third was Federal Express, the number one air carrier." Owades herself took responsibility for maintaining these relationships. She often telephoned or visited growers to overcome problems that had arisen, to negotiate seasonal prices, or simply to further strengthen healthy relationships. She also maintained direct contact with Federal Express representatives to maintain and improve their service.

Although Calyx & Corolla was by far the most successful of the "new wave" of mail order flower retailers, other companies with slightly different concepts were arising. The most direct competitor, a very well financed venture capital-backed start-up called "Floral Gift Express," had recently failed and Calyx & Corolla had acquired some of its assets. "Stillwater," another yet-unproven competitor, had recently entered the market. It was a division of a large, well-capitalized Japanese conglomerate.

Calyx & Corolla was not without problems, either. As Owades suggested:

Did we have problems? Of course. How about the coldest December on record for our first Christmas? Where even our California and Florida growers were in a deep freeze (not to mention our customers in Minneapolis and Boston). Did we deliver their holiday bouquets? Of course. How? With numerous sleepless nights and with the extraordinary combined efforts of that strong partnership I spoke about—of Calyx & Corolla, our growers, and Federal Express, a partnership getting stronger and more solid with each challenge.

—Excerpt from Owades speech

CALYX & COROLLA OPERATIONS

The headquarters of Calyx & Corolla were in modest offices just south of downtown San Francisco. Four thousand square feet housed the three senior executives, middle management, computers and fax machines, and all supporting functions, including the sales and customer service staff that took orders and answered customer inquiries or complaints respectively. Because the number of sales and customer service staff could rise from a normal complement of 5 to as many as 60 (full-time equivalents) before Mother's Day and other holidays, the company was squeezed for space at peak periods.

Apart from these offices, the company also occupied about 6,000 square feet of nearby warehouse space. Vases, wreaths, and dried flowers plus other nonperishable items and packaging supplies used by growers were kept there.

Owades and her colleagues recognized that the sales staff and customer service representatives were key components of the entire Calyx & Corolla system. For these positions they hired service-oriented people who demonstrated a real interest in flowers and plants. Their remuneration, which was about average for equivalent positions in the Bay area, was supplemented by various contests and incentive programs to reward them for exceptional quantitative and qualitative performance. Senior management maintained a very personal role in training and working with these individuals.

RELATIONSHIP WITH GROWERS

She provided an answer to what growers perceived as a problem. The industry and market needs had changed. Flower importing had greatly increased, as had domestic production. But although supply, and thus competition, had increased, consumption hadn't kept up. What Owades offered was a new—and needed—outlet for selling flowers. "We had toyed with mail order, and even tested it. But we're growers, not marketers" (said a grower).

Working Woman, February 1991

Initially convincing growers to support Calyx & Corolla was one of Owades' toughest tasks.

She faced the challenge of recruiting growers whose business for generations had consisted of packing 500 or 1,000 stems in large cartons and shipping them by truck across the country. They were being asked to carefully pack 11 perfect stems in special cartons, packaged according to stringent aesthetic specifications, and to include a neatly handwritten gift card.

Working Woman, February 1991

She had, however, become acquainted with several growers through her previous work.

Together we worked through the logistics of how we might make Calyx & Corolla happen. We tested flowers for longevity and shipability and packaging. We tested various packing materials that would protect the flowers, keep them cool, keep them wet, maintain a constant temperature, and that would look good and be environmentally sound.

—Excerpt from Owades speech

Owades' relationships with the growers, combined with a lot of hard work, had resulted in the current network of 30 quality flower suppliers. For these growers, Calyx & Corolla represented an exciting new distribution opportunity that could increase sales and help offset the seasonality of their business.

Calyx & Corolla's growers were located primarily in California, Florida, and Hawaii. Although most were smaller operations with sales of under $1 million, several had sales of over $5 million. The largest had sales of $100 million. The eight largest growers combined supplied 80% of Calyx & Corolla's product. Sales to the company represented no more than 25% of any one grower's business. Calyx & Corolla had contracts with the growers that prohibited them from supplying any other mail order retailers.

The Sunbay Company was typical of the larger growers. Located about two hours south of San Francisco, this family-operated grower/ distributor/ wholesaler had sales of $6 million and carried 300 items. Of those, it grew 90, representing 20% of its revenues. The balance were flowers purchased from other local growers, imported, or purchased from other distant distributors, to complete the selection they offered local florists. Calyx & Corolla purchased only locally grown flowers from Sunbay.

In addition to educating growers to execute their retail responsibilities accurately and quickly, Calyx & Corolla provided growers with shipping boxes, cards, labels, vases, etc., and also sent them demand forecasts. The growers, in turn, notified Calyx & Corolla of low stock positions so substitute suppliers could be utilized or alternate selections offered at or after the time of customer ordering. Growers also informed Calyx & Corolla of excess stocks so special offers could be communicated by supplementary selling when taking incoming orders or by outbound telemarketing.

Two or more times daily, depending on the season and the grower, Calyx & Corolla transmitted orders by modem to its growers. There, the Calyx & Corolla account manager employed by the grower would supervise the printing of orders, selection and packing of flowers, handwriting of gift messages, and preparation of Federal Express shipping manifests. Although during the slow seasons several people could handle the volume, during peak holidays such as Mother's Day, up to 50 workers might be dedicated to fulfilling Calyx & Corolla orders at a particular grower.

The price Calyx & Corolla paid to growers was really a combination of two factors. While Calyx & Corolla was a big volume purchaser, it had to reimburse growers for the additional retail functions which they performed. As a consequence, Calyx & Corolla paid growers wholesale prices plus a surcharge to cover extra labor and other added costs associated with their orders. Despite this premium, Calyx & Corolla was able to achieve gross margins of almost 80% of sales.

Other expenses incurred by Calyx & Corolla included Sales and Marketing and General and Administrative expenses (G&A). Sales and Marketing expenses mainly consisted of catalog production and mailing ($.32 per catalog), mailing list rental ($.08 per name), freight out ($9.00 per order), and order processing and fulfillment ($5.00 per order). G & A included management salaries, depreciation, rent, and office supplies and other miscellaneous expenses.

RELATIONSHIP WITH FEDERAL EXPRESS

Owades knew that her next challenge would be winning an overnight-delivery service to her side. Ideally, she wanted the industry giant Federal Express Corporation, since, Owades says, customers feel it has the most reliable service. And without quality service, Calyx & Corolla would not be able to do business. But Owades knew that Federal Express had rigid operating procedures, and she would need exceptions for her start-up.

Working Woman, *February 1991*

Well, the Calyx & Corolla concept epitomized time-sensitivity. Here was the first mail order business in America that would promise exact-day delivery. The most important question we ask our customers is "When would you **like** *that delivered?"...*

But, my objective from the start was to establish a relationship where they would work **with** *us—a partnership, together we would create and execute this novel means of marketing and distributing fresh flowers.*

—Excerpt from Owades speech

Pricing was certainly one important issue, but such subjects as dealing with several seasonal peaks and deliveries on freezing days when flower recipients were not home were critical as well. Calyx & Corolla used Federal Express exclusively for shipping perishable products. For less-perishable products such as dried flowers or vases, it sometimes used United Parcel Service.

The relationship with Federal Express had matured over several years. At first, Federal Express considered Calyx & Corolla a minor account that required special attention. By 1991, however, the relationship had vastly improved. Owades had negotiated a price that varied little by weight. During peak periods, Federal Express now left trailers at the various growers to be filled and replaced when full. Many delivery drivers had also become aware of Calyx & Corolla and when no one was at home, would not leave packages to freeze on a cold day. Frozen flowers did not encourage customer repeat orders from Calyx & Corolla. Saturday deliveries were now offered as well, although Sunday and holiday deliveries were still an unresolved issue. Since few conventional florists delivered on Sundays and holidays, this service could represent a major competitive advantage for Calyx & Corolla. Federal Express had even placed computer terminals in the Calyx & Corolla offices and at the major growers to allow on-line tracking of shipments. This equipment permitted Calyx & Corolla customer service representatives to respond immediately to customer inquiries concerning the whereabouts of an order.

THE CALYX & COROLLA PRODUCT LINE

The Calyx & Corolla catalog included fresh and dried flowers, a selection of plants such as bonsai, and a variety of vases and other floral accessories. (See **Exhibit 6** for selected pages from catalogs.) Prices for fresh flowers, including delivery, ranged from $23 for a single stem of protea to $60 or $70 dollars for bouquets of several dozen flowers. In addition, Calyx & Corolla offered vases and accessories starting at $12. The catalog also included continuity programs such as "a Year of Orchids" for $450, which included a selection of orchids to be delivered the first week of every month. Continuity programs comprised a significant portion of Calyx & Corolla sales. Most single items ranged from $30 to $60.

Although Calyx & Corolla did a substantial everyday business, seasonality was pronounced. Summer was slow and holiday spikes big. (See **Exhibit 7** for a graph of monthly sales for the year ending June 30, 1990.) Continuity programs were, however, less seasonal, since they were usually gifts for the regular delivery of flowers over a number of months. Calyx & Corolla and its growers favored this business because it helped offset peaks and valleys.

Owades took an active role in developing the product line and the content of each catalog. She worked closely with Ann Lee and with the growers to create new and exciting bouquets to reflect changing tastes, seasonal variation, or to introduce new products.

CUSTOMERS AND COMMUNICATION

If the catalog format offered Calyx & Corolla a leg up on the competition, the flowers and arrangements pictured still had to look appealing, "like they belong in your home," says Owades, "or you would be proud to give them as gifts." Because flowers are "emotional," her presentation was all the more challenging. "Poets throughout the ages have known that when words don't communicate, flowers do."

Yet no matter how beautiful the photographs, Owades feared that page after page of flowers and vases could get boring fast. So in addition to the cost and color choices in each selection's accompanying copy, she hit on the strategy of weaving in some educational trivia ("The curled flower of the petite calla lily is actually a modified leaf"); consumer information ("Protea stay fresh in water for up to two weeks; after that, they dry beautifully"); and arrangement suggestions ("Glads are especially striking when displayed in a tall vase").

Working Woman, February 1991

Seventy percent of Calyx & Corolla's revenues were derived directly from the catalog, while 20% were derived from corporate clients and promotional "tie-ins." The remaining 10% was from outgoing telemarketing to previous flower recipients and existing customers.

The catalog was the main form of advertising. Six catalogs were produced every year and mailed out under eight to nine covers. In fiscal 1991 one hundred thousand prior customers received one catalog per month, which provided 60,000 orders. Recipients of Calyx & Corolla flowers and others who had called to inquire about Calyx & Corolla flowers, who cumulatively totaled 500,000, received six catalogs each per year. The balance of the 12,055,000 catalogs mailed in fiscal 1991 were to 7,855,000 rented mailing-list names. Response rates varied significantly. Prior customer mailings yielded about 5% to 10%, while recipient and rented mailing lists only yielded between 1% and 2%. The recent rise in postal rates added materially to the expense of obtaining the attention of consumers who already received an avalanche of catalogs from other retailers.

Ann Lee characterized active buyers as those who had purchased at least two times a year, although she added that some purchased as many as 10 times a year. Eighty-five percent of these customers were women, mostly ranging in age from 30 to 55. Most worked and had substantial disposable income. Sophisticated information systems allowed Calyx & Corolla executives to analyze and manipulate the extensive database of customers, recipients, and prospects, allowing them to understand better their customers and to target their mailings more precisely. The largest group of potential buyers, however, were people who patronized florists or other retailers and were unaccustomed to buying anything by mail order.

Lee, in addition to her other responsibilities, marketed flowers to corporate clients who used them for reception areas, conference rooms, incentive programs, and customer gift programs. But by far the greatest proportion of corporate flower purchases were for promotional tie-ins, a segment of the business which management considered a major opportunity for incremental sales, and, more important, new mail order customers.

> *Promotions and incentives, corporate gifts, joint marketing approaches with specific partners and consumer brands—all these offer exciting potential both for revenues, for generating new customers, and for expanding awareness of our service and our product.*

> —Excerpt from Owades speech

Lee maintained a frequently referred-to list of objectives for proposed promotional programs. Each program had to (1) coincide with available resources, (2) fit with the Calyx & Corolla image, (3) open doors for new business opportunities, (4) be profitable, (5) not aggravate seasonal peaks, and (6) permit Calyx & Corolla to do a good job. Several such programs are described below.

Bloomingdale's used Calyx & Corolla flowers to help promote a selection of vases on Mother's Day. Advertised at Bloomingdale's expense through a full-page advertisement in the *New Yorker* (**Exhibit 8**) and other upscale regional publications, five dendrobium orchids were offered free with the purchase of any vase. A point-of-sale display greeted customers at each store, featuring a variety of vases complete with flowers. The vases were priced between $150 and $1,000. When purchasing a vase, the customer designated the recipient of the bouquet. Calyx & Corolla provided the flowers, which normally sold in the catalog for $34, at a discount to Bloomingdale's.

The program was a success. Lee believed that it opened the door for similar opportunities with other upscale retailers.

Another tie-in program was with SmithKline Beecham (SB) for a Mother's Day promotion of Contac 12-hour caplets for allergy relief. This program comprised four stages: (1) flowers were sent to SB retailers to spruce up stores and to promote Contac; (2) $10 coupons usable for discounts on purchase of Calyx & Corolla flowers were offered to store employees to generate excitement; (3) newspaper freestanding insert coupons were placed (see **Exhibit 9**) to gain exposure to 50 million readers, with coupons for $5 off an order to Calyx & Corolla without a Contac purchase and two coupons at $10 each for discounts on two different flower orders with proof of purchase of Contac (a special 800 number with a telemarketing agency was used for Calyx & Corolla orders), and (4) at its conclusion, SB purchased and sent bouquets to all distributors and key store personnel for contributing to the program's success.

The program was very profitable. Three out of four stages performed well, while sales from the consumer stage missed plan. The experience of creating and implementing this complex multi-level program was a valuable education and created a foundation for future promotions of this type.

Discussions were currently under way with other consumer product manufacturers for future programs. Other types of programs were being considered as well. A major mail order retailer was committed to including several pages of a forthcoming catalog to a selection of Calyx & Corolla flowers. Also under consideration was what was termed an "affinity group promotion." This program would offer discounts on flowers to doctors who were members of the Voluntary Hospitals of America (VHA), a trade organization that, among other services, arranged for discounts to doctors on the purchase of office and other supplies. Lee had, however, not yet committed Calyx & Corolla to these programs.

The last, and considered one of the most important, communications efforts was an active public relations initiative which Owades herself led. Considerable positive press, including articles in *Time* magazine, the *Wall Street Journal*, and the *International Herald Tribune,* had been generated, which had resulted in both new catalog and corporate customers (see **Exhibit 10** for a partial list of media attention to Calyx & Corolla and copies of selected articles).

CALYX & COROLLA'S ULTIMATE POSITIONING

It was in this context that Owades and other members of the top management team were assessing their options for growing the business. One option was for Calyx & Corolla to capture more gift business from traditional florists and possibly even increase total flower sales. The idea would be to sell also to customers who ordinarily did not buy much of anything by mail order.

One experiment under consideration was a test advertising campaign prior to at least one major holiday in the Minneapolis/St. Paul market. The following table summarizes demographic information.

Table A
Minneapolis/St. Paul TV Market Area—Estimates

Population	3,610,700
Households	1,352,400
Age	
Over 50	873,100
35–49	737,400
25–34	655,600
Less than 25	1,344,600
After-tax disposable income	
Median	$30,800
$10–20,000	17.9%
20–35	26.9%
35–40	21.9%
50+	21.3%

Source: Reprinted by permission of Sales Marketing Management. Copyright: Survey of Buying Power Part II, November 13, 1989

This campaign was planned, if it lasted 12 months, to at least double the annual FTD advertising budget of 21¢ per household ($24 million ÷ 114,000,000 households in the United States). The second year would taper to one and a half times the FTD budget and remain at parity thereafter. For the test to be successful, Calyx & Corolla management thought that the cost to acquire a new customer using this medium should not exceed the cost of current methods. Television advertising would emphasize the freshness and longevity of Calyx & Corolla flowers, with an 800 number to call to order either a specifically promoted floral arrangement or the catalog. Newspaper and magazine advertisements would consist of inserting "mini-catalogs" into Sunday newspaper supplements and run-of-press (ROP) promotions for a $34 seasonal bouquet. Printing costs for the mini-catalogs would cost about 9¢ each. What sort of response, Calyx & Corolla executives questioned, would they have to generate in order to justify expanding the advertising program beyond the test area? What would be the value of the names generated? Should Calyx & Corolla time the campaign to coincide with a holiday and confront FTD head on, or choose a less-competitive season and promote everyday floral purchases?

In the opinion of Ruth Owades and the other members of the top management team, Calyx & Corolla was an exceptionally promising, yet still only partly proven, start-up venture. Given the skills, values, and aspirations of the entrepreneurs and the investors, and the externalities which confronted them, what changes in their current strategy and positioning should Calyx & Corolla undertake? What might be the financial and organizational implications of a much more aggressive growth strategy, especially if they had to approach external financial markets to fund the advertising program under consideration?

Exhibit 1

Five-Year Summary P&L Statements and Projections for the Fiscal Years Ending on January 31, of the Succeeding Year (in thousands of dollars)[a]

	Actual FYI 1988–1989	Actual FY2 1989–1990	Actual FY3 1990–1991	Projected FY4 1991–1992	Projected FY5 1992–1993
Sales	$ 756	$4,018	$10,259	$15,163	$24,431
Cost of goods sold	189	972	2,452	3,487	5,496
Gross margin	567	3,046	7,807	11,676	18,935
Sales and marketing[b]	1,223	4,466	7,021	10,104	15,375
General and administrative[c]	374	752	1,213	1,459	2,263
Net profit (loss)	(1,030)	(2,172)	(427)	113	1,297

a Numbers have been disguised

b Sales and Marketing includes catalog production and mailing, list rental, and freight out (at approximately $9 per order). Order processing and fulfillment, also included, averaged $5 per order in 1990.

c General and Administrative includes management salaries, depreciation, rent, and other miscellaneous expenses.

Exhibit 2
Letters to Calyx & Corolla from Customers

Dear Recipient,

I am 13 years old. I found your catalog on the table and thought it would be a great idea for Mother's Day since I will be on a camping trip.

Sincerely,

P.S. Forty dollars cash is enclosed as payment. Please accept this.

* * * * *

Dear Calyx & Corolla:

In the beginning of December, I ordered a box of enchantment lilies for my parents to be delivered on December 22nd, just in time for the holidays.

The flowers were in bud stage when they arrived, they opened within a few days, and lasted for almost two weeks.

Your sales help was top notch on the phone when I placed my order, the flowers were delivered on time, in perfect condition, exactly as advertised. Congratulations on your terrific service and product. I will tell all my friends, and definitely be a repeat customer.

* * * * *

Dear Ms. Owades:

Since I'd long been given to understand that my mother-in-law prefers flowers to remain in gardens, I purposely avoided sending cut bouquets. But I decided to take a chance when your spring catalog arrived and ordered the Pink-Fringed Carnations which she said looked almost like silk and, more to the point, lasted several weeks—much to her delight and astonishment. [She did mention that her housekeeper changed the water and snipped the ends daily). And these were sent from your shop to Illinois!

I'm keeping your catalog for future surprises for her. It's sooo nice to know that for once advertising lives up to its name, as your brochure and service attest!

Thank you again.

* * * * *

Dear Calyx & Corolla:

I wish to compliment you on your fine packaging, of my lovely roses, that I received this morning.

I am saving your address, so that I can use it as the occasion arises that I must send flowers.

They "made my day." They arrived on my 86th birthday and 66th wedding anniversary.

* * * * *

Dear Ms. Owades:

I live in a remote town in Northern Vermont—population 1,200. We don't even have house numbers on our streets. When I saw the Federal Express truck drive up yesterday, my neighbors and I all came out to see who it was for.

Well, it was for me! The driver followed the directions perfectly: Go "Past the Church in the Square, second street on the right, red brick house, third from the end." We'd never seen a Federal Express truck on our street before— what excitement!

I certainly hope we see him again, the orchids are gorgeous!

* * * * *

Exhibit 3
1987 Florists' Transworld Delivery Operating Survey (all responding U.S. shops)

	Typical	Middle Range		
Income Statement ($ of total revenues)				
Net sales from inventory	93.7%	90.3	–	99.8%
Total other operating revenues	6.3	0.2	–	9.5
Total revenues	100.0%	100.0	–	100.0
Cost of goods sold	39.4	33.3	–	45.1
Total gross profit on operations	60.6	54.9	–	66.6
Operating expenses:				
Salaries and wages—owners, partners and officers	14.6	6.6	–	22.5
Other salaries, wages, bonuses and commissions				
(excluding owners, partners and officers)	10.6	0.0	–	19.2
Occupancy (rent, utilities, maintenance, etc.)	7.0	4.0	–	9.4
Delivery expense	2.6	1.4	–	3.5
Telephone and transmission	1.8	1.0	–	2.2
Advertising and promotion	2.8	1.4	–	3.8
All wire service fees, dues, commissions and expenses	4.2	0.9	–	5.8
General and administrative and other	11.1	6.1	–	14.9
Total operating expense	54.6	47.3	–	61.9
Operating profit	6.0	1.4	–	10.5
Nonoperating income/expense	-0.5	-0.7	–	0.0
Profit before tax	5.5	1.3	–	9.8
Profit after tax	4.6	1.2	–	7.6
Order and Delivery Charge Data				
Average order size[a]	$25.00	$20.00	–	28.00
Percentage of shops charging for delivery	90.90%			
Average delivery charge (if charged separately)	$ 2.25	$ 2.00	–	3.00
Delivery charge revenues as a % of total				
revenues (if charged separately)	3.2%	2.1	–	4.4%

a Average order size reflects all orders. Incoming and outgoing wire (FTD) orders represented 40% of member shop holiday orders and 33% of nonholiday orders. The average order for FTD orders was $39 including transmission and delivery service fees. By 1990, the average of all orders had grown to over $32.

Source: FTD Retail Florist Operating Survey, 1987. (The last such survey was in 1987.)

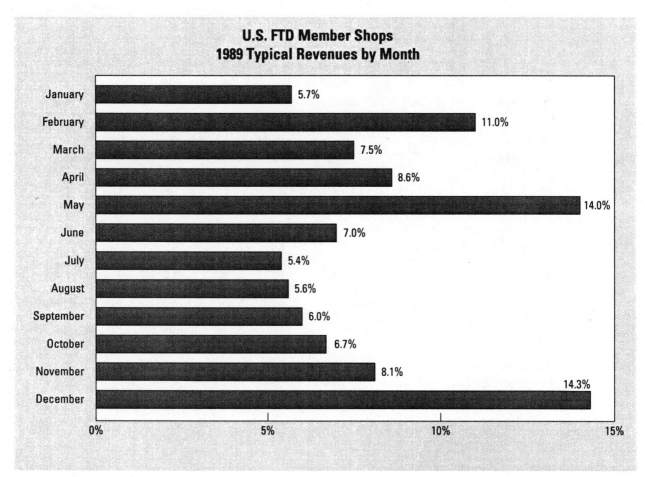

**U.S. FTD Member Shops
1989 Typical Revenues by Month**

Month	%
January	5.7%
February	11.0%
March	7.5%
April	8.6%
May	14.0%
June	7.0%
July	5.4%
August	5.6%
September	6.0%
October	6.7%
November	8.1%
December	14.3%

Source: *1990/91 FTD Flower Business Fact Book*

Exhibit 3, continued

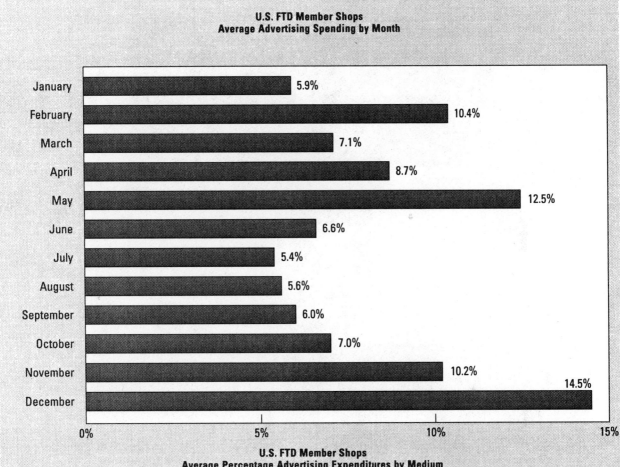

U.S. FTD Member Shops
Average Advertising Spending by Month

Month	Percent
January	5.9%
February	10.4%
March	7.1%
April	8.7%
May	12.5%
June	6.6%
July	5.4%
August	5.6%
September	6.0%
October	7.0%
November	10.2%
December	14.5%

U.S. FTD Member Shops
Average Percentage Advertising Expenditures by Medium

Medium	All Shops 1990	All Shops 1985
Yellow Pages	35%	32%
Newspaper	22	32
Radio	10	13
Product Donations	8	—
Direct Mail	8	7
Calenders	3	5
School Newspaper	2	—
Church Bulletin	2	—
Television	2	2
Fliers/Handouts	2	—
Pens & Giveaways	1	—
Outdoor Billboard	1	1
Other	4	8
Total Advertising	100%	100%

Source: *1990/91 FTD Flower Business Fact Book*

Exhibit 4
Sample Advertisements of FTD

Television

Video	Audio
Open on animated sun rising on the horizon. The sun is frowning and has a thermometer in its mouth. The Chicken Soup Bowl Bouquet appears.	MUSIC: (up) SINGERS: Send a hug from far away.
SUPER: Chicken Soup Bowl Bouquet.	
The sun smiles as puffy clouds form and it begins raining. The Pick-Me-Up Bouquet appears. SUPER: Pick-Me-Up Bouquet.	Brighten up a rainy day. Flowers say what words can't say.
Clouds change into a stork carrying a baby. The Bundle of Joy Bouquet appears. SUPER: Bundle of Joy Bouquet.	It's as easy as FTD.
The animation breaks up forming the Tickler as the Tickler Bouquet appears. SUPER: Tickler Bouquet	MERLIN: Whatever you need to say. . .
A balloon and confetti move around Merlin as he holds the Birthday Party Bouquet.	Your FTD Florist can send the right bouquet. And remember. . .
The animated logo swirls past Merlin and onto the screeen as the theme "It's as easy as FTD" appears.	SINGERS: It's as easy as FTD.

Radio

SINGER:	Send a hug from far away Brighten up a rainy day Flowers say what words can't say It's as easy as FTD (music goes down under)
MERLIN:	Now your FTD Florist has more ways than ever to show you care. Introducing the new FTD Affection Collection. Show your love with the Big Hug Bouquet. Show your appreciation with the Thanks a Bunch Bouquet. Or say way to go with the Congrats to You Bouquet. . . .It's never been easier to express all your affection. Just ask for these or any of the other bouquets form the new FTD Affection Collection. (music back up)
SINGER:	It's as easy as FTD As thoughtful as a gift can be From me to you From you to me It's as easy as FTD

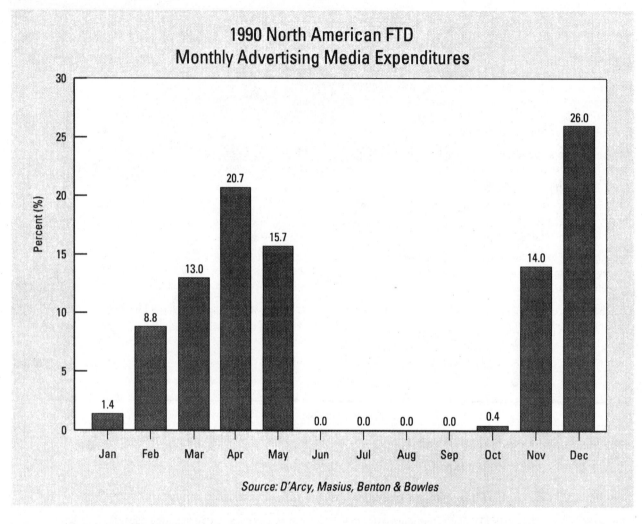

1990 North American FTD Monthly Advertising Media Expenditures

Source: D'Arcy, Masius, Benton & Bowles

Source: *1990/91 FTD Flower Business Fact Book*

Exhibit 6
Selected Pages from Catalogs

𝓕OR MEMORABLE GIFT GIVING, OUR   *FRESH FLOWERS MAKE A LASTING IMPRESSION!*

"I have ordered four different arrangements from Calyx & Corolla…without exception, everyone has commented on the beauty of their gifts and the exquisite care with which they were packaged…you offer real value in your very reasonable pricing…"
— **William E. Beal**

■ *When was the last time you bought flowers that lasted five weeks? Or even two weeks? If you bought them from a wire service, the supermarket, or a florist, chances are they lasted only a few days in the vase. That's because by the time you brought them home, they had already spent a lifetime (in flower terms) in warehouses, trucks and storerooms.*

■ *Calyx & Corolla flowers don't take detours. Our flowers are cut in the field and immediately flown by Federal Express to your doorstep.*

■ *"Last year, I ordered a bouquet of orange and yellow gladioli…everyone was impressed with the quality of the flowers as well as the beauty…the flowers lasted for two weeks."*
—**Barbara H. Young**

■ *Our customers tell us how easy we make it to give flowers with confidence. You may pick the varieties and colors you want. No more of those flowers-by-wire disappointments. We'll even help you select the appropriate vase.*

■ *"Just a note to let you know how pleased I am with your services. It is great to know there are companies out there committed to excellence!"*
—**Kathryn A. Lalla**

■ *Compare Calyx & Corolla with any other way of buying flowers, and we think you'll agree with these happy customers that we offer not just exceptional flowers…but exceptional value.*

Sincerely,

Ruth M. Owades, President

𝓐BOUT OUR COVER…

Our exclusive Christmas Orchid Bouquet is an exciting new interpretation of traditional holiday colors of red, white and green. For more information, please see page 21.

Holiday Parallels

Parallel lines converge in a sophisticated and inviting arrangement inspired by contemporary French dried floral designs. Our miniature terrace has been "cultivated" with a row of preserved red roses behind a "fence" of cinnamon sticks and a "hedge" of crimson gypsy grass. Silvery bear grass and white roita ti leaves add distinctive levels of interest. This artful design stands 16" tall and is contained in a woven basket accented with crossed cinnamon sticks and a sumptuous red moiré ribbon.

D918 **$89.00** postpaid

A Year of Roses

For that unforgettable gift for
yourself or someone else, we offer
12 monthly deliveries of our
exquisite roses.

A Year of Roses RS1Y **$595.00**

Sleeved and beribboned single roses
are perfect for party or wedding
favors. Call for quantity prices.

Call toll-free: 1-800-877-0998.

Bi-Color Roses

Our coral and cream long-stemmed
roses are especially welcome during the
holiday season because of their warm,
sun-kissed colors. Each freshly picked
stem comes in a vial of flower food and
water. The bouquet is enveloped in
lavender tissue and tied with a bow. Air-
shipped overnight, these lovely flowers will
open to open pastel blooms.

12 stems	RS12	**$59.00**
12 stems with classic glass vase	RSVX	**$69.00**
18 stems	RS18	**$79.00**

Cut crystal vase (as shown), 7½" high, RS52
$89.00 *postpaid*

Hydrangea Wreath

Our exclusive fashionable, yet romantic wreath is hand-crafted completely of preserved hydrangea blossoms. This lush, old-fashioned look is much admired among decorators both in Europe and America. Our design blends muted shades of blue, burgundy and green, handsomely complemented by a swath of French ribbon. Easy to hang from its attached hook, the wreath measures 14" in diameter. Each wreath is unique, and color patterns will vary.

WR10 **$89.00** *postpaid*

Fire Fragrance Logs

Lovely as a hearth decoration, delightful as additions to your fire, these mini logs designed exclusively for Calyx & Corolla are made of dried herbs and flowers grown in Northern California. Five 6"-long bundles tied together with jute are charming when hung by your hearth. When your fire has burned to the smoldering stage, top it with an herb-and-flower log and enjoy the delicate perfume. You may also use the logs as kindling when you start your fire. Colors will vary.

1 set of five DE02 **$36.00** *postpaid*
2 sets of five DE03 **$64.00** *postpaid (to same address)*

Freesia

If you admire flowers as much for their scent as for their beauty, you will surely love freesia. A bouquet can perfume an entire room. Let us choose from cream, butter-yellow, lavender and pink — we'll send the mix that looks best the day we pick your order.

25 stems FR25	**$44.00**
25 stems with classic glass vase FR05	**$58.00**
25 stems with Verdigris urn (as shown) FR5T	**$79.00**
50 stems FR50	**$64.00**
Verdigris urn, 8" high V007	**$39.00** *postpaid*

All flower prices include air delivery

When you place your order, ask about our Weekly Specials.

25

How To Order

By Phone...just call our toll-free number to place your credit card orders:

1-800-800-7788

Our sales representatives are at your service. Pacific Time

Mon.–Fri. 6 am–6 pm
Sat. and Sun. 7 am–2 pm

Holiday Orders...for your convenience, we extend our order taking hours before most major holidays.

Mon.–Fri. 5 am–9 pm
Sat. and Sun. 6 am–6 pm

For best selection, please place holiday orders early.

Just a reminder...

Holiday	Date	Holiday	Date
Halloween	*Oct. 31*	*Easter*	*Apr. 11*
Thanksgiving	*Nov. 26*	*Secretaries' Week*	*Apr. 19*
Hanukkah (begins)	*Dec. 20*	*Mother's Day*	*May 9*
Christmas	*Dec. 25*	*Father's Day*	*Jun. 20*
Valentine's Day	*Feb. 14*	*Fourth of July*	*Jul. 4*
St. Patrick's Day	*Mar. 17*	*Grandparents' Day*	*Sep. 13*
Passover	*Apr. 6*	*Rosh Hashanah*	*Sep. 28*

But, if you forget or have waited until the last minute... call us, we will do whatever we can to rescue you.

By Mail...fill out the order form and send it to us. Be sure to give us a <u>complete street address</u> (including apartment number) when ordering for yourself or sending a gift. Sorry, we cannot deliver to a P.O. Box. Please include a daytime phone number.

By Fax...fax us your credit card order any time of day or night and we'll deliver as you request. **Fax 1-415-626-3781.**

The Calyx & Corolla Plant Doctor

Though we include care cards with our flowers and plants, many of you have expressed a desire for more information about the care or history of your Calyx & Corolla purchases. With this in mind, we have established a service to answer your questions. Please call the Plant Doctor, 1-415-431-2273.

Corporate Gift Services

Use Calyx & Corolla's corporate gift services as a year round image builder and sales tool.

Our flowers and plants make a lasting impression that will attest to your company's style and taste. Flowers are particularly appropriate for client gifts, promotions, incentives and business events.

We offer corporate gift-planning services to businesses large and small. If you are interested in a corporate account, gifts in quantity or flowers at work and would like to receive our 1992–1993 corporate gift catalog please call us at 1-800-800-7788.

Shipping and Super Rush

Fresh Flowers and Plants...are delivered by air via Federal Express. You will receive them within 1–5 working days, depending on the variety and origin. For birthdays, holidays and other special events, we will ship to arrive on the exact date whenever possible. (Sorry, we cannot deliver on Sundays.) Our prices include packing and air express. There is a $3.95 handling charge for each address.

Dried floral designs and bulb kits...are shipped via UPS within 48 hours of your order. There is a $3.95 handling charge for each address.

Super Rush Service...we also offer exact day, extra fast deliveries for dried designs and bulb kits for an additional charge of $9.95.

Please Note

We are not able to make deliveries to Puerto Rico, Mexico, Canada, or to an APO or FPO address. There is a $10.00 surcharge on shipments to Alaska and Hawaii. Plants cannot be shipped to Hawaii.

Substitutions and Returns

If, due to crop failures or poor weather conditions, a particular flower is not suitable for shipping, we will send a fresh selection of equal or greater value. For items other than flowers and plants, please return via UPS or prepaid U.S. mail within three weeks of receipt. If there is shipping damage to any merchandise please retain the box and all packing materials and contact our Customer Service Department at 1-800-877-0998.

About Our Mailings

Mail Preference Service...from time to time, we make our customer list available to carefully selected reputable companies whose products we feel may be of interest to you. Should you not wish to receive such mailings, please send an exact copy of your mailing label to: Calyx & Corolla Mail Preference Service, 1550 Bryant Street #900, San Francisco, California 94103.

Duplicate Mailings...if you receive duplicates of our catalog, please copy exactly and/or enclose the mailing labels from all of them, indicating the proper name and address, and we will correct the situation. Please send to the address listed above.

Customer Service and Flower Consultant

We are here to serve you. If you have any questions regarding your order, need information about a particular flower or need help in selecting appropriate flowers and vases for any occasion, please call during the following hours, Pacific Time: 6 am–6 pm Mon.–Fri. 1-800-877-0998.

Our Guarantee

We cut and ship only the finest and freshest flowers. If for some reason you are not satisfied with your order, we will replace it promptly or refund your money.

Exhibit 7
Graph of Calyx & Corolla Monthly Sales for the Year Ending June 30, 1990

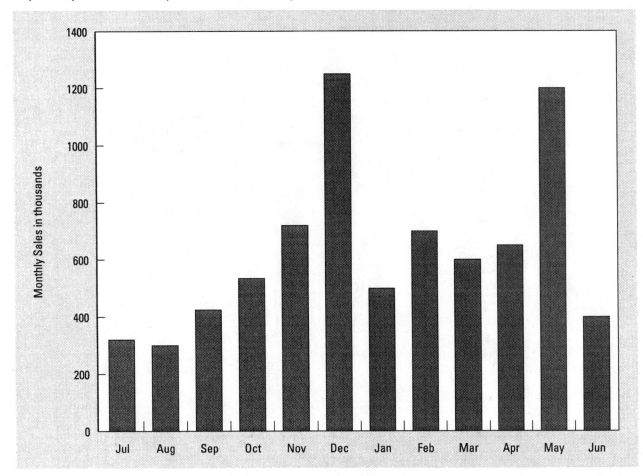

Exhibit 8
Bloomingdale's Advertisement in the *New Yorker*

Give Mother The Vase, And We'll Send Orchids

Complimentary Orchid Bouquet—a gift from Calyx & Corolla of San Francisco
with any Baccarat, Lalique, Waterford, Orrefors or Kosta Boda Vase
Purchase of $150 or More.

(Crystal on 6, New York. And in all our stores.)

WATERFORD
Introducing the new
Ashbourne 10" vase,
exclusively ours. 225.00

KOSTA BODA
Sails 11¾" vase,
exclusively ours, designed
by Goran Wärff, 150.00

LALIQUE
Sylvie 8" vase,
designed in 1956 by Marc Lalique.
690.00

BACCARAT
Presenting the new
Giverny 10" vase, exclusively ours,
designed by Robert Rigot. 285.00

ORREFORS
Denise 8" vase,
exclusively ours, designed
by Erika Lagerbielke. 150.00

MOTHER'S DAY MAY TWELFTH

bloomingdale's

TO ORDER PHONE TOLL FREE 24 HOURS A DAY, 7 DAYS A WEEK (800) 777-4999 REF. NO CM22. CALL 355-5900 FOR CUSTOMER SERVICE ONLY.

 Complimentary Bouquet With Any Baccarat, Lalique, Waterford, Orrefors or Kosta Boda Vase Purchase of $150 Or More

A dendrobium orchid bouquet from Calyx & Corolla (reg. 34.00) will be sent anywhere in the continental U.S. as our gift
in time for Mother's Day if your order is placed by May 7th. (Later purchases will receive Calyx & Corolla gift certificates.)

Exhibit 9
Newspaper Freestanding Insert Coupons of SmithKline Beecham

Exhibit 10
Partial List of Media Attention to Calyx & Corolla

"A Scripps Education Goes to Work"	*Scripps College Bulletin*, Summer 1989
"Hot People"	*Metropolitan Home*, February 1990
"Fortune People—A Harvard Study"	*Fortune*, November 5, 1990
"Hearts and Flowers: The Nosegay Express"	*Wall Street Journal*, February 14, 1991
"Just Picked Flowers: A Fresh Idea Pays"	*International Herald Tribune*, February 9-10, 1991
"The Truth About Ruth"	*Entrepreneurial Woman*, July/August 1990
"Stamping Out Mail-Order Misbeliefs"	*Los Angeles Times*, May 4, 1990
"Bouquet of the Month"	*Detroit Free Press*, July 1, 1990
"Floral Catalog Blooms with Exotic, Hard-to-Find Greenery"	*Rocky Mountain News*, January 25, 1990
"Of Wreaths and Flowers"	*San Francisco Chronicle*, November 29, 1989
"Flower Power"	*Business Week*, February 19, 1990
"Flowers, Fresh from the Growers to You"	*Gannett Westchester Newspapers*, August 24, 1989
"What's Hot: Flowers, Fresh and Fast"	*San Jose Mercury News*, August 29, 1989
"Fresh Flowers by Catalog"	*San Francisco Chronicle*, October 18, 1989
"Catalog Bazaar"	*Harper's Bazaar*, June 1991
"Business is Blooming"	*Catalog Age*, January 1991
"News Break"	*ELLE*, February 1991
"Profits in Bloom"	*TIME*, February 18, 1991
"Growing a New Market Niche"	*Working Woman*, February 1991
Television interview	Business Marketplace, ABC TV San Francisco, California September 15, 1991
Television interview	The Morning Exchange, ABC TV Cleveland, Ohio October 9, 1991

THE WALL STREET JOURNAL THURSDAY, FEBRUARY 14, 1991.

Hearts and Flowers: The Nosegay Express

BY PATTI HAGAN

Here we are, V-Day 1991, and a flowery mail-order catalog has saved me from the lists of Valentine's procrastinators. Otherwise, I might have made my valentine flower arrangements on the subway yesterday, humored by a supposed New York Post story blown up on a poster. "300 LB. QUEENS MAN MOVED BY 800 FLOWERS," and bylined Iris Inavase. "A 300 lb. Queens man, 52, was reduced to tears today by 800 Flowers," Ms. Inavase wrote. "To look at him, you would have thought it would take a professional moving company to budge him. But all it took was a $29.95 floral arrangement sent by 1-800-Flowers, the 24-hour-anytime-to-anyone floral delivery service." Amusing as I found the teary-eyed Ferdinand, hankie in one hand, 800 Flowers nosegay in the other, I'd long since dialed another floral 800 (1-800-877-7836) to reach Calyx & Corolla, in California.

A few months ago a friend had slipped me the catalog, figuring I'd appreciate the botanical name and the upscale difference. Calyx & Corolla does not ride the subway; C&C uses no weepy fat men. Calyx & Corolla instead runs 32 pages of flower pictures, only, on the theory that flowers best sell flowers, quite unassisted by kittens, Dalmatians, golden retrievers, Snoopy or Snow

Gardening

Calyx & Corolla

White and the Seven Dwarfs. Calyx & Corolla relies on flowers whose ancient good design makes them virtually fashion-proof: roses, daffodils, tulips, lilies ($395 for a year of lilies, orchids ($450 a year), protea. ("Botanists tell us that protea are one of the oldest flowers on the earth," the C&C care card informs. "Known to exist in prehistoric times, they survived the trials of evolution far better than the dinosaur.")

Something about the catalog reminded me of Eden—Gardener's Eden, the upscale gardening catalog—and sure enough Calyx & Corolla, which now operates at the cutting edge of the cut-flower business, is the latest eureka of floral entrepreneuse Ruth Owades, the Harvard MBA. Her alma mater immortalized hear in a widely taught 1982 Business School case study of her travails, in 1978, in founding Gardener's Eden (one Jeremiah told her: "Gardening is a blue-collar hobby, it'll never fly. There is no way in the world that people will buy things for their garden. If this was such a good idea, dearie, some man would have already done it.").

In 1982 she sold Boston-based Gardener's Eden to Williams-Sonoma for a cool million but stayed on for five years to manage G. Eden out West. By 1987, she had noticed an empty horticultural niche in the cut-flower industry. Her idea was to make possible a fast, fresh, FedExed flower valentine any time of the year by brokering a computer marriage of convenience between two industries that had heretofore never even been engaged: mail-order catalogs and fresh cut flowers. Though her research told her the U.S. cut-flower industry had been growing about 10% a year since the mid-80s, she found "an industry still stuck in the '50s."

She persuaded 25 flower growers to sign on to her computer network. She got them to install computers, modems for talking to the C&C mainframe in San Francisco, fax machines. And she taught them to cut flowers to order and pack them with aesthetic TLC. Roses would be dethorned by hand and travel with "ice pillows under their heads." Wood excelsior would cushion their every blow. "What we go through with gerberas is pretty amazing," Ms. Owades admits. "First of all they are capped with net caps in the fields where they're grown. Then because their stems tend to be weak, the grower puts [each of] them in thick straws."

Then, to deliver the critical Freshness Dividend, Ms. Owades prevailed on Federal Express to add Calyx & Corolla's natural brown boxes to its "brown box business," and fly the fresh cut flowers direct from grower to customer, guaranteeing arrival on the exact day requested. FedEx was the crucial link in Ms. Owades's new floral-delivery short-circuit service. In her catalog she explains that Calyx & Corolla "fresh" means "five to 10 days fresher than any other flowers you can buy!" Her research had revealed the "most flowers that we buy at a florist or certainly at a Korean grocer are at least seven to 10 days old." For her business, "I knew that the benefit had to be FRESHNESS. We cut to order. You receive a flower that was cut 24 to 48 hours previously. You get the seven to 10 days in your vase, instead of on a truck or in a distributor's warehouse."

Though this is Calyx & Corolla's biggest day of the year, Americans are floral underconsumers. Ms. Owades believes she's still battling the Puritan ethic. "It's not only that we're puritanical and feel that we don't deserve flowers on a regular basis, I also think that we are quite intimidated by flowers." However, this may be changing thanks to the puritanical American capacity for guilt. A spring 1990 Gallup Poll, "Americans on Gift Giving," found that for 51% of Americans "when feeling guilty, flowers and plants are the likely gift." Ms. Owades says of subscribers to Calyx & Corolla's flowers by the year, half-year and quarter: "That's for someone who

either loves flowers or else it's a gift from someone who feels really guilty about what he did." And in fact C&C offers a sort of rescue service for the guilty, volunteering on the order form "if you forget or have waited until the last minute...call us, we will do whatever we can to rescue you." And then the Calyx & Corolla Plant Doctor is on call to help survivors baby their plants and flowers. "People call back and say "it works! My gardenia is thriving!" Ms. Owades notes. "They're so happy they want to send him things. They're all trying to bake him chocolate cakes. We've had to limit it. They can send recipes." Others simply write: "If only your catalog had existed five years ago, my wife wouldn't have left me!" They send color snapshots of week-old bouquets *still fresh*. "I'm writing to thank you for giving me 'points' with my mother-in-law," one California woman wrote. "I'd long been given to understand that she prefers flowers to remain in gardens, I purposely avoided sending out bouquets." But the Pink Fringed Carnations bouquet changed everything.

Last Feb. 14 an irate Philadelphian wrote in the accusative: "Dear Calyx & Corolla: You've ruined my love life! How could you not have shipped the Valentine's Day tulips to my girlfriend?!" An apology followed two days later: "I guess 'polite thank yous' are no longer a way of life. But at least I am no longer in the doghouse."

In January Ms. Owades sent her flower catalog to war, addressing a special message to American servicemen and women in the Persian Gulf: "As Valentine's Day approaches, we would like to help you remember those that you love back home. Although the distance to your loved ones may be great, you can surprise them by sending them fresh, beautiful flowers this Valentine's Day." Wishing them all home soon, she asked, "Please identify yourself as a part of Operation Desert Storm in order to receive your discount." 20%.

On Jan. 16, the day the U.S. began bombing, Calyx & Corolla received a fax from a soldier on duty in Saudia Arabia. He requested that "Love" cards and bouquets be dispatched to five valentines in five different towns in three states: Lori, Melissa, Dee, Beth and Georgeanne. Once again Calyx & Corolla gave new meaning to the word fresh.

This article first appeared in The Wall Street Journal *of February 14, 1991. It is reprinted with the permission of Patti Hagan,* WSJ *Gardening Columnist.*

Just-Picked Flowers: A Fresh Idea Pays

by Lawrence Malkin

NEW YORK—Recession may be deepening and war fears rising, but the animal spirits in some American businesses show no signs of wilting yet. Think flowers. Think phone or fax to order them, picked the same day by their growers. Then think Federal Express to deliver them overnight.

Two years ago Ruth M. Owades assembled all these disparate elements and created a brand new business that is definitely greater than the sum of its parts.

Calyx & Corolla, as she named her company with floral terminology, grossed $10 million last year and is growing by about 10 percent a month against the slumping U.S. business tide.

A staff replying to a toll-free number in San Francisco takes an average of about 25,000 orders a month, collates them by computer and then forwards them on-line to computers at the company's contract growers in California and Florida.

The flowers are packed in specially insulated boxes and accompanied by the sender's greetings, done in calligraphy. At peak times such as Valentine's Day and Mother's Day Federal Express has to send 18-wheel trucks to move the orders from flower farm to airport.

Current specials range from 24 miniature carnations for $32.50 to 25 daffodils for $47, to a dozen long-stemmed roses for $68. Prices include delivery of flowers that are 24 hours old instead of several days old - as they would be after going through middlemen in the retail delivery chain.

The catalogue also offers tropical flowers, special wreaths, bonsai trees, and even monthly subscriptions for the business person too busy to remember. The trade publication *Catalog Age* rates Ms. Owades one of the best in the mail-order business.

Calyx & Corolla has sent flowers to celebrities including Henry Kissinger and Ivana Trump, and one of Rose Kennedy's great grandchildren ordered one hundred flowers from the company for Mrs. Kennedy's centenary.

Never one to miss a market opportunity, Ms. Owades also shipped catalogs to military personnel in Saudi Arabia offering them a 20 percent discount. A score of orders from troops in Operation Desert Storm have

> **The flowers are packed in insulated boxes, with the sender's greetings in calligraphy. At peak times, 18-wheel trucks move the flowers from farm to airport.**

already been dispatched to loved ones at home.

Calyx & Corolla and Federal Express are waiting at least until more customs barriers come down in 1992 to consider deliveries within Europe, where the logistics would be even more complex than they were in the United States.

Ms. Owades, 44, had already made her first million creating a mail-order firm selling high-priced garden equipment to upmarket buyers; the imponderables of starting up Gardener's Eden is now a case study at her alma mater, Harvard Business School.

She sold out to a big catalog firm and moved to California to run the business for the new owners. Her husband, Joseph Owades, who creates special beer recipes for large companies, moved from Boston with her, and she started looking for another start-up as ominous signs appeared in the U.S. economy. "I discovered that chocolates, ice cream, beer, and flowers are relatively recession-proof," Ms. Owades said.

"People send flowers in recession to apologize for the vacation they have to cancel," she said. Corporate clients have also boosted their orders to make up for canceling company parties and, Ms. Owades said, to help lift the war blues in the office.

Five years ago, not enough of the elements would have been in place with enough sophistication to make Calyx & Corolla work. She needed absolutely reliable airfreight service, an inexpensive computer network, special packaging such as iced bud-holders for roses, and, she says, "consumer confidence in the reliability of mail order."

Most of all, she said, the industry had to have confidence that it could improve on its traditional flowers-by-wire delivery system.

The single most important link in the chain was Federal Express, which had to help design the packaging, devise a special rate structure and install a computer tracking system at each of the contract growers.

Dick Metzler, the airfreight company's U.S. marketing chief, acknowledges that he was reluctant at first to gamble with an untried business to make the kinds of adjustments that Federal Express provides its regular clients.

"But we rolled the dice with Ruth, and we're not sorry," he said. "She has carved out a very clever niche for herself, and she's going to own it for a long time to come."

Walter Salmon, professor of retailing at Harvard Business School, says Calyx & Corolla is a perfect example of how to look at an industry as a whole and develop a new way of selling.

In fact, he's thinking of making Ms. Owades's second business start-up into another case study.

THE KING-SIZE COMPANY

—•—

Jessie Bourneuf (HBS '75), President of The King-Size Company, was reviewing statistics on her "big guy" customers. King-Size, an apparel and accessories mail order firm, catered to the needs of the big and tall man. Bourneuf wondered how she could continue to serve her existing customer base, offering new, branded products in larger sizes and, how she could reach out to the millions of other men who might be interested in King-Size's merchandise. Recently, the company had diverged from its traditional marketing strategy and tested a 60 second spot on cable television. The preliminary results seemed promising but were not yet conclusive. She mused about the advantages of cable television advertising over other formats King-Size was using.

On another front, Bourneuf contemplated her competitive environment. With the withdrawal of the Sears Catalog in the spring of 1993, a major gap was left in the mail order environment. In particular, the Sears Big and Tall Catalog that had been estimated to produce $150 million in annual sales was now extinct. What steps should she take to gain advantage from Sears' departure?

COMPANY BACKGROUND

The King-Size Company, with annual sales of approximately $22 million was a division of the WearGuard Company (sales of $160 million), a direct marketer of men's work clothes. King-Size, however, was originally founded as part of the Knapp Shoe company in the 1950's, but had gone through a number of different ownerships prior to its purchase by WearGuard. In 1986, The King-Size Company purchased Jerry Leonard retail stores with the stores retaining the Jerry Leonard name. By the late 1980s, the company consisted of both the King-Size catalog and a number of these Jerry Leonard retail stores. In 1989, WearGuard purchased the catalog and the company's list of mail order customers. (Jerry Leonard King-Size stores were ultimately sold to another company which had recently filed for bankruptcy.) See **Exhibit 1** for selected financial information about The King-Size company.

In the summer of 1992, the WearGuard Corporation, including its King-Size and E.T. Wright divisions (E. T. Wright was an executive shoe direct mailer) were purchased by ARA services, a $5 billion food services corporation. According to King-Size management the relationship with ARA had been very amicable and successful, with the parent company maintaining an arms length relationship with WearGuard and its divisions.

THE KING-SIZE COMPANY

WearGuard purchased the King-Size company after many months of searching for an acquisition. Bourneuf spearheaded this search and when the purchase was finalized she became president of the division. Both Bourneuf and the President of WearGuard, Bruce Humphrey, wanted to find and purchase a direct mail company that would benefit from the marketing know-how and

This case was prepared by Research Associate Dinny Starr Gordon under the supervision of Professor David Bell as the basis for class discussion rather than to illustrate either effective or ineffective handling of an administrative situation.

technological advancements of the WearGuard Corporation. They believed that the King-Size catalog was just such an operation; presenting significant opportunities for better management and expansion.

When purchased, the King-Size in-house mailing list included 450,000 names. After four years as a division of the WearGuard company, there were now 1.3 million names on the list. Of those customer names, 400,000 had bought products at some point in the past ten years, 120,000 had bought merchandise in the previous 12 months and an additional 60,000 had bought merchandise in the 12 months prior to that.

UNDERSTANDING THE KING-SIZE BUSINESS

After acquiring the King-Size business, Bourneuf took several steps to understand this new market and to revitalize the company. First, Bourneuf and Cindy Connelly, the company's Advertising Manager, conducted a number of focus groups of customers. In these sessions many issues became clear. According to Connelly, the management team was really surprised at the "emotional well-being of these really big guys—not like women, who would rather be on a diet." The participants in these initial focus groups made clear that they believed that the manufacturers and retailers had fallen short in their ability to service the Big and Tall man's apparel and accessory needs. One of their biggest criticisms was the lack of choice. Customers thought that the product line should be fresher and more comprehensive, and that the catalog needed updating. They believed that King-Size should be able to select and manufacture merchandise that suited their larger and taller frames, and that they should be able to provide both basic and fashion items that were of high quality and at prices that reflected the value of the product.

As part of the initial understanding of the business, Bourneuf also established an on-going advisory panel of customers so that management could hear on a regular basis what customers thought about King-Size products and services. According to Connelly, King-Size management was able to get a clearer picture of their customer base as well as receive both new product suggestions and product modifications from this advisory group. As a result of these initial conversations, in the first year of operations the King-Size catalog format was changed, the product line was expanded, merchandise quality was improved, and prices were raised. **Exhibit 2** shows pages from old and new catalogs.

THE KING-SIZE CUSTOMER

King-Size defined its potential customer as any man at least six feet two inches tall, weighing 225 pounds or more, or both. In 1993, approximately 12%–15% of the male population of the United States (about 10 million men) were in this category. From a survey, performed each year, some general information about the King-Size customer was extrapolated by the company. The King-Size customer tended to be older (over 40) although there was representation from all age groups. About one third tended to fall into the "big and tall" category, while about one quarter were considered "big" and one eighth were considered "tall." Over 60% of customers were married. The customer's average income was approximately $45,000 per year. The customer read a lot and was involved in a number of hobbies such as gardening, fishing and hunting. Bourneuf described the typical King-Size customer as follows: "He's white collar, he's in sales or management, he drives an American car, he reads a lot, he has above-average investments, he probably went to college, his kids go to college, he's married. So he's Mr. America, but with above-average income and disposable income."[1] For more information on Big and Tall men in the United States see **Exhibit 3**.

KING-SIZE PRODUCTS

King-Size carried an array of branded and private label men's apparel, accessories, and shoes. This included casual shirts, pants and shorts; dress shirts (with monogramming available) pants, suits, blazers, and ties; athletic clothing and sneakers; dress and casual shoes; and, accessories and gifts such as sunglasses, umbrellas, and suitcases. The branded products included labels such as Dockers, Cutter & Buck, Boston Trader, Arrow, Reebok, LA Gear, etc. All products were manufactured with the requirements of the larger sized man in mind. The products were designed according to body shape, either Tall or Big, allowing for extra length in the tall merchandise and extra breadth in the big items. T-Shirts, for instance, were available in TALL sizes (the numbers refer to chest size in inches); L(44–46), XL(48–50),

---

1 From *DNR: The Men's Wear Fashion/News Magazine*, Vol. 22 No. 30 Monday, Feb. 15, 1993.

2XL(52–54), 3XL(56–58), and 4XL(60–62), and in BIG sizes; 2XL(52–54), 3XL(56–58), 4XL(60–62), 5XL(64–66), 6XL(68–70), 7XL(72–74), and 8XL(76–78). If a customer was unsure of his exact size or if he had unusual sizing requirements, telephone order representatives had sizing charts for all products in the catalog to assist the customer in making his merchandise selection. (**Exhibit 4** shows size charts for two products.) In addition, in-seams on some pants, and sleeve lengths on dress shirts, were custom tailored for each customer. The most frequently purchased items from the King-Size catalog included various types of shirts and pants. Other important categories were shoes, underwear, outerwear and socks.

THE TELEPHONE ORDER SYSTEM

The in-house order entry department received an average of 250 orders a day on a slow day in July to 2,000 orders a day ten days before Christmas. Of these, approximately 75% were received via the telephone or fax machine, and the rest came in by mail. The telephone lines were open from 7:00 am to 12:00 midnight, seven days a week. The company had an 800 number to service its customers placing orders. The number was printed on all catalogs. There was a separate 800 number to service inquiries about damages and returns. About 40 telephone representatives were on the King-Size payroll with about 75% of these employees working on a part-time basis. The seasonal nature of the catalog business forced swells in the telephone order taking work force to about 100 people just before the Christmas holiday period. Telephone order representatives received about 25 hours of classroom training and 10–15 hours of training with a partner on the telephone before assuming the responsibility for their own phone line. The representatives were paid on an hourly basis but could augment their salary by selling weekly promoted goods.

The telephone system permitted a supervisor automatically to monitor the length of a given operator's conversation and the status of the order. The total number and dollar amount of orders could be monitored by hour and by day. Traditionally, the Monday and Tuesday after a catalog drop were high volume days on the order taking floor. The busiest hours tended to be around lunch time, from 11:00 am–2:00 pm. A summary of order taking results for a one-week period, called the Daily Tally report, is shown in **Exhibit 5**.

When a customer called, a telephone representative greeted the customer and asked for their customer number listed on the back of the catalog. The customer was also asked for the catalog number. This six digit number identified not only the particular catalog that the customer was looking at but also the marketing basis on which that customer received it. Inventory and pricing information for that specific catalog came up on the order entry screen as the order was taken.

As the telephone representative continued through the order taking process, much information was available on her screen. Customer height and weight specifications, purchase history including total amount of purchases over time, most recent purchase amount, and past orders in detail could be accessed as necessary. In addition, the telephone representatives could change any "ship to" or "bill to" data that was incorrect. According to Mary Sullivan, Sales and Customer Service Manager, it was very important for the telephone representatives to be cordial and expedient when taking orders.

THE MERCHANDISING DEPARTMENT

Given the recent growth in the business, the merchandising area at King-Size was undergoing some changes. In the past, the buying responsibilities had been divided by category of product, with buyers purchasing groupings such as all tops, all bottoms, or all accessories. In the current restructuring, however, products were bought on a more "ensemble" basis, (for example, button down shirts and matching khaki pants manufactured by the same vendor were purchased together), where merchandise categories were delineated by branded or private label product, or by fabrication. There were three buyers, or product managers, as they were called at King-Size. One product manager was responsible for shoes, accessories, all branded product, and outer-wear. The second product manager purchased the King-Size private label brand of casual knit and woven tops and bottoms (pants and shorts). These items were considered the "bread and butter" of the full product line. The third product manager took care of the "dress apparel"; better, higher end clothing and accessories such as sports coats, dress shirts, and ties. This third area included both private label and nationally branded merchandise.

The product manager's responsibilities at King-Size were numerous. They included understanding the unusual size requirements of their customers; educating suppliers about their big and tall business; finding new, and better, resources for their products; creating successful working relationships with their vendors; and, negotiating prices and quantities with these vendors.

King-Size's experience was that its relatively low buying power combined with what manufacturers perceived as an unattractive category of business made it difficult to obtain attractive prices and terms.

The product managers also had to stay on top of what was going on in the men's fashion environment by visiting men's apparel and accessory stores, the fashion markets in New York, and vendors from around the world. When merchandise arrived at King-Size, it was also the product manager's responsibility to check the quality and size specifications of the items and highlight the features and benefits to the customer service representative so they could better serve the customers.

One aspect of the product manager's position which was unique to a catalog company was understanding the critical issues of timing and forecasting. Unlike a retail environment where no commitment was made up front to the customer about the products available in the store, mail order houses had shown their merchandise, in print and with unalterable prices, well before the merchandise arrived in their warehouse. This made forecasting customer demand essential to the company's buying decision. A product manager, therefore, had to have a keen sense of her product's appeal to the customer.

Working with the three product managers were two other supportive positions. One was an analytical inventory management job, which included interfacing and assisting with warehouse operations as well as forecasting inventory needs. The other was a position focusing on assisting the product managers in an analysis of the performance of their products and the reordering of their merchandise.

The whole merchandising area was overseen by the Merchandise Manager, Colleen Cheney, who, outside of her supervisory responsibilities of the department, bought the swimwear and pocket T-shirt lines of clothing. She had chosen to keep these lines of products as her responsibility because they had "hard to deal with" vendors. She also had several support and data entry personnel reporting to her. These people were in charge of entering, maintaining, and updating the data in the inventory computer system. Among other tasks this included entering purchase orders, item style and size specifications by product, prices, and catalog copy into the computer.

CATALOG\BUYING CYCLES

For King-Size, like most mail order companies, the catalog and merchandise buying cycles were a critical driver in the operations of the business. Products pictured in any given catalog might be purchased up to 12 months or more in advance, forcing everybody to think at least one year out. For example, private label flannel shirts, an indispensable offering in the King-Size catalog, had to be purchased a full year in advance of sell date because the fabric was manufactured overseas and required a year's lead time. Other items, however, such as basic slacks which were available from a domestic manufacturer, could be ordered only a month or two before the selling season. Because of these differences, it was important for all members of the merchandising department to understand the distinct procurement cycles of all products.

For an additional reason, the King-Size purchasing cycle was different than other apparel mail order companies. Unlike regular men's apparel, the fashion elements of the big and tall men's business were generally a year behind that of his "regular sized" counterpart. This allowed the merchandise group at King-Size to evaluate current trends in the men's apparel environment and develop ideas for the following season. As the King-Size customer became more demanding, however, more timely evaluation and decision making by the merchandise group might be necessary.

THE CALENDAR

The King-Size year, in general, was divided into two seasons, Spring and Fall, and catalog development and merchandise purchases fell into either one of these time frames. To understand the buying process at King-Size, Cheney outlined the typical sequence of events using the fall catalog as her example. First, in the previous fall the buying group would spend time shopping men's stores, catalogs, outlets, etc., to pick up samples of the latest fashion trends that they believed might be an appropriate product for their customers. (One year this evaluation process included a trip to the Mall of America in Minneapolis.) The merchandising department would also consult recent research by The Fashion Association in New York. By January, the product managers would also attend several men's apparel trade shows (the Big and Tall Man Trade Show, "BATMAN," took place in the last week of January) and talk to a number of vendors to ascertain what merchandise would be available in the market for the fall.

Once all of this information gathering was done, usually by mid-to-late February, each product manager put together her proposals for the fall. The expected growth for the company as a whole and the development of each product category individually were made in conjunction with these product ideas. These efforts culminated in the Fall Line Review. The Line Review encompassed a number of meetings, over a two or three week period, where product managers presented their merchandise plans for the coming fall season. All members of the merchandising department, as well as the creative director, the marketing people, Connelly and Glenda Fishman (HBS '75), Marketing Manager, and Bourneuf attended the discussions. Together, they reviewed all the product categories, their product samples, Product Sheets (which outlined the items' features, fabrication and size specifications), and color swatches. The group decided which products would become part of the fall season product line. The overall strategy in recent years had been to limit the number of SKUs offered in the catalog by reducing the number of color choices. Included as part of the discussion were last year's sales figures, by category, style, color, etc.; the costs of the merchandise and any discounts available; delivery information as estimated by the suppliers; and, any relevant minimum order requirements for the products. Two or three product categories were reviewed each day.

Once the Fall Line Review was complete, product category decisions made, and general quantities and color schemes for merchandise outlined, the actual purchasing began. At this point, starting around mid-March and continuing through April, product managers drafted purchased orders detailing quantities to order, size distributions and specifications, delivery dates of merchandise, etc. Although these were the official purchase documents, dialogue and negotiation with King-Sizes' suppliers had been in process for many months prior to the submission of the final purchase orders. Once commitments were made to the vendors, either through earlier conversations or ultimately in these later purchase order documents, there was some flexibility, but not much, to alter or cancel the orders. It was critical, therefore, that the merchandising team was confident of their product selections and quantities made for the coming season. For about 60%–70% of the products King-Size could reorder the merchandise during the season. If a product was not successful, King-Size traditionally put it on sale or at clearance prices at the end of the season and still covered their costs.

As the spring and summer progressed, the product managers stayed in constant touch with their vendors in order to resolve any issues or questions that they might have about the purchase orders. They also monitored all expected merchandise delivery dates. Most fall products would arrive at the King-Size warehouse at the end of August or beginning of September. This would insure that inventory was available for sale when the first fall catalogs reached the customers. In total, therefore, it took close to a year for the merchandising department to research and analyze sales trends, receive sample products from vendors, choose product lines, colors and styles, negotiate prices and minimum quantities, finalize purchases, and ultimately receive merchandise for the fall season.

For the spring season, the Spring Line Review was scheduled for September. The sequence of events leading up to and following after the Spring Line Review were essentially the same as they were for the fall season. In fact, elements of preparation of each season were always running concurrently, making operations more complex. A product manager in March, for example, would simultaneously be negotiating prices and quantities with a supplier for fall merchandise while at the same time she might be dealing with a mis-shipped delivery on current spring merchandise.

All merchandising decisions were made in conjunction with the creation of the King-Size catalog. The development of the catalog started with the Line Review, where broad, general choices were made about the layout of the fall catalog, and continued for the next five to six months until the catalog boards and film were finally sent to the printer. To understand the catalog development process see **Exhibit 6**.

The first fall catalog was printed and distributed, "dropped," in mid-to-late August. A full size catalog usually had around 70 to 100 pages, whereas a prospect catalog might have as few as 36 pages. Normally, only the cover pages and a few critical interior pages were changed during a season. If, however, items had sold out during the season, that would be noted in the next printing of the catalog. For the schedule of catalog drop dates see **Table 1**. For a breakdown of Fall 1993 catalog costs see **Exhibit 7**.

MARKETING RESEARCH

Since the acquisition of the company in 1989, King-Size management had used a number of ways to understand and stay in touch with their customers. As mentioned above, the company established an advisory council of key customers and King-Size executives. The board was made up of at least eight customers and was convened

Table 1
Catalog Drop Dates

Catalog#	Drop Date	Circulation[1]
Fall Preview & Spring II Clearance	August	239,000
Fall Full Book	September	328,000
Fall II Full Book	October	479,000
Christmas Book	November	336,000
Christmas II Book	Late November	282,000
Winter Clearance	January	174,000
Spring Preview & Winter II Clearance	February	226,000
Spring Full Book	March	578,000
Spring II Full Book	April	207,000
Father's Day Book	May	486,000
Spring Clearance	July	249,000

1 Circulation indicates the number of catalogs sent out. The amounts are planned figures for Fall 1993 and Spring 1994. The figures exclude two prospect books not in the original plan, one for Fall '93 with circulation of 145,000 and the other for Spring '94 with circulation of 200,000.

twice a year. Board membership changed each year depending on where the meetings were to take place. The group was made up of better customers with an emphasis on achieving a cross-section of customer type such as varying clothing sizes, income levels, and psychographic characteristics. The purpose of the meetings were to let decision makers at King-Size get closer to the customer, as well as allowing for customer feedback on product and service issues. Some ideas that had been generated from the advisory board meetings included: (1) New product suggestions—sunglasses for larger size heads; (2) Enhancements to existing products—additional belt loops for bigger waist pants; and, (3) Suggestions on how to feature clothes in the catalog —showing models wearing a polo shirt with a denim shirt over it like a light-weight jacket.

Another way that King-Size received feedback from its customers was through a written survey sent out in customer packages. This survey attempted to identify customer demographics and customer opinions about King-Size products and services. Questions asked included issues of merchandise satisfaction, other places they shop, new product ideas, favorite activities, magazines read, TV programs watched, and occupations.

For the previous three summers, King-Size had contracted an outside research firm to conduct a telephone survey of a number of its customers. The objectives of the survey were: to try to predict general sales trends for the remainder of the year and the coming 12 months; to track buying patterns of key customer types; to identify dimensions on which company changes in the past had had a positive impact; and, to isolate areas where improvements were still needed. For the survey 229 customers were identified and contacted. About two thirds of those surveyed (169 customers) were chosen because they had made purchases since January 1993. The other 60 people, considered an "augment sample," were included to ensure base sizes for key subgroups of customers, including customers with marginal sizes (those with very tall/big sizes such as 7XL or 8XL); those with key attitudinal profiles; and, sale buyers. A summary of some of the results of the survey can be found in **Exhibit 8**.

Another focus of the telephone survey was to better understand King-Size's competitors. The telephone survey asked where else they shopped for their apparel and accessory needs. From the survey and other sources it was clear that King-Size competitors included JC Penney, Sears, and several Big and Tall retail stores. The principal specialty retail chain was Casual Male (called simply "Big & Tall" in some parts of the U.S.) with about 250 locations. Recently Edison Brothers had been acquiring many smaller Big and Tall retailers including King-Size's own one-time outlets. See **Exhibit 9** for additional survey information on King-Size competitors.

CUSTOMER ACQUISITION

King-Size used both conventional and more creative mail order acquisition techniques for finding new customers. Traditionally, catalog companies acquired customer names from lists of other mail order company customer names. These acquisitions were usually made through a list broker who tried to segment the characteristics of the purchasers. Some list brokers tailored lists based on a company's specific requests. A mail order house rented a list and paid for each name that converted into a sale. Lists were usually rented on a one-time basis.

For King-Size renting lists was uneconomic since there was no way to segment the names by height or weight. An exception was that state Registry of Vehicles recorded height and weight information for inclusion on drivers licenses. About twenty state registries had made this information available for purchase. The last time King-Size rented this information, in October 1992, the company spent $30,000 for about 100,000 new names. Each was sent a postcard offering to send a King-Size catalog. Of the 6,600 people who requested a catalog, 12% made an order.

King-Size also had package insert programs with several mail order companies including, among others, their fellow divisions, WearGuard and E.T. Wright. Other exchanges were with non-competitive catalogs thought to have a similar customer base, such as the Omaha Steaks, Hanover House, or Hammacher Schlemmer catalogs. In programs such as these, King-Size would either exchange package insert programs with the other catalog company or would pay to have their marketing materials inserted into the other company's packages. In 1993, King-Size spent $350,000 on package insert programs.

An alternate method for finding customers was through "card deck" advertising. In 1993, for instance, card decks accounted for almost $224,000 of King-Size's budget. Card Decks were postcard size advertisements that were mailed to consumers homes in packages of 30-60 cards at a time. **Figure 1**, below, shows a typical King-Size card deck advertisement. Each card usually was an advertisement or request form for a company's catalog or product. The marketing companies that put together these card decks could segment the demographic and buying characteristics, and area of interests, of the recipient consumers. This allowed the mail order company to designate who they thought would be interested in their catalog.

Figure 1
King-Size Card Deck Advertisement

Similar to a card deck was a "Valpak" advertisement. Like card decks, Valpaks (value packages) were sent directly to customers in their homes. Valpaks tended to be more coupon oriented than a card deck package, offering some amount off a purchase if the card was filled out and sent in. Valpaks were considered part of the King-Size card deck budget.

Another avenue for reaching potential customers was through space advertising in magazines and newspapers. King-Size promotions, usually block advertisements, were often found in the back pages of magazines such as *The New Yorker, Smithsonian, Golf Illustrated* and *American Gardener*, and newspapers such as *USA Today* and *The Wall Street Journal*. The ads were usually a brief description of the merchandise available and offered a toll-free number to call to request a catalog. Space advertising represented about $140,000 of the 1993 advertising budget. Sunday Supplements, such as *Parade Magazine* and *The New York Times Magazine*, were another advertising option for King-Size and were purchased every few months. In 1993, $97,000 was spent on Sunday Supplement campaigns.

The 1993 budget also included approximately $105,000 for public relations. Public relations materials included: press releases to various industry journals and trade publications; information created for trade shows and other events; and, a newsletter sent out to King-Size customers on a quarterly basis. For more information on advertising expenditures for 1993, see **Table 2**, below.

Table 2
Advertising Schedule—Mail Order Business[1] YTD 12/93

Public Relations	$ 105,752
Advertising Agency	0
Space Advertising	137,199
Sunday Supplements	97,674
Card Decks	223,949
Package Inserts	484,623
Market Research	55,451
Other	53,178
Total Mail Order	$ 1,157,827

---

1 In addition, King-Size spent $18,071 on advertising for their retail outlet in 1993.

CUSTOMER RETENTION

When a customer contacted King-Size to request a catalog, either via a mailed in card, or from an 800 number listed in an advertisement, the customer's information was entered into the computer system and then he was sent a copy of the most recent catalog. From that time forward, that customer's name was always associated with the way it was acquired. This let King-Size track the value over time of the media used to reach potential customers. For instance, a customer name that was obtained through a space advertisement in the *Wall Street Journal* might be more valuable in the long term than a customer reached via a card deck advertisement.

After the initial catalog request, King-Size sent new customer names two or three more catalogs during the first twelve months on the mailing list. Following that, customer names were evaluated based on the frequency and amount of purchases made during that time. If a customer did not buy often or at all, or the value of their purchases was low, they might receive fewer catalogs than a better customer during the same time frame. King-Size frequently experimented with its mailing strategy, sending catalogs to specific groups of customers to see how to more efficiently and effectively increase sales. To date, King-Size had not purged any names from their in-house customer list.

THE CABLE TV EXPERIMENT

In the beginning of 1992, King-Size conducted its first foray into video advertising. At that time, with the help of an ad agency, Bourneuf and Connelly developed a promotional video whose primary objective was to familiarize men's fashion editors and the press with King-Size. The secondary goal was to create a video piece that presented merchandise to customers in a different format than normal. They hoped that the video would stimulate interest in and trial of King-Size products. The videos were promoted in the 1992 spring catalogs. They could be purchased for $10 which was then credited towards a customer's purchase of merchandise. According to King-Size, the cost of the venture was low, and, because the business was growing quickly, presented little risk. Although the video was not very successful, ("thousands of videos were left over" according to one executive), it was considered an important step for the company. It was, in fact, the precursor to the development of King-Size cable advertising the following year.

The cable venture, started in the spring of 1993, was Bourneuf's special project. She had seen some other retailers promoting product through cable television and thought that it might be a good and viable advertising medium for King-Size. Furthermore, King-Size's penetration of the mass market was very small. She believed the potential number of customers, however, given the huge population of men who fell into the "big and tall" category, was great. The obstacle remained; how to reach a large portion of these men in an economical way. Traditional mass market vehicles such as *People* or *Newsweek*, were much too expensive for a company like King-Size. Bourneuf, therefore was searching for an alternative.

Bourneuf, Connelly, and the advertising agency which had produced the 1992 video, met to discuss the cable option. Together, they developed the idea for the commercial and then the ad agency established a proposed budget and media buying plan. The preliminary budget is shown in **Table 3** below. With this information, Bourneuf came to the following conclusions about cable advertising; first of all, she found that producing a cable TV advertisement could be done with a small budget, especially if the commercial was not too fancy or complex; second, unlike other advertising mediums, cable TV spots could be purchased in small units, limiting the up-front investment and risk; and third, the ability to reach a much larger mass market than other mediums such as package inserts or magazine space advertising was greatly increased. With these compelling reasons and the proposed budget in hand, Bourneuf approached ARA senior management with a plan for a King-Size Cable TV test promotion. Once they understood both the potential and the ability to discontinue the venture, and thereby minimize exposure, they agreed to the funding.

The television spot was designed to promote trial of the King-Size catalog. The commercial showed a man talking about King-Size merchandise and flipping through the most recent catalog. The spot stressed the extensive selection of big and tall sizes, the wide variety of branded and private label merchandise, the range of apparel, shoes, and accessories available, and the ease and privacy of shopping from home. The commercial was very straightforward, appealing to the customer to call the toll free number on their TV screen to receive a free King-Size catalog. The commercial was aired on five stations, TBS, ESPN, CNN, A&E and Family.

The initial results of the cable experiment were very positive. The number of catalog requests received over the six-week period exceeded 66,000. **Figure 2**, below, compares catalog requests by source for 1992 and 1993. In addition to the sheer number of respondents, the program was designed to capture as much information as was possible from these potential customers. For instance, each cable network had its own specific 800 number, helping King-Size identify which TV programs were the most successful for attracting customers. When the customer called to order the catalog the telephone representatives asked not only his name and address information, but also his height and weight. When the Cable TV promotion was complete it had cost King-Size approximately $144,000 to develop and run the commercial over a five-week period in September and October 1993. Preliminary results and costs breakdown of the campaign can be seen in **Exhibit 10**.

Table 3
King-Size Cable TV Campaign: Budget Summary

Production

TV Commercial Production	$ 48,000
Talent (session + 13 week cycle)[1]	4,212
Travel Expenses	1,436
Customized Edit (5 phone numbers)	1,880
Dubs	762
Music	150
	$ 56,440

Media

4 week schedule National Cable	$144,200

1 Talent costs for each additional 13 week cycle is $2003 (1st year).

Figure 2
Catalog Requests by Source

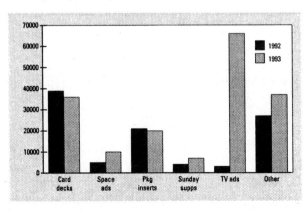

In order to handle the flood of calls generated from the cable promotion, King-Size contracted an outside service bureau to answer the telephone calls and fulfill the catalog requests. In addition, King-Size created a special "prospect" catalog for these customers. This catalog was only 36 pages in length, shortened so that it could be mailed quickly via first class mail. The costs for order processing and fulfillment can be seen in **Table 4**, below.

Table 4
Service Bureau Charges

Labor—Taking Call[1]	$1.35
Postage—1st Class	.98
Fulfillment	.12
Catalog Printing Cost—Prospect	.20

1 This figure included an additional $.35 which King-Size was charged by the service bureau to record and transmit the height and weight information of the callers.

CABLE PROMOTION—1994

King-Size believed that the Fall 1993 cable campaign was successful. When compared to other promotions and advertising occurring at the same time, the results seemed very positive. (**Exhibit 11** shows the breakdown of the costs, the number of requests, and conversion rates of the cable campaign and other media used at the same time.) King-Size also compared and analyzed the socio-economic differences between a sample group of the cable TV catalog requesters and the traditional print media catalog requesters at the same time. The results of this investigation, which were based on the ZIP codes of those who requested catalogs, can be seen in **Exhibit 12**.

There were some other issues about cable, moreover, that needed to be better understood. For one, because the prospect catalog was short and stated that a full size catalog would be mailed soon, it is possible that many customers were waiting until they received the full catalog to place orders. Two, because of the volume of calls generated from cable, King-Size could not handle the requests for catalogs or fulfillment in-house. This created an inability to control all of the process. And three, although the conversion rates on cable were good, it was not clear yet how loyal these customers would be over time. Industry averages suggested that a catalog company could expect to lose permanently half of its existing active customer base each year.

OTHER INITIATIVES

Jessie had often wondered if it would make sense to approach a chain like Casual Male with a view to a strategic alliance. Casual Male could extend to King-Size its buying clout with manufacturers in return for King-Size's help in running a Casual Male customer catalog.

Finally, Bourneuf had taken no action about Sears abrupt departure from the catalog business. Though their "Sears Big and Tall" catalog featured noticeably less-expensive goods, it was reasonable to suppose that many of their "abandoned" customers could be coaxed into buying from King-Size. Jessie wondered what her priorities should be at this point.

Exhibit 1
King-Size Selected Financial Information

Balance Sheet (As of October 1, 1993)

Assets		Liabilities	
Cash and cash equiv.	$ 564	Interdivisional payable	$ 4,135,885
Accounts receivable	(17,109)	Accts. payable—trade	1,943,828
Inventories	6,524,130	Accrued expenses	519,167
Prepaid catalog	685,884	Accrued catalog expense	239,333
Prepaid expenses	82,427		
Total current assets	7,275,897	Total current liabilities	6,838,213
Property and equipment	851,413		
Less accumulated depr. and amort.	(139,281)	Retained earnings	4,241,306
Net fixed assets	712,131		
Deferred charges and other assets	3,091,491		
Total assets	$11,079,519	Total liabilities and retained earnings	$11,079,519

Statement of Income (For twelve month period ended October 1, 1993)

Sales	
Mail Order	$21,702,896
Retail	495,091
List Income	38,287
Reserve against returns	(32,000)
Total Sales	**22,204,274**
Cost of Goods Sold	12,065,238
Gross Profit	10,139,035
SG & A	8,773,923
Earnings before interest, tax, depr. & amort.	1,365,112

Gross Profit

YTD 12/93
Percent to net sales

	%
List sales	93.31
Discounts	-1.62
Net Merchandise Sales	91.69
Personalization revenue	.96
Shipping revenue	7.17
Contract revenue	0.00
List income	0.18
Total sales	100.00
Material @ Std.	50.35
Freight	0.58
Other	1.00
Total material	51.92
Tailor shop	1.02
Screen print	0.00
Shrink	0.02
Non-continued merchandise	0.82
Liquidations	0.27
LIFO provisions	0.28
Total other costs	2.41
Subtotal	54.34
Total Cost of Goods Sold	54.34
Gross Profit	45.66

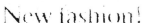

Exhibit 2A

Page from King-Size Spring 1990 Catalog

New fashion!

(1) EASY GOOD LOOKS FROM NEW "BANDED" BOTTOM TO KNIT COLLAR. Black and white pullover by Members Only* (logo on hidden pocket) teams knit and woven textures in 60% cotton/40% polyester blend. Striped sleeves with rib knit finish. Machine-care. Import.

TALL & EXTRA TALL

SHORT SLEEVES (FULL-CUT)
No. 2639 Black/White/Grey
Sizes L(16-16½) XL(17-17½) 2XL(18-18½) 3XL(19-20)
Price $47.95

BIG & EXTRA BIG

SHORT SLEEVES (FULL-CUT)
No. 2640 Black/White/Grey
Sizes XL(17-17½) 2XL(18-18½)
Price $47.95

SHORT SLEEVES (FULL-CUT)
No. 2641 Black/White/Grey
Sizes 3XL(19-20) 4XL(21-22)
Price $49.95

(2) "BANDED" IS THE BOTTOM LINE ON THIS SEASON'S HOT FASHION SPORT SHIRT. Full-cut two tone woven and knit pullover sports stripe chest with fashion label over inside zipper pocket and neat banded bottom. Machine-care polyester and cotton. Import by Colorworks.*

TALL & EXTRA TALL

SHORT SLEEVES (FULL-CUT)
No. 2648 Turquoise/Black
Sizes L(16-16½) XL(17-17½) 2XL(18-18½)
Price $26.95

BIG & EXTRA BIG

SHORT SLEEVES (FULL-CUT)
No. 2649 Turquoise/Black
Sizes XL(17-17½) 2XL(18-18½)
Price $28.95

SHORT SLEEVES (FULL-CUT)
No. 2650 Turquoise/Black
Sizes 3XL(19-20)
Price $29.95

(3) EASY-ON PULLOVER WITH SMART "BANDED" BOTTOM IS THE NEW LOOK FOR LEISURE. Two-tone woven and knit combination with black pinstripe collar, drop shoulders, welt pocket and screen-printed crest. Machine-care blend of 65% polyester-35% cotton. Full-cut body. Import by Colorworks.*

TALL & EXTRA TALL

SHORT SLEEVES (FULL-CUT)
No. 2642 White/Black Trim
Sizes L(16-16½) XL(17-17½) 2XL(18-18½)
Price $28.95

BIG & EXTRA BIG

SHORT SLEEVES (FULL-CUT)
No. 2643 White
Sizes XL(17-17½) 2XL(18-18½)
Price $28.95

SHORT SLEEVES (FULL-CUT)
No. 2644 White
Sizes 3XL(19-20)
Price $29.95

(4) PULL-ON EASE AND STYLING GIVE THIS "BANDED" BOTTOM SPORT SHIRT A NEW LOOK. Chest stripe is acid-washed with 2 bellows pockets and embossed crest. Regular collar, placket front, two-tone full-cut body. Machine-wash and dry cotton. Import by Colorworks.*

TALL & EXTRA TALL

SHORT SLEEVES (FULL-CUT)
No. 2645 White/Blue
Sizes L(16-16½) XL(17-17½) 2XL(18-18½)
Price $36.95

BIG & EXTRA BIG

SHORT SLEEVES (FULL-CUT)
No. 2646 White/Blue
Sizes XL(17-17½) 2XL(18-18½)
Price $38.95

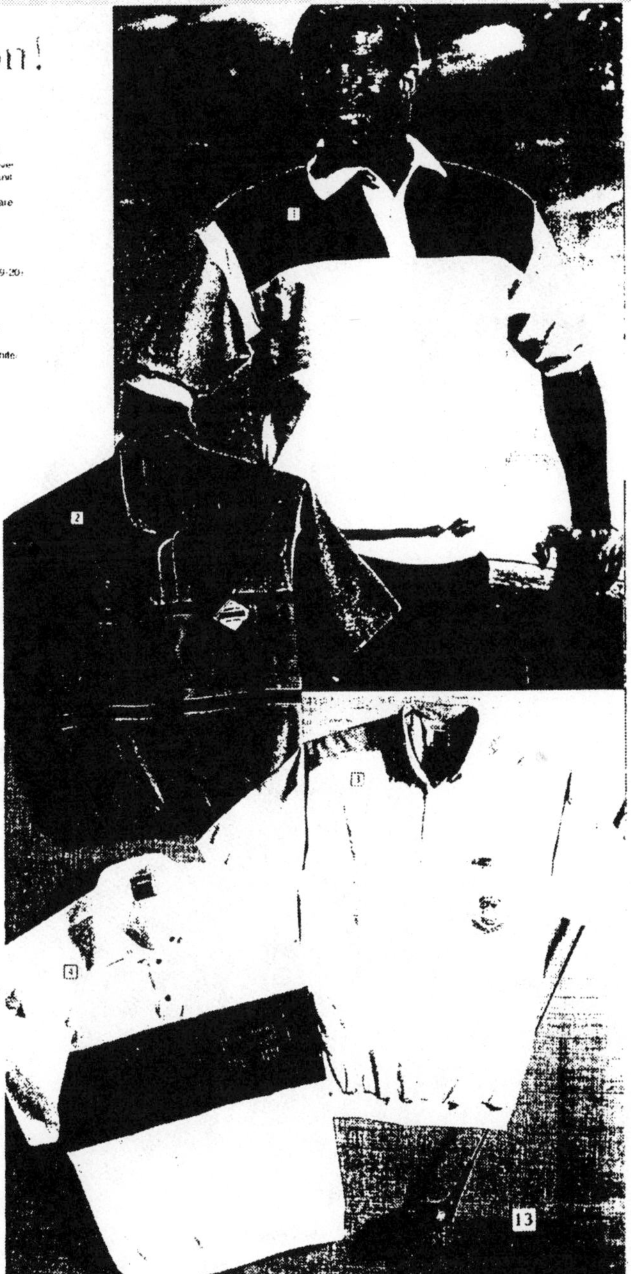

The quintessential wear for the weekend. A comfortable and creative approach to sophisticated sportswear. Fabrics engineered exclusively for Cutter & Buck®. High-quality and superior detailing. Roomy silhouettes. Luminous colors. Intricate embroidery. Cutter & Buck's New styles that will become your old favorites.

A CUTTER & BUCK HALF-SLEEVE JERSEY KNIT SHIRTS Elbow-length sleeves are stylish and extra-comfortable. Your choice of a rich, yarn-dyed stripe or solids with contrasting ribbed trim on collar and sleeve. Full-cut. Full taped collar and 3 button placket lined with sturdy cotton twill. Hemmed bottom. 100% cotton. Machine wash, dry low. USA made.
Solid Colors: Blue Jade — BLJ, White — WHT, Mets Orange — ORG.
Stripe Color:
Mets Orange/White/Deep Royal — OGS.
Tall: L(44-46), XL(48-50), 2XL(52-54), 3XL(56-58)
Big: XL(48-50), 2XL(52-54), 3XL (56-58), 4XL(60-62), 5XL(64-66)
        STYLE #1598 .... **$59.95**

B CUTTER & BUCK COTTON CANVAS SHORTS Roomy, classic-cut pleated shorts in cool, crisp 100% cotton canvas. Side on-seam pockets, 2 back pockets (1 button-flap, 1 with welted.) Belt loops. Machine wash, dry low. Imported.
Colors: Blue Jade — BLJ, Sand — SND, White — WHT, Blue Jay Stripe — BJS
Tall: Even Waist Sizes 38 to 44.
Big: Even Waist Sizes 44 to 56.
        STYLE #2535 .... **$59.95**

C CUTTER & BUCK HALF-SLEEVE BUTTON DOWN SHIRTS 100% cotton twill comfort in colorful solids and printed stripes. Full-cut, 1 chest button-flap pocket. Fine quality single and double needle detail. Machine wash, dry low. Imported.
Solid Colors: Blue Jade — BLJ, White — WHT, Mets Orange — ORG
Stripe Colors: Blue Jade/White — BJS, Mets Orange/White — OGS
Tall: L(16-16½), XL(17-17½), 2XL(18-18½), 3XL(19-20)
Big: XL(17-17½), 2XL(18-18½), 3XL(19-20), 4XL(21-22), 5XL(23-24)
        STYLE #1166 $59.95

Exhibit 3
1993 King-Size Press Release

Big And Tall Facts

- Today, more than 13 million men fall into the category of Big & Tall

- This means, they are 6'2" tall or taller, and weigh 225 lbs. or more, or BOTH

- By the year 2000, 1 out of every 5 men will fit this description

- 61% of adults in the U.S. weigh more than their ideal weight

- Of the 71.5 million men in the U.S., 18.7 million are obese by medical standards

- 31% of all men between the ages of 45 to 54 are overweight

- This age group is projected to double in the next ten years

- Between 1960 and 1980 the average adult weight increased by 6 pounds

- 75% of big and tall adults have big and tall relatives and offspring

- In the past century men have grown, on average, 6" taller

- When you think of it, many of the country's leading role models and celebrities (past and present), also happen to be big and tall:

Norman Schwarzkopf	Willard Scott
Ken Olsen	John Candy
John Kenneth Galbraith	Orson Wells
John Wayne	John Goodman
Larry Bird	Michael Jordan
Arnold Schwarzenegger	Harry Smith

All of the NFL!
All of the NBA!

Exhibit 4A
Style: 1022—Long-Sleeved Dress Shirt

Fabric content: Mixed—60% cotton, 40% polyester/55% cotton, 45% polyester
Care instructions: Machine wash, machine dry

Label: The King-Size Co.

BIG	17	17 ½	18	18 ½	19	20	22	24
Chest	54	56	58	60	62	64	68	72
Waist	54	56	58	60	62	64	68	72
Hip	54	56	58	60	62	64	68	72
Body length	33	33	33	33	34	34	34	34
Neck	17	17½	18	18½	19	20	22	24
Upper arm	19	19½	20	20½	21	21½	22	22½
Sleeve length	33–36	33–36	33–36	33–36	33–36	33–36	33–36	33–36
Cuff opening	9	10	10¼	10½	10	11	11½	12

TALL	15 ½	16	16 ½	17	17 ½	18	18 ½	19	20
Chest	47	49	51	53	56	58	60	62	64
Waist	42	45	47	51	54	56	58	60	62
Hip	47	49	51	53	56	58	60	62	64
Body length	36	36	36	36	36	36	36	36	36
Neck	15½	16	16½	17	17½	18	18½	19	20
Upper arm	17½	18	18½	19	19½	20	20½	21	21½
Sleeve length	34–38[a]	34–38[a]	34–38[a]	34–38[a]	34–38[a]	34–38[a]	34–38[a]	34–38[a]	34–38[a]
Cuff opening	9	9¼	9½	9	10	10¼	10½	10	11

a WHT and LBL sleeves to 40.
  Two-button adjustable cuffs, one chest pocket, regular collar
  Six buttons on BIGS; seven buttons on TALLS

Exhibit 4B
Style: 2100 Levi's Dockers

Fabric content: 100% washed cotton twill

Care instructions: Machine wash, machine dry

Label: Levi's Dockers

			BIG			
	44	46	48	50	52	54
Waist	44 $\frac{1}{4}$	46 $\frac{1}{4}$	48 $\frac{1}{4}$	50 $\frac{1}{4}$	52 $\frac{1}{4}$	54 $\frac{1}{4}$
Front rise	14 $\frac{5}{8}$	14 $\frac{7}{8}$	15 $\frac{1}{8}$	15 $\frac{3}{8}$	15 $\frac{5}{8}$	15 $\frac{7}{8}$
Back rise	19 $\frac{7}{8}$	20 $\frac{1}{8}$	20 $\frac{3}{8}$	20 $\frac{5}{8}$	20 $\frac{7}{8}$	21 $\frac{1}{8}$
Seat/hip	54 $\frac{1}{4}$	56 $\frac{1}{4}$	58 $\frac{1}{4}$	60 $\frac{1}{4}$	62 $\frac{1}{4}$	64 $\frac{1}{4}$
Thigh	33	34	35	36	37	38
Knee	23 $\frac{1}{4}$	23 $\frac{1}{2}$	23	24	24 $\frac{1}{4}$	24 $\frac{1}{2}$
Calf	20	21	21 $\frac{1}{4}$	21 $\frac{1}{2}$	21	22
Inseam—finished	34	34	34	32	32	32
Ankle opening	18 $\frac{1}{4}$	18 $\frac{1}{2}$	18	19	19 $\frac{1}{4}$	19 $\frac{1}{2}$

		TALL		
	36	38	40	42
Waist	36 $\frac{1}{4}$	38 $\frac{1}{4}$	40 $\frac{1}{4}$	42 $\frac{1}{4}$
Front rise	13 $\frac{1}{4}$	13 $\frac{1}{2}$	13	14
Back rise	17 $\frac{1}{4}$	17 $\frac{1}{2}$	17	18
Seat/hip	47 $\frac{1}{2}$	49 $\frac{1}{2}$	51 $\frac{1}{2}$	53 $\frac{1}{2}$
Thigh	29 $\frac{1}{2}$	30 $\frac{1}{2}$	31 $\frac{1}{2}$	32 $\frac{1}{2}$
Knee	23	24 $\frac{1}{4}$	24	25 $\frac{1}{4}$
Calf	20	21	21 $\frac{1}{4}$	21 $\frac{1}{2}$
Inseam—finished	38	38	36	36
Ankle opening	16 $\frac{1}{2}$	17	17 $\frac{1}{2}$	18

Exhibit 5
King-Size Daily Tally (For week ending Friday, December 10, 1993)

		Saturday, Dec. 4	Sunday, Dec. 5	Monday, Dec. 6	Tuesday, Dec. 7	Wednesday, Dec. 8	Thursday, Dec. 9	Friday, Dec. 10	W-T-D	% CHG
M	Received	352	0	497	240	158	300	326	1,873	
A	Keyed	352	0	497	240	158	300	326	1,873	
I	Carryover	0	0	0	0	0	0	0	0	
L	Unreleased batches	0	0	0	0	0	0	0	0	
C	Projected department	1,274	743	2,711	2,322	2,269	2,166	1,987	13,472	
A	Actual department	1,340	1,096	2,638	2,273	2,003	1,970	2,004	13,324	128%
L	% of projection	105%	148%	97%	98%	88%	91%	101%	99%	
L	Actual 1992	1,198	870	2,206	1,795	1,606	1,427	1,339	10,441	
S	Total abandoned	35	63	171	135	96	57	102	659	
	Abandon rate	3%	6%	6%	6%	5%	3%	5%	5%	
	Worst hour	6%	16%	18%	15%	11%	14%	21%		
O	Phone orders	804	658	1,361	1,197	1,101	1,067	935	7,123	112%
R	Average phone order	$ 113.36	$ 115.22	$ 119.54	$ 121.64	$ 117.98	$ 123.87	$ 118.01	$ 119.00	
D	Order/call %	60%	60%	52%	53%	55%	54%	47%	53%	
E	Orders 1992	802	579	1,352	1,062	938	867	769	6,369	
R	Mail orders	352	0	497	240	158	300	326	1,873	
S	Average mail order	$ 107.93	$ 0	$ 92.37	$ 124.46	$ 117.77	$ 101.34	$ 96.17	$ 103.65	
	Total orders	1,156	658	1,858	1,437	1,259	1,367	1,261	8,996	
	$ on hold		$ 17,863		$ 13,157	$ 13,527	$ 12,051	$ 12,372	$ 11,495	
$	Phone revenue	$ 91,138	$ 75,814	$ 162,696	$ 145,602	$ 129,893	$ 132,173	$ 110,341	$ 847,657	
$	Mail revenue	37,992	0	45,907	29,870	18,607	30,403	31,352	194,131	
$	Total Revenue	$ 129,130	$ 75,814	$ 208,603	$ 175,472	$ 148,500	$ 162,576	$ 141,693	$ 1,041,788	

Exhibit 6
Catalog Development Time Line

	Merchandising	Catalog Development
1)	Line Review (Feb. or Sept.)	Broad choices for catalog layout • number of pages • order of merchandise • front & back cover items • which models to use • colors highlighted for specific items Creative team receives Product Sheets—must understand features and specifications of merchandise
2)	Purchase Orders Written (During the next month)	Hand drawn catalog layout created Received samples to photograph from product managers Merchandising changes/input to layout
3)	Purchase Orders Monitored/ Product Delivery Dates Updated (Next two–three months)	Photography for catalog taken. Two months allocated for Fall catalog (done locally). Two weeks allocated for Spring catalog (done on location in Florida).
4)	Merchandise Arriving	Final catalog boards with copy and photographs delivered to printer (mid-August for Fall catalog, mid-January for Spring catalog)

Exhibit 7
King-Size Actual Catalog Costs—Fall 1993

	Vol. 50	Vol. 51	Vol. 52	Vol. 53	Vol. 54
No. of pages	36	112	120	116	72
No. of plates	24	64	72	72	40
No. printed	121,203	598,586	360,598	299,340	173,868
No. mailed		489,270	268,248	220,012	148,768
Paper cost—50#	38.88	38.88	38.88	35.79	38.88
Paper cost—40#	39.14	42.75	42.75	40.69	40.69
Weight of book		0.4846	0.5145	0.4969	0.3220

MANUFACTURING

Fixed Costs:
Plates/make-readies
Repack blankets
Paper make-ready
Miscellaneous preparation, etc.
Other binding
Mailing
Freight/packing
Order form plates

	Vol. 50	Vol. 51	Vol. 52	Vol. 53	Vol. 54
Total Fixed Costs	7,049	37,592	26,475	24,230	11,406

Variable Costs/1,000
Press run
Ink
Ink jetting
Binding

	Vol. 50	Vol. 51	Vol. 52	Vol. 53	Vol. 54
Subtotal	45.11	124.04	135.06	129.73	90.40
Order forms		17.55	18.64	19.65	25.34
Paper	71.13	237.56	254.39	232.73	147.08
Total Variable (excl. postage)	116.24	379.15	408.09	382.11	262.82
Total postage	24,100	148,219	88,092	69,293	33,150
Total Costs	21,137	442,357	261,725	207,905	90,252
Discounts	980	7,900	5,208	4,455	2,031
Net cost	44,257	434,457	256,516	203,450	88,221
Net cost/catalog	0.40	0.73	0.71	0.68	0.51

Exhibit 8

Selected 1993 Results of King-Size Telephone Survey—Demographics (based on sample of 169 customers)

Age Distribution	%
20s or younger	4
30s	13
40s	26
50s	27
60s or older	27
Refused	4

Body Type—Self Classification		Spouse
Big	25	11
Tall	12	10
Both big and tall	57	5
Neither	—	43
Hard-to-fit feature	8	—
Average size range	1	—
Don't know/Not sure	2	32

Marital Status	%
Single	24
Married	66
Other	10

Income	
Under $20,000	8
$20,000–$29,000	8
$30,000–$39,000	13
$40,000–$49,000	11
$50,000–$59,000	11
$60,000 or more	24
Refused	24

Exhibit 9
Selected 1993 Results of King-Size Telephone Survey—Competition (based on sample of 169 customers)

Other Sources of Clothing and Shoes	%	Other Sources for Clothing Only	%
(Unaided response)		(Unaided response)	
Casual Male/Big & Tall	24		
Sears/Sears Big & Tall Catalog	18	Big & Tall Casual Male	24
JCPenney/Penney Big & Tall Cat.	17	Sears	18
Various local big & tall shops	13	JCPenney/Penney Big & Tall Cat.	17
L.L Bean	5	Other or No Response	41
Land's End	4		
Phoenix	4	**Other Sources for Shoes**	**%**
Kmart	3	(Unaided response)	
WearGuard	2	Local stores/retailers (general)	31
Haband	2	Florsheim's	6
Macy's	2	Mason shoe catalog/Mason's	5
Eagleson's	1	JCPenney	3
Cabella's	1	Sears	2
Eddie Bauer	1	Various local big & tall shops	2
		Hitchcock	2
		Other or No Response	49

Other Catalogs that Carried Big & Tall Clothing (1991–1993)

(Unaided response)

	Base	1991 (150) %	1992 (159) %	1993 (169) %
Sears		27	38	35
JCPenney's		23	28	24
Big & Tall		—	—	8
Phoenix		—	—	.5
WearGuard		5	6	4
L.L. Bean		6	3	4
Montgomery Wards		—	—	3
Eddie Bauer		3	6	2
Land's End		3	4	1
Folley's		—	4	—
Cabella's		—	3	—
Haband		3	3	—

Exhibit 10
Cost and Lead Breakdown, September 13, 1993—October 31, 1993

Network	Week of 9/13	Week of 9/20	Week of 9/27	Week of 10/4	Week of 10/11	Drags[c] Week of 10/18 & 10/25	Total
ESPN	$17,500	$14,500	$16,000	$17,500	$ 4,950		$70,450
Total leads	5,579	4,278	5,043	5,654	2,710	467	23,731
Men	4,852	3,670	4,265	4,724	2,319		19,830 (85% men)
Women	727	608	778	930	391		3,434
CPL[a] (total schedule)							$ 2.97
CNN I	$ 3,575	$ 3,850	—	$ 3,850	$ 3,850		$15,125
Total leads	2,656	3,134	357	2,674	3,007	385	12,213
Men	2,104	2,330	251	1,989	2,271		8,945 (76% men)
Women	552	804	106	685	736		2,883
Total CPL							$ 1.24
CNN II[b]	$ 3,575	$ 3,850	—	$ 3,850	$ 3,850		$15,125
Total leads	3,000	3,546	268	3,024	3,440	479	13,757
Men	2,326	2,645	251	2,242	2,631		10,095 (76% men)
Women	674	901	17	782	809		3,183
Total CPL							$ 1.10
TBS	—	$12,900	$12,900	—	—		$25,800
Total leads	—	3,457	3,606	134	57	50	7,304
Men	—	2,188	2,182	78	31		4,479 (62% men)
Women	—	1,269	1,424	56	26		2,775
Total CPL							$ 3.53
A&E	—	—	—	—	$15,300		$15,300
Total leads	—	—	—	—	7,047	875	7,922
Men	—	—	—	—	5,011		5,011 (71% men)
Women	—	—	—	—	2,036		2,036
Total CPL							$ 1.93
Family	—	—	$ 1,600	$ 800			$ 2,400
Total leads	—	—	963	380	153	46	1,542
Men	—	—	828	283	111		1,222 (82% men)
Women	—	—	135	97	42		274
Total CPL							$ 1.56

Total campaign media expenditure—$144,200
Total # of leads—66,469
Total CPL—$2.17

a Cost per lead
b $10 offer
c This total does not affect percentages of men and women

Exhibit 11
King-Size Sample Fall 1993 Media Results

	Media Cost	# of Requests	$ per Request	Initial Orders	% Conv.	% Multi- buyers	Total Demand $	Total $/ Media Cost	Demand $ per Customer
ESPN	70,450	24,082	2.93	1,471	6.11%	16.5%	235,652	3.3	$160
CNN	15,125	12,192	1.24	627	5.14	17.5	98,958	6.5	158
CNN—$10 off	15,125	13,651	1.11	756	5.54	11.9	100,276	6.6	133
TBS	25,800	7,317	3.53	310	4.24	13.2	41,239	1.6	133
Family	2,400	1,586	1.51	107	6.75	17.8	16,006	6.7	150
A&E	15,300	7,956	1.92	310	3.90	12.6	37,116	2.4	120
Total TV	144,200	66,784	2.16	3,581	5.36%	15.1%	529,247	3.7	$148
Wall Street Journal	1,122	488	2.30	25	5.12%	24.0%	3,626	3.2	$145
Am Gardener card deck	3,000	1,326	2.26	85	6.41	23.5	13,113	4.4	154
Hamm Schlem (pkg ins.)	3,000	348	8.62	26	7.47	11.5	5,483	1.8	211
Val Pak—phone	7,000	1,838	3.81	93	5.06	19.4	14,551	2.1	156
Val Pak—no phone	35,000	8,270	4.23	424	5.13	15.6	59,154	1.7	140
Sub Newspaper Net	25,000	2,140	11.68	108	5.05	13.9	15,247	0.6	141
Public relations (9/93)		1,652		160	9.69	15.6	25,367		159

Exhibit 12
TV and Print Responders Versus Base of US: 1993 Households

Group	PRIZM #	CLUSTERS Nickname	BASE Count	BASE % Comp	TV RESPONDERS Count	TV RESPONDERS % Comp	TV RESPONDERS % Pen	TV RESPONDERS Index	PRINT RESPONDERS Count	PRINT RESPONDERS % Comp	PRINT RESPONDERS % Pen	PRINT RESPONDERS Index
S1	28	Blue Blood Estates	783,501	0.82	247	0.62	0.03	76	804	2.24	0.10	274
S1	8	Money & Brains	821,074	0.86	184	0.46	0.02	54	680	1.89	0.08	221
S1	5	Furs & Station Wagons	3,741,347	3.90	1,440	3.64	0.04	93	4,340	12.09	0.12	310
S2	7	Pools & Patio	3,129,876	3.26	1,072	2.71	0.03	83	1,894	5.28	0.06	162
S2	25	Two More Rungs	579,954	0.60	146	0.37	0.03	61	324	0.90	0.06	149
S2	20	Young Influentials	2,914,400	3.04	813	2.05	0.03	68	1,601	4.46	0.05	147
S3	24	Young Suburbia	6,109,272	6.37	2,598	6.56	0.04	103	4,090	11.39	0.07	179
S3	30	Blue-Chip Blues	5,827,931	6.08	2,227	5.62	0.04	93	2,398	6.68	0.04	110
U1	21	Urban Gold Coast	389,343	0.41	77	0.19	0.02	48	128	0.36	0.03	88
U1	37	Bohemian Mix	1,009,577	1.05	173	0.44	0.02	41	328	0.91	0.03	87
U1	31	Black Enterprise	655,412	0.68	264	0.67	0.04	98	309	0.86	0.05	126
U1	23	New Beginnings	4,381,621	4.57	1,099	2.77	0.03	61	1,322	3.68	0.03	81
T1	1	God's Country	3,701,075	3.86	2,089	5.27	0.06	137	1,800	5.01	0.05	130
T1	17	New Homesteaders	4,722,660	4.93	2,458	6.21	0.05	126	1,260	3.51	0.03	71
T1	12	Towns & Gowns	1,111,033	1.16	734	1.85	0.07	160	307	0.86	0.03	74
S4	27	Levittown, U.S.A.	2,591,320	2.70	1,053	2.66	0.04	98	927	2.58	0.04	96
S4	39	Gray Power	2,726,435	2.84	873	2.20	0.03	78	749	2.09	0.03	73
S4	2	Rank & File	1,238,110	1.29	401	1.01	0.03	78	351	0.98	0.03	76
T2	40	Blue-Collar Nursery	2,264,070	2.36	1,099	2.77	0.05	118	781	2.18	0.03	92
T2	16	Middle America	3,107,571	3.24	1,411	3.56	0.05	110	797	2.22	0.03	68
T2	29	Coalburg & Corntown	1,985,496	2.07	1,153	2.91	0.06	141	662	1.84	0.03	89
U2	3	New Melting Pot	767,547	0.80	112	0.28	0.01	35	153	0.43	0.02	53
U2	36	Old Yankee Rows	1,319,268	1.38	405	1.02	0.03	74	378	1.05	0.03	77
U2	14	Emergent Minorities	1,592,124	1.66	533	1.35	0.03	81	404	1.13	0.03	68
U2	26	Single City Blues	3,135,853	3.27	684	1.73	0.02	53	594	1.65	0.02	51
R1	19	Shotguns & Pickups	1,844,533	1.92	838	2.12	0.05	110	608	1.69	0.03	88
R1	34	Agri-Business	1,993,766	2.08	930	2.35	0.05	113	643	1.79	0.03	86
R1	35	Grain Belt	793,965	0.82	236	0.60	0.03	73	244	0.68	0.03	83
T3	33	Golden Ponds	533,036	5.56	3,204	8.09	0.06	145	1,550	4.32	0.03	78
T3	22	Mines & Mills	2,924,924	3.05	1,545	3.90	0.05	128	724	2.02	0.02	66
T3	13	Norma Rae-Ville	2,375,354	2.48	1,397	3.53	0.06	142	548	1.53	0.02	62
T3	18	Smalltown Downtown	2,166,127	2.26	739	1.87	0.03	83	449	1.25	0.02	55
R2	10	Back-Country Folks	3,436,297	3.58	1,909	4.82	0.06	134	867	2.41	0.03	67
R2	38	Share Croppers	3,676,212	3.83	2,027	5.12	0.06	133	915	2.55	0.02	66
R2	15	Tobacco Roads	884,207	0.92	545	1.38	0.06	149	185	0.52	0.02	56
R2	6	Hard Scrabble	1,275,371	1.33	618	1.56	0.05	117	317	0.88	0.02	66
U3	4	Heavy Industry	2,197,254	2.29	674	1.70	0.03	74	427	1.19	0.02	52
U3	11	Downtown Dixie-Style	2,840,266	2.96	950	2.40	0.03	81	533	1.48	0.02	50
U3	9	Hispanic Mix	1,588,477	1.66	239	0.60	0.02	36	191	0.53	0.01	32
U3	32	Public Assistance	1,957,460	2.04	411	1.04	0.02	51	320	0.89	0.02	44
Total			95,883,119	100.00	39,607	100.00	0.04	100	35,902	100.00	0.04	100

Case 28

TOUPARGEL

INTRODUCTION

Roland Tchénio parked his Mercedes and walked into Toupargel's brand new distribution center, a few miles down the road from Toupargel's headquarters in Lyon, France. He sat at his desk and once again read the acquisition proposal he was about to send to Mr. Robart, the owner of Organization Plus, a small frozen food retail business in Marseilles, France. Acquiring Organization Plus would open new possibilities for the growth of Toupargel's frozen food business in southern France. Organization Plus was located in a region in which Toupargel did not yet compete. It conducted all its business through home delivery, a retailing method on which Toupargel had built its 700% growth over the last 10 years. This seemed too good an opportunity to pass up.

Yet Tchénio and Toupargel's bankers were wary about buying out another competitor, the thirty-first since he had acquired Toupargel 10 years earlier. 1992 had been a difficult year. Results had been hurt by the completion of the new distribution center in Lyon and by the difficult turnaround of the recently acquired Brittany branches. These difficulties were compounded by the recession France was experiencing. Cash was scarce and Tchénio had initially planned to spend 1993 consolidating the existing business. He had not intended buying out any competitor, focusing instead on strengthening Toupargel's existing branches with the help of his newly hired marketing vice president.

THE FRENCH FROZEN FOOD MARKET

Toupargel was a small player in the huge French frozen foods market. Total retail sales of frozen foods in France represented 25 billion francs (Fr)[1] in 1991, for a volume of 1.43 million tons. The market was one of the main growth areas of the French food market, with an increase in volume sales of 6.5% in 1991 over 1990 (versus 0.4% for the total food market). Yet this growth had been slowing down and no longer reached the exceptional double digit increases of the 1980s, when the market multiplied by 2.36 in volume in 10 years (1981–91). On a per capita basis, consumption was equivalent to 24.4 kilograms of food plus 5.5 liters[2] of ice cream, putting France at, respectively, fourth and ninth rank in Europe, far behind the biggest consumers, the Danish. (See **Exhibit 1** for European figures.)

Frozen foods available in France included a wide range of products. The main categories, besides ice creams, were prepared foods (31% of sales in volume), potato-based products (25%), vegetables (21%), and seafood (10%). (See detailed figures in **Exhibit 2**.) Reflecting changes in

This case was prepared by David Vennin, MBA '93, under the supervision of Professor David E. Bell as the basis for class discussion rather than to illustrate either effective or ineffective handling of an administrative situation.

1 1 franc (Fr) = .18 US dollars
2 1 kilogram = 2.2 pounds; 1 liter = 1.06 quarts

consumption patterns, prepared foods were growing at a much faster pace than the average, with volumes increasing by 155% over the last five years.

Food retailing channels in France were quite different from most other countries. The industry was dominated by a small number of giant chains of hypermarkets. Hypermarkets were mega stores with a selling area that was often around 10,000 square meters.[3] They sold a wide assortment of most products. Sales for a single hypermarket exceeded 500 million Fr. Hypermarket chains used their considerable buying power to negotiate important buyer discounts with suppliers, allowing them to sell at what was recognized to be the lowest prices. Depending on the product category (hardware, soft goods, food, leisure), they usually represented somewhere between 20%–60% of total sales of each product category in France. In 1991 their market share was 52% for total food sales and 28% for frozen foods. They were playing a more and more important role in the frozen foods market, trying to expand their offering in this growth area. It was estimated that hypermarkets had increased the number of frozen food product references (stock keeping units or SKUs) they sold by 14.5% between 1987 and 1991, reaching a total assortment of 396 SKUs on average.

Other players in the frozen foods retailing market included supermarkets (30% of sales with 246 SKUs on average), convenience stores (5%), and two channels that were specific to frozen foods: freezer centers (18%) and home delivery (19%). Freezer centers were specialized chains of stores which sold only frozen foods. Located in urban areas, their main attraction was their wide assortment, with usually 800 to 850 SKUs available in the store. This segment of the market was dominated by three main players which had a total of 1,000 stores, representing a market share of 80% within this segment.

Toupargel was competing in the last segment of the market, home delivery. Home delivery in the French frozen foods market arose because after World War II, most French people did not have a refrigerator at home. They needed to make daily trips to the store to buy foods that had to be kept cold, (e.g., milk, butter, and cheese). Another solution was to buy from independent truck drivers who would drive around towns with their refrigerated trucks full of a wide assortment of products. These drivers would park their trucks at a street corner, honk and wait for housewives to stop by and shop. As their

customers slowly equipped themselves with refrigerators in the '50s and '60s, some of these drivers added frozen foods to their assortment. At the time, frozen foods were not commonly found in retail stores. The drivers developed regular customers that they would serve on a periodic basis through a system of established routes. By 1991, home delivery still represented 19% of sales of frozen foods, mainly from routes in remote areas.

Exhibit 3 shows the evolution of the market share of different retailing channels in the frozen foods market.

Frozen foods were sold to most French households. By 1993, only a minority of households (8%) did not eat frozen foods. Forty percent of households had a stand-alone freezer, while another 40% had a combined refrigerator/freezer. Combined refrigerator/freezer units usually had less space available for frozen food storage. Sometimes the freezer compartment could not keep food frozen for more than a few days. Consumption of frozen foods was not only correlated to freezer equipment but also to ownership of a microwave oven. Twenty-five percent of French households had a microwave oven and their numbers were growing fast. Usually, households with four people or more were the biggest frozen food consumers, with purchases 65% higher than the average.

TOUPARGEL'S HISTORY

When he took over Toupargel in 1982 for 4 million Fr (50% of which was in the form of assumed debt), Roland Tchénio bought an established local frozen food retailer. The firm was created in 1947 as a wholesaler of food products that needed to be kept refrigerated. Its customer base mainly included food services to which food was delivered in bulk. In 1968–69, Toupargel's owner decided to change the firm's main target market to households. It started a delivery service of cold and frozen foods to families in the Lyon area. Business in this market was brisk and it quickly represented the majority of sales.

In 1982, Toupargel was for sale. Its owner was not sure how to expand his business and was afraid that the economy would slump because of the change of government in 1981 which gave the power to the French Socialist Party. At the time, sales to households represented 80% of total sales of 50 million Fr. The market was

---

3 1 square meter = 10.8 square feet

serviced by 30 delivery trucks and six freezer centers, which sold frozen food exclusively. Each truck had 20 established routes that were serviced on a monthly basis to deliver to the existing customer base. Sales were made from the trucks on a cash & carry basis. The remaining sales were made on a wholesale basis to some of the major hypermarkets in the region, which at the time did not have a centralized buying organization. The firm had 60 employees and possessed a state of the art computer system with extensive databases. The databases were used to mail customers information a few days before the truck would come to service their area.

Roland Tchénio was a complete newcomer to retailing and frozen foods. After receiving his MBA from Harvard Business School, he had for the next 10 years been pursuing a successful career for a major French conglomerate. He had had a variety of responsibilities, including his latest position as general manager of a major toy manufacturer. He was now looking for an acquisition opportunity to start on his own. His targeting criteria included firms in the consumer goods retailing business, in a growing market segment, with potential for marketing leverage. He wanted a business with very low working capital needs so that it could be developed without financial pressure.

Toupargel matched most of his criteria. All customers paid cash. Accounts receivable were almost nil. The frozen food market was growing quickly. French households were buying huge freezers to store an increasing variety of frozen food products. The home delivery segment of the market was very fragmented. Most of the frozen food delivery businesses in France (about 250 at the time) were local distributors with little management expertise and very limited financial means.

Over the next ten years, Tchénio implemented an aggressive external growth strategy. He bought out over 30 competitors. (See **Exhibit 4** for a list of the main acquisitions.) In the first few years, most companies taken over were small but healthy local businesses. Beginning in 1987, Toupargel started to buy out small distributors operating under the French bankruptcy laws or about to go bankrupt. They varied in size, with sales anywhere between 3 million Fr and 60 million Fr. Sometimes the only activity of the distributor would be home delivery, while in other cases the distributor would also own freezer centers. All the acquired distributors met three conditions: they were geographically complementary to the existing Toupargel network; home delivery of frozen food was their main business, and they maintained a good-quality customer base. Toupargel would take them over for a very low price. The new branches were restructured. Logistics were improved and integrated into the Toupargel system of centralized warehouses with daily deliveries to local branches. Marketing was revamped. The existing product range was replaced by Toupargel's to lever its buying power. A unified Toupargel catalog was used.

By January 1993, Toupargel had become a significant player in the home delivery market of the frozen food retailing industry. Its sales in 1992 totaled 350 million Fr, representing a 7% market share of sales of frozen food through home delivery. Toupargel employed 620 people. Its assets included two major cold storage distribution centers (in Lyon for the eastern region and in Poitiers for the other regions), 230 refrigerated trucks, and 27 sales office/branches. These branches allowed Toupargel to serve a significant part of the French market. (See **Exhibit 5** for a map of France with all the branches.)

CUSTOMER BASE

Toupargel's active customer base included over 300,000 households. Most had become customers due to the takeover of their prior supplier by Toupargel. Although their profile was very varied, a few common characteristics could be identified. They generally lived in relatively rural areas or in midsize towns. They tended to eat more frozen food than the French average—usually more than 30 kilograms of food and 10 liters of ice cream per year. Being heavy frozen food consumers, they usually owned a large freezer and a microwave oven. Most of them lived in individual houses (people living in flats would not have room for a large freezer).

Reasons for using Toupargel's home delivery service changed depending on the customer's lifestyle, geographical locations, and personal priorities. Four main advantages of the Toupargel service were usually quoted:

Delivery: The food was delivered at home. There was no need for a car to drive to the store. The selection could be made at home at the consumer's convenience. This was particularly important considering the fact that French business hours for food stores were usually limited to 8 a.m. to 8 p.m., Monday through Saturday.

Respect of Cold Storage Standards: Toupargel's only business was frozen food. The food was professionally handled and always stored in controlled-temperature cold rooms. It was delivered by refrigerator truck and went straight to the consumer's freezer. It did not thaw in a car or shopping cart. This argument was thought to be of particular importance to heavy consumers of frozen food, who stored their purchases for extended periods of time.

Choice: Toupargel carried over 700 different frozen food products. Only specialized freezer-center stores offered as wide a choice. Those stores were not always convenient to the consumer, particularly in rural areas.

Service: All products were tested by the quality control department for taste and health checks. Sales agents were trained to help the consumer in cooking and choosing products.

Different customers had varied ordering patterns. Though the average order was nearly 300 Fr, the size of each order changed a lot with the customer and the season. Perhaps because there was a minimum order size of 150 Fr, not every customer ordered every time his or her route was serviced (i.e., 12.5 times a year). Customers who had ordered at least once during the last four months were called "active customers." Active customers were responsible for 95% of Toupargel's sales.

PRODUCT RANGE

Toupargel offered its customers one of the broadest selections of frozen foods available in France. Its product line included over 700 different products. It spanned all the main food product categories, including appetizers (salads, soups, patés), complete prepared dishes (lasagnas, pizzas, cooked fish or meat with a sauce), seafood, meats (including pet food), vegetables, seasoning herbs, fruits, pastries, ice creams, snacks, and regional specialties. Hypermarkets and supermarkets offered a similar range of raw foods and individual servings of prepared foods. The main difference came from Toupargel's wider assortment of high-quality, traditionally prepared, ready-to-eat foods. Products were either branded with well-known national brands, not branded, or branded with the "Toupargel Surgelés" name.

Before being offered to customers, products were quality controlled. They also underwent blind taste tests with the help of consumer panels and specialists. Each month the product range was revised. The catalogs (one for home sales, one for telesales) were edited on a monthly basis. They included many pictures of the food presented ready to be served (see **Exhibit 6** for a sample page of the catalog) as well as some cooking advice.

Buying was generally channeled through a cooperative buying organization. This organization grouped together many frozen food retailers and pooled their purchases to increase their bargaining power with suppliers to get better prices. Such organizations were very common in the French retailing industry. They generally achieved significant price breaks, depending on their buying power. This was one of the main reasons for the increasing concentration of retailing in France. The buying organization Toupargel used was one of the three biggest in the country. It grouped many frozen food retailers and local wholesalers. Its purchases represented around 10% of the French frozen food market. Toupargel was its second-biggest member. As was customary in the French retailing industry, suppliers were generally paid on a 60 days end-of-month basis (i.e., for delivery on April 12, payment was made at the end of June).

SELLING METHODS

For historical reasons, Toupargel was organized around two different selling methods: telesales and home sales. Both methods had one thing in common: deliveries were organized around a delivery route system. Each customer was on a truck route which was serviced once every four weeks. Each truck serviced the same 20 routes every four weeks. Deliveries were not made on demand. A customer could expect delivery only on the day the truck was scheduled to service his or her route. Toupargel and the customer agreed on a rough time for delivery (for example, before 10 a.m. or between 2 and 4 p.m.). The absence of the customer when the delivery truck arrived was not frequent but was a real problem when it occurred. Sometimes, in the countryside, when a driver had built a good relationship with his or her customers, some customers might leave a check written for the amount of the delivery in an agreed-upon hiding place while the driver would leave the box on the doorstep. In other cases, neighbors might agree to receive and pay for the food. Depending on the route and the driver, deliveries could be scheduled either during a 7:30 a.m.– 2 p.m. shift or during a 12 noon–8 p.m. shift.

The difference between both selling and delivery methods lay in the way the order was taken. In branches organized for home sales, the sales were made by the truck driver. The driver stopped by each customer at a regular time and day every four weeks. The truck carried approximately 350 different SKUs. The sale was made, paid and delivered on the spot, without the intervention of anybody else. With this organization, one truck driver could sell about 1.5 million Fr of frozen food a year. There were two main advantages to this method. First, the consumer saw the product. It was in his or her hands immediately, in a similar fashion to store shopping. Second, the logistics involved were much more limited and thus cost was lower. Indeed, orders were not individually prepared and shipped. The number of SKUs was smaller, and, since decentralized stocks were maintained in the trucks, the delivery system did not need to be as sophisticated. But there were several problems with this method. The major issue was the heavy reliance of the system on the truck driver. The sales volume depended on his or her selling skills and personal relationships with customers. The truck driver managed his or her own business and became Toupargel's customer, creating an additional intermediary between the firm and its customers. Since the process was far less structured, it was difficult to control what was sold to whom and at what prices. It reduced Toupargel's knowledge of its customer base. The driver might overcharge customers. He or she could also quit and start his or her own competing business, servicing the existing customer base along the delivery route, sourcing the products from a wholesaler. The maintenance of decentralized stocks in the trucks was another issue. It was harder to control and required higher inventories. Finally, the range of product offered to customers was smaller for obvious reasons of space and stock management in the trucks.

The process for telesales was quite different. A telesales agent phoned a customer four days before a truck would service his or her area. The telesales agent took the order based on the catalog which had been left with the customer four weeks prior. Some customers also mailed in an order stub or input their order in the French videotext system (Minitel). The catalog included over 700 SKUs. The order was entered on a PC by the agent. The customer was told the price of his or her total order and a delivery time was agreed on. The following night the order was downloaded to one of two central warehouse computers. At the warehouse the next day, the order was printed out and the items individually prepared and packaged. An invoice was edited. The second day, all the orders for this route were shipped from the central warehouse to the branch. The third day, orders were individually delivered along the established route. As the order was delivered, the invoice was given to the customer and payment was made. Payments were in cash, checks, or credit cards. No credit was given. With this process, all stocks were centralized in the warehouses. Cash transactions could easily be controlled by matching them to invoices. Although taking orders for one scheduled route on a determined day represented the equivalent of one full day of work for one telesales agent, most of the time the actual order taking spanned over two days (i.e., telesales agents always worked on taking orders for routes on two consecutive dates). This allowed callbacks to be made to customers who were not at home on the first day of order taking. One telesales agent generated on average 3 million Fr of sales a year.

Finally, although Tchénio had decided to exit the store retailing business, Toupargel was still operating a few stores in the freezer center format. Six stores were kept in major urban areas, with a view to potentially being used as flagships for a delivery system in major metropolitan centers. In 1991, one store had been closed down and seven others were sold to a freezer center operator.

Table A
Distribution of Sales Across Distribution Channels

	1989	1990	1991	1992
Home sales	105	130	118	91
Telesales	114	127	162	244
Stores	31	32	26	16
Total	250	289	306	351

Note: Figures in million Fr.

ORGANIZATION

Toupargel's headquarters were located in Dardilly, one of Lyon's suburbs. The main staff functions were located here. There were three staff vice presidents in charge of three functional areas (marketing, purchasing, administration). Besides Roland Tchénio, 26 people worked in Dardilly (17 in administration and finance, 3 in purchasing, and 6 in marketing). Centralized functions included logistics, the creation of catalogs, purchasing and quality control, the computer system, human resources, finance and marketing programs. A new marketing vice president had been hired a few months earlier to strengthen Toupargel's marketing programs. A person with extensive experience in the mail order business had been specially chosen.

Two area vice presidents (East and West) supervised the 27 branches and the two distribution centers. Each branch was organized as an independent profit center. It was staffed with a manager, a secretary, truck drivers and, in the case of telesales, telesales people. All branches had a small cold storage area. Their sales ranged from 3.5 million to 34 million Fr. Most were located in the suburbs of a mid-size city and covered the surrounding areas within 50 miles. Branches organized under the telesales method could service a bigger area with the same number of trucks since the delivery process with the customer was faster, leaving more driving time available for each truck. From a logistics point of view, it was the company policy to keep branches within a four-hour drive from one of the central warehouses. Indeed, French regulations prohibited truck drivers to drive more than four hours without stopping for a two-hour rest period. Delivering goods on a daily basis to a branch located further than four hours would require the presence of a second driver in the truck. In the absence of another driver, the trip would be lengthened by the two-hour rest period, making it impossible to return to the warehouse the same day. The profitability of a branch was judged by its contribution to headquarters. Contributions were calculated based on the gross margin generated by the branch sales minus the direct costs of the branch. Branch managers were held responsible for their total sales and their direct costs. They were financially interested in their total sales and received a bonus based on achieving their target contribution level.

Branch managers reported to one of the two area vice presidents. Each area vice president was assisted by a controller and a warehouse manager. Additionally, although the truck drivers reported to the branch managers, each area had a person in charge of training and motivating the truck drivers, as they were a key link with the customer. (**Exhibit 7** presents an organization chart.)

One management tool was the "rapport de récence." (See **Exhibit 8** for a sample report.) This report segmented the customer base into classes according to the date of their last purchase. Within each class, customers were further segmented based on the amount of their orders since the beginning of the year. For each class, the report gave the number of customers in the class, the number of orders they placed, the average value of their orders, and the total amount of business represented by this class. This report could be printed out on a monthly and per-branch basis. Other critical reports included analyses of sales and gross margin, depending on the product and geographical areas (region, branches, delivery route).

Toupargel's history of growth through acquisitions had required skillful integration of the new branches into the firm. Toupargel had a quarterly internal newsletter that was given to all employees. It was supplemented by additional letters from Tchénio on an as-needed basis. Tchénio himself was on the road approximately eight days every month to visit the branches. Toupargel held off-site management meetings regularly with all the branch managers. Training to reinforce the Toupargel unity and qualifications of the personnel was another key aspect of this work. In 1991, 138 employees had gone through an average of five days' training each. The total cost had been 1.2 million Fr. In 1987, Toupargel also had its logotype redesigned to reinforce the visual identity of the firm. The logotype and the brand "Toupargel Surgelés" (meaning Toupargel frozen foods) were prominently displayed on all company information and trucks. Finally, a short booklet describing company activities had been written. It was given out to every new employee. Part of this six-page booklet was a mission statement for Toupargel, affirming the goals of the company. (See **Exhibit 9** for a translated extract.)

ECONOMICS OF TOUPARGEL

Pricing was set upon publication of each monthly catalog. The level of prices was based on a range of criteria with no set formula. The main factors were gross margin, historical levels, and competitors' prices. Depending on the product categories, there could be some loss leaders. Tchénio personally approved all pricing decisions. Prices per piece and per weight or volume unit (as required by French laws) were printed next to the

Table B
Sales and Average Order Sizes by Region

Region	Home Sales			Telesales	
	Sales (millions Fr)	Avg. Order (Fr)		Sales (millions Fr)	Avg. Order (Fr)
East	62	267		103	295
West	—	—		81	286
South West	29	285		—	—
Brittany	—	—		60	300
Total	91	273		244	295

product description. Each page of the catalog included several price specials that were highlighted in bright yellow. Although frozen foods retail prices varied across the country, Tchénio estimated that, for similar products, Toupargel's prices were equivalent to those of freezer-center chains and roughly 10% above hypermarkets' prices.

The size of the average order had been constant over the last few years. This stability was the result of several conflicting trends:

- Customers were ordering products in smaller quantities.
- The mix of products sold was slowly shifting toward basic products, at the expense of the more expensive prepared foods.
- Frozen food prices on the French market were tending to go down.
- Toupargel salespeople were working, with moderate success, toward increasing the number of lines per order.

Costs fell in four main categories. (See **Exhibit 10** for financial information.) The most important one, of course, was cost of goods sold. Most purchases were made through a cooperative buying organization. Significant end-of-year rebates were obtained depending on the volume purchased from each manufacturer. Labor charges were also a significant expense. They included both actual pay and all the benefits required under French law. French labor regulations had changed in 1987 so that laying people off no longer required government authorization. Lay-offs were not considered a daily management tool but more a last resort for a firm. The third important category was what was grouped under the general heading "other purchases." It included every service Toupargel purchased from outside suppliers, except for products for resale and labor. It included energy, maintenance, rent, communications budget, telecommunications, and so forth. Finally, depreciation covered investments in cold rooms and other equipment that was not leased. In 1991, Toupargel had a new central warehouse built in Lyon's suburbs for a total cost of 15 million Fr, of which 11 million was for building expenses (financed through leasing) and 4 million was for fixtures (purchased by Toupargel). The new cold warehouse had a volume of 12,000 cubic meters. It was thought that it would bring significant savings, thanks to improved productivity and stock management. Order preparation was automated with state of the art optical reading devices and computers. Tchénio estimated that it cost 15 Fr to prepare an order and ship to the branch—half of which was a variable cost, the other half being fixed due to the equipment. The warehouse had the capacity to handle up to 7,000 orders a day, or roughly 500 million Fr a year in sales.

Toupargel had financed its growth without new capital. Short-term credit lines were arranged with various banks. The sale of most stores had generated significant capital gains. Toupargel also used an accelerated depreciation method that significantly reduced its tax exposure.

A TYPICAL BRANCH: ANNECY

Annecy was a mid-size city located in eastern France, in the Alps mountain range. The surrounding area included many small towns located in the valleys. The closest major French city, Grenoble, was over 100 kilometers away. Toupargel moved into the area in 1983 by buying out an existing distributor, Adigel. Annecy could be reached in two and a half hours by truck from Lyon.

In 1992, the Annecy branch sales represented 34 million Fr. and 100,000 orders had been processed. The economics and were as follows:

Sales	34,000	
Cost of goods	19,720	
Gross margin	14,280	
Total branch direct cost	8,800	(including 3,000 for direct delivery cost)
Contribution to headquarters	5,480	

Sales were seasonal. December was the peak month.

The staffing of the branch was kept level throughout the year. Toupargel Annecy had 12 trucks making deliveries 250 days a year. They drove on average 170 kms per route. There were 25,000 active customers whose average order size was 321 Fr. Labor and occupancy-related costs represented most of the branch direct costs.

GROWING TOUPARGEL

There were three possibilities to increase Toupargel home delivery sales:

- Toupargel could try to increase sales of existing branches.
- New branches could be created in geographical areas not covered by the existing network.
- Existing competing distributors could be bought out.

Growing the Existing Branches. Toupargel could try to increase sales to its customer base. For example, one promotion included giveaways for customers reaching specified buying levels over a three-month period. Gifts were offered depending on the purchase level reached between January and March 1993. See **Table D.**

Toupargel could also aim at selling to new customers. Ten thousand stable new customers represented around 20 million Fr of sales on an annual basis. On top of the traditional word of mouth, Toupargel used telemarketing. There were 20 dedicated telemarketers who contacted people on the phone based on a purchased database. The best criteria on the propensity to become a Toupargel customer were found to be the size of the freezer, the type of living arrangements (apartment versus house), and the number of people in the household. A typical telemarketer could sell to 70 new customers a month, including 50 that would stay as regular customers. A telemarketer cost approximately 12,500 Fr per month if prospecting was done locally and 16,000 Fr if it was long distance (excluding management and overhead costs).

Creating New Branches. New branches could be set up in different parts of France to expand Toupargel's coverage of the French market. The smallest branch required at least an office and a cold storage room, a manager and a secretary plus the necessary telesales and delivery people. A truck and its driver cost around 500,000 Fr a year, depending on the length of the routes. Setting up a new branch was a time-consuming and expensive operation. It took an extensive period of time to build up a satisfactory customer base. Initially customers would be spread over a wide area and required very long delivery routes.

Acquiring a Competitor. Data on competitors in the home delivery market was scarce. Most competitors were exclusively organized for home sales. Tchénio thought

---

Table C
Monthly Sales of the Annecy Branch in 1992

Jan	Feb	Mar	Apr	May	Jun	Jul	Aug	Sep	Oct	Nov	Dec
2,500	2,600	2,900	2,900	2,500	3,100	3,000	2,200	2,500	2,700	2,800	4,200

Note: All numbers in thousands of Fr.

Table D
Characteristics of the Winter 1993 Promotion

Purchasing level	Gift	Gift value	Number awarded
1,000–1,499 Fr	Cordless hand-held vacuum cleaner	9 Fr	15,000
1,500–2,000 Fr	Toupargel watch	40 Fr	2,000
2,000–2,500 Fr	Kitchen accessory	40 Fr	1,500
2,500+	Water-resistant camera	80 Fr	700

that Toupargel was the sales leader for telesales. There were five major competitors, including Toupargel. Each had sales ranging from 300 million to 900 million Fr and numerous branches, although none covered the whole country. Besides those major players, there were an important number of small firms. The small firms were family-owned, small size distributors, usually with one or two branches only. Many were in financial difficulty.

Organization Plus was a division of one of these family-owned frozen food businesses. It was the home delivery division of Force 5. Force 5 had frozen food sales of 60 million Fr, mostly in its food service division. The food service division was heavily in loss. Force 5 could not find a buyer for the food service division and so decided to sell Organization Plus and use the proceeds to turn the food service division around. Organization Plus delivered 18 million Fr of frozen foods in 1992, all from one big branch in Marseilles, with a profit of 520,000 Fr. (See **Exhibit 11** for financial information.)

Tchénio's plan was to convert Organization Plus into a regular Toupargel branch. He estimated that Toupargel could improve the contribution of the branch by more than a million francs. Most of the savings would come from improved logistics and buying, lower overhead and purchasing delivery trucks (instead of leasing). Organization Plus seemed to represent a golden opportunity to expand in new geographical markets. Southern France was particularly attractive as a new market because it was densely populated and was close enough to Lyon to be served by the existing distribution center.

Organization Plus was for sale for 2.5 million francs. The price was reasonable for 7,500 active customers but Tchénio was not sure Toupargel could afford it. Financial results over the last few years had not been up to his expectations. They had been hampered by losses of the newly integrated branches.

CONCLUSION

Roland Tchénio had to decide whether or not he should pursue the Organization Plus opportunity. He had planned to focus his energy in 1993 on consolidating the existing Toupargel. France was in the midst of a severe recession—probably the worst since the oil crisis in 1973–74. But a Toupargel branch in Marseilles was a new step toward a nationwide Toupargel. It would also allow increased utilization of the new Lyon distribution center. Yet Toupargel's results in 1992 were far from its target profit before tax of 5%. Tchénio thought that there might be significant contribution improvement to be made by increasing the sales of existing branches. Would it be possible to integrate a new branch while consolidating the results of the existing branches?

Table E
Toupargel's Net Income after Tax (millions of Fr)

	1990	1991	1992
Branches bought out in 1990	(3.2)		
Branches bought out in 1991		(4.2)	
Branches bought out in 1992			(4.0)
Pre-existing branches	1.7	4.3	3.0
Groupe Toupargel	(1.5)	0.1	(1.0)

Exhibit 1
Frozen Food and Ice Cream Consumption in Europe (1991)

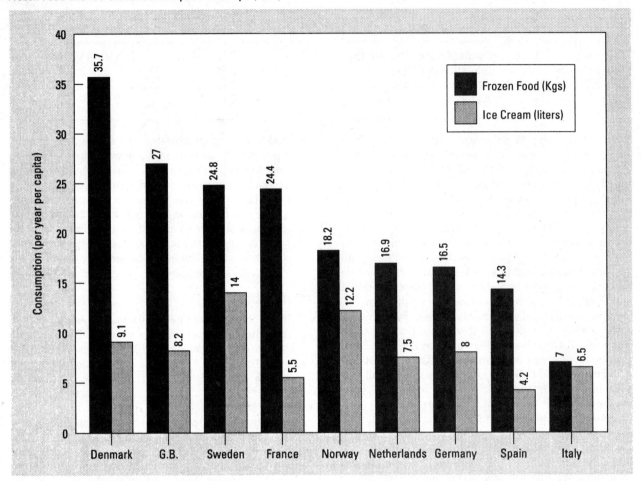

Source: Syndicats Professionnels des Glaces et Surgelés

Exhibit 2
Volume of the French Frozen Food Market by Product Type

	Vegetables	Fruits	Fruit Juices	Meats	Seafood	Crust	Prepared Entrees	Potatoes and Fries	Dessert	Milk	Poultry	Total
1990	294	5	3	145	165	217	138	336	0.2	2	37	1,343
1991	296	6	3	140	146	299	143	360	0.6	3	31	1,430

Notes:
All quantities in thousands of metric tons
Crust: Includes all products with a crust (pizza, pies)
Potatoes: Includes all products made from potatoes
Milk: Includes all products with a milk base (cheese, butter) except for ice cream

Source: La Surgélation, September 1992.

Exhibit 3
Frozen Foods Retailing Channels

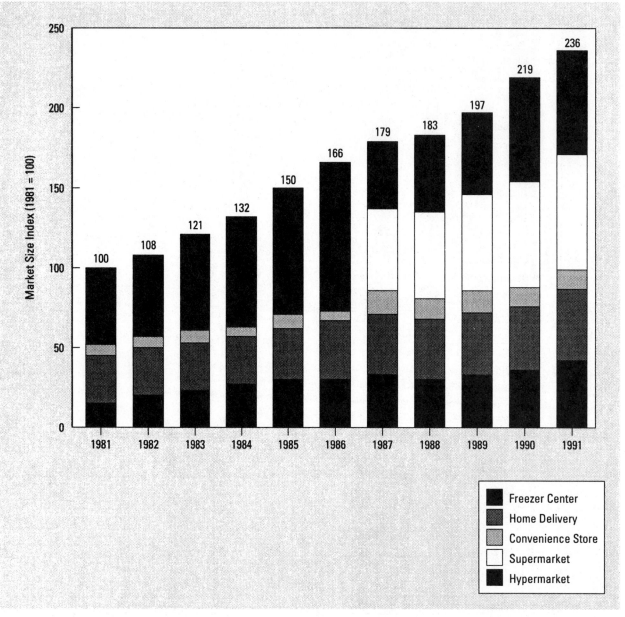

Source: La Surgélation, Sept. 1992

Exhibit 4
List of Toupargel's Main Acquisitions (1982-1992)

Date	Company	Location	Sales (millions of Fr) (at time of acquisition)
1983	Aligel	Annecy	20
1984	Gel Isère	Grenoble	15
1985	Janogel	Annemasse	5
	Alidogel	Poitiers	25
	Fermière de Montlouis	Tours	8
1986	Geldom	Clermont Ferrand	8
	Somagel	Valence	40
1989	Rural Service	Strasbourg/Wasselonne	8
	Villargel	La Rochelle	4
1990	Friscop	Alencon	12
1991	Gel Guyenne	Bordeaux (St. Astier)	33
	Kerdigel	Ploufragan	19
	Surgel Comtois	Besancon	5
1992	Gelarmor	Brest	55
	Segror	Besancon-Sochaux	18
		TOTAL	**275**

Exhibit 5
Map of Toupargel Branches

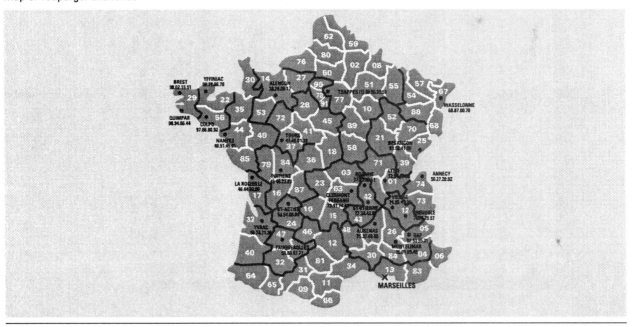

Exhibit 6
Sample Page of Toupargel Catalog

Exhibit 7
Organization Chart

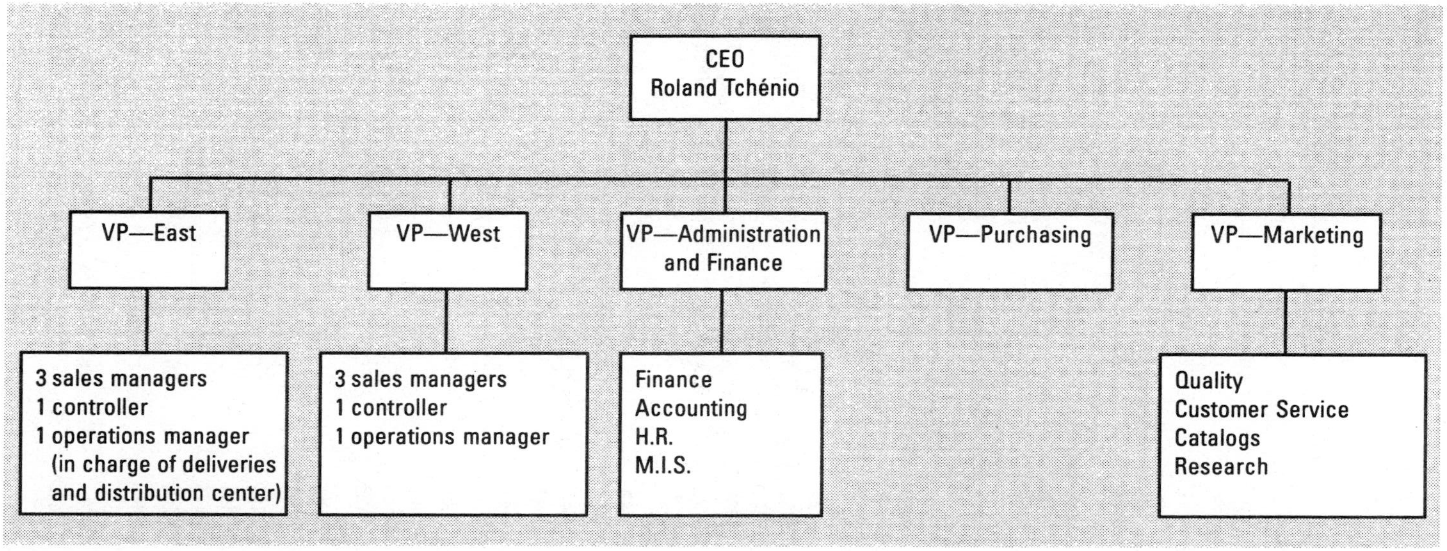

CEO
Roland Tchénio

VP—East

3 sales managers
1 controller
1 operations manager
(in charge of deliveries
and distribution center)

VP—West

3 sales managers
1 controller
1 operations manager

**VP—Administration
and Finance**

Finance
Accounting
H.R.
M.I.S.

VP—Purchasing

VP—Marketing

Quality
Customer Service
Catalogs
Research

Exhibit 8
Example of a "Rapport de Récence" for a Branch

	<1000	1000–1500	1500–3000	3000–4500	4500–6000	>6000	TOTAL
12/91	**2796**	**2538**	**6281**	**2735**	**1066**	**714**	**16130**
AC 91	9084	14372	48512	26073	11149	7983	117173
CA 91	1784254	3169156	13697227	9926999	5498948	5650093	39726678
PM 91	196	221	282	381	493	708	339
AC 90	8598	12750	43799	23863	10139	7369	106518
CA 90	1805602	2941978	12558464	8923090	4834123	4914306	35977563
PM 90	210	231	287	374	477	667	338
AC 89	8318	11928	40706	22124	9395	6816	99287
CA 89	1867284	2842261	11896225	8317697	4409904	4424477	33757846
PM 89	224	238	292	376	469	649	340
11/91	**1368**	**1076**	**1893**	**465**	**145**	**64**	**5011**
AC 91	4322	5377	12046	3459	1213	551	26968
CA 91	806949	1215444	3642630	1492203	674100	454154	8285481
PM 91	187	226	302	431	556	824	307
AC 90	3834	5079	11505	3337	1154	505	25414
CA 90	751642	1192653	3489752	1391417	642021	367012	7834497
PM 90	196	235	303	417	556	727	308
AC 89	3805	4864	10680	3006	1048	455	23858
CA 89	813292	1201788	3316003	1280822	559497	317742	7489144
PM 89	214	247	310	426	534	698	314
10/91	**934**	**464**	**600**	**125**	**28**	**17**	**2168**
AC 91	2524	1977	3183	833	196	124	8837
CA 91	485645	482460	1017448	369458	116857	106356	2578224
PM 91	192	244	320	444	596	858	292
AC 90	2379	2034	3350	829	194	119	8905
CA 90	492652	505222	1060773	359537	98101	97083	2613368
PM 90	207	248	317	434	506	816	293
AC 89	2305	1996	3242	685	172	104	8504
CA 89	519945	522332	1075776	300645	95760	87584	2602042
PM 89	226	262	332	439	557	842	306
09/91	**691**	**269**	**328**	**64**	**16**	**11**	**1379**
AC 91	1684	1047	1591	388	109	81	4900
CA 91	339252	258333	522922	171450	57672	57239	1406867
PM 91	201	247	329	442	529	707	287
AC 90	1562	1115	1760	445	126	91	5099
CA 90	325118	277590	574298	188230	80224	64127	1509587
PM 90	208	249	326	423	637	705	296
AC 89	1591	1044	1629	365	124	86	4839
CA 89	365313	265453	555745	158255	74428	55940	1475133
PM 89	230	254	341	434	600	650	305

Exhibit 9
Extracts from Toupargel's Presentation Booklet[a]

OUR GOALS

Toupargel's goal was to become a nationwide retailer within five years. We aim at a 25% market share, achieved through home delivery of quality frozen food, priced competitively, sold based on a catalog.

Toupargel will reach its goals thanks to internal growth and acquisitions. Our profitability target was of 5% of sales (before tax).

To reach these goals, Toupargel has developed an ambitious strategy that includes all aspects of its business:

CONSUMERS

- We want to be perceived as specialists
- We want to serve our customers through various delivery methods (home sales, telesales, mail-order, videotext, . . .)
- Increase our awareness
- Improve our customers' fidelity and broaden our customer base

PRODUCTS

- Offer only the best quality products
- Offer a very wide choice
- Price our products attractively
- Foster innovation

PEOPLE

- Rely on skilled people
- Develop training and promotion from within
- Improve internal communication
- Promote an atmosphere that favors worker satisfaction and personal development

TECHNOLOGY

- Respect cold food standards
- Invest to ensure the delivery of quality products
- A lean organization
- Look for advanced technologies, especially in computers.

a Translation by the casewriter.

Exhibit 10
Financial Information on Toupargel (thousands of Fr)

Balance Sheet	1987	1988	1989	1990	1991	1992
Assets	**81,923**	**88,865**	**85,724**	**98,415**	**99,130**	**122,065**
Cash and equivalents	10,160	15,456	7,796	5,863	15,433	13,538
Inventory	24,367	24,765	27,209	28,031	25,828	24,895
Accounts receivable	2,041	1,126	1,046	3,056	3,050	2,187
Others[a]	7,472	8,283	12,253	11,055	11,047	15,167
Total current assets	44,040	49,630	48,304	48,005	55,358	55,787
Net P. P. & E.	26,065	27,691	25,635	26,532	22,100	34,318
Goodwill - Intangibles	10,341	9,973	11,048	16,941	20,768	30,437
Shareholdings and loans[b]	1,477	1,571	737	6,937	904	1,523
Total fixed assets	37,883	39,235	37,420	50,410	43,772	66,278
Liabilities	69,903	75,351	70,538	83,874	84,814	109,616
Accounts payable	32,828	41,048	38,249	44,446	44,863	45,905
Bank debt	2,244	1,837	1,794	2,214	4,349	13,616
Other current liabilities[c]	13,024	12,690	12,982	15,719	12,972	16,367
Total current liabilities	48,096	55,575	53,025	62,379	62,184	75,888
Provisions	1,151	1,225	604	507	1,032	750
Long-term debt[d]	20,656	18,551	16,909	20,988	21,598	32,978
Shareholder equity	12,020	13,514	15,186	14,541	14,316	12,449

a Includes: sales tax refund expected from the government (1/3) and end-of-year rebates from suppliers (2/3).
b Includes shareholdings in branches in which Toupargel does not own 100% of the capital.
c Includes sales tax and social security due but not paid yet.
d Includes leasing obligations.

Exhibit 10, continued

Income Statement	1987	1988	1989	1990	1991	1992
Total sales	244,312	264,186	253,515	293,840	312,376	359,411
Cost of merchandise	140,567	152,922	142,088	161,174	169,576	194,889
Labor cost[a]	48,426	51,426	52,271	67,015	71,492	87,168
Purchase of outside services[b]	31,006	35,170	37,329	43,146	49,874	55,185
Taxes	3,456	4,416	4,382	5,169	6,076	6,779
Depreciation	10,073	12,815	13,552	14,593	12,772	15,085
Other costs	283	240	141	598	873	633
Operating profits	10,501	7,197	3,752	2,145	1,713	(328)
Interest income	599	634	453	58	13	259
Capital gains	143	317	284	266	130	226
Interest charges	1,784	2,417	2,021	2,321	3,183	4,285
Capital losses	—	—	—	—	—	—
Net financial results	(1,042)	(1,466)	(1,284)	(1,997)	(3,040)	(3,800)
Exceptional Revenue[c]	1,835	1,797	1,969	2,067	9,460	7,522
Exceptional Charges[c]	1,780	2,883	2,241	2,219	8,100	5,184
Net income before tax	9,514	4,645	2,196	(6)	32	(1,790)
Tax	2,933	2,554	(292)	1,385	(86)	(124)
Profit sharing distribution	—	—	303	—	—	—
Net income	6,581	2,091	2,488	(1,694)	118	(1,666)

a Includes exceptional costs for lay-offs in new branches in 1989, 1990 and 1991.
b Includes: 25% for catalog, 16% for energy (power and gas), 11% for rents, 8% for travel expenses, 7% for telephone.
c Gains and losses on assets sales.

Exhibit 11
Financial Information on Organization Plus—Balance Sheet 1992

Assets	**2,390**
Cash and equivalents	66
Inventory	1,437
Accounts receivable	397
Total current assets	1,900
P P & E	276
Goodwill - Intangibles	208
Shareholdings and loans	6
Total fixed assets	490
Liabilities	**1,442**
Accounts payable	956
Bank debt	176
Other current liabilities	310
Total current liabilities	1,442
Long-term debt	0
Shareholder Equity	**948**

Income Statement	**10/1/91–12/31/92**	**(15 months)**
Total sales	23,598	
Cost of merchandise	15,766	
Labor cost	2,724	
Purchase of outside services	3,845	
Depreciation	361	
Other costs	234	
Operating Profits	**668**	
Interest income	0	
Capital gains	0	
Interest charges	58	
Capital losses	0	
Net Financial Results	**(58)**	
Exceptional revenue	289	
Exceptional charges	215	
Tax	22	
Profit sharing distribution	0	
Net Income	**662**	

Note: All data in thousands of Fr

Case 29

CUC INTERNATIONAL: SHOPPERS ADVANTAGE

"Twenty years is a long time to wait to be an overnight success, but it does now seem that interactive home shopping has finally caught on." Walter A. Forbes, chairman and CEO of CUC International, was reflecting on the growing importance of home shopping via the television set. In August 1993, a substantial number of companies were developing and testing various approaches to interactive shopping. CUC had been a pioneer in the computer home shopping field, but its growth had come from providing a wide variety of member services, and by means other than computer.

CUC provided services to more than 28 million members. The company's original service was *Shoppers Advantage*. By accessing CUC's database, members could obtain product information and buy merchandise at low prices and then have it delivered to their home or office. In essence, CUC provided merchandise without stores or inventory. The consumer traded convenience (on-line information and purchasing capability from home) for delivery time.

In return for a $49 annual fee, a member of *Shoppers Advantage* could call a toll-free number (800-TEL-SHOP) and obtain information on, or buy, any of 250,000 products (such as televisions, cameras, towels, and automobiles). Some callers simply wanted a price quote, or were doing some "pre-shopping" by discovering what products and features were available within a particular category. If a member wanted to buy a product, CUC took a check or credit card information and then notified the relevant vendor who shipped the product directly to the customer, usually via UPS. CUC offered several separate programs (requiring their own membership fees) including *Travelers Advantage* (a travel agency) and *Auto Vantage* (new and used car evaluations, parts and service discounts). See **Exhibit 4** for a more complete description of company products.

BACKGROUND

In 1968, Walter Forbes graduated with an MBA from Harvard Business School and joined MAC Enterprises, a venture capital subsidiary of the MAC Consulting Group (now absorbed into Gemini Consulting) in Cambridge, Massachusetts. In 1973 he and a group of friends founded Comp-U-Card (the corporate name was changed to CUC International in 1982). As with a number of other companies existing at the time, the business idea was to provide members with a referral service for consumer products. Members could learn what products were available, at what stores, and at what price. The key to Comp-U-Card's success, however, would be that members would access the company's database directly over the phone lines via a modem and their own computer.

The young company quickly learned that it would need to make adaptations to its original concept. First,

This case was prepared by Professor David E. Bell as the basis for class discussion rather than to illustrate either effective or ineffective handling of an administrative situation.

the number of people willing and able to access the company's database by computer was far lower than thought. Second, it became clear that members were unlikely to develop a loyalty to the company (and renew their subscriptions) unless they actually made *purchases* through Comp-U- Card.

It was a relatively simple matter to address the first issue by providing non-computer access to the data (members could call a toll-free number and talk to an operator who then accessed the database on the member's behalf). However, setting up the capability to offer products rather than purely the information was quite another matter.

Manufacturers were reluctant to deal with what amounted to a consumer buying group whose declared intention was to offer the nation's lowest prices. They feared that such a service, if successful, could lead to erosions of retail margins and discontent among established channels of distribution, such as dealers and retailers.

Despite early reversals and the judgment of the retailing gurus of the time who said it couldn't be done, Forbes became increasingly convinced that the service would be successful. He left MAC in 1976 to become Comp-U-Card's chief executive officer. By 1983 the company had only 114 employees (of whom 38 staffed the phones), revenues of $4 million, and expenses of $7 million. An Initial Public Offering that year raised $20 million.

Time and persistence paid off, however. Manufacturers *did* start dealing with CUC, though sometimes indirectly, such as by subsidizing sales through one of their own dealers.

The membership grew dramatically when CUC targeted affinity groups as a source of new members, most notably holders of Citibank's Visa card. Citibank and CUC agreed on a program under which CUC could offer its memberships directly to Citibank's cardholders *but in Citibank's name*. Thus, cardholders were members of the *CitiShopper* Program, which in all but minor ways was identical to *Shoppers Advantage*. In exchange for this access and implied endorsement, CUC paid Citibank 15% to 20% of the resulting membership fees, including renewals.

SHOPPERS ADVANTAGE

By 1993 *Shoppers Advantage* (and associated affinity programs) had 3 million members and represented about one-fifth of CUC's revenues. CUC as a whole had 28 million members. The company employed 6,000 people, of which 3,000 were telephone operators. *Shoppers Advantage* was managed by Vincent D'Agostino, a senior vice president of the company and a Harvard Business School graduate (MBA '81).

The Customer's Perspective

A prospective subscriber to *Shoppers Advantage* (or *CitiShopper*) could join by returning a solicitation card or by calling 1-800-TEL-SHOP and paying the $49 membership fee. (All payments were in the form of check, money order, or credit card, but a credit card was the fastest, most convenient, and most usual form of payment.) The member then had the right to call CUC as often as he or she desired. A new member received a welcoming package that included a membership card and number, materials explaining the services offered, and a coupon good for $10 off the member's first purchase. CUC also sent members a monthly catalog featuring about 500 of the company's available items. All warrantable items bought through *Shoppers Advantage* with a manufacturer's warranty running for less than two years had the warranty extended automatically by CUC to bring it up to two full years. A customer had the right to cancel an order at any time and to return an item thought to be unsatisfactory. Returns were subject to a 15% "restocking fee" plus the additional shipping cost. Returns represented less than 5% of all orders. A member could cancel the membership at any time and receive a full refund of the then-current annual fee. For this reason the company recognized fee income as it was earned rather than when it was received.

A *Shoppers Advantage* member calling the toll-free number was first asked for a membership number and then asked to confirm his or her name and address. The member might wish to purchase a specific item seen in the catalog or in a retail store, or might simply be seeking more information about a general product category of interest (e.g., camcorders). In the latter instance, the operator would use the computer database to extract a list of items within that particular category and then probe the member about desired product features (Preferred manufacturer? Size? Color? Price range? . . .), until the list of available products had been narrowed to two or three. The operator might then read a detailed description of the remaining products. If the member decided to buy a product, the operator asked for a credit card number (these numbers were not saved as part of the member's file) and delivery address. The operator quoted the total delivered price (including delivery charges and taxes, if any) and provided an estimated delivery window (typically 1–2 weeks).

While most members called from their homes, many called from their places of work. Some members even called from retail stores, checking to see whether the store's price was acceptably low. Members were said to have called using cellular telephones while talking to a retail store salesperson, and used CUC's quote as leverage in a negotiation about the retail price.

After making a purchase, a member received a purchase confirmation notice in the mail. This notice served not only as a reminder but also as a proof of purchase in case there was a need to invoke CUC's warranty. An active record of the transaction was maintained in CUC's database for approximately six months, after which it was transferred to microfiche. Customers seeking to change their orders or to make inquiries about delivery delays or any other concerns about the transaction were asked to call a separate toll-free number. There, an operator reviewed the customer's computer record and took whatever action might be required to satisfy the customer, such as sending a message to the vendor or shipping agent, or approving a refund. About 17% of transactions led to one or more such calls. Most frequently the call was simply to ask for an update on the likely delivery date. Most vendors informed CUC when an order had been shipped and also supplied the UPS tracking number. In some cases CUC could confirm the order had been shipped only when the vendor billed CUC.

CUC forwarded an order electronically to vendors only after a check had cleared or a credit card authorization had been received. Credit checks were performed overnight after the order had been received. Vendors averaged seven days fulfilling an order. The package spent an average of three days in transit. The average time between order and delivery was 11.5 days although many more than half of all orders took less than that time.

Computer On-line memberships were relatively rare. Only 100,000 members were capable of accessing the database directly, including those who arrived "indirectly" through a network service such as Prodigy, CompuServe, Source Telecomputing Corporation, or the Dow Jones News Retrieval service. Few individual on-line members used the service during the day, but as many as 200 users might call in at night.

Vendor Relations

CUC's attempts to establish a low price direct channel to the customer were originally viewed antagonistically by most manufacturers. As late as 1988 some manufacturers refused to deal with any discount channels. Little by little, however, the dam began to break. Some manufacturers were happy to deal with CUC if sales goals were not being met. If a manufacturer was not cooperative, CUC would approach one or more of the manufacturer's dealers, or even a retailer. Price quotes from various sources were kept current on the database, and a member was automatically quoted the lowest delivered cost. If a manufacturer discovered that one of its dealers was working with CUC, the manufacturer might threaten to cancel the dealer's franchise and the dealer would usually withdraw from the CUC relationship. But tacit agreements gradually arose. In one variation, CUC would cycle from one dealer to the next as manufacturer pressure caused dealers to withdraw. In a second, the manufacturer would turn a blind eye to a dealer's association with CUC, sometimes giving off-invoice discounts to the dealer to ensure the competitiveness of the company's products against manufacturers dealing with CUC directly. A manufacturer might be in daily contact with CUC about new products, sales of existing products, and competitive conditions, while professing publicly what was technically true—that it did not *ship* for CUC.

In a 1988 sales pitch to a major manufacturer, CUC argued that sales through its channel were largely incremental to the manufacturer's retail business rather than cannibalizing it. "In fact, there are many advantages for a manufacturer who deals with us," said Keith Raiff, vice president for merchandising. "They have the convenience of dealing with a single buyer at a single site. Moreover, we carry their entire line, rather than cherry-picking the hottest items. The manufacturer gets great marketing research data from us, since the customer is comparing across the entire line. And of course, reaction to a new item can be measured within days rather than months."

One example of CUC's potential as a volume channel came in 1989 when *Shoppers Advantage* featured an AT&T phone handset on the catalog cover; 15,000 units were sold within 10 weeks. This was 25% of AT&T's U.S. inventory of the product. Impressed by this demonstration, AT&T actively cooperated with CUC, which by 1992 had become the company's second-largest special markets channel (with 45,000 units shipped).

Even in 1993, manufacturer cooperation was uneven. Most manufacturers were unable to give the needed attention to shipping a single unit when they were used to shipping by the truckload. Nor were they equipped to follow up if an order was lost or canceled. Particularly frustrating for CUC, and customers, were stockouts. Customers were notified by telephone or by mail if it became clear that an item was out of stock or if delivery was likely to exceed 30 days. AT&T was a rare example of a manufacturer who took on the responsibility of updating CUC's database directly with current information on product availability.

Pricing

CUC believed it obtained manufacturer prices that were roughly on par with those given to dealers. If CUC obtained a product through a dealer rather than the manufacturer, this might add another 5%–9% to CUC's offered price. Huge retailers like Sears could buy at perhaps 7%–14% less than CUC; this was due, in part, to Sears' willingness to guarantee large purchases well in advance of their manufacture, even providing associated letters of credit if necessary. Figuring that retailers needed at least a 25% gross margin in sales to consumers, CUC estimated the comparative economics to the consumer in **Table 1**. (The table uses CUC's purchase price as the base of 100.)

These price differentials were somewhat confirmed by prices listed in several advertisements in May 1993. **Table 2** shows the prices of identical items as shown in (a) the Shoppers Advantage catalog (the catalog does not show delivery price; the prices below include a quoted delivery charge to Boston, Massachusetts), (b) a Boston newspaper insert for Circuit City at a time when the retailer was entering that city, and (c) a Sears newspaper insert prior to the Memorial Day holiday. (**Exhibit 6** has more price information.)

Table 1

	CUC	Sears	Smaller Retailer
Manufacturer price	100	90	100
Wholesale markup	0	0	10
Retail gross margin	7	30	36
Retail price	107	120	46
Sales tax (at 5%)	0	6	7
Delivery	12 (varies)	0	0
Total cost	119	126	153

Table 2

	SA Catalog	Circuit City	Sears
JVC Car Cassette Stereo	$156.95	$ 199.97	
JVC Radio/Cassette/CD	199.95	219.97	
Toshiba 32" Color TV	955.50	1,199.97*	
VCR Plus Programmer	39.85		$47.24
Epson Printer	201.95		209.99
"Rival" Yogurt Maker	24.95		19.94

* Circuit City also provided customers a $100 US Savings Bond with this product.

CUC relied for its income almost exclusively on the membership fees. There were usually minor surpluses from shipping and handling costs (shipping costs quoted to the customer were estimated, not actual) and a gross margin on sales of about 7%.

Buyer Analysis

Though CUC had determined that its members were demographically similar to credit card holders as a whole, Keith Raiff explained that *Shoppers Advantage* members could be thought of as two extremes of the shopping public.

The "sophisticated" shopper uses us because of our comprehensive selection. This shopper is not particularly concerned about price but trusts that CUC is delivering good value. Our advantage with respect to selection is unbeatable. A typical retailer might carry only 5% of a manufacturer's line. For example, Toshiba makes 35 varieties of television sets; a typical retailer carries at most five of these. We offer all 35. Sears carries only two of Panasonic's 11 camcorders; we offer all 11. The sophisticated buyer understands that CUC offers superior selection, at competitive prices, and with the utmost convenience.

At the other extreme we have members who use us primarily because of our prices and because the buying process is simple. These customers are not so brand loyal, and so our vast selection enables them to find the lowest prices in a product category. These customers are especially attracted by our polite and helpful operators. Since neither they nor we get a commission from our sales, there is no pressuring the customer to purchase a particular item or brand. CUC can be said to be "brand neutral."

Five years ago I'd say about 80% of our customers were using us primarily because of our low prices. But now nearly a third of our customers use us because of the convenience. As the societal trend towards working couples continues, it seems to me the demand for convenience can only increase.

"We were slow to realize the importance of catalogs to our members," said Vince D'Agostino.

In 1990 we expanded our catalog to about 300 items and distributed it monthly. About half of all items purchased are from the catalog; in the week or so following the mailing of a catalog this proportion reaches 75%. This has cost advantages to us since our operations can process catalog purchases in much less time than one that involves searching the database and reading out product descriptions. In the last five years, the percentage of our members who purchase from any given catalog has risen from 1.4% to 6%, with a response rate of 15% from our Christmas catalog among members who have made at least one previous purchase. Another extraordinarily positive result from our own customer research: 95% of our members whom we interview after they have made a purchase say that they intend to buy from us again. I believe this exceeds even L.L. Bean's level of customer loyalty.

Though our membership levels have remained fairly constant over the last few years, the volume of products sold has been increasing rapidly. Some days we do a million dollars worth of business. Even so, the average transaction has fallen from $260 in the old days to around $160 now. This may be due to the influence of low-priced items in the catalog, but it may also be due to increasing acceptance of ourselves as a channel for routine purchases.

Marketing

In 1992 CUC sent over 200 million mail solicitations and made over 40 million telemarketing phone calls. Marketing costs of $328 million for the financial year ending in January 1993 represented 45% of revenues and resulted in the companywide addition of 2.5 million new subscriptions. Membership cancellations had represented 25% of gross membership fees for each of the last three years, amounting to $213 million for the financial year ending January 1992 (**Exhibit 1** shows fee revenue for 1992 at $739 million. Therefore, gross fee revenue was $952 million). Membership renewals had also been steady at about 65%, that is, of those members who did not cancel their subscriptions, 65% renewed.

But Vince D'Agostino cautioned that the renewal rates were skewed. "After a member has made two purchases through us, and so long as his or her credit card remains valid, then renewal is virtually assured. The other side of this coin is that members who never do make an initial purchase are not that likely to renew. Even those members who use us, but only as a referral service, have a renewal rate barely higher than a member who never calls at all. The key then is to make sure a member uses us for *some* purchase."

Each new member was given a one-time $10 off coupon, and the catalog included a number of low-priced items, some at exceptional values. Each caller, whether making a purchase or not, was invited to consider buying a daily special. On one day this consisted of a 5-pack of blank video tapes for a delivered price of $14.84.

Attrition of established members tended to occur only in cases of severe dissatisfaction. In a typical (but not frequent) example, a member might call about a missing package. The operator might not be able to get through to UPS while the member was on the phone and so would promise to follow up and call back. If the operator failed to make a note of this conversation on the member's order file, no follow-up might occur.

CUC had an additional 6,000,000 members through a marketing program known as "Enhancement Packages." Banks and other financial institutions were constantly seeking low-cost ways to create loyalty among their account holders. They might offer free checking, a free VISA card, or other such inducements. CUC had agreements with nearly 6,000 such institutions whereby it provided shopping and/or travel services to a bank's customers in exchange for a fee of about $1 per customer per month. Although the fee for "bulk members" was substantially lower than for regular members, bulk members' usage of CUC services was considerably lower, and of course, there were no marketing expenses involved.

The Information System

CUC maintained its own bank of Digital VAX computers at its Trumbull, Connecticut, facility. Great care was taken to ensure that the system remained "up." All land cables were laid in parallel, and all data were saved simultaneously on two disks, with additional backups made frequently.

The core system was expandable by the simple means of adding additional computers. CUC decided at an early stage not to rush headlong into new technologies; as a result, the underlying computer technology had changed only gradually over the years. The principal changes that occurred related more to I/O hardware, such as for the rapid scanning of applications and automatic backups. These reduced the labor needs of the operation and led to increased accuracy.

During a busy period the system handled simultaneous inquiries from about 1,000 users, most of whom were company operators.

A typical product entry is shown as **Exhibit 2**. A user might find this entry by typing the model number, if known, or through "feature shopping," a system by which an entry was defined as the answer to a series of computer inquiries.

Once a purchase was made, the computer would perform the credit check (overnight), notify the appropriate vendor (only 5% of orders could not be processed online), and then prepare to track delivery. As vendors notified CUC of a shipping date (or billed CUC, which was presumed to imply shipment), the customer's file was updated. If a customer called in later, an operator could give any tracking information that was available or cancel the order. Notations were appended to the customer's file, summarizing customer calls. If action was to be taken, the computer would notify the appropriate party. If delivery did not occur within 30 days, the computer generated a notification to the member (a notification required by law).

Six months after a purchase file was last accessed, the computer printed out copies of the file for transfer to microfiche.

Personnel

The operators, whose interaction with the members was of paramount importance to the success of the company, were carefully recruited and trained. CUC had deliberately adopted a policy of opening telephone centers in different regions of the country so as not to exhaust the supply of potential employees in any one location. By August 1993 there were 10 such centers.

In addition to competitive wages, employees participated in profit sharing (after six months), and could attend special seminars and health fairs. Turnover was around 3% per month, a figure that D'Agostino thought was low for this type of work. Operators developed great skill in using the database, not only because they became familiar with the items in it but also because they became adept with the keywords required to manipulate data retrieval.

In time, some operators moved to the "customer satisfaction" department. These calls were often more complex and potentially stressful. (See **Exhibit 3** for examples of the kinds of calls received.) CUC's goal was to answer 80% of all calls within 20 seconds. The average time until response during early 1993 was 15 seconds.

The Future of Shoppers Advantage

Vince D'Agostino was satisfied with the continued and rapid progress *Shoppers Advantage* was making. With renewal rates rising, CUC was becoming an increasingly significant player in the retail marketplace. As manager of *Shoppers Advantage* though, he had a number of continuing concerns about how to modify and improve the product.

Delivery. The average delivery time of 11½ days could clearly be improved, especially as 7 days of this represented the time taken by the vendor to ship the product. Perhaps as CUC's market share increased, suppliers would become more sensitive to the demands of customer service. Failing this, could *Shoppers Advantage* afford to source more through dealers, or even retailers, who were more accustomed to providing customer satisfaction, including faster delivery?

Operator Costs. With much of the operating budget consumed by operator salaries, this was a prime candidate for economies. Since catalog orders were so much easier to process, Vince had considered setting up a network phone prompter that would screen incoming callers according to whether or not they were ordering from the catalog. (A separate toll-free number for the catalog would achieve the same result.) Catalog orders could be processed by less-experienced operators, some of whom could be hired on a temporary basis to meet peak load demands. Catalog sales might even be automated, with customers entering their orders and credit card numbers directly over a touch-tone phone.

Inventory. Part of what made the *Shoppers Advantage* so simple was that it carried no inventory of its own. Yet with delivery times so poor on certain items, might it make sense for the company to set up its own warehouse for high-volume items? This would also help CUC in its relations with some manufacturers who seemed reluctant to deal with CUC unless negotiations resulted in a "purchase order."

Manufacturer Maintenance of the Database. Very few manufacturers took on the responsibility of keeping the CUC database up to date on product availability. There was good reason to suppose that manufacturers could benefit from keeping all of the information relating to their products up to date. In addition to product availability, such information included comprehensive product descriptions, new models, and price.

Merchandise Carried. There were many items that CUC did *not* carry. Heavy items such as refrigerators were a problem because of the shipping costs. To be more competitive on heavy items CUC would have to maintain data on vendors at least in each state, and perhaps even in each city. Items without a manufacturer identification number (jewelry, for example) were impossible to define precisely enough for mail-order selling, except perhaps, through the catalog. Short-life-span items (fads, fashionable clothing) were excluded because of the difficulty one had in judging their value and the frequency with which the database would need to be modified. Finally, items were not carried if CUC could not compete with the price available in ordinary retail channels. For example, toys were rarely carried in CUC because of the domination of Toys R Us; with a 30% market share, Toys R Us heavily discounted all high-volume items. Nintendo game equipment was invariably sold as a loss leader by all toy outlets. D'Agostino wondered whether *Shoppers Advantage* was taking too limited a view of what his network could sell.

Home Shopping Technologies

Despite CUC's attitude of "wait and see" on the question of technology, it was clear in August 1993 that the world of home shopping was heating up.

Home television shopping (through cable channels such as Home Shopping Network and QVC) had already achieved substantial success as an avenue for moving large quantities of merchandise in short intervals of time. While jewelry had been an early favorite of these networks, Saks Fifth Avenue had recently had some success in an experimental offering of apparel; one author sold 12,000 copies of his book in 30 minutes. As a result of successes such as these, Macy's had recently announced a joint venture with Cablevision to start a 24-hour 7-day per week shopping channel featuring Macy's own merchandise. "TV Macy's" was expected to reach 15 million to 20 million viewers when introduced in the fall of 1994.

But these ventures still required customers to pick up the telephone in order to purchase the merchandise. Another major development that had been much discussed was interactive TV. GTE Main Street was a venture that already operated an interactive cable channel in three markets, including Needham, Massachusetts. AT&T had an active interest in interactive cable. It had bought a 49% share in Sierra Online, a company recognized as a master of graphical user interface (GUI). Sierra Online had developed primarily as a medium through which members could talk to one another and play on-line games. AT&T hoped to be able to deliver full motion video through interactive TV by 1994. Many other companies were planning their own entry to this market.

Richard Leegant was head of Interactive Services for CUC and kept a close eye on those developments. He noted that there were various ideas on how best to "connect with the home." In December 1992 US West (one of the former regional Bell Telephone companies) announced that it would begin laying fiber optic cables to 13 million homes starting in 1994. Fiber optic cables could handle much more data than conventional metal cables.

Fiber optics offered two distinct solutions to one of the major problems confronting TV shopping: that of providing selection. At present, viewers could see only what the channel chose to show, and the pace was not rapid. One solution would be to offer many hundreds of channels with each channel corresponding to some subcategory of product, such as sporting goods. A second solution was interactive television. At a minimum, interactive television could simply allow someone to use the TV screen for access to a database, much as one of CUC's on-line subscribers did now. For example, Time Warner was already delivering 150 channels to 5,000 homes in Queens, New York, and was planning a 4,000-home test of interactive TV for Orlando in 1994. Interactive television might permit someone to call up full motion video of a product of interest. With fiber optics this was a possibility, but over conventional phone lines it was not.

Bellcore, the research group of the former Bell telephone companies, was actively developing technology to improve the capability of telephone lines to handle video, in support of screen-based telephones. As of August 1993, the transmission of even "still" full color pictures over telephone lines remained slow. In a related development, Bell Atlantic was working with Blockbuster Video to be able to download television programs and videos into the home on demand over regular telephone lines.

Copper wire and fiber optics were not the only possible access routes to the home. Hughes Communications expected to offer 150 video channels via satellite by 1994. In February 1992 Hewlett-Packard announced it would collaborate with TV Answer Inc., a consortium of Mexican investors, to develop a national interactive television system. Their device, expected to retail for less than $1,000, was described as a specialized computer that would transmit over a cellular-like system of receivers. A pilot program was to be unveiled later in 1993 in Washington, D.C. Another venture planned to communicate with TV sets over the FM radio band, a use already sanctioned by the FCC.

The interactive computer networks such as Prodigy and CompuServe were also interested in connecting with television. They, like CUC, already relied upon a third party to provide communication between themselves and their members (currently the telephone network). Would this dependency be viable if the television became a primary communication device with the consumer? Or should they form an alliance with a player who would have direct access to the consumer?

However the technology played out, and no matter who proved to be the winners and losers, if CUC wanted to participate more extensively in this sector, it would need to develop a library of video images to match its product offerings and improve the interactive capabilities of its database. A key issue facing CUC management was whether to proceed at once or wait until the competition and technological picture became clearer.

The Future of CUC

In light of CUC's increasing resources and cash flow, Walter Forbes knew he would soon be in a position, if need be, to make substantial investments in technology, marketing, or logistical infrastructure. The company that he had founded 20 years earlier had been based on the vision of home shopping that some very big players were now embracing.

There are a couple of reasons why I think CUC will benefit from all of this sudden activity. First, when interactive TV becomes a reality, there is going to be a demand for substantive services with which to interact. Even if interactive TV is available, the telephone may still prove to be the best way for customers to buy what they see on TV. Second, as soon as there are 6 or 7 TV shopping channels, the consumer will start making price comparisons across channels and pretty soon they'll want an independent shopping service such as is now provided by CUC.

With millions of dollars being thrown into technology, people sometimes observe that it would be simple for a Time-Warner or US West to set up their own version of CUC. It's not likely to happen. We have 27 million members over which to spread our fixed costs. That's not easy to replicate, and it can't be done overnight—except by buying us.

The issues we have to think about going forward include

1. Should we begin marketing ourselves directly to the public? We do accept individual memberships now, but we have never sought members except through a sponsor.

2. What services will be easier to obtain via interactive TV than over the phone?

3. Should CUC align itself with one of the technology or programming giants, or should we remain independent?

As Forbes edged his BMW onto the Merritt Parkway, he thought about where he should be placing his bets.

Exhibit 1
CUC International, Inc., & Subsidiaries Consolidated Statement of Income ($ in thousands except per share amounts)

	Year Ended January 31		
	1993	1992	1991
Revenues			
Membership and service fees	$738,948	$641,287	$543,215
Other	3,332	2,968	2,746
Total revenues	742,280	644,255	545,961
Operating Costs and Expenses			
Operating	196,867	170,902	144,225
Marketing	328,389	288,423	246,030
General and administrative	108,676	98,448	88,908
Interest	8,734	15,979	20,020
Amortization of deferred financing costs and restricted stock compensation	3,512	4,634	4,629
Merger integration and restructuring charges attributable to the merger with Entertainment Publishing Corp. [a]		20,737	
Total costs and expenses	646,178	599,123	503,812
Income before income taxes	96,102	45,132	42,149
Provision for income taxes	37,259	20,002	16,256
Net Income	$ 58,843	$ 25,130	$ 25,893
Net Income per Common Share	$0.85	$0.37	$0.39

a Represents costs in connection with the Company's plan to integrate the operations of CUC International, Inc., and Entertainment Publishing Inc. and costs of professional fees and other expenses related to the merger. The after-tax effect of these charges was $15 million ($.22 per share).

Exhibit 1, continued
Condensed Consolidated Balance Sheet ($ in thousands)

| | January 31, | |
	1993	1992
Assets		
Current Assets		
Cash and cash equivalents	$ 28,602	$ 14,400
Receivables	130,175	106,714
Membership solicitations in process	40,054	41,101
Prepaid membership materials	16,040	13,027
Prepaid expenses, deferred taxes and other	28,486	29,270
Total current assets	243,357	204,512
Contract renewal rights and intangible assets, net	179,120	67,616
Properties, net	23,971	23,104
Deferred income taxes	21,338	14,915
Other	10,794	11,654
	$478,580	$321,801
Liabilities and Shareholders' Equity		
Current Liabilities		
Accounts payable and accrued expenses	$106,104	$106,173
Revolving credit facility	15,182	26,725
Note payable, acquisition related	6,000	
Total current liabilities	127,286	132,898
Deferred membership income, net	158,350	110,283
Zero coupon convertible notes (net of unamortized original issue discount of $17,363 and $44,489)	37,295	69,228
Other	5,459	10,359
Shareholders' equity (deficiency)	150,190	(967)
	$478,580	$321,801

Exhibit 2
Sample Usage of Database

```
AQS>help

Valid entries are:
BArgains [ptype [mfg]]          - Find bargains
BCategory [bcat#]               - Displays bargain category information
CAtegory [cat#]                 - Displays product category information
CHeckout                        - Proceed to checkout cycle
COmment Display                 - Displays member's profile comments
COmment Entry                   - Allows entry of profile comments
EXIT                            - Exit the Shopping Service
FF ptype [mfg]                  - Find by Features
FM mfg [[*]model #]             - Find by Manufacturer
FP ptype [mfg [*][model #]]     - Find by Product Type
FS [recno]                      - Find Similar Models
List                            - Displays basic information including features
MAnufacturer [ptype]            - Lists manufacturers for selection
MEMber                          - Go to member # prompt
MESsage [code]                  - Displays messages on various topics
MList                           - Displays basic information including title
Order                           - Review current order
PRIce [[minamt] maxamt]         - Narrow selection set by Price Range
PROfile Display                 - Displays member's profile
PROfile Entry                   - Allows entry of profile information
PType [mfg]                     - Lists product types for selection
Quicklist                       - Short display of basic information
SHip                            - Change ship-to state
STate                           - Same as SHIP
Who                             - Displays member's name and address
X model#[model#...model#]       - Express model # find

Valid Disposition Codes Are:
        PRC PRICE TOO HIGH
        DES NOT ENOUGH DESCRIPTION
        DEL EXPECTED DELIVERY TIME TOO LONG
        SHP SHIPPING CHARGE TOO HIGH
        PLT WILL PURCHASE LATER
        LOC CHECK LOCALLY

AQS>ff tvcr

Format/style?
        1) No preference
        2) Vhs
        3) Eight millimeter
        4) Super-vhs
        5) Vhs-c & full size

Enter selection>2
```

Number of heads?
      1) No preference
      2) 2 heads
      3) 3 or 4 heads
      4) 5 or more heads

Enter selection>3,4

Sound system?
      1) No preference
      2) Stereo decoder
      3) Hi-fi
      4) Stereo and hi-fi
      5) Monaural

Enter selection>1

Built-in 'vcr-plus'?
      1) No preference
      2) Yes
      3) No

Enter selection>1

Center loading style?
      1) No preference
      2) Yes
      3) No

Enter selection>2

What's the most you will spend?
Enter $ limit or <ENTER> for all models >400
      21 products selected

AQS>quicklist

1)	TVCR CRAG PX7462	190.95	2) TVCR EMRS VCR4000	214.95
3)	TVCR FSHR FVH4909	305.95	4) TVCR GDST GVRC447	230.95
5)	TVCR GDST GVRC467	299.95	6) TVCR PANA PV4301	227.09
7)	TVCR PANA PV4314	260.95	8) TVCR PANA PV4351	310.95
9)	TVCR PANA PV4361	370.95	10) TVCR RCA VR501	241.62
11)	TVCR RCA VR667HF	389.27	12) TVCR SHRP VCA46U	266.52
13)	TVCR SHRP VCC56U	330.09	14) TVCR SNYO VHR9413	290.95
15)	TVCR TSHB C-M468	260.95	16) TVCR TSHB M449	230.95
17)	TVCR TSHB M468	250.95	18) TVCR TSHB M658	350.95
19)	TVCR TSHB M668	350.95	20) TVCR ZNTH VR2410	253.95
21)	TVCR ZNTH VR2420	330.95		

Enter HELP for instructions for product comparisons

Enter selection(s)>6

Video cassette recorders (TVCR) PANASONIC (PANA)
Model #: PV4301 Title: 4-HEAD VHS W/PROGRAM DIRECTOR

List Price: open
Our Price: 215.14
Color surcharge: .00

FDC for Regular Delivery: 227.09
 (delivery in 2-3 weeks)

THIS HIGH PERFORMANCE 4-HEAD VHS VCR FEATURES A PROGRAM DIRECTOR REMOTE, EASY-TO-READ ON-SCREEN
DISPLAY FOR PROGRAMMING AND A/V SELECTIONS, 1-MONTH/8-PROGRAM CALENDAR/TIMER, 181-CHANNEL CABLE
COMPATIBLE TUNER, DIGITAL AUTO PICTURE, DIGITAL AUTO TRACKING, ALL CHANNEL AUTO SET, QUICK PLAY, MULTI-
FUNCTION/CLOCK DISPLAY, TIME SEARCH, REAL TIME COUNTER, AUTO DAYLIGHT SAVING TIME, AUTO OPERATION, AND A
1-MIN. TIMER BACK-UP.
WARRANTY: 1-YEAR PARTS AND 90-DAY LABOR.

Want to order (Y or N)? >n

Enter Disposition Code>plt

Exhibit 3

The casewriter spent about half an hour listening to calls taken by one operator, and another half hour with a customer satisfaction operator. The reader should recognize that this sample is not statistically representative, nor are the calls necessarily judged by CUC to have been typical.

GENERAL OPERATOR

Caller 1 Member had ordered some earphones in late 1992 and wished to buy the same item for her mother. Member could only remember that the item had cost about $60. Operator brought up the earphone category and read out manufacturer names. Member recognized one of the names. Further discussion identified which of the two models had been purchased. Member ordered the product and had it shipped to her mother. The member then inquired about the availability of a component of the earphones. The operator could not find the component listed separately. The member then ordered another related product (from the catalog) for herself. The call lasted nearly 11 minutes.

Caller 2 The caller asked about a VCR and cited the model number. She asked about delivery time and was quoted 2–3 weeks. Member said she was leaving the country in two weeks. Operator suggested consideration of a tactic by which the member orders the product and then calls back in a week to see if the product has been shipped. If no, the member could cancel the order at that time. The caller said she would think about it and rang off.

Caller 3 The caller cited a model number of a computer, and asked the price. Operator described two pricing options, one with a supplementary package of software and printer, and the other without. After some discussion of features, the caller asked about credit terms. He was told that the purchase price could be spread across more than one credit card, or personal check or money order, but that the computer could not be shipped until payment was received. The caller said he would think about it and rang off.

The computer screen seen by the operator continuously displayed the member's name, basis of affiliation and membership date.

CUSTOMER SATISFACTION OPERATOR

Caller 1 Caller inquired about a package that had not arrived. Operator saw on file that the member had said he would send a check but apparently had not done so. Therefore the package had not yet been shipped. Member said he would send the check.

Caller 2 Caller asked about a product that was not carried by *Shoppers Advantage*. Operator transferred him to the Product Research Department (which looks into whether such an item can be obtained for the customer and if it should be carried in the future).

Caller 3 Caller inquired about an undelivered item. Operator noted that the delay had been caused by the manufacturer backordering the item. The item had now been shipped, however.

Caller 4 The customer had called many times before and was known to this particular operator. The order had been for three items. The difficulty seemed to center around a lost address. Operator transferred the call to her supervisor (who sat at the next desk).

Caller 5 Customer had received notice of a backorder but had already received the shipment. Operator apologized for the confusion.

Caller 6 A trucking company called, saying it could not deliver an item. Operator checked customer's file and found an alternate telephone number where the member might be reached.

Caller 7 Caller had received her shipment but had been billed the full amount, instead of receiving credit for a $15 gift certificate. Operator apologized for the mistake and said she would notify the accounting department to send the member $15. (Operator did this by making a notation on customer's file.)

Exhibit 4
CUC Program & Channel Descriptions

Channel/Program	Description	Member Fee	Members (000)
Retail Channel			
Shopping ("Shoppers Advantage")	Database price, product information, and discount purchasing capability on over 250,000 items. Regular Catalogs. Access via "800" phone lines and on-line PC.	$49	3,250
Travel ("Travelers Advantage")	Database information, reservations for discount air travel, hotels, auto rentals, tours, cruises, and short-notice travel. Access via "800" phone lines and on-line PC.	$49	2,900
Automotive ("AutoVantage")	New car price/performance summaries, used car valuations, parts and service discounts, lease deals. Access via "800" phone line, on-line PC, and national vendor network.	$49	1,800
Dining ("Premier Dining")	Two-for-one dining at mid-scale restaurants in major U.S. cities.	$49	1,250
Insurance	Accidental death and disability insurance (procured from third party)	$50	1,485
Travel Exchange ("Interval")	International travel accommodations through exchange of member-owned resort lodging.	$60 plus $89 per exchange	400
Wholesale Channel			
Enhancement Packages	Customized combinations of CUC's retail services sold as enhancements to credit cards and checking accounts.	$13	6,250
Insurance	Accidental death and disability insurance (procured from third party). Sold to credit unions and banks.	$35	1,000
Consignment Channel			
Entertainment Publishing	Coupon books featuring substantial savings on dining, theater, and merchant services. Individualized editions target 115 local markets.	$35 ("Entertainment") $10 ("Gold C")	3,900 4,400
Sally Foster Giftwraps	Premium gift wrap sold through fund-raisers (primarily schools).	$7 per roll	13,000

Source: Robertson, Shepleas and Company

Exhibit 5
New Technologies and Participatory Companies

Technology	Players
TV top "Computer"	TV Guide, 3DO, Silicon Graphics, HP/TV Answer, Microsoft/Intel/General Instrument
CD Enhanced TV	GTE Imagitrek/Discovery Channel Kaleida (Apple/IBM) ECA/GEC Marconi (Airplane Entertainment)
Wireless Personal Communications	Apple, Sun Microsystems
Video Telephone	Huntington National Bank, Bellcore, Bell South, NYNEX
Interactive Programming	QVC, GTE Main Street, Sierra Online/AT&T, AT&T/Sega, Interactive Network Inc.
Interactive TV via Computer	Minitel, Prodigy, CompuServe, Dow Jones Retrieval, America On-line
Interactive TV via:	
Satellite	Hughes Communications
FM Radio	TV Answer, Interactive Network Inc.
Fiber Optic Cable	US West, Time Warner, TCI
Wire Cable	Bell Atlantic/Blockbuster Video, AT&T
Cellular	HP/TV Answer

Exhibit 6
CUC Comparative Prices for Selected Products+ - As of July 7, 1993

Products	Model No.	CUC Delivered*	Lechmere	Sears	Fretter	Circuit City#
Televisions						
32" TOSHIBA TV	CF3272B	$955.50 C				$1,199.97
27" RCA TVs	F27120WN	$450.50 C	S $469.98 / R $499.99	DNC		DNC
	F27202FT			S $499.88		OS/1 $549.99
20" RCA TVs	F2057EM		S $289.98 / R $349.99		$315.97	$329.97
	F20600			S $349.99	$337.97	
20" SHARP TV	20CM100	$251.50 C				DNC
Computer Equipment						
Lotus 1-2-3	Release 2.4	$332.95	$309.99	$299.99	DNC	DNC
Epson Printer	AP3250	$201.95 C		$209.99		
Stereo Equipment						
Sharp Boombox	GK-CD610	$180.95	$139.98 / $169.99		DNC	
JVC Radio/Cass/CD	PCX100J	$199.95 C				$219.97
Sony Boombox	CFD757 (Disc) / CFD758 / CFD767	$285.50 C	$279.00 / $329.00	$299.99	$297.97	$328.00
JVC Car Cassette Stereo	KE1700QR	$156.95 C				$199.97
Sony Cassette Stereo	CFS-200	$47.95 C	$39.88	$44.99	DNC	$44.97
Sony Walkman	WMFX45	$74.95 C	OS/1 S $79.99 / R $89.00	DNC	DNC	$84.97
Appliances						
Braun 12 Cup Coffee Maker	KF800BGF / KF850	$87.67 / $86.95 C	$89.99	$44.99**	DNC	DNC
Panasonic Bread Bakery	SD-BT55P	$208.95 C	$249.99@	$169.99**		
Panasonic Bread Bakery	SD-BT65P	$290.95 C	$349.99@			
"Rival" Yogurt Maker	8200W	$24.95 C		$19.94		

Exhibit 6, continued

Products	Model No.	CUC Delivered*	Lechmere	Sears	Fretter	Circuit City#
Hoover Vacuum—Legacy	U4537-930 (New)	$134.95 C	S $179.98	DNC		$189.97
	U4537-910 (Old)		R $199.99	DNC		
	U4731-910		S $189.99	$199.99		
			R $219.99			
Hoover Vacuum—5.0 HP	S3551	$165.95				
Hoover Vacuum—Encore	S3395	$135.95 C				
Cameras						
Nikon 35 MM	Zoom Touch 500 (Disc.)	$185.95 C	DNC	DNC	DNC	DNC
Minolta 35 MM	Freedom Action	$145.95 C	$169.00			
Color Film						
MULTIPACK***	ASA 100	$29.84 C	$37.71	DNC	DNC	DNC
	ASA 200	$32.99 C	$46.11			
	ASA 400	$35.10 C	$54.81			
Telephones						
AT&T Cordless Phone	5515	$151.41	$169.99	$149.99	DNC	OS/3 $150.00
	5510					
AT&T Cordless Phone	5400					$79.98

S = Sale Price
R = Regular Price
DNC = Do Not Carry
OS/X wks = Out Of Stock/Expecting Delivery in X weeks

* A "C" next to the CUC price indicates that the product was listed in the Shoppers Advantage Catalog. Pricing on non-catalog products could be requested over the telephone. Shoppers Advantage offered an extended two-year warranty on its products, including parts and labor. Most products took 3-4 weeks to deliver. Delivery prices were to Boston, MA.

@ Lechmere planned to run a "20% off" sale on all bread baking machines the following weekend.

Circuit City guaranteed that it had the lowest prices. If a customer found the same product for a lower price, Circuit City would pay the customer the difference plus 10% of the difference. This applied to local stores only. On the Epson Printer, Circuit City also provided customers with a $100 U.S. Savings Bond.

** Sears often carried its own private label products. These private label or similar products were selected for the price comparison.

*** CUC Multipacks consisted of 6 rolls of 24-exposure and 3 rolls of 36-exposure film. Lechmere film is sold individually; however, the price indicated represents the cost of an equivalent multipack.

Index

of bankruptcy. . . . In his writings he visualizes a man with qualities of average measurement, physical and mental (*l'homme moyen*), and shows how all other men, in respect of any particular organ or character, can be ranged about the mean of all the observations. Hence he concluded that the methods of Probability, which are so effective in discussing errors of observation, could be used also in Statistics, and that deviations from the mean in both cases would be subject to the binomial law.

If we are to do justice to the claims of a calculus of exploration, we must therefore ask in what sense probability is indeed so effective in discussing errors of observation and in what sense, if any, are Quetelet's authentic deviations from a non-existent population mean comparable to the Gaussian deviation of a measurement from its putatively authentic value. We shall then envisage the present crisis in statistical theory as an invitation to a more exacting re-examination of its foundations than contemporary controversy has hitherto encompassed. After the appearance of his treatise on probability by Keynes, who dismisses Quetelet as a charlatan with less than charity towards so many highly esteemed contemporaries and successors seduced by his teaching, an open conspiracy of silence has seemingly exempted a younger generation from familiarity with the thought of the most influential of all writers on the claims of statistical theory in the world of affairs. Since his views will occupy our attention again and again in what follows, a few remarks upon his career, culled from Joseph Lottin's biography and from other sources, will be appropriate at the outset.

From 1820 onwards Quetelet was director of the Royal Belgian Observatory which he founded. In the 'twenties he professed astronomy and geodesy at the *Ecole Militaire*. The year following the publication (1835) of his portentous *Essai de Physique Sociale*, their uncle King Leopold committed to his care Albert of Saxe-Coburg and his brother Ernest for a brief course of instruction on the principles of probability. Correspondence continued between Quetelet and the Prince, who remained his enthusiastic disciple, affirming his devotion to the doctrine of the *Essai* both as president of the 1859 meeting of the British Association in Aberdeen when Maxwell first announced his stochastic interpretation of the gas laws and in the next year as president of the International Statistical Congress held (1860) in London. As official Belgian delegate, Quetelet himself had attended (1832) the third annual meeting of the British Association at Cambridge. There he conferred with Malthus and Babbage, then Lucasian professor of the Newtonian succession and the inventor of the first automatic computer, also famous as author of the *Economy of Manufacture* and of the *Decline of Science in England*. The outcome of their deliberations was the decision of the General Committee to set up a statistical section.

An incident in the course of Quetelet's relations with Albert is revealing and not without entertainment value. Gossart (1919) tells of it thus in the *Bulletin de la Classe des Lettres*, etc., of the Royal Belgian Academy.

Quetelet peu après la publication de ses lettres; presenta à l'Academie un mémoire *Sur la Statistique morale et les principes qui doivent en former la base*. . . . Par une fâcheuse coincidence, le volume dans lequel les théories de Quetelet touchaient à l'art de gouverne-ment paraissait à Paris au moment on éclatait la révolution de février 1848 et allait "se perdre au milieu des barricades" si bien que quelques exemplaires seulement furent alors distribués. En voyant ce que se passait en France et bientôt dans une partie de l'Europe, le prince Albert ne put s'empêcher de remarquer avec une certaine pointe de malice que le système social était "bien dérangé," que les "causes accidentelles" jouaient un grand rôle. "Le malheur," ajoutait il, "est que la loi qui les gouverne n'a pas été decouverte jusqu'à ce moment."

Quetelet's belief in eternal laws of human society was *en rapport* with a social philosophy unruffled by such mishaps as the Commune; and its Calvinistic temper is hard to reconcile with the libertarian *credo* for which Eddington finds sanction by appeal to the principle of uncertainty lately propounded by the exponents of statistical mechanics. "Tout en déplorant les maux que font à la société 'les changements brusque et les théories des rêveurs'," says Gossart, he attained *la resignation*. To be sure, "des fleaux frappent l'humanité au morale comme au physique," as he admits; but "quelque destructifs que soient leurs effets, il est au moins consolant de penser qu'ils ne peuvent altérer en rien les lois éternelles qui nous régissent. Leur action est passagere et le temps a bientôt cicatrisé les plaies du corps social."

(iv) *A Calculus of Judgments*, as here defined, ostensibly embraces a regimen of correct inference with respect to the credentials of hypotheses. This form of words is advisedly vague, because it is impossible to prescribe its terms of reference more explicitly without prejudging the outcome of the contemporary controversy we are about to examine. If one states that it includes both the theory of significance and of decision tests and the theory of interval estimation in terms of confidence or fiducial limits, the reader will infer all that we need say definitively and with propriety at this stage.

As such, the calculus of judgments subsumes a programme which is almost exclusively a product of our own century; but the emergence of the aspiration the programme endorses is traceable to the doctrine of inverse probability adumbrated in the posthumous publication of Bayes (1763) and propounded more explicitly by Laplace. The end Laplace himself had in view was to vindicate the credentials of inductive reasoning conceived in retrospective terms consistent with his own cosmogony and hence likewise in terms of dubious relevance to verification in the domain of experimental design. Most statisticians now reject the doctrine in its original form; but its essentially retrospective orientation is profoundly relevant to the contemporary crisis in statistical theory.

At what level the theory of probability can appropriately intrude in a prescription for reasoning rightly is an issue which we can discuss with profit if, and only if, we can arrive at agreement about the relevance of the theory of probability to induction in the traditional sense of the term. This is not the exclusive prerogative of the mathematician. It is the birthright and duty of every self-respecting scientific worker who subjects his data to the type of analysis prescribed by one or other school of statistical inference. That fundamental differences with respect to the relevance of the mathematical theory to the world of real decisions have come into focus so lately is not surprising, when we reflect on the circumstances that its application to the technique of interpretation basks in the reflected glory of the pragmatic triumphs of Maxwell, Mendel and their successors.

In the deductive unfolding of a theory which must stand or fall with the operational requirements of laboratory practice, we are entitled to start from any axioms however arbitrary. We should therefore scrutinise with some suspicion the following remarks about statistical methods by Wilks (1944):

The test of the applicability of the mathematics in this field as in any other branch of mathematics consists in comparing the predictions as calculated from the mathematical model with what actually happens experimentally. (*Mathematical Statistics*, Chapter 1, p. 1.)

This assertion would be unexceptionable, if statisticians invoked the algebra of Professor Wilks only in connexion with the genetical theory of populations, Brownian movement of visible particles, the collisions of gas molecules, the emission of photons, and with cognate themes which constitute the scope of a calculus of aggregates; but such topics have no direct relevance to what we imply by statistical theory in the context of a calculus of judgments. In the calculus of aggregates we invoke the theory of probability to prescribe a hypothesis; but a calculus of judgments does not undertake to prescribe hypotheses. It claims only to prescribe a rule which will entitle us to arbitrate on their merits. One may hence ask with propriety what controlled experiment prosecuted on either side of what iron curtain over what number of centuries would settle the dispute between Jeffreys and Fisher concerning the legitimacy of Bayes's postulate or the contest between Fisher and Neyman over test procedure. When the terrain of combat is the realm of means, experience and experience alone should dictate the outcome. When it is in the realm of ends we cannot invoke pragmatic sanctions with the assurance of an acceptable decision.

*   *   *

In the chapters which follow it will be the writer's aim to set forth the terms of reference of the classical theory in some detail at the outset and thereafter to examine its bearing on the four main themes distinguished in the foregoing paragraphs. First, I shall invite the reader to agree with me that my sub-title does not overstate what is a real intellectual dilemma of our time.

Crisis is a word which has become tarnished by misuse; and some of my readers may well wish me to justify the statement that there is indeed a contemporary crisis in statistical theory. Poincaré cites a remark that everyone believes in the normal law of error, the physicists because they think that the mathematicians have proved it to be a logical necessity, the mathematicians because they believe that physicists have established it by laboratory demonstration. The gap between theory and practice has vastly deepened since his time, as is evident from the concluding remarks of E. S. Pearson (1944)* in the following excerpt:

That the frequency concept is not generally accepted in the interpretation of statistical tests is of course well known. With his characteristic forcefulness R. A. Fisher (1945b) has recently written: "In recent times one often repeated exposition of the tests of significance, by J. Neyman, a writer not closely associated with the development of these tests, seems liable to lead mathematical readers astray, through laying down axiomatically, what is not agreed or generally true, that the level of significance must be equal to the frequency with which the hypothesis is rejected in repeated sampling of any fixed population allowed by hypothesis. This intrusive axiom, which is foreign to the reasoning on which the tests of significance were in fact based, seems to be a real bar to progress. . . ."

But the subject of criticism seems to me less an intrusive mathematical axiom than a mathematical formulation of a practical requirement which statisticians of many schools of thought have deliberately advanced. Prof. Fisher's contributions to the development of tests of significance have been outstanding, but such tests, if under another name, were discovered before his day and are being derived far and wide to meet new needs. To claim what seems to amount to patent rights over their interpretation can hardly be his serious intention. Many of us, as statisticians, fall into the all too easy habit of making authoritative statements as to how probability theory should be used as a guide to judgment, but ultimately it is likely that the method of application which finds greatest favour will be that which through its simplicity and directness appeals most to the common scientific user's understanding. *Hitherto the user has been accustomed to accept the function of probability theory laid down by the mathematicians; but it would be good if he could take a larger*

* *Biometrika*, Vol. 34, p. 142.

share in formulating himself what are the practical requirements that the theory should satisfy in application." (Italics inserted.)

Meanwhile the user, as Pearson calls him, continues to perform an elaborate ritual of calculations quite regardless of the fact that there are now at least three schools of theoretical doctrine with no common ground concerning what justification we have for applying a calculus of probability to real situations and with little agreement about how we should proceed to do so. Lest some readers should regard this as an overstatement, it will not be amiss to quote from a recent symposium following a paper read before the Royal Statistical Society* by Anscombe (1948) who undertook the courageous assignment of an impartial appraisal of the views respectively advanced during the last decade by R. A. Fisher, by H. Jeffreys and by J. Neyman and E. S. Pearson. Dr. J. O. Irwin (p. 201) who opened the discussion said:

I think all students of statistics should learn something about probability from a frequency point of view. When teaching students with mature minds who are yet new or almost new to the subject, I usually give an outline of the different theories of the subject, tell them that they will find the frequency theory the most useful in practice, and to suspend judgment on which theory they will ultimately prefer as a basis until they have had more opportunity of study.

Practically minded people with no great taste for logical and philosophical speculation need not probe too deeply. They will probably be just as good statisticians if they don't. More theoretically profound minds will gain much insight if they do and will be able to help the others on critical occasions. But we must admit that what level we agree to call axiomatic is largely a matter of taste.

Professor G. A. Barnard, who followed Dr. Irwin, said in a more explicitly accommodating vein (pp. 201–2):

All three main theories of statistical inference seem to have their proper sphere of application. What we should ask is, not so much which is right, but to what sort of field each theory should be applied; which framework is better in certain circumstances. For

* Discussion of Mr. Anscombe's Paper, *J. Roy. Stat. Soc.* (Series A), 1948, Vol. CXI.

example, in considering industrial inspection Dodge and Romig, two engineers, evolved the notions of producer's risk and consumer's risk, and these have been practically useful in statistical inspection. They are identical in content with the Pearson notion of errors of first and second kind. Again, during the war we had occasion to deal with other sorts of inspection problems, and in this connection we introduced the idea of the process curve, which is nothing but the *a priori* distribution of Professor Jeffreys. I must admit that in my own experience so far, cases where Professor Fisher's theory would have been most suitable have not been very frequent. I think that is because most of my problems have been those where it is necessary to make an administrative decision, rather than those in which one is concerned to establish or disprove a scientific theory. Our work is more concerned with immediate practical decisions, but I do not doubt that with wider experience I should have been able to quote practical cases for that also.

We are, then, left with three theories—the Jeffreys theory, the Pearson theory, and the Fisher theory. I think when we are discussing the foundations of statistics we should draw attention to the fact that this discussion is really, from a practical point of view, a discussion of the fine points of detail. All statisticians agree about what should be done in practical problems. The situation in statistics is really quite like the problem in mathematics. The foundations of mathematics have been discussed and queried for a long time. These discussions are now so broad and widespread that there is a journal devoted to them entirely. Yet no mathematician doubts that any of the mathematics are sound. . . . We have also to remember that a significance test, interpreted somewhat narrowly, as it must be, only allows us to say what is not true, but that does not involve proving a general proposition. In this connection a remark of Professor Jeffreys is worth quoting—that the methods of significance tests used in this way seem to enable us to disprove a great deal but never to prove anything. . . . I should like finally to make it clear that I disagree with all four parties to the controversy. The snag in Professor Jeffreys' theory is that to work it one has to specify a probability distribution for a class of alternative hypotheses and the whole of the probability has to be distributed. One must when interpreting one's experiments be able to think of all possible explanations of the data, and that, I think, none of us believe that we can do. It is always possible for someone to produce later an entirely new explanation we had never thought of, and which would not be represented in the hypothesis nor in the alternatives we had tested.

Taking that criterion it does suggest that in talking about inference from the probability point of view, leaving aside the rigorous ground of the randomization test, we ought to formulate our ideas, not in terms of probability, but in terms of odds. Bayes's theorem, in terms of odds, says that *a posteriori* odds = likelihood ratio (A) × *a priori* odds. We can separate out the two factors on the right-hand side, and it seems to me that along these lines it is possible to reconcile to some extent the various theories. Professor Jeffreys takes the second factor as equal to one by a special axiom or assumption. Professor Fisher seems to say we ought to neglect the second factor; but that is equivalent to saying that A times 1 is equal to A. Finally, Neyman and Pearson say that A itself is a frequency probability of errors, and this is so provided that the reference set used is that of the sequential probability ratio test.

Reported in *oratio obliqua*, Professor E. S. Pearson (pp. 203–4) said with more insight into the consumer's viewpoint:

It has yet to be shown that a mathematical theory could make possible their assimilation into the process of inference on a numerical basis. In balancing these elements to reach conclusions leading to action the power of judgment was called into play; it was something which might be intuitive, a quality which scientific training aimed at developing, but whose possession was no monopoly of the statistician. The judgment might be an individual one or it might be a collective one according to the magnitude of the problem. The question which he raised was whether it was possible to lay down usefully any formal rules of induction, specifying how the various aspects of the problem needing review could be brought together to reach a balanced decision.

None of the contributors to this symposium advanced the most usual excuse for renouncing the traditional obligation of the man of science to understand what he is doing, i.e. the assertion that the procedures described by statistical theories work [*sic*] in spite of the fact that there is so exiguous a basis of agreement about their credentials. It is gratifying to record doubts about its cogency expressed by one of them in another context, if only because the consumer with no appetite for methodological disputation all too readily succumbs to reassurance on such terms. Acceptability of a statistically *significant* result of an experiment on animal behaviour in contradistinction to a result which the investigator can repeat before a critical audience naturally promotes a high output of publication. Hence the argument that the techniques *work* has a tempting appeal to young biologists, if harassed by their seniors to produce results, or if admonished by editors to conform to a prescribed ritual of analysis before publication. A reminder that the plea for justification by works derives its sanction from a different domain of statistical theory is therefore likely to fall on deaf ears, unless we reinstate reflective thinking in the university curriculum. Meanwhile, the views of E. S. Pearson* on the teaching of statistics will commend themselves to the reflective few who entertain a pardonable scepticism about the allegedly useful contribution of current theories in so-called operational research:

Probably there are several of us who can recall a considerable number of reports, or appendices to reports, written on both sides of the Atlantic by mathematically trained statisticians, which were hardly more than a waste of the paper on which they were written. There were cases where the results of statistical analyses were simply put on one side because the practical man, whether scientist or service technician, shrewdly sensed that the theoretical treatment was either not needed, or was actually leading to conclusions which the data could not possibly warrant. The trouble usually arose because the mathematical enthusiast had allowed his theory to run away with his common sense, or, perhaps, because he had never received an adequate training in the application of theory. It was true that biologists did extremely well in operational research; but their success often seemed due to the way in which an experimental training had taught them to handle data rather than to the fact that they mastered statistical technique quickly.

I hope that these citations will dispel any doubt about whether there are very fundamental differences within the hierarchy of theoretical statistics concerning what the theory of probability can contribute to a regimen of scientific inference. They also disclose a widespread disposition on the part of the makers of the theory to disclaim at all costs any relevance of their differences to the requirements of those who use it.

* Discussion on Dr. Wishart's Paper (*The Teaching of Statistics*), *J. Roy. Stat. Soc.*, 1948, Vol. CXI, p. 218.

Kendall (1949), who is deeply disturbed by the clamour the contemporary controversy has assumed, attempts in a recent paper "On the reconciliation of theories of Probability" to resolve disagreement by making explicit on what axioms widely current techniques in use depend; but his approach is essentially that of the pure mathematician seeking to remove *internal* inconsistencies of an otherwise satisfactory calculus. From the standpoint of the user, this accomplishes nothing unless he can also show that otherwise arbitrary postulates have any verifiable foundation in *external* experience. The engaging humour of his final remarks, which I shall now quote, suggest that Kendall himself is not wholly satisfied with the outcome of his pacific negotiations:

A friend of mine once remarked to me that if some people asserted that the earth rotated from east to west and others that it rotated from west to east, there would always be a few well-meaning citizens to suggest that perhaps there was something to be said for both sides, and that maybe it did a little of one and a little of the other; or that the truth probably lay between the extremes and perhaps it did not rotate at all.

It would be less necessary to insist that the issues at stake are of the utmost importance to the user, especially to the vast class of users who take the techniques on trust, if theoretical statisticians were content to arbitrate on the value of conclusions advanced by research workers on the basis of enquiries designed *ad hoc* and with due regard to background knowledge of the enquiry. Of late, more especially during the last fifteen years, they have in fact advanced claims with much wider terms of reference, as illustrated by the following citation from R. A. Fisher (*Design of Experiments*, 5th edn., pp. 7–9):

Inductive inference is the only process known to us by which essentially new knowledge comes into the world. To make clear the authentic conditions of its validity is the kind of contribution to the intellectual development of mankind which we should expect experimental science would ultimately supply. . . .
It is as well to remember in this connection that the principles and method of even *deductive* reasoning were probably unknown for several thousand years after the establishment of prosperous and cultured civilisations.

THE UNCERTAINTIES OF UNCERTAIN INFERENCE

... The liberation of the human intellect must, however, remain incomplete so long as it is free only to work out the consequences of a prescribed body of dogmatic data, and is denied the access to unsuspected truths, which only direct observation can give. ...

... The chapters which follow are designed to illustrate the principles which are *common to all experimentation*, by means of examples chosen for the simplicity with which these principles are brought out. Next, to exhibit the principal designs which have been found successful in that field of experimentation, namely agriculture, in which questions of design have been most thoroughly studied, and to illustrate their applicability to other fields of work. (*Italics inserted.*)

This passage is instructive more because of what it implies than because of what it explicitly asserts. We get the impression that recourse to statistical methods is prerequisite to the design of experiments of any sort whatever. In that event, the whole creation of experimental scientists from Gilbert and Hooke to J. J. Thomson and Morgan has been groaning and travailing in fruitless pain together; and the biologist of today has nothing to learn from well-tried methods which have led to the spectacular advances of the several branches of experimental science during the last three centuries. Nor is this all. We learn that we shall find the pattern of new and more powerful methods in a procedure for carrying out agricultural field trials prescribed, though Fisher does not say so, by one school of statisticians, and one alone.

What we then naturally ask is whether consequent advances of our knowledge of the soil, if any, have been commensurate with such a claim. In the parallel domain of marine biology, our knowledge of how to reproduce all relevant conditions for the culture of sea creatures has made great strides by recourse to entirely traditional principles of experimentation, while our theoretical knowledge of the growth needs of plants has not conspicuously broadened as the outcome of experiments designed in conformity with the demands of Greco-Latin Squares or randomised blocks. In the latter domain the claim that the theoretical statistician knows better than the man on the job how to do it is one which derives its sanction from a particular theory of statistical inference; and Fisher himself would be first to admit this. If the theory turns out to be false, the result of increasingly widespread use of methods prescribed to design experiments must result both in curbing the ingenuity of the investigator at stupendous cost of time and in deterioration of standards of good workmanship in the laboratory. I believe we can already detect signs of such deterioration in the growing volume of published papers—especially in the domain of animal behaviour—recording so-called significant conclusions which an earlier vintage would have regarded merely as private clues for further exploration. Be that as it may, the fact that such methods are now in general use signifies that it is not merely an academic exercise to clarify the credentials of current views on statistical inference. Least of all is it merely a matter of moment to the trained mathematician at a time when trained mathematicians cannot reach agreement about them among themselves.

Should our adjudication lead us to embrace, with all its as yet half-formulated implications, the viewpoint of the new American school, the consequences will be far more drastic than many of our island contemporaries as yet recognise. In the closing words of his essay *Of the Academical or Sceptical Philosophy* Hume asks: "when we run over libraries persuaded of these principles, what havoc must we make?" Such havoc I suggest that little if anything in the cookery books will remain. We may have to reinstate statistics as continental demographers use the term. Laboratory experiments will have to stand on their own feet without protection from a façade of irrelevant computations. Sociologists will have to use their brains. In my view, science will not suffer.

PART I

The Founding
Fathers

CHAPTER TWO

THE FOUNDING FATHERS AND THE NATURAL HISTORY OF GAMBLING

THE CURRENT DISPOSITION to regard stochastic* considerations as prerequisite to the formulation of scientific laws derives its plausibility from two circumstances: (*a*) contemporary statistical theory embraces diverse domains of discourse into which the calculus of probability has intruded; (*b*) the laboratory worker too lightly assumes that there is general agreement about the relation of the calculus of probability to external events. The relation of the algebraic theory of probability to the real world is indeed more than ever before a topic of keen controversy. It therefore calls for critical re-examination at the outset; and we shall handicap ourselves unduly if we undertake our task on the optimistic assumption that all men of science are logically consistent. At the level of applied theory, we find in one and the same camp representatives of widely divergent views about when and in what sense the theory of probability can help us to interpret experience of the real world in a useful way. The core of the dispute is neither mathematical nor empirical. It is primarily a semantic issue which involves a fundamental dichotomy of attitudes with respect to the nature of valid judgment. As such it concerns us all. Were it not for the fact that most statisticians of middle age had already invested moral and intellectual capital in the Yule–Fisher tradition before existing differences became too acute to overlook, it would be hard to understand how British leaders of statistics, as cited in the last chapter, adroitly maintain an aspect of benevolent and seemingly nonchalant, though one may suspect uneasy, neutrality to the contestants.

Bacon somewhere speaks of man's inveterate habit of dwelling on abstractions. With equal propriety we may deplore a pernicious predilection of many highly intelligent people for *double-talk*. Rapid advances in the sciences of biology and chemistry after the mid-eighteenth century were in no small

* *See* Chapter 5, p. 118.

measure made possible by a deliberate discipline to curb it. With experience of substantial progress during the preceding century behind them, men of science then had an object lesson before their eyes. The substitution of the word *gas* for *spirits* had exorcised a host of unclean superstitions at about the time when mathematics also annexed from common speech a word as redolent as spirits with emotive misconceptions. In seeking a relation between the calculus of *probability* and human action we thus encounter a difficulty which will dog our steps at every ensuing stage of our examination of the history of the topic. The word probability, like *bias, random, population, significance, likelihood, confidence*, and so many other terms in the vocabulary of statistics, carries over from common speech a miasma of irrelevant associations. While there is general agreement about the algebraic rules of the game, there is therefore still much controversy about the relevance of the rules to what we care to call *probability* in so far as the concept is referable to inference or to decision.

"Fundamentally the term probable," says Miss David (*Probability for Statistical Methods*, p. 1), "can only apply to the state of mind of the person who uses the word"; but she goes on to say that "the mathematical theory of probability is concerned, however, with building a bridge . . . between the sharply defined but artificial country of mathematical logic and the nebulous shadowy country of what is often termed the real world." In spite of her Platonic feelings about the real world, the ensuing discussion is essentially behaviouristic and one concludes that *fundamentally* in this context signifies "in everyday life." To a considerable school, however, *fundamentally* would here signify an article of faith which is through and through Platonic. To such, probability is a measure of the *legitimate intensity* of our conviction that a body of evidence justifies certain conclusions. This is the stand which Jeffreys and Carnap take. Kendall follows them when he speaks (Vol. I, p. 164) of the "attitudes of mind to which we relate the concept of probability."

The idealistic doctrine has a symbolism of its own (*vide infra* p. 51). Those who adopt it speak of: (i) the certainty that hypothesis H on data q is true as $P(H/q) = 1$; (ii) the cer-

THE FOUNDING FATHERS AND THE NATURAL HISTORY OF GAMBLING

tainty that it is false on the same basis as $P(H/q) = 0$; (iii) any other "state of mind" as $P(H/q) = p$ such that $0 < p < 1$. If nothing we may infer from q has any bearing on H, proponents of the idealistic doctrine proceed in accordance with the axiom $P(H/q) = \frac{1}{2}$ to build up a cumulative measure of conviction by iterative invocation of ignorance. Such is the *principle of insufficient reason*. To decide how contestants with different states of mind can agree about what particular value of p in a particular situation makes it a *legitimate* measure of our confidence in the truth of the hypothesis, we must either—as do Jeffreys and Carnap—fall back on such supposedly self-evident axioms or reinterpret our definitions in terms of observable occurrences.

If we follow the latter course, we shall speak only of the frequency with which our assertions consistent with a rule of assessing such and such evidence in such and such a way correspond with reality in the long run. It is in such strictly behaviourist terms that the experimentalist will presumably prefer to participate in the discussion of the relevance of the algebraic theory of probability to the real world. A sufficient objection to the alternative is the existence of a very large number of intelligent people, including not a few professional mathematicians, to whom the postulates invoked by the axiomatic school are by no means self-evident. In the commonly accepted sense of both terms, they are indeed amenable to proof or to disproof only if we can translate them into a frequency idiom referable to observable occurrences in contradistinction to inaccessibly individual states of mind.

Happily, we do sometimes have the opportunity to observe mental processes to which a formal calculus of probability conceived in terms of the principle of insufficient reason, or in any other terms divorced from experience, should have a peculiar relevance if we have also good reason for subscribing to the faith of the axiomatic school. Levy and Roth (*Elements of Probability*, p. 14) cite an instructive example of such situations:

If 100 persons each have to choose a number between 0 and 9 inclusive, how often will the numbers 0, 1, 2 . . . be chosen? The abstraction which a mathematician *might* make from this problem

35

would leave him with a purely mathematical question concerning arrangements, the answer to which is, that each of the numbers will "probably" be chosen ten times. But this is not the real question; what we want to know is how people *actually choose*, and here we are faced by considerations of a psychological and social nature. In point of fact it has been found by actual testing of a large number of individuals that 7 and 3 are much more frequently chosen than any other number; these numbers both, of course, have a long historical and religious tradition behind them. As we see from such an example, the question whether the abstraction may be validly applied in a given case is not to be begged. The mathematical problem deals with the number of arrangements that can be conceived as possible in the circumstances, the physical problem with the groups of these which actually come into play. We can develop a mathematical theory of arrangements but a separate justification has to be found for it if it is to have practical applications. Thus, the mathematician may postulate that "an event can happen in two different ways"; whereas the physicist knows that it does happen in one way only.

The last sentence puts the spotlight on the main theme of this chapter. I here propose to deal with three questions in the following order:

(*a*) in what sense did the architects of the algebraic theory of probability themselves conceive it to be relevant to the real world?

(*b*) in what terms did they formulate the rules of the calculus and what latent assumptions about the relevance of the rules to reality do their axioms endorse?

(*c*) to what extent does experience confirm the factual relevance of the rules in the native domain of their application?

Our first question then is: *in what sense did the architects of the algebraic theory of probability themselves conceive it to be relevant to the real world?* This at least is answerable in non-controversial terms. An algebraic calculus of probability takes its origin from a correspondence between Pascal and Fermat over the fortunes and misfortunes of the Chevalier de Méré, a great gambler and by that token *très bon esprit*, but alas (wrote Pascal) *il n'est pas géomètre*. Alas indeed. The Chevalier had made his pile by always betting small favourable odds on getting at least one six in 4 tosses of a die, and had then lost it by always betting small odds on getting at least one double six in 24 double tosses. Thus the problem out of which the calculus took shape was eminently practical, viz. *how to adjust the stakes in a game of chance in accordance with a rule which ensures success if applied consistently regardless of the fortunes of the session.* This is the theme song of the later treatise by James Bernoulli, and the major pre-occupation of all the writers of the classical period, including de Moivre, D. Bernoulli, d'Alembert and Euler.

Thus there is no ambiguity about what the Founding Fathers conceived to be the type specimen of real situations in which a calculus of probability is usefully applicable. Their formal statement of the fundamental operations of such a calculus is essentially identical with what is now current, though different schools of doctrine verbalise the initial assumptions in different terms. The end they had in view is beyond dispute; but the relevance of the assumptions implicit in the solution they offered is still highly debatable. Despite such obscurities not yet resolved by common consent, we may conceivably be satisfied that theory correctly prescribes a regimen of practice consistent with the intentions of writers in the classical period. If so, we may decently refrain from participation in the controversy without relinquishing the right to apply the rules of the calculus in strictly comparable situations. Our concern will then be to assess the claim that any one of the multitudinous applications of the calculus endorsed by the current theory of statistics is truly identifiable as a situation on all fours with the prescription of a reliable rule for division of stakes in a game of chance.

The ideological climate of our time is not propitious to success if we undertake the task with a light heart. Many of us, including the writer, have a puritan distaste for gambling and at best a superficial familiarity with the type of problems Pascal and his immediate successors tackled. At the outset, we should therefore be very clear about what we here mean by a betting rule. Let us accordingly scrutinise a situation analogous to the dilemma of the Chevalier through the eyes of his own generation. Our task will be to state a rule for division of stakes to ensure success to a gambler who bets on the outcome of taking 5 cards *simultaneously* from a well-shuffled pack. We shall assume his bet to be that 3 of the cards will be pictures and that 2 will be aces. Without comment on the rationale of the rule, we shall first illustrate what the operations of the calculus are, and then how we prescribe the rule deemed to be consistent with the outcome. If we approach our problem in the mood of the Founding Fathers of the algebraic theory, we shall reason intuitively as follows.

In a full deck of 52 there are $52^{(5)}$ ways* in which the disposition of the cards *may* occur, this being the number of linear permutations of 52 objects taken 5 at a time without replacement. Out of these $52^{(5)} = 311,853,201$ ways in which the cards might occur, the number of ways in which the disposition is consistent with the bet is $5_{(2)} \cdot 4^{(2)} \cdot 12^{(3)} = 158,400$, this being (*vide infra*, p. 41) the number of recognisably different linear permutations of 5 things taken from 52 when: (*a*) we regard 4 of the 52 as identical members of class Q and 12 as identical members of class P; (*b*) the sample consists of 2 members of Q and 3 members of P. Without here pausing to examine the relation between such usage and what probability signifies in everyday speech, we shall now arbitrarily define the *algebraic* probability of a *success*, i.e. of the specified 5-fold choice, and hence of the truth of the assertion the gambler proposes to make, in the classical manner, that is to say, the ratio $5_{(2)} \cdot 4^{(2)} \cdot 12^{(3)} \div 52^{(5)} = 1 : 1,969$.

To get the terms of reference of the operations of the calculus vividly into focus in its initial domain of practice before making them more explicit, we may then postulate fictitiously that *exactly* one in every 1,969 games justifies the gambler's assertion. In this fictitious set-up, we shall suppose that:

(*a*) the gambler A bets that the result will be a success and agrees to pay on each occasion if wrong a penalty of £x to his opponent B;

(*b*) his opponent likewise bets that the result will be a failure and agrees to pay to A a penalty of £y if wrong;

(*c*) each gambler adheres to his system throughout a sequence of 1,969 withdrawals.

* Here, as elsewhere, I adopt Aitken's economical symbolism: $r_{(x)} = r! \div x! \, (r-x)!$ The symbol $r^{(x)}$ has the usual meaning, i.e. $r^{(x)} = r! \div (r-x)!$

If $x = 1$ and $y = 1,968$, A will part with £1 on 1,968 occasions or £1,968 in all and B will part with £1,968 on only one occasion. Thus neither will lose or gain in any completed 1,969-fold sequence. If $x = 1 \cdot 05$, so that A parts with a guinea whenever wrong and $y = 1,968$ as before, A will part with £2,066 8s. od. in a complete 1,969-fold sequence and B will gain £98 8s. od. at his expense. If $x = 1$ but $y = 2,000$, A will gain £32 in each such sequence and B will lose that amount. On the foregoing assumption, therefore, A will always gain if two conditions hold good:

(i) A consistently follows the rule of asserting that the result of a 5-fold withdrawal will be a success;

(ii) B agrees to pay a forfeit somewhat greater than £1,968 when A is right, on the understanding that A agrees to pay a forfeit of £1 if wrong.

Needless to say, the Founding Fathers did *not* postulate that the gambler A would score exactly one success in every 1,969-fold sequence. What they did claim is that the ratio of success to failure, i.e. of true to false assertion, would be 1 : 1,968, if he went on making the same bet consistently in a sufficiently extended succession of games. Such then are the odds in favour of success in the idiom of the game. In so far as the classical formulation has any bearing on a calculus of truth and falsehood, it thus refers to the long-run frequency of correct assertion in conformity with a rule *stated in advance*. We are then *looking forwards*. Nothing we observe on any single occasion entitles us to deviate from adherence to it. Nothing we claim for the usefulness of the calculus confers a numerical valuation on a *retrospective judgment* referable to information derived from observing the outcome of a particular game.

In stating the foregoing rule and its application, we have identified the long-run ratio of the number of successes which *will* occur to the number of failures which *will* also occur with the ratio of the number of different ways in which success *may* occur to the number of different ways in which failure *may* occur. The italicised auxiliaries suffice to show that this calls for justification; but the proponents of the classical theory seem to have been quite satisfied to embrace the identification as a self-evident principle. Even so, we shall see that it does not suffice to prescribe the circumstances in which the calculus actually specifies long-term experience of situations to which they applied it, or even to prescribe any class of situations to which the rule might conceivably be relevant. This will emerge more clearly if we now formulate the definition of the concept and the rules it endorses more explicitly.

We thus come to the second question we have set ourselves to answer: *in what terms did the Founding Fathers formulate the rules of the calculus and what latent assumptions about the relevance of the rules to reality do the axioms condone?* To do justice to this, we shall first need to distinguish between two ways in which we may choose 5 cards: (*a*) *exhaustively*, i.e. simultaneously or successively without replacement of any one of the 5 cards chosen before picking its successor; (*b*) *repetitively*, i.e. picking the cards successively and *replacing* each card after recording its denomination before picking a successor, or cutting successively and recording each time the bottom card exposed before reassembling the pack.

If we now speak provisionally of our card pack in more general terms as the *universe of choice*, we may formally state as follows a comprehensive algebraic definition of probability consistent with the classical approach in the discrete domain of the game of chance:

If x_j or $x_{(j)}$ denote the number of different linear permutations of r items from an n-fold universe consistent with the specification of the way of choosing a sample of class J and $x_{r.n}$ or $x_{(r.n)}$ is the corresponding number of all different linear r-fold permutations from the same n-fold universe in conformity with the *same rule of exclusion*, the probability of observing the specified sample class is the ratio of $x_j : x_{r.n}$ or $x_{(j)} : x_{(r.n)}$.

The insertion of the words italicised leaves open the alternative prescription of sampling exhaustively (i.e. *without* replacement) or repetitively (i.e. *with* replacement as defined); and the use of the brackets in $x_{(j)}$ and $x_{(r.n)}$ signifies that sampling occurs without replacement. Such a definition subsumes all the elementary rules of the calculus of probability in what Macmahon calls the *Master Theorem* of permutations. This is as follows. If an n-fold universe is exhaustively and exclusively classifiable as a items of class A, b of class B, c of class C, etc., the number of r-fold linear permutations containing u items of class A, v of class B, w of class C, etc., is:

with replacement:

$$x_j = \frac{r!}{u!\,v!\,w!\,\dots}\,a^u \cdot b^v \cdot c^w. \qquad \dots \quad \text{(i)}$$

without replacement:

$$x_{(j)} = \frac{r!}{u!\,v!\,w!\,\dots}\,a^{(u)} \cdot b^{(v)} \cdot c^{(w)} \quad \dots \quad \text{(ii)}$$

The alternative assumptions w.r.t. the rule of exclusion respectively prescribe $x_{r.n} = n^r$ and $x_{(r.n)} = n^{(r)}$, whence the appropriate probabilities referable to the r-fold sample of type J defined as such by $a, b, c, \dots u, v, w$, etc., are:

with replacement:

$$P_j = \frac{r!}{u!\,v!\,w!\,\dots}\,\left(\frac{a}{n}\right)^u \left(\frac{b}{n}\right)^v \left(\frac{c}{n}\right)^w \quad \dots \quad \text{(iii)}$$

without replacement:

$$P_{(j)} = \frac{r!}{u!\,v!\,w!\,\dots}\,\frac{a^{(u)}\,b^{(v)}\,c^{(w)}\,\dots}{n^{(r)}} \quad \dots \quad \text{(iv)}$$

These expressions respectively correspond to the general term of the multinomial theorem in its customary form and in the form of which Vandermonde's theorem is a special case. Each defines the distribution law appropriate to the type of sampling specified, and each subsumes the two fundamental laws of the calculus. It will suffice to state the latter in the simplest form as below, i.e. for two score values, whence the more general statement follows by iteration:

The Multiplicative Property. If p_b is the unconditional probability of first recording a score b and $p_{c.b}$ is the conditional probability of then recording a score c, the joint probability of recording both b and c in that order is $p_{bc} = p_b.p_{c.b}$.

The Additive Property. If b and c are among possible score values, only one of which one may record on any one occasion, the

*

probability that the score will be either b or c on such an occasion is $P(\text{b } or \text{ c}) = p_b + p_c$.

A single illustration will suffice to show that (iii) and (iv) do indeed subsume both rules. The probability of the compound choice J specified as the extraction of 2 spades and 1 red card in a 3-fold exhaustive (with removal) trial is $3_{(2)} \cdot 13^{(2)} \cdot 26^{(1)} \div 52^{(3)}$. This is also the probability of getting any one of the sequences S S R, S R S or R S S, and we may write in the foregoing notation:

$$\frac{3_{(2)} \cdot 13^{(2)} \cdot 26^{(1)}}{52^{(3)}} = \frac{13}{52} \cdot \frac{12}{51} \cdot \frac{26}{50} + \frac{13}{52} \cdot \frac{26}{51} \cdot \frac{12}{50} + \frac{26}{52} \cdot \frac{13}{51} \cdot \frac{12}{50}$$

$$= p_s \cdot p_{s.s} \cdot p_{r.ss} + p_s \cdot p_{r.s} \cdot p_{s.sr} + p_r \cdot p_{s.r} \cdot p_{s.rs}$$

$$= p_{ss} \cdot p_{r.ss} + p_{sr} \cdot p_{s.sr} + p_{rs} \cdot p_{s.rs}$$

When sampling is repetitive (with replacement or without removal), $p_{s.s} = p_s = p_{s.ss}$, etc., and the foregoing reduces to

$$3_{(2)} \cdot \left(\frac{13}{52}\right)^2 \left(\frac{26}{52}\right) = p_s^2 \cdot p_r + p_s \cdot p_r \cdot p_s + p_r \cdot p_s^2 = 3p_s^2 \cdot p_r$$

To exhibit these expressions as terms of the appropriate multinomial, we recall that spades and reds together with clubs constitute an exclusive system, as follows:

Spades	Red	Clubs	Total
13	26	13	$n = 52$
2	1	0	$r = 3$

In full, since $13^0 = 1 = 13^{(0)}$ and $0! = 1$:

$$3_{(2)} \cdot \frac{13^{(2)} \cdot 26^{(1)}}{52^{(3)}} = \frac{3!}{2! \, 1! \, 0!} \cdot \frac{13^{(2)} \cdot 26^{(1)} \cdot 13^{(0)}}{52^{(3)}}$$

$$3_{(2)} \cdot \left(\frac{13}{52}\right)^2 \cdot \frac{26}{52} = \frac{3!}{2! \, 1! \, 0!} \left(\frac{13}{52}\right)^2 \left(\frac{26}{52}\right)^1 \left(\frac{13}{52}\right)^0$$

These are respectively the appropriate terms of:

$$(13 + 26 + 13)^{(3)} \div 52^{(3)}$$

and

$$\left(\tfrac{1}{4} + \tfrac{1}{2} + \tfrac{1}{4}\right)^3 = (13 + 26 + 13)^3 \div 52^3$$

Actually, (iii) and (iv) subsume the rules of the calculus in a more comprehensive way than any formulation of the classical period, here defined as that which antedates the writings of Laplace; but the idiom of choice in the foregoing definition is wholly consistent with the usage of the Founding Fathers. The terms used call for careful scrutiny, if we wish to be clear about their relevance to the frequency of success in games of chance. At the outset, we have identified *all possible ways* of choosing 5 cards specified in a particular way with all *linear permutations* consistent with the specification, i.e. referable to a particular combination. This identification of our unit of choice with a single linear arrangement will prove to be highly suggestive, when we later explore circumstances in which our formal definition is itself identifiable as a frequency ratio; but a blunder of D'Alembert in his article on probability in the first edition of the *Encyclopédie* reminds us how liberally writers of the classical period relied on their own intuitions to assign to the combination and to its constituent permutations their agreed role in the theory.

*   *   *   *

In the classical context of the gaming table, the factual application of the rules of the calculus presupposes the existence of: (*a*) an *agent*, the player and/or dealer; (*b*) an *apparatus*, card pack, die or lottery; (*c*) a *programme of instructions*; (*d*) a wager, i.e. an unchangeable *assertion* of the outcome of each trial. If the apparatus is a card pack or lottery urn, the programme of instruction will include a specification of the act of choice in the most literal sense of the term. One difficulty which confronts a confident evaluation of the viewpoint of the Founding Fathers arises from the circumstance that verbal specification of different methods of choice in textbook expositions of combinations and permutations leaves much to the imagination of the reader. Before trying to get to grips with a theory of chance which relies on a calculus of choice, it may therefore be profitable to sharpen the outline of situations in which expressions for the enumeration of all possible acts of choice consistent with a particular prescription are also in fact consistent with the range of realisable possibilities. The reader who regards the undertaking as trivial may skip what precedes the next row of asterisks.

At this stage, we shall refrain from asking whether such considerations have any bearing on how *often* the gambler actually chooses a sample of one or other class specified as a particular combination in this context. The word *actually* as used by Levy and Roth in the passage cited above has indeed other implications worthy of notice as a qualifier of the verb which follows it. For specification of the particular *unit of choice* in our foregoing definition imposes unstated factual restrictions on any conceivable relevance of probability so defined to what we may literally or metaphorically mean by choice in successive games of chance. We may usefully examine such restrictions in this context because it is easy to overlook them when theory invokes the sanction of the classical doctrine to identify the hypothetical infinite population of Laplace with what we here refer to provisionally, and somewhat ambiguously, as the universe of choice. The meaning we can rightly assign to our universe of choice, and the sense in which we can usefully conceive it as finite or otherwise, depends on the system of choice we prescribe.

In the formal calculus of choice we mean by all linear permutations of 5 cards of a particular specification all the different ways in which we can lay them out face upwards in a line, if free to do anything we like with a single pack or with a sufficient number of identical packs but with due regard to the explicit alternative conditions customarily distinguished as *with* and *without* replacement. Choice *without* replacement then merely means that no card of a particular denomination may be present more than once in one and the same sequence. Choice with replacement signifies that cards of one and the same denomination may occur any number of times from o to r inclusive in one and the same r-fold sequence. Though this broad distinction between sampling without and sampling with replacement suffices to specify appropriately all possible ways of choosing our cards when we are free to handle the packs face upwards, it emphatically does not suffice to specify appropriately all possible ways of doing so when we are choosing cards face downwards from one or even from an

44

indefinitely large number of identical packs. We then have to prescribe factual safeguards which the foregoing definition of *algebraic* probability does not make explicit.

Whether or no our definition has any justifiable relevance to the frequency of success in games of chance, it certainly cannot claim to have any relevance to a succession of games in which the possibilities it specifies are *not* realisable. Clearly, therefore, some safeguards must be explicit if our calculus is to describe what the gambler *actually* chooses. If we specify all different linear permutations of cards in a pack or sample sequences consistent with the criterion of success as information relevant to long-term experience of sampling in conformity with the prescription of such a game, we imply the actuality of making their acquaintance if we go on playing the same game long enough. That this need not be so, unless we prescribe the rules appropriately, will be sufficiently evident if we distinguish as follows between two different ways of actually choosing blindfold *without* replacement:

(i) we take each card of the *r*-fold pack without restriction from any part of the pack;

(ii) we extract them simultaneously, i.e. we pick out *with one hand* an *r*-fold sequence of cards lying consecutively in the deck *held by the other*.

If we adopt the latter procedure, there will be only (*n-r* + 1) ways of selecting an *r*-fold sample from one and the same finite *n*-fold universe identified as such with any particular pack. Thus there will be 48 different ways of choosing 5 cards, and none of these will include 2 aces and 3 pictures if we pick the 5 from the middle of a pack with all aces at the bottom of the deck or all the pictures at the top. If we always use a new pack stacked in the same way, we shall therefore never meet more than 48 different 5-fold sequences. We can hope eventually to meet all the possible ways implicit in our initial algebraic definition of probability only if we *shuffle* the same pack before each game or use different packs stacked in every possible order. Either way, what we have here provisionally called *the* universe of choice changes from sample to sample, and the definite article is justifiable only in so far as the composition of any full pack specifies all the *numerical* information relevant to our definition.

If we adopt the alternative stated above, we are free to choose each card of the r-fold sample from any part of the pack. On the assumption that we fully exploit this freedom to choose each card from *any* part of the pack, we may eventually hope to meet all possible $n^{(r)}$ different r-fold samples of exhaustive choice and all $x_{(j)}$ different r-fold samples of the particular class J in successive r-fold withdrawals from n-fold card packs stacked in exactly the same way and hence identical in all respects. None the less, we cannot speak with propriety of sampling without replacement from *a* finite universe with the implication that we are talking about one and the same card pack throughout. Neither sampling successively without replacement nor sampling simultaneously is consistent with the identification of the universe of choice with a single particular card pack.

When we speak of choosing cards from a pack, we do not necessarily imply that we remove them. If the cards lie face downwards, choosing *with replacement* subsumes any method of choice which leaves us free to record any card of a particular denomination from o to r times. For instance, we may cut the pack and turn the top set face upwards. The presumption then is that we might equally well entrust the task to a dealer. Thus we need not interpret the term choice in the most literal way. To say that we may choose 52^5 different sequences of 5 cards if allowed to record the result of cutting 5 times anywhere or of picking out 5 cards in succession, replacing each one except the last before taking the next, merely states that there are 52^5 different ways in which *anyone* may arrange 5 cards, face upwards in a row, if free to take one card from *any* part of 5 identical full packs, and hence 52^5 distinguishable hands which we might receive from the dealer who picked out a single card from *any* position in each deck of cards. On the other hand, there would be only one possible way of dealing the 5 cards singly from the 5 packs, if the dealer took each card from the top or from any preassigned level in the deck in an assigned order. If we therefore assert that all possible ways of *choosing* with replacement 5 cards from a full pack correspond to all possible ways of *dealing* one card from each of 5 packs, we implicitly impose some plan of action on the dealer.

More than one such plan is consistent with the same formal statement of the choice. This will be clear if we think of 6 packs each consisting of the ace, 2, 3, 4, 5 and 6 of spades. If we score a sequence by adding up the number of pips on the constituent cards and distinguish a class of 3 selections by the fact that the score is 5, the class itself subsumes 6 different sequences:

$$113, 131, 311 \; ; \; 122, 212, 221$$

In the same set-up all possible 3-fold sequences that we may distinguish are $6^3 = 216$. If we speak accordingly of $6 \div 6^3 = \frac{1}{36}$ as the *probability* of scoring 5 in sampling with replacement from the 6-fold pack, the classical prescription embraces several factually different situations:

(i) the player or the dealer removes 3 cards singly in succession from *anywhere* in the same pack and replaces each card *anywhere* after recording the scores before drawing another;

(ii) the player or the dealer cuts 3 times the same pack *anywhere* replacing the cards in their original position after recording the exposed card;

(iii) the player or dealer cuts *anywhere* each of 3 identical packs recording each result and replacing the cards in their original order;

(iv) the player or dealer removes a single card from *anywhere* in each of 3 packs, recording the result and replacing each card *anywhere* in its own pack.

Inasmuch as we have defined probability with reference to all possible sequences we may encounter, the word *anywhere* in this context has therefore a special meaning. It endorses the possibility that we may eventually meet all possible sequences, the implication being that we follow no set plan w.r.t. the level from which we take a card, the level at which we replace it, or the level at which we cut the pack, in a sufficiently protracted succession of games. It is irrelevant to make this explicit if we alternatively prescribe:

(*a*) a *reshuffle* of the pack of (i) or (ii) between taking from it an individual card and replacing it;

(*b*) a reshuffle of each of the 3 packs in (iii) and (iv) between successive games.

What we thus mean by choice with replacement in the face-upward setting of the algebra of permutations and combinations embraces a diversity of factual situations in which all possible ways of actually choosing a particular hand in a game of chance will not necessarily correspond to all possible ways prescribed by a formal calculus of choice, unless our programme of instructions prescribes how we actually choose them. How *often* we actually choose them is another matter which will be the theme of Chapter 3. Nothing we have said so far suffices to justify the conviction that the ratio of all different ways of scoring a factually realisable success to all different methods of scoring either a success or a failure on the same assumption will be the same as the ratio of actual successes to successes and failures in a long enough sequence of games.

On this understanding, we are free to extend our definition to games of chance other than card games. By putting the dealer into the picture, we have absolved ourselves from the need to interpret the term choice in its most usual sense. The score the player records when the dealer, as the *agent*, cuts the pack is in no sense more literally an act of choice than the score the player records when the cubical die comes to rest on the floor. The specification of all different ways in which a cubical die may lie uppermost in a 3-fold toss and all different ways in which we may score 5 in a 3-fold toss is thus formally identical with the foregoing specification for the deck of six spades, if we also postulate that each face will at some time lie uppermost in a sufficiently prolonged succession of tosses; but we have not absolved ourselves from the need to make explicit the circumstances in which we can confidently assert that it will do so, except in so far as we assume that the act of tossing is comparable to cutting *anywhere*. We can then speak of the die as an unchanging finite universe of choice in the sense that the pack from which we cut *anywhere* is an unchanging (finite) universe of choice if the dealer restores the deck to its original arrangement after recording the cut; but we have still to satisfy ourselves that the dealer's utmost efforts will suffice to justify the rule for the division of the stakes. We shall later see that the manufacturer of the die must share some of the responsibility with the dealer.

*   *   *   *

The foregoing digression to clarify the factual content of the term *choice* in the context of the game of chance will not have been fruitless, if it forces us to recognise that an alternative formulation of the basic concept, now more fashionable than the foregoing, itself discloses no explicit indications of circumstances which endorse the factual relevance of the rules of the calculus to the prescription of a reliable betting rule, still less to the wider terrain of situations annexed by contemporary statistical theory. The restatement of the classical doctrine in the symbolism of the modern theory of sets is indeed merely a refinement of the classical notation. It owes its appeal to the mathematician because the theory of sets can accommodate points as well as discrete objects and hence annexes the continuum as its legitimate territory.

In the discrete domain of the game of chance, we think of a *set* S as a collection of $n(S)$ items with an attribute A_s which each of its members possesses, and say that an object O is in S if it has the attribute A_s. An object may be in more than one set, and we say that it is in the set PQ of $n(PQ)$ items if it has A_p and A_q. We say that it is in the set $(Q + P) = (P + Q)$ if it has A_q without A_p, A_p without A_q or A_p with A_q, i.e. is in the set made up of the sets P and Q alone, whence $n(P + Q) = n(P) + n(Q) - n(PQ)$. If all members of P are members of S, we speak of P as a subset of S, and of S as the *universal set* if it includes every other set in the field of discourse as a subset. Thus the set H of all hearts is a subset of the universal set F of the full pack, as is also the subset E of all cards with an even number of pips. The set HE = EH of all hearts with an even number of pips is a subset of the set $(E + H)$ which includes all hearts, all cards (including hearts) with an even number of pips and no others, and the set $(E + H)$ is itself a subset of F. Thus $n(F) = 52$, $n(E) = 20$, $n(H) = 13$, $n(EH) = 5$, $n(E + H) = 13 + 15 = 28 = n(E) + n(H) - n(EH)$. Those

49

who use the set theory symbolism define the probability that O in the set M has A_q as

$$P(Q/M) = n(MQ) \div n(M).$$

Whence we get for O in F interpreted as above

$$P(\overline{E + H}/F) = P(E/F) + P(H/F) - P(HE/F) \qquad \text{(v)}$$

$$P(HE/E) \cdot P(E/F) = P(HE/F) = P(HE/H) \cdot P(H/F) \qquad \text{(vi)}$$

The above are the two fundamental theorems of addition and multiplication each in its most general form for 2 criteria of classification of the event. They are easily adaptable to accommodate more than 2 criteria by simple iteration. Thus the reader should be able to derive:

$$P(\overline{A + B + C}/S) = P(A/S) + P(B/S) + P(C/S)$$
$$- P(AB/S) - P(AC/S) - P(BC/S) + P(ABC/S)$$

In this idiom, we say that two sets H and K are *exclusive* if no object is in both, so that $n(HK) = O$ and $P(\overline{H + K}/F) = P(H/F) + P(K/F)$. Thus if K is the set of black aces, $n(K) = 2$, $n(H + K) = 15$, $n(HK) = O$ and $P(H + K/F) = 15/52$. We say that two subsets H and K of F are *independent* if $n(HK) \div n(K) = n(H) \div n(F)$ and $n(HK) \div n(H) = n(K) \div n(F)$. Thus if $K = E$, so that $n(KH) = 5$, $n(H) = 13$, $n(E) = 20$ and $n(F) = 52$, we have $P(HE/F) = P(H/F) \cdot P(E/F)$. In this more restricted form, the rule of addition is implicit in (iii) and (iv) above.

In the foregoing example, we have defined an object illustratively as a single card from the full pack which is the universal set, called also the *fundamental probability set* (F.P.S.). Thus O is a unit sample and F is the universe of choice. The fundamental rules of the calculus embodied in (v) and (vi) still hold good if we define an object as an r-fold sample for $r > 1$, and the F.P.S. as the set of all different r-fold samples distinguishable in terms of the relevant criteria of classification applicable to each constituent event and the sequence of events so distinguished. We thus get back to the classical definition in terms of linear permutations. All we have achieved is that we have made the addition rule in its most general form explicit at the outset with a formal endorsement to extend the terms of reference of the calculus into the continuum.

The explicitly idealistic symbolism mentioned above (p. 34) is an adaptation of the foregoing. Those who use it, define the assertion O in Q is $also$ in M, i.e. O with the attribute A_q has also the attribute A_m, as the hypothesis H_m on data q. They then write $P(M/Q) = P(H_m/q)$. In either domain of symbolism we assign the probability $\frac{1}{2}$ to heads in single tosses of a penny because $n(M) = \frac{1}{2}n(Q)$ if A_q characterises the set of all properly minted pennies after a toss and A_m the set of all pennies which *supposedly* lie heads uppermost. When they assign this value some proponents of the set-theory definition, e.g. Neyman, seemingly do so (*vide infra p.* 55) on the understanding that the identity stated suffices to endorse a *prospective* rule about betting on the outcome of a long sequence of tosses; but those who use the $H ./ q$ symbolism make no such prospective claim.

As I understand it, their convention extends to the following situation. A normal penny lies under the mat. Before lifting the mat I know nothing about the penny other than that it has 2 faces, i.e. $n(F) = 2$, one only classified as a tail, i.e. $n(TF) = 1$. Since $n(TF) = \frac{1}{2}n(F)$, on these data "q" we assign to the hypothesis H, viz. to the value of the *retrospective* verdict that the unseen penny lies tail uppermost, the probability $P(H_t/q) = \frac{1}{2}$; but what we mean by probability in this setting is equally consistent with the assertion that the penny fell on its face after a spin or that someone placed it tails up before placing the mat on top of it. If we therefore try to translate our symbols into the public idiom of frequency, we merely get back to admission of ignorance. It may well be that I here misinterpret what Jeffreys or Carnap conceive as the proper interpretation of this $H . q$ notation. If so, I must plead that the numerical assessment of states of ignorance about numismatic data at the level of individual judgment conveys nothing intelligible to me.

It will now be clear that the set-theory restatement of the calculus embraces exactly the same set of operations as the classical statement, as does also the explicitly idealistic interpretation of the initial concepts in the restatement of Jeffreys or Carnap. Different conventions of symbolism are current and different interpretations of the symbols at the verbal level endorse different types of statement about their conceivable relevance to practical affairs. What we mean by the *operations* of a calculus of probability thus admits no difference of opinion; but we are as yet no nearer to understanding the factual relevance of the rules to the class of situations in which the Founding Fathers invoked them. No algebraic definition of probability so far stated in terms of what *may* occur or of what *has* occurred endorses an indisputable warrant for a rule of conduct conceived in terms of how *often* it *will* occur.

The reader may therefore forgivably feel that an answer to our third question is overdue: *to what extent does experience endorse the factual relevance of the rules in the original domain of their application?* Let us admit that few of us seriously doubt the reality of some factual basis for the faith of the Founding Fathers, and the relevance of their faith to the fate and fortunes of the Chevalier. A few investigations recorded in more recent times will indeed encourage us still to explore hopefully the credentials of a doctrine with so little ostensible relevance to its applications at the most elementary level. All we shall ask of the theory at this stage is that it *works*, if the gambler goes on *long* enough. We here interpret this to mean that:

(*a*) over 1,000 is a *large enough* number of games in the context;

(*b*) as a criterion of what *works*, we shall be satisfied with a correspondence between theory and observation if it conforms to the familiar standard set by the tabular content of any current textbook of physical chemistry.

Karl Pearson (*Biometrika* 16) cites the following counts for 3,400 hands (of 13 cards) at whist with corresponding probabilities calculated in accordance with the distribution defined by the terms of $(13 + 39)^{(13)} \div 52^{(13)}$:

No. of Trumps per hand	No. of hands observed	No. of hands expected
under 3	1,021	1,016
3-4	1,788	1,785
over 4	591	599

Uspensky (*Introduction to Mathematical Probability*) records two experiments of this type. The first records 7 experiments each based on 1,000 games in which the score is a success if a card of each suit occurs in a 4-fold simultaneous withdrawal from a pack without picture cards. The probability of success is thus:

$$\frac{4!}{1!\,1!\,1!\,1!} \cdot \frac{10^{(1)}\,10^{(1)}\,10^{(1)}\,10^{(1)}}{40^{(4)}} = 0\cdot1094$$

The outcome for the seven successive 1,000-fold trials (I-VII) was as follows:

I	II	III	IV	V	VI	VII
0·113	0·113	0·103	0·105	0·105	0·118	0·108

A second experiment subsumes 1,000 games in which the score for the 5-fold withdrawal from a full pack is the number of different denominations cited below with the corresponding theoretical and observed proportions correct to 3 places:

	1+1+1+1+1	2+1+1+1	2+2+1
Observed	0·503	0·436	0·045
Expected	0·507	0·423	0·048

	3+1+1	3+2	4+1
Observed	0·014	0·002	0·000
Expected	0·021	0·001	0·000

Many experiments purporting to vindicate the calculus merely show that the mean proportion of successes in large trials lies close to what the classical writers would call the proportion of favourable cases, viz. 0·5, if we score each head as a success in a long sequence of coin tosses. Good agreement then merely shows that assumptions consistent with a naïve adherence to the set theory definition of the probability of success in a *single* trial are acceptable. For reasons discussed below (p. 62), they do not necessarily vindicate the claim of the calculus to prescribe the long run frequency of the *r*-fold trial for values of *r* other than unity.

In the domain of die models, results obtained from experiments on the *needle problem* of the eighteenth-century French naturalist Buffon are both relevant and arresting. The gamester drops a needle of length *l* on a flat surface ruled with parallel lines at a distance (h) apart, scoring a success if it falls across and a failure if it falls between them. Theory prescribes that the ratio of success to failure involves π, the probability of success being $2l/h\pi$. If we equate this to the proportionate frequency of success, we may thus be able to give a more or less satisfactory evaluation for π, and its correspondence with the known value will then be a criterion of the adequacy of the calculus. Uspensky (*loc. cit.*) cites two such:

Investigator	No. of throws	Estimate of π	Error
Wolf 1849–53	5,000	3·1596	<0·019
Smith 1855	3,204	3·1412–3·155	<0·015

The alternative figures in the second line of the table take doubtful intersections into account. In 1901, an Italian mathematician (cited by Kasner and Newman, *Mathematics and the Imagination*) carried out an experiment involving 3,408 tosses of the needle. Lazzerini obtained the value $\pi \simeq 3\cdot 1415929$, an error of only 0·0000003.

The theory of this experiment need not concern us here; but the nature of the game calls for comment because the model set-up is seemingly more comparable to that of the Chevalier's die than are some situations cited above. In the context elsewhere cited Uspensky refers to records of Bancroft Brown on experience of American dice in the game of *craps*. The caster wins if he scores a *natural* (7 or 11) at the initial double toss, loses if he scores *craps* (2, 3 or 12) and otherwise has the right to toss his two dice till the score is the same on 2 successive occasions, in which event he wins, or till the score for the double toss is 7, in which event he loses. Correct to 3 places, the probability of winning is 0·493 and of scoring craps is 0·111. In 9,900 games recorded by Brown the corresponding frequencies were 0·492 and 0·106.

This is admittedly impressive. None the less, much more prolonged trials summarised by Keynes (*vide infra*) have dispelled the belief that a calculus conceived in the foregoing terms is consistent with any reasonable expectation of an equally spectacular correspondence between theory and the behaviour of European dice in commercial production at an earlier date. Admittedly, the discrepancies are not formidable in terms of a division of stakes congenial to the gaming companions of *de Meré* in their cups; but we may dismiss the objection that they are attributable to lack of perseverance. Unless we equate the word *ordinary* to twentieth-century American, Neyman has therefore chosen a singularly unsatisfactory exhibit to vindicate the adequacy of the set theory formulation, when he declares in his recent *Introduction to Probability and Statistics* (p. 16):

An ordinary die has six sides. Hence the F.P.S. is composed of $n(A) = 6$ elements. Only one of the sides has six dots on it. Hence $n(AB) = 1$. Hence $P_1 \ldots = \frac{1}{6}$.

A customary rejoinder to objections of this sort is that the definition refers to an *unbiased* die; but this is merely abuse of the plaintiff's counsel if it carries with it no specification of how to construct a die which has no bias, i.e. one which does in fact conform to the rules of the calculus. In Neyman's system the F.P.S. of the penny has 2 elements, and the probability of scoring r heads in an r-fold toss is $\frac{1}{2}$. If it happens that 10,000 tosses yield a head score of 4,800, we might plausibly guess that our penny will subsequently behave in close accord with the long-run outcome of cutting cards from a 100-fold pack of which 48 were red and 52 black; but we should need experience of an endless series of trials to specify precisely the F.P.S. of our second-order model in the appropriate way. We are thus no nearer to our goal, i.e. how to prescribe the factual conditions relevant to the validity of a rule we have already undertaken to state *in advance*.

In a comprehensive survey of factual investigations into what actually happens in games of chance, Keynes draws attention to the delusion that the outcome has a special relevance to J. Bernoulli's *deductive* theorem (p. 86) of large numbers. All they can in fact do is to reinforce confidence in the empirical principle of statistical equilibrium in large-scale trials and exhibit how far the classical statement of the theory suffices to state in advance a reliable rule for large-scale operations. "We can seldom be certain," writes Keynes, "that the conditions assumed in Bernoulli's Theorem are fulfilled . . . the theorem predicts not what will happen but only what is, on certain evidence, likely to happen. Thus even where our results do not verify Bernoulli's Theorem, the theorem is not thereby discredited." Keynes thus describes the outcome of experiments on die models.

The earliest recorded experiment was carried out by Buffon, who, assisted by a child tossing a coin into the air, played 2,048 *partis* of the Petersburg game, in which a coin is thrown successively until the *parti* is brought to an end by the appearance of heads. The same experiment was repeated by a young pupil of De Morgan's "for his own satisfaction." In Buffon's trials there were 1,992 tails to 2,048 heads; in Mr. H.'s (De Morgan's pupil) 2,044 tails to 2,048 heads. . . . Following in this same tradition is the experiment of Jevons, who made 2,048 throws of ten coins at a time, recording the proportion of heads at each throw and the proportion of heads altogether. In the whole number of 20,480 single throws, he obtained heads 10,353 times. . . . All these experiments, however, are thrown completely into the shade by the enormously extensive investigations of the Swiss astronomer Wolf, the earliest of which were published in 1850 and the latest in 1893. In his first set of experiments Wolf completed 1,000 sets of tosses with two dice, each set continuing until every one of the 21 possible combinations had occurred at least once. This involved altogether 97,899 tosses, and he then completed a total of 100,000. These *data* enabled him to work out a great number of calculations, of which Czuber quotes the following, namely a proportion of .83533 of unlike pairs, as against the theoretical value .83333, i.e. $\frac{5}{6}$. In his second set of experiments Wolf used two dice, one white and one red (in the first set the dice were indistinguishable), and completed 20,000 tosses. . . . He studied particularly the number of sequences with each die, and the relative frequency of each of the 36 possible combinations of the two dice. The sequences were somewhat fewer than they ought to have been, and the relative frequency of the different combinations very different indeed from what theory would predict. The explanation of this is easily found; for the records of the relative frequency of each face show that the dice must have been very irregular, the six face of the white die, for example, falling 38 per cent more often than the four face of the same die. This, then, is the sole conclusion of these immensely laborious experiments—that Wolf's dice were very ill made. . . . But ten years later Wolf embarked upon one more series of experiments, using *four* distinguishable dice—white, yellow, red, and blue—and tossing this set of four 10,000 times.

Wolf recorded altogether, therefore, in the course of his life 280,000 results of tossing individual dice. It is not clear that Wolf had any well-defined object in view in making these records, which are published in curious conjunction with various astronomical results, and they afford a wonderful example of the pure love of experiment and observation.

Of lotteries Keynes records the following particulars:

Czuber has made calculations based on the lotteries of Prague (2,854 drawings) and Brünn (2,703 drawings) between the years 1754 and 1886, in which the actual results agree very well with theoretical predictions. Fechner employed the lists of the ten State lotteries of Saxony between the years 1843 and 1852. Of a rather more interesting character are Professor Karl Pearson's investigations into the results of Monte Carlo Roulette as recorded in *Le Monaco* in the course of eight weeks . . . on the hypothesis of the equi-probability of all the compartments throughout the investigation, he found that the actually recorded proportions of red and black were not unexpected, but that alternations and long runs were so much in excess that . . . *a priori* odds were at least a thousand millions to one against some of the recorded deviations. Professor Pearson concluded, therefore, that Monte Carlo Roulette is not objectively a game of chance in the sense that the tables on which it is played are absolutely devoid of bias. Here also, as in the case of Wolf's dice, the conclusion is solely relevant, not to the theory or philosophy of chance, but to the material shapes of the tools of the experiment.

*   *   *   *

We may now summarise the outcome of our enquiry at this stage in the following terms:

(i) The practical problem which gave rise to a formal calculus of probability is that of devising a rule for division of stakes in a game of chance with a view to ensuring a net gain in the long run to the gambler who adheres consistently thereto. The rule so conceived is a deduction from the premises assumed in the initial definitions of the concepts the calculus invokes. We can operate it only if we state it in advance, in which event we are *looking forwards*. In the initial formulation of the calculus we therefore have no sanction for *retrospective* judgments.

(ii) In the domain of games of chance, the Founding Fathers relied on their own intuitions to supply the missing link between numerical calculations derived from the algebra of choice and *observable frequencies* implicit in the assumed reliability of any rule conceived in the foregoing terms. The justification for their faith is amenable to empirical enquiry, if we circumscribe the terms of reference of the algebraic calculus in this way. If we invoke it to justify retrospective judgments, we raise a new issue which did not emerge in the context of the classical period, i.e. before Laplace propounded the doctrine of insufficient reason and therewith identified the algebraic concept with the subjective usage of the term probability in daily speech.

(iii) If we locate our definition of probability "in the mind" or define it without reference to external events, we have no firm foothold for asserting any class of factual situations to which the operations of the calculus are relevant. We may none the less formulate the operations of such a calculus with a conceivably useful outcome, if we embrace a responsibility which is the theme of Chapter 3, viz. that of investigating the property or properties common to the class of all situations in which it more or less correctly describes frequencies of observable occurrences in large-scale trials.

CHAPTER THREE

RANDOMNESS AND THE RELEVANCE
OF THE RULE

IN THE FOREGOING CHAPTER we sought an answer to three questions:

(a) To what class of problems did the Founding Fathers of the algebraic theory of probability conceive it to be relevant?

(b) In what terms did they formulate the rules of the calculus and with what relevance to the end in view?

(c) To what extent does experience of games of chance endorse their expectations?

We may summarise the outcome of our enquiry as follows:

(i) the end in view is consistent with the terms of reference of the calculus, if, and only if, the definition of algebraic probability is factually identifiable with the long run *frequency* of the gambler's score;

(ii) the concord of experience and theory vindicates the intuitions of the Founding Fathers that this is so in some situations, but not conspicuously in others;

(iii) their explicit formulation of the theory fails to exhibit what characteristics of a situation endorse it as a more or less reliable code of conduct.

Our next task must therefore be to ask how to recognise such situations when we meet them. Here again we shall have reason to deplore how assuredly the clarification of statistical theory has been bogged down from the start by the emotive force of a vocabulary recruited from common speech. Otherwise, it would be difficult to explain the invocation of *bias* as an absolution for the failure of the theory to prescribe a reliable rule for division of stakes when experience does indeed discredit its claims; but the popularity of this verbal device does not belong to the classical milieu. Long after Laplace had given the algebraic theory a new orientation, writers on the algebraic theory of probability accepted the factual credentials of the calculus at face value; and the experiments referred to in the preceding chapter belong to a period long after that of Laplace himself.

This hiatus between theory and practice provoked little concern till the mid-nineteenth century. Maybe, the invocation of bias to accommodate fact and fancy had already begun to provoke misgivings about the adequacy of the classical formulation; but the gambler had by then retired from the stage. While claiming new factual territories for occupation, writers on the mathematical theory of probability continued to rely on their intuitions about its relevance to the real world till Quetelet's programme (p. 18) of imperial stochastic expansion claimed the sanction of the empirical Law of the Constancy of Great Numbers, and thereby forced the inadequacies of the classical definition into the open. An intuitive formal approach in terms of the calculus of choice then made way for an ostensibly empirical definition of probability widely adopted after the publication of Venn's *Logic of Chance*, and more appropriate than the classical statement to the new use of the calculus by Maxwell. An earlier explicit formulation occurs in two contributions of Lewis Ellis, more especially "Remarks on the Fundamental Principles of the Theory of Probabilities" (*Trans. Camb. Phil. Soc.*, 1854). Keynes (*Treatise on Probability*) cites the last-named author's views as follows: "if the probability of an event be correctly determined the event will on a long series of trials tend to recur with frequency proportional to its probability."

If we are to approach the present crisis in statistical theory with a clear understanding of the relevance of the algebraic theory of probability to the long-term frequency of observable events, we must therefore digress from the historical sequence of its successive claims by seeking an answer to the question: *in what terms did mathematicians of the latter half of the nineteenth century seek to make the relevance of the rules more explicit by re-definition of the concept?* We here drop the idiom of the calculus of choice. Watching our gambler A who consistently sets his stake in accordance with a rule, we envisage a sequence of occasions (*trials*) at each of which an onlooker may make an observation recording one or other outcome as an *event* E_1, E_2, etc. Venn speaks of the sequence as the *series of the event*. I shall speak of it more often as the framework of repetition. Among all trials of the sequence, we shall suppose that P_x is the proportion at which the onlooker correctly records the particular event E_x. We may suppose that A stakes to win in conformity with the rule: claim that the observed event is E_x at each trial. Then P_x will also be the proportion of truthful assertions the gambler will make if he consistently adheres to the rule regardless of the outcome of any run of trials in the sequence. In Venn's formulation P_x is the probability of the event. Chrystal, with a host of imitators, advances the following definition as substantially the view which Venn champions:

We are thus led to the following abstract definition of the Probability or Chance of an Event: If on taking any very large number (N) out of a series of cases in which an event A is in question, A happens on pN occasions, the probability of the event A is said to be p. (*Text Book of Algebra*, Vol. II, 2nd edn., p. 567.)

In fairness to Venn and to Chrystal, one must add that *very large* in this context is a picturesque simplification of what is implicit in their usage of the definition. More precisely they signify by implication that p is the limit of a ratio $s : N$ as N approaches ∞, if s is the actual number of occasions on which A occurs. Thereafter basic rules of addition and multiplication, etc., intrude ostensibly as corollaries. The numerous objections Keynes (pp. 104–6 *op. cit.*) puts forward and the particular criticism advanced by Aitken (*op. cit. infra*, p. 8) suffice to dispose of their claims as such.

Arguments commonly advanced against the Venn–Chrystal approach are formal; but we may dismiss it on other grounds. Since the intention of the concept is factual, it must embrace any actual situation consistent with the specification. Before we get to the corollaries, we find that Chrystal, as is true of any who follow Venn literally, has unobtrusively introduced factual qualifications and elaborations which are quite alien to his own definition as cited above, *inter alia* the following:

If for example, we assert regarding the tossing of a halfpenny, that out of a large number of trials heads will come up nearly as often as tails—in other words, that the probability of heads is $\frac{1}{2}$, what we mean thereby is that all the causes that tend to bring up heads neutralise all the causes that tend to bring up tails. In every series of cases in question, the assumption, well or ill-justified, is made that the counter-balancing of causes takes place. That this is really the right point of view will be best brought home to us, if we reflect that undoubtedly a machine could be constructed which would infallibly toss a halfpenny so as always to land it head-up on a thickly sanded floor, provided the coin were always placed the same way into the machine; also, that the coin might have two heads or two tails; and so on. (*Op. cit.*, p. 568.)

The Gaussian gloss, i.e. the concept of causal neutralisation, superimposed on the Venn prescription in this context does not obviously guarantee that the behaviour of the penny conforms to the rules of a calculus of probabilities. It puts no restriction on the material composition of the halfpenny which might be of magnetised iron, copper-plated, to all appearances genuine and with faces of opposite polarity. Undoubtedly, we could then construct a machine to ensure that the penny would alternately fall heads and tails upwards. We have merely to suppose that the trials occur in a powerful magnetic field the polarity of which changes at each toss by photoelectric (or other appropriate) control. Clearly the ratio of heads to tails in this set-up approaches the 50 per cent limit more and more closely as the number of trials increases; and the gratuitously inserted concept of causal neutralisation holds good for a large enough sequence of trials, considered as a whole. Just as clearly, the rules of the calculus of probability, including the corollaries inconsequentially appended to the Venn–Chrystal formula, do not give a remotely correct description of the observable sequence of events, since the proportion of heads would be the same ($\frac{1}{2}$) in every sequence of $2r$ unit trials. To ensure that the end result is consistent with the corollaries, i.e. with the laws of addition and multiplication of probabilities, we have to postulate that the Gaussian principle of causal neutralisation operates at every *single* trial; but we have then added to our definition a new concept, that essential *lawlessness* which is characteristic of situations to which the so-called laws of probability are applicable.

From the classical viewpoint, the identification of probability with frequency at the level of definition in such terms is objectionable for another reason. We have undertaken to state in advance a rule which will be valid in an endless succession of trials, if the probability assigned to the event correctly specifies its limiting frequency in a sequence of games conceived as such. Now our definition identifies probability with a limiting frequency which it specifies on the implicit assumption that we either have at our disposal experience of an endless sequence, or may justifiably infer what will happen in such a sequence from other sources. Needless to say, our definition does not take such sources within its terms of reference.

In short, a definition of probability presupposing what Venn calls the *series of the event* must explicitly or implicitly contain something more than the postulate of a limiting ratio of observed occurrences of the series. Otherwise, and as Keynes rightly recognised, the derivation of the elementary rules of the calculus of probability entails a *non sequitur*. Contrariwise, the purely formal definition of probability in terms of what we now call the theory of sets is open to Venn's objection (*Logic of Chance*, p. 87) examined at length in the last chapter. Keynes (p. 94, *op. cit.*) states it more briefly thus:

When probability is divorced from direct reference to objects, as it substantially is by not being founded on experience, it simply resolves itself into the common algebraical doctrine of Permutations and Combinations.

We must now therefore come to grips with an issue which is more challenging than any we have so far faced. The question for which we must seek an answer is: *what initial assumptions must we endorse, if we wish to define the class of factual situations to which the rules of the calculus are indeed relevant?* In relying on intuitions consistent with long experience of the game, we must assume, for reasons already stated, that the Founding Fathers recognised that factual conditions such as the instruction to cut *anywhere* or to *shuffle* the pack are prerequisite to a fully explicit prescription of a betting rule for a card game. That such conditions also have implications not as yet disclosed will now emerge, if we re-examine what we do when we define the probability of the event $E_{x,r}$ referable to an r-fold sample as the ratio of all linear permutations of single events consistent with its specification to all r-fold linear permutations of single events in the infinite series of the event.

If we visualise how we can best set out all possible results of a 3-fold toss of a common die or of cutting our card pack (p. 47) of 6 spades (A, 2, 3, 4, 5, 6) three times, we may proceed as follows. First lay out, in each row of a square grid of 36 cells, dice or cards with 1, 2, 3 . . . 6 pips face upwards in ascending order from left to right, one to each cell. Next side by side with, and consistently left of or right of, one of the foregoing in each cell we also place in descending order in each cell of each column a die or card with 1, 2, 3 . . . 6 pips face upwards. We have now set out all $6^2 = 36$ linear permutations of 6 distinguishable objects recorded 2 at a time without restriction on the repeated use of any one. In the same way, we may now lay out a new grid of 36×6 cells, allocating to each cell of a row one of the 36 pairs and to each cell of a column one of the 6 cards or die-faces we may encounter at the third trial. We have then exhibited each of the $6^3 = 216$ linear permutations of 6 distinguishable objects taken 3 at a time with replacement.

Evidently we can specify the 4-fold, 5-fold and in general r-fold choice by successive applications of this procedure. In following the iterative plan of the grid, we have then exhibited the two fundamental rules of the calculus implicit in the definition of p. 40. Thus there will be one way of scoring 18 in a 3-fold trial with probability $\frac{1}{216} = \frac{1}{6} \cdot \frac{1}{6} \cdot \frac{1}{6}$ in accordance with the theorem of multiplication. There will be 3 ways of scoring 2 twos and an ace each with probability $\frac{1}{216}$, and the probability of the event so defined is also by definition $\frac{3}{216} = \frac{1}{216} + \frac{1}{216} + \frac{1}{216}$ in accordance with the rule of addition for exclusive events. There are also 3 ways of scoring two aces and a three. These 6 sequences exhaust the possibility of getting a total score of 5, whence by definition the probability of getting a score of 5 in the 3-fold toss is $\frac{3}{216} + \frac{3}{216} = \frac{1}{36}$ in accordance with the addition rule.

Now what we do, when we thus exhibit the basic rules of the calculus of probability, i.e. the theorems of multiplication and addition, as implicit in the classical definition of probability also discloses another implication we have not as yet examined. At each stage in the build-up of the r-fold sample we have conferred on every possible $(r\text{-}1)$-fold sample an equal opportunity of associating with each possible 1-fold sample. Regardless of the alternative methods of sampling we may postulate, specification of the correct number of different linear permutations consistent with a given sample structure thus signifies that *we allocate to each item an equal opportunity to associate in successive stages of the build-up of the sample with each residual item of the universe of choice.* We may speak of this assertion, which embodies the possibility of visualising the build-up of linear permutations by successive applications of a grid layout as the *principle of equipartition of associative opportunity.* In so far as a sequence of events in the real world guarantees such equipartition of associative opportunity, *if continued long enough,* we may speak of it as a *random* system; and in so far as it is a random system in this sense the probability assigned by the calculus to the event will prescribe its long-run frequency.

The relevance of our formal definitions to the sort of practical judgments with which we associate the word probability, then raises two questions:

(i) whether there are any situations in which observation of a protracted sequence of events justifies the belief that the principle of equipartition adequately describes the limiting state of equilibrium;

(ii) what characteristics of such situations, if they do indeed exist, are relevant to their recognition as such in real life?

When the Founding Fathers identified games of chance as one such class of situations, they had more than guesswork to go on. If the game involves a pack of cards, their intuitive conviction embraces the unstated assumption that we reshuffle the pack again and again lest previous disposition of the cards and inclination of the player to draw a card more or less near the top (or bottom) of the pack leads to unequal partition of opportunity for choice of one card rather than another. It is not obvious that this procedure will guarantee *randomness,* i.e. what

C

we have here referred to as equipartition of associative opportunity, if continued long enough; but it is at least a plausible assumption that it will do so. As it happens, experiments on card packs such as that of Pearson (p. 52) give the assumption a favourable verdict.

If we prefer to define the concepts of our calculus in formal terms unrelated to events, we may thus argue as follows: (*a*) experience vindicates the claim that probabilities assigned by the calculus closely tally with corresponding frequencies in long-term experience of an historical sequence of events in certain model situations; (*b*) in so far as we can impose on a system or predicate of it the relevant peculiarities of such model situations, we may justifiably extend its terms of reference to other situations. We then accept the obligation to impose randomness on, or at least to identify randomness as a property of, such situations. The distinction between imposing and identifying randomness will assume importance at a later stage, when we come to examine the concept of the infinite hypothetical population. Earlier remarks about the analogy between repetitive sampling from a card pack and the tossing of a die have anticipated it, but we must now accept the responsibility of scrutinising the analogy more closely.

In the domain of card packs or urn models we implicitly or explicitly recognise the need to take action, i.e. randomisation, on behalf of the calculus. In the domain of lotteries and die models, including the penny or the needle of Buffon, we are seemingly more reluctant to do so. Otherwise, it is difficult to explain the expenditure of so much industry (*vide infra*, p. 56) in a fruitless quest to vindicate the adequacy of the calculus to describe with equally conspicuous precision the long-run behaviour of an ordinary cubical die and that of Buffon's needle. The challenge evaded by blaming the die for its bias is not easy to rebut, if we retain the role of the passive spectator who accepts a toy in commercial production as a *fait accompli*; but we can carry our enquiry a step forward if we approach the issue in a more positive temper. We shall then gratefully dedicate ourselves to helping the calculus to work in return for so much work our contemporaries demand of it on our behalf.

At the outset, let us be clear about which of two questions

66

we are asking. To assert that the die behaves in a random way does not necessarily mean that it behaves in accordance with random sampling from a rectangular universe of six score classes; but it will at least be difficult to prove conclusively that it does so unless we can make this assumption with propriety. In any event, we shall require to specify the parent universe appropriately in advance, if the end in view is to prescribe a rule for the division of the stakes. We shall therefore interpret the challenge we have here accepted on the understanding that the specification of the six faces must indeed prescribe all the numerical information the classical definition incorporates. If no rule prescribed for the dealer then suffices to justify the use to which we put the definition, we may still entertain the possibility of enlisting a little co-operation from the manufacturer. Indeed, J. Bernoulli (*Ars Conjectandi*, Cap. IV) implicitly does so in disclosing the intuitive approach of his contemporaries:

. . . Evidently there are as many cases for each die as there are faces, and all these cases have an equal chance to materialize. For, by virtue of the similitude of faces and the *uniform distribution of weight* in a die, there is no reason why one face should show up more readily than another, as there would be if the faces had a different shape or if one part of a die were made of heavier material than another. (*Italics inserted.*)

We shall accordingly concede that there is an essential difference between Buffon's needle and the Chevalier's die. In either situation, we are observing the behaviour of a ponderable object heavier than air in a gravitational field. This of itself is entirely irrelevant to whether a needle will fall between or across the lines of Buffon's board. Unless the speed of the spin is exceedingly high, it is not irrelevant to the way in which a solid polyhedron will fall. The position of the centre of gravity will certainly influence the way in which it will most often come to rest unless located appropriately, and the construction of a homogeneous die with *indented* pips to make the article more durable certainly confronts the manufacturer with a very difficult task of location, if the end in view is to equalise the gravitational pull on the faces.

A trained investigator who set out to clarify the relevance of the calculus to a game of craps would not therefore design experiments of the sort summarised in Keynes's *Treatise*. *Inter alia*, he would carry out long-term trials to compare: (*a*) the results of spinning ordinary dice by machinery at very high speeds, letting ordinary dice roll gently to rest and tossing them negligently by hand in accordance with the gambler's practice; (*b*) the results of spinning in the ordinary way an ordinary die and a die with arbitrarily numbered faces distinguishable only by a thin homogeneous film of pigment of appropriate thickness and density;* (*c*) the results when such dice and ordinary dice made to spin at the same speeds fall on smooth and on rough surfaces. In restating the problem of the die in this way, we have translated the risk of passively detecting properties which confer randomness on a system into the idiom of randomisation, conceived as an outcome of deliberate human interference. Our approach to a definition of randomness is then consistent with that of Peirce (*Theory of Probable Inference*) cited by Keynes (p. 290, *op. cit.*). A random sample is one "taken according to a precept or method which, being applied over and over again indefinitely, would in the long run result in the drawing of any one set of instances as often as any other set of the same number."

From a behaviourist viewpoint, the adequacy of our initial definition of probability or of our subsequent prescription of the relevance of the rules of the calculus in the real world is thus largely referable to how far and in what terms they make explicit both the concept of *randomness* and the situations of which it is a characteristic. Reluctance to get to grips with the issue in the formative stage of the mathematical theory of probability is perhaps explicable in its own setting. In the social context of Pascal and Fermat, probability was a calculus of the gaming table at which the nobility made or lost fortunes on the genteel understanding that the contest was truly a game of chance, and that intelligent specification of the correct wager would ensure eventual success. In conformity with the *mores* of

---

* Alternatively, to make the article more durable each face might have six indents of equal capacity appropriately filled with white and black paint of equal density.

polite society and the dictates of good breeding, a gentleman did not probe too deeply into the unspeakable mystery of fair play; and a mathematician, if also a gentleman, could conveniently entrust the custody of the concept of randomness to his own conscience.

Such amiable conventions do not explain why some mathematicians of high repute and good judgment still decline the exacting invitation to clarify the semantic content of the word random by tinkering with the definition of probability in the hope that a supplementary and circular tautology will evacuate latent factual potentialities. Thus they permit us to define it in terms of a universe of choice only if it is *equally likely* that any residual item therein will occur in sample appropriately specified, or to define it in terms of a limiting frequency in the series of the event only if it is *equally likely* that any admissible subsequent event will follow any one specified antecedent. Textbooks still extant in the twenties of our century abounded in such emendations and evasions. Indeed Aitken (1939) finds it necessary to forewarn his readers against them, when he charitably states

Criticism is easy. The logician will not fail to pounce upon the words "equally likely," pointing out that they are synonymous with "equally probable" and that therefore probability is being defined by what is probable, a *circulus in definiendo.*" (*Statistical Mathematics,* pp. 6–11.)

For expository convenience, Aitken himself prefers to confer axiomatic status on the concept of randomness. Concerning his own definition of probability he confesses

Something has been glossed over here; there is the tacit assumption that the initial phases are "equally likely"... The inclusion of the words ... in a definition is in fact a concession: it *puts the reader more gently at terms with the abstract formulation* by anticipating its chief future application. The usage is not uncommon. ... If a straight line is defined as "lying evenly" between its extreme points, what else does "evenly" mean but "in a straight line"? Every definition which is not pure abstraction must appeal somewhere to intuition or experience by using some such verbal counter ... under the stigma of seeming to commit a circle in definition." (*Italics inserted.*)

This is a candid and admissible viewpoint within its own terms of reference, i.e. class-room usage; but we are under no obligation to shirk the issue on that account. If we do indeed cherish the inclination to make the concept of randomness more explicit, it will be necessary to sidestep the snare of current idiom. When we use the expression *in the mind* the preposition unobtrusively identifies the dynamics of mental processes with mind conceived as a static object in three dimensional space. When we likewise speak elliptically of a *random sample* in contradistinction to *a sample taken at random*, we unwittingly predicate randomness as a property of an event in contradistinction to a property assignable to the series of the event. Within such a framework of discourse we must interpret the statement that events are *equally likely* to mean that they occur as often in the long run. We may then approach the terms of reference of the calculus from a different viewpoint.

We have seen that Venn's definition of the probability of an event in terms of frequency is inadequate because it fails to define what properties of the series of the event endorse the rules of the calculus. A definition which invokes the concept of frequency can indeed be adequate in that sense only if it takes within its scope an appropriate specification of the series itself. Accordingly, an algebraic theory consistently formulated in frequency terms must incorporate the concept of randomness in the initial definition of the series. Such is the comparatively recent restatement of the calculus by von Mises whose *Irregular Kollektiv* includes the notion of a limiting ratio in the empirical definition of Venn and adds the missing link in Venn's series of events, viz. the property we have here called the equipartition of associative opportunity. The concept embraces a sequence in which the number of distinguishable events may be finite or infinite. For illustrative purposes, it will suffice to conceive it in terms of 3 only: *a b b a c a a b c c a b b b c c a c a c a b* . . ., etc.

If n_c here enumerates the event c in the first n_t events of the series, the ratio $n_c : n_t$ becomes p_c when n_t becomes infinite in accordance with Venn's definition, but this of itself is consistent with an orderly arrangement of the series. The new principle of disorder imposed on the series of the event by von Mises takes advantage of a conceptualisation of denumerable infinities not as yet widely current in Venn's time, viz. we can accommodate an infinity of even, an infinity of odd, an infinity of perfect squares, or an infinity of perfect cubes in one to one correspondence with the infinity of all integers, which specify the position (rank) of the event in the series. Thus one such infinite subsequence of n_5 events is the subsequence of rank 5, 10, 15, 20 and so on. More generally, we say that there are $n_{c.r}$ events specified as c in the finite subsequence of n_r events of rank r, $2r$, $3r$ and so on. For any value of r we care to assign, the definition of von Mises specifies: $n_{c.r} : n_r = p_c$. Similarly, we might define n_s events of rank 1, 4, 9, 16, 25 and so on, n_p events of rank 1, 3, 5, 7, 11, 13, 17, 19, 23 and so on, and more generally n_0 events selected in accordance with any orderly procedure. We still postulate $n_{c.0} : n_0 = p_c$.

Thus the proportionate contribution of the event c to the denumerable infinity of any prescribed subsequence is fixed. It is therefore entirely undetermined by its prescription; and this indeed we convey by the statement that the series of the event is *orderless*. The algebraic properties of the orderless series are formally identical with the operations of the calculus conceived in terms of set theory or of the classical concept of choice; but the initial definition of probability explicitly identifies it with frequency and also makes explicit the class of situations to which the rules are relevant, i.e. orderless systems of events. That it does indeed accommodate fundamental rules of multiplication and addition subsumed by the general term of the multinomial theorem in its alternative forms (p. 41) in conformity with the classical definition, will be evident from what follows.

We shall consider a sequence of n_t events, divisible into $(n_t\text{-}1)$ pairs of consecutive events. Within this sequence of n_t events, the particular event x occurs n_x times; and by definition $p_x \simeq n_x \div n_t$ as n_t becomes indefinitely large, if p_x is the probability that x is the score at a unit trial. If x may denote any one of the score values b, c, d, we may write $n_x = n_b + n_c + n_d$. In the limit $(n_b + n_c + n_d) \div n_t$ is then the probability that x

71

will be one of the scores b, c, d. More explicitly we may then
write $p_x = P(\text{b } or \text{ c } or \text{ d})$, so that:

$$P(\text{b } or \text{ c } or \text{ d}) = \frac{n_b}{n_t} + \frac{n_c}{n_t} + \frac{n_d}{n_t} = p_b + p_c + p_d$$

This relation exhibits the additive property for unit trials,
and we may extend it to compound trials by iteration. Thus
we conceive n_{xyz} consecutive triplets (3-fold trials) out of
$(n_t\text{-2})$ consecutive triplets of every sort in the n_t-fold sequence
of single events. The probability that the triple event will be
one of the score sequences abc, abd or bcd is the limiting value of
$(n_{abc} + n_{abd} + n_{bcd}) \div (n_t\text{-2})$. In the limit we may write
$(n_t\text{-2}) = n_t$, and

$$P(\text{abc } or \text{ abd } or \text{ bcd}) = \frac{n_{abc}}{n_t} + \frac{n_{abd}}{n_t} + \frac{n_{bcd}}{n_t} = p_{abc} + p_{abd} + p_{bcd}$$

The derivation of the multiplicative property involves some
circumlocution (*vide infra*), if we assume sampling without
replacement from a finite universe. Otherwise, we may develop
it iteratively from considerations of two consecutive events, of
which $(n_t\text{-1})$ is the total number in the sequence of n_t single
events. If n_{cx} is the number of pairs of which c is the initial
event, $n_{cx} = n_c$ unless c is the terminal event of the whole
sequence, in which case $n_{cx} = (n_c\text{-1})$. The probability (p_{cx})
that the pair will have c as its initial member is by definition the
limit of $n_{cx} \div (n_t\text{-1})$ and this is $(n_c \div n_t) = p_c$. The conditional
probability $(p_{b.c})$ that $x = b$ is its successor if c is the initial
event is also by definition the limit of $(n_{cb} \div n_{cx}) = (n_{cb} \div n_c)$;
and the unconditional probability (p_{cb}) that a consecutive pair
is c followed by b is the limit of $n_{cb} \div (n_t\text{-1})$, which is $n_{cb} \div n_t$.
We may thus write

$$p_{bc} = \frac{n_{cb}}{n_t} = \frac{n_c}{n_t} \cdot \frac{n_{cb}}{n_c} = p_c \cdot p_{b.c}$$

We may now reverse the order of procedure adopted in our
last chapter to show that the general expressions cited on p. 41
follow from the additive and multiplicative properties of
probability defined in the foregoing terms. We shall accordingly
denote by $p_{(s)}$ and p_s the probabilities of picking out a particular

score sequence S in exhaustive and repetitive sampling respectively; and may illustrate the build-up by reference to 3-fold sequences (AAB) in which two events of class A precede an event of class B. The multiplicative property then states that $p_a \cdot p_{a.a} \cdot p_{b.aa} = p_{(s)}$ or p_s if we define $p_{a.a}$ and $p_{b.aa}$ appropriately. If sampling is without replacement from a finite universe of n items, of which a and b are respectively of classes A and B,

$$p_{(s)} = \frac{a}{n} \cdot \frac{a-1}{n-1} \cdot \frac{b}{n-2} = \frac{a^{(2)} \cdot b}{n^{(3)}}$$

If sampling involves no removal, $p_{a.a} = p_a$ and $p_{b.aa} = p_b$ so that

$$p_s = \frac{a^2 b}{n^3} = \left(\frac{a}{n}\right)^2 \left(\frac{b}{n}\right) = p_a^2 \cdot p_b$$

The probability that a sample will contain two items of class A and one of class B is that of getting any one of the sequences *AAB, ABA, BAA* for each of which $p_{(s)}$ or p_s has the same value as above. By the addition theorem we therefore derive for the probability that the 3-fold score will be $2A + B$ is

without replacement $3 \cdot \dfrac{a^{(2)} \cdot b}{n^{(3)}}$; *with replacement* $3 p_a^2 \cdot p_b$

More generally, we may assume that n items consist of a of class A, b of class B, c of class C, etc., and that a sample of r items consists of u of class A, v of class B, w of class C, etc. For each sequence consistent with the specification, the theorem of multiplication means that

$$p_s = p_a^u \cdot p_b^v \cdot p_c^w \cdots \; ; \; p_{(s)} = \frac{a^{(u)} \cdot b^{(v)} \cdot c^{(w)} \cdots}{n^{(r)}}$$

There are $r! \div (u!\; v!\; w! \dots)$ sequences consistent with each specification of u, v, w, etc. Whence we derive (iii) and (iv) of Chapter Two.

Such a restatement involves an expository difficulty which is not necessarily a disadvantage. In terms of the calculus of choice, the problem of sampling without replacement from a finite universe is on all fours with the problem of sampling with replacement, and we may indeed exhibit the latter as a limiting case of the former when the universe becomes indefinitely large in comparison with the sample. The beginner who gets his first empirical ideas about probability from what happens in the allocation of hands of cards at whist or comparable situations, is therefore on familiar ground at the start. To conceptualise non-replacement sampling against the background of the irregular collective (I.K.) calls for some circumlocution which creates a difficulty for the beginner, but forces us to scrutinise the sampling process with greater circumspection. In effect, we regard each item taken from the static universe of choice as a lottery ticket which entitles us to identify the sampling procedure for a subsequent draw with a newly constructed I.K. My own staircase model of non-replacement sampling (*Chance and Choice*, Vol. I) is a visualisation of the combination of one I.K. with another in this way.

The tidiness of the formulation of a calculus of probability by von Mises is indisputably attractive; but the initial definition of the concept in terms of a frequency limit does not disclose any clue to an empirical criterion for its numerical evaluation by recourse to experience of a finite sequence of occurrences. This limitation, too easily overlooked, leads to verbal difficulties from which we can extricate ourselves only by the exercise of considerable circumlocution. If we embrace the classical or set theory definition on the understanding that we thereby undertake the obligation to provide experimental evidence of its relevance to the outcome of large-scale trials such as those cited in Chapter Two, we can readily attach a meaning to what Uspensky and other writers call the *constant probability of the event at each trial*, this being uniquely determined by the structure of a putatively fixed universe of choice. As defined by von Mises, the probability of the event is assignable as a property of the infinite collective of trials themselves; and it is difficult to compress the content of the words last cited in a compact form consistent with the definition of the concept.

As a basis for a betting rule for the benefit or comfort of the *individual* gambler, we have to conceive the orderless series of the event as a *temporal framework of repetition*, the specification of which is adequate to the task only if we have both: (*a*) some reliable means of assigning in advance correct numerical values of the relevant basic parameters (p_a, p_b, etc., in the foregoing exposition); (*b*) sufficient reason for assuming that the successive component unit scores of each game in an endless sequence of such games recur in an orderless succession. By accommodating the concept of randomness explicitly in his definition of probability, the algebraist has admittedly made explicit the class of situations with respect to which the calculus can claim to endorse a reliable code of conduct; but it is not the business of the algebraist to tell us how to recognise such situations when we meet them or whether we have at our disposal the requisite additional information prerequisite to a reliable rule for division of the stakes when we do so. Each of the conditions stated is essential. Thus we may satisfy ourselves that a particular system of successive shuffling ensures the prescribed disorder; but we cannot usefully apply this knowledge unless we also know the number of cards of each relevant class in the pack.

It is all too easy to lose sight of our equal obligation to equip ourselves with knowledge of both sorts when we interpret the *Kollektiv* in terms more relevant to anything we may legitimately or otherwise convey by assigning a probability to the truth of a scientific judgment. To speak of an individual field trial as one of an infinite succession of games is merely a figure of speech. Unless content to converse in metaphors, we must therefore leave behind us the temporal framework of repetition when we invoke stochastic theory in such situations. One way in which we can dispose of the need to interpret the series of the event as an historical sequence is to conceptualise the beneficiaries of the rule as an infinite team of gamblers each one simultaneously playing one game only with one of an infinitude of essentially identical packs, dice, etc., but the mere fact that the number of such dice, packs, etc., is accordingly limitless does not suffice to impose the condition of disorder on the system. The word *essentially* in this context will indeed be a danger signal, unless the reader has dismissed as trivial an earlier digression (pp. 44–47) on the analogy between the card pack and the die. As we there saw, our calculus will work if each player takes a sequence of *r* consecutive cards from his assigned pack, only if we assume an adequate preliminary shuffle of each such pack.

Nor do we impose the condition of disorder on the conduct of the game, if we relinquish the right to discuss simultaneous sampling in a finite universe by conceding to each member of the infinite team of players the right to pick r cards simultaneously from one and the same pack containing a denumerable infinitude of cards suitably placed face downwards. We shall later see that this way of disposing of the inconvenience of conceptualising our *Kollektiv* exclusively in terms of an historic sequence has acquired the status of a widely current axiom, which doubtless derives a spurious cogency from the misinterpretation of an algebraic identity. Its correct interpretation in the domain of fact will not deceive us, if we are fully alert to the issues raised by the subversively over-simplified distinction between sampling with and without replacement.

We have seen that it is possible to subsume under two expressions (p. 41) the content of the classical definition of the probability of extracting an r-fold sample of specified constitution from a finite n-fold universe. Let us here recall them:

without replacement

$$P_{(u, v, w \ldots)} = \frac{r!}{u!\, v!\, w! \ldots} \cdot \frac{a^{(u)} \cdot b^{(v)} \cdot c^{(w)} \ldots}{n^{(r)}}$$

with replacement

$$P_{u, v, w \ldots} = \frac{r!}{u!\, v!\, w! \ldots} \left(\frac{a}{n}\right)^u \left(\frac{b}{n}\right)^v \left(\frac{c}{n}\right)^w \ldots$$

The formal identity of the two expressions if we substitute ordinary for factorial exponents or *vice versa* is an irresistible invitation to extensive generalisation. If n is very large in comparison with r, we may write $a^{(u)} \div n^{(r)} \simeq a^u \div n^r$, etc., and the two foregoing expressions become identical in the limit, i.e. for finite values of r when n is infinite. Actually, the prescribed probability of taking randomwise 5 specified cards simultaneously from a composite card pack of 200 ordinary full packs of 52 is assignable with a trivial error, if we specify it as that of recording the same 5 specified cards in a 5-fold cut without removal; but the convenience of this approximation as a computing device does not dispose of a factual limitation fully discussed (pp. 43–49) in Chapter Two. If we cut 5 times randomwise, replacing the cards in their original order after each cut, the pack remains the same throughout the series of the event, and the formula holds good. If we pick a sequence of 5 cards simultaneously, we can do so randomwise only if we shuffle the pack before each game.

When our concern is with the 5-fold cut, the probability assigned to the compound event depends only on the proportions (p_a = a/n of class A, p_b = b/n of class B, etc.) of cards of relevant denomination in the pack. Thus the outcome of so-called replacement sampling is independent of the actual size of the pack; and the results of sampling in the infinite card pack without removal as commonly prescribed are the same as the results of such sampling in the 52-fold card pack, if the corresponding relevant parameters p_a, p_b, etc., have identical values for each. By the same token, we may think of recording the toss of a hypothetical unbiased cubical die as comparable to cutting the pack of six cards on p. 47 or cutting an infinite pack containing cards with 1, 2, 3 . . . 6 pips in equal proportions. Having conceptualised our pack in this way, we are free to regard it as a widow's cruse from which we can continue indefinitely to extract finite samples without exhausting it, i.e. without changing the proportions of cards severally denoted by p_a, p_b, etc.

Can we then say that taking a sequence of 5 cards simultaneously from any part of an infinite card pack is strictly comparable to cutting the pack anywhere five times? If we do so, we allow ourselves to be deluded by an algebraic trick. That it is indeed a trick becomes manifest, if we visualise how we actually choose the cards in the two situations. When we speak of cutting anywhere, the understood connotation of the adverb is that we cut in an orderless way. The act of cutting so prescribed thus imposes on the infinite series of the event the essential property of the *Kollektiv*, and we do not need to make any additional assumption about the arrangement of the cards in the pack, infinite or otherwise. As we have seen, we are free to regard the arrangement as fixed throughout, if we replace the cards in the same order after cutting. That allowing n to become infinite does not restore this freedom, which we relinquish by prescribing a reshuffle of the n-fold card pack between each game defined as the extraction of an r-fold sequence of cards, is evident, if we specify one way of building up such a pack.

We have seen that we can choose blindfold with our two hands only 48 different 5-fold simultaneous sequences from one and the same full deck of 52 cards. If we now place on it a second full deck of cards arranged in the same order, we can actually choose 52, but we can never actually choose more than 52 different ones, if we pile on 3, 4, 5, etc., decks stacked in the same order. Our pack may become infinite, and we can still actually choose only 52 out of the 52^5 different sequences we could actually choose if free to shuffle the pack between each of a limitless sequence of games. On the assumption that the re-shuffle imposes the essential property of the *Kollektiv* on the act of choice, we should then legitimately deem the *replacement* formula to be appropriate to the situation. Otherwise, we must assume that each of the 52^5 different sequences occurs with equal frequency in the infinite stack.

To regard simultaneous sampling without removal as rightly equivalent to sampling with removal when the pack is infinite, does not therefore suffice to prescribe the way in which we choose the cards. We have also to introduce a new assumption about the arrangement of the cards in the pack. It is not enough to instruct the members of our infinite team to play the game in accordance with a rule of randomisation. We have also to equip them with an infinite card pack which has the unique property of randomness. As a model of sampling in field work, the infinite card pack does not, in short, exonerate us from the obligation to identify circumstances which endorse the putative relevance of the calculus of probability to the real world. Even if our statement of its initial terms of relevance incorporate the concept of randomness, we have still to settle the question: how can we prescribe randomness or recognise it when we meet it? So far, we have merely gleaned a clue to the first half of the question.

In so far as extensive experiments on games of chance have

subsequently vindicated the intuitions of the Founding Fathers, they do so only where human interference imposes the properties of randomness on a system; and it is at least difficult to see how such confirmation can endorse the intrusion of the calculus into the domain of retrospective judgment. Nor is it easy to derive from what we know about the manufacture of the die or of the lottery wheel, any sufficient empirical basis for detecting a system of complete disorder in nature. If we approach the factual credentials of the classical theory with due regard to the evidence assembled by Keynes, we shall not lightly assume that an organism or a society is comparable to a Prague lottery in 1754 or to a Brünn lottery in 1886 when what we also know about Monte Carlo is inconsistent with what we should prefer to believe about the habits of lotteries in general. Still less shall we complacently invoke the properties of such models to confer innate stochastic properties on natural phenomena for no better reason than our ignorance of what determines their vagaries.

The full statement of the views of von Mises first appeared in 1936. An English translation (*Probability, Statistics and Truth*) of the German text became available in 1939. With the introduction of the *Kollektiv* we thus arrive at the most recent attempt to make explicit the assumptions latent in the doctrine of the Founding Fathers with due regard to the end they had in view. Our enquiry has brought into focus the need to distinguish between what our contemporaries refer to as *randomisation* in the context of experimental design and *randomness* conceived as an innate characteristic of natural phenomena in the domain of statistical theory elsewhere referred to as a calculus of exploration. When we speak of randomisation we connote a property imposed by a plan of conduct on the collection of data, as when we prescribe the need to shuffle the card pack, shake the urn or spin the die. If we speak of randomness as the characteristic of a set-up in which we ourselves are passive spectators, nothing we have so far learned from classical models, i.e. games of chance, has given us a clue to its recognition.

If we do conceive randomness as an innate property of a die on all fours with its density or thermal conductivity, and seemingly von Mises does so, we have to admit that the concept is factually meaningful only in so far as it is possible to prescribe how to construct a die whose long-term behaviour conforms to the requirements of the algebraic calculus. Experiment may well justify the belief that it is possible to do so; but the relevance of any such prescription to the recognition of randomness in nature is debatable. If it is possible to recognise randomness in nature, we must go to nature for our clues. That the outcome of doing so has not been wholly satisfactory to date sufficiently explains a widespread contemporary readiness to probe more deeply into the historical foundations of the algebraic theory. Meanwhile, the nostalgia with which our contemporaries turn to the writings of the Founding Fathers to reinforce their several claims as custodians of the classical tradition need not surprise us.

If our attempt to find in their own experience an unstated rationale for the intuitive convictions of Pascal, J. Bernoulli, de Moivre, Euler and their following has not been wholly successful, one reason may be that they would face an embarrassing dilemma, if asked to bestow their benediction on their successors of any persuasion. If called on to state the end in view, the answer they would have given would be unquestionably consistent with Neyman's interpretation of their intentions, that is to say the deduction of a rule which would ensure eventual success to the gambler if stated in advance and scrupulously obeyed thereafter. This intention does not encompass the right to evaluate a judgment referable to any isolated past event; and it is wholly unintelligible unless we conceive the formal definition of probability of an event in terms of the observable frequency of the event in a limitless number of trials. To that extent the outlook of the classical period is inconsistent with the repudiation of the notion of frequency by the school of Jeffreys and Carnap, and cannot accommodate the concept of fiducial probability (p. 441) embraced by the school of R. A. Fisher.

If asked to state explicitly why they believed that the formal identification of choice and chance is a sufficient basis for the deduction of any such rule, we can at best guess what answer the Founding Fathers would have given. No doubt, they would have conceded that each successively possible act of choice must occur with equal frequency in the long run; but if forced to justify this faith one may well suspect that they would have been able to enter no better plea in defence than our ignorance of the outcome. The gratuitous assumption that events which are equally likely are events about which we know nothing is the penalty we pay for imposing a numerical specification in a technical context on a word which signalises by daily and long association an unquantifiable measure of uncertainty. To that extent, the Founding Fathers might well have felt themselves on familiar ground in discussing the fundamentals of the theory in the idiom of Jeffreys and Carnap. Though he consistently restricts his theme to an examination of the observable long run frequency of external events, Bernoulli, in whose *Ars Conjectandi* the classical theory as set forth in the first half of the preceding paragraph first takes shape in its entirety, equates in several places the conviction that a die will behave in a particular way to the assertion that we have no reason for believing the contrary.

In the restatement of the theory by von Mises this axiom drops out; and we must concede that his definition of probability, unlike any previously put forward by a professional mathematician, formally specifies the class of situations to which the calculus is truly relevant. Unluckily, the specification is not sufficiently explicit at the factual level to disclose how to set about identifying such situations when we meet them. Nor is it easy to give a confident prescription for doing so by relying on what is factually common to situations in which the calculus does work as well as we have reason to hope. Any such situations so far examined involve an agent and a repetitive programme of action. If, as is true of card pack and urn model situations, the trial involves an act of choice in the most literal sense of the term, the instructions embodied in the programme must include an explicit specification of the act itself; but in any case they will embrace instructions for shuffling, tossing or spinning with the ostensible aim of imposing disorder, as von Mises uses the term, on what Venn calls the series of the event. The execution of such instructions constitutes the putative randomising process. The identification of such a programme of instruction with the concept of randomisation forces us therefore to carry our enquiry a step further by asking: what is common to all such programmes?

At this stage, we can plausibly predicate only three features shared by all of them. All impose the condition that the sensory discrimination of the agent is impotent to influence the outcome of the programme. All embrace the possibility that strict adherence to the programme is consistent with the realisable occurrence of any conceptually possible outcome in a single trial. All exclude the possibility that any orderly rhythm of external agencies intervene to impose a periodicity on the series of the event. Whether these three features suffice to specify a randomising process as such is difficult, if not impossible, to prove; but the indisputable relevance of the first to a satisfactory specification confers no sanction on the principle of insufficient reason. The latter endows the subjective judgment of the passive spectator with the property of generating randomness without active participation in promoting the series of the event.

CHAPTER FOUR

DIVISION OF THE STAKES AND
THE LOTTERY OF LIFE AND DEATH

THROUGHOUT THE CLASSICAL PERIOD, i.e. from the correspondence of Pascal with Fermat to the enunciation of the doctrine of inverse probability by Laplace, the hazards of the gaming table were the major preoccupation of mathematicians who contributed to the formulation of a stochastic calculus. Whatever views we may entertain about the relevance of the calculus of probability to scientific enquiry and in whatsoever way we may now choose to define probability in their context, there can thus be no doubt about the intentions of the Founding Fathers. Their practical aim was to prescribe a betting *rule* to ensure a profit to the gambler who consistently applies it. A rule so conceived is a rule the gambler must continue to apply in spite of a run of bad luck. It therefore dictates inexorably the proper form of the assertion which specifies the gambler's bet, even if the fortunes of the gambler himself tempt him to doubt its reliability. Only on that understanding can we assign a probability to the truth of his assertion. Clearly, therefore, the proper use of the theory conceived in such terms cannot accommodate the right to assign a probability to an assertion ostensibly justified by the occurrence of a particular event in the past; but it would not be true to state that all of the predecessors of Laplace invariably recognised this limitation of the classical formula. In a prize essay of the *Academie Royale des Sciences*, D. Bernoulli (1734) discusses at length whether the narrow zone in which the orbits of the planets lie around the ecliptic is attributable (in Todhunter's words) to hazard. If we sustain the Forward Look, this is a meaningless query. The planets lie where they do lie.

Such lapses are exceptional. Nor did they fail to provoke intelligent protest at the time. Even in the treatment of a new theme which intrudes as we approach the grand climacteric of the classical theory, the end in view is seemingly consistent with the programme stated in the preceding paragraph; and if the justification for extending the terms of reference of the theory to embrace it is exceptionable, objections which now seem self-evident invoke factual considerations far less familiar at the time. This new theme which now invites our scrutiny is a class of problems which to writers of the century antecedent to the promulgation of his eternal law of population by parson Malthus might well seem to be cognate to the hazards of the gambler. In the sixteenth century the practice of insurance had indeed grown gradually out of a traffic in wagers at mediaeval fairs. It expanded briskly in the eighteenth century against the background of Halley's Life Table published in the *Philosophical Transactions of the Royal Society* (1693). As a Huguenot refugee after the Revocation of the Edict of Nantes, de Moivre undertook actuarial work to support himself, and annuity expectations make their appearance in his *Doctrine of Chances* (1718) in the same milieu as the fortunes of the gaming saloon. The treatise itself deals largely with the latter; but the identification of insurance risks with the hazards of gambling asserts itself more obtrusively in later writings of the classical period, including in particular the works of Euler and of d'Alembert.

In what sense, if any, the classical theory of the gambler's risk offers a rationale for the costing of an insurance corporation will be the more easy to recognise, if we examine the implications of a theorem announced by J. Bernoulli (1713) in the *Ars Conjectandi*. To set forth the theorem in formal terms, we may specify the probability that the sample mean score (M_0) referable to a distribution whose true mean is M lies in the range $M \pm \epsilon$ as: $P(M - \epsilon \leqslant M_0 \leqslant M + \epsilon) = (1 - \alpha)$. Then α is the probability that a deviation is numerically greater than ϵ; and the value assignable to α depends both on ϵ and on the size (r) of the sample. For a fixed value of r, deviations numerically greater than $\epsilon = u$ will be more frequent than deviations numerically greater than $\epsilon = v$ if $v > u$; and we must assign a lower value to α if we assign a higher value to ϵ. For one and the same value of ϵ we may assign a lower value to α if we assign a higher value to r; and the probability that M_0 will lie inside a range specified as above will approach unity as r approaches infinity. The theorem states that this is true for any value of ϵ *however small*.

So stated, it admits of a more or less general proof by several methods; but it will here be convenient to approach it in a way which facilitates numerical calculations illustrative of its bearing on one factual preoccupation of its author. We shall then see more clearly what it does *not* mean. Accordingly, we shall take advantage of the fact that the normal curve provides a close fit for the random sampling distribution of the mean score of the r-fold sample from any n-fold discrete universe of choice, if r is very large but also a small fraction of n (Appendix I). On this understanding, we shall denote by σ_m^2 the variance of the r-fold sample mean score distribution and by $\sigma^2 = r\sigma_m^2$ the fixed variance of the unit score distribution. We then define a normally distributed standard score of unit variance by $h = (M_0 - M) \div \sigma_m$, whence if $h\sigma_m = \epsilon = (M_0 - M)$, we may write:

$$P(M - \epsilon \leqslant M_0 \leqslant M + \epsilon) = (1 - \alpha)$$
$$= P(M - h \cdot \sigma_m \leqslant M_0 \leqslant M + h \cdot \sigma_m) \quad \text{(i)}$$

For the probability that M_0 lies within the limits $(M \pm h\sigma_m)$ when h is positive, we may write:

$$P(M - h \cdot \sigma_m \leqslant M_0 \leqslant M + h \cdot \sigma_m)$$
$$= (1 - \alpha) = (2\pi)^{-\frac{1}{2}} \int_{-h}^{h} e^{-\frac{1}{2}c^2} \cdot dc$$

$$P(M_0 < M - h\sigma_m) = \tfrac{1}{2}\alpha = P(M_0 > M + h\sigma_m)$$
$$P(M_0 > M - h\sigma_m) = (1 - \tfrac{1}{2}\alpha) = P(M_0 < M + h\sigma_m)$$

For illustrative use in what follows, we may obtain from the table of the normal integral the following values for α in terms of h:

h	$(1 - \alpha)$	$\tfrac{1}{2}\alpha$	$(1 - \tfrac{1}{2}\alpha)$
1·64	0·8990	0·0505	0·9495
1·96	0·950	0·0250	0·9750
2·43	0·985	0·0075	0·9925
2·81	0·995	0·0025	0·9975
3·08	0·998	0·0010	0·9990
3·20	0·9986	0·0007	0·9994

In (i) above we have defined ϵ in terms of h and σ_m, but we may define it alternatively in terms of the fixed constant σ and r, viz. :

$$\epsilon = \frac{h\sigma}{\sqrt{r}} \quad and \quad r = \frac{h^2\sigma^2}{\epsilon^2}$$

The formal meaning of the theorem is now clear. We can fix α in (i) at any level, however small, by making h sufficiently large, e.g. $\alpha = 0\cdot005$ if $h = 2\cdot81$, $\alpha = 0\cdot002$ if $h = 3\cdot08$ and if $h = 3\cdot2$, $\alpha \simeq 0\cdot0014$, as shown in the foregoing table. Having thus fixed α, we may then make ϵ as small as we like by increasing r sufficiently. On the assumption that the calculus is in fact consistent with the natural history of the game, we can thus ensure that the frequency of a deviation of the sample mean score (M_0) from the true mean (M) numerically greater than any minute quantity ϵ however small will itself be inappreciably small, if we make the size of the sample, i.e. the number of unit trials per game, sufficiently large.

The statement last made emphatically does not mean that enlarging the size of a finite sample will ensure that deviations numerically larger than ϵ will *never* occur. Thus it is difficult to see why so many writers exhibit results such as those set forth on pp. 52–57 above as empirical verification of Bernoulli's theorem. We shall prefer to regard them as positive evidence for the belief that the operations of the stochastic calculus do creditably conform to the long-run luck of the game; and to that extent they are justification for using the theorem as a factually legitimate extension of its terms of reference. As Keynes remarks, the theorem in its own right is amenable neither to proof nor to disproof, the record of a large deviation in a single large-scale experiment being consistent with what the theorem states may occasionally, albeit very rarely, happen.

What the theorem rightly signifies in the social context of the *Ars Conjectandi* will become more clear if we examine a model situation. We suppose that a lottery wheel:

    (*a*) has 10 sectors of equal area, nine black and one red;
    (*b*) each sector comes to rest against a pointer with equal frequency in the long run;
    (*c*) a gambler A scores 1 when the red sector comes to rest against it and zero otherwise.

In this set-up the true mean score of the distribution is $M = 0 \cdot 1$ and $\sigma = \sqrt{(0 \cdot 1)(0 \cdot 9)} = 0 \cdot 3$ for the unit trial distribution. Successive terms of the binomial $(0 \cdot 9 + 0 \cdot 1)^r$ exactly specify the sampling distribution of the mean score (M_0) of the r-fold spin with variance $\sigma_m^2 = (0 \cdot 3)^2 \cdot r^{-1}$. If $r > 300$, the normal quadrature will be very close and we may then regard $h = (M_0 - M) \div \sigma_m$ as a normal score of unit variance. By definition therefore

$$(M_0 - M) = \epsilon \; ; \; \epsilon = h\sigma_m = -\frac{3h}{10\sqrt{r}}$$

$$\therefore r = \frac{9h^2}{100\epsilon^2} \; and \; h = \frac{10\epsilon\sqrt{r}}{3} \tag{ii}$$

Thus we may first suppose that $\epsilon = 0 \cdot 03$, so that α is the probability that the player's mean score lies outside the range $0 \cdot 07 \leqslant M_0 \leqslant 0 \cdot 13$ and $r = 100h^2$. From the foregoing figures citing α in terms of h, we then derive

h	α	r
$1 \cdot 96$	$0 \cdot 05$	384
$2 \cdot 81$	$0 \cdot 005$	790
$3 \cdot 08$	$0 \cdot 002$	949
$3 \cdot 2$	$0 \cdot 0014$	$1,024$

The theorem acquires a new interest if we use (i) and (ii) above to formalise a rule for division of the stakes, invoking the notion of the gambler's *expectation* of gain and the *risk* associated with a specified gain or loss. We suppose that A agrees at each spin to pay $\$y$ forfeit if the score is zero, receiving $\$x$ compensation if his bet is right, i.e. if the score is unity. Thus he either gains $\$x$ or loses $\$y$ at each spin. If M_0 is the proportion of successes in a game of r spins, the net gain is

$$G = r \cdot M_0 \cdot x - r(1 - M_0)y$$

For brevity we may write $M = p = (1 - q)$ and $\epsilon = (M_0 - M)$

$$\therefore G = r(px - qy) + r\epsilon(x + y) \tag{iii}$$

The theorem implies that ϵ approaches zero with a probability ever nearer unity as r approaches infinity. In the limit therefore

$$G_r \simeq r(px - qy)$$

87

We speak of $E = (px - qy)$ as the gambler's expectation of gain per game, and may write (iii) as

$$G = r\,[E + \epsilon(x + y)] \qquad \text{(iv)}$$

When $\epsilon = 0$ so that $M_0 = M$, the total gain is rE and

$$P(G < rE) = 0.5 = P(M_0 < M) \qquad \text{(v)}$$

Now the gambler must lose in the long run, if the expectation is negative, i.e. if $E < 0$ so that $px < qy$. If his opponent agrees to pay 10 dollars for each success A scores, A will thus win in the long run if $10p > qy$ and lose if $10p < qy$. In the set-up referred to above, $p = 0.1$ and $q = 0.9$. Thus the forfeit A will agree to pay must be $y < 1.1$, if he hopes to win in the long run. If $y = 1.1$, so that $G = 0$ for $\epsilon = 0$, the probability of eventually losing the game is therefore 0.5; but if A sets his stake with his opponent's consent at 1 dollar ($y = 1$), so that $E = 0.1$, he has a 50 per cent chance of making at least $(0.1)r$ dollars in a game of r spins. Nor will he necessarily lose in the long run if $M_0 < M$, so that ϵ in (iv) is negative. So long as E is numerically greater than $\epsilon(x + y)$, his net gain will be positive. If we write $\epsilon = -k = h\sigma_m$ the risk of losing the game is then

$$P(M_0 < M - k) = \tfrac{1}{2}\alpha = P(M_0 < M - h\sigma_m)$$

When $\tfrac{1}{2}\alpha = 0.001$, $h = 3.08$, so that

$$k = \frac{3(3.08)}{10\sqrt{r}} \quad and \quad r = \frac{0.853776}{\epsilon^2}$$

If A wants to keep the risk of losing the game at the 0.001 level for the stakes, $x = 10, y = 1$, in which event $k = 0.009 \simeq (110)^{-1}$, the duration of the game (number of spins) will be

$$r = (110)^2(0.853776) \simeq 10,331$$

We shall now suppose that the rule fixes the duration of the game as $r = 625$, so that

$$k = \frac{3(3.08)}{250} = 0.03696 \quad and \quad 11k \simeq 0.4065$$

Since $(x + y) = 11$ for the stakes $x = 10$ and $y = 1$, his net gain for $11k = 0·4065$ is

$$r(0·1 - 0·4065) = -625(0·3065) = -192$$

Thus $0·001$ is the risk that he will lose at least 192 dollars if the game lasts for only 625 spins. To keep the risk of loss at the same level he must therefore get his opponent to agree to an offer of a lower stake y for the same stake $x = 10$. Accordingly, we may write:

$$E = 1 - (0·9)y \quad and \quad (x + y) = (10 + y)$$

Hence A neither gains nor loses if $E = - \epsilon(10 + y)$ and $\epsilon = - k$ is negative, so that

$$k = \frac{1 - (0·9)y}{10 + y}$$

The probability that he will not win is

$$P(E \leqslant 10k + ky) = \tfrac{1}{2}\alpha = P(M_0 \leqslant M - k)$$

If $k = h\sigma_m$ and $r = 625$, $k = 3h \div 250$ and $h = 3·08$ if $\tfrac{1}{2}\alpha = 0·001$, so that $k = 0·03696$ if the risk is $0·001$

$$\therefore (0·03696)(10 + y) = 1 - (0·9)y$$
$$\therefore y \simeq 0·673$$

So far we have assumed that he fixes the stake in accordance with a pre-assigned risk of not winning the game. We may also fix the stake at a pre-assigned risk on the assumption that he will gain at least m dollars or lose less than d dollars. If he wishes the risk to be $0·001$ that he will not make at least 250 dollars, we may illustratively* proceed to evaluate y for $x = 10$ as follows. To win 250 dollars we must assume:

$$625 \left[1 - (0·9)y - k(10 + y)\right] = 250$$
$$P(G < 250) = 0·001 = P(M_0 < M - k)$$

---

* At the level $h = 3$ for $r = 625$ the normal quadrature is by no means reliable when $p = 0·01$.

If $\frac{1}{2}\alpha = 0\cdot001$, $h = 3\cdot08$ as before and $k = 0\cdot03696$, so that

$$625\,[0\cdot6304 - 0\cdot937\cdot y] = 250$$
$$\therefore y \simeq 0\cdot246$$

Thus his stake will be roughly a quarter dollar.

We may thus summarise as follows the general theory of the division of the stakes, when we may assume that the normal quadrature is sufficient. If G is the gain of gambler A in a game of r unit trials, x the stake his opponent B pays up if A wins his bet, y the forfeit A pays up if he loses it, $p = M = (1 - q)$ the probability that A will win in a single trial:

$$G = rE + r\,.\,\epsilon\,(x + y) \quad in\ which \quad E = px - qy$$

In this expression p and q are constants assigned by the nature of the game, and we may also assume that the opponent fixes the stake x in advance. We may then consider r, y and ϵ as unknown. We may specify the risk that A will not win as much as a fixed sum m in the form:

$$P(G < m) = \tfrac{1}{2}\alpha = P(M_0 < M - k) \qquad \text{(vi)}$$

The relation between k and m is then

$$m = rE - rk(x + y) \qquad \text{(vii)}$$

If we write $k = h\sigma_m$, we may evaluate $\frac{1}{2}\alpha$ by recourse to the identity $\sigma_m^2 = r^{-1}p(1 - p)$ which fixes h. Conversely we may fix $\frac{1}{2}\alpha$ at any assigned level by first fixing h. Thus the probability of not winning as much as m is assignable as a known function of h, r and y, i.e.

$$P(G < m) = F(h, r, y)$$

If we wish to assign the risk $(\frac{1}{2}\alpha)$ for fixed stakes (x, y) and fixed duration (r) of game for less than a fixed gain m, we solve (vii) for k and hence for h, having pre-assigned x, y and r. If we wish to specify the stake y for a fixed risk in a game of fixed duration, we pre-assign h, x, r and likewise appropriately for $\frac{1}{2}\alpha$, whence also k, to solve (vii) for y. If we wish to determine the appropriate duration of the game for fixed stakes at a pre-assigned risk, we solve (vii) for r having pre-assigned x, y and h, whence k.

The rule for the division of the stakes assumes a new interest if we introduce a third gambler to underwrite A. We have seen that A's risk of losing the game of 625 spins is about 0·001, if he stakes 67·3 cents against 10 dollars. In that event he cannot lose more than $625(0·673) = 421$ dollars per game. In n games he stands to lose at most 421 n dollars and to gain as much as 6,250 n. We may suppose that his capital is 105,250 dollars. He will therefore remain solvent, if he plays no more than 250 games with a possibility of winning as much as 1,562,500 and of thereby increasing his capital to 1,667,750 dollars. We may also suppose that a third gambler C with more capital and many such clients agrees to pay any debts A may incur, if A pays him 5 dollars a game. Thus A may lose $(421 + 5)$ dollars per game or $426n$ in n games. He must then remain solvent if he plays less than 248 games with the possibility of increasing his capital by 1,542,515 dollars. In this set-up, C may have to pay up as much as $(247)(416) = 102,752$ dollars and may add as much as $5(247) = 1,235$ dollars to his capital.

Let us now regard C as a corporation with enough capital to take on 10,000 clients on the same terms as A without the possibility of insolvency. In that event, we may put its gain per successful game as $x = 5$ and its loss at a figure never exceeding $y = 416$. If the stake were exactly 416, we might write the expectation accordingly as:

$$E = 5(0·999) - 0·001(416) = 4·579$$

On the same assumption, there are therefore equal odds that C will gain more or less than 45,790 dollars; but the figure 416 is not the actual stake which C forfeits for a failure, being the greatest forfeit C can ever pay in a game with a variable forfeit (y) for a fixed return (x). Even so, the risk that C will not substantially gain is small.

For illustrative purposes, we shall thus put the plight of C *at its worst*, if we assume that C always pays up 416 dollars when A loses. We shall then think of C as standing to lose 416 dollars with probability 0·001 and to gain 5 dollars with probability 0·999 in each of 10,000 unit trials. The net gain in 10,000 games (one per client) is accordingly specifiable as:

$$45,790 + 10,000\epsilon \, (421)$$

For $p = 0\cdot001$ and $r = 10,000$, $\sigma_m \simeq 0\cdot0003162$.

If $h = 1\cdot64$ so that $\tfrac{1}{2}\alpha = 0\cdot05$, we set 5 per cent as the risk that C will gain less than

$$45,790 - 10,000(421) \, (0\cdot0005186) \simeq 43,607$$

Needless to say, this is a gross underestimate of what C stands to gain with 5 per cent risk of failure. In any event, the possible loss the corporation might incur is $(102,752) \times (10,000) = 1,027,520,000$ dollars, and without danger of insolvency if this is indeed its capital. Having less capital, it may insure itself against insolvency by restricting the number of its clients and paying 50 cents per client to a more wealthy corporation D to cover all possible loss. It can then take on c clients with no possibility of insolvency if

$$(0\cdot5)c + (102,752)c = 1,027,520,000$$

Thus C may still accept nearly 10,000 clients with complete protection against insolvency if it pays to D a premium of 10 per cent on all premiums received from gamblers who operate in the same way as A.

The foregoing is more than a parable. During the latter half of the eighteenth century the government of Royalist France reaped a handsome revenue from a lottery which throws light on the predilection of Laplace for the urn model. Other European governments operated similar state lotteries in the following century. A French citizen of the earlier period could purchase one or more *billets* numbered from 1 to 90 inclusive. At appointed intervals an official drew randomwise 5 tickets of a complete set of 90. On the announcement of the result the holder of one or more tickets bearing the same number as a ticket drawn could claim compensation. Uspensky tells us that the holder of one or more tickets with the same winning number could claim 15 times the cost of each, of one or more pairs with 2 different winning numbers 270 times the cost of each, and so on. For each claim so specified, the government set its stake to gain in the long run. If N is the number on a single ticket, the probability that one of 5 taken from 90 will be N is $\frac{5}{90} = p = \frac{1}{18}$. If the holder pays t francs for it, the government thus gains t with probability $\frac{17}{18}$ if N is not one of the winning numbers and otherwise loses $(15 - 1)\, t$ with probability $q = \frac{1}{18}$. The expectation of the government is therefore positive, being

$$E = \frac{17}{18}\,t - \frac{14}{18}\,t = \frac{1}{6}\,t$$

If the holder has two tickets with different numbers N and M, the probability that the second is a winner if the first is also is the probability that it is one of 4 out of 89 tickets and $p = \dfrac{5 \times 4}{90 \times 89} = \dfrac{2}{801}$, and this is the probability that the government will have to pay $2t(270)$ losing $2t(270) - 2t = 538t$, whence

$$E = \frac{(799)2t}{801} - \frac{2 \cdot 538t}{801} = \frac{58}{89}\,t$$

If the government sold single tickets to 100,000 different holders at 10 francs, its net gain in francs in accordance with (iii) above would be

$$G = 1{,}000{,}000 \left(\frac{1}{6} + 15\epsilon \right)$$

For this set-up $p = \dfrac{17}{18}$ and

$$\sigma_m = \frac{\sqrt{17}}{1800\sqrt{10}} \simeq 0 \cdot 000724$$

Whence $\epsilon \simeq -0 \cdot 002231 = h\sigma_m$ if $h = 3 \cdot 08$ and we put $\frac{1}{2}\alpha = 0 \cdot 001$ as the risk of making less than

$$1{,}000{,}000 \left(\frac{1}{6} - 0 \cdot 0335 \right) = 133{,}200 \text{ francs}$$

The risk of making no profit is $\frac{1}{2}\alpha = P\left(15k > \dfrac{1}{6} \right)$ and $15k > \dfrac{1}{6}$ if $h > 15 \cdot 3$, whence $\frac{1}{2}\alpha < 0 \cdot 0000000001$.

Till abandoned in 1789, the enterprise proved profitable to the regal gambler. Had the monarch chosen to limit the issue of tickets and to seek coverage against insolvency like Gambler A in the foregoing parable, we may suppose that an insurance company C with more capital than the treasury might also have profited by underwriting possible loss and have covered itself against insolvency by a comparable arrangement with one of the big banking houses (D) in a period when a banking family could (and did) in effect underwrite the risk that Wellington would lose the Battle of Waterloo. Such then was the setting in which one of the first surviving Life Insurance corporations, the *Equitable*, came into being (1762).

There had been earlier and unsuccessful ventures. If they had conducted business solely with lottery proprietors, Bernoulli's theorem might supply a rationale for success of one or failure of the other. A gambler with more capital can play more games without risk of insolvency and play them for higher stakes. More often then, but not necessarily so, the firm with more capital will increase its capital and less often will become insolvent than a smaller one, meanwhile improving its prospect of continuing in business with greater rewards, if it does not fail. This interpretation of the theorem presumes that the firm does in fact operate in circumstances strictly comparable to the relation between the corporation C and the gambler A. That gambling on the lives of one's clients is strictly comparable to gambling on the success of a lottery or of a gamester at the card table will seem plausible enough if we equate what is probable to what is not quite certain, whence and by merely verbal association extending the terms of reference of the algebraic concept of probability to embrace any situations about which our information is inadequate to sustain a firm assertion. The author of the theorem (Cap IV) does indeed anticipate such a use of it when he thus foreshadows a stochastic rationale of the Life Table:

... who can say how much more easily one disease than another— plague than dropsy, dropsy than fever—can kill a man, to enable us to make conjectures about the future state of life or death? ... such and similar things depend upon completely hidden causes, which, besides, by reason of the innumerable variety of combinations will forever escape our efforts to detect them. . . . However, there is another way to obtain what we want. And what is impossible to get a priori, at least can be found a posteriori; that is, by registering the results of observations performed a great many times.

To assess rightly the relevance of the theorem to the prospects of the *Equitable* corporation, we may usefully recall Uspensky's verdict, and his two criteria of its legitimate application

. . . little, if any, value can be attached to practical applications of Bernoulli's theorem, unless the conditions presupposed in this theorem are at least approximately fulfilled: independence of trials and constant probability of an event for every trial. And in questions of application it is not easy to be sure whether one is entitled to make use of Bernoulli's theorem; consequently, it is too often used illegitimately.

That year to year variation of death rates referable to particular diseases is strictly independent in the stochastic sense of the term is a postulate to which biologists in general and epidemiologists in particular could now advance formidable objections. To assert that the probability of the event is fixed from year to year is flagrantly inconsistent with mortality experience of all civilised communities in the century and a half dating from the eclipse of the classical tradition, but such an assumption was by no means repugnant to common experience in the historic context of the *Ars Conjectandi*. If therefore the historical tie-up between insurance and gambling helps us to understand how easily this identification could gain universal assent, a necessary logical relation between the classical calculus of probability and the empirical rule of thumb which dictates actuarial practice is today less easy to detect.

In our own social context, it is surely difficult to see why computations referable to empirical confidence in the short-term stability of the vital statistics of populations requires any explicit introduction of the classical theory. The entire argument on which Euler (1760) bases his formulae for life annuities in *Récherches sur la mortalité*, etc., is presentable, like those for the construction of the life table itself, without recourse to any considerations other than experience and simple arithmetic.

Indeed, this is how Todhunter expounds it. Todhunter himself expresses an unwitting uneasiness when he declares

This history of the investigations on the laws of mortality and of the calculations of life insurances is sufficiently important and extensive to demand a separate work; these subjects were originally connected with the Theory of Probability but may now be considered to form an independent kingdom in mathematical science . . .

Nor is Todhunter alone in his misgivings. Though intensive study of algebraic probability has been compulsory till recently as a vocational discipline only in the training of Actuaries, and still occupies a place of honour in the actuarial curriculum, an influential body of actuarial mathematicians subscribe to the conclusion last stated, as the reader may infer from the pages of the *Journal of the Institute of Actuaries* (1945). A report on papers written for the Twelfth International Congress of Actuaries with the heading *The Theory of Probability in Insurance*, expresses the view:

The part that the theory of probability plays in insurance is regarded as important by Baptiste, de Finetti, Berger, doubtful by Hammon and Clarke, Lah, and of little consequence by Hagstroem, Shannon, ten Pas.

The most we can say about the relevance of the classical theory to the task of the Actuary is that the arithmetical operations which we may carry out with confidence as a prescription of long-term policy when we can legitimately presume that Uspensky's two-fold condition does hold good suggest a rough and ready pattern for short-term policy in a changing situation when the firm fixes its stake with a sufficiently generous safety margin. The fate of the *Equitable* indeed vindicates the merit of such a margin.

The *Equitable* felicitously based its early premiums on the Northampton Life Table, the author of which grossly underestimated the population at risk by using the data of baptismal registers in a township with a large dissenting community. By this error the firm added a vast sum to its capital assets. By the same error the British government at that time lost heavily on annuity outpayments to its pensioners. If the actuaries of the *Equitable* did in fact shape its policy in conformity with Bernoulli's theorem and with Bernoulli's own recipe for a *posteriori* ascertainment of the putatively constant probability of the event at each trial, the efficacy of their recommendations confers its sanction neither on the theorem nor on the recipe.

How powerfully the analogy between insurance risks and those of the gambler was to influence statistical thinking, the now technical connotation of the word *expectation* sufficiently attests. A remarkable contribution of D. Bernoulli (1760) contemporaneous with the *Recherches* of Euler and entitled *Essai d'une novelle analyse de la mortalité causée par la petite Vérole*, etc., provides a direct link between actuarial preoccupations and Quetelet's identification of the so-called laws of chance with the laws of population. At a time when the Turkish practice of inoculation had newly reached Western Europe, the vital statistics of smallpox had already enlisted the attention of D'Alembert. In the *Essai* mentioned, D. Bernoulli set out how the incidence of a disease (*smallpox*) which confers immunity, will decline as age advances. Though this, for its time so remarkable feat of analysis, seems to have passed unnoticed by British epidemiologists till Greenwood drew our attention to it, it may well have provoked interest on the Continent, where there appeared in 1840 the first noteworthy book about medical statistics, namely *Principes généraux de Statistique Médicale* by Jules Gavarret. Bernoulli's essay on smallpox is itself justly noteworthy as a landmark in the history of epidemiology; but it can stand on its own feet without the crutches of a stochastic calculus to support its weight.

The formal identification of the risk of dying with the risks of casting a double six in two tosses of a die becomes more explicit when Laplace introduces the entirely Platonic notion of the infinite hypothetical population, expounded by Todhunter as follows:

Laplace then considers the probability of the results founded on tables of mortality: he supposes that if we had observations of the extent of life of an infinite number of infants the tables would be perfect, and he estimates the probability that the tables formed from a finite number of infants will deviate to an assigned extent from the theoretically perfect tables.

Two new concepts emerge in the treatment of the problem by Laplace. Initially and explicitly, he asks us to conceive an infinite and hypothetical population of which any actual population is an imperfect sample. Next, in effect, he asks us to conceive our observed sample as a sample taken randomwise therefrom. The assumption last stated is the kingpin of the theory of statistical inference expounded by R. A. Fisher, who follows in the tradition of Karl Pearson when he asserts (1925) unequivocally:

any body of numerical observation or qualitative data, thrown into a numerical form as frequencies may be interpreted as a random sample of some infinite hypothetical population of possible values. (*Proc. Camb. Phil. Soc.*, XXII.)

To do justice to the *infinite hypothetical population* it will be useful to examine separately the implications of its infinite contents and its hypothetical attributes. Its model was the urn of the Royal Lottery. It is not wholly an accident of fate that the urn model invoked in the promulgation of the doctrine of Laplace was also the funeral urn of the Forward Look. No familiar conventions of daily life inhibit an inclination prompted by a theoretical prepossession to enlarge both its size and the number of *billets* or balls it contains; but a so seemingly innocent materialisation seemingly also confers the licence to dispense with the temporal series of the event, as we conceive it for the benefit of the gambler who perseveres in quest of his winnings. Our universe of choice is a *bran tub universe* into which each of an infinitude of children is at liberty to dip and to withdraw therefrom a single r-fold sample at one and the same instant of time. Thus the Forward Look has now become a fixed stare. The framework of repetition is no longer historic; and its conceptualisation in a static imagery invites us to forget an essential property of the new model. If our model justifiably endows the event with constant probability at each trial, what we predicate of such sampling will be more or less relevant to what will happen at next year's Christmas Party only if the bran tub of today is in all relevant particulars identical with the bran tub of tomorrow.

Before we can persuade ourselves that any sample from this

bran tub universe is indeed what Fisher calls a random sample, and hence that we can speak of the constant probability of the event at each trial, we encounter a difficulty discussed in an earlier chapter (p. 75). The mere fact that our card pack is infinite does not dispense with the need to prescribe a rule to ensure randomwise removal of samples therefrom. If we concede that the observed population of the village of Glynceiriog in the year 1953 is in some transcendental sense a sample of some infinite hypothetical population, the assumption that the latter is also, as such, an unchanging universe of choice does not suffice to endorse the relevance of the classical calculus to the process of sampling therefrom. We must equip it with all the essential properties of the *Irregular Kollektiv*; and it is by no means easy to discern a single adequate reason for doing so. Kendall, who subscribes to the enlistment of a new term with a so highly emotive content when asserting (p. 19) that "the population conceived of as parental to an observed distribution is fundamental to statistical inference," likewise concedes with commendable candour that the concept of the infinite hypothetical population:

. . . is not required (and indeed has been explicitly rejected by Jeffreys) in the approach which takes probability as an undefinable measurement of attitudes of doubt. But if we take probability as a relative frequency, then to speak of the probability of a sample such as that given by throwing a die or growing wheat on a plot of soil, we must consider the sample against the background of a population. There are obvious logical difficulties in regarding such a sample as a selection—it is a selection without a choice—and still greater difficulties about supposing the selection to be random; for to do so we must try to imagine that all the other members of the population, themselves imaginary, had an equal probability of assuming the mantle of reality, and that in some way the actual event was chosen to do so. This is, to me at all events, a most baffling conception. (*The Advanced Theory of Statistics*, Vol. I.)

The popularisation of the term population for what we may now call the *Irregular Kollektiv*, with less risk of the self-deception incident to use of common speech in a highly technical context, was largely due to Quetelet, whose *niche* in the history of statistical theory we have already noticed (pp. 18-20). Quetelet wrote in the context of Gauss, and we must therefore defer a full consideration of the misconceptions embedded in the *mystique* he bequeathed to posterity. As they concern the theme of this chapter, what is most relevant emerges from the following citation from Keynes who elsewhere remarks "there is scarcely any permanent accurate contribution to knowledge which can be associated with his name":

> Quetelet very much increased the number of instances of the Law of Great Numbers and also brought into prominence a slightly variant type of it, of which a characteristic example is the law of heights, according to which the heights of any considerable sample of a population tend to group themselves according to a certain well-known curve. His instances were chiefly drawn from social statistics and many of them were of a kind well calculated to strike the imagination—the regularity of the number of suicides, *l'effrayante exactitude avec laquelle les crimes se reproduisent* and so forth. Quetelet writes with an almost religious awe of these mysterious laws, and certainly makes the mistake of treating them as being adequate and complete in themselves like the laws of physics and as little needing any further analysis or explanation. Quetelet's sensational language may have given a considerable impetus to the collection of social statistics but it also involved statistics in a slight element of suspicion. . . . The suspicion of quackery has not yet disappeared. (*Treatise on Probability*, p. 335.)

In this context, we must interpret the *Law of Great Numbers* in an empirical sense. Experience commonly shows that social indices of a large population fluctuate less widely than those of small ones as will commonly be true if: (*a*) the latter are its constituents; (*b*) they do not all fluctuate in the same direction at the same time. We can imagine many reasons for this, if we fix our attention on any particular rate and explore the secular or local operation of known agencies which determine its magnitude; but there is no *prima facie* reason for regarding a principle of statistical equilibrium formulated in such terms as an outcome of circumstances to which the so-called laws of large numbers severally identified with later elaborations of Bernoulli's theorem by Poisson, Tchebyshev, Cantelli and Markhov are pertinent. Nor did Quetelet himself rely on the algebra of Bernoulli or of Poisson to interpret it in stochastic terms.

We can do full justice to Quetelet's reasoning, only if we first acquaint ourselves with the postulates and proper scope of the Gaussian calculus. The well-known curve referred to by Keynes is indeed the Gaussian Curve of Error, thereafter endorsed as the *normal* distribution; and Quetelet's major error arises from a still too widespread belief that we can legitimately infer an interpretative law of nature from the applicability of an algebraic formula to the contour of a fitting curve. Fortunately, this misconception was less prevalent at the beginning of the nineteenth century, when the formal equivalence of the partial differential equations for conduction of heat and for diffusion of fluids might otherwise have endowed the *caloric* with a longer lease of life. At an early stage, the student of physics now gratefully welcomes the same familiar graphical representations of metrical relations in a diversity of otherwise dissimilar physical phenomena with no disposition to draw false or gratuitous conclusions about what they may have in common; but Quetelet's eagerness to descry curves which recall sampling distributions assumed as the basis of the Gaussian theory of errors in a range of studies less attuned to such coincidences gave a powerful and lasting impetus to the gratuitous intrusion of a stochastic theory of errors of observation into the domain of structural variation. The confusion is still with us. Thus R. A. Fisher, in a passage elsewhere cited (p. 501) from the *Design of Experiments* (p. 195), refers to the *theory of errors* in a context which unequivocally identifies the relevant distribution of a test procedure with that of an infinite population on all fours with that of Quetelet's so-called law of heights. Even more explicitly (p. 56 *op. cit.*) he declares that

the mean square corresponding to 28 degrees of freedom ascribed to *error*, is available as an estimate of the variance of a single plot due to the uncontrolled causes which constitute the errors of our determinations.

If we take this step, we have in fact transferred the responsibility for consistent adherence to the rules of the classical calculus of probabilities from the shoulders of the Chevalier de

Méré to those of Nature disguised as the Divine Dealer. Against the background of his usually urbane comments on other writers, his subsequent criticism of the Galton–Pearson measure of correlation in social enquiries and his final conclusions that the calculus of aggregates alone remains intact amidst the wreckage, the ferocity of Keynes when dealing with Quetelet thus becomes intelligible and fully consistent with his antagonism to the then nascent claims of statistical inference in the domain of the social sciences. For the classical framework of repeated trials is not the way in which Nature makes history.

In the domain of the deductive genetical theory of population Quetelet's much-quoted metaphor about Nature's urn need not lead us far astray; and we can invoke a stochastic interpretation of erroneous observation in the experimental sciences without excessive violence to the classical tradition. In laboratory work, we can postulate a protracted framework of repetition on the explicit assumption that we have the relevant variables under control; but in large measure, the subject-matter of the social sciences consists of unique historical situations which (as such) are unrepeatable in any sense unless we regard the shadow world of human experience as a sample of an infinite stock laid up in the Platonic heaven of universals. Anything we do in the laboratory of government changes the structure of the apparatus and the materials involved in the experiment. The bran-tub universe is an illusion, because the bran-tub at the Christmas party next year will be a new one.

None the less, we cannot concur with Keynes in dismissing Quetelet as an addle-pated and rhetorical enthusiast without likewise condemning a generation which embraced his *mystique*. To understand its appeal, we must recreate the intellectual climate of the period. We have then to remind ourselves that the discussion of annuities in the classical context had attuned the ears of the generation to whom Quetelet and de Morgan addressed themselves to the acceptance of a stable rate of birth and death as a law of Nature proclaimed with the fervour of the pulpit by the parson Malthus and endorsed by Darwin with the status of an article of faith. How else can we explain that all extant books in actuarial practice exhibit the simple arithmetic of the construction of a life table, which is in fact a summary of current events in a rapidly changing situation, as an exercise in probability in contradistinction to an exercise in the Rule of Three? Those of us who are near sixty take for granted a steadily falling infant death rate over the period of a lifetime; and reliable statistics inform us that the mean duration of life in our community has increased steadily since 1837. None the less, the craft guild of actuaries still maintains its privileged position by imposing on candidates for admission a discipline which has had little relevance to the *modus operandi* of the insurance business since the office of the Government Actuary came into being.

It is therefore a circumstance of no mean significance that Karl Pearson's school, which built on the foundations laid by Quetelet and by his disciple Galton opposed with every spurious syllogism endorsed by a basically false theory of inheritance the claim that considerable improvement in the health of the community unaccompanied by selective breeding could be other than an ephemeral event. On any other view, it is impossible to conceive *successive* statistics of a population as samples extracted from one and the same *Irregular Kollektiv*. The tenacity of Pearson's belief in the stability of human populations is thus easy to understand, if difficult to condone. It re-asserts itself today as a deeply religious anxiety to resurrect the doctrine of the gloomy parson after its ceremonial crucifixion in the writings of R. R. Kuczynski and Enid Charles, as when Sir Charles Darwin invites us to look wistfully and hopefully to the Far East from whence cometh our Malthusian damnation.

Kendall concludes the passage last cited from his works by remarking:

At the same time, it has to be admitted that certain events such as dice-throwing do happen as if the constituents were chosen at random from an existent population, and it accordingly seems that the concept of the hypothetical population can be justified empirically.

We may indeed concede that the concept is meaningful and tailored to the requirements of a stochastic calculus in the domain of American dice which behave like the dice of Uspensky (p. 53). If so, we then conceive the infinite population in terms of an historic framework of endless repetition; and the stochastic propriety of the behaviour of the die will suffice to justify the concept as "fundamental" in the wider domain of statistical inference only in so far as we can justifiably endow natural phenomena with its relevant properties. In particular, and needless to say, we implicitly concede that the probability of the event remains constant at each trial. How Quetelet accomplished the feat of proving to the satisfaction of his contemporaries that variation in the domain of biological and sociological enquiry is indeed the manifestation of a self-randomising process, we shall examine more closely in the Gaussian *milieu*. Here it suffices to remark that the exclusion of this principle, as a precondition to the tie-up of the algebraic law of great numbers with the empirical stability of large units of population, also and inexorably excludes from the proper domain of stochastic theory a theme which has lately become another fashionable playground for algebraic exploits. A single quotation will suffice to show that the present writer is not alone in affirming this conviction. In *The Theory and Measurement of Demand* (pp. 214–15), Henry Schultz (1938) declares:

Now time series, especially those relating to social and economic phenomena, are likely to violate in a marked degree the fundamental assumption . . . that not only the successive items in the series but also the successive parts into which the series may be divided must be random selections from the *same* universe. Time series are, in fact, a group of successive items with a characteristic conformation. Such series . . . cannot be considered as a random sample of any definable universe except in a very unreal sense. Nor are the successive items in the series independent of one another. . . . The fact is that the "universe" of our time series does not "stay put," and the "relevant conditions" under which the sampling must be carried out cannot be recreated. . . . It is clear, then, that standard errors derived from time series relating to social and economic phenomena do not have the same heuristic properties that they have, or are supposed to have, in the natural sciences.

Aside from a legitimate objection to the licence conferred on gratuitous extension of stochastic principles to unique historical situations by the use of the word population ambiguously both for what we have elsewhere called the fixed universe of choice and for the dynamic orderless collective of von Mises, its prevalence in statistical literature is exceptionable because it has added a new difficulty to the exposition of the theory of probability by depriving a *frequency distribution* of any single clear-cut meaning. Thus current statistical textbooks exhibit results of experiments on tossing dice side by side with records of rainfall and weights of beans. In one and the same context, a frequency distribution may thus mean:

(i) a precise specification (elsewhere called a unit sample distribution) of actual or relative frequencies of discrete score values in either an infinite or a finite known universe of choice such as an urn;

(ii) a comparable specification of relative frequencies in a hypothetical continuum of score values;

(iii) a deductive algebraic specification of the relative frequencies of an infinitude of r-fold samples taken randomwise from the appropriate universe of choice, if specifiable in terms of (i) or (ii);

(iv) an empirical specification of numbers or proportions of individual numbers of any finite assemblage classifiable with respect to some numerically specifiable attribute by a system of scores which may stand for counts (e.g. deaths per thousand, red blood cells per *cmm*) or for measurements (e.g. heights) grouped in discrete intervals;

(v) a descriptive curve of best fit for (iv) supposedly exhibiting the composition of a parent assemblage w.r.t. which (iv) itself is a sample.

It is therefore all too easy for the beginner to assume that a hypothetical construct such as (ii) can rightly claim the same factual credentials as (i) or that (iv) stands in the same relation to (v) as (iii) to (i). That the legitimacy of such assumptions is highly debatable will have sufficiently emerged from our examination of the classical heritage. Whether considerations which emerge in a later context can substantiate them will dictate a rational assessment of the enduring contribution statistical theory can make to the advancement of science.

When we do examine in greater detail the arguments Quetelet advanced to sustain the thesis that empirical distributions such as the so-called law of heights are the outward and visible sign of a natural shuffling process, the circumstance that he was the foremost Belgian astronomer and meteorologist in the thirties of the nineteenth century will disclose more than one intelligible clue to the genesis of his monumental *non sequitur*. Here it will suffice to refer to the attitude Quetelet adopted to scientific law. By no means the amateur and the playboy portrayed by Keynes, Quetelet was indeed an academician of high esteem. As founder of the Belgian national observatory, he was a custodian of the Newton–Laplace cosmogony with a peculiar interest in natural periodicities, meteorological and ecological. If we subscribe both to the view that some unique verbal formulation can embrace every situation in which men of science speak of a law of nature and to the eighteenth-century belief that Newton's law of universal gravitation is its supreme paradigm, what experimental science must now dismiss as an absurdity assumes the aspect of a truism in the highly respectable tradition extending from Aristarchus and Hipparchus to Ptolemy, from Ptolemy to Kepler and from Kepler to Einstein.

In the proper domain of celestial periodicities beyond man's power to control, the identification of the discovery of such a law with an exercise in curve-fitting is consistent with what we do in fact commonly agree to call a law of nature in the same context. In asserting Kepler's laws of the planets as in asserting Calvin's laws of God, we ourselves occupy the role of passive spectators impotent to set aside what the Almighty predestined and foreordained in the beginning. That all scientific laws are expressible in such terms is likewise consistent with a social doctrine which extends from Kepler's contemporary Calvin through Adam Smith and Malthus to Darwin, to Galton, the father of the political cult variously named *eugenics* or *Rassenhygiene*, to Galton's disciple Karl Pearson and to Dr. Malan. Thus Quetelet, Malthus and Galton alike conceived a law of society in terms entirely consistent with the prevailing concept of natural law as the statement of an unchangeable regularity which man's own frail and sinful nature can never gainsay.

Though himself confessedly an impenitent devotee of Malthus, Keynes derides the awe with which Quetelet proclaims these eternal verities; but a concept of natural law so widely acknowledged, and one which Karl Pearson took as the text of his *Grammar*, has inspired others of the same persuasion, notably Galton, to utterances equally in tune with those of Calvinistic theologians proclaiming the inscrutable exclusion of all the sons of Ham from the benefits of the New Dispensation of Grace. If one endorses the identification of all scientific law with statements on all fours with charts of the unchanging periodicities of the heavenly bodies, one can complain with little justice about the melancholy earnestness of Quetelet's declaration:

We pass from one year to another with the sad perspective of seeing the same crimes reproduced in the same order and calling down the same punishments in the same proportions. Sad condition of humanity. . . . We might enumerate in advance how many individuals will stain their hands in the blood of their fellows, how many will be forgers, how many will be poisoners, almost we can enumerate in advance how many births and deaths there should occur. There is a budget we pay with a frightful regularity; it is that of prisons, chains and the scaffold.

Quetelet had at least one excuse which we cannot plead in exoneration of Galton's equally rhetorical relapses. All the thinking in his *Essai de Physique Sociale* had already taken shape before a laboratory demonstration of the first law of thermo-dynamics by Joule vindicated the common sense of British engineers in the following of James Watt. Here, admittedly, is law conceived in terms no less inexorable than the law of universal gravitation; but the intention is wholly different. The emphasis is henceforth on law conceived as a recipe for action in man's exercise of his power to make all things new. Quetelet's teaching also antedated the controversy over evolu-tion. Here we must adjust our sights again. Like the law delivered on tables of stone, what is law is now the written word of the record of the rocks. Eventually, we have thus three concepts of law to accommodate, that of the Nautical Almanac, that of the Cookery Book and that of the Statute Book. Whether J. S. Mill or Karl Pearson succeeded in finding a formula for scientific method able to subsume all three or even any two of them is still debatable.

Perhaps the worst we may say of Quetelet is that he was consistent in the worst sense of the term. No less than his professional preoccupation with a prescription of natural law dictated by the teaching of the Newtonian era, Quetelet's nostalgia for the *ancien régime* in the stormy setting of 1848 is the hallmark of one of two conflicting ideologies which reappear in a new guise at times congenial to innovation. We fail to recognise the peculiar strength of its appeal to the individual, if we disregard the vigour with which many innovators of the past have assumed the role of champions of ancient liberties. In different places and at different times the partisans of over-privilege and the pamphleteers of the have-nots may vigorously espouse a dogmatic determinism or a euphoric libertarianism for reasons to which logic alone furnishes no clue.

In Quetelet's boyhood a united front against clerical authority had little inclination to recognise a dichotomy, which will emerge again and again as we proceed with our examination of current statistical doctrine. It does not assert itself in the contemporary writings of Whewell and Mill. It could enlist little attention in the climate of the third session of the British Association, when Quetelet brought the evangel of *Physique Sociale* to Cambridge. In the following of the *École Polytechnique*, the exhilaration of successfully imposing on every admissible branch of human knowledge a discipline congenial to the cosmogony of Laplace and Lagrange was a sentiment shared by strange bedfellows. Of necessity the undertaking had to accommodate itself to two streams of humanistic thinking. In the setting of the 18*th Brumaire*, Comte is the pilot of one, Quetelet of the other. The successors of both are with us; but few among those whose preferences lean to the conservative and descriptive rather than to the perfectionist and experimentalist tradition would now care to subscribe to the rationale of Quetelet's conservatism. We still know little about how to diminish crime; but a programme of research with that end in view is by no means meet for contemptuous dismissal as an unscientific aspiration engendered in the enthusiasm of the English Evangelical revival and the French Revolution.

We do not err too widely from the track of our assigned enquiry, if we thus pause to see Quetelet and his enthusiastic following in the milieu of the 1848 Commune and the Great Exhibition of 1851. As the parent of what we have elsewhere called the *calculus of exploration*, he was more than the inventor of a technique. He was the architect of a system of values and of an epistemology later inflicted by Karl Pearson on a generation still surviving. The intellectual climate of Quetelet's generation thus forces on our attention an issue which we shall have to face in more than one form, if we intend to carry out an exhaustive revaluation of the claims and credentials of current statistical theory. At a later stage, we shall see how prominent a part Pearson's unique formula for enquiry subsumed by the expression *scientific method* and by any unique definition of *law* suitable to all the uses of scientific enquiry plays in the background of the theory of regression. If we hope to pass judgment with wisdom on conflicting current claims of statistical inference, we shall also find ourselves forced to re-examine Mill's attempt to disclose a common denominator for the reflective and retrospective disciplines on the one hand and for the activist and prospective disciplines on the other.

CHAPTER FIVE

THE BACKWARD LOOK AND THE
BALANCE SHEET OF THOMAS BAYES

WE MAY DIVIDE what we have called the classical period into two phases. The first culminates in the publication of the *Ars Conjectandi*. At this stage, the calculus of probability makes only one claim to topical relevance. Inasmuch as it endorses a rationale for the division of stakes in games of chance, it can supply to court circles a new theme for conversational entertainment; but it can offer to a thrifty bourgeoisie no certain recipe for swelling a bank balance. It has as yet no solid foothold in the world of affairs. Were it not for what followed shortly after, it would have accomplished little to engage the interest of posterity.

In the background of the second phase we discern the juncture of two circumstances. An effete dynasty, otherwise unable to endow the whims of its mistresses from a treasury which supported the largest standing army of the time, had successfully commercialised the art of gambling to beguile the surrender of their savings from subjects sullenly rebellious against the salt tax. Meanwhile, the practice of life insurance had gained a firm foothold with new prospects of gain for merchants of substance. In this setting, there was a new public eager enough to give ear to the popularisation of the theory of probability. Diderot's co-editor of the greatest popular work of all time was none other than d'Alembert, himself a prominent exponent of the theory.

If the identification of insurance risks with the hazards of the gaming table is exceptionable from our own viewpoint, it committed the contemporaries of d'Alembert to no rupture with the doctrine of their predecessors. The latter had relied exclusively on their own intuitions to prescribe when the concept of *random* choice is admissible. If those who succeeded them indulged in the same liberty, they did not violate the explicit teaching of their teachers. To be sure, a generation less tolerant of Platonic notions might have rejected the infinite hypothetical population of Laplace as a gratuitous meta-physical abstraction; but its intrinsically stochastic properties will be repugnant to our inclinations only if we have accepted the obligation to define circumstances relevant to our recognition of random occurrence. We have already seen that no writer on probability before von Mises paid much attention to this issue; and what now seems to us to be a formidable factual obstacle to the acceptance of the infinite hypothetical population in the context of life insurance provoked no remonstrance from the many adherents to Quetelet's belief in a fixed norm about which births and deaths fluctuate in accordance with a law comparable to the Gaussian law of error.

In short, de Moivre, Euler and d'Alembert and D. Bernoulli did not overtly deviate from the *Forward Look* of their predecessors, when they turned their attention to the theory of the Life Table. What signalises a manifest break with the past is the announcement of the doctrine of *inverse probability*. The principal proponent of the doctrine, commonly associated with the name of an English dissenting divine in the circle of Joseph Priestley, was Laplace himself; but no account of it is complete if we fail to mention a theorem which has kept posterity guessing for nearly two centuries. In 1763 the Royal Society published in its *Philosophical Transactions* a posthumous contribution of the Rev. Thomas Bayes. Dr. Richard Price, himself like Bayes and Priestley a Unitarian minister and like the latter a Fellow, communicated it to the Society. Price prepared for publication the script from the author's unrevised relicta. Were it not for the fact that Laplace later acknowledged it as the spiritual parent of his own *mystique*, few of us would have heard of it. As matters stand, most subsequent writers on statistical theory up to and including the present time recognise the *Essay towards solving a Problem in the Doctrine of Chance* as a landmark, and its contents as a challenge or programme, according to taste. ●

Price merits comment *en passant* on his own account. From a *View of the Rise and Progress of the Equitable Society* (1828) by its actuary, William Morgan, F.R.S., we learn that the promoters of the *Equitable*, when first incorporated (1762), gained much "profit by the advice and instruction of such a person as

Dr. Price" who "communicated to the court of directors some observations on the proper method of keeping the accounts and determining from year to year the state of the society." We also read that

this invaluable communication contained three plans for that purpose detailed at considerable length:—the first, by ascertaining the proportion of the claims to the premiums; the second, by comparing the decrements of life in the Society with those in the Table, from which its premiums were computed; the third, by making a separate computation of the values of all the different policies of assurance, and comparing the amount with the capital of the Society. In addition to these plans, Dr. Price, among other important advice, urged the necessity of altering the tables of premiums then published in the *Short Account* of the Society, not only as being exorbitant, but absurd, and inconsistent with the result of all observations—alluding particularly to the female and youth hazards. These extraordinary charges were, in consequence, immediately abolished, and each of the three plans above mentioned was adopted for ascertaining the state of the Society from the year 1768 to the year 1776 inclusive. By the first of these plans it appeared that, on an average, during the nine preceding years, the annual surplus had been about 3000 £. By the second plan, that the probabilities of life in the Society had been higher than those in Mr. Dodson's Table, from which its premiums were computed, in the proportion of three to two. And by the third plan, that the whole surplus stock amounted nearly to 30,000 £. In consequence of results so highly favourable to the Society, the premiums were reduced *one-tenth*: which does not, however, appear to have had any great effect, either in increasing the business or in lessening the annual surplus; for the continual accession of new members, by adding to the number of the old ones, fully supplied the deficiency produced in the surplus by the reduction of the premiums, and thus made it increase very nearly in the same proportion as in the two or three preceding years.

It appears that Price was directly responsible for the adoption of the Northampton Life Table already mentioned (p. 96).

In the year 1780, Dr. Price had formed a great number of tables deduced from the probabilities of life at Sweden, Chester, Northampton, and other places, preparatory to the fourth edition of his work on Reversionary Payments. These tables he considered as more correct than any hitherto published, and recommended the adoption either of the Chester or the Northampton to the Society, in lieu of the very imperfect table from which its premiums had hitherto been computed. This, like every other measure recommended by Dr. Price, was agreed to without hesitation, and before the end of the year 1781, a complete set of tables was formed from the Northampton observations, consisting of more than 20,000 computations, and containing the values of single and joint lives of all ages, and the single and annual premiums of assurance of every description; but the latter, though computed at 3 per cent, were so far below the premiums then in use, that it was thought proper to make an addition of 15 per cent to them, to prevent too sudden a reduction in the annual income of the Society. By the adoption of these new tables, the annual premiums, which would then have been 36,000 £, if the old tables had been continued, were reduced to little more than 32,000 £, and in order to compensate the members then existing, for having contributed to the success of the Society by the payment of higher premiums than were necessary, an addition was made to each 100 £ assured by them of thirty shillings for every payment which had been made prior to the 1st of January 1782. During this and the three following years, the number of new assurances annually increased about *one half* of their former number, and the annual income in the same proportion. This rapid growth of the Society, added to the circumstance of no particular investigation having been made of its actual state since the year 1776, led to the resolution for making a fresh investigation before any measures should be adopted that had a tendency to affect the finances of the Society. In the course of the year 1785, this laborious work was accomplished, and the result proved so highly favourable that it was determined not only to take off the charge of 15 per cent on the premiums, but to make a further addition of 1 to each 100 £ for every payment made prior to the 1st of January 1786. By these operations the surplus of 164,000 £ was reduced to 110,000, and every person assured prior to 1772, had 30 per cent added to the sum originally assured.

To any careful reader of Morgan's pamphlet, it will be clear that Dr. Price was not the obsessional gambler who adheres to a rule regardless of the consequences; and the hard-headed business men who benefited from his advice and instruction had no scruples about changing the rules of the game as good luck enjoined. A break with the classical tradition was therefore inevitable, if the stochastic calculus was henceforth to annex a territory with so promising a prospect of full employment for the algebraist, and the more so when the immediate successors of Price began to entertain misgivings about the constancy of the *billets* in the mortality lottery. It was soon clear that a malignant fate changes the contents of the funeral urn:

Ever since the promulgation of Mr. Malthus's system, a general alarm has been excited among all ranks and conditions of men in the United Kingdom, that the population increases so fast, and the life of man is extended to such a length, that the fruits of the earth will soon be insufficient to preserve us from perishing by famine. . . . The tables also which formerly denoted the probabilities of life, are now said to be no longer applicable to the improved health and constitutions of the present race, a circumstance which is rendered the more remarkable from the acknowledged increase of pauperism among the greater number of them.

In the first Report of the Committee of the House of Commons on Friendly Societies, a large collection of tables is inserted; which, if we judged from the long line of decimals to which the values are extended, might be considered as a work of uncommon accuracy, and founded on documents which did not even admit of error. But of these documents we have not sufficient information, nor is it indeed a matter of much consequence—the tables themselves, though computed to the millionth part of a *farthing*, being so wrong in the *pounds*, especially in the case of female lives, as to deserve little or no regard. By the assistance of these tables, the notable discovery has been made of the loss sustained by the public of many thousands every week, for several years past, by granting annuities on lives, computed from the Northampton Table of Observations, which had the surprising effect of alarming the House of Commons into a vote for immediately repealing the law which authorized that measure.

The document is worthy of study in its entirety, if the reader still entertains any illusions about the possibility of regulating the affairs of a successful life insurance corporation by strict adherence to the principles of J. Bernoulli. *Inter alia* it is a useful source of information about the early practice of life assurance. Before 1762, the *Amicable* "which had existed from the beginning of the century was the only society formed for the express purpose of making assurances on single lives. . . . Although the *Royal Exchange* and the *London* assurance office were empowered by their characters to assure lives, they seldom availed themselves of that power." It does not appear that Dr. Price enriched himself in his capacity as consultant to the Equitable. Nor is it likely that he did so. In his time, the Anglican Church was still the custodian of what social security the masses enjoyed; and dissent could successfully challenge the prerogative of the parish council as the dispenser of public charity only by showing that thrift pays in the long run. Henceforth paid-up premiums conferred on the *paterfamilias* of the non-conformist household a certificate of piety. As the familiar name of the *Wesleyan and General* reminds us, the chapel vestry remained the recruiting station of the insurance company throughout the nineteenth century. We may therefore charitably assume that the advice and instruction by which the court of the Equitable derived such signal profit, no less than the work of editing the mathematical relicta of his ministerial colleague the Rev. Thomas Bayes, was a labour of love.

Though Bayes's theorem and Bayes's postulate or scholium meet the eye in every contemporary controversial contribution to theoretical statistics, it will rarely happen that three statisticians chosen randomwise will wholly agree about what precisely Bayes did say. Nor will they necessarily agree about which of two different propositions constitute his theorem. In justice to Bayes, one may say that one form of the theorem attributed to him certainly does not occur in his works, and the other, which is a modern interpretation of the *ipsissima verba*, is dubiously consistent with the author's intentions. Such misunderstanding would be merely of lexicographical interest, were it not also true that later generations have chosen to identify, fairly or falsely, the views of Laplace with those of Bayes himself; but we need not wonder why there can be so much confusion about the issue when all the relevant source material is accessible in any creditable university library. Bayes employed in his own notes a symbolism of an older vintage than that of his French contemporaries, being himself steeped in the Newtonian method. That his language is excessively obscure, we may tolerantly condone, since he had no opportunity to assemble the material for publication. Nor need we blame his literary executor who confessedly indulged himself so freely in footnotes and addenda not necessarily consistent with the author's intentions.

However, these circumstances do not throw much light on one novel feature of the memoir, and one which has also been contributory to subsequent mystification. Pascal, pre-eminent among the founding fathers, was likewise the author of a treatise on discrete figurate number series which have a special significance in the elementary calculus of choice; and it would be fair to say that the notion of a continuum, except as a background for performing computations which would otherwise be intolerably laborious, does not intrude aggressively in the classical period. In the *Essay* of Bayes, we are no longer counting discrete pips and discrete faces. We find ourselves in a non-enumerable domain of Platonic points, where summation is quadrature in the most literal sense of the term. In defiance of the, not as yet established, first law of thermodynamics, perfectly spherical and perfectly smooth billiard balls roll at the behest of the author's pen on frictionless planes as the theme of Euclidean demonstrations in the grand manner of the *Principia*.

It is possible to terminate otherwise unending theological disputation about what is real Christianity or about what Karl Marx really meant, if one restricts the opportunity for self-indulgence in phantasy by also limiting the field of discourse to what the gospels actually record or to what *Das Kapital* does indeed state. We shall therefore do well to study closely the text of the *Philosophical Transactions* for the year 1763, interpreting the *ipsissima verba* with due regard to the idiom of the author's contemporaries. The posthumous memoir has two parts. The first sets out as Euclidean propositions, in a style still current when Loney's textbooks of dynamics, statics and hydrostatics became obsolete long after my own schooldays, a few school certificate level tautologies of the classical theory. It is notable only because one of them, one which prompted the editor to comments seemingly inconsistent with the author's intention and one which prompts the first historian of probability to bewildered reflection on its ostensible novelty and possible self-evidence, plays an important role in the section which follows. It there provides a platform for a highly sophisticated pun; and its examination will help us to see the pitfalls of a symbolism which does service to those who locate probability *in* the mind.

To convey the gist of Proposition V, we may suppose that we have several dice to toss so many (r) times or several urns from which to extract randomwise so many (r) balls, recording the score of an r-fold trial as x. One of these dice or one of the urns we shall call an urn of type H. If we follow an appropriate recipe to ensure randomwise choice of urn or die, we may state comprehensively the elementary theorem of multiplication of probabilities for a situation involving *two* acts of choice by recourse to appropriate symbols as follows:

$P_{h.r}$ is the unconditional probability that we *shall* first choose an urn or die of type H;

$P_{x.r}$ is the unconditional probability that the score of the r-fold trial *will* be x;

$L_{x.hr}$ is the conditional probability that the r-fold trial score *will* be x if we do in fact first choose an urn or die of type H;

$L_{h.xr}$ is the conditional probability that we *shall* choose an urn or die of type H in the infinite sub-set of r-fold trials which yield the particular score x;

$P_{h.xr}$ is the unconditional probability of the compound event that we shall both score x and choose an urn or die of type H.

The elementary multiplication theorem then takes the comprehensive form

$$P_{x.r} \cdot L_{h.xr} = P_{h.xr} = P_{h.r} \cdot L_{x.hr}$$

Thus we may write with equal propriety:

$$L_{h.xr} = \frac{P_{h.r} \cdot L_{x.hr}}{P_{x.r}} \ or \ L_{x.hr} = \frac{P_{x.r} \cdot L_{h.xr}}{P_{h.r}} \tag{i}$$

Now there is nothing new in the identity on the left, which is in fact Proposition V of Section I of the Bayes memoir; but one can read into it something foreign to the thought of the classical period in the light of what use Bayes makes of it in Section II. There the author advances, intentionally or otherwise, a new idea. We think of multiplication as an operation to which division is the corresponding *inverse* operation; and our algebraic jargon here becomes entangled in our daily habits of verbal discourse. Bayes may have thought, and Price certainly did think, that the division theorem set forth as (i) above confers the licence to look backwards as well as forwards, when we specify a rule of procedure within the framework of the classical theory of risks in games of chance; but the intentional insertion of the italicised future auxiliary in the foregoing specification of our symbols should suffice to remind us that this is a verbal trick. From his own words, which Todhunter complains of as obscure, there is no indication that Bayes intended to exploit the punning potentialities of a trivial tautology for rhetorical effect in this context. It may help to clarify what follows if we here recall his own idiom:

If there be two subsequent events, the probability of the 2nd b/N and the probability of both together P/N, and it being first discovered that the 2nd event has happened, from hence I guess that the 1st event has also happened, the probability I am in the right is P/b.

The use of the verb *guess* by Bayes in this context is instructive. It recalls the literal derivation of a word current in English long before it became part of the jargon of statistical theory, as when Dean Swift* writes: "I am master of the stockastic art; and by virtue of that, I divine that those Greek words in that discourse have crept from the margin into the text otherwise than the author intended." In the classical theory of wagers, every bet is a guess; and the probability that the guess will be right is the probability that the event specified by the guess will occur in the endless sequence of the event. In the classical tradition, we can assign a probability to our guesswork in this sense only if we confine our statements to guesses dictated by a rule stated in advance; and the use of the past tense in this citation entails no explicit renunciation of the

---

* In *Right of Precedence between Physicians and Civilians enquired into*. Misc. Works 1720.

Forward Look, if we interpret the terms of reference of the probability assignable to a guess on this understanding. Seemingly, Bayes did recognise a nicety which is at the very core of what is most controversial at the present time, viz. the distinction between statements about the probability of events and statements about the probability of making correct assertions about events. Whatever we may justly say in criticism of Bayes, this much is certain. He never explicitly locates probability in the nebulous domain of the *mind*.

So far, there is nothing new in Section I of the memoir; and if we choose to verbalise (p. 117) the fifth proposition in terms of hypotheses rather than events, no confusion need arise when there is a factually realisable event corresponding to each hypothesis involved in the specification of a trial which involves *two* independent performances of randomwise sampling. One may indeed dismiss the likelihood that the statement of the *division* theorem would have led to any misunderstanding, were it not for the part it plays in Section II. The theme of the latter is the following model situation. Two balls successively come to rest on a smooth rectangular table at some point [*sic*]; and at this point we may discard the *ipsissima verba* of the author, if we wish to extract any intelligible message from the model. The truth is that this non-Euclidean and very real ball does not make contact with a Euclidean point. It comes to a standstill resting on a finite area of the surface of the said table. We may therefore convey the legitimate intentions of the author in the classical idiom, if we here interpret them against the background of a comparable, but factually realisable, situation unencumbered by Euclidean prepossessions.

Accordingly, we shall suppose that the table has equally spaced holes in rows and columns, the number of holes per row (i.e. number of columns) being a, numbered from the edge as $1, 2, 3 \ldots a$. If the number of holes per column (i.e. number of rows) is b, the total number of holes is $n = ab$. In accordance with Postulate 1 at the head of Section II of the memoir,* we suppose that a ball released on the table will drop into any

* Postulate 1. I suppose the square table or plane ABCD to be so made and levelled, that if either of the balls O or W be thrown upon it, there shall be the same probability that it rests upon any one equal part of the plane as another, and that it must necessarily come to rest.

single hole in the long run as often as it drops into any other, also that the ball will not rest till it falls into one of them. We may then write:

$P_{kh} = n^{-1}$ the probability that a ball will drop into the kth hole of the hth row in a unit trial;

$P_h = b^{-1}$ the probability that a ball will drop into one or other of the a holes of the hth row in a unit trial;

$p_h = h \cdot b^{-1}$ the probability that a ball will drop into one of the h rows 1, 2 ... h at a single trial.

We are now ready to undertake the 2-*stage* experiment which is the topic of Proposition VIII at the beginning of Section II. We take two balls A and B, release A first recording the row (h) in which it comes to rest as the A-score, withdraw it and then release B successively r times recording x as the B-score of the r-fold trial if it comes to rest x times in one of the h rows 1, 2, 3 ... h. The probability that the B-score will be x is accordingly

$$L_{x.hr} = r_{(x)} \cdot p_h^x \cdot (1 - p_h)^{r-x} = \frac{r_{(x)} \cdot h^x \cdot (b-h)^{r-x}}{b^r} \quad \text{(ii)}$$

We now ask: what is the probability of the compound event that the A-score will be h and the B-score will be x? By the elementary theorem of multiplication this is:

$$P_{hx} = P_h \cdot L_{x.hr} = \frac{r_{(x)} \cdot h^x \cdot (b-h)^{r-x}}{b^{r+1}} \quad . \quad . \quad \text{(iii)}$$

Such is a fair translation of the factual content of Proposition VIII*; and it registers no innovation. We shall now frame a different question, which is indeed novel. We postulate the following situation. We shall confine our attention to an infinite *sub-sequence* of trials in which the B-score is x as already defined. We shall then *guess* that the A-score in any such trial will be h. Stated in terms consistent with the Forward Look, the topic of Proposition IX is: *how often will our guess be right, if we consistently follow such a prescription for guessing?* In effect, the answer Bayes gives is the ratio of the infinite number of all

---

* In the Euclidean continuum of Bayes the probability here defined by P_h will be infinitesimal. Bayes actually specifies a row-score lying between u and v; and gives the result somewhat portentously as an area.

compound trials in which the A-score is h when the B-score is x to the infinite number of all compound trials in which the B-score is x. In the foregoing symbolism this is

$$L_{h.xr} = \frac{P_{h.r} \cdot L_{x.hr}}{P_{x.r}}$$

In this expression $P_{x.r}$ is the unconditional probability that the B-score will be x for the whole range of A-scores 1, 2, 3 . . . b, inclusive. Whence by the elementary theorem of addition

$$P_{x.r} = \sum_{m=1}^{m=b} P_{m.r} \cdot L_{x.mr}$$

We may now state our result in terms uniquely defined by x as

$$L_{h.xr} = \frac{P_{h.r} \cdot L_{x.hr}}{\sum\limits_{m=1}^{m=b} P_{m.r} \cdot L_{x.mr}} \qquad \cdots \cdots \quad \text{(iv)}$$

In this expression $P_{h.r}$, the probability that the first ball falls in row h, is independent of h, because that is the prescription of the model embodied in Postulate 1 at the beginning of Section II of the memoir. Whence, $P_{h.r} = P_{m.r}$; and the foregoing reduces to the likelihood ratio:

$$L_{h.xr} = \frac{L_{x.hr}}{\sum\limits_{m=1}^{m=b} L_{x.mr}} \qquad \cdots \cdots \quad \text{(v)}$$

Some writers refer to (iv) and some to (v) as Bayes's theorem. Confusion arises, partly because either form is consistent with the prescription of the model and partly because of the archaic geometrical symbolism in which Bayes states the solution of the Problem. The issue would be of trivial interest but for an after-thought tacked on to Proposition IX as the famous *Scholium* also called Bayes's Postulate, a name more properly reserved for the postulate explicitly and legitimately specifying that the Model has the property which guarantees the identity of (iv) and (v). In the Scholium, Bayes says:

I shall take for granted the rule given concerning the event M in prop. 9 is also the rule to be used in relation to *any event* concerning the probability of which nothing at all is known antecedently to any trials made or observed concerning it. And such an event, I shall call an unknown event. (*Italics inserted.*)

So far, we have kept close to the actual situation in which Bayes applies his theorem, deviating therefrom only in as much as we reject the concept of rest at a point as logically irrelevant and factually inappropriate. Factually, the rule given in Proposition IX of the memoir refers to a situation in which every possible outcome of the first two events is *equally probable* whence we may interpret with equal propriety either (iv) or (v) as the translation in modern symbolism of the theorem embodied in Proposition IX. Here we may break off to clarify the foregoing argument by recourse to a model situation more appropriate, if the end in view is to exhibit the factual implications of (iv) and (v) respectively. Our new model will be a box which contains six *unbiased* tetrahedral dice, which we shall specify as follows:

(*a*) three such dice (*A*) having on one face 1 pip, on each of two faces 2 pips and 3 pips on the fourth face;

(*b*) one such die (*B*) having on the four faces 1, 2, 3 and 4 pips respectively;

(*c*) two such dice (*C*) having on each of three faces 2 pips and 1 pip on the fourth.

To make all the relevant information explicit, we may set out the data as follows, specifying score values as x and probabilities as y:

Type of Die	No. of Dice	Unit sample distribution
A	3	$x = 1 \ 2 \ 3 \ 4$ $y = \frac{1}{4} \ \frac{1}{2} \ \frac{1}{4} \ 0$
B	1	$x = 1 \ 2 \ 3 \ 4$ $y = \frac{1}{4} \ \frac{1}{4} \ \frac{1}{4} \ \frac{1}{4}$
C	2	$x = 1 \ 2 \ 3 \ 4$ $y = \frac{1}{4} \ \frac{3}{4} \ 0 \ 0$

By recourse to a chessboard lay-out we may derive the 2-fold toss score-sum (s_2) distributions thus:

Type of Die	2	3	4	5	6	7	8
A	$\frac{1}{16}$	$\frac{1}{4}$	$\frac{3}{8}$	$\frac{1}{4}$	$\frac{1}{16}$	0	0
B	$\frac{1}{16}$	$\frac{1}{8}$	$\frac{3}{16}$	$\frac{1}{4}$	$\frac{3}{16}$	$\frac{1}{8}$	$\frac{1}{16}$
C	$\frac{1}{16}$	$\frac{3}{8}$	$\frac{9}{16}$	0	0	0	0

We may classify the outcome of the 2-fold toss in several ways of which one will suffice for our purpose, viz.: (i) $s_2 < 4$; (ii) $s_2 \geqslant 4$. The corresponding probabilities for the three types of dice are then:

Die	(i) $s_2 < 4$	(ii) $s_2 \geqslant 4$
A	$L_{i.a} = \frac{5}{16}$	$L_{ii.a} = \frac{11}{16}$
B	$L_{i.b} = \frac{3}{16}$	$L_{ii.b} = \frac{13}{16}$
C	$L_{i.c} = \frac{7}{16}$	$L_{ii.c} = \frac{9}{16}$

We now define a *trial* in the following terms. A blind umpire shakes the box thoroughly to ensure random choice, selects a single die for a player who tosses it *twice*, records the joint score and replaces the die in the box. We may conceive an indefinitely large number of trials conducted in this way, the implications of the prescription being that the player's chance of getting a die of a particular type at a single trial is specifiable in terms of their relative numbers as follows:

TABLE I

Type	Chance of getting same
A	$P_a = \frac{1}{2}$
B	$P_b = \frac{1}{6}$
C	$P_c = \frac{1}{3}$

The entries P_a, P_b, P_c so defined are the so-called *prior probabilities* of the Bayes balance sheet. By the elementary rules of probability we can now set out as below the joint probabilities of: (*a*) getting a score $s_2 < 4$ and $s_2 \geqslant 4$; (*b*) choosing a die of one or other type:

TABLE II

Die	$s_2 < 4$	$s_2 \geqslant 4$	*Total*
A	$\frac{1}{2} \cdot \frac{5}{16} = \frac{5}{32}$	$\frac{1}{2} \cdot \frac{11}{16} = \frac{11}{32}$	$\frac{1}{2}$
B	$\frac{1}{6} \cdot \frac{3}{16} = \frac{1}{32}$	$\frac{1}{6} \cdot \frac{13}{16} = \frac{13}{96}$	$\frac{1}{6}$
C	$\frac{1}{3} \cdot \frac{7}{16} = \frac{7}{48}$	$\frac{1}{3} \cdot \frac{9}{16} = \frac{3}{16}$	$\frac{1}{3}$
Total	$\frac{1}{3}$	$\frac{2}{3}$	I

We have now classified the outcome of all trials which result in a score $s_2 < 4$ under three headings w.r.t. the die selected by the player, viz.:

(*a*) $s_2 < 4$ with die of type A;

(*b*) $s_2 < 4$ with die of type B;

(*c*) $s_2 < 4$ with die of type C.

In conformity with the prescription of the game the long run frequencies associated with the three events are *in the same ratio* as the probabilities in the left-hand column of Table II. Their sum is $\frac{1}{3}$. If we confine our attention to the class of results defined by $s_2 < 4$, we may therefore assert that the long-run proportionate frequencies of such a score referable to each of the three types of dice are:

$$\text{A} \quad \frac{5}{32} \div \frac{1}{3} = \frac{15}{32}$$
$$\text{B} \quad \frac{1}{32} \div \frac{1}{3} = \frac{3}{32}$$
$$\text{C} \quad \frac{7}{48} \div \frac{1}{3} = \frac{14}{32}$$
$$\textit{Total} \qquad \text{I}$$

In the phraseology of Bayes's successors, the adjusted frequencies in the right-hand column are the *posterior probabilities* of our balance sheet. In more general terms, they represent the long-run proportionate frequencies of samples whose source is one or other die in the class of all samples whose score has a particular value. Symbolically, we may label the items of the final balance sheet as follows:

$P_{h.r}$ the *prior* probability that any r-fold sample will come from a die of class H.

$L_{x.hr}$ the *conditional* probability that the r-fold sample score will be x, if the die is of class H.

$L_{h.xr}$ the *conditional* (so-called *posterior*) probability that the r-fold sample whose score is x will come from a die of class H.

By the elementary theorem of multiplication, $P_{h.r}.L_{x.hr}$ is the joint probability that the sample score will be x and that the source will be a die of class H. By the elementary theorem of addition, the unconditional probability that the sample score will be x is the sum of such products for all values of h. The law of the balance sheet is then in agreement with (iv):

$$L_{h.xr} = \frac{P_{h.r}.L_{x.hr}}{\sum\limits_{s=1}^{s=\infty} P_{s.r}.L_{x.sr}} \qquad \ldots \quad \text{(vi)}$$

Let us now suppose that we decide to act in accordance with the following rule: whenever the score of the r-fold sample is x we shall say that the source of the sample is a die of class H; but we shall *reserve judgment* if the r-fold trial score is not x. In an indefinitely protracted sequence of trials, the proportion of samples referable to a die of type H among all samples whose score is x is $L_{h.r}$. Thus $L_{h.r}$ is the long-run proportion of correct statements we shall make if we consistently follow the prescribed rule. If we specify as hypothesis H the particular assertion that the die is of class H, we may then say that $L_{h.r}$ is the probability of choosing hypothesis H correctly by pursuing a prescribed course of behaviour regardless of the outcome of any single trial. Most assuredly, this is not the same thing as saying that $L_{h.r}$ is the probability that hypothesis H is true if the score at a particular trial happens to be x. Likewise, and most assuredly, Bayes never employs this idiom, subsequently accredited to him by implication, in the exposition of Prop. IX in his memoir.

In the foregoing set-up we specify as hypothesis A the

assertion that the die cast is of type A. We may then choose to make the following rule: say that hypothesis A is true *whenever* the score $x = s_2$ of the 2-fold toss is less than 4. Our balance sheet then shows that $\frac{15}{32}$ is the proportion of trials in which we select the die A if we confine our verdicts to the infinite class of trials which yield score values $x < 4$ and reserve judgment about the die chosen in the infinite class of trials which yield score values $x \geqslant 4$. Thus $\frac{15}{32}$ is the probability of correctly choosing hypothesis A if we follow the prescribed rule consistently and $\frac{17}{32}$ is the probability of choosing it wrongly.

Alternatively, among a great number of conceivable rules of this sort, we may choose the following: say hypothesis B (i.e. the die is of class B) is true whenever the score of the 2-fold toss is at least 4. Within this infinite class of trials the proportion of trials in which we select the die B is

$$\frac{1}{6} \cdot \frac{13}{16} \div \left(\frac{1}{2} \cdot \frac{11}{16} + \frac{1}{6} \cdot \frac{13}{16} + \frac{1}{3} \cdot \frac{9}{16} \right) = \frac{13}{64} \simeq 0 \cdot 20$$

In this case, the risk of falsely saying that the die cast is a die of type B is thus approximately $(1 - 0 \cdot 20)$ or 80 per cent. The reader will thus see what the so-called *posterior* probability of the event in the Bayes Balance Sheet means in terms of the classical theory of risk. We may speak of $P_f = (1 - L_{h.x})$ as the risk of falsely choosing hypothesis H as the true one, if we follow the rule of saying that it is specified in advance. We may likewise call $P_t = L_{h.x}$ the *stochastic credibility* of such a rule; and $P_f = (1 - P_t)$ the *uncertainty safeguard* of the rule; but we shall deviate from the classical and behaviouristic approach referable to observable frequencies of external occurrences if we conceive $L_{h.x}$ as the stochastic credibility of the hypothesis H or if we use a form of words assigning a probability $P_f = (1 - L_{h.x})$ to its falsity.

The last model illustrates the implications of what many writers refer to as Bayes's theorem in its most general form, that is to say (iv) above. We could bring it into line with the actual model of Bayes by putting 9 dice, three of each type, in the box. The so-called prior probabilities $(P_a = P_b = P_c = \frac{1}{3})$ are then equal. This imposes on the model the particular restriction embodied in the first postulate of Section II of the

Essay, and the equivalent but more general principle put forward in the Scholium. The reader may adjust the balance sheet accordingly. The expression for $L_{h.x}$ now reduces to (v) which suffices for the Bayes model. For the class of 2-fold samples defined by $x < 4$ we now have

$$L_{x.a} = \frac{5}{16} \; ; \; L_{x.b} = \frac{3}{16} \; ; \; L_{x.c} = \frac{7}{16}$$

$$\sum_{s=1}^{s=\infty} L_{x.s} = \frac{5 + 3 + 7}{16} = \frac{15}{16}$$

$$\therefore L_{h.a} = \frac{1}{3} \; ; \; L_{h.b} = \frac{1}{5} \; ; \; L_{h.c} = \frac{7}{15}$$

Let us now make the rule: say Hypothesis A is true when $x < 4$, otherwise say nothing. Our uncertainty safeguard for the rule so stated is now $\frac{2}{3}$, instead of $\frac{17}{32}$ as for the preceding set-up.

Models of the type so far discussed are remote from the world's work. To get their relevance—if any—to practical affairs into focus, let us now see how we can bring this type of decision into workmanlike relationship to laboratory experience. So we now suppose that a laboratory stock of 1,000 female rats consists of: (*a*) healthy females which carry a sex-linked lethal gene; (*b*) normal healthy females. Accordingly, the probabilities that the individual offspring will itself be female are

$$p_a = \frac{2}{3} \text{ if the mother is a carrier}$$

$$p_b = \frac{1}{2} \text{ if the mother is normal}$$

For heuristic purposes, we may assume with sufficient plausibility that the elimination of male progeny by the lethal gene does not appreciably affect the total number of live-born rats, since there is commonly in rodents a considerable mortality of embryos owing to production in excess of uterine capacity. Let us then ask what long-run proportion of mothers of eight offspring, all female, are respectively carriers and normal. In the foregoing symbolism we state the probability of each event on the appropriate assumption as:

$$L_{8.a} = \left(\frac{2}{3}\right)^8 \simeq 0 \cdot 039 \; ; \; L_{8.b} = \left(\frac{1}{2}\right)^8 \simeq 0 \cdot 0039$$

If we suppose that 5 per cent of the females are carriers, the prior probabilities are:

$$P_a = 0 \cdot 05 \; ; \; P_b = 0 \cdot 95$$

In accordance with (vi) we can thus state as follows the so-called posterior probability of the two events, viz. that the mother of eight all female is a carrier and that the mother of eight all female is normal as

$$L_{a.8} \simeq \frac{(0 \cdot 05) \, (0 \cdot 039)}{(0 \cdot 05) \, (0 \cdot 039) + (0 \cdot 95) \, (0 \cdot 0039)} \simeq 0 \cdot 345$$

$$L_{b.8} \simeq \frac{(0 \cdot 95) \, (0 \cdot 0039)}{(0 \cdot 05) \, (0 \cdot 039) + (0 \cdot 95) \, (0 \cdot 0039)} \simeq 0 \cdot 655$$

Of rat colonies with the prescribed composition, we may thus say elliptically: the probability of correctly asserting that a mother of eight all female is a carrier is $P_t \simeq 0 \cdot 345$; and the probability that such an assertion is false is $P_f = (1 - P_t) \simeq 0 \cdot 655$; but this form of words is legitimate only in so far as we assign the probabilities stated to the operation of the rule and then only if we suppose that we consistently follow some *randomisation recipe* for picking the rat-mother out of the colony. Moreover, we are not legitimately assigning a probability to an *individual verdict*. On that understanding, our judgments will be nearly twice as often wrong as right, if we do consistently follow the rule stated. Alternatively, we may decide to deem a female rat to be normal in the same set-up, if it has eight offspring all female. If so, our uncertainty safeguard will be $0 \cdot 345$ and the stochastic credibility of our assertion will be $0 \cdot 655$. In the long run we shall be about twice as often right as wrong.

Such a specification of so-called *posterior probabilities* in the current idiom of a calculus of judgments presupposes that we know the actual values of the prior probabilities P_a and P_b. In many comparable situations we might know that the colony contained female rats of each of these two classes *alone* without knowing how many of each. Can our Bayes' balance sheet then lead us to formulate a rule with an assignable risk of error? Price thought, and Laplace thought, that the words italicised in the foregoing citation (p. 121) from the notorious Scholium suggest a way out of the difficulty, though it is not wholly clear that Bayes himself confidently proffered the suggestion for model situations to which the initial postulate of Section I has no relevance. The recipe known as the *Bayes' Postulate* is that we here assign equal probability $(P_a = \frac{1}{2} = P_b)$ to the choice of a sample from one or other class of rats when we are wholly ignorant of the true values. If we apply this convention to the foregoing problem, we derive

$$P_{a.8} = \frac{\frac{1}{2}(0 \cdot 039)}{\frac{1}{2}(0 \cdot 039) + \frac{1}{2}(0 \cdot 0039)} \simeq 0 \cdot 91$$

$$P_{b.8} = \frac{\frac{1}{2}(0 \cdot 0039)}{\frac{1}{2}(0 \cdot 039) + \frac{1}{2}(0 \cdot 0039)} \simeq 0 \cdot 09$$

The application of the Bayes' postulate thus confers the value $0 \cdot 09$ as the long-run frequency of false assertion referable to consistent application of the first rule stated above; but we know that the long-run frequency of false assertion in this situation is actually $0 \cdot 655$. Reliance on the Scholium here leads to a result inconsistent with the classical theory. Nor is this surprising, since it entails the vulgar error of *neglecting the population at risk*.

Our difficulties do not end here, if we assume, as do so many writers on statistical theory, that Bayes's theorem in one form or another embraces the terms of reference of a calculus of judgments. That we can rarely give numerical flesh and blood to the algebraic dry bones of the prior probabilities in a set-up of the sort last *discussed* is only one horn of the dilemma with which the invocation of the Scholium confronts us. There is another. We have here presumed the knowledge that the colony contains rat mothers of two sorts; but if we adopt the Scholium as a universal principle of statistical inference, we have to provide for four situations in which the problem of identification may arise:

(a) we both know that the colony contains two sorts of rats, and how many there are of each;

(b) we know that the colony contains rats of both sorts, but we do not know how many there are of each;

(c) for anything we do know to the contrary, the colony consists of one sort only;

(d) we know that it does consist of one sort only, but we do not know which.

From the viewpoint of the mathematician we may say that the statement $P_a = (1-P_b)$ subsumes all four situations, if we allow P_a to have every value from 0 to 1 inclusive; but this evades a highly relevant *factual* aspect of the situation. If we say that $0 < P_a < 1$ as in (a) and (b), we postulate a system of *randomwise* sampling in *two stages* in conformity with the model situation to which the balance sheet is factually relevant. If we say that $P_a = 0$ or $P_a = 1$ in conformity with (d), we say in effect that sampling occurs *in one stage*, in which event the Balance Sheet is irrelevant to the formulation of any rule of procedure consistent with the Forward Look, and the allocation of equal prior probabilities, i.e. the assumption of equal populations at risk, is inconsistent with what we already know about the situation.

Such inconsistencies will emerge more clearly when we have examined the model situation which led Laplace to break decisively with the classical tradition. Meanwhile, it may help us to sidestep some sources of confusion in contemporary controversy, if we here attempt a judicious assessment of what Bayes actually attempted to do without prejudging his intentions unduly. We may accordingly summarise the foregoing examination of his memoir as follows:

(i) The theorem especially associated with the name of Thomas Bayes deals with *two* randomwise sampling processes, the outcome of *only one* of which is open to inspection.

(ii) In the model situation to which the theorem explicitly refers any possible outcome of the first sampling process is as probable as any other.

(iii) For such a model situation, the result Bayes gives is entirely consistent with the classical theory of risks in games of chance, and the *ipsissima verba* of the author, if at times obscure, are not inconsistent with what we have elsewhere designated the *Forward Look*.

(iv) Bayes admittedly, but with some hesitation, advances the suggestion that we may assign equal probabilities to each possible outcome of the first sampling process when we have no certain information to the contrary; but he does so on the implicit assumption that the first sampling process is referable to *external occurrences*.

(v) We must allocate to Dr. Price alone the credit or discredit for extending the principle of insufficient reason to situations in which only one outcome of the first sampling process is realisable and to Price alone the responsibility for identifying the latter with a *subjective choice* in favour of one or other among different conceptual possibilities.

(vi) By this extension and identification, Price raised two issues which do not emerge in the model situation dealt with by the author:

(*a*) whether the choice between conceptually admissible hypotheses, only one of which can be applicable to a given situation, is factually on all fours with the concept of choice in the setting of the classical theory;

(*b*) whether there is any intelligible sense in which we can speak of such a process of sifting hypotheses as *random*, and as such relevant to the proper terms of reference of a stochastic calculus.

Of Bayes's suggestion, which invokes the principle of insufficient reason when the prior probabilities are severally referable to existential populations at risk, we may say that it is certainly reliable only when the populations at risk are equal; and there would be no need to invoke the principle if we had any means of knowing that this is so. Of his editor's implicit assumption that mental decisions made in total ignorance are random occurrences, it suffices to say that no one has hitherto been able to advance any conclusive evidence in favour of a contention which is not amenable to experimental enquiry; but if we cannot plan an experiment to justify or to discredit it, we can at least devise experiments to test the validity of a more restricted contingent proposition, viz. do we actually make decisions of one sort or another with equal frequency when nothing we know about a situation furnishes any rational grounds for preferring one verdict to another?

Experiments of the sort referred to last are indeed easy enough to plan or to conduct. For example, we may: (a) tell each of a large group of people that the number of balls in a box is at least one and less than ten; (b) ask each member of the group to guess how many balls the box contains; (c) record the frequency with which individuals guess each of the numbers from 1 to 9 inclusive. To the writer's knowledge, no one has recorded a large-scale experiment of this type, perhaps because experience has taught us that threes, fives and sevens would turn up too often.

CHAPTER SIX

THE PLACE OF LAPLACE
AND THE GRAND CLIMACTERIC
OF THE CLASSICAL TRADITION

NOTABLE CONTRIBUTORS to knowledge in any age suffer from a double disability at the hands of history. Hero worshippers read into their authorities intentions that the authors themselves would not have dreamed of; and this is not necessarily flattering, since there is no one to one relation between hero-worship and intellectual good taste. Contrariwise, a chance remark wrested from its context for controversial advantage becomes the trademark of a philosophical system which critics can attack from the advantage of safe distance; and this is a rude sort of justice since contra-suggestible critics are not unduly willing to undertake a charitable appraisal of an opponent's viewpoint. So was it with David Hume. So may it well be with Bayes who did not explicitly state the theorem we associate with his name exhibited either as in (iv) of Chapter Four or in the particular form (v) which embodies the highly debatable axiom (p. 121) in the Scholium. The *fons et origo* of inverse probability is Laplace. For good or ill, the ideas commonly identified with the name of Bayes are largely his.

A demonstration, extensively discussed by Karl Pearson in the *Grammar of Science*, signalises both the explicit formulation of what we now choose to call Bayes's theorem and the use of the Scholium to validate judgments about the course of events. It appears in the *Memoire sur la Probabilité des causes par les événements*, "remarkable in the history of the subject," says Todhunter, "as being the first which distinctly enunciated the principle for estimating the probabilities of the causes by which an observed event may have been produced." The problem which Laplace there proposes is as follows. A player takes *with replacement r* balls* from an urn known to contain white balls

---

* Laplace actually speaks of *billets*, presumably thinking of the Royal lotteries referred to in Chapter Four. This may be the explanation of the vogue the urn model enjoyed.

and/or black ones. He observes that x of the r balls are white and $(r-x)$ are black. According to Laplace, he may then conclude that the chance $P_{(x+1.)r}$ of getting a white ball at the $(r + 1)$th draw is

$$P_{(x+1).r} = \frac{x + 1}{r + 2} \qquad \ldots \ldots \quad \text{(i)}$$

It will be easier to get into focus what are exceptionable assumptions in the derivation of this rule by Laplace himself, if we now construct a model which admissibly does lead to the solution he offers. We suppose that we have $(n + 1)$ urns each containing n balls, of which 0, 1, 2, 3 ... n are white. Thus the proportions of white balls are 0, n^{-1}, $2n^{-1}$ ... 1; and in general for the kth urn the probability of drawing a white ball in a single trial is $p_k = kn^{-1}$. In this set-up consecutive values of p_k differ by the same increment, viz.:

$$\Delta p_k = n^{-1}$$

Since there are $(n + 1)$ urns in all, the prior probability (P_k) of choosing any one urn randomwise is $(n + 1)^{-1}$ for all values of k. If n is large we may therefore write

$$P_k \simeq \Delta p_k$$

We shall now denote by $L_{k.x}$ what we may loosely and provisionally, but advisedly (see p. 143) here designate in the language of Laplace as the probability that the urn contains k white balls if the r-fold sample score is x white balls. Bayes's theorem gives:

$$L_{k.x} = \frac{P_k . L_{x.k}}{\sum\limits_{k=0}^{k=n} P_k . L_{x.k}} \simeq \frac{L_{x.k} . \Delta p_k}{\sum\limits_{k=0}^{k=n} L_{x.k} . \Delta p_k}$$

In this ratio:

$$L_{x.k} = r_{(x)} . p_k^x (1 - p_k)^{r-x}$$

In the last expression $r_{(x)}$ is a constant, since we are talking about a specified *particular* sample size and a specified score.

If the sample is finite and we sample with replacement, n being in any case very large in comparison with r:

$$\sum_{k=0}^{k=n} r_{(x)} \cdot p_k^x (1 - p_k)^{r-x} \cdot \Delta p_k \simeq r_{(x)} \int_{p=0}^{p=1} p_x (1 - p)^{r-x} \cdot dp$$

$$\therefore L_{k.x} \simeq \frac{p_k^x (1 - p_k)^{r-x} \cdot \Delta p_k}{\displaystyle\int_0^1 p^x (1 - p)^{r-x} \cdot dp}$$

The conditional probability of getting a white ball at the $(r + 1)$th trial is p_k, if the urn is the kth. The conditional probability that the urn contains k white balls if the r-fold sample score is x is $L_{k.x}$ as above. In conformity with our assumption that n is very large, the conditional probability of getting a white ball from an urn containing k white balls at the next trial after getting x white balls in r trials from the same urn is therefore:

$$P_{(x+1).kr} = L_{k.x} \cdot p_k \simeq \frac{p_k^{x+1} (1 - p_k)^{r-x} \cdot \Delta p_k}{\displaystyle\int_0^1 p^x (1 - p)^{r-x} \cdot dp}$$

The unconditional probability of getting a white ball at the $(r + 1)$th trial follows from the addition theorem, viz.:

$$P_{(x+1).r} = \sum_{k=0}^{k=n} P_{(x+1).kr}$$

$$\simeq \frac{\displaystyle\int_0^1 p^{x+1} (1 - p)^{r-x} \cdot dp}{\displaystyle\int_0^1 p^x (1 - p)^{r-x} \cdot dp}$$

$$\simeq \frac{B(x + 2, r - x + 1)}{B(x + 1, r - x + 1)}$$

The ratio of the two Beta functions above is:

$$\frac{\Gamma(x + 2) \cdot \Gamma(r - x + 1)}{\Gamma(r + 3)} \cdot \frac{\Gamma(r + 2)}{\Gamma(x + 1) \cdot \Gamma(r - x + 1)}$$

$$= \frac{(x + 1)! \, (r + 1)!}{(r+2)! \, x!} = \frac{x + 1}{r + 2} \quad . \quad \text{(ii)}$$

So far the algebra. We have still to divulge what this charity is in aid of, and if the reader is perplexed, it is not without good reason. Equation (ii) is identical with (i) above, but the problem of which it is the solution is not the problem Laplace himself sets out to solve. The latter is a problem about *one urn and only one*. Its statement admits no preliminary random choice of the urn from which we draw the $(r + 1)$ balls. It is therefore not a situation which we can discuss in terms to which the balance sheet of Bayes is factually relevant, unless we know everything relevant about its contents, in which event we already know the solution.

This confusion of topic would scarcely call for comment, if Laplace had offered the solution of the problem as a *jeu d'esprit* to entertain the wits of a Paris salon. It is, it happens, the foundation-stone of a new system of thought. The urn from which we are to draw the white and black balls is no less than the one to which Quetelet refers when he epitomises a novel interpretation of scientific reasoning in the assertion "*l'urne que nous interrogeons c'est la nature.*" Pearson speaks of it (*Grammar of Science*, 2nd edn., p. 147) as the *nature bag*. Among other consolations he extracted therefrom, Laplace conceived it as possible to provide a long overdue rationale for inductive reasoning and a rebuttal of Hume's so often misconstrued scepticism. Thus he uses it to solve to his own satisfaction a problem cited in the appendix Price wrote to the *Essay* of Bayes as a proper application of the Scholium. Can we assign a probability to the assertion that the sun will rise tomorrow? On the understanding that it has done so daily for 5,000 years (1,826,213 days), the formula of Laplace assigns $P_{r+1} = \frac{1826214}{1826215}$ or betting odds of 1826214 : 1 in favour of the event.

In the context of contemporary discussion, this use of his theorem has a lighter side with which Karl Pearson deals earnestly and at length. Following Eddington, recent writers on scientific method have welcomed the reformulation of scientific laws in statistical terms which supposedly dispense with the eminently operational concept of causality and the shadow of an absolute, if none the less unattainable, truth in the background. The implication is that miracles can happen, and hence that a long-standing antagonism between the laboratory and the vestry admits of a happy ending.

Unhappily, Laplace is no longer able to comment on this engaging prognosis of his labours; and Pearson's major pre-occupation with the exposition of his views when he speaks of the nature bag will not help the zealous seeker after truth to find in (i) above the spiritual solace which Eddington wistfully proffers. His ensuing remarks (*op. cit.*, pp. 142–3) are therefore worthy of reproduction:

Laplace has even enabled us to take account of possible "miracles," anomalies, or breaches of routine in the sequence of perceptions. He tells us that if an event has happened p times and failed q times, then the probability that it will happen the next time is $\dfrac{p+1}{p+q+2}$, or the odds in favour of its happening are $p+1$ to $q+1$. Now if we are as generous as we possibly can be to the reporters of the miraculous, we can hardly assert that a well-authenticated breach of the routine of perceptions has happened *once* in past experience for every 1,000 million cases of routine. In other words, we must take p equal to 1,000 million times q, or the odds against a miracle happening in the next sequence of perceptions would be about 1,000 millions to one. It is clear from this that any belief that the miraculous will occur in our immediate experience cannot possibly form a factor in the conduct of practical life. Indeed the odds against a miracle occurring are so great, the percentage of permanently diseased or temporarily disordered perceptive faculties so large as compared with the percentage of asserted breaches of routine, and the advantage to mankind of evolving an absolutely certain basis of knowledge so great, that we are justified in saying that miracles have been *proved* incredible—the word *proved* being used in the sense in which alone it has meaning when applied to the field of perceptions.

The system of thought which Laplace thus introduced departs from the pre-existing tradition explicitly at three levels; and the theorem under discussion illustrates them all. To the writer's knowledge only one exponent of the theory of probability has explicitly pointed out all the debatable issues involved. In *Probability, Statistics and Truth*, p. 175, R. von Mises writes as follows:

Nearly all the older textbooks were agreed that these problems involve a special kind of probability. They called it the *probability of causes*, or the *probability of hypotheses*, and assumed it to be different from the usual probability of events. The word "cause" can, in fact, be easily introduced into the description of the Bayes' problem. We just say that the "cause" of result n_1 6's in n trials is a special value of x, where x is the probability for a given die showing a 6 when thrown. Since we wish to know the probability of different values of x, we can say that we are examining the probabilities of different causes. This is nothing but an idle play upon words. We actually calculate the probability of a certain event in a certain collective. . . . Its elements are *experiments carried out in two stages*; drawing a stone from an urn, and throwing it out n times from a dice box. The probability is defined in this case, exactly as in all the others, as the limiting value of the relative frequency. No excuse can be given for speaking of a special kind of *probability of causes* or *probability of hypotheses*, since all that is determined is, as always, the probability of an event in a collective.

In what follows, I shall deal separately with the debatable issues on which von Mises puts the spotlight in the preceding citation, viz.:

    (*a*) in what class of situations is the concept of *prior* probability factually relevant;

    (*b*) in what sense, if any, can we legitimately identify the concept of *posterior* probability with the probability of *causes*;

    (*c*) what meaningful content can we convey by the term probability of *hypotheses* within the framework of a behaviouristic attitude?

The Concept of Prior Probability. We have seen that the actual model which leads to the solution given by (i) is an infinitude of urns to which we assign different relevant parameter values

p_k equally spaced and all different. Thus it is a property of our stratified universe of urns that the distribution of prior probabilities is both rectangular and continuous. The introduction of the assumption of continuity in this context is not without interest, because the differential calculus had no function in the classical theory except as a convenient computing device to sidestep laborious calculation in the domain of finite differences. Its utility so conceived is purely empirical; and its legitimate use presupposes *ad hoc* investigation to justify the assumption that the order of error in the appropriate summation of relevant terms of a discrete probability series does not contravene the operational intention. Henceforward, theoretical distributions of this or allied types, here the so-called incomplete beta function (Type II of Pearson's system), acquire an indispensable theoretical status in virtue of the principle which prompted Laplace to formulate a distribution of prior probabilities as stated. The distribution of p must be continuous to allow for the possibility that the unknown p_k may have any value if we start with no background information about the model set-up. Likewise, it must be rectangular to accommodate the postulate that all prior probabilities are equal when we know nothing relevant about the source of a sample other than its definitive score.

The two issues last stated invite separate consideration. The second alone has been, and still is, the pivot of a controversy which might be more profitable if it took within its scope the first. In assigning equal prior probabilities to the sources of the sample when we start with no background knowledge, Laplace takes over what is most exceptionable in Bayes's Scholium, henceforth referred to as the *principle of insufficient reason*. He proffers it as a new law of thought, commonly accepted till the time of Boole, but subsequently contested for different reasons by Boole's successors. The usual arguments advanced against the principle of insufficient reason as a self-evident axiom of stochastic inference in the domain of factual research are:

(*a*) that we do not commonly investigate the credentials of a hypothesis unless we either have good initial reasons for supposing that it is faulty or have good initial reasons to commend its claims*;

(b) even if the investigator undertakes an enquiry with an *open mind*, i.e. a mind uninformed by relevant knowledge of his materials in contradistinction to a mind disciplined to accept the verdict of ineluctable new fact, there is no particular reason to assume that his or her mental valuations have any relation to the complexities of natural phenomena.

Few hard-headed investigators will contest the first contention; but the second concedes to the opposition an unnecessary advantage which will be easy to recognise, if we now focus attention on a type of problem which has lately become a playground for stochastic test and estimation procedures, viz. the therapeutic trial. If one asks whether treatment B is more efficacious than treatment A, the orthodox perception sets out in effect to explore three *conceptual* possibilities:

(i) B is in fact better than A;

(ii) A is in fact better than B;

(iii) A and B are equally good.

In this context, *good* is referable to a population and has no relevance to the individual as such; but this limitation need not concern us here. When we then say that the end in view is to arbitrate on the merits of these conceivably correct hypotheses, we imply that one, *and only one*, of these hypotheses is

* F. J. Anscombe (1948) states it thus:

It is highly unusual for an experiment to be conducted without some prior knowledge of expectation of the result, and the case of complete ignorance should be merely a stepping-stone in the development of the theory. The special virtue of a theory of rational belief is surely that it can take account of even the vaguest prior knowledge. Some such knowledge generally exists even when a hypothesis is first propounded by an experimenter, before it has been tested; since some conceivable results of an experiment carried out to test it would be classed by him as "reasonable" or expected, and others as utterly unlikely. (*Journ. Roy. Stat. Soc.*, CXI, p. 193.) Elsewhere (*Mind*, Vol. 60) the same author rightly comments in the same vein as follows:

As soon as any proposition or hypothesis has been formulated which is worth testing experimentally, there is already evidence as to its truth derived from existing accepted knowledge and from considerations of analogy or "consilience." A question to which we have no grounds whatever for hazarding an answer is an idle question and would not be the subject of scientific investigation.

correct. It is equally implicit in the second objection to the Bayes' postulate, and in the viewpoint of those who subscribe to it, that a decision of this sort is on all fours with a decision about which of the three types of dice we have taken from the box in the model situation of p. 122. Now this assumption leads to a manifest inconsistency. If we look more closely at the problem of the therapeutic trial we may say that there exist in the box two sorts of dice which we label as A and B without knowing whether the fact that we do label them in this way has any relevance to the long-run mean score we get from tossing a die of either sort. The very fact that we admit as a topic of enquiry Hypothesis (iii) above, viz. that treatment A and treatment B are equally good, is also an admission of the possibility that our classification has no factual bearing on the long-run mean score of the r-fold toss, i.e. that all the dice in the box are of one and the same type in any sense relevant to the classical calculus of risk in games of chance.

In Damon Runyon's vivid idiom there is clearly no percentage in looking at the problem of the trial in this way. In the real world only one hypothesis, as here stated, can be right. If so, every type of die we conjure into our model to specify an additional and false hypothesis exists only in the eye of the beholder. By the same token, probability is a state of mind and prior probability is merely a device for registering a purely subjective evaluation. If so, we exclude the possibility of defining the proper terms of reference of a calculus of judgments unless we first embrace philosophical idealism; but we limit the scope of profitable discussion in this way merely because we have chosen the wrong classical model for the problem in hand. It is wrong for the reason stated by von Mises. The concept of prior probability is factually relevant only to *experiments carried out in two stages*.

Once we lose grip of this elementary consideration, as indeed we do if we invoke the concept of prior probability in the domain of the therapeutic trial, we depart from a behaviourist viewpoint, because we have ceased to communicate within the framework of observable events. In the Bayes' model each hypothesis to which we assign a finite prior probability is referable to an *existent* population at risk; and we audit the balance sheet on the assumption that we are free to choose randomwise a die of a particular type in a box *before* tossing it or a particular urn or bag *before* drawing balls from it. In the set-up of the trial we have no such *preliminary act of random choice*. We have to take nature on her own terms.

That so simple a consideration does indeed merit emphasis will be evident if I cite a passage in which Karl Pearson expounds the Laplace theorem discussed above. There we have one bag with two sorts of balls, albeit in the original publication an urn with two sorts of tickets, but in what proportions we do not know. As the tale unfolds, this mysterious bag turns out to be an infinitude of bags, all except one of which exists only in the mind of the Maestro; but it miraculously regains its status as the one bag of the problem for which Laplace offers (i) as the correct solution. Thus Pearson says*

We are now in a position to return to our bag of white and black balls, but we can no longer suppose an equal number of both kinds, or that routine and breach of routine are equally probable. We must assume our "nature bag" to have every possible constitution or every possible ratio of black to white balls to be equally likely; to do this we suppose an infinitely great number of balls in all. We may then calculate the probability that with each of these constitutions the observed result, say p white balls and q black balls (or, p cases of routine and q anomalies) would arise in $p + q$ drawings.† This will determine, by Laplace's principle, the probability that each hypothetical constitution is the real constitution of the bag.

The reader will not be slow to detect that nothing about this surprisingly one and indivisible *nature-bag* remains constant throughout the syntactical operations of the previous paragraph except—and then only by implication—the material used in its manufacture before insertion of its appropriate but none the less mutable contents. Possibly also its shape remains the same, if we assume that the said material is fairly stiff. In that event the author of the *Grammar of Science* might have referred more felicitously, if more sepulchrally, to the original urn. In so far as it is relevant to the argument, all that we learn about our

* *Grammar of Science*, 2nd edn., p. 147.
† The reader may suppose the ball returned to the bag after each drawing.

bag with its *two*-fold equipment of balls is that its contents change from sentence to sentence with a teasing disregard for the plural flexion of the English noun. So stupendous an exploit of stochastic conjuring should suffice to emphasise the importance of what von Mises means when he speaks of an *experiment carried out in two stages*. The absurdities into which the principle of insufficient reason leads us arise less from the circumstance that it is gratuitous than because it is wholly irrelevant to most situations in which even its opponents would readily concede its convenience if susceptible of proof. This will emerge more clearly when we examine the properties of a model situation discussed below.

The Probability of Causes. We have seen that contemporary writers who repudiate with abhorrence the doctrine of inverse probability commonly do so because the allocation of equal prior probabilities is uncongenial to the outlook of the laboratory worker with first-hand knowledge of his materials. However, they rarely do so with explicit recognition of the factual relevance of the concept itself to most situations which prompt the theoretician to condone its invocation. Still less do they reject the doctrine of inverse probability for reasons foreshadowed in the foregoing discussion of Bayes's *Essay*. Thus those who knowingly reject it, relinquish the principle of insufficient reason somewhat wistfully, seemingly unaware of the most insidious departure from the classical tradition implicit in the exposition of the doctrine by Laplace himself.

For expository purposes, let us now assume for the time being that our infinite collection of urns is indeed a model relevant to the identification of a correct hypothesis. Can we then say that $L_{h.x}$ is the probability of a *cause* in the sense that we have loosely, provisionally and admittedly in the language of Laplace himself, specified it (p. 134) as the probability that the source is the kth urn if the score is x? This form of statement is highly elliptical, and conveys something which is inconsistent with the Forward Look. It suggests that we first look at a sample, then make an assessment of a probability on the basis of the evidence it supplies, an implication inherent in the misleading designation *posterior* applied thereto. Now we can give no meaning to the probability we are attempting to assess when we look at the issue in this way unless we abandon the factual historic framework of the classical theory of risks. Within that framework we must interpret $P_f = (1 - L_{k.x})$ as the *uncertainty safeguard* of a rule of procedure stated in advance and consistently followed regardless of the outcome of any individual trial.

So conceived $L_{k.x}$ is not the probability of a cause inferred from an isolated event. It is the probability of correctly identifying a cause, if we pursue throughout an endless succession of a particular class of events one and the same rule specified *in advance* by the occurrence of a particular score value. To me, it thus seems that so much emphasis on the credibility of the principle of insufficient reason has diverted attention from a highly exceptionable innovation which alone endorses the literal meaning of the epithet *inverse* in the doctrine of Laplace. If we concede to tradition by identifying the stochastic credibility of a rule with a *posterior* assessment of probability conceived in terms of *weighing the evidence* when we already know the sample score, we have taken with Laplace a decisive backward step. We have abandoned the Forward Look of the Founding Fathers.

The Probability of a Hypothesis. Having taken this step, our descent into a nebulous domain of mental images is swift. We can speak of the probability of correctly guessing that hypothesis K is the right one in strictly behaviourist terms, only if we confine our statements to the verbo-factual level at which we can assign a limiting ratio to the frequency of two classes of external events within a framework of consistent conduct. Our concern is then with: (*a*) statements we make to the effect that hypothesis K is correct whenever we encounter a score x; (*b*) trials of which it is both true that hypothesis K correctly identifies the source of the sample and true that x is also the sample score. Needless to say, this presupposes a correct factual specification of our statistical model. If we invoke Bayes's theorem we then do so on the understanding that our sampling procedure is factually consistent with the choice of a sample with score x from a source specified by hypothesis K in the endless sequence of such trials.

When we speak of the probability that hypothesis K is true on data k in the idiom of Carnap and Jeffreys, we implicitly abandon the attempt to locate in the world of affairs this preliminary act of choice in a 2-stage experiment for which the balance sheet of Bayes is unexceptionable in terms of the classical theory of risks. The sources specified by our hypotheses—of which we may postulate, as does Laplace in the above treatment, an enumerable infinitude each one equally admissible—are no longer observable entities with respect to which each relevant prior probability is referable to an existent population at risk. They are now conceptual images concerning which the classical theory of risks is entirely silent. Accordingly, we then formulate Bayes's theorem in terms such as the following:

Suppose, in fact that an event can be explained on the mutually exclusive hypotheses $q_1 \ldots q_n$ and let H be the data known before the event happens, so that H is the basis on which we first judge the relative probabilities of the q's. Now suppose the event to happen. Then Bayes' theorem states that the probability of q_r *after it has happened* (i.e. on data H and p) varies as the probability *before it happened* multiplied by the probability that it happens on data q_r and H. The probability $P(q_r/pH)$ is therefore called the *posterior* probability, $P(q_r/H)$ the prior probability, and $P(p/q_rH)$ will be called the *likelihood*. (Kendall's *Treatise*, Vol. I, p. 176.)

I do not cite this passage (*italics* inserted) to score a debating point by placing on record the difficulty of understanding what an event is unless it happens. Nor is it necessary to reiterate that the event which has or has not happened, as the case may be, is in this context two totally different events referable to different stages of a 2-stage experiment. I do so especially because I want to emphasise that some current writers who decline to endorse the principle of insufficient reason subscribe both: (*a*) to the misconception that the concept of prior probability is essential to the definition of the terms of reference of a calculus of judgments; (*b*) to the belief that the theory of probability endorses posterior judgments on the basis of isolated events. This misconception of the legitimate status both of prior probability and of posterior probability in the classical theory of risks is indeed inherent in the symbolism adopted by Jeffreys, by Carnap and by other writers who more candidly disclaim the attempt to define probability in terms consistent with a behaviouristic outlook.

A Generalised Model of Stochastic Inference. We have seen that the formula (p. 134) which epitomises the announcement of the doctrine of inverse probability is not indeed a solution relevant to the properties of the factual model situation Laplace proposes to explore and to expound. We have also seen that his approach is inconsistent with a behaviouristic— or as a previous generation would have said, an objective— attitude towards the relevance of an axiomatic theory of probability to the real world. We shall be able to get the issues raised above in clearer perspective if we now examine, both from his own viewpoint and from one which is consistent with the behaviourist approach, a model situation mentioned by Laplace himself.

In the *Introduction a Théorie analytique des Probabilités* (1820) Laplace proposes the following problem. An urn contains two balls. Initially, one knows that both may be white, both may be black or that there may be one ball of each sort. A player draws out one ball randomwise, replaces it and draws again. If the ball is white at each draw, what is the probability that it will be white at the third after replacement of the ball extracted at the second?

Laplace argues as follows. One need here advance only two hypotheses: (*a*) neither of the balls is black; (*b*) one only is black. On hypothesis (*a*) the likelihood of drawing two white balls in a double draw is 1, on hypothesis (*b*) it is $\frac{1}{4}$. He regards it as both meaningful to assign prior probabilities to hypotheses as such and legitimate to equate prior probabilities when we have no information to discredit the assumption. Accordingly, he assigns to the truth of hypothesis (*a*), in accordance with (iv) in Chapter 5, the probability

$$\frac{(\frac{1}{2})\,(1)}{\frac{1}{2}\,(1) + \frac{1}{2}\,(\frac{1}{4})} = \frac{4}{5}$$

Similarly, he assigns to the truth of hypothesis (b)

$$\frac{\frac{1}{2}\left(\frac{1}{4}\right)}{\frac{1}{2}\left(1\right) + \frac{1}{2}\left(\frac{1}{4}\right)} = \frac{1}{5}$$

Laplace speaks of each such ratio as the probability of the *cause*. Having done so, he invokes a retrospective interpretation of the addition theorem in the following terms (7th Principle). At the third trial the probability of drawing a white ball will be 1 if hypothesis (a) is correct and $\frac{1}{2}$ if hypothesis (b) is correct. The joint probability that (a) specifies the cause correctly and that the ball will be white is for Laplace $\left(\frac{4}{5}\right)\left(1\right)$. The alternative that (b) specifies the cause correctly and the ball will be white he cites by the same token as $\left(\frac{1}{5}\right)\left(\frac{1}{2}\right)$. Since one or other hypothesis must correctly specify the cause of the event, he derives the probability of getting a white ball as:

$$\left(\tfrac{4}{5}\right)\left(1\right) + \left(\tfrac{1}{5}\right)\left(\tfrac{1}{2}\right) = 0\cdot9$$

In the idiom of Chapter Five, we may say that Laplace here assigns an uncertainty safeguard $P_f = 0\cdot1$ to the rule of consistently betting that the third ball is white, when the first two of a 3-fold trial are also white. Let us now look at the problem in terms consistent with the Forward Look. The results of two particular unit trials admittedly leave us with only two hypotheses, as stated; but the divulged result of one 2-fold trial will merely restrict the verbal form of the bets we may choose to make from three to two. If hypothesis (a) is true, the probability that the ball will be white in each of an unending sequence of single trials is unity. If it is false, the probability is $\frac{1}{2}$. All we know is that it is either true or false. Hence we can say that at least 50 per cent of our guesses will be right if we bet on white. Alternatively, the uncertainty safeguard of the rule is $P_f \leqslant 0\cdot5$.

Let us next suppose that we can draw *six* balls successively and randomwise with replacement, equipped as before with the knowledge that one 2-fold trial yielded two white balls, and hence with only two relevant hypotheses. We are free to make the rule: say that hypothesis A (that neither of the balls is black) is true when all six balls are white, otherwise reject it as false. Three situations then arise:

(i) we rightly reject hypothesis A when there is at least one black ball in the sequence of six;

(ii) we wrongly accept hypothesis A when all six balls are white;

(iii) we rightly accept hypothesis A when all six balls are white.

By definition, we do not err if (i) holds good, and we do not err if (iii) holds good. The probability assignable to a run of 6 white if hypothesis (b) is true is 2^{-6}, and in that event we wrongly accept hypothesis (a). Since (i) and (iii) entail no risk, our risk cannot be greater than $2^{-6} = 0 \cdot 015625$, and we shall accordingly assign the uncertainty safeguard of our rule as $P_f \leqslant 0 \cdot 015625$. More generally, we may state our rule in the form: reject hypothesis A if at least one black ball turns up in the r-fold trial and accept it if all the balls are white. We may then tabulate as follows the risk associated with trials of 1, 2, etc.:

r	P_f	r	P_f
1	0·500	4	0·062500
2	0·250	5	0·031250
3	0·125	6	0·015625

Should a player, who bets in conformity with the rule last stated, wish to guarantee himself against bankruptcy without incurring a risk greater than 5 per cent, he must therefore: (a) fix his stake and the maximum number of r-fold trials on which he will bet in accordance with his capital resources at the start; (b) get his opponent to agree *in advance* that the number (r) of unit trials per game is not less than 5.

If we thus dispose of the problem as stated by Laplace in terms consistent with the classical theory for division of stakes, the only legitimate use of our knowledge about the outcome of an antecedent 2-fold trial is to exclude the hypothesis that both the balls in the urn are black, and limit accordingly the form our rule will take. The reader may therefore ask whether the contingency we are discussing is not in fact reducible to the question: what is the probability that we shall pick three white balls in succession? In one sense this is so, but if so, we can incorporate the prescription of the outcome of the first two of the three unit trials in a rule *stated in advance* as above, only if we also take the risk of never being able to make a bet. In terms of the classical theory we then interpret the problem of the two balls as the problem of assigning the risk of betting that the third ball drawn in a 3-fold trial will be white, if: (*a*) the first two are also white; (*b*) our only initial information is that either ball may be either white or black. It remains true that the risk of erroneous statement is $P_f \leqslant$ 0·125, if we bet consistently to that effect; but we have now conceded the possibility that both balls may be black. In that event our rule is useless, in so far as it deprives us of the right to make a bet on the outcome of *every* 3-fold trial.

To cover the contingency last stated we must extend the terms of reference of the rule. For instance, we may:

(i) say that both the balls in the urn are white, whenever all three balls drawn in a 3-fold trial are white;

(ii) say that both the balls in the urn are black, whenever all three balls drawn in the 3-fold trial are black;

(iii) otherwise, say that one of the balls in the urn is white, the other black.

If both balls are black or if both are white, our rule will never lead us astray. If one is white and one is black, the probability of getting three white balls or three black balls is $2(2^{-3}) =$ 0·25, in which event our verdict will be wrong. Whence the probability of error cannot exceed 0·25.

The inconsistency of the classical theory and the solution of Laplace emerges more clearly if we elaborate the problem he himself states, e.g. what is the probability that the next five balls we draw will be white, if the two balls previously drawn are white. The answer Laplace would give is:

$$\left(\tfrac{4}{5}\right)(1) + \tfrac{1}{5}\left(\tfrac{1}{32}\right) = \tfrac{129}{160} \simeq 0\cdot8065$$

Thus the risk of betting accordingly is $P_f \simeq$ 0·1935. The only answer consistent with the classical approach is that the risk cannot be greater than 2^{-7}. Whereas the classical theory thus assigns a risk $P_f \leqslant 0 \cdot 5$ on the outcome of betting on white at the third draw when the *Théorie Analytique* assigns $P_f = 0 \cdot 1$, the classical theory assigns to betting on white at the third, fourth, fifth, sixth and seventh draw when the first and second are white a risk $P_f \leqslant 0 \cdot 0078125$ and the *Théorie Analytique* assigns $P_f = 0 \cdot 1935$.

In the solution of this problem proffered by Laplace, three principles alien to the classical theory intrude. In terms of the classical theory, we must interpret Bayes's theorem as a rule of guessing with an assignable risk referable to an endless sequence of trials. Laplace interprets it as a *retrospective evaluation of the result of an individual trial divorced from the series of the event.* In terms of the classical theory Bayes's theorem refers to a two-stage sampling process in the domain of external events. In the use Laplace makes of it, the first stage is a mental arte-fact which has no reference to observable occurrences. In so far as it is meaningful in the context of the classical theory to speak of the probability that a particular hypothesis is true, i.e. that we shall win our bet that it is true, the only values assignable to the prior probabilities in this set-up are zero or unity. Laplace himself assigns to each of two conceptually admissible hypotheses a prior probability of $0 \cdot 5$ and to the third zero prior probability on the basis of information the appropriate betting rule cannot anticipate, if stated before the game begins.

Interpreted as in Chapter Five in terms consistent with the For-ward Look, and formally embracing as a limiting case situations in which the first stage of the sampling process is non-existent, Bayes's theorem leads to no inconsistencies or paradoxes which we encounter in the *Théorie Analytique*. This will be clear if we now *frame a rule which takes within its scope situations to which Bayes's theorem is factually relevant, doubtfully relevant or irrelevant.* We shall be able to do so only if we content ourselves with defining the upper limit of the uncertainty safeguard.

We shall assume that a bag contains pennies which *may* be of three sorts only: (a) with the Queen's head on both sides; (b) with Britannia on both sides; (c) with the Queen's head on one side and Britannia on the other. We shall further assume that (c) are "unbiased," i.e. that $p = \frac{1}{2} = 1-q$ is the probability of scoring a head at a single toss. The use of the word italicised in the first sentence is intentional to cover four of the possibilities w.r.t. our background knowledge of the situation:

(i) we know both that the bag contains pennies of each sort and how many of each sort it contains;

(ii) we know that the bag contains pennies of each sort but we do not know how many of each it contains;

(iii) we do not know whether the bag contains pennies of all three sorts, two only or one only;

(iv) we know that the bag contains pennies of only one sort but we do not know which sort.

Of these admissible situations (i) alone fulfils the condition to which Bayes's theorem, as defined by (v) in Chapter Five is unquestionably relevant in the domain of action, i.e. in the sense that all the relevant numerical data are at our disposal. The definition of (iv) excludes the factual possibility of sampling conceived as a two-stage process. If we conceive it *formally* in this way as a limiting case of (i), we can do so only if we say that one of the three prior probabilities must be unity, the other two being zero. This is inconsistent with the principle of insufficient reason, which would assign the numerical value $0 \cdot \dot{3}$ to each. Of the remainder, (ii) is the only one to which the Scholium has factual relevance if admissible; but in real life we shall rarely encounter situations in which we can distinguish (ii) from (iii) which embraces both (ii) and (iv) as limiting cases. Clearly, (iv) is inconsistent with the Scholium, and we must also regard (iii) as inconsistent therewith.

Thus we have before us four situations to only one of which the principle of insufficient reason is intelligibly relevant; but in real life we cannot say that this is necessarily true of the third. It may happen that we start with some knowledge of the source of the pennies in the bag, knowing also that errors of minting which give rise to the bad pennies of classes (a) and (b) are extremely rare. If so, our background knowledge, though inadequate to prescribe an exact figure for the corresponding prior probabilities P_a, P_b, P_c, may fully justify our conviction that P_c is much greater than $0 \cdot 3$; and this again is inconsistent with the principle of insufficient reason.

Let us now presume that an observer chooses randomwise at each trial one penny from the bag, tosses it r times, observes the head score x and records his conviction that it is a penny of one of the three specified types (a), (b), (c) above. We may then use a model bag from which we *may* extract (in the general sense defined) a penny belonging to one of these three classes to illustrate the statement of a comprehensive rule which usefully covers all the situations specified by (i)–(iv) above. We shall initially suppose that the bag contains 100 pennies as follows:

No. of Pennies	Type	Corresponding Hypothesis (H)	Prior Probability (P_h)
5	(a) with two heads	A	$P_a = 0 \cdot 05$
20	(b) with two tails	B	$P_b = 0 \cdot 20$
75	(c) normal unbiased	C	$P_c = 0 \cdot 75$

We may set out as below the conditional probability (likelihood) for a score of 0, 1–3 and 4 heads in a 4-fold toss:

For Penny of Type	Conditional Probability of Score of		
	0	1–3	4
A	0	0	1
B	1	0	0
C	$\frac{1}{16} = 0 \cdot 0625$	$\frac{7}{8} = 0 \cdot 875$	$\frac{1}{16} = 0 \cdot 0625$

The complete Bayes Balance Sheet for the 4-fold toss is therefore:

Type of Penny	Probability of a score of		
	0	1–3	4
A	$(0 \cdot 05)(0) = 0$	$(0 \cdot 05)(0) = 0$	$(0 \cdot 05)(1) = 0 \cdot 05$
B	$(0 \cdot 20)(1) = 0 \cdot 20$	$(0 \cdot 20)(0) = 0$	$(0 \cdot 20)(0) = 0$
C	$(0 \cdot 75)(0 \cdot 0625)$	$(0 \cdot 75)(0 \cdot 875)$	$(0 \cdot 75)(0 \cdot 0625)$
	$= 0 \cdot 046875$	$= 0 \cdot 65625$	$= 0 \cdot 046875$

Let us now suppose that we consistently operate the following *comprehensive* rule:

(*a*) whenever the score is 4, we say that the penny is of class A.

(*b*) whenever the score is 0, we say that the penny is of class B.

(*c*) whenever the score is 1–3, we say that the penny is of class C.

Our assertions thus constitute an exclusive and exhaustive set of events to each of which we can assign a probability of truthful statement:

(*a*) 0·05 ; (*b*) 0·20 ; (*c*) 0·65625

Since the set is exclusive and exhaustive, we can apply the fundamental addition rule to derive the overall probability of truthful assertion, i.e.

$$P_t = 0·05 + 0·20 + 0·65625 = 0·90625$$
$$\therefore P_f = (1 - P_t) = 0·09375$$

If we look at the balance sheet in its entirety, as in this example, we get a new slant on the misleading implications of the word *posterior*. Our posterior probabilities are of use only when we define a rule which *limits a verdict to situations in which a certain score class henceforth turns up.* Thus we pass by easy stages from thinking of the probabilities so defined as probabilities referable to one class of situations in our *total* experience to thinking of them as probabilities which are definable only in terms of what we have *already* experienced. That the last step is a step in the dark is evident when we explore the possibility of formulating rules which are not comprehensive in the sense that the foregoing rule is comprehensive.

If we confine ourselves to statements to the effect that the penny is *not* phoney (class A or B), we might operate within the framework of the rule: say that the penny is normal whenever the score is 1–3 and otherwise say nothing. We then restrict our procedure to 0·65625 of all the trials we encounter, and our balance sheet then shows that the probability of correct statement in conformity with the understanding that we operate the rule consistently is what common sense tells us, viz. :

$$P_{t.c} = \frac{0}{0 \cdot 65625} + \frac{0}{0 \cdot 65625} + \frac{0 \cdot 65625}{0 \cdot 65625} = 1 \ and \ P_{f.c} = 0$$

Let us now examine the consequences of another rule of restricted applicability: say that the penny is *not* normal if the score is either 0 or 4, and otherwise say nothing. The relevant figures of our complete balance sheet are then

	Score 0 or 4	Score 1–3
A	0·05000	0
B	0·20000	0
C	0·09375	0·65625
Total	0·34375	0·65625

The so-called posterior probability of the event that the penny is of class C when the score is 0 or 4 is here

$$\frac{0 \cdot 09375}{0 \cdot 34375} \simeq 0 \cdot 273$$

Within the framework of the rule last stated, this represents the probability of *erroneously* stating that the penny is phoney, i.e. $P_{f.ab} \simeq 0 \cdot 273$. There is, of course, no inconsistency between the statements $P_{f.ab} \simeq 0 \cdot 273$ and $P_{f.c} = 0$, since each endorses statements referable to a rule applicable to the outcome of only a limited class of trials, and each as such is referable to a different body of experience. The consistent operation of either rule last stated has at least a limited usefulness only because we know that each prior probability of the balance sheet is referable to an existential population at risk. If all the pennies in the bag were phoney, the first of the two would be useless, being inapplicable. The same would be true of the second if all the pennies were normal.

So far, we have assumed that we know how many pennies of each sort the bag contains. Let us next assume that we are dealing with a situation in which we know that there are three sorts of pennies in the bag without knowing how many of each. To explore what we can then truly say about the long-run value of the 3-fold comprehensive rule of p. 153 we need to formalise it:

$$P_t = P_a(1) + P_b(1) + P_c(0 \cdot 875)$$
$$= P_a + P_b + P_c - (0 \cdot 125)P_c = 1 - (0 \cdot 125)P_c$$
$$\therefore P_f = (0 \cdot 125)P_c$$

Now P_c by definition lies in the range $0 - 1$ inclusive, i.e. $P_c \leqslant 1$

$$\therefore P_f \leqslant 0 \cdot 125$$

If we endorse the principle of insufficient reason, we shall set $P_a = P_b = P_c = \frac{1}{3}$, and derive $P_f = 0 \cdot 0416$, a result which will be inconsistent with the entries of our balance sheet if the composition of the bag is as specified above; but the fact that we invoke the principle implies that we cannot certainly exclude such a possibility. If we speak of the probability (P_f) of wrong assertion when we operate the rule consistently, as the *uncertainty safeguard* of the rule, we may thus say of situations to which Bayes's theorem is factually relevant:

(i) when we can assign the true values of the prior probabilities, we can frame a rule to which we can also assign an *exact* uncertainty safeguard;

(ii) when we cannot assign the true values of the prior probabilities, we can merely state an upper limit to the uncertainty safeguard of the rule which we operate.

We are now in a position to cover the situations specified by (iii) and (iv) on p. 151. We have stated a rule to which we can assign an uncertainty safeguard with a specifiable *upper limit* for *all* values of the prior probabilities including as a limiting case the possibility that the value of one is unity and that of all others is zero. This covers case (iii) which is consistent with the possibility that the value of any or all except one of the prior probabilities is zero, and case (iv) of which we know in advance that the value of one is indeed unity and that of all others is zero. We can thus resolve the antinomy inherent in our initial statement. From the viewpoint of the practical man, there is an essential factual distinction between (i) and (iv), because (i) alone is literally an experiment carried out in two stages. From that of the mathematician, (iv) is merely a special case of (i), because the first stage of the experiment is irrelevant, if we assign unity as the value of one of the prior probabilities. The conflict no longer exists if we state our rule in a form applicable to the situation regardless of any numerical values we may assign to them.

Hitherto, we have directed our attention to the formal statement of the rule without reference to its operational content, if any; but it serves no useful end to frame a rule of procedure which specifies the risk of error unless the risk of error is acceptable, i.e. does not exceed a specified limit. Thus no one would be enthusiastic about a rule which would merely ensure 50 per cent or less correct decisions and 50 per cent or more false ones. Let us then suppose that we are content that 95 per cent of our decisions will be true in the long run, if we consistently do follow a rule stated in advance of any particular trial, i.e. our uncertainty safeguard must not exceed $0 \cdot 05$. How shall we accomplish our task, if we choose the 3-fold comprehensive rule under discussion? For the 4-fold trial the probability of getting 0 or 4 heads when the penny is normal is $(0 \cdot 5)^3 = 0 \cdot 125$. More generally for an r-fold trial it is $(0 \cdot 5)^{r-1}$. For the r-fold trial we may therefore write

$$P_f = P_c (0 \cdot 5)^{r-1} \leqslant (0 \cdot 5)^{r-1}$$

Since $(0 \cdot 5)^4 > 0 \cdot 05 > (0 \cdot 5)^5$ we must make r at least 6 to ensure that $P_f \leqslant 0 \cdot 05$. In other words, we can interpret a rule consistent with the Forward Look to accomplish the end in view, i.e. to satisfy a preassigned level of acceptability, if (and only if) the rule includes *in advance a specification of the size of the sample chosen.* At the operational level this is what the classical theory demands. It cannot prescribe a rule for the division of the stakes with an assignable risk of loss or gain, unless the prescription encompasses a specification of the number of unit trials per game. We shall see later that this limitation is the core of the current controversy concerning the credentials of the significance test.

PART II

The Calculus of Error and the Calculus of Exploration

CHAPTER SEVEN

THE NORMAL LAW COMES INTO THE PICTURE

WE HAVE NOW behind us the grand climacteric of the classical period. We stand on the threshold of a new phase. In tracing the origins and assumptions peculiar to a *Calculus of Errors*, one part of our task will be to separate what are: (*a*) purely mathematical issues within a consistent calculus; (*b*) logical and factual issues relevant to the use of the calculus in everyday life.

The reader who stumbles on statements to the effect that Laplace or Gosset discovered, and Liapounoff or R. A. Fisher first proved rigorously, such and such a theorem is apt to conclude that: (*a*) proof in this context has something to do with the validity or usefulness of the application; (*b*) the notion implicit in the mathematician's conception of rigour is necessarily connected with the relevance of the axioms of the calculus to the world's work. The need to draw this distinction emerges so soon as we first invoke the continuum as a useful computing device to sidestep the labour of deriving a solution which, if exact in every sense, is inconsistent with the assumption of continuity.

In the eighteenth century a major preoccupation of mathematicians was the derivation of infinite series which facilitate computations for astronomy and navigation. In that context the exploration of approximate methods for solving with as much accuracy as need be summations of terms of an unwieldy binomial series involved no departure from the outlook of the Founding Fathers. It was thus that de Moivre, Bernoulli and Laplace hit on the result sometimes pretentiously called the theorem of Laplace, viz. that the normal curve closely tallies with the contour of the histogram or so-called frequency polygon for successive terms of the binomial $(q + p)^r$ when r is large in comparison with the reciprocal of both p and $q = (1-p)$.

This demonstration is a piece of pure algebra. It has no necessary relevance to the uses of a calculus of probability, if only because its invocation as a device for quadrature of sufficient precision for practical purposes demands numerical investigation. Which of several more or less elementary procedures the pure mathematician regards as a more or less rigorous justification for the conclusion that the theorem is true in the limit is of little interest in practical situations. Our concern is then to assign particular numerical values to r, p, q sufficient to ensure the precision we demand of the computation. Here it will suffice to say that the correspondence over a range of 95 per cent of the area of the histogram will be as close as we are likely to want it to be for all values of r, p and q, if rp and rq both exceed 10.

Empirical investigation alone can justify our confidence in any empirical use to which we may put the result stated. In any event, its derivation as a limiting case has its proper domain in the natural history of the binomial theorem rather than in that of the art of gambling or of naturalistic applications of statistical theory. In so far as an applied theory of probability makes use of the binomial theorem, it does so when the topic is an enumerable collection of objects, i.e. when the postulate of continuity is factually irrelevant to the situation. To Laplace and to his immediate predecessors it would scarcely seem necessary to make this concession explicit, because the modern concept of the number continuum had not taken shape. When it did take shape the calculus of probability provided a playground in which the pure mathematician could develop a calculus on the basis of initial assumptions more general than those from which the validity of the calculus in the domain of scientific research derives its sanction. By then, as we have now seen, the doctrine of inverse probability had firmly but unobtrusively installed a continuum of suppositious prior probabilities in the sepulchral regions where mental images have their place of abiding.

Part of the task of putting the new orientation of statistical theory into its rightful historical perspective is thus to disentangle axioms introduced to exercise the ingenuity of mathematicians from axioms which have some connexion with the practical utility of their pursuits. Two circumstances in particular conspired to give the infinitesimal calculus a status which the thought of the classical period could scarcely endorse. One I have mentioned, the introduction by Laplace of the Type II Beta Function as the keystone of the doctrine of inverse probability. I cannot do better than quote Brunt (*The Combination of Observations*) with respect to the other:

Gauss (Werke, IV, p. 116) took Bessel's reduction of 470 observations of the right ascensions of Procyon and Altair made by Bradley, and compared the distribution of errors with the theoretical curve obtained by evaluating h by the above formula. He calculated the numbers of observations whose errors should be numerically between $0''\cdot0$ and $0''\cdot1$, between $0''\cdot1$ and $0''\cdot2$, etc., and compared them with the actual numbers obtained from Bradley's observations. The results are given in the following table.

Errors		Theoretical number	Actual number
$0''\cdot0$ to $0''\cdot1$		$94\cdot8$	94
$0''\cdot1$	$0''\cdot2$	$88\cdot8$	88
$0''\cdot2$	$0''\cdot3$	$78\cdot3$	78
$0''\cdot3$	$0''\cdot4$	$64\cdot1$	58
$0''\cdot4$	$0''\cdot5$	$49\cdot5$	51
$0''\cdot5$	$0''\cdot6$	$35\cdot8$	36
$0''\cdot6$	$0''\cdot7$	$24\cdot2$	26
$0''\cdot7$	$0''\cdot8$	$15\cdot4$	14
$0''\cdot8$	$0''\cdot9$	$9\cdot1$	10
$0''\cdot9$	$1''\cdot0$	$5\cdot0$	7
above	$1''\cdot0$	$5\cdot0$	8

The table shows a remarkable correspondence between the theory and the observational data. There is, however, a slight discrepancy in the number of large errors, the number occurring in practice exceeding the theoretical number.

The major contributions of Gauss relevant to our present theme appeared in the twenties and thirties of the nineteenth century. In the development of the theory associated with his name a contribution of outstanding interest is the *Grundzuge der Wahrscheinlichkeits Rechnung* of Hagen (1837), published two years after Quetelet's notorious *Essai de Physique Sociale*. Hagen

sought to explain the remarkable correspondence between the figures of the foregoing table and the requirements of what we now call the normal law as the limit of a binomial series of frequency terms in conformity with a situation to which the classical theory of probability is truly relevant. His explicit postulates are as follows:*

1. An observed error (m) is the algebraic sum of a very large number of minute elementary errors of equal magnitude (ϵ).

2. Positive and negative errors $(+\epsilon$ and $-\epsilon)$ occur with equal frequency in the long run. From this it follows that:

(a) if $(r-x)$ out of r elementary errors whose algebraic sum is m are positive and x are negative

$$(r-x)\,\epsilon + x\,(-\epsilon) = m = (r-2x)\,\epsilon \quad . \quad . \quad \text{(i)}$$

(b) the mean value of m in an indefinitely large number of trials is zero, whence if v_t is the true value of the measurement and v_o the observed one:

$$v_t = v_0 + m \; ; \; E(v_0) = E(v_t - m)$$
$$\therefore E(v_0) = v_t - E(m) = v_t \quad . \quad . \quad . \quad \text{(ii)}$$

If we wish to bring the above into harmony with the classical calculus of probability, we need to invoke the principle of *equipartition of associative opportunity*, i.e. that of the *Irregular Kollektiv*. We must thus add a third implicit postulate to the foregoing:

3. If the assumed fixed value of contributory errors to the observed error m_k at the kth trial is r the probability $(P_{x.k})$ that $m_k = (r-2x)\epsilon$ is *independent* of k, being uniquely determined by x, i.e.

$$P_{x.k} = r_{(x)} \cdot 2^{-r}$$

Given (1) — (3) above Hagen's argument is translatable in terms of the gaming idiom of the founders of classical theory by reference to the following model. We toss an unbiased

* Since we do not here initially invoke the continuum in the foregoing statement, it is pertinent to quote Brunt (p. 11):

"Hagen based his proof on the assumption that an accidental error consists of the algebraic sum of a *very large number* of infinitesimal errors of equal magnitude, and as likely to be positive as negative." (Italics inserted.)

penny r times. At each unit trial we record the score as $+ \epsilon$ if it falls head upwards and $- \epsilon$ if it falls tail upwards. If x is the taxonomical* tail-score, the total score (m) in the domain of representative scoring adopted in this context is:

$$(r - x)\epsilon + x(- \epsilon) = m = (r - 2x)\epsilon$$

The mean of the x-score distribution is $\frac{1}{2}r$ and that of the m distribution is $E(m) = 0$. The variances of the two distributions are respectively:

$$\sigma_x^2 = \frac{r}{4} \ and \ \sigma_m^2 = 4\sigma_x^2\epsilon^2 \quad . \quad . \quad . \quad \text{(iii)}\dagger$$

The probability of getting a tail-score x is

$$P_x = \frac{r!}{x!(r - x)!} 2^{-r} \quad . \quad . \quad . \quad . \quad \text{(iv)}$$

If r is very large we may write:

$$P_x \simeq \frac{1}{\sigma_x \sqrt{2\pi}} \ exp \ \frac{- (x - \frac{1}{2}r)^2}{2\sigma_x^2} \quad . \quad . \quad . \quad \text{(v)}$$

With appropriate change of scale the ordinate equation of the corresponding fitting curve of the m-distribution is

$$y_m = \frac{1}{\sigma_m \sqrt{2\pi}} \ exp \ \frac{- m^2}{2\sigma_m^2} \quad . \quad . \quad . \quad . \quad \text{(vi)}$$

The probability of getting a value of m in the interval $m \pm \frac{1}{2} \Delta m$ is then

$$\Delta P_m \simeq \frac{1}{\sigma_m \sqrt{2\pi}} \cdot exp \ \frac{- m^2}{2\sigma_m^2} \cdot \Delta m$$

* The distinction between taxonomical and representative scoring here and elsewhere made is the writer's own usage. Taxonomical scoring enumerates objects or classes, representative scoring records totals and averages of assigned score values.

† The scale of the x-distribution is $\Delta x = 1$. For the 2-fold toss we may score $(-\epsilon, -\epsilon)$; $(-\epsilon, +\epsilon)$, $(+\epsilon, -\epsilon)$; $(+\epsilon, +\epsilon)$ so that possible values of m are -2ϵ, 0, $+2\epsilon$. Similarly, $m = -3\epsilon$, $-\epsilon$, $+\epsilon$, $+3\epsilon$ for the 3-fold toss. Thus the scale of the m-distribution is $\Delta m = 2\epsilon$. To derive (vi) we note that the area of the histogram column of height y_x is $y_x\Delta x = y_x$ for the interval $x \pm \frac{1}{2}\Delta x$ on the x-score scale. On the m-score scale the width of the interval is $\pm \epsilon$ for the corresponding score $m = (r - 2x)\epsilon$. If y_m is the height of the column whose area is $y_x\Delta x = y_x$, we may write $y_x = y_m\Delta m$ whence $y_x = 2\epsilon \cdot y_m$ in the derivation of (iii).

If we seek to relate the theory of the model to practice, we do not know the numerical values of r or of ϵ. Hence we do not know the value of σ_m. In accordance with (iii) above, the earlier writers put:

$$\frac{1}{2\sigma_m^2} = h^2 = \frac{1}{2r\epsilon^2} \quad \cdots \quad \text{(vii)}$$

Thus the ordinate equation assumes the form:

$$y_m \simeq \frac{h}{\sqrt{\pi}} e^{-h^2 m^2} \quad \cdots \quad \text{(viii)}$$

In this expression, the so-called *precision index* (h) is a constant to be determined approximately by the data of a sufficiently large experiment. The probability that an error will be as great as $+ a$ is

$$P(m \leqslant a) \simeq \frac{h}{\sqrt{\pi}} \int_{-\infty}^{a} e^{-h^2 m^2} . dm \quad \cdots \quad \text{(ix)}$$

For purposes of tabulation we may write $hm = t$, so that:

$$P(m \leqslant a) \simeq \frac{1}{\sqrt{\pi}} \int_{-\infty}^{ha} e^{-t^2} . dt \quad \cdots \quad \text{(x)}$$

One speaks of the table of the definite integral (x) as the table of the *Error Function*, sometimes written *Erf(ha)*, still cited in handbooks for the use of physicists, surveyors and astronomers. It is, of course, equivalent to the table of the normal integral of unit variance and of zero mean with suitable change of scale. For the latter our standard score (k) is

$$k = \frac{a}{\sigma_m} \quad \text{and} \quad P(m \leqslant a) \simeq \frac{1}{\sqrt{2\pi}} \int_{0}^{k} e^{-\frac{1}{2}c^2} . dc \quad \text{(xi)}$$

The definite integral on the right of (xi) is that of the normal curve of unit variance as tabulated for use in modern textbooks of statistical theory. It is more convenient, since the unbiased estimate (s_m) of the unknown σ_m has a simpler relation to the empirical data. By definition $v_0 = v_t - m$ as in the derivation of (ii) above. Thus the distribution of m and v_0 the observed value of the measurement involves only a shift of origin when the variance of the distribution of the individual measurements (v_0) is that of the distribution of errors (m). The mean of the former is v_t of which the unbiased estimate based on n successive observations is

$$M_0 = \frac{1}{n} \sum_{x=1}^{x=n} v_{0.x} \quad . \quad . \quad . \quad . \quad . \quad \text{(xii)}$$

The unbiased estimate of the unknown variance of the distribution is:

$$s_m^2 = \frac{1}{n-1} \sum_{x=1}^{x=n} (v_{0.x} - M_0)^2 \quad . \quad . \quad . \quad \text{(xiii)}$$

When we test the theory we rely on the hope that $\sigma_m \simeq s_m$ if n is large in accordance with the first postulate of Hagen's so-called proof; and we may then invoke Bernoulli's theorem to justify our confidence that the error involved in the approximation will very rarely be sensible if n is sufficiently large.

Our statistical model gives a *possible* explanation of a correspondence which Bradley's data illustrate. This does not conclusively prove that the two explicit postulates are correct; and it presupposes that the approximation in substituting (v) for (iv) is valid. The numerical correspondence between the latter is indeed very close if $r > 16$. The derivation given above implies that there will be $(r + 1)$ different values of m whose relative frequencies tally with successive terms of $(\frac{1}{2} + \frac{1}{2})^r$. We shall therefore not expect good correspondence unless the recorded observation may be referable to at least 17 different scale divisions of the instrument. In the example cited from Gauss, we have before us 21.

Such a spread is by no means a universal experience and the background of the experiment Gauss cites is therefore instructive. A modern observatory is a highly complex mechanism in which large numbers of cog wheels engage in the process of setting an instrument in position for any single recorded observation. Thus all the combined effect of sources of relevant variability may be considerable when we have eliminated all systematic errors. In many types of experiment this is manifestly untrue. If we repeatedly titrate from the same solution with the same burette and with the same pipette, we do not expect successive observations performed with competence to deviate by more than one scale division—or at most two—on either side of a central value. Thus the relevance of Hagen's postulates or of any deductions we may draw from them to an experimental situation depends on the nature of the latter, and no particular verification in one domain of experiment is necessarily relevant to any other.

Let us therefore examine the postulates more closely. Our Hagen model embodies three quite arbitrary assumptions which call for separate consideration:

(*a*) the elementary errors are of *equal* magnitude;

(*b*) the particular combination of elementary errors collectively equivalent to the deviation of an observed from its true value is the outcome of a native *randomising* process;

(*c*) negative and positive errors occur with *equal frequency* in the long run.

Of the first and second of these, it suffices to say that neither is amenable to empirical verification. The second implies a symmetrical distribution of observed measurements repeated on a sufficiently large scale. The preceding tabulation does not in fact exhibit whether the original distribution was more or less skew or not.

Though together *sufficient*, no one of the two explicit postulates is indeed a *necessary* condition that the normal curve should be a good descriptive device for the distribution of repeated measurements; but (*b*) and (*c*) are of basic importance to the classical theory of error *per se*. If we reject (*a*) as unnecessarily arbitrary, we can conserve the peculiar status of the arithmetic mean in the Gaussian system only by rephrasing (*c*) in a more general form, viz.: *the mean of the distribution of elementary errors is zero*. It then follows that their combined effect will cancel out in the mean of a sufficiently large number of observations, i.e. that the arithmetic mean of our experimental values (v_0) approaches the unknown putatively true value (v_t) more and more closely as we enlarge the number of observations recorded. This is implicit in any intelligible theory of error *sensu stricto*.

That the third postulate is irrelevant to the derivation of the so-called law itself is deducible from elementary considerations which antedate the Gaussian Theory. In our model set-up, there is equal probability of scoring heads $(+ \epsilon)$ or tails $(- \epsilon)$ at each toss contributory to the r-fold trial. In the customary symbolism, we may denote by p and q respectively the probabilities of one or other event in the unit trial. We should then write more generally for (iv) and (iii) above respectively

$$P_x = \frac{r!}{x!\,(r-x)!}\, p^{r-x} q^x \; and \; \sigma_x^2 = rpq$$

As already stated (p. 160), numerical investigation then shows that the approximation specified by (v) holds good if rq and rp both exceed 10. The rest of the demonstration is valid with due regard to the reinterpretation of σ_m in terms of σ_x defined as above.

If we regard the number of elementary errors contributory to the total error and the probabilities p and q as consistent with the criterion stated immediately above, the first and second explicit postulates of our model set-up together furnish a sufficient condition for reliance on the normal curve as a descriptive device. That the third is not a necessary one is less obvious than its arbitrariness. Advanced textbooks of statistics show how it is possible to arrive at the same result without assuming that the elementary errors are of equal magnitude. Laplace foreshadowed this derivation known as the *Central Limit Theorem* which has played a very large part in the background of what we shall later call the *Quetelet mystique*. Kendall defines the theorem as follows: "under certain conditions the sum of n independent random variables distributed in whatever form tends, when expressed in standard measure to the normal form as n tends to infinity."

The search for what mathematicians call a rigorous proof of the theorem has provoked much discussion and leads us into unnecessarily deep waters, if we arbitrarily assume a truly continuous distribution of elementary errors of different magnitude. If we stick to the firm ground of a model we can visualise, we shall suppose that a lottery wheel has some number of sectors N each labelled with some score value

$\epsilon_{0.1}$, $\epsilon_{0.2}$, $\epsilon_{0.3}$, etc., not necessarily of the same sign. We shall spin the wheel r times, record at each spin the particular value $\epsilon_{0.x}$ of the sector which stops against a fixed pointer and define the score-sum (s_0) of the r single trials as our total "error" of observation, i.e.

$$s_0 = \sum_{x=1}^{x=r} \epsilon_{0.x} \quad . \quad . \quad . \quad . \quad (xiv)$$

Since we might record at a single trial r values of the numerically highest negative or positive value of $\epsilon_{0.x}$, the range of the distribution of $\epsilon_{0.x}$ will be small in comparison with that of s_0, if r is large. *En passant* we note that we have dispensed with the second postulate, as given above, or in the alternative form which alone endows the arithmetic mean with the special meaning it enjoys in the Gaussian theory, i.e. we do not assume that the distribution of elementary errors is symmetrical about zero mean or even that the mean is zero.

The student, who has an elementary acquaintance with the notion of *moments* as descriptive measures of the contour of a distribution, will be content if we assume that two distributions are identical when all corresponding moments about the mean when expressed in standard measure are identical. It then suffices to establish the following result which relies only on elementary algebra, if we invoke our implicit assumption, i.e. statistical independence of unit trials: the standardised mean moments of the distribution of the r-fold score sum referable to any discrete score distribution approach those of the normal distribution of unit variance more and more closely as we increase the value of r.*

The *Central Limit Theorem* occupies a pivotal, if unobtrusive, place in statistical thought from the time of Laplace to that of Liapounoff (1901) who first gave what a pure mathematician of today would concede to be a rigorous proof. This may be partly because it proceeds from less arbitrary postulates than those of Hagen to a possible explanation of why the normal law gives a tolerably satisfactory description of the outcome of repeated observations in some types of physical experimentation. If so, it illustrates how much relevance we may sacrifice

* *See* Appendix I.

or greater generality in the algebraic sense of the term. Unless we assume a distribution of elementary errors about zero mean, we have no justification for interpreting the limiting value of the mean of our observations or that of any other parameter of their distribution as the *true one;* and we have no solid foot-hold for a concept of error, if we jettison the concept of a true value as the goal of our endeavours. Whatever bearing on scientific enquiry the theory of probability may or may not rightly have, no one fully informed will deny that: (*a*) the attempt to formulate a stochastic theory of error was its first considerable claim to recognition as such; (*b*) the founders of the theory took the view last stated, as did their immediate successors. Thus Brunt (1917) says:

> This relation* is of such importance that it is necessary to consider it in some detail. The residuals v_1, v_2, etc., are the deviations of the observed values from the A.M., and if the A.M. could be definitely regarded as the *true* value of the unknown, the (M.S.E.)^2 ought to be equal to $\dfrac{[vv]}{n}$. (*Italics inserted.*)

On any terms, the Gaussian theory of error, and the vast superstructure erected thereon, is indeed an entirely meaning-less algebraic exercise, unless we conceive the attempt to arrive at a *true* value as the reason for making repeated observations. What endows the central limit theorem with a more special interest is that it tempts us to carry into quite a different domain from that of the combination of observations the formal algebra of the Gaussian theory without probing into its relevance too deeply. This development begins with Quetelet. It was he who first drew attention to the distribution of heights of adults in a comparatively homogeneous population, and advanced the proposition that its form is a manifestation of (his words) the *binomial law.* In short, nature is an urn which shakes out numbered *billets* at random. The individual is a packet of such *billets.* His or her score—height or whatnot—is the numerical sum of the numbers of the constituent *billets.*

We may seek a rationale for Quetelet's so-called law of

---

* Unbiased estimate of variance. In the symbolism of Brunt [vv] at the end of the citation stands for the sum of the squares of the residuals v_1, v_2, etc.

height at very different levels. If we disregard the role of environment, we can nowadays invoke stochastic principles from the domain of the genetical theory of populations. With some plausibility we can then identify a pool of elementary entities with a system of supposedly *additive* multiple factors each assigned a hypothetical score $\epsilon_{0.x}$ in an assumed framework of random mating. To give this hypothetical score any substance from a genetical viewpoint, we have to think of it in terms of gene substitution, i.e. against the background of a reconstructed ancestral "wild type." In a standard environment, we thus conceptualise each elementary score as a deviation of so many units of relevant measurement. However, the ancestral wild type which we invoke is beyond recall.

Quetelet's following, in particular Galton and K. Pearson, had no such empirically validated stochastic theory to discipline their speculations. They took over from Darwin a vague particulate hypothesis, which leaves us with no origin of reference for the hypothetical elementary score value $\epsilon_{0.x}$ unless we arbitrarily define it as the *norm* of the population. In that event, we become involved in the comic obligation to decide arbitrarily what parameter of the population distribution is the true norm. Indeed, discussion about whether to plump for the arithmetic mean, the geometric mean, the harmonic mean, the mode or the median filled pages of statistical textbooks issued in the heyday of the singular cult of biometrics. It should be—but alas is not even yet—needless to say that the issue is meaningless. Only the assumed existence of a true value which we may hope to approach more closely by taking the mean of an ever larger number of observations endows the arithmetic mean or any other parameter of their distribution with a unique semantic content in contradistinction to what claims it may have if we wish to specify a descriptive curve in the most convenient way.

That it is still necessary to state this truism is evident from the fact that contemporary literature on significance tests follows the practice of Yule by ascribing a special status to the probability that the deviation of an observed measurement from the true mean of the parent population [*sic*] will attain a certain magnitude. To keep up the illusion we still speak of the mean as the *expected* value of a statistic and denote by E (or ϵ) the operation of extracting the arithmetic mean of a sampling procedure; and we may readily forgive the pure mathematician who walks into the trap, when the same symbolism serves to specify both a *deviation* from a non-existent norm and an *error* in determining the *true value* of a measurement. What is not easy to understand is how this formal identity can hoodwink anyone accustomed to naturalistic pursuits.

This will be clear if we examine what we really mean when we say that 75 per cent is the *expected* proportion of peas with yellow seeds from *a* mating of yellow-green hybrid parent plants. The italicised indefinite article in the last sentence is operative. The calculus of probability does not and cannot entitle us to speak of *a* mating. In this context it can merely provide the basis for a verifiable theory about a particular class of matings *in the long run*. It does not even justify the statement that we shall encounter 75 per cent more often than any other proportion of yellow peas in an indefinitely protracted number of trials. Unless the sample size (r) in the sequence of trials is an exact multiple of 4 an observed proportion of 75 per cent yellow seeds is an event we can never expect to encounter in *any* such trial.

The last consideration puts the spotlight on what is perhaps the most puzzling consequence of the formal identification of a natural deviation from a suppositious norm with an error as Gauss conceived it. In a scrupulously careful repetition of matings from inbred stocks no error as Gauss conceived error need arise, if we employ reliable mechanical aids to *enumeration*. In the system of Gauss, the deviations from the limiting value of the mean signifies man's fallibility in the apprehension of natural law, and as such we deem it to be irrelevant to the precise formulation of a law of nature. In the so-called law of height our observed deviations from the norm, if recorded with sufficient precision, embody the content of the so-called law itself.

In the last two paragraphs I have deliberately anticipated an intrusion of the calculus of probability into the domain of experimental science at a different level from that of Gauss, and after a lapse of nearly a century. I have felt it necessary to do so to get into focus an issue raised by Brunt (*vide infra*). In one sense, the Central Limit Theorem offers us the algebraic apparatus for an explanation of a class of occurrences, but not as men of science commonly use the word *explanation*. It is evidently consistent with any particulate theory of inheritance, right or wrong, in situations which admit of explanation in terms of inheritance alone. It might well be likewise possible with a little ingenuity to bring earlier speculations which invoke humours, fluids, essences *et hoc genus omne* within the scope of its catholic terms of reference; but what have we gained by doing so? Can it specifically lead us to a deeper understanding of nature, by disclosing hitherto unsuspected phenomena? The answer is that any confidence in stochastic reasoning we now derive from the advancement of knowledge concerning heredity arises from circumstances to which the Gaussian theory of error is irrelevant.

The influence of Quetelet on subsequent thought is the more remarkable because the legacy of absurdities he bequeathed to posterity were fully recognised by writers on probability in the middle of the nineteenth century; and physicists who endorse the Gaussian theory of error have been highly critical of the uses to which Quetelet's followers have put it. In the preface of his book already cited, Brunt expressly warns his readers against the folly of confusing unavoidable human error with natural variation; but the cardinal absurdity of doing so is condoned by implication in any current treatise on statistical theory for research workers in the biological and social sciences.

It is therefore both gratifying and instructive to recall the engaging summary of Quetelet's views by Bertrand* in his *Calcul des Probabilités* (1888). Bertrand does not fail to anticipate how heavily the superstructure of regression theory erected on the foundations Quetelet laid leans on a scaffolding of Platonism:

... The world of universals seemed talked out and quite forgotten. M. Quetelet, without reviving this ancient problem, seriously believes he has resolved it and, in a book stuffed full of judiciously

---

* I must thank Dr. Richard Padley for a translation which does justice to the Voltairean flavour of the original.

collected facts, would have us accept a precise definition of the word Man, independently of human beings whose particularity can be considered accidental. With as little discussion as subtlety, the painstaking author defines his specimen, attributing to him the arithmetic mean of every element that varies from one man to another. After a survey, for example, of the heights of 20,000 soldiers, the mean has been determined at 1 m 75; such then is the height of the average man. Around it in the scale of measurement are grouped greater or lesser statures, exactly graduated according to the law of error. Nothing distinguishes the heights of the conscripts from 20,000 successive measurements which an incompetent observer would have taken on a man 1 m 75 tall if we suppose the work to have been carried out with instruments which, though crude enough, were corrected for any constant error.

In this comparison M. Quetelet sees an identity. Our inequalities of height are, in his eyes, the result of inept measurements taken by Nature on an immutable model in whom alone she reveals her secrets. 1 m 75 is the normal height. A little more makes no less a man, but the surplus or deficit in each individual is nature's error, and thus monstrous.

Abelard, if set to this disputation, would have presented the argument in formal terms, but such subtlety no longer holds sway. Wandering over the schoolmen's ancient battlefield, M. Quetelet has fallen in with neither ally nor foe.

The Thesis has, however, more than one inconvenience. The ideal man, we shall say, represents in all things the arithmetic mean of humanity. This sounds very simple and very clear, but how are we to compute these measurements defined within the limitations of ruler and compasses. Mean height of head, for example, can be computed in two ways; we can take the mean of head lengths, or for each individual, the relationship between head and body length and then the mean of these ratios. The results are different; how should they be brought together.

The difficulty is serious and shipwreck certain. To show this in a model situation let us examine the mean of two spheres. The first has unit radius and we shall choose a scale such that surface area and volume are also unity. The second, I will suppose, has radius 3 and, necessarily, will have a surface area of 9 and volume 27. Means of 2, 5 and 14 are incompatible; a sphere of radius 2 would have a surface area 4 and volume 8 exactly; no concession is possible, a sphere can have no other shape. Men's shapes unfortunately can vary, and M. Quetelet profits therefrom. By combining the mean weight of 20,000 conscripts with their mean height, we should

STATISTICAL THEORY

produce an absurdly fat man and, whatever Reynolds might have
said, a poor model for an artist. This eminent painter, in his
Lectures on the Fine Arts preceded Quetelet in setting up the
average man as the type of perfect beauty. If such were the case,
suggested Sir John Herschel, ugliness would be the exception. I
cannot follow his argument. The individual traits of perfect beauty
would not be rare; indecorously jumbled together they would lack
merit. Grace stems from harmony. Chance doubtless would summon
few elect and, despite Sir John Herschel, in the ill assorted assembly,
if ugliness formed the exception, the grotesque would become the
rule.

In the body of the average man our Belgian author sets an
average soul. To summarize the moral qualities it is necessary to
cast 20,000 characters in one. The specimen man would be without
passion or vice, not foolish, not wise, not ignorant, not knowledgeable, generally dozing, for it is the average between wakefulness and
sleep; he would answer neither yes nor no, and be in all things
mediocre. After remaining alive for 38 years on the average ration
of a healthy soldier, he would die, not of old age, but of an average
disease which statistics would discover for him.

But for Galton, this and other epitaphs on the views of
Quetelet by exponents of the theory of probability in the latter
half of the nineteenth century should have buried the author
of the *Essai* with appropriate honours. *Natural Inheritance*
appeared in 1889, a year after Bertrand's *Calcul*. Among other
diversions of a country gentleman Galton took to photography,
and was able to give verisimilitude to the Quetelet norm by
producing composite snapshots of the judge, the criminal and
the leading counsel as visual aids to the hitherto nebulous
domain of Plato's universals. The following passage (*italics
inserted*) illustrates how the Gaussian law of *instrumental error*
henceforth becomes the *normal* law of *nature:*

I need hardly remind the reader that the Law of Error upon
which these Normal Values are based, was excogitated for the use
of astronomers and others who are concerned with extreme accuracy
of measurement, and without the slightest idea until the time of
Quetelet that they might be applicable to human measures. But
Errors, Differences, Deviations, Divergences, Dispersions, and
individual Variations, all spring from the same kind of causes.
Objects that bear the same name, or can be described by the same

174

THE NORMAL LAW COMES INTO THE PICTURE

phrase, are thereby acknowledged to have common points of resemblance, and to rank as members of the same species, class, or whatever else we may please to call the group. On the other hand, every object has Differences peculiar to itself, by which it is distinguished from others.

This general statement is applicable to thousands of instances. *The Law of Error finds a footing wherever the individual peculiarities are wholly due to the combined influence of a multitude of "accidents," in the sense in which that word has already been defined. All persons conversant with statistics are aware that this supposition brings Variability within the grasp of the laws of Chance,* with the result that the relative frequency of Deviations of different amounts admits of being calculated, when those amounts are measured in terms of any self-contained unit of variability, such as our Q. (pp. 54–5).

Starting with this misconception of the proper terms of reference of a calculus of error, Galton speaks (pp. 16–17) in the following passage concerning the *Variety of Petty Influences.*

The incalculable number of petty accidents that concur to produce variability among brothers, make it impossible to predict the exact qualities of any individual from hereditary data. But we may predict average results with great certainty, as will be seen further on, and we can also obtain precise information concerning the penumbra of uncertainty that attaches itself to single predications.

Thus we learn at the end (p. 193):

A brief account of the chief hereditary processes occupies the first part of the book. It was inserted principally in order to show that a reasonable *a priori* probability existed, of the law of Frequency of Error being found to apply to them. It was not necessary for that purpose to embarrass ourselves with any details of theories of heredity beyond the fact that descent either was particulate or acted as if it were so. I need hardly say that the idea, though not the phrase of particulate inheritance, is borrowed from Darwin's provisional theory of Pangenesis, but there is no need in the present enquiry to borrow more from it.

For the reader who does not probe too deeply into "what all persons conversant with statistics are aware" of, the outcome of the enquiry is not less arresting because the author expresses his more dramatic conclusions with becoming modesty. Elsewhere, we learn (p. 48):

175

My data were very lax, but this method of treatment got all the good out of them that they possessed. In the present case, it appears that towards the foremost of the successful men within fifteen years of taking their degrees, stood the three Professors of Anatomy at Oxford, Cambridge, and Edinburgh; that towards the bottom of the failures, lay two men who committed suicide under circumstances of great disgrace, and lowest of all Palmer, the Rugeley murderer, who was hanged.

We need scarcely recall that K. Pearson's flair for ancestor worship had ample scope for self-expression in his partnership with the founder of the Eugenic cult. He took over from Galton the term *regression* and sponsored a novel extension of the Gaussian technique of statistical estimation in publications which successfully concealed the biological postulates and implications of Galton's so-called *Law of Ancestral Inheritance* behind a forbidding façade of symbolic inconsequence. An issue which was essentially mathematical thus became the battleground of a biological controversy conducted with an output of heat totally disproportionate to the illumination conferred. When the shouting and the tumult died, the older generation of mathematicians had lost interest in the origins of the concept and were all too ready to accept at face value a now allegedly indispensable "tool" of biological enquiry as a means of providing full employment for their younger colleagues. How this came about we shall see more fully, when we have looked a little more closely into the Gaussian *Method of Least Squares* and the concept of covariance which emerges therefrom.

In this context our main concern is to trace to its origins the peculiar status which the normal distribution enjoys in contemporary statistical theory. The rationale of Quetelet's binomial law, espoused by Galton and thereafter endorsed as the kingpin of the theory of regression, is the suppositious relevance of Hagen's model; and the best one can say of Hagen's model in this context is that it is an attractive expository device. Its relevance to the contour of graphs defining certain empirical distributions of measurements made on populations of living beings and its relevance to observed distributions of instrumental errors are alike amenable neither to proof nor to disproof. Thus Brunt (p. 17 *op. cit.*) concludes his exposition of attempts of Hagen and others to provide a *proof* of the Normal Law of Error in the following salutary terms (*italics inserted*):

The proofs of the Normal Error Law given above are based on certain definite hypotheses concerning the nature of accidental errors. It has been shown that, if the accidental errors to which a series of observations is liable satisfy these hypotheses, the errors of observation will be distributed according to the normal law. The final justification of the use of Gauss's Error Curve rests upon the fact that it works well in practice, and yields curves which in very many cases agree very closely with the observed frequency curves. The normal law is to be regarded as *proved by experiment*, and *explained* by Hagen's hypothesis. When the curve of frequency of the actual errors is not of the form of the normal curve, we may safely conclude that the nature of the accidental errors concerned is not in accordance with Hagen's hypothesis.

As we have seen, Hagen's model is one of many models entirely consistent with the classical theory of risks in games of chance. Each can lay claim with as much and as little plausibility to furnish an *explanation* of the distribution of errors, when the distribution accords closely with the normal curve; but close correspondence between distributions of error in the Gaussian sense of the term is one which we shall expect to encounter, and shall indeed encounter, only in a limited class of experimental enquiries. Aside from the arbitrariness of the assumptions embodied in the specification of the Gaussian law of error, this reflection alone suffices to dispose of the misconception that the classical theory of risks can indeed furnish any rationale for error distributions in general.

When we transgress the boundaries of the domain of experimental error to contemplate the baffling intricacies of natural variation, no person conversant with the content of the classical theory of risks can condone the identification of the variety of petty influences with "accidents" which bring "variability within the grasp of the laws of chance" so defined. The belief that the *Central Limit Theorem* endorses such an identification is groundless for two reasons, each sufficient to dispose of the claim. One is the formal assumption that we are dealing with elementary scores whose gross effects are both *independent* and *additive*, both suppositions certainly false in many situations, and especially in the Galtonian context of the nature-nurture issue. The other is that its acceptance as a law of nature excludes the possibility that natural variation interpretable in terms of an infinitude of such additive petty influences can ever be skew.

If unfamiliar with the history of statistical theory, the reader might well suppose that the foregoing citations from Galton exaggerate the role of the normal man in the superstructure of contemporary theory raised on the foundations Quetelet laid. If so, two citations should dispel them. The first is from a polemic note in *Biometrika* (Vol. 8, p. 249, 1912). Replying with characteristic vigour to a criticism to the effect that "we can only speak of a typical individual when we are dealing with one measurable feature at a time," Pearson asks:

> Can Professor Lloyd have the least conception of what are the leading features of a multiple frequency surface? Has he never heard of the "mean man" of Quetelet, or of Edgworth's defence of that *"mean man's"* actuality? (*Italics inserted.*)

What meaning we may attach to actuality in Pearson's Platonic universe of perceptions will appear from Edgworth's own words in a publication entitled *Statistical Correlation between Natural Phenomena* (*Journ. Stat. Soc.*, Vol. 56, 1893). He therein promulgates the bivariate normal distribution:

> Let it be required to construct a budget . . . representing the expenditure of a typical workman's family upon several articles of food, rent, etc. . . .
> Here, as elsewhere, sociology may derive instruction from the experience of her elder sister, physical science. The case before us is analogous to that which Quetelet treated when he sought to construct a *Mean Man* by measuring the limbs or organs of a great number of men, and taking the mean of the measurements relating to each part as the type of that part. It has been objected to this method that the parts thus determined might not fit each other. . . .
> It is with great diffidence that I venture to differ slightly from such high authorities; by submitting that their objection, though valid in the abstract, is much weakened by a circumstance which prevails *in rerum natura*, the fulfilment of the law of error. I need not

remind students of statistics that very generally the members of a species, e.g. men or shrimps, range with respect to any measurable attribute, such as the length of an organ, under a curve of which the equation is of the form $y = Ke^{-ax^2}$, . . . I have now to introduce a more general law of error, expressing the frequency of the concurrence between two, or more, attributes. . . . If, as in a former paper, we compare the curve of error to the outline of a *gendarme's* hat, we may now compare the surface of error to the top of a "pot" or "billicock" hat.

It is wonderful how accurately this double law of error is fulfilled in the case of animal organisms, as shown by the observations of Mr. Galton on men (Royal Society, 1888), and those of Professor Weldon on shrimps (*Ib.*, 1892); . . .

. . . There exists a mathematical, as well as an artistic, proportion between the parts of the human frame. . . . P_1, P_2 being any points on the axis of x, if planes be drawn through them perpendicular to that axis, the highest points of the curves traced out on these planes by their intersection with the error-surface will lie on a plane perpendicular to the plane of xy, and passing through a certain straight line OR.

A case of this proposition, which particularly concerns us, is when $x = 0$. In that case the average, which is also the greatest ordinate or centre of greatest frequency, for one attribute corresponds to or, is in the long run most frequently associated with, the average, or greatest ordinate value, of the other attribute. Our hat has one rounded summit; it is not puckered up into irregular projections like the soft felt hats now sometimes worn.

Here is the answer to the Cournot–Westergaard objection that the average value of one organ may be inapt to coexist with the average value of the other organ. The exact contrary proves to be true. Considering the average of one organ, we see that the value of the other organ which most frequently in experience—most probably in expectation—is associated with the average of that one is the average of the other.

These propositions may be transferred from animal to social organisms; in virtue of the presumption that the compound law of error prevails in the latter, as well as in the former, department. This presumption is based upon these two premises: (1) The compound, as well as the simple, law of error is apt to be fulfilled by phenomena which depend upon a variety of independent elements or agencies. . . . (2) Social phenomena are largely of this character; as is shown, (α) generally by the constancy of statistics, a constancy which seems best explained by the play of an immense number of influences whose fluctuations compensate each other; (β) in particular by the prevalence of the simple law of error in social phenomena . . . which can hardly be accounted for otherwise than by such a combination of agencies as would equally tend to fulfil the compound law; (γ) by actual verification in the particular case of correlation between the marks in Greek and Latin at the India Civil Service Examinations for 1874 and 1875—Candidates who are above or below the average mark in Greek prove to be above or below the Latin average to about the extent which the theory predicts.

No doubt in acting upon this presumption—as generally in applying mathematical ideas to social phenomena—regard must be had to the degree of irregularity which may be expected in the subject-matter. One abnormality which often characterises a group of quantities which cannot sink below zero, but may rise ever so high, is an elongation of the upper limits of the theoretically symmetrical curve of error. I have noticed this incident in the fluctuation of prices. . . .

We may extend the province of the foregoing argument to accommodate as many measurable or enumerable attributes as anatomists, physiologists and psychologists can specify. Our bivariate universe conceived in 3-dimensional space as a policeman's helmet then becomes a multivariate universe in the abstract domain of multidimensional geometry. It thus turns out that the *actuality* of the normal man is the distance of a point from an arbitrary origin in a non-visualisable hyperspace having an infinitude of dimensions. In the gospel of Pearson the just man made perfect is in short an arbitrarily selected constant definitive of what is actually an arbitrarily selected population.

Having identified the angelic choir in the Platonic empyrean of universals with an infinite population of the Normal Man, we must needs furnish it for his occupation, if we are to do justice to the nature-nurture issue conceived in such terms. By implication* in his attempt to evaluate the roles of nature and nurture interpreted gratuitously, and in manifest contrariety to facts sufficiently familiar to the biologist, as additive and independent components of growth, R. A. Fisher does indeed invoke the concept of an environmental norm—the mean of

* And explicitly in a private communication (1933) to the writer.

all environments. Within what geographical limits we shall
locate the source of our data and within what geographical
limits such data are available are questions to which no answer
is conceivably attainable, the more so because we should need
to be able to specify every variation of nurture relevant to
development before we could list what data we require.
Assuredly, we need not traverse the argument of Bertrand's
exposure of the Normal Man to convince ourselves that the
normal environment is a figment of the imagination devoid of
any intelligible interpretation in the domain of conduct.

CHAPTER EIGHT

THE METHOD OF LEAST SQUARES AND THE CONCEPT OF POINT ESTIMATION

IN THE CLASSICAL THEORY of the division of the stakes our concern is with systems on which we can impose randomness, or at least aspire to do so, by prescribing appropriate precautions, e.g. thorough shuffling between successive deals. As we approach the climax of the classical period, there emerges with the doctrine of inverse probability an innovation which has exerted a more lasting influence and one which has provoked far less controversy. The concept of the infinite hypothetical population embraces the postulate that blindfold selection therefrom is necessarily randomwise; and this postulate is the keystone of a calculus of exploration propounded by Quetelet in the social milieu both of a new public concern for the collection of reliable statistics of human welfare and of a new impetus to formulate an acceptable regimen for the assessment of instrumental errors of observation.

That none of Quetelet's contemporary critics cast doubt on it is not remarkable in the context of the emergence of an ostensibly stochastic rationale for the combination of observations on physical phenomena. The same assumption is inherent in the latter, and enjoys the sanction of Gauss. To do justice to the Gaussian theory in its own domain, it is indeed necessary to distinguish two levels at which it invokes the calculus of probability. First, it invites our assent to the proposition that uncontrollable errors of observation are the outcome of the allocation of intangible additive components by a randomising process inherent in the process of measurement. It likewise invites our assent to the proposition that uncontrollable errors referable to consecutive gross measurements of the same entity are themselves the outcome of a self-randomising process. The first of these two propositions has been the topic of Chapter Seven. Only the second, which will be the theme of this, is strictly essential to the claims of the stochastic calculus of error. We can get the distinction here stated into focus more clearly, if we now formulate two model situations.

Let us first imagine an urn A containing an infinitude of tickets each with a number, either negative or positive. We conceive that an umpire draws k tickets and records as the *gross trial score* the result of adding the sum of all the numbers thereon to a fixed constant (M). At this stage the ballot is secret. The onlookers have no opportunity to scrutinise the draw. They cannot see the face of the umpire. They neither know how many (k) tickets he draws at each trial nor what numbers the individual tickets bear. All the onlooker can observe is the outcome of a very large number of trials, viz. the frequency with which different values of the k-fold gross trial score occur. We may speak of this as the *unit sample distribution of observable errors*. In so far as it confers any special status on the mean of *all* trial scores, we must at least assume that it is symmetrical about M, i.e. that the sum of all the negative ticket numbers in the urn is numerically equal to that of all positive ticket numbers. Such is the stochastic model which endorses the first of the two propositions on which the calculus of error relies, if we also assume that the fictitious umpire shakes the urn thoroughly before each trial.

We now conceive the construction of a second urn B containing an infinitude of counters each with a number corresponding to a trial score of a k-fold draw from urn A. We shall also suppose that the relative frequencies of the counter score values tally with the unit sample distribution of gross trial scores referable to the outcome of the previous ballot. A second umpire now draws r counters from urn B. This time, we recognise the face of the umpire as that of an existent investigator. We can see how many counters he withdraws at each r-fold trial, and we can recognise the score on each of the r counters at each trial. What we cannot see is whether he shakes the urn thoroughly between trials. Such is the model the calculus of error invokes to justify the second proposition stated above, if we charitably assume thorough shaking.

Now the only reason for believing that the fictitious umpire withdrawing the *billets* bearing numbers definitive of suppositious elementary components of error does indeed shake urn A thoroughly before each k-fold trial is that the unit sample distribution of observable errors as here defined, sometimes accords with a type of sampling distribution, the normal, deducible from assumptions consistent with the postulate of randomisation. The most we can therefore claim for our first proposition is that it is not inconsistent with anything we know about how uncontrollable—so-called *accidental*—errors arise. Nothing we know from direct observation or from background information conclusively endorses the postulate.

Whether the unit sample distribution of observable and uncontrollable errors does indeed conform to the normal prescription is irrelevant to the truth or falsehood of our second proposition; but if we invoke the classical theory to interpret the result of successive r-fold trials in sampling from urn B we must assume* that any particular value the counter score may have at a single trial will turn up with the same frequency in juxtaposition to each possible value its predecessor or successor may have. This may well be so; but one seeks in vain for evidence of large-scale trials which confer any plausibility on the truth of the assertion. If we assume it to be true, the central limit theorem will justify our confidence that the mean distribution of the r-fold sample will be approximately normal for sufficiently large values of r; but the mere fact that the normal curve proves to give a good fit does not suffice to justify the postulate that the process of successive measurement is random in the classical sense.

At this point the reader may rightly say that the validity of the postulate is irrelevant. What matters is whether the system behaves as if the postulate does hold good; and this contention is surely admissible, if we also accept the obligation to examine each system on its own merits. So far as the writer can discover, there has been little intensive study of the natural history of error with that end in view; but recent work of Wootton and King (*Lancet*, March 7, 1953) casts grave doubts on the propriety of using the normal curve as a descriptive device for distributions of sample means of chemical tests for human

---

* The condition here stated does not suffice to prove that the endless series of the event is strictly without pattern; but its verification in large-scale trials would go far to reinforce our faith in the postulate of randomness.

blood constituents. We therefore arrive at the following conclusions: (i) the properties of classical models can give us no conclusive assurance that stochastic algebra will correctly describe the distribution of sample means; (ii) the use of stochastic algebra to assign frequency limits to errors of observation entails the obligation to undertake an *ad hoc* enquiry into the error distribution referable to any method of determination, when we do indeed invoke it.

The use of a statistical model such as urn A to interpret the approximately normal distribution of observations in certain types of physical enquiry is admittedly not inconsistent with the terms of reference of the classical theory, though the facts of the case furnish no reason for preferring one model to another; but if we ask why the normal distribution occupied so pre-eminent a place in the theory of error which Gauss and Hagen propounded, we come face to face with an innovation for which the classical theory furnishes no self-evident rationale. Though we shall later see that Gauss justified it by recourse to other considerations, the prominence it assumed in the exposition of the theory by the successors of Gauss was undoubtedly due to their belief that it endorses a new principle for combining observations in accordance with the outcome of randomwise sampling from urn B.

The new principle known as the *Method of Least Squares* signalises the intrusion of a concept which we now speak of as *point estimation*, and the enlistment of the theory of probability in a domain of application different from that of interpreting error distributions of the type exhibited on p. 161 in terms consistent with stochastic models. The formulation of the method itself antedates Gauss, and many expositions of the basic assumptions current from that of Gauss to our own time interpret them *en rapport* with the viewpoint of Legendre and of Laplace. It took shape during a period of outstanding refinements in the design of measuring instruments, a circumstance which throws light on its ready welcome. An earlier generation might have lazily and cheerfully hoped that instruments of greater precision would eliminate discrepancies between successive determinations of the same entity; but the introduction of vast improvements of observatory equipment leading to the detection of the annual parallax of a star, alone sufficed to dispel any grounds for believing that mechanical procedures could extricate the observer from the need to formulate some guiding principle or universal convention for minimising the error entailed in any method of arriving at an average. Better measuring devices reduce the range of valuation but on a more refined scale. Thus they do not necessarily reduce the number of scale divisions consistent with competent observation of the same physical dimension.

Most of us will be well content to give equal weight to every observation of a single entity, as when we adopt the arithmetic mean for successive measurements of the same physical dimensions, e.g. a height or a weight; but few, if any, of us could confidently furnish a wholly convincing justification for this preference. In many situations, few of us would indeed pause to challenge the propriety of the custom; but the issue assumes a more provocative aspect for two reasons when we combine different measurements to *estimate*, i.e. determine *as best we can*, such a single entity. For example, we may use the angle of elevation (a_1 and a_2) at each extremity of a base line of length (b) to determine the height (h) of a mountain. Each such combined observation entails errors of three sorts, or at least of two, if we reject the possibility that one of the three measurements (b) is liable to error. In that event any single pair of observations will yield one and the same estimate of h, but the attempt to accomplish greater precision by making more observations will lead us to different estimates referable to different paired values of a_1 and a_2. Nor do our difficulties end here. If we record a_1 and a_2 alternatively we come face to face with the question: shall we take the mean of each estimate based on a particular pair of values $a_{1,r}$ and $a_{2,r}$, or shall we make an estimate based on the mean value of $a_{1,r}$ and $a_{2,r}$? Since the results will not necessarily tally, an intuitive and unreflective preference for the mean leaves unsolved the problem of combining observations in the best way.

This simple illustration of the problem subsumed in the title of more than one standard text on the *Combination of Observations* is pertinent to the historic context in which the theory emerges. In the half-century from 1780–1830, the introduction of achromatic lenses, a new technique of glass polishing and new machine tools for wheel-cutting in the wake of emergent steam power contributed alike to improved design of the telescope, the microscope and the theodolite. Incident to these improvements, and coincident with the demonstration by Gauss of the normal law of error as a remarkably good fitting curve for Bradley's observations on Altair and Procyon (p. 161) came the final vindication of Kepler, the detection of the annual parallax of the star 61 *Cygni* by Bessel (1837–40). Hitherto the only co-ordinates of the map of the celestial sphere beyond the solar system had been angular. Star map-making now enters on a new phase in which the determination of interstellar distances calls for ever-increasing refinement of measurement.

In the same milieu, earth map-making embraces a new programme by taking advantage of new means, a new motive and a new opportunity to explore the earth's crust. Advances in the technology of the observatory immediately followed extensive surveying for the canal system and synchronised both with still more extensive surveying for the new railroads and with a concomitant efflorescence of geological enquiry. A theory of error which could lead to agreement about the best method of combining observations was thus a keenly felt need in the domain of geodesics. Indeed, textbooks of surveying give us the best insight into the use of the new principle on its original terms of reference. Thus it is not without interest that the author of the *Essai de Physique Sociale* was both an astronomer in charge of the national observatory and professor of geodesics in the Brussels military academy.

When we do combine different observations (x_1, x_2, x_3, etc.) to determine one or more physical dimensions or constants (p_1, p_2, etc.), different methods of doing so may commend themselves to common sense; and these may lead us to assign somewhat different values to what we may here call the required parameters (p_1, etc.). In the Gaussian theory of error different values of the parameters will entail different deviations of x_1, x_2, etc., from their putative true values (t_1, t_2, etc.). The probability assigned by the classical theory to the compound event of recording the particular set deemed to be a sample chosen randomwise from all possible observations of the same sort within an assumed fixed framework of repetition will thus depend on whether we adopt one or other set of parameter values. For reasons which are by no means obvious nor exempt from criticism, Legendre and Laplace invoked this consideration to justify a method of combining observations individually liable to instrumental error in the widest sense of the term. In the thought of the period which antedates Gauss, the fundamental postulates of the method are two:

(i) of all sets of values we might choose as estimates of the parameters, we shall deem that set as best, if it assigns the highest probability to the compound occurrence;

(ii) the values which satisfy the criterion of preference so prescribed are those which make the sum of the squares of the residuals, i.e. $(x_1 - t_1)^2$, $(x_2 - t_2)^2$, etc., as small as possible.

As shown below, (ii) is an algebraic tautology, if a normal distribution of independent errors holds good, i.e.: (a) the normal law prescribes the probability of a given deviation $\epsilon_r = (x_r - t_r)$ of an individual observation from its true value; (b) the individual observations are themselves statistically independent. This indeed is what most early expositions of the Method of Least Squares proffer as a proof of it on the explicit assumption that the criterion of preference defined by (i) is also admissible; but the prescription of the criterion of preference embodied in (i), hereinafter referred to as the Legendre–Laplace Axiom, has no obvious connexion with the classical theory. Nor did Gauss himself invoke it. It calls for comment, because it has left a lasting imprint on the discussion of the place of *point estimation* in the applications of the theory of probability.

The derivation of the normal curve as an approximate description in accordance with the Hagen model or with any more generalised model of observed measurements which present themselves as *discrete* quantities in terms of scale divisions leads us to an expression for the probability of a deviation (X) of a particular observation from its mean value on unit scale as

$$P_x = \frac{h}{\sqrt{\pi}} e^{-h^2 X^2}$$

For a set of independent deviations (U, V, W) subject to the *same dispersion* due to the same sources of so-called accidental error, we may regard h as constant and the probability of the particular sequence of values as:

$$P_s = K \, exp - h^2 \, (U^2 + V^2 + W^2)$$

This expression will be a maximum, if the sum of the square deviations $(U^2 + V^2 + W^2)$ is a minimum. We may write the sum more explicitly in terms of the actual observations u, v, w and their corresponding true (long-run *mean*) values as

$$(u - M_u)^2 + (v - M_v)^2 + (w - M_w)^2 = E_s$$

The values of M_u, M_v, M_w which will confer on P_s its maximum value must thus satisfy the identities

$$\frac{\partial E_s}{\partial M_u} = \frac{\partial E_s}{\partial M_v} = \frac{\partial E_s}{\partial M_w} = 0$$

If all the observations refer to the same quantity, we may put $M = M_u = M_v = M_w$ and

$$\frac{\partial E_s}{\partial M} = 0$$

$$(2M - 2u) + (2M - 2v) + (2M - 2w) = 0$$

$$\therefore M = \frac{u + v + w}{3}$$

This result merely states that the mean is the *best* value of independent observations on the same quantity, if the method of least squares is the method which leads us to the best value. It throws no light on what we mean by *best* in this context.

THE METHOD OF LEAST SQUARES. That the mean is an *un-*

*biased estimator** of the true value when each observation is referable to one and the same physical dimension is deducible from elementary considerations without invoking the normal or any other distribution of errors. This we shall presently see; but some readers may first wish to familiarise themselves with the type of physical situation in which the physicist invokes the method of least squares itself.

The sort of situation which first commended the use of the method of least squares to the contemporaries and immediate successors of Gauss arises when we seek to combine information from observations referable to *two* different quantities. A simple illustration from elementary physics will suffice to indicate the problem of the combination of observations at this level. We shall suppose that we wish to determine the resistance (x) of a bridge wire, in which event our external circuit will make a fixed contribution (y) to the measured resistance (m). If we could determine the latter without error it would suffice to make two determinations, one (m_1) referable to a particular fraction (f_1) of the length of the bridge wire included in the circuit and a second (m_2) referable to a different fraction (f_2). We should then have

$$m_1 = f_1 x + y \; ; \; m_2 = f_2 x + y \; ; \; x = (m_1 - m_2) \div (f_1 - f_2)$$

In practice, the problem of combination arises because a third observation m_3 referable to f_3, if paired off with m_1 or m_2, will not yield exactly the same value of x. Accordingly, we regard any such measurement as subject to an *error*, which we denote as ϵ_j for the jth of a sequence of such measurements, so that

$$\epsilon_j = (f_j . x + y) - m_j \; or \; m_j = f_j . x + y - \epsilon_j \quad . \quad \text{(i)}$$

It is customary to speak of each such equation on the right as one of our *observational equations*. If we make n measurements we shall define the sum of the squares of the errors as

$$E = \sum_{j=1}^{j=n} \epsilon_j^2 \quad . \quad . \quad . \quad . \quad \text{(ii)}$$

---

* i.e. that the mean of a sufficiently large number of estimates based thereon is the true value we seek.

The method of least squares prescribes that we shall choose as our values of x and of y those which minimise E, i.e. those for which

$$\frac{\partial E}{\partial x} = 0 = \frac{\partial E}{\partial y} \qquad \cdots \qquad \text{(iii)}$$

If ϵ_j does *not** depend on the particular value of f_j, we may write:

$$\frac{\partial \epsilon_j^2}{\partial x} = 2f_j\,(f_j.x + y - m_j) \; ; \; \frac{\partial \epsilon_j^2}{\partial y} = 2\,(f_j.x + y - m_j)$$

Whence we obtain from (ii) and (iii)

$$\sum_1^n f_j\,(f_j.x + y - m_j) = 0 = \sum_1^n (f_j.x + y - m_j) \quad \text{(iv)}$$

We may write this result in the form

$$\sum_1^n f_j\,(f_j.x + y) = \sum_1^n f_j.m_j \qquad \cdots \qquad \text{(v)}$$

$$\sum_1^n (f_j.x + y) = \sum_1^n m_j \qquad \cdots \qquad \text{(vi)}$$

We have thus two equations involving observed values of m_j and the unknown values of x and y. The numerical example given below exhibits the most convenient computing scheme for the solution; but an alternative way of writing down the solution will prove instructive at a later stage. The formal relation between the statistical procedure known as *regression* and the theory of the combination of observations will then be apparent if we proceed as follows. For brevity, we may write the mean values of f_j and m_j as M_f and M_m; and

$$\Sigma f_j = nM_f \; ; \; \Sigma m_j = nM_m \; ; \; \Sigma f_j^2 = nQ_f \; ; \; \Sigma f_j.m_j = n.C_{fm}$$

Whence we derive:

$$\Sigma (f_j - M_f)^2 = nQ_f - nM_f^2;$$
$$\Sigma (f_j - M_f)\,(m_j - M_m) = nC_{fm} - nM_f.M_m$$

Our equations are then

$$(n.Q_f)x + (nM_f)y = nC_{fm} \; and \; (n.M_f)x + ny = nM_m$$

---

* This assumption is amenable to experimental verification in the domain of physical measurement, but it is gratuitous in the domain of natural variation.

The solution for x is therefore:

$$x = \frac{C_{fm} - M_m M_f}{Q_f - M_f^2} = \frac{\Sigma \, (f_j - M_f) \, (m_j - M_m)}{\Sigma \, (f_j - M_f)^2} \quad . \quad \text{(vii)}$$

More generally, for a series of measurements in linear relation to three unknown quantities, we may write our observation equations in the form:

$$m_j = a_j . x + b_j . y + c_j . z - \epsilon_j$$

The reader will easily derive the least squares solution as that of the three equations

$$\left. \begin{aligned} \Sigma \, a_j \, (a_j . x + b_j . y + c_j . z) &= \Sigma \, a_j . m_j \\ \Sigma \, b_j \, (a_j . x + b_j . y + c_j . z) &= \Sigma \, b_j . m_j \\ \Sigma \, c_j \, (a_j . x + b_j . y + c_j . z) &= \Sigma \, c_j . m_j \end{aligned} \right\} \quad . \quad \text{(viii)}$$

In this set-up, we need vary only the contributions of two unknown components by assigning different values to the corresponding constants (e.g. a_j and b_j) so that we can fix the third (e.g. $c_j = 1$). The method cannot yield more equations of the form shown in (viii) than the number of unknown quantities involved. Hence, it cannot lead to inconsistent estimates of the latter.

Numerical Example: If we here use data of a Wheatstone Bridge experiment of the type described above, as cited by Wald (*Theory of Errors and Least Squares*), to illustrate the computation in accordance with the pattern exhibited in (vi)–(viii), we should pause to ask ourselves whether we have not exceeded the terms of reference of the normal law of error. For we are now working with a null point instrument; and it is unlikely that repeated determinations of the total resistance of the circuit for the same fixed length of the bridge wire would transgress the boundaries of 5 scale divisions. The data of our experiment will be as follows for a bridge wire of 100 cm.

Length (l) of Bridge Wire included (cm.)	Total Resistance (ohms.)
10	0·116
30	0·295
50	0·503
80	0·760

Here our observations $(r_{0.1})$ refer to the total resistance $(r_{t.1})$ and we wish to estimate the resistance (u) of the bridge wire alone; but to do this we have to eliminate the resistance (v) of the external circuit. If l is the length of the bridge wire included in the circuit, the fraction of u which contributes to the total resistance is $0 \cdot 01 l = a_l$. Thus

$$r_{t.1} = a_1 . u + v$$

$$\epsilon_1 = a_1 . u + v - r_{0.1}$$

The so-called normal equations prescribed by (iv) in this case will be:

$$\sum a_1(a_1 . u + v - r_{0.1}) = 0 = \sum (a_1 . u + v - r_{0.1})$$

The computation is as follows:

$0 \cdot 01u + 0 \cdot 1v - 0 \cdot 0116 = 0$	$0 \cdot 1u + v - 0 \cdot 116 = 0$
$0 \cdot 09u + 0 \cdot 3v - 0 \cdot 0885 = 0$	$0 \cdot 3u + v - 0 \cdot 295 = 0$
$0 \cdot 25u + 0 \cdot 5v - 0 \cdot 2515 = 0$	$0 \cdot 5u + v - 0 \cdot 503 = 0$
$0 \cdot 64u + 0 \cdot 8v - 0 \cdot 6080 = 0$	$0 \cdot 8u + v - 0 \cdot 760 = 0$

Total $0 \cdot 99u + 1 \cdot 7v - 0 \cdot 9596 = 0 \qquad 1 \cdot 7u + 4v - 1 \cdot 674 = 0$

Thus our normal equations are:

$$0 \cdot 99u + 1 \cdot 7v - 0 \cdot 9596 = 0$$

$$1 \cdot 7u + 4v - 1 \cdot 674 = 0$$

The solution is

$$u = 0 \cdot 9277 \; ; \; v = 0 \cdot 0243$$

If we employ the method of least squares we thus take $0 \cdot 9277$ ohms as our estimate of the resistance of the bridge wire itself.

The Legendre–Laplace Axiom. We have now acquainted ourselves with one class of problems, the earliest, in which it is customary to invoke the Method of Least Squares. At least we can here say that the river of theory has not overflown its banks, i.e. our sole concern is with *error* in the Gaussian sense. We have, however, postponed the examination of the stochastic credentials of the criterion of preference (p. 188) which led the immediate predecessors of Gauss to endorse the method. We must now scrutinise it, because the Legendre–Laplace

Axiom, as we may call it, recurs in expositions of the method widely current throughout the nineteenth century; and it has emerged in a new guise during the past generation. First, it will be instructive to cite Merriman (*Introduction to Geodetic Surveying*, 1893):

The Method of Least Squares sets forth the processes by which the *most probable values of observed quantities* are derived from the observations. The foundation of the method is the following principle:

In observations of equal precision the most probable values of observed quantities are those that render the sum of the squares of the residual errors a minimum.

This principle was first enunciated by Legendre in 1805, and has since been universally accepted and used as the basis of the science of the adjustment of observations. The proof of the principle from the theory of mathematical probability requires more space than can be here given, and the plan will be adopted of taking it for granted. Indeed some writers have regarded the principle as axiomatic. (*Italics inserted.*)

This citation is of two-fold interest. First, it emphasises a minor postulate which is of major consequence if we transport the algebra of the theory of error into the domain of natural variation, where equal precision connotes the highly debatable assumption of equal dispersion of observed values about a suppositious norm. What is more relevant to our present purpose is that the obscurity of the idiom serves to conceal the irrelevance of anything in the classical theory to the postulate definitive of our best choice of a parameter value, viz. that (if true) it would assign maximum probability to the observed set of observations.

This irrelevance becomes apparent when we explore its implications in the set-up of a 2-stage classical model. We postulate five types of urns, A, B, C, D, E, the total number being N and the numbers of each type being N_a, N_b, etc., respectively. Thus we assign prior probabilities $P_a = N_a \div N, P_b = N_b \div N$, etc., to the initial act of choice. We shall refer to the number of red balls in a 4-fold replacement sample from one such urn as our observed quantity (*score*), and shall postulate $p_a = 0$, $p_b = \frac{1}{4} p_c = \frac{1}{2}, p_d = \frac{3}{4}, p_e = 1$ as the proportions of red balls in the several types of urn. Below we see the 4-fold sample distributions for each type of urn.

Score	0	1	2	3	4	Total
A	256	0	0	0	0	256
B	81	108	54	12	1	256
C	16	64	96	64	16	256
D	1	12	54	108	81	256
E	0	0	0	0	256	256
Total	354	184	204	184	354	1280

If we adopt the Legendre–Laplace axiom, the rule of conduct we shall consistently pursue is as follows:

If the score is 0, say that $p = 0$
,, ,, 1, ,, ,, $p = \frac{1}{4}$
,, ,, 2, ,, ,, $p = \frac{1}{2}$
,, ,, 3, ,, ,, $p = \frac{3}{4}$
,, ,, 4, ,, ,, $p = 1$

If we postulate that there are five urns in all, one of each type, so that the prior probabilities are equal, we may tabulate as follows the probability of correctly asserting that a given hypothesis is correct on the basis of the evidence supplied by the four-fold sample score in accordance with the prescribed rule.

Score	$p = 0$	$p = \frac{1}{4}$	$p = \frac{1}{2}$	$p = \frac{3}{4}$	$p = 1$
0	$\frac{256}{354}$	0	0	0	0
1	$\frac{81}{354}$	$\frac{108}{184}$	$\frac{54}{204}$	$\frac{12}{184}$	$\frac{1}{354}$
2	$\frac{16}{354}$	$\frac{64}{184}$	$\frac{96}{204}$	$\frac{64}{184}$	$\frac{16}{354}$
3	$\frac{1}{354}$	$\frac{12}{184}$	$\frac{54}{204}$	$\frac{108}{184}$	$\frac{81}{354}$
4	0	0	0	0	$\frac{256}{354}$

In this table the diagonal terms downwards from left to right assign the probability of correct identification for any given value of the score. In each column the highest term lies on this diagonal; but the highest term may be appreciably less than a half. In accordance with the viewpoint of Laplace, i.e. against the background of a Bayes model w.r.t. which the relevant prior probabilities are equal, the rule of procedure implicit in the axiom thus means: (a) the probability of choosing the correct hypothesis is greater than that of choosing any single alternative to it; (b) the probability of choosing the correct hypothesis is not necessarily greater than the probability of choosing a wrong one.

The second conclusion suffices to exclude the axiom from any formidable claim to consideration as a useful tool of inductive reasoning. The preceding one might have claims to consideration as a mere convention *en rapport* with the interpretation suggested at the end of this chapter (p. 206), if it were possible to justify it without invoking a factually irrelevant 2-stage model upholstered with an entirely arbitrary postulate inconsistent with the Forward Look. One example suffices to show that it has no general validity unless we do so. Without disclosing the trick to the player, we shall now add to our system another urn of type C ($p = \frac{1}{2}$), and we may set out the arithmetic of the sampling system in the following schema:

Score	0	1	2	3	4	Total
A	256	0	0	0	0	256
B	81	108	54	12	1	256
C	16	64	96	64	16	256
C	16	64	96	64	16	256
D	1	12	54	108	81	256
E	0	0	0	0	256	256
Total	370	248	300	248	370	1536

Only one column of this table need now concern us. When the 4-fold sample score is unity the probability that the sample will come from an urn of type B is $\frac{108}{248}$. That it will come from an urn of type C is $\frac{64+64}{248} = \frac{128}{248}$. Now the axiom prescribes that we shall say that the sample comes from an urn of type B whenever the score is unity; but classical theory prescribes that such 4-fold samples containing a single red ball will turn up more often from an urn of type C. Within the framework of a suppositious 2-stage model approach, the criterion of preference embodied in the Legendre–Laplace axiom thus entitles

196

us to frame a rule for the choice of a particular parameter with an uncertainty safeguard less than what we should properly assign to the operation of the rule for the identification of any single admissible alternative parameter value as the true one, if (and only if) we embrace the principle of insufficient reason as an act of faith.

Since we shall see that Gauss repudiated it, the fact that the Legendre–Laplace axiom is intelligible only if we invoke the notion of inverse probability current in the historic context of the two authors would be merely a matter of historic interest, were it also true that the method of least squares is the only accepted recipe for *point-estimation*, i.e. for specifying some unique value of a parameter as the best one on the basis of information supplied by a finite sample of observations. The method of least squares is not in fact a unique prescription for doing so. It is one of special applicability in the domain of *measurement* (representative scoring). An alternative procedure with more relevance to the domain of *enumeration* (taxonomic scoring) adopted in our last model is the *Method of Maximum Likelihood* which relies on the same postulate, as we shall now see. The formal statement of the *Method of Maximum Likelihood* in no way involves the assumption of a normal—or of any particular—distribution law, a circumstance which may account for its appeal to theoreticians, albeit this is equally true (*vide infra*) of the Method of Least Squares; but its author commits us to the same profession of faith as the Legendre–Laplace axiom. As Kendall (*Biometrika*, Vol. XXXVI, 1949) remarks:

it states that we are to proceed on the assumption that the most likely event has happened. Now, why?

Why, indeed, unless we invoke the doctrine of inverse probability?

THE METHOD OF MAXIMUM LIKELIHOOD. The simplest of all model situations will serve to illustrate the alternative method of point estimation referred to by Kendall in the passage cited. Our supposition is that we take at random one penny from a bag containing pennies all of which have not the same *bias*.*

* As defined by v. Mises, see however p. 460.

We toss it four times, and record the result. Our problem is to identify the penny taken as one of a particular class of pennies in the bag, specifiable as such by its *bias*.

If p is the probability that a penny turns up heads in a single trial the long run frequency (y) distribution for the number (x) of heads in a 4-fold trial is:

x	0	1	2	3	4
y	q^4	$4pq^3$	$6p^2q^2$	$4p^3q$	p^4

We may speak of b as the bias in favour of heads if we write $p = (\frac{1}{2} + b)$. The above then becomes

x	0	1	2
y	$\dfrac{(1 - 2b)^4}{2^4}$	$\dfrac{4\,(1 - 2b)^3\,(1 + 2b)}{2^4}$	$\dfrac{6\,(1 - 4b^2)^2}{2^4}$

x	3	4
y	$\dfrac{4\,(1 - 2b)\,(1 + 2b)^3}{2^4}$	$\dfrac{(1 + 2b)^4}{2^4}$

If therefore the observed score of a single 4-fold toss is 3, the unknown probability of the event is

$$p_{3.4} = \frac{(1 - 2b)\,(1 + 2b)^3}{4}$$

Evidently, $p_{3.4}$ will have two minima, viz. zero probability, when $b = +\frac{1}{2}$ or $-\frac{1}{2}$, i.e. when $p = 0$ or $p = 1$, to get three heads and one tail being impossible on either assumption, and by tabulating $p_{3.4} = 4p^3\,(1 - p)$ for different values of p and b as in the table on page 199, we see that it has a maximum value at or in the neighbourhood of $p = 0·75$, $b = 0·25$.

We can get the value of b corresponding to the *exact* maximum of $p_{3.4}$ in the usual way by equating the first derivative to zero, i.e.:

$$\frac{dp_{3.4}}{db} = \frac{6\,(1 + 2b)^2\,(1 - 2b) - 2\,(1 + 2b)^3}{4} = 0$$

$$\therefore\ 6\,(1 + 2b)^2\,(1 - 2b) = 2\,(1 + 2b)^3$$

$$\therefore\ b = 0·25\ \ and\ \ p = 0·75$$

On the basis of the evidence, viz. a score of three heads in a single 4-fold toss, we speak of the particular value $b = 0.25$ as the maximum likelihood point-estimate of the bias in favour of heads and of the particular value $p = 0.75$ as the maximum likelihood point estimate of the probability of the coin turning

p	b	$P_{3.4} = 4p^3(1-p)$
0	-0.5	0
0.05	-0.45	0.0005
0.10	-0.40	0.0036
0.15	-0.35	0.011
0.20	-0.30	0.026
0.25	-0.25	0.047
0.30	-0.2	0.076
0.35	-0.15	0.111
0.40	-0.10	0.154
0.45	-0.05	0.200
0.50	0	0.250
0.55	$+0.05$	0.299
0.60	$+0.10$	0.346
0.65	$+0.15$	0.384
0.70	$+0.20$	0.412
0.75	$+0.25$	0.422
0.80	$+0.30$	0.410
0.85	$+0.35$	0.368
0.90	$+0.40$	0.292
0.95	$+0.45$	0.171
1.00	$+0.50$	0

up heads in a single trial. We may generalise the foregoing procedure for situations in which the score is x in an r-fold trial so that

$$P_{x.r} = 2^{-r} . r_{(x)}(1 - 2b)^{r-x} (1 + 2b)^x$$

$$\frac{dp_{x.r}}{db} = 2^{-r} . r_{(x)} 2x (1 + 2b)^{x-1} (1 - 2b)^{r-x}$$
$$- 2^{-r} . r_{(x)} 2 (r - x)(1 - 2b)^{r-x-1} (1 + 2b)^x$$

On equating the last expression to zero, we get:

$$b = \frac{2x - r}{2r} \quad and \quad p = \frac{x}{r}$$

For 4-fold sample scores of 0, 1, 2, 3, 4 in the model situation invoked to illustrate the implications of the Legendre–Laplace axiom, the maximum likelihood estimates of p will therefore be as there cited: $p = 0$, $p = \frac{1}{4}$, $p = \frac{1}{2}$, $p = \frac{3}{4}$, $p = 1$. What we have already had occasion to infer thus applies with equal force to the method of maximum likelihood. The axiom cited by Kendall is a meaningful rule of conduct against the background of the doctrine of inverse probability; but if we relinquish the latter, it is devoid of any intelligible justification.

The Principle of Minimum Variance. If neither the method of least squares nor any other method of point estimation such as that of maximum likelihood can guarantee that the risk of accepting the value assigned by it to the unknown quantity is less than the risk of accepting any other *single* value, still less that the risk is necessarily small, we have to face the question: is there any special reason for adopting any such procedure? Accordingly, we have now to examine an alternative interpretation of the method of least squares, and one which does *not* invoke the Legendre–Laplace axiom. It is in fact that of Gauss with whose name later generations have come to associate the method of least squares, although current literature on the theory of errors still largely proceeds from assumptions which Gauss repudiated.

Misunderstanding concerning what Gauss proved is easy to understand. He wrote his *magnum opus* (1821) on the method in Latin, and in classical Latin at that. Bertrand's translation did not appear till many years after expositors of the principle had associated his name with the earlier views of Laplace; and it is still customary to give credit to Markhof (1912) for a theorem which Gauss proved three-quarters of a century before him.* As stated, this theorem does not invoke the Legendre–

---

* In an informative *Historical Note* on the Method, R. L. Plackett (*Biometrika*, 1949) states: "Gauss was the first who justified least squares as giving those *linear estimates which are unbiased of minimum variance* . . . (he) presented his justification in 1821. The paper is written in Latin, but a French translation was published by

Laplace axiom or any considerations which necessarily rely on the Bayes' scholium in the background. It does not indeed invoke a normal distribution of errors. It merely asserts that the method of least squares leads to an *unbiased estimate whose sampling variance is minimal.* The advantages of choosing an estimate with this end in view still raise controversial issues which Gauss could scarcely foresee; and we shall leave the discussion of them till a later stage. First, let us acquaint ourselves with what Gauss did indeed establish.

To justify the assertion that the method of least squares leads to an unbiased estimate of minimal variance when we use it to assign a value to component measurements of which we vary at least one as in the numerical illustration following (viii) above, it will suffice to disclose the pattern of the proof. Accordingly, we shall confine our attention to such a simple situation in which we wish to assign a value to a fixed component x, i.e. the resistance of the bridge wire on the basis of direct measurements m, depending on x and a second fixed component y. In the absence of any error, we postulate the theoretical relation

$$m_r = k_r x + y \quad . \quad . \quad . \quad . \quad \text{(ix)}$$

In this expression we are free to vary k_r on the assumption that any error involved in recording its value (the fraction of the length of the bridge wire) appears in our observation equations as a quantity independent of k_r. The observation equations then take the form

$$m_r = k_r x + y - \epsilon_r \quad . \quad . \quad . \quad \text{(x)}$$

Our observation equations will be consistent if we have only two values of m_r, and we need postulate only three values to exhibit the principle under discussion, i.e.

$$m_1 = k_1 x + y - \epsilon_1 \; ; \; m_2 = k_2 x + y - \epsilon_2 \; ;$$
$$m_3 = k_3 x + y - \epsilon_3 \quad \text{(xi)}$$

Our aim will first be to show how we can obtain an unbiased estimate (X) of x having minimal sampling variance by

Bertrand in 1855 and the fundamental theorem incorporated in Bertrand's own book (*Calcul des Probabilites*) of 1888 . . . Gauss's proof is valid for all values of n, entirely free from any assumption of normality."

suitably weighting our observations (m_1, etc.). Accordingly, we write*:

$$X = C_1m_1 + C_2m_2 + C_3m_3 \quad . \quad . \quad . \quad \text{(xii)}$$

If our estimate is to be unbiased $E(X) = x$, so that

$$E\,(C_1m_1 + C_2m_2 + C_3m_3) = x$$

$$\therefore \quad C_1.E\,(m_1) + C_2.E\,(m_2) + C_3.E\,(m_3) = x$$

We are assuming that the errors cancel out in the long run, i.e.:

$$E\,(m_r) = k_rx + y$$

$$\therefore \quad C_1\,(k_1x + y) + C_2\,(k_2x + y) + C_3\,(k_3x + y) = x$$

$$x = (C_1k_1 + C_2k_2 + C_3k_3)x + (C_1 + C_2 + C_3)y$$

To satisfy this relation and hence to ensure that X in (xii) is an unbiased estimate:

$$(C_1k_1 + C_2k_2 + C_3k_3) = 1 \; and \; (C_1 + C_2 + C_3) = 0 \quad \text{(xiii)}$$

From (xiii) we obtain:

$$C_3 = \frac{1 - C_1k_1 + C_1k_2}{k_3 - k_2} \; ; \; C_2 = \frac{1 - C_1k_1 + C_1k_3}{k_2 - k_3} \quad \text{(xiv)}$$

The last equation defines the condition that X is an unbiased estimate of x. To say that it has minimal variance is to say that $V_x = E\,(X - x)^2$ is as small as possible. Now the variance σ_r^2 of the distribution of m_r depends only on the error distribution assumed to be independent of the particular value of k_r, i.e.:

$$\sigma_1^2 = \sigma_2^2 = \sigma_3^2 = \sigma^2$$

If we adopt (xii) as our definition of X:

$$V_x = C_1^2\,\sigma_1^2 + C_2^2\,\sigma_2^2 + C_3^2\,\sigma_3^2 = (C_1^2 + C_2^2 + C_3^2)\,\sigma^2 \quad \text{(xv)}$$

* We here assume that the estimate X is to be a linear function of m_1, m_2, etc. This assumption calls for comment. One may argue as follows. Let $X = f$ $(m_1, m_2, \ldots)$, any continuous function of our observations, i.e. such that we can expand it as a power series, w.r.t. m_1, m_2, etc. By hypothesis the mean of first powers of the error terms will vanish, but the mean of even powers of the error terms will be positive. Hence X will be an unbiased estimate of x only if expressible in first powers of m_1, m_2, etc.

Having defined X in this way, we wish to specify C_1, C_3, etc., so that V_x is a minimum, i.e.

$$\frac{\partial V_x}{\partial C_1} = \frac{\partial V_x}{\partial C_2} = \frac{\partial V_x}{\partial C_3} = 0 \qquad \cdot \quad \cdot \quad \cdot \quad \text{(xvi)}$$

In this set of equations:

$$\frac{\partial V_x}{\partial C_1} = \left(\frac{\partial C_1^2}{\partial C_1} + \frac{\partial C_2^2}{\partial C_1} + \frac{\partial C_3^2}{\partial C_1} \right) \sigma^2$$

The condition of minimum variance for the choice of C_1 is therefore

$$\frac{\partial C_1^2}{\partial C_1} + \frac{\partial C_2^2}{\partial C_1} + \frac{\partial C_3^2}{\partial C_1} = 0 = 2C_1 + 2C_2 \frac{\partial C_2}{\partial C_1} + 2C_3 \frac{\partial C_3}{\partial C_1}$$

$$\therefore \quad C_1 + C_2 \frac{\partial C_2}{\partial C_1} + C_3 \frac{\partial C_3}{\partial C_1} = 0 \qquad \cdot \quad \cdot \quad \text{(xvii)}$$

To satisfy (xiv), we must put

$$C_2 \frac{\partial C_2}{\partial C_1} = \frac{(1 - C_1 k_1 + C_1 k_3)(k_3 - k_1)}{(k_2 - k_3)^2} \quad and$$

$$C_3 \frac{\partial C_3}{\partial C_1} = \frac{(1 - C_1 k_1 + C_1 k_2)(k_2 - k_1)}{(k_3 - k_2)^2}$$

Whence (xvii) becomes:

$$(k_2 - k_3)^2 C_1 + (k_3 - k_1)(1 - C_1 k_1 + C_1 k_3)$$
$$+ (k_2 - k_1)(1 - C_1 k_1 + C_1 k_2) = 0$$
$$\therefore \quad 2(k_1^2 + k_2^2 + k_3^2 - k_1 k_2 - k_1 k_3 - k_2 k_3)C_1 = 2k_1 - k_2 - k_3$$
$$\qquad \qquad \cdot \quad \cdot \quad \cdot \quad \cdot \quad \text{(xviii)}$$

We can simplify (xviii) by introducing M_k the mean value of k_r, i.e.:

$$3M_k = (k_1 + k_2 + k_3) \; so \; that \; 3(k_1 - M_k) = 2k_1 - k_2 - k_3$$
$$\qquad \qquad \cdot \quad \cdot \quad \cdot \quad \cdot \quad \text{(xix)}$$

$$9(k_1 - M_k)^2 = 4k_1^2 + k_2^2 + k_3^2 - 4k_1 k_2 - 4k_1 k_3 + 2k_2 k_3$$
$$9(k_2 - M_k)^2 = k_1^2 + 4k_2^2 + k_3^2 - 4k_1 k_2 + 2k_1 k_3 - 4k_2 k_3$$
$$9(k_3 - M_k)^2 = k_1^2 + k_2^2 + 4k_3^2 + 2k_1 k_2 - 4k_1 k_3 - 4k_2 k_3$$

$$\therefore \quad 3 \sum_{r=1}^{r=3} (k_r - M_k)^2 = 2(k_1^2 + k_2^2 + k_3^2 - k_1 k_2 - k_1 k_3 - k_2 k_3)$$
$$\qquad \qquad \qquad \qquad \qquad \text{(xx)}$$

By substitution from (xx) and (xix) in (xviii) we now obtain

$$C_1 = \frac{k_1 - M_k}{\sum\limits_{r=1}^{r=3} (k_r - M_k)^2} \quad \cdots \quad \text{(xxi)}$$

From the build-up of the equations, we can write down by inspection the corresponding identities which satisfy (xiii) and (xiv) as

$$C_2 = \frac{k_2 - M_k}{\sum\limits_{r=1}^{r=3} (k_r - M_k)^2} \quad and \quad C_3 = \frac{k_3 - M_k}{\sum\limits_{r=1}^{r=3} (k_r - M_k)^2} \quad \text{(xxii)}$$

By substitution of these weights in (xii) we thus obtain

$$X = \frac{\sum\limits_{r=1}^{r=3} m_r (k_r - M_k)}{\sum\limits_{r=1}^{r=3} (k_r - M_k)^2}$$

We may express this relation in another form. If M_m is the sample mean value of m_r:

$$3M_m = \sum\limits_{r=1}^{r=3} m_r \quad and$$

$$(m_r - M_m)(k_r - M_k) = m_r(k_r - M_k) - M_m k_r + M_m M_k$$

$$\therefore \sum\limits_{r=1}^{r=3} (m_r - M_m)(k_r - M_k)$$

$$= \sum\limits_{r=1}^{r=3} m_r (k_r - M_k) - M_m \sum\limits_{r=1}^{r=3} k_r + 3M_m M_k$$

$$\therefore \sum\limits_{r=1}^{r=3} (m_r - M_m)(k_r - M_k) = \sum\limits_{r=1}^{r=3} m_r (k_r - M_k) \quad \text{(xxiii)}$$

Whence we may write our unbiased estimate of minimal variance for n observational equations in the alternative form:

$$X = \frac{\sum\limits_{r=1}^{r=n} (m_r - M_m)(k_r - M_k)}{\sum\limits_{r=1}^{r=n} (k_r - M_k)^2} \quad \cdots \quad \text{(xxiv)}$$

*   *   *   *

The foregoing derivation sufficiently illustrates the Gaussian rationale of the Method of Least Squares for combinations of observations in geodesy, astronomy and many situations which arise in the physical laboratory. Of more relevance to its uses in later statistical theory is the situation which arises when we wish to determine one or more physical constants. This will be the topic of our next chapter. Here we may pause with profit to recall the peculiar circumstances which impelled Gauss to confer on the theory of error subsequently associated with his name the prestige of a mathematician of such outstanding originality and foresight.

There is a topical piquancy in the association of his name with that of Bradley (p. 161) in this setting. With Bradley's (1728) observations on γ *Draconis* and with his own interpretation we now associate the discovery of a phenomenon provoking a new synthesis of theoretical optics and Galilean mechanics. From this fusion we may trace the origin of the dilemma which Lorentz and Einstein have successfully resolved to the satisfaction of their own contemporaries; and we think of Gauss first and foremost in the context of the theory of relativity as a pioneer of Non-Euclidean geometry. Gauss himself did indeed entertain a hope that later research seems to have vindicated. He turned to Bradley's careful and extensive observations on the stars Altair and Procyon for evidence of the inadequacy of the relevant Euclidean postulate with full appreciation that a true discrepancy would not have hitherto defeated recognition, unless of an order commensurate with the error of observation. Since it was not his primary concern to disclose a universal pattern for the combination of observations, still less to enunciate the basic principles of a calculus of judgments, we shall not denigrate his genius if we now ask what indeed was the outcome of an undertaking with no reward for his own expectations in his own time.

Point Estimation as a Stochastic Procedure. In this chapter, we have explored two different ways in which we may seek justification for the combination of observations by the Method of Least Squares. One invokes an axiom. As such, it is not susceptible of proof and its implications disclose no intelligible merits of the Method at an operational level, if we reject the doctrine of inverse probability. We have also seen that the same axiom intrudes into the prescription of an alternative and lately more fashionable procedure for point estimation, i.e. for assigning a unique value of a metric or parameter* on the basis of a pool of data from which it is possible to extract different estimates thereof. So far we have not asked what advantages the alternative approach confers. Before doing so, it is pertinent to remark that point-estimates derived by the method of maximum likelihood satisfy the requirement of minimum variance, if they also satisfy Fisher's criterion of sufficiency (p. 446), i.e. if a sufficient statistic exists.

To get the operational content of the question last stated into focus, let us recall the historical situation in which the theory of error took shape. If our concern, like that of the astronomer or of the surveyor, is to make a map of the heavens for the navigator or a map of a territory for the railway engineer, we shall need to specify each of a set of points uniquely. Thus some standard convention which everyone observes is a social discipline essential to geodesic or to astronomical enquiry. If content to look at the procedure of point estimation unpretentiously as a social undertaking, we may therefore state our criterion of preference for a method of agreement so conceived in the following terms:

(i) different observers make at different times observations of one and the same thing by one and the same method;

(ii) individual sets of observations so conceived are independent samples of possible observations consistent with a framework of competence, and as such we may tentatively conceptualise the performance of successive sets as a stochastic process;

(iii) we shall then prefer any method of combining

---

* In geodesics we may illustrate the use of the Method to estimate by an indirect procedure which necessarily relies on more than one observation, an unknown distance, itself at least conceivably amenable to estimation by recourse to a single observation. In the next chapter our concern will be with the use of the Method to estimate the constant of a physical law deemed to be true on the basis of prior experience. By its definition, such a constant (here referred to as a *parameter*) is not amenable to direct observation.

constituents of observations, if it is such as to ensure a higher probability of agreement between successive sets, as the size of the sample enlarges in accordance with the assumption that we should thereby reach the true value of the unknown quantity in the limit;

(iv) for a given sample size, we shall also prefer a method of combination which guarantees minimum dispersion of values obtainable by different observers within the framework of (i) above.

In the long run, the convention last stated guarantees that there will be minimum disagreement between the observations of different observers, if they all pursue the same rule consistently. On the same understanding, the previous requirement specified by (iii) guarantees a procedure that will lead them to agree correctly, if they carry out a sufficiently large number of observations. In stating our programme of action in terms thus consistent with the Forward Look, we invoke no considerations of inverse probability; but we have brought into focus two issues which call for additional comment.

First, we have undertaken to operate within a fixed framework of repetition. This is an assumption which is intelligible in the domain of surveying, of astronomy or of experimental physics. How far it is meaningful in the domain of biology and whether it is ever meaningful in the domain of the social sciences are questions which we cannot lightly dismiss by the emotive appeal of the success or usefulness of statistical methods in the observatory, in the physical laboratory and in the cartographer's office. Aside from this, the foregoing considerations suggest a rationale of the Method of Least Squares *en rapport* with the Gaussian approach only if we identify minimum dispersion with minimum variance. Now variance is a unique measure of dispersion if we postulate a normal distribution of errors; but it is easy to construct distributions of which this statement is not true, and variance has then no special claims to commend it in preference to other measures of dispersion. Thus we have achieved little by renouncing the assumption (see footnote p. 200) that the Gaussian Law of Error is necessarily applicable to situations in which the preference for an unbiased estimate of minimal variance is interpretable as a useful social convention.

If we do invoke the normal curve as a plausible description of the distribution of repeated observations subject to accidental (p. 205) errors alone, we expose ourselves to a temptation to err from the straight and narrow path of the classical theory of risks at a different level. Can we assign an uncertainty safeguard to the statement that an estimate x_m of the true value x_t lies within an interval $x_t \pm c$? This is the form of a class of questions which are the theme of Chapter 18 on interval estimation. We shall there see reason to doubt that the specification of an unbiased point estimate of minimal sampling variance fulfils all the prescribed conditions; and if it does not, the disciplinary approach to point estimation is seemingly the only one consistent with the classical theory of risks.

If we adopt a consistently behaviourist approach, the terms of reference of a rationale of point estimation conceived simply in the foregoing terms as a social discipline essential to the art of map-making, celestial or terrestrial alike, encompass only the class of situations in which it is necessary to *locate putatively real points for further reference in a stable situation*. This is not the intention when we invoke the Method of Least Squares in anthropometric and social studies to prescribe fitting curves passing as nearly as may be through points referable to no assumed *true* values unless we identify the latter with some hypothetical non-existent norm. Our next task will therefore be to assess the relevance, if any, of the Gaussian theory of error to the current statistical procedure subsumed by the terms Regression, Multivariate Analysis and Analysis of Covariance.

The last remarks do not signify that point estimation is pointless in domains of enquiry other than astronomy, cartography and physics. In one branch of biological science its use is strictly on all fours with its use in surveying. No less than a map of Kentucky, a chromosome map of a species embodies information for future use in a definable framework of repetition; and the application of the Method of Maximum Likelihood by R. A. Fisher to the combination of observations which contribute to its construction accounts in no small measure for the disposition of biologists to condone its use in enquiries which endorse no intention of future application at the level of numerical tabulation and no opportunities for using such tabulated information in comparable situations.

The view here stated is somewhat less iconoclastic than that of so eminent a theoretical physicist as the late Norman Campbell (1928):

I reject, then, the Gaussian theory of error, without qualification and with the utmost possible emphasis; and with it go all theoretical grounds for adopting the rules that are based on it. But the rules themselves are not necessarily worthless; confidence in them may be restored if some less fragile support is found. (*Measurement and Calculation*, p. 162.)

CHAPTER NINE

ERROR, VARIATION AND NATURAL LAW

IN CHAPTER ONE we have deferred the obligation to define sharply the terms of reference of the type of statistical procedures there called the *Calculus of Exploration*. As now seen, it emerges in the same historic *milieu* as the Calculus of Errors; when new precision instruments were available for use in astronomy and geodesics; but the end in view was wholly different. Ostensibly it was to fashion a new instrument for the discovery of scientific laws pertaining to human society. Its parent was Quetelet, by training an astronomer and a student of geodesics. He it was who first drew attention to the similarity between: (*a*) certain empirical distributions of variation w.r.t. measurable characteristics of individual members of a population; (*b*) the Gaussian distribution of instrumental errors in an observatory. Quetelet himself did not invite the ridicule of Bertrand and of other contemporary mathematicians by exploiting the algebraic opportunities of a metaphor with so luxuriant a subsequent overgrowth of portentous symbolism. The adaptation of the formal theory of the combination of instrumental observations to the study of individual variation in nature and in society was the outcome of the partnership between his disciples Francis Galton and Karl Pearson.

By the Calculus of Exploration in our own setting I here refer to the types of statistical procedure respectively called *regression* or *multivariate analysis* on the one hand and *factor analysis* on the other. The statistical concept common to both is *covariance*, a name which describes the mean of the products of the deviations of paired measurements or numbers (e.g. load and stretch of spring) from a putative true mean or from a non-existent norm (e.g. that of birth weights of babies and duration of pregnancy). As such, the mean value of the numerator of (xxiv) in Chapter 8 or in (iii) below defines its sample value. In this chapter and in the next we shall deal with regression only. Its formal relation to the theory of error is more obvious than that of factor analysis; and it brings more readily into focus the additional assumptions we must invoke when we transgress from the proper domain of observational error into the uncharted terrain of natural variation.

We have now familiarised ourselves with the use of the method of least squares to determine the true value of a measurement in a situation comparable to those in which the problem of combining observations most commonly arises, i.e. in astronomy and in geodesics. Throughout the nineteenth century such was indeed the principal domain of its application. From a formal viewpoint, the procedure is precisely equivalent to a use of the method with supposedly far wider terms of reference, as when the end in view is to determine the slope constant of a simple linear physical law involving only two variable measurements. Hooke's law of the spring (*ut tensio sic vis*) will suffice to illustrate such a situation. That the law is linear does not restrict its interest unduly from the viewpoint of the laboratory worker, who commonly seeks a suitable formula by choosing a score transformation to give a good linear fit. Thus we can investigate Boyle's law ($pv = k$) relating the volume (v) to the pressure (p) of a gas at fixed temperature by plotting pressure against density (d) in accordance with the substitution $kv^{-1} = Kd$ so that $p = Kd$.

If x is the weight applied and y is the length of the spring the customary school textbook statement of the law of the spring for the range in which it holds good is:

$$y = k.x + C$$

More precisely, what we mean is that the result of a sufficiently large number of determinations of y for one and the same value of x will yield a mean ($M_{y.x}$) which satisfies the linear relation

$$M_{y.x} = k.x + C \quad . \quad . \quad . \quad . \quad \text{(i)}$$

That the value of the constant k depends on the dimensions and material of the spring we may make explicit by labelling it as k_s. When the end in view is to determine k_s for a particular spring, we may regard the weight (x) in the scale-pan as subject to no error of observation, if we make repetitive determinations of the length (y) referable to one and the same value of x. More fully then, our *observational* equation referable to the jth measurement of y for a fixed (ith) value of x is:

$$y_{ij.s} = k_s . x_{i.s} + C - \epsilon_{ij.s} \quad . \quad . \quad . \quad . \quad \text{(ii)}$$

In this expression we have merely interchanged our specification of k_s and x in (ix) of Chapter Seven as constants respectively referable to a particular experiment and to all experiments undertaken in situations to which the only sources of error are *accidental* in a sense to be defined more precisely at a later stage. In accordance with (xxiv) in Chapter Eight, the method of least squares prescribes as our estimate of k_s based on n paired values of x and y, each referable to a different value of x:

$$k_s = \frac{\sum_{i=1}^{i=n} (y_{i.s} - M_{y.s})(x_{i.s} - M_{x.s})}{\sum_{i=1}^{i=n} (x_{i.s} - M_{x.s})^2} \quad . \quad . \quad \text{(iii)}$$

As stated above, we speak of the *mean value* of the products in the numerator of (iii) as the covariance of x and y, written *Cov* (x, y). If m values of y are available for each of n values of x, so that the number of paired values is nm we must adjust (iii) accordingly, viz.:

$$k_s = \frac{\sum_{i=1}^{i=n} \sum_{j=1}^{j=m} (y_{ij.s} - M_{ij.s})(x_{i.s} - M_{x.s})}{m \sum_{i=1}^{i=n} (x_{i.s} - M_{x.s})^2} \quad . \quad . \quad \text{(iv)}$$

In current textbooks of statistics for research workers in biology or in the social sciences it is customary to write (iv) in the form:

$$k_{xy} = \frac{Cov\ (x,\ y)}{V_x}$$

Numerical Illustration. To keep a foothold on the solid earth of the Gaussian domain, we may use the numerical data of a high school class experiment on the determination of the elastic constant within the range of tension prescribed by Hooke's law to illustrate the foregoing use of the method of least squares:

Load (grams)	Mean stretch (mm.)
x_i	M_i
1	0·4
2	1·1
3	1·4
4	2·1

Any two of these pairs of values will suffice to yield an estimate of k, but we can derive six different estimates of k_{xy} by taking different pairs of paired values alone. To combine our observations with a view to choosing the unbiased estimate of minimal variance, we proceed as follows:

$$M_x = \tfrac{1}{4}(1 + 2 + 3 + 4) = 2\cdot5$$

$$M_y = \tfrac{1}{4}(0\cdot4 + 1\cdot1 + 1\cdot4 + 2\cdot1) = 1\cdot25$$

$$V_x = \tfrac{1}{4}(1 + 4 + 9 + 16) - (2\cdot5)^2 = 1\cdot25$$

$$Cov\ (x, y) = \frac{1(0\cdot4) + 2(1\cdot1) + 3(1\cdot4) + 4(2\cdot1)}{4}$$
$$- (1\cdot25)(2\cdot5) = 0\cdot675$$

$$k_{xy} = \frac{0\cdot675}{1\cdot25} = 0\cdot54$$

This illustration of the use of the method raises no new issues in the context of the Gaussian theory. What gives it special interest is that it emerges in the Galton–Pearson partnership in a factually new setting. The *elastic* coefficient of the foregoing example is now grandiloquently the *Coefficient of Regression* of y on x. As such, it is the keystone of the imposing edifice currently referred to as multivariate analysis. For this reason, a comprehensive examination of the credentials of the Calculus of Exploration would be incomplete without a preliminary re-examination of the factual assumptions which justify the use of the Method of Least Squares to estimate a linear constant in the domain of physical experiment. Such is the theme of what follows. In Chapter Ten, I shall discuss the meaning of regression from a more formal viewpoint with the help of relevant stochastic models.

If we are to do justice to our theme, three issues will invite clarification:

(i) what do we mean by *error* in this context;

(ii) what do we imply when we say that k_s is a constant *definitive of the law* as applied to a particular spring;

(iii) within what *framework of repetition* do we conceive a stochastic model to be relevant to our specification of k_s?

The Meaning of Error. I cannot convey to the reader a correct view of the use of the term *accidental* error in a preceding paragraph better than by quoting at length from a book in the hope that any reader with erroneous ideas about the proper terms of reference of the Gaussian Theory of Errors will read it. In his authoritative text on *The Combination of Observations*, Brunt (1917) defines two classes of errors of observation as follows:

As we shall frequently have to refer to constant and systematic errors in the sequel, it will be well to have a clear conception of the meaning of these terms. A *constant error* is one which has the same effect upon all the observations in a series. It has the same magnitude and sign in all observations. A *systematic error* is one whose sign and magnitude bear a fixed relation to one or more of the conditions of observation. It should be noted that neither of these types of error fulfils the laws of accidental errors given. . . .

Errors of the types here referred to are not therefore errors which fall within the province of the theory of combination of observations. We assume that the investigator knows his job sufficiently well to eliminate all known sources of constant or of systematic error so defined, in particular to control external conditions to the best of his ability, to exclude personal bias and to make the appropriate correction for instrumental defects. The classical theory of Error does not take over till the research worker has shouldered this responsibility. Brunt defines its proper domain as follows (*italics inserted*):

If a series of observations be made, and corrected in each case for the errors due to the three factors* considered above, it will in

---

* (Instrument, observer, external conditions.)

general be found that the corrected measurements differ among themselves. These individual differences are ascribed to a fourth class of error, known as the accidental error.

Accidental errors are due to no known cause of systematic or constant error. They are irregular, and more or less unavoidable. The term "accidental" is not used here in its ordinary significance of "chance." Strictly speaking, an observation of any kind is affected by the state of the whole universe at the time of observation. But as an observer cannot take account of the whole universe and its changes of condition during the time occupied by his observations, he has to limit his attention to those operative causes which he regards as affecting his observations in a measureable degree; i.e. he limits his attention to the "essential conditions." If an observation could be repeated a number of times, and corrected in each case for changes in the essential conditions, the results of all the observations should be identical. But in practice it is found that the individual observations in a series differ among themselves. These differences may be ascribed to the fact that the so-called "essential conditions" do not include all the effective operative causes. There will be other operative causes of error, whose laws of action are unknown, or too complex to be investigated. These causes will introduce errors which will appear to the observer to be accidental.

. . . when all the systematic errors traceable to the instrument, the external conditions, or the observer, have been corrected, no observation can be regarded as perfect. It will *miss perfection on account of the presence of accidental errors.* The effect of the accidental errors will differ for different observations in the same series. It is thus impossible to attain certainty in the result of an observation. In practice a series of observations is made in the hope that the discussion of the series will eliminate the effect of the accidental errors. The problem which we have to solve is that of deciding the best method of conducting this discussion. . . . In what follows, accidental errors will be regarded as obeying the following laws:

(i) A large number of very small accidental errors are present in any observation.

(ii) A positive error and an equal negative error are equally frequent.

(iii) The total error cannot exceed a certain reasonably small amount.

(iv) The probability of a small error is greater than the probability of a large error.

On a minor issue, I think that the last remarks are incomplete. In so far as any manageable theory of error invokes stochastic considerations, it implies a fifth postulate, i.e. that the errors are independent of one another and of the true value of the relevant metric. However, that is immaterial in this context. I have italicised one remark in the foregoing, because it has a special bearing on (iii) in the preceding statement of the postulated laws of accidental errors. Brunt's wholesome use of the term perfection confers no licence for the recurrently stated contemporary *credo* that statistics have freed science from the tyrannical chimera of absolute truth as the goal of enquiry. On the contrary, we rely on such a concept as the only tangible basis for a definition of what is erroneous, and the postulate mentioned makes this explicit. Why must we assign equal probability to negative and to positive errors? The answer is that the long-run mean error must be zero, if we are to endorse the possibility of approaching the true value as our accepted goal more closely as we enlarge the content of our experience.

Within the framework of the assumption that there is a true law, and that this true law would be specifiable in all relevant numerical particulars if our fallible methods of observation did not handicap our efforts, the concept of the mean is therefore something more than a convenient parameter of a stochastic distribution. *The mean of a sufficiently large number of observations on one and the same metric is the unique observation we are seeking imperfectly to record.* If this savours of metaphysics to the evangelists of the new doctrine of free stochastic grace, I am content to remark that they cannot have it both ways. If they appeal to the dominant role of statistical theory in contemporary science, they rest their case in no small measure on the reliance of the laboratory worker on statistical models in situations which can endorse a stochastic model with intelligible relevance if, and only if, we take truth seriously in the manner of our forefathers.

The definitive parameter. Let us now seek an answer to our second query: in what sense is k_s a constant definitive of the law of a spring of specified materials and dimensions? In the practice of the laboratory, we assuredly presuppose what our examination of the foregoing question has brought into focus.

We do not invoke the Method of Least Squares, to establish the law. It comes into the picture *when we have already satisfied ourselves that the law is sound*. We start by comparing the outcome of repeated experiments which we perform with every possible precaution to eliminate (or correct for) personal, instrumental or environmental errors of the sort Brunt refers to as *constant* or *systematic*. We observe that each such experiment referable to the same range of x values yields a scatter of corresponding y co-ordinates on either side of a straight line. We likewise observe that the points on our scatter diagram do indeed cluster as closely round a straight line as our *prior knowledge* of the range of uncontrollable (*accidental*) error would entitle us to expect, if a straight line does indeed pass through the assumed *true values* of the relevant points whose co-ordinates (x_i, y_{ij}) are definitive of a particular (ith) value of x and the corresponding j values of y referable thereto.

Having decided that a straight line is in this sense a satisfactory descriptive device for prescribing the result of stretching a spring in an assigned range of x values under carefully controlled conditions, we may then usefully incorporate our conviction in the corpus of scientific knowledge by tabulating for future use in appropriately defined situations the definitive parameter k_s for springs of specified materials and dimensions, and thereby forestall unnecessary effort, e.g. when our aim is to prescribe the design of a spring balance. Only when we undertake this task of tabulation do we call on the Method of Least Squares, i.e. we do so to endorse what particular numerical values of k_s appear *in our tables of physical constants*.

Whatever justification, if any, there may be for the Pearsonian reliance on the Method of Least Squares to define the straight line of best fit for the so-called linear regression of heights of brothers on heights of sisters, bodyweight of sons on bodyweight of mother or of family income on tuberculosis rates, it assuredly signalises an innovation on which the Gaussian theory of error confers no licence; and the more so if we invoke significance tests to justify our preference for a straight line rather than for one of an infinitude of other descriptive curves. If we then designate a *deviation* as the displacement of a point about some straight line around which our plotted points appear to cluster, we most certainly repudiate the hope that any such line would go through every point if faultlessly determined. Faultless determination is indeed practicable in small scale undertakings involving enumerative data in both dimensions. In that event our deviations will certainly not be errors in the Gaussian sense of the term.

What then are such deviations which we find on our hands when we have indeed eliminated all error of observation? The answer is as inescapable as it is also simple. They record the failure of a straight line or some other descriptive fitting curve to tell us where a uniquely true value of y corresponding to a particular value of x lies, or vice versa. Their existence thus signalises the certainty that the selected descriptive curve is not a true law of nature as the astronomer or the experimental physicist interprets the term *law* in situations which provoke him to make use of the Method of Least Squares as a method of combining observations. The deviations we are discussing are not the outcome of human frailty. The points about which we are talking are not unique natural events that we are seeking to locate in our frail human way. The deviations are nature's errors, the failure of nature to get to the point. The point itself is a *norm* imposed on nature by the edict of a realm which is supernatural in any intelligible sense of the term.

In the grand manner of Bertrand (p. 172) we may answer the question proposed at the beginning of the last paragraph more picturesquely as follows. If we plot the tuberculosis rate against preassigned values of family income, each point the line goes through specifies a *normal* tuberculosis rate, not too tragic nor too encouraging to complacency. If we plot the heights of sisters against a fixed median height interval of the brothers, the point our line goes through specifies the height of the *normal* sister not too tall nor too short, not too domineering nor too clinging, not too glamorous nor too homely. If we plot the body weight of mothers against that of sons, the line goes through the body weight of the *normal* mother, neither too stout nor too skinny, neither too strict nor too indulgent, neither too flighty nor too immersed in domestic routine, not too dowdy nor too chic, neither passionate nor frigid. So we might continue with our catalogue of laws laid up in the

218

felicitous heaven of Plato's universals but devoid of conceivable content in the dismal terrain of the efforts of living men to come to grips with inexorable nature.

Whereas the practice of the ordnance survey, the observatory or the physical laboratory, relies on the Method to tabulate for *future use* without recourse to direct observation a parameter definitive of a law deemed to be the true one for reasons which have nothing to do with the method, too many who invoke it in the domain of anthropometry and social studies do so indeed to confer the status of law on a generalisation which is not a law of nature as laboratory workers speak of one. They do so, as we shall now see, in circumstances which preclude the possibility of ever making any practical use of the estimated parameter k prescribed within a definable framework of repetition. That such is at least a novel use of the Gaussian Theory of Error has not escaped the attention of writers on the uses of the theory within the framework of its original terms of reference. Thus Brunt remarks apropos its alleged utility in connexion with biological enquiry: "it is thus in no way justifiable to regard Least Squares as a magical instrument applicable to all problems."

The Framework of Repetition. We have seen how and why the laboratory worker, the astronomer or the surveyor may wish to determine a physical constant formally equivalent to what is in its latest reincarnation the *regression* coefficient, a neologism concocted to communicate Galton's erroneous beliefs about inheritance. The assumption is that we can define the circumstances in which an experiment or set of observations is *repeatable*. Otherwise the tabulation of values appropriate to particular statistics (e.g. elastic coefficients for springs of standard dimensions but different metals) would be valueless. All this presupposes that we can control the situation. It is implicit in what we here mean by saying that a law of experimental physics presumes a causal or, if we are too fastidious to use a word so *démodé*, a *consequential* relationship.

When we apply the Gaussian method of line fitting to measurements referable to concomitant variation of collateral relatives (e.g. heights of first cousins), it is obvious that no consequential relationship is conceivable. More generally in sociology, we may hope or suspect that our data disclose a consequential relationship; but only controlled experiment in the most literal sense of both terms can disclose whether this is so or whether the relationship involved is *concurrent*, i.e. referable to a common antecedent. Perhaps Karl Pearson appreciated this uncertainty when he borrowed from Edgworth (p. 178) a mathematical device which is meaningless in the setting of Gauss and has no bearing on the dilemma of geodesics. Partly because it is indeed so irrelevant to the combination of physical observations and partly because change of name by deed poll through publication of the main thesis in Series B of the *Transctions of the Royal Society* as a new rationale of Darwin's doctrine, the concept of Regression evaded the searchlight of Bertrand's critique. If sceptical about its practical value which they could assess, biologists were willing to concede its mathematical respectability on which they could not pass judgment with equally good grace. In such a setting, a new tribal ritual which derives no sanction from the admissible claims of point estimation in the world of affairs became fashionable by default.

The device we here recall is the *bivariate normal* universe. In a situation such as Hooke's law of the spring serves to illustrate, the investigator commonly records equal numbers (j) of observations y_{ij} referable to each fixed value (x_i) of the controlled variable, which does indeed then enjoy a special factual status in the formal statement of the law as the independent variable of the definitive equation. If we then postulate the normal law of accidental error, the universe of our sampling system conceived in stochastic terms against the background of a unique historical framework of repetition is a *normal-rectangular* universe. This convention is not inexorable; but in no thinkable circumstances consistent with the design of a physical experiment is it possible to conceive the chosen values of the fixed x-set as a sample taken randomwise from a normal universe of x-scores. To assert the contrary is indeed inconsistent with the identification of the independent variable with the variable subject to the control of the investigator.

Needless to say, brother's height has no priority w.r.t. sister's height or vice versa as the independent, i.e. controlled variable of our scatter diagrams for regression of one on the other. To give verisimilitude to a framework of repetition prerequisite to a stochastic theory of sampling, and to accommodate the convenient fiction that height conforms to the normal law, we have thus to postulate a universe which is normal in two dimensions. The formal dilemma which arises out of this ambiguity of interpretation has recently prompted a statistician to propound the question: *are there two regressions?** It emerges because: (*a*) the choice of the so-called independent variable involves no *prima facie* priority when we plot two such variates as heights of brothers and sisters; (*b*) the same method leads to different values of the so-called regression coefficient if we substitute one for the other as the variable deemed to be independent.

The same dilemma does not arise in a controlled laboratory experiment. In plotting the results of such experiments we may distinguish between two procedures: (*a*) each value of the so-called *dependent* variate, e.g. the *stretch* of a spring, plotted against a particular value of the other (e.g. *tension* applied), may truly correspond to one value of the latter, as when we successively measure the stretch (y_{ij}) produced by adding one and the same load (x_i) to the scale-pan in a consistent environment; (*b*) each value of the dependent variate (e.g. *blood sugar*) plotted against one and the same value of the other variate (e.g. *insulin dosage*) involves an *unacknowledged* error of observation in the measurement of the latter. Either way, the customary procedure in the conduct of an experiment entails what we tacitly assume, as then formally admissible, when fitting a line to our observations by the method of least squares, viz. that all the errors of observation arise in assigning a value to the so-called dependent variate.

In the laboratory there is also commonly a clear-cut operational distinction between the variate we choose to designate as the dependent (e.g. *volume*) and the alternative one, i.e. the one which is more amenable to direct control (e.g. *pressure*). In applying the Gaussian method to laboratory data we may not indeed be free to make a choice between the two ways of fitting a line, though this is not always so. It may be possible

* J. Berkson (1950). *Journ. Amer. Stat. Ass.*, 45, 164.

to adopt either of two procedures: (*a*) to measure the stimulus requisite to produce a fixed response; (*b*) to measure the response evoked by a fixed stimulus. In whichever way we do proceed, the value of the so-called independent variable may in fact be subject to experimental error, neglected as such by the way in which we plot our data. Customarily, the physicist allocates all sources of error to the side of the balance sheet identified with what he elects to call the dependent variate.

In laboratory enquiry, the mere fact that one variable is under the control of the investigator signifies that the relation sought is consequential; and the legitimate implications of the use of curve-fitting by least squares do not admit of any formidable dangers if we approach our task as an obligation to agree upon a social convention for reasons stated at the conclusion of Chapter Eight. That the method of least squares transplanted into the field of biology and sociology by Karl Pearson was indeed originally a device for use in the domain of a *theory of error*, thus imposes upon us the duty to scrutinise two basic assumptions we take for granted legitimately in laboratory practice: (*a*) the physicist can *control* every relevant variable in an experimental set-up other than variability of the type specified on p. 215 above; (*b*) all such deviations occur *random-wise* in repeated determinations.

In experimental biology, one must always and at all times also take stock of individual variation attributable to nature and to nurture; but the biologist with justifiable intention of propounding a law, as physicists use the term, e.g. the linear alignment of the genes, implicitly assumes the possibility of repeating observations based on different individuals without introducing a systematic source of variability referable to either. If he can specify the extent to which he has standardised the genetic make-up and culture of his stocks, there is then an intelligible framework of repetition within which the law is valid. It is scarcely in doubt that admissible postulates of physical experimentation and those the biologist may adopt with justifiable confidence on the understanding last stated are gratuitous in many situations which prompt sociologists and psychologists to employ regression equations.

In such enquiries, what is usually a more important source

of variation is a complex of external agencies we have no power to control. Were it otherwise, our residual variance, i.e. deviations from what our selected so-called law prescribes, would be simply a measure of the failure of our powers of observation to detect an explicitly definable and inflexible regularity of nature. As it is, our residual variance is, and to no small extent, a record both of the inadequacy of any simple law as a description of our observations purged of all error in the Gaussian sense and of our powerlessness to recreate a *unique historic event*. Thus the mortality experience of the Borough of Tottenham (Middlesex) 1952, summarised (inadequately) as a frequency distribution by age and income, defines a 3-dimensional unit sample distribution which has almost certainly never existed as a specification of the mortality experience of any pre-existing community and almost certainly can specify that of no community in the future. If we seek to formulate a rule of procedure in accord with the forward look, we have therefore no realisable prospect of opportunities for making any statements to which we can assign an upper limit of uncertainty consistent with the classical theory of risks.

Needless to say, this dilemma will not inhibit our industrious computations, if we have taken the decisive backward step which was the theme of Chapter Four, i.e. the identification of an ever-changing population of living creatures with a universe which remains constant within the indefinitely protracted framework of repetition prescribed by the classical theory. We can then locate in the Pearsonian manner, and in the Platonic heaven of universals, the 3-dimensional distribution of Tottenham mortality in the year 1952 as a sample of an infinite hypothetical trivariate normal universe from which (alas) only the hypothetical normal man with hypothetically normal opportunities presumptively enjoys the right to extract more than one sample.

To make the foregoing criterion more tangible, let us recall the law of the stretched spring. When we give assent to such a law, our presumptive aim is to state in advance how much we can extend a spring under specified loads, if we measure the extension with sufficient accuracy under specified conditions. A latent postulate is therefore that our laboratory is static, since the results would be quite different in virtue of variations w.r.t. the gravitational constant *g*, if we made our observations in an aeroplane at different (and unknown) heights above sea-level. The best we could then hope for is that we could distribute our observations on the stretch with respect to a specified tension so that differences with respect to elevation would be uniformly distributed. Even in the absence of error inherent in the technique of observation as such, our line of best fit could then tally with the one definitive of the physical law of the static laboratory only in so far as it describes the trend of averages which have no definable bearing on future experience.

This parable gives us a new slant on the line which goes through the normal, as opposed to an *actual*, point of the Pearsonian regression graph. Figuratively speaking, the laboratory of the social scientist and of the vital statistician is most often an aeroplane at unknown and changing height above sea-level; and it is possible to formulate the implications of the foregoing remarks with reference to the assumed framework of repetition in which we conceptualise the sampling process at a more elementary level of discourse, if we recall a commonplace universally admitted as a canon of scientific method, viz. any statement of a scientific law is complete only in so far as it incorporates the recognition of its own limitations. To be sure, the laboratory worker familiar with such limitations may, and customarily does, forget to make them explicit; but he can commonly do so without compromising the usefulness of conclusions drawn from the law itself. For example, any bright boy who has passed through a high school course of physics can safely use an equation prescribing how the density of water varies in relation to temperature at sea-level pressure without succumbing to the temptation to invoke its aid to prescribe the density of steam at 120° C. and 730 mm. atmospheric pressure. Again, we all learn at school that Hooke's law breaks down, if the extension approaches breaking-point; and that van de Waals' equation must replace Boyle's simpler, and for many purposes good enough, rule in the neighbourhood of absolute zero or of the critical pressure.

That the *explicit* algebraic formulation of a physical law is always incomplete from this viewpoint is innocuous, because the experimentalist translates it in the domain of action with the reservation that the correct interpretation carries with it a supplementary specification of the *boundary conditions* of its validity. To say this, is to say that the legitimate use of an equation definitive of a structural law in physics lies within the domain of *interpolation*, i.e. within the domain of a clearly conceived historic framework of repetition; and the teaching of elementary physics familiarises us with the absurdities which arise when we use such a law for *extrapolation* beyond the boundaries of its applicability. The teaching of sociology impresses the same lesson less firmly on the beginner. Extrapolation beyond its legitimate terms of reference is indeed precisely comparable to what we do, if we succumb to the temptation of using a regression equation as a basis for predicting how a wage increase will affect fertility or infantile mortality.

What is a sufficiently well-recognised truism in experimental science is a *caveat* we too easily ignore in sociology and vital statistics. We cannot legitimately infer from the regression of completed family size on family income what the completed family size would be, if we stabilised all incomes at a fixed level, thereby changing the framework of conditions in which the regression relation is valid. Statistical literature of the last fifty years abounds with generalisations of this sort; but it is not difficult to detect the fallacy in such reasoning, if we recall a fundamental difference between experimental investigation and statistical description, as already mentioned. We have previously had occasion to recognise that there is a clear-cut distinction in experimental science between what we commonly call the dependent and the independent, or as we might more informatively say, *consequent* and *antecedent*, variates. The antecedent (so-called independent) is the one which the investigator has under his direct and deliberate control; and commonly, though not always, it is the only one within his power to control. Thus one cannot fill an injection syringe with adrenaline solution by raising the blood pressure of the patient; but one can raise the blood pressure of the patient by injection of the contents of a syringe containing adrenaline in solution.

H
225

We recognise such a relationship as consequential because, and only because, we are able to interfere actively with the course of events; but we are not recording the result of any such active interference when we plot a regression graph of maternal morbidity on completed family size at a particular time in a particular place or of heights of first cousins referable to a particular and historically unique human population. At least as likely as not, the relationship involved is concurrent, and necessarily so w.r.t. the second example last mentioned. In any event, our plotted data can give us no assurance to the contrary. A little reflection on a simple suppositious situation will serve to clarify one set of limitations imposed on the use of statistical methods in sociological enquiry when we do indeed take the trouble to clarify the historical framework in which the enquiry itself proceeds.

We may imagine a set-up not uncommon in Asia or in Africa. A population subject to malaria lies spread over a dry hillside and over the swampy lowlands around it, the more prosperous house-holders having settled on the heights. In the nature of the case, we should then expect to find a correlation between mean income and malaria incidence in the various precincts. It would not then be surprising if we found that we could plot our statistics plausibly as a linear regression graph. In this situation, raising the income of the less prosperous sections of the community might admittedly permit more migration from the swampy lowlands and hence less risk of malaria; but only if there were still land available for building on the uplands and only if there were no commensurate increase in the value of house property. In the absence of any information about the availability of alternative accommodation and about the prospects of the building market, we therefore lack sufficient reason for inferring what effect an all-round increase of income would have. A vigorous planning policy to make available inadequately utilised housing accommodation might well produce beneficial results; but our regression equation contains no precise information relevant to this possibility. In any case, it cannot legitimately lead us to forecast the effects of a change defined uniquely in terms of the only relevant variable, i.e. income as such.

THE TYRANNY OF AVERAGES. The technique of simple regression suffices to illustrate all the essential features of multivariate analysis. In common with factor analysis, its initial programme is the description of populations of organisms in terms which exclude a prescription for the *control* of individual behaviour. Figuratively speaking, we might say much the same about the kinetic theory of gases; but the comparison would be superficial. At an operational level, the individual molecule, atom, electron and the like is merely a convenience for interpreting the behaviour of matter in bulk. In so far as we may speak of a gas as a population of molecules, it is the special task of the experimental physicist to teach us how to handle such populations with the assurance that we can define conditions relevant to the identification of other such populations alike in all relevant particulars. In large measure, the problems of greatest practical interest to the biologist and to the psychologist are problems of individual behaviour, and the end in view is to define conditions relevant to the identification of circumstances in which different individuals behave. The only proven method of achieving this is the Baconian recipe, i.e. successive elimination of relevant variables by punctilious regard for the canons of controlled experimentation.

Such is the issue which the great physiologist Claude Bernard, provoked by the influence of Gavarret (p. 97) and other of Quetelet's disciples inspired with the new evangel of averages, raises in one of his lectures posthumously published as *Introduction to the Study of Experimental Medicine*. I quote him at length, because the experimentalist is at least entitled to the last word on what class of problems he prefers to investigate:

By destroying the biological character of phenomena, the use of *averages* in physiology and medicine usually gives only apparent accuracy to the results. From our point of view, we may distinguish between several kinds of averages: physical averages, chemical averages and physiological and pathological averages. If, for instance, we observe the number of pulsations and the degree of blood pressure by means of the oscillations of a manometer throughout one day, and if we take the average of all our figures to get the true or average blood pressure and to learn the true or average number of pulsations, we shall simply have wrong numbers. In fact, the pulse decreases in number and intensity when we are fasting and increases during digestion or under different influences of movement and rest; all the biological characteristics of the phenomena disappear in the average. Chemical averages are also often used. If we collect a man's urine to analyse the average, we get an analysis of a urine which simply does not exist; for urine, when fasting, is different from urine during digestion. A startling instance of this kind was invented by a physiologist who took urine from a railroad station urinal where people of all nations passed, and who believed he could thus present an analysis of *average* European urine! Aside from physical and chemical, there are physiological averages, or what we might call average descriptions of phenomena, which are even more false. Let me assume that a physician collects a great many individual observations of a disease and that he makes an average description of symptoms observed in the individual cases; he will thus have a description that will never be matched in nature. So in physiology, we must never make average descriptions of experiments, because the true relations of phenomena disappear in the average; when dealing with complex and variable experiments, we must study their various circumstances, and then present our most perfect experiment as a type, which, however, still stands for true facts. In the cases just considered, averages must therefore be rejected, because they confuse, while aiming to unify, and distort while aiming to simplify. Averages are applicable only to reducing very slightly varying numerical data about clearly defined and *absolutely simple cases*. . . . I acknowledge my inability to understand why results taken from statistics are called *laws*: for in my opinion scientific law can be based only on certainty, on absolute determinism, not on probability. . . . In every science, we must recognise two classes of phenomena, first, those whose cause is already defined; next, those whose cause is still undefined. With phenomena whose cause is defined, statistics have nothing to do; they would even be absurd. As soon as the circumstances of an experiment are well known, we stop gathering statistics: we should not gather cases to learn how often water is made of oxygen and hydrogen; or when cutting the sciatic nerve, to learn how often the muscles to which it leads will be paralysed. The effect will occur always without exception, because the cause of the phenomena is accurately defined. . . . Certain experimenters, as we shall later see, have published experiments by which they found that the anterior spinal roots are insensitive; other experimenters have published experiments by which they found that the same roots were sensitive. These cases seemed as comparable as possible; here was the same operation done by the same method on the same spinal roots. Should we therefore have counted the positive and negative cases and said: the law is that anterior roots are sensitive, for instance, 25 times out of a 100? Or should we have admitted, according to the theory called the law of large numbers, that in an immense number of experiments we should find the roots equally often sensitive and insensitive? Such statistics would be ridiculous, for there is a reason for the roots being insensitive and another reason for their being sensitive; this reason had to be defined; I looked for it, and I found it; so that we can now say: the spinal roots are always sensitive in given conditions, and always insensitive in other equally definite conditions.

How far statistical methods can indeed contribute to the initial stage of an investigation by screening likely clues is not the issue which Claude Bernard raises in this context. In contemporary terms, what he rightly rejects is the now widely current practice of publishing as a discovery what is at best an encouragement to further examination. If his comments on the use of averages were salutary in his own time, they are still more so in ours. In his day, the statistician was content to assert a modest claim to the supervision of interpretation. In ours, he claims the prerogative of prescribing the *Design of Experiments*, i.e. the conduct of experiments to supply figures which certain test and estimation procedures can, or purport to be able to, accommodate. Indeed one contemporary publication,* referring to the use of factor analysis in physiological enquiry, goes so far as to say:

Although it is true that any experimental statistical design permits one to look for a law in the relation between certain variables, without entering the experiment with too definite a hypothesis as to what form the law must take, *factor analysis is unique in demanding no prior hypothesis and in being automatically productive of a hypothesis. (Italics inserted.)*

Though the acceptance of such claims is the repudiation of the methods by which the experimental sciences have attained their present status, no experimental scientist of Bernard's standing has hitherto accepted the challenge publicly. It is

*Cattell, R. B., and Williams, N. F. V. M. (1953). *Brit. Journ. Prev. Soc. Med.*, Vol. VII.

therefore pertinent to state that the issue is essentially a matter of scientific method on which mathematicians as such have no prior claim to arbitrate. If statistics is indeed the science of averages, the statistician has a special claim to our attention when the end in view is to record averages, as is true of demographic studies and administrative enquiries which do not concern themselves with individuals as such; but it is for the biologist, for the psychologist and for the clinician themselves to decide whether an average can be a satisfactory answer to questions they ask about the individual organism. The statement that a solution of iodine in KI makes starch paste blue in $75 \pm 1 \cdot 5$ per cent of samples examined will not commend itself to a chemist. He will wish to know what impurities or what range of pH values, etc., determine when the reaction does or does not occur. Such has been the attitude in which physiologists have hitherto undertaken the investigation of animal behaviour. If we abandon it, we are lowering our standards. We are concealing our retreat from a position of hard-won advantage behind an impressive smoke screen of irrelevant algebra.

What commonly evades recognition when the statistician advances such claims is that terms such as *law* and *hypothesis* have a totally different connotation in the operational domain of experimental enquiry and in the descriptive domain of computing indices referable to natural populations or to the variable states of single individuals. This will become more apparent in the next two chapters when we have examined both the origin of the term regression against the background of Galton's attempt to create a science of genetics without recourse to the safeguards of controlled experimentation and the subsequent contribution of factor analysis to our present knowledge of human behaviour. Meanwhile, the reader needs no intimate knowledge of the theoretical basis of the P-technique to appreciate what the writers last cited do in fact mean by a *hypothesis*. In the summary of Cattell and Williams we find that:

The correlation of 36 physiological variables and nineteen psychological variables measured on a normal 23-year-old male for 110 successive days has yielded clusters of significant correlation coefficients which indicate that a considerable fraction of the day-to-day variation of measurement is due to fluctuation of unitary underlying functions rather than experimental error of measurement. . . .

In general, these results show that factor analysis is capable of structuring a wide array of physiological manifestations in a way not possible by any other method. *Controlled experiments, however, are desirable, if these findings by the exploratory, factor-analytic method are to be followed up to give causal explanation of the associations.* They also show substantial relations between the physiological patterns and some of the factor patterns previously recognised in psychological (total behaviour) variables. It is to be hoped that physiologists specialising in particular fields may be able to suggest more detailed explanations for some of these observed correlations. (*Italics inserted.*)

Thus the outcome is to *classify* certain phenomena which may prove to be worthy of the attention of the laboratory worker; but this is admittedly useful only in so far as it furnishes the latter with a clue. In what sense then do the writers use the term *hypothesis*? As I see it, they do so in the sense that the systematic botanist might so speak of the choice of the number of ridges on the ovary of an *Umbellifer* as a marker-characteristic to sort out genera embracing species with many common characteristics. That such taxonomical industry has its uses, no experimental biologist would deny; but classificatory systems as such have no intrinsic validity. All one can say about a taxonomy is that it is more or less useful as a means of identifying entities with common characteristics or as an impetus to investigate otherwise unrecognised similarities. Since no recipe for classification can anticipate what class of similarities will prove to be a fruitful theme for experimental enquiry, the use of the word *hypothesis* to signify a taxonomical convention is admissible only if we recognise that the word has a totally different meaning in the context of the laboratory.

CHAPTER TEN

STOCHASTIC MODELS FOR SIMPLE REGRESSION

IN WHAT has gone before I have assumed that the reader understands the contemporary connotation of the term *regression*, in so far as it is a procedure prescribed for fitting a line—not necessarily straight—to a scatter diagram of points defining paired score-values plotted on a 2-way Cartesian grid—or more generally a specification of the definitive parameters of a formula involving sets of n corresponding connected score-values. Thus we may choose to plot in a 3-dimensional grid family income, completed size of family and mortality rates as an assemblage of 3 corresponding connected score values. We have seen that the prescribed procedure, including the use of the familiar covariance formula for simple linear regression involving only two such variates, enlists the method of least squares originally invoked for use in situations essentially different from those which prompt sociologists and agricultural scientists to rely on it. We have also acquainted ourselves with the social setting in which the Method of Least Squares gained a footing in the laboratory at a time when the normal curve attained a peculiar status in descriptive statistics of populations; but we have not as yet examined the circumstances in which the Gaussian concept of point estimation first intruded into the domain of descriptive statistics.

It will help us to get into focus a distinction emphasised in Chapter Eight and to view it from a fresh angle, if we now retrace our steps to the historical background of the innovation signalised by Pearson's partnership with Galton. It may also be profitable to do so for another reason. We shall be better able to see how the tyranny of averages checked the progress of biological science at a time when new experimental methods (*vide* Chapter XIII) had laid the sure foundations for spectacular advances on a wide front. First, it will be necessary to explain how the definitive constant of a linear physical law such as the elastic coefficient of a spring has acquired so singular a designation as the *regression coefficient*, the more so since at least nine contemporary biologists out of ten, if under 50 years of age, and perhaps 99 sociologists out of a hundred, appear to believe that regression signifies the comparatively recent introduction of an algebraic manipulation peculiar to the realm of biological and/or sociological investigation. Nor are there many sources to enlighten those who cannot recall, as can the writer, the intellectual climate of the college or campus in 1912, when lectures on what we now call genetics impressed on the beginner that there are two sorts of heredity, severally designated alternating, qualitative or Mendelian and statistical, quantitative or biometric.

In another context I have referred to Galton's *Natural Inheritance* as source material for the genesis of the Quetelet *mystique*. Here our concern is to elucidate the origin of the word *regression* which makes its first appearance therein. Like Quetelet, Galton collected data w.r.t. such human measurements as heights, but with a different end in view. He industriously made scatter diagrams exhibiting values referable to pairs of individuals at a particular level of family relationship. For instance, he tabulated heights of sons against those of all fathers whose heights lie within a certain interval, e.g. $0 \cdot 5$ *in*. Having done so, he recorded with a rapture commensurate with the ambiguity of the outcome that the mean heights of sons lie very close to a straight line. Seemingly, he had expected that the grand mean of all sons in such a set-up would be the same as that of all the corresponding fathers. It turned out to be nearer the mean of the population, whence he discerned a universal drift of the hereditary process to what we may faithfully call in his own words *mediocrity*.

Galton christened the drift *regression*, a name which has outlived its original connotation and now signalises any exploits of draughtsmanship directed to exhibit the mean of a set of measurements plotted against particular values of another connected set, more especially perhaps when the draughtsman himself is not quite clear about what he is doing. Galton himself thought about the matter more deeply; and his second thoughts accommodated the circumstance that boys also have mothers. Being a gentleman, he was willing to apportion the

*

233

blame equally. He allocated to each parent a 25 per cent contribution to their son's height with a joint contribution of 50 per cent to his mediocrity. It was thus that there came to him the revelation embodied in a generalisation which incorporates a felicitously elementary arithmetical operation already beatified in the doctrine of Malthus. If a quarter of our inheritance comes from our Victorian father and a quarter from the weaker vessel, each of our four grandparents must contribute an eighth. Thus we arrive by easy stages at the quaint geometric series released to an expectant world as the *Law of Ancestral Inheritance*. Galton summarises it in the following passage cited from *The Average Contribution of each several Ancestor to the total Heritage of the Offspring*. (*Proc. Roy. Soc.*, 1897, Vol. LXI, pp. 401–5):

The law to be verified may seem at first sight too artificial to be true, but a closer examination shows that prejudice arising from the cursory impression is unfounded. This subject will be alluded to again, in the meantime the law shall be stated. It is that the two parents contribute between them on the average one-half, or $(0 \cdot 5)$ of the total heritage of the offspring; the four grandparents, one quarter or $(0 \cdot 5)^2$; the eight great-grandparents, one-eighth, or $(0 \cdot 5)^3$, and so on. Thus the sum of the ancestral contributions is expressed by the series $(0 \cdot 5) + (0 \cdot 5)^2 + (0 \cdot 5)^3$, etc., which, being equal to 1, accounts for the whole heritage.

The same statement may be put into a different form, in which a parent, grandparent, etc., is spoken of without reference to sex, by saying that each parent contributes on an average one-quarter or $(0 \cdot 5)^2$, each grandparent one-sixteenth, or $(0 \cdot 5)^4$, and so on, and that generally the occupier of each ancestral place in the nth degree, whatever be the value of n, contributes $(0 \cdot 5)^{2n}$ of the heritage.

The law to be verified supposes all the ancestors to be known, or to be known for so many generations back that the effects of the unknown residue are too small for consideration. The amount of the residual effect, beyond any given generation, is easily determined by the fact that in the series $\frac{1}{2} + \frac{1}{4} + \frac{1}{8}$, etc., each term is equal to the sum of all its successors. Now in the two sets of cases to be dealt with the larger refers to only two generations, therefore as the effect of the second generation is $\frac{1}{4}$, that of the unknown residue is $\frac{1}{4}$ also. The smaller set refers to three generations, leaving an unknown residual effect of $\frac{1}{8}$. These large residues cannot be ignored, amounting, as they do, to 25 and 12·5 per cent respectively. We have, therefore, to determine fixed and reasonable rules by which they should be apportioned.

It will be convenient to use the following nomenclature in calculations:

a_0 stands for a single member of the offspring.

a_1 for a single parent; a_2 for a single grandparent, and so on, the suffix denoting the number of the generation. A parallel nomenclature, using capital letters, is:

A_0 stands for all the offspring of the same ancestry.

A_1 for the two parents; A_2 for all the four grandparents, and so on. Consequently A_n contains 2^n individuals, each of the form a_n, and A_n contributes $(0·5)^n$ to the heritage of each a_0; while each a_n contributes $(0·5)^{2n}$ to it.

The analytical profundities of the foregoing train of reasoning do not take within their scope the possibility that the human family hands on a physical and cultural environment as well as an assemblage of what we now call *genes*. So we need not break a long since defunct butterfly on the wheel with the sledgehammer blows of a generation instructed in the art of conducting genetic experiments in standard culture conditions. It will suffice to recall the gratitude of the undergraduate of 1912 when his teachers abandoned this half of their assigned schedule with evident relief. The time had now come to talk of Mendelism, as they then said. Throughout the rest of the course one never lost the feeling that the prison gates were at last open. In those days, it was my own privilege to sit at the feet of Leonard Doncaster who discovered sex-linked inheritance, a phenomenon inconsistent with the half-and-half law briefly expounded above.

The vindication of Mendel in 1902 might have been the death-blow to the so-called law of ancestral inheritance, if the spiritual marriage of Galton and Pearson had not already produced a large progeny of mathematical contributions. As already stated, Pearson published these under a biological title in the *Philosophical Transactions of the Royal Society*, and on that account exempt from exposure to the scrutiny of mathematical colleagues sufficiently familiar with the theory of the combination of observations to recognise its abuse as well as its uses. Pearson had already discerned in Galton's data a formal similarity between a graph exhibiting the several heights of sons of fathers of the same height and a graph exhibiting the several observations of the stretch of a spring when we apply the same load thereto. Accordingly, he proceeded to adapt the formal algebra of the nineteenth century theory of error to the requirements of an entirely new class of situations. Being a skilful manipulative mathematician equipped with a vigorous command of the English language, he had no difficulty in recruiting a militant following to spread a gospel which handicapped the progress of experimental genetics in Britain for at least half a generation.

Let us then be clear about what we mean by regression. When we plot pairs of measurements and discern a drift, regression is merely a name to signify what we discern. For the time being, we need not ask whither we are then drifting. If the drift suggests a straight line we speak of it as linear. More precisely, we may define *simple linear regression* as follows, in accordance with (i) of Chapter Nine. For j values of observations y_{ij} associated with a particular value of an associated measurement x_i, we may define a mean value $M_{y.i}$. If $M_{y.i}$ increases by equal increments corresponding to equal increments of x_i, we may write $M_{y.i} = k_{yx}.x_i + C$. We then say that linear regression is exact and speak of k_{yx} as the coefficient of regression of y on x.

A Stochastic Model of the Gaussian Theory. At one level we have seen that the nineteenth century theory of error is neither inconsistent with the eighteenth century theory of risks in games of chance nor necessarily cognate thereto. One can make different models such as the Hagen model to show that the normal is a good fitting curve for an empirical frequency distribution of repeated measurements of one and the same physical entity; but it is impossible to prove the validity of the postulates peculiar to one or other model and equally impossible to deny with a good grace the inadequacy of the normal law to describe all error distributions which arise in experimental enquiry.

At a different level, we may say that the Gaussian Theory invokes a stochastic model whose properties are unique. They

236

fully satisfy the requirements of the classical theory if we concede that a fixed randomwise distribution of accidental errors is consistent with the presumptive framework of repetition. This postulate of the theory is not amenable to conclusive demonstration; but it is not repugnant to common sense; and it derives sanction from laboratory experience as an at least plausible assessment of the outcome of repeated efforts to measure the same entity in comparable circumstances. To get into focus the affinity of the Theory of Error with the classical theory of risks in games of chance at this level, it will therefore be profitable to discuss a model game to which we may indeed prescribe the rules in accordance with the gentlemanly convention that both players have an equal chance of winning. The model appropriate to the Gaussian Theory will then help us to see how much factually relevant information we sacrifice on the altar of algebraic generalisation when we invoke such devices as the bivariate normal distribution to interpret or to misinterpret seemingly linear relationships in sociological enquiry.

The game we shall prescribe is one we may call the *Player-Bonus Model*. Player A tosses twice an ordinary cubical die and records his 2-fold score sum (x_a). Player B then tosses 3 times a tetrahedral die as before with face scores $-$ 1, 0, 0, $+$ 1, adds the score sum $(x_{b.0})$ of his own 3-fold toss to 3 times the score of player A at each trial and records as his gross score:

$$x_b = 3x_a + x_{b.0}$$

Player B wins if his mean score is greater than 3 times that of player A. Player A wins if his mean score is more than a third of that of player B.

By recourse to a simple chessboard diagram we obtain the frequency (f_a) distribution of the score of player A as below:

Distribution of A score

x_a	2	3	4	5	6	7	8	9	10	11	12
$f_a \times 36$	1	2	3	4	5	6	5	4	3	2	1
Bonus $(3x_a)$ of Player B	6	9	12	15	18	21	24	27	30	33	36

The distribution of the individual score of player B before addition of the trial-bonus is deducible in the same way as:

Distribution of B's individual score

$x_{b.0}$	-3	-2	-1	0	$+1$	$+2$	$+3$
$f_{b.0} \times 64$	1	6	15	20	15	6	1

To construct a so-called correlation table which exhibits the relevant data of a scatter diagram referable to all possible samples and specifying their long run frequencies, we then proceed as follows. For A scores of 2, the distribution of B scores is that of $6 + x_{b.0}$, i.e.:

x_b	3	4	5	6	7	8	9
Relative frequency	1	6	15	20	15	6	1

Similarly for $x_a = 3$ we have:

x_b	6	7	8	9	10	11	12
Relative frequency	1	6	15	20	15	6	1

To combine our entries of corresponding A-scores and B-scores with due regard to the distribution of the former, we must weight them accordingly by recourse to the relative frequencies of the A-scores themselves as given above. We then obtain the composite table shown opposite (page 239):

Inspection of this table shows that $M_{b.a}$, the mean B-score for a fixed value of the A-score, increases by equal increments $\Delta M_{b.a} = 3$ for unit change of x_a in the range $x_a = 2$ to $x_a = 12$ and $M_{b.a} = 6$ to $M_{b.a} = 36$. If $C = 0$ and $k_{ba} = 3$, we may therefore write

$$M_{b.a} = k_{ba} \cdot x_a + C$$

This is the type of relationship already defined as *exact linear regression*. Let us now look at the way in which it arises. We started with the relation:

$$x_b = 3x_a + x_{b.0}$$

B-score	2	3	4	5	6	7	8	9	10	11	12
3	1	..	..								
4	6	..	..								
5	15	..	..								
6	20	2	..								
7	15	12	..								
8	6	30	..								
9	1	40	3	..							
10	..	30	18	..							
11	..	12	45	..							
12	..	2	60	4	..						
13	..	..	45	24	..						
14	..	..	18	60	..						
15	..	..	3	80	5	..					
16	..	..	..	60	30	..					
17	..	..	..	24	75	..					
18	..	..	..	4	100	6	..				
19	..	..	..	..	75	36	..				
20	..	..	..	..	30	90	..				
21	..	..	..	..	5	120	5	..			
22	..	..	..	..	..	90	30	..			
23	..	..	..	..	..	36	75	..			
24	..	..	..	..	..	6	100	4	..		
25						..	75	24	..		
26						..	30	60	..	..	..
27						..	5	80	3	..	..
28							..	60	18	..	..
29							..	24	45	..	..
30							..	4	60	2	..
31								..	45	12	..
32								..	18	30	..
33								..	3	40	1
34									..	30	6
35									..	12	15
36									..	2	20
37										..	15
38										..	6
39										..	1
Mean B-score ($M_{b.a}$)	6	9	12	15	18	21	24	27	30	33	36
Variance $\sigma^2_{b.a}$	1·5	1·5	1·5	1·5	1·5	1·5	1·5	1·5	1·5	1·5	1·5

In the foregoing expression x_b signifies a single observation on the gross score of player B within the framework of a limitless game. In this game, the long-run mean value of $x_{b.0}$ is zero for all values x_a may assume. The outcome is that the long-run mean value of the gross score of player B is three times that of player A in an indefinitely protracted sequence of trials specified by any particular score player A may record. The result would be just the same if the individual score contribution $(x_{b.0})$ were zero at each trial, i.e. if the die of player B had zero score on each face.

Our parable is now complete. We may exhibit the correspondence between the score components of this set-up, and the variables of a physical experiment referable to a linear law involving 2 variables as below:

Stochastic Model	Symbol	Physical Experiment
Score of Player A.	x_a	Antecedent (independent) variable.
Trial bonus allocated to Player B.	$k_{ba} \cdot x_a$	True value of the consequent (dependent) variable.
Individual Score of Player B.	$x_{b.0}$	Error of observation.
Gross score of Player B.	$x_b = k_{ba} \cdot x_a + x_{b.0}$	Observed value of the consequent.
Mean value of the individual B-score for fixed value of the A-score.	$M_{b.0} = 0$	Zero mean of error distribution for each value of the antecedent.
Mean value of gross B-score for fixed value of the A-score.	$M_{b.a} = k_{ba} \cdot x_a$	True value of the consequent for fixed value of antecedent.

Needless to say, our final table of p. 239 does not summarise the results of a particular game. It summarises the long-run outcome of an endless sequence of games. In so far as our model is a model relevant to the assumptions inherent in the

Gaussian Theory of Error, our table is therefore a summary of a sample distribution referable to sampling randomwise from a bivariate universe of paired scores. In one respect, it is artificial, and inevitably so. No fixed rule prescribes the equivalent A-score distribution of repeated trials in the conduct of experimental enquiry. All that we can say about it is that it would never be normal, and perhaps there is too much of a soupçon of normality about the A-score distribution the rule of our game prescribes. It is at least unimodal and symmetrical, but a rectangular distribution of the A-scores as interpreted above is, as elsewhere stated, more consistent with the practice of the laboratory worker. However, this is immaterial to our undertaking. We can impose the condition last stated by a slight modification of the rule of the game, i.e. we may allow player A to toss the cubical die once only at each trial.

A Modernised Stochastic Model of Galton's Regression. In the foregoing exposition of a classical model which incorporates the essentials of the Theory of Error, we have initially stated the rules of a game of chance, and subsequently exhibited the correspondence between the formal prescription of the rules and the postulates of the Gaussian Theory in the domain of a linear physical law involving only two variables. Let us now change our tactics by: (*a*) first formulating the Pearson concept of linear regression in its original setting in terms of a scoring system; (*b*) next specifying the rules of a game consistent with the scoring system so prescribed.

As regards (*a*), we first recall that the term regression came into use to accommodate Galton's ill-starred superstitions about inheritance. So we may profitably choose the correlation of height of brother with height of sister. Since nothing human interference can do to a brother necessarily affects the height of a sister, we cannot speak of either variable in terms of antecedent and consequent. Thus the scatter diagram in this situation is necessarily referable to a *concurrent* relationship. Fortunately, we can approach our problem with information derived from a field of research which Pearson valiantly obstructed during his lifetime. We shall thus speak of different *genes* and different *environments* in which the same gene complex is consistent with unique manifestations of structure and/or behaviour. Accordingly, we may schematically postulate component scores contributory to resemblance or "regression" as follows:

(i) *Contributory to resemblance.*

x_a the autosomal genes common to the gene complex of both sibs

x_m the equipment of *maternal* X-borne genes which brothers of the same parents share with their sisters

x_n the contribution attributable to environmental agencies (nurture) operating on both sibs in the same way.

(ii) *Contributory to so-called regression.*

$x_{a.b}$, $x_{a.s}$ autosomal genes respectively peculiar to the gene complex of the brother and the sister

$x_{m.b}$, $x_{m.s}$ *maternal* X-borne genes *ditto*

x_p the paternal X-borne gene equipment of the sister *only*

$x_{n.b}$, $x_{n.s}$ the contribution of *differential* environmental agencies operating on the two sibs

$x_{e.b}$, $x_{e.s}$ independent errors of measurement w.r.t. the observed characteristic, here assumed to be *height*.

*　　　　*　　　　*　　　　*

The foregoing will suffice for our purpose, if we collect our data as did Galton. If we also include unlikesex twin pairs in our pool, we shall need to distinguish two other components of resemblances: x_u to specify what they owe to the fact that they share the same *uterine* environment at one and the same time and x_b to specify that they turn up in the same stage of the family fortunes by virtue of identical birth rank. If we include brothers and sisters singly or both adopted into different foster homes, we shall also need to distinguish common score components: x_f for sibs brought up together and x_s for sibs reared apart in homes at the same social level.

The refinements last mentioned need not detain us here. If we interpret the addition sign *with due safeguards* as below, we may specify the total paired scores of our scatter diagram, i.e.

the height of a boy $(x_{h.b})$ and that of his sister $(x_{h.s})$ by the equations:

$$x_{h.b} = (x_a + x_m + x_n) + (x_{a.b} + x_{m.b} + x_{n.b} + x_{e.b})$$

$$x_{h.s} = (x_a + x_m + x_n) + (x_{a.s} + x_{m.s} + x_{n.s} + x_p + x_{e.s})$$

In this context, the invocation of the genotypically normal sib conceived in a normal womb, reared on normal milk in a normal home will not assist us to interpret the assumed *additive* property in realistic biological terms consistent with what we now know. We are at liberty to consider: (*a*) each of the components $x_{n.b}$, $x_{n.s}$ as a (positive or negative) *increment* of height referable to the result of rearing the same pair of sibs in one and the same environment; (*b*) the components $x_{a.b}$, $x_{a.s}$, $x_{m.b}$, $x_{m.s}$ as increments referable to the substitution of a common gene complex for the entire assemblage of genes w.r.t. each of which one or both parents of a sib pair are heterozygous. Now no unique framework of substitution accommodates either class. Each such interpretation of the additive property embraces an infinitude of possibilities. Unless we dismiss the indisputable reality both of *interaction* between genes and of interaction between gene substitutions and specific environmental agencies, the effect of standardising either our environment or our gene complex in any one such way will determine what increment we can predicate of our common score components x_a, x_m, x_n.

Needless to say, Galton's approach to inheritance took no stock of such interaction. If we are to interpret correlation of relatives in his way, we shall therefore regard our paired total scores as the simple sum of two components x_c and $x_{d.b}$ or $x_{d.s}$ defined as follows:

$$x_c = x_a + x_m + x_n$$

$$x_{d.b} = x_{a.b} + x_{m.b} + x_{n.b} + x_{e.b}$$

$$x_{d.s} = x_{a.s} + x_{m.s} + x_p + x_{n.b} + x_{e.b}$$

Our equations definitive of score components now become:

$$x_{h.b} = x_c + x_{d.b}$$

$$x_{h.s} = x_c + x_{d.s}$$

On the assumption that we gratuitously (and erroneously)

interpret the additive sign in the usual way, we may speak of the above as *linear equations of concomitant variation*. With due regard to the reservations stated above, and neglecting inter-action by assuming the independence of x_c, $x_{d.b}$, $x_{d.s}$, we may then define a stochastic model which precisely embodies the formal assumptions of our nature-nurture-error schema. It is the one I have called the *Umpire Bonus Model*. As a game which endorses the equal chance of success to each player, the prescription is as follows:

(i) At each trial the players A and B each toss different dice, the number of tosses (r_a and r_b) allocated being such as to guarantee the same mean value of the trial score sum in the long run, so that $r_a = r_b$ if the two dice are alike;

(ii) At each trial an umpire C tosses a third die r_c times, and each player records as his total score (x_a or x_b) the score sum of his own toss ($x_{a.0}$ or $x_{b.0}$) added to that (x_c) of C.

With this prescription, we can set out a table for the bivariate universe of the sampling process like that of p. 239, if we specify r_a, r_b, r_c and the types of dice respectively allocated to A, B and C. In the Pearsonian jargon we then say that:

(i) there is linear regression of the B-score on the A-score (x_a), if the mean B scores ($M_{b.a}$) associated with particular values of the A-score increase by equal increments corre-sponding to equal increments of the latter (x_a);

(ii) there is linear regression of the A-score on the B-score (x_b) if the mean A-scores ($M_{a.b}$) associated with particular values of x_b increase by equal increments corresponding to equal increments of x_b itself.

Before proceeding, we may usefully recall the true role of the umpire (C) in the game. The game itself is a game within the terms of reference of the classical theory of risks only if it is repeatable, i.e. relevant to the conduct of an experiment only in culture conditions of which we can predicate a distribu-tion independent of and constant throughout a putatively randomwise sampling process. The umpire's score x_c is by definition what sibs of a pair owe both to a common ancestry and to a common environment. Hence it is not surprising that samples* of identical twins respectively reared in the same families and apart may (and do) yield different Pearsonian measures of correlation. Our umpire bonus is not a measure of genetic identity *per se* and has therefore no necessary bearing on the recognition of laws pertaining to inheritance. However, it is not our main concern in this context to conduct an autopsy on a defunct biological superstition. What is more relevant to the credentials of statistical procedures is why Galton or Pearson believed that any intelligible interpretation of the correlation of relatives implies a law of linear regression.

Elderton (*Frequency Curves and Correlation*) first propounded this model for a limited class of situations consistent with the specification I have given above, i.e. when all the dice are alike. It then happens that regression is linear in both dimensions as above, i.e.

$$M_{b.a} = k_{ba}.x_a + C_b \quad and \quad M_{a.b} = k_{ab}.x_b + C_a$$

If $r_a = r_b$, we shall find that $k_{ba} = k_{ab}$; but otherwise there will be, as Berkson would say, two regressions. Now neither Elderton, who specifies this model in numerical terms without formal treatment of the postulates, nor Rietz† (1920) who later makes unnecessarily heavy weather of the algebra, appears to have noticed what is most instructive about its properties. If the dice are not identical, four situations may arise: linear regression in both dimensions of the scatter diagram, linear regression in one dimension only or in the other only and linear regression in *neither* dimension. That linear concomitant variation, as defined above for two concurrent variates, does not necessarily imply linear regression of either w.r.t. either, a single example serves to put beyond dispute.

The game we shall now play is in all respects like the one

* In terms of the supplementary components specified above but neglected in the foregoing and with due regard to the limited meaning we here attach to the addition symbol, we may specify

Ordinary sibs reared together:	$x_c = x_a + x_m + x_f,$
,, ,, apart, same social level:	$x_c = x_a + x_m + x_s$
,, ,, apart, different social level:	$x_c = x_a + x_m$
Twins reared together	$x_c = x_a + x_m + x_u + x_f,$
,, ,, apart, same social level:	$x_c = x_a + x_m + x_u + x_s,$
,, ,, apart, different social level:	$x_c = x_a + x_m + x_u$

† *Ann. Maths.*, Vol. 21, 1920.

last prescribed. The only details to fill in are the specifications of the dice and numbers of tosses at each trial, viz.:

(i) the umpire C tosses twice a flat unbiased circular die with 2 pips on one face and 1 pip only on the other;

(ii) player A tosses once an unbiased tetrahedral die with face scores of 1, 2, 3 and 4 pips respectively;

(iii) player B tosses once an unbiased tetrahedral die with 2 pips on each of three faces and 1 pip on the fourth.

We may proceed effortlessly as follows. Our grid of concomitant A-scores and B-scores before addition of the umpire's bonus is at each trial as below, the frequency of each bivariate cell score $(x_{a.0}, x_{b.0})$ in that order being equal in accordance with the lay-out:

A-score $(x_{a.0})$
before addition of bonus

		1	2	3	4
	1	1,1	2,1	3,1	4,1
B-score $(x_{b.0})$	2	1,2	2,2	3,2	4,2
before addition of bonus	2	1,2	2,2	3,2	4,2
	2	1,2	2,2	3,2	4,2

Our umpire bonus score (x_c) distribution for the 2-fold toss is 2, 3, 3, 4. Accordingly, we construct 4 corresponding grids of bivariate scores as below:

$x_c = 2$				$x_c = 3$			
3,3	4,3	5,3	6,3	4,4	5,4	6,4	7,4
3,4	4,4	5,4	6,4	4,5	5,5	6,5	7,5
3,4	4,4	5,4	6,4	4,5	5,5	6,5	7,5
3,4	4,4	5,4	6,4	4,5	5,5	6,5	7,5

$x_c = 3$				$x_c = 4$			
4,4	5,4	6,4	7,4	5,5	6,5	7,5	8,5
4,5	5,5	6,5	7,5	5,6	6,6	7,6	8,6
4,5	5,5	6,5	7,5	5,6	6,6	7,6	8,6
4,5	5,5	6,5	7,5	5,6	6,6	7,6	8,6

We now condense our 64 entries in a frequency grid as follows:

Total A-score (x_a)

	3	4	5	6	7	8	$M_{a.b}$
Total B-score (x_b) 3	I	I	I	I	0	0	$\frac{1890}{420}$
4	3	5	5	5	2	0	$\frac{2058}{420}$
5	0	6	7	7	7	I	$\frac{2370}{420}$
6	0	0	3	3	3	3	$\frac{2730}{420}$
$M_{b.a}$	$\frac{405}{108}$	$\frac{477}{108}$	$\frac{513}{108}$	$\frac{513}{108}$	$\frac{549}{108}$	$\frac{621}{108}$	

*   *   *   *

Here it is neither true that $M_{a.b}$ increases by equal increments when x_b also increases by equal increments, nor that $M_{b.a}$ increases by equal increments when x_a does so. Even if our highly schematic interpretation of the correlation of brother's height with sister's height—front stall exhibit in Pearson's rationale of Galton's so-called Law of Ancestral Inheritance—is defensible in all particulars, we thus see that stochastic theory gives us no guarantee of linear regression unless we invoke some additional and exceptionable assumptions. This raises the question: what distribution of the component variates x_c, $x_{d.b}$, $x_{d.s}$ in our schematic definitive equations of $x_{h.b}$, $x_{h.s}$ will ensure that linear regression is a necessary consequence of linear concomitant variation? Evelyn Fick (1945)* has lately defined the necessary and sufficient condition in the domain of continuous variates. It appears that regression will then be linear if, and only if, x_c, $x_{a.b}$, $x_{d.s}$ are normally distributed variates.

The consideration last stated makes Pearson's bivariate normal distribution an attractive playground for exhibiting a so-called Law of Inheritance which has not stood the test of

* *Proc. Berkeley Symposium on Mathematical Statistics and Probability.* Edit. J. Neyman.

carefully controlled experimental studies of animal and plant breeding; but we have seen that the bivariate normal distribution does not—and cannot—describe a universe consistent with the proper terms of reference of the Theory of Error *sensu stricto*. Nor is it consistent with the considerations which led Pearson to propound his system of curve fitting by moments in a memoir ostensibly devoted to the theory of evolution. Why he chose this medium of publication is relevant to earlier remarks on the irrelevant invocation of the Central Limit Theorem, at least by implication, in Galton's own defence of his speculations and computations.

We have seen two reasons why this theorem is irrelevant to the contention that nature operates on stochastic principles applicable to an indefinitely large number of "contributory causes." We then have to assume that their effects on the growth process of a living being or of a society are independent and additive, a postulate which is indisputably false in a large variety of relevant situations. Furthermore, the endorsement of this supposition excludes the possibility of meeting skew distributions of characteristics of populations to which the theorem is supposedly relevant. Seemingly, Pearson did not appreciate the force of the first objection. Indeed, the superstition that we can rightly regard the effects of gene substitutions and of the multiplicity of interchangeable external agencies contributory to development as both independent and additive still persists, being inherent in Fisher's use of *Analysis of Variance* to assess the role of nature and nurture. What did profoundly disturb Karl Pearson is the fact that skew distributions do commonly occur in nature.

This is the theme of the latter part of (9) and the beginning of (11) in the second of the *Contributions to the Mathematical Theory of Evolution* with the sub-title *Skew Variation in Homogeneous Material*. It appeared in the Biological Series of the *Philosophical Transactions of the Royal Society* in the year 1895. The title and the content of the passages referred to explain what would otherwise be enigmatic. Why did the Pearson system of moment fitting curves see the light in a biological publication? Why does Pearson derive the parent differential equation of his Type system from considerations based on the hypergeometric distribution, and why accordingly does a fitting curve for sampling without replacement from a finite binomial appear as head of the list as Type I?

A simple answer resolves these questions. If nature's urn of innumerable contributory small, and supposedly independent, causes whose effect is additive is also infinite, algebra offers us only the solution which the Central Limit Theorem endorses; but then we have to explain away the fact that empirical frequency distributions of population parameters are not necessarily—or even commonly—symmetrical. Happily it seems, we can sidestep this discouraging reflection by conceding that the contents of our nature-bag, if relevant to any particular make-believe sampling process congenial to the presumptions of Quetelet's *mystique*, is indeed finite and that the sample our suppositious supernatural gamester takes therefrom is a relatively large fraction of the whole.

It thus turns out that the bivariate normal frequency surface is not adequate to shoulder the burden of heredity on Galton's own terms; but the history of this engaging mathematical toy is of interest *vis-à-vis* the contemporary revaluation of statistical procedures from another viewpoint. When we formulate a stochastic model in the factual language of the discrete universe of scores which circumscribe the programme of the classical theory of risks in games of chance, we can make explicit the factual relevance of our algebraic conventions to the causal *nexus* which is the focus of interest to the naturalist and man of affairs. For instance, we can then see in what circumstances linear regressions may arise; and the examples cited above illustrate but two among many for which it is possible to specify an appropriate model game. When we transfer the issue to the continuous domain, our geometrical conventions give us no clue whatever to the diverse ways in which seemingly identical statistical patterns may arise in nature. A dominant *motif* of theoretical statistics for more than a century has been this disposition to sacrifice factual relevance to the dictates of mathematical tidiness.

As an index of resemblance between relatives, Pearson sidestepped the ambiguity of the two regressions by recourse to the *product-moment* coefficient of correlation. When regression is indeed linear in both dimensions, this is the *geometric mean of the two coefficients*. By definition in accordance with (iv) of Chapter Nine

$$k_{ab} = \frac{Cov\ (x_a, x_b)}{V_b}\ ;\ k_{ba} = \frac{Cov\ (x_a, x_b)}{V_a}$$

As shown in Appendix 2, this is a tautology true of any set of paired scores which satisfy the condition that the row and column means of one set increase by equal steps for equal increments of the corresponding border scores of the alternative set. Whence we define the correlation coefficient (r_{ab}) as

$$r_{ab} = \frac{Cov\ (x_a, x_b)}{\sqrt{V_a \cdot V_b}}$$

As a summarising index, the product moment coefficient has the useful property that its value is either $+1$ (positive correlation) or -1 (negative correlation) if there is one-to-one linear correspondence between x_a and x_b. When this is so, $x_a = M_{a.b}$ for a fixed value of x_b and $x_b = M_{b.a}$ for a fixed value of x_a. If $M_{b.a}$ is constant for all values of x_a and $M_{b.a}$ is constant for all values of x_b or if the row and column means $(M_{b.a}, M_{a.b})$ vary periodically and symmetrically with the border scores (x_a, x_b) its value is zero.

As also shown in Appendix 2, the fundamental property of the foregoing model when each player receives the same bonus from the umpire is that the variance (V_c) of the umpire score distribution is equal to the covariance of the players' joint score distribution. If we write V_b and V_s respectively for the variances of the distribution of heights of brothers and heights of sisters, the product-moment coefficient for height on the foregoing arbitrary assumptions will thus be

$$r_{bs} = \frac{V_c}{\sqrt{V_b \cdot V_s}}$$

In deriving this expression, we assume that the score components x_c, $x_{d.b}$, $x_{d.s}$ with sampling variances V_c, $V_{d.b}$, $V_{d.s}$ are independent, so that

$$V_b = V_c + V_{d.b}\ \ and\ \ V_s = V_c + V_{d.s}$$

If regression is linear in both dimensions and $k_{bs} \simeq k_{sb}$, it follows from the definition of the regression coefficients that $V_b \simeq V_s$ and $r_{bs} \simeq V_c \div V_b$, so that $r_{bs} \simeq V_c \div (V_c + V_{d.b})$. Pearson found that $r_{bs} \simeq 0 \cdot 5$. This implies that $V_{d.b} \simeq V_c \simeq V_{d.s}$, if, as stated, the two coefficients are nearly equal; but there is no known reason why this should be so. Thus it is difficult to see how an appropriate stochastic model can endorse the arithmetic of the so-called law of ancestral inheritance. Still less is it easy to justify one assumption we have so far taken for granted. Our score components are conceptual entities about which we claim to know nothing more, in Galton's statement of the problem, than that x_c is referable to some assemblage of particles. By what sanction do we then claim that the components r_c, $x_{h.b}$, $x_{h.s}$ are random variables? The only possible answer is a novel extension of the principle of insufficient reason. We have to assume randomness because we know nothing to the contrary. By the same token, a philosopher unacquainted with the railway timetable might admissibly assume that trains move in all directions randomwise throughout the course of the day.

The same gratuitous assumption is inherent in subsequent use of the product-moment coefficient as the keystone of the edifice called factor analysis. That it does indeed underlie much of contemporary thought gives the formal concept of the Irregular Kollektiv advanced by von Mises a special interest. If we take the contribution of von Mises seriously, we commit ourselves to the assertion that randomness is a *knowable* property of a system of scores. At least, it is a property whose existence we cannot conclusively demonstrate, but one we can infer with legitimate confidence against the background of large-scale experience. Thus the invocation of the concept in the domain of the statistical theory of the combination of instrumental observations is not on all fours with its intrusion in the domain of intangible hypothetical particles unless it leads to the construction of a unique hypothesis amenable to independent verification in the domain of experiment. The astronomer with long experience of his observatory may draw on a fund of factual information about how successive uncontrollable errors turn up in the course of his work; but the score components which a stochastic model of regression or factor analysis (*vide infra*) must accommodate are fictions about whose distribution we can have no immediate experience.

We may now sum up in the following terms the outcome of our examination of the terms of reference of the theory of regression in this chapter and in its predecessor:

(1) The Gaussian calculus prescribes a discipline to promote agreement about the true values of physical measurements and of physical constants of laws inferred to be true for reasons to which the calculus is irrelevant; and the end in view is to place on record numerical values for future use in strictly comparable circumstances, endorsed either by experience of inexorable natural periodicities such as the movements of celestial bodies or by confirmatory experience of independent observations made daily in the laboratory or in the factory.

(2) The theory of regression prescribes a method of locating averages or specifying parameters of descriptive formulae referable to such averages; but the deviation of any individual score from such an average has no more title to be more or less near to a *true* value than any other; and the descriptive formula which embraces them can rightly claim the title of law as the physicist uses the term only if we have some assurance that we shall meet a population described in terms of such averages in definable circumstances. In fact, we are rarely, if ever, able to do so in branches of enquiry relying on this procedure.

(3) Laboratory or observatory experience may endorse with some plausibility the assumption that successive uncontrollable instrumental errors turn up randomwise; but the assumption that deviations of population scores from a fictitious mean are random variables derives its sanction wholly from the arbitrary and Platonic concept of the infinite hypothetical population. This concept has not gained universal acceptance, being indeed rejected by the school most antagonistic to a behaviourist approach to the theory of probability.

(4) Though the theory of regression makes use of the same

formal algebra as the Gaussian theory of error, it derives
no sanction from whatever claims to usefulness we concede
to the latter. Its aim is different. The concept of law which
it embraces is different. Its factual assumptions are
different.

The Grammar of Science. If we enlist in the undertaking to
which the calculus of exploration commits us, all we can thus
hope to gain at the end of the journey is a relation between
averages referable to populations beyond our powers to
recreate. In the domain of social relations, the methods it
prescribes can never give us the assurance of unmasking a
causal nexus; and the recognition of such a causal nexus is a
necessary basis for applying our knowledge constructively.
Under a pretentious edifice of mathematical sophistication, we
inter the hope of changing our world. We resign ourselves
to the role of the passive and helpless spectator. Having buried
the Baconian formula, we must then doctor our definition of
scientific law accordingly, and regression takes its place in a
formalised ideology. What might otherwise seem to be misconceptions too trivial to merit rebuttal are indeed by-products
of such an ideology set forth in Pearson's *Grammar of Science.*

As one of the last survivors of a generation which received
it as a new evangel, I find it hard to discover any rational
ingredients in an enthusiasm which I once shared with so many
others. As one sees it at a more mature age, Pearson's message is
consistent with what the rising generation now interpret as
its main thesis. Briefly, this is:

(*a*) the raw data of science are individual mental images in
a static framework which excludes the recognition of unique
historical events as a proper theme for intelligent reflection;

(*b*) the concept of scientific law is reducible to one "brief
statement or formula which resumes the relationship between
a group of facts."

On a generation whose Victorian elders welcomed the late
Professor Henry Drummond's *Natural Law in the Spiritual World*
as a challenging contribution to human thought, the brevity
of the aforesaid statement exerted an appeal a younger generation can never recapture. In these days we hear enough, and it

may be too much, about *operational* research. So we do not commonly expect to specify a particular assemblage of facts by a relationship which is unique in the sense that it is independent of considerations relevant to the chosen framework of classification. How then are we to specify the terms of reference of the relationship expressed by the brief statement or formula? The student of today will no longer be content with the answer that the formula must be short. He or she will ask: what can it do for us? If the answer we seek is Pearson's own view, we may well infer that the composite photograph of the deserving recipient is Quetelet's normal man at home by his normal fireside with his normal wife and normal offspring at the end of a normal day; but we shall certainly not make his acquaintance in a world outside and antecedent to ourselves. We shall locate him (p. 110, *vide infra*) in the Platonic domain of our individual *perceptions*.

Even the definition of *brief* in this context is vague. Pearson nowhere explicitly asserts that the terms of reference of his brief formula are necessarily numerical; but he is very clearly of one mind with Kelvin when the latter declares:

When you can measure what you are talking about and express it in numbers, you know something about it; but when you cannot measure it, when you cannot express it in numbers, your knowledge is of a meagre and unsatisfactory kind, it may be the beginning of knowledge but you have scarcely in your thoughts advanced to the stage of science whatever the matter may be.

The concluding remarks of his discussion of the content of natural, in contradistinction to civil or spiritual, law affirm an out-and-out idealistic viewpoint *en rapport* with his adherence to the principle of insufficient reason, as quoted elsewhere. He there defines the *Weltanschauung* of Pearsonian man in the following terms (p. 110):

He recognises that the so-called law of nature is but a simple *résumé*, a brief description of a wide range of his own perceptions and that the harmony between his perceptive and reasoning faculties is not incapable of being traced to its origin. Natural law appears to him an intellectual product of man, and not a routine inherent in "dead matter." The progress of science is thus reduced to a more and more complete analysis of the perceptive faculty—an analysis which unconsciously and not unnaturally, if illogically, we too often treat as an analysis of something beyond sense-impression. Thus both the material and the laws of science are inherent in ourselves rather than in an outside world.

A view of science so conceived can readily accommodate such artefacts as the normal man and the normal environment cheek by jowl with Ricardo's economic man, the eternal verities of Malthus and such scholastic generalisations as the so-called law of supply and demand. Thus it extends the benefits of free grace on Kelvin's terms to the newer disciplines, which the great grammarian woos with temporary disregard for the foregoing renunciation of the external world, as when he declares (p. 12):

The unity of all science consists alone in its method, not in its material. The man who classifies facts of any kind whatever, who sees their mutual relation and describes their sequence, is applying the scientific method and is a man of science. The facts may belong to the past history of mankind, to the social statistics of our great cities, to the atmosphere of the most distant stars, to the digestive organs of a worm, or to the life of a scarcely visible bacillus. It is not the facts themselves which form science, but the method in which they are dealt with. The material of science is co-extensive with the whole physical universe, not only that universe as it now exists, but with its past history and the past history of all life therein.

In such temporary lapses into a conciliatory attitude towards the claims of non-quantitative historical studies, Pearson does not disclose how the chronologically closed field of our perceptions is able to accommodate what antedated their existence; and indeed part of his appeal resides in an eclecticism which entitles the reader of any persuasion to find in the *Grammar*, as in Engels' *Anti-Duehring*, something to his or her taste. At a time when the 1902 Education Act had rekindled the embers of the Religious Tests Controversy, he is able to allay our suspicion that he is defending a metaphysic in the tradition of so staunch a churchman as Berkeley by a disarming bouquet to the bishop's opponents in the same context (p. 109):

It may seem to the reader that we have been discussing at unjustifiable length the nature of scientific law. Yet therein we have reached a point of primary importance, a point over which the battles of systems and creeds have been long and bitter. Here the materialists have thrown down the gauntlet to the natural theologians, and the latter in their turn have endeavoured to deck dogma with the mantle of science.

No doubt many other circumstances were propitious to the uncritical welcome the book received from the Edwardian left and right. One is certainly the fact that the author had a magnificent command of pungent English; and his early volume of essays entitled *The Ethic of Free Thought* is still readable as a model of prose style. Above all, a generation of biologists weary of reckless and fruitless speculations about phylogeny in the wake of the Darwinian controversy and goaded by Kelvin's challenge in the setting of spectacular inventions traceable to discoveries of physicists, was eager enough to welcome any prospect of exalting the claims of its own field of enquiry to rank as *exact* science. Pearson's repudiation of the Baconian viewpoint extended to biology and to sociology the benefits of mathematical free grace at his own price. What price psychology has paid for the privilege will be the theme of the next chapter.

CHAPTER ELEVEN

THE IMPASSE OF FACTOR ANALYSIS

A RETROSPECTIVE GLANCE at the pages of *The Grammar of Science* is a fitting introduction to factor analysis, as will appear from the following profession of faith by Thurstone (*The Vectors of the Mind*):

A scientific law is not to be thought of as having an independent existence which some scientist is fortunate to stumble on. A scientific law is not a part of nature. It is only a way of comprehending nature . . . the chief object of science is to minimalise mental effort. . . . It is in the nature of science that no scientific law can ever be proved to be right. It can only be shown to be plausible. The laws of science are not immutable. They are only human efforts towards *parsimony in the comprehension of nature.* (*Italics inserted.*)

Here we have the Pearsonian evangel in its entirety. Of two or more descriptions of natural phenomena, we shall deem to be acceptable the one which is most *economical.* It will thus be less difficult for the reader to discern how largely the Pearsonian formula for natural law derives its urgency from the inclination to equip the Pearsonian calculus of exploration with a plausible rationale. By a familiar feat of metalepsis congenial to the professional mathematician, the most parsimonious form of statement is that which embraces a *minimal* solution. The method of least squares will lead us to the true description of concomitant variation of tuberculosis rates and of housing density, because it *minimalises* the variance of the deviations around a line fitted to a scatter diagram. Accordingly, we abandon the obligation to ask what useful outcome, if any, is the reward of our labours or to subject the conclusions to which the method leads us to the arbitrament of verification by recourse to other procedures.

It is one of time's ironies that the statistical technique most heavily indebted to the essentially novel feature of Pearson's contributions to statistical theory, namely the *product-moment*

STATISTICAL THEORY

index of concomitant variation, has led after forty years of
fruitless wandering in the wilderness of matrix algebra to a
cul de sac in which its practitioners are at length asking: is
there indeed any unique sense in which a statement summarising our acquaintance with natural phenomena is as economical
as may be? Meanwhile, the influence of Pearson has extended
over a far wider field. We necessarily think of algebraic formulae as more economical than verbal statements because in one
sense they are so. Accordingly, observations upholstered with
sufficient algebraic sophistication are *ipso facto* praiseworthy on
that account. By the same token, we discount the contribution
of the naturalist or of the physician with clinical judgment,
unless the presentation of the observational record conforms
to a ritual whose credentials lie outside the curriculum of his
training. More and more, he thus learns to rely on interpretation by recourse to methods which he understands less and
less.

Thus the influence of Pearson has brought about a new orientation of values. When the *Grammar of Science* came out in its first
edition, T. H. Huxley and his influential following could still
boast that the man of science takes nothing on trust. To the
naturalist smarting under clerical antagonism to assertion of
the right to indulge in the luxury of speculation unlicensed by
scriptural sanction and contrary to the customary interpretation of the *ipsissima verba* of Holy Writ, there was nothing
incongruous in this claim; but no reflective person of our own
generation could regard it as now true. Indeed, few of the
younger men of science would endorse it as the statement of a
congenial ideal. A vast literature on *Factor Analysis* accumulated
in the last forty years bears witness to the role of Pearson as the
parent of a methodology fitting to the authoritarian temper of
our time. In every, or almost every, teachers' training college
throughout the English-speaking world, students whose mathematical equipment rarely transgresses the boundaries of the
high school curriculum listen to glib parables about the rotation
of axes in hyperspace with docile anticipation of examinations
conducted in a temper as likely to encourage a rational scepticism as did the forced repetition of the lesser catechism to
Scottish children of an earlier generation.

The impact of this peculiar private language of so-called *factor-space* on the uninitiated recalls the bewilderment of schoolboys of an earlier generation when their instructors failed to distinguish between the ether as a convenient fiction to accommodate the algebra appropriate to the description of actual wave motion and the ether as a self-contradictory metaphor for the actual medium in which propagation amenable to description in such terms takes place. Nearly all current accounts of factor analysis presuppose some elementary acquaintance with matrices and determinants or start with an exposition of grid algebra, leaving the initiate with the impression that the credentials of the procedure are incomprehensible in any other idiom. The truth is that every logical issue raised by the claims of factor analysis is understandable, and the more readily so, if we keep a firm foothold in classical models for which high school algebra suffices. The need for an alternative notation arises only when the work of computation otherwise becomes excessively laborious, and then only for that reason.

In this chapter, we shall trace to its origin the *impasse* into which factor analysis has led contemporary psychologists who have followed this trail. It will not be necessary to presume a knowledge of matrix algebra, but it will be necessary at the outset to introduce a few terms to avoid periphrasis in what follows. By the *correlation coefficient* we shall consistently signify the Pearsonian covariance (*product-moment*) formula, denoted r_{ab} for paired measurements of attributes A and B (e.g. height of son and height of father or the A-test score of an individual and the B-test score of the same individual). In general terms, Factor Analysis is the attempt to interpret observations which disclose an appreciable measure of correlation, in the sense that $r_{ab} \neq 0$, when our data embrace several pairs of such attributes.

From variable measurements referable to attributes A, B, C, D . . ., etc., we may calculate correlation (product-moment) coefficients r_{ab}, r_{ac}, r_{ad}, r_{bc}, r_{bd}, r_{cd} . . . If we lay these out gridwise in accordance with the pattern shown overleaf, it is customary to speak of the symmetrical arrangement as the *correlation matrix* for the set of attributes.

By a suitable choice of what we choose to label as A, B, etc., it may then be possible to lay out such a symmetrically ordered grid with successive cell entries of each column (from top to bottom) and successive cell entries of each row (from left to right) in ascending numerical order. If this is indeed possible, we say that the correlated attributes conform to the *hierarchical*

	A	B	C	D	...
A	...	r_{ba}	r_{ca}	r_{da}	
B	r_{ab}	...	r_{cb}	r_{db}	
C	r_{ac}	r_{bc}	...	r_{dc}	
D	r_{ad}	r_{bd}	r_{cd}	...	
...	...	...	...	...	

principle. From data w.r.t. paired scores of groups of individuals each subjected to a set of educational tests A, B, C, etc., Spearman (1912) claimed that it was possible to exhibit such a hierarchical pattern; and advanced the view that the inter-correlations then arise from concomitant variation assignable to a single source or factor, which he named g and identified as *general intelligence*.

Of itself, the fact that r_{ab}, r_{ac} and r_{bc} appreciably exceed zero, as is implicit in the statement that A, B, C are intercorrelated variables, merely signifies that the scores x_a, x_b, x_c of one and the same individual for tests A, B, C agree too closely to be consistent with randomwise distribution. We may regard this as indicative of the existence of some source of individual variation common to any pair of tests; but this is consistent with the possibility that there are as many common sources (*factors*) as the number of different pairs, i.e. $^nC_2$ for n tests. Factor Analysis starts from the assumption that the correct interpretation of the properties of the correlation matrix is that which is consistent with postulating the *minimum* number of factors common to one or more pairs. Accordingly, it seeks an answer to two questions: (*a*) what is the minimum number of factors we require on that understanding; (*b*) how can we assess the contributions of each of them to variation w.r.t. the individual's score for each test?

If we can say that *one* common factor, e.g. Spearman's g, provides the answer to the first question last stated, we can answer the second decisively in terms consistent with the arbitrary choice of an appropriate stochastic model. Otherwise, no stochastic model can certainly lead us to the goal we seek. There is indeed more than one current prescription for *multiple* factor analysis, and different prescriptions lead us to assign different values to the contribution of the several factors of the minimum set. Thus Spearman's original formulation, if applicable in practice and acceptable in theory, confers no licence on the subsequent development of the statistical theory he propounded.

When the factor pattern is as described above, the stochastic model which fulfils the expectations implicit in Spearman's interpretation of the correlation matrix for a set of inter-correlated test scores with a single common factor is a more general case of the *umpire bonus model* than the one discussed in our last chapter. There each player receives the same bonus from the umpire. As before, we shall postulate that each player tosses a die and that the umpire does likewise at each game; but we shall suppose that the bonus each player incorporates with his individual score ($x_{a.0}$, $x_{b.0}$, etc.) in his final score (x_a, x_b, etc.) is some multiple of the umpire's score, such that the actual bonus any one player receives in one and the same game is different from that which any other receives.

For a set-up involving one umpire and four players (A, B, C, D) the definitive equations of the score are thus

$$x_a = A \cdot x_u + x_{a.0}$$
$$x_b = B \cdot x_u + x_{b.0}$$
$$x_c = C \cdot x_u + x_{c.0}$$
$$x_d = D \cdot x_u + x_{d.0}$$

If V_u and V_a respectively denote the variance of the umpire score distribution and that of the final score of player A, the properties of the model relevant to our theme are, as derived in *Appendix II*:

$$r_{ab} = r_{au} \cdot r_{bu} \; ; \; r_{au} = A \cdot V_u^{\frac{1}{2}} \cdot V_a^{-\frac{1}{2}} \; ; \; V_a = A^2 V_u + V_{a.0} \quad \cdot \text{ (i)}$$

Thus the fraction (so-called *communality*) of the variance of the distribution of the final score of player A contributed by the umpire bonus is:

$$\frac{A^2 V_u}{V_a} = r_{au}^2 \qquad \cdots \cdots \quad \text{(ii)}$$

In virtue of the relation $r_{ab} = r_{au} \cdot r_{bu}$, we may write

$$r_{ab} \cdot r_{cd} = r_{au} \cdot r_{bu} \cdot r_{cu} \cdot r_{du}$$
$$r_{ac} \cdot r_{bd} = r_{au} \cdot r_{cu} \cdot r_{bu} \cdot r_{du}$$
$$r_{ad} \cdot r_{bc} = r_{au} \cdot r_{du} \cdot r_{bu} \cdot r_{cu}$$

$$\therefore \quad r_{ab} \cdot r_{cd} = r_{ac} \cdot r_{bd} = r_{ad} \cdot r_{bc} \quad \cdots \quad \text{(iii)}$$

If $r_{au} < r_{bu} < r_{cu} < r_{du}$, it follows that

$$r_{ab} < r_{ac} < r_{ad}$$
$$r_{ab} < r_{bc} < r_{bd}$$
$$r_{ac} < r_{bc} < r_{cd}$$
$$r_{ad} < r_{bd} < r_{cd}$$

This is Spearman's *hierarchical principle*.

We may now recognise the following rule: r_{au}^2 is the ratio of the sum of all the products of pairs of observed correlations involving the A-score to the sum of all the correlations which do not involve the A-score. Thus

$$r_{ab} \cdot r_{ac} + r_{ab} \cdot r_{ad} + r_{ac} \cdot r_{ad} = r_{au}^2 (r_{bu} \cdot r_{cu} + r_{bu} \cdot r_{du} + r_{cu} \cdot r_{du})$$
$$r_{bc} + r_{bd} + r_{cd} = r_{bu} \cdot r_{cu} + r_{bu} \cdot r_{du} + r_{cu} \cdot r_{du}$$

From this relation we can get a pooled estimate of r_{au} and in the same way of r_{bu}, r_{cu}, etc. From these estimates we may then reconstruct a correlation matrix of *estimated* values of r_{ab}, r_{ac}, etc., as shown opposite.

The identity embodied in (iii) embraces a more general rule when we have before us the scores of more than 3 players, as in the foregoing exemplary correlation matrix. For any pair of columns we can pick out two rows without zero entries, e.g.:

$$\frac{r_{ac} \ r_{bc}}{r_{ad} \ r_{bd}} \ ; \quad \frac{r_{ab} \ r_{cb}}{r_{ad} \ r_{cd}} \ ; \quad \frac{r_{ab} \ r_{bd}}{r_{ac} \ r_{cd}} \ ; \quad \frac{r_{ab} \ r_{ac}}{r_{bd} \ r_{cd}} \ \cdots\cdots$$

For each of these *tetrads* (Spearman), spoken of as a *determinant minor of order* 2 in the idiom of matrix algebra, the difference

	r_{au}	r_{bu}	r_{cu}	r_{du}
r_{au}	$\ldots$	$r_{au} \cdot r_{bu}$ $= r_{ab}$	$r_{au} \cdot r_{cu}$ $= r_{ac}$	$r_{au} \cdot r_{du}$ $= r_{ad}$
r_{bu}	$r_{au} \cdot r_{bu}$ $= r_{ab}$	$\ldots$	$r_{bu} \cdot r_{cu}$ $= r_{bc}$	$r_{bu} \cdot r_{du}$ $= r_{bd}$
r_{cu}	$r_{au} \cdot r_{cu}$ $= r_{ac}$	$r_{bu} \cdot r_{cu}$ $= r_{bc}$	$\ldots$	$r_{cu} \cdot r_{du}$ $= r_{cd}$
r_{du}	$r_{au} \cdot r_{du}$ $= r_{ad}$	$r_{bu} \cdot r_{du}$ $= r_{bd}$	$r_{cu} \cdot r_{du}$ $= r_{cd}$	$\ldots$

between the cross products is zero in accordance with (iii) above. For instance,

$$r_{ac} \cdot r_{bd} = r_{au} \cdot r_{bu} \cdot r_{cu} \cdot r_{du} = r_{bc} \cdot r_{ad}$$

$$\therefore \quad r_{ac} \cdot r_{bd} - r_{bc} \cdot r_{ad} = 0 \quad . \quad . \quad . \quad . \quad \text{(iv)}$$

In the language of matrix algebra, we express this formulation of the hierarchical principle by saying that *every second order minor of the correlation matrix vanishes*.

In so far as r_{au}, r_{bu}, etc., are adequate summarising indices the cell entries of the foregoing grid should tally closely with the observed values of r_{ab}, r_{ac}, etc. To get the relevance of our model to the use of factor analysis into focus, we shall now suppose that:

(*a*) we are able to observe a very large number of games in which the 4 players A–D participate;

(*b*) we are able to record the final score of each player on each occasion, but know neither what bonus the umpire contributes to each nor what are the individual scores of the players;

(*c*) we regard the final scores of any two players at one

and the same game as a pair for the purpose of determining score correlations r_{ab}, r_{bc}, etc.;

(*d*) the calculation yields a set of values consistent with the hierarchical principle, and the values of $r_{ab} \cdot r_{cd}$, $r_{ac} \cdot r_{bd}$ and $r_{ad} \cdot r_{bc}$ are approximately equal;

(*e*) the cell entries of the correlation matrix reconstructed from our estimates of r_{au}, etc., tally closely with the observed values of r_{ab}, etc.

(*f*) our estimated communalities conform to the order

$$r_{au} < r_{bu} < r_{cu} < r_{du}.$$

In this situation, the fact that the scores of any two players are correlated indicates that each receives a bonus which varies from game to game, but not necessarily randomwise. That the score tetrads are approximately equal, and that the hierarchical principle holds good, point to the existence of a single source of the bonus each player receives and to its randomwise distribution from game to game. What then may we also infer from the border factors of our grid? From (ii) we see that r_{au}^2 represents the proportionate contribution of the umpire's bonus to the variance of the score distribution of player A. The statement that r_{au} is the smallest of the factors means that the withdrawal of the umpire's bonus would proportionately diminish the dispersion of the score of A *less* than that of the other players. Conversely, the statement that r_{du} is the greatest of the factors signifies that the withdrawal of the umpire's bonus would proportionately diminish the dispersion of the score of D more than that of any of the other players.

Let us now assume that our model reproduces the essential features of the application of 4 tests A–D to a large number of boys and girls. Each boy or girl then corresponds to a game. The test score A and the test score D of one and the same boy or girl corresponds to a pair of players' final scores in a particular game of the sequence. We deem the umpire bonus to represent the common ability which tests A and D assess, and the players' individual scores to represent the specific abilities which the tests respectively assess and/or *error*. The term error in this context is equivocal, meaning the unreliability of the test in terms of: (a) mistakes the record may contain; (b) inconsistencies w.r.t. individual response to one and the same stimulus on different occasions.

Thus r_{au}^2 signifies the proportionate contribution of the common ability to the dispersion of the A test score in the population tested. If r_{au} is less than r_{bu}, r_{cu}, r_{du}, this signifies that the common ability assessed by the 4 tests contributes proportionately least to the variation of the A test score in the population as a whole. By the same token we regard the A-test as a less sensitive measure of individual variability w.r.t. the assumed common ability.

If we concede all the assumptions provisionally adopted, we may thus state the ostensible uses of the procedure outlined. It claims to tell us:

(i) whether the correlation between three or more measurements is referable to a single common component;

(ii) whether one test which putatively assesses such a single common component is more or less sensitive in the sense that it yields results less influenced by other sources of variation.

The second of the foregoing is of theoretical interest only as a more or less useful means of sharpening the tools of the research worker. What precisely we may achieve by the first is an empirical issue, since the procedure under discussion does not guarantee to label the common component usefully. As stated, it led Spearman to conclude that there is a single component ability (g) contributory to the individual's rating referable to different types of scholastic tests deemed to assess what we commonly call intelligence. We may interpret this conclusion, if true, by saying that there is some meaningful nucleus in the use of the adjective *intelligent*. If so, we may deem it desirable to make a linguistic recommendation in favour of restricting the use of the word intelligent to the individual's rating on a so-called g-saturated test, i.e. a test T such that the g-communality r_{tg}^2 accounts for a very high percentage of the test-score variance.

What is not clear is whether we have accomplished more than refinement of our terminology by doing so. That such refinement may be eminently useful at a certain stage in the development of any science, especially a young science, is not disputable; but the usefulness of a procedure to promote refinement of a taxonomy does not suffice to justify the claim that it automatically generates a correct hypothesis without demanding any initial statement of the job assigned to it. What we shall deem to be useful in an operational sense on all fours with the criteria we adopt in experimental physiology will be what leads us to the recognition of regularities of human behaviour verifiable by other means. Only if susceptible to independent verification, can the conclusions to which our selected stochastic model leads us, justify its endorsement, as when we justifiably accept the postulate of randomwise association of the gametes to interpret hereditary transmission.

Be this as it may, we may concede that the stochastic interpretation of a hierarchical factor pattern is an attractive one, and is not one we should lightly dismiss as a clue to follow up, if such patterns turned up commonly in the course of statistical investigations on intra-group variation. The truth is that subsequent research on the lines first explored by Spearman has led to the conclusion that a recognisably and consistently hierarchical pattern rarely, if ever, emerges from comparison of scores referable to different tests or to measurements referable to different attributes of different individuals or—Cattell's P-technique (p. 229)—to successive states of the same individual. While some workers in the same field have recorded plausible examples of bi-factor patterns, i.e. hierarchical systems of intercorrelations interpretable in terms of one factor common to all test scores and other factors common to discrete groups of test scores in a battery, the procedures subsumed under the term *multiple factor analysis* derive no such plausibility from immediate inspection of the data. As stated, their aim is to assign *loadings*, such as r_{au}^2, r_{bu}^2 in the foregoing, to components of test score variance without invoking the assumption that any such loading exceeds zero for all classes of scores involved.

Before we ask how far any unique stochastic model can endow this pursuit with some similitude of cogency, let us elaborate the foregoing model situation. We shall now suppose that each of more than two umpires (U_1, U_2, etc.) contributes to some multiple of each player's individual score some multiple of his own (x_1, x_2, etc.); but we shall not exclude the possibility that any multiplicative constant (F_1, F_2, etc.) may be zero. The player's individual score on the Fth test will therefore be

$$x_f = F_1 \cdot x_1 + F_2 \cdot x_2 \ldots \ldots + F_0 \cdot x_{f.0} \quad . \quad . \quad \text{(v)}$$

By the same reasoning (*Appendix II*) employed in deriving the formal relations implicit in the rule of the game when there is only one umpire bonus, we then derive for the set-up involving two umpires the following relations involving the observable correlation (r_{fg}) between the player's score on two tests (F, G) and the correlation between either test score of the player and that of either umpire:

$$r_{f1} \cdot r_{g1} + r_{f2} \cdot r_{g2} = r_{fg}$$

$$F_1^2 \cdot V_1 + F_2^2 \cdot V_2 + F_0^2 \cdot V_{f.0} = V_f$$

$$r_{f1}^2 + r_{f2}^2 + \frac{F_0^2 \cdot V_{f.0}}{V_f} = 1$$

More generally for *n* umpires we may write:

$$r_{fg} = \sum_{x=1}^{x=n} r_{fx} \cdot r_{gx} \ and \ V_f = F_0^2 \cdot V_{f.0} + \sum_{x=1}^{x=n} F_x^2 \cdot V_x \quad . \quad \text{(vi)}$$

By recourse to the expression on the left hand in (vi) we may derive without much labour a formula analogous to (iv) for the correlation matrix when only two umpires participate, viz.:

$$r_{ad} (r_{bc} \cdot r_{cf} - r_{bf} \cdot r_{ce}) - r_{ac} (r_{bd} \cdot r_{cf} - r_{bf} \cdot r_{cd})$$
$$+ r_{af} (r_{bd} \cdot r_{ce} - r_{cd} \cdot r_{be}) = 0 \quad . \quad \text{(vii)}$$

The last equation cited does not obviously conform to a pattern of which (iv) is a special case, unless the reader is familiar with the notation of matrix algebra. In the idiom of matrix algebra (*Appendix III*), it signifies that all determinant minors of order 3 in the correlation matrix vanish for 2 umpires as all determinant minors of order 2 vanish for the foregoing case of one umpire; and more generally we may derive from

(v) by recourse to determinants the rule that all minors of order $(n + 1)$ vanish when there are n umpires.

With the enunciation of this rule by Thurstone, theory loses all foothold in the comparatively firm soil of the classical model, and we thread our way through a maze of algebraic metaphors invoked to describe subsequent symbolic manipulations rather than the properties of the model itself. Since but a small fraction of research workers who rely on multiple factor analysis as a so-called tool of research are at home in the hyperspace of the matrix notation, the ensuing confusion of thought is what one might well anticipate. Albeit the labour involved in discussing more than two common factors by recourse to schoolbook algebra is a sufficient justification for preferring the use of matrices, the invocation of three or more factors involves no logically new issue which the unrestricted invocation of two wholly or partially common factors in place of Spearman's single one cannot bring clearly into focus.

Accordingly, we shall now relinquish the privilege of taking a backstage view of the game. All we shall permit ourselves to know is the final test score of each player; and our task in the Spearman tradition will be both to decide how many umpires participate and what contribution the variance of the score distribution of each umpire makes to that of the distribution of the final score of each player. Even if we then have the assurance that the rules of the game are correctly subsumed in (v) above, we are in a quandary. The principle last stated may satisfy our requirements for the first part of our task; but we then find that the evaluation of the loadings (r_{f1}^2, r_{f2}^2, etc.) admits of no unique solution, unless we rely on assumptions deriving no sanction from the observations themselves.

This will be sufficiently clear, if we now divert our attention from the putatively appropriate model to the test situation. We then have to take cognisance of our initial arbitrary assumption that the score components are strictly additive as well as the equally arbitrary assumption that their distribution is randomwise. It is difficult to see why the possibility that all minors of order n in a correlation matrix vanish in theory and have negligible numerical values in practice should endorse either the one or the other; but if we grant the assumption that we really know the rules of the game in general terms as stated above, we come face to face with difficulties more disturbing to the docile practitioner. It will suffice to mention one of them.

In Spearman's original formulation there are two factors only, one common to all test scores, the other unique and putatively referable to a specific attribute measured by a given test after correction of the test scores for error in Spearman's sense, i.e. reliability of the test procedure. Now the foregoing formulation places *no* restriction on the value of the constant F_0. Thus we are free to reject the proposition that any test score has a truly *specific* component; and it is here that prescriptions for evaluating the loadings respectively given by Thurstone's following and that of Hotelling diverge radically. Thurstone endows every test score with, and Hotelling deprives every test of, a specific component.

Hotelling's position is wide open to criticism for two reasons. Of minor importance is the fact that any test must be subject to independent variability unless perfectly reliable, and we have therefore to assume without opportunity for verification that correction for unreliability, being itself a statistical device and therefore fallible on its own terms, removes all sources of error in the widest sense of the term. From the viewpoint of the pure mathematician this has the merit of empowering us to extract a tidy solution implicit in the right-hand expression of (v) above. Since all the variance of the test score is referable to the communalities in the absence of specifics, the variance of the score distribution for each test is exhaustively expressible in terms of them. To guarantee a unique evaluation of the communalities, we then make the further assumption that the total number of wholly or partially common factors assessed by r_{f1}^2, r_{2f}^2, etc., is equal to the number of tests. The addition of another test to the battery must then change, and may grossly change, our previous evaluation of each test as a gauge for the abilities referable to the factors.

Godfrey Thomson (*Factorial Analysis of Human Ability*, p. 68) refers to this quandary in the following remarks (*italics inserted*):

... If there are, say twenty tests, there will be twenty principal axes ranging from longest to shortest, and twenty Hotelling components. But the first four or five of these will go a long way towards defining a man's position in the tests, and will do so better than any other equally numerous set of factors, whether of Hotelling's or of any other system. In this respect Hotelling's factors undoubtedly stand foremost. They will not, however, reproduce the *correlations* exactly unless they are all used, whereas in Thurstone's system a few common factors can, theoretically, do this, though in actual practice the difference of the two systems in this respect is not great. *The chief disadvantage of Hotelling's components is that they change when a new test is added to the battery.*

The gentleness of the rebuke in the last sentence cited will reinforce its cogency, if read in a reflective temper. One might with equal propriety say that a method of analysis is admissible if it yields consistent figures for percentage composition in repeated titrations of *x* cc. of a solution, but with the trifling drawback of yielding a totally different estimate based on repeated titrations of *y* cc. of one and the same solution. We need therefore record no despondency if another school of factor theory repudiates both assumptions on which Hotelling relies.

From the foregoing it should be clear that Hotelling's formulation does not embrace Spearman's as a special case. That of Thurstone admits no test F for which $F_0 = 0$ and embraces Spearman's hierarchical pattern when the value of F_x, etc., for all values of x from 1 to n is zero for every test score component other than the particular (*rth*) common component to which F_r is referable; but the endorsement of a component specific to each test does not lead to a unique evaluation of the loadings, nor does it clearly guarantee that addition of a new test to the battery leaves our previous evaluation of loadings intact. Again I quote from Godfrey Thomson (*op. cit.*) :

Whether Thurstone's common factors will remain invariant in augmented batteries, and if so under what conditions, is a question we shall consider at a later stage in this book. Though such invariance seems unlikely, it is not obviously inconceivable. . . . The Hotelling components . . . can be calculated exactly from a man's scores, whereas Spearman or Thurstone factors can only be estimated. This is because the Hotelling components are never more numerous than the tests, whereas the Thurstone or Spearman factors, including the specifics, are always more numerous than the tests. For the Hotelling components, therefore, we always have just the same number of equations as unknowns, whereas we have more unknowns than equations in the Spearman–Thurstone system.

To formulate his own rule for the evaluation of the loadings Thurstone relies on a somewhat personal interpretation of the familiar dictum of William of Occam, whence the special relevance of the citation at the beginning of this chapter. One way of stating the Thurstone principle of economy is as defined by Godfrey Thomson, viz. that the most economical evaluation maximises the contribution of the specifics and minimises the number of contributory common factors in the balance sheet of the test score variance. Burt expresses Thurstone's approach in different terms (*The Factors of the Mind*, p. 162):

His interpretation of the "law of parsimony in scientific description" requires, not (as mine does) that each factor in turn should account for the greatest possible amount of the variance, but that: (*a*) the total number of factors entering into the whole set of traits and (*b*) the number of factors entering into each sample trait should be as small as possible. . . . He therefore seeks a factorial matrix in which every factor shall have at least one zero coefficient for at least one of the tests.

The controversy between the different schools of factor theory as revealed in the passage last quoted thus lays bare an issue raised elsewhere and at the beginning of this chapter. The *Grammar* of Karl Pearson propounded an ideology tailored to the requirements of his conviction that the edifice he erected on the foundations laid by Quetelet could accommodate all the future requirements of truly scientific enquiry pertaining to evolution, man's nature and human society. The keystone of the edifice was the author's own interpretation of *entia non multiplicanda praeter necessitatem*, a counsel of modest prudence and salutary enough unless beatified as an article of faith. The truth is that there are as many criteria of economically interpreting nature as there are different frameworks of interpretation dictated by different ways in which we may seek to bind nature in the service of man. The present dilemma of factor analysis arises from the fact that its initial terms of reference embrace a classificatory task without explicit formulation of the end in view, an explicit admission of protagonists* anxious to promote its claims to consideration in the domain of experimental science.

That the real dilemma arises from the impossibility of uniquely defining a universal criterion of economy or parsimony in the interpretation of nature is at least evident to one contemporary, who has devoted many years to evaluating the credentials of factor analysis, as when Godfrey Thomson (*op. cit.*, pp. 133–34) writes:

Shorthand descriptions. It is to be observed that an analysis using the minimal number of common factors, and with maximised specific variance, is capable of reproducing the correlation coefficients exactly by means of these few common factors, and in the case of an artificial example will actually do so; while in the case of an experimental example including errors, it will do so at least as well as any other method. If this is our sole purpose, therefore, the Thurstone type of analysis is best, since it uses fewest factors.

But the few common factors of a Thurstone analysis do not enable us to reproduce the original test scores from which we began, they do not enable us to describe all the powers of our population of persons very well. With the same number of Hotelling's "principal components" as Thurstone has of common factors we could arrive at a better description of the scores, though a worse one of the correlations. The reader may reply that he does not want factors for the purpose of reproducing either the original scores or the original correlations, for he possesses these already! But what we really mean, and what it is very convenient to have, is a concise shorthand description, and the system we prefer will depend largely on our motives, whether we have a practical end in view or are urged by theoretical curiosity. The chief practical incentive is the hope that factors will somehow enable better vocational and educational predictions to be made. Mathematically, however, as we have seen, this is impossible. If the use of factors turns out to improve vocational advance it will be for some other reason than a mathematical one. For vocational or educational prediction means, mathematically, projecting a point given by n oblique co-ordinate axes called tests on to a vector representing the occupation, whose angles with the tests are known, but which is not in the n-space of the tests. The use

* See Cattell and Williams, p. 229.

of factors merely means referring the point in question to a new set of co-ordinate axes called factors, a procedure which cannot define the point any better, and, unless care is taken, may define it worse, nor does the change of axes in any way facilitate the projection on to the occupation vector.

Against the background of these remarks it is suggestive to contrast the role of economy with the role of analogy in the search for truth. Most of us will agree that reasoning from analogy in matters pertaining to human affairs often leads to gross error and rarely, if ever, to a profitable outcome. None the less, the progress of experimental physics during the four centuries which have followed the exposition of Gilbert's *terella* is in large measure due to the exploitation of daring metaphors whose initial plausibility we cannot easily discern at a distance. Thus we may well ask why analogy which is so good a servant of natural philosophy is so bad a master of humanistic enquiry. If we approach the issue from what G. P. Meredith calls the epistemic viewpoint the question admits of more than one answer, but an answer relevant to our present theme is not far to seek. The physicist follows an analogy only in so far as it leads him to conclusions susceptible to factual verification. Where two analogies suggest different conclusions, he designs the *experimentum crucis* to adjudicate on their respective merits. I have yet to discover that comparisons between the State and the organism or between the nervous system and the self-guided missile have led to conclusions sufficiently free from ambiguity to succumb to disproof, if false.

To me it seems that the peculiar status of the principle of parsimony in Pearson's system is on all fours with the misuse of analogy. Few of us, if any, will prefer a more laborious interpretation of a physical event to a more simple one, when both conform to factual requirements; but if such was indeed the motivation of those who first explored the consequences of the heliocentric interpretation of planetary motion, it would be false to say that the world of science rejected the Ptolemaic view for this reason only. In his own time, Hipparchus rejected the heliocentric viewpoint endorsed by Aristarchus, because no annual parallax of a star was detectable by methods then available. The doubt remained

(p. 187) till the thirties of the last century, but the view of Aristarchus meanwhile gained strength from a succession of other discoveries, made after Copernicus revived it, viz. the existence of Jupiter's moons, the retardation of the pendulum by latitude, the flattening of the earth at the poles and the phenomenon of stellar aberration.

Thus it is not true to declare that astronomers rejected the Ptolemaic system by reliance on any rule of thumb application of the renowned razor of Occam. Were it otherwise, they would have done so with some misgivings. For the decision to do so raises a dilemma of the sort disclosed in the foregoing citation from Godfrey Thomson. Admittedly, the heliocentric postulates lead to a simpler method for tracking the course of the planets, a consideration of some practical interest in the milieu of Copernicus, when navigators had to rely on planetary conjunctions and occultations for determining the longitude of a ship at sea. Contrariwise, the geocentric view leads to a simpler method of representing the position of the fixed stars on which the mariner still relies to fix his latitude. Accordingly, all current books on nautical astronomy still adhere to the Ptolemaic conception of the celestial sphere, except in the chapter or chapters devoted to planetary motion.

In so far as a proponent of multiple factor analysis may, as does Thurstone, invoke the history of astronomy to endorse the principle of parsimony, he cannot therefore evade the question: with what end in view does a particular hypothesis *minimalise human effort?* The question has no singular answer in the domain of astronomy and no singular answer in the domain of psychology. If the record of astronomical discovery has any lesson for the humanistic disciplines, it should surely remind us that many millenia of patient and unpretentious observations on the night sky and the sun's shadow antedated the useful enlistment of higher mathematics in the study of the motion of the celestial bodies. A technique which automatically accelerates the tempo of relevant fact-finding in the formative phase of a science would doubtless be a godsend to the psychologist; but the present impasse does not encourage us to be confident that factor analysis fulfils this role.

The following would thus seem to be a just assessment of the claims of factor analysis as a so-called tool of research at the present time:

(i) Because its raw data emerge from the domain of *concomitant* variation, factor analysis, like multivariate analysis, is legitimately at best descriptive. Of itself, it can at best lead to a more satisfactory taxonomy, but then only if we are clear about what and why we want to classify. It cannot disclose a causal nexus; and we must judge its usefulness as a means for unmasking unsuspected regularities of nature, of personality or of society by its fruits alone.

(ii) So far the fruitage has been disappointing in the domain of its widest application, and the assertion of its claims in other fields of enquiry may well leave us with the suspicion that its advocates are less reluctant to exploit new markets than to guarantee the intrinsic value of the export.

(iii) At the most elementary level of theory, the invocation of a stochastic model to endorse a recognisable factor-pattern would be unexceptionable if undertaken on the understanding that experiment alone can validify the interpretation suggested by the model; but it is difficult to cite examples of interpretations both consonant with the theory of a suitable stochastic model and also amenable to the verdict of another court of justice.

(iv) Once we abandon the hope of disclosing a unique factor pattern, we can hope to interpret a system of inter-correlations only if content to fall back on an ambiguous principle of parsimony. That any such principle is indeed ambiguous is the sufficient explanation of the existence of different recipes advanced by different schools with no prospect of endorsing the same balance sheet.

(v) Whatsoever be the preferred principle of parsimony, the incorporation of the classical theory of probability in the initial postulates is arbitrary in more ways than one, and involves assumptions which can never be amenable to direct proof. Like Hagen's model of the so-called law of error, any classical model we press into the service of the theory may explain how certain numerical regularities *might* arise but cannot suffice to prove that in fact they *do* so.

PART III

The Calculus of Aggregates

CHAPTER TWELVE

MAXWELL AND THE URN OF NATURE

THE ORIGINAL POPULATION of the, now for us notorious, urn of Laplace was a population of *billets*. At what stage the inhabitants of *l'urne que nous interrogeons* became balls the writer has been unable to trace in the literature. Maybe the change occurred *pari passu* with the intrusion of statistical theory into the particulate domain of nineteenth-century experimental science; or possibly it preceded and prepared the way for it. In either event, it signalises the definition of a model peculiarly appropriate to the uses of research when the current conception of atoms and molecules identified them with elastic spheres subject to the Newtonian laws of impact. With this identification before us, we stand on the threshold of what is indisputably to date the most powerful use of the theory of probability; and we shall do well to recall previous remarks on the diversity of its actual or suppositious uses.

In Chapter One we have seen that the word statistics has many uses and that its use in the context of statistical theory alone subsumes four themes which are different at least in the sense that exponents of one or the other respectively operate in watertight compartments of exposition. Thus it is worthy of comment that Kendall's treatise in two volumes on the *Advanced Theory of Statistics* (1943–1946) gives no consideration to the Kinetic Theory of Gases, to Quantum Mechanics or to the Genetical Theory of Populations. It devotes doubtless adequate, perhaps more than adequate, space to Gram-Charlier Series, Tetrachoric functions, Factorial Moments, Tchebychev–Hermite polynomials and Sampling Cumulants of k-statistics; but it is silent with respect to Maxwell–Boltzmann, Einstein–Bose and Fermi–Dirac statistics. Indeed, the index cites neither the name of Maxwell nor that of Mendel.

To say this, explicitly carries with it no oblique criticism of Kendall's extremely useful work. I mention these omissions merely to emphasise the fact that a considerable body of specialists in the theory of statistics refrain from disclosing the relevance of their work to the class of problems here referred to as the *Calculus of Aggregates*. None the less, expositors of the contemporary reorientation of physical concepts unquestionably refer to the construction of hypotheses *en rapport* with recipes which date from Maxwell and Mendel, when they assure us that the statistical is now the canonical formulation of a scientific law. Presumably also theoretical statisticians themselves refer more especially to the domain of such hypotheses when they assure us, if legitimately, that experiment vindicates the success of statistical methods.

Before we can accept the appeal to experience with an easy mind on these terms, we shall need to be clear about the common content of the epithet *statistical* in current usage; and this is now possible only if our reading roams over a wide territory. It is scarcely an exaggeration to say that a course on theoretical statistics delivered to physicists in the department of applied mathematics of any contemporary university would scarcely traverse a single theme dealt with in a course offered to research workers in agricultural science, to students of production engineering or to sociologists. To be sure, the normal distribution would have its niche in both; but the introduction of simple harmonic motion into the treatment of elementary optics, acoustics, the theory of the alternating current and the dynamics of the pendulum does not entitle us to dismiss the obligation to discuss on their own merits problems peculiar to phenomena so diverse. Nor does the use of Fourier series in the treatment of crystal structure, of the conduction of heat and of the diffusion of a solute seduce any reasonable student into believing that the three domains of enquiry have in common anything other than the convenience of exploiting in different situations, and for different reasons, the same algebraic techniques.

If there is indeed any common ground for equating the term statistics as the physicist uses the term when he speaks of Maxwell's Kinetic Theory of Gases as a statistical hypothesis with statistics as R. A. Fisher uses the term in *Statistical Methods for Research Workers*, the student anxious to locate it will get little guidance from any textbooks now in circulation. It is worthy of note that the book last mentioned, though planned primarily for the use of biologists, does not deal with the genetical theory of populations, an outstanding achievement of the Calculus of Aggregates, the only example of its kind in the terrain of biological research, and a topic to which Fisher himself has contributed. Nor does the same author's *Design of Experiments* set forth the Theory of Error as it emerges in the practice of the observatory and of the physical laboratory.

What I have previously said with reference to Kendall's treatise applies equally to the foregoing remarks. The intention is not to criticise the books here mentioned, because they contain no reference to topics the authors prefer to exclude. I cite such omissions as case material. The naturalist who wishes to understand the contemporary content of the word statistics will wish to know what problems occupy the attention of professional statisticians. If one consults a library with this end in view, one soon becomes aware of an iron curtain between: (*a*) the Theory of Regression as set forth for the benefit of sociologists, biometricians and educational psychologists; (*b*) the traditional domain of the *Calculus of Error*, as set forth for astronomers and surveyors. Still more is it true that there is an iron curtain between what I have elsewhere called the *Calculus of Judgments* and the construction of hypotheses which fall within the scope of the *Calculus of Aggregates*.

To define the scope of the latter and the implications of the epithet *statistical* in that context is the theme of this chapter and the next one. It will not be possible to do justice to the task unless we now retrace our steps to the milieu of the Pascal–Fermat correspondence. We must then adjust ourselves to the intellectual climate of a century in which the recognition of the gaseous condition as the third estate of matter was an adventure in wholly uncharted territory. The speculations of Leucippus and Democritus, immortalised in the poem of Lucretius, derided by Aristotle for frivolously fallacious reasons and banned by the Mediaeval Schools on that account, became again widely known in the seventeenth century through the publication of Gassendi's commentaries on Epicurus. The *Commentaries* profoundly influenced the thought of the Newtonian age. The particulate view then re-emerges with the final vindication of the gaseous state of matter as such in the same setting as the exposure of Aristotle's misconceptions about gravity and buoyancy against the background of the way in which the common pump works. Though seventeenth-century thought failed to incorporate a particulate view of matter in a system of quantitative generalisations concerning combination of gases by weight and volume, Hooke himself invoked nitro-aerial particles to offer an explanation of oxidation entirely consistent with the one which Dalton elaborated at the beginning of the nineteenth century.

Gassendi's atoms move in all directions freely. Such motion accounts for the free diffusion of the gaseous state in apparent violation of gravitation. The particles have mass, and particles of like matter are of equal mass. So the density of a gas at a particular pressure depends only on the mean number present in unit space. Being free to move in all directions, they will collide with any partition which obstructs their egress from a vessel. If we move the partition in the direction which lessens the space available to their movements, the number of such collisions will increase. Additional force will thus be necessary to oppose their impact. As its author himself seems to have divined, this brings them into the picture disclosed by Hooke's (so-called Boyle's) law connecting pressure and volume. Daniel Bernoulli, himself a pioneer of stochastic theory in the classical setting, explicitly incorporates the conception in his *Hydrodynamica* (1738).

Before the century ends, we see the stage set for a wider recognition of its usefulness when Charles announced the law connecting the temperature of a gas with its pressure and volume. The work of Black and of James Watt is leading to the recognition of heat as a form of energy. So we can now envisage the possibility of interpreting heat in terms of motion. In everyday life, collision signifies friction, and friction signifies heat. By easy stages we therefore reach the interpretation of temperature in the idiom of *averages*, i.e. in terms of the *mean* incidence of collisions per unit space in unit time, and of conduction as a process of attaining a higher *mean* speed by collision of invading and more swiftly moving particles in a space containing particles in motion at a lower tempo.

If we say that *atomism* is the keynote of naturalistic thought in the nineteenth century, we do not therefore signify that the particulate interpretation of matter was still novel. All we can truly mean is that the particulate view of matter now becomes a background for the construction of hypotheses leading to unique quantitative conclusions susceptible to verification. In the speculations of Dalton, Avogadro, Williamson and Mendel-ejev the discussion proceeds on the assumption that the gross structure of matter is referable to the *additive* effects of classes of particles *individually alike and endowed with the tangible properties of matter in bulk*. In the intellectual climate at the turn of the half-century, a different picture of the molecule takes shape. We approach its behaviour in the setting of the Gaussian theory of error and its overflow into the domain of vital statistics through the influence of Quetelet's evangel. In short, we identify atoms and molecules with the infinitude of black and white balls in the urn of Nature. The time is ripe for the reception of two generalisations which signalise a new use of the particulate concept and an entirely novel recipe for the prescription of quantitative verifiable hypotheses.

In the background of one we discern a phenomenon which endows the new orientation with a compelling plausibility. Though the germ of the notion is in Gassendi's teaching, the study of Brownian movement in the context of greatly improved microscopic technique during the first half of the nineteenth century made it more easy to visualise the molecules of Avo-gadro as entities in a state of constant *haphazard* motion. To say as much in the same setting provokes us to seek some connexion between their capricious movements and the concept of randomness implicit in the classical theory of risks in games of chance. The exploitation of this notion explicitly by Clausius (1857) and by Maxwell (1859) necessarily invokes a postulate which is foreign to the Dalton–Mendelejev tradition; and the implications of its invocation still trouble those who demand from science a monolithic statue of nature.

The *individual* particle—atom or molecule—of classical chemistry has such properties of matter in bulk as are relevant to the terms of reference of the theory, and such properties alone. The particles of Clausius and Maxwell are in constant collision and are therefore losing momentum or gaining it by impact. Their speeds vary *inter se* and that of an individual particle itself varies in less than a twinkling of an eye. If we seek to interpret the gas laws of temperature, pressure and volume in terms of their behaviour, what we can thus postulate about their properties as most relevant to properties of matter in bulk is reducible to averages. Nothing we can know about the *individual* particle is relevant to the behaviour of the aggregate. Though in one sense Maxwell's model of the structure of matter is *en rapport* with a long tradition of thought and with the English tradition of map-making initiated by Gilbert, the relation between the model and the experimental situation has on this account an unfamiliar aspect. If we speak of its essentially novel content as a statistical concept, we can find an intelligible meaning for the otherwise tiresome caption that statistics is the science of averages.

This is not the place in which to do justice to an issue so controversial as the status of the *Principle of Uncertainty* or of *Indeterminacy* in the world-outlook of twentieth-century science, but it may be forgivable if we here pause to remark that certain limitations in what we can say with propriety about individual particles within the framework of a hypothesis stated in such terms are doubtless inherent in our initial assumptions about the model. It is therefore permissible to express a lingering doubt concerning the legitimacy of deriving what spiritual consolations so many contemporary expositors of science do indeed derive from Heisenberg's principle at a macroscopic level before we have conclusively rejected reasonable grounds for supposing that the paradox arises at the level of admissible recipes for constructing hypotheses acceptable or otherwise in virtue of their adequacy in the domain of practice.

Indeed, Jeans (*Dynamical Theory of Gases*) anticipates the paradox as a corollary of the restrictions inherent in the initial assumptions, when he declares:

In the gas of the Kinetic Theory we do not know anything as to the co-ordinates of the individual molecules . . . the problem we have to attack is virtually that of finding as much as we can about the behaviour of a dynamical system without knowing in which of the paths in our generalised space its representative point is moving.

It is the writer's view that the professional logician has the last word in the following passage from John Laird's *Recent Philosophy* (pp. 163–5):

The claim that Heisenberg's "uncertainty principle" knocks the bottom out of determinism seems to be a simple-minded mistake. Everything in nature is what it is, that is, cannot be vague. If precision in the measurement of position is unfriendly towards precision in the measurement of momentum, the trouble lies in the measurement, and is in itself a proof that accuracy of measurement is not the same thing as natural reality unless, indeed, particles do *not* have position, and do *not* have momentum.

In any case, it is an elementary confusion to confound this alleged indefiniteness of nature with "free will," that is, with "indeterminism." The indeterminist holds, say, that he moves his arm freely, but never dreams of denying that his free movements are perfectly definite. What he does deny is that they were inevitably determined by antecedent causes.

Accordingly, if there really is sub-atomic "freewill" quite different arguments must be adduced; and it is plausible to argue, as many modern physicists do, that the macroscopic determinism that astronomers and others assume regarding eclipses and the like does not necessarily imply microscopic determinism, even granting that the macroscopic is composed of the microscopic. For if the macroscopic is a statistical aggregate, it is illogical to apply aggregate-principles forthwith to the components of the aggregate. In life-insurance the death-rate for large numbers is the important matter, and such statistical aggregates do not yield direct information about the chances of survival of some particular insured person.

On the other hand, the difference between aggregates and their components does not even make it plausible to suggest that the former are wholly determined by causes and the latter not at all. There are causes for the death of insured persons (as detectives know) whether or not actuaries concern themselves with any of these particular causes. Again, if the components are determined it is not unreasonable to assume that statistical regularities will continue if no new causes enter, and that they will change if new causes do enter (as the death-rate changes when there is a war). If, however, the components acted quite capriciously, why should there be aggregate constancy?

If and so far as our measurements yield statistical aggregates only we cannot argue that because we know the (macroscopic) past and cannot infer the (microscopic) future, therefore we should abandon determinism. For, by hypothesis, we do not know the *microscopic* past. Moreover "randomness" is irrelevant. It could be induced in a pack of cards by a shuffling-machine without the faintest denial of determinism. Again, if "randomness" be the opposite of organisation, the human will, being highly organised, ought to be *less* free than most other natural entities.

Improvement of the microscope responsible for the discovery (1827) of Brownian movement also stimulated a new interest in the cellular structure of tissues, the recognition of the role of gametes in sexual generation* and the study of micro-organisms as agents of fermentation or disease during the last three decades of the first half of the nineteenth century. The discovery of numerical constancy of the chromosomes followed soon after. At more than one level the particulate concept was thus invading biological thought. We encounter it in Darwin's *pangens* incorporated in Galton's erroneous speculations on natural inheritance. What is more important is its role in a now familiar publication which appeared (1866) within seven years of Maxwell's first contribution to the Kinetic Theory of Gases. In this memoir Mendel records no experimental results which signalise an addition to factual knowledge of inheritance based on methods essentially different from those already employed by Thomas Knight, by Gärtner, by Naudin and by his contemporary Laxton during the course of nearly a century of experimental hybridisation. What is noteworthy is a wholly novel interpretation of results substantially identical with those of his predecessors and contemporaries.

The novelty of Mendel's contribution resides partly in the introduction of a particulate concept (designated a *factor* in the days before Drosophila, but now the *gene*), and partly in the postulate that fertilisation is comparable to randomwise choice of pairs of balls each member of a pair from one of two urns, though the author does not explicitly exploit the metaphor. At the most elementary level—unit character differences in the idiom of the childhood of modern genetics— we may conceive the balls in the urn to be of two sorts: black and white. We identify those of one urn as male gametes, those

---

* Brown was a botanist. Amici (1821) who first recorded the fertilisation of the ovule by a single pollen grain was a physicist.

of the other as female. We score the pair as a success if black-black or black-white and as a failure if white-white is the zygote. Mendel carried this conception further to interpret with equal acceptability the outcome of his own crosses involving two so-called unit character differences. We then conceive that each urn contains balls of four sorts and adapt our scoring system accordingly.

Unlike that of Maxwell, Mendel's theory failed to attract recognition from his contemporaries. When it engaged the attention of a later generation several circumstances were propitious to its reception. One of these recalls the part played by the study of Brownian movement in the background of Maxwell's own innovation. Mendel knew that only one pollen grain unites with the ovum of the seed plant; but the essentials of animal breeding were still obscure and controversial in his own time. In 1875 Hertwig and Fol first observed the fertilisa-tion of the egg of an Echinoderm. This observation brought the study of animal inheritance within the terms of reference of Mendel's hypothesis, but it is here of special interest for another reason. That only one sperm penetrates the egg is not the only noteworthy feature of a process we now regard as the keystone of bisexual inheritance. What is also remarkable is the fact that spermatozoa execute movements hither and thither in all directions like the movements of Brownian particles. Seemingly reasonable betting odds on the successful attainment of its goal are the same for any one sperm as for any other. All that we can see through the microscope is thus consistent with the conclusion that a drop of seminal fluid is one of nature's urns.

The reader should not conclude that such new knowledge of the material basis of inheritance led to any immediate and explicit formulation of hereditary transmission in terms of a stochastic model. What makes the Mendelian hypothesis of special relevance to our attempt to clarify the diverse current meanings of such words as probability and statistics is that Mendel himself never explicitly invoked the classical doctrine, and his foremost expositors developed the theory for more than a decade in opposition to Pearson's assertion of the claims of statistical methods without realising that the theory of the gene is a statistical hypothesis in the same sense that the Kinetic Theory of Gases is also a statistical hypothesis. That the theory of the gene did so develop without explicit recognition of the formal identity of the operations invoked and the basic theorems of the classical theory is instructive for reasons we shall examine in the next chapter. Here it suffices to indicate one relevant difference between the problems which Maxwell and Mendel respectively assailed.

In the initial stages of the growth of what we now call the theory of the gene, the main preoccupation of the investigator in the field was with clear-cut qualitative differences between varieties with a view to testing the relevance of the principle of segregation for a wide range of structural features definable in such terms and for a wide range of species, plant or animal. In such enquiries, the method of scoring is that of simple enumeration, and it is possible to exploit the initial assumptions by recourse to simple algorithms without importing a tailor-made algebra to accomplish the end in view. From one point of view, this simplicity of the formal apparatus gives the theory a unique interest in the context of our theme. For we can explore the implications of the use of the word *statistical* in a calculus of aggregates without the additional distraction of traversing a formidable terrain of mathematical operations. On that account I shall devote the next chapter to the theory of the gene as case material.

From another viewpoint, the compelling simplicity of the initial assumptions we make in the theory of the gene has a drawback. When the scope of the theory enlarges, and we then feel the need to interpret our algorithms in the idiom of the classical theory of probability, we do so with no disposition to examine our preference for the stochastic model we enlist. Nowadays, every biological student who attends a vacation course at Woods Hole, at Plymouth or at Naples, sees with his or her own eyes what Hertwig and Fol saw, as indeed did all the author's first-year students in the University of Cape Town. When we translate Mendel's interpretation into the idiom of the urn model, we do so effortlessly with little disposition to ask why we have chosen a model with the properties peculiar to it.

Our approach to the sister theory is necessarily different. Maxwell's concern was to explore the implications of the movements of particles *vis-à-vis* the relation of the gas laws to the physical phenomena contingent on chemical reaction involving molecular recombinations. Initially, then, we are dealing with a system of scores referable to speeds. We are thus in the domain of representative scoring, and indeed of distributions which admit of an infinitude of score values. All our particles—in a homogeneous gas—have the same mass, but their speeds are variable in virtue of the collisions. The initial problem is to define what we can say about the distribution of particle speed referable to a particular gas at a particular temperature and pressure within the framework of the assumption that the particles behave like elastic spheres subject to the Newtonian laws of impact.

In his memorable paper delivered to the British Association in Aberdeen, Maxwell (1857) attacked this problem by assuming that the molecules of a gas at a given instant may be anywhere. He endows the velocity of each particle with three Cartesian co-ordinates (u, v, w) to each of which he assigns a function which specifies a frequency definitive of its particular value referable to an arbitrary origin. He then cites the following conclusion. If $f(u)$ is the relative frequency of particles with speed u after unit interval of time in the appropriate axis of the Cartesian space:

$$f(u) = Ce^{-Ku^2} \quad and \quad f(u,v,w) = C^3 e^{-K(u^2+v^2+w^2)}$$

This relation is the foundation-stone of the theory associated especially with the names of Maxwell and Boltzmann; but the original publication does not make explicit all the steps in the reasoning which led Maxwell to advance it. Its importance resides in the fact that it embodies a *principle of equilibrium*, i.e. it asserts, without invoking any restriction on the initial state, what proportion of particles are moving at the end of a unit interval of time with an assigned velocity in a particular direction specified by the elementary rule for composition of velocities expressed in terms of Cartesian components. It is scarcely necessary to point out that this principle has a familiar aspect. The algebraic function which it embodies is one which had emerged from the soil of the classical theory of probability in the writings of Laplace. Hagen had dramatised its convenience in a domain of models conceived in terms strictly consistent with the classical theory.

Thus Maxwell had to hand a system of formal algebra uniquely associated with the term probability as used by the physicists of his time; whence his much-quoted aphorism "the true logic for this world is the calculus of probability, the only mathematics for practical men." A saying so strongly entrenched by oft-repetition would be less exceptionable if we could justifiably equate the practical man with the physicist of Maxwell's time. Even so, the form of words is mischievous, because most practical men, including many physicists, use the word probability, if at all, to describe a personal sentiment to which considerations suggesting the construction of models in the Hagen tradition have no compelling relevance.

We have had occasion to note that Hagen's choice of a classical model was quite arbitrary. It was not obvious in Maxwell's time that an explicit formulation of a model which incorporates all the assumptions appropriate to the dynamics of a system of particles is equally arbitrary, though the outcome has more comprehensive claims to usefulness. Few, if any, would now assert that Maxwell's formulation of the distribution law referred to above is a satisfactory proof in this sense. Indeed, a single citation from Jeans (*Dynamical Theory of Gases*, pp. 56–7) will suffice to disclose a lack of unanimity about the validity of the postulates he and others have invoked. Referring to objections w.r.t. his original deductive statement of the theory, Jeans remarks:

This proof must be admitted to be unsatisfactory, because it *assumes* the three velocity components to be independent. The velocities do not, however, enter independently into the dynamical equations of collisions between molecules, so that until the contrary has been proved, we should expect to find correlation between these velocities.

On account of this defect, Maxwell attempted a second proof, which after emendations by Boltzmann and Lorentz assumes the form given in Chapter II. It is, however, very doubtful whether this proof can claim any superiority on grounds of logical consistency or completeness over Maxwell's original proof. The later proof finds it necessary to assume that there is no correlation between the velocity and space co-ordinates, while the earlier proof merely assumed that there was no correlation between the separate velocity components *inter se*. In each case the dynamical conditions equally suggest correlation until the contrary has been proved, and it would be hard to give reasons why one assumption of no correlation is more justifiable than the other. It should be mentioned that Burbury was always of opinion that the later proof of Maxwell was not only logically unsound, but led to an inaccurate result. . . .

A second class of proof of the law is represented by the proof which has been given in this chapter. . . . As important examples of this class of proof may be mentioned a proof due to Kirchhoff, given in his lectures, and one due to Meyer and Pirogoff, given in Meyer's *Kinetic Theory of Gases*. Both these proofs are found on analysis to depend upon a use of the calculus of probabilities which cannot be justified. The proof given in this chapter is my own: it also has been criticised by Burbury.

It is not here necessary to examine such subsequent attempts to provide a better justification of the normal law of molecular speed components than that of Maxwell himself. By enlisting the same type of reasoning to describe the behaviour of a new battery of particles, more recent developments of physical theory have brought into focus more clearly than hitherto what assumptions we then have to make. The dilemma arising from one such set of assumptions is easy to grasp without recourse to dynamical concepts. If we speak of a randomwise distribution of particles in space, we imply that we assign equal probability to each of all possible configurations appropriately specified. This leaves open the question: how shall we specify such configurations? If we then conceive our space as a grid of cells to each of which we can allocate one or more balls, we may seek in more than one way an answer to the question at the level of stochastic theory conceived in terms of proportionate choice.

Given a grid of n cells, we may specify the number of ways of allocating r balls to the cells in accordance with different suppositions of which only 3 need concern us:

(*a*) the balls are distinguishable, and there is no restriction on the number 0, 1 . . . r allocated to one and the same cell;

(b) the balls are indistinguishable, and there is no restriction on the number per cell as before;

(c) the balls are indistinguishable, and one cell can accommodate only one ball.

If our problem is (a), the number of different allocations is n^r since we can put the first ball in any one of n cells and so forth. In the formal definition (p. 41) of algebraic probability in terms of proportionate choice, we shall say that any one of the n^r different patterns of allocation has therefore a probability n^{-r}. Now each of these n^r different configurations is one of a class of different linear arrangements of balls in the individual cells of one and the same cell-set in the same way. All members of such a class would be indistinguishable, if the balls were alike as in (b); but we cannot assign to every such distinguishable group an equal probability, without abandoning the foregoing specification of the probability assigned to each member (n^{-r}), since different groups will contain a different number of members. Thus the class of allocations specified by the fact that the hth cell contains r balls consists of one member. The class specified by the allocation of 1 ball each to the first r cells consists of $r!$ members. For the 7-cell and 6-ball set-up specified by the class represented in terms of balls (B) per cell and empty cells (O) as BOBBBOOBBO, the number of different members is $6! \div (1!3!2!) = 60$, if each ball is distinguishable and the probability of getting such a class specification is therefore $60 \cdot 7^{-6} \simeq \frac{1}{2000}$.

Specification of all possible ways of making the second type of allocation, (b) above, is not so obvious, unless we think of the n-fold grid laid out in a row, with one or more balls (B) in a cell separated from its neighbour by a partition (P), some cells being empty (O). For a grid of 8 cells to which we allocate balls, our pattern of one such allocation will then be:

$$P O P B B P O P B B B P O P O P B P O P$$

Only $7 = (n-1)$ partitions separate adjacent cells, and our problem is thus to state how many linear arrangements of $(n-1)$ partitions and r balls are possible. This is the familiar problem of the number of permutations of $m = (n + r - 1)$

things all taken, r being alike of one kind and $(n - 1)$ alike of another, i.e. $(n + r - 1)! \div (n - 1)! . r!$. In the sense defined above, we may then assign to any of the allocations specified by (b) the probability:

$$P_b = \frac{(n - 1)! r!}{(n + r - 1)!} \qquad . \qquad . \qquad . \qquad (i)$$

Our third type of allocation offers no difficulty, if we first assume that the balls are distinguishable. Then we can allocate one of the r to any of n cells, one of the remaining $(r - 1)$ to any one of $(n - 1)$ cells and so on. There will thus be $n^{(r)}$ different ways of making the allocation, but each such allocation involves $r!$ different linear arrangements of r objects taken all at a time. If the balls are indistinguishable, the number of distinguishable allocations will therefore be $n^{(r)} \div r!$ We may accordingly assign to any one of the allocations defined by (c) above a probability:

$$P_c = \frac{r! (n - r)!}{n!} \qquad . \qquad . \qquad . \qquad (ii)$$

Whereas we have seen that the specification of the probability of the particular allocation for a set-up of 7 cells and 6 balls as BOBBBOOBBO in accordance with (a) is approximately $\frac{1}{2000}$, we obtain from the definition of the event in accordance with (b) from (i) and in accordance with (c) from (ii)

$$(b) \quad \frac{6! \ 6!}{12!} = \frac{1}{924} \quad ; \quad (c) \quad \frac{6! \ 1!}{7!} = \frac{1}{7}$$

The three foregoing methods of scoring the event of allocating r balls to n cells of a grid as a prerequisite to definition of the probability of a specified grid distribution of the balls correspond to three different systems of scoring the position of a system of particles in space; and the initial choice of the scoring system leads to different formulations referred to respectively as: (a) Maxwell–Boltzmann statistics; (b) Einstein–Bose statistics; (c) Fermi–Dirac statistics mentioned on page 279. The formulations lead to different results. Einstein–Bose statistics give a satisfactory account of photons, nuclei and atoms with an even number of elementary particles. Fermi–

Dirac statistics lead to a satisfactory description of phenomena involving electrons, protons and neutrons. Maxwell–Boltzmann statistics are not wholly satisfactory for particles of any sort. "We have here," says Feller rightly, "an instructive example of the impossibility of selecting or justifying probability models by *a priori* arguments. In fact, *no pure reasoning* could tell us that photons and protons could not obey the same probability laws."

In the next chapter we shall examine the Mendelian theory of populations more fully to clarify the terms of reference of a statistical hypothesis as we use the term *statistical* in the experimental sciences without blurring semantic issues by introducing kinematical algebra irrelevant to the stochastic assumptions. At this stage it is already permissible to anticipate the main conclusions which emerge against the background of the foregoing historical narration. Accordingly, we shall define a statistical hypothesis in the framework of the Calculus of Aggregates as a hypothesis which explicitly invokes, or is interpretable in terms of a model of the die, urn, card pack or lottery wheel type in the sense that its properties are not specifiable in terms of the unique properties of a particular face, ball, card or sector. Though we may make certain initial assertions, e.g. about the shape or mass of all our particles, as we may make certain assertions about the colour or shape of balls in an urn, we shall otherwise confine ourselves to statements about the distribution of the scores assigned to the components on the assumption that such statements hold good, if, and only if, the sample is very large. When we interpret the behaviour of matter in the bulk in terms of particles outside the range of immediate inspection, the assumption last stated is trivial. For we are clear enough about the end in view. On this understanding, we may make the following assertions:

(i) the choice of a stochastic model endorses reliance on the algebraic theory of probability only in so far as we deem the algebraic theory of probability to describe its relevant properties in terms of observable external events;

(ii) the choice of any such model is arbitrary, as is the choice of any non-stochastic model which physicists of the seventeenth and eighteenth century invoked, e.g. waves on the surface of a pond or elastic springs in a viscous jelly;

(iii) what justification we deem to be adequate for such a choice is the same as adequate justification for preferring any one non-stochastic model to any other, i.e. the outcome is *both* capable of accommodating what we know about a certain range of phenomena *and* of pointing to new hitherto unsuspected regularities of nature.

From the foregoing summary two other conclusions are inescapable:

(*a*) what we do when we invoke the formal algebra of the classical theory has at no stage from the initial step in the construction of a statistical hypothesis to its final confirmation any necessary relevance to a concept of probability defined as the measure of our legitimate conviction concerning the truth of a proposition;

(*b*) what we mean by justifying the choice of an appropriate model is neither more nor less than what we mean by confirming the hypothesis itself.

The first of the two conclusions last stated signifies that we cannot legitimately invoke the success of the foregoing recipe for law-making as a justification for faith in a calculus of judgments conceived in terms of a definition of probability referable to legitimate intensity of conviction, unless we also define the word legitimate in a particular way. We must then define it in the strictly behaviourist framework of verbo-factual parallelism. Our definition of probability as a measure of our legitimate conviction that a statement is correct will then convey no more than the assertion that: (i) we make a statement in conformity with a prescribed rule; (ii) an assignable proportion of our statements will be correct in the long run if we adhere to the rule consistently.

If we restrict the proper domain of the calculus of probability to a particular class of external events, i.e. long-run score frequencies definitive of the behaviour of particular model situations, we are using the same language in the domains I have distinguished at the outset as a *Calculus of Judgments* and as a *Calculus of Aggregrates*; but the terms on which we invoke the formal algebra of the classical theory or the model to which we deem it to be appropriate will still be different. In the domain of the latter we justify an arbitrary prior choice of the model by whether it works; and a single *experimentum crucis* suffices to relegate it to the limbo of profitless speculation, if it does not work. In the domain of the former we can endorse the rule we operate only by correct prior choice of the model. We can entertain no hope of justification by works, because the rule permits us to make a mistake on any single occasion, and the criterion of its relevance must be the outcome of an *endless* sequence of experiments. We must then concede to Bacon that radical errors in the first concoction cannot be mended by subsequent remedies, however excellent.

CHAPTER THIRTEEN

MENDELISM AND THE TWO MEANINGS
OF PROBABILITY

THOUGH WE NOW recognise Mendel's theory and the super-structure raised on its foundations as an outstanding example of a statistical hypothesis in the same sense that Maxwell's Kinetic Theory of Gases is a statistical hypothesis, no one would have suggested the inclusion of a course on the theory of probability in a curriculum of biological instruction pre-requisite to the study of experimental genetics in 1913, when the writer attended Punnet's course at Cambridge—in that year the only one of its kind in Britain. The early stages of testing and extending Mendel's hypothesis after the inde-pendent rediscovery of the principle by Tschermak, by Correns and by de Vries (1900), followed shortly by the work of Bateson and of Cuenot (1902) who independently demonstrated the applicability of the principle of segregation to bisexual inheri-tance of animals, recall a story in the memoirs of Sherlock Holmes about the dog that barked in the night. The clue is (my dear Watson) that the dog did not bark.

As I have elsewhere said, our more conciliatory instructors in such days conceded the existence of two sorts of inheritance—statistical or *regression* and experimental or *alternating*. Otherwise, they advised us, and with good reason, that statistics had done a lot of harm. Should any reader of this book regard my *commentar* in Chapters Seven to Nine as irresponsibly facetious or as unjust to the memory of the redoubtable founders of the Eugenic cult, a citation from Bateson's book *Mendel's Principles of Heredity* (1913) will dispel the illusion. In the passage which follows we see the Galton–Pearson episode from the viewpoint of the outstanding pioneer of genetics as an experimental science in Britain:

Of the so-called investigations of heredity pursued by extensions of Galton's non-analytical method and promoted by Professor Pearson and the English Biometrical school it is now scarcely necessary to speak. That such work may ultimately contribute to the development of statistical theory cannot be denied, but as applied to the problems of heredity the effort has resulted only in the concealment of that order which it was ostensibly undertaken to reveal. A preliminary acquaintance with the natural history of heredity and variation was sufficient to throw doubt on the foundations of these elaborate researches. *To those who hereafter may study this episode in the history of biological science it will appear inexplicable that work so unsound in construction should have been respectfully received by the scientific world.* (Italics inserted.)

The index of Bateson's noteworthy exposition in which this passage occurs does not list the word probability or the word chance; and I have not been able to find either in the text. The following citation in which the idiom of *averages* is consistent with that of the author's argument throughout does indeed contain an explicit reference to *chance* in the English translation of Mendel's own original memoir; but it scarcely justifies the assumption that he used it with any awareness of its meaning in the context of the classical calculus:

In individual flowers and in individual plants, however, the ratios in which the forms of the series are produced may suffer not inconsiderable fluctuations. Apart from the fact that the numbers in which both sorts of egg cells occur in the seed vessels can only be regarded as equal on the average, it remains purely a *matter of chance* which of the two sorts of pollen may fertilise each separate egg cell. For this reason the separate values must necessarily be subject to fluctuations, and there are even extreme cases possible, as were described earlier in connection with the experiments on the form of the seed and the colour of the albumen. The true ratios of the numbers can only be ascertained by an average reduced from the sum of as many single values as possible; the greater the number the more are merely *chance* effects eliminated. (*Italics inserted.*)

We may seek an explanation of this reticence at more than one level. One, which has been the subject of comment *en passant* in Chapter Ten, is that the convenience of an algebraic formulation of the theory of the relevant models does not become imperative till: (*a*) the theory of hybridisation takes within its scope quantitative differences referable to many gene substitutions: (*b*) the genetical theory of populations advances beyond the level at which Mendel left it. Another relevant circumstance emerges from one of the foregoing citations. During the first two decades of the Mendelian renaissance, biologists in the following of Bateson and Morgan were mostly familiar with the calculus of probability, if at all, through the writings of Pearson, himself a staunch advocate of the backward look and of the identification of the concept of probability with a state of mind. For one reason or another, the pioneers of the Mendelian renaissance were one and all content, and well content, to interpret their findings by recourse to simple algorithms to which the Pearson–Laplace doctrine of inverse probability has no relevance whatsoever.

The bearing of these reflections on the present crisis of theoretical statistics will become more apparent, if we now set forth Mendel's hypothesis first in the idiom of the classical theory and then in the idiom of his earliest expositors. With that end in view, we may conveniently distinguish two levels of discussion in Mendel's own memoir. At one, he deals with the interpretation of his own experiments on what Knight had called in the closing years of the eighteenth century the *Law of the Splitting of Hybrids*. At the other, he asks and correctly answers the question: how does it come about that close in-breeding results in producing the pure stocks necessary for the conduct of such experiments? His approach to the first issue suffices to specify a stochastic model for the theory of the gene conceived in structural terms. I shall call this the *First Order Model*. His approach to the second foreshadows models of a different order as a basis for the genetical theory of populations. I shall call these *Models of the Second and of the Third Order*.

The First Order Model. Our first-order model will be two types of urn (A and B), the contents of which we identify respectively with the gametes of the father (A) and of the mother (B). Each urn contains an infinitude of balls, and we choose random-wise one ball from one of each type of urn. We identify the 2-fold sample (pair chosen) as a zygote. If we now appropriately prescribe the contents of each urn, we have all the data for specifying the relevant constitution of a zygote in terms consistent with the eighteenth-century theory of probability. That is to say, we can state what proportion of zygotes will have the specified constitution, if we continue the sampling process long enough, in other words, if we rear a large enough progeny of two parents with the prescribed equipment of genes.

To accommodate all possibilities which arise when our concern is with only *one* gene substitution, we shall admit two ways of specifying the urn contents consistent with normal chromosome behaviour:

(*a*) each urn may contain white balls only, black balls only or black and white in equal numbers (*autosomal* case);

(*b*) urn B may contain white balls only, black balls only or white and black in equal numbers, but urn A must contain either white balls and grey balls in equal numbers or black and grey balls in equal numbers (*X-linked* case).

A single example will suffice to illustrate how we accommodate situations involving more than one gene substitution. If we put two autosomal gene substitutions in the picture, we shall have to admit the possibility that both our urns contain balls of 1, 2, 3 or 4 sorts (blue, green, yellow and red). Mendel's own experiments at this level constitute a special case of a more general pattern which will emerge if we now specify the probabilities appropriate to the relevant unit sample distribution of the urn.

If we denote by p the probability of drawing a white ball and $q = (1 - p)$ that of drawing a black ball from either urn of (*a*) above, the admissible values of p are 0, $\frac{1}{2}$, 1 for all possible specifications of either A or B appropriate to the interpretation of Mendel's monohybrid experiments. When we also allow for the possibility (*b*) of sex-linked inheritance $p = \frac{1}{2}$ or 0 for urn A and 0, $\frac{1}{2}$ and 1 for urn B. We have then completely specified the problem for a given pair of parents or for parents of specified genotypes.

When there are two autosomal gene substitutions to consider, we shall have to specify the probabilities of drawing a blue (*AB*), green (*Ab*), yellow (*aB*) or red (*ab*) ball respectively by p, q, r and $s = (1 - p - q - r)$ with the restriction that $(p + q)$ can have values 0, $\frac{1}{2}$ or 1 only and $(r + s)$ can have values of 0, $\frac{1}{2}$ or 1 only as prescribed by the constitution of the urn, i.e. parental genotype. For the most generalised situation disclosed by the elucidation of linkage either $(p + s) = c$ or $(q + r) = c$ in which $c \leqslant \frac{1}{2}$ is a constant for the particular pair of gene substitutions. For the particular case $c = \frac{1}{2}$ we have $p = q = r = s = \frac{1}{4}$. This is a formal statement of Mendel's so-called second law.

To proceed, we have merely to agree about the specification of p, q, etc., and how to score the two-fold sample. We may then subsume as follows all the results of Mendel's monohybrid experiment by the following frequency distribution of pairs of white balls (WW), mixed balls (BW) and pairs of black balls (BB), if we distinguish p_a and p_b as the proportions of white balls in urns of type A and type B respectively:

WW	BW	BB
$p_a p_b$	$p_a q_b + p_b q_a$	$q_a q_b$

Since this expression is symmetrical with respect to $p_a = (1 - q_a)$ and $p_b = (1 - q_b)$, six situations arise. We may explicitly identify them by classifying our genotypes as R = WW, H = BW and D = BB, the matings then being specified uniquely by the numerical values of p_a and p_b:

RR $\qquad$ $p_a = 1 = p_b$

RH or HR $\qquad$ $p_a = 1$; $p_b = \frac{1}{2}$ or $p_a = \frac{1}{2}$; $p_b = 1$

RD or DR $\qquad$ $p_a = 1$; $p_b = 0$ or $p_a = 0$; $p_b = 1$

HH $\qquad$ $p_a = \frac{1}{2} = p_b$

HD or DH $\qquad$ $p_a = \frac{1}{2}$; $p_b = 0$ or $p_a = 0$; $p_b = \frac{1}{2}$

DD $\qquad$ $p_a = 0 = p_b$

The foregoing define all possible constitutions of the urn model of our mating system, and the general expression cited above then yields the following in agreement with Mendel's results:

Offspring:	R	H	D
Mating			
RR	1	0	0
RH or HR	$\frac{1}{2}$	$\frac{1}{2}$	0
RD or DR	0	1	0
HH	$\frac{1}{4}$	$\frac{1}{2}$	$\frac{1}{4}$
HD or DH	0	$\frac{1}{2}$	$\frac{1}{2}$
DD	0	0	1

Other possibilities are obtainable in the same way; and the only necessary elaboration of the foregoing model to accommodate the theory of the gene in the absence of mutation arises when there is an abnormal chromosome complex, e.g. a cross between heterozygous eyeless (*EEe*) of triploid stock and the normal heterozygote (*Ee*). Here $p = \frac{1}{3}$ for one urn and $p = \frac{1}{2}$ for the other. Thus the 2-fold sample frequency of the class eyeless (*ee*) is $\frac{1}{6}$, a ratio of 5 dominants to 1 recessive.

The Model of the Second and Third Order. In the domain of the model of the first order we ask the following question: if we can specify the genotypes of the parents, what is the frequency distribution of genotypes referable to their offspring? In the domain of a class of models we shall now deal with in less detail we ask: if we can specify the frequency distribution of genotypes in a generation of parents, what is the corresponding distribution referable to their offspring? We can make the last question meaningful only if we can also specify the mating system, i.e. the relevant conditions which prescribe how a male parent of a specified genotype mates with a female parent of a specified genotype. The outcome is the way the genotype structure of a population changes if we impose on it a particular mating system or selection. For any specified genotype, we express this by citing the general $(n + r)$th term of a series exhibiting its frequency in the $(n + r)$th generation in terms of its initial frequency, that of the nth. The necessary preliminaries may end, if we can express the genotypic frequencies of one generation uniquely in terms of those of its predecessor, in which case we shall require what we shall define as a model of the *second order*. It may be necessary to specify the grand-parental, as well as the parental, generation in which event we shall encounter *recurrent* series, and our model will be a *third-order model*.

For present purposes it will suffice, if we illustrate the specification of a second order model by reference to the particular situation which arises when our concern is with only one autosomal gene substitution. We shall then postulate:

(*a*) a pack containing N cards of nine types marked as such by the letters A, B, C . . . I, the numbers of cards of the several types being respectively a_0N, b_0N ... i_0N, so that a_0 is the probability of drawing a card of type A, b_0 of drawing a card of type B, and so on, in a single trial;

(*b*) a series of urns likewise labelled A–I, each constituted as follows:

A	white balls only;
B and C	white and grey balls in equal numbers;
D and E	grey balls only;
F	white, grey and black balls in the ratio 1 : 2 : 1;
G and H	grey and black balls in equal numbers;
I	black balls only;

The rules of the game are as follows:

(*a*) at each trial, draw one card from the pack, record its type, replace and reshuffle;

(*b*) draw *one* ball from the urn bearing the label corresponding to the type of card chosen;

(*c*) record the result as W, G or B in terms of the specification of the ball chosen.

Here the nine card types (A–I) stand for matings: RR, RH, HR, RD, DR, HH, HD, DH and DD respectively. Accordingly, the parental (*n*th) generation has the following genotypic frequency distribution:

$$\left.\begin{array}{l} R_n = a_0 + \tfrac{1}{2}b_0 + \tfrac{1}{2}c_0 + \tfrac{1}{2}d_0 + \tfrac{1}{2}e_0 = u_n \\ H_n = f_0 + \tfrac{1}{2}b_0 + \tfrac{1}{2}c_0 + \tfrac{1}{2}g_0 + \tfrac{1}{2}h_0 = 2v_n \\ D_n = i_0 + \tfrac{1}{2}d_0 + \tfrac{1}{2}e_0 + \tfrac{1}{2}g_0 + \tfrac{1}{2}h_0 = w_n \end{array}\right\} \quad . \quad \text{(ii)}$$

By definition $(u_n + 2v_n + w_n) = 1$, in the foregoing. We interpret our three classes of balls as the three genotypic classes of the offspring of the matings, viz. white as R, grey as H and black as D. We can then specify their frequencies by recourse to the multiplicative rule. Thus the probability that we shall sample in urn F is f_0 and the unconditional probabilities of getting a white, grey or black ball from urn F are $\tfrac{1}{4}f_0$, $\tfrac{1}{2}f_0$ and $\tfrac{1}{4}f_0$ respectively. We may then audit the complete balance sheet of the 2-stage sampling process by recourse to the addition theorem:

Mating	*Offspring*		
	R	H	D
RR	a_0	o	o
RH	$\frac{1}{2}b_0$	$\frac{1}{2}b_0$	o
HR	$\frac{1}{2}c_0$	$\frac{1}{2}c_0$	o
RD	o	d_0	o
DR	o	e_0	o
HH	$\frac{1}{4}f_0$	$\frac{1}{2}f_0$	$\frac{1}{4}f_0$
HD	o	$\frac{1}{2}g_0$	$\frac{1}{2}g_0$
DH	o	$\frac{1}{2}h_0$	$\frac{1}{2}h_0$
DD	o	o	i_0

Thus the genotypic frequency distribution (*g.f.d*) of the generation of offspring is:

$$\left.\begin{array}{l} R_{n+1} = a_0 + \frac{1}{2}b_0 + \frac{1}{2}c_0 + \frac{1}{4}f_0 = u_{n+1} \\ H_{n+1} = d_0 + e_0 + \frac{1}{2}b_0 + \frac{1}{2}c_0 + \frac{1}{2}f_0 + \frac{1}{2}g_0 + \frac{1}{2}h_0 = 2v_{n+1} \\ D_{n+1} = i_0 + \frac{1}{2}h_0 + \frac{1}{2}g_0 + \frac{1}{4}f_0 = w_{n+1} \end{array}\right\} \text{(iii)}$$

Here by definition $(u_{n+1} + 2v_{n+1} + w_{n+1}) = 1$. By giving a_0, b_0, c_0, etc., appropriate values we can now define the results of several systems of mating. For illustrative purposes, two will suffice.

(i) There is no restriction on the randomwise choice of parents, i.e. mating is *non-assortative*. For a parental distribution of R_n, H_n, D_n, specified as u_n, $2v_n$ and w_n in (ii) above, the probabilities of mating R_nR_n, R_nH_n, H_nR_n, etc., are u_n^2, $2u_nv_n$, $2u_nv_n$, etc., i.e.:

$$a_0 = u_n^2 \; ; \; b_0 = 2u_nv_n \; ; \; c_0 = 2u_nv_n$$
$$d_0 = u_nw_n \; ; \; e_0 = u_nw_n \; ; \; f_0 = 4v_n^2$$
$$g_0 = 2v_nw_n \; ; \; h_0 = 2v_nw_n \; ; \; i_0 = w_n^2$$

304

If we now paint these values into (iii) we get:

$$\left.\begin{array}{l} u_{n+1} = u_n^2 + 2u_nv_n + v_n^2 = (u_n + v_n)^2 \\ 2v_{n+1} = 2u_nw_n + 2u_nv_n + 2v_nw_n + 2v_n^2 \\ \qquad\qquad = 2\,(u_n + v_n)\,(v_n + w_n) \\ w_{n+1} = w_n^2 + 2v_nw_n + v_n^2 = (v_n + w_n)^2 \end{array}\right\} \quad (iv)$$

If these offspring mate randomwise without restriction, we start a new cycle and must accordingly redefine the constitution of our new card pack as:

$$a_1 = (u_n + v_n)^4 \; ; \; b_1 = 2\,(u_n + v_n)^3\,(v_n + w_n) = c_1$$
$$d_1 = (u_n + v_n)^2\,(v_n + w_n)^2 = e_1 \; ;$$
$$f_1 = 4\,(u_n + v_n)^2\,(v_n + w_n)^2$$
$$g_1 = 2\,(u_n + v_n)\,(v_n + w_n)^3 \; ; \; i_1 = (v_n + w_n)^4$$

The definition of the g.f.d. for the offspring will then be in accordance with (iii), e.g.:

$$\begin{aligned} u_{n+2} &= a_1 + \tfrac{1}{2}b_1 + \tfrac{1}{2}c_1 + \tfrac{1}{4}f_1 \\ &= (u_n + v_n)^4 + 2\,(u_n + v_n)^3\,(v_n + w_n) \\ &\qquad\qquad + (u_n + v_n)^2\,(v_n + w_n)^2 \\ &= (u_n + v_n)^2\,[(u_n + v_n)^2 \\ &\qquad + 2\,(u_n + v_n)\,(v_n + w_n) + (v_n + w_n)^2] \\ &= (u_n + v_n)^2\,(u_n + 2v_n + w_n)^2 \\ &= (u_n + v_n)^2 \end{aligned}$$

Whence from (iv):

$$u_{n+2} = u_{n+1}$$

Similarly $v_{n+2} = v_{n+1}$ and $w_{n+2} = w_{n+1}$. Thus the genetic structure of the population attains a constant state after one generation of mating randomwise without restriction. We express this by saying that non-assortative mating in a population classified w.r.t. a single autosomal gene substitution attains equilibrium in one generation.

(ii) Let us now suppose that only like genotypes can mate *inter se* as is true if there is only *self-fertilisation* or if there is *complete positive assortative mating without dominance*. We then admit only matings RR, HH and DD so that $b_0 = c_0 = d_0 = e_0 = g_0 = h_0 = 0$. Whence we obtain from (ii) and (iii) at one step the genotypic frequency distributions:

	R	H	D	
Parents from (ii)	a_0	f_0	i_0	(v)
Offspring from (iii)	$(a_0 + \tfrac{1}{4}f_0)$	$\tfrac{1}{2}f_0$	$(i_0 + \tfrac{1}{4}f_0)$	

If we now repeat the process by reconstituting our card pack accordingly as in the previous example, we get:

R_{n+2}	H_{n+2}	D_{n+2}
$a_0 + \tfrac{1}{2}f_0$	$\tfrac{1}{4}f_0$	$i_0 + \tfrac{1}{2}f_0$

Thus the proportion of heterozygotes falls off 50 per cent in each generation, a result Mendel himself gives, i.e.:

$$H_{n+1} = \tfrac{1}{2}H_n \; ; \; H_{n+2} = \tfrac{1}{4}H_n^- \; ;$$
$$H_{n+3} = \tfrac{1}{8}H_n ; \ldots H_{n+r} = 2^{-r}.H_n$$

*   *   *   *

The foregoing examples do not exhaust the uses of the second order model; but it may be necessary to introduce a 3-stage sampling programme, in which event we arrive at recurrent series such as (v) involving two antecedent terms, i.e.:

$$S_{n+2} = a.S_{n+1} + b.S_n$$

A single example will suffice. If we follow a system of in-breeding by brother-sister mating in a population classified w.r.t. a single autosomal gene substitution, all mating sub-populations will be:

I   *For parents* RR   RR
II *For parents* RH or HR $\tfrac{1}{4}$RR; $\tfrac{1}{2}$RH or HR; $\tfrac{1}{4}$HH
III *For parents* RD or DR   HH
IV *For parents* HH $\tfrac{1}{16}$RR; $\tfrac{1}{4}$RH or HR; $\tfrac{1}{8}$RD or DR; $\tfrac{1}{4}$HH; $\tfrac{1}{4}$DH or HD; $\tfrac{1}{16}$DD
V   *For parents* HD or DH $\tfrac{1}{4}$DD; $\tfrac{1}{2}$DH or HD; $\tfrac{1}{4}$HH
VI *For parents* DD   DD

For each of these types we require a separate card pack with appropriately specified values of $a_{0.t}$, $b_{0.t}$, $c_{0.t}$, etc., above, e.g. for IV $a_{0.4} = \frac{1}{16} = i_{0.4} = d_{0.4} = e_{0.4}$; $b_{0.4} = c_{0.4} = \frac{1}{8} = g_{0.4} = h_{0.4}$; and $f_{0.4} = \frac{1}{4}$. We shall also need to express the relative frequencies of fraternities I–IV by $f_t = f_1, f_2, \ldots f_6$. These assign the probability of choosing at random a card pack of the appropriate type (*first stage*), before choosing a card (*second stage*) as a ticket of entry to the appropriate urn (A–F) from which (*third stage*) we extract a single ball.

The Frequency Approach. As stated, Mendel cites the result embodied in (v); but he reached it by reasoning at a much less formal level. He says in effect: let us put the case at its worst, starting with a generation in which there are *no* homozygous genotypes. Then all matings are HH and half the next generation must be heterozygotes. The rest will be homozygotes. So only half of the subsequent generation can have any heterozygous offspring and only half of such offspring will in fact be heterozygous. In this generation the proportion of heterozygotes will thus be $\frac{1}{4}$. If we denote by $H_0 = 1$ the proportion of heterozygotes in the initial generation, $H_1 = \frac{1}{2}$ in the next, $H_2 = \frac{1}{4}$ in the next, and so on, we may therefore put $H_n = 2^{-n}$ as the proportion of heterozygotes in the nth or less than one in a thousand after 10 generations of self-fertilisation.

There was no noteworthy advance of this aspect of theoretical genetics till the publication of a memoir by Jennings (1917), disclosing remarkable results, including genotypic series for brother-sister mating and simple assortative mating. Like Mendel, Jennings proceeds from an arbitrary origin of population structure and, also like Mendel, invokes no calculus more elaborate than common-sense arithmetic. His memoir is the foundation of later and more formal developments of the genetical theory of population by Haldane, Sewall Wright, Dahlberg, Hogben and others, all of whom explicitly enlist the classical theory of probability. That Jennings could travel so far without its help raises the question: in what sense is the formal calculus of probability essential and with what end in view do we usefully invoke classical models such as the foregoing. The answer to the second part of the question is unequivocal. We do so, more or less profitably, to steer our way with as little effort as need be through a sequence of otherwise confusing operations; but the mere fact that we may then be talking about urns or card packs does not supply an answer to the first part.

To find one, let us now go back to the earliest class of problems which geneticists had to tackle. With no evidence to the contrary, we may assume that Mendel had not made a study of the algebraic theory of probability, his casual reference to *chance* being no more than current idiom. In any event, a corresponding statement would certainly be true of some of his foremost expositors among the pioneers of modern genetics, as the writer knew them in his student days. One has at least ample material for studying how they did in fact approach as teachers the class of problems subsumed in the epoch-making publication of the *Mechanism of Mendelian Inheritance* (1915) by Morgan, Muller, Sturtevant and Bridges; and we can retrace all their steps. We do not then start at the abstract level of Darwin's pangens. We proceed from a background of factual experience, more especially:

(*a*) that small samples of progeny may depart widely from the Mendelian ratios which provide a satisfactory description of a large pool of such samples;

(*b*) no visible characteristics of spermatozoa suggest that the genetic equipment of one class of sperms produced by a father has any influence on the relative frequency with which sperms so specified fertilise the egg;

(*c*) for all differences referable to autosomal gene substitutions the results of reciprocal crosses are identical.

We shall now advance the following postulates as a basis for a hypothesis which must stand or fall by the issue of experiment.

Postulate 1. In accordance with (*a*), we shall concede that statements we make are conceptually precise in the limit only;

Postulate 2. In accordance with (*b*), we shall assert that any two spermatozoa have the same opportunity to fertilise one and the same egg;

Postulate 3. We shall likewise assert that one and the same sperm has the same opportunity of fertilising any two ova to which it has simultaneous access.

For heuristic purposes we may temporarily disregard our first postulate. We shall assume a set-up in which there are three eggs A_1, A_2, and a_1 available to five sperms A_3, A_4, A_5, a_2 and a_3. If we lay out all possibilities gridwise, our picture of what *may* happen in fertilisation takes shape as below:

	A_3	A_4	A_5	a_2	a_3
A_1	A_1A_3	A_1A_4	A_1A_5	A_1a_2	A_1a_3
A_2	A_2A_3	A_2A_4	A_2A_5	A_2a_2	A_2a_3
a_1	a_1A_3	a_1A_4	a_1A_5	a_1a_2	a_1a_3

If our only concern is with the class designation A and a, we may condense our grid of equal opportunity by assigning to each cell a score of unity as follows:

	A	a
A	AA	Aa
a	aA	aa

	A	a
A	6	4
a	3	2

We then see that we can represent the *proportionate possibilities* consistent with the equipartition of opportunity for association for the 15 different zygotes in the original table, as on the left below. On the right, we attach to each class a border score specifying its proportionate contribution to the appropriate total population (sperm or egg).

	A	a
A	$AA = \frac{6}{15}$	$Aa = \frac{4}{15}$
a	$aA = \frac{3}{15}$	$aa = \frac{2}{15}$

	$\frac{3}{5}$	$\frac{2}{5}$
$\frac{2}{3}$	$\frac{6}{15}$	$\frac{4}{15}$
$\frac{1}{3}$	$\frac{3}{15}$	$\frac{2}{15}$

We have now exhibited one of the two fundamental operations of our calculus. The other emerges, if we set out the result as below:

AA	Aa or aA	aa	$Total$
$\frac{6}{15}$	$\frac{7}{15}$	$\frac{2}{15}$	1

With due regard to Postulate 1, such, in the context of Mendel's monohybrid experiments, is the genesis of what we call the theorems of multiplication and addition in the calculus of probability; but we have reached our goal without using a word redolent with subjective associations. We have done so by recourse to postulates referable only to external events completely independent of our convictions and sentiments. If we care to designate as probabilities the proportionate possibilities defined as above, we must therefore renounce any disposition to locate probability so conceived in the mind. Whether the earliest expositors of genetical theory relied on the visual aid of the grid to exhibit the operations appropriate to the postulates because they were unfamiliar with the algebraic theory of probability, because they rightly assumed that most of their pupils would be, or because the word probability had become tarnished by the metaphysical doctrine of insufficient reason, are questions to which we need not seek a definite answer. What is more material to the choice of our theme is that the foregoing schema records how they actually did expound the theory of the gene. With appropriate emendations it contains all the necessary ingredients for a genetical theory of populations. It is therefore not surprising that the latter developed so far without explicit identification of its operations with those of the classical theory of risks in games of chance.

Without asking any more of our grid than it can do for us, we shall now examine another consequence of Mendel's hypothesis. With this end in view, we may usefully make explicit a postulate which we might otherwise regard as redundant. We shall say:

Postulate 4. For parents of given genotype the proportions of offspring of a specified genotype are the same for all birth ranks.

For illustrative purposes, we may then apply our grid procedure to the situation in which the parental mating is RH, referable to a single autosomal gene substitution. In the long run, half the offspring will then be R and half will be H.

For 2-fold fraternities classified w.r.t. both genotype and birth rank, we may set out the table as follows:

1st birth

		R	H
	R	$\frac{1}{4}$	$\frac{1}{4}$
2nd birth			
	H	$\frac{1}{4}$	$\frac{1}{4}$

HH	RH. or HR.	RR
$\frac{1}{4}$	$\frac{1}{2}$	$\frac{1}{4}$

Alternatively, we may score the result in terms of numbers of recessives per 2-fold fraternity as:

R-score	0	1	2
Frequency	$\frac{1}{4}$	$\frac{1}{2}$	$\frac{1}{4}$

Our fourth postulate implies that each result for the first two birth ranks will be equally often associated with either possibility for the third. We may set this out fully thus:

	HH $\frac{1}{4}$	RH $\frac{1}{4}$	HR $\frac{1}{4}$	RR $\frac{1}{4}$
H $\frac{1}{2}$	HHH $\frac{1}{8}$	HRH $\frac{1}{8}$	HHR $\frac{1}{8}$	HRR $\frac{1}{8}$
R $\frac{1}{2}$	RHH $\frac{1}{8}$	RRH $\frac{1}{8}$	RHR $\frac{1}{8}$	RRR $\frac{1}{8}$

R-score	0	1	2	3
Frequency	$\frac{1}{8}$	$\frac{3}{8}$	$\frac{3}{8}$	$\frac{1}{8}$

More economically, we may now set out our grid for the result of a *fourth* birth with appropriate border R-scores as:

	0	1	2	3
0	0 $\frac{1}{16}$	1 $\frac{3}{16}$	2 $\frac{3}{16}$	3 $\frac{1}{16}$
1	1 $\frac{1}{16}$	2 $\frac{3}{16}$	3 $\frac{3}{16}$	4 $\frac{1}{16}$

Whence for the 4-fold fraternity we have:

R-score	0	1	2	3	4
Frequency	$\frac{1}{16}$	$\frac{4}{16}$	$\frac{6}{16}$	$\frac{4}{16}$	$\frac{1}{16}$

If we summarise the foregoing results, we have now the pattern for the *r*-fold fraternity:

	0	1	2	3	4
1-*fold fraternity*	$\frac{1}{2}$	$\frac{1}{2}$	..	..	..
2-*fold* ,,	$\frac{1}{4}$	$\frac{1}{2}$	$\frac{1}{4}$	..	..
3-*fold* ,,	$\frac{1}{8}$	$\frac{3}{8}$	$\frac{3}{8}$	$\frac{1}{8}$	..
4-*fold* ,,	$\frac{1}{16}$	$\frac{4}{16}$	$\frac{6}{16}$	$\frac{4}{16}$	$\frac{1}{16}$

Thus for *r*-fold fraternities of matings RH, the long-run frequency of fraternities with 0, 1, 2 .... *r* recessives are successive terms of $(\frac{1}{2} + \frac{1}{2})^r$, i.e.:

0	1	2	3	....
$\frac{1}{2^r}$	$\frac{r}{2^r}$	$\frac{r(r-1)}{2 \cdot 2^r}$	$\frac{r(r-1)(r-2)}{3 \cdot 2 \cdot 2^r}$	....

For fraternities of 10 this yields:

0	1	2	3	4	5	6	7	8	9	10
$\frac{1}{1024}$	$\frac{10}{1024}$	$\frac{45}{1024}$	$\frac{120}{1024}$	$\frac{210}{1024}$	$\frac{252}{1024}$	$\frac{210}{1024}$	$\frac{120}{1024}$	$\frac{45}{1024}$	$\frac{10}{1024}$	$\frac{1}{1024}$

We now recall Postulate 1. We shall talk only about what happens when our numbers are very large, or *in the limit,* if we need to be fastidious. With that reservation, we shall say of a sufficiently large number of fraternities of ten with parents R.H: one out of every 1,024 of such fraternities will contain *no* recessive members. Let us then suppose we have before us a 10-fold fraternity with no recessive members. If we actually know that the parents are R.H. we also know that we are the privileged spectators of an event we have roughly a one in a thousand chance of witnessing. We may agreeably suppose that we now imbibe two or three tots of Scotch at the bar, lose our notes and no longer feel quite so sure that the parents were indeed R.H. Are we to dismiss the possibility that we may be the recipients of this privileged opportunity? The answer is that we cannot do so, unless we hypostatise our own ignorance as the pacemaker of the external situation. Otherwise, nothing which our postulates imply gives us the slightest justification for making any such stupendously irrelevant decision. Our hypothesis must stand or fall within the framework of its original terms of reference which include Postulate 1; and this excludes our title to make any statement about a *single* 10-fold fraternity in contradistinction to a denumerable infinitude of 10-fold fraternities, i.e. for practical purposes a very large number. We are then accepting the hypothesis on its own terms—as indeed did Mendel and his first exponents— by pooling the results of individual matings.

By itself, the outcome of such pooling does not suffice to justify the assertion that the hypothesis works. To say that a hypothesis works in the experimental sciences means more than asserting its consistency with known facts, especially if we rely on such facts to suggest the background model. We ask also that it shall lead us to new and unforeseen consequences which are verifiable. The theory of the gene has abundantly vindicated its claim to inclusion in the corpus of scientific knowledge by providing practical recipes for establishing new stocks of guaranteed purity by procedures previously unknown to practitioners of animal and plant breeding.

In the same way, we accept a physical hypothesis on its own terms whether the model enlisted in its construction is a stochastic model or a non-stochastic model; and I have yet to learn that the physical chemist consults one of the new departments for the Design of Experiments in a University to help him to decide whether the Kinetic Theory gives or does not give a satisfactory account of the phenomena of freezing-point depression. If we seek a criterion for acceptance or rejection of any hypothesis in terms of the rarity of an event it can admittedly accommodate, we have indeed stepped into another domain, that of the Calculus of Judgments; and we have raised a new issue which invites enquiry on its own merits. Such will be the theme of our next chapter.

The Two Probabilities. A just assessment of the use of the theory of probability in the domain of the Calculus of Aggregates will clarify the task we shall then undertake. To get into focus the relevant issues which have emerged in this chapter, let us recall the argument of Chapter Two. We there distinguished between two ways of defining probability, the *formal* and the *empirical*. If we rely on experience to justify the choice of the model to which the formal definition is relevant, a preference for one or the other is equally consistent with a behaviourist outlook; and convenience for expository usage will dictate our choice. If we do not explicitly state the need for such verification of the relevance of the formal definition, the distinction becomes a challenge.

In the preface to the first volume of his treatise on the theory Carnap does indeed distinguish between different *probabilities*, one formal and ostensibly relevant to matters of judgment, one empirical and relevant to external events such as those which our present theme subsumes. The behaviourist will not dispute the contention that a distinction is necessary to describe two domains of verbal behaviour; and will even advance a plea for the substitution of separate vocables for Carnap's *probability one* and *probability two*; but the behaviourist will not be able to accept the compromise Carnap proposes. It is exceptionable, if only because theoretical statisticians (p. 22), are all too ready to invoke the successful application of a stochastic calculus in the domain of events to justify their claims to dictate rules of inference appropriate to the interpretation of experimental data. Thus the consumer naturally concludes that such self-justification derives its sanction from one and the same usage of the term probability.

I have already cited Wilks to show how easily misunderstanding of this sort may arise; and I disclaim any intention of blame if I here cite another example. Referring explicitly to the contemporary controversy concerning the credentials of modern statistics with a bouquet *en passant* to Kolmogorov's "complete axiomatic treatment of the foundations of probability theory," Feller (1950),* also a distinguished American mathematician, complains that "an *unfortunate publicity*" has been "given to discussions of the so-called foundations of probability and thus the erroneous impression was created that essential disagreement *can* exist among mathematicians" (*italics inserted*). He then assures us that "there exists no disagreement concerning mathematical facts" (pp. 6–7), an assertion which is not open to debate, if we choose to regard the theory of probability as a branch of pure mathematics. In that event, any axioms are admissible, if the outcome is self-consistent.

Such a view of its scope is difficult to square with the same author's claims for "the success of the modern mathematical theory" in the domain of practice, unless the criterion of success is the verifiability of the *end-product*. If so, the only domain in which the end manifestly justifies the means is the domain of Maxwell and Mendel. Contrariwise, the consumer should have the last word about whether experience justifies the *initial* axioms when the statistician claims the right to prescribe how to interpret and design his experiments. In that event, the consumer will be wise to examine such claims unmoved by the emotive appeal of Feller's plea (*op. cit.*, p. 7):

It is easy to decry theories as impractical. The foundations of practical things of today were so decried only yesterday, and the theories which will be practical tomorrow are branded as valueless abstract games by the practical men of today.

If it happens that the consumer has no disposition to rely on recipes of inference deriving no sanction from experience,

* *Probability Theory and its Applications,* Vol. **I.**

it is his right both to know whether such recipes are or are not referable to a definition of probability consistent with his requirements and to know that recipes referable to a purely subjective definition of probability have no title to share the spoils of the hard-won victories of a calculus conceived in empirical terms. From one viewpoint, Carnap's contribution is therefore salutary. If it receives the publicity it deserves, its only effect will be to infect the investigator in the laboratory and in the field with a sceptical temper towards the claims of statistical theory, a temper more in keeping with the traditional claim that science is the last defence of intellectual freedom in its perennial conflict with arbitrary authority.

PART IV

The Calculus of Judgments

CHAPTER FOURTEEN

STATISTICAL PRUDENCE AND STATISTICAL INFERENCE

TOWARDS THE CLOSE of the last chapter we touched on a question at the core of contemporary controversy in statistical theory: what bearing, if any, has the rarity of an observable occurrence as prescribed by an appropriate stochastic hypothesis on our legitimate grounds for accepting or rejecting the latter when we have already witnessed the former? The form of the answer we deem to be appropriate will define what we here conceive to be the proper terms of reference of a Calculus of Judgments, i.e. *statistical inference* as some contemporary writers use the term. Such is the theme of this chapter and of those that follow.

At the outset, it will forestall misunderstanding if we concede that some contemporary writers use the term statistical inference in a wider sense than as defined above, embracing any sort of reasoning which takes within its scope considerations referable to a calculus of probability. Such usage is regrettable, because the form of words suggests a more radical difference. By inference in the traditional sense of the term as used by the logicians of science from Bacon to Mill and Jevons, we signify rules which *unreservedly* lead to correct conclusions. By statistical inference, or, as we shall later say, *stochastic induction*, we here imply rules of reasoning which lead to correct conclusions subject to a reservation expressible in stochastic terms. We relinquish the claim that any such rule *always* leads to a correct conclusion. All we claim for such a rule is that it guarantees an assignable probability of correct or false assertion, if we apply it consistently to the relevant class of situations.

By an assignable probability we then mean the proportion of true or false assertions to which the rule will lead us in an endless sequence of such situations, and the theory of probability can endorse such a rule if, and only if, the assemblage of data for our observational record is the outcome of randomwise sampling. For the time being, I shall assume that this is so, and shall reserve till Chapter 19 an examination of what obligations the assumption imposes. On that understanding, we may specify the proportion of false assertions as the *uncertainty safeguard* (P_f) of the rule with an upper acceptable limit $P_f \leqslant \alpha$. Alternatively, we may assign a lower acceptable limit $P_t = (1 - P_f) \geqslant (1 - \alpha)$ to the proportion of true statements which consistent application of the rule will endorse in the long run. We may then speak of such a lower limit as the *stochastic credibility* of the rule. What limit we deem to be acceptable in this context is not a logical issue. If we commonly set $\alpha = 0 \cdot 05$ for illustrative purposes in the course of the chapters which follow, we do so because it is a widely current convention which will help some readers to feel at home in familiar territory.

In pursuing our theme on this understanding and historically as heretofore, we may conveniently distinguish between two sorts of statistical inference as *test procedure* and *interval estimation*. The dichotomy is provisional. For we shall later see that interval estimation embraces test procedure as a special case. Meanwhile, two difficulties beset our task. One arises from the circumstance that a strictly behaviourist formulation of the terms of reference of a stochastic calculus of judgments, as in the preceding paragraph, is wholly consistent with the attitude to test procedure adopted by only one of two different schools of doctrine; and its implications have come clearly into focus only since the contemporary controversy touched on in Chapter 1 has forced the contestants to make explicit latent assumptions lazily embraced by their predecessors. Contemporaneously, claims put forward by exponents of the alternative school have changed in response to criticism not previously anticipated. Thus our foothold on fact is insecure when we seek to evaluate the original intentions of the authors with due regard to the way in which the consumer has meanwhile interpreted them.

Since emphasis on differences of test prescription and on what each type of test can accomplish has shifted in the turmoil of discussion, it is not easy to circumscribe acceptably the connotation of the term *decision test* as defined by Wald on the basis of views first advanced by J. Neyman and E. S. Pearson in contradistinction to the term *significance test* as prescribed by the school of R. A. Fisher in the older tradition of Karl Pearson and Udny Yule. In this chapter, we shall therefore disclaim any attempt to verbalise the distinction with finality. Instead, we shall restrict our attention to the historical background of the controversy. Against this background, we may formulate a preliminary statement of what a significance test is and of what are its claims to usefulness, deferring a definition of the decision test as such to Chapter 15 in the context of an examination of appropriate model situations. Comments here stated *en passant* will therefore anticipate formal reasoning advanced more fully in what follows. Accordingly the reader may find it advantageous to defer careful reading of this chapter to a later stage.

We may trace the beginnings of a view of test procedure widely current during the twenties and the thirties of this century to the practice of citing with point-estimates in surveying and in the physical sciences an *empirical* assessment *either* of the precision index (h) prescribed by the Gaussian, as we now say *normal*, law of error *or* of some parameter of the distribution related thereto, more especially the so-called *probable error*. For a normal error distribution of known precision (p. 164), the probable error ($p.e.$) defines a continuous class of corresponding negative and positive deviations from the mean bounding half its total area. In sampling randomwise, equal probability thus attaches to the occurrence of deviations numerically less than and deviations numerically greater than the $p.e.$ The probability that a deviation from the mean will numerically exceed no more than three times the $p.e.$ is about 0·95.

Throughout the nineteenth century, those who followed this procedure did so with little disposition to claim that it embodies a major innovation of scientific reasoning. Nor did they need to do so. In the domain of precision instruments and of mechanical defects, it would be easy to cite a variety of situations in which the specification of a deviation from the putative true value of a dimension or constant has a utility none the less admissible because no professional logician would endorse its title to disclose a new formula for scientific induction. A single fictitious and over-simplified example from the contemporary setting of quality control (statistical inspection) at its most elementary (p-chart) level will suffice to clarify what we can legitimately and usefully say about a probable error in the Gaussian domain.

We shall suppose that: (a) a machine turns out lengths of metal wire of thickness guaranteed to lie within 0·98 and 1·02 mm.; (b) the variation of the thickness under normal working conditions is approximately normal with a probable error 0·004 mm. about mean 1·0 mm. Thus values which numerically exceed the mean by more than the guaranteed 0·02 mm. will turn up in only about one four hundredth of a very long sequence of samples during the normal production process. So long as the machine delivers the guaranteed product there is no need to interfere with it; but it may well run off a length of wire 1·025 mm. thick. The production engineer has then to face a dilemma. In which of two ways is he to interpret the event? He will know that the mishap may well be an extreme example of the uncontrollable vagaries of the mechanical set-up. He may also legitimately suspect that the machine has developed a fault which calls for repair. Without incurring the risk of having a large consignment of defective products on his hands, he can immediately settle the issue by an overhaul; but this spells needless loss of time if his suspicion is groundless. A plausible rationalisation of his choice therefore presupposes the possibility of balancing the cost of taking a wise precaution which may be unnecessary against the possible penalty of failing to do so.

His predicament is indeed on all fours with that of the reflective householder whose dog does not habitually bark in the night. There may be no burglar, when the dog does indeed bark. On the other hand, the risk may be worth the effort of getting out of bed, if there is enough portable property of value to conserve. Neither the householder who justifies his decision to make a search on these terms, i.e. as a wise rule of conduct, nor the engineer, who justifies the procedure of overhauling the machine as the less calamitous of two acts of choice, necessarily commits himself to an *inference* in the sense in which logicians traditionally use the term. To be sure, we might say of the householder and of the production engineer that each is testing the truth of alternative hypotheses; but the recognition of the rarity of the relevant event as a danger signal rather than the interpretation of its outcome dictates the choice of the test procedure; and the finality of the selected test has nothing to do with the rarity of the event which prompts its choice. If the dog's bark evokes the decision of the householder to go downstairs, he will admittedly be able to infer the truth or falsity of the hypothesis that a burglar is on the premises; but if he decides to remain in bed, he will also know before breakfast whether there has been an entry.

It suffices to speak of the engineer's rule as a rule of *statistical prudence;* but we may reasonably conclude that the theoretical statistician means something more than this when he uses a form of words so portentous as *statistical inference.* Indeed, some contemporary writers pinpoint such a distinction by using the term *conditional,* in contradistinction to unconditional, inference for what we here refer to as statistical prudence. Contrariwise, others make no such distinction and seemingly claim for what a test procedure can accomplish little more than the prescription of a wholesome discipline. If so, the research worker who embraces a test procedure presumably undertakes what may be a time-consuming programme of laborious computations in the mistaken belief that the statistician has much more to offer.

When we speak of testing a hypothesis, the form of words suggests a procedure for endorsing a valid verdict for or against its title to subsume new information worthy to take its place in the enduring corpus of scientific knowledge. The consumer has therefore the right to know that he is doing nothing of the sort, if the test is merely a *screening* convention to check rash decisions or to arbitrate on the advisability of following up a plausible hunch. An experienced investigator, with no illusions about the practicability of formulating risks relevant to further effort in numerically intelligible terms consistent with the professional ethic of scientific research, may accordingly prefer to rely on common sense, if statistical theory has nothing better to confer. The truth is that the distinction between statistical inference as an interpretative device defined at the beginning of this chapter and statistical prudence conceived as a discipline to forestall rash judgments did not become clear till Fisher repudiated the scholium of Bayes in his *Mathematical Foundations of Theoretical Statistics* (1921). This evoked a vigorous rejoinder from Jeffreys, whose confessedly idealistic approach to the theory of probability would not otherwise fall within the scope of an assessment of the present crisis from a behaviourist viewpoint.

Jeffreys propounded what Anscombe (*op. cit.*, p. 24) calls a *proper theory of induction*, i.e. a system of which the terms of reference are at least intelligible to those who find the initial assumptions acceptable. In controversy with him, Fisher consistently refused to commit himself explicitly to a definition of probability located in the mind, and, by so doing, enlisted the sympathy of contemporaries to whom such a formulation would be repugnant; and nothing in his earlier publications unequivocally advances the claims of test procedure as an innovation of logical technique. As controversy over the scholium sharpened, we can trace the emergence of a new *motif* in his writings. In his *Mathematical Foundations* referred to above, he elaborates the formal algebra of a test procedure essentially *en rapport* with that of his predecessors in the tradition of Karl Pearson, and in an idiom which does not provoke the professional logician to assent or denial. Only when controversy with Jeffreys had clarified some of the cruder implications of abandoning the doctrine of Laplace did his assertion of the claims of *uncertain inference* explicitly annex a procedure which the logician might reasonably have regarded as the more fitting preserve of a disciplinary precaution.

The treatise of Jules Gavarret mentioned elsewhere, signalises what seems to be the earliest intrusion of the probable error into the domain of natural variation. Therein Gavarret propounds a statistical approach to the evaluation of the efficacy of a treatment. It is in essence the significance test as commonly conceived in the twenties and thirties of our own century; but it seems to have exercised little influence on medical research in the author's own lifetime, perhaps because overshadowed by spectacular contemporaneous advances in experimental physiology. Meanwhile, there was a soil more favourable than medicine for the seed of the word. In the domain of natural variation, comparative anatomy was in the ascendant. Under the impact of the Darwinian doctrine in the setting of Galton's racialist creed and of the controversy over slavery in America, anthropometry became a fashionable academic playground. Thus we find one of the earliest examples of the use of the terms *test* and *significant* in their now current meaning in a memoir by J. Venn (1888) in the *Journal of the Anthropological Institute* (pp. 147–8):

But something more than this must be attempted. When we are dealing with statistics, we ought to be able not merely to say vaguely that the difference does or does not seem significant to us, but we ought to have some test as to what difference would be significant. For this purpose appeal must be made to the theory of Probability. Suppose that we have a large number of measures of any kind, grouping themselves about their mean in the way familiar to every statistician, their degree of dispersion about this mean being assigned by the determination of their "probable error." . . . For instance, the difference in the mean length of clear vision between the A's and the C's is about an inch and a quarter; that between the same classes, of the age of 24, is slightly more, viz. about an inch and one-third. But the former is the difference between the means of 258 and 361, the latter that between means of 25 and 13. By the formula above given we find that the respective probable errors of the differences between these means are one-twelfth and one-third of 3·7 inches, i.e. about 0·3 inches and 1·2 inches. The latter is almost exactly the observed difference, which is therefore seen to be quite insignificant. The former is about one-quarter of the observed difference, which is therefore highly significant; for the odds are about 25 to 1 that a measure of any kind shall not deviate by three times its probable error.

The above remarks are somewhat technical, but their gist is readily comprehensible. They inform us which of the differences in the above tables are permanent and significant, in the sense that we may be tolerably confident that if we took another similar batch we should find a similar difference; and which of them are merely transient and insignificant, in the sense that another similar batch is about as likely as not to reverse the conclusion we have obtained.

All this adds up to little in terms of the world's work, because anthropometry had then (as now) scanty, if any, practical value other than for manufacturers of ready-made wearing apparel or of school furniture. That reliance on test procedures so conceived suddenly becomes so universally *de rigueur* among experimental biologists in the twenties and thirties of our own century is an enigma which admits of no wholly satisfactory solution; but one clue to the mystery may be the fact that the influence of men such as Farr had already popularised interest in descriptive medical statistics in anticipation of public legislation to enforce immunisation procedures. By the end of the nineteenth century, the vaccination issue had indeed become the focus of a vehement public debate which provided a propitious setting for the reception of the views Gavarret had earlier expressed. Had it been true that men of science were themselves of one accord in the polemics of the last decade of the nineteenth and of the first decade of the twentieth century, the outcome might have been otherwise; but the opponents of vaccination could themselves claim enthusiastic supporters among biologists, for instance Alfred Russel Wallace. In such circumstances, a counsel of moderation could prevail against reckless washing of dirty linen in public only by taking the issue to a higher court of appeal with a better prospect of assembling a unanimous bench of respected judges.

Such was the situation when Yule and Greenwood published a memoir which was the curtain-raiser to the appearance on the stage of the statistician as arbitrator on matters about which trained observers disagree. The publication (*Proc. Roy. Soc. Med.*, Vol. VIII) of the last named authors bore the title *The Statistics of Anti-typhoid and Anti-cholera Inoculations and the Interpretation of such Statistics in general*. It appeared (1915) in the middle of a world catastrophe, at the end of which the notion of significance becomes for the first time prominent in a new *genre* of statistical textbooks, such as those of Bowley and of Caradog Jones. Meanwhile a generation suckled on the *Grammar of Science* and attuned to the controversies of *Biometrika* were rising to positions of influence in the biological world. Of such were Raymond Pearl in America and in England Major Greenwood himself.

By then, food shortage at the end of the First World War had catalysed interest both in deficiency diseases and in agricultural output. The former merits comment because research on the vitamins enlisted methods of bio-assay which rely on group averages in contradistinction to one-to-one correspondence of stimulus and response of one and the same individual. Food production is especially relevant because there was now a ready audience for the honest broker of the vaccination controversy, when R. A. Fisher (1925), then engrossed in fertiliser records, published a well-known textbook ostensibly addressed to research workers in general, though in fact almost exclusively concerned with the agricultural field trial. Almost overnight it became a best seller. In America, agricultural statisticians, there led by Snedecor, became the most enthusiastic converts to an evangel which is indeed a still unanswered challenge to Bernard's teaching and to the Baconian recipe.

Pari passu throughout the thirties, the use of statistical tests in the experimental sciences became more fashionable; but there was little inclination to probe their several claims in the domains of error and of natural variation. Meanwhile medicine remained aloof from the statistical approach to the therapeutic or to the prophylactic trial until unprecedented production of new synthetic drugs and of antibiotics on the eve of, and during, a second world war. An informed public now eagerly awaited a verdict on their merits. By that time, controversy concerning the current statistical recipes had become vocal and vigorous in mathematical circles; but its echoes did not penetrate the pathological laboratory. It would be unnecessary to write this book, if many men of science did as yet realise how little the College of Cardinals can agree about the rubric.

I have deliberately used the term *field trial* in the foregoing remarks. Such at first, and rightly, was the designation of what the statistician of a later vintage refers to as *experiment*; but the acceptability of the new title is instructive, because it focuses attention on a confusion of aims. The twenties and thirties witnessed rapid advances in techniques of bio-assay first as tools of pure research in dietetics and in endocrinology, later as the means of accrediting the reliability of products in commercial production. Juxtaposition of statistical tests employed in comparable circumstances in the milieu of the new pharmacy seemingly encouraged the belief that there is a common denominator for the objectives which a commercial corporation and a disinterested scientific worker pursue. As Abraham Wald explicitly defines it, and as several expositors of Fisher's methods for the use of pharmacologists define it by implication, statistical inference is this common denominator.

Perusal of the earliest prescriptions for the testing of hypotheses may well leave the reader in considerable doubt about what the pioneers did claim. What is clear is that they carried over from the proper domain of the Gaussian theory of point-estimation a body of concepts with disputable relevance to a new class of situations, when the immunisation controversy recruited the statistician as the arbitrator of truth and falsehood. The ill-fated marriage of the Gaussian theory of error with the empirical study of populations had already generated a sturdy progeny of misconceptions dealt with elsewhere. Hence we may record the event without bewilderment, even if the *ipsissima verba* of Karl Pearson, who played a leading role in the background of the debate, do not greatly help us to formulate a clear distinction between the scope of scientific induction as interpreted in the English tradition from Bacon to J. S. Mill and induction restated in terms of stochastic theory. We encounter an early use of the now familiar expression *significant difference* in a discussion (*Biometrika*, Vol. 8, 1911, p. 250) on the *Probability that two Independent Distributions of Frequency are really Samples from the same Population*; and it would be difficult to select a more forceful illustration of the *Backward Look* than in the following citation therefrom:

In a memoir contributed to the *Phil. Mag.*, 1900 (Vol. 50, p. 157), I have dealt with the problem of the probability that a given distribution of frequency was a sample from a *known* population. That investigation was the basis of my treatment of the "goodness of fit" of theory and frequency samples. The present problem is of a somewhat different kind, but is essentially as important in character. We have two samples, and *a priori* they may be of the same population or of different populations; we desire to find out what is the probability that they are random samples of the same population. This population is one, however, of which we have no *a priori* experience. It is quite easy to state innumerable problems in which such knowledge is desirable. We have two records of the number of rooms in houses where (i) a case of cancer has occurred, (ii) a case of tuberculosis has occurred; the number of cases of each disease may be quite different, and we may not be acquainted with the frequency distribution of the number of rooms in the given district. *What is the chance that there is a significant difference in the tuberculosis and the cancer houses?* Or again, we have a frequency distribution of the interval in days between bite and onset of rabies in two populations of bitten persons (i) who have been and (ii) who have not been inoculated in the interval. What is the probability that the inoculation has modified the interval? Many other illustrations will occur to those who are dealing with statistics, but the above will suffice to indicate the nature of the problems I have in view. (*Italics inserted.*)

For Pearson, as for Venn (p. 61), a difference is *significant*, in the sense that it casts doubt on a hypothesis, if the chance of its occurrence is very small on the assumption that the hypothesis is true. Thus it would not be easy to confuse so many issues with so few words as those of the query: "what is the chance that there is a significant difference in the tuberculosis and the cancer houses?" The publication of Yule and Greenwood (1915)* cited above, defines significance in the same way. At the outset, the authors give their own interpretation of the question: "is there a significant difference between the attack or fatality rates of the two classes?" To them—as to a subsequent generation of consumers—this is strictly equivalent to asking: "is the observed difference greater than we could fairly attribute to the action of chance?" The answer they seek, but without attempting a definition of *fairly* in this context, is indeed an answer to a different question: how often "errors of sampling would lead to as great a discrepancy as or a greater discrepancy than that actually observed between *theory* and observation." (*Italics inserted.*)

One implication of the foregoing is that we can first look at

* The first edition of Yule's *Theory of Statistics* published in 1911 devotes no more than three pages to illustrations of a method of testing the significance of a difference, i.e. the truth of the hypothesis that the universes from which different samples come are in all relevant particulars alike. The rest of the book deals with summarising indices devised in accordance with stochastic considerations in the manner of Quetelet with no explicit recognition of the need to distinguish between a rule of decision and a law of nature.

our sample and then decide what rule to apply. This we have already seen (p. 39, *et seq.*) to be wholly inconsistent with a behaviourist approach. Remarks on p. 171 have anticipated another objection, which we can get into focus more readily if we examine test prescription through the spectacles of the Forward Look. In effect, we then say that we shall reject a particular hypothesis if the deviation (X) of the sample score from the mean (M_x) of the distribution *numerically* exceeds a certain value X_r, so chosen that the probability assigned by the same hypothesis to sample scores in the range $M_x \pm X_r$ is $P_t = (1 - P_f) = (1 - \alpha)$. The choice of a *score rejection criterion*, so defined, raises a debatable issue at the outset. If the rarity of an observed occurrence as prescribed by a particular hypothesis can indeed endorse any intelligible grounds for rejecting it, there is still no obvious reason, other than the culture-lag of the Quetelet mystique, to compel us to define a score rejection criterion in this *two-sided* way. If our real concern is with the possibility that inoculation may lower the attack rate, our criterion of rarity will be relevant to the end in view only if we define it in a *one*-sided way, i.e. in terms of score values less than one which we may denote alternatively as x_r if the origin of the distribution is the least value (here zero) x may have, or $- X_r$ if we transfer the origin to the mean for algebraic convenience.

The distinction is worthy of emphasis, because writers in the Yule–Fisher tradition, though commonly disposed to adopt the *modular* (two-sided) rejection criterion when the sampling distribution is symmetrical, otherwise employ a *vector* (one-sided) rejection criterion without explicitly disclosing the relevance of the algebraic properties of a particular sampling distribution to the factual content of the decision involved. The use of the word *theory* in the foregoing citation from Yule and Greenwood helps us to trace this confusion of aim to its source. What they here *signify* by theory is the long-run mean value of the sample difference, i.e. *zero* if the universes from which two samples come are alike w.r.t. all relevant particulars; but in this context the word is an unwarranted intruder from the proper domain of precision instruments. We cannot here assume that any universe parameter has a *true* value which would suffice to define the sample structure if we did not make mistakes.

The situation to which Yule and Greenwood refer is in no relevant respect comparable to the class of problems we discuss in the Gaussian domain. No parameter of the distribution has any special claim to dictate how to delimit from the class of all samples a particular sub-class to which we may be able to assign a very low frequency. Indeed, we shall see that the repudiation of such an arbitrary choice is an essential feature of the theory of test procedure expounded by E. S. Pearson, Neyman and Wald.

It goes without saying that the adverb *fairly*, as used by Yule and Greenwood, begs the whole question at issue. The algebra which the test invokes tells us how often we should encounter a certain and arbitrarily defined range of observed values on the conditional assumption that the samples come from like universes. Thus the mere fact that a particular observation is one of an arbitrarily delimited class of values, themselves collectively rare, is *ipso facto* consistent with the possibility that the hypothesis is true. In short, the so-called laws of chance provide for the very contingency which Yule and Greenwood invite us to regard as inconsistent with the truth of the test hypothesis. This being so, one may find it difficult to sympathise with Greenwood's dignified expression of grief in response to the ensuing and pertinent comment of his doughty clinical opponent Sir Almroth Wright:

It cannot be too clearly understood that the mathematical statistician has no such secret wells of wisdom to draw from, and that his science does not justify his going one step beyond the purely numerical statement that—as computed by him from the data he has selected as suitable for his purposes—the probabilities in favour of a particular difference being or not being due to the operation of chance are such and such. There need, therefore, be no hesitation in saying that when the mathematical statistician makes free with the terms *significant* and *non-significant*, he is simply taking upon himself a function to which he can lay no claim in his capacity as a mathematician.

It is thus equally impossible to extract any intelligible definition of test procedure from Karl Pearson's earlier pronouncements or to pin down the expressed views of Yule and Greenwood in the publication last cited to a decisive statement which would confer on the term statistical inference any intention not implicit in the suggested alternative statistical prudence. The same is true of the book (see *Appendix IV*, p. 487, *et seq.*) which introduced statistical test procedure to a wider audience of investigators. In *Statistical Methods for Research Workers* (1925), destined to be the parent of a large fraternity of manuals setting forth the same techniques with exemplary material for the benefit of readers willing—and as it transpired, only too anxious—to take them on trust, Fisher's formulation of the rationale of the significance test neither discloses a new outlook explicitly nor clarifies views expressed by his predecessors. All that is novel is a refinement of the algebraic theory of the sampling distributions—with one notable exception embraced by Pearson's (1895) system of moment-fitting curves.

Without reading into the words of R. A. Fisher or of the authors cited above more than they would have conceded on second thoughts, we may none the less fairly define in broad outline under three headings the essential features of the *significance*, in contradistinction to the *decision*, test:

(i) we set up a single, the so-called null, hypothesis that one or more samples come from a hypothetical infinite population whose random sampling distribution is specifiable;

(ii) we decide to *reject* the hypothesis whenever the deviation of the sample score (X) from the *mean* of the distribution so prescribed is such that $P_f = \alpha$, if P_f is the probability of meeting a score deviation numerically* equal to or greater than X.

(iii) our reliance on the foregoing procedure places on us *no* obligation to specify in advance the size (r) of the samples to which we propose to apply the test, and hence no pre-assigned rejection score criterion X_r consistent with the agreed value of α.

---

* We shall return to this issue in Chapter Fifteen (p. 350 *et seq.*). As stated on p. 330, exponents of the test procedure are not wholly consistent w.r.t. the use of a 2-sided criterion here implicit in the word *numerically* in accordance with the choice of the mean as origin; but they give no factual reasons for adopting a one-sided criterion, when they do so.

For relevant source material with reference to (i) and (ii) the reader may consult *Appendix IV* on *Significance as Interpreted by the School of R. A. Fisher.* The third heading which draws attention to the most essential difference between the terms of reference of a significance, in contradistinction to a decision, test will occupy our attention in the ensuing chapter. There it will be necessary to examine the definition of the rejection criterion specified by (ii) in a more formal way than in what follows. Here our concern will be the content of (i) and (ii) in so far as they involve a still largely inarticulate conflict of interest intensified by amendments explicitly adopted to forestall criticism of the theoretical foundations of the test procedure without reconsideration of the saleability of the final product to a consumer fully acquainted with what the producer can now guarantee.

From this viewpoint, an issue raised in (ii) claims prior attention. We have assumed that the test merely prescribes when to *reject* the null hypothesis. Actually, the earliest exponents of the significance concept are by no means definite about this; and what seems to be the first wholly unequivocal pronouncement of R. A. Fisher (p. 500) is in the *Design of Experiments.* This first appeared after publications which prescribe another view of test procedure had already raised the question: when and in what sense can we legitimately accept the alternative to the null hypothesis? In the context referred to, Fisher's statement that the test outcome can sometimes disprove but never prove the truth of the null hypothesis is, to say the least, obscure; and it evades the sixty-four dollar question: what do we mean by proof in the domain of statistical inference? The reason for the afterthought will be clear enough at a later stage, when we shall examine (Chapter 15) the concept of test power.

If we do explicitly limit the terms of reference of our test procedure to rejection, it seems to me that we may interpret it in terms consistent with a behaviourist viewpoint in either of two ways:

(*a*) in the phraseology of p. 346, we shall assign an uncertainty safeguard to a rule which is not *comprehensive.* In effect we say: in some situations we shall reserve judgment and in others we shall make a decisive statement in accordance with a prescribed rule. We can then assign an uncertainty safeguard $(P_f \leqslant \alpha)$ which defines the probability of erroneous decision in a restricted class of situations; but we do so with no means of knowing how often the test will fail in the sense that we arrive at no decision at all.

(b) we shall impose on ourselves the self-denying ordinance of relinquishing the prescribed hypothesis only in exceptional circumstances as a disciplinary precaution against too ready acceptance.

Only the first of the two views here stated merits to rank as a technique of statistical inference in contradisdinction to what we might more appropriately designate statistical prudence. Either way, the utility claimed for the performance of the test raises the question: have we any more reason for deciding when it is important to reject than for deciding when it is important to accept a particular hypothesis? This at least is an issue on which the consumer may rightly claim to voice an opinion; and it is scarcely deniable that the laboratory worker who invokes a test procedure conceived in terms of a unique null hypothesis commonly assumes that the test procedure justifies acceptance or rejection on equal terms. Indeed, the present writer can see no reason why the investigator should shoulder the responsibility of performing an elaborate drill of statistical computations, unless fortified by this belief. A few citations (*italics inserted*) from the good books which have taught the laboratory worker to do so will show that he has ample encouragement for his faith:

(i) Many scientific investigations involve the employment of the method of framing working hypotheses and testing them experimentally. As long as the experiments fail to disprove them, so long are the hypotheses accepted. This is the general method by which statistical inferences are made . . . the probability level of the observed difference is calculated accordingly. . . . The hypothesis is *accepted* if the level is fairly high and . . . if the level is low (say below 0·05) the hypothesis is rejected. (Tippett, *The Methods of Statistics*, 1931, pp. 69–70.)

(ii) In presenting the results of any test of significance the probability itself should be given. The reader is then in a position

STATISTICAL PRUDENCE AND STATISTICAL INFERENCE

to form his own opinion as to the justification of the *acceptance or rejection* of the hypothesis in question. (Mather, *Statistical Analysis in Biology*, 1942, p. 21.)

The last source is of special interest, since the book carries the *nihil obstat et imprimatur* of a Foreword by R. A. Fisher; and it is therefore pertinent to quote (2nd ed., 1946, p. 194) the author in a context* which exhibits the investigator in the act of interpretation:

(iii) . . . which for 1 degree of freedom has a probability of $0\cdot30$–$0\cdot20$, *showing that there is no interaction* between the classifications, i.e. that the type of water does *not* affect germination.

Snedecor, the most widely read exponent of the Fisher test battery, is less explicit, but does not dispel the belief that acceptance of something is the presumptive alternative to rejection of the null hypothesis:

(iv) Statistical evidence is not proof. Even after extensive sampling the investigator may not reject the null hypothesis when in fact the hypothesis is false. For example, m may not be zero in the population, yet natural variation may be great enough to confine t to a moderate value in any practicable size of sample. Therefore when one fails to reject the hypothesis he does not thereby conclude that m is zero. He decides only that m is *so small as to be unimportant to his investigation.* (Snedecor, *Statistical Methods*, 4th edn., 1946, p. 47.)

In Chapter 15 we shall see why we can legitimately draw no such conclusion as the one last stated without due regard to what Neyman calls the *power* of the test. In that event, what we deem to be small depends more on the size of the sample than on its importance to the investigator. The writer disowns any intention of carping criticism if seemingly implicit in citing twice from Mather's book. Mather writes less as a logician interested in the test credentials than as an investigator concerned with its utility. His attitude is of interest in this context mainly because his words make explicit the only terms in which a hard-headed investigator will presumably welcome a significance test procedure as an instrument for validifying

* Here the null hypothesis is that there is no interaction.

conclusions reached in the laboratory or in the field. Should the laboratory worker turn to treatises written from the viewpoint of the mathematician, he will not necessarily find an interpretation of the use of the test inconsistent with the understanding that failure to reject is equivalent to acceptance:

> (v) We begin by asserting that the hypothesis to be tested is true. . . . We may calculate the probability $P(D > D_0)$ that the deviation D will exceed any given quantity D_0. . . . Let us choose $P(D > D_0) = \epsilon$ where ϵ is so small that we are prepared to regard it as *practically certain that an event of probability ϵ will not occur in one single trial.* . . . If we find a value $D > D_0$ this means that an event of probability ϵ has presented itself. However, on our hypothesis such an event ought to be practically impossible in one single trial, and thus we must come to the conclusion that in this case our hypothesis has been *disproved by experience.* On the other hand, if we find a value $D \leqslant D_0$ we shall be willing to *accept the hypothesis* as a reasonable interpretation of our data. . . . (Cramer, *Mathematical Methods of Statistics*, 1946.)
>
> (vi) Improbable arrangements give clues to assignable causes; and excess of runs points to intentional mixing, a paucity of runs to intentional clustering. It is true that these conclusions are never foolproof. Even with perfect randomness improbable situations occur and may mislead us into a search for assignable causes. However this will be a rarity, and with an appropriate criterion we shall in actual practice be misled once in 100 times and *find* assignable causes 99 out of 100 times. (Feller, *An Introduction to Probability Theory and its Applications.* 1950.)

*　　　*　　　*　　　*

These citations suffice to show that expositors of the significance test give the laboratory or field worker enough encouragement for overlooking the reservation specified in (ii) above (p. 332). That the investigator would indeed less readily embrace the type of test procedure they expound if fully aware of its implications will be clear enough if we now examine (i) against the background of the situation discussed by Yule and Greenwood in the publication already cited. The null hypothesis (H_0) which circumscribes the prescription of the test procedure in accordance with (i) on p. 332 is that our two groups (treated and untreated) come from the *same infinite hypothetical population.* This is the negation of the assertion that prophylactic inoculation is efficacious; but the main preoccupation of the investigator, who will commonly approach the task of carrying out the trial with a good hunch about the outcome, a hunch derived from preliminary experiments on related animals, from laboratory culture of bacteria or of viruses or from clinical observation, is in practice to establish the affirmative, i.e. to vindicate the credentials of a new instrument of preventive medicine. For what reason then should he or she be eager to take advantage of a test which can merely assign a low probability to erroneously asserting that the treatment is useless, but with no guarantee that the most likely result of applying it will be an open verdict, i.e. no verdict at all? We can justify the choice of our null hypothesis on such terms only from the disciplinary viewpoint defined by (*b*) on p. 334; but we are then using the idiom of statistical prudence rather than that of statistical inference. As Keynes (*op. cit.*, p. 300) remarks, the assumption

that it is a positive advantage to approach statistical evidence *without* preconceptions based on general grounds, because the temptation to "cook" the evidence will prove otherwise to be irresistible, has no *logical* basis and need only be considered when the partiality of an investigator is in doubt.

All procedures of the type under discussion, including the entire test battery of *Analysis of Variance* and *Analysis of Covariance* elaborated by R. A. Fisher and by his pupils, are referable in the last resort to the hypothesis that samples come from one and the same specified population in accordance with (i) of p. 332. If we ask why, the only reason offered is the reason given by Fisher in the context referred to above. So specified, the null hypothesis is seemingly unambiguous and on that account its algebraic formulation is tractable; but this butters no parsnips from the viewpoint of the laboratory worker who understands what he is doing. In an oblique reply (p. 498) to criticism of the significance test in these terms, Fisher admittedly invites the research worker to be the arbiter of the choice of the null hypothesis; but the motives which have promoted his own exploration of sampling distributions and the models set forth by all his expositors are inconsistent with such freedom and with his own unequivocal expression of faith in the infinite hypothetical population as the keystone of the test theory edifice.

In the set-up of the clinical trial, choice of a null hypothesis appropriate to the operational intent is never consistent with (i), since it implies that the two samples come from different populations; and the only hypothesis consistent with (i) is that the mean (M_d) of the sample score difference (d_m) in randomwise extraction is zero $(M_d = 0)$. The intelligible alternative to our prescribed null hypothesis will be unambiguous, only if our main concern is to make a terminal statement of the form $M_d \geqslant k$, i.e. to the effect that prophylactic treatment lowers the proportion who succumb to attack by a target figure (k per cent) deemed sufficient to justify its adoption. As we shall later see, we must then define our uncertainty safeguard in the limiting form $P_f \leqslant \alpha$ in contradistinction to the form specified in (ii) on p. 332; and this is true of any test prescription referable to a *discrete* sampling distribution, if we claim the right to prescribe a preassigned rejection criterion at any acceptable level.

The intelligible alternative $(M_d \geqslant k)$ to the null hypothesis that both treatment groups are samples from a single infinite hypothetical situation, signifies that each is a sample from a unique population; but Fisher's explicit statements· proscribe the choice of a null hypothesis conceived in such terms. What thus emerges from the pivotal role of the infinite hypothetical population in the theoretical superstructure of the significance test is a curious restriction. The terminal statement which the test procedure ostensibly endorses provides an answer (if any) devoid of operational value in the context of an experiment rightly undertaken to confirm a positive assertion suggested by prior information. Since the test procedure merely endorses the negation of a null hypothesis conceived within the straitjacket of the single infinite hypothetical population, the outcome will thus be an irrelevant decision or no decision at all.

The clinical trial sheds light on the legitimate claims of a significance test for another reason. It encourages us to probe more deeply into the structure of the alleged single infinite hypothetical population from which we extract two groups subjected to equally efficacious treatments. The truth is that the attack rate of a group of persons does not merely depend on what we associate with the treatment criterion. It will depend on age, medical history, nutrition and innumerable other changing circumstances. Thus our assumed infinite hypothetical population is not a fixture; though we may here concede that we can extract a very large number of samples from a factually finite population during a period in which relevant change is negligible. If we merely propose to apply the conclusion which the test endorses to situations in which relevant change is indeed negligible, we shall indeed do no violence to the canon of the fixed historical framework of repetition. Unless new circumstances conspire to make operative an otherwise latent difference with respect to the efficacy of two treatments, we may therefore reasonably continue to believe that their efficacy is constant if previous experience of an infinite hypothetical population conceived in the foregoing terms has justifiably convinced us that this is true; but then we must ask ourselves what we mean by *justifiably* in this context. For the judgment it implies, we assume some rational basis outside the framework of the test procedure dealt with; and the test procedure itself disclaims the title to justify such a conclusion, if the prescribed alternatives are reservation of judgment and rejection of the null hypothesis that our two samples, in Fisher's own words, come from the same infinite hypothetical population.

A new issue arises if we take courage from Fisher's second thoughts (p. 498) and choose a null hypothesis appropriate to the end in view. We then formulate it in terms of a target value k on the assumption that: (a) we do not wish to relinquish lightly the benefit of substituting treatment B for treatment A; (b) a difference as great as k is our criterion of minimal efficacy when we use the word *lightly* in this context. With appropriate choice of a one-sided criterion of rejection we may adopt as our null hypothesis either that $M_d \geqslant k$ or that $M_d < k$. If we choose and reject the latter our equivalent assertion is the former. In the set-up of the Yule-Greenwood trial, we are then saying that the adoption of treatment B (*inoculation*) will ensure a reduction of the attack rate by at least 100 k per cent, the alternative (treatment A) being *no* inoculation. This at least would seem to be a useful statement, if true; but closer examination raises doubt both about its usefulness and about its credibility.

For the sake of argument we have conceded the claim that the biologist, if convinced that treatment B has no effect in one milieu, may have good grounds for dismissing the possibility that it will be efficacious in a new one; but his legitimate assurance that $M_d \geqslant k$ is not on the same footing. Experience has taught him that epidemic diseases may disappear dramatically in response to changes of the social environment without intervention of the sort here signified as treatment. Hence he may well find that the advantage of treatment B has become negligible after lapse of a comparatively short time interval. Though we may define a framework of repetition in terms which plausibly accommodate the formal credentials of the test procedure with the theory of a stochastic model, we are therefore on shifting sands, when we seek to define our framework of repetition in terms of future conduct.

Nor does the mere fact that treatment A in a prophylactic trial of the type dealt with by Yule and Greenwood commonly means *no treatment at all*, restrict the relevance of the difficulty here disclosed. In therapeutic trials now zealously conducted on the same prescription, the dilemma is at least equally real. We have much evidence that: (*a*) otherwise indistinguishable bacteria may be more or less resistant to the sulphonamides; (*b*) widespread use of sulphonamides—especially in low dosage —results in selection of resistant strains. Thus experience of sulphonamide therapy which was much more efficacious than $KMnO_4$ or $HgOCN$ for treatment of gonorrhoea at the time of its introduction in the mid-thirties proved to be highly disappointing when used for British troops (1944) in Italy, where the German authorities had already distributed sulfa-drugs freely as a preventive measure to the prostitute population.

If we dismiss all the foregoing considerations, we have still to dispose of a formidable objection to the use of a statistical test procedure in the conduct of the clinical trial, and it is an objection which confronts the decision test of Neyman, E. S. Pearson and Wald (Chapter 15) no less than the Yule–Fisher significance test. It is now customary to assume that the problem of the *prophylactic* trial (e.g. whether vaccination is efficacious against attack), is formally identical with that of the *therapeutic* trial (e.g. is penicillin more efficacious than sulphonamides for the treatment of gonorrhoea?) The identification is admissible, only if we lose sight of the end in view. In the practice of preventive medicine our concern is with numbers, and the framework of our problem is essentially one of social accountancy. In the practice of curative medicine our concern is with the sick individual, and unreflective reliance on averages as a criterion of preference may lead us to recommendations inconsistent with the end in view.

That this is so will be immediately apparent if we look at the problem through the spectacles of Claude Bernard (p. 227). Let us therefore consider a fictitious situation. We may suppose: (i) that a disease D is incurable if untreated; (ii) that a clinical trial of the usual type leads us to assess the recovery-rate under treatment A as about 25 per cent and the recovery-rate under treatment B as about 50 per cent. In such circumstances we too easily then content ourselves with a recommendation to step up the recovery rate 25 per cent by substituting treatment B for treatment A. If so, our preoccupation with averages has blinded us to biological realities. If we are alert to the manifold interaction of nature and nurture, the outcome invites us to ask the question: what peculiarities are common to individuals who respectively respond or fail to respond to one or other treatment?

For heuristic reasons, let us now assume that: (*a*) persons with grey or brown eyes invariably respond to treatment B and fail to respond to treatment A; (*b*) persons with blue eyes invariably respond to treatment A but do not respond to treatment B; (*c*) blue-eyed individuals and individuals with grey or brown eyes occur in the population in the ratio 25 : 50; (*d*) our clinical trial groups are representative in the sense that the ratio of blue-eyed persons to persons with grey or dark eyes is also close to 25 : 50. On these assumptions the recovery rate would be 100 per cent if all D patients with blue eyes continued to receive treatment A and all D patients with grey or brown eyes henceforth received treatment B.

Doubtless, such reflections will not greatly trouble the mind of the true believer. If they do, the true believer may gain what reassurance the circumstances solicit from one of Fisher's most recent pronouncements. He states his matured views on the composition, location and duration of the infinite hypothetical population in terms which are worthy of citation* because the choice of phraseology suggests that the concept is less the reason for the faith that is in them than the *result* of the application of his method by the militant church of his following:

Briefly, the hypothetical population is a *conceptual resultant* of the conditions we study.

If such considerations are not wholly negligible in the set-up of the therapeutic trial, they are of compelling relevance to the task of the field worker in the social sciences; and it is agreeable to be able to cite one exponent of social statistics alert to the pitfalls which beset reliance on the concept of an infinite hypothetical population. Margaret Jarman Hagood's discussion of its status in *Statistics for Sociologists* (Second Edition, 1947, pp. 429–31) is worthy of citation at length:

In any test of significance there is a testing of some hypothesis about a universe from which the set of observations (a limited universe itself in this case) may be considered a random sample. That is, the logical structure of a superuniverse and the variation expected in random samples from it is the same for the observer sociologist as for the experimentalist. Imagining any experimental counterpart of the logical model is a more difficult matter, however. It is easy enough for the experimentalist to imagine repeated experiments under identical conditions, whether or not he can actually perfect his technique to the degree that he can reproduce conditions identically. His universe of possibilities can therefore be put into meaningful terms; it can at least be imagined, even if it cannot actually be produced. It is not so easy for the sociologist

* *Proc. Camb. Phil. Soc.*, 22, p. 700.

to imagine a set of observations repeated under conditions identical with those of one date. The fact of change in social and cultural phenomena renders unrealistic any conception of identical repetition of the complex of factors conditioning characteristics such as fertility and level of living. . . . To what, then, does the variation expected from random sampling from such a universe of possibilities correspond? Only a feat of imagination involving an infinite prolongation of a present moment, where conditioning factors remain the same but "chance" factors continue to produce random variation can supply the answer. With this done, the observer sociologist along with the experimentalist still faces the problem of interpretation of the chance variation—with the alternatives of ascribing it to the present limitations in knowledge or to the statistical nature of the occurrence of events. . . . It has been suggested that the limited universe of measures on all of a series of demographic units as of a certain date be considered a sample in time; that the random variations of sampling from a superuniverse have their counterpart in the fluctuations which would be observed if we made observations on successive days, or for successive years, while the general influencing conditions would not have altered appreciably. It is evident, however, that such successive fluctuations would not be independent, nor could they be thought of as being produced by forces independent of each other, and therefore they would not be expected to have the same distribution as those produced by chance factors in random sampling (as in fact can be shown to be the case). . . . Another suggestion is that the measures on demographic units may be conceived of as one of an infinite set of such measures secured by dividing the total area surveyed into different series of areal units by shifting of boundaries under certain conditions of contiguity and uniformity of size. The matter of the arbitrary nature of the "lumps" in which our demographic information is secured, and the possible variations to be expected by recombining the information into different lumps has not been explored adequately. While the matter needs attention, it is probably not the answer to the search for a realistic counterpart of the universe of possibilities and to the random variation expected in samples from such a universe. . . . At present, the sociologist must face the fact that the postulated, hypothetical, infinite universe of possibilities, concerning which he tests hypotheses to establish the "significance" of his results, is merely a logical structure, for which he can offer no real counterpart in his research situation. Then what is the utility of such a construct and of the tests of significance based upon it? The answer to this question is not perfectly clear at the present stage of the application of statistical methods to sociological research.

I shall not comment on Margaret Hagood's concluding remarks concerning the possibility that "a case for the use of such a construct may be made," because it is not the obligation of the research worker to bow to the dictates of statistical theory until he or she has conclusively established its relevance to the technique of enquiry. On the contrary, the onus lies on the exponent of statistical theory to furnish irresistible reasons for adopting procedures which have still to prove their worth against a background of three centuries of progress in scientific discovery accomplished without their aid.

CHAPTER FIFTEEN

DECISION, INDECISION AND
SAMPLE ECONOMY

IN CHAPTER FIVE (pp. 150–56) we have explored a type of test procedure which embraces model situations to which Bayes's theorem is factually relevant, model situations to which it may be factually relevant for anything we know to the contrary, and model situations to which it can have no factual relevance. Since the theorem of Bayes still casts a pall of irrelevant gloom over controversy concerning the credentials of test procedure, I shall now examine two different current views against the background of a situation which we may approach in accordance with the same three assumptions. Our model will be a fruitfly culture. We shall assume that it contains females of not more than two sorts when classified with respect to all particulars relevant to the question we shall ask, i.e. the alternative hypotheses we propose to test:

(a) they are normal in the sense that they carry no sex-linked lethal;

(b) they are heterozygous w.r.t. such a gene.

In accordance with the strictly stochastic modern theory of the gene, we denote the probability that an offspring of a female of type (a) is male by $p_a = \frac{1}{2} = (1 - q_a)$, and the probability that an offspring of a female of type (b) is male by $p_b = \frac{1}{3} = (1 - q_b)$. We shall assume that we are able to record how many of the r progeny of females chosen random-wise are males, and we shall seek to formulate a rule of procedure for deciding whether female flies with r offspring are of type (a) or of type (b) on the understanding that we can set a long-run upper limit (our *uncertainty safeguard*) to the frequency of erroneous assertion, if we follow the rule consistently. If we specify Hypothesis A as the assertion that the female is of type (a) and Hypothesis B as the assertion that the

345

female is of type (b), our assertion on any single occasion may be:

either Hypothesis A true and B false

or Hypothesis B true and A false.

Such a rule is a *decision test* in the most literal sense of the term; but it will help us to clarify the credentials of the *significance* test procedure of the opposing school, if we here speak of the former as a *comprehensive* test in the sense that it commits us to an equally definite assertion about the outcome of *every* trial in the assumed framework of repetition. As we have already seen (p. 332), we can make a more restricted type of rule to which we can meaningfully assign an upper limit of statistical uncertainty. For instance, we may say: (a) if the outcome of the unit trial conforms to a prescribed specification, assert that Hypothesis A is false; (b) if the outcome of the unit trial does not conform to the prescribed condition, say nothing at all. We may speak of a rule conceived in these terms as a *partial* test, because the assigned uncertainty safeguard is referable only to assertions about the outcome of a limited class of situations consistent with the sampling process. Since exponents of the significance test have lately (p. 333) found it convenient to accept this limitation, it will be instructive to examine the implications of such a partial test in the context of the model situation specified above before proceeding to formulate a rule which is comprehensive in the sense already defined.

All we have said about our model situation so far is consistent with three possibilities which we shall separately examine:

(a) we know that the culture contains flies of both sorts, and we also know how many of each it contains;

(b) we know that the culture contains flies of only one sort, but we do not know which sort;

(c) for anything we know to the contrary, the culture may contain flies of both sorts or of one sort only.

To define any decision rule—comprehensive or partial alike —in terms consistent with the argument of Chapters Four and Five, we must specify in advance both an acceptable uncertainty safeguard and the size of the class of samples subsumed by the test procedure as a basis for the definition of our criterion of decision—acceptance and rejection, if comprehensive, or rejection and reservation of judgment, if partial. For illustrative purposes we shall here restrict our discussion to individual female fruitflies with 22 offspring. The probability that the number of males in an r-fold fraternity will be x is:

$$r_{(x)}p_a^x(1 - p_a)^{r-x} = 22_{(x)}2^{-22}, \qquad \text{if Hypothesis A}$$
$$(p_a = \tfrac{1}{2}) \text{ is true}$$

$$r_{(x)}p_b^x(1 - p_b)^{r-x} = 22_{(x)}2^{22-x} \cdot 3^{-22}, \qquad \text{if Hypothesis B}$$
$$(p_b = \tfrac{1}{3}) \text{ is true.}$$

From tables of the Binomial Distribution prepared by Dr. Churchill Eisenhart and his co-workers* we thus obtain the following data relevant to the types of test prescription we shall now explore w.r.t. 22-fold samples, denoting respectively by P_a and P_b the probabilities assigned by the hypotheses A and B to a specified range of x:

$$\sum_{16}^{22} 22_{(x)} \cdot 2^{-22} = P_a(x > 15) \qquad \sum_{16}^{22} 22_{(x)} \cdot 2^{22-x} \cdot 3^{-22} = P_b(x > 15)$$
$$= 0 \cdot 0262 \qquad\qquad \simeq 0 \cdot 0002$$

. . . .

$$\sum_{7}^{15} 22_{(x)} \cdot 2^{-22} = P_a(6 < x \leqslant 15) \qquad \sum_{7}^{15} 22_{(x)} 2^{22-x} \cdot 3^{-22} =$$
$$P_b(6 < x \leqslant 15)$$
$$= 0 \cdot 9476 \qquad\qquad \simeq 0 \cdot 6380$$

. . . .

$$\sum_{0}^{6} 22_{(x)} \cdot 2^{-22} = P_a(x \leqslant 6) \qquad \sum_{0}^{6} 22_{(x)} \cdot 2^{22-x} \cdot 3^{-22} = P_b(x \leqslant 6)$$
$$= 0 \cdot 0262 \qquad\qquad = 0 \cdot 3618$$

We may thus arbitrarily split our range of sample score

* *Tables of the Binomial Probability Distribution.* U.S. Dept. of Commerce, National Bureau of Standards, Applied Mathematics Series No. 6. Washington, 1949.

values (0, 1 . . . . 21, 22 males) with probabilities assignable on the alternative prescribed hypotheses as below:

On Hypothesis A

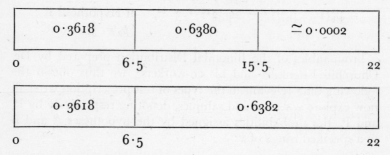

0·0262	0·9476	0·0262

0   6·5   15·5   22

On Hypothesis B

0·3618	0·6380	≃ 0·0002

0   6·5   15·5   22

0·3618	0·6382

0   6·5   22

Our sole reason for making the split in this way is that we can examine the implications of the Fisher test theory without relinquishing the 5 per cent feeling it confers. On Hypothesis A, the mean of the distribution is 11 and the range of scores from 7 to 15, i.e. all admissible scores in the range $11 \pm 4·5$, defines a class of samples which conform to the 2-fold condition that they: (a) lie symmetrically about the mean; (b) include nearly 95 per cent of those which we meet in an endless sequence of randomwise trials. In the situation before us there is no compelling reason why we should prefer Hypothesis A to Hypothesis B as our null hypothesis in Fisher's sense, since neither is ambiguous and one is just as tractable as the other in terms of algebra or computation. If we here choose Hypothesis A, we do so because: (i) most laboratory workers brought up on the good books are apt to identify the null hypothesis with the more conservative hypothesis; (ii) neither Fisher nor his disciples clearly specify the criterion for preferring a modular (two-sided) criterion of rejection rather than a vector (one-sided) when the distribution happens, as is prescribed by Hypothesis B, to be skew.

If we now proceed as we should proceed in accordance with the prescribed significance test drill, we have already made an important concession to the Forward Look by stating our rule in the form:

(a) reject Hypothesis A if the score lies outside the range 7 to 15 inclusive *for the 22-fold sample*,

(b) otherwise reserve judgment.

The rule so stated prescribes that we shall reject the null hypothesis when true only in $5 \cdot 2$ per cent of the situations we encounter; and this may sound like the same thing as saying that we reject it at the $5 \cdot 2$ per cent significance level; but by stating the rule as above, we have relinquished the right to look at the sample before we specify the score rejection criterion. Contrariwise, the customary significance test procedure endorses our right to say that we shall reject the null hypothesis, if:

(a) the score is $X_r = \pm (x - M)$ if the sample contains x males

(b) $P(M \pm \overline{x - 1}) \geqslant 0 \cdot 948$, i.e. a deviation from the mean of the distribution numerically *as great as* X_r has a probability of $0 \cdot 052$ for samples of the same size as the observed one.

In accordance with decision test procedure, we here say that *not more* than $5 \cdot 2$ per cent of our assertions will be false *about samples of 22 offspring* if we reject the null hypothesis (here Hypothesis A) when x is less than 7 or more than 15. Thus we have implicitly shouldered the obligation to specify the size of the sample, and hence a score rejection criterion *before* we examine the evidence. At this stage, some reader may regard this as a distinction without a difference; but a fuller examination of our model situation will disclose an eminently practical reason for insistence on preliminary specification of sample size other than an unduly fastidious concern for the statement of a formula consistent with the Forward Look.

First let us examine our rule against the background of the alternative admissible assumptions on the understanding that our rule permits us only to say that Hypothesis A is false and otherwise to reserve judgment. If Hypothesis A is actually true, this means that roughly 5 per cent of our assertions will be false; but if Hypothesis B is true, none of our statements will be false, since we have excluded our right to say that Hypothesis A is the correct one. Thus at most, not more than about 5 per cent (more closely 5·2 per cent) of any statements we make within the framework of the rule can be erroneous.

Before scrutinising more closely a so seemingly gratifying conclusion, we shall do well to notice *en passant* that we have picked up an unnecessary encumbrance in our wanderings within the shadowy domain of the infinite hypothetical population. We are much less likely to meet scores of over 15 if Hypothesis B is true than otherwise. All that is relevant to the rule of decision to which we seek to attach an uncertainty safeguard at an acceptable level (here assumed to be 5·2 per cent) is that the number of males in the sample will be greater in the long run if Hypothesis A is true than it will be if Hypothesis B is true. Why therefore should we carry over from the Gaussian domain the inclination to use a 2-sided rejection criterion referable to an irrelevant mean value? Why should we not more boldly state that we shall reject Hypothesis A if $x < 6$ and otherwise reserve judgment? Since $P_f \simeq 0.026$, we are then entitled to attach an upper limit of approximately 2·6 per cent to the uncertainty safeguard of the rule.

Let us now look at the issue, as we have seen from the citations on pp. 334–335 that the consumer customarily does look at it, and with every encouragement from the good books. We may reasonably assume that we need not go to great trouble to gratify the whims of a particular school of statistical theory without the assurance that it provides a recipe for arriving at a decision one way or the other. We shall accordingly modify the statement of the foregoing by substituting the words *accept Hypothesis B* for the words *reserve judgment*. We must then adopt a one-sided rejection criterion, and may formulate a comprehensive rule in the following terms:

(i) reject Hypothesis A (and hence accept Hypothesis B) if $x \leqslant 6$,

(ii) accept Hypothesis A (and hence reject Hypothesis B) if $x > 6$.

In the terminology of Neyman and of E. S. Pearson (*Proc. Camb. Phil. Soc.* 29, 1933) we may here make errors of two kinds:

A. We may reject Hypothesis A when it is true, thus accepting Hypothesis B when it is false with conditional probability α.

B. We may accept Hypothesis A when it is false, thus rejecting Hypothesis B when it is true with conditional probability β.

When we designate Hypothesis A as the null hypothesis, the sample score as x and the rejection score criterion as x_r, we may write:

$P_{x.a}(x \leqslant x_r) = \alpha$ as the conditional probability of making an *error of the first kind*

$P_{x.b}(x > x_r) = \beta$ as the conditional probability of making an *error of the second kind*.

For the comprehensive rule last stated, x is the number of males, $r = 22$ and we set:

$x_r = 6$; $P_{x.a}(x \leqslant 6) = \alpha = 0\cdot0262$; $P_{x.b}(x > 6) = \beta = 0\cdot6382$

We may cover all three possibilities embraced by picking out from our culture *at random* female fruitflies with 22 offspring, if we postulate that: (*a*) the proportion of normal females is P_a, that of lethal carriers being $P_b = (1 - P_a)$; (*b*) the value of P_a lies in the range $0 - 1$ inclusive, being unity when all the flies are normal and zero if all are carriers. The probability of all possible results of the test procedure then follows from the multiplication theorem, viz.:

(i) Hypothesis A is true and we accept it: $P_a(1 - \alpha)$

(ii)   *ditto*   but we reject it: $P_a \cdot \alpha$

(iii) Hypothesis B is true and we accept it: $P_b(1 - \beta)$

(iv)   *ditto*   but we reject it: $P_b \cdot \beta$

By the addition theorem we thus derive:

Probability of *True* assertion:

$$P_t = P_a(1 - \alpha) + (1 - P_a)(1 - \beta) = 1 - \beta + P_a(\beta - \alpha) \quad (i)$$

Probability of *False* assertion:

$$P_f = P_a \cdot \alpha + (1 - P_a)\beta = \beta + P_a(\alpha - \beta) \quad . \quad (ii)$$

In the foregoing situation $\alpha = 0 \cdot 0262$ and $\beta = 0 \cdot 6382$, $(1 - \beta) = 0 \cdot 3618$ and $(\alpha - \beta) = -0 \cdot 6120$, so that

$$P_f = 0 \cdot 6382 - P_a(0 \cdot 6120)$$

We may now tabulate the uncertainty safeguard of the rule for different possible proportions of normal flies in the culture, i.e. different prior probabilities which we can assign to the null hypothesis in accordance with our assumption that the culture contains each of these two sorts of female fruitflies, one chosen randomwise for each test performance

$P_a =$	$P_f \simeq$
0·999	0·027
0·990	0·032
0·900	0·087
0·500	0·332
0·200	0·516
0·050	0·608
0·001	0·638

We see from this what is formally evident from (ii):

(i) As P_a approaches unity, i.e. when nearly all the females conform to the specification of the null hypothesis (Hypothesis A), P_f approaches α more and more closely;

(ii) as P_a approaches zero, i.e. when nearly all the females are lethal carriers and thus do *not* conform to the null hypothesis, P_f approaches more and more closely to β.

It is now easy to state the result of the test procedure, when we conceive the situation in terms of *sampling in one stage:* i.e. we know that the culture contains only one sort of fly, but not which sort. This is the situation in which we commonly find ourselves, when we talk about testing the truth of a hypothesis. If Hypothesis A is true, we cannot make an error of the second kind and $P_f = \alpha$. If Hypothesis B is true, we cannot make an error of the first kind and $P_f = \beta$. All we can say is that $\beta \geqslant P_j \geqslant \alpha$ (if $\beta > \alpha$) or $\alpha \geqslant P_j \geqslant \beta$ (if $\alpha > \beta$). This interpretation of the rule covers the case which arises when we do not know whether the culture contains both sorts of fruitflies or one only, since we then assume that P_a can have any value in the range o to 1 as above.

The reader will now see why it is necessary for the exponents of the significance test conceived as such in terms of a single null hypothesis without reference to any alternative must needs insist that the outcome of their test prescription does not entitle the performer to *accept* it. In this case the adoption of a rejection criterion, which confers on a *partial* decision rule with this restriction an uncertainty safeguard $\alpha \leqslant 0 \cdot 026$, entitles us to say no more about the result of operating the corresponding comprehensive rule, i.e. acceptance of the null hypothesis when we do not reject it, than that nearly 64 per cent of the assertions the rule endorses might be false in the long run.

To operate a comprehensive decision rule which takes stock of admissible alternative hypotheses, we have therefore to choose our rejection criterion with due regard to the conditional probability (β) of error of the second kind as well as to the so-called significance level (α) referable to the error of the first kind. From inspection of (ii) we see that $P_j = \alpha$, if $\beta = \alpha$, and we cannot decrease β for a prescribed sample size unless we increase α. For example, our tables show that $P_{x.a}(x \leqslant 9) \simeq 0 \cdot 462$ and $P_{x.b}(x > 9) \simeq 0 \cdot 162$ for 22-fold samples. If we choose to reject the null hypothesis when the score (male offspring) is less than 10, we shall reject Hypothesis B if true in only about 16 per cent of samples which we shall then encounter; but we shall now reject Hypothesis A if true in about 46 per cent of samples we shall then encounter. To prescribe a comprehensive test procedure consistent with a preassigned acceptable uncertainty safeguard we must thus define our sample size (r) in advance.

This will be a laborious procedure, if we use the tables of

the binomial, but we can define a standard score of unit variance with an approximately normal distribution if r is fairly large (see p. 160), i.e. for the hypotheses under consideration $r > 30$. If $p_h = (1 - q_h)$ is the long-run proportion of male offspring on hypothesis H, and x is the actual number in the r-fold sample, the corresponding square standard score is

$$\frac{(x - r \cdot p_h)^2}{r \cdot p_h \cdot q_h} = c_h^2$$

In the situation we here examine for illustrative purposes, we have

$$p_a = \tfrac{1}{2} \; ; \; c_a = \frac{2x - r}{\sqrt{r}} \qquad \cdots \qquad \text{(iii)}$$

$$p_b = \tfrac{1}{3} \; ; \; c_b = \frac{3x - r}{\sqrt{2r}} \qquad \cdots \qquad \text{(iv)}$$

If we wish to make $P_f = \alpha$, in which event $\alpha = \beta$, we shall choose our rejection score criterion (x_r) so that $c_b = -c_a$, whence

$$x_r = \frac{(1 + \sqrt{2})r}{3 + 2\sqrt{2}} \simeq 0 \cdot 414r \qquad \cdots \qquad \text{(v)}$$

Let us then assign as our acceptable uncertainty safeguard $P_f \leqslant 0 \cdot 05$. The table of the integral shows that $0 \cdot 05$ of the normal curve lies in the region from $-\infty$ to $c_h = -1 \cdot 64$ or from $c_h = +1 \cdot 64$ to $+\infty$. Whence by substitution in (iii), we get

$$\sqrt{r} = \frac{1 \cdot 64}{0 \cdot 182} \simeq 9 \cdot 01$$

$$r \simeq 81 \cdot 2$$

Also from (v), $x = 33 \cdot 9$. We shall thus guarantee $P_f < 0 \cdot 05$ if we confine our attention to samples of 82 and:

reject Hypothesis A in favour of Hypothesis B if $\; x < 34$

reject Hypothesis B in favour of Hypothesis A if $\; x > 33$

By examining only samples of larger size, we can of course

reduce the upper limit of uncertainty. As before, we have only to choose our score rejection criterion to satisfy the foregoing criterion $\alpha = \beta$, so that $- c_a = c_b$.

At this stage, the reader may ask the following question: is there any essential difference between a partial decision rule and a significance test in the Yule–Fisher tradition? One answer to this is that a decision test of any sort, as we have defined it, imposes on us the obligation to state in advance the size of the sample to which the test prescription applies. I have elsewhere contended that such a consistently behaviourist interpretation of the test procedure as a rule of conduct does indeed impose on us this obligation. The laboratory worker, not as yet restored to self-confidence after the traumatic discovery that he can no longer accept with propriety a null hypothesis seductively irrelevant to his main preoccupations, and therefore all too ready for belated assurance concerning the utility of the test prescription, may be less impressed by such formal considerations than by the practical consequences of performing tests without a preliminary examination of the bearing of sample size on any realisable reward for much expended arithmetical toil.

If anxious to find a formula for compromise, we may indeed gracefully yield to the temptation to state that we make an error of the second kind only if we accept the null hypothesis when false, and hence that we cannot make the error of the second kind within the framework of a rule to reserve judgment when our sample score does not lie outside the chosen limit or limits definitive of α, i.e. the conditional probability of wrongly rejecting the null hypothesis. We may therefore all too readily welcome the disclosure that we can at least say something directly relevant to the truth or falsehood of our decisions, if we restrict the verdict to rejection and reservation of judgment. At its face value, this contention is admissible; but it entails devastating consequences to highly publicised claims which have been largely responsible for the popularity of the significance test formula.

It has been the plea of R. A. Fisher and of his followers that the tests elaborated by them have special advantages on grounds of economy; and an imposing edifice of *small sample theory* has arisen on this understanding. Indeed, some devotees have lapsed into the idiom of poetic diction appropriate to the magnitude of their benefits so conceived. In one context, we hear that they are "exquisitely sensitive." In another, Darlington is content to use the idiom of ballistics with pardonably patriotic exaltation, when he assures us that:

Modern statistical methods, largely developed by Englishmen, have transformed our knowledge of how to extract information from numbers. They have become in recent years one of our most powerful and most general instruments of discovery. Our great Government departments are busy collecting for us numbers, so-called statistics, on a vast scale. . . . Modern statistical methods would demand new activities of explosive violence.

What the school of R. A. Fisher defines as the appropriate criterion of *economy* in the context of small sample theory need not detain us, because the concepts of efficiency and sufficiency* as Fisher first defined them, emerged in the domain of *point*-estimation. In any event, we can presume to know what the consumer will reasonably expect of it. If told that a test is economical in its demand on sample size, he or she will reasonably expect that its design will commonly guarantee the possibility of arriving at the only sort of decision it does endorse; but our foregoing model situation shows that this is a hope forlorn. If all our fruitfly mothers of 22 offspring are lethal carriers, the decision to reserve judgment or to reject the null hypothesis at the $2 \cdot 6$ per cent significance level on the basis of a one-sided criterion, and approximately 5 per cent if we adopt a 2-sided criterion, signified that 64 per cent of all the tests we shall carry out will be indecisive.

It is revealing to consider how the Fisher test procedure works out, when the size of the fruitfly fraternity is 9. We need not here rely on the tables. In the foregoing symbolism

$$\text{(i) } P_{x.a}(x \leqslant 1) = \frac{1 + 9}{2^9} < 0 \cdot 02$$

$$\text{(ii) } P_{x.b}(x > 1) = 1 - \frac{11 \cdot 2^8}{3^9} > 0 \cdot 85$$

* R. A. Fisher (1922). *"Foundations of Theoretical Statistics."* Phil. Trans. Roy. Soc. A., ccxxii.

In words, what this means is that: (i) the probability of meeting 9-fold samples containing 0 or 1 males is less than 0·02 when Hypothesis A is true; (ii) more than 85 per cent of all samples we shall meet will actually contain as many as 2 males if Hypothesis B is true. On this understanding, we may therefore frame a partial decision rule referable to a unique null hypothesis in the following terms: if the 9-fold sample contains less than two males, reject Hypothesis A and otherwise reserve judgment if it contains 2 or more males. We may then admittedly assign an uncertainty safeguard $P_f < 0·02$ to any positive assertions to which we commit ourselves. The fact remains that Hypothesis B may be true, in which event more than 85 per cent of our samples will contain 2 or more males. If, therefore, Hypothesis B is true, our rule enjoins on us to reserve judgment about 85 per cent of the samples we meet. To sidestep the error of the second kind by a verbal afterthought, we thus arrive at the alarming conclusion that the test prescription is consistent with the possibility that the result of applying it will be inconclusive in about 85 per cent of all opportunities we may have for doing so.

Thus rejection of the null hypothesis at the one-sided 2 per cent (or at the two-sided 4 per cent) significance level means that we may have nothing positive to show for the labour of performing some 85 per cent of all tests we carry out. In this context, the labour is admittedly a trivial issue; but it is by no means a trivial undertaking to ring the changes on the test battery of an Analysis of Covariance. The investigator who shoulders the obligation to do so, and accordingly relinquishes his own prerogative of experimental design to fit the assembly of data in the mould prescribed by the test prescription, must therefore reluctantly abandon the hope that a significance test accomplishes what little R. A. Fisher (p. 500) claims for it in his later pronouncements *ex cathedra*.

In any event, it is now clear that the consumer will not know how much of the effort is fruitless unless he can give a more precise meaning to Snedecor's statement (p. 335) expressing a somewhat lax view of the implications of rejection, viz. that the relevant parameter is "so small as to be unimportant to his investigator." We can indeed do this only if we set an upper limit to what we deem to be small. If our null hypothesis is $p_a = \frac{1}{2}$, we shall then say that we ask the test to guarantee that we shall rarely suspend judgment when

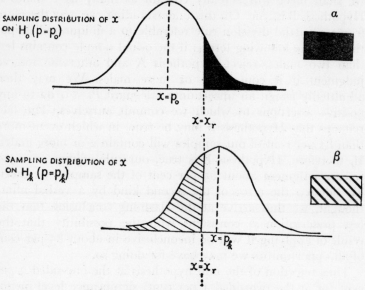

FIG. 1.—*Decision—partial and comprehensive*

Above.—Sampling distribution of a score x in accordance with the Hypothesis H_0 that $p = p_0$.

Below.—Sampling distribution of a score x in accordance with the Hypothesis H_k that $p = p_k$.

Rejection Criterion	Partial Rule	Comprehensive Rule
If $x > x_r$	Say H_0 is false	Say H_0 is false and H_k is true
If $x \leqslant x_r$	Say nothing	Say H_k is false and H_0 is true
α	Probability of rejecting H_0 when H_0 is true	Probability of rejecting H_0 when H_0 is true
β	Probability of suspending judgment when H_k is true	Probability of rejecting H_k when H_k is true

the true value (p_b) of the parameter has some limiting value (k) which we may define in a one-sided or two-sided way as:

(i) $p_b < k_2$; (ii) $k_2 > p_b > k_1$; (iii) $p_b > k_1$

358

Thus we cannot confer any intelligible connotation on the economy of the test procedure from the viewpoint of the consumer who has nothing to show for a non-committal test result unless we can set up some clear-cut alternative to the hypothesis we propose to discredit. In the fruitfly model situation discussed above, only one alternative to the null hypothesis is admissible; but the issue raised by Snedecor demands a different fomulation in the set-up of the prophylactic trial. If we denote by p_a and p_b respectively attack (or mortality) rates for treatments A and B, having reason to expect that treatment B is the more efficacious, our concern will be to decide whether the difference $(p_a - p_b = M_d)$ attains a certain target value (k), i.e. $M_d \geqslant k$. To be sure, this hypothesis is ambiguous in the sense that it is consistent with an infinitude of sampling distributions, but we can dispose of this objection if we proceed as follows.

We shall suppose that our null hypothesis (H_k) is $M_d = k$, and that we shall reject it when the observed attack rate difference (d) is less than d_r, the latter being itself less than k. Our error of the first kind will be

$$P_{d.k}(d < d_r) = \alpha$$

For any other hypothesis (H_m) such that $M_d = m > k$, we may write:

$$P_{d.m}(d < d_r) < \alpha$$

If α is the probability that we shall reject the hypothesis $M_d = k$ when it is true, the probability that we shall reject the range of hypotheses $M_d \geqslant k$ is thus $P_f \leqslant \alpha$. Hence the hypothesis $M_d \geqslant k$ is unambiguous if we: (a) choose a *vector* rejection score criterion to satisfy the acceptable level of uncertainty $P_f = \alpha$ when $M_d = k$; (b) content ourselves with stating the uncertainty safeguard of the rule in the form $P_f \leqslant k$. On this understanding, we can view the claims of small sample theory from a new aspect, if we take a *back stage* view of a 2 × 2 table (proportionate score difference or so-called 1 d.f. Chi Square test) prescribed by Fisher for trials of the sort discussed by Yule and Greenwood and indeed used by the latter.

Accordingly, we shall assume: (i) that we know the true value of p_a which is the attack rate in an infinite population specified by treatment A; (ii) that we agree about the target value k which defines $p_b = (p_a - k)$ as that of a population specified by treatment B; (iii) that k so specified is the least operational advantage we choose to regard as important. In the last expression $(p_b - p_a) = 0 = k$ if the two populations are identical in accordance with the Yule–Fisher test prescription.

We may then define the variance of the distribution of an observed proportionate difference $d = (p_{a.s} - p_{b.s})$ referable to observed attack rates $p_{a.s}$ and $p_{b.s}$ of equal (r-fold) samples as:

$$\sigma_d^2 = \frac{p_a(1 - p_a)}{r} + \frac{p_b(1 - p_b)}{r}$$

$$= \frac{2p_a(1 - p_a) - k(1 - 2p_a + k)}{r} \qquad . \quad \text{(vi)}$$

If both p_a and p_b lie in the range $0 \cdot 4 - 0 \cdot 6$, the normal curve of unit variance will describe adequately for our purpose the distribution of the standard score of 50-fold samples:

$$c_k = \frac{(d - k)}{\sigma_d} \qquad . \quad . \quad . \quad . \quad \text{(vii)}$$

Since we are here taking a back-stage view by assuming that we have a firm value p_a for treatment A, we may set $p_a = 0 \cdot 5$ for illustrative purposes and shall then define a square normal score of unit variance (i.e. a Chi Square variate of 1 d.f.) by

$$c_k^2 = \frac{2r(d - k)^2}{1 - 2k^2}$$

We shall now consider the alternative hypotheses: (a) H_0 if $k = 0$; (b) H_k, if $k = 0 \cdot 10$. In words, this means: (a) the true attack rates for both treatments are 50 per cent, the two treatments thus being equally efficacious on H_0; (b) the attack rates for treatments A and B are respectively 50 per cent and 40 per cent, treatment B being therefore 10 per cent more efficacious than treatment A on H_k. We shall then write the standard scores of the two sampling difference distributions as:

$$c_0 = + d\sqrt{2r} \; ; \; c_k = \frac{(10d - 1)\sqrt{r}}{7} \qquad . \quad \text{(viii)}$$

Since a large positive difference d will be more rare than otherwise if H_0 is true, we shall choose a one-sided rejection criterion $d_r > 0$ such that $P_{d.0}\,(d > d_r) = \alpha$ and set $\alpha = 0\cdot05$. A partial decision rule is then rejection of H_0 if $d > d_r$ with an uncertainty safeguard $P_f = 0\cdot05 = \alpha$. Accordingly, we choose d_r so that $d_r = d = (p_{a.s} - p_{b.s})$ when $c_0 = + 1\cdot64$, since 5 per cent of all sample values lie in the range of standard scores (c_h) from $+ 1\cdot64$ to $+ \infty$. We have then fixed c_h in (viii) for any specified value of r and are able to give a more definite form to the issue Snedecor states in the passage cited. Our rejection criterion means that we suspend judgment when $c_0 < + 1\cdot64$; and if $r = 50$ this means that $d < 0\cdot164$ and $c_k < 0\cdot65$. If we suppose that H_k is true, we shall thus suspend judgment whenever the score deviation $(d - k)$ lies in the range from $- \infty$ up to $+ 0\cdot65$, as is true of 74 per cent of the samples that we shall encounter. Had we chosen as our target value of minimum acceptable efficacy 5 per cent advantage $(k = 0\cdot05)$, we should obtain $c_k = + 1\cdot14$. This bounds 87 per cent of the area of the normal distribution. Thus we shall suspend judgment about 87 per cent of samples we encounter, if we carry out the usual drill at the 5 per cent significance level on equal samples of 50 when there is a real advantage of 5 per cent.

By defining k as our target value of minimal efficacy, we have said that any difference $M_d = (p_a - p_b)$ less than k is unimportant, or, in Snedecor's own (p. 335) words "so small as to be unimportant for our investigation." We thus arrive at the following conclusions with reference to the Fisher Chi Square test for the 2×2 table of the clinical trial:

(i) if we interpret the alternative to rejection in the sense endorsed by Snedecor, the overwhelming majority of our judgments may be wrong:

*

(ii) if we stand fast by Fisher's injunction to suspend judgment, an overwhelming majority of the tests we carry out may be indecisive *vis-à-vis* the only type of decision which justifies recourse to the procedure.

In any event, we shall not know how much expended effort may well be fruitless, unless we explore what Neyman calls the *power* of the test procedure. This we shall now define. Having chosen some unique hypothesis H_0 referable to a unique parameter p_0 as the basis of a partial decision rule or significance test rehabilitated in such terms, we are free to consider what would happen if any hypothesis H_k referable to the corresponding parameter p_k is admissible in the range $p_k > p_0$. We must then preassign a score rejection criterion x_r, so that P_0 $(x > x_r) = \alpha$ defines an acceptable uncertainty safeguard against *wrongly* rejecting H_0. If any admissible alternative hypotheses H_k is true the probability that we shall suspend judgment is $P_k(x < x_r) = \beta_k$, being numerically identical with the error of the second kind, if we operate the corresponding comprehensive test. The power of the test is then $(1 - \beta_k)$, being the probability that we shall reject H_0 when H_k is true.

For illustrative purposes we may return to the foregoing discussion of a normally distributed difference $(p_a - p_b) = k$. It will suffice to consider two admissible alternatives to the null hypothesis H_0, viz.:

$$H_0 \qquad \text{that} \qquad k = 0$$
$$H_1 \qquad \text{that} \qquad k = 0\cdot05$$
$$H_2 \qquad \text{that} \qquad k = 0\cdot10$$

By using (viii) above, we then obtain for $c_0 = 1\cdot64$ so that $\alpha = 0\cdot05$ the following values of $(1 - \beta_k)$

r	H_1 true	H_2 true
50	0·13	0·26
100	0·18	0·45
200	0·26	0·64
400	0·41	0·88

.   .   .   .   .

Ceteris paribus, the power of the test increases as we increase the size (r) of the sample or increase k. If we postulate that $k = e$ is positive but infinitesimal, we shall require indefinitely large samples to ensure a high power test procedure in Neyman's sense; but this form of words is liable to conceal the essential lesson the table of the so-called power function conveys. If the value of $(1 - \beta_k)$ is high, that of β_k is low and *vice versa*. To say that the power of a test is low for any sizeable specification of the sample thus means that β_k is high; but if H_k is true, β_k is the proportion of indecisive partial decision tests we shall perform on the basis of the null hypothesis H_0. We thus reach the following conclusion: if the null hypothesis $(k = 0)$ is false, no specification of sample size, however large, can guarantee the opportunity of arriving at a definite decision as the outcome of an appreciable proportion of test applications.

One hopes that the force of the foregoing considerations will commend themselves to any reader who has not a heavy emotional investment in the performance of the significance test ritual. If so, some will have begun to wonder: (*a*) how the plea of small sample economy advanced by Fisher's disciples gained such widespread assent; (*b*) why there has been so belated a recognition of logical issues within easy grasp of the consumer with little mathematical knowledge. The first question claims attention, if only because intellectual modesty forbids us to dismiss lightly the views of others possibly more clever than ourselves. When we have arrived at contrary convictions by a different route, it is therefore seemly to ask how misunderstanding may well have arisen.

The source of misunderstanding in this setting is not far to seek, and illustrates a disposition we have already recognised as a perennial source of confusion. When the theoretician speaks of the rigorous proof of a theorem, we should be at all times alert to the distinction between: (i) clarification of the logical credentials of a statistical procedure in the domain of action; (ii) refinement of a cognate algebraic technique in conformity with the requirements of the pure mathematician. If we examine the sense in which Fisher gave the first rigorous proof of the *t*-distribution, we have an answer to the first of the two questions stated above. Let us therefore do so.

The null hypothesis of the significance test procedure commonly invokes the assumption that the unit sample distribution of the universe of choice is normal. In fact it never is, and never can be; but the assertion may be sufficiently near to the truth to justify recourse to an appropriate sampling distribution referable thereto. If so, we may say that the distribution of the mean of r-fold samples from a universe whose definitive parameters are M and σ is normal with definitive parameters M and $\sigma_m = \sigma \div \sqrt{r}$. Now in practice, we do not know the true value of σ; but we may be content to assume that the sample root-mean-square deviation s is a sufficiently reliable estimate of σ and that $s_m = s \div \sqrt{r}$ is accordingly a sufficiently reliable estimate of σ_m if r is large enough. Practitioners in the domain of the theory of error from Gauss well into the first half of the subsequent century consistently made the best of a bad job in this way when they cited the precision index h or probable error of a point estimate; and the school of K. Pearson adopted the practice when applying the theory to a new class of problems.

Under the pen-name *Student*, W. H. Gossett (1908) published what is a purely algebraic theorem to the effect that the distribution of the ratio of the deviation of the sample mean from its true value to the estimated standard deviation (s_m) is definable for a normal universe without reference to the unknown parameter σ for all values of r. At the time, this attracted little attention, partly because the author's proof is fallacious, and perhaps partly also because his symbolism is very obscure. In 1923 Burnside (*Proc. Camb. Phil. Soc.*, Vol. 21) took up the issue for the Gaussian domain in a paper which explicitly refers to, and disclaims, what we have elsewhere (p. 193) called the Legendre–Laplace axiom: "it would be difficult to justify the assumption that because a particular value of the precision constant makes the probability of the observed event as great as possible, the precision constant necessarily has that value." The reader will recall that the precision constant h in this context is $(\sigma\sqrt{2})^{-1}$ in the symbolism of statistical tests; and on that understanding Burnside derives a distribution closely related to the t-distribution of Gossett.

In the same year and in the same journal, the publication

of Burnside's paper prompted R. A. Fisher (1923) to direct attention to the neglect of "the brilliant work of Student," asserting that it "is so fundamental from the theoretical standpoint and has so direct a bearing on the practical conclusions to be drawn *from small samples*." Fisher's communication has attracted more attention than that of Burnside for two reasons, and with some justice.* He announced his intention of publishing, as indeed he did subsequently publish, a table of the integral with a foolproof explanation of how to use it for the benefit of consumers with no mathematical pretensions to understand its derivation. He also invoked a new algebraic technique cognate to contemporary preoccupation with the theory of relativity, and later exploited the same method to derive distributions of other statistics—notably the ratio of different variance estimates—referable to sampling in a putative normal universe.

In the sense that the distributions of the *t*-ratio and of other sample statistics of the Fisher test battery do not depend on the unknown σ of the putative normal universe, they are equally *exact* for samples of any size; and we may invoke them without the reservation that they are valid only for large samples, if we have good reason to invoke them at all. When we say that the Fisher test prescriptions are valid for small samples, all we therefore rightly mean is that the theoretical distributions on which they rely are valid in the foregoing sense; but this assertion has no direct bearing on the claim that such tests are intrinsically economical in the sense that they satisfy the consumer's demand for a decisive outcome of their use.

Let us now turn to the second question stated above. How

---

* In a review (*Scientific Monthly*, LXII, 1951) of the memorial volume referred to in *Appendix IV*, Neyman delivers what may well be the verdict of the next generation in the following terms:

A very able "manipulative" mathematician, Fisher enjoys a real mastery in evaluating complicated multiple integrals. In addition, he has a remarkable talent in the most difficult field of approaching problems of empirical research. As a result, his lifework includes a series of valuable contributions giving exact distributions of a variety of statistics, such as the correlation coefficient, the central χ^2 with due allowance for degrees of freedom, the noncentral χ^2, the quotient of two χ^2 etc. etc. These distributions are bound to stay on the books and be used continuously.

can we explain the belated recognition of considerations first advanced by Neyman and E. S. Pearson more than twenty years ago? We may seek an answer to this on more than one level. Here we shall consider two. While it seems clear that the view of test procedure elaborated by Neyman and E. S. Pearson is traceable to the period in which tests recommended by R. A. Fisher were still widely accepted as novel, we must also recall that the only claim of the latter to novelty is the invocation of new algebraic techniques to specify more or less relevant advantages of invoking particular sample distributions. In fact, they signalise no essential break with a long tradition transmitted by Quetelet through Galton to Pearson and incorporated in postulates defined in all essential particulars by Yule and Greenwood. Inescapably, therefore, the emergent concept of a decision rule had to fit as best it could into a pre-existing framework of custom thought.

Thus the concept of test power which usefully calls attention to our obligation to define the size of the sample, if we wish to confer any intelligible rationale on a test procedure, succumbed to a period of arrested development. To woo their elders and contemporaries, Neyman and Pearson almost succeeded in disposing of an unwanted child by a concession which invalidates reasonable grounds for a hopeful attitude towards its survival. They introduced the concept of a unique *uniformly most powerful* (U.M.P.) test, i.e. a partial decision test which is as powerful as possible in the sense defined above. For the reason mentioned above, this was a decisively backward step, since the most powerful test definable cannot necessarily satisfy one presumptive demand of the consumer, i.e. that he will commonly be able to arrive at a definite decision. Till Wald, as a newcomer in the field, interpreted the power concept with few preoccupations traceable to the Quetelet *mystique*, the contemporaries of Neyman and Pearson could pardonably regard it as a new refinement of an old technique, and indeed as a programme for promoting better and brighter significance test procedures.

Another reason for belated appreciation of the trail blazed by the Neyman–Pearson partnership emerges from a new use Wald —acclaimed by many as America's leading theoretical statistician of our own generation*—found for the comprehensive decision test procedure. Though the logical credentials of the comprehensive decision test must exert a compelling appeal to any student who approaches the issues involved with a fresh mind, it has a limited usefulness for a reason not yet discussed. In our fruitfly model set-up, we can reasonably limit our admissible hypotheses if appropriately fortified with background knowledge of the culture; but comparable situations are rare in comparison with those which the traditionalist significance test prescription claimed as its province. For instance, the general pattern of a hypothesis we might deem to be appropriate to the clinical trial is $M_d \geqslant k$ and k may conceivably have any value in the range ± 1, if we have no prior knowledge of the parameter (p_a above) definitive of our yardstick treatment group (A).

In such a situation as that of the Yule–Greenwood trial, we can indeed specify two exclusive alternatives in terms of a target value k as $M_d < k$ and $M_d \geqslant k$; but we have then seen that the power of the test—even if the test is a U.M.P. test—may be negligible for samples of any obtainable size. More generally, we may formulate this dilemma as follows. We suppose: (*a*) that the only admissible alternative to the null hypothesis $p = p_0$ is $p \geqslant p_h$; (*b*) that the rejection criterion assigns a probability α to wrong rejection of the null hypothesis and β to wrong rejection of the particular alternative $p = p_h$. If the difference between p_h and p_0 is infinitesimal, $\beta \simeq 1 - \alpha$ (see Fig. 1) for any sample of finite size, and the uncertainty safeguard of the test procedure will be $P_f \leqslant \beta$ if α itself conforms to any acceptable criterion of conditional risk, e.g. $P_f \leqslant 0 \cdot 95$ if $\alpha = 0 \cdot 05$. Thus prescription of sample size to ensure any acceptable uncertainty safeguard for decision test procedure is possible only if there is a finite difference between p_0 and p_h.

Wald first pointed out the foregoing implications of the attempt to discriminate between exclusive alternative hypotheses consistent with a continuous range of admissible values of p from p_o to p_h, and proffered a recipe for dealing with a limited class of situations which then arise. If we may legiti-

---

* *Journ. Amer. Stat. Ass.*, Vol. 46, 1951, pp. 242–4.

mately relinquish the attempt to discriminate between *exclusive* alternatives, we may sidestep this disability as follows. We assume two hypotheses H_a and H_b referable to definitive parameters M_a and $M_b = (M_a + k)$. If k is positive, our comprehensive test prescription is then as follows. We first define a rejection score x_r and sample size r to ensure acceptable values of α and β such that

$$P_a(x \geqslant x_r) = \alpha \quad and \quad P_b(x < x_r) = \beta$$

For any hypothesis H_i that $M_d < M_a$, and for any hypothesis H_j that $M_d > M_b$ we may then say:

$$P_i(x \geqslant x_r) < \alpha \quad and \quad P_j(x < x_r) < \beta$$

We can then assign to a specifiable rule an uncertainty safeguard $\alpha \leqslant P_f \leqslant \beta$ if $\beta > \alpha$, $\alpha \geqslant P_f \geqslant \beta$ if $\beta < \alpha$ and $P \leqslant \alpha$ if $\alpha = \beta$, i.e. $P_f \leqslant 0 \cdot 05$ if $\alpha = 0 \cdot 05 = \beta$. The rule is as follows:

    (i) If $x \geqslant x_r$ reject H_a, i.e. say that $M > M_a$

    (ii) If $x < x_r$ reject H_b, i.e. say that $M < M_b$

In the context of the clinical trial, we might then choose as our hypotheses $M_d = 0 \cdot 05$ and $M_d = 0 \cdot 10$. In that event the outcome of the test would be to make either of the two following terminal statements:

    (*a*) the advantage of treatment B is greater than 5 per cent.

    (*b*) the advantage of treatment A is less than 10 per cent.

Now the statement that the advantage is less than 10 per cent does not exclude the possibility that it is also less than 5 per cent. Consequently, the test prescription does not provide a formula for a situation in which the only type of terminal statement consistent with the operational intention must take the form $M \geqslant k$. What it can do is to provide a formula for the commercial situation in which we assume: (i) that the consumer will tolerate a proportion of defective articles in excess of the producer's guarantee; (ii) the producer wishes to insure both against the risk of losing the consumer's good will and against the risk of discarding consignments up to guaranteed standard.

Evidently a dilemma of this sort involves an ethical issue; and it is difficult to conceive situations confronting the research worker with a comparable choice which is also consistent with the ethic of science. If so, we may gratefully record the fact that the American way of life has provided a milieu in which it has been possible to explore fully the implications of the theory of the decision test. In so far as the undertaking has any bearing on its role as an instrument of statistical inference in scientific investigation, the outcome is that:

(*a*) any test procedure with an assignable and acceptable upper limit of uncertainty and the prospect of arriving at a decision on most occasions when applied is one which we can hope to prescribe for a very limited class of situations;

(*b*) no test procedure which conforms to both requirements last stated is relevant to the class of situations which the test batteries of the Analysis of Variance and the Analysis of Covariance claim as their province.

In this context, it is pertinent to state a third conclusion which will forestall the criticism that later chapters contain no detailed treatment of two such now fashionable procedures as last named. If we regard both requirements above stated as prerequisite to a consistently behaviourist approach to the usefulness of statistical procedures, neither of them calls for further comment in subsequent discussion of the terms of reference of a Calculus of Judgments. Indeed, we shall see (p. 420) that they rely on sampling distributions which fail to satisfy an additional and compelling requirement, not as yet explicitly stated.

CHAPTER SIXTEEN

INDUCTION AND DESIGN
STOCHASTIC AND NON-STOCHASTIC

IN THE EXPOSITION of his own views on *The Design of Experiments*, R. A. Fisher declares that "the statistician cannot excuse himself from the duty of getting his head clear on the principles of scientific inference, but equally no other thinking man can avoid a like obligation." Here at least, we have grounds for agreement. We cannot indeed do justice to the claims of statistical inference if we refrain from asking: what is the role of any procedure referable to testing hypotheses as an instrument of scientific reasoning? This question, which we shall now scrutinise in conformity with Fisher's admirable counsel, imperatively raises others. What do we imply when we speak of the scientific method as inductive? What do we imply when we distinguish between *deduction* and *induction?*

Off-guard in a local brains trust with only a few seconds in which to frame a suitable reply, most scientific workers would answer the last question by defining: (*a*) deduction as reasoning from an assumed or known cause or set of axioms to an undiscerned effect or conclusion; (*b*) induction as reasoning from a known effect to an undiscerned cause. Alternatively, he or she might say in accord with the Concise Oxford Dictionary that: deduction is "inference from general to particular" and induction is "inferring of general law from particular instances." Either way, we are prone to regard induction as a reversal of the logical processes subsumed by the term deduction, whence by an all too common exercise of metonymy we identify it with the Backward Look.

The Oxford Dictionary definition is consistent with Mill's usage when he declared that "induction is inferring a proposition from propositions less general than itself." Professional logicians of a later vintage have been less preoccupied with the inadequacy of Mill's exposition of the process of scientific investigation than with the laxity of his concept of *cause* and with the irrelevance of the syllogistic formula to deduc-

tions incident to the interpretation of data. They have
therefore done little to clarify the reorientation signalised
by Neyman's use of the expression *inductive behaviour* and by
what we have called the Forward Look in foregoing chapters.
A brief reference to Mill's views is therefore pertinent to our
theme. As is true of other philosophers of a past generation,
it is easy to find in his writings anticipations of modern views.
In one context, Mill defines induction unexceptionably but
uninformatively as: "the operation of discovering and proving
general propositions"; and we can concur readily with his
view that a prerequisite to understanding the operation is
"sufficient acquaintance with the process by which science has
actually succeeded in establishing general truth." None the
less, we must be wary of assuming either that the practice of
scientific enquiry in his own time could provide the basis for
such sufficient acquaintance or that a now acceptable interpretation of the term *general truth* as applied to a hypothesis is
entirely consistent with the usage of Mill's contemporaries.

Mill's insistence on the unity of the scientific method had
a wide emotive appeal to a contemporary popular front of
secular opposition to ecclesiastical control of education; and
the meaning he attaches to a general truth is wholly consistent
with his message. There was as yet little provision for scientific
research as a profession, and public pronouncements of the
leaders of science, eloquent in the defence of unfettered
curiosity and of conscientious fact-finding, disclose few agenda
for a programme of enquiry on a level of discussion now likely
to enlighten or to enlist the interest of the professional logician.
For two reasons, the statement of a single formula for the
scientific method embracing Biblical criticism, the study of
history and social institutions, the theory of organic evolution,
Newton's laws of motion and the discovery of lately unknown
electromagnetic phenomena was indeed an easier undertaking
for Mill and for his immediate following than it can now be
for us. In the more mature sciences, hit-and-miss methods of
the brilliant amateur exploring unknown territories in the
domain of electricity or of animal behaviour have increasingly
made way for a professional regimen of planned experimentation. Meanwhile, we think of the framework of interpretation

less as a photograph of nature in glorious technicolour than as an expanding code of recipes for human action. What endures and expands, as the building called science gains in breadth and stature, is not the scaffolding of metaphor. It is man's command over nature.

To make a just appraisal of Mill's viewpoint with due regard both to his immense erudition and to his indisputable sagacity, we must judge him in his own context, equally that of Landseer, of the traveller naturalists and of the Great Exhibition. In Mill's day and generation, the current view of the wonders of science was a Royal Academy view, an unfinished but ever unfolding landscape picture of a universe into which man is a recent, somewhat pitiable and becomingly apologetic intruder. Swinburne was nearer to the temper of our own time when he ended his memorable hymn with the lines "Glory to Man in the Highest, for Man is the master of things." So indeed was Bacon, when he proclaimed that the roads to human power and to human knowledge lie close together.

More than two centuries before Mill, the author of the *Novum Organum* had indeed pleaded with unsurpassed eloquence for an operational approach to the terms of reference of scientific enquiry *en rapport* with the reorientation of our own time; but the experimental method was then on trial. Like Bacon, Mill exalted its merits, but the essence of the experimental method, as he expounds it, is active interference with nature. His canons for the interpretation of the outcome of such interference scarcely transgress the boundaries of common sense, and shed no new light on the terms of reference of the undertaking. In so far as he had any prevision of what we now call the *Design of Experiments*, his main concern was to point out the dangers of reliance on what he called the *Hypothetical Method* in the search for a unique and final specification of cause and effect. He might well have had a less discouraging view of its usefulness if he had also had less inclination to announce a formula to fit all methods of investigation worthy of respect.

In what follows I shall use some terms introduced by Wrighton* in a recent and thought-provoking statement

* *Acta Genetica et Statistica Medica*, 1953.

of a novel approach to the scope of statistical inference. Accordingly, we shall distinguish between experiments of two kinds as *exploratory* and *holonomic*. In the latter we proceed from a limited set of hypotheses to deduce consequences which are factually verifiable and select a hypothesis or sub-set of hypotheses uniquely consistent with observation. We might speak of this as Mill's hypothetical method; but we shall not expose ourselves to his legitimate objections to its misuse if we undertake it with no illusions concerning our obligation to furnish in advance reasons for the choice of a uniquely admissible set of hypotheses. We shall also be able to appreciate why Mill's own generation had not "sufficient acquaintance with the process by which science has succeeded in establishing general truth," if we first explore its use in a field of enquiries which prompted Mill himself to express a very conservative—and, as now appears, factually unjustifiable—opinion about the usefulness of the experimental method.

The writer here deliberately selects an investigation into animal behaviour carried out under his own direction, because it will illustrate how the biologist himself approaches the problem of design when his aim is to solve a biological problem rather than to collect data suitable for demonstrating computations invoked by a significance test procedure. Conceding to Mill that our definition of the admissible set must itself have a factual basis, we assume that flies of the species *Drosophila melanogaster* have *hygro-receptors*, i.e. sense organs by which they recognise moisture, and *chemo-receptors*, i.e. sense organs by which they recognise specific chemical compounds. Our factual basis for this assumption is that normal flies of the species released in a closed space with choice of entering: (i) a dry or a moist, but otherwise similar, chamber congregate in the latter (positive h-response); (ii) a chamber containing dilute acetic acid and an otherwise similar chamber containing pure water congregate in the former (positive c-response). Let us also concede to Mill a second factual prerequisite to the design proposed, viz. that casual observation on the movements of the antennae of flies in search of food or of a sufficiently moist environment suggests the localisation of such receptors therein. Against this background information we may postulate a uniquely admissible set of axioms or hypotheses embracing *all* factual possibilities:

H.1 Both hygro-receptors and chemo-receptors of *D. melanogaster* are *exclusively* located in the antennae.

H.2 The chemo-receptors are *exclusively* located in the antennae, but the hygro-receptors are not.

H.3 The hygro-receptors are located *exclusively* in the antennae, but the chemo-receptors are not.

H.4 Receptors of *neither* sort are exclusively (if at all) located in the antennae.

If we appropriately define our criterion of *negative* response, i.e. partition of released flies in approximately equal numbers in alternative choice-chambers, we may also classify *all* possible observations on a choice-chamber set-up involving flies of both sorts thus:

O.1 normal flies give both a positive *h*-response and a positive *c*-response, but antennaless flies give both a negative *h*-response and a negative *c*-response;

O.2 normal flies as before, antennaless giving a positive *h*-response and a negative *c*-response;

O.3 normal flies as before, antennaless being *c*-positive and *h*-negative;

O.4 both normal and antennaless *c*-positive and *h*-positive.

Having stated both a comprehensive set of hypotheses and a comprehensive set of observations, we may now make the following deductions:

(i) If H.1 is true, normal flies will give both a positive *h*-response and a positive *c*-response, but antennaless flies will give both a negative *h*-response and a negative *c*-response.

(ii) If H.2 is true, normal flies will give both positive responses, but antennaless flies will give a positive *h*-response and a negative *c*-response.

(iii) If H.3 is true, normal flies will give both positive responses, but antennaless will give a positive *c*-response and a negative *h*-response.

(iv) If H.4 is true, normal flies will give both positive responses and antennaless will give both positive responses.

Up to this point, it is immaterial whether we speak of H.1–H.4 as axioms or hypotheses. Our next step is possible because each deduction (i)–(iv) is uniquely endorsed by an actual observation of a unique event or fact, if we can obtain by surgical or other procedure flies deemed to be healthy and comparable in all particulars other than lack of the antennae. Accordingly, we may exhibit a set of all conceivable observations and corresponding admissible hypotheses as below in a table with a + sign to indicate which observation is alone consistent with each hypothesis, and if recorded as such endorses one of four *terminal statements* T.1–T.4 consistent with our deductions (i)–(iv) above:

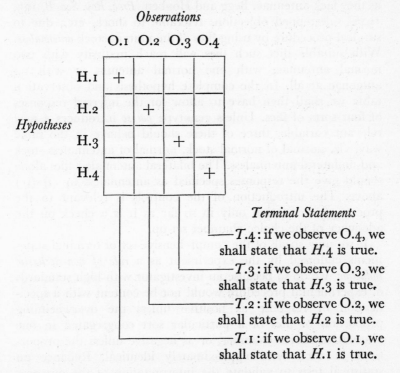

Observations

O.1 O.2 O.3 O.4

Hypotheses

H.1 +

H.2   +

H.3   +

H.4   +

Terminal Statements

———*T*.4 : if we observe O.4, we shall state that *H*.4 is true.

———*T*.3 : if we observe O.3, we shall state that *H*.3 is true.

———*T*.2 : if we observe O.2, we shall state that *H*.2 is true.

———*T*.1 : if we observe O.1, we shall state that *H*.1 is true.

The reader may here note the deliberate use of the future auxiliary in the formula of the terminal statement, emphasising the Forward Look which anticipates the final step called *verification*. Subsequently, we may agree to drop it for brevity, when clear about what we are doing. The final step of *verification* itself is: (*a*) to release flies of both sorts with appropriate choice chambers for detection of the *h*-response only and flies of both sorts with appropriate choice chambers for detection of the *c*-response only; (*b*) to count the flies of each sort in each sort of choice chamber after a suitable lapse or—better still—at regular intervals.

In a perfectly designed experiment of this type, we shall need to forestall a legitimate objection of Mill to the hypothetical method by assuring ourselves that the *experimental* flies are in all relevant particulars like the *controls* except in so far as they lack antennae. Begg and Hogben (*Proc. Roy. Soc. B*, 133, 1946) sidestepped objections referable to shock, etc., due to surgical procedure by using flies of the mutant stock *antennaless*. With suitable diet such flies will reach maturity with two normal antennae, with one normal antenna or with no antennae at all. In the complete hypothesis and observation table we shall then have to allow for the inferred responses of four sorts of flies. Unless genotype *per se* introduces a new relevant variable, three of these should behave in the same way, viz. normal of normal stock, normal of antennaless stock and unilateral antennaless. The bilateral antennaless flies alone should give the responses specified as antennaless by (i)–(iv) above. The introduction of the controls is relevant to the process of verification only in so far as it is a check on the adequacy of the choice chamber set-up.

If we now speak of the comprehensive set of terminal statements endorsed by the experiment as a *rule of non-stochastic induction*, we do so because an investigator with high standards of experimental procedure would not be content with a specification of response as positive unless the overwhelming proportion of flies of a particular sort congregated in one alternative choice chamber, or as negative unless the proportions in each were approximately identical. Reliance on statistical tests to validate the interpretation of the outcome would indeed signify either or both of two defects of design: (*a*) lack of relevant genetical background information implicit in the claim that the final assertion (Wrighton's *terminal state-*

ment) embraces flies of the species as a whole; (*b*) lack of a satisfactory response criterion for the type of receptivity under investigation. In any event, our procedure is throughout consistent with the Forward Look. *Our induction is anticipatory deduction subject to the discipline of ineluctable fact.*

Before we now ask what is indeed characteristic of stochastic in contradistinction to non-stochastic induction, we may here usefully note that we can speak of interference with nature at more than one level. In many experiments of this sort we might legitimately adopt a surgical procedure instead of taking advantage of the fact that nature has provided us with two sorts of flies. Here therefore we interfere at the level of nurture alone. In studies on human behaviour we may take advantage of the fact that society arranges for the adoption of children; and we can set out reactions of fraternal or of identical co-twins brought up in the same or in different families in a hypothesis-observation table derivable without recourse to active interference at either the level of nature or the level of nurture. This suggests a possible programme of enquiry which may eventually bring within the same framework of interpretation disciplines whose conduct is consistent with the Forward Look and some disciplines in which we take the necessity of the Backward Look for granted. Be that as it may, the common disposition to assume that scientific enquiry on human beings in circumstances which exclude the active interference Mill so lightly regards as the hall-mark of the experimental method is essentially statistical—and less precise on that account—rests on a misunderstanding of what is an essential characteristic of designed experimentation.

Having defined a *holonomic* experiment as above, it is scarcely necessary to define the alternative category, except to say that some of the most noteworthy discoveries of the past—and this is largely true of discoveries in the domain of electricity, magnetism or physiology in Mill's time—were the outcome of experimentation undertaken to enlarge our factual knowledge rather than to interpret facts already known in a new way. The discovery of radioactivity and of radium should make us hesitate to dismiss the usefulness of such *exploratory* experimentation or to regard it as a thing of the past; and indeed it is difficult to believe that designed enquiry can lead to the discovery of previously unsuspected natural phenomena except in so far as the investigator is alert to events which do not appear as entries in the hypothesis-observation table of the holonomic experiment. What makes experimentation here called holonomic of special interest is not that it is necessarily destined to supersede the alternative. It is instructive in this context because it has a special relevance to an intelligible distinction between non-stochastic and stochastic induction.

To get the distinction into sharper focus it is useful to divide experiments of the holonomic type into two categories, those which *may* and those which *must* lead to a conclusive outcome. In terms of design, Wrighton speaks of them respectively as *a posteriori* adequate and *a priori* adequate. Our last example was *a priori* adequate in the sense that there is a single positive sign in each column of the hypothesis-observation table, whence one and the same observation endorses only one of the set of terminal statements which justify the design. One example will suffice to specify the alternative class. We first predicate the following as background information. In fowls:

(*a*) one dominant gene substitution is responsible for the difference between the pea comb of the Partridge Cochins and the single comb of the Mediterranean breeds (leghorns, anconas, etc.);

(*b*) one dominant gene substitution is responsible for the difference between the rose comb of the Wyandottes or Hamburghs and the single comb;

(*c*) the interaction of both dominant genes in a gene complex otherwise like that of the single comb breeds leads to the development of the walnut comb of the Malay breeds. Accordingly, we may classify genotypes w.r.t. the four sorts of combs mentioned as:

(i) *Single* pp.rr
(ii) *Pea* PP.rr *or* Pp.rr
(iii) *Rose* pp.RR *or* pp.Rr
(iv) *Walnut* PP.RR; Pp.RR; PP.Rr; Pp.Rr

Thus we can set out the possible types to which we may assign a *single* offspring of all possible matings between two fowls *each* with the walnut comb in a hypothesis-observation grid (H.O.G.) as below:

	Hypotheses (Matings are:)	Observations (Offspring are):			
		O.1 Walnut	O.2 Pea	O.3 Rose	O.4 Single
1.	PP.RR × PP.RR	+			
2.	PP.RR × PP.Rr	+			
3.	PP.RR × Pp.RR	+			
4.	PP.RR × Pp.Rr	+			
5.	PP.Rr × Pp.RR	+			
6.	PP.Rr × PP.Rr	+	+		
7.	PP.Rr × Pp.Rr	+	+		
8.	Pp.RR × Pp.RR	+		+	
9.	Pp.RR × Pp.Rr	+		+	
10.	Pp.Rr × Pp.Rr	+	+	+	+

We may speak of each one of the comprehensive set of 10 hypotheses here disclosed as an *elementary* hypothesis. We make our table more compact by combining nine of them in three *composite* hypotheses which with the last in the foregoing make up the following 4-fold comprehensive set:

H.1. The parental pair is any one of the following: PP.RR × PP.RR; PP.RR × Pp.RR; PP.RR × PP.Rr; PP.RR × Pp.Rr; PP.Rr × Pp.RR.

379

H.2. The parental pair is *either*: PP.Rr × PP.Rr *or* PP.Rr × Pp.Rr.

H.3. The parental pair is *either*: Pp.RR × Pp.RR *or* Pp.RR × Pp.Rr.

H.4. The parental pair is: Pp.Rr × Pp.Rr.

Our H.O.G. of hypotheses referable to parental pairs of fowls with the walnut comb (regardless of sex) and of observations referable to one *individual* offspring, then assumes the form:

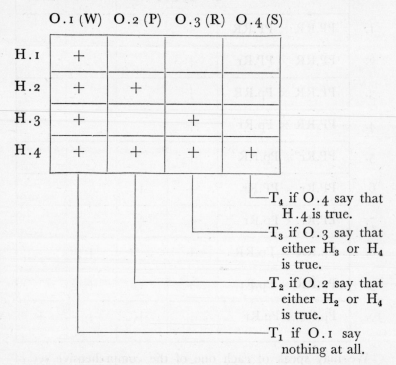

O.1 (W)   O.2 (P)   O.3 (R)   O.4 (S)

	O.1 (W)	O.2 (P)	O.3 (R)	O.4 (S)
H.1	+			
H.2	+	+		
H.3	+		+	
H.4	+	+	+	+

T₄ if O.4 say that H.4 is true.

T₃ if O.3 say that either H₃ or H₄ is true.

T₂ if O.2 say that either H₂ or H₄ is true.

T₁ if O.1 say nothing at all.

In this table only one column O.4 (S) contains one cell marked with the positive sign; and hence only one observation is consistent with a single hypothesis. Should it happen that only one chick comes to maturity, we can thus justify a terminal statement in favour of a single hypothesis of the 4-fold comprehensive set only if the chick also happens to have the single comb. The result then justifies the design; but no other result

380

could do so, if the intention is a terminal statement asserting that one of the four hypotheses is correct. In such a situation, Wrighton speaks of the design of the experiment as *a posteriori* adequate for the observation O.4.

En passant we may here note that our legitimate scope of inference is exactly the same if we look at the issue *retrospectively*, i.e. if asked to make a terminal statement of the same sort on the basis of information about two fowls each with the walnut comb. Though we are reasoning about a *past* event, our reasoning follows the path we traverse with eyes *forward* when we design an experiment to test the same set of hypotheses; and this may give us a clue to an acceptable answer to the question: how, if at all, is it possible to find a formula to embrace both acceptable reasoning about past events beyond the range of human interference and acceptable reasoning about situations we can control?

In the preceding discussion we have assumed that we can get information about only one offspring of the cross between two fowls with walnut combs classified in four possible categories as defined above. If we conceive the possibility of obtaining a large enough number of offspring to ensure representation of all possible phenotypes consistent with the parental mating class, we can classify conceivably observations on progeny of a single mating comprehensively as:

O.1   walnut only (W)
O.2   both walnut and pea but no other (W + P)
O.3   both walnut and rose but no other (W + R)
O.4   all four phenotypes (W + P + R + S)

On the assumption stated, it would thus be possible to make, as on page 382, the H.O.G. of an *a priori* adequate design in terms of the foregoing 4-fold comprehensive set of hypotheses.

We might speak of such a schema as *asymptotically* adequate *a priori* since there is a finite probability that the experiment will *not* fulfil our expectations, if r itself is finite as indeed it must be. That this is so, makes it a model of an alternative procedure of formulating a set of terminal statements in a *rule of stochastic induction.* Accordingly, we shall refer to it henceforth as *Model I.*

Model I. Since the number (r) of offspring two fowls with the walnut comb may produce is finite, each hypothesis is consistent with the occurrence of fraternities exclusively made up of W alone; but such occurrences will be rare when r is large unless H.1 is true. If H.2 is true, we may expect to meet fraternities of phenotypes W alone, P alone or W and P

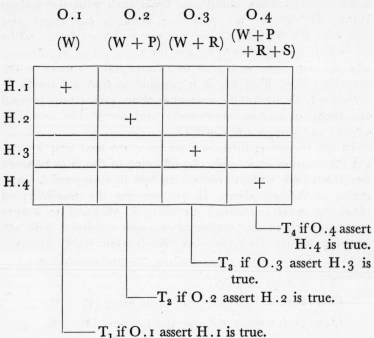

	O.1 (W)	O.2 (W + P)	O.3 (W + R)	O.4 (W + P + R + S)
H.1	+			
H.2		+		
H.3			+	
H.4				+

T₄ if O.4 assert H.4 is true.

T₃ if O.3 assert H.3 is true.

T₂ if O.2 assert H.2 is true.

T₁ if O.1 assert H.1 is true.

together, the last most often. If H.3 is true, we may expect to meet W alone, R alone or W and R together, the last most often. If H.4 is true, we may expect to meet fraternities of W, P, R or S alone, any pair (W + P, W + R, W + S, P + R, P + S, R + S) of the four phenotypes alone, any three alone (W + P + R, W + P + S, W + R + S, P + R + S) or all four (W + P + R + S). With due regard to what we shall indeed most commonly meet in the totality of our experience, we are free to classify all possible observations on an *r*-fold fraternity with parents both of phenotype W as containing:

O.1 W only.

O.2 At least one P but no R and no S.

O.3 At least one R but no P and no S.

O.4 Either at least one S or at least one of *both* R and P.

The probability assigned by the Theory of the Gene to the four possible phenotypes to which an individual offspring of each class of matings is itself assignable are

	W	P	R	S
H.1	1	0	0	0
H.2	$\frac{3}{4}$	$\frac{1}{4}$	0	0
H.3	$\frac{3}{4}$	0	$\frac{1}{4}$	0
H.4	$\frac{9}{16}$	$\frac{3}{16}$	$\frac{3}{16}$	$\frac{1}{16}$

Here we note that each of the four hypotheses, heretofore specified in *qualitative* terms, of our comprehensive set is also distinguishable by a numerical specification, viz. the three (one being redundant) parameters definitive of the randomwise sampling distribution of phenotypes among the offspring of the relevant mating. Only when it is possible to identify each hypothesis of the comprehensive set uniquely by a parameter or parameters definitive of a unique sampling distribution can we take the first step from the domain of a rule of non-

	O.1 (W only)	O.2 (at least one P, but no R and no S)	O.3 (at least one R, but no P and no S)	O.4 At least one S or at least one R and at least one P also
H.1	1	0	0	0
H.2	$(\frac{3}{4})^r$	$1 - (\frac{3}{4})^r$	0	0
H.3	$(\frac{3}{4})^r$	0	$1 - (\frac{3}{4})^r$	0
H.4	$(\frac{9}{16})^r$	$(\frac{3}{4})^r - (\frac{9}{16})^r$	$(\frac{3}{4})^r - (\frac{9}{16})^r$	$1 - 2(\frac{3}{4})^r + (\frac{9}{16})^r$

stochastic to a rule of stochastic induction. We may then take the next step. We lay out an H.O.G. (leaving blank the specification of the terminal statements) with probability entries in place of the + sign for concurrence of hypothesis and observation. From the parameters shown above we easily derive the H.O.G. shown at foot of page 383.

This design is not *a priori* adequate as it stands, since r is finite; but we can imagine what it would imply if r became indefinitely large, so that each diagonal cell would contain a unit and every other cell a zero. It would then look like the table (p. 382) of an a priori adequate set-up; and we should be able to operate the rule of induction which subsumes the exhaustive 4-fold set of terminal statements.

Let us now imagine that r is so large that each diagonal entry is numerically well above 0.5. We may then say that

T.1 if all the offspring are W, we *shall* assert that H.1 is true;

T.2 if the offspring include at least one P but no R or S, we *shall* assert that H.2 is true;

T.3 if the offspring include at least one R but no P or S, we *shall* assert that H.3 is true;

T.4 if the offspring either include at least one S or at least one R *and* at least one P also, we *shall* assert that H.4 is true.

More than 50 per cent of the observations we shall meet in a long enough sequence of trials will be specifiable as:

O.1 if H.1 is true
O.2 if H.2 is true
O.3 if H.3 is true
O.4 if H.4 is true

If we consistently follow the rule last stated, we shall say that H.1 is true only if we make the observation O.1 and this we shall do in more than 50 per cent of the situations we shall encounter if H.1 is indeed true. In more than 50 per cent of the situations we shall encounter when H.1 is true the assertion we shall make will be true, i.e. more than 50 per cent of the assertions we make will be true, if we adhere to the rule regardless of the outcome. Similar remarks apply *mutatis mutandis* to H.2, H.3 and H.4. *Whichever* hypothesis is true, more than 50 per cent of our assertions will therefore be true, if we follow the rule consistently. At the risk of being wrong sometimes, we can thus frame a rule which will guarantee both that we: (*a*) make a decisive judgment; (*b*) do so correctly more often than otherwise.

To do so we have: (*a*) to agree about what risk of erroneous statement we are prepared to take; (*b*) to fix accordingly the size (*r*) of fraternities w.r.t. which we record the relevant observations. First, we note that the lowest probability cited as a diagonal cell entry refers to an observation which will *least* often lead us to identify the correct hypothesis correctly. In the last table this is the entry on the right at the foot. If we denote by P_t the proportion of our assertions which will be right in the long run, we can therefore write:

$$P_t \geqslant 1 - 2(\tfrac{3}{4})^r + (\tfrac{9}{16})^r$$

For the values $r = 12, 13, 14$, we may thus tabulate the relevant expressions thus

r	$1 - (\tfrac{3}{4})^r$	$1 - 2(\tfrac{3}{4})^r + (\tfrac{9}{16})^r$
12	0·969	0·937
13	0·976	0·953
14	0·982	0·965

To make the probability of correct assertion at least 95 per cent, we must thus confine our attention to fraternities of $r \geqslant 14$. If we denote the risk of erroneous statement by $P_f = (1-P_t)$ we may say that $P_f < 0.05$ if $r \geqslant 14$ for the *rule of stochastic induction* subsumed under the foregoing statements. We have elsewhere spoken of this risk as the *uncertainty safeguard* of the rule. We now see more explicitly that it is *a property of the rule in its entirety*. It is not the probability that we shall be right, if we restrict our verdicts to observations deemed to endorse any individual terminal statement. If H.4 is true, we shall always be wrong, if we assert H.1 is true when we observe O.1; and all we can legitimately say about the probability that the *individual* terminal statement will be true is that it may be either zero or unity.

In one respect, the Model I design is highly artificial. We have approached the distinction between a stochastic and a non-stochastic rule of induction by tracing the steps traversed in a *designed* experiment, but we have not asked ourselves: what end in view has the design? We have provisionally distinguished between a terminal statement which is the assertion that a hypothesis is actually true and a hypothesis which is the assertion of a statement conceivably true in the absence of evidence to the contrary; and we have provisionally defined *a priori adequacy* of design in terms of one to one correspondence between terminal statements and hypotheses. We have also quite arbitrarily exercised the liberty of combining elementary in composite hypotheses to ensure the possibility of *a priori* adequacy; but such liberty is inconsistent with the notion of design unless the comprehensive set of terminal statements is *acceptable* in the sense that it supplies answers consistent with a presumptive operational intent. More explicitly therefore, we should speak of an experiment as *a priori* adequate only if there is one to one correspondence between the members of the comprehensive set of hypotheses—composite or otherwise—and a comprehensive set of *acceptable terminal statements*.

If we then ask whether the definition of a 4-fold comprehensive set of hypotheses and of terminal statements adopted in the foregoing model situation is consistent with an intelligible criterion of acceptability, the answer must be *no*. A practical poultry breeder having read so far might with justice protest that we have butchered the presumptive operational intent of the experiment to indulge in a statistical holiday. We have defined hypothesis IV in terms of a unique mating which specifies uniquely the genotype of each parent regardless of sex, but hypotheses I–III each embrace more than one mating, only one such mating (PP.RR × PP.RR) being unique w.r.t. the sex of the parents. If we had specified all the ten different hypotheses each referable to a unique mating on the assumption that the operational end in view is to identify a unique parental *pair* of genotypes or all the sixteen different hypotheses each referable to a unique mating if our aim is to identify the genotype of cock and hen *separately*, no classification of possible observations based on a mating of the cock and the hen *inter se* would have been consistent with an *a priori* adequate design. We have indeed invoked a 4-fold comprehensive set of hypotheses, and hence of admissible terminal statements, to illustrate a theoretical nicety without asking whether it accomplishes any useful result in the realm of action.

The writer here concedes the deliberate commission for expository purposes of an error which is a serious, but by no means the only serious, ground for criticism of the unique null hypothesis drill for the therapeutic, prophylactic or agricultural field trial. The truth is that the experiment under discussion has no intelligible operational intent with which the design is consistent. If we really want to know the genotype of a cock and of a hen each with a walnut comb, we shall not mate them *inter se*. We shall mate each with a fowl of opposite sex and of the single comb type. In that event, and only so, our design will be *a priori* adequate to the presumptive operational intent.

In so far as the design of an experiment is consistent with the proper uses alike of stochastic or of non-stochastic induction, we may now set out the steps thus:

(i) to what *question* or questions do we seek an answer or answers?

(ii) what *background knowledge* of the situation in which we seek an answer or answers is initially available?

(iii) what opportunities of *relevant observation* does the proposed situation offer?

(iv) what form must the set of *terminal statements* have to be acceptable in terms of (i) and attainable in terms of (ii) and (iii)?

(v) what *comprehensive set of hypotheses* is consistent as a whole with (ii)?

(vi) what specification of the members of the comprehensive set of hypotheses is *a priori* adequate to the design in terms of (iii) and (iv)?

Model II. To illustrate the place of each of these in the design of an experiment, let us now examine a model set-up of the sort we commonly invoke to illustrate the uses of the theory of probability, though we shall do so without actually transgressing the boundaries of non-stochastic induction.

1. To what question do we seek an answer?

The mean cash value (M) of the tickets in an urn.

2. What background knowledge may we assume?

(a) the urn contains N tickets of cash value £ x, $x + 1, x + 2 \ldots x + N - 1$, x being an integer;

(b) there are not less than three nor more than six tickets in the urn $(3 \leqslant N \leqslant 6)$;

(c) the cash value of no ticket exceeds £7, i.e. $(x + N - 1) \leqslant 7$.

3. What observations shall we be free to make?

The mean cash value (m) of two tickets removed simultaneously from the urn.

Before examining what terminal statements are acceptable in terms of the operational intent (1) and attainable in terms of our observations (3) interpreted against our background knowledge (2), let us set out as below the construction of the Hypothesis-observation table and the conclusions we can derive from it.

N	All possible sequences consistent with postulates						M	m (in intervals of $0\cdot5$)
6	2	3	4	5	6	7	$4\cdot5$	$2\cdot5 - 6\cdot5$
5	2	3	4	5	6	.	$4\cdot0$	$2\cdot5 - 5\cdot5$
	3	4	5	6	7	.	$5\cdot0$	$3\cdot5 - 6\cdot5$
4	2	3	4	5	.	.	$3\cdot5$	$2\cdot5 - 4\cdot5$
	3	4	5	6	.	.	$4\cdot5$	$3\cdot5 - 5\cdot5$
	4	5	6	7	.	.	$5\cdot5$	$4\cdot5 - 6\cdot5$
3	2	3	4	.	.	.	$3\cdot0$	$2\cdot5 - 3\cdot5$
	3	4	5	.	.	.	$4\cdot0$	$3\cdot5 - 4\cdot5$
	4	5	6	.	.	.	$5\cdot0$	$4\cdot5 - 5\cdot5$
	5	6	7	.	.	.	$6\cdot0$	$5\cdot5 - 6\cdot5$

Hypothesis Observation Grid

Hypothesis	Observations (m)								
(M)	2·5	3·0	3·5	4·0	4·5	5·0	5·5	6·0	6·5
3	+	+	+						
3·5	+	+	+	+	+				
4·0	+	+	+	+	+	+	+		
4·5	+	+	+	+	+	+	+	+	+
5·0			+	+	+	+	+	+	+
5·5					+	+	+	+	+
6·0							+	+	+

Permissible Terminal Statements

Observation (m)	Lower Limit of M	Upper Limit of M
2·5	3·0	4·5
3·0	3·0	4·5
3·5	3·0	5·0
4·0	3·5	5·0
4·5	3·5	5·5
5·0	4·0	5·5
5·5	4·0	6·0
6·0	4·5	6·0
6·5	4·5	6·0

Evidently, we cannot give an exact answer to the question stated in 1 above, but if we are content to accept the most *precise* answer the data of any one experiment can ever endorse, our acceptable terminal statement will take the form:

$$M = m \pm 2$$

If we decline to pass judgment on the result of the experiment unless the score (m) is a whole number, we could always assert truthfully that

$$M = m \pm 1 \cdot 5$$

389

We may thus say that the design of the experiment is *a priori* adequate if we deem a terminal statement of the form $M = m \pm 2$ to be acceptable. If the end in view is to make the more precise statement $M = m \pm 1 \cdot 5$ the design of the experiment does not fulfil the requirement of *a priori* adequacy but it is *a posteriori* adequate for situations in which the observed score is an integer. In short, the best answer we can guarantee to give in all circumstances is a terminal statement which picks out the smallest number of individual hypotheses consistent with each possible observation we may make.

This criterion of choice has no special interest in the domain of Model I, because no numerical specification of our hypotheses is there meaningful *vis-à-vis* a rule of non-stochastic induction; and no hypothesis is specifiable for the purposes of stochastic induction by a single parameter. Here one number suffices to label an elementary hypothesis, and the comprehensive set of elementary hypotheses are meaningfully presentable as an ordered set within which we can make a more parsimonious disposition of composite hypotheses each definable as an *interval*. If the longest interval specified by any such composite hypothesis endorsed by any one of the corresponding set of terminal statements is consistent with the *precision* which defines our criterion of acceptability, the classification of our hypotheses satisfies the requirements of *a priori* adequacy.

Though we have introduced no stochastic considerations in our discussion of the foregoing model, we have here reached a conclusion which points the way to an extension of the terms of reference of a calculus of judgments consistent with the Forward Look, embracing the theory of the decision test as a special case and resolving the dilemma arising from its limited usefulness. A third set-up much like the last but simpler for our purpose will serve to bring into sharper focus both the line of demarcation between stochastic and non-stochastic induction and also to clarify some of the essential features of the type of stochastic induction subsumed by the term *interval estimation*.

Model III. For what follows we may briefly state the data relevant to the initial problem thus:

(a) *Background Knowledge*

An urn contains six tickets of cash value £p, $p + 1$, $p + 2 \ldots p + 5$ on the understanding that p is an integer in the range $1 \leqslant p \leqslant 6$.

(b) *Permissible Observations*

We take two tickets successively, replacing the first and shaking up the urn thoroughly before taking the second and record the mean cash value (x_m).

(c) *Required Information*

What is the least cash value (p) of any ticket?

We shall approach the problem last stated both in terms of non-stochastic and of stochastic induction. A rule of stochastic induction must invoke a preliminary prescription of the sampling distribution referable to each hypothesis endorsed by a terminal statement. This we shall first do. For any value of p, we easily obtain the following random distribution of the mean score of 2-fold samples by recourse to a chessboard diagram:

Distribution of 2-fold sample mean (with replacement)

Frequency	$\frac{1}{36}$	$\frac{2}{36}$	$\frac{3}{36}$	$\frac{4}{36}$	$\frac{5}{36}$	$\frac{6}{36}$
Sample score	p	$p + \frac{1}{2}$	$p + 1$	$p + 1\frac{1}{2}$	$p + 2$	$p + 2\frac{1}{2}$

Frequency	$\frac{5}{36}$	$\frac{4}{36}$	$\frac{3}{36}$	$\frac{2}{36}$	$\frac{1}{36}$
Sample score	$p + 3$	$p + 3\frac{1}{2}$	$p + 4$	$p + 4\frac{1}{2}$	$p + 5$

We may accordingly lay out a hypothesis-observation table for values of p in the range $1 \geqslant p \geqslant 6$ as below; but we shall not signify concurrence of observation and hypothesis by a $+$ sign. Instead we enter in each cell entitled to the sign of consent a number (>1) which expresses as a multiple of 6^{-2} the long-run frequency of each observation consistent with a particular hypothesis specifying a unique value of p; and we may speak of all cells so labelled as the *region endorsed* by the background information. If we look at the experiment in the domain of non-stochastic induction, inspection of the table

391

then shows that the most general form of acceptable terminal statement consistent with the specification of requisite information (c) by the endorsed region of the H.O.G. is:

$$x_m \geqslant p \geqslant x_m - 5$$

This statement is *always* true and embodies as much as we can ever hope to say on the basis of the permitted class of observations, if we seek to frame a rule of decision with the intention implicit in the italicised adverb. Now different hypotheses (values of p) here assign different long-run frequencies to one and the same observation (x_m). From the foregoing set-up of the sample distribution we see that 34 (6^{-2}) is the proportion of all observations in the range $(p + 0 \cdot 5) \leqslant x_m \leqslant (p + 4 \cdot 5)$ for all values of p, i.e. we retain $94 \cdot \dot{4}$ per cent of the background information consistent with our long-run experience, if we exclude observations outside this range from the *endorsed region*. In that event, $94 \cdot 4$ per cent of our assertions will be correct for any value p may have, if we always assert that

$$x_m - 0 \cdot 5 \geqslant p \geqslant x_m - 4 \cdot 5$$

Thus we may narrow the interval in which we deem p to lie thereby achieving a higher level of terminal acceptability, i.e. a more precise answer to our question, if we are content to take an assignable risk that the rule will sometimes fail to give a true answer. If a stochastic procedure cannot guarantee a more precise answer than a rule of non-stochastic induction can endorse in the same set of situations, the risk we thus take is fruitless. We cannot then meaningfully speak of the statements it endorses as acceptable.

Before we travel further, let us scrutinise more closely what we *can* legitimately say and what we *cannot* legitimately say about the H.O.G. in the stochastic domain. We may set out the two rules of procedure in terms of the comprehensive set of possible observations we may make and the corresponding terminal statements subsumed by each rule as in the table on p. 394.

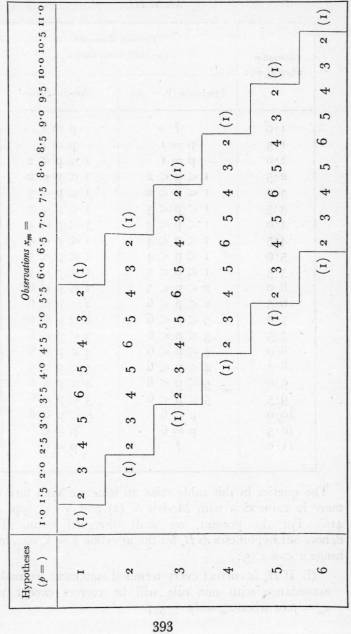

Model III

(The cell entries are *relative* frequencies)

Model III

Observation (when x_m is):	Terminal Statements (we shall assert that):	
	Stochastic ($P_f = \frac{1}{18}$)	Non-Stochastic
1·0	?	p = 1
1·5	p = 1	p = 1
2·0	p = 1	1 ⩽ p ⩽ 2
2·5	1 ⩽ p ⩽ 2	1 ⩽ p ⩽ 2
3·0	1 ⩽ p ⩽ 2	1 ⩽ p ⩽ 3
3·5	1 ⩽ p ⩽ 3	1 ⩽ p ⩽ 3
4·0	1 ⩽ p ⩽ 3	1 ⩽ p ⩽ 4
4·5	1 ⩽ p ⩽ 4	1 ⩽ p ⩽ 4
5·0	1 ⩽ p ⩽ 4	1 ⩽ p ⩽ 5
5·5	1 ⩽ p ⩽ 5	1 ⩽ p ⩽ 5
6·0	2 ⩽ p ⩽ 5	1 ⩽ p ⩽ 6
6·5	2 ⩽ p ⩽ 6	2 ⩽ p ⩽ 6
7·0	3 ⩽ p ⩽ 6	2 ⩽ p ⩽ 6
7·5	3 ⩽ p ⩽ 6	3 ⩽ p ⩽ 6
8·0	4 ⩽ p ⩽ 6	3 ⩽ p ⩽ 6
8·5	4 ⩽ p ⩽ 6	4 ⩽ p ⩽ 6
9·0	5 ⩽ p ⩽ 6	4 ⩽ p ⩽ 6
9·5	5 ⩽ p ⩽ 6	5 ⩽ p ⩽ 6
10·0	p = 6	5 ⩽ p ⩽ 6
10·5	p = 6	p = 6
11·0	?	p = 6

The queries in this table raise an issue we shall face once more in connexion with Models V (*a*) and V (*b*) (pp. 407–416). For the present, we shall disregard them. If we denote our hypotheses as H_n for the assertion $p = n$, etc., in the range $2 \leqslant n \leqslant 5$:

(i) If H_n is correct every terminal statement we make in accordance with our rule will be correct except when $x_m = p$ or when $x_m = (p + 5)$;

(ii) situations in which $x_m = p$ or $x_m = (p + 5)$ make up $\frac{1}{18} = P_f$, of the totality of our experience within the assumed framework of unending repetition;

(iii) if therefore we make a terminal statement consonant with the rule whenever we take a sample regardless of its value, only $\frac{1}{18}$ of our assertions will be false in the long run.

Now consider the case when $n = 1$ or $n = 6$. As it stands, the table will entitle us to make no statement. If we refrain from doing so, the numbers in the corresponding rows specify $\frac{35}{36}$ of our total experience, and we can err in our terminal statements

if H_1 is true when $x_m = 6 \cdot 0$ with probability $\frac{1}{35} < P_f$

if H_6 is true when $x_m = 11 \cdot 0$ with probability $\frac{1}{35} < P_f$

Alternatively, we may modify the rule by the addendum

Say $p = 1$ if $x_m = 1$, $1 \cdot 5$ or $2 \cdot 0$ with probability $1 \cdot 0$

Say $p = 6$ if $x_m = 10$, $10 \cdot 5$ or $11 \cdot 0$ with probability $1 \cdot 0$

Again, we shall err only if $x_m = 6 \cdot 0$ when $p = 1$ and $x_m = 6 \cdot 0$ when $p = 6$, and

If H_1 is true $x_m = 6 \cdot 0$ with probability $\frac{1}{36} < P_f$

If H_6 is true $x_m = 11 \cdot 0$ with probability $\frac{1}{36} < P_f$

In either event, every admissible hypothesis prescribes that the proportion of false terminal statements will be equal to or less than $P_f = \frac{1}{18}$. Thus we can say that at least $\frac{17}{18}$ of our assertions will be true in the long run, if we operate the rule consistently. This is what we mean by saying that the uncertainty safeguard $P_f \leqslant \frac{1}{18}$ specifies the risk of error incurred by following the rule.

It is most important to have no illusions about what we rightly mean by following the rule *consistently* in this context. We are talking about the *totality* of our experience in the repetitive framework of randomwise sampling. We are not talking about a fraction of this totality such as the class of situations which arise when $x_m = 4 \cdot 0$. Thus we cannot say that the risk of false assertion is $P_f \leqslant \frac{1}{18}$ when we make the particular assertion $1 \leqslant p \leqslant 3$ if $x_m = 4 \cdot 0$, implying thereby that the probability that such an assertion is true is $P_t \geqslant \frac{17}{18}$. Our table shows that x_m may indeed be $4 \cdot 0$ when $p = 4$, and we are exploring a range of admissible possibilities in which p actually has a particular value which may be $p = 4$. Should it happen that H_4 is true, we should always be wrong in asserting that $1 \leqslant p \leqslant 3$ when $x_m = 4 \cdot 0$, and we may write $P_{f.n} = 1$, so that $P_{t.n} = 0$ respectively for the *conditional* uncertainty safeguard and conditional stochastic credibility of the assertions embodied in our rule for all *particular* situations arising when $x_m = n$ in the range $1 \leqslant p \leqslant 5$.

This distinction brings out a fundamental difference between what is meaningful, if we adopt the *Forward Look* which embraces the outcome of a rule conceived in behaviourist terms, and what we deem to be meaningful, if we adopt the *Backward Look* consistent with the location of probability "in the mind." Of the endorsed region of our table it is true to say w.r.t. any *conceivable* particular value of p

$$(p + 0 \cdot 5) \leqslant x_m \leqslant (p + 4 \cdot 5)$$

$$\text{with probability } (1 - P_f) \geqslant \tfrac{17}{18} \qquad (i)$$

We may express this symbolically as

$$P(p + 0 \cdot 5 \leqslant m \leqslant p + 4 \cdot 5) \geqslant \tfrac{17}{18} \qquad . \qquad (ii)$$

Of our table *as a whole*, we can also rightly say for all values of p:

$$(x_m - 0 \cdot 5) \geqslant p \geqslant (x_m - 4 \cdot 5) \qquad . \qquad . \qquad (iii)$$

The formal identity of (i) and (iii) conceals a factual difference. Actually, we shall encounter in the totality of our experience any value of x_m consistent with the value of p we insert; but we can meet only one value of p in the same framework of repetition, since only one hypothesis of our admissible set is true of the assumed homogeneous universe (our urn) of choice. Thus we might speak of x_m as a factual variable and p as a conceptual variable. Of one we can make statements in the domain of events to the effect: x_m is ... if p is ... We have left the domain of events if we say: p is . . . if x_m is . . . In the domain of events, p is a constant for whatsoever value of x_m we observe. If we interpret it retrospectively as a statement about the probability that p lies in a particular range when we already know that x_m has a particular value, we therefore retreat into the shadowy domains of probabilities in the mind. We do so explicitly if we embody (iii) in a statement analogous to (ii), viz.:

$$P\,(x_m - 0\cdot5 \geqslant p \geqslant x_m - 4\cdot5) \geqslant (1 - P_f)$$

In any meaningful sense consistent with the behaviourist outlook, the above refers only to the long-run frequency of correct assertion within the framework of a rule which we operate without knowing what value of x_m we may meet on any single occasion for its application. It follows that the design must be *a priori adequate* for the form of terminal statement deemed to be acceptable and this is inconsistent with a procedure which puts no restriction on what form of terminal statement is indeed acceptable. In the domain of *interval estimation* illustrated by our Model III, this implies a statement of the length of the interval we deem to be satisfactory. Only then can we define the size of sample consistent with an assigned upper limit of acceptable risk.

For Model III the procedure is as follows. Instead of assuming arbitrarily for expository purposes that we are content with a terminal statement to the effect that p lies in the range from $(x_m - 4\cdot5)$ to $(x_m - 0\cdot5)$ if we can assign an uncertainty safeguard $P_f < 0\cdot06$ to our rule, we shall now assume that no terminal statement will be acceptably precise unless our rule places p in the interval $(x_m - 4)$ to $(x_m - 1)$ with an uncertainty safeguard $P_f \leqslant 0\cdot05$. Our first step is to tabulate distributions of the score mean (x_m) 3-fold, 4-fold, 5-fold, etc., samples. This we can do by successive application of the chessboard device which we invoked to define the 2-fold sample mean score distribution on page 393. We may then make a more condensed table of probabilities as shown in the table on page 398.

To say that p lies in the range $(x_m - 4)$ to $(x_m - 1)$ inclusive is formally equivalent to the statement that x_m lies in the range

$(p + 1)$ to $(p + 4)$, if we interpret the identity as valid for the operation of the rule in its entirety. Our uncertainty safeguard to the former assertion is thus the probability that x_m will lie outside the range $(p + 1)$ to $(p + 4)$; and our table shows that this exceeds $0·05$ unless $r > 4$. Thus we shall be able to design a procedure which accomplishes the end in view, only if we base our assertions on the outcome of taking with replacement

	Probability that x_m lies				
Outside the Range (inclusive)	For samples of				
	2	3	4	5	6
p + 0·5 to p + 4·5	0·056	0·037	0·008	0·005	0·001
p + 1·0 to p + 4·0	0·167	0·093	0·054	0·032	0·020
p + 1·5 to p + 3·5	0·333	0·324	0·194	0·196	0·122
p + 2·0 to p + 3·0	0·556	0·519	0·478	0·443	0·412

5-fold or larger samples randomwise from the urn. It is worthy of comment that we cannot here express an uncertainty safeguard by the identity $P_f = \epsilon$ in terms of a preassigned level (ϵ) of acceptability. All we can say is $P_f < \epsilon$, or $P_f \leqslant \epsilon$. This is because we are dealing in this context realistically with a discrete distribution. $P_f = \epsilon$ is justifiable only if we can justifiably invoke a continuous distribution of sample score values.

CHAPTER SEVENTEEN

RECIPE AND RULE IN STOCHASTIC INDUCTION

WITHIN WHAT WE may regard as the legitimate terms of reference of a calculus of judgments consonant with a behaviourist outlook, it has been customary to make a sharp distinction between *test* procedures and *interval*—in contradistinction to *point*—estimation. We have examined the credentials of two views of test procedure in Chapter Fifteen; and in current use the term interval estimation also subsumes divergent views propounded by the same opposing schools. The divergence between Neyman's *Theory of Confidence* and R. A. Fisher's doctrine of *Fiducial Probability* did not become apparent to many writers on statistical theory till many years after the appearance of the original publication of their views. This is partly because the arithmetical recipes prescribed by them are in many situations identical; but if we probe more deeply we may discern another source of misunderstanding. We have seen that the disputable issues involved in test procedure did not come sharply into focus till Wald expounded the views of Neyman and E. S. Pearson. If we now adopt the approach to stochastic induction in a publication (*op. cit.*) by Wrighton,* we shall see that a comparable reorientation of the problem of interval estimation is overdue.

Several circumstances have conspired to retard such a reorientation. One of these is the disposition to emphasise the distinction between test procedure and interval estimation at the wrong level, as when we identify the former with the domain of situations admitting discretely bounded alternative hypotheses and the latter with that of situations consistent with a continuum of parameter values each conceptually definitive of an initially admissible elementary hypothesis. What is more important emerges in the distinction Wrighton draws between exploratory and holonomic experimentation. If we take seriously Neyman's own interpretation of a rule

* *Acta Genetica et Statistica Medica*, 1953.

of stochastic induction as a rule stated in advance and consistently followed regardless of the outcome, we shall too readily overlook some of its more challenging implications unless we also ask what task the rule accomplishes. We must then impose a criterion of acceptability on the terminal statements subsumed by the rule. If we likewise concur in the full implications of Neyman's interpretation of the uncertainty safeguard as a risk associated with the operation of the rule *in its entirety*, we must also concede that: (*a*) each of a comprehensive set of *acceptable* terminal statements must endorse one, and only one, of a comprehensive set of hypotheses; (*b*) there must be a corresponding terminal statement to endorse each member of the comprehensive set of hypotheses.

Such is the principle of *a priori adequacy* which Wrighton postulates as an essential property of the stochastic hypothesis-observation grid, and his approach by way of the H.O.G. of a holonomic experiment in the non-stochastic domain suggests a sufficient reason for Neyman's failure to recognise its relevance to the Confidence controversy which is the topic of a later chapter. If we accustom ourselves to regard the H.O.G. as a visualisation of stochastic induction in the discrete domain of classical models such as Model III of the last chapter, it is easy to conceive each cell as an infinitesimal element of area and hence an effortless step to regard a graph exhibiting interval estimation in the continuum as a recipe— adequate or otherwise—for making a rule of procedure consistent with the Forward Look. Contrariwise, it is all too easy to overlook the elementary logic of the procedures we adopt, if we follow the historic path, *i.e.* if we start with the theory of interval estimation in the factually nebulous domain of an infinity of hypotheses w.r.t. each of which the relevant sampling distribution admits an infinity of score values.

Accordingly, we shall now explore a set of model situations which will disclose essential features of stochastic induction with a view to:

(*a*) exhibiting test procedure and interval estimation as variants of a common pattern of reasoning;

(*b*) making explicit certain canons prerequisite to the complete definition and prescription of a rule of stochastic induction.

Models IV (a) and IV (b). Consider the following model situations:

(a) Two pennies come from a bag containing pennies of 3 sorts:

> A minted with 2 heads
> B minted with 2 tails
> C normal

(b) Two pennies come from *one* of 2 bags, respectively containing:

> (i) normal pennies (C) and pennies with 2 heads (A);
> (ii) normal pennies (C) and pennies with 2 tails (B).

We shall suppose that the acceptable terminal statement of an experimental design is to identify the *pair* itself. In that event our comprehensive set of hypotheses need take no stock of order. For the Model IV (a) set-up, we may specify our elementary hypothesis in qualitative terms as: AA, AB, AC, CC, CB, BB. For the Model IV (b) set-up they are: AA, AC, CC, CB, BB. For either, we may specify all the relevant information for a stochastic design based on 4 tosses of each penny chosen as in Table I below:

TABLE I

Type	Actual No. of Heads in the pair	No. of Heads *observed* in the 4-fold joint toss								
		0	1	2	3	4	5	6	7	8
AA	4	0	0	0	0	0	0	0	0	1
AC	3	0	0	0	0	$\frac{1}{16}$	$\frac{4}{16}$	$\frac{6}{16}$	$\frac{4}{16}$	$\frac{1}{16}$
AB	2	0	0	0	0	1	0	0	0	0
CC	2	$\frac{1}{256}$	$\frac{8}{256}$	$\frac{28}{256}$	$\frac{56}{256}$	$\frac{70}{256}$	$\frac{56}{256}$	$\frac{28}{256}$	$\frac{8}{256}$	$\frac{1}{256}$
BC	1	$\frac{1}{16}$	$\frac{4}{16}$	$\frac{6}{16}$	$\frac{4}{16}$	$\frac{1}{16}$	0	0	0	0
BB	0	1	0	0	0	0	0	0	0	0

This method of specifying our hypotheses is valid for either model; and is alone adequate to label each distinctively in the Model IV (*a*) set-up; but it is not the only way in which we can do so in the Model IV (*b*) set-up, where we exclude AB in

TABLE II

First Rule of Exclusion

Hypothesis		Observation (*Heads*)								
Type	No of *Heads*	0	1	2	3	4	5	6	7	8
AA	4									+
AC	3					+	+	+	+	−
CC	2	−	−	+	+	+	+	+	−	−
BC	1	−	+	+	+	+				
BB	0	+								

Second Rule of Exclusion

Hypothesis		Observation (*Heads*)								
Type	No. of *Heads*	0	1	2	3	4	5	6	7	8
AA	4									+
AC	3					−	+	+	+	+
CC	2	−	−	+	+	+	+	+	−	−
BC	1	+	+	+	+	−				
BB	0	+								

virtue of additional *prior* information. We can thus identify each qualitatively specifiable elementary hypothesis by a unique number referable to a unique sampling distribution, viz. the total number of heads on the 4 faces of the two pennies chosen. Accordingly, we can lay out our hypotheses as an *ordered* set.

The Model IV (*b*) situation will here suffice to illustrate an essential step in the prescription of a proper recipe for stochastic induction, namely the discovery of an appropriate rule of exclusion and endorsement. The reader may find it helpful to explore the Model IV (*a*) situation in the same way. We shall assume that $P_f < \frac{1}{14}$ is an acceptable uncertainty safeguard. Of itself, this is consistent with more than one rule of exclusion, as will be seen by comparison of Table I (in which the line corresponding to AB is irrelevant) with Table II in which the *positive* sign indicates a hypothesis retained as consistent with a particular set of observations and the *negative* sign indicates a hypothesis rejected as such because the risk of meeting such an observation if the hypothesis is true does not exceed $\frac{1}{14}$. In the phraseology of p. 392 the cells with the plus sign define the *endorsed* region of the stochastic H.O.G., the endorsed region of the non-stochastic grid including *also* the *excluded* cells labelled as such by the minus sign. For no hypothesis do the cells excluded by either rule specify more than a fraction equivalent to $\frac{18}{256}$ (slightly less than $\frac{1}{14}$) of our total experience consistent with its truth.

Table III, which summarises the outcome of two designs based on different rules of exclusion and endorsement, also shows what the outcome of the experiment may be in the non-stochastic domain. At a first glance we might yield to the temptation to say:

    (i) if our primary concern is to satisfy ourselves that neither penny is normal, we shall prefer the first rule of exclusion;

    (ii) if our primary concern is to satisfy ourselves that both pennies are normal, we shall choose the second.

If we did indeed base our preference on such considerations, we should not be interpreting the terms of reference of the uncertainty safeguard consistently. The latter applies to the rule in its

TABLE III

Observation No. of Heads	Non-Stochastic Type	Non-Stochastic (No. of Heads)	Stochastic ($P_f < \frac{1}{14}$) 1st Rule of Exclusion Type	1st Rule of Exclusion No. of Heads	2nd Rule of Exclusion Type	2nd Rule of Exclusion No. of Heads
0	CC, BC, BB	2, 1, 0	BB	0	BC, BB	0, 1
1	CC, BC	2, 1	BC	1	BC	1
2	CC, BC	2, 1	CC, BC	1, 2	CC, BC	1, 2
3	CC, BC	2, 1	CC, BC	1, 2	CC, BC	1, 2
4	BC, CC, AC	1, 2, 3	BC, CC, AC	1, 2, 3	CC	2
5	CC, AC	2, 3	CC, AC	2, 3	CC, AC	2, 3
6	CC, AC	2, 3	CC, AC	2	CC, AC	2, 3
7	CC, AC	2, 3	AC	3	AC	3
8	CC, AC, AA	2, 3, 4	AA	4	AC, AA	3, 4

entirety and has no bearing on the frequency of correct assertions limited to particular terminal statements. To discover a legitimate basis for preference we must therefore ask what the rule does accomplish in its entirety. Now Rule 2 ensures that no terminal statement endorses a composite hypothesis embodying more than 2 consecutive members of the comprehensive set of elementary hypotheses. Since the non-stochastic procedure is not *a priori adequate* to accomplish this, we may say that Rule 2 is conceivably acceptable in the *minimal* sense defined on p. 449; but Rule 1, like the non-stochastic procedure, does endorse a terminal statement referable to a composite hypothesis which encompasses 3 elementary hypotheses, viz. the assertion which goes with the observation of 4 heads in the 4-fold joint toss. Thus one lesson we learn from our model is that a prerequisite to prescription of a proper rule of stochastic induction is a Rule of Exclusion and Endorsement (R.E.E.) consistent *both* with the acceptable level of uncertainty which circumscribes its validity, *and* with the acceptable form of terminal statements it subsumes.

We shall also recognise an implication of the principle of *a priori adequacy* if we modify the foregoing procedure. Either rule of exclusion and endorsement we have explored is comprehensive in the sense defined on p. 346, i.e. we commit ourselves to a terminal statement referable to every observation we may make. If we are content to take the risk that as many as $\frac{70}{256}$—roughly a quarter—of our experiments will be fruitless in the long run, if 4 is the actual number of heads on the 4 faces of the 2 coins chosen in the Model IV (b) set-up and that *all* our experiments will then be fruitless in the Model IV (a) set-up, we are entitled to explore the possibility of prescribing a new design based on a greater number of joint tosses but still consistent with the condition $P_f < \frac{1}{14}$. What we cannot safely do is to adapt a comprehensive design to satisfy the requirements of *a priori* adequacy by disregarding a particular class of observations.

Since Rule 1 would guarantee the same overall precision of statement as Rule 2, in the Model IV (b) setting if we refrained from making any terminal statement referable to a head-score of 4 in the 4-fold joint toss, it is instructive to examine the consequences of making our test non-comprehensive w.r.t. Rule I. Without changing the prescription in any other way, we shall suppose that we confine our attention to trials of which the outcome is any number of heads other than 4. If AA or BB correctly describe our choice the situation remains the same. If either AC or BC truly specifies our choice we shall confine our positive terminal statements to 15 out of 16 situations in our total experience. If the pair chosen is CC we decline to make a statement in 70 out of 256 situations and confine our positive terminal statement to 186 out of 256 in

TABLE IV

Hypothesis		Observation (No. of *Heads*)							
Type	No. of *Heads*	0	1	2	3	5	6	7	8
AA	4	0	0	0	0	0	0	0	1
AC	3	0	0	0	0	$\frac{4}{15}$	$\frac{6}{15}$	$\frac{4}{15}$	$\frac{1}{15}$
CC	2	$\frac{1}{186}$	$\frac{8}{186}$	$\frac{28}{186}$	$\frac{56}{186}$	$\frac{56}{186}$	$\frac{28}{186}$	$\frac{8}{186}$	$\frac{1}{186}$
BC	1	$\frac{1}{15}$	$\frac{4}{15}$	$\frac{6}{15}$	$\frac{4}{15}$	0	0	0	0
BB	0	1	0	0	0	0	0	0	0

our total experience. Accordingly, we must readjust the relevant figures of Table I, as in Table IV. We then see that 18 in 186 of our assertions will be false if the correct specification of the pair is CC. The overall operation of the rule now signifies that it is not inconsistent with $\frac{1}{14}$ of total experience within the framework of the assumption that any single hypothesis may be true. Thus $\frac{18}{186} > P_f$ as defined by the comprehensive rule. So the design will not be consistent with the acceptable level of uncertainty, if we reserve the right to restrict the terms of reference of the rule to observations consistent with the pre-sumptive operational intent.

Models V (a) and V (b). So far, we have seen that different rules of exclusion and endorsement may be consistent with one and the same level of uncertainty, but only one of the two discussed above is also consistent with the criterion of *acceptable terminal statement.* That different laws of exclusion may fulfil both conditions will emerge from a study of two model situations with respect to each of which we shall postulate the following common features:

(*a*) a lottery wheel has N equal sectors each of which is black or red;

(*b*) the single-spin (unit trial) score depends on whether the sector which comes to rest opposite a fixed pointer is black (*zero* score) or red (*unit* score);

(*c*) we do not know the number (Np) of red sectors or the number $(Nq = N.1\text{-}p)$ of black ones;

(*d*) we spin the wheel 400 times, and record the 400-fold *mean* score.

We now distinguish wheels of 2 sorts:

Model V (a): We know that:
  (i) $N = 10$;
  (ii) at least one sector is red;
  (iii) at least one sector is black.

Model V (b): We know that:
  (i) $N = 100$;
  (ii) at least 10 sectors are red;
  (iii) at least 10 sectors are black.

In either set-up we are sampling in a 2-class universe and successive terms of the binomial $(q + p)^{400}$ define the sample mean score distribution. Of either set, we may also say that neither $rq = 400q$ nor $rp = 400p$ is less than 10, whence we may invoke (p. 160) the normal distribution as a satisfactory descriptive device. The essential difference between the two models is this. Of Model V (a) we know that p has one of a set of 9 *discrete* values from 0·1 to 0·9 in intervals of 0·1. Of Model V (b) we know that p has one of a set of 81 discrete values from 0·1 to 0·9 in intervals of 0·01.

Without assuming that we can actually design an experiment unless we assign in advance the sample size (r) consistent with an acceptable set of terminal statements at an acceptable level of uncertainty, let us here examine the implications of arbitrarily fixing $r = 400$ in terms of the adequacy of a design to endorse a statement about p. First we express in standard form the mean score values ($p_{0.1}$ and $p_{0.2}$) which define a range in which 95 per cent of all score values lie symmetrically about the mean p, viz.:

$$\frac{(p - p_{0.1})^2}{\sigma_p^2} = 4 = \frac{(p - p_{0.2})^2}{\sigma_p^2} \ \text{and} \ \sigma_p^2 = \frac{p(1-p)}{400}$$

Thus $p_{0.1} = 0 \cdot 45$ and $p_{0.2} = 0 \cdot 55$ if $p = 0 \cdot 5$. For any value of p other than $0 \cdot 5$ the interval consistent with the 5 per cent level of uncertainty will be shorter. Thus the probability that a mean score lies inside the range $0 \cdot 35$ to $0 \cdot 45$ when $p = 0 \cdot 4$ is less than $0 \cdot 05$.

In either set-up, the arbitrarily assumed value $r = 400$ thus ensures that *more than* 95 per cent of all score values will lie inside the range specified below for each value of p cited:

range of mean score (p_0)	p
$0 \cdot 05 - 0 \cdot 15$	$0 \cdot 1$
$0 \cdot 15 - 0 \cdot 25$	$0 \cdot 2$
$0 \cdot 25 - 0 \cdot 35$	$0 \cdot 3$
$0 \cdot 35 - 0 \cdot 45$	$0 \cdot 4$
$0 \cdot 45 - 0 \cdot 55$	$0 \cdot 5$
$0 \cdot 55 - 0 \cdot 65$	$0 \cdot 6$
$0 \cdot 65 - 0 \cdot 75$	$0 \cdot 7$
$0 \cdot 75 - 0 \cdot 85$	$0 \cdot 8$
$0 \cdot 85 - 0 \cdot 95$	$0 \cdot 9$

In the Model V (a) set-up these 9 values of p constitute a discrete comprehensive set of hypotheses and score values in the range defined by a rule of exclusion consistent with the uncertainty safeguard $P_f \leqslant 0 \cdot 05$ for each admissible hypothesis do not overlap. For Model V (a) we may thus make one rule of induction *en rapport* with decision test procedure embracing a comprehensive set of 9 admissible hypotheses with an uncertainty safeguard $P_f \leqslant 0 \cdot 05$, viz.:

If p_0 is *inside* the range $0 \cdot 05 - 0 \cdot 15$ we shall assert that $p = 0 \cdot 1$.

If p_0 is *inside* the range $0 \cdot 15 - 0 \cdot 25$ we shall assert that $p = 0 \cdot 2$.

If p_0 is *inside* the range $0 \cdot 25 - 0 \cdot 35$ we shall assert that $p = 0 \cdot 3$.

etc. etc. etc.

For two reasons recognisable by reference to Fig. 2 the rule so stated is not comprehensive in the sense defined on p. 346:

(i) since the distribution of score values is discrete with fixed interval $\Delta p_0 = 0 \cdot 0025$ in the range 0 to 1, the restriction implied by *inside* in our statement of the rule excludes our right to make a statement when the value of p_0 is an exact multiple of $0 \cdot 05$;

(ii) the rule permits us to make no statement if $p_0 \leqslant 0 \cdot 05$ or $p_0 \geqslant 0 \cdot 95$.

Since the truth of any one of the 9 admissible hypotheses excludes the possibility that more than 5 per cent of samples we meet in the long run will be *null*, i.e. that we shall have to refrain from making statements about them, it happens that the disadvantages of (i) and (ii) in terms of economical design are trivial; but we can remove this minor disability in more than one way. First we recall that the interval which symmetrically circumscribes 95 per cent of all sample scores for all admissible values of p other than $0 \cdot 5$ is less than $0 \cdot 1$. Thus we shall not violate our uncertainty safeguard if we define our score interval for $p = 0 \cdot 5$ as $0 \cdot 45 - 0 \cdot 55$ inclusive and each interval on either side symmetrically of length $0 \cdot 1 - 2\Delta p_0 = 0 \cdot 995$. Since the 95 per cent score range falls off from $p = 0 \cdot 5$ to $p = 0 \cdot 1$ and from $p = 0 \cdot 5$ to $p = 0 \cdot 9$, we are free to accommodate the otherwise null score values in many *other* ways, each being an R.E.E. consistent with $P_f \leqslant 0 \cdot 05$. Next we note that scores outside the range $p_0 \leqslant 0 \cdot 05$ or $p_0 \geqslant 0 \cdot 95$ must occur in less than $2 \cdot 5$ per cent of all samples even when $p = 0 \cdot 1$ or $p = 0 \cdot 9$. So we shall not violate our uncertainty

safeguard if we define our terminal intervals with limits at
$p_0 = 0$ and $p_0 = 1$. Accordingly, we might state *one* rule
consistent with an uncertainty safeguard $P_f \leqslant 0 \cdot 05$ and
admitting no *null* observations as:

If p_0 lies *inclusively* in the range	Assert that p is
$0 \cdot 00 - 0 \cdot 1475$	$0 \cdot 1$
$0 \cdot 15 - 0 \cdot 2475$	$0 \cdot 2$
$0 \cdot 25 - 0 \cdot 3475$	$0 \cdot 3$
$0 \cdot 35 - 0 \cdot 4475$	$0 \cdot 4$
$0 \cdot 45 - 0 \cdot 55$	$0 \cdot 5$
$0 \cdot 5525 - 0 \cdot 65$	$0 \cdot 6$
$0 \cdot 6525 - 0 \cdot 75$	$0 \cdot 7$
$0 \cdot 7525 - 0 \cdot 85$	$0 \cdot 8$
$0 \cdot 8525 - 1 \cdot 0$	$0 \cdot 9$

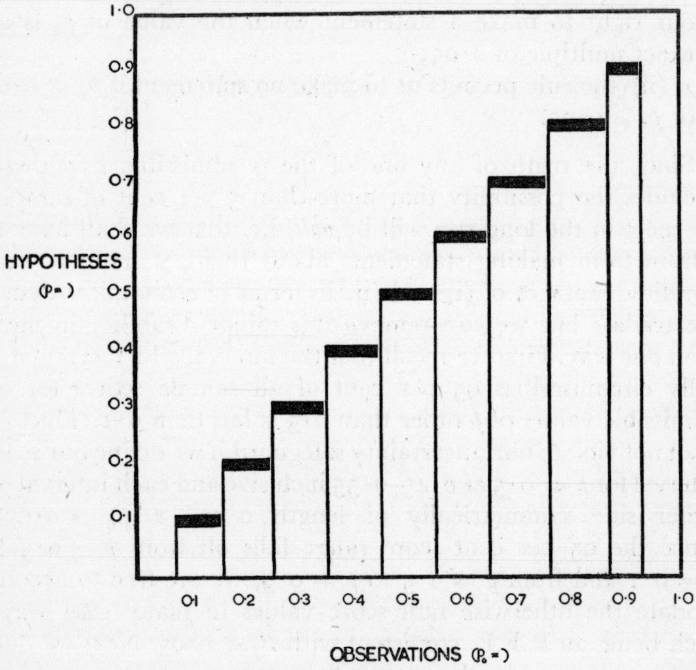

FIG. 2. Model V (a)

The length of each thick black horizontal line represents a 95 per cent range of
all observations consistent with the corresponding hypothesis.

410

In the foregoing discussion of Model V (*a*) it has not been necessary to discuss what is an acceptable terminal statement. We have tacitly assumed that we wish to specify the exact value of p within the framework of an acceptable risk of error, and it transpires that the sample size $r = 400$ satisfies the condition that our error risk is $P_f \leqslant 0.05$, i.e. does not exceed the conventionally prescribed level of uncertainty. If we demand the same precision of statement in the set-up of Model V (*b*), we shall need to prescribe r for a comparable test procedure, so that 95 per cent of score values lie symmetrically in an interval of 0.01 when $p = 0.5$, i.e. for a range bounded by $p_0 = 0.495$ and $p_0 = 0.505$.

Whence we must define r so that

$$\frac{(0.5 - 0.505)^2}{\sigma_p^2} = 4 \quad and \quad \sigma_p^2 = \frac{1}{4r}$$

$$\therefore \quad r = 40,000$$

An essential difference between the two models is therefore that a design to ensure correct acceptance of each admissible *elementary* hypothesis with an uncertainty safeguard $P_f \leqslant 0.05$ prescribes recourse to samples 100 times as large for a Model V (*b*) as for a Model V (*a*) set-up. A sample size so large as 40,000 is too large to handle in almost any conceivable designed experiment. Accordingly, we must abandon hope if we identify each acceptable terminal statement as the assertion that a particular elementary hypothesis (discrete value of p) is the true one; but we are then asking our design to guarantee a much higher level of numerical precision than the design for Model V (*a*) prescribed. In effect, we were then content to say that p lies in an *interval* of length 0.1. Let us therefore now assume that assertions about p consistent with this precision level are acceptable terminal statements. Our set of *composite* hypotheses corresponding to 401 possible observations (p_0) will then constitute a comprehensive set of 9 *consecutive overlapping intervals* in the sense defined above; and our procedure will offer no difficulty if we visualise these 401 possible observations and 81 elementary hypotheses laid out gridwise as a hypothesis-observation table with cell entries of a given row referable to a particular elementary hypothesis and cell entries of a particular column referable to a particular observation (mean score), as for Type III of p. 428 below.

Each elementary hypothesis specified by one of the ordered set of parameter (p) values in the range $0 \cdot 1$ to $0 \cdot 9$ with an interval $\Delta p = 0 \cdot 01$ admits the occurrence of an observation in each cell of the corresponding row labelled by mean score values (p_0) of the 400-fold spin from 0 to 1 with an interval $\Delta p_0 = 0 \cdot 0025$. Thus every cell of the grid would carry a positive sign, if we labelled it as for an experiment in the non-stochastic domain. No rule referable to single observations (mean score of 400-fold spin) in the domain of non-stochastic induction could then give us any information whatsoever about p. We may, however, take advantage of the fact that observations consistent with any elementary hypothesis are not of equal value in terms of the totality of our experience. Some are far more common than others, and we may black-out a class of rare ones according to a rule of exclusion which guarantees the same risk of erroneously stating that such and such a set of observations are inconsistent with the truth of such and such a hypothesis.

There will be many different ways of doing this, but the one which leads to the most tractable outcome is to exclude all values of p_0 outside the symmetrical range $p_i \pm h\sigma_{p.i}$ for every value of i which labels one or other of the elementary hypotheses. Our cell entries marked with the positive sign collectively then occupy a lozenge shaped (*endorsed*) region with a jagged outline running diagonally across the grid. If we interpret this as we should interpret a similar hypothesis-observation table for a non-stochastic domain, the column of marked cells corresponding to a particular score value will delimit the row marginal p values (elementary hypothesis) deemed to be consistent with the observation on the dual assumption that: (*a*) we operate the rule itself consistently; (*b*) we accept the assigned risk.

As before, we shall assign as an acceptable risk $P_f \leqslant 0 \cdot 05$, so that $h = 2$ above. To operate the rule consistently we must then ensure that it will guarantee the acceptable terminal statement, here expressible as a precision level. If we call the marginal value of p referable to the uppermost cell of the jth column $p_{v.j}$ and the one referable to the lowermost cell $p_{u.j}$, our precision level for the particular score value $p_{0.j}$ will be $(p_{v.j} - p_{u.j})$. To define our rule in terms of an acceptable terminal statement we must specify an interval i_p so that $(p_{v.j} - p_{u.j}) \leqslant i_p$; and this will be possible only if we define r appropriately for the r-fold spin. Thus we cannot arbitrarily

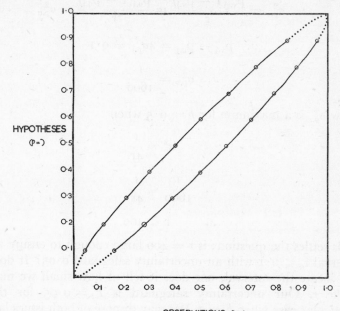

OBSERVATIONS $(\mathscr{Q} =)$

Fig. 3.   Model V (b).

The Neyman solution.

assume that $r = 400$ satisfies the criterion of acceptable terminal statement defined by $i_p = 0 \cdot 1$. If we prescribe this as our criterion, we must seek to specify r appropriately.

When r is large—as we can satisfy ourselves by preliminary examination—we may provisionally regard the jagged outline of the *endorsed* region enclosing all admissible observations consistent with the prescribed rule of exclusion as two curves defined by the equations

$$p_{u.j} + 2\sigma_{p.v} = p_{0.j} = p_{v.j} - 2\sigma_{p.v} \quad . \quad . \quad . \quad (i)$$

413

As we know, $\sigma_{p.j}$ has its maximum value when $p = p_i = 0 \cdot 5$ and the horizontal width of the endorsed region is greatest at this level. From Fig. 3 we see that the vertical width is also greatest for $p_0 = 0 \cdot 5$. It will therefore suffice if we prescribe r to ensure that $i_p \leqslant 0 \cdot 1$ when $p_0 = 0 \cdot 5$ so that $(p_{v.j} + p_{u.j}) = 1$, whence $p_{u.j} = (1 - p_{v.j})$ and $(1 - p_{u.j}) = p_{v.j}$

$$\therefore \quad \sigma_{p.v}^2 = \frac{p_{v.j}(1 - p_{v.j})}{r} = \frac{p_{u.j}(1 - p_{u.j})}{r} = \sigma_{p.u}^2$$

$$\therefore \quad p_{v.j} - p_{u.j} = 4\sigma_{p.v} = 0 \cdot 1$$

$$\therefore \quad \sigma_{p.v}^2 = \frac{1}{1600}$$

Now $\sigma_{p.v}^2$ is a maximum for $p = 0 \cdot 5$ when

$$\sigma_p^2 = \frac{1}{4r}$$

$$\therefore \quad \frac{1}{1600} \leqslant \frac{1}{4r}$$

$$\therefore \quad r \leqslant 400$$

This settles the question: is $r = 400$ large enough to ensure an interval $i_p \leqslant 0 \cdot 1$ with an uncertainty safeguard $0 \cdot 05$? It does not locate the interval, nor does it tell us how small we may make r. Our uncertainty safeguard is $P_f = 0 \cdot 05$ for the particular case when $h = 2$. We may dispose of both issues last stated in more general terms than above, if we define P_f in terms of $h\sigma$. In that event we may write (i) above as

$$(p_{v.j} - p_{u.j})^2 = h^2\sigma_{p.v}^2 \quad and \quad (p_{u.j} - p_{0.j})^2 = h^2\sigma_{p.u}^2$$

$$\therefore \quad (r + h^2)p_{v.j}^2 - (2rp_{0.j} + h^2)p_{v.j} + rp_{0.j}^2 = 0$$

$$and$$

$$(r + h^2)p_{u.j}^2 - (2rp_{0.j} + h^2)p_{u.j} + rp_{0.j}^2 = 0$$

Formally, the last two equations are identical and their two roots are the roots of

$$(r + h^2)p^2 - (2rp_0 + h^2)p + rp_0^2 = 0$$

414

Thus we obtain

$$p_{v.j} = \frac{(2rp_{0.j} + h^2) + \sqrt{(2rp_{0.j} + h^2)^2 - 4r(r + h^2)p_{0.j}^2}}{2(r + h^2)} \quad \text{(ii)}$$

$$p_{u.j} = \frac{(2rp_{0.j} + h^2) - \sqrt{(2rp_{0.j} + h^2)^2 - 4r(r + h^2)p_{0.j}^2}}{2(r + h^2)} \quad \text{(iii)}$$

We wish to make $(p_{v.j} - p_{u.j}) = 0 \cdot 1$ when $p_0 = 0 \cdot 5$, whence

$$\frac{1}{100} = \frac{4}{r + 4}$$

$$\therefore \ r = 396$$

For a given value of $p_{0.j}$, (ii) and (iii) give the appropriate limits of p consistent with the uncertainty safeguard. The solution of (ii) and (iii) for values of $p_{0.j}$ other than $0 \cdot 5$ and a fixed value of r determined in this way to ensure the prescribed precision level, yields so-called confidence intervals $(p_{v.j} - p_{u.j})$ of different length for each value of $p_{0.j}$ on either side of $p_{0.j} = 0 \cdot 5$. If p may have any values in the range from o to 1, we are therefore entitled to say that (ii) and (iii) subsume a rule consistent with an acceptable form of terminal statement and an uncertainty safeguard $P_f = 0 \cdot 05$ at the prescribed acceptable level. This is indeed the statement of the procedure advanced by Neyman's school; but it is open to three (see also p. 451) objections, two of which our Model IV brings sharply into focus.

First we note that rp and rq will both exceed 10, our criterion (p. 160) of an adequate normal fit, only if p lies in the range $0 \cdot 025 - 0 \cdot 975$, whence a method of assigning intervals of length less than the precision level (here $0 \cdot 1$) prescribed as the allowable maximum for $p_{0.j} = 0 \cdot 5$ will not be valid at the limit of the range of values $p_{0.j}$ may assume. Next, let us ask what the consistent use of a rule circumscribed by (ii) and (iii) implies when $p_{0.j}$ lies in the neighbourhood of zero or unity. For $p_{0.j} = 0$, $p_{v.j} = 0 \cdot 01$ and $p_{u.j} = 0$, so that our terminal statement corresponding to the observation $p_{0.f} = 0$ will be $0 \leqslant p \leqslant 0 \cdot 01$. Similarly, we find $0 \cdot 99 \leqslant p \leqslant 1 \cdot 0$ for $p_{0.j} = 1$. Both assertions are false in the Model V situation, since we know that $0 \cdot 1 \leqslant p \leqslant 0 \cdot 9$, and in general consistent adherence to (ii) and (iii) must lead to false statements for some values of $p_{0.j}$ if background knowledge of prior possibilities limits the admissible range of the comprehensive set of hypotheses specified by values of p. That we shall always be wrong when we make terminal statements referable to observations outside the range stated is not inconsistent with what we can claim for the operation of the rule in its entirety; but it is not a circumstance which commends the rule to our good judgment.

Model VI. The two issues last stated do not explicitly force themselves on our attention when we assume that the universe of choice is normal. We shall defer their consideration to Chapter 18 in which we shall examine the need for a modification of the theory of interval estimation prescribed by Neyman. First, we may clarify some implications of a rule of stochastic induction when we assume a randomwise sampling process in a putative normal universe by exploring the following set-up.

A lottery wheel has 1024 sectors labelled with scores x, $(x + 1)$, $(x + 2)$, $(x + 3)$ ... $(x + 9)$, $(x + 10)$ respectively allocated to 1, 10, 45, 120, 210, 252, 210, 120, 45, 10, 1 sectors. We do not know the numerical value of x, but know that it is any one of a set of consecutive positive numbers in the range $0 - 10$ with fixed interval $\Delta x = 0 \cdot 01$. The long-run mean value (M) of the score of any sample is, of course $(x + 5)$; and the terms of $(\frac{1}{2} + \frac{1}{2})^{10}$ define the unit sample distribution of the universe with variance $\sigma^2 = 2 \cdot 5$, whence that of the distribution of the 40-fold sample mean is

$$\sigma_m^2 = \frac{\sigma^2}{40} = \frac{1}{16}$$

Thus $\sigma_m = 0 \cdot 25$; and the error involved in a normal quadrature for the distribution of the sample means is trivial. We can thus say that

(a) the mean (M_x) of $2 \cdot 5$ per cent of all samples in the long run will exceed $M + 2\sigma_m = M + 0 \cdot 5$;

(b) the mean of $2 \cdot 5$ per cent of all samples in the long run will be less than $M - 2\sigma_m = M - 0 \cdot 5$;

(c) the mean of 95 per cent of all samples will lie in the range $M \pm 2\sigma_m = M \pm 0 \cdot 5$.

In this set-up the slightly jagged outlines of the region of the H.O.G. endorsed by the rule closely follow two parallel straight lines, whence the length of the interval (vertical width of the endorsed region) referable to each admissible observation will be the same for each, as illustrated in Fig. 4. There we see that the slope of the two bounding lines is unity, whence the vertical and horizontal widths of the endorsed region are identical. In this set-up an R.E.E. consistent with $P_f \leqslant 0 \cdot 05$ is also consistent

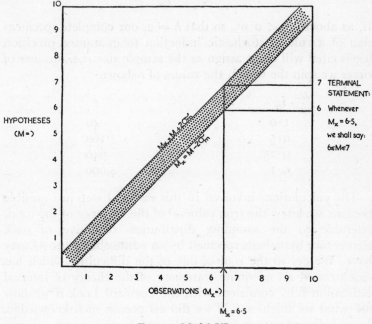

FIG. 4. Model VI.

with the assumption that our criterion of acceptability w.r.t. the set of terminal statements is the precision level $i_m = 1 \cdot 0$. If the sampling distributions were truly normal, we could set no limits on the range of our observations, and we could disregard extreme values of M_x with impunity. It would then be possible to write $P_f = 0 \cdot 05$ in this context.

Now the choice of our criterion of acceptability $(i_m = 1 \cdot 0)$ is quite arbitrary. If we are to acquaint ourselves *with all the steps we must traverse* when we seek to prescribe a proper rule of stochastic induction, we must therefore ask how we should define the numerical value of r appropriate to any agreeable criterion of acceptability w.r.t. both the risk and the precision level. We then write

$$i_m = 2h\sigma_m \quad and \quad \sigma_m^2 = \frac{\sigma^2}{r} = \frac{2\cdot 5}{r}$$

$$\therefore r = \frac{10h^2}{i_m^2}$$

If, as above, $P_f \leqslant 0\cdot 05$, so that $h = 2$, our complete specification of a rule of stochastic induction to guarantee precision levels cited will be to assign as the sample size (i.e. number of times we spin the wheel) the values of r shown

i_m	r
$1\cdot 0$	40
$0\cdot 5$	160
$0\cdot 25$	640
$0\cdot 1$	4,000

The calculations involved in this essential step are possible because we know the true value σ^2 of the variance of the u.s.d. referable to the sampling distribution definitive of each elementary hypothesis specified by an admissible value M may have. We get to the root of one of the difficulties which has embarrassed an adequate statement of the theory of interval estimation fully consistent with the Forward Look if we now ask what we might say, if we did *not* possess such knowledge. In such circumstances each sample we take gives us an estimate s_n of σ_m. From the t-distribution we then have:

(i) $\quad \dfrac{M_x - M}{s_m} = t \; ;$ (ii) $\quad s_m^2 = \dfrac{1}{r(r-1)} \sum_{u=1}^{u=r} (x_u - M_x)^2$

(iii) $\quad P\,(M - h.s_m \leqslant M_x \leqslant M + h.s_m) = \displaystyle\int_{-h}^{h} F(t)dt$

When $r = 12$ the t-table, i.e. the table of the integral of $F(t)$, gives $h = 2\cdot 2$ for $P(M - h.s_m \leqslant M_x \leqslant M + h.s_m) = 0\cdot 95$.

It is therefore tempting to say that $P_f = 0.05$ is the uncertainty safeguard for the operation of the rule:

say that $M_x + 2.2s_m \geqslant M \geqslant M_x - 2.2s_m$ whenever we take a 12-fold sample for whatever values of M_x we may encounter.

If so, our calculation will proceed as follows for a 12-fold sample of score values:

$$2, \quad 7, \quad 9, \quad 9, \quad 12, \quad 18, \quad 21, \quad 33, \quad 37, \quad 44, \quad 51, \quad 80$$

These yield $M_x = 26.92$ and $s_m \simeq 6.64$. Seemingly, our so-called rule will therefore lead us to assert: $12.31 \leqslant M \leqslant 41.53$ with uncertainty safeguard 0.05 when $M_x = 26.92$. Let us now suppose we take a second sample constituted thus:

$$1, \quad 3, \quad 8, \quad 8, \quad 8, \quad 10, \quad 20, \quad 25, \quad 29, \quad 32, \quad 49, \quad 130$$

Again $M_x = 26.92$ but $s_m \simeq 10.22$ and our so-called rule leads us to assert $4.44 \leqslant M \leqslant 49.40$.

At first sight, we may be inclined to dismiss this discrepancy since: (a) the two values of M_x are referable to samples of different make-up; (b) the use of the statistic s_m in the definition incorporates the relevant difference. What is not at once apparent is that our reliance on the latter excludes our right to prescribe a one-stage trial for which we can preassign the sample size r consistent *both* with the acceptable level of uncertainty *and* with a criterion of acceptable terminal statement. Though M_x and s_m incorporate all the information a sample can contribute to our knowledge of the parent universe, they do not incorporate singly or jointly the information we require if we are to complete the formulation of a rule of stochastic induction in its entirety.

In the ideally normal domain of the pure mathematician an infinitude of values of σ are consistent with a single value of M, and for each of these the single r-fold distribution of $(M_x - M)$ in the row of infinitesimal elements our hypothesis-observation grid can accommodate will be different. In this ideally normal domain, s_m^- and M_x are independent variables and each admits an infinitude of values. Whence the range of the t-ratio for each pair of admissible values of M and σ for a fixed value of r

is also infinite. In short, the mathematical theory of the *t*-distribution, albeit admittedly and at best a rough and ready approximation to experience of the real world, endorses no guarantee that our confidence interval, as defined by Neyman (p. 437) or the fiducial interval as defined by R. A. Fisher below (p. 441), will necessarily be finite. If not, our so-called rule violates the criterion of minimal acceptability of terminal statement stated on p. 449. That is to say, it cannot ensure that the outcome of applying it will endorse a more precise statement than we might justify by reasoning in the domain of non-stochastic induction.

Against the background of the lottery wheel of the Model VI set-up, we may clarify the inadequacy of the *t*-distribution to provide a basis for interval estimation in a one-stage trial in the following terms. To prescribe a rule of stochastic induction involving a comprehensive set of acceptable terminal statements referable to composite hypotheses, two steps are necessary:

(i) to define a rule of exclusion and endorsement which will guarantee either of the two following:

(*a*) an acceptable uncertainty safeguard for a fixed sample size when we have not as yet fixed our criterion of acceptable terminal statement;

(*b*) an acceptable precision level when we have not as yet fixed our risk of erroneous statement;

(ii) to define the size (*r*) of sample requisite to ensure the acceptable precision level when we have formally stated an R.E.E. consistent with a criterion of acceptability w.r.t. the set of terminal statements.

There is as yet no general principle which subsumes (i) and (ii) for all appropriate situations. Nor is it likely that we shall be able to accomplish the end in view without recourse to hit-and-miss procedures, when we come to grips with a new one. Be that as it may, the inadequacy of the *t*-distribution resides in the circumstance that it provides an exploratory basis only for (*a*) stated above as only one of two essential steps in the prescription of a rule of stochastic induction. It cannot help us to proceed by the alternative route and it cannot help us to take the second equally essential step.

Patterns of Stochastic Induction. The device of the H.O.G. sheds a new light on a familiar type of graph such as Fig. 3 illustrating Neyman's theory of interval estimation for a fixed sample size. We can interpret it rightly as a visualisation of the *first* step towards the prescription of a rule of procedure which is complete only when we take the next step by prescribing the size of sample consistent with an acceptable criterion of terminal statement. In the enumerative domain the number of cells is necessarily finite; but we can make the transition from grid to graph with little effort, when we pass into the domain of continuous sampling distributions. Accordingly, it may be instructive if we pause at this stage to examine the guises the H.O.G. may assume both in the domain of non-stochastic and of stochastic induction.

PATTERNS OF STOCHASTIC INDUCTION. We have seen that we can specify the elementary hypotheses of the Model IV (*b*) set-up in purely qualitative terms or in numerical terms consistent with the lay-out of an ordered set. When we can do so, we may helpfully distinguish between two situations in a set-up which does admit of a precise qualitative definition of hypotheses: (*a*) the ordered set is arbitrary in the sense that the qualitative specification of the hypotheses admits of no intelligible and/or useful corresponding arrangement; (*b*) the ordered set at least corresponds to an intelligible and/or useful system of *rank* scoring, e.g. black, brown, yellow, cream, white. If (*b*) holds good, the problem of experimental design is on all fours with what arises in situations admitting no qualitative specification of elementary hypotheses, as is true of the urn model introduced on p. 390 to illustrate how stochastic differs from non-stochastic induction. That is to say, we can define composite hypotheses with each of which we can associate a terminal statement referable to a range or interval.

Whenever we can make an intelligible and/or useful ordered sub-classification of elementary hypotheses, we can draw an intelligibly sharp distinction between two ways in which we can do so: (i) no members of a sub-set corresponding to a particular acceptable terminal statement occur in any other such subset; (ii) each acceptable terminal statement refers to a subset of which some members occur in others. We may then speak of the composite hypothesis corresponding to each terminal statement as a *consecutive discrete interval*. If (ii) is admissible, it may be possible to grade the subsets so that successive subsets contain an ordered terminal sequence in common with an ordered terminal sequence of a successor and predecessor. We may then speak of the composite hypothesis corresponding to each terminal statement as a *consecutive overlapping interval*. Among possible patterns of the hypothesis-observation table of an experimental design distinguishable in terms of (i) and (ii) above for 8 elementary hypotheses and 4 observations (score values) are those shown in Fig. 5. Only the upper two labelled as (i) are consistent with *a priori* adequacy of design in the non-stochastic domain.

The two types of arrangement shown opposite do not exhaust all ways in which we might conceivably combine elementary hypotheses into composite hypotheses corresponding to acceptable terminal statements. The usefulness of grouping elementary hypotheses in one way or another depends on the acceptable terminal statements consistent with the design; but a stochastic design gives us a greater freedom to combine elementary hypotheses into subsets consistent with the whole operational intent. The reason for this is that the rule of exclusion consistent with the acceptable level of uncertainty permits us to disregard some elementary hypotheses consistent with a particular observation. Thus it is often possible to design an experiment which is *a priori adequate* in the stochastic domain for *a particular set* of acceptable terminal statements when it would not be possible to do so otherwise. In the domains of Models V (*a*) and (*b*) and of VI, every possible observation is—if only very rarely—realisable within the framework of the presumptive truth of every admissible elementary hypothesis. Thus no rule of non-stochastic induction is admissible since no admissible terminal statements could ever be acceptable.

If we now look at possible patterns more explicitly in terms

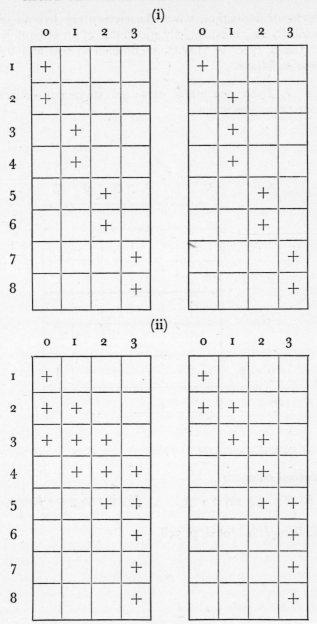

FIG. 5

of stochastic induction, when the elementary hypotheses are numerically and meaningfully specifiable as an ordered set, we may classify types of H.O.G. mentioned in this and the last chapter as follows.

Type I. Each acceptable terminal statement endorses a discrete parameter value.

(a)

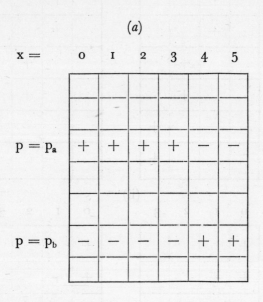

x =	0	1	2	3	4	5
$p = p_a$	+	+	+	+	−	−
$p = p_b$	−	−	−	−	+	+

Rule of Exclusion one-sided

Terminal statements:

(i) if $x \leqslant 3$ say $p = p_a$,   (ii) if $x > 3$ say $p = p_b$.

Cf. *Drosophila* Model, p. 348.

(b)

$x =$	0	1	2	3	4	5	6	7	8	9
$p = p_1$	−	+	+	+	−	−	−	−	−	−
$p = p_2$	−	−	−	−	+	+	+	+	+	−
$p = p_3$	−	−	−	−	−	−	−	−	−	+
$p = p_4$	−	−	−	−	−	−	−	−	−	−

$x =$	10	11	12	13	14	15	16	17	18
$p = p_1$	−	−	−	−	−	−	−	−	−
$p = p_2$	−	−	−	−	−	−	−	−	−
$p = p_3$	+	+	+	−	−	−	−	−	−
$p = p_4$	−	−	−	+	+	+	+	−	−

Rule of Exclusion two-sided
  Terminal statements:

(i) if $x \leqslant 3$ say $p = p_1$, (iii) if $8 < x \leqslant 12$ say $p = p_3$,
(ii) if $3 < x \leqslant 8$ say $p = p_2$, (iv) if $x \geqslant 13$ say $p = p_4$.

Cf. Model V (a) above.

Type II. The acceptable terminal statements endorse alternative composite hypotheses and each acceptable terminal statement is consistent with a range of different observational values.

(a)

x =	0	1	2	3	4	5	6
p₁	+	+	+	+	−	−	−
p₂	+	+	+	+	−	−	−
p₃	+	+	+	+	−	−	−
p₄	+	+	+	+	−	−	−
p₅	+	+	+	+	−	−	−
p₆	−	−	−	−	+	+	+
p₇	−	−	−	−	+	+	+
p₈	−	−	−	−	+	+	+

Rule of Exclusion one-sided
Hypothesis H_1: p has one of the values

$$p_1, p_2, p_3, p_4, p_5$$

Hypothesis H_2: p has one of the values

$$p_6, p_7, p_8$$

Terminal statements:
  (i) If $x \leqslant 3$ assert H_1 is true,
  (ii) If $x > 3$ assert H_2 is true.

(Cf. the dilemma of test procedure in the domain of the clinical trial, p. 367.)

(b)

x =	0	1	2	3	4	5	6	7
p_1	+	+	+	+	−	−	−	−
p_2	+	+	+	+	−	−	−	−
p_3	+	+	+	+	−	−	−	−
p_4	+	+	+	+	−	−	−	−
p_5	+	+	+	+	+	+	+	+
p_6	+	+	+	+	+	+	+	+
p_7	+	+	+	+	+	+	+	+
p_8	−	−	−	−	+	+	+	+
p_9	−	−	−	−	+	+	+	+
p_{10}	−	−	−	−	+	+	+	+

Rule of Exclusion one-sided

Hypothesis H_1: p has one of the values

$$p_1, p_2, p_3, p_4, p_5, p_6, p_7$$

Hypothesis H_2: p has one of the values

$$p_5, p_6, p_7, p_8, p_9, p_{10}$$

Terminal statements:

(i) If $x \leqslant 3$ assert H_1 is true,

(ii) If $x > 3$ assert H_2 is true.

(Cf. Wald's consumer-producer risk procedure, pp. 367–8.)

(c)

x =	0	1	2	3	4	5	6
p_1	+	+	−	−			
p_2	−	−	+	+	+	−	−
p_3				−	−	+	+

Rule of Exclusion two-sided

  Terminal statements:

    (i) if $x \leqslant 1$ say $p = p_1$,

    (ii) if $2 \leqslant x \leqslant 4$ say $p = p_2$,

    (iii) if $x > 4$ say $p = p_3$.

(Cf. Model IV (b) above.)

Type III. The acceptable terminal statements are composite hypotheses and each observation is referable to a different set of elementary hypotheses (see opposite page).

    .   .   .   .   .

Types I to III do not exhaust all possible patterns of the stochastic hypothesis-observation grid conceived in terms of discrete score values (observations) and discrete values of p (hypotheses). As a condition of a manageable size of sample to endorse a commonly acceptable level of uncertainty, Type I presupposes that the interval between any two successive values of p is small. If p has only 2 admissible values, the appropriate rule of exclusion is necessarily one-sided. If p has more than 2 admissible values, a two-sided rule of exclusion will commonly be most easy to explore as for the urn model of p. 151 and for Model III in this context; but Model II in this context invokes both methods of exclusion. Type II (a) embraces Type I (a) as a special case. Its interest arises from the fact that it is unworkable when p admits a continuous range of values, since no acceptable sample size (r) is then consistent with an acceptable level of uncertainty. Type II (a)

$x =$	0	1	2	3	4	5	6	7	8	9	10	11	12
p_1							−	−	−	+	+	−	
p_2							−	−	−	+	+	−	
p_3						−	−	−	+	+	+	−	
p_4				−	−	+	+	+	+	+	+	−	
p_5				−	−	+	+	+	+	+	+	−	−
p_6				−	−	+	+	+	+	+	+	−	−
p_7			−	−	+	+	+	+	+	+	−	−	
p_8			−	−	+	+	+	+	+	+	−	−	−
p_9	−	−	+	+	+	+	+	+	−	−	−	−	
p_{10}	−	−	+	+	+	+	+	−	−	−	−	−	
p_{11}	−	−	+	+	+	+	+	−	−	−	−	−	
p_{12}	−	−	+	+	+	+	−	−	−	−			
p_{13}	−	+	+	+	+	−	−	−	−	−			
p_{14}	−	+	+	−	−	−	−	−	−	−			

Rule of Exclusion two-sided

Comprehensive (minimal) terminal statement:

If the interval $p_{h+1} - p_h = \Delta p$, and p_x is the median value of p_h corresponding to a particular observation (x_h):

$$\text{if } x - x_h \text{ say } p_x - 4\Delta p < p_h < p_x + 4\Delta p$$

. . . .

429

which is Wald's overlapping dual test procedure (p. 368) side-steps this difficulty by defining the upper limit of p for one composite hypothesis and the lower limit of p for the alternative at the price of excluding the possibility of making a statement asserting that p lies between these limits. Type III is the pattern of what we commonly mean by interval estimation. The rule of exclusion is necessarily 2-sided. If we compare Types I (b) referable to such a model as V (a) above with Type III referable to Models V (b) or VI or Type I (a) with Type II (b), we are entitled to regard the distinction between test procedure and interval estimation as less important than the distinction between procedures which involve one-sided, two-sided or mixed rules of exclusion and endorsement.

Rules of Induction. We shall more readily face our next task (Chapter 17), if we now recapitulate the outcome of our examination of induction, whether stochastic or non-stochastic, in this chapter and in the last. Induction of either sort subsumes rules which endorse a decisive outcome whenever applied, if and only if: (a) the hypotheses are comprehensive in the sense that they embrace all admissible contingencies in the domain of observation; (b) the blueprint is *a priori adequate* in the sense that each observation endorses only one of a unique comprehensive set of acceptable terminal statements each of which itself endorses only one of a unique comprehensive set of hypotheses. In the non-stochastic domain, the specification of hypotheses which constitute a comprehensive set for design of a holonomic experiment may be expressible only in qualitative terms. In the stochastic domain they may be definable in such terms, but they *must* always be also expressible, if distinguishable, in terms of unique parameter values relevant to the specification of an appropriate sample distribution. What we may prefer to speak of as an elementary hypothesis or as a composite hypothesis in either domain is a matter of no importance except in so far as the distinction is relevant to: (a) specification of the class of terminal statements deemed to justify the design of the experiment; (b) the uniqueness of the relevant sample distribution.

In non-stochastic induction we formulate a rule of procedure which should: (a) never lead to a false conclusion; (b) always lead to a definite and acceptable conclusion, if the design is *a priori* adequate. In stochastic induction we formulate a rule of procedure with which we can associate a numerically specifiable upper limit to the risk of erroneous statement if the design is *a priori* adequate; but the design must then encompass a specification of the number of requisite observations, if we wish to fix the risk at a level agreed as acceptable. This risk is not referable to *any individual* terminal statement or class of terminal statement. It is referable only to the consequences of applying the rule *in its entirety*. To speak of a rule which we must operate in its *entirety* presupposes:

(*a*) that the set of hypotheses we are exploring is in fact comprehensive;

(*b*) that the design is *a priori adequate* for the set of terminal statements the rule endorses.

It goes without saying that we accomplish nothing by accepting a risk of error, if we can thereby say no more than our observations would otherwise entitle us to say. Consequently, we may enlarge our previous comparison in the following terms:

(i) In the domain of non-stochastic induction, we can explore situations which suggest new hypotheses to test *pari passu* a comprehensive set of hypotheses. In stochastic induction we must state the set *in advance*. Whence non-stochastic induction embraces experiments which are exploratory as well as experiments which are holonomic. Contrariwise, stochastic induction is admissible only in the holonomic domain.

(ii) In the domain of non-stochastic induction, we may be content if the enquiry leads to any addition to our knowledge, whether by design or luck. In the domain of stochastic induction, our criterion of an acceptable terminal statement must at least guarantee at the outset a verdict which is more informative than whatever verdict we might reach by relying on non-stochastic induction.

Having given reasons which seem to me to be sufficiently compelling, I shall now put forward dogmatically the following canons illustrated by our discussion of model situations in this chapter and in the last.

Canon 1

A necessary condition for prescribing a rule of stochastic induction is that we can specify for each elementary hypothesis endorsed as admissible by one of the set of acceptable terminal statements a *unique* sampling distribution of admissible observations.

Canon 2

The legitimate use of a rule of stochastic induction in terms of an assigned and acceptable risk of error presupposes its operation in its entirety; and excludes the right to make any statement of the form: if we meet the *particular* observation x the probability that the particular elementary or composite hypothesis H_p is true is P_t. Instead we say: $P_f = (1 - P_t)$ is the risk of erroneous statement if we *always* adhere to the rule regardless of whatever value x may have on a particular occasion.

Canon 3

That more than one rule of stochastic induction with one and the same uncertainty safeguard may be consistent with the same comprehensive set of elementary hypotheses and with the same set of acceptable statements is fully consistent with the acceptance of the preceding canons, and is a necessary consequence of our freedom to prescribe different rules of exclusion at the same level of risk.

Canon 4

The complete statement of a rule of stochastic induction must embrace:

(*a*) a criterion of *acceptability* for the entire class of terminal statements subsumed;

(*b*) an *acceptable risk* of erroneous statement;

When sampling occurs in one stage, (*a*) and (*b*) jointly signify that the rule must embrace a specification of the *size of the sample*.

CHAPTER EIGHTEEN

THE CONFIDENCE CONTROVERSY
AND THE FIFTH CANON

IN THE LAST TWO CHAPTERS I have discussed at length a novel
viewpoint of Wrighton, because it will help us to retrace
our steps from a quagmire of controversy over interval estimation to a solid foothold for a new approach. That writers
on statistical theory continued to speak of Fiducial limits and
Confidence limits interchangeably throughout a decade after
the relevant original publications first appeared should not
surprise us, if we realise the difficulty of the task of extricating
a novel restatement of principle from an overgrowth of custom
thought embodied in current practice. With respect to the
formal issue which divides the followers of Neyman from those
of Fisher, the approach we have explored in the last two
chapters is unequivocally opposite to the fiducial argument,
and starts from the same premises as the theory of Confidence
intervals; but it leads us to conclusions which do not emerge
explicitly in Neyman's own writings, and the outcome will be
to accommodate some objections which his critics have legitimately advanced.

It will help us to do justice to the disputants in the current
controversy before we proceed to examine more closely
Wrighton's own recent restatement, if I cite at length an
exposition of his own position by Neyman himself.

In *Foundations of the General Theory of Statistical Estimation*,*
Neyman says:

. . . a brief summary of the general ideas underlying the theory
of statistical estimation which I developed about 1930 and which,
more recently, were brilliantly extended and generalized by
Abraham Wald and by many other authors . . . it may be useful
to mention briefly in what ways the new theory of estimation, or,
more precisely, the theory of estimation which was new in the
1930's, differs from the earlier methods of attacking the problem.
This difference may be symbolized by the change in labels.

* xviii *Congrès Intern. Phil. Sci.* (1949).

Previously, attempts to build up a theory of statistical estimation went under the label "inductive reasoning." On the other hand, my own attempt was characterized by the label "theory of inductive behavior." The difference behind these two labels is primarily a difference in attitude towards the problem of estimation. . . . The approach to the theory of estimation characterized by the label of inductive reasoning consists in the search for such values ascribable to the parameters to be estimated, which, for one reason or another, are supposed to inspire the greatest possible confidence. The typical question asked would be:

> in these circumstances, when these particular values of the random variables under consideration have been observed, what are the most probable (or the most likely) values of the unknown parameters?

Contrary to this, the more recent approach to the problem of estimation does not deal with the relative probability or likelihood of the various values ascribable to the unknown parameters but with the frequency of errors which will be committed if this or that particular method of estimation is consistently applied. In order to formulate the typical questions of this theory we introduce some notation. Let one letter X stand for the whole system of observable random variables with their joint distribution depending upon an unknown parameter θ and let $f(X) \leqslant g(X)$ be some two functions of X. The original approach to the problem of estimation from the point of view of inductive behaviour contemplates a process of estimation which consists (a) in observing the values, say x, of the random variables X and (b) in asserting that the true value of the parameter satisfies the double inequality $f(x) \leqslant \theta \leqslant g(x)$. The typical questions of the new theory are asked *before* the values x of the random variables X are observed. The first question is:

> (i) Given the distribution of X and given the two functions $f(X)$ and $g(X)$, what is the probability that the assertion $f(X) \leqslant \theta \leqslant g(X)$ will be correct?

The second question is more important and much more interesting:

> (ii) Given the distribution of X and given a number θ between zero and unity, can one determine the two functions $f(X)$ and $g(X)$ so that the probability that the assertion $f(X) \leqslant \theta \leqslant g(X)$ is true equals α (or is at least equal to α), irrespective of the unknown value of the parameters and also irrespective of other parameters on which the distribution of X may depend?

434

. . . If the two functions f(X) and g(X) satisfy the conditions described in question (ii) then they are called *confidence limits* for estimating θ, corresponding to the confidence coefficient α. Also the random interval [f(X), g(X)] is called the *confidence interval*. . . . The reason for abandoning the old point of view on the problem of estimation should have been apparent for about the last century and a half, since the time when the formula of Bayes was discovered. The reason is that in order to obtain the *a posteriori* most probable values of the unknown parameters one must use the formula of Bayes which depends explicitly on probabilities *a priori* which are not implied by the circumstances of many problems where statistical estimation is needed. . . . To remedy the situation, some authors tried, and still try, to conjure the missing probabilities *a priori* out of a specially devised postulate, which I prefer to call a dogma. Some other authors dislike this particular postulate and give up the idea of "most probable" values of the parameters. Instead, they produce a recipe for constructing a function to measure our confidence in any stated value ascribable to a parameter, given the results of the observations, and then look for "optimum" values of the parameter.

Such methods of attack appear to me as evasions rather than solutions of the problem of estimation. Since about 1930, it was clear to me that, in order to attain the solution, only two methods were open: either find an error in the formula of Bayes (and I most sincerely believe that this is impossible) or modify the mathematical problem behind the methods of estimation so as to make it soluble in more general cases.

The reader will recognise that the formulation of Neyman's concept of inductive behaviour is fully *en rapport* with the viewpoint referred to as the *Forward Look* throughout this book; and registers a reorientation towards the proper terms of reference of a calculus of judgments explicitly stated in terms consistent with a behaviourist outlook. To Neyman first and foremost is due the credit for this reorientation; but it is singularly unfortunate that his views took shape at a time when the engaging algebraic properties of the *t*-distribution (p. 419) occupied the centre of the arena of statistical discussion, and seemed to offer a prospect of sidestepping uncertainties which had previously dogged the discussion of estimation and test procedure. Had he initially explored the implications of a behaviourist viewpoint in the discrete domain of classical models, as in his recently published volume elsewhere cited, he would have seen what we have seen in Chapter 17. To speak of an act of will involved in following a rule of stochastic induction conveys little unless we assume a target of our endeavours. It is then necessary both to formulate a procedure with which we can associate an acceptable risk and one which guarantees an acceptable set of terminal statements. Neyman's formulation cited in this context violates our Canon 4 (p. 432), because it defines the rule to follow in terms of the acceptable risk alone; and this leads to an impasse in the field of the first application of his theory of interval estimation, viz. a hypothesis-observation set-up in which:

(a) the comprehensive set of hypotheses is a continuum of values the true mean (M) of a normal universe may conceivably have;

(b) the observations constitute a continuum of sample mean values (M_x);

(c) the terminal statements vindicate composite hypotheses, each embodying a particular range of values of M_x within which M lies.

We have indeed (pp. 419–420) already explored the implications of the Forward Look *vis-à-vis* the usefulness or otherwise of the *t*-distribution to accomplish (c) on the assumption that the parent universe is normal; but it will not be profitless if we now re-examine it as case material to illustrate the *casus belli* of the confidence controversy. In the symbolism of p. 418, we may express in the most general form as below the probability that the sample mean (M_x) lies in an interval uniquely determined by the unknown true mean (M), the unbiased sample estimate (s_m) of the variance of the mean and two arbitrary constants $(h$ and $k)$ which we are free to fix at will:

$$P(M + k \cdot s_m \leqslant M_x \leqslant M + h \ s_m) = \int_k^h F(t) \cdot dt \quad . \quad \text{(i)}$$

In this equation the expression on the right is the tabulated integral of the *t*-distribution. If we wish to make our interval

436

symmetrical about the mean, we shall then write $k = -h$, so that

$$P(M - h.s_m \leqslant M_x \leqslant M + h.s_m) = \int_{-h}^{h} F(t).dt = P_t \quad (ii)$$

Alternatively, we may wish to specify the probability that M_x will not exceed the limit determined by h for samples specified by the independent statistic s_m, i.e.

$$P(M_x \leqslant M + h.s_m) = \int_{-\infty}^{h} F(t).dt \quad . \quad . \quad (iii)$$

The foregoing statements involve no departure from the classical approach. In Neyman's statement of the problem of interval estimation, we proceed therefrom as follows:

(*a*) when $(M - s_m.h \leqslant M_x \leqslant M + s_m.h)$ it will be true that $(M_x - s_m.h \leqslant M \leqslant M_x + s_m.h)$, since the two assertions are formally equivalent;

(*b*) if I consistently assert that $(M - s_m.h \leqslant M_x \leqslant M + s_m.h)$ the long run frequency of correct assertions I shall make will be P_t as defined in (ii) for all corresponding sample values M_x and s_m and for any single value the unknown parameter M may have;

(*c*) I may therefore associate an uncertainty safeguard $P_j = (1 - P_t)$ with the rule:

for samples of which the relevant definite sample statistics are M_x and s_m, I shall always assert that $(M_x - s_m.h \leqslant M \leqslant M_x + s_m.h)$.

In this formulation we do not make any self-contradictory assertion assigning a probability to the range of values in which a putatively unique parameter lies. Instead, we confine ourselves to prescribing a rule to which we can assign a long-run frequency of correspondence between our own statements and observed events. So far as it goes, this formulation is therefore entirely consistent with the Forward Look; but if we ask what the rule can do for us, we disclose an inadequacy. To set any preassigned precision level to our terminal statements about M, we need to know s_m as well as h, and we can do so only if we have first looked at the sample. Thus a rule stated in advance and followed consistently regardless of the outcome cannot guarantee that the outcome will be useful. It is either useless or inconsistent with the Forward Look.

Up to a point, Neyman concedes this in a recent discussion on a contribution by Stein. Stein has attempted to evade one horn of the dilemma by prescribing a two-stage procedure, which in effect provides the possibility of working within the framework of a normal universe for which σ has a fixed value; but Neyman's own candid comment (*Lectures and Conferences on Mathematical Statistics and Probability*, 1952) exonerates us from the need to refer to his sequential method more explicitly in this context:

> Brilliant as his result is . . . its practical applications involve a new difficulty just as insuperable as that complained of by Berkson.*

Wrighton's principle of *a priori adequacy* epitomises all that need be said from a formal viewpoint about the issue to which Berkson drew attention. Of itself the interval assigned by fixing an acceptable uncertainty safeguard by recourse to (ii) is not a proper rule of stochastic induction. To make it such we must take another step by assigning the size of sample sufficient to ensure in advance an interval length concordant with an acceptable level of precision. None the less, it is appropriate here to state the issue in another way, because the formulation of Confidence theory in the foregoing citation is equally inadequate when the relevant sampling distribution endorses the statement of a rule which conforms both to the formal requirements of a behaviourist outlook and the presumptive operational intention of a rule worth stating at all.

If we are to retain a useful place for the t-distribution as an instrument of interval estimation in the domain of representative scoring, we can do so only if we claim the right to rely on the evidence of a single sample when consistent with

---

* J. Berkson first drew attention to the inconvenience of the fact that a confidence interval determined as above may exceed a precision level consistent with any conceivable practical requirements (*vide* pp. 418–420 above).

the terminal statement we deem to be acceptable. If we adopt the new orientation, we are then reserving the luxury to look at the sample before we decide whether to operate a rule which implicitly guarantees a particular set of terminal statements in advance. In mixed metaphor we have brought back the Backward Look by the back door. We are claiming the right to make the class of statements Confidence theory disclaims* and—as we shall later see—the Fiducial argument condones.

Should any doubts remain about the propriety of this procedure, we may dispel them by soliciting the co-operation of the always serviceable Martian observer. We shall suppose that we set the problem of Model V (b) in Chapter 15 to a very large number of observers each with limited resources, which we may signify by allowing them to operate once with a sample of 100. We shall assume that the acceptable terminal statement places p in an interval of length $i_c \leqslant 0 \cdot 1$ as before with a risk of error $P_f \leqslant 0 \cdot 05$. Now we have seen that a rule which guarantees this in all circumstances in its entirety calls for samples of 396 or more; but the terminal statements it permits places the value of p in an interval much shorter than $0 \cdot 1$ for observed values of p_0 near the limits there assumed to be $0 \cdot 1 - 0 \cdot 9$. Indeed, a corresponding rule will prescribe an interval of the required length for outsize values of p when r is much less than 396. As an exercise, the reader may apply the algebraic reasoning invoked on p. 413 to ascertain what values of p_0 would place p in an interval $i_c \leqslant 0 \cdot 1$ when $r = 100$ as we here assume; and to show how much the interval prescribed by consistent operation of the rule given on p. 415 would exceed the acceptable precision level for sample scores in the neighbourhood of 50 ($p_0 \simeq 0 \cdot 5$).

* As the title of their paper *The Use of Confidence or Fiducial Limits* implies, Clopper and E. S. Pearson (1934) explicitly stated the most essential issue w.r.t. which Fisher's fiducial concept and Neyman's theory of Confidence part company long before their contemporaries recognised that a fundamental difference was at issue. Thus they say (*Biometrika*, 26):

. . . the percentage of wrong judgments differs according to the value of x, from 100 to 0. We cannot therefore say that for any specified value of x the probability that the confidence interval will include p is $\cdot 95$ or more. The probability must be associated with the whole belt, that is to say with the result of the continued application of a method of procedure to all values of x met with in our statistical experience.

If our observers take the stand that one is free to make statements when acceptable and otherwise refrain, they will therefore make statements to the effect that p lies within acceptable limits consistent only if they observe such outside values of p_0. From his backstage viewpoint, the Martian umpire would notice that each observer who recorded a score sum of e.g. 50 ($p_0 = 0 \cdot 5$) at a particular trial would omit to record the score, thus falsifying the balance sheet which correctly describes the outcome of their observations considered as a whole. If he understands the rule, and knows that p does not fall within the limits assigned by the recorded scores, he will not be fooled by the plea of poverty as an excuse for cheating. The assigned risk $P_f \leqslant 0 \cdot 05$ is relevant if and only if we follow the rule regardless of the outcome of any single trial.

This is why Wrighton's criterion of *a priori adequacy* is so indispensable to a statement of the problem of interval estimation wholly consistent with the Forward Look. Whereas Neyman is content to demand that the size of the sample shall ensure a form of statement consistent with an acceptable level (α) of risk, Wrighton insists that the form of statement also must conform to a criterion of acceptability. Otherwise, we may either end by saying nothing new or break the rule of the game by declining to follow it unless the result of doing so is congenial to our hopes and fears. While we must thus acknowledge a debt to Neyman for first stating what a rule of stochastic induction consistent with a behaviourist viewpoint implies at a verbal level, his successors who build on the foundations he laid will record that his algebraic formulation does not suffice to prescribe such a rule. It merely prescribes an important step in the process of devising one.

It happens that the numerical prescription for assigning fiducial limits within which M lies by recourse to the t-distribution is precisely the same as Neyman's numerical prescription for defining confidence limits in the same class of situations. It is mainly for this reason that many statisticians in the late 'thirties and early 'forties continued to regard the two theories of interval estimation as identical. At this level indeed the only difference between the two is a form of words. R. A. Fisher explicitly speaks of the probability that μ (our M) lies between certain limits when $\bar{x}$ (our M_x) has a particular value. He inserts the epithet fiducial in the statement merely to emphasise his repudiation of inverse probability as Laplace propounds it, i.e. reliance on the scholium of Bayes. The reason why the t-distribution permits us to take this step is in his view:

"That the two quantities, the sum and the sum of the squares calculated from the data, together contain all the information supplied by the data concerning the mean and variance of the hypothetical normal curve. Statistics possessing this remarkable property are said to be *sufficient*, because no other can, in these cases, add anything to our information. The peculiarities presented by t which give it its unique value for this type of problem are:

(i) Its distribution is known with exactitude, without any supplementary assumptions or approximations.

(ii) It is expressible in terms of the single unknown parameter μ together with unknown statistics only.

(iii) The statistics involved in this expression are sufficient."

(*Design of Experiments*, pp. 205–6, *First Edition*.)

Before examining what Fisher means by a sufficient statistic, let us examine his own verbal formulation of the problem discussed above. In Neyman's statement of the case, we do not speak of the probability that M lies within a particular range of values. In the domain of observable events this probability is in fact zero or unity and can have no other meaning. An essential step in the fiducial argument is the one we have indeed repudiated as inconsistent with a behaviourist viewpoint in our discussion of Model III on p. 397. Since the statement $(M_x \leqslant M + h . s_m)$ is formally equivalent to the statement $(M \geqslant M_x - h . s_m)$, we assume the right to state (iii) above in the form

$$P(M \geqslant M_x - h . s_m) = \int_{-\infty}^{h} F(t) . dt \quad . \quad . \quad \text{(iv)}$$

For observed values M_x and s_m referable to a sample we have observed, we may then construct a Fiducial Probability Distribution. The example cited on p. 418 will suffice to illustrate the procedure. There we observe $M_x = 26 \cdot 92$ and

$s_m = 6 \cdot 64$ for a 12-fold sample. From the table of the t-integral we obtain for $h = 2 \cdot 2$:

$$P(M_x \leqslant M - h.s_m) = \int_{-\infty}^{-h} F(t)dt = 0 \cdot 025$$

$$P(M_x \leqslant M + h.s_m) = \int_{-\infty}^{h} F(t)dt = 0 \cdot 975$$

$$\therefore \quad P(M - h.s_m \leqslant M_x \leqslant M + h.s_m) = 0 \cdot 950$$

By recourse to the table we obtain in the same way when $M_x = 26 \cdot 92$ and $s_m = 6 \cdot 64$:

h	$P(M \geqslant M_x - h.s_m)$	$M_x - h.s_m$
$- 3 \cdot 11$	$0 \cdot 005$	$6 \cdot 27$
$- 2 \cdot 72$	$0 \cdot 010$	$8 \cdot 86$
$- 2 \cdot 20$	$0 \cdot 025$	$12 \cdot 31$
$- 1 \cdot 80$	$0 \cdot 050$	$14 \cdot 97$
$- 0 \cdot 70$	$0 \cdot 250$	$22 \cdot 27$
$0 \cdot 00$	$0 \cdot 500$	$26 \cdot 92$
$+ 0 \cdot 70$	$0 \cdot 750$	$31 \cdot 57$
$+ 1 \cdot 80$	$0 \cdot 950$	$38 \cdot 87$
$+ 2 \cdot 20$	$0 \cdot 975$	$41 \cdot 53$
$+ 2 \cdot 70$	$0 \cdot 990$	$44 \cdot 98$
$+ 3 \cdot 11$	$0 \cdot 995$	$47 \cdot 57$

For an observed sample in terms of relevant sample statistics (here M_x and s_m,) such a fiducial distribution of a parameter (p) cites the probability that p will exceed an assigned value, and hence that it will lie within specified limits. If it is admissible to apply the rules of the classical calculus of probability in this context, it is then right and proper to state that

$$P(M_x - s_m.h \leqslant M \leqslant M_x + s_m.h)$$
$$= P(M \leqslant M_x + s_m.h) - P(M \leqslant M_x - s_m.h) \quad \text{(v)}$$

The table of the t-integral gives:

$$P(M_x - 2 \cdot 2.s_m \leqslant M \leqslant M_x + 2 \cdot 2.s_m) = 0 \cdot 975 - 0 \cdot 025$$

When $M_x = 26 \cdot 92$ and $s_m = 6 \cdot 64$ the foregoing table of the fiducial distribution then gives

$$P(12 \cdot 31 \leqslant M \leqslant 41 \cdot 53) = 0 \cdot 95$$

In Fisher's theory these are the 95 per cent fiducial limits of M for the observed sample whose definitive statistics are $M_x = 26 \cdot 92$ and $s_m = 6 \cdot 64$. Numerically, they are identical with the confidence limits prescribed by Neyman's theory. The essential divergence is the step incorporated in (iv) above; and if we admit this step we might obtain the same result less circuitously by writing (ii) as

$$P(M_x - h.s_m \leqslant M \leqslant M_x) = \int_{-h}^{h} F(t).dt$$

If we do admit the step incorporated in (iv), and hence the possibility of constructing a fiducial probability distribution, we may proceed to use it in accordance with the rules of the classical calculus and the difference between the two formulations then assumes a more challenging aspect. This occurred when Fisher prescribed a recipe for interval estimation of the difference $(M_b - M_a)$ between the mean of two hypothetical universes A and B each normal but with different unknown parameters σ_a and σ_b. In the derivation, he takes a step which is certainly not consistent with Neyman's procedure which works within the framework of sampling distributions prescribed by the classical theory. A fiducial probability distribution is not a sampling distribution in the classical domain of events. The unknown parameter (p) is merely a conceptual variable presumed to have a fixed value in the factual domain. In treating it as a variable, Fisher followed his own intuitions as his apologists have to concede, and the details of the controversy over the so-called Behrens test need not greatly concern us. Yates, who has the last word to date in defence of the Fiducial Argument, concedes (see *Appendix IV*, p. 506) that it is possible to justify it only if we invoke a new law of thought. Seemingly, this undertaking is not uncongenial to the converted. Others may harbour honest doubts about the difficulty of accommodating a customary minimum of intellectual rectitude with the invocation of a new law of thought to rehabilitate an otherwise indefensible proposition in the absence of any ostensible additional advantages.*

We are now in a position to recognise two circumstances which delayed recognition of a difference which now divides exponents of statistical theory into irreconcilable factions. One is that the *t*-distribution which provided the pivotal illustrative material for Neyman's original statement of his viewpoint cannot endorse the useful outcome of a rule stated before examining a sample and consistently pursued regardless of what structure any individual sample may have. The other is that the fiducial argument leads to numerical results inconsistent with the alternative approach only when we claim the freedom to operate with so-called fiducial probability distributions in accordance with the classical recipe for deriving the sampling distribution of a joint score of components with specifiable distributions referable to different universes of experience.

None the less, an essential difference expressly stated in a paper by Clopper and Pearson (1934) divides the two forms of statement at the outset. That a parameter definitive of a fixed framework of sampling has one value, that it therefore either does or does not lie within a particular range of values specified by an interval estimate, and that it is accordingly meaningless to assign any probability other than zero or unity to the statement that it does so in the domain of events, are niceties of verbal usage which we might well transgress, if a rule conceived in terms of the Forward Look could assign a probability to the truth of assertions based on particular observations. We might then regard the fiducial distribution of p referable to a particular observed value p_0 as an elliptical way of describing

---

* Kendall's summing-up of the Behrens test controversy is quotable, because the final remarks (*italics* inserted) have a much wider range of relevance to current statistical controversies:

> So far as concerns problems of estimation, the Behrens test is accurate both in fiducial theory and in the theory of probability propounded by Jeffreys. But the test does not hold in the theory of confidence intervals. In fact the latter fails to provide an exact solution of the problem. . . . Fisher has criticised Confidence intervals on the grounds that they do not give an answer to what is admittedly an important question; but *it appears possible to maintain consistently that some questions may not have an answer.*

the probability of making correct assertions about p when our source of information is indeed p_0. What Neyman calls a rule of inductive behaviour does not in fact justify statements of this sort. The probability which we denote as the uncertainty safeguard of the rule pertains only to the entire class of statements subsumed thereby when we operate the rule consistently in its entirety.

From this point of view, the concept of sufficiency which occupies so prominent a place in the fiducial argument is irrelevant to the theory of interval estimation explored in the last two chapters. An air of mystery envelops the sufficiency concept, because current standard textbooks commonly illustrate it by reference to continuous distributions and hence enlist manipulative skill for dealing with multiple integrals beyond the range of readers who are not trained mathematicians. Actually, the essentials are easy to grasp in the terrain of classical models, such as the following. We assume two universes from which we may sample:

A. A full card pack for which we assign zero score if a card is black and unit score if a card is red;

B. A full card pack for which we assign scores of 0, 1, 2, 3 respectively to cards specified by suit as clubs, diamonds, hearts and spades.

We shall now consider the result of extracting *successively* from each universe 5 cards without replacement. We may then denote the component unit scores as $x_1, x_2 \ldots x_5$ and the probability that the sample is a given sequence as $P_s(x_1, x_2 \ldots x_5)$. Of many ways in which we may score the 5-fold trial one is to record the mean value of x, and we shall assume that the mean score $x_{m.5}$ of the 5-fold trial is $0 \cdot 6$. If the sample comes from universe A, we then know that it consists of 3 red and 2 black cards. Whence from (iv) of p. 41 we may write

$$P_s(x_1, x_2 \ldots x_5) = 26^{(3)} . 26^{(2)} \div 52^{(5)}$$

Thus the mean score suffices to specify the probability of meeting a sample of relevant specified make-up. More generally for a 2-class universe of s objects to which we assign

445

a score b, the mean score of the r-fold non-replacement sample suffices to specify the probability of getting the score sequence $x_1, x_2, x_3 \ldots x_r$, since any unit score x_u in the sequence must have the value a or b and $x_{m.r}$ therefore suffices to evaluate u and $v = (r - u)$ in the expression:

$$P_s(x_1, x_2, x_3 \ldots x_r) = (s^{(u)}.f^{(v)}) \div n^{(r)}$$

In this sense we may say that the statistic $x_{m,r}$ contains all the relevant information a sample from a 2-class universe can contain; but this is not true of the mean score referable to the alternative 4-class universe B above. If $r = 5$ all we may infer from the information $x_{m,5} = 0 \cdot 6$ is that the composition of the sample may be any of the following:

Unit Trials	Probability of the observed sequence
$4(0) + 1(3)$	$13^{(4)}.13 \div 52^{(5)}$
$3(0) + 1(1) + 1(2)$	$13^{(3)}.13^2 \div 52^{(5)}$
$2(0) + 3(1)$	$13^{(2)}.13^3 \div 52^{(5)}$

As we see from the above, each unique *combination* of unit trial scores here assigns a different probability to the observed event, i.e. particular combination in a particular sequence.

This example exhibits the meaning we may attach to the terms when we say that $x_{m.r}$ is a *sufficient* statistic when we sample in universe A and an insufficient statistic when we sample in universe B; and the formal distinction is easy to infer from it. For samples from universe A, the probability assignable to $x_{m.5} = 0 \cdot 6$ is:

$$P_{s.m}(x_1, x_2 \ldots x_5) = \frac{3! \, 2!}{5!}$$

If P_m is the probability of getting a unique score combination:

$$P_s(x_1, x_2 \ldots x_5) = P_{s.m}(x_1, x_2 \ldots x_5).P_m$$

$$= \frac{3! \, 2!}{5!} \cdot \frac{5!}{3! \, 2!} \cdot 13^{(2)}13^{(3)} \div 52^{(5)}$$

$$= 13^{(2)} \cdot 13^{(3)} \div 52^{(5)}$$

446

Thus we may here split the expression for the probability of extracting a sample completely specified as a unique ordered sequence into 2 factors, one being the probability that the sufficient statistic will have its observed value, the other being the conditional probability of the observed event if the sufficient statistic has this value. Now we cannot do this with the insufficient statistic $x_{m.r}$ referable to sampling in universe B. We then have for $r = 5$ and $x_{m.5} = 0 \cdot 6$

$$52^{(5)} \cdot P_m = \frac{5!}{4! \, 1!} \, 13^{(4)}13 + \frac{5!}{3! \, 1! \, 1!} \, 13^{(3)}13^2 + \frac{5!}{2! \, 3!} \, 13^{(2)}13^3$$

If it happens that the sample consists of 4 clubs and 1 spade, we may write

$$52^{(5)} \cdot P_s(x_1, x_2 \ldots x_5) = 13^{(4)}13 \;\; and \;\; P_{s.m}(x_1, x_2 \ldots x_5) = \frac{4! \, 1!}{5!}$$

Whence it is clearly false to write as above:

$$P_s(x_1, x_2 \ldots x_5) = P_{s.m}(x_1, x_2 \ldots x_5) \cdot P_m$$

The possibility of factorisation in this way does indeed furnish the formal conditions which define whether a sample statistic is sufficient; but the status of the concept of sufficiency in the theory of interval estimation is amenable to discussion at a less formal level. The important difference between $x_{m.r}$ as a sample statistic of universe A and $x_{m.r}$ as a sample statistic of universe B resides in the fact that the former alone embodies every relevant particular referable to the individual sample. If then we claim the right to assign a probability to statements about a source on the evidence which a sample of specified make-up supplies, we shall employ statistics which summarise all the evidence a sample can indeed supply, whence we shall invoke only sampling distributions referable to sufficient statistics. If we claim no more than the right to associate a probability to correct assertion within the framework of consistent adherence to a rule stated in advance, there is no obvious reason why we should conform to any such restriction.

The controversy over the Behrens distribution and the search for sufficient sampling statistics has provoked an extensive literature at a high level of mathematical sophistication, but the *casus belli*, like the *t*-distribution dilemma disclosed in our earlier discussion of Model VI (p. 416) involves logical issues which are not difficult to grasp if we keep our feet on the solid ground of situations for which we can prescribe *discrete* distributions as in Chapter 14 and 15. The dilemma raised in the Model VI set-up does not arise, if we endorse Wrighton's principle of *a priori adequacy* as an inescapable obligation to those who adopt the Forward Look. The *t*-distribution relies exclusively on sufficient statistics; but it cannot provide a sufficient basis for the interval estimation of the mean of a normal distribution in terms consistent with a behaviourist viewpoint, since the rule prescribed admits of no restriction to the set of terminal statements it endorses. Meanwhile, controversy continues in a progressively more rarefied atmosphere of symbolic conventions remote from the real world. So far the outcome has been to provide pure mathematics with a new crop of problems. That the illumination conferred will prove to be proportionate to the output of heat generated seems less certain. It is the writer's view that further progress awaits a vigorous restatement of first principles, and that such restatement will reveal both the need for refinement of the original terms of reference of Neyman's theory and the impossibility of accommodating the Fiducial Argument to an interpretation of the terms of reference of a calculus of probabilities in the domain of observable occurrences.

Kendall (*op. cit.* Vol. II, p. 90) clearly recognises the difficulty of accommodating Fisher's formulation with the behaviourist viewpoint, when he states

. . . Fisher considers the distribution of values of θ for which t can be regarded as a representative estimate-representative, that is to say, in the sense that it could have arisen by random sampling from the population specified by θ. As pointed out above, this does not mean that we are regarding the true value of θ as a member of an existing population. Rather, we are considering the possible values of θ and attaching to each value a measure of our confidence in it, based on the probability that it could have given rise to the observed t.

If I interpret him correctly, Fisher would regard a fiducial distribution as a frequency-distribution. This implies that θ is regarded as a random variable. It appears to me, however, that it is not a random variable in the ordinary sense of the frequency theory of probability, in which values of θ either are or can be generated by an actual sampling process. We can never test whether the fiducial distribution holds in the frequency sense by drawing a number of values and comparing observation with theory. Nor, in calculating fiducial limits of the type $\theta = t + h(\alpha)$, do we imply that the proportion of cases for which $\theta \leqslant t + h$ is true will be α in the long run.

We have sufficiently acquainted ourselves with the inadequacy of Neyman's original statement of the problem if we accept the principle of *a priori* adequacy. Wrighton specifies a second restriction likely to call for more drastic innovations of procedure if it commends itself to our good judgment. This is the *principle of the minimal set*. The principle of *a priori* adequacy signifies that the rule must guarantee the possibility of making terminal statements which are acceptable at the lowest level in the sense that we must always be in a position to say more than the outcome of non-stochastic reasoning in the same class of situations. The principle of the minimal set imposes a three-fold limitation. If less compelling than the principle of *a priori* adequacy, it does at least link the theory of estimation more closely to the real world. A set of acceptable statements is minimal in Wrighton's sense, if it conforms to three requirements:

(i) *No terminal statement may be null in the sense that it implies reservation of judgment.*

(ii) *No terminal statement may be inconsistent with background knowledge of prior possibilities.*

(iii) *No terminal statement may imply a higher level of precision than the rule in its entirety can endorse.*

The null condition is trivial in the domain of interval estimation and merely prescribes that the rule of stochastic induction should be comprehensive in the sense defined on p. 346. Some would deny that it is a logical necessity, but the practical inconvenience of relinquishing the requirement in the domain of the alternative test procedure should be sufficiently clear in

P

the light of the discussion on pp. 359–362 of Chapter 15. Disregard of (ii) above, viz. the requirement that no terminal statement should necessarily be false, might likewise seem to be logically consistent with what we claim for the rule as a whole; but it is inconsistent with the principle of design implicit in the interpretation of a confidence chart like that of Fig. 3 as a visualisation of the hypothesis-observation grid in the two-way continuum. This emerges clearly from our discussion of Models V (a) and V (b) and IV in Chapter 15.

The incorporation of (ii) as a fifth (see p. 432) canon of stochastic induction in an adequate restatement of the theory of confidence intervals will remove a widely felt objection to Neyman's original theory and one which has prompted the criticism that Neyman dispenses with the prior probabilities of Bayes by an ingenious trick. We have seen sufficient reason to exonerate Neyman from this charge, since Bayes's prior probabilities are assignable to hypotheses in a meaningful sense only in the domain of what von Mises speaks of (p. 138) an experiment carried out in two stages, i.e. when each of the hypotheses of the comprehensive set is referable to a real population at risk. The form of the objection so stated thus arises from failure to distinguish between the *prior probabilities* of Bayes and the *prior possibilities* which delimit the comprehensive set of hypotheses, whence also the rightly conceived boundaries of the hypothesis-observation grid. None the less, the need for a realistic formulation of any rule of stochastic induction with due regard to the latter remains, as Kendall (*Biometrika XXXVI*, 1949) recognises:

Suppose I assume that a sampling process is such as to reproduce a binomial distribution—there is a good deal of evidence for this in the case of births. I observe a value of 0·60 as the ratio of male to total births in a sample of 10,000. The theory of confidence intervals says that I may assert that the proportion p lies between 0·59 and 0·61 with the probability that, if I make this type of assertion systematically in all similar cases, I shall be about 95 per cent right in the long run. But I do not then make such an assertion because I know too much about birth-rates to believe any such thing. The theory of confidence intervals gives no place to prior knowledge of the situation. How, then, can that theory provide a guide to conduct in making decisions?

The third requirement embodied in Wrighton's principle of a *minimal* set of acceptable terminal statements confers a special relevance on the italicised epithet. Its importance emerges only when the terminal statement specifies an interval $(p_a - p_b) = i_{p.0}$. In some model situations, e.g. that of p. 359 in Chapter 15, a rule which endorses the statement $M_a = k$ at an acceptable uncertainty level $P_f \leqslant \epsilon$ for a particular observation endorses the same identity for all situations; but this need not be so. It is not true of the Model III at the end of Chapter 14; nor is it true of Model V (*b*) in Chapter 16. There we saw that if $i_c = k$ for $p_0 = 0 \cdot 5$, $i_c < k$ for all other values of p_0 in the admissible range.

Now it is not necessarily inconsistent with the operation of the rule in its entirety to allow that different observations may prescribe different values $k_{p.0} < k$, the requisite precision level which determines the requisite size (*r*) of sample consistent with the assigned uncertainty safeguard $P_f \leqslant \epsilon$; and we have adopted this procedure in the discussion of Model V (*a*) in conformity with Neyman's formulation. On the other hand, there are good reasons for relinquishing the obligation to do so, and if we do dispense with it we embrace certain advantages, in particular the possibility of handling otherwise intractable situations. We are then free to formulate rules of interval estimation, which are not identical with those prescribed by Neyman's formal definitions, and rules which also incorporate (ii) above.

Wrighton's argument is as follows. Presumptively our end in view, when we operate within the framework of the hypothesis-observation grid either in non-stochastic or stochastic terms, is to decide whether a statement is admissible within the corpus of knowledge; and our precision level (*k*), being in this context our criterion of acceptability, defines the eligibility of a terminal statement to admission within the corpus of knowledge. If we take the concept of such a corpus of knowledge seriously, the admission of terminal statements to the effect $k_{p.0} < k$ when p_0 has particular values other than the value which endorses $k_{p.0} = k$ would seem to imply a *second* corpus of knowledge with which we associate more exacting standards of precision than the operation of the rule in its entirety can guarantee. If so, the experimental design violates the principle of *a priori adequacy* relative thereto. The argument so stated is subtle. In more simple terms, we may state it interrogatively thus: if I say that I ask no more of my rule in its entirety than the right to assert $k_{p.0} = k$, have I really gained anything by reserving the right to say $k_{p.0} < k$ in particular situations?

Though this does not call for restatement of the method of determining the interval in the domain of Model VI (p. 416) of Chapter 17, it will lead us to a different procedure in the situation of Model V (*b*). In the case which arises when the binomial parameter *p* of Model IV may admissibly have any value in the range $0 - 1 \cdot 0$, two parallel straight lines like those of Fig. 4 in our treatment of Model VI enclosing the lozenge shaped region of Fig. 3 will define all the intervals corresponding to our set of acceptable terminal statements. Consequently, the numerical computation of confidence limits prescribed by the adoption of the Principle of the Minimal Set will not be as for Neyman's theory of confidence intervals.

Wrighton's restatement differs from Neyman's in another way. As we have consistently maintained, Neyman insists that a rule of induction referable to the terms of reference of the classical theory is a rule stated in advance. Thus the calculus of judgments cannot prescribe how we should weigh the evidence which a single sample supplies. It can merely endorse a procedure for weighing the way in which we weigh the evidence. None the less, it would seem that Neyman still experiences a nostalgia for retrospective judgments in so far as he seemingly condones the practice of examining previously accumulated data as if they are accumulating in the course of an experiment designed in accordance with what he calls a rule of inductive behaviour. At first sight, Wrighton's principle of the minimal set might seem to make this licence more defensible, since it excludes our right to make statements prescribing a precision level more refined than the size of sample can endorse. Wrighton repudiates this deviation from the Forward Look. Any such appeal to the restriction the principle imposes is illusory, if we consistently interpret the true terms of reference of a rule stated in advance. As Clopper and Pearson remind us, we relinquish more than the certainty of being right when we operate a rule of stochastic induction with an assignable risk of error. We confer on the totality of our assertions a greater precision, but we can assign no acceptable risk to the possibility that any individual assertion is false. We cannot admit the right to examine isolated samples of past experience as if we were performing experiments in accordance with a rule which disclaims any title to evaluate the verdict we may pass on any single one of them.

A communication (see p. 24) of Anscombe on the Analysis of Variance was the occasion for a discussion which forced the current controversy over the credentials of statistical inference into the open. Anscombe was content to point out that the null hypotheses of the test battery are factually ambiguous. Wald's restatement of test procedure as prescribed by Neyman and E. S. Pearson seemingly deprives the battery of any intelligible rationale. What then remains of the technique we now identify with statistical design of experiments? In one of the few thought-provoking discussions of the Analysis of Variance, Churchill Eisenhart has advanced the view that its main usefulness lies in the domain of interval estimation. If we adopt Wrighton's restatement of Neyman's Confidence theory, we must abandon the hope of rehabilitating its credentials as such. What I have said, and what Neyman himself now concedes, concerning the limitations of the Gosset sample distribution as a device for assigning an interval estimate to the mean proscribes the Analysis of Variance as a procedure for so doing.

CHAPTER NINETEEN

EPILOGUE

IN THIS BOOK our concern has been to trace disputable claims
of statistical theory to their sources. We have seen that the
calculus on which current statistical theory relies took shape
when the only practical preoccupation of the pioneers was a
regimen for gambling in games of chance. With the rise of life
insurance the emergence of a new *motif* signalises two innovations equally alien to any such undertaking. In effect, the
calculus of probability henceforth claimed as its province
situations in which the toy changes during the course of the
game and the player is at liberty to change his bet as the
game progresses. In the background of every contemporary
issue, we may detect an uneasy but not fully articulate recognition that the calculus has no necessary relevance to situations
of either sort. Having striven to make this twofold dilemma
explicit it remains for me to summarise the outcome of the
foregoing discussion as I now see it. I propose to do so by
asserting three theses.

1. Unless we rely on axioms which are not susceptible of
proof, we must concede that a calculus of probability is relevant
to the real world; (*a*) only in so far as it specifies frequencies
of observable occurrences in an indefinitely protracted sequence
of trials; (*b*) only if also such occurrences (e_1, e_2, e_3, etc.)
collectively constitute a sequence wholly devoid of order.

2. If we take the view last stated, it is improper to speak
of the probability that a verdict on the outcome of a single
trial is true. We can speak with propriety only of the frequency
of correct assertion in an unending sequence of trials, and then
only if we adhere consistently to the same rule. Since the theory
of probability conceived in the foregoing terms does not
sanction the right to vary the rules of the game in accordance
with the player's luck, we then shoulder the obligation of
stating in advance the rule in its entirety.

3. If we concede 1 (*a*) above, any proper terms of reference
we may claim for a stochastic calculus of error, for a stochastic

calculus of exploration or for a stochastic calculus of judgments restricts their legitimate use to situations of which we can predicate a fixed framework of repetition.

1. *Unless we rely on axioms which are not susceptible of proof, we must concede that a calculus of probability is relevant to the real world: (a) only in so far as it specifies frequencies of observable occurrences in an indefinitely protracted sequence of trials: (b) only if also such occurrences collectively constitute a sequence wholly devoid of order.*

At the outset we may dismiss any objection to an axiomatic approach when we invoke the calculus of probability to construct hypotheses subsumed by the subject-matter of Chapters Twelve and Thirteen. From the viewpoint of scientific method, the hypothesis that particles of matter behave in accordance with a stochastic model is on all fours with the hypothesis that matter is particulate. We accept or reject such hypotheses because they lead us to conclusions which are or are not *independently* verifiable; and a single accredited experiment of which the outcome is conclusively inconsistent with the axioms suffices to compromise their further usefulness irremediably. Thus none of the foregoing theses impinge on the credentials of what I have called a stochastic Calculus of Aggregates. Contrariwise, the admitted usefulness of stochastic models in contemporary physics and genetics has no bearing on the claims of the theory of probability in situations which offer us no opportunity for testing the validity of our initial assumptions in the light of their practical consequences.

If we invoke the calculus of probability in such situations, my first thesis signifies that we implicitly accept the responsibility of defining circumstances in which we can either identify randomness as a property of a system of occurrences or conduct our observations within a framework of randomisation which we ourselves impose. Now the only domain of action in which it has hitherto been possible both to test the credentials of the calculus and to record an outcome favourable to its claims is the classical domain of games of chance. We may justifiably invoke it in other domains of action, only if we are able to specify what is common to all the procedures subsumed by games of chance. In all such games, we recognise an inextricably three-fold relation between an agent, an apparatus and a randomising procedure. We have seen no sufficient grounds for predicating randomness as something which the apparatus generates except in so far as an agent conforms to the programme of active interference subsumed by the randomising procedure; and all we have been able to say with confidence about the latter is that the task it sets transcends the limits of sensory discrimination of the agent.

It is thus clear that the stochastic Calculus of Error stands on a firmer foundation than its offspring which I have referred to elsewhere as the stochastic Calculus of Exploration. Though the latter derives its formal symbolic outfit with only trivial refinements from the former, it relegates to Nature the responsibility which the player undertakes in the classical situation. Contrariwise, the player takes his proper place in a stochastic calculus of error as the observer. In the same idiom, *accidental* error is precisely equivalent to a score component associated with that part of the player's assigned task beyond possibility of fulfilment in virtue of the limits of sensory discrimination. *Mutatis mutandis*, we may say the same about certain statistical procedures employed in production engineering.

As it bears on the status of what I have called a stochastic Calculus of Judgments, my first thesis raises an issue not as yet examined in these pages. Throughout the foregoing discussion, we have assumed a system of randomwise sampling without discussing what circumstances justify the identification of such a system with situations in which we apply a test procedure or undertake an interval estimation. The contemporary attitude to this task is puzzling. In one context we read that we can legitimately regard any sample (*vide*, p. 489) as a random sample from an infinite hypothetical population, and in another context one and the same author will advocate recourse to random numbers to ensure truly randomwise sampling. If we reject the proposition that mere ignorance is a sufficient guarantee of random selection and decline to assume that the Divine Dealer shuffles the *billets* in Nature's urn before each draw, we must indeed accept the obligation to employ some randomising device when we apply procedure discussed in the last four chapters.

Our examination of the credentials of a calculus of judgments will therefore be incomplete unless we seek an answer to the question: how can we guarantee that a system of sampling is truly random? All statisticians hold that artificial randomness is attainable. Most of them subscribe to the use of *random numbers* as an appropriate device for attaining the end in view; but few consumers are alert to the implications of their use. Since some readers may be unfamiliar with a table of such numbers, a few preliminary remarks on the prescribed usage will not here be out of place. A table of random numbers is a table of c cyphers (0–9) in each of r rows selected in various ways (*vide infra*). If the table is extensive enough, we may expect to meet any of the first hundred integers (labelled 00–99) in the first two columns, any one of the first thousand (labelled 000–999) in the first three, and so on. The way in which we use the table depends on the size of the total sample (N) and the number of groups into which we seek to divide it ostensibly randomwise.

To illustrate the prescribed procedure, we may here suppose that $N = 96$ and that we wish to divide an n-fold sample of persons into three subsamples of 32 each. We may then decide to label the three groups by the numbers:

$$00\text{–}32 \text{ A} : 33\text{–}65 \text{ B} : 66\text{–}99 \text{ C}$$

To allocate our 96 persons to the groups, we first label the individuals as P_1, P_2, P_3, . . . P_n quite arbitrarily. Having done so we say that the random number for P_1 is the first pair of cyphers in the first column, that of P_2 is the second, and so on. The following example will make this clear. As we go from top to bottom, the first two columns in one set of tables read: 03, 97, 16, 12, 55, 16, 84, 63. . . . Thus we award to the person (P_8) whose rank order is 8, the number 63, which places him in group B. In proceeding thus, we shall not expect the groups to accumulate their quota simultaneously. Thus the first 24 rows of the first two columns of the table cited would lead to the allocation of 11 persons to A, 7 to B and 6 to C.

*   457

There will come a stage when we have allocated 32 to one group, let us say A. We then neglect any table entry which assigns a number in the range 00–32 and pass on to the next, till we have filled up the quota for a second group, let us say B. In that event we allocate all the rest to C.

The validity of any such procedure raises several issues, including whether the make-up of the table sufficiently guarantees an Irregular Kollektiv of cypher sequences. Kendall cites three methods of constructing one;

(i) *Use of Mathematical Tables.* Fisher and Yates derived theirs from the 15th to the 19th digits of A. J. Thompson's table of logarithms;

(ii) *Use of Census Figures.* The assumption is that the final digits of large numbers taken from demographic data in no preassigned order will turn up randomwise. Tippett adopted this plan.

(iii) *Mechanical.* By definition, an ideal lottery wheel with 100 sectors labelled 00–99 will generate a random sequence of paired cyphers. On this assumption, Kendall and Babington Smith have tabulated such number sequences by specially constructed machines.

If we ask why successive final digits or pairs, etc., of digits in a table of logarithms should constitute a random sequence, one answer we may get appeals to the fact that a logarithm is a transcendental number; but the fact that such a number cannot be the solution of an algebraic equation in the current sense of the term does not obviously imply that the sequence of cyphers by which we represent it constitutes an Irregular Kollektiv as von Mises uses the term. Moreover, the method is open to a formidable objection of another sort. Kendall expresses it thus:

Here again, however, the use of such tables requires care—they may have been compiled by an observer with number preferences, and some rounding up may have taken place.

More explicitly, Kendall comments on the tables of Fisher and Yates in the following terms:

These numbers were obtained from the 15th–19th digits in A. J. Thompson's tables of logarithms and were subsequently adjusted, it having been found that there were too many sixes.

The procedure followed by Tippett depends on the appeal to insufficient reason. We are then back to the axiom that blindfold selection from Nature's urn is *ipso facto* randomwise. If we accept it, we have exonerated ourselves from the obligation to enlist an artificial randomising device. If we reject it because we have insufficient reason for believing it to be true, there is nothing more to be said in favour of Tippett's method. It is justifiable only if also redundant.

The third method has a more attractive aspect, but Kendall himself concedes:

Thus, it is to be expected that in a table of Random Sampling Numbers there will occur patches which are not suitable for use by themselves. The unusual must be given a chance of occurring in its due proportion, however small. Kendall and Babington Smith attempted to deal with this problem by indicating the portions of their table (5 thousands out of 100) which it would be better to avoid in sampling experiments requiring fewer than 1,000 digits.

The mechanical procedure is attractive because we are at home in a familiar situation. We entrust the making of the table to a lottery, and we can all agree that a lottery situation is the type of situation in which it is indeed possible to generate a sequence as nearly random as we connive in the conduct of tests of the credentials of the calculus of probability hitherto undertaken. With the reservation last stated, we may therefore say that a table of r numbers consisting of c cyphers compiled in accordance with the outcome of r spins of a wheel with c sectors should record *one* r-fold sample in the unending random sequence. None the less, there remains a doubt about the relevance of the assertion to the task of allocating our N individuals randomwise to three groups, A, B and C? Surely, the task so stated implies a procedure which will justify itself only by continual repetition. If so, would not the correct course be to operate the lottery procedure anew whenever we make such an allocation?

The issue last raised focuses attention on an exceptionable

feature of *any* method of allocation which relies on a table of so-called random numbers; but the seemingly unexceptionable alternative suggested in the final query of the last paragraph evades a difficulty. When we use such a table our aim is not merely to allocate individuals in conformity with a random sequence. The end in view is also to ensure that every one of N individuals has an equal chance of allocation to one of the subsamples and that any assemblage of n individuals we may allocate to a particular subsample has the same chance of allocation thereto as any other assemblage of n individuals. Thus the task of prescribing randomwise allocation and that of recognising situations in which the calculus is operative bring us face to face with the same dilemma. If the behaviour of an ordinary cubical die or of a lottery wheel is inconsistent with the assumption of a rectangular distribution of unit trial score values, are we to conclude that: (*a*) the behaviour of the system fails to conform to the requirements of the Irregular Kollektiv; (*b*) though the score sequence is truly random, there is a bias in the sense that our specification of its definitive sampling parameters is erroneous?

If the series of the event is truly random, we require information about the outcome of an infinite sequence of unit trials before we can decide what the bias is. Experience of a finite sequence can merely endorse the upper limit of uncertainty to a statement concerning the limits between which the numerical value of a parameter must lie. To be sure, we can make both the limits and the associated uncertainty safeguard trivial if we conduct a sufficiently prolonged sequence of trials; but we cannot resolve the dilemma last stated by appeal to experience *a posteriori*. Any precise statement about limits endorsed by the calculus of probability is valid only if we can first assure ourselves that the series of the event is truly random.

In this context, the word *bias* as commonly used is a pitfall. We have no sufficient reason for assuming that any formal definition of probability, e.g. in terms of set theory (p. 49), embraces the specification of the true numerical values of parameters definitive of a sampling distribution. Nor have we sufficient reason for assuming that the exclusive source of any departure from values assigned *a priori* is some mechanical defect of the apparatus, in contradistinction to minor variations of procedure consistent with the *explicit* programme of instructions. If we say that the probability (p) of tossing a head lies in the range $\frac{1}{2} \pm b$, we cannot therefore legitimately imply assent to the proposition that p has a unique limiting value fixed by the agent's instructions and the construction of the penny.

If we could confidently assume that the programme of instructions guarantees a truly random sequence in which p has a unique limiting value, it would be possible to score the results of trials to compensate for *bias* in the customary and naïve sense of the term, e.g. by alternately scoring heads as 0 or 1 and tails likewise. We should then have a random sequence with equiprobability of scoring unity or zero. We might accomplish the end in view in many other ways. For heuristic reasons, it will be helpful to take a backstage view of a particular system of compensatory scoring on this assumption. Our rule will be: if the number of tails in an r-fold trial is odd, score the result as 0, otherwise as 1. For $r = 2$ we shall then set out our results thus:

Result	HH	HT or TH	TT
Score	1	0	1
Probability	p^2	$2p(1-p)$	$(1-p)^2$

Similarly for $r = 3$ we should have:

HHH	HHT, HTH, THH	TTH, THT, HTT	TTT
1	0	1	0
p^3	$3p^2(1-p)$	$3p(1-p)^2$	$(1-p)^3$

On the naïve view under consideration, we may assume a fixed proportionate bias b from the ideal value $\frac{1}{2}$, such that $p = \frac{1}{2}(1 + b)$. Thus for $r = 2$, the probability of scoring 1 is $\frac{1}{2}(1 + b^2)$, for $r = 3$ the probability of scoring 1 is $\frac{1}{2}(1 + b^3)$.

461

If the proportionate bias thus naïvely defined is 0·2, so that $p = 0·6$, it follows that the probability of scoring 1 in a single trial is 0·6, in a double trial 0·52, in a 3-fold trial 0·508, and so on. More generally, the probability of scoring 1 in an r-fold trial would be $\frac{1}{2}(1 + b^r)$. On the assumption that b is fixed and does not exceed an agreed figure, we should therefore be able to make the probability of scoring 0 in an r-fold trial as small as need be by prescribing a sufficiently large value of r.

We have here assumed that the outcome of successive individual tosses is a truly random sequence. Now the assumption that it will be so involves the agent's intervention and the programme of instructions as well as the construction of the penny. Alas we have little reason to believe that it is possible to frame a programme which does not admit minor variations, any one of which will lead to a unique value of p in the long run if the agent follows the same plan at every trial. Some of them might favour heads, others tails uppermost at a toss, and if aware of the outcome, the agent might use his or her knowledge to vary the programme in an orderly way. In what follows, therefore, we shall no longer assume that the penny has a fixed bias as writers on the theory of probability commonly use the term. We shall also need to examine what are the consequences of withholding knowledge of the outcome from the agent.

All we shall then be able to say about the limits of bias will concede that the agent may be free to act both in a way which favours heads and in a way which favours tails. We suppose that one way of consistently behaving leads in the long run to an upper value $p_1 = \frac{1}{2}(1 + b_1)$ and another to a lowest value $p_2 = \frac{1}{2}(1 - b_2)$. It will not affect the ensuing argument if we put $b_1 = b = b_2$ for the outside limits. Accordingly, we may write $p_1 = (1 - p_2)$ and $p_2 = (1 - p_1)$. We are then ready to appreciate in outline the rationale of a method of randomisation with equiprobability advanced by Wrighton (in the press). As a method of allocation, it is not open to the objection already advanced against the use of a table. It invokes the randomising procedure anew for every allocation of a group, and the randomising procedure itself has three essential innovations:

(*a*) a blindfold agent tosses a penny in accordance with precise instructions with reference to the way in which he must toss it;

(*b*) an umpire records the score at each toss without divulging it to the agent;

(*c*) the scoring of the composite (*r*-fold) trial which determines the allocation of each individual follows the prescription already explored, viz. score o if the number of tails in the *r*-fold trial is odd, otherwise score 1.

The importance of withholding knowledge of the outcome of the toss from the agent will be clear, if we consider the 2-fold composite trial. For brevity we may put $p_1 = \frac{1}{2}(1 + b)$ and $p_2 = \frac{1}{2}(1 - b)$ for the definitive parameters of the two most-biased ways of interpreting the programme of instructions. If the agent does not know the outcome, he or she may operate either plan consistently or vary them without reference thereto; and we may prescribe possible results within limits set by regularly alternating or consistently adopting one or the other. We may then lay them out thus:

	HH	HT or TH	TT
	1	0	1
Plan 1	p_1^2	$2p_1(1 - p_1)$	$(1 - p_1)^2$
Plan 2	p_2^2	$2p_2(1 - p_2)$	$(1 - p_2)^2$
Alternating	p_1p_2	$p_1^2 + p_2^2$	p_2p_1

If the agent follows either plan consistently, the result will be the same. The probability of scoring 1 will be $\frac{1}{2}(1 + b^2)$. If the two plans alternate, it will be $\frac{1}{2}(1 - b^2)$. Thus the limits between which probability of scoring 1 must lie will be $\frac{1}{2}(1 \pm b^2)$. More generally for an *r*-fold trial, this will be $\frac{1}{2}(1 \pm b^r)$. Thus the system of scoring ensures that the probabilities of scoring 0 or 1 approach equality as *r* increases.

Now this is not necessarily so, if knowledge of the result of the toss empowers the agent to vary the plan of action in an *orderly* way. For instance, the agent would then be free to operate plan 1 consistently if the result of the first toss of the 2-fold trial proved to be a head, but to operate plan 1 at the first and plan 2 at the second if the first proved to be a tail. Our schema thus becomes:

HH	HT	TH	TT
1	0	0	1
p_1^2	$p_1(1-p_1)$	$p_2(1-p_2)$	$(1-p_1)(1-p_2)$

On this showing the probability of scoring 1 would be $\frac{1}{2}(1+b)$, i.e. the departure from equiprobability would be as great as if the agent scored the result in the usual way.

Without here defining our criterion for deciding on the number (r) of tosses in the composite trial scored as 0 or 1 with probability as nearly 0·5 as we care to make it, we may now outline the method of allocation. To do so, we may speak of any such composite r-fold trial based on the primary sequence of tosses as a unit secondary trial, and of any k successive unit secondary trials as a k-fold secondary trial. The outcome of any one of these will be one of 2^k different sequences of unit scores 0 or 1. We may imagine that each of an assemblage of 2^k individuals receives a different ticket bearing one or other of these sequences. If we wish to allocate him to two groups of equal size, we may place any individual in Group A if the result of a k-fold secondary trial tallies with his ticket, continuing the process till Group A holds half the assemblage of 2^k individuals. The remainder will then constitute Group B. If the size of the assemblage is N, it will not commonly be possible to fix k so that $N = 2^k$. All that matters is that each individual holds a unique ticket recording a score sequence which has approximately the same probability of turning up as any other. Thus 2^k must be at least as great as N and our criterion for choosing k will be $2^{k-1} < N \leqslant 2^k$.

We have still to define how to fix r. If the end in view is that the ticket held by every individual is to have approximately the same chance of recording the score sequence of one of the k-fold secondary trials we may argue as follows. Absolute equiprobability implies that the chance of meeting any such sequence is 2^{-k}; but we cannot hope to achieve this. All we can hope to achieve is that:

(a) it will lie in a range $\dfrac{1 \pm \epsilon}{2^k}$;

(b) the maximum proportionate bias ϵ will not exceed an agreed limit, e.g. $0 \cdot 01$ (1 per cent).

Now the probability of scoring 1 or 0 at a single trial lies in the range $\frac{1}{2}(1 \pm b^r)$. So the worst that can happen is that the probability of getting a particular k-fold sequence lies in the range:

$$\left(\frac{1 \pm b^r}{2}\right)^k \simeq \frac{1 \pm kb^r}{2^k}$$

Thus the condition we seek is that $(1 + \epsilon) \simeq (1 + kb^r)$ or $\epsilon \simeq kb^r$.

Illustratively, we may suppose that

(a) the size of the group is $N = 73$ so that $2^6 < N \leqslant 2^7$ and $k = 7$;

(b) we are confident that p lies between $0 \cdot 6$ and $0 \cdot 4$, in the sense that the maximum single toss bias allowable is 20 per cent, i.e. $b = 0 \cdot 2$;

(c) we are satisfied if the maximum proportionate bias of the k-fold sequence is 1 per cent, i.e. $\epsilon = 0 \cdot 01$.

In that event we shall choose r so that $0 \cdot 01 = 7 \ (0 \cdot 2)^r$. Since $7 \ (0 \cdot 2)^3 = 0 \cdot 016$ and $7 \ (0 \cdot 2)^4 = 0 \cdot 00224$, it will ensure that $\epsilon \leqslant 0 \cdot 01$, if $r = 4$, and the allocation of an individual will involve $4 \ (7) = 28$ tosses of the coin.

2. *It is improper to speak of the probability that a verdict on the outcome of a single trial is true. We can speak with propriety only of the frequency of correct assertion in an unending sequence of trials, and then only if we adhere consistently to the same rule. Since the theory of probability conceived in the foregoing terms does not sanction the right to vary the rules of the game in accordance with the player's luck, we then shoulder the obligation to state in advance the rule in its entirety.*

The second thesis I have proposed carries with it a corollary that has only very lately gained recognition, and by no means universally. In so far as we can claim any usefulness for a rule of the type under discussion, the statement of it must include a specification of the size of the sample. Now the self-same property which bestows on such sample distributions as the t and the F (or Fisher's z) a peculiar fascination from the viewpoint of the mathematician deprives us of the opportunity of doing so. If we accept my second thesis, we have thus to admit that we have as yet no means at our disposal for assigning a meaningful confidence interval: (*a*) to a Gaussian point-estimate in its proper domain of the calculus of error; (*b*) to a mean or other parameter of a table set out in accordance with the Fisher prescription for *Analysis of Variance*. By the same token, the test battery of the technique designated *Analysis of Covariance* forfeits any claims to usefulness endorsed by a calculus of judgments consistent with the Forward Look.

In short, the attempt of Neyman and of Wald to rehabilitate the theory of test procedure and of interval estimation in terms consistent with what Neyman himself calls inductive behaviour has led to an admitted (p. 438) *impasse*. It forced Wald to enunciate the *Minimax* solution which is wholly arbitrary, embodying a concept of decision ostensibly behaviouristic but on closer examination consistent only with the view which locates probability in the mind. I do not venture to express any opinion about whether mathematical ingenuity will eventually surmount the difficulty Neyman himself concedes; but it seems to me that we have now before us a simple choice. If we decline to relinquish the mathematical apparatus of current test and interval estimation, we must retreat from a behaviourist approach to the credentials of statistical theory. In that event, we shall embrace arbitrary axioms the truth of which we can never hope to prove conclusively. If we decline a profession of faith without justification by works, we must abandon the mathematical apparatus of sampling distributions now in vogue. In that event we must dig more secure foundations on which to build a new edifice of theory.

The choice here stated raises issues of which the implications extend far beyond the confines of current statistical controversy. We have seen (p. 443) that one writer prefers to announce a new law of thought rather than to abandon Fisher's concept of a fiducial distribution. Among those who embrace the new law of thought no single exponent has come forward to vindicate its claim to consideration for any reason other than the plenary absolution it confers on adherence to a calculus conceived in solipsistic terms. Thus the dilemma forced on us by the attempt to accommodate the algebraic convenience of the t-distribution with the logical requirements of a concept of confidence consistent with an empiricist viewpoint has brought into sharper relief an as yet unresolved antinomy between the traditional outlook of the experimental scientist and the current metaphysic of the professional statistician. The antinomy itself is not new. It was latent in the entire tradition of thought which Quetelet, Galton and Pearson bequeathed to our generation. In his own day, Claude Bernard recognised it as such.

3. *Any proper terms of reference we may claim for a calculus of error, for a calculus of exploration or for a calculus of judgments restricts their legitimate use to situations of which we can predicate a fixed framework of repetition.*

That such a postulate is admissible in the domain of error *sensu stricto* is not open to question; but the family likeness of the Gaussian algebra and that of multivariate or of factor analysis tempts us to forget that a common algebraic symbolism furnishes no safeguard for conserving a necessarily implicit, if not actually explicit, assumption of the stochastic calculus of error. In the new role which Quetelet, Galton and Pearson found for the Gaussian algebra, we have to relegate the randomising procedure to Nature; and we have to abandon the opportunity of recording the same observation in precisely the same circumstances on successive occasions. For the classical theory of wagers we can define randomness in a meaningful way only if we also predicate a temporal framework of limitless repetition. This may be admissible in the domain of populations of living beings when we are dealing with highly inbred stocks in an ideally standardized environment, though then only if we neglect mutation as a second order effect. Otherwise, our opportunities of observation refer only to events which are historically unique.

The *raison d'être* of the infinite hypothetical population bequeathed by Laplace to Quetelet's successors including the contemporary school of R. A. Fisher, is the search for a formula to sidestep this dilemma. The undertaking fails at two levels. One is that the conceptually static and infinite population endorses the gratuitous belief that blindfold selection is *ipso facto* randomwise; but the construction or use of tables of random numbers by those who subscribe to it sufficiently shows that they entertain grave doubts about it. This is confessedly an argument *ad hominem*; but the concept of a static infinite population is also exceptionable at an operational level. Any conclusions to which statistical procedures may lead us are useful only if we can legitimately identify situations in which we propose to apply them with the entire class of situations subsumed by the putative fixed framework of repetition. Needless to say, it is commonly, if not invariably, impossible to conceive of an infinite actual population which we can pin down to such definite requirements.

*　　　*　　　*　　　*　　　*

The foregoing theses epitomise the positive outcome of the task undertaken in this book; but they do not impinge on the issue: what light can statistical studies based as such on populations shed on the mechanism of *individual* behaviour? If we abandon the claim to assign a probability to the truth of a particular verdict as inconsistent with a behaviourist approach, we must regard a calculus of judgments as a prescription for a collective discipline of interpretation in contradistinction to a sanction for individual conviction. We may still concede the possibility of building an edifice of new theory on foundations more secure than the infinite hypothetical population; but we have then to ask: what useful role can such a calculus fulfil in the biological or social sciences? For my part, I should hesitate to say *none at all*; but we shall be wise to refrain from indulging in unjustifiable expectations about the situations in which it may be helpful to enquiry. We shall be still wiser, if our revaluation of the claims of a calculus of judgments encompasses a re-examination of the type of situations to which it has no relevance.

To do justice to the foregoing query, we must first ask ourselves: to what class of questions do we seek an answer when we invoke such procedures as statistical tests and interval estimation? A foregoing citation (p. 227) from Claude Bernard in the context of the clinical trial forewarns us of and forearms us against one widely current delusion about their relevance. If it is proper to say that statistics is the science of averages, we should be hesitant about enlisting statistics in experimental enquiry before asking: is the answer to our question usefully expressible in terms of an average? Otherwise, undue reliance on statistics must impede the march of science by encouraging us to ask useless questions or to refrain from asking the most useful ones.

Fisher's oft-quoted parable about the lady and the tea-cup is an instructive text for this theme, since it illustrates an issue of fundamental importance to the study of animal or human behaviour and one with topical relevance *vis à vis* latter-day claims concerning the existence of so-called *extrasensory perception*. As R. A. Fisher states it, the problem is as follows. A lady declares that she can distinguish by taste whether her hostess puts milk in the cup before the tea or *vice versa*. He proposes to test the truth of her assertion by allowing her to taste 8 cups after telling her that he has mixed four in one way and four in the other. From the writer's viewpoint, this form of words is exceptionable, if we reject the relevance of stochastic induction to the outcome of single trials; but this need not here detain us. The possible answers the lady may give, when asked to classify the 8 cups on the assumption stated, subsume $(8! \div 4!\ 4!) = 70$ permutations, only one of which can correspond to actuality. If we deem denial of her claim to discriminate as equivalent to correct assessment with a long-run frequency consistent with truly random choice, the denial of her claim (Fisher's null hypothesis) will occur with a frequency of one in seventy. If she discriminates consistently, she will always be right. In effect, therefore, Fisher proposes the rule: say that she can discriminate if the outcome is correct assignment. Then 70^{-1} is the probability of error, if she cannot discriminate at all, and zero is the probability of error, if she can. Thus $P_f \leqslant 70^{-1}$.

If the only admissible alternatives are as stated, the positive outcome of several such experiments without a failure will presumably satisfy the sceptic to whom the investigator submits his findings, and he will not need to lean on the statistician for support; but Fisher himself envisages a lady content to claim "not that she could draw the distinction with invariable certainty, but that, though sometimes mistaken, she would be right more often than not." Evidently, this claim is not susceptible to discussion in statistical terms, unless we add one or both of two emendations: (*a*) she can herself state her claims with more precision; (*b*) the jury can agree about what numerical level of long-run success is worthy of consideration.

Neyman makes this point vigorously in a critique of Fisher's treatment of the problem. For him, as for Fisher, the probability of correctly identifying a single cup is $p = \frac{1}{2} = p_0$, if she has no discrimination at all; but we can assign the appropriate sample size to endorse an acceptable uncertainty safeguard for a rule of procedure only if we assign a positive number $k < \frac{1}{2}$, being content to deny that she can discriminate unless $p \geqslant p_0 + k = p_k$. In short, the lady then supposedly behaves like a biased penny, and we can formulate a decision rule to test its bias (k) only if we first decide to dismiss certain values of k as trivial.

If we adopt a somewhat naïve view about a biased penny, this disposes of the dilemma; but any such conceptualisation of a *degree of sensory perception* forces Neymann to postulate "identity of conditions and the complete independence of the n successive classifications of pairs of cups of tea." Some of my readers will therefore share Wrighton's misgivings, when he asks: "If conditions were in fact identical, what factor would intervene to make the lady's response vary?" Wrighton himself answers it as follows:

The only formal explanation is that in this respect the lady's sensory equipment operates in a fashion characteristic of the roulette board. Alternatively, following Fisher's treatment of other problems, we may identify *the lady as she is at the time of the experiment* with a conceptual lady out of whose infinitely protracted tea-tasting the experience of the experiment is regarded as a random sample. The idea may be attractive, but it carries with it an embarrassing consequence (if we pursue Neyman's illustration). If the experiment demonstrates the phenomenon, it is the conceptual lady who must in fairness be rewarded, and if not, it is the conceptual lady whose pretensions must be exposed.

For Neyman, however, the p appears to be real. The successive trials of the lady are specifically postulated as independent and she is axiomatically endowed with an unvarying p. It is difficult to imagine a justification which would obtain general acceptance among biologists and experimental psychologists for either of these postulates.

Some may feel that the remarks last cited do less than justice to Neyman's treatment of the problem. In my view, we shall do justice to it only if we recognise a confusion of aims, when we enlist a decision rule procedure in this context. To me as a biologist, Neyman's procedure is intelligible only if the end in view is *personnel selection*, in this context picking out ladies who can invariably discriminate from a group containing others who cannot. We thus come back to the issue: to what class of questions do we seek an answer when we invoke statistical procedures?

When discussing populations our concern may be: (*a*) to classify the constituent individuals in a rough and ready way for convenience of administrative book-keeping; (*b*) to arrive at a deeper understanding of the laws of individual behaviour, i.e. a confident prescription for evoking particular responses. If the end in view is a piece of social accountancy, the answer we shall seek will be an average or will be justifiable in terms of a criterion of average success. An average level of perfor-mance may then be consonant with the operational intention. If the end in view is to arrive at a useful understanding of individual behaviour, what peculiarities of nature and previous nurture determine whether different individuals respond to the same stimulus in different ways, or what internal states and external circumstances determine the different responses of one and the same individual to one and the same stimulus are the questions to which we rightly seek an answer. We have indeed accomplished our objective only if we can say of such and such an individual that the probability of responding in such and such a way and in such and such circumstances does not appreciably differ from unity or from zero. In the context of research on the mechanism of behaviour, Neyman's p lying somewhere between 0·5 and 1·0 is a tiresome distraction which contributes nothing to the business in hand.

Such is the glamour of statistics, that the oncoming generation too readily overlook this distinction. Procedures which might be defensible as screening devices thus become an encouragement to evade reality and an excuse for curbing curiosity about fundamental issues. In short, a calculus of uncertainty is becoming the creed of a cult which disdains to press forward to greater certainty when certainty is indeed attainable, and when nothing short of certainty constitutes a useful addition to the enduring corpus of scientific knowledge. In part, the appeal of its doctrine is due to the prestige which mathematics, however irrelevant, confers on those who use it as a tool of interpretation. In part, it results from a failure to distinguish between the permanent factual bricks continually added to the ever-growing edifice of scientific knowledge and a temporary scaffolding of metaphors which the builders discard at their own convenience.

What most helps to perpetuate the confusion last stated is a monistic prejudice which demands a unitary formula for scientific method. Having found no such formula, I have resigned myself to an eclectic acceptance of a diversity of scientific methods; and I believe that it is high time to unmask the semantic implications of using terms such as law, theory, hypothesis in the diverse domains of the retrospective and prospective disciplines. That it leads to confusion of thought, the reader will readily enough concede if he or she reflects on a few familiar examples of their use. Thus the Cell *theory* in biology subsumes merely the factual content of our observational record; but the Wave *theory* of light subsumes a metaphor congenial to the exposition of the metrical relations we encounter in the study of optical interference and the phenomenon of double refraction. Mendel's *law* of segregation is a recipe for action in the practice of plant breeding and runs the gauntlet of possible disproof whenever we apply it. The *law* of evolution is an obituary notice, interpreting *past* change in the light of *current* experience. As such, it offers us no opportunity to test its validity in the domain of action.

One might multiply such examples indefinitely, and if we draw what seems to me to be the inescapable conclusion, it will be very difficult to see how a stochastic calculus of exploration consistent with the Forward Look can claim an enduring place among scientific methods of proven usefulness. Briefly, then, the outcome of our examination of the present crisis in statistical theory from a behaviourist viewpoint which encompasses no axioms unwarranted by the practical experience of mankind is as follows:

(*a*) the credentials of a stochastic calculus of aggregates stand secure from the impact of any contemporary debatable issues arising from disagreement concerning the proper terms of reference of a theory of probability;

(*b*) in its legitimate and original domain of error, the procedure of point estimation is at least a meaningful convention;

(*c*) the factual basis for the assumptions inherent in such exploratory and descriptive procedures as multivariate analysis and factor analysis is exiguous and the ostensible rationale is difficult if not impossible to reconcile with any definable historic framework of randomwise repetition;

(*d*) the available theory of sampling distributions does not suffice to endorse a non-subjective theory of test procedure or of interval estimation in situations which admit of recourse to randomising devices;

(*e*) if it proves possible to rehabilitate a stochastic calculus of judgments in terms consistent with the full implications of a behaviourist outlook, it will be the more necessary to remind ourselves that it can merely endorse assertions which encourage us to probe more deeply, and without reliance thereon, into nature's secrets;

(*f*) the claim of the statistician to prescribe the design of experiments in accordance with the requirements of significance test procedures and of fiducial estimates is consistent neither with a behaviourist view of the proper scope of stochastic induction nor with what should presumably be the primary intentions of the investigator.

There will assuredly be few to whom so iconoclastic a verdict will be palatable; and the writer himself has reached it reluctantly with all the mental discomfort of discarding a weighty incrustation of prevalent custom-thought. In following to what now seems to me to be the bitter end of a trail which others, more especially J. Neyman, E. S. Pearson and A. Wald, have blazed, I have at all times hoped that the prospect of the promised land would prove to be more fertile. It is not agreeable to cherish opinions which isolate one from the bulk of one's intellectual contemporaries; but if one is to enjoy the privileges of intellectual adventure, one must resign oneself to a little isolation as the price of self-indulgence in so exotic a luxury as intellectual rectitude. If I am in error, I can at least hope that the issues I have brought before my readers will compel others wiser than myself to formulate more clearly than heretofore a rational basis for convictions which my own reflections have forced me to abandon. Statistical theory will then enlarge its claim to our respect by relinquishing authoritarian pretensions uncongenial to the temper of science. Contrariwise, the possibility that I may be right in the main does not discourage me. Only when their elders have cleared the site for new foundations will a younger generation be intellectually free to undertake truly creative work now neglected and denigrated.

Persuaded of this conviction, I conclude by citing a challenge for rebuttal or otherwise. In his *Cours de Philosophie Positive*, Auguste Comte (1839), who led the contemporary revolt against Quetelet's *physique sociale*, expresses himself in the following terms:

La seule aberration de ce genre qui eût pu mériter quelque discussion sérieuse, si l'ensemble de ce Traité ne nous en avait d'avance radicalement dispensé, c'est la vaine prétention d'un grand nombre de géomètres à rendre positives les études sociales d'après une subordination chimérique a l'illusoire théorie mathématique des chances. C'est là l'illusion propre des géomètres en philosophie politique, comme celle des biologistes y consiste surtout,

ainsi que je l'ai ci-dessus expliquée, à vouloir ériger la sociologie
en simple corollaire ou appendice de la biologie, en y supprimant,
dans l'un et l'autre cas, l'indispensable prépondérance de l'analyse
historique. Il faut néanmoins convenir que l'aberration des géomètres
est, à tous égards, infiniment plus vicieuse et beaucoup plus nuisible
que l'autre; outre que les erreurs philosophiques quelconques sont,
en général, bien autrement tenaces chez les géomètres, directement
affranchis, par la haute abstraction de leurs travaux de toute
subordination rigoureuse à l'étude réelle de la nature. . . . Serait-il
possible, en effet, d'imaginer une conception plus radicalement
irrationnelle que celle qui consiste à donner pour base philo-
sophique, ou pour principal moyen d'élaboration finale, à l'ensemble
de la science sociale, une prétendue théorie mathématique, où,
prenant habituellement des signes pour des idées, suivant le caractère
usuel des spéculations purement métaphysiques, on s'efforce
d'assujétir au calcul la notion necessairement sophistique de la
probabilité numérique, qui conduit directement à donner notre
propre ignorance réelle pour la mesure naturelle du degré de
vraisemblance de nos diverses opinions? Aussi aucun homme sensé
n'a-t-il été, dans la pratique sociale, effectivement converti de nos
jours à cette étrange aberration, quoique sans pouvoir en démêler
le sophisme fondamental. Tandis que les vraies théories mathé-
matiques ont fait, depuis un siècle, de si grands et si utiles progrès,
cette absurde doctrine, sauf les occasions de calcul abstrait qu'elle
a pu susciter, n'a véritablement subi, pendant le même temps,
malgré de nombreux et importans essais, aucune amélioration
essentielle, et se retrouve aujourd'hui placée dans le même cercle
d'erreurs primitives, quoique la fécondité des conceptions constitue
certainement, à l'égard d'une science quelconque, le symptôme le
moins équivoque de la réalité des spéculations.

If Comte is right in this declaration, what does the future
hold for the practitioner of statistics as an academic discipline
in the domain of the biological and of the social sciences? The
question admits of no simple and, to most of my contemporaries, of no agreeable answer. The stochastic theory of
genetical populations remains an outstanding achievement of
experimental biology, and time may conceivably come when
a calculus of aggregates can usefully embrace other cellular
phenomena. As yet we can discern no prospect of this in the
social sciences. Unless it is possible to rebuild a calculus of
judgments on a firmer basis it may well be that the future

of statistics in the social sciences is what Anscombe (p. 14) contemptuously calls statistics as the term is used by some continental demographers.

If so, it may still claim a modest field of usefulness by prescribing techniques of summarisation appropriate to different types of problems which arise in the study of populations. The first volume of Yule's treatise claimed to do little more. Stochastic models may still suggest recipes for summarising indices which do indeed summarise as do the rank coefficients of Spearman and of Kendall; but a more parsimonious view of the relevance of the calculus of probability to social occurrence is not likely to offer attractive opportunities for the exercise of mathematical subtlety of a high order. The focus of contemporary controversy has been the nature of statistical inference subsumed by what I have called a calculus of judgments; and the vehemence of the debate has demonstrated its vulnerability. What has emerged from these pages is that the stochastic theory of curve fitting subsumed by what I have called a calculus of exploration is even more vulnerable, if we scrutinise its credentials on the same footing. That graduating devices have a limited usefulness in the study of populations as first aids in the search for deeper insight we may well concede; but those who adhere to a behaviourist view will be willing to endorse a stochastic rationale for their prescription only if it is possible to rehabilitate their credentials without recourse to such Platonic constructs as the infinite hypothetical population, the normal man and the normal environment.

CENTRAL LIMIT THEOREM

BY DEFINITION, we speak of a score x whose mean value is M as a normal variate, if the equation of its frequency (y) in the interval $x \pm \frac{1}{2}dx$ is

$$y_x = \frac{1}{\sqrt{2\pi V}} \, exp\left[-\frac{(x - M)^2}{2V} \right] \cdot dx$$

In this expression the constant V is the variance (*second* mean moment) of the distribution. If we denote by $X = (x - M)$ the deviation of x from its mean value, there will correspond to each value of x with the same frequency in the appropriate interval a *standard* score $(X \div \sqrt{V}) = c$. The equation for the frequency of c in the interval $c \pm \frac{1}{2}dc$ is

$$y_c = \frac{1}{\sqrt{2\pi}} \, exp\left(-\tfrac{1}{2}c^2\right) . dc$$

For any *discrete* distribution of a *standard score* $c = (X \div \sqrt{V})$ we define the kth mean moment in terms of f_c the frequency of c in the interval $c \pm \frac{1}{2}dc$ as the mean value of the kth power of c, viz.:

$$M_k = \sum_{-\infty}^{+\infty} f_c . c^k = E(c^k) \quad . \quad . \quad . \quad . \quad (i)$$

Whence, alternatively:

$$M_k = V^{-\frac{1}{2}k} . E(X^k)$$

If $f_c = y_c . dc$ for a continuous variate, we write

$$M_k = \int_{-\infty}^{+\infty} y_c . c^k . dc$$

For a normal variate

$$M_k = \frac{1}{\sqrt{2\pi}} \int_{-\infty}^{+\infty} e^{-\frac{1}{2}c^2} . c^k . dc$$

$$= \frac{2}{\sqrt{2\pi}} \int_{0}^{\infty} e^{-\frac{1}{2}c^2} . c^k . dc \text{ (if } k \text{ is even) } or \text{ zero (if } k \text{ is odd)}$$

477

To evaluate this integral, we may substitute $c^2 = Q$, so that $dc = \frac{1}{2}Q^{-\frac{1}{2}}.dQ$, and

$$M_k = \frac{I}{\sqrt{2\pi}}\int_0^\infty e^{-\frac{1}{2}Q}.Q^{\frac{1}{2}(k-1)}.dQ$$

This is a Gamma function whose value is zero for *odd* values of k, and its value for even values of k is the product $1 . 3 . 5 \ldots (k - 1)$. For the normal distribution we therefore have:

$$\left. \begin{array}{l} M_1 = 0 \; ; \; M_3 = 0 \; ; \; M_5 = 0 \;\; ; \; M_7 = 0 \\ M_2 = 1 \; ; \; M_4 = 3 \; ; \; M_6 = 15 \; ; \; M_8 = 105 \end{array} \right\} \quad . \quad \text{(ii)}$$

Let us now consider a discrete distribution of unit trial scores (x) about mean M with variance $V = M_2(1)$ which is by definition the mean value of $(x - M)^2 = X^2$. We shall assume that unit trials are independent. For the r-fold sample score sum we shall write x_r and the corresponding deviation $X_r = (x_r - rM)$ whose mean value is zero. For the $(r + 1)$th unit trial score we shall write x_1 and for the $(r + 1)$-fold sample score sum x_{r+1}, so that $X_{r+1} = (x_r + x_1) - (rM + M) = X_r + X_1$. The kth mean moment of the $(r + 1)$-fold sample score sum is then by definition

$$m_k(r + 1) = E(X_r + X_1)^k$$
$$= \sum_{p=0}^{p=k} E(k_{(p)}.X_r^{k-p}.X_1^p)$$

In virtue of independence of the unit trial scores, therefore

$$m_k(r + 1) = \sum_{p=0}^{p=k} k_{(p)}.E(X_r^{k-p}).E(X_1^p)$$
$$\therefore \quad m_k(r + 1) = \sum_{p=0}^{p=k} k_{(p)}.m_{k-p}(r).m_p(1)$$

When $p = 1$, $m_p(1) = 0$ and when $(k - p) = 1$, $m_{k-p}(r) = 0$. Whence we have

$$m_2(r + 1) = m_2(r) + m_2(1)$$
$$m_3(r + 1) = m_3(r) + m_3(1)$$
$$m_4(r + 1) = m_4(r) + 6m_2(r).m_2(1) + m_4(1)$$

etc. etc.

478

By successively putting $r = 1, 2, 3$, etc., in the above we derive:

$$m_2(2) = 2m_2(1) \qquad ; m_2(3) = 3m_2(1) \quad \text{etc.}$$

$$m_3(2) = 2m_3(1) \qquad ; m_3(3) = 3m_3(1) \quad \text{etc.}$$

$$m_4(2) = 2m_4(1) + 6m_2^2(1) ; m_4(3) = 3m_4(1) + 18m_2^2(1) \quad \text{etc.}$$

$$m_4(4) = 4m_4(1) + 36m_2^2(1) \ldots \text{etc.}$$

Thus more generally:

$$m_2(r) = r \cdot m_2(1) ; m_3(r) = r \cdot m_3(1)$$

$$m_4(r) = r \cdot m_4(1) + 3r^{(2)} \cdot m_2^2(1)$$

By definition, $m_2(1) = V$ in the above is the variance of the unit sample distribution and $m_2(r) = V_r$ that of the r-fold score sum. The kth mean moment of the r-fold score sum distribution in standard form is by definition

$$M_k(r) = V_r^{-\frac{1}{2}k} \cdot m_k(r)$$

$$\therefore \quad M_2(r) = 1 ; M_3(r) = \frac{m_3(1)}{\sqrt{rV^3}}$$

$$M_4(r) = \frac{m_4(1)}{rV^2} + \frac{3(r-1)}{r}$$

For large values of r, we therefore have

$$M_2(r) = 1 ; M_3(r) \simeq 0 ; M_4(r) \simeq 3$$

In the same way, we can show that for large values of r higher moments approach the corresponding values for the normal distribution:

$$M_5(r) \simeq 0 \simeq M_7(r) ; M_6(r) \simeq 15 ; M_8(r) \simeq 105 \quad \text{etc.}$$

THE UMPIRE BONUS MODEL

CERTAIN RELATIONS between a system of paired scores x_a, x_b are tautologies which do not depend on stochastic considerations. They are easily deducible by recourse to the operators

$E_{a.b}(f_{a.b})$ arithmetic mean of any function f_a, of x_a for a fixed value of x_b.

$E_{b.a}(f_{b.a})$ ditto f_b of x_b for a fixed value of x_a.

$E_a(f_{ab})$ arithmetic mean of any function f_{ab} of both x_a and x_b for all values of x_a.

$E_b(f_{ab})$ ditto for all values of x_b.

$E(f_{ab})$ ditto for all values of both x_a and x_b.

From the definition of the arithmetic mean:

$$E_a . E_{b.a}(f_{ab}) = E(f_{ab}) = E_b . E_{a.b}(f_{ab})$$

$$E(f_a) = E_a(f_a) \; ; \; E(f_b) = E_b(f_b)$$

The following definitions of summarising indices in this notation are necessary for what follows.

Means:

$$E_a(x_a) = M_a \; ; \; E_{a.b}(x_a) = M_{a.b} \; ; \; E_b(x_b) = M_b \; ; \; E_{b.a}(x_b) = M_{b.a}$$

$$E_a(M_{b.a}) = M_b \quad and \quad E_b(M_{a.b}) = M_a$$

Variances:

$$E_a(x_a - M_a)^2 = V_a = E_a(x_a^2) - 2M_a . E_a(x_a) + M_a^2 = E_a(x_a^2) - M_a^2$$

Similarly:

$$E_{a.b}(x_a - M_{a.b})^2 = V_{a.b} = E_{a.b}(x_a^2) - M_{a.b}^2$$

$$E_{b.a}(x_b - M_{b.a})^2 = V_{b.a} = E_{b.a}(x_b^2) - M_{b.a}^2$$

$$E_b(x_b - M_b)^2 = V_b = E_b(x_b^2) - M_b^2$$

For brevity, it is convenient to write:

$$X_a = x_a - M_a \quad ; \quad X_{a.b} = x_{a.b} - M_{a.b} \quad \text{etc.}$$

If $x_k = kx_a$, so that $M_k = kM_a$, it follows that

$$V_k = E(x_k - M_k)^2 = k^2 V_a$$

Covariance:

$$Cov \ (x_a, x_b) = E(X_a . X_b) = E(x_a . x_b) - M_a . M_b$$

$$E(x_a . x_b) = E_a . E_{b.a}(x_a . x_b) = E_a(x_a . M_{b.a})$$

$$\therefore \quad E_a(x_a . M_{b.a}) = Cov \ (x_a, x_b) + M_a . M_b = E_b(x_b . M_{a.b})$$

Linear Regression of x_a on x_b

$$M_{a.b} = k_{ab} . x_b + C \quad . \quad . \quad . \quad . \quad \text{(i)}$$

$$M_a = E_b(M_{a.b}) = k_{ab} . E_b(x_b) + C = k_{ab} . M_b + C$$

$$\therefore \quad (M_{a.b} - M_a) = k_{ab} . X_b \quad . \quad . \quad . \quad \text{(ii)}$$

$$\therefore \quad E_b(X_b . M_{a.b}) - M_a . E_b(X_b) = k_{ab} . E(X_b^2)$$

Since $E_b(X_b) = 0$ by definition

$$k_{ab} . V_b = Cov \ (x_a, x_b) \quad and \quad k_{ab} = \frac{Cov \ (x_a, x_b)}{V_b} \quad \text{(iii)}$$

Linear Regression of x_b on x_a

$$M_{b.a} - M_b = k_{ba} . X_a$$

$$k_{ba} . V_a = Cov \ (x_a, x_b) \quad and \quad k_{ba} = \frac{Cov \ (x_a, x_b)}{V_a} \quad \text{(iv)}$$

Whence, if $V_a = V_b$, $k_{ba} = k_{ab}$.

Product-Moment Correlation Coefficient.

$$r_{ab} = \frac{Cov \ (x_a, x_b)}{\sqrt{V_a . V_b}} \quad . \quad . \quad . \quad . \quad \text{(v)}$$

When regression is linear in both dimensions:

$$r_{ab}^2 = k_{ab} . k_{ba} \quad . \quad . \quad . \quad . \quad \text{(vi)}$$

If $k_{ba} = k_{ab}$, $k_{ab} = r_{ab} = k_{ba}$

. . . . . .

The Umpire Bonus Model: We now postulate a system of scores x_u, $x_{a.0}$ and $x_{b.0}$ which are independent stochastic variables, so that

$$Cov\ (\mathrm{x}_{a.0}, \mathrm{x}_u) = Cov\ (\mathrm{x}_{b.0}, \mathrm{x}_u) = 0 = Cov\ (\mathrm{x}_{a.0}, \mathrm{x}_{b.0})$$

We then define

$$\mathrm{x}_a = A.\mathrm{x}_u + \mathrm{x}_{a.0} \quad and \quad \mathrm{x}_b = B.\mathrm{x}_u + \mathrm{x}_{b.0} \ . \quad \text{(vii)}$$

It follows that:

$$M_a = A.M_u + M_{a.0} \quad and \quad M_b = B.M_u + M_{b.0}$$

$$\therefore\ \ X_a = A.X_u + X_{a.0} \quad and \quad X_b = B.X_u + X_{b.0}$$

$$E(X_a.X_u) = A.E(X_u^2) + E(X_u.X_{a.0})$$

$$E(X_b.X_u) = B.E(X_u^2) + E(X_u.X_{b.0})$$

$$E(X_a.X_b) = AB.E(X_u^2) + A.E(X_u.X_{b.0})$$
$$+ B.E(X_u.X_{a.0}) + E(X_{a.0}.X_{b.0})$$

Whence we obtain:

$$Cov\ (\mathrm{x}_a, \mathrm{x}_u) = A.V_u\ ;\ Cov\ (\mathrm{x}_b, \mathrm{x}_u) = B.V_u\ ;$$
$$Cov\ (\mathrm{x}_a, \mathrm{x}_b) = AB.V_u$$

$$\therefore\ \ r_{au} = \frac{A.V_u}{\sqrt{V_a.V_u}} = A\sqrt{V_u \div V_a}\ ;$$

$$r_{bu} = \frac{B.V_u}{\sqrt{V_b.V_u}} = B\sqrt{V_u \div V_b}\ ;\ r_{ab} = \frac{AB.V_u}{\sqrt{V_a.V_b}} \quad \text{(ix)}$$

$$\therefore\ r_{ab} = r_{au}.r_{bu} \quad . \quad . \quad . \quad . \quad \text{(x)}$$

If $A = 1 = B$, $r_{ab} = 0 \cdot 5$ when $V_a = V_b$ and $V_{a.0} = V_u$; and if regression is also linear in both dimensions $k_{ab} = 0 \cdot 5 = k_{ba}$.

Statistical Independence. The mean of the score sum $x_s = x_a + x_b$ is $M_s = M_a + M_b$ and its variance is by definition

$$E(x_s - M_s)^2 = E(x_a^2 + x_b^2 + 2x_a . x_b - 2x_a . M_b - 2x_b . M_a$$
$$- 2x_a M_a - 2x_b M_b + M_a^2 + M_b^2 + 2M_a M_b)$$
$$= E(x_a^2) - M_a^2 + E(x_b^2) - M_b^2 + 2E(x_a . x_b) - 2M_a M_b$$
$$= V_a + V_b + 2 \, Cov \, (x_a, x_b)$$

When x_a and x_b are independent stochastic variates:

$$E(x_a . x_b) = E(x_a) . E(x_b) = M_a . M_b$$
$$\therefore \quad Cov \, (x_a, x_b) = 0$$

Whence for two independent variates x_a, x_b the variance (V_s) of the score sum is:

$$V_s = V_a + V_b \quad . \quad . \quad . \quad . \quad . \quad \text{(xi)}$$

From (xi) we see that

$$V_a = A^2 V_u + V_{a.0} \; ; \; V_b = B^2 V_u + V_{b.0}$$

Accordingly, we may write:

$$\frac{A^2 V_u}{V_a} + \frac{V_{a.0}}{V_a} = 1 = r_{au}^2 + \frac{V_{a.0}}{V_a}$$

$$\frac{B^2 V_u}{V_b} + \frac{V_{b.0}}{V_b} = 1 = r_{bu}^2 + \frac{V_{b.0}}{V_b}$$

We may therefore speak of r_{au}^2 and r_{bu}^2 respectively as the contribution of the umpire bonus to the total variance of the score of player A and of player B.

If either A or B is zero or if both are zero $x_a = x_{a.0}$, the numerator of r_{ab} in (ix) is zero, whence $r_{ab} = 0$. In that event x_a and x_b are independent. For any two independent variates x_a and x_b, the product-moment coefficient r_{ab} must be zero, since in that event also $Cov \, (x_a, x_b) = 0$. If $x_{a.0} = 0 = x_{b.0}$, so that $B . x_a = A . x_b$ there is perfect linear correspondence between the scores of the players, and

$$V_a = A^2 V_u \; ; \; V_b = B^2 V_u \; ; \; \sqrt{V_a . V_b} = AB . V_u$$

Thus $r_{ab} = +1$ if the signs of A and B are alike and $r_{ab} = -1$ if the signs are unlike. These limits necessarily hold good if x_a is a perfect linear function of x_b, i.e. $x_a = kx_b$ in which event $Cov\ (x_a\,x_b) = E(kb^2) - kM_b^2 = kV_b$ and $V_a = k^2V_b$, so that $\sqrt{V_a \cdot V_b} = kV_b$.

DETERMINANT NOTATION

WE DEFINE A DETERMINANT of order n as a set of n^2 numbers laid out gridwise in n rows and n columns; and define the numerical value of the determinant of order 2 as

$$\begin{vmatrix} a_1 & b_1 \\ a_2 & b_2 \end{vmatrix} = a_1b_2 - a_2b_1$$

The definition of the numerical value of any determinant of order higher than 2 depends on the application of a rule for expressing a determinant of order n in terms of determinants of order $(n-1)$ and hence by iteration in terms of determinants of order 2. Corresponding to each of the n elements in the top row, we speak of the *minor* of order $(n-1)$ as the residual determinant formed by eliminating the elements of the top row and of the corresponding column. The rule for reduction is as follows: proceeding from left to right multiply each minor by the corresponding element in the top row assigning positive and negative values to the products alternately. To represent the rule compactly it is convenient to label a determinant by its diagonal terms thus

$$\begin{vmatrix} a_1 & b_1 & c_1 & d_1 \\ a_2 & b_2 & c_2 & d_2 \\ a_3 & b_3 & c_3 & d_3 \\ a_4 & b_4 & c_4 & d_4 \end{vmatrix} = \Delta(a_1 . b_2 . c_3 . d_4)$$

The rule for reduction is then:

$$a_1 . \Delta(b_2 c_3 d_4) - b_1 . \Delta(a_2 c_3 d_4) + c_1 . \Delta(a_2 b_3 d_4) - d_1 . \Delta(a_2 b_3 c_4)$$

We expand each of the minors of order 3 in the same way, e.g.

$$\begin{vmatrix} b_2 & c_2 & d_2 \\ b_3 & c_3 & d_3 \\ b_4 & c_4 & d_4 \end{vmatrix} = b_2 . \Delta(c_3 d_4) - c_2 . \Delta(b_3 . d_4) + d_2 . \Delta(b_3 c_4)$$

$$= b_2(c_3 d_4 - d_3 c_4) - c_2(b_3 d_4 - d_3 b_4)$$
$$+ d_2(b_3 c_4 - c_3 b_4)$$

Thus the 4th order determinant reduces to a sum of 12 products involving an element from each of the first two rows and a determinant of order 2. Similarly a 5th order determinant reduces to a sum of 60 products involving an element in each of the first three rows and a determinant of order 2.

In practice, the evaluation of a determinant of high order does not involve the evaluation of many terms. Instead one applies a set of straightforward rules of elimination, subsumed in Aitken's *pivotal condensation* (*vide* Aitken, *Determinants and Matrices*, Oliver and Boyd).

SIGNIFICANCE AS INTERPRETED BY THE SCHOOL OF R. A. FISHER

OF THREE WIDELY DIVERGENT VIEWS about the nature of statistical inference, two have hitherto attracted little attention except among professional mathematicians, and have had few protagonists among practical statisticians except—as is true of Neyman's school—in connexion with new recipes for statistical inspection in commerce and manufacture. Contrariwise, the overwhelming majority of research workers in the biological field (including medicine and agriculture), as also a growing body of workers in the social sciences, rely largely on rule of thumb procedures set forth in a succession of manuals modelled on *Statistical Methods for Research Workers* by R. A. Fisher. This publication, which disclaims any attempt to set forth comprehensive derivations to justify the rationale of the author's methods, some of them first announced therein without formal proof, has thus become the bible of a world sect. It has a special importance because the author refers to it in a highly controversial context as a source book of his own *Weltanschauung*.

Some of Fisher's ideas took shape in the context of the early developments of the theory of relativity; and he learnt to move with ease and grace in the empyrean of the hypersphere when abstract multidimensional geometry was still an uncharted domain to theoretical statisticians of an earlier vintage. None of his many self-confessed expositors has attempted the task of interpreting the mathematical techniques involved on a plane intelligible to the investigator with no better equipment than a good practical grasp of the elements of the infinitesimal calculus or to analyse the logical content of the concepts invoked *vis-à-vis* the classical theory of probability. The consumer who is not a trained mathematician has therefore to learn the jargon of *degrees of freedom*, an expression which is meaningful only to those so fortunate as to be familiar with such branches of applied mathematics as the theory of the gyrostat or the development of thermodynamics in the tradition of Willard Gibbs.

Thus the controversy provoked by the more recent writings of Neyman, Wald, von Mises and others is essentially a challenge to the adequacy of statistical procedures already invoked by most laboratory workers who make much use of statistics; and those who use them most have so far had little opportunity to contribute to a discussion the outcome of which is highly relevant to their day's work. A temperate appraisal of the content of the controversy therefore calls for a more detailed examination of the views of R. A. Fisher and of his disciples than of the more concisely and explicitly stated opinions of his opponents.

To do justice to an evolving system of thought with lexico-graphical punctiliousness is commonly difficult, if only because it is by no means to the discredit of any philosopher to say that he has changed his views in the course of a prolific career. Happily, we may sidestep this obstacle. Fate has not deprived us of an up-to-date assessment of his mature views, since no sentiment of false modesty has deterred R. A. Fisher from taking the unusual precaution of collecting what he regards as his hitherto major contributions in an impressive quasi-memorial volume with a biographical introduction, with a portrait in photogravure of the author and with his own respectfully retrospective comments on the outstanding importance of each of the literary landmarks re-erected therein.

In these collected *Contributions* (1950) Fisher (35.173a) refers explicitly to the core of the current controversy in the following words:

Pearson and Neyman have laid it down axiomatically that the level of significance of a test must be equated to the frequency of a wrong decision "in repeated samples from the same population." This idea was foreign to the development of tests of significance given by the author in 1925, for the experimenter's experience does not consist in repeated samples from the same population, although in simple cases the numerical values are often the same; and it was, I believe, this coincidence of values in simple cases which misled Pearson and Neyman, who were not very familiar with the ideas of "Student" and the author.

In the references which follow, Fisher quotes under his own name only a short paper (1937) "on a point raised by M. S. Bartlett," his book (1925, 1st edition) *Statistical Methods for Research Workers* and a third as above. Before we consult this source, we may pause to anticipate a curious implication of the foregoing remarks. Our next citation asserts that the static population of the experimenter's experience is also infinite. If so, we exclude the treatment of sampling without replacement from a finite universe from the domain of discourse at the outset, a limitation which is certainly inconsistent with the practice of Fisher's disciples and with the much-quoted tea cup test (*vide infra*) in his later book *Design of Experiments*. Fisher's own analysis of the lady and the tea-cup problem involves a non-replacement situation with reference to which the only conceivable meaning one can give to his infinite population is precisely the postulate he repudiates in the passage cited above, viz. an infinite succession of 4-fold trials without replacement from 2-class universes of 8 objects.

The index of the 1948 edition of the *Statistical Methods* does not cite any page reference against *significance*, *null* or *hypothesis*, but gives p. 41 under *Tests, Significance of*. With this clue and from elsewhere in the same source we may try to get a clear idea of a theory of decision test procedure and/or estimation alternative to that of Neyman and Pearson. I shall first cite the only relevant (p. 41) indication the index supplies:

(i) The idea of an infinite population distributed in a *frequency distribution* in respect of one or more characters is fundamental to all statistical work. From a limited experience, for example, of individuals of a species, or of the weather of a locality, we may obtain some idea of the infinite hypothetical population from which our sample is drawn, and so of the probable nature of future samples to which our conclusions are to be applied. If a second sample belies this expectation we infer that it is, in the language of statistics, drawn from a different population; that the treatment to which the second sample of organisms had been exposed did in fact make a material difference, or that the climate (or the methods of measuring it) had materially altered. Critical tests of this kind may be called tests of significance, and when such tests are available we may discover whether a second sample is or is not significantly different from the first.

*

Since we have here no definitive criterion of when a sample score belies our expectation, we must seek further afield for an elucidation of what a decision test can accomplish. Three pages later we come to the next unequivocally relevant statement which follows a definition of a normal score deviation in any infinitesimal range dx.

(ii) In practical applications we do not so often want to know the frequency at any distance from the centre as the total frequency beyond that distance; this is represented by the area of the tail of the curve cut off at any point. Tables of this total frequency, or probability integral, have been constructed from which, for any value of $(x - \mu)/\sigma$, we can find what fraction of the total population has a larger deviation; or, in other words, what is the probability that a value so distributed, chosen at random, shall exceed a given deviation. Tables I and II have been constructed to show the deviations corresponding to different values of this probability. The rapidity with which the probability falls off as the deviation increases is well shown in these tables. A deviation exceeding the standard deviation occurs about once in three trials. Twice the standard deviation is exceeded only about once in 22 trials, thrice the standard deviation only once in 370 trials, while Table II shows that to exceed the standard deviation sixfold would need nearly a thousand million trials. The value for which $P=0\cdot05$, or 1 in 20 is $1\cdot96$ or nearly 2; it is convenient to take this point as a limit in judging whether a deviation is to be considered significant or not. Deviations exceeding twice the standard deviation are thus formally regarded as significant. Using this criterion we should be led to follow up a false indication only once in 22 trials, even if the statistics were the only guide available. Small effects will still escape notice if the data are insufficiently numerous to bring them out, but no lowering of the standard of significance would meet this difficulty.

Evidently, it is difficult to confer any meaning on the expressions "about once in 22 trials" or "only once in 370 trials" unless we postulate the extraction as a repetitive process in conformity with the Neyman–Pearson axiom. We might thus conclude that Fisher's objection to the axiom cited arises from the circumstance that it interprets significance levels in terms of frequency of wrong decisions. There is in fact nothing in either of the preceding paragraphs to suggest an alternative view. The criterion which would lead us "to follow up a false indication only once in 22 trials" presupposes that the sample does in fact come from a particular infinite population; but has no bearing whatsoever on how often we should follow a false indication if the sample came from some other infinite population. The sort of decision to which the test leads us is therefore useful if, and only if, our sole concern is to set a fixed limit to the conditional risk of rejecting the unique proposition implicit in the null hypothesis, viz. that the infinite population from which the sample comes has a certain structure.

The choice of an appropriate null hypothesis then presupposes: (*a*) that the main preoccupation of the investigator is to safeguard himself or herself against the risk of rejecting as the source of the sample a population with a particular structure; (*b*) there exists a convenient distribution function definitive of repeated sampling from such a population. If so, the numerous manuals devoted to the exposition of the Fisher battery of tests display a truly astonishing prescience concerning the preoccupations of the research worker or indifference to what they are. Thus a prodigious literature on therapeutic trials records the outcome of a Chi Square ld.f. test for the 2×2 table in conformity with the null hypothesis that one treatment is as good as another. Actually, the risk the research worker may be most anxious to avoid is that of rejecting a new treatment which is better than the old one, in which event the procedure prescribed by Fisher's pupils and expositors has then no bearing on the presumptive reason for carrying out the test. Clearly, the considerations which dictate the null hypothesis implicit in the test procedures advocated in the many manuals which expound Fisher's methods are mainly referable to what is an essential desideratum of any test procedure, viz. that the sample distribution of the population specified by the hypothesis chosen is definable and amenable to tabulation for ready reckoning. No less evidently, the fact that it may have this desirable property has no necessary connexion with any risk the laboratory or field worker is unwilling to incur.

There is another puzzling feature of the passage first cited, when we interpret it side by side with the second. In the former

Fisher refers to an infinite population as a fundamental postulate of his theory of statistical work. In the latter he elucidates his views about significance levels in terms of a particular population which is *ex hypothesi* infinite; but we could pair off each statement with appropriate verbal changes with a corresponding statement about the risk of following up a false indication about the structure of an urn containing 25 balls some red and some black on the basis of our knowledge that 3 out of 5 balls extracted from it without replacement are red. Surely the reason for introducing the concept of infinity has therefore no special relevance to the population of objects to which the score values of the frequency distribution refer. Its convenience can arise only in a conceptual framework of infinite repetition indispensable to the formulation of a correspondence between assertions and the occurrences falsely or truly described by them.

The rest of the chapter beginning on p. 41 sheds no new light on what Fisher claims for a decision test or on his views about statistical inference in general. On p. 96 we come on the following statement which encourages us to hope for more:

The treatment of frequencies by means of χ^2 is an approximation, which is useful for the comparative simplicity of the calculations. The exact treatment is somewhat more laborious, though necessary in cases of doubt, and valuable as displaying the true nature of the inferences which the method of χ^2 is designed to draw.

There follows an exposition of a treatment of 2×2 tables to test the hypothesis of proportionality, i.e. that two small samples are samples from populations with the same definitive parameter p.* The conclusion is:

Without any assumption or approximation, therefore, the table observed may be judged significantly to contradict the hypothesis of proportionality if

$$\frac{18! \; 13!}{30!} (2992 + 102 + 1)$$

* Fisher himself does not explicitly in this context make the important semantic distinction between the statement that the two samples come from the same infinite population and the statement that they come from populations which are alike in terms of the classificatory criterion relevant to the methods of sampling.

is a small quantity. This amounts to 619/1330665, or about 1 in 2150 showing that if the hypothesis of proportionality were true, observations of the kind recorded would be highly exceptional.

In this example, the reader will note that Fisher disclaims the necessity to formulate a criterion of rejection before undertaking a decision test; and calculates the frequency with which a particular range of score values, including the sample score itself will turn up, if the null hypothesis is true. No one can take exception to the deduction that "observations of the kind recorded are highly exceptional"; but the logician will wish to know if this conclusion has any necessary bearing on the type of inference relevant to the aim and nature of the test. Kendall's comment on a comparable distribution summarises the most we can say in such a situation:

> If this probability is small we have the choice of three possibilities:
>
> (a) An improbable event has occurred.
> (b) The hypothesis is not true, i.e. the proportion of A's in the population is not $\bar{\omega}$.
> (c) The sampling process is not random.

The calculation cited from p. 97 of *Statistical Methods* refers to "the probabilities of the set of frequencies observed and the two possible more extreme sets of frequencies which might have been observed." If we have so far failed to clarify what role Fisher confers on a significance test as a tool of statistical inference, this *accouplement* at least gets into focus a fundamental difference between his own attitude to the theory of test procedure and that of Neyman, Pearson, Wald, and the Columbia Research Group. Their view is that a decision test embodies a rule with statistically specifiable consequences if followed consistently. The kingpin of the rule is a rejection criterion which is independent of the particular sample under examination. The criterion prescribes a range of sample scores deemed to be inadmissible if the population prescribed by the test hypothesis correctly describes the source of a sample. If the sample score (x_0) lies in a *critical region* defined by the vector rejection criterion $x > x_r$ any possible value of x greater than the observed one will also lie in it. If x_0 lies in a critical region defined by the vector rejection criterion $x < x_r$ any possible value of x less than x_0 will also lie in it.

The prestatement of the rejection criterion thus gives an intelligible meaning to the quadrature which defines the probability (α) of rejecting the hypothesis if true; but Fisher offers no alternative justification for the association with x_0 of all values of x greater than x_0 in the summation cited above, though the exposition of the test procedure is clearly inconsistent with any such prestatement of a uniform rejection criterion. This circumstance seemingly throws more light than does anything elsewhere stated on Fisher's insistent refusal to identify significance levels with frequency of wrong decisions. All he offers in the source he himself cites as a basis for decision is a range of inadmissible score values specified *after* observing the sample on the basis of an intuitive evaluation of its likeability.

The Design of Experiments, first published some ten years later than the source cited, gives us an opportunity for exploring the author's second thoughts on significance and on estimation. In the index of the fifth edition (1949) we find the following relevant entries:

Significance: 13, 33, 55, 73, 105, 113, 182
Null Hypothesis: 15–17, 182–208
Fiducial Probability: 182, 195

Of the entries under significance only one explicitly throws further light on the author's viewpoint. In the citation (pp. 13–14) which follows, three different concepts seemingly compete for mastery and somewhat inconclusively.

It is open to the experimenter to be more or less *exacting* in respect of the smallness of the probability he would require before he would be willing to admit that his observations have demonstrated a positive result. It is obvious that an experiment would be useless of which no possible result would satisfy him. Thus, if he wishes to ignore results having probabilities as high as 1 in 20—the probabilities being of course reckoned from the hypothesis that *the phenomenon to be demonstrated is in fact absent*—then it would be useless for him to experiment with only 3 cups of tea of each kind. For 3 objects can be chosen out of 6 in only 20 ways, and therefore complete success in the test would be achieved without sensory discrimination, i.e. by "pure chance," in an average of 5 trials out of 100. It is usual and convenient for experiments to take 5 per cent as a standard level of significance, in the sense that they are prepared to ignore all results which fail to reach this standard, and, by this means, to eliminate from further discussion the greater part of the fluctuations which chance causes have introduced into their experimental results. No such selection can eliminate the whole of the possible effects of chance coincidence, and if we accept this convenient contention, and agree that an event which would occur by chance only once in 70 trials is decidedly "significant," in the statistical sense, we thereby admit that no isolated experiment, however significant in itself, can suffice for the experimental demonstration of any natural phenomenon; for the "one chance in a million" will undoubtedly occur, with no less and no more than its appropriate frequency, however surprised we may be that it should occur to us. *In order to assert that a natural phenomenon is experimentally demonstrable we need, not an isolated record, but a reliable method of procedure. In relation to the test of significance, we may say that a phenomenon is experimentally demonstrable when we know how to conduct an experiment which will rarely fail to give us a statistically significant result.* (*Italics inserted.*)

Initial remarks about how exacting the experimenter needs to be re-echo the impression that a significance test as conceived by the author is primarily a disciplinary regimen to discourage rash judgments. The statement that it is *usual* for research workers to adopt a 5 per cent significance level in the same context is true only of those who rely on the many rule of thumb manuals expounding Fisher's own test prescriptions. The explicit admission that we reckon the probabilities on the basis of the truth of *the hypothesis that the phenomenon to be demonstrated is in fact absent* implies that the only type of statement justified by the outcome of the test is conditional on the assumption that the hypothesis is true. In its own context the assertion that we need a *reliable method of procedure* in contradistinction to an isolated record seems to be consistent with the framework of indefinitely protracted repetition postulated by Neyman, von Mises and Wald; but it is the final statement which provokes our attention more especially.

As it stands, its literal form might legitimately convey the author's intention of introducing a new definition of *demonstrability*; but we do not in fact repeat experiments to see whether they fail to give a significant result in Fisher's sense of the term, or in any other. Accordingly, we must interpret it in its own context *vis-à-vis* the sentence italicised in the preceding paragraph, i.e.: (*a*) the so-called *null* hypothesis we select as a basis of test procedure is the *negation of the hypothesis which asserts the reality of the phenomenon*; (*b*) we decline to abandon our suspicion that the alternative hypothesis is true, i.e. that the phenomenon exists, if the null hypothesis assigns an *arbitrarily* low enough probability of occurrence to a specified class of score values including the unique score our single record yields. In any case, we here presume, though in contrariety to the author's apparent intention cited above, a conceptual repetitive framework in which the test procedure operates. Each of the assertions (*a*) and (*b*) above thus invite closer scrutiny, to which the author's failure to distinguish a phenomenon from a hypothesis about a phenomenon and his catholic use of the term *variation* adds a special difficulty arising out of the important distinction to which Kendall directs attention, viz: (*a*) the rarity of the prescribed event in virtue of the hypothetical random distribution implicit in the chosen null hypothesis, *if true*; (*b*) the rarity of the prescribed event in virtue of departures from randomisation in the assembly of data; (*c*) the rarity of the prescribed event in virtue of the inapplicability of the null hypothesis to the occurrence.

As regards the author's view of the proper criterion of choice for a unique null hypothesis, several difficulties arise when we ask what form the denial must take, i.e. what precisely do we mean if we assert that the phenomenon to be demonstrated *is in fact absent*? This is indeed the theme (p. 470) of a lengthy and entertaining analysis by Neyman of the lady and the teacup parable referred to for illustrative use in the passage under discussion. The two major difficulties are these: (*a*) many situations in which the author's expositors could certainly advocate a Fisher test procedure admit of no singular statement of the denial appropriate to the situation; (*b*) the object of an experiment may be to assess the validity of equally commendable alternatives each being the denial of the other.

A single example will suffice to elucidate (*a*). We suppose that rival schools, as indeed in the days of the controversy between Weldon and Bateson, assert of a particular class of experiments; (i) a ratio of the most elementary type prescribed by Mendel's hypothesis (3 : 1) holds good; (ii) such a ratio does not hold good w.r.t. the phenomenon under dispute. Proponents of (ii) may adopt (i) as the denial of their assertion. Proponents of (i) can formulate no such unique denial satisfactory to proponents of (ii). To be sure, they can place themselves in the position of their contestants; but this then imposes the same impracticable obligation on the latter. Few who follow Fisher's test prescriptions appear to realise that there never can be a unique denial of a hypothesis itself formulated, like the theory of the gene, in statistical terms, nor that a 20 to 1 convention can have any relevance to one's assessment of its truth.

In any case, the form of the denial must necessarily satisfy one criterion of adequacy and should rightly satisfy a second. Since a stochastic null hypothesis must prescribe a sample distribution of score values, mathematical tractability of the implicit assumptions in terms of sampling theory will in practice dictate the form that the denial will take. It is therefore of interest to note that the several components of the impressive battery of significance tests associated with Fisher's name consistently imply that the universe of choice is homogeneous w.r.t. the relevant dimension of classification, i.e. that any manifest discrepancy associated with the relevant taxonomical criterion (or criteria) is such as would arise in random sampling from one and the same infinite hypothetical population. Admittedly, this makes the prescription of a test more tractable from the viewpoint of the mathematician; but if there is any other intelligible reason for adopting such a postulate, it is difficult to find an equally intelligible reason for the silence of Fisher's expositors with respect to the operational intention of the denial. Contemporary literature of therapeutic and prophylactic trials is an uninterrupted record of Chi Square tests for 2×2 tables to test the null hypothesis that there is no treatment difference, when the question of real interest is the putative existence of a difference sufficient to justify replacement of one treatment by another.

No doubt Fisher would concede that this is an issue of estimation; but this scarcely explains the object in view when performing the so-called exact test cited in his own words above. In practice, the overwhelming majority of biologists and sociologists who employ Fisher's battery of tests have learned the routine as an army drill from the many manuals following the same method of presentation as his *Statistical Methods*. As stated, this gives no derivation of the sampling distributions invoked and no adequate survey of what principles of statistical inference accredit their use. As also stated, the prescribed null hypothesis conforms to a set pattern in which the idea of randomisation is paramount; but Anscombe (1948) has rightly pointed out that this concept admits of interpretation at no less than three semantic levels when conceived in terms of the assertion that *the phenomenon to be demonstrated is not present*.

In the *Design*, the last passage cited is the only one in which the author expounds his fundamental attitude to significance explicitly or at length. As we have seen, it endows the null hypothesis with a unique status which would be less difficult to interpret if the test battery itself supplied the investigator with a range of choice adequate to what denials may be appropriate to the experimental set-up. We therefore turn with bewilderment to what the author has to say (p. 138, *op. cit.*) on this topic in a seemingly oblique reference to the Neyman–Pearson theory of alternative test procedure:

The notion that different tests of significance are appropriate to test different features of the same null hypothesis presents no difficulty to workers engaged in practical experimentation, but has been the occasion of much theoretical discussion among statisticians. The reason for this diversity of viewpoint is perhaps that the experimenter is thinking in terms of observational values, and is aware of what observational discrepancy it is which interests him, and which he thinks may be statistically significant, before he enquires what test of significance, if any, is available appropriate to his needs. He is, therefore, not usually concerned with the question: To what observational feature should a test of significance be applied? This question, when the answer to it is not already known, can be fruitfully discussed only when the experimenter has in view, not a single null hypothesis, but a class of such hypotheses, in the significance of deviations from each of which he is equally interested. We shall, later, discuss in more detail the logical situation created when this is the case. It should not, however, be thought that such an elaborate theoretical background is a normal condition of experimentation, or that it is needed for the competent and effective use of tests of significance.

Lack of a clear-cut distinction between observational discrepancy and the hypothesis in seeming contrariety to the recorded observation is at this stage a familiar idiom and need not detain us. The passage is quotable since it implies that the laboratory or field worker has no doubts about what is the appropriate null hypothesis to select and has at his or her disposal no lack of appropriate test prescriptions presumably equipped with suitable tables in one of the good books. We have seen that this is not so, and there is no need to add anything to foregoing comments bearing on this charitable interpretation of the consumer's choice and custom. It is not without interest that Fisher's assertion (cited from pp. 13–14) of the unique form the null hypothesis must take is not easy to reconcile with the above and retires from the field on pp. 15–16.

Our examination of the possible results of the experiment has therefore led us to a statistical test of significance, by which these results are divided into two classes with opposed interpretations. Tests of significance are of many different kinds, which need not be considered here. Here we are only concerned with the fact that the easy calculation in permutations which we encountered, and which gave us our test of significance, stands for something present in every possible experimental arrangement; or, at least, for something required in its interpretation. The two classes of results which are distinguished by our test of significance are, on the one hand, those which show a significant discrepancy from a certain hypothesis; namely, in this case, the hypothesis that the judgments given are in no way influenced by the order in which the ingredients have been added; and on the other hand, results which show no significant discrepancy from this hypothesis. This hypothesis, which may or may not be impugned by the result of an experiment, is again characteristic of all experimentation. Much confusion would often be avoided if it were explicitly formulated when the experiment is designed. In relation to any experiment we may speak of this hypothesis as the "null hypothesis," and it should be noted that the *null hypothesis is never proved or established, but is possibly disproved, in the course of experimentation.* Every experiment may be said to exist only in order to give the facts a chance of disproving the null hypothesis. (*Italics inserted.*)

In the light of these remarks and more especially with due regard to the content of the citation from p. 138 of the *Design*, it is permissible to entertain the possibility that Fisher did not initially intend to limit (as on pp. 13–14) the null hypothesis appropriate to every situation by a form of words implying that *the phenomenon to be demonstrated is not present.* Since we cannot explicitly formulate any unique hypothesis conceived as the negation of a particular genetic hypothesis of the Mendelian type, let us therefore explore the consequences of regarding the proper null hypothesis as the Mendelian interpretation itself. Following the prescription of Fisher's school, we should then say that a deviation of $\pm 2\sigma$ from expectation would be a rare event, but a deviation of $\pm 3\sigma$ would be more so. Indeed, any deviation numerically greater than $0 \cdot 675\sigma$ would be less common than the residual score class. Thus the more exacting we make our significance criterion, the greater will be the chance that a true discrepancy between hypothesis and fact will escape detection. All we can say is: (*a*) if the hypothesis is true, score deviations within the range $\pm 0 \cdot 675\sigma$ will occur as often as score deviations outside this range; (*b*) if our rejection score criterion x_0 is numerically greater than $0 \cdot 675\sigma$ our procedure will more often lead us to correct than to wrong decisions in the long run, *if the hypothesis is* true. Surely it is clear that the conditional risk so specified by the procedure is not necessarily the risk against which the investigator wishes to protect his judgment. Nor is it clear that investigators with opposite views about the *phenomenon to be demonstrated* will assign priority to one and the same alternative risks of recording an erroneous verdict.

This interpretation of an isolated test turns the spotlight on the last words italicised in the citation from pp. 15–16. For reasons set forth in Chapter Thirteen, the assertion that the test cannot demonstrate the truth of the hypothesis, an assertion difficult to dovetail into the intention of the last sentence of the citation from pp. 13–14, deprives it of any usefulness unless conceived as a disciplinary device; but what precisely entitles us to hope that we have *possibly disproved* it? Within the strait-jacket of the unique null hypothesis, we have merely made a reason for rejecting it dictated by considerations relevant to the penalties of doing so when it happens to be true. In any event, the considerations advanced at the end of the last paragraph suggest that the use of the probable error by a generation with no prescience of the 5 per cent feeling scarcely merits the stricture (*Statistical Methods*, 10th edn., 1948, p. 45).

The value of the deviation beyond which half the observations lie is called the *quartile* distance, and bears to the standard deviation the ratio 0·67449. It was formerly a common practice to calculate the standard error and then, multiplying it by this factor, to obtain the *probable error*. The probable error is thus about two-thirds of the standard error, and as a test of significance a deviation of three times the probable error is effectively equivalent to one of twice the standard error. The common use of the probable error is its only recommendation; when any critical test is required the deviation must be expressed in terms of the standard error in using the tables of normal deviates.

The insertion of italics in this citation is not relevant at this stage. In striking contrast to the pervasive assumption of homogeneity within the framework of test decision is the form of words Fisher uses when he introduces readers of the *Design* (pp. 195–6) to the *fiducial concept of probability that the unknown parameters . . . should be within specified limits*. For the real universe of estimation is in such situations the homogeneous universe of what we elsewhere refer to as Model I; and the probability assignable to a parameter in connexion with anything we say about the interval in which it lies can have only two values, viz. zero and unity.

It is the circumstance that statistics sufficient for the estimation of these two quantities are obtained merely from the sum and the sum of squares of the observations, that gives a peculiar simplicity to problems for which the theory of errors is appropriate. This simplicity appears in an alternative form of statement, which is legitimate in these cases, namely, statements of the *probability that*

the unknown parameters, such as μ and σ, *should lie within specified limits.*
Such statements are termed statements of *fiducial* probability, to
distinguish them from the statements of *inverse* probability, by which
mathematicians formerly attempted to express the results of inductive inference. Statements of inverse probability have a different
logical content from statements of fiducial probability, in spite of
their similarity of form, and require for their truth the postulation
of knowledge beyond that obtained by direct observation.

In this context it is tempting to cite the curious reasons
Fisher gives for restricting the fiducial argument to situations
in which we may conceptually invoke a continuous, in contradistinction to a discrete, distribution:

. . . With discontinuous data, however, the fiducial argument
only leads to the result that this probability does not exceed 0·01.
We have a statement of inequality, and not one of equality. It is
not obvious, in such cases, that, of the two forms of statement
possible, the one explicitly framed in terms of probability has any
practical advantage. The reason why the fiducial statement loses
its precision with discontinuous data is that the frequencies in our
table make no distinction between a case in which the 2 dizygotic
convicts were only just convicted, perhaps on venial charges, or
as first offenders, while the remaining 15 had characters above
suspicion, and an equally possible case in which the 2 convicts
were hardened offenders, and some at least of the remaining 15
had barely escaped conviction. (*The Logic of Inductive Inference.*
J. Roy. Stat. Soc., Vol. XCVIII, Pt. I, pp. 50–1, 1935.)

Some of the enigmas and seeming inconsistencies exhibited
in previous citations take on a new aspect when we recall:
(*a*) how largely R. A. Fisher by his own admission relies on
intuition; (*b*) how much his later views owe to his early
experience, assigned as Statistician to an Agricultural Research
Institute with the task of extracting any grain reclaimable
from a long-standing accumulation of inexpertly designed field
trials. This suffices to explain his preoccupation with *sufficiency*,
a concept which has so much less prominence in theories
advanced by the opposing school. Insistent concern for what
his own school refer to as *Amount of Information* and disdain for
excessive consistency go hand in hand in the following from

502

The Logic of Inductive Inference (1935) reprinted in the collected works as 26.47:

. . . One could, therefore, develop a mathematical theory of quantity of information from these properties as postulates, and this would be the normal mathematical procedure. It is, perhaps, only a personal preference that I am more inclined to examine the quantity as it emerges from mathematical investigations, and to judge of its utility by the free use of common sense, rather than to impose it by a formal definition. As a mathematical quantity information is strikingly similar to *entropy* in the mathematical theory of thermodynamics. You will notice especially that reversible processes, changes of notation, mathematical transformations if single-valued, translation of the data into foreign languages, or rewriting them in code, cannot be accompanied by loss of information; but that the irreversible processes involved in statistical estimation, where we cannot reconstruct the original data from the estimate we calculate from it, may be accompanied by a loss, but never by a gain.

The importance of this preoccupation with *amount of information* lies in a basically different orientation of Fisher's sect when we set his views in juxtaposition to those of the alternative school. One mode of thought proposes the question: what rules must we impose on our reasoning before we have permitted the data to influence our views? That of Fisher and his followers asks: what course shall we pursue when we have weighed up all the relevant evidence inherent in the data? Thus we find the following in *Uncertain Inference* (27.254–27.255 *op. cit.*):

. . . There is one peculiarity of uncertain inference which often presents a difficulty to mathematicians trained only in the technique of rigorous deductive argument, namely, that our conclusions are arbitrary, and therefore invalid, unless all the data, exhaustively, are taken into account. In rigorous deductive reasoning we may make any selection from the data, and any certain conclusions which may be deduced from this selection will be valid, whatever additional data we may have at our disposal. . . . This consideration is vital to the fiducial type of argument, which purports to infer exact statements of the probabilities that unknown hypothetical quantities, or that future observations, shall lie within assigned limits, on the basis of a body of observational experience. No such process could be justified unless the relevant information latent in this experience were exhaustively mobilized and incorporated in our inference.

The special difficulty that arises from Fisher's robust and seemingly contagious confidence in his own intuitions appears in the two following citations, the first of which is from *The Foundations of Theoretical Statistics* (1922) reprinted in the collected works (10.323):

> ... For the solution of problems of estimation we require a method which for each particular problem will lead us automatically to the statistic by which the criterion of sufficiency is satisfied. Such a method is, I believe, provided by the Method of Maximum Likelihood, although I am not satisfied as to the mathematical rigour of any proof which I can put forward to that effect. Readers of the ensuing pages are invited to form their own opinion as to the possibility of the method of the maximum likelihood leading in any case to an insufficient statistic. For my own part I should gladly have withheld publication until a rigorously complete proof could have been formulated; but the number and variety of the new results which the method discloses press for publication, and at the same time I am not insensible of the advantage which accrues to Applied Mathematics from the co-operation of the Pure Mathematician, and this co-operation is not infrequently called forth by the very imperfections of writers on Applied Mathematics.

This intrepid belief in what he disarmingly calls common sense, as a substitute for a system of communicably acceptable rules of procedure, has led Fisher, in a source elsewhere cited, to advance a battery of concepts for the semantic credentials of which neither he nor his disciples offer any justification *en rapport* with generally accepted tenets of the classical theory of probability. Thus an operation which appears in the derivation of Behrens' test as a simple error in terms of the classical theory reappears as a novel and *ad hoc* rule of thought (*vide infra* Yates) described as fiducial inference in Fisher's own treatment of the same issue. Again and again, we seem to sidestep the notion of inverse probability or the invocation of the highly exceptionable Bayes's scholium either by using a new name for the same reasoning process or by ignoring the issue involved.

Thus we come on the following in *Foundations of Theoretical Statistics* reprinted in the collected works (10.326):

There would be no need to emphasize the baseless character of the assumptions made under the titles of inverse probability and BAYES' theorem in view of the decisive criticism to which they have been exposed at the hands of BOOLE, VENN and CHRYSTAL, were it not for the fact that the older writers, such as LAPLACE and POISSON, who accepted these assumptions, also laid the foundations of the modern theory of statistics, and have introduced into their discussions of this subject ideas of a similar character. I must indeed plead guilty in my original statement of the Method of the Maximum Likelihood to having based my argument upon the principle of inverse probability; in the same paper, it is true, I emphasized the fact that such inverse probabilities were relative only. That is to say, that while we might speak of one value of p as having an inverse probability three times that of another value of p, we might on no account introduce the differential element dp, so as to be able to say that it was three times as probable that p should lie in one rather than the other of two equal elements. Upon consideration, therefore, I perceive that the word probability is wrongly used in such a connection; probability is a ratio of frequencies, and about the frequencies of such values we can know nothing whatever. We must return to the actual fact that one value of p, of the frequency of which we know nothing, would yield the observed result three times as frequently as would another value of p. If we need a word to characterize this relative property of different values of p, I suggest that we may speak without confusion of the *likelihood* of one value of p being thrice the likelihood of another, bearing always in mind that likelihood is not here used loosely as a synonym of probability, but simply to express the relative frequencies with which such values of the hypothetical quantity p would in fact yield the observed sample.

We thus build up a battery of concepts which constitute the exclusive *mystique* of the sect; and a secret language which excludes intercommunication with heretics or schismatics, as in the following from *Inverse Probability* (1930) reprinted in the source already cited (22.532):

... The process of maximizing $\pi (\phi)$ or S (log ϕ) is a method of estimation known as the "method of maximum likelihood"; it has in fact no logical connection with inverse probability at all.

The fact that it has been accidentally associated with inverse probability, and that when it is examined objectively in respect of the properties in random sampling of the estimates to which it gives rise, it has shown itself to be of supreme value, are perhaps the sole remaining reasons why that theory is still treated with respect. The function of the θ's maximized is not, however, a probability and does not obey the laws of probability; it involves no differential element $d\theta_1\,d\theta_2\,d\theta_3\,.\,.\,.\,.\,.\,.$; it does none the less afford a rational basis for preferring some values of θ, or combination of values of the θ's, to others. It is, just as much as a probability, a numerical measure of rational belief, and for that reason is called the *likelihood* of $\theta_1\,\theta_2\,\theta_3\,.\,.\,.$ having given values, to distinguish it from the probability that $\theta_1\,\theta_2\,\theta_3\,.\,.\,.$ lie within assigned limits, since in common speech both terms are loosely used to cover both types of logical situation.

The only notably valiant attempt of one of the apostles of the sect to interpret the teaching of the Leader as a system of logic is that of Yates. In his paper (1939) on *An Apparent Inconsistency arising from Tests of Significance based on Fiducial Distributions of Unknown Parameters* (*Proc. Camb. Phil. Soc.*, Vol. 35) Yates concedes that in Fisher's extension of the Behrens' integral:

We must frankly recognize that we have here introduced a new concept into our methods of inductive inference, which cannot be deduced by the rules of logic from already accepted methods, but which itself requires formal definition.

What follows is less recognisable as a new concept than as a sequence of *ad hoc* assumptions relevant to a particular test prescription. In simple words, the contention is that: (*a*) the fiducial argument would be invalid if we did not introduce the new concept; (*b*) the acceptance of the new principle leads to no "inconsistencies" if the estimates are sufficient in Fisher's sense; (*c*) if we wish to retain the fiducial argument, we may therefore embrace the new concept with a clear conscience. If there is any ulterior reason for doing so, Yates does not explicitly disclose it.

INDEX